HANDBOOK OF NORTH AMERICAN INDUSTRY

HANDBOOK OF NORTH AMERICAN INDUSTRY:

NAFTA AND THE ECONOMIES OF ITS MEMBER NATIONS

FIRST EDITION

EDITED BY:
JOHN E. CREMEANS

BERNAN PRESS
LANHAM, MD

Published 1998 by Bernan Press, an imprint of Bernan Associates, a division of The Kraus Organization Limited

Printed in the United States of America

99   98   4 3 2 1

Bernan Press
4611-F Assembly Drive
Lanham, MD 20706-4391
(800) 274-4447
e-mail: info@bernan.com

ISBN: 0-89059-073-7

TABLE OF CONTENTS

ACKNOWLEDGEMENTS

The majority of the statistical data in this book are from Canadian, U.S., and Mexican government sources. In all cases, sources for the data are given in the notes. Those data from the U.S. government are in the public domain. Data from Canadian and Mexican government sources are printed with permission and may be subject to copyright restrictions. Some data are from private sources and may also be subject to restrictions. The presentations of data and the text portions of this book (except as noted) are protected by copyright.

Sources of data include:

Canada: All Statistics Canada data are reproduced by authority of the Minister of Industry, 1997. Readers wishing further information on data provided through the cooperation of Statistics Canada may obtain copies of related publications from: Publications Sales, Statistics Canada, Ottawa, Ontario K1A OT6, or by calling 1-613-951-7277 or toll-free 1-800-267-6677. Readers may also facsimile their order by dialing 1-613-951-1684.

The United States: Data and information in the book was obtained from the following U.S. government agencies:

The U.S. Department of Agriculture
   Foreign Agricultural Service
   National Agricultural Statistics Service
The U.S. Department of Commerce:
   Bureau of the Census
   Bureau of Economic Analysis
   International Trade Administration
   National Oceanic and Atmospheric Administration
The U.S. Department of Energy, Energy Information Administration
The U.S. Department of Health and Human Services, Health Care Financing Administration
The U.S. Department of Labor
   Bureau of Labor Statistics
   Office of Trade Adjustment Assistance
Federal Reserve Board of Governors
National Science Foundation
Office of the U.S. Trade Representative

Mexico: All Mexican statistics are reproduced by permission; additional information may be obtained from:

The National Institute of Statistics, Geography and Information (INEGI)
Av. Heroe de Nacozari 2301
Fracc. Jardines del Parque
C.P. 20270
Aguascalientes, Ags.
Mexico
Internet http//www.inegi.gob.mx.

Other sources: A number of trade associations and other sources also supplied information, for which the editor and publisher are very grateful. Among these sources are:

Air Transport Association of America
American Council of Life Insurance
American Farm Bureau Federation
American Feed Industry Association
American Forest and Paper Association
American Furniture Manufacturers Association
AMT—The Association for Manufacturing Technology
American Textile Manufacturers Institute
American Trucking Associations
Association of International Automobile Manufacturers
Chemical Manufacturers Association
Conference Board of Canada
Construction Industry Manufacturers Association
Edison Electric Institute
Health Insurance Association of America
National Association of Realtors
National League of Cities
National Restaurant Association
Printing Industries of America

The data in this volume meet established publication standards for statistical data. Every effort was made to select data that are accurate, meaningful, and useful. All statistical data are subject to error arising from sampling variability, reporting errors, incomplete coverage, imputation, and other sources. The responsibility of the editor and publisher of this volume is limited to reasonable care in the reproduction and presentation of data obtained from established sources.

The editor is very grateful to all those who assisted in the preparation of this volume. Beverly Horsley wrote most of the text for the industry chapters in a clear, concise way that will be appreciated by readers. Steven Thomas prepared most of the tables, used his fluent Spanish to converse directly with sources in Mexico, and to ensure that the technical points written in Spanish were fully understood; he also wrote the article on Chile, a country with which he has particular familiarity. Eric Hosken wrote several industry chapters and helped in preparing tables. Cornelia Strawser was our intrepid fact-checker—no one is happy to be told they have made an error, but the editor is very grateful for her meticulous reviews and unwavering insistence on clarity and accuracy. George Hall helped with lots of encouragement and good common sense. The editor is especially obliged to Dr. Courtenay Slater, Manager of Economic Publications; she kept the project on course and up to speed with excellent judgment, good cheer, and an occasional needed correction. Finally, special thanks are due to many people in Statistics Canada, the U.S. Federal statistical agencies, INEGI, and the Conference Board, Canada; they gave generously of their time, knowledge, and talent in responding to our frequent requests for data and general information.

PREFACE

The Handbook of North American Industry-NAFTA and the Economies of its Member Nations is a basic reference book for everyone working in, competing in, selling to, buying from, or just interested in NAFTA and the very large area it covers. The many economic and political controversies surrounding it are to be expected because NAFTA affects almost everyone—consumers, workers and their unions, environmentalists, businessmen, and politicians. Important decisions on the management and expansion of the agreement are made with increasing frequency and, in some cases, serious dispute. Comprehensive, accurate, and detailed information is essential to understanding and participating in these decisions and to working within the new system. The Handbook was created to fill those needs.

BASIC CONCEPTS

Every effort has been made to provide the necessary information in an unbiased, comprehensive, and, above all, useful reference book that is accessible to everyone. To that end, the Handbook was prepared based on the following concepts:

1. *North American coverage.* The Handbook covers Canada, the United States, and Mexico. Coverage of the United States is usually more detailed because the U.S. economy is the largest of the three and because more detail is to be had. But the relevant data from Canada and Mexico are presented, as well.

2. *Industry detail.* This is essential to the understanding of the North American market and the evaluation of NAFTA. Summaries and averages can be helpful, but their use may hide important information. Industry-level detail facilitates analysis and encourages insight. The focus of the Handbook is on individual industries.

3. *Words follow numbers.* Verbal analysis and evaluation is very useful, but only if based on facts and figures. Also, many readers will want to pursue points of special interest that require numeric data, not someone else's summary. The text is concise and comprehensive, but will always be based on the facts, mainly as presented in tables and charts. The Handbook's motto is, "Show me the numbers!"

4. *Broad and comprehensive coverage.* The Handbook contains a collection of the most useful statistics on the North American economy. The Handbook has data from Statistics Canada and from Instituto Nacional de Estadistica, Geografia e Informatica (INEGI) of Mexico; among U.S. sources, data are included from the International Trade Administration, the Census Bureau, and the Bureau of Economic Analysis of the U.S. Department of Commerce; the Bureau of Labor Statistics and the Office of Trade Adjustment Assistance of the Department of Labor; the Federal Reserve Board of Governors; the National Science Foundation; the Health Care Finance Administration; and many industry sources.

5. *Comparability.* The data are presented in similar ways for the three countries to facilitate comparisons. There are many difficulties in comparing industry data for the three NAFTA countries—but such comparisons are important. Every effort is made to reduce or eliminate these difficulties, which, in all cases, are discussed and explained.

6. *Standardization.* The industry chapters use a standard format; each chapter's text and statistics present data in an organized way so that industry-to-industry and country-to-country comparisons can be made. The chapter texts follow a standard format so that discussion of topics, such as employment or industry shipments, quickly can be found. Readers, once familiar with the format, can move from industry to industry without having to adjust to differing presentations.

ORGANIZATION

Part I contains feature articles about the North American Free Trade Agreement (NAFTA), the North American economy as a whole, and specific areas of interest. The lead article, "NAFTA— The First Four Years," discusses the steps leading to the agreement, the details of its contents, and consequences as we can discern them now. Other articles focus on specific problems and issues. These include articles about:

- the "peso crisis" and Mexico's crash and recovery;

- employment, wages, and benefits in each of the three members, with detailed tables comparing U.S., Canadian, and Mexican hourly labor costs by industry;

- the proposed addition of Chile to the agreement and the negotiations with other countries of the Western Hemisphere toward a Free Trade Area of the Americas (FTAA);

- Mexico's Maquiladora program, a duty-free manufacturing and re-export program that preceded NAFTA by more than 20 years but set the stage for the economic integration of North America now being realized under NAFTA;

- the prospect of an independent Quebec and what it might mean to Quebec, Canada, and the rest of North America; and

- the problems caused by illegal drugs—the uncounted, multibillion-dollar "industry," whose impact extends from the largest cities to the smallest and most remote towns and villages of North America.

Part II contains standardized chapters covering industries in the agriculture, mining, construction, manufacturing, trade, and service-producing industries. With a few exceptions, each chapter contains 11 standard tables covering specific topics and four standard figures. The chapters also bring together a broad range of authoritative data for the United States and provide significantly more industry data than available from some reference books devoted to the U.S. economy.

The appendixes include the full text of a number of documents helpful, if not essential, to understanding NAFTA and how it affects business. Included are:

- The Executive Summary of the Administration's Report to the Congress on NAFTA;

- The official summary of the NAFTA Agreement;

- An explanation of the new North American Industry Classification System and how it will affect data users.

Every effort has been made to make the Handbook a most useful tool for the analysis and understanding of this very important subject.

How To Use This Book

This section is meant to help the reader get the most out of *The Handbook of North American Industry*. It describes the standard chapter organization, describes and explains the standard figures and tables, and provides technical details on the classification of data and the calculation of the analytical measures. Note that the Preface describes the plan of the book and explains its organizing concepts. This section is intended to answer questions that the reader may have about the sources of the data and how they can be used.

Part I

Part I of the *Handbook* focuses on the North American Free Trade Agreement (NAFTA); policies, programs, and agreements leading up to it; and some of the major issues and problems facing NAFTA members today. The lead article, "NAFTA—the First Four Years," summarizes and reviews NAFTA: what it is, how it came about, the size and nature of the trade area, its results so far, and its future as can now be discerned. Other articles in this section take a look at employment, wages, and benefits in the three member countries; Mexico's long-standing duty-free Maquiladora program; the prospect of an independent Quebec; progress made toward further enlargement of NAFTA and the creation of a Free Trade Area of the Americas (FTAA); and the huge and daunting illegal drug trade. Part I also contains statistical information on the North American market as a whole and on its member countries. Readers are encouraged to read all these articles, but those who wish may go directly to topics of particular interest.

Part II

Standard Chapter Outline.

Chapters in Part II cover the major North American industries as defined in the U.S. Standard Industrial Classification System (SIC), described later in this article. For comparison purposes, we have grouped industries in Canada and Mexico to conform as closely as possible to those in the United States. In the manufacturing section, most chapters consist of four standard sections and 11 subsections, four figures (charts), and 11 tables designed to answer specific questions about each industry. In some chapters, certain of the standard tables are missing, owing to a lack of data or the inclusion of pertinent data in other industry groups (e.g., financial information on tobacco is included in the Food and Beverages chapter). In several of the nonmanufacturing chapters (for example, those on mining, agriculture, fishing, and health services), nonstandard tables are used because of data differences and limitations.

The standard sections, the figures and tables referred to in each, and the questions they answer are listed below, along with the titles of the figures and tables for each, using the chemical industry as an example:

The United States

- **Products and Processes.** How large and important is this industry relative to the national economy? What products/services are produced by the industry, and what processes are used? What is the regional distribution of the industry?

  Table 1: United States: Component Industries of Chemicals and Allied Products (SIC 28), 1992

  Table 2: U.S. Employment and Earnings: Chemicals and Allied Products

  Figure 1: U.S. Employment in Chemicals

- **What's New.** What recent events, laws, regulations, or trends are significant to this industry?

- **Output.** Has the output of this industry grown or declined, and what has been the cyclical pattern?

  Figure 2: U.S. Employment and Shipments, Chemicals and Allied Products

  Table 3: U.S. Output, Investment, and Prices: Chemicals and Allied Products

- **Investment.** How much does this industry invest; is its capacity utilization increasing; how much is spent on research and development?

- **Prices.** Are industry prices rising or falling and how rapidly?

- **Workforce and employment.** Is employment increasing or decreasing, and how have production workers and women fared during the past decade? What are hourly and weekly earnings in the industry and have they kept pace with inflation? How does the change in corporate earnings compare to the change in earnings of employees? What is the industry's occupational distribution? What are the prospects for future employment growth?

  Table 4: U.S. Employment, Hours, and Earnings: Chemicals and Allied Products

  Table 5: U.S. Employment Projections By Major Occupational Group: Chemicals and Allied Products

  Figure 3: U.S. Occupational Injury and Illness Rates: Chemicals and Allied Products, 1995

- **Finance.** What is the financial condition of the industry? How are industries doing in terms of corporate sales, profits, assets, profit-to-sales ratios, and other key measures of financial health?

  Figure 4: U.S. Corporate Income and Worker Earnings: Chemicals

  Table 6: U.S. Corporate Income and Assets: Chemicals

Canada. What are the major industry components? What are the patterns of growth in output and employment?

Table 7: Canada: Component Industries of Chemicals and Chemical Products (CSIC 37), 1993

Table 8: Canadian Employment and Shipments: Chemical Industries, 1987-1994

Mexico. What are the major industry components? What are the patterns of growth in output and employment?

Table 9: Mexico: Component Industries of Chemicals and Petroleum (CMAP 35), 1993

Table 10: Mexican Gross Domestic Product and Employment: Chemicals, Derivatives of Petroleum, Rubber and Plastic, 1988-1995

International Trade

- **United States.** How have the products of the U.S. industry fared in international trade during the 1989-1996 period, both globally (with all other countries) and specifically with Canada and Mexico?

- **Canada.** How have products of the Canadian industry fared in bilateral trade with the U.S. and with Mexico during 1989-1996?

- **Mexico.** How have products of the Mexican industry fared in bilateral trade with the United States and Canada during 1989-1996?

- **NAFTA.** What are the trade patterns within NAFTA and how have they changed since 1989 and since enactment of the agreement in 1994?

  Table 11: International Trade, Chemicals and Allied Products

Industry Classification

In order to collect, tabulate, and analyze industry data, it is first necessary to classify establishments by industry based on the activity in which they are engaged and what they produce. Most national statistical organizations have classification systems that reflect their nation's preferences and peculiarities. The Canadian, Mexican, and U.S. systems are no exceptions; the three systems have many similarities, but are nonetheless distinct.

The industry classification schemes of Canada, Mexico, and the United States are hierarchical. In the United States, economic activity is classified by "division" (e.g. mining, construction, manufacturing, etc.) and within divisions by major groups referred to as "2-digit" industries because the approximately 80 major industries are identified by their 2-digit code; for example, Food and Kindred Products manufacturing is SIC 20. Within major industries, there are 3-digit industry groups; for example, Grain Mill Products (SIC 204) in the food industry. The industry groups are further subdivided into 4-digit categories; for example, Dog and Cat Food (SIC 2047). Data are typically tabulated initially at the industry (4-digit) level and, when "larger" groupings are required, accumulated into 3- or 2-digit classifications.

The Canadian and Mexican classification schemes are similar in structure to the U.S. SIC; Canadian codes have 4 digits; Mexican codes have 6. In the *Handbook*, major industries and subindustries of all three countries are sometimes referred to as 2-digit, 3-digit, and 4-digit industries, respectively.[1]

The governments of Canada, Mexico, and the United States have developed the "North American Industry Classification System" (NAICS), which eventually will be the universal classification scheme for each of the three countries in place of their current systems. U.S. statistical agencies will implement NAICS incrementally: the Census Bureau will begin with the 1997 Economic Censuses (to be collected in 1998 and released in 1999), but the Bureau of Labor Statistics (BLS) does not expect to use it in the Producer Price and Productivity Indexes until 2004.[2] Statistics Canada has already begun implementing NAICS and expects to have completed the conversion early in the next century. Mexico expects to collect data on a NAICS basis beginning with the reference year 1998.

In the meantime, comparisons of the industries of the three NAFTA countries will have to be based on a matching of the existing industry classifications. Matching the industry classifications, particularly at the 3- and 4-digit levels, can be very difficult and complex,[3] but alignment of industries at the 2-digit level is less difficult.

The *Handbook*'s industry chapters are organized on the basis of the U.S. 2-digit industry classifications (in a few cases several 2-digit industries are combined): Canadian and Mexican industries and subindustries are aligned for comparison. By and large, the U.S. and Canadian industries can be easily aligned at the 2-digit level, but alignment of the Mexican system requires that some industry categories be separated and assigned to different Canadian-U.S. 2-digit categories. The Handbook editors have made diligent efforts to match the industries of Canada, Mexico, and the United States correctly, but in some cases the disparity is too great to overcome. All 3- and 4-digit industries included for each nation are identified in Tables 1, 7, and 9.

Establishments and Enterprises

The establishment is the primary unit used in the collection of much economic data. The official definition of an establishment is: "an economic unit, generally at a single physical location, where business is conducted or where services of industrial operations are performed; for example, a factory, mill, store, hotel, movie theater, mine, farm, ranch, bank, rail-

---

[1] The U.S. Census Bureau tabulates some information at greater levels of detail (5- and 7-digit), but this level of detail is not used in the Handbook.

[2] See Appendix B for a more detailed discussion of NAICS.

[3] An example of a meticulous effort to make such matches at the lowest level of classification is the "International Concordance between the Industrial Classifications of the United Nations and Canada, the European Union, and the United States," Office of Management and Budget, et al, July 1994.

road depot, airline terminal, sales office, warehouse, or central administrative office."[4] The industrial classifications described earlier are applied to establishments and data collected are identified by industry. In some cases, distinct and separate economic activities are performed at the same physical location, in which case two or more "establishments" may be identified and different classification codes applied.

While employment and shipments can be collected at the establishment level and tabulated by specific 4-digit industry, financial and some other data are only available at the enterprise level because enterprises operating in more than one industry cannot fully separate certain accounting values, such as profits made and certain expenses incurred, at the establishment level. Although financial data thus are not perfectly classified, imperfect financial data are preferable to no financial data at all.

Industry and Product Data

For each manufacturing industry, there are two output classifications: "industry shipments" (the total of all products produced in industry establishments) and "product shipments" (the total of specific products classified as primary to the industry). Shipments data are collected at the establishment, rather than the company level, since establishments often produce items classified in more than one industry. For example, 80 percent of a factory's production might consist of motor vehicle parts with the remaining 20 percent aircraft parts. For industry shipment data, the factory would be classified according to its principal products, so all data for the factory (shipments, hourly earnings, etc.) would be classified as Motor Vehicle Parts and Accessories (SIC 3714) under Motor Vehicles and Motor Vehicle Equipment (SIC 371). For product shipments, the 80 percent that is motor vehicle parts would be charged to SIC 3714 and the 20 percent that is aircraft parts would be charged to Aircraft Parts and Auxiliary Equipment, n.e.c.[5] (SIC 3728).

Growth Rates

Growth rates are useful summary measures for many time series, including revenues, employment, shipments, wages and profits. A growth rate answers the question: Given the starting value, at what annual percent rate would the variable have grown each year to achieve the ending value? Growth rates are valuable because they can be used to compare growth between different variables, such as shipments and employment, and, if care is taken, between like series of different lengths. For example, employment growth during one period of expansion may be compared with that of similar periods of expansion with different lengths.[6] In the *Handbook*, annual rates are calculated as compound annual growth rates, the standard practice for economic time series.

STANDARD FIGURES

Most chapters contain four standard figures (charts). Two of them (Figures 2 and 4) are based on indexes in which 1993 is the base year; i.e., 1993 = 100. In addition, many other indexes in the tables have been adjusted to make 1993 equal 100. The editors chose 1993 as the base year because it was the last year before the implementation of NAFTA; it was not a peak or a trough year in Canada, the United States, or Mexico; and detailed data are available for that year in all three countries (in particular, the Mexican Censos Economicos provides detailed industry data for that year). Sample figures are included near the sections that describe them.

---

[4] *Standard Industrial Classification Manual*, Executive Office of the President, Office of Management and Budget (OMB), Washington, DC, U.S. Government Printing Office, 1988.

[5] Not elsewhere classified.

[6] In these cases, great care must be taken in selecting end-points in order to be certain the two periods are comparable.

Figure 1 is a map of the United States showing the percent of total industry employment located in each of eight geographic regions. The employment percentages are based on 1995 data from the Bureau of Economic Analysis (BEA), and the regions shown are as defined by BEA, except that The *Handbook* uses the term "Mid-Atlantic" for the region that BEA calls the "Mideast."

The regions vary in population and employment size, with the Southeast being the largest in both categories. The regions, their shares of U.S. employment, and the states they include are shown below:

REGION	EMPLOYMENT SHARE (PERCENT)	STATES INCLUDED
New England	5.4	Connecticut, Maine, Massachusetts, New Hampshire, Rhode Island, Vermont
Mid-Atlantic	16.5	Delaware, District of Columbia, Maryland, New Jersey, New York, Pennsylvania
Great Lakes	16.7	Illinois, Indiana, Michigan, Ohio, Wisconsin
Plains	7.8	Iowa, Kansas, Minnesota, Missouri, Nebraska, North Dakota, South Dakota
Southeast	23.7	Alabama, Arkansas, Florida, Georgia, Kentucky, Louisiana, Mississippi, North Carolina, South Carolina, Tennessee, Virginia, West Virginia
Southwest	10.4	Arizona, New Mexico, Oklahoma, Texas
Rocky Mountain	3.4	Colorado, Idaho, Montana, Utah, Wyoming
Pacific	16.1	Alaska, California, Hawaii, Nevada, Oregon, Washington

The distribution of employment in each industry should be interpreted with this distribution of total employment in mind. Thus, the fact that the Southeast accounts for 24 percent of employment in rubber and plastic products indicates only that the Southeast has a proportionate share of industry employment, while the Southeast's 12 percent share of employment in instruments indicates a less than proportionate share, even though it exceeds the share of four other regions.

FIGURE 1

TOTAL U.S. EMPLOYMENT

Percent distribution by region, 1995

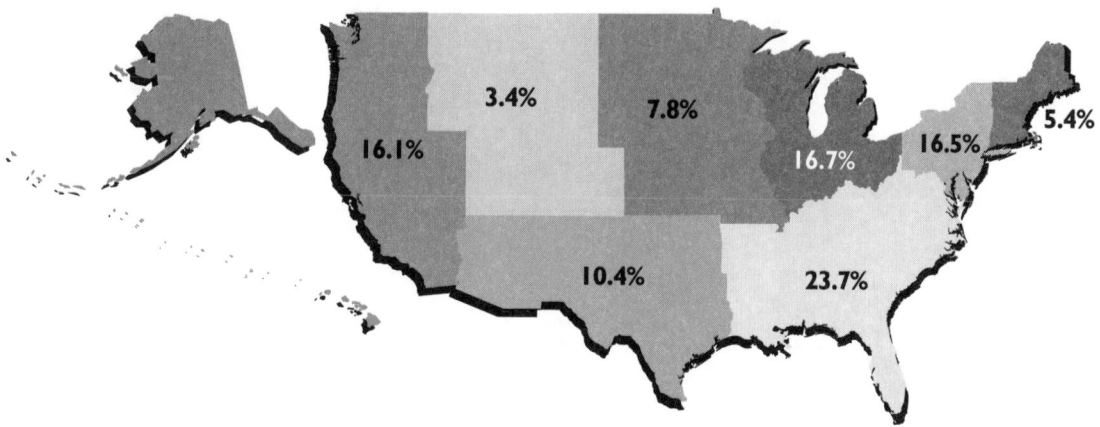

Source: U.S. Department of Commerce, Bureau of Economic Analysis.

Figure 2 is a bar graph comparing real output and employment from 1987 through 1996, or the portion of that period for which suitable data are available for a particular industry. For manufacturing, the output measure is industry shipments adjusted for inflation. Outside manufacturing, the output measure is receipts, revenue, or, in some cases, gross domestic product originating in that industry. In all cases the output measures have been adjusted for inflation. The notes below about Table 3 provide additional detail on the output measures available for each industry.

The employment data are total payroll employment as published by the Bureau of Labor Statistics. Both the output and employment measures have been converted to indexes based on 1993=100.

FIGURE 2

U.S. EMPLOYMENT AND SHIPMENTS, CHEMICALS AND ALLIED PRODUCTS

Total payroll employment and manufacturers' inflation-adjusted shipments

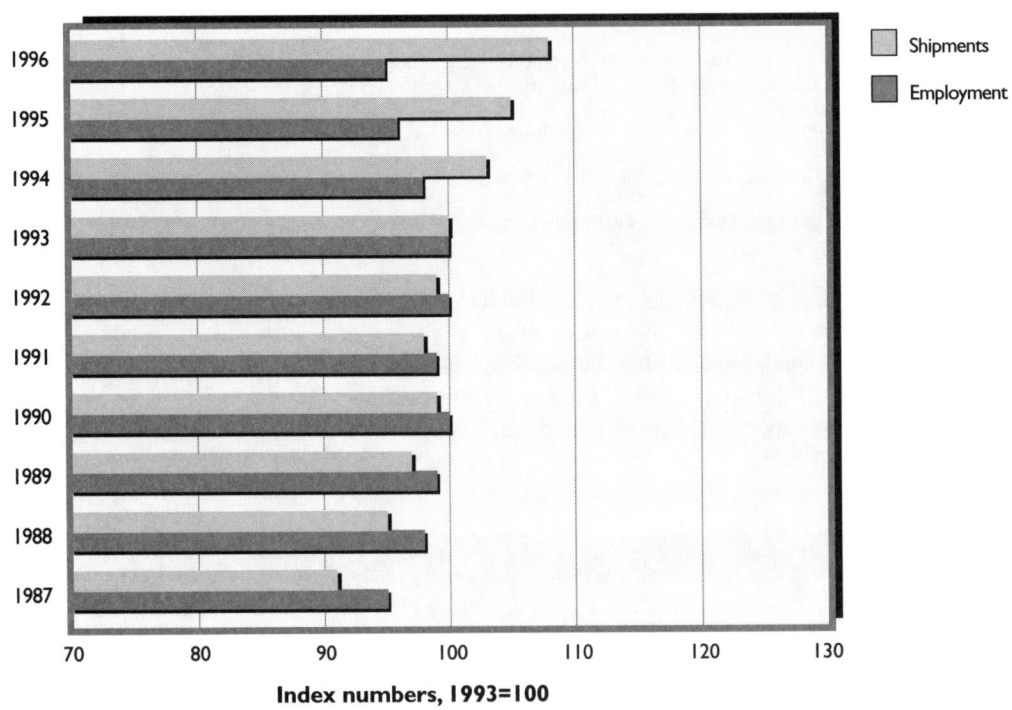

Index numbers, 1993=100

Source: U.S. Bureau of Labor Statistics, U.S. Department of Commerce, and estimates by the editors.

Figure 3 shows the 1995 incidence of nonfatal injuries and illnesses per 100 workers. The data are from the Bureau of Labor Statistics. A bar representing the industry is compared to a line representing the private economy as a whole and, for industries within manufacturing, to a second line representing the average for manufacturing as a whole. The injury and illness rate may vary widely among the components of a 2-digit industry. The transportation equipment industry is a particularly striking example. The average rate for the industry as a whole is 18.6 cases per hundred, but rates for the component 3-digit industries range from 4.0 in missiles and space vehicles to 27.3 in ships and boats.

FIGURE 3

U.S. OCCUPATIONAL INJURY AND ILLNESS RATES:

CHEMICALS AND ALLIED PRODUCTS, 1995

Incidence of nonfatal injuries and illnesses per 100 full-time workers

In 1995, the chemical industry averaged 5.5 cases of nonfatal occupational illnesses and injuries per 100 workers, one of the lowest levels in manufacturing.

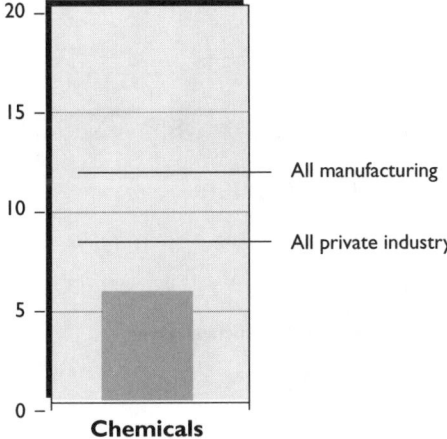

Source: U.S. Bureau of Labor Statistics.

Figure 4 is a bar graph comparing corporate operating income with total production worker earnings in the same industry (or industries) for 1988 through 1996. The corporate operating income is taken from the Quarterly Financial Reports published by the U.S. Bureau of the Census. Complete and separate data for all 2-digit industries are not available. In some cases, the data for two industries (e.g., food and beverages and tobacco) are available only in combination; in some cases (e.g., lumber and wood products) data are available only beginning with 1992; and in some cases, data for a particular industry are not available at all. The notes below about Table 6 provide additional information about the data from the Quarterly Financial Reports. Total production worker earnings have been estimated by multiplying average weekly earnings of production workers by the number of production workers. Both of these data series are from the U.S. Bureau of Labor Statistics and both are shown in Table 4. The notes below about Table 4 provide background information about these data. Both corporate operating income and production worker earnings have been converted to indexes based on 1993=100.

In interpreting this figure, it should be kept in mind that corporate earnings are a residual and tend to be both more volatile and more sensitive to the business cycle than are the earnings of production workers. Corporate earnings, in fact, can be negative (losses), whereas earnings of production workers are variable, but never negative.

FIGURE 4

U.S. CORPORATE INCOME AND WORKER EARNINGS: CHEMICALS AND ALLIED PRODUCTS

Corporate operating income and aggregate production worker earnings

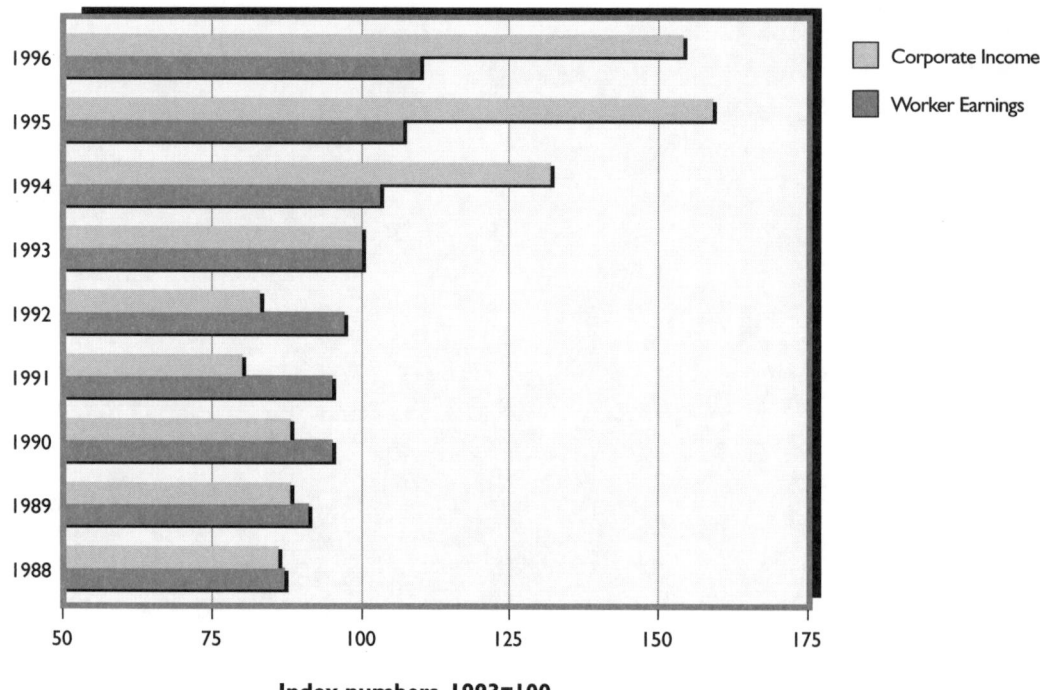

Index numbers, 1993=100

Source: U.S. Bureau of Labor Statistics, U.S. Bureau of the Census, and estimates by the editors.

STANDARD TABLES

In general, much more detailed information is available for manufacturing industries than for other industries. For example, "shipments" is a standard measure of output for manufacturing industries that is not available for nonmanufacturing. "Revenues" or "sales" is the measure usually associated with nonmanufacturing, particularly trade and services. Revenues, sales, and shipments are not generally comparable across industries, because of the wide variability in the value of purchased materials and services incorporated therein.

The following sections describe the 11 standard tables and include samples of each table. The columns or rows are **numbered** in both the **descriptions** and the **sample tables** to facilitate comparisons. Some of the standard tables used in the *Handbook* are different for manufacturing and nonmanufacturing industries, and the key differences are noted.

Table 1: United States: Component Industries. . .

Table 1 completes the definition of the chapter industry (2-digit) by listing all its component 3- and 4-digit subindustries. For each subindustry, it shows the number of establishments, the value of shipments, the percent of total shipments accounted for by the four largest companies, value added, new capital expenditures, employment, and payroll. Except for the chapters on agriculture and on health services, all data for Table 1 are from the 1992 Economic Censuses: the Censuses of Manufacturing; Mining; Construction; Retail Trade; Wholesale Trade; Finance, Insurance, and Real Estate; or Services, as appropriate. In most cases these are the most recent data providing the level of detail shown, and the use of the common base year 1992 facilitates comparisons across industries. Note, however, that Census Bureau employment data from Table 1 are not directly comparable to those in Table 2, which are from the Bureau of Labor Statistics (BLS), because the Census and BLS use different classification schemes for establishments and parts thereof.[7]

TABLE 1

UNITED STATES: COMPONENT INDUSTRIES OF CHEMICALS AND ALLIED PRODUCTS (SIC 28), 1992

(Monetary values in millions of U.S. dollars)

❶ INDUSTRY	❷ SIC	❸ ESTABLISH-MENTS	❹ SHIPMENTS VALUE	❺ PERCENT BY 4 LARGEST COMPANIES	❻ VALUE ADDED BY MANUFACTURE	❼ NEW CAPITAL EXPENDI-TURES	❽ EMPLOY-MENT[1]	❾ PAYROLL
CHEMICALS AND ALLIED PRODUCTS	28	12,004	$305,420.1	....	$164,346.2	$16,380.9	848,600	$32,501.9
Industrial inorganic chemicals	281	1,422	27,331.4	....	16,723.7	1,553.2	103,400	4,214.4
Alkalies and chlorine	2812	51	2,786.9	75	1,408.1	176.2	8,000	353.3
Industrial gases	2813	592	3,095.7	78	2,076.2	146.3	7,700	261.8
Inorganic pigments	2816	89	3,320.0	69	2,027.4	509.1	8,700	333.7
Industrial inorganic chemicals, n.e.c.	2819	690	18,128.9	39	11,212.0	721.6	78,900	3,265.7

The following descriptions correspond with the numbered columns shown here in Sample Table 1.

---

[7] The Census Bureau assigns establishments to industries based on their classification of "principal" products; they also classify some units—e.g., accounting, sales, etc.—at the 2-digit level only. By law, because of privacy concerns, BLS does not have access to the Census list and must prepare its own in cooperation with state authorities. As a result, figures for employment, especially at the 3- and 4-digit levels, can be very different. Users are cautioned not to mix these two data series.

Columns

1. *Industry*: The subindustry name (in some cases slightly modified for brevity and clarity) from the 1987 standard industrial classification.[8] Many of these names will change as the North American Industry Classification System (NAICS) replaces the SIC system.[9]

2. *SIC:* The numeric SIC code, again from the 1987 SIC Manual, corresponding to the industry name.

3. *Establishments:* The number of establishments in the industry.

4. *Value of Shipments, Sales, or Revenues:* The value of shipments, sales, or revenues for the industry in millions of U.S. dollars. The shipments, sales, or revenue values are annual totals covering all establishments in business at any time during the year. For construction, net value of construction is shown rather than gross revenue. For manufacturing, aggregate shipments values include large amounts of duplication, since the products of some industries are used as materials by others. For services, the data do not include the receipts of firms not subject to Federal tax (i.e. not-for-profit service providers).

5. *Percent of shipments by 4 largest companies:* The percent of shipments accounted for by the four largest companies in the industry is a frequently used measure of the concentration of economic power in an industry. These data are not shown for mining, construction, agriculture, or health services.

6. *Value added by industry:* The value (in millions of U.S. dollars) of shipments less purchased intermediate materials, supplies, containers, fuel, electricity, and contract work, as calculated by the Census Bureau. This item is shown only for manufacturing, mining, and construction. It is related but not identical to "gross product originating" calculated by the Bureau of Economic Analysis and presented in a later table, the principal difference being that "gross product originating" also excludes purchased services, such as advertising and computer services, that cannot be attributed easily at the establishment level. Gross product originating is equivalent, in concept, to the sum of employee compensation, capital compensation (net interest paid and profits), depreciation, and indirect business taxes.

7. *New capital expenditures:* The value of expenditures for new capital goods for the industry in millions of U.S. dollars. They do not include land but do include equipment, buildings, and improvements. This item is shown only for manufacturing, mining, and construction.

8. *Employment:* For manufacturing and mining, the employment data are the average of production worker employment at 4 times during the year (the pay periods including the 12th of March, May, August, and November) plus the number of other employees in mid-March. Employees of auxiliary units of multi-establishment manufacturing firms, such as administrative offices and R&D facilities, are not included. For construction, the data are the average of all employees on the payroll during the pay periods including the 12th of March, May, August, and November. For the other non-manufacturing industries, employment is the total number of payroll employees during the pay period including March 12th.

9. *Payroll:* The annual payroll for the industry in millions of U.S. dollars. It includes wages, salaries, bonuses, and other cash and in-kind labor payments and in general corresponds to the definition used for calculating Federal withholding tax. It does not include "supplemental" labor costs such as the employer's share of payroll taxes, pension costs, insurance premiums, or workers' compensation. As with employment, auxilary establishments are not included.

---

[8] OMB, Op. Cit.

[9] See Appendix B, "The North American Industry Classification System"

Table 2: U.S. Employment and Earnings. . .

Table 2 provides a snapshot of employment in the chapter industry and its subindustries. It is based on Bureau of Labor Statistics (BLS) estimates and contains data for almost all 3-digit subindustries plus some important 4-digit industries for which data are available.[10] Table 2 shows the number of persons employed, the percent of total employment in the 2-digit industry accounted for by the 3- or 4-digit industry, the average hourly earnings of production or nonsupervisory workers, and the BLS "moderate" projection of employment in 2005.[11] There are no differences in the table between manufacturing and nonmanufacturing industries. As noted earlier, data in Tables 1 and 2 are not comparable because they are based on different classification schemes.

TABLE 2

U.S. EMPLOYMENT AND EARNINGS: CHEMICALS AND ALLIED PRODUCTS

❶ INDUSTRY	❷ SIC	1993 ❸ EMPLOYMENT[1] ❹		❺ AVERAGE HOURLY EARNINGS (U.S. DOLLARS)[2]	2005 ❻ PROJECTED EMPLOYMENT[3]
		NUMBER OF PERSONS	PERCENT OF INDUSTRY TOTAL		
CHEMICALS AND ALLIED PRODUCTS	28	1,080,500	100.0	$14.82	1,067,000
Industrial inorganic chemicals	281	135,000	12.5	16.37	122,170
Industrial inorganic chemicals, n.e.c.	2819	87,000	8.1	16.83	....
Plastics materials and synthetics	282	166,700	15.4	15.22	142,500
Plastics materials and resins	2821	79,900	7.4	16.47	....
Organic fibers, noncellulosic	2824	56,900	5.3	13.98	....

The numbered columns in Sample Table 2 correspond with the numbered descriptions that follow.

Columns

1 Industry: The subindustry name (in some cases slightly modified for brevity and clarity) from the 1987 Standard Industrial Classification Manual (SIC).

2. SIC: The numeric SIC code, from the 1987 SIC Manual, corresponding to the name.

3. Employment: The monthly average number of persons employed in the subindustry in 1993 as estimated by BLS. This is "total payroll employment" and so covers all paid employees from company officers to part-time production workers.

4. Percent of industry total: The percent of total employment for the chapter industry accounted for in 1993 by the 3- or 4-digit industry shown.

5. Average hourly earnings: The average earnings per hour paid for production or nonsupervisory workers in 1993 in the 3- or 4-digit industry in U.S. dollars. See the notes below about Table 4 for additional information.

6. Projected employment: The number of persons projected by the BLS to be employed in the 3- or 4-digit industry in 2005.

---

[10] The year 1993 was chosen for this table in order to make comparisons with Canadian and Mexican data easier; Table 1 contains data from the 1992 economic censuses, which occur every 5 years. BLS does not prepare estimates for all 4-digit industries. Table 2 contains all industries covered by BLS.

[11] For an explanation of the BLS projections, see "Table 5" in this section.

Table 3: U.S. Output, Investment, and Prices. . .

Table 3 shows recent trends in the industry's output and investment, and in the prices of its products for the years 1987 to 1996. Manufacturing output is measured as both industry shipments and product shipments (shown in current and constant dollars.) For nonmanufacturing industries, revenues or sales are the basic available measure, although there are a few industry-specific measures, such as housing starts. The index of industrial production (a measure provided by the Federal Reserve Board) is available for all manufacturing industries, mining, and utilities. Gross domestic product is also shown in current and constant dollars for all major industries. The Producer Price Index, prepared by BLS, shows prices for many industries; for others, the Implicit Price Deflator, prepared by BEA, is available.

TABLE 3

U.S. OUTPUT, INVESTMENT, AND PRICES: CHEMICALS AND ALLIED PRODUCTS

(Millions of U.S. dollars, except as noted)

	1987	1988	1989	1990	1991	1992	1993	1994	1995	1996	GROWTH RATE 1987-1996[1]
VALUE OF SHIPMENTS:											
BY INDUSTRY:											
❶ Current dollars	229,546	261,238	283,196	292,803	298,544	305,420	314,907	333,905	362,127	376,104	5.64
❷ Constant 1992 dollars	279,866	292,278	299,184	305,527	302,217	305,420	307,610	317,570	323,643	330,856	1.88
BY PRODUCT:											
❸ Current dollars	214,618	244,515	260,649	268,505	268,935	282,242	292,416	309,592	338,065	351,113	5.62
❹ Constant 1992 dollars	259,639	271,412	273,211	278,547	271,466	282,242	285,755	294,562	301,340	308,056	1.92
OTHER OUTPUT MEASURES:											
❺ Industrial production, 1993=100	86.1	91.3	94.2	96.3	95.4	99.0	100.0	103.1	105.4	107.8	2.53
Gross domestic product:											
❻ Current dollars	85,112	96,982	104,922	110,348	114,148	120,457	126,492	132,375	....	....	....
❼ Percent of total GDP	1.8	1.9	1.9	1.9	1.9	1.9	1.9	1.9	....	....	....
❽ Rank in manufacturing	3	3	3	2	1	1	1	1	....	....	....
❾ Chained (1992) dollars	110,397	110,440	111,401	117,260	115,814	120,457	122,100	125,128	....	....	....
INVESTMENT-RELATED MEASURES:											
❿ Capacity utilization, percent	81.3	84.0	83.7	83.0	80.1	80.3	78.8	79.1	79.1	78.6	....
⓫ New capital expenditures	8,711	11,006	13,775	15,645	16,599	16,381	15,690	15,411	17,627	....	....
⓬ Research and development spending	9,445	10,828	11,943	13,168	14,439	15,091	16,658	16,559	....	....	....
⓭ Producer prices, 1993=100[2]	81.5	88.8	94.1	95.2	97.8	98.9	100.0	102.2	112.8	114.6	3.86

1. Compound annual growth rate.

2. Prices received by domestic producers.

Sources: Shipments and new capital expenditures: U.S. Department of Commerce for 1987-1995, editor's estimates for constant dollar data for 1987-88 and all shipments data for 1996; Industrial production and capacity utilization: Federal Reserve Board of Governors; GDP: Bureau of Economic Analysis; Research and development spending: National Science Foundation; Producer prices: Bureau of Labor Statistics.

Columns

The first column of Table 3 contains the description of the row. The next 10 columns are for the years 1987 to 1996, and the last column shows the compound annual rate of growth over the years shown. Descriptions of the rows follow:

Rows

Manufacturing

Value of shipments:

By *industry*:

1. *Current dollars*: The current dollar value of all shipments made from establishments classified in the specified industry. (See the discussion under "Industry and Product Data" of industry versus product shipments.)

2 *Constant 1992 dollars*: A calculation of the value of industry shipments after adjustment for price changes, with 1992 as the base year.

By *product*:

3. *Current dollars*: The current dollar value of shipments of products classified in the industry, wherever made.

4. *Constant 1992 dollars*: The inflation-adjusted value of product shipments, based on 1992 dollars.

Sources and estimating proceedures: Where available, current and constant dollar estimates for both industry and product shipments were obtained from the International Trade Administration, U.S. Department of Commerce (ITA). For years for which ITA estimates were not available, the current dollar shipments series were extended by applying the percent changes in Bureau of the Census data to the beginning or ending years of the ITA series, as appropriate. Constant dollar estimates, where not available from ITA, were obtained using the Producer Price Index for the industry to extend the deflator.

Other output measures:

5. *Industrial production* (1993=100): The index of industrial production prepared by the Federal Reserve Board (if available.) The Board has estimated physical output for many major industries for many years in the form of an index. The Board publishes its index as 1992 =100, but the index has been converted to 1993=100 for this book in order to facilitate comparison with Canadian and Mexican data.

Gross domestic product: Rows 6 through 9 contain aspects of GDP by industry[12]—a standard measure prepared by BEA of an industry's contribution to the economy. It is the sum of payrolls and supplemental labor costs (moneys paid for labor input), profits and interest, capital consumption allowances, and indirect taxes.[13] The basic concept of this measure is that it eliminates double counting. For example, the value of bread sold includes the farmer's wheat, the miner's salt, the trucker's charge for transportation, and the utility company's charge for gas and electricity, as well as the baker's wages and profit. "Gross product originating" eliminates those "outside" inputs so that "GDP by industry" for all industries adds up to total national GDP.

---

[12] Also called, "gross product originating."

[13] Indirect taxes are included because they are a part of the value of products and services that consumers pay for that is not an input from another industry.

6. *Current dollars*: The industry's GDP in current dollars.

7. *Percent of total GDP*: The percent of national current dollar GDP accounted for by the industry.

8. *Rank in manufacturing*: The industry's rank within manufacturing based on current dollar GDP.

9. Chained (1992) dollars: GDP for the industry in constant (chained) 1992 dollars.[14]

Investment-related measures:

10. Capacity utilization, percent: The percent of the industry's physical plant capacity being utilized, as measured by the Federal Reserve Board. This measure is designed to be used in conjunction with the Index of Industrial Production shown above. It is a measure of utilization of sustainable practical capacity and is considered by many to be a measure of both the pressure on prices and the need for investment.

11. New capital expenditures: The Census Bureau's estimates of expenditures in the industry for new capital purchases (equipment and buildings but not land.) These data are not available for all industries.

12. Research and development spending: National Science Foundation estimates of industry spending for research and development. Federally-supported industry R&D spending is not included.

13. Producer Prices: The Producer Price Index from BLS. The PPI measures average changes in the selling prices received by domestic producers for their output. Producer Price Indexes are among the nation's oldest continuous statistics (first published in 1902) and were called the Wholesale Price Indexes until 1978. However, producer prices for the net output of industries, as shown in the Handbook, typically are available only from the mid-1980s. The PPI's are converted to 1993=100 for this book.

Nonmanufacturing

Revenues or sales: For nonmanufacturing, those measures of activity that are available are shown. In general these include revenues (sales, receipts, etc.). In most cases, GDP originating is available and shown. In others, there are special measures of activity; for example, in finance, assets, loans and leases, and deposits are useful measures. For measures of price and price change, the Implicit Price Deflator prepared by BEA or a relevant Consumer Price Index is shown for some industries for which Producer Price Indexes are not available. For wholesale and retail trade the Implicit Price Deflators for nonfarm inventories are used as proxies for deflators for sales.

---

[14] See *Survey of Current Business*, May 1997, pp. 58-68, for an explanation of chained constant dollar measures.

Table 4: U.S. Employment, Hours and Earnings. . .

Table 4 contains employment, hours, and average earnings for the years 1987 to 1996 for the 2-digit industries, plus the annual rate of growth over the 1987 to 1996 period.

TABLE 4

U.S. EMPLOYMENT, HOURS, AND EARNINGS: CHEMICALS AND ALLIED PRODUCTS

(Monetary values in U.S. dollars)

	1987	1988	1989	1990	1991	1992	1993	1994	1995	1996	CHANGE[1]
NUMBER OF EMPLOYEES, IN THOUSANDS:											
① Total	1,025	1,057	1,074	1,086	1,076	1,084	1,081	1,057	1,038	1,032	0.08
② Production workers	575	596	603	600	580	567	573	578	580	575	0.01
③ Percent of total	56.1	56.4	56.2	55.2	53.9	52.3	53.0	54.6	55.9	55.7	....
④ Women	294	308	318	328	327	335	339	334	330	327	1.19
⑤ Percent of total	28.7	29.1	29.6	30.2	30.4	30.9	31.4	31.6	31.8	31.7	....
HOURS AND EARNINGS OF PRODUCTION WORKERS:											
AVERAGE HOURLY EARNINGS[2]											
⑥ Current dollars	12.37	12.71	13.09	13.54	14.04	14.51	14.82	15.13	15.62	16.17	3.02
⑦ 1992 dollars[3]	15.20	15.01	14.76	14.51	14.44	14.51	14.42	14.35	14.41	14.50	-0.52
⑧ Average weekly hours	42.3	42.2	42.4	42.6	42.9	43.1	43.1	43.2	43.2	43.2	0.23
⑨ Average weekly earnings, current U.S. dollars	523.25	536.36	555.02	576.80	602.32	625.38	638.74	653.62	674.78	698.54	3.26

1. Compound annual growth rate, 1987-1996.

2. Including overtime.

3. Converted to 1992 dollars using Consumer Price Index for Urban Wage Earners and Clerical Workers.

Source: Bureau of Labor Statistics.

Columns: The first column of Table 4 contains the description of the row. The remaining columns are the years 1987 to 1996 and the last column shows the compound annual rate of growth over the period.

Rows

Number of employees, in thousands:

1. *Total:* The monthly average number of persons (in thousands) employed in the industry, as reported by BLS. For each month, BLS counts all persons who received pay for any part of the payroll period including the 12th of the month. This is "total payroll employment" and so covers all paid employees, from company officers to part-time production workers. Note that these are "wage and salary" workers. Owners, proprietors, unpaid family workers, and self-employed persons not on the payroll are not included. For example, "total employment" for hospitals would not include physicians or technicians who are compensated by fee-for-service, rather than by wages or salaries, and may not include personnel hired through temporary help and similar contracting organizations. (Employment at such personnel supply services is included in the "Business Services" industry.)

2. *Production or nonsupervisory workers:* Total full and part-time production workers in the industry in thousands. Production workers in mining, manufacturing, and construction are defined as working supervisors and nonsupervisory workers engaged in production. In other industries, working supervisors and all nonsupervisory employees are included.

3. *Percent of total:* Production or nonsupervisory workers as a percent of total employment. Note that this ratio usually changes slowly if at all. If this percentage is increasing, it may indicate that the number of technical and supervisory employees is decreasing in proportion to the total and so suggest that "middle management" jobs are in decline in the industry.

4. *Women workers:* Total full and part-time women workers, including production workers and others.

5. *Percent of total:* Women workers as a percent of total employees in the industry. Again, this figure changes slowly if at all.

Hours and earnings of production or nonsupervisory workers:

Average hourly earnings:

6. *Current dollar:* The average hourly earnings of production workers calculated as total annual wages (and other monetary compensation) divided by annual hours paid. Overtime hours and wages are included, as are late-shift or piece-work premiums, but not irregular bonuses, other special payments, or supplemental labor costs such as the employer share of payroll taxes and the costs of "fringe benefits".

7. *1992 dollars:* Average hourly earnings in "constant 1992 dollars." These constant wages are calculated from the current dollars in the preceding row using the national "All City Urban Wage & Clerical Workers Consumer Price Index" (CPI-W), prepared by the BLS. This standard procedure is less than perfect since workers for any particular industry are not uniformly distributed over the country, but are often concentrated in various regions, as is shown in Figure 1. A more accurate method would be to weight the CPI for specific regions by the number of employees of the industry in that region. However, the difference in most cases is probably quite small.

8. *Average weekly hours:* Average weekly hours for which pay was received, which may not be the same as "scheduled" or "regular" hours. Hours paid include overtime and paid vacations and holidays.

9. *Average weekly earnings:* Weekly earnings of production workers in current dollars.

Table 5: U.S. Employment Projections by Major Occupational Group. . .

Table 5 projects growth in employment to the year 2005 for the 2-digit industries by major occupational classifications. Three projections are shown for each classification corresponding to a range of demographic and economic possibilities—low, moderate, and high. Employment by occupation and the percent of total employment for the industry in that occupation are shown for 1994 for comparison. These projections are prepared by the Employment Projections Division of the Bureau of Labor Statistics.

All three projections use the same underlying assumptions about population birth and death rates, which come from the Census Bureau's middle-growth population projections. However, the high economic growth projection assumes higher net immigration and therefore a greater total population and potential labor force than in the other two employment projections. The supplementary explanation at the end of this section gives further details.

Table 5 has the same format for all industries. The columns are described in the following section.

TABLE 5

U.S. EMPLOYMENT PROJECTIONS BY MAJOR OCCUPATIONAL GROUP: CHEMICALS AND ALLIED PRODUCTS

① OCCUPATION	② 1994 NUMBER OF EMPLOYEES	③ PERCENT OF INDUSTRY TOTAL	PROJECTIONS, 2005			⑦ PERCENT OF INDUSTRY TOTAL, MODERATE PROJECTIONS
			④ NUMBER OF EMPLOYEES LOW	⑤ MODERATE	⑥ HIGH	
Total, all occupations	1,060,700	100.0	1,032,100	1,067,000	1,089,400	100.0
Executive, administrative, and managerial	138,875	13.1	141,161	145,955	149,123	13.7
Professional specialties	129,314	12.2	151,830	157,495	161,231	14.8
Technicians and related support	67,500	6.4	66,561	68,944	70,470	6.5
Marketing and sales	47,247	4.5	47,380	49,108	50,371	4.6
Administrative support including clerical	150,142	14.2	133,271	137,681	140,668	12.9
Service	18,883	1.8	17,070	17,673	18,071	1.7
Agriculture, forestry, and fisheries occupations	2,139	0.2	2,214	2,319	2,392	0.2
Precision production, craft, and repair	202,596	19.1	190,100	196,242	199,645	18.4
Operators, fabricators, assemblers	304,003	28.7	282,511	291,584	297,429	27.3

Source: Bureau of Labor Statistics, November 1995.

Columns

1. *Occupation:* The names of nine major occupational groupings and the total for all occupations in the specified industry.

1994:

2. *Number of employees:* 1994 employment in the industry, by occupational group, as estimated at the time the projections were made. These figures may differ from the latest 1994 numbers for the industry shown in Table 4.

3. *Percent of industry total:* The percent of total employment in the industry for each occupational group.

Projections, 2005:

Number of employees:

4. *Low:* Projected employment for the major occupational groups in the year 2005, based on the low growth assumptions.

5. *Moderate:* Projected employment based on the moderate growth assumptions.

6. *High:* Projected employment based on the high growth assumptions.

7. *Percent of industry's total:* Each occupational group's percentage share of total employment projected for 2005 under the moderate assumptions.

Table 6: U.S. Corporate Income and Assets. . .

Table 6 provides detailed financial data for the industry. These data are a subset of the Census Bureau's "Quarterly Financial Report for Manufacturing Corporations."

It is important to note that these data are collected and tabulated on an "enterprise" (or "company") basis. That is, each reporting corporation is classified by 2-digit industry and its results are incorporated into the summary figures for that industry. It is not at all unusual for a single enterprise to have establishments (plants or branches) that make products defined as those from several different industries.[15] For example, the U.S. Steel Corporation bought the Marathon Oil Company some years ago and became the USX Corporation. How should we classify its financial report? We could classify it in SIC 33, Primary Metals, or perhaps, SIC13, Oil and Gas Extraction, or SIC 29, Petroleum Refining and related industries, or

TABLE 6

U.S. CORPORATE INCOME AND ASSETS: CHEMICALS AND ALLIED PRODUCTS

(Monetary values in millions of U.S. dollars)

INCOME AND EXPENSES	1988	1989	1990	1991	1992	1993	1994	1995	1996	CHANGE OR AVERAGE[1]
1 Sales and receipts	261,616	278,300	287,568	297,841	315,534	325,074	357,581	397,699	415,863	5.96
2 Depreciation and amortization	(11,027)	(12,104)	(12,947)	(13,689)	(14,783)	(15,300)	(16,155)	(17,107)	(17,733)	6.12
3 Other operating costs	(225,361)	(240,436)	(249,029)	(260,766)	(276,583)	(280,621)	(302,822)	(334,130)	(353,265)	5.78
4 Income from operations	25,229	25,759	25,591	23,386	24,166	29,152	38,602	46,462	44,867	7.46
5 Nonoperating income (expenditures)	8,321	8,130	7,236	4,575	(7,350)	(8,169)	2,537	3,868	13,057	....
6 Income before taxes	33,551	33,889	32,826	27,961	16,818	20,983	41,139	50,332	57,924	7.06
7 Income after taxes	23,651	24,523	23,393	19,997	12,996	15,550	30,447	36,878	45,300	8.46
8 Cash dividends	9,835	10,846	13,422	12,478	14,204	14,673	15,316	20,544	19,960	9.25
9 Income retained in business	13,816	13,677	9,972	7,520	(1,208)	877	15,131	16,334	25,341	7.88
10 Direct credits (charges)	(1,580)	(8,659)	(2,197)	(4,254)	(4,714)	(2,980)	(5,594)	(1,518)	(18,686)	....
11 Ending retained earnings	92,072	96,932	102,074	104,835	100,435	98,255	103,591	121,352	125,652	3.96
ASSETS, END OF YEAR:										
12 Total	277,582	293,317	325,370	357,665	385,374	418,285	462,321	516,968	537,221	8.60
13 Accounts receivable	37,614	39,103	41,260	41,421	42,361	44,254	49,635	53,547	55,353	4.95
14 Inventories	34,731	35,688	37,505	38,197	39,160	40,541	42,530	47,400	48,250	4.20
15 Net property, plant and equipment	92,835	100,219	114,586	129,785	141,857	147,292	156,416	164,849	163,108	7.30
RATIOS, PERCENT: INCOME TO SALES:										
16 Before tax	12.82	12.18	11.42	9.39	5.33	6.45	11.50	12.66	13.93	10.63
17 After tax	9.04	8.81	8.13	6.71	4.12	4.78	8.51	9.27	10.89	7.81
INCOME TO STOCKHOLDERS' EQUITY:										
18 Before tax	27.84	26.52	23.75	18.70	11.26	13.72	25.67	28.36	28.92	22.75
19 After tax	19.62	19.19	16.92	13.38	8.70	10.17	19.00	20.78	22.62	16.71
INCOME TO TOTAL ASSETS:										
20 Before tax	12.09	11.55	10.09	7.82	4.36	5.02	8.90	9.74	10.78	8.93
21 After tax	8.52	8.36	7.19	5.59	3.37	3.72	6.59	7.13	8.43	6.54
AS A PERCENT OF TOTAL ASSETS:										
22 Property, plant and equipment	33.44	34.17	35.22	36.29	36.81	35.21	33.83	31.89	30.36	34.14
23 Short-term debt	4.94	5.98	5.06	4.25	5.08	4.10	5.05	4.53	5.07	4.90
24 Long-term debt	21.21	22.03	23.05	23.48	21.35	20.92	21.83	21.76	20.79	21.82
25 Stockholders' equity	43.42	43.57	42.48	41.80	38.77	36.56	34.66	34.32	37.28	39.21

1. For income and asset amounts, compound annual growth rate; for ratios, average of ratios for the years shown.

Source: U.S. Bureau of the Census, Quarterly Financial Report.

Notes: Parentheses ( ) indicate negative items, e.g., net expenses, charges, or losses. Net property, plant, and equipment is net of accumulated depreciation. Because the samples used to collect the data change, retained earnings at the end of a given year will not exactly equal the previous year's retained earnings plus the current year's retained income and credits.

---

[15] See "Establishments and Enterprises" above for an explanation of this problem.

maybe SIC 55, Automotive Dealers and Gasoline Service Stations. The Census Bureau places industries in the SIC reflecting their "primary" activity[16]. Thus, the financial reports must be recognized as being not strictly comparable to the sum of the establishment data shown in Tables 2 through 4. However, financial data are of such importance to many people that they much prefer to use these data with their known faults than to have no financial data at the industry level at all.

Manufacturing

Columns

The first column gives the name of the item shown in the row. Columns 2 through 10 contain the values for the activity (in millions of U.S. dollars) for the years 1987 to 1996. Column 11 provides the compound annual rate of change from 1987 to 1996 for the income and expenses group and the assets group and averages for the ratios, described further in the following section.

Rows

Income and expenses:

1. *Sales and receipts:* The total sales and receipts reported by corporations classified in the industry.

2. *Depreciation and amortization:* The total depreciation and amortization reported.

3. *Other operating costs:* The sum of other operating costs.

4. *Income from operations:* Sales and receipts (row 1) less depreciation (row 2) and other operating costs (row 3).

5. *Nonoperating income:* Income or charges not resulting from "normal operations;" e.g., sales of assets or charges for unusual or one-time expenses, such as the expenses associated with closing a plant or branch.

6. *Income before taxes:* Income from operations (row 4) plus nonoperating income (row 5)

7. *Income after taxes:* Income before taxes (row 6) less corporate income taxes paid.

8. *Cash dividends:* The sum of cash dividends paid to stockholders.

9. *Income retained in business:* Income after taxes less cash dividends.

10. *Direct credits (charges):* Direct credits received or charges paid by the corporation. Charges are shown in parentheses.

11. *Ending retained earnings:* Cumulative earnings retained in the industry. They may not be equal to the previous year's retained earnings plus income retained and direct credits because the sample changes in most years.

Assets, end of year:

12. *Total.* Assets of the corporations in the industry at the end of the year. Note that the following 3 rows are selected from all assets and will not add to the total.

13. *Accounts receivable:* Total accounts receivable for the industry.

14. *Inventories:* The value of inventories for corporations in the industry.

---

[16] The Census Bureau follows a predetermined set of rules for classification but their actual classifications of individual companies are confidential by law. We don't know how the USX corporation, for example, is classified.

15. *Net property, plant, and equipment*: The book value of all property, plant, and equipment in the corporation.

Ratios, percent:

Income to sales: Income as a of percent of sales.

16. Before tax.

17. After tax.

Income to stockholders equity: Income as a percent of stockholders' equity.

18. Before tax.

19. After tax.

Income to total assets: Income as a percent of total assets.

20. Before tax.

21. After tax.

As a percent of total assets:

22. Property, plant and equipment.

23. Short-term debt.

24. Long-term debt.

25. Stockholders' equity.

Table 7: Canada: Component Industries. . .

Table 7 defines the chapter industry by detailing its 3- and 4-digit subindustries. All data shown are 1993 estimates from Statistics Canada. Shown are the number of establishments, employment, shipments, and average hourly earnings for the chapter industry and its subindustries. Canadian and U.S. industry classifications correspond reasonably well at the 2-digit level, but often diverge at the more detailed levels. The columns are described in the following section.

Manufacturing

Columns

1. *Industry name*: The official name of the industry and its components (some are shortened to fit the space available.)

2. CSIC: The numeric Canadian Standard Industry Classification code.

3. *Establishments*: The number of establishments in the industry and subindustries.

Employment:

4. *Number*: The number of persons employed in the subindustry in 1993.

5. *Percent of industry total*: The percent of total employment for the chapter industry account-ed for in 1993 by the 3- or 4-digit industry shown.

6. *Value of shipments*: The value of shipments for the industry and subindustries in 1993, in millions of Canadian dollars; for nonmanufacturing industries, revenues are given.

TABLE 7

CANADA: COMPONENT INDUSTRIES OF CHEMICALS AND CHEMICAL PRODUCTS (CSIC 37), 1993

(Monetary values in Canadian dollars)

❶ INDUSTRY NAME	❷ CSIC	❸ ESTABLISH- MENTS (NUMBER)	❹ EMPLOYMENT NUMBER	❺ PERCENT OF INDUSTRY TOTAL	❻ VALUE OF SHIPMENTS (MILLIONS)	❼ AVERAGE HOURLY EARNINGS[1]
CHEMICAL AND CHEMICAL PRODUCTS INDUSTRIES	37	1,248	87,453	100.0	CAN$22,609.5	CAN$17.66
Industrial chemicals, n.e.c.	371	195	16,768	19.2	6,446.1	23.24
Industrial inorganic chemicals, n.e.c.	3711	135	9,035	10.3	2,494.6	21.45
Industrial organic chemicals	3712	60	7,733	8.8	3,951.5	25.06
Agricultural chemicals	372	150	4,164	4.8	1,532.4	19.15
Chemical fertilizers	3721	15	1,693	1.9	812.6	26.44
Mixed fertilizers	3722	124	1,905	2.2	423.8	13.21
Other agricultural chemicals	3729	11	566	0.6	296.0	13.83
Plastic and synthetic resins	373	91	8,819	10.1	3,319.5	20.94
Pharmaceuticals and medicines	374	119	20,584	23.5	4,544.0	16.47
Paint and varnish	375	127	7,314	8.4	1,482.6	14.28
Soap and cleaning compounds	376	118	8,014	9.2	1,601.6	15.70
Toilet preparations	377	74	7,208	8.2	967.2	12.07
Other chemical products	379	374	14,582	16.7	2,716.2	14.90
Printing ink	3791	62	1,686	1.9	291.8	14.92
Adhesives	3792	38	1,929	2.2	309.5	14.24
Other chemical products, n.e.c.	3799	274	10,967	12.5	2,114.9	15.01

1. Including overtime.

Source: Adapted from Statistics Canada, *Manufacturing Industries of Canada* (Cat. No. 31-203).

7. *Average hourly earnings*: The average hourly earnings of production workers, calculated as total annual wages paid divided by hours paid; wages and hours include holiday, vacation, and overtime pay. Production workers include working supervisors and all nonsupervisory workers engaged in fabricating, processing, assembling, inspecting, handling, packing, warehousing, maintenance, repair, janitorial, guard services, and other services closely associated with production operations.

Nonmanufacturing

Table 7 for nonmanufacturing industries does not contain shipments, nor does it contain average hourly earnings. However, Table 8, described next, contains revenues or sales (where available) and <u>weekly</u> earnings.

Table 8: Canadian Employment and Shipments. . .

Table 8 provides detailed employment, earnings, and shipments or receipts information for the (2-digit) chapter industry. All manufacturing data are from Statistics Canada: *Manufacturing Industries of Canada* (Cat.No. 31-203); data for nonmanufacturing come from CAN-SIM, the Statistics Canada electronic data source. All monetary values are in Canadian dollars. Data for nonmanufacturing industries are more limited than those for manufacturing.

TABLE 8

CANADIAN EMPLOYMENT AND SHIPMENTS: CHEMICAL INDUSTRIES, 1987-1994

(Monetary values in Canadian dollars)

	1987	1988	1989	1990	1991	1992	1993	1994	CHANGE[1]
① All employees	89,030	93,860	95,403	94,888	91,527	91,149	87,453	84,273	-0.78
② Establishments	1,306	1,438	1,443	1,450	1,320	1,283	1,248	1,248	-0.65
③ Employees per establishment	68	65	66	65	69	71	70	68	-0.14
④ Production workers per establishment	.....	777	786	771	696	695	699	698	-1.77
PRODUCTION WORKERS:									
⑤ Total	.....	50,733	51,955	50,464	48,243	49,390	48,974	47,157	-1.21
⑥ Percent of all employees	.....	54.1	54.5	53.2	52.7	54.2	56.0	56.0	.....
⑦ Male	.....	38,985	40,087	39,345	38,013	49,390	48,974	47,157	.....
⑧ Female	.....	11,748	11,868	11,119	10,230	.....	.....	.....	.....
⑨ Percent of total production workers	.....	23.2	22.8	22.0	21.2	.....	.....	.....	.....
⑩ Average hourly earnings	.....	14.50	15.17	16.27	16.83	16.80	17.66	18.27	3.93
⑪ Average weekly earnings	.....	592.29	618.49	657.42	673.65	683.80	710.97	749.79	4.01
⑫ Average weekly hours	.....	40.9	40.8	40.4	40.0	40.7	40.3	41.1	0.08
⑬ Shipments (millions)	20,267	22,775	23,668	23,118	21,297	21,489	22,609	25,598	3.39

1. Compound annual growth rate.

Source: Adapted from Statistics Canada, *Manufacturing Industries of Canada* (Cat. No. 31-203).

Manufacturing

Columns

The first column of Table 8 contains the description of the row. The next eight columns of the table are the years 1987 to 1994. Column 10, change, is the compound annual growth rate for the row. The rows are described in the following section.

Rows

1. *All employees*: The total number of employees for the chapter industry. This is "total payroll employment" and so covers all paid employees, from company officers to part-time production workers.

2. *Establishments*: The number of establishments in the chapter industry.

3. *Employees per establishment*: The result of dividing Row 1 by Row 2.

4. *Production workers per establishment*: The result of dividing Row 5 (total number of production workers) by Row 2.

Production workers: Production workers are defined as workers engaged in processing and assembling activities, including employees engaged in storing, inspecting, handling, packing, warehousing, maintenance, repair, janitorial and watchmen services, etc. , as well as working foremen doing similar work to that of employees they supervise.

5. *Total*: The total number of production workers in the chapter industry.

6. *Percent of all employees*: The result of dividing Row 5 by Row 1.

7. *Male*: The number of male production workers in the chapter industry; available only through 1991.

8. *Female*: The number of female production workers in the chapter industry, available only through 1991. Note that these values are not comparable to U.S. Table 4, "Women," which refers to all women in the industry—production workers and others.

9. *Percentage of total production workers*: The result of dividing Row 8 by Row 5.

10. *Average hourly earnings*: Total annual wages paid production workers divided by hours paid, which include holidays, vacation, and overtime.

11. *Average weekly earnings*: Wages paid to production workers in the chapter industry divided by 52.

12. *Average weekly hours*: Weekly hours for which pay was received.

13. *Shipments*: The industry's shipments, in millions of Canadian dollars.

Nonmanufacturing

In general, the total number of employees, the number of nonsupervisory workers, average weekly earnings of nonsupervisory workers, and total receipts in millions of Canadian dollars are shown for nonmanufacturing industries.

Table 9: Mexico: Component Industries. . .

Table 9 provides a summary of employment, remuneration, and benefits in the Mexican chapter industry. The source of the data is the INEGI *Censos Economicos*, 1994 (the data are for 1993).

The table is essentially the same for manufacturing and nonmanufacturing industries. However, there are many differences between the data in this table and those in Tables 4 and 7—the roughly comparable tables for the United States and Canada. Some are due to definitional and classification differences in the collection of the data, but most are fundamental differences in business and employment practices in Mexico compared with the United States and Canada.

The subindustries (4-digit level of the Mexican Standard Industry Classification (CMAP)) are shown in order to define the industry more closely and to provide detail. Some 2-digit classifications are comparable to the corresponding U.S. and Canadian 2-digit industries, but in many cases industries must be combined at the 4-digit level in order to obtain reasonable matches with U.S. and Canadian 2-digit industries. Even then, perfect matches are not always achieved. The columns are described in the following section.

TABLE 9

MEXICO: COMPONENT INDUSTRIES OF CHEMICALS AND PETROLEUM (CMAP 35), 1993

(Monetary values in 1993 Mexican New Pesos)

			ALL WORKERS									
								PAID WORKERS				
							PRODUCTION WORKERS		NONPRODUCTION EMPLOYEES		BENEFITS	UNPAID
(1)	(2)	(3) NUMBER OF UNITS	(4) NUMBER	(5) PERCENT OF INDUSTRY TOTAL	(6) AVERAGE DAYS WORKED	(7) REMUN- ERATION[1]	(8) NUMBER	(9) WAGES AND SALARIES	(10) NUMBER	(11) WAGES AND SALARIES	(12) PER PAID EMPLOYEE	(13) WORKERS, NUMBER
INDUSTRY	CMAP											
Chemicals and petroleum	35	7,091	380,140	100	276	36,607	259,834	17,367	114,910	43,751	11,150	5,396
Basic petrochemistry	3511	18	19,311	5	304	46,995	16,504	29,069	2,807	63,049	12,987	0
Manufacture of basic chemicals	3512	667	44,887	12	292	49,322	27,263	22,103	17,404	48,855	16,795	220
Artificial and synthetic fibers	3513	22	14,475	4	318	44,879	11,469	18,334	3,003	55,525	18,828	3
Pharmaceutical industry	3521	394	39,099	10	267	51,626	18,641	16,878	20,227	54,378	15,233	231
Other substances and chemicals	3522	1,738	74,153	20	266	39,915	40,957	17,730	31,696	41,874	11,652	1,500
Petroleum refining	3530	6	19,818	5	365	52,309	17,553	33,835	2,265	65,840	14,816	0
Coke, coal, and oil by-products	3540	205	10,114	3	278	36,636	6,933	15,926	3,094	43,158	12,307	87
Rubber industry	3550	792	33,265	9	276	34,936	25,700	19,607	6,919	37,345	11,566	646
Plastics products	3560	3,249	125,018	33	278	20,507	94,814	10,239	27,495	31,468	5,495	2,709

1. Average annual remuneration including benefits, excluding profit sharing.

Source: INEGI, Censos Economicos 1994.

Columns

1. *Industry*: The names of the 2-digit industry and its 4-digit subindustries.

2. CMAP: The numeric industry classification code (CMAP) for the row.

3. *Number of units*. The total number of units (establishments) in the industry or subindustry.

All workers:

4. *Number*: The average number of all employees—paid and unpaid—at work. A major difference between Mexico and the United States and Canada is that there are generally a large number of unpaid employees in Mexico. These are proprietors, partners, and unpaid family members who work in the enterprise, but are compensated in ways other than through wages or salaries.[17]

5. *Percent of industry total*: The relative importance of the subindustry in terms of its share of total industry employment.

6. *Average days worked*: The average number of days that establishments in the industry are open and work is being done.

Paid workers:

7. *Remuneration*: The average of annual wages or salaries, *plus benefits*, paid to all (paid) employees, including production workers and others.

---

[17] See, "Employment, Wages, and Benefits," for more details on unpaid workers.

Production workers:

8. *Number:* The average number of production workers (*obreros*) at work. The definition of *obreros* may not match the BLS or Statistics Canada definitions of production workers exactly.

9. *Wages and salaries:* The average annual wages paid to production workers—benefits are not included.

Nonproduction employees: These *empleados* include supervisors, technicians, sales, and some clerical employees.

10. *Number:* The average number of nonproduction employees at work.

11. *Wages and salaries:* The average annual salary paid to nonproduction workers—benefits are not included.

12. *Benefits per paid employee:* The average benefits (*prestaciones social*) paid per employee. These include such things as payroll taxes covering government benefits: an 18.3 percent payroll tax on employers provides health care, compensation for the disabled, and old age pensions (employees making more than the minimum wage pay an additional 4.8 percent, <u>not included</u>); a 1 percent tax on employers to provide child care; a 5 percent tax on employers for the national low-cost housing fund; and a 2 percent mandatory tax on employers for an individual retirement savings plan. Mexican workers may also receive other benefits, which may or may not be included in the data in Table 9. There is no unemployment insurance, but employers are required to compensate workers dismissed without cause based on length of service; the worker is also eligible for health care for six months following termination. Workers' compensation for injury or job-related illness is included in the general "social security package." There is also a mandatory profit sharing plan: 10 percent of taxable profits must be distributed to employees based on the number of days worked during the year and wage/salary rates. There may be additional benefits distributed by the employer to individual employees included. See "Employment, Wages, and Benefits," for more detail.

13. *Unpaid workers, number:* The number of persons who work in the enterprise but do not receive compensation in the form of wages or salaries. These are proprietors, partners, and unpaid family members who work in the enterprise, but are compensated in other ways. Typically, unpaid workers account for a large proportion of the staff in small establishments and a small proportion in large ones.

Table 10: Mexican Gross Domestic Product and Employment. . .

Table 10 provides a picture of recent trends in the chapter industry in terms of employment and GDP originating in the industry. The source of the data is the Sistema de Cuentas Nacionales de Mexico, INEGI, 1996.

National Accounts data were used in Table 10 because they have been benchmarked to the 1993 *Censos Economicos* and are generally comparable to Table 9. There are differences between employment for 1993 in the two tables; in most cases—but not all—these differences are small. Some differences are due to adjustments to the numbers of unpaid workers counted in the census. For example, unpaid workers who work less than 15 hours per week are not included in the national accounts data, and hence not in Table 10, but are included in Table 9. On the other hand, for some industries, the employment figure in Table 10 is larger than in Table 9.

GDP originating is used in Table 10 because these are the best and most useful data available for Mexico. They are comparable to constant dollar GDP originating in Table 3 and do provide an inflation-adjusted measure of industry growth. The columns and rows are described in the following section.

TABLE 10

MEXICAN GROSS DOMESTIC PRODUCT AND EMPLOYMENT: CHEMICALS, DERIVATIVES OF PETROLEUM, RUBBER AND PLASTIC, 1988-1995

	1988	1989	1990	1991	1992	1993	1994	1995	CHANGE[1]
GROSS DOMESTIC PRODUCT:									
❶ Millions of constant 1993 new pesos	30,417.9	33,279.1	34,724.7	35,060.4	35,684.2	35,075.2	36,270.1	35,953.9	2.42
❷ Millions of constant 1993 U.S. dollars[2]	9,737.8	10,653.8	11,116.5	11,224.0	11,423.7	11,228.7	11,611.3	11,510.0	2.42
TOTAL EMPLOYMENT:									
❸ Chemicals, derivatives of petroleum, et al	370,230	380,425	393,831	401,902	395,282	383,933	370,978	349,721	-0.81
Petroleum	53,548	49,861	50,944	46,858	41,015	35,528	32,703	32,691	-6.81
Chemicals and allied products	196,234	200,741	206,213	211,912	204,258	190,895	177,988	167,750	-2.22
Rubber and plastic	120,448	129,823	136,674	143,132	150,009	157,510	160,287	149,280	3.11

1. Compound annual growth rate.
2. Converted at 3.1237 new pesos to the U.S. dollar.
Source: Sistema de Cuentas Nacionales de Mexico, INEGI.

Columns

The first column contains the row name. Columns 2 through 9 contain data for 1988 through 1995; and Column 10 contains the compound annual growth rate for the row.

Rows

Gross domestic product (not available for all industries):

1. *Millions of constant 1993 new pesos*: The 1993 constant new peso value of GDP originating in the industry.

2. *Millions of constant 1993 U.S. dollars*: The results of converting Row 1 to U.S. dollars using the 1993 exchange rate of 3.1237 new pesos to the dollar.

3. *Total employment*: This and any following rows contain employment for the chapter industry and its subindustries.

Table 11: International Trade. . .

Table 11 provides a picture of global trade for the chapter industry for the United States and bilateral trade among the three NAFTA countries.

U.S. global trade data come from the International Trade Administration, U.S. Department of Commerce; U.S.—Canada and U.S.—Mexico bilateral trade data are from the U.S. Bureau of the Census; and Canada—Mexico trade data are from Statistics Canada.[18] Data from Statistics Canada were in Canadian dollars and have been converted to U.S. dollars by the editors using exchange rates shown in Part I, Facts and Figures. Bilateral trade data for U.S.—Canada and U.S.—Mexico for 1996 are preliminary. All values are in millions of U.S. dollars.

TABLE 11

INTERNATIONAL TRADE, CHEMICALS AND ALLIED PRODUCTS

(Millions of U.S. dollars)

	1989[1]	1990	1991	1992	1993	1994	1995	1996
GLOBAL TRADE, U.S.								
IMPORTS								
❶ Value	20,215.4	21,732.0	23,138.4	26,006.2	27,258.9	31,696.9	38,079.0	42,825.7
❷ Ratio to new supply[2]	7.4	7.7	8.1	8.7	8.8	9.6	.....	.....
❸ Ratio to apparent consumption[3]	8.6	8.9	9.5	10.1	10.1	11.2	.....	.....
EXPORTS								
❹ Value	35,993.1	38,056.3	41,669.0	42,129.0	42,741.9	48,950.1	57,896.6	58,502.7
❺ Ratio to comparable domestic shipments	14.3	14.7	15.9	15.4	15.0	16.3	.....	.....
❻ TRADE BALANCE	15,777.7	16,324.3	18,530.6	16,122.8	15,483.0	17,253.2	19,817.6	15,677.0
BILATERAL TRADE: NAFTA[4]								
❼ U.S. exports to Canada	4,413.0	5,692.3	6,344.8	6,902.3	7,976.8	9,123.8	10,114.5	11,051.5
❽ Canadian exports to U.S.	3,924.2	4,062.3	4,094.0	4,621.9	5,171.3	6,290.3	7,653.7	7,916.9
❾ U.S. exports to Mexico	2,022.0	2,160.5	2,408.4	2,766.0	3,035.8	3,829.3	3,754.5	4,573.8
❿ Mexican exports to U.S.	611.5	651.6	692.8	806.4	780.0	1,064.9	1,368.8	1,407.1
⓫ Canadian exports to Mexico	9.5	12.1	7.6	11.6	12.4	23.7	26.8	50.6
⓬ Mexican exports to Canada	14.9	13.0	13.7	14.8	22.3	36.1	76.9	78.7
TRADE BALANCES WITHIN NAFTA[5]								
⓭ Canada	(494.2)	(1,630.9)	(2,256.9)	(2,283.6)	(2,815.4)	(2,845.9)	(2,510.9)	(3,162.7)
⓮ Mexico	(1,405.1)	(1,508.0)	(1,709.5)	(1,956.4)	(2,245.9)	(2,752.0)	(2,335.6)	(3,138.6)
⓯ United States	1,899.3	3,138.9	3,966.3	4,240.1	5,061.3	5,597.9	4,846.5	6,301.3

1. 1989 and earlier data on U.S. exports to Canada for manufacturing total and manufacturing industries are not comparable with data for 1990 and later years because of a change in the reporting system. The NAFTA trade balances for the U.S. and Canada also are affected.

2. New supply equals comparable domestic shipments plus imports for consumption.

3. Apparent consumption equals comparable domestic shipments plus imports for consumption less exports.

4. Amounts less than U.S. $100,000 shown as zero.

5. Parentheses indicate an excess of imports over exports. Because of commodity coding and other data differences among the three countries, these trade balances are only rough estimates and should be used with caution.

Source for U.S. Global Trade: U.S. Department of Commerce, International Trade Administration.

Source for U.S. -Canada and U.S.-Mexico Bilateral Trade: U.S. Bureau of the Census.

Source for Canada-Mexico and Mexico-Canada Bilateral Trade: Statistics Canada, Foreign Trade Division, Special tabulation, March 1997, converted to U.S. dollars by the editors.

---

[18] Canada—Mexico bilateral trade data were adapted from Statistics Canada, Foreign Trade Division, Special Tabulation, April 1997.

Note that all values, imports and exports, are more comparable to "product" shipments in Table 3 than to "industry" shipments in the same table. That is, U.S.—Canadian and U.S.—Mexican trade data are based on the U.S. "Harmonized Tariff Schedule" codes for imports and the Schedule B codes for exports; the Canada—Mexico trade data are based on similar Canadian systems. Thus, exported products are classified without regard to their industry of origin. See the "Industry and Product Data" section for descriptions of the differences in the two sets of data.

Because the Canada-Mexico data are from a different source than the U.S. data and may reflect some differences in classification practices, the trade balances calculated must be treated as approximations only. They are provided, in spite of the difficulties, because this information is of great interest and no better estimates appear to be available. The following section includes descriptions of the columns and rows.

Columns

The first column contains the name or description of the row values. Columns 2 through 9 contain values for the years 1989 to 1996. Data begin in 1989 rather than in 1987, as in other tables, because most data were derived from special tabulations prepared for the *Handbook* and necessary data were not available for key series prior to 1989. Data for 1989 for U.S. exports to Canada and trade balances are not comparable to data from later years because of a change in reporting systems.

Rows

Global trade, U.S.: Rows 1 through 6 contain the total U.S. global trade (trade with all countries) for the chapter industry.

Imports:

1. *Value*: The value of total U.S. imports.

2. *Ratio to new supply*: The result of the division of Row 1 by "new supply"— comparable domestic shipments plus imports for consumption— expressed as a percent.[19]

3. *Ratio to apparent consumption*: The result of the division of Row 1 by "apparent consumption"—comparable domestic shipments, plus imports for consumption, less exports— expressed as a percent.[19]

Exports:

4. *Value*: The value of total U.S. exports.

5. *Ratio to comparable domestic shipments*: The result of the division of Row 4 by shipments of goods of comparable types, expressed as a percent. The idea is to provide a measure of the percentage of domestic shipments that are exported.

6. *Trade balance*: Row 4 minus Row 1.

Bilateral trade: NAFTA: As with the global trade figures above, all values below are of exports or imports of products usually associated with the chapter industry.

7. *U.S. exports to Canada*: The value of U.S. exports to Canada (imports into Canada from the United States).

8. *Canadian exports to U.S.*: The value of Canadian exports to the United States (imports into the United States from Canada).

---

[19] The idea here is to provide a comparison between domestic and imported goods that are rough substitutes for each other and thus in competition. To prepare "comparable domestic shipments," the Census Bureau matches imports to domestic shipments by their corresponding product codes. Imports for consumption are all imports less those not entering the U.S. consumption stream; e.g., goods sent to bonded warehouses, foreign trade zones, etc.

9. U.S. *exports to Mexico*: The value of U.S. exports to Mexico (Mexican imports from the United States).

10. *Mexican exports to the U.S.*: The value of Mexican exports to the United States (U.S. imports from Mexico).

11. *Canadian exports to Mexico*: The value of Canadian exports to Mexico (Mexican imports from Canada).

12. *Mexican exports to Canada*: The value of Mexican exports to Canada (Canadian imports from Mexico).

Trade balances within NAFTA:

13. *Canada*: The sum of Canadian exports to Mexico and the United States less the sum of Mexican and U.S. exports to Canada.

14. *Mexico*: The sum of Mexican exports to Canada and the United States less the sum of Canadian and U.S. exports to Mexico.

15. *U.S.*: The sum of U.S. exports to Canada and Mexico less the sum of Canadian and Mexican exports to the United States.

Nonmanufacturing

For nonmanufacturing industries, trade data may not be as complete as for manufacturing, but are shown in each chapter as available.

Some nonmanufacturing industries, by their nature or definition, are not directly involved in foreign trade, and import and export data for such industries do not exist. Examples are construction and trade. Imports of construction materials are classified according to the comparable manufacturing industry (e.g., lumber or structural steel); and by definition, actual construction as measured in U.S. statistics takes place in the U.S. However, U.S. construction firms do export their services, which are measured in the Business and Professional Services industry.

Both wholesale and retail trade buy and sell imported products, and wholesale trade firms may export goods as well. Again, however, these products are classified in the original manufacturing or mining industry. Sales by retailers to foreign tourists are classified as exports of "travel" and shown in the Transportation chapter.

Separate industry-specific data on international trade in health and consumer services are generally not available. In many such industries (e.g., most consumer services), transactions with foreigners may be negligible, and will be included in "travel".

SUPPLEMENTARY EXPLANATION TO TABLE 5.

Table 5 projects future growth in employment for the major industries and industry groups by the major occupational classifications. For each group and classification, three different projections are shown, corresponding to a range of demographic and economic possibilities— low, moderate, and high growth.

All three projections use the same underlying assumptions about population birth and death rates, which come from the Census middle-growth population projections. However, the high economic growth projection assumes higher net immigration and therefore a greater total population and potential labor force than in the other two employment projections.

Economic strength and the composition of demand differ among all three scenarios.

- *Low growth* features supply constraints in energy, higher inflation, a more restrictive Federal Reserve policy leading to higher interest rates, a stronger dollar, and relatively deep and prolonged recessions. Employment growth and labor force participation are low and the unemployment rate in 2005 is 7.0 percent. In each of the three scenarios, the year 2005 is projected to be just on the long-term growth path calculated for the particular set of economic assumptions, not at either a cyclical peak nor in a recession trough. Recent modest productivity gains continue. Continued growth in Federal health and welfare spending and low revenues from the weak economy combine to produce a rising Federal deficit. The stronger dollar limits exports and the trade deficit rises.

- *Moderate growth.* Productivity growth is stepped up to 1.4 percent per year from a recent history of 1.2 percent. Foreign trade grows, especially in services, and the trade deficit declines. Federal entitlement spending is slowed and the budget deficit remains low. The unemployment rate in 2005 is 5.7 percent.

- *High growth.* This path features lower energy prices and inflation, higher immigration, and higher labor force participation, capital spending, and productivity growth. Monetary policy is easier, the dollar has lower value, export growth is stronger, and the trade deficit is lower. With higher revenues, the Federal budget comes into balance. The economy has growth slowdowns rather than recessions and the unemployment rate falls to 4.0 percent.

Compared with the moderate projections for 2005, most industries have higher employment in the "high" economic path and lower employment in the "low" path. But because of differences in certain specific assumptions among the three projections, this is not true for every industry. Notably, the mining and petroleum refining industries have higher employment in the low economic projection, reflecting the stimulus of higher energy prices to domestic production of crude oil and its products. Agriculture and food and tobacco manufacturing also display such anomalies, reflecting differing foreign trade and consumer demand conditions.

For further information on the employment projections, see *Monthly Labor Review*, November 1995.

GLOSSARY, ABBREVIATIONS, AND DATA SOURCES

American Council of Life Insurance—Trade association representing legal reserve life insurance companies doing business in the United States. It is the source of data for life insurance companies in the Finance, Insurance, and Real Estate chapter.

Apparent consumption—Product shipments plus imports for consumption minus exports. Imports for consumption are all imports less those not entering the U.S. consumption stream; e.g., goods sent to bonded warehouses, foreign trade zones, etc.

Board of Governors of the Federal Reserve System (FRB)—Institution responsible for setting monetary policy. It is the source of *Handbook* data on commercial bank assets and liabilities, money stock, industrial production, and capacity utilization.

Bureau of Economic Analysis (BEA)—The U.S. Department of Commerce bureau that prepares the U.S. National and International Accounts and other analytical measures of the economy. It is the source of *Handbook* data on gross product by industry and international trade in services.

Bureau of Labor Statistics (BLS)—The U.S. Department of Labor bureau that prepares employment, unemployment, price, and other analytical measures of economic activity. It is the source for *Handbook* data on U.S. employment, hours, earnings, employment projections, producer prices, and consumer prices.

Bureau of the Census—A bureau of the Commerce Department whose mission is to provide timely, relevant demographic and economic data about the United States. It is the source for *Handbook* data in Table 1 of almost every chapter, all financial data for Table 6, and U.S.-Canada and U.S.-Mexico bilateral trade data.

Caribbean Basin Initiative (CBA)—An inter-American program, led by the United States, of increased economic assistance and trade preferences to Caribbean and Central American countries. CBI provides duty-free access to the United States for most products from the region and promotes private sector development in the region.

CARICOM—Caribbean Community and Common Market. Formed in 1973 to replace the Caribbean Free Trade Area, Caricom, in spite of its name, is a customs union rather than a common market. Members are Antigua and Barbuda, Bahamas, Barbados, Belize, Dominica, Grenada, Guyana, Jamaica, Montserrat, Saint Kitts and Nevis, Saint Lucia, Saint Vincent and Grenadines, Suriname, and Trinidad and Tobago. A CET (Common External Tariff) was proposed in 1973, but little progress has been made toward implementation. Caricom has about 6.3 million people and a combined GDP of about $16 billion.

CACM (Central American Region)—Created in 1960 and effective in 1963, CACM members are Guatemala, El Salvador, Honduras, Costa Rica, and Nicaragua; Panama has observer status and Belize participates in CACM summits. CACM has about 30 million people and a combined GDP of about $40 billion.

Canada-U.S. Free Trade Agreement (CUSFTA) —It was implemented in January 1989 to eliminate all tariffs on U.S. and Canadian goods by January 1998 and to reduce or eliminate many nontariff barriers.

Capacity utilization—Output as a percent of capacity. Indexes by industry are published by the Board of Governors of the Federal Reserve System.

Compound Annual Growth Rate (CAGR)—A method of calculating the representative annual percentage growth over a period of years. See "How to Use this Book" for a detailed description.

CET—Common External Tariff.

CMAP—Clasificacíon Mexicana de Actividads y Productos. The Mexican standard classification system for industries and products.

Cost, insurance, and freight (c.i.f.)—The usual method of valuing imports. (See also "Customs import value.")

Conference Board—A nonprofit, nonpolitical business group in New York City that specializes in analysis of the U.S. economy, and the collection, analysis, and reporting of worldwide management practices and policies.

Conference Board—Canada—The Canadian Conference Board located in Ottawa—a licensed disseminator of data from Statistics Canada from whom most of the Canadian data in the *Handbook* were obtained.

Constant dollars (or "real" dollars)—Output values converted to a base price, calculated by dividing current dollars by a deflator. Use of constant dollars eliminates the effect of price changes between the year of measurement and the base year and allows calculation of real changes in output.

Consumer Price Index (CPI)—Measures the price level of the average market basket of various goods and services purchased by urban consumers, relative to the price in a base period. It is prepared by the Bureau of Labor Statistics.

Council for Labor Cooperation (CLC)—The council set up by the "side agreements" to monitor NAFTA's effect on labor issues and to make recommendations for improvement. Source of some *Handbook* information on employment, wages, and benefits.

Council for Environmental Cooperation—The council set up by the "side agreements" to monitor NAFTA's effect on environmental issues and to make recommendations for improvement.

Countervailing duty—A retaliatory charge that a country places on imported goods to counter the subsidies or bounties granted to the exporters of the goods by their home governments.

Current dollars—The dollar amount of sales, wages, or other monetary measures—i.e. not adjusted for inflation.

Customs import value—Alternative method of determining import value as appraised by the U.S. Customs Service in accordance with legal requirements. (See Cost, insurance, and freight.)

Dumping—A term used in international trade that refers to the sale of a product in export markets below the selling price for the same product in domestic markets.

Durable goods (durables)—Items with normal life expectancy of three years or more, such as automobiles, furniture, and major household appliances. Sales of durable goods are often postponable and therefore are the most volatile component of consumer and business expenditures.

Energy Information Administration (EIA)—An organization within the U.S. Department of Energy that prepares statistical information about, and economic analysis of, the energy sector. It is an information source for the *Handbook* sections on oil and gas extraction and petroleum products.

Establishment—An economic activity involving one or more persons at a single location. A company, or economic enterprise, may consist of one or more establishments.

Eurodollars—Deposits held in denominations of U.S. dollars in commercial banks outside the United States.

European Community (EC)—The organization for the European common market, merged into the European Union in 1992.

European Union—A large regional economic/political organization with a population of about 345 million. Its 15 members, as of 1997, are Austria, Belgium, Denmark, Finland, France, Germany, Greece, Ireland, Italy, Luxembourg, the Netherlands, Portugal, Spain, Sweden, and the United Kingdom. The EC (above) became the European Union (EU) on November 1, 1993, as a result of the Maastrict Treaty. If fully implemented, it will be the world's first economic union, with additional political and military ties.

Export-Import Bank (Eximbank)—An independent agency of the U.S. Government, created in 1934 to facilitate the export trade of the United States.

Fast Track —A procedure for the negotiation of trade agreements in which the U.S. Congress grants the President permission to proceed under special conditions. The executive branch agrees to consult with the Congress during all phases, thereby permitting a "yea" or "nay" congressional vote on the final implementing legislation without amendments. Past and current Presidents have argued that it would be very difficult to negotiate a trade treaty without it since the Congress could revise and amend an agreement after the President had signed a pact with a foreign country or countries.

Federal Home Loan Mortgage Corporation (Freddie Mac)—The recently renamed corporation is a government-mandated public company that purchases residential mortgages from banks and mortgage bankers and generates fee and interest income on the mortgages through sale or investment. It is the source of data on the mortgage interest rate in the Finance, Insurance, and Real Estate chapter of the *Handbook*.

Fiscal Year (FY)—Designation of a year for budget and accounting purposes. The U.S. Government's fiscal year is from October 1 to September 30.

Foreign trade zones (FTZs)—Designated areas in the United States, usually near ports of entry, considered to be outside the customs territory of the United States. Also known as free trade zones.

Forest Service of America (FSA)—Organization within the Department of Agriculture charged with protecting the forests and related fauna. It is the source of data in the *Handbook* on the forestry industry.

Free alongside ship (f.a.s.)—The transaction price of an export product, including freight, insurance, and other charges incurred in placing the merchandise alongside the carrier in the U.S. port.

Free on board (f.o.b.)—Without charge for delivery of export merchandise to and placing on board a carrier at a specified point.

Free Trade Area of the Americas (FTAA)—A Free Trade Area proposed by 34 democratically elected leaders of Western Hemisphere countries at the "Summit of the Americas" in Miami in 1994 and proposed to take effect in 2005.

G-7 (Group of Seven)—Seven industrial countries: the United States, Japan, Germany, France, the United Kingdom, Italy, and Canada. G-7 leaders meet at annual economic summits to coordinate their economic policies.

General Agreement on Tariffs and Trade (GATT)—A trade agreement signed by the United States and 22 other countries in Geneva, Switzerland, in 1947. Since implementation in 1948, 128 nations (as of 1997) have signed this agreement—accounting for more than 80 percent of current world trade. GATT was grounded in a uniform system of rules to promote world trade expansion based on tariff reductions. As a result of these reductions, the average tariff rate on imports into the United States has dropped from 30 percent, just after WWII, to the present level of around 5 percent. See also World Trade Organization.

Generalized System of Preferences (GSP)—A system approved by GATT in 1971 that authorizes developed countries to give preferential tariff treatment to developing countries.

Gross domestic product (GDP)—The value of all goods and services produced in a country. The measure of a nation's output now most used throughout the world.

Gross national product (GNP)—The value of all goods and services produced in a country plus income earned in foreign countries less income payable to foreign sources.

Harmonized System—An international convention, implemented by the United States in 1989, for classifying imports and exports so that trade data from different countries are comparable.

Health Care Finance Administration (HCFA)—Organization within the Department of Health and Human Services administering Medicare and Medicaid. It is a source for health industry information in the *Handbook*.

Health Canada— Canadian governmental organization that disseminates health information, conducts research on medicines, and inspects health care centers. It is a source of Canadian health care data in the *Handbook*.

Imports for consumption—All imports less those not entering the U.S. consumption stream; e.g., goods sent to bonded warehouses, foreign trade zones, etc.

IN—Internet.

Industrial production—In the United States, measures of the constant dollar value of the output of manufacturing, mining, and utility industries, relative to a base period, prepared by the Board of Governors, Federal Reserve System.

Instituto Nacional de Estadistica, Geografia e Informatica (INEGI)—Institute for Statistics, Geography and Information; Mexico's central agency for statistics, national accounts, and census functions. It is the source for almost all *Handbook* data on Mexican industries.

Intellectual property—Includes trademarks, copyrights, patents, and trade secrets.

International Monetary Fund (IMF)—Established in 1945, the IMF is a permanent forum for its member countries to coordinate economic and financial policies. It monitors compliance with agreements to maintain orderly exchange rates, provides resources to members facing balance-of-payments difficulties, and offers technical and policy assistance.

Joint venture—An international business undertaking, usually between foreign interests and private parties from the host country, or between foreign interests and the host government.

Just-in-time (JIT) delivery—A management technique in which a manufacturer works closely with its suppliers to assure that critical components are delivered as needed to avoid disruptions of the production process and the costs of maintaining excessive inventories.

Manufacturers' shipments by industry—The total value of products shipped by manufacturing establishments classified as being in an industry, plus receipts for miscellaneous activities; e.g., repair and maintenance.

Maquila (maquiladora)—Mexico's in-bond export manufacturing sector. Under the Maquiladora program, components and raw materials are imported to Mexico from abroad without duty, held in-bond by the manufacturer while further processing takes place, and then re-exported abroad with no (Mexican) duties or taxes except on the value added. Most such plants are owned by U.S. corporations, and most production is exported to the United States.

Mercosur (Mercosul) (Southern Common Market)—The Southern Common Market (Mercosur in Spanish, Mercosul in Portuguese) established in 1994 by the treaty of Asuncion. It is the largest preferential trade agreement in Latin America and consists of Argentina, Brazil, Paraguay, and Uruguay. Mercosur has a combined GDP of just over $1 trillion, more than half of Latin America's GDP. U.S.-Mercosur trade was $30 billion in 1996. Both Chile and Bolivia have signed agreements with Mercosur calling for elimination of tariffs between those countries and Mercosur.

Most-favored-nation (MFN) trade status—An arrangement in which GATT countries must extend to all other members the most favorable treatment granted to any trading partner, thus assuring that any tariff reductions or other trade concessions are automatically extended to all GATT parties.

Multifiber Arrangement (MFA)—Trade agreements, under GATT auspices, between major textile importing and exporting countries covering most of the world trade in textiles and apparel. The MFA was in effect through December 1993, pending completion of the Uruguay Round.

National Association of Realtors (NAR)—World's largest trade association, the NAR is composed of residential and commercial realtors. Source of *Handbook* data for existing home sales.

National Science Foundation—U.S. government organization founded to provide research, investment, education, and infrastructure to advance the state of knowledge about science and engineering. It is the source for *Handbook* data on research and development spending by industry.

NEC (or n.e.c.)—Not elsewhere classified.

NIC—Newly industrialized (or industrializing) country. Developing countries that have experienced rapid growth in GDP, industrial production, and exports in recent years..

Nondurable goods (nondurables)—Items which last for less than three years, such as food, beverages, and clothing. Nondurables purchases are relatively stable from year to year, compared with purchases of durables.

North American Free Trade Agreement (NAFTA)—Agreement to create a free trade area among the United States, Canada, and Mexico. Implementation was effective January 1, 1994.

North American Industry Classification System (NAICS)—The industrial classification system designed to apply to the North American economy (U.S., Canada, Mexico) as a whole and to account for national peculiarities and recently developed industries. Scheduled to be phased into use over the period 1998-2005.

Organization for Economic Cooperation and Development (OECD)—Group of 29 (as of December 1997) industrialized, market economy countries of North America, Europe, Asia, and the South Pacific. The OECD, which has headquarters in Paris, was established in 1961 to promote economic development and international trade. It is the source of considerable statistical data about and economic analysis of its member countries.

Organization of Petroleum Exporting Countries (OPEC)—An association of important oil-exporting countries that are highly dependent on oil revenues. Formed in 1960, its major purpose is to coordinate the petroleum production and pricing of its members.

Pacific Rim—A term that technically means all countries adjoining the Pacific Ocean, although it often refers only to East Asian countries.

Producer Price Index (PPI)—Measures the price levels of commodities and some services in the United States, at the producer level, relative to a base period. It is prepared by Bureau of Labor Statistics.

Product shipments—The total value of specific products, classified as primary to an industry, that are shipped by all establishments, irrespective of the industry classification of these establishments.

Purchasing Power Parity (PPP) —A Purchasing Power Parity (PPP) is the rate of currency conversion which eliminates the differences in price levels between two countries. This means that a given sum of money when converted into a different currency at these rates will buy the same basket of goods and services in the other country. PPP rates in the Handbook are given in national currency units per U.S. dollar. For example, the PPP rate for Mexico in 1994 (as estimated by the OECD) is 1.95. This means that in 1994 it took 1.95 New Pesos to buy the same "bundle of goods" in Mexico as could be bought in the United States that year for $1.00.

Real dollars—See constant dollars.

Shipments— See manufacturer's shipments, product shipments.

Standard Industrial Classification (SIC) system—The standard established by the U.S. government for defining industries and classifying individual establishments by industry. Canada's version (CSIC) and Mexico's (CMAP) are not identical with the U.S. SIC. Over the next several years, the three NAFTA countries will be converting to the new North American Industry Classification System (NAICS). See North American Industry Classification System.

Statistics Canada—Canada's central agency for statistics, national accounting, and census functions. The source of most data on Canada in the *Handbook*.

TCF—Trillion cubic feet (usually of natural gas).

Total quality management (TQM)—A management technique to improve the quality of goods and services, reduce operating costs, and increase customer satisfaction.

United States Department of Agriculture (USDA)—U.S. department charged with developing and administering U.S. agricultural, food, and nutrition policy; representing U.S. agricultural interests abroad; and collecting data about the agricultural industry. It is the source of most U.S. statistics in the agricultural chapter of the *Handbook*.

United States Department of Commerce—U..S. department charged with promotion of domestic and foreign U.S. commercial interests, enforcement of relevant laws, and collection of census and other economic data. The Bureau of the Census and the Bureau of Economic Analysis are parts of Commerce.

Uruguay Round—Eighth round of multilateral trade negotiations held under GATT auspices, named for the country where initial discussions began in September 1986. Most of the negotiations have taken place in Geneva, Switzerland.

Value added—The difference between the value of goods produced and the cost of materials and services purchased to produce them. This is equivalent in concept to the labor share of production (wages, salaries, and supplements) plus the capital share (profits, interest, depreciation, etc.). "Census value added," as defined and measured by the U.S. Bureau of the Census, does not subtract all purchased services and therefore is greater than the industry's contributions to GDP. See "How to Use this Book" for additional information.

Voluntary restraint agreement (VRA)— An import relief device to limit foreign trade in a particular commodity and protect domestic industry from injury by foreign competition. Sometimes referred to as a "voluntary export restraint" or an "orderly marketing agreement."

World Bank—The International Bank for Reconstruction and Development (IBRD), the most important member of the World Bank Group, was created in 1945 as a companion organization to the IMF. The main purposes of the IBRD are to lend funds and provide technical and policy assistance to foster the economic development of its poorer member countries.

World Trade Organization (WTO)—Created by the Uruguay Round of negotiations (1986-1994), the WTO has 132 member countries as of September 1997. The WTO administers GATT trade agreements, provides technical assistance and training for developing countries, and handles trade disputes.

PART I:
THE NORTH AMERICAN ECONOMY

NAFTA—THE FIRST FOUR YEARS

BY JOHN E. CREMEANS

An active North American trade area has existed for centuries, with patterns and relationships well established long before the North American Free Trade Agreement (NAFTA) was conceived. The history of relationships among the three countries of North America is one of both disagreement and cooperation, reflecting political and economic conditions of the moment. From protectionism and distrust in the not-too-distant past, these relationships have evolved into unprecedented cooperation, culminating in implementation of NAFTA in January 1994.

Trilateral trade grew rapidly in the decade preceding NAFTA as cheaper transportation, greatly improved communications, and the end of the cold war made trade easier and more important for everyone. Thus, in a sense, NAFTA has only formalized trends that were well established, while focusing increased attention on existing problems (e.g. worker dislocation and cross-border environmental deterioration.)

All the same, NAFTA is a radical new departure in trade and cooperation that affects everyone—consumers, workers, and businesses in all three countries. It is an unprecedented agreement in which a developing country joins with two of the world's most highly industrialized countries. Until the defeat of fast-track legislation in the United States, it appeared that NAFTA might expand quickly to include Chile and that a Free Trade Area of the Americas might be in the near future. Although those possibilities are now stalled, it is clear that NAFTA has greatly influenced trade patterns in the Western Hemisphere and throughout the world.

This article provides a summary and review of NAFTA: what it is, how it came about, the size and nature of the trade area, its results so far, and its future as can be discerned now. The article is organized into topics, all of which provide relevant information and insights into NAFTA and its workings. Readers are encouraged to read all the parts, but those who wish may pick and choose. Other articles in Part I of the Handbook address related topics and issues, including employment, wages, and benefits in the three countries, Mexico's long-standing duty-free Maquiladora program, the prospect of an independent Quebec, and the huge and daunting illegal drug trade.

NAFTA: THE POLITICAL BACKGROUND

In retrospect, it is surprising that NAFTA was ratified. If national polls are to be believed, the one thing that Canadians, Mexicans, and Americans are united in believing is that NAFTA has been good for the other two, but not their own country. The Canadian–U.S. Free Trade Agreement (CUSFTA) was the essential precursor, and that agreement seems to have been opposed continuously by a majority of Canadians (except for the day the electorate approved it). In Mexico, President Carlos Salinas de Gortari sold NAFTA to Mexicans as the means to escape "underdevelopment," but less than two years after its implementation, his brother Raul was in jail, and Carlos himself was in exile in Ireland. In the United States, NAFTA's major proponent, George Bush, was defeated before the Senate approved it; his successor, Bill Clinton, seemed against it as a candidate and as President seemed lukewarm at first even after his "side agreements" were incorporated.[1] So how did NAFTA come to be approved?

---

[1] Bradsher, Keith, "3 Nations Resolve Issues Holding up Trade Pact Vote," *New York Times*, August 14, 1993, p A-1.

Mexico. Whatever else Carlos Salinas may have been, he was a true believer in an open, capitalist economy for Mexico. Salinas made the first move toward NAFTA,[2] and in June 1990—shortly after the CUSFTA took effect—Presidents Salinas and Bush issued a joint statement endorsing a U.S.-Mexico free trade agreement.

Salinas then sold the idea to a majority of his countrymen. How did he do it? He presented NAFTA less as a means to open markets to Mexican exports than as a means to access almost-limitless foreign capital. He had already prepared the way for the agreement by reducing tariffs and eliminating laws against foreign ownership of Mexican companies. But with Mexico's still-huge foreign debt and its underdeveloped economy, massive foreign investment was desperately needed. NAFTA would give investors the confidence to go ahead. The agreement would also provide a measure of prestige to Mexico and to Salinas himself. Formal association with the United States and Canada would give Mexico special status, especially with its Latin American neighbors.

Salinas persuaded his country to abandon more than 50 years of protectionist policies and fear of *el coloso del norte*, to embrace openness and enter virtual economic union with the United States. He agreed to eliminate tariffs and other barriers to trade, to permit foreigners to hold majority ownership of Mexican companies, to open the banking system to foreign banks, and to renounce expropriation of foreign assets without just compensation. It was, perhaps, one of the more significant national policy reversals in history.

Canada. Brian Mulroney had been re-elected Prime Minister in 1988 by what seemed to some a fluke, and by 1992 his popularity had fallen to new lows. Professors, analysts, and international businessmen thought CUSFTA had been a success, but most ordinary Canadians thought otherwise. Trade with the United States had increased quite briskly and, after a rocky first year, the positive Canadian balance of payments continued to grow. But Canada's overall economy slowed, and friends or relatives who lose jobs when plants move south make a much greater impression than those who gain jobs in export industries. Both ordinary Canadians and their leaders continued to believe that the United States used its economic power to keep Canada down.[3] Despite these attitudes, there was no serious movement to abrogate CUSFTA.

NAFTA represented an entirely different opportunity to Canada from that afforded to its two counterparts. Canadians had little to gain or lose. Canadian-Mexican trade was less than 2 percent of Canadian-U.S. trade. Canada's leaders and its people generally saw the NAFTA negotiations as an opportunity to renegotiate the faults they found in CUSFTA. First Mulroney, then his successor, Kim Campbell, skillfully exploited the desire of the other two parties to complete the agreement to gain their own ends. The Canadian politicians also used the opportunity to improve their own political situations by "standing up to the Americans."[4]

United States. Of the three leaders, George Bush had the least personal stake in the negotiations. His popularity was at its high following Desert Storm, and there was no pressing need to open up trade with Mexico.[5] There seemed to be advantages, nonetheless. NAFTA explicitly gave greater security for American investors, particularly in Mexico: the agreement committed Mexico both to opening previously closed industries to foreign investment and

---

[2] This was after he traveled to Europe in search of investors and found West Europeans preoccupied with newly opened Eastern Europe.

[3] Clyde Farnsworth, "U.S. Trade Pact a Spur to Canada: But Adding Mexico Meets Opposition," *New York Times*, July 22, 1992, p. D-1.

[4] Farnsworth, "A Gamble by Campbell Earns Praise and Points," *New York Times*, August 14, 1993, p A-45.

[5] The average Mexican tariff on U.S. imports was about 12 percent (U.S. tariffs on Mexican goods, about 4 percent), and imports from the United States were almost 70 percent of the Mexican total.

to forswearing the expropriation of foreign assets. More importantly, NAFTA seemed a sure way of securing privileged access to the Mexican market of 93 million potential consumers, and Mexico's economic growth of 3.9 and 4.0 percent in 1990 and 1991 suggested that the Mexican economy was poised for dramatic improvement.

Another factor was that an independent, strong, and economically healthy Mexico is a fundamental U.S. interest.[6] Salinas was committed to NAFTA, and the U.S. Government wanted to support a progressive and successful Latin American leader. Moreover, a thriving Mexican economy seemed the best and most desirable way to curb illegal immigration. The agreement was signed, but its approval became one of the issues in the 1992 election.

As a presidential candidate, Bill Clinton said he was for NAFTA in principle, but that there were inadequate protections against environmental abuses and that American labor was not protected against sweatshops and other labor abuses. He said he would correct it by making "side agreements" with Canada and Mexico that would cover the flaws of the agreement negotiated by President Bush. Third party candidate Ross Perot made the now-famous comment that he could already hear "a giant sucking sound" as American jobs went south to Mexico.

NORTH AMERICAN FREE TRADE AGREEMENT CHRONOLOGY[1]

November 6, 1987. Establishment of principles concerning trade and investment relations between Mexico and the United States.

February 1988. Formal negotiations begin under the U.S. Mexico Framework Agreement.

June 10, 1990. President Bush and Mexican President Salinas issue a joint statement endorsing the idea of a comprehensive free trade agreement between the United States and Mexico and direct their trade ministers to undertake consultations and preparatory work.

February 1991. President Bush, President Salinas, and Prime Minister Brian Mulroney announce their intentions to pursue a North American Free Trade Agreement (NAFTA).

June 12, 1991. NAFTA negotiations formally launched in Toronto with trilateral meeting of trade ministers. Nineteen working groups convene.

August 12, 1992. Negotiators initial a Tentative North American Free Trade Agreement

September 8, 1992. Draft legal text of NAFTA is published.

September 18, 1992. President Bush notifies Congress of his intention to sign NAFTA. Congress has 90 days to study the agreement and recommend changes.

December 17, 1992. NAFTA is signed.

May 27 and June 23, 1993. Canada's Parliament first to ratify NAFTA.

September 14, 1993. NAFTA "side agreements" are signed.

November 1993. NAFTA is ratified by the Senate and House of Representatives of the United States and the Senate of Mexico.

January 1, 1994. The North American Free Trade Agreement takes effect.

1 Lillian Dayan, York University, Canada, 2/9/95 (IN).

[6] For example, the "Enterprise for the Americas Initiative," proposed by George Bush in 1989, included all the Americas, but encompassed the idea that free trade in the Latin American countries would increase stability and represent a gain for the United States.

THE SIDE AGREEMENTS

Following the U.S. Presidential election, congressional approval of NAFTA was by no means certain. President Clinton was unable to get the tough labor and environmental agreements he wanted because neither the Mexicans nor the Canadians wanted to give up their authority over these sensitive issues.[7] He did get two side agreements that created commissions with authority to "monitor" and "recommend," but not to enforce. These new agreements created a Commission on Environmental Cooperation (CEC) and a Commission on Labor Cooperation (CLC). Ironically, these agreements were viewed as "tame" by many of those Clinton wanted to persuade, while a few NAFTA supporters grumbled that the commissions weakened U.S. sovereignty. Whether because of or in spite of the side agreements, NAFTA was approved by the U.S. Congress in November 1993.

In the years since implementation, both commissions have been active and have assisted in trilateral cooperation outside the scope of the agreement itself. The CLC's three commissioners have met several times, and the CLC recently published its first report, *North American Labor Markets: A Comparative Profile*." [8]

The Commission for Environmental Cooperation has been active also and has received a number of "enforcement petitions" to be investigated. Environmental organizations opposed NAFTA almost unanimously at the beginning, and organized opposition re-emerged when fast-track legislation was submitted to Congress in September 1997. However, the creation of CEC did reduce contention a bit and the mechanism of the CEC has actually been used in several cases to bring attention to environmental problems.[9]

In short, the side agreements have proved to be less effective than their supporters hoped, and more useful than their critics feared.

THE AGREEMENT ITSELF[10]

> The objectives of the Agreement are to eliminate barriers to trade, promote conditions of fair competition, increase investment opportunities, provide adequate protection for intellectual property rights, establish effective procedures for the implementation and application of the Agreement and for the resolution of disputes and to further trilateral, regional and multilateral cooperation.[11]

The above-stated objectives of the agreement involve five major concepts:

- *The elimination of tariffs, licenses, and other trade barriers.* NAFTA provides for elimination of most tariffs in five or 10 equal annual decrements, with those on some sensitive products (e.g., household glassware) eliminated over 15 years. Special sections on agriculture, textiles and apparel, automotive products, energy, land transportation, and telecommunications are included. Detailed "rules of origin" ensure that "fourth country" firms cannot set up establishments in one of the three countries in order to gain preferred "NAFTA status" for their products.

---

[7] President Salinas did promise to look into raising the minimum wage.

[8] Published by Bernan Press. Information from this report is used extensively in the "Employment, Wages, and Benefits" article in this book.

[9] In at least one case, a U.S. environmental group has used the CEC to address an alleged problem in the United States. Earthlaw, an organization within the University of Denver Law School, has filed two petitions, one against the Hutchison Rider that would curb enforcement of the endangered species act and another against U.S. Army (Fort Huachucha) use of water from the San Pedro River (IN).

[10] The reader is cautioned not to rely on this brief summary, but to read the actual agreement and consult an expert before investing or taking other action based on a view of the agreement. Complete copies of the Agreement are available on several websites; e.g., http://garnet.berkeley.edu., and the official summary of the agreement is included as Appendix D of the *Handbook*.

[11] "Synopsis of the proposed North American Free Trade Agreement," prepared by the Governments of Canada, Mexico, and the United States, August 12, 1992 (IN).

- *Standardization and simplification of paperwork and other procedures and protection of specific rights and rules.* The agreement encourages standardization, but acknowledges each country's right to protect its citizens by establishing technical rules and standards, as long as they are not discriminatory. Citizens and firms of each NAFTA country are to be treated in a nondiscriminatory way by the governments of the other countries. Intellectual property rights are explicitly protected.

- *Simplification of procedures for resolving disputes or differences of interpretation.* Citizens or firms of one NAFTA country may not be discriminated against in another. The right of each country to protect its environment and the health and safety of its citizens at levels of its own choosing is explicitly affirmed so long as these concerns do not disguise discriminatory treatment of goods or services from outside.

- *Basic protection for* NAFTA *investors and removal of barriers to investment.* The agreement also provides a mechanism for the settlement of disputes between such investors and a NAFTA country. For example, Mexico has already opened a number of industries, formerly reserved exclusively to its own citizens, to investment by foreigners. Each of the three countries agrees never to expropriate the assets of a foreign (NAFTA) firm without full compensation.

- *Opening up of cross-border service opportunities.* Banks and other financial firms may establish branches in other NAFTA countries or may own interests in domestic institutions. In the year 2000 (six years after the Agreement went into effect), the United States will provide cross-border access to its entire territory to trucking firms from Mexico. Mexico will provide the same treatment to trucking firms from Canada and the United States.

Major Changes Under NAFTA

One might argue that there is less to NAFTA than meets the eye. Prior to the implementation of CUSFTA in 1989, the average Canadian and Mexican tariffs on U.S. products were about 10 percent. More importantly, the average U.S. tariff on Canadian goods was 3.3 percent; on Mexican goods, 4 percent. Of course, tariffs on both sides of the border were higher on specific goods (such as automobiles and apparel). However, the trend had been down for many years and, under GATT and the World Trade Organization (WTO), would likely have continued down. It is hard to argue—in terms of specific tariff barriers—that NAFTA has "opened the gates" to foreign goods; the gates were already ajar. Nonetheless, NAFTA has resulted and will result in substantially greater trilateral trade and has and will put pressure on unskilled, poorly educated workers in the United States and Canada.

In the long run, the most important effect of NAFTA will probably be institutional and psychological. The elimination of tariffs and other barriers to trade is important, but the fact of a trilateral agreement to support and encourage economic trade and cooperation may in itself have great significance. For example, the agreement explicitly permits trucks and tour buses of each member country to operate in the other countries. Firms of each country are explicitly guaranteed nondiscriminatory treatment throughout the region. It is difficult to avoid the conclusion that businesses (and ordinary citizens) in each of the countries will soon identify the entire region as their market and their competition. The economies of the three countries will be integrated, and as a result, more low-skilled manufacturing jobs will move south.

THE NORTH AMERICAN (NAFTA) MARKET

The free trade area of Canada, the United States, and Mexico is the largest such area in the world, with 20 million square kilometers, 391 million people, and a combined gross domestic product (GDP) of $8 trillion.[12] It is dominated by the United States. The central U.S. location, with easy land transport to each of the other countries, is by itself an important advantage. In addition, this country has 68 percent of the North American population, 84 percent of the GDP, 73 percent of the labor force, and 49 percent of the trade in goods.[13] The United States also has the highest per capita GDP and the highest employment/population ratio. Mexico has only 9 percent of the total GDP, and Canada, only 8 percent (see "NAFTA Countries and the European Union" in "Facts and Figures"). The United States is an economic and military superpower, whereas Canada's and Mexico's military forces are small.

As a free trade area, NAFTA eventually will have no tariffs on goods shipped from any NAFTA country to any other. However, goods imported into any one country from outside NAFTA will be subject to the tariffs in force in that country and will not qualify for "preferred" NAFTA tariff treatment if re-exported to another NAFTA member. The "rules of origin" established under NAFTA were explicitly intended to prevent a "fourth country" firm from establishing an export platform in one NAFTA country so as to benefit from the NAFTA preferences.

The European Union (EU), in contrast, is not a free trade zone, but a customs union, with uniform "external" tariffs established for all imports from outside the union into any country within the union. Once imported, goods may be freely shipped from any member country to any other member country without additional charge. It is argued by some that free trade zones such as NAFTA are designed to give members of the zone protection from the outside world and to encourage the development of trade within the zone only, whereas customs unions encourage world trade.[14]

On the other hand, the EU arrangement has tended to encourage intra-EU trade at the expense of the outside world through relatively high external tariffs, nontariff barriers, and export subsidies (to offset the high costs of production, particularly of agricultural products). Internally, the EU has gone far beyond the trade liberalization plans of NAFTA. It has eliminated restrictions on the movement of labor and capital among its members, has agreed to coordinate economic policies, and has established a number of governing bodies for both economic and social activities. In addition, the EU plans to initiate a monetary union in 1999 and a common currency—the "euro"—in 2002.

Both NAFTA and the EU envision some integration of their members' economies, but the EU has involved much greater integration, political and cultural, as well as economic. The EU has a legislative body that may pass laws for the entire union; each member country has given up a portion of its sovereignty. Nothing like this has been proposed for NAFTA, but it is conceivable that it might be drawn in this direction if the present system leads to full and successful economic integration of the three countries. For example, a coordinated monetary policy or fiscal policy might seem desirable; the recent experience with the peso crisis makes it clear that monetary problems in one NAFTA country can have important effects in the others. However, such a change would require a significantly revised agreement and new legislation.

---

[12] See the NAFTA tables in "Facts and Figures." The European Union, with 371 million people and $8.5 trillion in GDP, is comparable in population and size of economy. China has a population of 1.2 billion and a GDP of $322 billion; India has a population of 891 million and a GDP of $252 billion; the Russian Federation has a population of 148 million and a GDP of $249 billion.

[13] Percent of trade calculated as the sum of exports and imports to the other NAFTA countries for each of them, divided by the sum of the exports and imports for all.

[14] Gantz, David A., "Maximizing the Regional Benefits of North American Economic Integration: Rules of Origin under NAFTA", Arizona State University (IN). Gantz argues that the NAFTA countries are protecting their markets on the North American continent from competition from the outside world.

AN EVALUATION

The first and most important thing to be said is that a four-year period is not long enough to tell us much about the ultimate success or failure of NAFTA, especially since only three years of detailed economic and trade data are now available. In addition, there are three exogenous events that complicate analysis of those years. A prolonged recession in Canada, a severe monetary crisis in Mexico, and an unusually long and strong recovery in the United States all have had strong impacts on trilateral trade. [15] Difficulties in Canada and Mexico have tended to reduce their imports, whereas U.S. growth and a strong dollar have encouraged its imports. Total employment growth in the United States has swamped any negative employment effects that NAFTA might have generated.

Although the CUSFTA was implemented eight years ago, all of its provisions have not yet been finalized, and longer term investment and reallocation effects have still to be realized. In the case of Mexico, all tariffs and other barriers to trade will not be removed until 2002. The lasting consequences of NAFTA will be the result of the reallocation of resources, and these effects will take a long time to reveal themselves fully. Nonetheless, some observations can be made.

TRADE IN GOODS

Canada. In the first quarter of 1990, Canada slipped into a severe recession that lasted about six quarters, followed by very slow growth until the fourth quarter of 1993. Canadian exports to the United States grew 9.4 percent annually from 1993 to 1997, compared with 6.0 percent in the comparable period preceding the agreement. U.S. exports to Canada have grown 9.8 percent annually, compared with a 6.3 percent rate earlier. Thus, trade has

FIGURE 1

CANADIAN-U.S. TRADE IN GOODS, 1989-1997

Billions of U.S. dollars

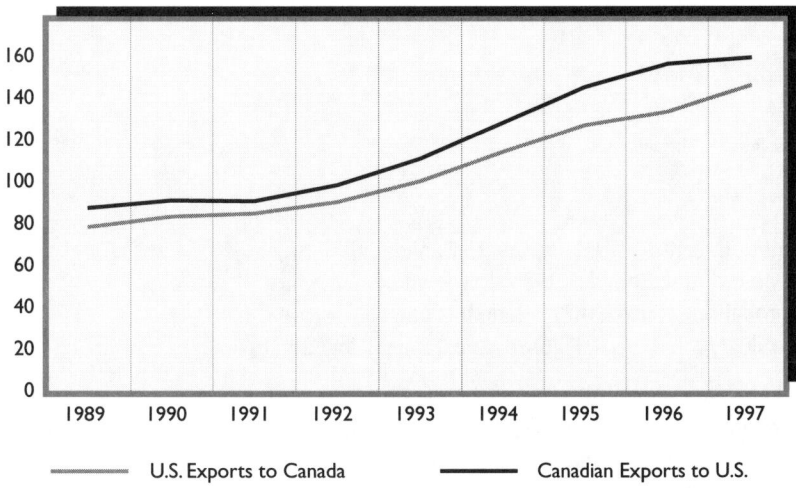

Source: U.S. Bureau of the Census and editors' estimates.

---

[15] The 1991-92 recession in the United States was relatively short and mild and was followed by a robust economy, whereas Canada's recession lingered.

TABLE 1

BILATERAL TRADE IN GOODS AMONG NAFTA COUNTRIES
(Millions of U.S. dollars)

	1989[1]	1990	1991	1992	1993	1994	1995	1996	1997[2]
BILATERAL TRADE: NAFTA									
U.S. Exports to Canada	78,809	83,674	85,150	90,594	100,444	114,439	127,226	133,668	146,079
Canadian Exports to U.S.	87,953	91,380	91,064	98,630	111,216	128,406	145,349	156,506	159,483
U.S. Exports to Mexico	24,982	28,279	33,277	40,592	41,581	50,844	46,292	56,761	69,482
Mexican Exports to U.S.	27,162	30,157	31,130	35,211	39,917	49,494	61,685	72,963	81,000
Canadian Exports to Mexico	524	551	492	662	619	772	810	856	1,048
Mexican Exports to Canada	1,442	1,498	2,251	2,294	2,876	3,313	3,898	4,394	4,878
TRADE BALANCES WITHIN NAFTA[3]									
Canada	8,225	6,759	4,155	6,404	8,515	11,427	15,035	19,300	9,574
Mexico	3,099	2,825	(388)	(3,749)	593	1,190	18,481	19,740	15,348
U.S.	(11,324)	(9,584)	(3,767)	(2,655)	(9,108)	(12,617)	(33,516)	(39,040)	(24,922)

1. 1989 and earlier data on U.S. exports to Canada are not comparable with data for 1990 and later years because of a change in the reporting system. The NAFTA trade balances for the U.S. and Canada also are affected.

2. 1997 figures are projections by the editors.

3. Parentheses indicate an excess of imports over exports. Because of commodity coding and other data differences among the three countries, these trade balances are only rough estimates and should be used with caution.

Source: U.S. Bureau of the Census and Statistics Canada.

TABLE 2

GROWTH IN BILATERAL GOODS TRADE BEFORE AND AFTER NAFTA
(Compound annual growth rate)

	1989-93	1993-97	PERCENTAGE POINT DIFFERENCE
U.S. exports to Canada	6.25	9.82	3.56
Canadian exports to U.S.	6.04	9.43	3.39
U.S. exports to Mexico	13.58	13.70	0.11
Mexican exports to U.S.	10.10	19.35	9.25
Canadian exports to Mexico	4.27	14.04	9.77
Mexican exports to Canada	18.83	14.12	(4.71)

Source: Calculated by the editors from trade data from the U.S. Bureau of the Census and Statistics Canada.

increased about evenly for both countries. In contrast, U.S. exports to Canada fell during the Canadian recession of 1982, as they did during Canada's 1986 slowdown. Canada has retained a trade surplus with NAFTA throughout. Thus, NAFTA trade has been a positive factor for Canada through an otherwise slow period. (See Figure 1, and Tables 1 and 2.)

One might expect that Canadians would be pleased—both imports and exports have continued to grow at greater rates than before. But a survey taken in 1992 indicates that only 6 percent of Canadians thought free trade a good idea.[16] Canadian trade with the United States did well during the 1994-1996 period, but the economy as a whole did not. Its growth declined to very low levels, and unemployment increased, averaging about 10 percent following the agreement. Brian Mulroney, Prime Minister and principal negotiator of

[16] Only 6 percent of Canadians believed (in the summer of 1992) that Canada had benefited from the Canada-U.S. FTA, according to an Angus Reed survey. Farnsworth, "U.S. Trade Pact Spur to Canada..."

the CUSFTA, became so unpopular that he stepped down early in favor of Kim Campbell, but his party lost badly in the next election anyway.

The Canadian economy has done better in 1997. Economic growth picked up in 1997 and is expected to continue at about 3 percent for the next three years. Unemployment is expected to decline by about a point over the same period.

Mexico. Mexican trade with both the United States and Canada has been enormously influenced by the monetary crisis that began in December 1994, when the peso dropped from about 3.4 to the U.S. dollar to 5.3 in just seven days. The peso continued to decline and the 8.25 pesos to the dollar rate prevailing by late-1997 cuts the cost of Mexican goods for U.S. and Canadian importers to less than half that before the crisis and doubles the cost of imports for Mexicans. Such a sharp change in effective price overwhelms any effect that lower tariffs required by NAFTA may have had. Moreover, the ratio of U.S. to Mexican hourly compensation costs in U.S. dollars has risen from 6.9 to 1 in 1993, prior to implementation of the agreement, to 11.8 to 1 in 1996. (See "Employment, Wages, and Benefits.") This not only increases the competition from Mexican imports, but makes it much more profitable to move production south. Seen in this light, it is remarkable that U.S. and Canadian trade deficits with Mexico are not larger.

FIGURE 2

MEXICAN-U.S. TRADE IN GOODS, 1989-1997

Billions of U.S. dollars

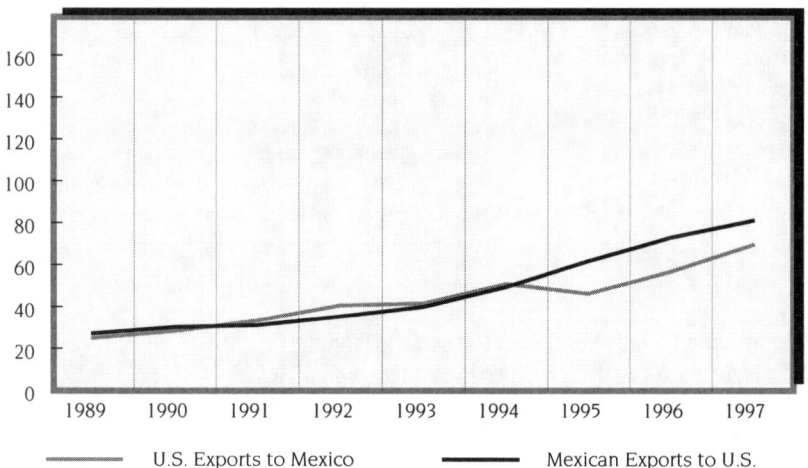

U.S. Exports to Mexico   Mexican Exports to U.S.

Source: U.S. Bureau of the Census and editors' estimates.

THE PESO CRISIS: "PETTY CRIME AND CRUEL PUNISHMENT"[1]

On January 1, 1994, the day NAFTA took effect, the "Zapatista" revolt began in Chiappas. The Government was able to contain it, but it was an unpleasant reminder that Mexico ". . . has one foot in central America and the other foot in North America."[2] No sooner was this crisis relieved, then PRI Presidential candidate, Luis Donaldo Colosio was assassinated (March 1994.) The PRI quickly nominated Ernesto Zedillo in his place.

Political instability and rising trade deficits made it apparent that the peso would have to be devalued, but the presidential election was not going well for the PRI, and President Salinas feared that devaluation might be the straw that broke the PRI's back. By late summer, pressure on the peso was increasing, and Mexico's reserves were rapidly diminishing.[3]

In September, Ru'z Massieu, a young PRI congressman and party secretary, was gunned down in Mexico City, and a clear connection to the Abrego drug cartel was soon established.[4] Zedillo was elected in November, but by one of the smallest margins in PRI's history. Zedillo had hoped that Salinas would devalue the peso before he left office, but instead, the new president began his administration with an overvalued peso and a world financial community seeing increasing instability in Mexico.

A key part of Mexico's anti-inflation program was to peg the peso to the U.S. dollar. The peg was allowed to "crawl" (to move) downward at the maximum rate of 0.0004 pesos a day. This proved to be insufficiently flexible. A peasant uprising and two political murders made investors very nervous. The peso survived a speculative attack in March and another in November, but only because the Bank of Mexico emptied its coffers of foreign exchange defending it.

On December 21, 1994, the new administration made its move. The peso, which had been trading at about 3.4 to the U.S. dollar, was devalued by 15 percent. The devaluation was widely expected and generally approved by international businessmen and economists.[5] But the market reacted sharply and with unexpected ferocity. The result was catastrophic for Mexico and its government. Suddenly, no one wanted to hold pesos. The Bank of Mexico ran out of hard currency reserves, the new administration was forced to float the peso, and in just seven days its value fell to 5.3 to the dollar. The decline continued throughout 1995, and by December, the peso was valued at only about 7.5 to the dollar.

The consequent recession was one of the sharpest and deepest in modern Mexican history. The Mexican stock and bond markets crashed, decimating investors who held peso-denominated bonds. The government and many Mexican corporations that had issued U.S. dollar-denominated bonds were stuck with crushing debt. The price of imported goods skyrocketed, and middle-class Mexicans with savings in pesos were impoverished. Inflation jumped, rising by 52 percent in 1995 and 27.7 percent in 1996. Industrial activity dropped by about 5.5 percent in the first quarter of 1995.

Early in 1995, President Clinton proposed a plan to guarantee up to $40 billion in loans to the Mexican Government to prevent default on outstanding bonds. The U.S. Congress would not go along, however, so the President developed a new plan under his emergency powers in which the United States loaned Mexico $20 billion for 3 to 5 years, the International Monetary Fund loaned $17.8 billion, and the Bank of International Settlements loaned $10 billion. This support calmed the immediate crisis and the peso stabilized, although at a substantially

Mexican exports to both the United States and Canada continued to rise following the implementation of NAFTA (Figure 2). Mexican exports to the United States grew at a 19.4 percent annual rate from 1993 to 1997, almost double the growth rate of the preceding four years; Mexican imports from the United States grew 13.7 percent annually over the same period, almost the same as in the comparable period prior to NAFTA.

Although percentage growth in Canadian-Mexican trade has been strong, Canada's trade with Mexico in 1996 was only about 2 percent of Canada-U.S. trade. It does seem to have been greatly influenced by the implementation of NAFTA.

U.S. exports to Mexico did fall immediately after the peso crisis (Table 1). But they fell far less in the 1994-1995 peso crisis than they did in the Mexican monetary crisis of 1982. U.S. exports to Mexico resumed their rapid growth in 1996, and the Mexican recovery is now well established. This suggests that the agreement may actually have helped ameliorate the effects of economic instability in Mexico. In previous Mexican economic crises, the government moved to restrict imports. In the 1994-95 crisis, the government did not restrict imports, and it carried out tariff reductions called for in the NAFTA agreement on schedule. U.S. exports to Mexico increased sharply in 1997 and exceeded U.S. exports to Japan in the first nine months of 1997.

reduced level. In October 1995, President Zedillo announced the repayment of $700 million of those loans and noted that $468 million in interest had already been paid.

Many observers argue that Mexico did not deserve the cruel punishment of a deep recession. The devastating drop in the peso was due more to the fears of the international financial community than to any fatal weakness in the Mexican economy. Prior to December 1994, Mexico was considered the very model of a developing economy benefiting from market-oriented reforms. The technocrats had accomplished a great deal. They had gained control of hyperinflation, brought the budget within bounds, privatized many inefficient government properties, opened the nation to foreign trade, and made the central bank independent of government. In the 1988-1993 period, foreign investment grew rapidly, making growth in consumer and producer imports possible and sparking modest growth in the economy. The economy had not yet "taken off" as hoped, but a number of observers thought Mexico was poised for sustained growth.

AND THE RECOVERY

The recession was relatively short. The peso devaluation effectively doubled import prices and cut export prices by more than half. Imports were sharply curtailed, but exports remained strong and actually accelerated. The largely foreign owned or operated plants in the duty-free Maquiladora manufacturing sector led the economy out of the recession. Maquiladora output—as measured by value added—showed no decline and actually accelerated with the fall of the peso as Mexican exports became cheaper. Manufacturing as a whole declined by about 3.75 percent in the first quarter of 1995, but recovered quickly. Workers' wages fell in both current and constant terms throughout the economy, but manufacturing wages regained their pre-recession peso level by the third quarter of 1996. Imports also picked up and reached their pre-recession level by about the same time. Even the con-

struction industry, which suffered sharply from the crash, had recovered by the second quarter of 1996.

The Mexican economy has now stabilized, but most Mexicans still are feeling the effects. Many families have lost their savings, have lower real earnings, and can no longer afford imported goods that were once considered necessities. Nonetheless, one of the worst recessions since the 1930s was also one of the shortest and the economy is again growing.[6] INEGI reports 5.1 percent real growth from the first quarter 1996 to first quarter of 1997, and unemployment reduced to 3.4 percent by June 1997.

1 The phrase comes from Calvo, Guillermo A. & Mendoza, Enrique G., "Petty Crime and Cruel Punishment: Lessons from the Mexican Debacle," *The American Economic Review*, May, 1996, pp. 170—175.

2 Carlos Fuentes, as quoted in: "Chiapas: Latin America's First Post-Communist Rebellion", *New Perspectives Quarterly* (NPQ), Spring 1994, Vol. 11, No. 2.

3 The pressure was applied by ordinary businessmen (Mexicans and foreigners alike) who kept their peso holdings to a minimum in anticipation of devaluation and by international speculators who borrowed pesos and immediately converted them to hard currency. To defend the peso, the Bank of Mexico had to buy pesos with its declining reserves of U.S. dollars and other hard currencies.

4 In February, 1995, Raul Salinas, the former President's brother, was arrested and charged with masterminding the assassination of Ruiz Massieu. In March 1995, charges were also filed against the brother of Ruiz Massieu for obstructing investigations into the murder. Since then both men have been accused of amassing fortunes in stolen funds abroad and Carlos Salinas has become something of an arch-villain in the minds of many Mexicans. U.S. Department of State, Background notes, 1997.

5 See, for example, Hanke, Steve H. & Walters, Alan, "The Wobbly Peso," *Forbes*, July 4, 1994.

6 See Inter-American Development Bank, "Mexico—Situacion economica reciente," Oct. 1997.

The United States. Critics predicted that NAFTA would bring factory closures, lost jobs, and falling wages. Imports from both Canada and Mexico did grow following the implementation of the respective free trade agreements, and at higher rates than in the comparable period preceding the agreements.[17] (See Tables 1 and 2.) Jobs have been lost, but not at the rates predicted. Overall employment growth has been strong, and the unemployment rate has been falling since 1993—it dropped to 4.6 percent in November, 1997.

U.S.-Canada trade has increased substantially. U.S. exports to Canada have grown at a 9.8 percent annual rate, and Canadian exports to the United States have grown at a 9.4 percent rate. (See Table 2.) The United States still has a trade deficit with Canada—projected to be about $13 billion in 1997, compared with about $8 billion in 1992.

U.S.-Mexico trade has also increased substantially. U.S. exports to Mexico have grown at a 13.7 percent rate (based on 1997 projections)—virtually unchanged from the pre-NAFTA rate, despite the depreciation of the peso. Mexican exports to the United States have grown

[17] This analysis reviews U.S. Canadian trade from the implementation of the CUSFTA in 1990; U.S.—Mexican trade is analyzed from the implementation of NAFTA in 1994 to 1996.

at a 19.4 percent rate—almost double the pre-NAFTA rate. (See Table 2.) The United States had a trade surplus with Mexico of about $5 billion in 1992; based on current projections, the 1997 trade balance will show a deficit of about $11 billion.

If one judges the value of NAFTA solely on the change in the U.S. trade balance since its implementation, as some of its opponents do, NAFTA has not been good for the U.S. The U.S. trade deficit within NAFTA rose from near balance at $2.7 billion in pre-NAFTA 1992 to $39.0 billion in 1996. (It is expected to fall to about $25 billion in 1997—see Table 1 and Figure 3.)

But the trade deficit should not be the sole measure of NAFTA, and it is clear that the agreement has not been the primary cause of this swing. The sharp decline in the Mexican peso—from US$0.32 in 1993 to US$0.12 in late 1997—and a milder decline in the Canadian dollar—from US$0.77 in 1993 to US$0.70 in late 1997—have completely overwhelmed the effects of tariff reductions as the result of NAFTA. "Price cuts" resulting from reduced tariffs have been minuscule in comparison to the "price cuts" brought about by movements in the rates of exchange.

The effects of the recession in Canada, the peso crisis in Mexico, and the strong U.S. recovery have made it difficult to evaluate NAFTA. The President's report on NAFTA, in noting that NAFTA has had a "... modest positive effect on U.S. exports, income, investment and jobs..."[18] seems premature.

FIGURE 3

TRADE BALANCES WITHIN NAFTA

Billions of U.S. dollars

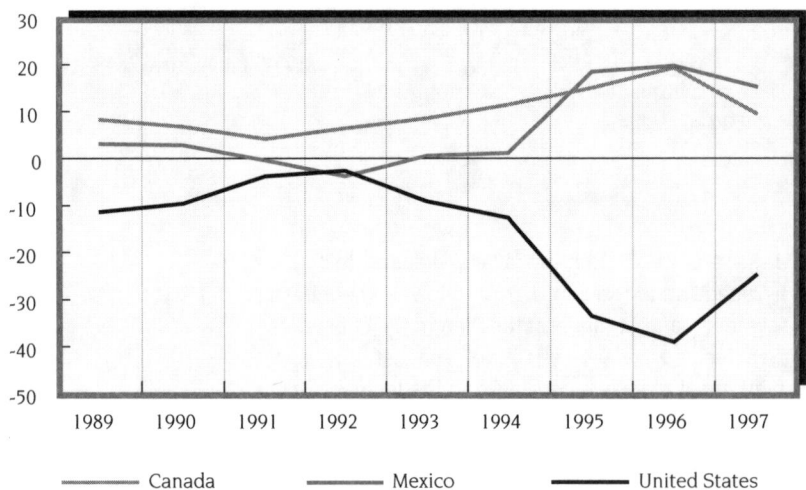

Sources: U.S. Bureau of the Census, Statistics Canada, and editors' estimates.

---

[18] Op. Cit. The President's Report to Congress.

TRADE IN SERVICES

New estimates of U.S. trade in services for 1993 through 1996, both worldwide and with NAFTA, have recently become available.[19] Worldwide, trade in services has become increasingly important to the United States, with an $80 billion surplus in 1996 partly offsetting a record $191 billion deficit in goods. Within NAFTA, the United States had a $2.5 billion surplus on trade in services in 1996, a combination of a $6.2 billion surplus with Canada and a $3.7 billion deficit with Mexico. (See Table 4)

The largest categories of U.S. trade in services are travel (expenditures of U.S. travelers abroad and foreign travelers in the United States) and "other private services," which includes educational, financial, telecommunications, business, professional and technical services. Of importance to the U.S. - Mexican trade figures, the "other private services" category also includes wages paid to cross-border commuters.

In 1996 the United States global surplus in travel exceeded $20 billion. The travel surpluses of the 1990s are a dramatic contrast to earlier decades, when spending by foreign visitors to the United States was far less than U.S. spending abroad. Within NAFTA, however, the United States had a small deficit in travel in 1996. This was in contrast to 1993 and reflects the impact of the peso devaluation on the relative costs of travel in Mexico and in the United States.

TABLE 3

U.S. GLOBAL TRADE IN SERVICES
(Billions of dollars)

	1993	1996	CHANGE
EXPORTS			
Total	172.4	221.2	48.8
Travel	57.9	69.9	12.0
Passenger fares	16.6	20.6	4.0
Other transportation	23.1	27.2	4.1
Royalties and license fees	20.3	30.0	9.7
Other private services	54.5	73.6	19.1
IMPORTS			
Total	111.9	143.1	31.2
Travel	40.7	48.7	8.0
Passenger fares	11.3	15.8	4.5
Other transportation	25.7	28.5	2.8
Royalties and license fees	4.8	7.3	2.5
Other private services	29.4	42.8	13.4

Source: U.S. Department of Commerce, Bureau of Economic Analysis.

As can be seen in Tables 3 and 4, the United States has experienced strong growth in exports of "other private services" within NAFTA (and globally as well), reflecting its competitive edge in business, professional, financial, and technical services. For U.S.–Mexican trade the "other private services" group is heavily influenced by the inclusion of the wages paid to cross-border commuting workers. In 1996, for the sub-category including these wages, U.S. payments to Mexico were $2.8 billion. Mexican payments to the U.S., at $1.6 billion, were also substantial.

---

[19] Michael A. Mann, et al, *Survey of Current Business*, Bureau of Economic Analysis, Oct. 1997, p. 95.

TABLE 4

U.S. TRADE IN SERVICES WITH CANADA AND MEXICO
(Billions of dollars)

	1993			1996		
	CANADA	MEXICO	TOTAL	CANADA	MEXICO	TOTAL
EXPORTS						
Total	17.4	9.3	26.9	20.0	7.9	27.9
Travel	7.5	5.1	12.6	6.8	3.0	9.8
Passenger fares	1.2	0.6	1.8	1.3	0.6	1.9
Other transportation	2.1	0.5	2.6	2.9	0.6	3.5
Royalties and license fees	1.2	0.5	1.7	1.4	0.5	1.9
Other private services	5.5	2.7	8.2	7.6	3.2	10.8
IMPORTS						
Total	10.3	9.8	20.1	13.8	11.6	25.4
Travel	3.7	5.2	8.9	4.6	6.0	10.6
Passenger fares	0.3	0.6	0.9	0.4	0.6	1.0
Other transportation	2.9	0.4	3.3	3.6	0.5	4.1
Royalties and license fees	0.1	0.1	0.2	0.2	0.1	0.3
Other private services	3.3	3.5	6.8	5.0	4.4	9.4

Source: U.S. Department of Commerce, Bureau of Economic Analysis.

NAFTA-TAA

For the United States, there is another way to evaluate the effects of NAFTA on the economy and especially on jobs. As a part of the NAFTA Implementation Act, the U.S. Congress created NAFTA-TAA (Trade Adjustment Assistance) administered by the Labor Department. NAFTA-TAA provides that companies, unions, or workers who believe jobs have been lost due to increased imports from the NAFTA countries may apply for assistance.[20] If a case is certified (if it is found that the workers did lose their jobs as a result of NAFTA), workers may receive assistance and training. Table 5, NAFTA-TAA Cases Certified, 1994-June 18, 1997, shows the results by two-digit Standard Industrial Classification (SIC) industries.

As of June 18, 1997, NAFTA-TAA had certified 1,102 cases involving 129,450 U.S. workers who lost their jobs due to NAFTA-related production shifts or increased imports. Certification was denied in 714 cases involving 81,532 workers. Since the system is based on self-reporting (the affected parties are responsible for bringing it to the attention of NAFTA-TAA), it is biased toward large companies and union-represented workers.[21] Professor Raul Hinojosa Ojeda of UCLA estimates that only about half the jobs actually lost are reported to NAFTA-TAA.[22] If this is correct, about 260,000 jobs have been lost in the United States as a result of NAFTA since its implementation. This is, of course, a "gross" figure since increased exports have clearly tended to increase employment, and the "net" figure would be smaller or perhaps would show a net job gain.[23]

Table 6 shows the 10 U.S. industries with the largest number of TAA-certified workers. Apparel, electronic and electrical equipment, and transportation equipment lead the list. Table 7 shows the results by state, and Table 8 shows the 10 states with the largest number of certified workers.

---

[20] NAFTA-TAA office, 202/219-5555.

[21] Ojeda, Raul Hinojosa, et al, "North American Integration Three Years After NAFTA," UCLA, School of Public Policy and Social Research, Dec. 1996, pp. 56-57. N.B. The President's report on NAFTA interprets the NAFTA-TAA figures differently. "Workers may be certified if the worker is at risk of losing his or her job due to trade or production shift in North America." (emphasis added.) The President's report suggests that actual jobs lost are fewer than the NAFTA-TAA data suggest.

[22] Ibid.

[23] It is clear that increased exports do increase employment, but not so clear that increased imports have the same "one-for-one" effect. For example, imports from Mexico may be substitutes for imports from other underdeveloped countries, and Maquiladora imports contain significant amounts of U.S. manufactured materials.

TABLE 5

WORKERS CERTIFIED FOR TRADE ADJUSTMENT ASSISTANCE BY INDUSTRY

SIC	INDUSTRY	NUMBER OF WORKERS	SOURCE OF JOB LOSS		
			MEXICO	CANADA	UNIDENTIFIED
1	Agricultural production-crops	2,212	2,150	.....	62
2	Agricultural production—livestock	105	.....	105	.....
10	Metal mining	1,208	.....	1,208	.....
13	Oil & gas extraction	1,054	.....	315	739
15	Building construction general contractors	19	.....	19	.....
17	Construction -special trades	50	.....	50	.....
20	Food & beverages	1,869	196	653	1,020
22	Textile mill products	4,529	1,807	659	2,063
23	Apparel & kindred products	28,362	21,504	186	6,672
24	Lumber & wood products ex furn	5,517	12	3,520	1,985
25	Furniture & fixtures	2,820	2,343	400	77
26	Paper & allied products	4,734	430	1,546	2,758
27	Printing & publishing	1,432	212	20	1,200
28	Chemicals & allied products	2,033	855	1,063	115
29	Petroleum refining	21	.....	21	.....
30	Rubber & miscellaneous plastic products	3,690	2,884	470	336
31	Leather & leather products	5,873	1,617	2,619	1,637
32	Stone, clay & glass	4,057	2,897	854	306
33	Primary metals	4,357	1,917	1,802	638
34	Fabricated metal products	6,595	3,706	2,641	248
35	Industrial & commercial machinery	4,830	4,180	473	177
36	Electronic & electric equipment	21,029	18,108	1,296	1,625
37	Transportation equipment	10,100	9,251	439	410
38	Instruments	4,823	3,121	293	1,409
39	Other manufacturing	2,539	2,497	42	.....
49	Electric, gas & sanitation services	4,062	.....	4,062	.....
50	Wholesale trade, durables	299	181	88	30
51	Wholesale trade, nondurables	697	465	170	62
73	Business services	474	319	155	.....
76	Miscellaneous repair services	56	56	.....	.....
87	Engineering, accounting & related	4	.....	4	.....
	Total	129,450	80,708	25,173	23,569

Source: Department of Labor, Office of Trade Adjustment Assistance, June 18, 1997; calculations by editor.

TABLE 6

TEN INDUSTRIES WITH THE MOST CERTIFIED WORKERS—1994 TO JUNE 18, 1997

SIC	INDUSTRY	NUMBER OF WORKERS	SOURCE OF JOB LOSS			PERCENT OF 1993 WORKERS[1]
			MEXICO	CANADA	UNIDENTIFIED	
23	Apparel	28,362	21,504	186	6,672	2.9
36	Electronic & electric equipment	21,029	18,108	1,296	1,625	1.4
37	Transportation equipment	10,100	9,251	439	410	0.6
34	Fabricated metal products	6,595	3,706	2,641	248	0.5
31	Leather & leather products	5,873	1,617	2,619	1,637	5.0
24	Lumber & wood products	5,517	12	3,520	1,985	0.8
35	Industrial & commercial machinery	4,830	4,180	473	177	0.3
38	Instruments	4,823	3,121	293	1,409	0.5
26	Paper & allied products	4,734	430	1,546	2,758	0.7
22	Textile mill products	4,529	1,807	659	2,063	0.7

1. Percent of total wage and salary employment in the industry.

Source: U.S. Department of Labor, Office of Trade Adjustment Assistance, calculations by editors.

TABLE 7

WORKERS CERTIFIED FOR TRADE ADJUSTMENT ASSISTANCE BY STATE

STATE	NUMBER OF WORKERS	SOURCE OF JOB LOSS		
		MEXICO	CANADA	UNIDENTIFIED
Alaska	780	.....	280	500
Alabama	1,383	1,133	.....	250
Arkansas	5,397	2,154	2,978	265
Arizona	684	684	.....	.....
California	7,351	6,085	761	505
Colorado	1,990	903	587	500
Connecticut	631	616	15	.....
Florida	2,804	2,777	5	22
Georgia	6,186	3,450	621	2,115
Iowa	83	83	.....	.....
Idaho	2,005	250	1,438	317
Illinois	2,902	1,890	924	88
Indiana	5,691	5,022	513	156
Kansas	1,184	484	.....	700
Kentucky	1,016	665	159	192
Louisiana	778	500	184	94
Massachusetts	1,315	837	378	100
Maryland	86	86	.....	.....
Maine	432	432	.....	.....
Michigan	3,783	1,428	1,926	429
Minnesota	336	176	160	.....
Missouri	3,049	2,404	-	645
Montana	613	32	579	2
North Carolina	13,272	10,918	416	1,938
North Dakota	300	.....	300	.....
Nebraska	220	220	.....	.....
New Hampshire	139	139	.....	.....
New Jersey	4,471	2,279	1,258	934
New Mexico	242	122	50	70
Nevada	76	76	.....	.....
New York	10,985	4,030	5,585	1,370
Ohio	3,989	3,235	478	276
Oklahoma	230	224	.....	6
Oregon	2,135	597	600	938
Pennsylvania	10,682	6,659	737	3,286
South Carolina	2,305	2,118	187	.....
South Dakota	65	.....	.....	65
Tennessee	5,493	3,624	122	1,747
Texas	12,018	9,893	512	1,613
Utah	292	175	75	42
Virginia	2,166	1,730	4	432
Vermont	361	276	85	.....
Washington	3,445	490	1,811	1,144
Wisconsin	4,405	1,259	668	2,478
West Virginia	1,288	498	470	320
Wyoming	392	55	307	30
Totals	129,450	80,708	25,173	23,569

Source: U.S. Department of Labor, Office of Trade Adjustment Assistance

TABLE 8

Ten States with Most Certified Workers

Rank	State	Number of Workers	Source of Job Loss			Percent of 1993 Workers[1]
			Mexico	Canada	Unidentified	
1	North Carolina	13,272	10,918	416	1,938	0.41
2	Texas	12,018	9,893	512	1,613	0.16
3	New York	10,985	4,030	5,585	1,370	0.14
4	Pennsylvania	10,682	6,659	737	3,286	0.21
5	California	7,351	6,085	761	505	0.06
6	Georgia	6,186	3,450	621	2,115	0.20
7	Indiana	5,691	5,022	513	156	0.22
8	Tennessee	5,493	3,624	122	1,747	0.24
9	Arkansas	5,397	2,154	2,978	265	0.54
10	New Jersey	4,471	2,279	1,258	934	0.13

1. Percent of total nonagricultural wage and salary employment in state.

Source: U.S. Department of Labor, Office of Trade Adjustment Assistance.

Even using the more pessimistic 260,000 estimate of job loss attributable to NAFTA, this is only 0.2 percent of total U.S. employment in 1996 and less than 3 percent of the employment growth from 1993 to 1997. But the job loss has been highly concentrated in a few industries and a few states (Tables 4 and 6.) North Carolina, which accounts for 28 percent of all U.S. earnings from textile manufacture, has had the greatest certified job loss. However, measured as a percent of total employment in each state, Arkansas has experienced the greatest impact. Even so, the certified job loss is equal to less than 0.4 percent of total Arkansas employment in 1996.

On the national level, the impact has been slight, but some localities have clearly suffered more than their share of NAFTA's adverse effects. Arkansas and North Carolina are states with per capita incomes below the U.S. average. NAFTA's impact on jobs, as measured by NAFTA-TAA certifications, has been most severe on a few, mostly poor, communities that have suffered job losses from low cost imports for a number of years. For many of these communities, workers losing jobs as a result of imports are often unable to take advantage of new jobs opening up in other locations or for other skills.

The relatively modest overall impact of NAFTA to date seems to be an eminently predictable result, in that the major changes in the factors that underlie trilateral trade—particularly Mexico-U.S. trade—were established well before NAFTA was signed. Some pertinent facts and conclusions include:

- Opportunities for U.S. firms to move south did not begin with NAFTA. The Maquiladora program permitted U.S. and Canadian firms to move most phases of production to Mexico with minimum duty on either side. NAFTA does make such moves somewhat easier in that foreign firms may now own a larger percentage of Mexican establishments than before, and financing may be more direct since foreign financial institutions are now permitted to operate in Mexico.

- The decline in U.S. tariffs required by NAFTA was small—U.S. tariffs were quite low before NAFTA was contemplated, averaging less than 4 percent. They had been virtually eliminated for Canada by the CUSFTA. For Mexico, a "most favored nation," U.S. tariffs on manufactured goods had averaged about 4 percent—less than the sales tax in many jurisdictions. For most products manufactured in Mexico, the pre-NAFTA tariffs were only a minor barrier.[24]

---

[24] U.S. tariffs averaged just above 4 percent prior to January 1994, then dropped to about 1 percent. Many goods enjoy tariffs substantially higher than the average. For example, textiles (about 20 percent), footwear (8.5 to 70 percent), color picture tubes (15 percent), and small trucks (25 percent). All tariffs are to be eliminated eventually.

- The United States appears to have gained more from NAFTA tariff reductions than did Mexico. (See Table 9.) Immediately prior to NAFTA, Mexican tariffs on U.S. goods, which once averaged nearly 50 percent, had been reduced to an average of about 12 percent, with many items in the 15-20 percent range. At the implementation of the agreement, Mexican tariffs came down, on average, about 7.5 percentage points. The drop in the five years before NAFTA was significantly greater than the decrease required by NAFTA. [25]

- NAFTA did not cause the Mexican peso crisis—if anything, the agreement made the future of Mexico's economy and its peso stronger not weaker. The sharp recession that followed, although punishing, was shorter and less painful than those in the past in which tariffs were raised and foreign trade languished. In fact, it could be argued that NAFTA has given Mexico's economy a resilience, and perhaps future stability, that will benefit its partners as well as itself.

TABLE 9

TARIFFS AND IMPORT SHARES—U.S. IMPORTS FROM MEXICO & MEXICAN IMPORTS FROM THE UNITED STATES

| | U. S. IMPORTS FROM MEXICO | | | | | MEXICAN IMPORTS FROM THE U.S. | | | | |
| | AVERAGE CUSTOMS DUTY | | PERCENTAGE POINT | MEXICAN SHARE OF TOTAL U.S. IMPORTS | | AVERAGE CUSTOMS DUTY | | PERCENTAGE POINT | U.S SHARE OF TOTAL MEXICAN IMPORTS | |
PRODUCT CATEGORY	1992	1996	REDUCTION	1996	CHANGE	1992	1996	REDUCTION	1996	CHANGE
I Animals & products	0.7	.....	0.7	5.7	(1.8)	6.5	4.4	2.1	61.0	0.4
II Vegetable products	5.6	2.8	2.8	22.5	0.4	4.1	1.7	2.5	83.5	6.5
III Waxes, fats & oils	2.5	1.0	1.5	3.5	0.5	12.0	8.3	3.7	59.7	3.5
IV Food, beverages, spirits & tabacco	3.6	2.2	1.4	6.9	1.8	15.2	9.6	5.6	69.0	(1.3)
V Minerial products	0.5	.....	0.4	9.3	0.6	3.3	1.7	1.6	77.3	2.4
VI Chemicals & products	1.0	0.5	0.6	2.7	0.3	10.2	4.0	6.2	60.3	3.2
VII Plastics, rubber & products	1.1	0.2	0.9	4.7	1.3	13.9	8.2	5.7	86.3	0.3
VIII Leather, travel goods, etc	5.5	1.7	3.8	3.7	0.9	8.8	5.1	3.7	82.5	9.9
IX Wood & related articles	0.3	0.1	0.3	3.3	(0.3)	14.4	5.0	9.4	82.8	0.1
X Pulp, paper & products	0.6	0.1	0.5	2.5	1.1	8.4	3.6	4.9	88.1	7.4
XI Textiles & apparel	9.1	1.3	7.8	9.6	5.2	16.0	5.3	10.7	86.4	17.2
XII Footwear, headgear & related	7.8	4.1	3.8	2.5	0.4	18.8	0.6	18.2	51.8	21.4
XIII Ceramics, glass, etc.	4.3	2.6	1.8	11.3	2.1	16.0	6.2	9.7	71.2	6.5
XIV Jewelry, precious metals & stones	0.1	.....	0.1	2.9	1.0	5.4	1.9	3.6	87.7	34.8
XV Base metals & articles	2.0	1.3	0.7	7.6	2.1	12.4	6.7	5.8	75.1	4.1
XVI Electronic goods & appliances	2.6	0.4	2.2	10.9	2.0	13.4	4.4	9.0	74.3	5.7
XVII Transport equipment	1.6	0.6	1.1	12.3	5.7	15.1	4.9	10.2	83.1	19.2
XVIII Scientific & other instruments	2.9	0.4	2.5	8.8	2.0	12.9	1.5	11.5	67.1	3.2
XIX Arms & ammunition	0.2	-	0.2	1.4	(1.0)	14.7	.....	14.7	28.0	(16.6)
XX Miscellaneous manufactured articles	1.1	0.1	1.0	9.4	2.2	18.3	6.0	12.3	73.1	4.8
XXI Art & antiques	.....	.....	.....	0.6	(0.2)	14.5	.....	14.5	48.5	(13.8)
Other	.....	.....	.....	10.5	1.1	9.8	6.9	2.9	46.0	(21.3)
Total, all product groups	.....	.....	1.7	9.2	2.3	.....	.....	7.2	75.5	6.2

1. These groupings are based on broad trade categories used in the U.S. Harmonized Tariff Schedule. They account for all goods traded between the United States and Mexico. Comparative differences in U.S. and Mexico tariff reductions for the product groupings during 1993-96 are based on constructed values using 1992 tariffs, 1993 trade flows, and staged tariff reductions under the NAFTA.

2. Percentage point difference between 1993 and 1996. Parentheses indicate decrease.

Source: Study on the Operation and Effects of the North American Free Trade Agreement, President's Report to the Congress, July 1997, Chapter 2, Tables 1, 2, and 3.

[25] Mexican tariffs averaged just above 12 percent prior to January 1994, then dropped to about 4 percent. Many goods enjoy tariffs substantially higher than the average. All tariffs are to be eliminated eventually. (See Table 7.)

FUTURE DEVELOPMENTS

NAFTA portends greater integration of the economies of Canada, the United States, and Mexico. Without tariffs and other barriers to trade, many aspects of the three economies will merge and function as one. In theory, only transportation costs (and perhaps cultural or language differences) would limit the market for any producer or service provider in any of the three countries. For example, a buyer living in Kansas City (or Winnipeg or Aguascalientes) will be sought after by producers in Toronto or Monterey in addition to producers closer to home. These changes, of course, could also mean that some nearby, but less efficient, producers would decline or go out of business. The North American continent will increasingly become an integrated whole with efficient producers reaching out to every corner. Time will tell how far integration will go. Critics will, no doubt, continue to be vocal in their opposition, but barring a major economic crisis, NAFTA members appear to be on course toward economic integration.

Already there are examples of integrated industries. The motor vehicle industry in Canada and the United States is integrated as a result of the Canadian-U.S Auto Free Trade Agreement; the Mexican-U.S. motor vehicle industry is rapidly moving toward the same status. Although not as far along, the textile and apparel industries of Canada, the United States, and Mexico are rapidly moving toward integration, as is the chemical industry. There will be many other examples in the near future.

For a time, it appeared that NAFTA might expand rapidly geographically. At the "Miami Summit of the Americas" in 1994, the Clinton Administration proposed to negotiate an expanded NAFTA incorporating all the nations of the Hemisphere by 2005. Speaker of the House Newt Gingrich spoke favorably of the proposed Free Trade Area of the Americas (FTAA) at a conference organized by former President Jimmy Carter at the Carter Center in Atlanta in the spring of 1997.[26] It was also proposed that Chile be added to NAFTA well in advance and that a Caribbean free trade area be established early.

In September 1997, President Clinton asked Congress to grant him "fast track" authority for negotiations leading to trade agreements. Particular future negotiations were not specified in the bill, but it was clear that Chile and other Latin American trade partners were on the horizon. Fast track would permit the President to negotiate trade agreements that would then be voted up or down by Congress, but not amended. All Presidents since Gerald Ford had been given this authority. The idea is that other countries do not want to negotiate detailed trade deals that may then be effectively renegotiated in Congress via the addition of numerous amendments protecting particular interests.

President Clinton worked hard to get fast track passed, but in the end the bill was withdrawn when it became apparent that he did not have the votes to win in the House of Representatives. The opposition was mainly from the President's own party, led by Minority Leader Richard Gephardt. In announcing the withdrawal, the President said he would reintroduce the bill in 1998, but many observers believe it has even less chance to succeed then.

The full consequences of this setback are not immediately clear. Some supporters of extended free trade suggest negotiations can proceed if President Clinton and the Republican Congressional leaders restate their commitment to fast track and the Free Trade Area of the Americas, and if a critical mass of Latin American countries want to continue negotiations.[27] A summit meeting on free trade in the Western Hemisphere is scheduled for Santiago, Chile, in April, but Chile's foreign minister, Jose Miquel Insulza, has been quoted as saying that the meeting "…won't move much of anything if the U.S. doesn't have [fast track] authority."[28]

---

[26] Rosenfeld, Stephen S., "Gingrich's Surprise," *The Washington Post*, May 2, 1997.

[27] Conversation with Robert Devlin of the Inter-American Development Bank, Nov. 14, 1997.

[28] "Defeat on Trade Bill May Weaken Clinton in Last Three Years," *Wall Street Journal*, Nov. 11, 1997.

An immediate consequence will be to strengthen Mercosur, the South American common market group consisting of Argentina, Brazil, Paraguay, and Uruguay. Brazil, the generally acknowledged leader, has long resisted the idea of FTAA as a simple expansion of NAFTA led by the United States. Thus, it is quite possible that future U.S. trade negotiations in South America will be with Mercosur rather than with individual countries such as Chile or Argentina.

Postponement of U.S. negotiations with Chile seems certain. Chile already has trade agreements with Canada and Mexico, but has refused to negotiate with the United States without fast track authority. Chile's Insulza said recently, "We now see free trade with the U.S. as a more remote possibility."[29]

The recent collapse of stock markets in Thailand, Hong Kong and elsewhere and the monetary crisis in several Far Eastern countries have strengthened the U.S. dollar as a store of value throughout the world. In fact, in mid-November 1997, the value of the U.S. dollar rose to 1.42 Canadian dollars and 8.25 Mexican new pesos. Of course, this makes U.S. exports to those nations still more expensive and imports from them still cheaper. The apparent recovery in the U.S. balance of trade with NAFTA in early 1997 could be slowed or reversed in 1998.

In the long run, the impact of NAFTA will reach beyond the Americas. Rather than simply a North American agreement, designed by North Americans for North Americans, NAFTA could become a model for future agreements elsewhere in the world. NAFTA is unique in that a less developed nation is joining two highly developed countries as an equal partner. It is an experiment that many are watching closely because NAFTA could set the pattern for similar agreements between developed and undeveloped countries throughout the world.

---

[29] Faiola, Anthony, "Fast Track Fallout Blankets S. America," *The Washington Post*, Nov. 12, 1997.

THE EVOLUTION OF NORTH AMERICAN TRADE POLICIES

North American trade policies have evolved erratically through the years, from extreme protectionism at times to the free trade and economic integration now being pursued under the North American Free Trade Agreement (NAFTA). In evaluating the results of NAFTA so far, and the prospects for its future, it is instructive to look at past relationships among the three members and the trade policies and trade arrangements that have grown out of these relationships.

CANADIAN TRADE POLICY

Canadian trade policy is very much influenced by its relationship with the United States. This relationship is characterized by four factors:[1]

Similarity: While not identical, there are few countries in the world with more shared characteristics than the United States and Canada. Politically they share British traditions of democracy, law, values, and customs. Majorities in both countries speak English. On both sides of the border, television viewers and radio listeners share programs.

Alliance: While Canada and the United States have their differences (e.g., Vietnam, Cuba), they have been allies in both world wars, Korea, and the cold war. Canada lacks the population or resources to defend its huge territory without the aid of the United States, and the United States would be hard put to defend itself without Canadian cooperation.

Interdependence: The two countries share the largest bilateral trade in the world. Canada sends 80 percent of its exports to the United States and receives 67 percent of its imports from the United States. The United States sends 22 percent of its exports to Canada, which supplies 19 percent of its imports. Three-quarters of Canadian citizens live within 100 miles of the United States, and many find it easier to travel, communicate, and trade with this country than with other Canadians to the east or west.

---

[1] Leyton-Brown, David, "Canada—U.S. Relations and the Quandary of Interdependence," The Strathrobyn Papers (IN).

A PRECURSOR TO NAFTA: THE CANADIAN-U.S. AUTO FREE TRADE AGREEMENT [1]

Although various free trade schemes have been proposed over the years, one of the first along modern lines was the Canadian-U.S. Auto Free Trade Agreement of 1965. Prior to that agreement, the major U.S. manufacturers dominated the Canadian new car market, but virtually all manufacturing was done in the United States. In the 1960s, the Canadian government threatened to raise tariffs and foster a Canadian auto industry if the U.S. industry didn't move to build some plants in Canada and integrate them with the U.S. industry.

The result of this pressure from Canada was an agreement—signed by President Johnson and Prime Minister Lester B. Pearson on January 16, 1965—that eliminated tariffs on motor vehicles and parts manufactured in both countries. Replacement parts were not covered. This agreement is referred to, at least by Canadians, as a great success in that many auto models and components of all American auto companies are now manufactured in Canada for sale in both countries. One might argue that the auto agreement set the pattern for the movement of U.S. production facilities to other countries.

---

[1] *New York Times*, 1/18/65, pp. 29-30. Interestingly, it notes that "...both Canadian and U.S. officials here say that...it would be a mistake to anticipate from Canada any great interest in economic union with the United States."

Asymmetry: Although Canada is slightly larger than the United States in territory, it is substantially smaller and less powerful in almost every other way. The United States has nine times the population of Canada, 10 times the GDP, and four times the arable land. The United States is the world's remaining superpower, whereas Canada is not a major military power. Canada's most important foreign policy consideration is its relationship with the United States, but to the United States, Canadian concerns are often secondary to other more pressing needs.

It is this last factor in Canada-U.S. relations that many Canadians seem to think of first. In fact, they often express fear of political and economic dominance by the United States. The *Encyclopedia Britannica* notes, "The most striking aspect of Canadian mining and manufacturing is the extent of foreign ownership or influence."[2] That ownership and influence is, of course, mostly American. Two-thirds of Canadian unions are affiliated with American organizations. Former Prime Minister Brian Mulroney, speaking of Canada's overwhelming economic dependence on the United States, once joked that being in bed with an elephant is terrific, but if he ever rolls over, you're a dead man.[3] Canadians are attracted by the economic benefits of the close association with the United States, but wary of the dangers of political and cultural domination.

A sampling of titles included in a Canadian Internet posting, "Selected Reading list on Canada-U.S. Relations," tells the story:

> "Take Back the Nation"
> "Dismantling a Nation: Canada and the New World Order"
> "The Fight for Canada: Four Centuries of Resistance to American Expansionism"
> "Canada and the United States: Differences that Count."

Former Prime Minister Pierre Trudeau ordered a systematic policy review of the Canada-U. S. relationship in the 1970s. The upshot was to launch an effort to diversify by expanding trade with Europe and Asia and to build a regulatory wall against cultural invasion by limiting access to foreign (American) books, magazines, and movies. Neither effort achieved much success. [4]

---

[2] *Encyclopedia Britannica*, 15th Edition, 1994.

[3] Bankers' Assoc. for Foreign Trade, "Trading & Prosperity: a Canadian Perspective," Boca Raton, FL., May 17, 1993 (IN).

[4] Leyton-Brown and Bankers' Assoc.

A PRECURSOR TO NAFTA: THE CANADIAN-U.S. FREE TRADE AGREEMENT, 1988.

Canadian Prime Minister Brian Mulroney proposed a free trade agreement between Canada and the United States in September 1985. The Canadian electorate had rejected various "free trade" proposals in the past, but Mulroney laid the groundwork by emphasizing that Canada had succeeded in maintaining its identity through many trials. His speeches often congratulated Canadians for their independence and stout support of Canadian culture and values in spite of the dominating presence of their neighbor to the south.

After long negotiation, the final text of an agreement was signed on January 2, 1988, and the U.S. Congress passed the implementation act in September 1988. But the Canadian Parliament had not approved the agreement, and many authorities on both sides of the border doubted that it would ever come about. Mulroney made the agreement the central issue of the parliamentary election of 1988: his party and his personal re-election as Prime Minister would stand or fall based on the electorate's reaction. As the November election approached, experts and opinion polls alike predicted that Mulroney's Conservatives and his trade agreement would be defeated.[1] In fact, the Conservatives won, and the new parliament ratified the agreement on December 30, 1988.

---

[1] The present writer went to lunch with five Canadian government officials in Ottawa in early November 1988; they were unanimous in their opinion that Mulroney and the agreement would go down to defeat. In contrast, the U.S. public seemed only mildly interested in the agreement at that time.

CANADIAN—U.S. FREE TRADE AGREEMENT CHRONOLOGY[1]

SEPTEMBER 26, 1985.	Canadian Prime Minister Brian Mulroney formally requests that the United States and Canada start negotiations on a U.S.- Canada Free Trade Agreement.
DECEMBER 10, 1985.	President Reagan notifies the U.S. Congress of his intention to enter into a bilateral negotiation with Canada
JUNE 17, 1986.	Negotiations begin to establish a free trade agreement.
OCTOBER 3, 1987.	A basic free trade agreement is initialed.
DECEMBER 9, 1987.	Final text is completed.
JANUARY 2, 1988.	President of the United States and Prime Minister of Canada sign the agreement.
SEPTEMBER 28, 1988.	The U.S. Congress passes, and the President signs, the U.S.-Canada Free Trade Agreement Implementation Act of 1988.
DECEMBER 30, 1988.	The Canadian Parliament approves the Agreement.
JANUARY 1, 1989.	The Canada-United States Free Trade Agreement takes effect.

[1] Lillian Dayan, York University, Canada, 2/9/95 (IN).

The Administration of Brian Mulroney took a different tack—he celebrated the distinctiveness of Canada and emphasized its strength and independence. Mulroney then surprised almost everyone by proposing the Canadian–American Free Trade Agreement and laid the groundwork for Canada's acceptance of NAFTA.

A factor influencing Canadian foreign policy is the status of Quebec. (See "An Independent Quebec?"). The status of Quebec is Canada's most important domestic policy matter and so affects Canada's relationship with the United States indirectly; Quebec's potential as a trading partner with the United States in the event the province becomes independent is a matter of concern to both sides in the debate.

MEXICAN TRADE POLICY

As in Canada, foreign policy in Mexico is heavily influenced by proximity to the United States. The U.S.-Mexico relationship has always been more important to Mexico than to the United States. The U.S. economy is about nine times the size of the Mexican economy. Historically, the United States has received about 85 percent of Mexican exports, while its exports to Mexico have averaged only about 5 percent of the U.S. total. Also, U.S. investors have long played a major role in Mexican industry and trade. In the19th and early 20th centuries, the United States often threatened armed intervention to protect those investments. It is, therefore, natural that relationships with the United States have been an overwhelming Mexican consideration in the formation of trade and economic policy, whereas the United States has often looked upon Mexican trade as important, but of secondary concern.

In the 19th century, raw materials were the principal Mexican export, and many of the mines, wells, and farms producing them were owned and managed by foreigners; for example, publisher William Randolph Hearst held title to 8 million acres in Mexico.[5] Mexico had to import most needed manufactured goods, particularly consumer and capital

[5] Ruiz, Ramon Eduardo, *Triumphs and Tragedy*, Norton 1992, p. 305.

durables. At the turn of the century, President Porfirio Diaz welcomed British, French, and American corporations to increase their investments in Mexico and open new manufacturing facilities. [6]

Diaz was deposed after the defeat of his army by a rebel force in 1911.[7] There followed a period of 18 years of military coups, short-term governments, and economic hardship. The worldwide depression of the late 1920s hit Mexico especially hard and was worsened by high U.S. tariffs and by drought in the early 1930s. Protracted economic hardship left the Mexican people and its government with a heightened awareness of foreign economic domination. In March 1938, the administration of President Lazaro Cardenas expropriated the oil holdings of foreign companies and established PEMEX (Petroleos Mexicanos) as a government monopoly. The United States did not object because the majority of these holdings were British or Dutch and it seemed likely that PEMEX would turn to U.S. firms for equipment and technical assistance. [8]

This action was followed by the enactment of high tariffs designed to encourage domestic industry. [9] In addition, Mexico passed laws to reduce foreign influence in the economy, making foreign control of companies in some industries illegal. In the 1945-1975 period, Mexico extended the policy of developing domestic industries to replace imported consumer goods and services with a growing emphasis on state owned and operated enterprises. The country imported intermediate goods for domestic production of consumer goods in a policy known as "Import Substituting Industrialization."[10] Communications, transportation, and a number of other industries became government monopolies, or were dominated by state enterprises. [11]

These policies essentially were failures. Overall growth was slow, and per capita growth even slower as population doubled from 1935 to 1955 and rose another 82 percent from 1955 to 1975. Social problems festered, and President Gustavo Diaz Ordaz (1964-1970) was forced to use repressive tactics, culminating in the violent suppression of protests preceding the 1968 Olympics.[12]

The Administration of President Jose Lopez Portillo (1976-1982) was marked by good fortune in the beginning as world oil prices jumped and Mexico's export revenues rose rapidly. Predictions of continued increases in oil prices permitted Mexico to borrow heavily against future revenues. This was the period of the "sovereign risk" concept, whereby nations were considered to be exempt from bankruptcy and large banks (particularly large U.S. banks) "recycled" petro-dollars by lending them to developing countries, including an eager Mexico. The oil revenues and loans permitted Mexico to maintain a large current account deficit and relieved social pressure on the government. Government expenditures increased by about one-third in 1979 and two-thirds in 1980. Mexico's external debt increased 10-fold between 1970 and 1980,[13] and the state sector became bloated and inefficient.

In 1982—an election year—Mexico's luck ran out when the oil market crashed. Incoming President Miquel de la Madrid was faced with a staggering US$85 billion in foreign debt. A

---

[6] La Botz, Dan, *Edward Doheny*, Praeger 1991 pp. 21–29.

[7] Ruiz, p 317.

[8] La Botz, pp. 21-29.

[9] Mexico was not alone; many other countries adopted similar policies at this time.

[10] Ojeda, Raul Hinojosa, *North American Integration Three Years After NAFTA*, UCLA, 1996.

[11] Nolan, James L., Mexico Business, World Trade Press, 1994.

[12] Ibid.

[13] "Mexico," *Encyclopedia Britannica*, 15th edition, 1994.

A PRECURSOR TO NAFTA: ECONOMIC GROWTH AND STABILIZATION IN MEXICO.

The 1982 financial crisis—precipitated by plunging oil prices and, in August 1982, by foreign banks' cessation of all lending to Mexico–was followed in 1985 by a devastating earthquake in Mexico City that left the country in desperate straits. Mexican foreign debt peaked in 1987 at US$107.4 billion, 76 percent of Mexico's GDP. Inflation soared, and real per capita income dropped by almost 50 percent. President de la Madrid initiated liberalization of industry and trade, including the Maquiladora program,[1] and pushed for full membership in GATT, which it achieved in 1986. (See: "The Maquiladora-9802 Program: A Forerunner to NAFTA" in this book.) A concerted effort was also made to increase non-oil exports in order to reduce dependence on oil prices. By 1988, non-oil exports had increased to 66 percent of the total.[2]

In January 1989, the new administration of Carlos Salinas de Gortari initiated "The Pact for Stabilization and Economic Growth," designed to reduce inflation and increase industrialization. Price and wage controls reduced profits and held wages in check. The program did reduce inflation, although it remained at rates that might be considered unacceptable elsewhere. Salinas also accelerated the privatization of government enterprises. By mid-1990, 845 state-owned businesses out of a total of 1,155 had been sold to private businesses, merged, or closed. Real economic growth reached 3.9 percent in 1990 and 4.0 percent in 1991. Mexico had seemingly transformed itself into a stable, modern economy and an attractive candidate for partnership with its neighbors to the north.

_____

[1] The Maquiladora program is not limited to U.S. or Mexican firms; in recent years, third-country firms, mostly from Asia, have been set up in Mexico to take advantage of the program and the proximity to the United States.

[2] U.S. Small Business Administration, "Opportunity in Mexico: A Small Business Guide," Chap. 1. 6/21/93 (NTDB).

serious and prolonged crisis followed, with a sharply falling peso and deep, long-term recession. Mexico declared a moratorium on debt repayments, demanded restructuring of its loans, nationalized the banking system, and intensified the protectionist approach to trade. De la Madrid struggled to overcome the resulting massive economic problems and growing social unrest, but the Mexico City earthquake of 1985 (estimated to have caused US$4 billion in damages) was yet another terrible blow.

President de la Madrid was himself a U.S.-educated economist, and he added many "technocrats" to his staff. These men, called "los perfumados" (the perfumed ones), also were largely U.S. educated economists who believed in the power of the free market. These men initiated a re-examination of Mexico's traditional protectionist policies. Their work led to the opening of the Mexican economy and a genuine industrialization program. Most significantly, under de la Madrid's administration, the Maquiladora program was accelerated and Mexico moved to join the General Agreement on Tariffs and Trade (GATT).

U.S. TRADE POLICY

In its early years, America was a "developing nation," and as with developing nations today, tariff policy was a major issue. Alexander Hamilton's famous "Report on Manufactures" recommended high tariffs to protect "infant" industries while they matured enough to be competitive with foreign imports. But the vast majority of the population made its living from agriculture and agricultural exports and favored low tariffs, both to encourage exports and to make manufactured products cheaper. Also, not all industrialists wanted high tariffs; for example, many U.S. railroads were built originally with British rails. But the fall of the South in the Civil War and the rapid industrialization in the last third of the 19th Century tipped the balance toward a high tariff policy.

In the early 20th century, the United States continued its high tariff policy designed to encourage domestic industry. When World War I broke out in 1914, the European nations flooded the American market with orders for munitions and other products as well. Most of these exports were purchased on credit—loans made by American banks and investors to foreign governments—or paid for in gold that piled up in Fort Knox. In the mid-1920s, foreign governments began to default, and many of these loans were never repaid.[14]

_____

[14] Samuelson, Paul A., _Economics_, McGraw-Hill, 1967, pp. 681-682. Some argued that the boom times in the previous 15 years had been worth the losses. Leon Fraser, President of the First National Bank of New York, quipped, "It is better to have lent and lost than never to have lent at all."

Americans were fond of complaining that "solemn obligations" were not being honored while simultaneously barring imports—the only path to repayment for the debtor nations.

The reaction to the worldwide depression that began in the late1920s was the Smoot-Hawley tariff of 1930, which averaged almost 60 percent. First imports and then exports were reduced to a trickle. Americans who earned their livings in the export trade were thrown out of work. The United States was not alone; many other countries raised tariffs in the belief they were saving jobs at home at the expense of foreigners. High tariffs in the United States and many other countries virtually eliminated international trade as a means to recovery. The Roosevelt Administration's Trade Agreements Act of 1934 did introduce a series of reciprocal trade agreements that accomplished some reduction in tariffs.

After almost a decade of depression, the U.S. economy rebounded with the advent of war in Europe. The Allies, especially the United Kingdom, again flooded the United States with orders for munitions and other products needed to fight the war. Initially, borrowing from the U.S. government, banks, and investors financed these exports, but after the United States entered the war, many of the "exports" were financed by grants. After the war, with much of the world in ruins, demand for U.S. exports continued, largely with the help of U.S. government financing. But this time, a more realistic policy was adopted. The United States forgave many of these loans and launched the Marshall Plan and other programs, largely financed with grants, to help rebuild Europe.

Perhaps more important in the long run, the United States continued the slow process of lowering its high tariff wall even before the end of the war. All post-war administrations thought of themselves as "free-traders," although some were more so than others. Average tariffs were gradually reduced beginning with the Cordell Hull reciprocal trade agreements, continuing with the Kennedy trade act, and more recently with the General Agreement on Tariffs and Trade (GATT).

In an important sense, the road to NAFTA began in the post World War II confidence that Americans felt in their country and their economy. The United States was the one large, modern economy undamaged by the war. The predicted post-war depression never came, and boom times seemed here to stay. U.S. exports boomed, and the threat of "job-stealing imports" seemed remote. The United States became the advocate of "free trade," and initiated several tariff-lowering programs. By the end of the 1960s, the United States had among the lowest tariffs in the world. [15]

---

[15] There were important exceptions; e.g., textiles and apparel.

THE MAQUILADORA-9802 PROGRAM:
A FORERUNNER TO NAFTA

One of the major complaints about NAFTA is that it seems to encourage the relocation of U.S. and Canadian companies to Mexico. In reality, however, this trend has been going on for more than 20 years under Maquiladora-9802, a duty-free manufacturing and re-export program that grew out of a U.S. customs initiative. NAFTA's main impact has been to extend duty-free trade to all industries in Mexico, which, ideally, should stimulate economic growth in non-Maquiladora areas and, concurrently, boost demand for higher value imports from the United States and Canada.

HOW MAQUILADORA WORKS

Under the Maquiladora program, components and raw materials are imported into Mexico from abroad without duty and held in bond by the manufacturer while further processing takes place. The resulting products are then re-exported, with only the value-added portion subject to Mexican taxes. The program was initiated by the Mexican government more than 20 years ago and has enjoyed steady support and growth since. Its name comes from the share of the flour the miller gets for grinding the grain.

The underlying idea was to give Mexico a "jump start" on industrialization by encouraging foreign companies to provide capital, build plants, and train workers for manufacturing. A large number of U.S., Asian, and other foreign companies have taken advantage of this program to open plants, often with Mexican partners, for the assembly or other processing of products for export. Mexican workers earn their fee, or "maquiladora," by processing foreign materials. Mexican businesses gain the experience needed to open independent manufacturing facilities on their own. Foreign companies benefit from inexpensive labor working in modern, often high-tech plants. Maquiladora is rarely mentioned in discussions of NAFTA, yet the major problem many critics find with NAFTA—the encouragement it gives to relocation of U.S. companies in Mexico—has been there all along.

Maquiladora is a Mexican program and a Mexican success, but it had earlier roots in U.S. trade policy. The U.S. Customs 806-807 program,[1] initiated in the early 1960s, permitted duty-free reimports of U.S. manufactured parts and products that had not been "transformed" in the course of off-shore assembly.[2] The Maquiladora program eliminated Mexican duties on imported components, and U.S. duties had already been eliminated on those components incorporated in off-shore assembly. The Maquiladora program was thus a step along the way to NAFTA—it required changes in both the Mexican and the U.S. tariff rules, thereby greatly increasing trade between the two countries.

---

[1] When the Harmonized Tariff Schedule (HTS) was introduced in 1988 re-imported components and materials were placed under code HTS 9802.00.80—hence the 806—807 program was renamed the 9802 program. Of course, its use is not limited to Maquiladora or to Mexico.

[2] The words "transformed" and "assembly" have never been precisely defined and are subject to interpretation, but the essential idea is that the exported materials are not raw materials to be changed into another material or product, but components to be put together with other parts by low or semiskilled workers.

THE PROGRAM'S CHANGING ROLE

The program has been a development and employment engine for Mexico, although its recent exports have not kept pace with the surge in total Mexican exports since implementation of NAFTA. In 1993, the year before NAFTA took effect, more than half a million people were employed in Maquiladora industries; this figure rose to 750,000 people by 1996. Yet Maquiladora industries' share of exports declined from 42 percent of all manufactures exported in 1993 to 38 percent in 1996. A part of this decline may be attributed to changes in the rules governing Maquiladora sales: under the pre-NAFTA rules, output of Maquiladora plants could not be sold in Mexico; NAFTA rules provide for the gradual lifting of that restriction for products with high U.S. and Canadian content.

In the early years, virtually all Maquiladora facilities were located in the frontier states immediately south of the U.S. border, and 86 percent are still located there (Table 1). However, states further south are gradually increasing their participation.

TABLE 1

LOCATION OF MAQUILADORA ESTABLISHMENTS, 1996

STATE	NUMBER OF ESTABLISHMENTS	NUMBER OF EMPLOYEES
Total, all states	2,411	754,858
Total, frontier states	1,974	651,344
Aguaucalientes	49	11,781
Baja California *	793	159,519
Baja California Sur	7	1,936
Coahuila *	212	62,984
Chihuahua *	371	215,423
Durango	79	20,677
Gaunajuato	40	8,868
Jalisco	59	13,725
Edo De Mexico YDF	55	8,851
Nuevo Leon *	99	32,032
Puebla	34	12,046
Sonora *	192	58,886
Tamaulipas *	307	122,500
Yucatan	41	8,031
All others	73	17,599

* Frontier states.

When fully implemented, the NAFTA agreement will make the Maquiladora special exception unnecessary for Canada and the United States since all tariffs will be eliminated. Its use appears to be decelerating already. Maquiladora establishments have increased at a 4.5 percent annual rate, and Maquiladora employment at a 5.5 percent rate, since the implementation of NAFTA. In a comparable period prior to NAFTA, Maquiladora establishments increased at a 7.5 percent annual rate, and employment rose at a 12.7 percent rate.[3]

The measures of Maquiladora activity shown in this article are thus declining in their value as year-to-year surrogate estimates of Mexican export activity or of U.S. corporate activity in Mexico. Maquiladora activity will not cease, however, because facilities of non-NAFTA countries—now primarily Asian—will continue to benefit and will likely use the program as

---

[3] INEGI, Industria Maquiladora de Exportacion, May 1997, 5, 8.

a platform for exports to the United States and other countries of the hemisphere.[4] As a result, Maquiladora activity in the future may be a more reliable measure of non-NAFTA foreign manufacturing in Mexico.

Table 2 shows Mexican imports and exports of manufactured goods from 1991 to 1996. In 1993, the year before NAFTA took effect, Maquiladora exports reached almost US$22 billion, or 42 percent of total Mexican manufacturing exports.[5] In 1996, such exports were just short of $37 billion, although they fell in percentage terms to 38 percent of all exports. Mexico's net Maquiladora trade (Maquiladora exports less Maquiladora imports) was positive in all years shown, but actually decelerated in 1994 and fell slightly in 1995.[6]

TABLE 2

IMPORTS AND EXPORTS OF MANUFACTURED GOODS, MAQUILADORA AND OTHER INDUSTRIES

(Millions of US dollars, f.o.b. values[1])

YEAR	EXPORTS			IMPORTS			NET[2]		
	TOTAL	MAQUILADORA	OTHER	TOTAL	MAQUILADORA	OTHER	TOTAL	MAQUILADORA	OTHER
1991	42,687.5	15,833.1	26,854.4	49,966.6	11,782.4	38,184.2	(7,279.1)	4,050.7	(11,329.8)
1992	46,195.6	18,680.1	27,515.6	62,129.3	13,936.7	48,192.6	(15,933.7)	4,743.4	(20,677.0)
1993	51,886.1	21,853.0	30,032.7	65,366.5	16,443.0	48,923.6	(13,480.4)	5,410.0	(18,890.9)
1994	60,882.2	26,269.2	34,613.0	79,345.9	20,466.2	58,879.7	(18,463.7)	5,803.0	(24,266.7)
1995	79,541.5	31,103.3	48,438.3	72,453.1	26,178.8	46,274.3	7,088.4	4,924.5	2,164.0
1996	95,999.7	36,920.3	59,079.4	89,468.8	30,504.7	58,964.1	6,530.9	6,415.6	115.3

1. Free on board.

2. Parentheses indicate a negative value, i.e. an excess of imports over exports.

Source: INEGI, *Cuaderno de Informacion Oportuna*, Agosto 1997, p. 146.

A breakdown of Maquiladora exports by country is not available. However, Table 3 shows estimates of Maquiladora exports to the United States.[7]

TABLE 3

MAQUILADORA EXPORTS TO AND IMPORTS FROM THE UNITED STATES

(Millions of U.S. dollars)

YEAR	EXPORTS	PERCENT OF MAQUILADORA TOTAL	IMPORTS	PERCENT OF MAQUILADORA TOTAL	NET EXPORTS
1991	14,334.3	91	7,254.8	62	7,079.5
1992	16,502.0	88	8,691.9	62	7,810.1
1993	18,967.7	87	9,871.9	60	9,095.8
1994	23,068.2	88	11,608.4	57	11,459.8
1995	24,962.3	80	12,832.8	49	12,129.5
1996	26,014.6	71	14,118.7	46	11,895.9

Source: INEGI, *Cuaderno de Informacion Oportuna*, Jan 1997, p. 126, and Ojeda, "North American Integration, Three Years After NAFTA", Dec. 1996, Table 3.5.

---

[4] Non-NAFTA countries will not gain tariff advantages for exports to the United States or Canada because the NAFTA rules of origin are specifically designed to prevent that.

[5] Manufactured goods accounted for about 94 percent of total Mexican exports in 1996.

[6] These results may be due to changes in data collection brought about by the implementation of the NAFTA agreement. See text and endnote.

[7] Ojeda, Raul Hinojosa, "North American Integration three years after NAFTA," UCLA, School of Public Policy and Social Research, December 1996. These estimates were made by tabulating the total HTS 9802.00.80 and 9802.00.60 imports from Mexico.

Although no breakdown by country is available, indications are that U.S. companies own and operate the majority of Maquiladora plants, which, in some sense, are "U.S. plants moved to Mexico." This may appear to be bad news from the perspective of U.S. workers in the affected industries, but there is some good news in that a portion of the production remains in the United States. Trade data in Table 3 show that imports of U.S. manufactured components have grown in tandem with exports. Such growth continued right through the peso crisis and the downturn in "other" Mexican imports of manufactured goods. To put it in another way, the gross exports above might not have been partially offset by (Maquiladora) imports from the United States if there had been no Maquiladora program or if the imports had come from a third country.

Before 1994, non-Maquiladora manufacturing exports grew at a slower rate than the Maquiladora exports. However, since NAFTA, their growth has picked up considerably while comparable imports have decelerated, actually declining in 1995.[8] As a result, Mexico in 1995 and 1996 had a net positive balance of trade in manufactures for perhaps the first time. This change was probably not due so much to the implementation of NAFTA as it was to the peso crisis and the resulting decline of the peso from about 3.5 to the U.S. dollar in late 1994 to around 8.25 to the dollar by late 1997. (See sidebar, "The Peso Crisis," in "NAFTA— The First Four Years.") This precipitous decline was effectively a price cut for Mexican goods to the United States and a price rise for U.S. goods to Mexico, which had a significant effect on exports and imports.

INDIVIDUAL MAQUILADORA INDUSTRIES

Table 4 is a summary of Maquiladora activity in all industries. All measures have steadily increased over the 1987-1996 period. Employment, perhaps the best available measure of activity, grew at a 10 percent annual rate from 1987 to 1993 and at 11.7 percent from 1993 to 1996.[9]

Table 5 is a summary of Maquiladora employment by industry. Note that INEGI classifies Maquiladora industry differently than it does non-Maquiladora industry. Throughout the period covered, the electrical and electronic materials and accessories industry has been the largest employer among the Maquiladora industries, followed by transportation equipment. From 1989 to 1993, the chemical industry had the fastest annual growth rate, at 43 percent, but this was because it started at a very low level. The food, furniture, and apparel industries had high rates of growth in the 1989-1993 period, at 27, 11, and 13 percent, respectively.

TABLE 4

MAQUILADORA FACILITIES: NATIONAL TOTALS

	1987	1988	1989	1990	1991	1992	1993	1994	1995	1996e
Number of establishments	1,125	1,396	1,655	1,703	1,914	2,075	2,114	2,085	2,130	2,411
Employees	305,253	369,489	429,725	446,436	467,352	505,698	542,074	583,044	648,263	754,858
Annual change, percent	22.2	21.0	16.3	3.9	4.7	8.2	7.2	7.6	11.2	16.4
Production workers	248,638	301,379	349,602	360,358	374,827	406,879	440,683	477,032	531,729	617,069
Percent female	66.0	63.2	61.4	60.9	60.3	60.4	59.5	59.5	59.0	58.1
Technicians	36,740	44,312	50,921	53,349	56,705	60,273	60,986	64,986	71,098	82,980
Clerical, supervisory, administrative	19,875	23,798	29,202	32,729	35,820	38,546	40,405	41,357	45,436	54,808

e Estimated 1996 figures by HNAI based on three quarters' data.

Source: INEGI, *Industria Maquiladora de Exportacion*, Noviembre 1996.

---

[8] It is possible that some of these "other" imports after 1994 would have been Maquiladora imports if NAFTA had not made the administrative processing required for Maquiladora and 9802 unnecessary.

[9] INEGI provides a measure, "Valor Agregado," often translated, "Value Added," but it is not comparable to value added as defined by the U.S. Census Bureau and other authorities. Valor Agregado contains both imported materials and purchased services; e.g., electricity, and is therefore neither a measure of the contribution of the facility or industry, nor is it a measure of domestic (Mexican) contribution.

TABLE 5

SUMMARY OF MAQUILADORA EMPLOYMENT BY INDUSTRY

(Number employed)

	1989	1990	1991	1992	1993	1994	1995	1996	GROWTH RATE[1]	
									1989-1993	1993-1996
Grand total	429,725	446,436	467,352	505,698	542,074	583,044	648,263	754,858	5.98	11.67
Food	4,361	7,862	8,789	10,002	11,436	7,407	7,730	11,277	27.25	-0.46
Apparel	39,077	42,464	46,324	53,729	63,999	75,296	99,476	131,820	13.13	27.23
Shoes	8,090	7,238	7,391	7,367	7,268	7,400	7,587	7,544	-2.64	1.25
Furniture	21,384	24,224	26,658	28,834	32,688	34,462	35,807	40,548	11.19	7.45
Chemicals	2,841	6,565	7,680	9,338	11,887	12,610	12,754	13,734	43.01	4.93
Transportation equipment	90,525	104,487	116,595	124,226	126,650	129,843	137,220	158,364	8.76	7.73
Tools	5,696	5,018	5,079	5,163	5,322	5,639	6,783	7,971	-1.68	14.41
Machines	63,201	51,891	50,269	54,167	57,796	63,768	67,269	71,470	-2.21	7.34
Electric and electronic	103,460	114,610	114,358	123,387	131,346	147,452	167,164	191,332	6.15	13.36
Toys and sports equipment	12,154	10,298	8,045	8,247	9,055	9,538	9,527	11,152	-7.10	7.19
Other manufacturing	60,114	48,956	51,429	54,424	56,715	63,922	69,193	78,532	-1.44	11.46

1. Compound annual growth rate.

Note: Detail will not add to totals because of components not shown.

Source: INEGI, *Industria Maquiladora de Exportacion*, Nov. 1996, and Banco de Datos [I].

Following implementation of NAFTA, employment in the Maquiladora apparel industry grew most rapidly (27.2 percent annually), moving the industry to third largest employer in 1996 from fifth in 1989. This was probably due to the substantial reduction in U.S. tariffs on apparel at implementation of NAFTA. Tool industry employment grew at a 14.4 percent rate during 1993-1996. Electric and electronics grew at 13.4 percent, and transportation equipment, at 7.7 percent. In the United States, on the other hand, employment in apparel manufacturing fell by 146,000 workers from December 1993 to March 1997, and that in tools was virtually unchanged. Yet U.S. electronic and other electrical and motor vehicles actually increased their employment by 100,000 workers each over the same period.[10]

Table 6 shows hourly compensation costs for Maquiladora industries, as estimated by the Foreign Labor Statistics Division of the Bureau of Labor Statistics (BLS). These are not direct hourly wages paid to workers, but direct wages plus all benefits. They include direct pay for hours worked; pay for holidays and days off; traditional Christmas bonuses (equal to 15 days' pay); profit sharing; social contributions (severance pay, medical services, scholarships, etc.); and employer contributions to social security, housing, and other funds. The benefits are substantial, amounting to 31.8 percent of direct earnings in 1987 and rising to 46.8 percent in 1993.[11]

Table 6 shows labor compensation costs both in U.S. dollars and in Purchasing Power Parity (PPP) adjusted dollars. Both measures are important. The U.S. dollar measure is a straight conversion of Mexican pesos to dollars at the standard exchange rate of the time. These figures are most useful if one's purpose is to compare manufacturing labor costs in Mexico with those in Canada or the United States, but are of little use in comparing the workers' ability to purchase goods and services.

Mexican wages expressed in U.S. dollars reflect the volatility of the international exchange market. The exchange rate was relatively stable during the 1988-1993 period, but rather unstable in periods both before and after. Also, exchange rates do not take into account the relative prices in the three countries—every tourist knows it is impossible to buy the same "basket of goods and services" in Canada, the United States, and Mexico with US$100,

---

[10] U.S. industry employment data from BLS.

[11] For a more complete discussion see the next section, "Employment, Wages, and Benefits."

TABLE 6

MAQUILADORA EXPORT INDUSTRIES: COMPENSATION PER HOUR IN U.S. DOLLARS

(Exchange rate and purchasing power parity bases)

	1988 BASED ON		1989 BASED ON		1990 BASED ON		1991 BASED ON		1992 BASED ON		1993 BASED ON	
	EXCHANGE RATE	PURCHASING POWER PARITY	EXCHANGE RATE	PURCHASING POWER PARITY	EXCHANGE RATE	PURCHASING POWER PARITY	EXCHANGE RATE	PURCHASING POWER PARITY	EXCHANGE RATE	PURCHASING POWER PARITY	EXCHANGE RATE	PURCHASING POWER PARITY
All non-Maquiladora manufacturing	$ 1.25	$ 2.68	$ 1.48	$2.82	$ 1.64	$ 2.92	$ 1.93	$ 3.08	$ 2.29	$ 4.14	$ 2.56	$ 4.34
All Maquiladora manufacturing	0.98	2.10	1.15	2.19	1.26	2.24	1.45	2.32	1.62	2.93	1.75	2.96
Food and related products	0.75	1.61	0.86	1.64	0.97	1.73	1.18	1.88	1.26	2.28	.....	.....
Apparel and other textile products	0.76	1.63	0.89	1.70	1.01	1.80	1.13	1.80	1.24	2.24	.....	.....
Footwear and leather products	0.89	1.91	0.97	1.85	1.10	1.96	1.25	2.00	1.47	2.66	.....	.....
Furniture and fixtures	1.01	2.17	1.14	2.17	1.25	2.23	1.38	2.20	1.56	2.82	.....	.....
Chemicals and chemical products	0.98	2.10	1.02	1.95	1.19	2.12	1.32	2.11	1.42	2.57	.....	.....
Machinery and equipment ex electric	1.15	2.47	1.50	2.86	1.59	2.83	1.98	3.16	2.17	3.93	.....	.....
Electric and electronic equipment	1.02	2.19	1.19	2.27	1.28	2.28	1.51	2.41	1.66	3.00	.....	.....
Transportation equipment	1.09	2.34	1.27	2.42	1.44	2.56	1.61	2.57	1.82	3.29	.....	.....
Toys and sporting goods	1.12	2.40	1.28	2.44	1.44	2.56	1.44	2.30	1.42	2.57	.....	.....
Other manufacturing	0.85	1.82	0.99	1.89	1.12	1.99	1.35	2.16	1.54	2.79	.....	.....
Maquiladora cost as a percent of non-Maquiladora manufacturing cost	78	78	78	78	77	77	75	75	71	71	68	68
Conversion factors for peso costs, new pesos per U.S. dollar:												
Exchange rate	2.273	.....	2.461	.....	2.813	.....	3.018	.....	3.095	.....	3.116	.....
Purchasing power parity (OECD)	.....	1.06	.....	1.29	.....	1.58	.....	1.89	.....	1.71	.....	1.84

Source: Office of Productivity and Technology, U.S. Bureau of Labor Statistics, Unpublished data.

converted to the appropriate currency in each country. But the PPP-adjusted rates (expressed in U.S. dollars) are designed to show the purchasing power of incomes in different countries. Thus, the PPP-adjusted rates in Table 6 show the "command over goods and services" that an hour's compensation yields, as measured in U.S. dollars.

Note that compensation of Maquiladora workers is significantly less than the average for all manufacturing in Mexico—78 percent in 1988, falling to 68 percent in 1993. (The ratios are the same for the exchange rate values and the PPP values.) This is puzzling because most Maquiladora facilities are located in the north, which is thought to be the more urban, more prosperous region of the country. In addition, Maquiladora employment has expanded substantially, up by 95,000 production workers from 1990 to 1993 and by 213,000 from 1993 to 1996. It seems unlikely that large numbers of new workers could be attracted if wage rates were not competitive.

It is not clear why this difference prevails, but it may reflect the fact that Maquiladora manufacturing is primarily (in some cases exclusively) assembly and therefore does not include the same proportion of higher skilled and higher paid workers. It also may reflect the fact that women make up a higher percentage of Maquiladora workers.

It is possible that a portion of the pay differential is due to the different mixes of industries in the two groups. In other words, the prevailing wages in the industries in Maquiladora may be lower—on the average—than those in all manufacturing. However, a rough calculation suggests this is not the case. An alternative Maquiladora average rate was calculated using the appropriate industry rate from outside Maquiladora, weighted by employment in each of the Maquiladora industries. The result was within a few pennies of the "all industry" rate, suggesting strongly that the wage differential is due to factors other than the industry mix.[12]

Table 7 shows the details available on each of the Maquiladora industries reported by INEGI.

---

[12] It should be noted that the INEGI survey of Maquiladora wages and employment is different from that used to determine those variables for all manufacturing; it is possible, although unlikely, that different definitions or methods contributed to the difference.

TABLE 7

PROFILES OF MAQUILADORA INDUSTRIES, 1989-1994

	1989	1990	1991	1992	1993	1994
FOOD AND KINDRED PRODUCTS						
Number of establishments	25	45	51	58	59	56
Percent in frontier states	.....	73.6	73.0	56.9	54.5	.....
Total employment	4,361	7,862	8,789	10,002	11,436	7,407
Percent in frontier states	86.3	50.5	48.4	31.0	24.3	.....
Production workers[1]	6,725	7,629	8,687	10,197	6,015	.....
Percent female	60.9	60.1	60.7	45.7	59.6	.....
Average weekly pay, new pesos	236.01	270.57	307.09	235.63	354.99	.....
APPAREL AND OTHER TEXTILE PRODUCTS						
Number of establishments	246	277	321	372	392	398
Percent in frontier states	.....	53.3	48.8	47.7	44.6	40.3
Total employment	39,077	42,464	46,324	53,729	63,999	75,296
Percent in frontier states	.....	49.2	44.1	41.3	37.3	34.7
Production workers[1]	.....	36,107	39,653	46,034	54,964	63,626
Percent female	.....	75.6	75.2	74.9	73.7	73.0
Average weekly pay, new pesos	.....	361.28	425.20	489.80	507.34	538.14
SHOES AND LEATHER						
Number of establishments	49	47	53	58	59	56
Percent in frontier states	.....	81.1	72.3	69.0	64.1	64.0
Total employment	8,090	7,238	7,391	7,367	7,268	7,400
Percent in frontier states	.....	84.8	79.0	76.2	79.5	77.0
Production workers[1]	.....	5,990	6,025	6,068	6,010	6,266
Percent female	.....	55.9	56.8	55.2	55.2	58.4
Average weekly pay, new pesos	.....	207.27	258.29	313.94	362.93	405.06
FURNITURE AND FIXTURES						
Number of establishments	219	219	257	284	291	277
Percent in frontier states	.....	91.3	89.2	90.6	89.6	89.8
Total employment	21,384	24,224	26,658	28,834	32,688	34,462
Percent in frontier states	.....	94.4	91.4	90.0	90.9	93.0
Production workers[1]	.....	19,838	21,747	23,581	27,153	28,755
Percent female	.....	29.3	28.8	29.0	28.7	31.1
Average weekly pay, new pesos	.....	164.73	194.99	221.96	237.46	275.25
CHEMICALS						
Number of establishments	55	75	94	115	124	113
Percent in frontier states	.....	79.7	78.7	80.8	80.7	78.7
Total employment	2,841	6,565	7,680	9,338	11,887	12,610
Percent in frontier states	.....	86.4	82.5	87.6	89.1	88.6
Production workers[1]	.....	5,536	6,418	7,820	10,052	10,631
Percent female	.....	53.1	54.3	53.6	55.8	55.4
Average weekly pay, new pesos	.....	235.77	278.36	326.30	375.83	418.68
TRANSPORTATION EQUIPMENT AND ACCESSORIES						
Number of establishments	141	156	166	165	169	165
Percent in frontier states	.....	73.9	72.2	72.7	72.0	71.7
Total employment	90,525	104,487	116,595	124,226	126,650	129,843
Percent in frontier states	.....	73.9	71.5	72.1	71.3	73.9
Production workers[1]	.....	82,987	91,732	97,494	100,629	104,729
Percent female	.....	52.6	51.4	52.1	51.2	51.0
Average weekly pay, new pesos	.....	229.35	264.03	305.72	339.23	388.43
TOOLS (EXCLUDING ELECTRIC)						
Number of establishments	35	39	42	45	45	42
Percent in frontier states	.....	84.6	85.7	88.9	86.7	85.7
Total employment	5,696	5,019	5,078	5,163	5,322	5,639
Percent in frontier states	.....	96.9	96.4	96.8	96.7	95.2
Production workers[1]	.....	4,051	4,126	4,182	4,380	4,702
Percent female	.....	35.7	33.0	32.1	37.8	39.0
Average weekly pay, new pesos	.....	234.88	277.57	321.22	365.14	416.45

TABLE 7 (CONTINUED)

PROFILES OF MAQUILADORA INDUSTRIES, 1989-1994

	1989	1990	1991	1992	1993	1994
MACHINERY AND EQUIPMENT (EXCLUDING ELECTRIC)						
Number of establishments	116	102	110	117	115	117
Percent in frontier states	.....	79.6	78.2	78.6	80.9	77.8
Total employment	63,201	51,891	50,269	54,167	57,796	63,768
Percent in frontier states	.....	89.8	87.4	81.4	78.8	78.4
Production workers[1]	.....	40,810	38,454	42,322	45,631	50,705
Percent female	.....	63.2	64.4	63.2	63.2	64.4
Average weekly pay, new pesos	.....	313.11	401.83	426.49	466.45	534.79
ELECTRIC AND ELECTRONIC EQUIPMENT						
Number of establishments	348	370	392	410	410	402
Percent in frontier states	.....	85.8	83.9	83.7	84.6	84.3
Total employment	103,460	114,610	114,358	123,387	131,346	147,452
Percent in frontier states	.....	83.5	84.4	83.6	83.8	84.8
Production workers[1]	.....	89,734	88,683	96,791	104,353	117,473
Percent female	.....	67.6	67.2	67.3	66.8	65.2
Average weekly pay, new pesos	.....	341.05	409.87	466.80	505.39	539.41
TOYS AND SPORTS EQUIPMENT						
Number of establishments	29	32	35	38	38	40
Percent in frontier states	.....	81.9	81.2	81.8	76.0	79.3
Total employment	12,154	10,298	8,045	8,247	9,055	9,538
Percent in frontier states	.....	95.6	92.3	91.4	91.8	81.9
Production workers[1]	.....	8,348	6,480	6,426	7,140	7,053
Percent female	.....	67.1	66.7	65.1	61.0	56.2
Average weekly pay, new pesos	.....	385.22	427.89	412.86	424.64	423.78
OTHER MANUFACTURING						
Number of establishments	321	264	300	308	301	315
Percent in frontier states	.....	73.5	69.4	70.4	71.7	73.0
Total employment	60,114	48,956	51,429	54,424	56,715	63,922
Percent in frontier states	.....	70.5	66.6	68.5	67.8	67.8
Production workers[1]	.....	39,968	42,092	44,086	45,996	51,861
Percent female	.....	59.5	59.5	60.0	59.4	57.3
Average weekly pay, new pesos	.....	270.15	324.83	386.73	426.13	447.81
SERVICES						
Number of establishments	71	79	94	105	110	104
Percent in frontier states	.....	73.3	73.5	74.2	74.3	74.1
Total employment	18,821	22,824	24,735	26,812	27,913	25,658
Percent in frontier states	.....	63.4	63.3	63.6	66.4	68.2
Production workers[1]	.....	20,264	21,788	23,387	24,178	22,287
Percent female	.....	75.0	74.9	72.8	70.7	71.0
Average weekly pay, new pesos	.....	417.49	483.16	507.68	540.36	605.92

1. The production worker figure is for "obreros," which may not be the precise equivalent of the U.S. production workers concept.

Source: INEGI, "Estadistica de la Industria Maquiladora de Exportacion," 1995.

EMPLOYMENT, WAGES, AND BENEFITS IN NORTH AMERICA

Much of the controversy surrounding NAFTA turns on its effect on employment, wages, and benefits, but comparing these variables in the three NAFTA countries is not a simple task. Reliable data are limited in important respects, and their comparability is often in doubt. Work environments and patterns of employment in the United States and Canada are similar, and the methods of classification and data collection used by the respective statistical agencies are comparable. But employment practices, standards, and methods of classification are different in Mexico.

These problems should lessen in the future. An important part of NAFTA covers efforts to standardize data collection, classification, and presentation among the three countries. The Commission for Labor Cooperation (established by the "side agreements") is already fostering cooperation in the collection of data on labor markets,[1] and the three governments have published a common industrial classification code, the North American Industry Classification System (NAICS). The statistical agencies of the NAFTA countries will phase in use of the new system beginning in 1999.

MEXICO'S LABOR MARKET

Most of the problems of comparison revolve around differences between Mexican data and those of the United States and Canada. There is, for example, a dual market for labor in Mexico. This duality can be seen in the wide differences in wages and benefits in the large cities versus the small towns and villages, the large companies and government enterprises versus small companies, and the industrialized northern tier states versus the agrarian south. But the principal division is between the "formal" and the "informal" sectors of the economy.

The term "informal" was first suggested by an International Labor Organization study of the 1970s to describe certain economic activities in developing countries in which technology and labor practices are "pre-industrial." For example, owners and workers are often closely related, and master-apprentice relationships are common. The Mexican statistical agency, Instituto Nacional de Estadistica Geografia e Informatica (INEGI), classifies many smaller enterprises as belonging to the informal, or micro-enterprise, part of the economy if they have six workers or less (including the owners and unpaid family members) and are operated by the owner. Offices of professionals and other technology-related enterprises are excluded.[2] It has been estimated that about 38 percent of total nonagricultural employment in Mexico is in the informal sector.[3]

---

[1] See, for example, Commission for Labor Cooperation, North American Agreement on Labor Cooperation, *North American Labor Markets: A Comparative Profile*, co-published by Bernan Press and the Commission for Labor Cooperation, First Edition, 1997.

[2] For surveys of small businesses conducted in 1976, 1988-1989, and 1992: Fleck, Susan, and Constance Sorrentino, "Employment and Unemployment in Mexico's Labor Force," *Monthly Labor Review*, November 1994, pp. 3-31.

[3] Fleck and Sorrentino, *Op. Cit.*, p. 12.

The significance of the informal sector is that it operates largely outside the established rules. An article in the November 1994 *Monthly Labor Review* describes it this way:

> Mexico has extensive labor legislation (laws pertaining to minimum wages, limits on hours worked, pay for overtime, and so on) that is applicable to all types of workers.... In addition, the local and central governments place health and safety requirements on enterprises. However, a high proportion of informal enterprises operate outside these boundaries, and a significant amount of informal employment occurs in large-scale formal enterprises. Trade unions and social security protection are rarely found in the informal sector. . . .The bulk of informal sector enterprises lie in an intermediate zone between the extremes of complete legality and illegality, selectively fulfilling some legal requirements while avoiding others.[4]

Table 1 provides a glimpse of the differences between large urban versus smaller areas from 1988 to 1993 (of course, many informal enterprises are not covered by government surveys). In 1993, wage and salary workers comprised 74.2 percent of all workers in the larger areas (the same as in 1988), but only 41.4 percent of workers in the smaller areas (and down from

TABLE 1

MEXICAN EMPLOYMENT BY STATUS

	1988		1991		1993	
CATEGORY	THOUSANDS OF WORKERS	PERCENT OF ADJUSTED EMPLOYMENT	THOUSANDS OF OF WORKERS	PERCENT OF ADJUSTED EMPLOYMENT	THOUSANDS OF WORKERS	PERCENT OF ADJUSTED EMPLOYMENT
ENTIRE COUNTRY:						
Total	28,128	.....	30,534	.....	32,833	.....
Wage and salary workers	15,861	58.4	16,878	56.7	18,102	56.9
Self-employed	6,371	23.5	7,283	24.5	8,817	27.7
Employers	1,690	6.2	2,396	8.0	1,349	4.2
Unpaid family workers[1]	4,057	.....	3,969	.....	4,560	.....
Working less than 15 hours/week	832	.....	741	.....	1,003	.....
Adjusted unpaid family workers	3,225	11.9	3,228	10.8	3,557	11.2
Not specified	148	.....	9	.....	4	.....
Employed[2]	27,148	100.0	29,784	100.0	31,826	100.0
LARGER URBAN AREAS:						
Total	12,848	.....	14,354	.....	15,214	.....
Wage and salary workers	9,412	74.2	10,604	74.6	11,149	74.2
Self-employed	2,145	16.9	2,398	16.9	2,552	17.0
Employers	589	4.6	693	4.9	734	4.9
Unpaid family workers[1]	697	.....	655	.....	780	.....
Working less than 15 hours/week	165	.....	141	.....	181	.....
Adjusted unpaid family workers	532	4.2	514	3.6	599	4.0
Not specified	4	.....	4	.....	.....	.....
Employed[2]	12,679	100.0	14,209	100.0	15,033	100.0
SMALLER AREAS:						
Total	15,280	.....	16,180	.....	17,618	.....
Wage and salary workers	6,449	44.9	6,274	40.3	6,954	41.4
Self-employed	4,226	29.4	4,886	31.4	6,266	37.3
Employers	1,101	7.7	1,703	10.9	614	3.7
Unpaid family workers[1]	3,360	22.0	3,313	.....	3,780	21.4
Working less than 15 hours/week	767	.....	599	.....	823	.....
Adjusted unpaid family workers	2,593	18.0	2,714	17.4	2,957	17.6
Not specified	144	.....	5	.....	4	.....
Employed[2]	14,369	100.0	15,576	100.0	16,791	100.0

1. Predominantly family but includes some non-family workers.

2. Adjusted to exclude family workers with less than 15 hours a week and not specified.

Source: Fleck and Sorrentino, Employment and unemployment in Mexico's labor force, *Monthly Labor Review*, Nov. 1994.

[4] Ibid.

44.9 percent in 1988). Unpaid family workers accounted for 22.5 percent of total workers in the smaller areas, slightly below the 1988 level. On the other hand, the proportion of self-employed persons in the smaller areas increased from 29.4 percent in 1988 to 37.3 percent in 1993.

All countries, including the large industrialized ones, have informal sectors and economic activities that operate on the fringes and outside strict compliance with labor law. For example, some domestic workers and illegal immigrants in the United States are not covered by Social Security, although the law requires it. However, the informal sector in Mexico and other developing countries is much larger, and this affects the impact of labor laws and regulations. A principle that emerges from any study of the labor markets within NAFTA countries is that averages alone can be quite misleading.[5]

EMPLOYMENT IN NORTH AMERICA

Table 2 shows labor characteristics as reported by the three countries, covering 1987 though 1996 for the United States and Canada and 1988, 1991, and 1993 for Mexico. With the exception of 1995-1996, reported unemployment is lowest in Mexico (but does not reflect the underemployed or the "unpaid worker" classification, usually family workers). Unemployment has been highest in Canada throughout the period.

United States. The U.S. unemployment rate averaged 6.1 percent annually from 1987 to 1996, with a high point of 7.5 percent in 1992. It dropped steadily after 1992, to 5.4 percent in 1996 and to under 5 percent in 1997, the lowest point in many years. The employment/population ratio for working-age persons rose from 61.5 percent in 1987 to 63.2 percent in 1996—the highest rate for the three countries.

Canada. The unemployment rate in Canada rose from 7.8 percent in 1988—the last year before implementation of the Canadian-U.S. Free Trade Agreement (CUSFTA)—to a high of 11.3 percent in 1992 before dropping to a still-high 9.7 percent in 1996. During the same period, labor force participation fell from 67.2 in 1988 to 64.9 in 1996. Thus, some people of working age in Canada have dropped out of the labor force, possibly discouraged by a lack of job opportunities. This could well be an important reason why recent polls show Canadians believing that free trade has benefited the United States more than Canada. Although the Canadian-U.S. balance of trade has been favorable to Canada throughout the period, the Canadian surplus did decline immediately after implementation of CUSFTA before rising slowly and by 1996 exceeding the 1989 level.[6]

Mexico. Unemployment in Mexico was low throughout the 10-year period until the peso crisis and the consequent sharp recession in 1995. An explanation often given for the low rate is the lack of government unemployment insurance: a worker out of a job in Mexico must take any available employment in order to survive.[7] This explanation is supported, some believe, by other data showing that the lowest rates of unemployment are found among those with the least education, the idea being that those with some savings or family support can afford to hold out for suitable jobs.

Another explanation sometimes offered is that differences in the way employment and unemployment are measured in Mexico may account for the relatively low rates reported. The underlying figures must be adjusted to conform to the concepts and definitions used in the United States and Canada if meaningful comparisons are to be made. Fortunately, the U.S. Bureau of Labor Statistics has meticulously made such adjustments. The results are

[5] Commission for Labor Cooperation (CLC), Op. Cit., p.1.

[6] The Canadian balance of trade with the United States was $19.7 billion in 1989; it fell to a low of $5.9 billion in 1991, then rose to US$22.8 billion in 1996.

[7] Mexican law requires employers to pay a lump sum of three months' pay, plus 20 days' pay for each year of service. Again, this law may not be honored in the informal sector.

shown in Table 3.[8] The adjustments are not large, and Mexico's adjusted rates are still the lowest of the three countries in the years for which figures are available.

INEGI has recognized that its definition of "open unemployment" (desempleo abierto) may not measure the need for additional employment opportunities. Alternative measures are provided by INEGI, and two of these are shown in Table 4. The column labeled "insufficient income" includes the unemployed plus employed persons (other than family workers) who earned less than the minimum daily wage. The column labeled "underemployed" includes those employed who worked (1) less than 35 hours a week for economic reasons, (2) more than 35 hours a week while earning less than the minimum wage, and (3) more than 48 hours a week while earning only one to two times the minimum wage.[9]

As shown in Table 2, employment in Mexico grew substantially faster in the 1988 to 1993 period (3.2 percent annually) than employment in either the United States or Canada in the same period (less than 1.0 percent in both). Table 2 also indicates that employment as a percentage of the working age population is lowest in Mexico and highest in the United States. However, one may legitimately question the validity of this comparison given the large informal sector in Mexico.

Some additional observations can be made:

- The Mexican labor force is significantly younger than in the United States and Canada; 18 percent of the labor force and 49 percent of the population are under 20 years of age.[10]

- In all three countries, there has been a dramatic and continuing shift in employment from goods-producing industries to service industries.

- In all three countries, wage and salary workers are the largest group. In Mexico, less than 60 percent of all workers are in this category. In the United States and Canada, the figure is about 80 percent, but declining as the number of self-employed persons grows.[11]

TABLE 2

EMPLOYMENT CHARACTERISTICS: CANADA, UNITED STATES, MEXICO

	Employment level (1000's)			Labor force participation rate[1] (%)			Unemployment rate[2] (%)			Employment-population ratio (%)		
	Canada	U.S.	Mexico	Canada	U.S.	Mexico	Canada	U.S.	Mexico	Canada	U.S.	Mexico
1987	12,422	112,439	.....	66.7	65.6	.....	8.9	6.2	3.9	60.8	61.5	.....
1988	12,819	114,974	27,148	67.2	65.9	53.2	7.8	5.5	3.6	62.0	62.3	50.0
1989	13,086	117,327	.....	67.5	66.5	.....	7.5	5.3	3.0	62.4	62.9	.....
1990	13,165	118,796	.....	67.3	66.4	.....	8.1	5.6	2.8	61.9	62.8	.....
1991	12,916	117,713	29,784	66.7	66.0	53.6	10.4	6.9	2.6	59.8	61.7	51.1
1992	12,842	118,488	.....	65.9	66.3	.....	11.3	7.5	2.8	58.4	61.5	.....
1993	13,015	120,259	31,826	65.5	66.2	55.2	11.2	6.9	3.4	58.2	61.7	52.2
1994	13,292	123,067	.....	65.3	66.6	.....	10.4	6.1	3.7	58.5	62.5	.....
1995	13,506	124,899	.....	64.8	66.6	.....	9.5	5.6	6.3	58.7	62.9	.....
1996	13,676	126,705	.....	64.9	66.8	.....	9.7	5.4	5.5	58.6	63.2	.....

1. Labor force as a percent of working age population.
2. As a percent of labor force.

Source: Statistics Canada and U.S. Bureau of Labor Statistics (BLS), as reported. Mexico data are from INEGI as reported by BLS.

---

[8] Fleck and Sorrentino, Op. Cit., p. 20.

[9] Note that in Mexico minimum wages are determined by region and are set as a rate per day.

[10] Fleck and Sorrentino, Op. Cit., p. 8.

[11] CLC, Op. Cit., p. 2.

- Most North American workers still have one full-time, permanent, paid job, but growth in "nonstandard" employment (part-time, self-employed, temporary, and contract work) is increasing.[12]

- In all three countries, there is growing polarization between the educated and highly skilled, on the one hand, and the uneducated and unskilled, on the other. NAFTA probably exacerbates that divide, at least in the two northern countries.

- Unionization rates in Canada and Mexico are substantially higher than in the United States. There was a significant decline in unionization in the United States from 1984 to 1995.[13] In Mexico, on the other hand, the informal sector generally does not work under labor rules. Moreover, many unions reportedly are government-controlled and used mainly to turn out votes at election time and to keep labor cheap, according to an article in the *New York Times International* (October 13, 1997).

TABLE 3

MEXICAN UNEMPLOYMENT RATES ADJUSTED TO U.S. CONCEPTS, LARGER URBAN AREAS, SECOND QUARTER 1988, 1991, AND 1993

Category	1988			1991			1993		
	Total	Men	Women	Total	Men	Women	Total	Men	Women
NUMBER UNEMPLOYED:									
Reported	494,316	266,862	227,454	352,114	209,144	142,970	490,941	306,703	184,238
Adjusted	723,936	413,170	310,768	586,566	360,850	225,716	776,104	494,227	281,877
NUMBER IN LABOR FORCE:									
Reported	13,342,433	8,834,563	4,507,870	14,706,007	9,617,006	5,089,001	15,705,194	10,220,312	5,484,882
Adjusted	13,181,341	8,763,614	4,417,727	14,565,209	9,559,108	5,006,101	15,524,775	10,142,372	5,382,403
UNEMPLOYMENT AS PERCENT OF LABOR FORCE:									
Reported	3.7	3.0	5.0	2.4	2.2	2.8	3.1	3.0	3.4
Adjusted	5.5	4.7	7.0	4.0	3.8	4.5	5.0	4.9	5.2

Source: Fleck and Sorrentino, *Monthly Labor Review*, Nov. 1994.

TABLE 4

UNEMPLOYMENT AND UNDEREMPLOYMENT IN MEXICO

(Percent of labor force)

YEAR	INSUFFICIENT INCOME AND UNEMPLOYMENT RATE[1]	UNDEREMPLOYMENT RATE[2]
1987	30.8	30.5
1988	21.8	22.9
1989	18.3	20.1
1990	14.6	16.8
1991	11.7	14.3
1992	10.7	13.9
1993	12.3	14.0
1994	11.1	12.8

1. Reported unemployed plus employed who earned less than the minimum wage, as a percent of labor force.

2. Persons working from one to 35 hours a week for economic reasons, working more than 35 hours a week while earning less than the minimum wage, and working more than 48 hours a week while earning between one and two times the minimum wage, as a percent of total employment

Source: Fleck and Sorrentino, *Monthly Labor Review*, Nov. 1994.

---

[12] Ibid.

[13] Ibid.

HOURLY COMPENSATION—U.S., CANADA, AND MEXICO

There are at least two ways to compare hourly labor compensation in the three NAFTA countries. One way is *direct hourly compensation*—wages, vacation and holiday pay, bonuses and other direct pay, and the cost of pay in kind. An alternative way of comparison is *total compensation*, which includes private benefit plans such as employer-paid health insurance and, perhaps, social insurance and other payroll taxes. Employers (and their accountants) certainly take the latter view, as must anyone who hires workers through one of the temporary service contractors, and it is of interest to workers and their unions as well. The following discussion considers both direct hourly compensation and total hourly compensation costs.

Another comparison choice has to do with the conversion of wages and salaries in the three countries to a common basis. If one is contemplating opening a factory in another country, or is concerned about competition from another country, then compensation converted via exchange rates is the appropriate method. But if one wants to compare the living standards of workers in the three countries (that is, their ability to purchase goods and services), exchange rates are not appropriate. Exchange rates do not reflect relative purchasing powers because they do not account for differences in prices in the three countries: a given amount of money converted to the various currencies will not buy the same basket of goods in the three countries. For example, the U.S.-Saudi Arabian exchange rate may be appropriate for oil, but would not reflect the cost of food in the two countries.

Fortunately, purchasing power parity (PPP) measures have been developed[14] and can be used to compare compensation of workers in the three countries in terms of how much their incomes will buy. When converted into different currencies at PPP rates, a given sum of money is expected to buy comparable baskets of goods and services in all countries. This method dampens, but does not eliminate, the most extreme effects of volatility in exchange rates. For Mexico especially, many manufactured consumer goods are imported, and so a decline in the value of the peso does directly affect workers' well being. In this section, we will consider direct compensation and hourly compensation costs on both an exchange rate and a PPP basis.

Table 5 shows both direct compensation and hourly compensation costs for production workers in manufacturing in the United States, Canada, and Mexico for selected years from 1975 to 1996.[15] Estimates are included in national currencies, in U.S. dollars, and on a PPP adjusted basis. [16]

Note that both direct compensation and hourly compensation costs in Mexico are quite volatile when converted to U.S. dollars at standard exchange rates. Average hourly compensation in 1975 was $1.33, rose to a high of $2.18 in 1994, then fell back to $1.33—its level 20 years before. Mexican compensation in U.S. dollars fell substantially in 1983 and again in 1995 because of monetary crises in Mexico. In 1982, the value of the peso fell dramatically against the dollar following the drop in international oil prices (oil was Mexico's principal export, and the country was deep in debt). In late 1994, the peso fell again as an attempted devaluation by the government went seriously out of control.

It is often noted that U.S. average hourly earnings in manufacturing have not kept up with inflation. Average hourly earnings for all manufacturing, when adjusted for inflation, have

---

[14] See Robert Summers and Alan Heston, "The Penn World Table (Mark 5), An Expanded Set of International Comparisons, 1950-1988," *The Quarterly Journal of Economics,* May 1991, pp. 327-368.

[15] The U.S. Bureau of Labor Statistics (BLS) regularly updates its estimates of both direct compensation and hourly compensation costs for production workers in manufacturing in a number of countries including the United States, Canada, and Mexico. Great care is taken to convert data from the various countries to the same conceptual basis. The data in Table 5 come from the supplementary tables released on June 27, 1997 (USDL 97-213).

[16] The rates used in this article come from the Organization for Economic Cooperation and Development (OECD) and have been calculated for GDP. It would be better to use PPP calculated for personal consumption expenditures (GDP includes producers' goods not usually purchased by individuals.) However, OECD (GDP) PPPs are the best currently available.

declined about 0.7 percent annually from 1985 to 1996.[17] (However, Alan Greenspan and others have argued that the U.S. consumer price index, used to calculate real earnings, overstates the rate of inflation by a point or more.) The comparable figures for Canada show that Canadian wages have risen about 0.2 percent annually over the same period. Mexican wages have risen about 4.3 percent annually.[18] It should not be surprising that Mexico's real wages have risen more rapidly than those of the two northern countries since Mexico has increased its level of industrialization significantly over the same period.

In 1985, U.S. wages were about 9 percent higher than those in Canada after conventional exchange rate conversion. In 1996, Canadian wages were about the same as those of the United States (using the same conversion method). Mexican real average hourly earnings in pesos have increased over the same period by more than 4 percent annually, but the sharp decline in value of the peso has resulted in an actual decline in dollar value. This difference suggests the difficulty of comparing NAFTA countries in dollar terms.

Table 5 also shows direct pay as a percent of hourly compensation costs. Indirect costs (benefits, social insurance, and some other payroll taxes) are a larger proportion of compensation costs in the United States than in Canada, and they are greater in Canada than in Mexico. In 1996, indirect costs were about 21.5 percent of the average compensation cost in the United States and only 17 percent in Canada. However, Canadian government health insurance is not financed by payroll taxes or employer contributions (nor, generally, is private health insurance), as in the United States and Mexico, but comes out of general revenues. (See the Health Services Chapter.) This difference in handling health costs—and the higher per capita cost of health insurance in the United States—could explain some of the difference between U.S. and Canadian hourly compensation costs.[19] These comparisons are for production workers only and differ from data on all employees presented in the section on benefits.

The last three lines of the table show the labor cost ratios for the three NAFTA countries. The United States generally has the highest rates. U.S. labor costs were slightly lower than in Canada in 1990-1992, one year following implementation of CUSFTA. The ratio rose again after 1993, reaching 1.07 in 1995 and 1996. Thus, U.S. costs have been higher in recent years, but not greatly higher.

Of course, the cost ratios reflect the variations in the exchange rate. In general, the Canadian/U.S. rate has been reasonably stable, whereas the Mexican/U.S. and Mexican/Canadian rates have not. The U.S./Mexico compensation ratio was a bit greater than four to one in 1975, grew to nine to one in 1990, fell back, and then rose to more than 11 to one in 1995 and 1996—its highest level for the years shown. The sharp increase in 1995 shows clearly why Mexican exports to the United States rose in that year and why the balance of trade is likely to continue to favor Mexico until the peso's exchange value rises. It is interesting to note that the United States maintained a favorable balance of trade with Mexico when the compensation ratio was almost seven to one. The ratio of Canadian to Mexican compensation costs behaved similarly, rising from 6.4 to one in 1994 to 11.1 to one in 1996.

Table 6 shows hourly compensation costs (total costs including direct and indirect compensation) for the United States, Canada, and Mexico for all manufacturing from 1987 to 1996 and by industry from 1987 to 1994.[20]

---

[17] The "flatness" of real wages was first noted in the mid-1970s.

[18] The "real" average hourly earnings were calculated by adjusting the rates in local currencies reported by BLS (USDL 97-213) and shown in Table 5, using the CPI (all wage and clerical workers—all items) from BLS, the CPI from Statistics Canada, and the Indice de Precios al Cumsumidor, Mexico, respectively.

[19] It is interesting to note that the 1994 ratio of U.S. to Canadian hourly compensation costs in Motor Vehicles and Equipment (SIC 371) is 1.28, compared to the all-manufacturing average of 1.06. The U.S. motor vehicles industry is known for its high, employer-paid health insurance costs.

[20] These estimates have been prepared by BLS from data supplied by the statistical agencies of the countries. BLS meticulously reviews the data, then adjusts for differences in coverage and definition to provide comparable estimates of compensation costs.

TABLE 5

HOURLY COMPENSATION COSTS FOR PRODUCTION WORKERS IN MANUFACTURING—U.S., CANADA, & MEXICO

	1975	1980	1983	1985	1990	1992	1993	1994	1995	1996
DIRECT HOURLY COMPENSATION										
IN NATIONAL CURRENCIES:										
United States, U.S. dollars	5.30	7.98	9.69	10.43	11.80	12.50	12.80	13.14	13.47	13.92
Canada, Canadian dollars	5.52	9.05	12.06	13.09	16.02	17.36	17.74	18.02	18.28	18.87
Mexico, new pesos*	0.017	0.046	0.150	0.365	3.956	5.967	6.630	7.37	8.51	10.09
CONVERTED TO U.S. DOLLARS USING EXCHANGE RATES:										
United States	5.30	7.98	9.69	10.43	11.80	12.50	12.80	13.14	13.47	13.92
Canada	5.43	7.74	9.79	9.58	13.73	14.36	13.75	13.19	13.31	13.93
Mexico	1.33	1.99	1.25	1.42	1.41	1.93	2.13	2.18	1.33	1.33
CONVERTED TO U.S. DOLLARS USING PURCHASING POWER PARITY:										
United States	5.30	7.98	9.69	10.43	11.80	12.50	12.80	13.14	13.47	13.92
Canada	4.52	7.24	9.28	10.23	12.32	13.67	14.08	14.42	14.86	15.47
Mexico	1.73	2.42	2.47	2.61	2.50	3.49	3.60	3.78	3.32	3.12
HOURLY COMPENSATION COSTS										
IN NATIONAL CURRENCIES:										
United States, U.S. dollars	6.36	9.87	12.14	13.01	14.91	16.09	16.51	16.87	17.19	17.74
Canada, Canadian dollars	6.07	10.13	13.71	14.94	18.49	20.59	21.21	21.66	22.02	22.73
Mexico, new pesos*	0.018	0.051	0.17	0.409	4.44	6.72	7.48	8.34	9.66	11.39
CONVERTED TO U.S. DOLLARS USING EXCHANGE RATES:										
United States	6.36	9.87	12.14	13.01	14.91	16.09	16.51	16.87	17.19	17.74
Canada	5.96	8.67	11.13	10.94	15.84	17.03	16.44	15.85	16.04	16.66
Mexico	1.47	2.21	1.42	1.59	1.58	2.17	2.40	2.47	1.51	1.50
CONVERTED TO U.S. DOLLARS USING PURCHASING POWER PARITY:										
United States	6.36	9.87	12.14	13.01	14.91	16.09	16.51	16.87	17.19	17.74
Canada	4.98	8.10	10.55	11.67	14.22	16.21	16.83	17.33	17.90	18.63
Mexico	1.84	2.68	2.80	2.92	2.81	3.93	4.07	4.28	3.77	3.53
DIRECT PAY AS PERCENT OF HOURLY COMPENSATION COST:										
United States	83.3	80.9	79.8	80.1	79.2	77.7	77.5	77.9	78.4	78.5
Canada	90.9	89.4	87.9	87.6	86.6	84.3	83.6	83.2	83.0	83.0
Mexico	92.3	89.7	88.2	89.2	89.1	88.9	88.6	88.4	88.1	88.5
RATIOS OF COMPENSATION COSTS IN U.S. DOLLARS, BASED ON EXCHANGE RATES:										
U.S.:Canada	1.07	1.14	1.09	1.19	0.94	0.95	1.00	1.06	1.07	1.07
U.S.: Mexico	4.33	4.47	8.55	8.18	9.44	7.42	6.88	6.83	11.38	11.83
Canada: Mexico	4.05	3.92	7.84	6.88	10.03	7.85	6.85	6.42	10.62	11.11

Source: Unpublished data from BLS (Susan Fleck, June, 1997).

Note that 1,000 old pesos were turned in for 1 Nuevo Peso in November 1993.

TABLE 6

UNITED STATES, CANADA AND MEXICO: HOURLY COMPENSATION COSTS FOR PRODUCTION WORKERS IN MANUFACTURING

(U.S. dollars)

	USSIC	1987	1988	1989	1990	1991	1992	1993	1994	1995	1996
ALL MANUFACTURING											
United States		13.52	13.91	14.32	14.91	15.58	16.09	16.51	16.86	17.20	17.74
Canada		12.04	13.50	14.77	15.83	17.16	17.03	16.43	15.87	16.03	16.66
Mexico		1.04	1.25	1.43	1.58	1.84	2.17	2.40	2.47	1.51	1.50
FOOD, BEVERAGE, AND TOBACCO[1]	20-21										
United States		12.55	12.85	13.15	13.58	14.14	14.76	15.12	15.48	.....	.....
Canada		11.21	12.50	13.59	14.42	15.40	14.89	14.79	14.18	.....	.....
Mexico		0.91	1.06	1.22	1.35	1.61	1.83	2.04	2.21	.....	.....
TEXTILE, APPAREL, AND LEATHER PRODUCTS[1]	20,23 & 31										
United States		8.27	8.54	8.87	9.23	9.56	10.07	10.26	10.60	.....	.....
Canada		7.49	8.30	9.23	9.77	10.58	10.56	9.81	9.59	.....	.....
Mexico		0.86	1.02	1.20	1.32	1.52	1.81	1.96	1.98	.....	.....
TEXTILE MILL PRODUCTS	22										
United States		9.11	9.44	9.86	10.34	10.73	11.46	11.63	11.97	.....	.....
Canada		8.98	9.97	11.23	11.88	12.80	13.02	12.06	11.58	.....	.....
Mexico		1.13	1.36	1.56	1.68	1.94	2.31	2.62	2.78	.....	.....
APPAREL AND OTHER TEXTILE PRODUCTS	23										
United States		7.64	7.88	8.14	8.43	8.69	9.04	9.22	9.53	.....	.....
Canada		6.68	7.35	8.21	8.73	9.26	9.06	8.51	8.25	.....	.....
Mexico		0.73	0.79	0.92	1.03	0.93	1.40	1.54	1.55	.....	.....
LEATHER AND LEATHER PRODUCTS	31										
United States		7.96	8.26	8.66	9.10	9.53	9.97	10.27	10.77	.....	.....
Canada		7.54	8.45	9.23	9.72	10.22	9.46	9.27	9.20	.....	.....
LEATHER FOOTWEAR	314										
United States		7.54	7.87	8.31	8.75	9.04	9.39	9.59	10.26	.....	.....
Mexico		0.61	0.79	1.04	1.34	1.60	2.10	2.16	2.18	.....	.....
LUMBER, WOOD, AND FURNITURE[2]	24 & 33										
United States		10.64	10.91	11.26	11.67	11.98	12.38	12.66	12.85	.....	.....
Canada		10.82	11.96	13.03	14.33	14.98	14.74	14.39	14.00	.....	.....
Mexico		0.68	0.75	0.85	0.98	1.14	1.33	1.54	1.49	.....	.....
LUMBER AND WOOD PRODUCTS	24										
United States		10.98	11.18	11.50	11.90	12.17	12.57	12.78	12.97	.....	.....
Canada		11.82	13.05	14.23	15.63	16.51	15.98	15.50	14.98	.....	.....
Mexico		0.67	0.75	0.85	0.96	1.12	1.30	1.49	1.43	.....	.....
FURNITURE AND FIXTURES	25										
United States		10.16	10.56	10.95	11.38	11.75	12.15	12.53	12.76	.....	.....
Canada		8.67	9.57	10.53	11.45	11.93	11.97	11.65	11.40	.....	.....
Mexico		0.68	0.75	0.84	1.00	1.16	1.36	1.58	1.53	.....	.....
PAPER, PRINTING AND PUBLISHING[1]	26 & 27										
United States		14.46	14.77	15.16	15.68	16.23	16.78	17.17	17.41	.....	.....
Canada		13.87	15.69	16.91	18.04	20.02	19.89	18.91	17.76	.....	.....
Mexico		1.04	1.23	1.43	1.57	1.88	2.28	2.51	2.50	.....	.....
PAPER AND ALLIED PRODUCTS	26										
United States		15.90	16.23	16.66	17.26	18.02	18.56	19.14	19.53	.....	.....
Canada		15.88	17.73	19.31	20.44	22.64	22.42	21.64	20.90	.....	.....
Mexico		1.24	1.44	1.67	1.84	2.18	2.49	2.81	2.75	.....	.....
PRINTING AND PUBLISHING	27										
United States		13.49	13.80	14.19	14.74	15.13	15.65	15.91	16.08	.....	.....
Canada		11.24	12.64	13.64	14.55	16.18	16.53	15.65	14.06	.....	.....
Mexico		0.87	1.05	1.23	1.36	1.65	2.12	2.31	2.34	.....	.....
CHEMICALS, RUBBER AND PLASTIC PRODUCTS[1]	28-30										
United States		15.05	15.46	16.08	16.66	17.44	18.03	18.35	18.55	.....	.....
Canada		12.54	13.95	15.03	15.70	16.68	16.64	15.86	15.34	.....	.....
Mexico		1.41	1.82	2.03	2.29	2.66	3.18	3.58	3.67	.....	.....

TABLE 6 (CONTINUED)

UNITED STATES, CANADA AND MEXICO: HOURLY COMPENSATION COSTS FOR PRODUCTION WORKERS IN MANUFACTURING

(U.S. dollars)

	USSIC	1987	1988	1989	1990	1991	1992	1993	1994	1995	1996
CHEMICALS AND ALLIED PRODUCTS	28										
United States		17.21	17.81	18.33	19.12	19.95	20.75	21.25	21.76	.....	.....
Canada		12.84	14.38	15.58	16.80	18.60	18.30	17.73	16.91	.....	.....
Mexico		1.56	2.05	2.34	2.60	3.10	3.72	4.24	4.42	.....	.....
PETROLEUM AND COAL PRODUCTS	29										
United States		20.18	20.72	21.48	22.96	24.32	25.45	26.63	27.48	.....	.....
Canada		19.58	22.14	24.29	24.47	19.67	18.36	21.23	20.53	.....	.....
RUBBER AND PLASTIC PRODUCTS	30										
United States		12.27	12.55	12.95	13.50	14.07	14.55	14.80	14.87	.....	.....
Canada		10.81	11.97	12.92	13.65	14.97	15.04	14.15	13.94	.....	.....
Mexico		1.04	1.22	1.38	1.58	1.90	2.24	2.50	2.50	.....	.....
RUBBER PRODUCTS	301-6										
United States		14.86	14.79	15.37	16.12	16.91	17.59	18.12	18.28	.....	.....
Canada		11.56	12.57	13.82	15.03	17.57	17.63	16.35	16.13	.....	.....
Mexico		1.91	2.32	2.51	2.93	3.55	4.21	4.63	4.62	.....	.....
PLASTICS AND PRODUCTS	308+										
United States		11.19	11.63	11.97	12.47	12.99	13.36	13.58	13.66	.....	.....
Canada		10.45	11.72	12.61	13.18	14.17	14.02	13.15	12.99	.....	.....
Mexico		0.77	0.90	1.06	1.20	1.46	1.72	1.98	1.98	.....	.....
STONE, CLAY AND GLASS	32										
United States		13.94	14.37	14.77	15.30	15.85	16.27	16.67	16.97	.....	.....
Canada		12.70	14.10	15.47	16.22	17.79	17.90	17.02	16.08	.....	.....
Mexico		1.02	1.19	1.39	1.54	1.79	2.12	2.46	2.52	.....	.....
GLASS AND GLASSWARE	321-3										
United States		15.28	15.44	15.84	16.53	17.15	17.73	18.39	18.77	.....	.....
Canada		12.52	14.01	15.04	15.92	17.38	16.97	16.08	15.21	.....	.....
Mexico		1.13	1.42	1.61	1.76	2.06	2.44	2.98	2.99	.....	.....
POTTERY AND RELATED PRODUCTS	326										
United States		12.26	12.88	13.16	13.63	13.94	14.24	14.38	14.82	.....	.....
Mexico		0.79	0.96	1.09	1.24	1.53	1.82	1.91	2.20	.....	.....
PRIMARY METALS	33										
United States		18.10	18.74	18.92	19.72	20.73	21.54	22.29	22.80	.....	.....
Canada		15.94	17.95	19.78	21.08	22.84	23.05	22.59	21.40	.....	.....
Mexico		1.60	1.89	2.45	2.63	2.76	3.44	3.66	3.79	.....	.....
IRON AND STEEL	331										
United States		22.53	23.72	23.60	24.28	25.76	26.98	28.92	30.25	.....	.....
Canada		16.98	18.63	20.08	21.21	23.27	23.25	22.83	21.99	.....	.....
NONFERROUS METAL, INCLUDING FOUNDRIES	333-6										
United States		15.68	15.99	16.42	17.17	17.99	18.66	18.83	18.93	.....	.....
Canada		15.00	17.51	19.92	21.44	22.76	23.24	22.78	21.23	.....	.....
Mexico		1.10	1.46	1.67	1.76	2.04	2.57	2.78	2.81	.....	.....
FABRICATED METAL PRODUCTS, MACHINERY AND EQUIPMENT[1]	34-38										
United States		15.78	15.47	15.93	16.59	17.46	17.97	18.51	19.74	.....	.....
Canada		12.68	14.28	15.53	16.85	18.38	18.42	17.71	17.30	.....	.....
Mexico		1.07	1.27	1.43	1.61	1.89	2.26	2.50	2.52	.....	.....
FABRICATED METAL PRODUCTS	34										
United States		13.77	14.17	14.59	15.10	15.76	16.13	16.49	16.65	.....	.....
Canada		11.69	13.15	14.48	15.55	16.70	16.68	15.38	14.76	.....	.....
Mexico		0.88	1.04	1.23	1.35	1.54	1.89	2.15	2.32	.....	.....
INDUSTRIAL AND COMMERCIAL MACHINERY AND EQUIPMENT	35										
United States		14.66	14.98	15.45	16.07	16.73	17.20	17.71	17.93	.....	.....
Canada		12.45	13.93	15.05	16.51	17.93	18.10	17.03	16.43	.....	.....
Mexico		1.00	1.20	1.43	1.53	1.90	2.30	2.69	2.80	.....	.....

TABLE 6 (CONTINUED)

UNITED STATES, CANADA AND MEXICO: HOURLY COMPENSATION COSTS FOR PRODUCTION WORKERS IN MANUFACTURING

(U.S. dollars)

	USSIC	1987	1988	1989	1990	1991	1992	1993	1994	1995	1996
ELECTRONIC AND ELECTRICAL EQUIPMENT	36										
United States		.....	13.51	13.85	14.31	15.05	15.50	15.89	16.19	.....	.....
Canada		11.54	12.77	13.91	15.47	16.50	16.89	16.28	15.44	.....	.....
Mexico		0.94	1.10	1.24	1.34	1.62	1.90	2.11	2.05	.....	.....
TRANSPORTATION EQUIPMENT	37										
United States		18.45	18.58	19.07	19.71	20.78	22.21	23.03	23.82	.....	.....
Canada		13.98	15.86	17.18	18.46	20.43	20.22	19.83	19.72	.....	.....
Mexico		1.60	1.93	2.03	2.44	2.76	3.45	3.83	3.87	.....	.....
MOTOR VEHICLES AND EQUIPMENT	371										
United States		20.40	20.80	21.39	22.48	24.28	24.70	25.52	26.56	.....	.....
Canada		14.49	16.41	17.88	19.09	21.06	20.95	20.72	20.72	.....	.....
Mexico		1.61	1.96	2.03	2.50	2.90	3.62	3.98	4.05	.....	.....
AIRCRAFT,	372 & 376										
United States		18.05	18.41	19.03	20.03	21.42	22.81	24.32	25.47	.....	.....
Canada		12.94	13.74	15.65	16.89	18.36	20.74	20.22	19.43	.....	.....
SHIP AND BOAT BUILDING AND REPAIR	373										
United States		14.36	14.52	14.82	15.56	16.66	17.58	18.26	18.08	.....	.....
Canada		10.75	12.58	14.42	16.18	17.69	17.53	15.93	14.95	.....	.....
INSTRUMENTS AND RELATED PRODUCTS	38										
United States		.....	14.72	15.10	15.89	16.58	17.00	17.60	17.87	.....	.....
MISCELLANEOUS MANUFACTURING	39										
United States		10.11	10.44	10.84	11.30	11.70	12.25	12.62	12.91	.....	.....
Canada		10.13	11.23	12.56	13.47	13.77	12.58	12.64	12.31	.....	.....
Mexico		0.84	0.94	1.11	1.15	1.36	1.59	1.86	1.76	.....	.....

1. Some categories combine two or more U.S. SIC codes to allow easier comparison to Canadian or Mexican practice.

2. Both wood and metal furniture are included, conforming to the U.S. system.

Source: Bureau of Labor Statistics, unpublished data, 6/96.

BENEFITS

Benefits vary considerably among the three NAFTA countries. "A Comparison of Legislated Employment Benefits in North America" has been prepared by the Commission for Labor Cooperation and is included in *North American Labor Markets: A Comparative Profile*.[21] It is reprinted below with permission.

TRENDS IN EMPLOYMENT BENEFITS

Overview

Each country in North America has a unique combination of publicly and privately funded employment benefits that reflect its economic and social policies. The main legislated employment benefits are summarized and compared below. Available information on nonlegislated employment benefits is also presented.

In Mexico and Canada, many employment benefits and standards, such as hours of work, vacation, and maternity leave, are defined by law. In the United States, most employment benefits are established by collective bargaining between labor organizations and employers, or by company policy in nonunion firms. Another significant difference among the three countries is the extent to which health care is considered an employment benefit. Health care in Canada is not an employment benefit; it is publicly financed and universally accessible to workers and nonworkers alike. Many larger firms provide dental benefits and supplementary health and medication plans, although those benefits are a small proportion of total employment benefits. As their name implies, they are intended as a supplement to the public system.

The IMSS[22], which is funded by employees, employers, and government contributions in Mexico, supports health care services for wage and salary workers. Other groups of workers, such as family workers, the self-employed, employers, and small collective landholders, are also eligible for these benefits. However, they are required to pay all contributions, and very few of them have taken advantage of this eligibility. Health care for employees in the public sector is provided by the ISSSTE[23].

In the United States, workers' health care is considered an employment benefit and is funded largely by employers and employees. Workers whose employers do not provide this benefit can purchase private insurance, obtain insurance under a spouse's plan, or remain uninsured. These distinctions are important to keep in mind when examining trends in employment benefits.

There are some important similarities in trends in employment benefits in all three countries. Benefits are gaining greater importance as a form of compensation as they grow relative to wages and salaries. The distribution of benefits among workers is being altered as growing numbers of workers in nonstandard jobs are provided with reduced benefits or none. Benefits are taking new forms as profit-sharing and other benefit mechanisms grow in popularity and the needs of aging populations are addressed. The challenge for North American countries is to improve the living standards of workers by encouraging the development of employment benefits that are transferable from one job to another, that can benefit workers in nonstandard jobs, and that can provide adequate, lifelong benefits in a cost-effective manner. In all three countries, many programs that legislate employment benefit are under review.

---

[21] CLC, *Op.Cit.*, pp.106-115.

[22] Instituto Mexicano del Seguro Social (Mexican Institute for Social Security).

[23] Instituto de Seguridad y Servicíos Sociales de los Trabajadores del Estado (Institute for Security and Social Services for Public Servants).

Comparison of Benefits

The main sources of information for Table 7, which compares legislated employment benefits in North America, are Human Resources Development Canada, the Mexican STPS[24], and the United States Department of Labor.

In Mexico, all legislated employment benefits fall under federal statutes, with enforcement shared by federal and state authorities. In Canada and the United States, these benefits are regulated by a combination of federal and either provincial or state statutes. In Canada, labor laws fall mainly within provincial authority (as property and civil rights legislation). However, federal jurisdiction over labor matters extends to areas that are national, international, or interprovincial in nature, such as railways, banks, radio and television broadcasting, and telephone and cable systems. Approximately 10 percent of the Canadian work force is covered by federal jurisdiction; the rest of the workers come under provincial law. In the United States, the federal jurisdiction prevails in the establishment of minimum standards in most areas of employment legislation, but states can set higher standards and often share in enforcement.

In all three countries, collective agreements may contain special provisions that enhance minimum legislated employment benefits.

Legislated Employment Benefits

The extent to which various benefits are legislated differs from country to country. Tables 7A-7E compare various types of benefits available to North American workers and notes the presence or absence of legislation regulating them.

Other Employment Benefits

Cost of Benefits

In all three North American countries, employment benefits are gaining in importance as a form of compensation.[24] Benefits accounted for 30.0 percent of manufacturing remuneration in Mexico in 1995. In 1992, benefits accounted for 40.3 percent of manufacturing payroll in the United States. In 1995, benefits represented 27.3 percent of total payroll in Canada and 28.4 percent of total compensation in the United States (note that the Canadian figure does not include health insurance, while the U.S. figure includes health insurance, which accounted for 6.2 percent of total compensation costs). While these data are not strictly comparable across countries, they provide an indication of benefit levels in each country.

The cost of benefits has grown significantly in all three countries over the past decade. In the United States, "other labor income," which includes employer contributions to social programs and additional private benefits, increased from 9.0 percent to 11.0 percent of total labor income between 1984 and 1994. In Canada, "supplementary labor income," which includes employer contributions to social programs and private benefits, increased from 10.0 percent to 13.0 percent during 1984-1994. In Mexico, benefit costs in manufacturing industries grew 17.8 percent in real terms during 1984-1995, and employer and employee payroll taxes for social security increased.

---

[24] Some of the data supporting this discussion of benefits as a form of compensation come from National Income and Expenditure Accounts, *Conference Board of Canada Compensation Planning Outlook*, 1996; Mexico's National Income and Expenditure Survey and Monthly Industrial Survey; U.S. National Income and Product Accounts; Bureau of National Affairs [an independent U.S. publisher of business and labor reports], *Benefit Costs and Practices*, 1995; and the U.S. Department of Labor, "Report on the American Workforce," 1994 and 1995.

Distribution of Benefits

The distribution of employment benefits among the working population in North America has been significantly altered as a result of the increase in nonstandard work, the numbers of workers in small firms, and the increasing cost of benefits.[25] Employment benefits in the United States, Mexico, and Canada have largely been designed for "standard" full-time wage and salary workers. Most private employer-provided benefits, such as vacations and company pension plans, improve with a worker's seniority. However, with a higher degree of flux in the labor market, fewer workers remain with the same employer for a significant length of time. Further, with the growth in nonstandard work and in employment in small firms with fewer than 100 employees, fewer workers are gaining access to benefits.

TABLE 7A

COMPARISON OF LEGISLATED EMPLOYMENT BENEFITS IN NORTH AMERICA:
VACATIONS, HOLIDAYS, AND WORK HOURS

TYPE OF BENEFITS	PAID VACATIONS	PAID HOLIDAYS	HOURS OF WORK
Canada	2 weeks of annual vacation after each completed year of employment at 4 percent of annual earnings; the federal and several provincial jurisdictions also provide for 3 weeks of vacation after 4-6 years of continuous employment with one employer at 6 percent of annual earnings.	Varies from 5 to 11 paid holidays annually with most provincial legislation requiring 8 or 9 days.	Standard is 8 hours/day, 40-48 hours/week with 44 hours/week being the most common. Maximum of 48 hours/week in most jurisdictions, after which overtime rates must be paid.
United States	No federally or state mandated vacation requirements. General practice: 1 week after 1 year, 2 weeks after 2 years, 3 weeks after 5-10 years, and 4 weeks after 10-20 years.	No federally mandated days off for holidays in private sector, though some states have such requirements.	Legislated standard is 40 hours/week after which overtime at a rate of 150 percent must be paid; no maximum.
Mexico	6 days of vacation after one year of employment. Two additional days/year for each year thereafter up to 12 days. After 5 years the employee is entitled to 14 vacation days, and two additional days for each subsequent 5-year interval. Seasonal or occasional workers are entitled to vacation time on a pro-rated basis, according to the number of days worked. Workers are entitled to a bonus of not less than 25 percent of pay for the vacation period.	7 mandatory statutory holidays.	A maximum of 8 hours per day, 7 hours/night and 6.5 hours for split shift work. Overtime limited to 3 hours/day for no more than 3 days/week at overtime premium rates (usually 150 percent).

---

[25] Some of the data supporting this discussion of the distribution of employment benefits come from Statistic Canada's National Income and Expenditure Accounts, *Conference Board of Canada Compensation Planning Outlook*, 1996; Human Resources Development Canada, *Statistics Canada Working Paper Series*, No. 71; Mexico's National Commission for Minimum Wages and INEGI, 1993, and the ENE; U.S. Department of Labor, Bureau of Labor Statistics, "Survey of Employee Benefits in Small Establishments," 1992; U.S. Department of Labor, Bureau of Labor Statistics, "Report on the American Workforce," 1994 and 1995; H. Stein and M. Foss, *The American Economy*, 1995, AEI Press; and Bureau of National Affairs, *Benefit Costs and Practices*, 1995.

TABLE 7B

COMPARISON OF LEGISLATED EMPLOYMENT BENEFITS IN NORTH AMERICA: REST AND LEAVES

TYPE OF BENEFITS	DAY(S) OF REST	MATERNITY/PARENTAL LEAVE	OTHER FAMILY-RELATED LEAVES
Canada	One full day of rest/week, preferably Sunday	17 weeks leave of absence without pay after anywhere from 1-26 weeks of employment service, depending on the province of residence as well as anywhere from 0-34 weeks of parental leave, depending on the province. Workers are entitled to be reinstated in the same or comparable position. The unemployment insurance program provides 15 weeks of maternity benefits, 10 weeks of parental benefits, and 15 weeks of sickness benefits for a maximum of 30 weeks at 55 percent of insurable earnings.	The federal and several provincial jurisdictions allow for bereavement leave for death in the immediate family, as well as unpaid sick leave and child-care leave.
United States	No general federal mandate. Some federal regulations for specific occupations; some state regulations.	No federal paid leave requirement, but federal law protects the right to return to a job after childbirth in firms with more than 50 employees. Maternity must be treated like any disability. If disability pay is provided for nonwork related injuries, it must be given for maternity leave. There is no unemployment insurance for maternity leave.	Family leave law allows workers in businesses with 50 or more employees to take up to 12 weeks of unpaid leave per year for family or medical emergencies
Mexico	One complete day of rest with full pay, preferably Sunday.	All employees are entitled to 3 months of fully paid maternity leave. They are entitled to free medical and hospital care and to medication supported by social security payments (see Social Security below).	

In Canada, legislated benefits such as a standard 40-48 hour work week and a certain number of vacation days apply only to full-time workers with one employer. These benefits do not apply to the 15.5 percent of the labor force who are self-employed, nor to many multiple part-time job holders. Close to half of full-time employees are covered by employer-sponsored pension plans, whereas only 10.0 percent of part-time workers are covered by such plans. Less than half of all workers were eligible for unemployment insurance in 1995 as a result of the growth in part-time workers (those working less than 15 hours per week were ineligible until recently) and the self-employed. Small firms, which between 1978 and 1992 created the majority of net jobs in Canada, tend to limit employment benefits. Flexible working hours, extended maternity leave, and special family leaves are offered by 60.0 percent of the largest firms (more than 2,000 employees), but just over one-third of smaller firms (fewer than 500 employees) offer such benefits.

TABLE 7C

COMPARISON OF LEGISLATED EMPLOYMENT BENEFITS IN NORTH AMERICA: PUBLIC PENSIONS

TYPE OF BENEFITS	SOCIAL SECURITY/PUBLIC PENSION PLANS
Canada	Canada/Quebec Pension Plans, disability income, and death benefits are financed by a 5.6 percent payroll tax paid in equal shares by employers and employees with maximum pensionable earnings of C$35,400. Pension benefits in 1996 were 25 percent of average monthly pensionable earnings during the contribution period. Individual Registered Retirement Savings Plans can be set up privately by workers to provide tax-deferred retirement savings.
United States	A 15.3 percent payroll tax is equally shared by employers and employees. The tax supports a public pension plan, disability insurance, death benefits, and health care for those over age 65 (Medicare) with maximum insurable earnings of U.S.$62,700 in 1996. Employers and employees can opt to establish private defined benefit or contribution pension plans, which may be tax deferred.
Mexico	Wage and salary workers at IMSS receive health and maternity care, compensation for the disabled, and old age dismissal and pensions supported by a 14.7 percent employer payroll, a 3.25 percent employee payroll (employer pays full cost for employees earning the minimum wage), and a government contribution. This fund covers about 11 million wage and salary workers in the private formal sector. Child care for working women is supported by a 1 percent payroll tax on employers. About 2.2 million federal government workers have a separate but similar social security plan. An employer payroll tax of 5 percent supports the National Housing Fund, which provides low-cost housing to private wage and salaried employees. A mandatory retirement savings plan for wage and salary workers was established in 1992 funded by a 2 percent employer payroll tax.

TABLE 7D

COMPARISON OF LEGISLATED EMPLOYMENT BENEFITS IN NORTH AMERICA: UNEMPLOYMENT INSURANCE AND PROFIT-SHARING

TYPE OF BENEFITS	UNEMPLOYMENT INSURANCE	PROFIT-SHARING
Canada	Benefits are 55 percent of insurable earnings to a maximum of C$413/ week, for up to 45 weeks. Minimum weeks of work to qualify varies between 12 and 20 weeks depending on regional unemployment rate. For new labor force entrants and reentrants 26 weeks are required. Payments are financed by employer payroll tax of 4.3 percent of insured earnings and an employee contribution of 3 percent of insured earnings. As of January 1997, minimum hours of work required will be 420-700 hours with 910 hours of work required for new entrants or reentrants. A family income supplement for low-income families will also be available. Less than half of the unemployed received benefits in 1994.	No requirement by employers to share profits with employees.
United States	State-based system provides for about 13 weeks, at 37 percent of pay on average (minimum 27 percent, maximum 52 percent) to a maximum of U.S.$180-354/ week, depending on the state. Duration can be extended to 26-39 weeks in states with high unemployment or for trade adjustment. Payments are financed by an employer payroll tax that ranges from 0.6 percent to 4.9 percent (average across states is 2.2 percent) with experience rating and a federal supplement from the General Treasury. About 35 percent of unemployed received benefits in 1995.	No requirement by employers to share profits with employees.
Mexico	There is no unemployment insurance program. Severance pay is provided to formal sector workers in the case of layoffs or closures and is based on length of service and circumstances surrounding the dismissal. Generally, a lump sum equal to 3 months' pay plus 20 days' pay for each year of service is provided to workers in the formal sector. Unemployed formal sector workers are eligible for health care benefits for up to 6 months after dismissal.	Enterprises are required by law to distribute 10 percent of annual taxable income to employees. Profits are allocated in two stages: first distribution is based on days worked/ year; second distribution is proportional to the workers' annual salary.

Among small firms (fewer than 100 employees) in the United States, which accounted for 39 percent of employment in 1991, 30 percent of full-time workers did not participate in employer-provided health care plans, 12 percent did not receive paid vacations, 18 percent did not receive paid holidays, and 47 percent did not receive paid sick leave. In 1992, 55 percent of full-time workers and 88 percent of part-time workers did not have retirement plans. Also in 1992, 72 percent of small employers did not provide unpaid maternity leave. In large and medium-sized firms, 8 percent of full-time workers did not receive paid vacations and holidays, 33 percent did not receive paid sick leave, 63 percent did not receive unpaid maternity leave, and 22 percent did not receive a retirement plan in 1992. About 50 percent of private wage and salary workers in the United States who work 1-20 hours per week lacked

TABLE 7E

COMPARISON OF LEGISLATED EMPLOYMENT BENEFITS IN NORTH AMERICA: WORKER'S COMPENSATION

TYPES OF BENEFITS	WORKER'S COMPENSATION
Canada	Provincially based systems provide no-fault worker's compensation benefits. Federal system, tied to provincial system, provides benefits for workers in the federal jurisdiction. Insurable earnings ranged from C$35,000 to C$55,600, and maximum benefit levels ranged from 75 percent to 90 percent of net insurable earnings in 1995. The system is supported by an employer payroll tax of between 1.4 percent and 3 percent, depending on the province.
United States	State-based system generally provides for two-thirds of salary for duration of disability and provides schedule of specified benefits for certain injuries. Maximum weekly benefit ranges from U.S.$275-846, depending on the state. Worker's compensation is optional in some states. The system is financed by employer payroll taxes with experience rating and uses no federal standards or funding.
Mexico	Compensation for job-related accidents and illnesses is supported through mandated employer contributions, which are part of the social security system.

Source: Canada, "Employment Standards Legislation," Human Resources Development Canada, 1995-1996; Mexico, IMSS and STPS; United States, Department of Labor, Bureau of National Affairs, and the AFL-CIO.

employer-sponsored health care coverage, compared with 26 percent working 21-34 hours per week and 3 percent of those working more than 35 hour per week. About 49 percent of employees working for temporary help agencies had health insurance available to them, although less than 10 percent actually participated in the plan. Similarly, 74 percent of these U.S. workers had holiday and vacation plans available to them, but fewer than 10 percent qualified for these benefits in 1994. Agencies typically require 1,000 hours of service in a year to qualify for benefits. In 1993, 58 percent of the population had employer-sponsored health insurance, compared with 66 percent in 1980, despite increases in employer expenditures on health care over this period.

In Mexico, 34 percent of the labor force received benefits in 1995, compared with 39 percent in 1991. This change was mainly because of the growth in the numbers of nonstandard and unpaid workers. About 63 percent of salary workers received social security benefits in 1993, down from 66 percent in 1991. Only 29 percent of piece workers had benefits in 1993. These workers have increased their share from 9 percent of all salary workers in 1991 to 11 percent of all salary workers in 1995. Among nonsalary workers such as the self-employed, employers, and unpaid workers, who in 1995 accounted for almost 45 percent of total employment, only 2 percent received employment benefits. Under the Social Insurance Law of the Mexican Institute for Social Security, these workers are permitted to join the obligatory insurance regime and receive social security services if they pay the total required contribution themselves. These workers rely on publicly financed systems for health care and other benefits.

Types of Workers

Greater benefits go to higher paid, more educated workers in professional occupations and in sectors such as manufacturing and public administration.[26]

In Canada, supplementary labor income (including employer paid benefits, such as pensions, Unemployment Insurance, Worker's Compensation, disability insurance, etc.) of manufacturing workers represented 15.3 percent of total labor income in 1994, compared with 9.0 percent for service workers. Professional and technical employees had the greatest access to family-supportive work arrangements, such as child care, family leave, and flexible

---

[26] Some of the data supporting this discussion of the relationship between education level and benefits come from Statistics Canada, National Income and Product Accounts; National Childcare Survey; "Decima Workplace Survey in Canada," 1992; Mexico's ENE; and the U.S. Department of Labor, Bureau of Labor Statistics, "Report on the American Workforce," 1995.

hours, while unskilled workers had the least access. Canadians least likely to be satisfied with their maternity and pension benefits are those who work in small firms, are under 35 years of age, and earn lower incomes. Those who are most satisfied tend to be in larger firms (more than 500 employees); in technical, professional, or managerial occupations; in a unionized firm; and in jobs earning higher incomes.

In Mexico, the percentage of professional, technical, and managerial workers with benefits dropped from 82 percent in 1991 to 76 percent in 1993, compared with a drop from 42 percent to 39 percent during that period for service and domestic workers with benefits. In 1995, the majority of workers in agriculture, hotels, restaurants, transportation, business, and other services had no benefits, while a majority of workers in manufacturing, utilities, and public administration had benefits. Access to benefits increased with earnings in Mexico for workers earning less than 10 times the minimum wage. For example, in 1995, 91 percent of workers earning less than the minimum wage had no benefits compared with 58 percent of workers earning one to two times the minimum wage.

In the United States, health care coverage for workers with a college degree dropped from 79 percent to 73 percent between 1979 and 1993, while coverage for workers with less than a high school education dropped from 52 percent to 36 percent coverage during the same period. Similarly in 1993, 27 percent of workers with family incomes below U.S.$10,000 were ineligible for or were denied employer-sponsored health care coverage, compared with 6 percent of workers with family incomes above U.S.$40,000.

Profit-Sharing and Pension Plans

One growing type of benefit is profit-sharing in the form of cash or deferred plans. Another important development is the growing popularity of defined contribution pension plans in Canada and the United States.[27]

In 1990, about 12 percent of Canadian employees participated in cash profit-sharing schemes, which were available in 15 percent of firms with more than 20 employees. Also in 1990, fewer than 8 percent of employees participated in the formal deferred profit-sharing plans offered by 4 percent of firms with more than 20 employees. Cash-based schemes increased by at least one-third in the 1980s, while deferred plans declined.

In Mexico, cash-based profit-sharing is obligatory by law for all enterprises, excluding new enterprises, the mining industry, private assistance institutions, public assistance institutions, and enterprises with less than a certain amount of capital. All workers, with the exception of directors, management, and domestic employees, are covered. Profit-sharing is fixed at 10 percent of annual taxable income.

In the United States in 1993, 3.0 percent of firms with more than 100 employees have cash-based profit-sharing plans, and 15.0 percent of firms with more than 100 employees have deferred profit-sharing plans. In contrast with Canada, there was no significant increase in cash-based plans in the United States during 1985-1989. However, deferred plans increased fourfold from 1969 to 1989. Only 0.4 percent of payroll was spent on profit-sharing in 1993, and 0.3 percent on stock bonus and employee stock ownership plans.

While defined benefit pension plans continue to be the dominant form of employer-provided pension plans in both Canada and the United States, defined contribution pension plans are growing in importance. In the United States during 1980-1987, the proportion of private-sector workers with defined benefit pension plans declined from 38 percent to 31 percent, while the proportion of these workers with defined contribution pension plans grew from 8 percent to 15 percent. In Canada, the shift has been less dramatic. In 1986-1994, the

---

[27] Some of the data supporting this discussion of profit-sharing and defined contribution pension plans come from the OECD Employment Outlook, 1995; U.S. Department of Labor, Bureau of Labor Statistics, 1992; and the U.S. Chamber of Commerce Study of Employer's 1993 Benefit Costs.

proportion of private-sector workers with defined benefit, registered pension plans dropped from 27 percent to 25 percent, while the proportion with defined contribution or hybrid registered plans grew from 4 percent to 5 percent.

In Mexico, the national pension system (SAR) was modified in 1996. By July 1997, the pension contributions that will be paid by employers, workers, and the government to Mexico's grant security agency will be redirected to individual accounts managed by private companies called AFORES (Administradoras de Fondos Para el Retiro de los Trabajadore). Under this new pension system, workers will have the option to chose among difference investment plans that are presented by the AFORES.

THE UNCOUNTED INDUSTRY—
A NORTH AMERICAN PROBLEM

No one knows exactly how large the North American trade in illegal drugs is, but it is surely a major industry and a very profitable one. It involves all three NAFTA countries—Mexico, primarily as the transshipper; the United States, primarily as the major consumer; and Canada, primarily as consumer. It is clear that illegal drugs are not just dropped north of the border: they are distributed to virtually every city, town, and village in North America. The transport, sale, and use of illegal drugs is a major North American industry and a serious problem everywhere on the continent.

North America has a 100-year history of smuggling at the U.S.-Mexican border (and at the U.S.-Canadian border as well). Guns moved south during Mexico's revolutions; beer, tequila, and whiskey, north during prohibition; appliances, cars, and heavy equipment, south in the 1970s; and illegal drugs (home-grown marijuana and imported cocaine), north in the 1980s and 1990s. Peter Lupska[1] reports that Juan Garcia Abrego,[2] an experienced marijuana smuggler, established the model for the industry when he offered to transship and deliver cocaine to any location in the United States—delivery guaranteed, losses replaced—for 50 percent of the total load. In other words, Abrego would take over the entire distribution system—warehousing, shipment, and insurance—for 50 percent of the gross. The deal was very attractive to the Colombian cartels, then suffering major interdiction losses to U.S. law enforcement. It is estimated that at least 75 percent of the street cocaine in the United States is now delivered via the "narcotics superhighway" from Mexico.[3]

Eduardo Valle Espinosa, a former special prosecutor (narcotics) for Mexico's Attorney General, estimates that the profits from that trade exceed those of Petroleos Mexicanos (PEMEX), Mexico's petroleum monopoly.[4] The National Autonomous University of Mexico estimates that the drug cartels spend $500 million on bribes annually.[5] The U.S. Justice Department has estimated that Mexico's illegal drug trade with the United States is valued at $27 to $30 billion.[6] Mexico's total legal exports of goods to the United States were $73 billion in 1996.

If the Justice Department estimates are roughly correct, the illegal drug trade is indeed one of the largest industries in Mexico; it is less important in the United States only because the legal economy is so much larger. If the Mexican cartel's revenues are 50 percent of the gross on imported and transshipped cocaine and all the gross on home-grown marijuana, then $13.5 billion (half the estimated $27 billion U.S.-Mexico illegal drug trade) seems a very

---

[1] Peter A. Lupska, "Under the volcano: Narco Investment in Mexico," *Transnational Organized Crime Journal*, 1995.

[2] Abrego is actually an American citizen of Mexican descent who grew up in Los Angeles. His family is alleged to have been involved in smuggling for generations. Abrego was recently convicted in Houston and is serving 11 life sentences in a U.S. prison. John Ward Anderson, Molly Moore, and Douglas Farah, "U.S. Probes Mexico's Role in Drugs," *The Washington Post*, 11 May 1997, A2ff. The distribution model established by Abrego has been followed by many others including Amado Carrillo Fuentes. See, for example, Douglas Farah, "Mexican Control of U.S. Cocaine Market Grows," *The Washington Post*, 15 August 1997, A11.

[3] Linda Robinson, "An Inferno Next Door," U.S. *News & World Report*, 24 Feb.1997, 36.

[4] Robert D. Kaplan, "History Moving North," *Atlantic Monthly*, February 1997, 21-31.

[5] Linda Robinson.

[6] Susan E. Reed, "Certifiable—Mexico's Corruption, Washington's Indifference," *The New Republic*, 17 March 1997. This is apparently an unpublished DEA estimate. It is not clear that it is for 1996 or some other year.

conservative estimate of the GDP originating in the industry. This puts the illegal drug industry ahead of Mexico's chemicals industry, which has a GDP originating of about $12.6 billion[7]. The GDP originating in the U.S. illegal drug industry must be at least as large, given the huge illegal imports and the fact that marijuana is a major crop in California and elsewhere in the United States.

Industry revenues are enormous. Were it a legal business, it would certainly rate a chapter of its own in this book and be publicly recognized as a major contributor to all three economies. Indeed, if this industry were legal, a most unlikely and questionable prospect, Mexico's status as an international borrower would be substantially improved. If the trade were subject to normal taxation, the international bankers would stand in line to get Mexico's business[8].

There can be little doubt that Mexico's government and law enforcement organizations are riddled with drug-money-induced corruption. But it is abundantly clear that Americans are involved in virtually every aspect of the trade and that the organization required to operate the U.S. distribution industry must be large and profitable. The U.S. Department of Justice's Public Integrity Section says 32 U.S. law enforcement officials have been indicted for border-related corruption and 18 have been convicted.[9] One has to assume that some of the $500 million in bribe money finds its way north and, indeed, that the indigenous industry has its own budget for bribes.

---

[7] Subsector 35, Chemicals and Products Derived from Petroleum, Charcoal, Rubber, and Plastic, CMAP (Mexican Classification of Activities and Products.) Estimates based on 1993 Producto Interno Bruto (PIB), *Anuario Estadistico* 95, INEGI, p. 246, and an exchange rate of 3.1 Nuevo Pesos to the U.S. dollar. All figures in this paragraph are U.S. dollars.

[8] Of course, if narcotics were legal, the Colombians would export directly, and far more marijuana would be grown in the United States.

[9] "The American Connection...", *Newsweek*, 24 Feb 1997.

An Independent Quebec?

Canada's ongoing debate on the status of Quebec significantly affects both its foreign and domestic policies. Parti Québécois (PQ) has had a majority in the provincial legislature for a number of years and is dedicated to independence. In a provincial referendum in October 1995, about 60 percent of Quebec's francophones voted for separation and 49.4 percent of all voters voted "oui" to sovereignty[1] The PQ lost, but by such a small margin that many knowledgeable observers now believe that Quebec will ultimately vote to separate.[2]

The Canadian government has been deeply concerned about this possibility over several administrations. Major efforts have been made to satisfy Quebec and keep it a part of Canada—most notably the "Meech Lake" constitutional package vetoed by Manitoba and Newfoundland. Most proposals have centered on recognizing Quebec as "a distinct society" and decentralizing federal functions to permit greater freedoms of choice to the Province of Quebec. But the federal government's ability to satisfy Quebec's demands is limited. Canada is already one of the most decentralized democracies in the world, and some Canadians, both to the east and west, are losing patience with Quebec's demands.

After the 1995 referendum, leaders of the PQ demanded a constitutional change that would declare Quebec a distinct society and give Quebec a veto over all future constitutional changes. In addition, the PQ wants Quebec to be "an equal partner to the rest of Canada" in many types of negotiations.[3] It is unlikely that the federal government can meet these demands. For one thing, an October 1995 survey found that 77 percent of Canadians outside of Quebec would insist that any offer made to Quebec apply equally to the other nine provinces.[4]

An independent Quebec would be a viable economic unit, at least in the long run. Its population is small (7.3 million), but it has substantial natural resources, three times the territory of France, greater total gross domestic product (GDP) than Austria or Denmark, and greater GDP per capita than Australia or Sweden. If it could enter into a favorable arrangement with the rest of Canada and with the other NAFTA countries, it would be within 600 miles of about 100 million potential customers.[5]

But an independent Quebec would be faced with some daunting economic problems. The province now carries an onerous debt burden of Can$11 billion, or 20 percent of gross provincial product. If it takes on its share of Canada's debt (about 20 percent), as would certainly be demanded, it would then carry the staggering burden of Can$190 billion, 112 percent of Quebec's gross provincial product. If Quebec were independent, its debt instruments might get a lower rating than the "A2" now given them by Moody's Investors Service, which would result in Quebec paying an even higher rate of interest. Quebec's economy then would suffer from higher interest rates. Its growth is already lower than that for the rest of Canada, and its unemployment rate is higher as well. It is also quite likely that full membership in NAFTA, the Canada-U.S. Auto Pact, and possibly the World Trade

[1] Fry, Earl H., "Quebec, Canada & the United States: the Economic Dimension," *American Review of Canadian Studies*, Winter 1995, pp. 497-517.

[2] See for example, Lamont, *The Coming End of Canada and the Stakes for America*, W. W. Norton, 1994.

[3] Fry.

[4] *Toronto Globe and Mail*, November 2, 1995, A6, as quoted by Fry.

[5] Fry.

Organization (WTO) would be subject to lengthy negotiation, making the first few years of independence a period of real hardship.[6]

The recent election did nothing to clarify this issue. Canadian Prime Minister Jean Chretien called early elections for June 2, 1997, in hopes of improving his majority in Parliament. In the end, the Liberal party clung to a bare majority as two of its cabinet ministers were defeated in individual races.[7] More important to the future of Quebec, the voting seems to have been sharply regional. The Liberal party has its greatest strength in Ontario and is the party most strongly committed to "unity." It won 155 seats in the 301-seat House of Commons. The Reform party, with its strength almost entirely in the western provinces, won 60 seats and became the official "opposition party." Parti Québécois maintained its base with 44 seats.[8]

In the view of some, Preston Manning, leader of the Reform party, set the tone for the election by insisting that the issue vis-á-vis Quebec is one of equality, "...this country will be united on the basis of equality of citizens and provinces or it is unlikely to be united at all." [9] His stand against "special status" for Quebec won him supporters in western Canada and equally strong antipathy in Quebec.[10] He seems certain to oppose any resolution of Quebec's status that involves special treatment or official recognition of Quebec as "a distinct society."

In another important decision, Canada's Supreme Court was expected to rule in the fall of 1997 on a federal government challenge to Quebec's self-declared right to declare independence unilaterally. Some observers expected the court to come down on Ottawa's side.[11]

However, it is by no means certain that Quebec will remain a part of Canada. If Quebec departs, the implications for the rest of Canada, for the United States, and for NAFTA are serious. A divided Canada would have extensive economic and political problems. Four of the remaining nine provinces would be cut off from land communication with the rest, except through Quebec or the United States. Canada's population and GDP would be reduced by nearly one-fourth. The high costs of the necessary adjustments and the uncertainty of outcome would probably lower the rating for Canada's debt instruments and drive up the cost of carrying the very large national debt. The result could be a significant drop in the exchange value of its currency. A rebound for both an independent Quebec and for a new smaller Canada would undoubtedly take place eventually, but there would be several years of reduced or negative growth and serious economic hardship for both countries.

The United States has much at stake. Trade with Canada accounts for a substantial number of U.S. jobs, and U.S. investments in Canada are significant. The U.S. economy would be adversely affected by a drop in the Canadian dollar or by a severe recession north of the border. The U.S. government position has always been that it prefers a united Canada but will not take sides in an internal debate. However, U.S. leaders may well view a possible breakup of Canada with far greater concern than their public statements would suggest.[12]

---

[6] Ibid.

[7] Schneider, Howard, "Liberals Win Canadian Vote by Slim Margin," *Washington Post*, June 3, 1997, p. A1.

[8] Wilson-Smith, Anthony, "Distinct Societies—The election leaves the nation splintered as never before," *MacLeans*, June 9, 1997.

[9] Eisler, Dale, "Prairie Pragmatist—The Opposition Leader Vows to Change Canadian Politics," *MacLeans*, June 16, 1997.

[10] Wilson-Smith, "Distinct..."

[11] Wilson-Smith, Anthony, "Millennium Man," *MacLeans*, June 16, 1997.

[12] David Jones, a former official of the U.S. Department of State, has written in a recent issue of the *Washington Monthly* that the Department has studied the possibility of an independent Quebec and found that the United States could "live with" an independent Quebec. However, State Department spokesman Nicholas Burns condemned Jones' statement as "outrageous and undisciplined."

CHILE: A FOURTH MEMBER OF NAFTA?

BY STEVEN G. THOMAS

In 1997, Chile's strong economy and stable democratic political system seemed to make it a logical candidate for participation in NAFTA, but the U.S. Congress refused to grant the President the Fast Track authority necessary to proceed. Chile is still a strong candidate—both Canada and Mexico have had free trade agreements with Chile since 1991. To many opponents of the expansion of NAFTA, however, Chile's economic and political strengths and weaknesses are not the important issue. Chile's candidacy may be most important to both sides of the Fast Track controversy as a symbol and a model for future expansion.

As Table 1 shows, Chile is quite small relative to NAFTA and its current members. Chile's population is less than 4 percent of NAFTA's total and its GDP (on an exchange rate basis) is less than 1 percent (see Table 1). But Chile is in South, not North America; thousands of miles from NAFTA's current borders and, in the view of some, an equally symbolic distance from the original concept of NAFTA.

Outstanding trade issues in the hemisphere remain, and legislation giving fast track authorization may come up again in 1998. Thus, the following information about Chile and its economy may be useful.

POLITICAL BACKGROUND

It is worth noting the history behind the making of the current political system of Chile, which has some democratic tradition, despite the extremes of the recent past. Until 1973, Chile was a democratic republic. It was marked by strong left and right parties and a relatively weak center. The last government from the political center of that era was that of Eduardo Frei, Sr. (father of the current president). The Frei government accomplished many of its goals, including improvement of the education system and unionization of rural workers, but found itself severely restricted by strong opposition from both political extremes. In 1970 Dr. Salvador Allende, a candidate from the leftist coalition, took power in a narrow victory. Allende's tenure was tumultuous, as strikes, riots, and shortages plagued the country. Allende aligned himself with Fidel Castro's Cuba, further alienating investors. Then, on September 11, 1973, a military coup overthrew Allende, who died under mysterious circumstances.

General Agosto Pinochet governed the country as a dictator from 1973 until 1990. The regime was marked by numerous documented human rights violations, and was a virtual police state. The right-leaning military sought to impose discipline on the previously tumultuous country by forcefully suppressing political conflict and civil unrest. It also imposed policies of economic austerity, receiving help in this effort from University of Chicago economists, and over time succeeded in bringing inflation under control and attracting investment. Eventually, the international outcries for a cessation of human rights abuses and a return to democracy were heeded. Chile returned to democracy in 1990 with the election of center-left engineer Patricio Alywin as president. The military, formerly under Pinochet, is still an active player in the political arena, mostly influencing the right-leaning parties. Pinochet himself stepped down from the military in 1997 but will become a Senator for life in March 1998.

TABLE 1

CHILE AND NAFTA: GEOGRAPHY, DEMOGRAPHY, AND ECONOMY

		CHILE	NAFTA
GEOGRAPHY	Land area, square kilometers	748,800	20,310,610
	Percent of NAFTA	3.7	100
	Coastline, kilometers	6,435	273,045
	Land use, percent of total land area:		
	Arable land	7	14.6
	Meadows and pastures	16	16.8
	Forest and woodlands	21	35.8
	Irrigated land	1.7	1.2
DEMOGRAPHY	Population, thousands of persons, July 1996	14,333	391,068
	As a percent of NAFTA	3.7	100
	Gender ratio (males/females)	0.97	.....
	Age structure, percent:		
	14 and younger	29	.....
	15 to 64	65	.....
	65 and older	6	.....
	Rates per thousand in population:		
	Births	18.09	.....
	Deaths	5.68	.....
	Net migration	0	.....
	Fertility rate, children born per woman	2.23	.....
	Labor force, thousands of persons	5,099	179,242
	Percent of NAFTA	2.8	100
ECONOMY	GDP, billions of U.S. dollars, current prices:		
	Exchange rate basis, 1995	67.3	7,794.1
	Percent of NAFTA	0.86	100.0
	Purchasing power parity basis, 1995	113.2	8,282.7
	Percent of NAFTA	1.37	100.0
	GDP per capita, 1995, U.S. dollars, current prices:		
	Exchange rate basis	4,695	20,857
	Purchasing power parity basis (e)	8,000	22,122
	Real growth, percent, 1995	8.5	.....
	Unemployment rate, May 1996	7.1	.....
	Gini coefficient[1]	0.57	.....
	Distribution of GDP by sector, percent of total:		
	Agriculture	7.4	.....
	Industry	36.4	.....
	Services	56.2	.....
	Distribution of employment by sector, percent of total:		
	Agriculture	19.2	.....
	Industry[2]	42.5	.....
	Services	38.3	.....
	Labor force (thousands)	5,099	179,242
	Participation rate, total, percent	53.7	.....
	Male	74.2	.....
	Female	34.2	.....
	Gross domestic investment (% of GDP)	27.7	.....
	Gross domestic savings (% of GDP)	25.5	.....
	Consumer prices (% change 1996)	5.3	.....
	Total external debt, billions of U.S. dollars	21.1	.....
	Debt to GDP, percent	49.5	.....
	Major markets for exports (percent):		
	European Union	26	.....
	Japan	18	.....
	U.S	14	.....
	U.K.	7	.....
	Brazil	6	.....
	South Korea	5	.....
	Germany	5	.....

e = Estimate.

1. A measure of income distribution; 1.00 would be perfect inequality, 0.00 perfect equality. Source is Inter-American Development Bank. Not comparable with Gini coefficients shown in the *Handbook* table "NAFTA Countries and the European Community: Geography, Demography, and Economy" because of differing income definitions. Coefficients on the IADB basis are not available for the U.S. and Canada. For Mexico, IADB reports 0.57, the same as Chile.

2. For Chile, includes "Commerce," which is classified as a service industry in other countries.

Source: CIA World Factbook, Inter-American Development Bank, Department of State (Background Notes).

Today, Chile is a democratic republic. Suffrage is mandatory and universal at age 18, thus making turnout near 100 percent of eligible voters. The current constitution took effect in 1981 and was amended in 1989 (after a referendum approving the current democratic system) and again in 1993. It provides for a strong directly elected president, a bicameral legislature (a half-appointed Senate and an elected Chamber of Deputies), and a judicial branch. The political center, led by President Eduardo Frei, has been active in recent years, winning every election in the 1990s. There are sizeable parties from the right and left. In 1997 an election was held which saw the Senate, whose composition includes many controversial appointed right-wing supporters of the military and General Pinochet, remain essentially unchanged, meaning efforts to amend the constitution will be postponed.

TABLE 2

CHILE: PHYSICAL AND HUMAN INFRASTRUCTURE

TRANSPORTATION AND UTILITIES	
ELECTRICITY:	
Capacity, million kilowatts	4.8
Production, billion kilowatt hours	22.0
Consumption per capita, kilowatt hours	1,499
TRANSPORTATION, KILOMETERS:	
Railways	6,782
Highways	79,593
Paved	10,984
Unpaved	68,609
Waterways	725
Pipelines:	
Oil and products	1,540
Natural gas	320
MERCHANT MARINE:	
Ships, 1,000 gross register tons or over	37
Total gross register tons, thousands	530
Paved airports, number	263
COMMUNICATIONS	
Telephones, millions	1.5
Phones per capita	0.1
Radio broadcast stations:	
AM	159
FM	na
Television broadcast stations	131
Television sets, millions	2.85
HEALTH	
Health, percent of government expenditures, 1994	12.2
Doctors per 10,000 population, 1993	12
EDUCATION	
Education, percent of government expenditures, 1993	13.9
Average years of schooling, persons 25 and older	6.7
Literacy rate	95.2

Source: CIA World Factbook, Inter-American Development Bank, Department of State (Background Notes)
na = not available

TABLE 3

CHILEAN INDUSTRIAL PRODUCTION, PRICES, AND EARNINGS, 1987-1994

	1987	1988	1989	1990	1991	1992	1993	1994	Change[1]
INDUSTRIAL PRODUCTION, 1993=100:									
Total	71.1	75.9	81.9	81.9	89.2	97.6	100.0	104.2	5.62
Mining	71.2	74.5	80.4	81.5	90.8	96.2	100.0	106.5	5.92
Manufacturing	71.0	76.8	83.2	82.6	87.7	98.1	100.0	101.9	5.31
Food, beverages, and tobacco	74.2	78.5	85.9	82.2	83.4	96.3	100.0	108.0	5.50
Textiles	108.3	103.3	105.0	98.3	108.3	104.2	100.0	91.7	-2.36
Chemicals and petroleum products	66.7	74.1	82.7	82.1	86.4	95.1	100.0	106.8	6.96
Basic metals	83.8	89.7	94.9	96.3	94.1	102.2	100.0	95.6	1.89
Metal products	57.7	61.7	69.8	70.5	71.1	89.9	100.0	102.0	8.48
Electricity	67.2	72.7	76.3	78.8	84.8	94.9	100.0	108.6	7.10
Producer prices, 1993=100: Domestic production	.....	46.4	53.6	66.2	80.8	92.7	100.0	107.9	15.13
Agricultural products	.....	44.0	54.0	66.7	82.0	93.3	100.0	108.7	16.26
Industrial products	.....	46.4	52.3	65.4	80.4	91.5	100.0	108.5	15.21
Average yearly earnings, manufacturing, Chilean pesos	409,644	497,964	605,184	773,364	1,006,896	1,230,168	1,423,344	.....	23.07
Per capita gross domestic product, U.S. dollars	1,655	1,900	2,179	2,310	2,571	3,143	3,302	3,685	12.11

1. Compound annual growth rate for years shown.

Sources: Industrial Production, per capita GDP: U.N. Statistical Yearbook, 1996; Producer prices, Average yearly earnings: Statistical Abstract of Latin America, 1996.

THE CHILEAN ECONOMY

The Chilean economy has been growing at an impressive rate, averaging 6-8 percent real growth of Gross Domestic Product per year for the last 13 years, and establishing a relatively low inflation rate (7 percent in 1996). GDP per capita has reached $4,700, which ranks Chile second only to Argentina among Latin American countries.

Chile has a small budget surplus, as well as substantial foreign capital reserves. These factors have contributed to a stable Chilean peso and enabled early and substantial debt repayment. Chile is one of the few countries in Latin America to make loan repayments ahead of schedule.

Key sectors of the economy are manufacturing (18.2 percent of GDP) and mining (15 percent), followed by the financial services, telecommunications and forestry industries[1]. For selected employment data, see Table 4. Chile is the world's leading supplier of copper, and copper comprises 40 percent of exports. For further data on the composition of Chile's foreign trade 1987-1993, see Table 5. Timber, iron ore, nitrates, and agriculture are other major industries. The financial sector has been developing rapidly (Standard and Poors' rates the Chilean banking system the most sound in Latin America[2]), helped by high levels of investment and savings. The internal rate of savings is approximately 28 percent and helps sustain high levels of domestic investment[3]. The high levels of private investment are aided by Chile's private pension system, which has assets worth over U.S. $24 billion[4].

[1] U.S. Embassy, Santiago, "Country Report: Chile"; U.S. Department of Commerce Country Reports.

[2] Ibid.

[3] U.S. Department of State, Background Notes.

[4] Ibid.

The stability brought about by improved labor conditions in Chile has also encouraged increased investment. Wages have risen 35 percent in the last six years, and continue to rise faster than inflation[5]. This reflects increased productivity and a tendency by management to share the benefits of growth with labor. The work week is generally 44 hours, on the average, and six-day weeks are not uncommon for supervisory and non-supervisory workers alike. Further, the Chilean peso is stable and has been for several years, backed by budget and current accounts surpluses.

TABLE 4

CHILE: EMPLOYMENT, TOTAL AND SELECTED INDUSTRIES, 1994

(Thousands of persons)

Total employment	4,988.3
Total agriculture	808.9
Mining	86.4
Total manufacturing	818.8
Utilities	33.6

Source: Statistical Abstract of Latin America.

TABLE 5

CHILE: COMMODITY COMPOSITION OF TOTAL IMPORTS AND EXPORTS, 1987-1993

(Percent)

	1987	1988	1989	1990	1991	1992	1993
Imports	100.0	100.0	100.0	100.0	100.0	100.0	100.0
Food and beverages	3.9	4.0	3.0	3.7	4.7	5.1	5.0
Industrial supplies	33.9	32.1	30.1	27.4	30.7	28.8	28.1
Fuels	12.2	12.1	12.3	15.6	14.8	11.5	8.9
Machinery	27.3	27.0	27.4	32.1	24.9	25.0	28.4
Transport equipment	12.3	14.0	16.2	11.8	12.7	16.2	15.1
Consumer goods	8.4	8.6	9.0	8.1	10.6	11.7	12.7
Other	2.0	2.1	2.0	1.3	1.6	1.6	1.7
Exports	100.0	100.0	100.0	100.0	100.0	100.0	100.0
Agriculture	16.7	15.2	13.5	16.2	17.1	17.2	18.4
Mining	13.5	12.8	13.4	11.1	14.4	14.3	13.0
Manufacturing	69.7	72.1	73.1	72.7	68.5	68.4	68.7
Food and beverages	12.9	11.3	11.2	9.9	12.3	13.2	12.6
Textiles	0.7	0.8	1.0	1.4	1.7	1.6	2.0
Wood	2.9	2.8	3.2	3.8	4.3	3.8	4.4
Paper	7.5	6.1	5.3	5.3	5.5	7.3	7.5
Chemicals	3.3	3.7	4.6	4.4	4.9	4.5	5.1
Non metal products	0.4	0.5	0.5	0.3	0.2	0.2	0.2
Basic metals	35.0	39.8	40.4	44.3	35.7	33.2	30.7
Metal products	6.1	6.3	5.9	1.8	2.1	2.7	3.7
Other	1.0	0.8	1.0	1.5	1.9	2.0	2.3

Source: Statistical Abstract of Latin America.

[5] U.S. Embassy, Santiago, Op. Cit.

NAFTA-CHILE TRADE

The NAFTA countries are among Chile's main trading partners, and Chile remains a principal recipient for North American investment. Combined, the three NAFTA states have more trade with Chile than any other economic entity, supplying 31 percent of Chile's imports and buying 16 percent of Chile's exports[6]. Imports to Chile are subject to an 11 percent tariff, in addition to the 18 percent value added tax. Chile has had free trade agreements with Canada and Mexico since 1991 as part of its general policy of promoting free trade with the rest of the world. Chile has a small current account surplus, and foreign capital reserves equal to one year's worth of imports. This is enabling early and substantial debt repayment. Foreign investment equaled U.S. $3.6 billion in 1996, with the U.S. and Canada, two potential NAFTA partners, being the two largest investor countries.

U.S.-CHILE TRADE

By itself, the United States supplies more of Chile's imports than any other country, and Chile exports more only to Japan[7]. U.S. exports to Chile primarily consist of finished goods, such as vehicles, capital goods, electronic equipment, petroleum, and machinery. This places the United States as a key trading partner for Chile, thereby spurring Chile's interest in joining NAFTA after already having signed free trade agreements with Canada and Mexico. Chile is a less important trading partner for the United States, although Chilean exports are generally concentrated in several important strategic commodities, such as copper, iron ore, timber, and nitrates. Chile also exports several less important commodities such as wine and salmon which are both high-quality and generally less expensive than their U.S. counterparts. This has triggered anti-Chile sentiment among some select interest groups in the United States, which seek to impose tariffs and quotas to limit the import of such goods.

Overall, the economy is diversifying with the aid of large-scale investment. Currently, the Chilean economy remains highly dependent on copper, forestry and other primary materials for export. The rapidly growing financial sector is buoying the economy, providing jobs for many of Chile's growing numbers of university graduates. Mining, services, and manufacturing have received the most foreign direct investment by far, with the greatest share going to mining. The service industries were the primary recipients of foreign investment in 1996, with financial services leading the way in growth, having received a major boost from foreign direct investment in recent years. With continued fiscal soundness and debt repayment, the economy should be able to sustain stable growth for the foreseeable future.

---

[6] Interamerican Development Bank Internet Database.

[7] Interamerican Development Bank, Op. Cit.

A FREE TRADE AREA OF THE AMERICAS?

The idea of a Free Trade Area of the Americas (FTAA) was formally proposed by President Clinton in December 1994 at the Miami "Summit of the Americas." Leaders from the 34 countries of the Western Hemisphere with democratically elected governments—Fidel Castro was not invited—resolved to "begin immediately to construct the FTAA, in which barriers to trade and investment will be progressively eliminated."

The declaration of principles for the FTAA may be summarized as: promoting prosperity through economic integration and free trade, working to eradicate poverty and discrimination in the Western Hemisphere, and conserving the natural environment for future generations.

On June 30, 1995, the FTAA held a second meeting in Denver for trade ministers of the 34 countries. At that meeting and in subsequent meetings, working groups were established with lead countries for each. They include:

Working Group	Lead Country
Market access	El Salvador
Customs procedures and rules of origin	Bolivia
Investment	Costa Rica
Standards and technical barriers to trade	Canada
Sanitary and phytosanitary measures	Mexico
Subsidies, antidumping, and countervailing duties	Argentina
Small economies	Jamaica
Government procurement	United States
Intellectual property rights	Honduras
Services	Chile
Competition policy	Peru
Dispute settlement	Uruguay

On March 21–22, 1996, another FTAA meeting was held in Cartagena, Colombia. This meeting was divided into workshops in which papers on the above and other subjects were presented and discussed.

The next meeting is to be held in Belo Horizonte, Brazil, on May 13, 1998. The workshop concept will be continued, and additional papers and bases for agreement will be presented.

An issue discussed but not resolved is the "path" by which FTAA is to be reached. The United States has favored bringing Latin American countries under the NAFTA umbrella one by one, so as to gain the advantage of a uniform set of rules and tested procedures and, of course, to put the United States firmly in control.

Brazil, the Latin American country with the largest gross domestic product (GDP), favors a different approach. The farther south one goes, the less dependence on trade with the United States there is and the more advantageous trade arrangements with immediate neighbors can be. Brazil is the acknowledged leader of the MERCOSUR free trade group, which consists of Brazil, Argentina, Paraguay, and Uruguay, with Chile as an associate member. Brazil proposes the continued development of regional agreements, such as

NAFTA and MERCOSUR, followed by links between them. The Miami conference and all meetings since have left the question unresolved.

It is improbable that either FTAA or any other hemisphere-wide trade agreement will come about without the consent of both the United States and Brazil. To resolve the conflict, some have proposed a third path—NAFTA and MERCOSUR might negotiate a trade agreement between themselves.[1] Nonmember nations might then join one of the free trade areas, or might form a new free trade area that could negotiate new links.

Of course, none of these paths will be clear soon. With the autumn 1997 failure of fast-track legislation to pass the Congress, U.S. trade policy is in disarray, and virtually everything about the FTAA must be rethought. Perhaps the most important consequences are that Brazil's hand has been strengthened and MERCOSUR will grow, whereas NAFTA's membership will remain unchanged at least until the United States resolves its internal disagreements on trade policy.

Some observers believe FTAA negotiations can proceed if three conditions are met: first, that the President and the Republican leaders of Congress restate their commitment to FTAA; second, that President Clinton shows enthusiasm for the process in the upcoming meetings; and third, that a critical mass of countries within the hemisphere is willing to proceed with negotiations.[2] Of course, negotiations will be fruitless if the United States fails to gain fast-track authority.

---

[1] For example, Sidney Weintraub, the Dean Rusk Professor of International Affairs at the University of Texas, Austin.

[2] Conversation with Robert Devlin, Inter-American Development Bank, November 14, 1997.

MAPS—CANADA, MEXICO AND THE UNITED STATES

CANADA

Mexico

Tijuana
Mexicali
Ensenada
Baja California Norte
Puerto Penasco
Nogales
Ciudad Juarez
San Quintin
Sonora
Hermosillo
Guaymas
Isla Cedros
Santa Rosalia
Cuidad Obregon
Chihuahua
Chihuahua
Ojinaga
Delicias
Piedras Negras
Coahuila
Hidalgo del Parral
Monclova
Nuevo Laredo
Gulf of California
Loreto
Los Mochis
Torreon
Saltillo
Nuevo Leon
Monterrey
Matamoros
Baja California Sur
La Paz
Culiacan
Durango
Durango
Sinaloa
Mazatlan
Zacatecas
Zacatecas
San Luis Potosi
Cuidad Victoria
Tamaulipas
Ciudad Mante
Gulf of Mexico
North Pacific Ocean
San Lucas
Aquascalientes
San Luis Potosi
Tampico
Nayarit
Islas Marias
Tepic
Guanajuato
Leon
Guadalajara
Jalisco
Queretaro
Pachuca
Poza Rica
Progreso
Merida
Yucatan
Isla de Cozumel
Colima
Colima
Manzanillo
Morelia
Michoacan
Mexico City
Toluca
Tlaxcala
Puebla
Xalapa
Veracruz
Orizaba
Bahia de Campeche
Campeche
Quintana Roo
Chetumal
Cuernavaca
Puebla
Veracruz
Coatzacoalcos
Villahermosa
Campeche
Lazaro Cardenas
Guerrero
Chilpancingo
Acapulco
Oaxaca
Oaxaca
Salina Cruz
Puerto Escondido
Tuxtla Gutierrez
Chiapas
Comitan
Golfo de Tehuantepec
Tapachula

UNITED STATES

INDUSTRY RANKINGS IN NAFTA COUNTRIES

This section of the Handbook looks at the relative performance of manufacturing and other commodity-producing industries in North America in terms of employment, wages, shipments, and various measures of trade. In the tables that follow, all rankings are of the primary, or "2-digit," industries, as defined in the industry classification systems of the United States, Canada, and Mexico.[1] These systems are the U.S. Standard Industrial Classification (U.S. SIC) System, the Canadian Standard Industrial Classification (CSIC) System, and the Mexican Classification of Activities and Products system (CMAP.) The U.S. SIC system is similar to the industry classification systems of Canada and Mexico, although there are some differences, particularly regarding Mexican 2-digit industries. Other ways of combining industries can lead to different results. For example, in Table 1, "Rankings of U.S. Manufacturing Industries," the food industry is ranked first in shipments and the electronics industry is ranked fifth. But a study commissioned by the American Electronics Association and the NASDAQ stock market grouped computer hardware and software with telecommunications and found that the redefined "high technology" industry was the No. 1 U.S. industry.[2] Additionally, each 2-digit industry is composed of one or more subindustries, which may vary markedly from one another, not only in terms of products but also in areas such as trade. For example, the United States is a heavy importer of motor vehicles, both globally and within NAFTA, and a heavy exporter of aircraft. Because motor vehicles and aircraft are grouped into the 2-digit transportation equipment industry, these differences are not reflected in the tables.

It is hard to come up with the leading North American industry, given the many different ways of ranking industries. However, two industries—transportation equipment and food and beverages— are in the forefront in many areas. The *transportation equipment* industry ranked first in Canada and second in the United States in terms of constant-dollar industry shipments in 1994 and 1995, respectively, and for the United States, it was first in terms of current-dollar 1996 shipments. It was the largest employer in Canada (in 1994) and the second largest in the United States (1996) and Mexico (1995). It also ranked first in 1996 U.S.-NAFTA trade and second in U.S. global exports. However, imports were even larger than exports, and transportation equipment ranked first among U.S. imports of manufactured products. The industry was third in the United States in 1996 inflation-adjusted hourly earnings, exceeded only by tobacco and petroleum products manufacturing. But, with a recent slowing of growth and stiffened competition in motor vehicle production, it was also one of the least profitable U.S. industries, ranking last in after-tax profits as a percentage of 1988-1996 sales and 17th out of 18 in the ratio of after-tax profits to stockholders' equity.

The *food and beverage industry* was first in the United States (1995) and second in Canada (1994) in terms of industry shipments and was the top Mexican industry in terms of gross domestic product. It also was first in Mexico (1995), second in Canada (1994) and third in the United States (1996) in terms of employment.

Industrial and commercial machinery (including computers) ranked first in 1996 U.S. employment, global U.S. exports, and in net U.S.-NAFTA exports. The U.S. *chemical* industry ranked first in growth of net U.S.-NAFTA exports; it also had the best ratio of after-tax profits to sales and

---

[1] See "How to Use This book" for an explanation of "2-digit" industries.

[2] Lohr, Steve, "Information Technology Field Is Rated Largest U.S. Industry," *New York Times*, Nov. 18, 1997.

was second, next to food, beverages and tobacco, in the ratio of profits to stockholders' equity over the 1988-1996 period. *Electronics* had the highest rate of growth in U.S. industry shipments from 1987 to 1995, and *rubber and plastics products* had the fastest employment growth during 1987-1996. A more detailed discussion of industry rankings follows.

EMPLOYMENT

Overall manufacturing employment has declined in the United States, Canada, and Mexico relative to employment in service-producing industries, although this may be a temporary situation in Mexico. As productivity continues to rise, more goods can be produced with fewer people. In contrast, service industries continue to grow rapidly in all three NAFTA countries. The shift from manufacturing to services also reflects increased affluence, greater reliance on computer technology and the increasing number of dual-income households that are able and willing to pay for time-saving or convenient services.

Because of the limitations of currently-available data and classifications systems, the rankings shown here are limited to manufacturing industries. As mentioned earlier, the food and beverage and the transportation equipment industries are among the top three employers in all three NAFTA countries. The top five U.S. industry employers in 1996 were industrial and commercial machinery, transportation equipment, food and beverages, electronics, and printing and publishing, respectively (Table 1). In Canada, the top five were transportation equipment, food and beverages, fabricated metals, printing and publishing, and wood (Table 2). In Mexico, they were food and beverages; transportation equipment; electrical equipment; garments; and fabricated metals, instruments, and metal furniture (Table 3).

When it comes to employment *growth*, the results are quite different. In the United States 11 of 20 industries had declining employment from 1987 to 1996. The five fastest growing industries in terms of employment were rubber and plastics, food and beverages, miscellaneous manufacturing, industrial and commercial machinery, and fabricated metals, in that order. In Canada, 19 of the 20 manufacturing industries had declining employment from 1987 to 1994. The one exception was rubber and plastics. Transportation equipment, wood products, printing and publishing, and industrial and commercial machinery, respectively, had the slowest rates of employment decline. Nine of Mexico's 18 manufacturing industries lost employment from 1988 to 1995. The highest growth rate was in "other" manufacturing, followed by transportation equipment and rubber and plastics (tied); electrical equipment; and food and beverages.

WAGES

Available data suggest that manufacturing wages are, on average, keeping up with inflation in Canada, but not in the United States or in Mexico.[3] In Canada, real manufacturing wages grew by 0.6 percent annually from 1988 to 1994. In the United States, real hourly earnings in manufacturing declined by 0.7 percent annually from 1987 to 1996.[4] In Mexico, real manufacturing wages declined by 5.4 percent annually from 1994 to 1996, reflecting in large part the peso crisis and subsequent recession of 1994 and 1995.

With respect to U.S. real wages, it is argued by some (notably Michael Boskin, former Chairman of the President's Council of Economic Advisers, and Alan Greenspan, Chairman of the Federal Reserve Board of Governors) that the U.S. Consumer Price Index (CPI-U) overstates cost-of-living increases in the United States by about 1 percentage point or more

---

[3] Data used in this analysis are for 1986-1994 for Canada, 1987-1996 for the United States, and 1994-1996 for Mexico. Readers are cautioned that these comparisons are subject to many potential problems as classifications, measures of inflation, and other factors may differ from country to country. For example, benefits are included under "Remuneration" in Mexico, but not in average hourly earnings in Canada or the United States.

[4] Real hourly earnings of production and nonsupervisory workers in the total U.S. private economy fell at a 0.4 percent annual rate over the 1987 to 1996 period.

annually.[5] This is subject to widespread dispute, but if inflation has been overstated by 1 percent, only lumber; stone, clay and glass; and printing and publishing would show negative wage growth over the 1987-1996 period.

In terms of wage *levels*, tobacco and petroleum are ranked first and second and primary metals in the top five in all three countries. In Canada, primary metals, paper, and transportation equipment are third through fifth, respectively. In the United States, transportation equipment, chemicals, and primary metals are third through fifth. In Mexico, chemicals, basic metals, and paper follow tobacco and petroleum. It is unclear why tobacco ranks first in all three countries, except that the cigarette manufacturing subindustry is highly automated, and employment has declined sharply in recent years. Having fewer, more senior employees in a generally profitable industry apparently results in higher average wages.

TABLE 1

RANKINGS OF U.S. MANUFACTURING INDUSTRIES

| | INDUSTRY | EMPLOYMENT, THOUSANDS OF PERSONS, 1996 | | EMPLOYMENT GROWTH, 1987-1996 | | PROJECTED EMPLOYMENT GROWTH, 1994-2005[2] | | AVERAGE HOURLY EARNINGS, PRODUCTION WORKERS, CONSTANT 1992 U.S. DOLLARS | | | | VALUE OF INDUSTRY SHIPMENTS, MILLIONS OF CONSTANT 1992 U.S. DOLLARS | | | |
| | | | | | | | | 1996 | | REAL GROWTH, 1987-1996 | | 1995 | | REAL GROWTH, 1987-1995[3] | |
SIC	NAME	LEVEL	RANK	RATE[1]	RANK	RATE[1]	RANK	LEVEL	RANK	RATE[1]	RANK	LEVEL	RANK	RATE[1]	RANK
23	Apparel	864	9	(2.62)	18	(2.05)	17	7.14	20	(0.24)	4	76,546	15	0.62	15
28	Chemicals	1,032	7	0.08	9	0.05	7	14.50	4	(0.52)	9	323,643	4	1.83	7
36	Electronics	1,651	4	(0.64)	13	(0.99)	11	10.92	12	(0.70)	10	302,252	5	6.66	1
34	Fabricated metals	1,448	6	0.38	5	(1.46)	14	11.23	11	(1.00)	16	193,322	6	1.63	11
20	Food and beverages	1,693	3	0.51	2	0.09	6	10.04	14	(0.97)	14	433,666	1	1.94	6
25	Furniture	504	16	(0.24)	10	0.23	4	9.10	17	(0.38)	8	49,358	17	1.64	10
35	Industrial and commercial machinery	2,112	1	0.45	4	(1.04)	13	12.19	7	(0.87)	13	382,339	3	6.65	2
38	Instruments	854	10	(1.86)	17	(0.72)	9	11.78	8	(0.75)	12	137,256	11	1.75	9
31	Leather	96	19	(4.33)	20	(4.94)	20	7.68	19	0.31	1	8,401	20	(3.01)	20
24	Lumber	780	11	0.37	6	(0.85)	10	9.36	15	(1.11)	19	88,002	13	0.26	18
39	Miscellaneous	387	17	0.50	3	0.30	3	9.31	16	(0.26)	5	44,274	18	2.23	5
26	Paper	681	13	0.11	8	0.22	5	13.16	6	(0.72)	11	141,416	10	1.81	8
29	Petroleum and coal products	142	18	(1.59)	15	(0.54)	8	17.33	2	(0.37)	7	157,489	8	0.73	14
33	Primary metals	711	12	(0.53)	12	(2.46)	18	13.43	5	(0.98)	15	155,576	9	3.02	4
27	Printing and publishing	1,538	5	0.26	7	0.49	2	11.35	10	(1.18)	20	168,855	7	(0.07)	19
30	Rubber and plastic products	981	8	1.71	1	0.72	1	10.08	13	(1.00)	16	135,238	12	4.36	3
32	Stone, clay, glass	541	15	(0.26)	11	(1.85)	16	11.50	9	(1.01)	18	68,844	16	0.55	16
22	Textiles	624	14	(1.65)	16	(1.53)	15	8.69	18	(0.15)	3	77,780	14	1.45	13
21	Tobacco	41	20	(3.21)	19	(4.35)	19	17.35	1	0.04	2	38,972	19	0.46	17
37	Transportation equipment	1,781	2	(1.43)	14	(0.99)	11	15.43	3	(0.33)	6	433,463	2	1.55	12

1. Compound annual growth rate for indicated years. Parentheses ( ) indicate decline.

2. BLS moderate projections.

3. 1995 is the most recent year for which shipments data are available for all industries.

Source: U.S. Bureau of Labor Statistics and Bureau of the Census. Rate calculations and rankings by the editors.

---

[5] Although the subject of recent widespread public attention, this is not a new concept to the economics profession. The heart of the argument is that the measurement of inflation depends on comparing the change in prices of like products, but in the present situation, where new products and services and radically improved existing products are regularly introduced, such measurement is extremely difficult. Proponents argue that the increases in prices are measured, but the improvements and increases in quality are not.

The available data show Canada doing substantially better than the United States or Mexico in real wage growth (although it also has the highest level of unemployment). Of Canada's 20 industries, 12 showed positive real wage growth for the 1988-1994 period. Machinery, tobacco, transportation equipment, chemicals, and leather led, in that order. In the United States, only two of the 20 SIC manufacturing industries—leather and tobacco—showed positive (but fractional) growth in real wages during 1987-1996, and these industries both have sharply declining employment levels (employment fell at annual rates of -4.3 and -3.2 percent, respectively). Again, the positive growth in average real wages probably reflects the fact that as more junior employees are released and less efficient establishments are closed, the average wage increases, primarily because the remaining employees were paid at higher rates all along. In leather, wages still are the second lowest in manufacturing, next to apparel, so any gain just moves them a little closer to the norm.

Comparable real wage data by industry are not available for Mexico. However, the 5.4 percent annual decline in real wages for all manufacturing (excluding the Maquiladora industry) from 1994 through 1996[6] was more severe than for any individual industry in the United States or Canada. Much, if not all, of this decline was due to the peso crisis and severe recession suffered by Mexico beginning in late 1994 and 1995. Although the Mexican economy has recovered in the sense that its real growth rate and manufacturing output have returned to pre-recession levels, manufacturing wages are still sharply depressed in real terms.

TABLE 2

RANKINGS OF CANADIAN MANUFACTURING INDUSTRIES

| | INDUSTRY | EMPLOYMENT, NUMBER OF PERSONS, 1994 | | EMPLOYMENT GROWTH, 1987-1994 | | AVERAGE HOURLY EARNINGS, PRODUCTION WORKERS, CONSTANT 1992 CANADIAN DOLLARS | | | | VALUE OF INDUSTRY SHIPMENTS, MILLIONS OF CURRENT CANADIAN DOLLARS | | | |
| | | | | | | 1994 | | REAL GROWTH, 1988-1994 | | 1994 | | GROWTH, 1987-1994 | |
CSIC	NAME	LEVEL	RANK	RATE[1]	RANK	LEVEL	RANK	RATE[1]	RANK	LEVEL	RANK	RATE[1]	RANK
37	Chemicals	84,273	9	(0.78)	7	17.91	6	0.77	4	25,598	4	3.39	8
24	Clothing	80,383	11	(4.63)	19	8.75	20	0.12	11	6,147	15	(0.70)	18
33-336	Electrical	101,230	7	(3.14)	14	15.27	11	0.67	7	18,366	7	4.37	6
30	Fabricated metals	140,452	3	(1.62)	11	14.47	12	0.61	8	17,815	9	0.88	15
10+11	Food and beverages	215,487	2	(0.84)	8	13.79	13	(0.24)	16	49,523	2	2.60	12
26	Furniture	46,960	13	(3.80)	17	11.16	18	0.03	12	4,523	16	0.43	16
16	Industrial and commercial machinery	95,485	8	(0.62)	5	15.51	9	1.64	1	17,871	8	7.91	2
391	Instruments	20,393	17	(0.76)	6	13.52	14	(0.63)	18	2,480	18	3.47	7
17	Leather	13,010	19	(7.10)	20	9.68	19	0.71	5	1,006	20	(4.10)	20
39-391	Misc manufacture	44,691	15	(0.97)	9	11.25	17	(0.04)	13	4,420	17	2.64	11
35	Non-metallic minerals	41,913	16	(4.25)	18	15.53	8	(0.24)	16	6,696	13	(1.50)	19
27	Paper	101,834	6	(2.24)	12	20.08	4	0.56	9	25,648	3	1.52	13
36	Petroleum	13,554	18	(1.58)	10	23.53	2	(0.70)	20	17,536	10	0.93	14
29	Primary metals	83,915	10	(3.03)	13	20.26	3	(0.05)	14	23,442	5	2.93	9
28	Printing and publishing	122,594	4	(0.56)	4	16.08	7	(0.67)	19	13,496	11	2.73	10
15+16	Rubber and plastic	76,970	12	1.60	1	12.93	15	(0.21)	15	10,514	12	4.80	5
18+19	Textile mill products	46,730	14	(3.67)	16	11.52	16	0.16	10	6,243	14	(0.30)	17
12	Tobacco	4,600	20	(3.60)	15	27.43	1	1.47	2	2,471	19	5.43	4
32	Transportation equipment	217,198	1	(0.08)	2	18.25	5	1.13	3	76,132	1	8.38	1
25	Wood	117,982	5	(0.44)	3	15.46	10	0.68	6	22,907	6	6.63	3

1. Compound annual growth rate for indicated years. Parentheses ( ) indicate decline.

Source: Adapted from Statistics Canada, Manufacturing Industries of Canada (Cat. 31-203) with rate calculations and rankings by the editors.

---

[6] "Cuaderno de Informacion Oportuna," INEGI, Julio 1997, p. 85.

SHIPMENTS

In terms of level of manufacturers' shipments, food and beverages, transportation equipment, industrial and commercial machinery (including computer equipment), chemicals, and electronics were the top U.S. industries in 1995, based on 1992-dollar shipments (Table 1). The top five Canadian industries in 1994 were transportation equipment, food and beverages, paper, chemicals, and primary metals, in that order (Table 2). This is based on current-dollar values; constant-dollar values were not available. Comparisons with Mexico are complicated by the lack of detailed shipments data for Mexico—several 2-digit industries are grouped into larger categories in the available Mexican statistics. The leading industries there in terms of gross domestic product are food and beverages; metal products, machinery, and equipment (including transportation equipment); chemicals, petroleum, rubber and plastics; textiles and garments; and nonmetallic minerals, in that order (Table 3).

In terms of *growth* in shipments—based on constant dollars for the U.S., but current dollars for Canada—industrial and commercial machinery and rubber and plastics are among the top five industries in both the United States and Canada. In the United States, electronics,

TABLE 3

RANKINGS OF MEXICAN MANUFACTURING INDUSTRIES

CMAP	Name	Employment, number of persons, 1995		Employment growth, 1988-1995		Average annual remuneration including benefits, all paid workers, new pesos, 1993		Gross domestic product, millions of constant 1993 U.S. dollars[2]			
								1995		Real growth, 1988-1995	
		Level	Rank	Rate[1]	Rank	Level	Rank	Level	Rank	Rate[1]	Rank
31	Food, beverages, and tobacco	650,911	.....	0.9	.....	21,951	10	19,612	1	3.7	3
311, 312, 313	Food and beverages	639,933	1	1.2	5	.....	.....				
314	Tobacco	10,978	18	(8.7)	17	48,763	1				
32	Textiles, garments, leather	481,961	.....	(1.1)	.....	16,258	12	5,838	4	0.7	8
321	Textiles	166,823	7	(2.0)	12						
322	Garments	231,619	4	0.9	6	11,720	.....	.....	.....	.....	.....
323, 324	Leather	83,519	14	(4.1)	15	.....	.....	.....	.....	.....	.....
33	Wood and wood products	137,231	11	(3.0)	14	13,149	13	2,151	8	(0.8)	9
34	Paper and printing	172,399	.....	0.4	.....	26,324	.....	3,448	6	2.5	5
341	Paper	54,756	15	0.1	9	30,438	5	.....	.....	.....	.....
342	Printing	117,643	12	0.6	7	24,159	8	.....	.....	.....	.....
35	Chemicals, petrol, rubber and plastic	349,721	.....	(0.8)	.....	36,607	.....	11,510	3	2.4	6
351, 352	Chemicals	167,750	6	(2.2)	13	45,588	3	.....	.....	.....	.....
353, 354	Petrol	32,691	17	(6.8)	16	47,013	2	.....	.....	.....	.....
355, 356	Rubber and plastics	149,280	10	3.1	2	23,539	9	.....	.....	.....	.....
36	Non-metallic minerals	150,304	9	(0.7)	10	26,487	6	5,195	5	2.2	7
37	Basic metals	52,724	16	(9.2)	18	38,682	4	3,425	7	2.7	4
38	Metal products, machinery & equipment	975,775	.....	1.7	.....	25,236	7	16,628	2	3.9	2
381, 385	Fabricated metals, instruments, and metal furniture	168,520	5	0.2	8	.....	.....	.....	.....	.....	.....
382	Machinery	165,813	8	(0.9)	11	.....	.....	.....	.....	.....	.....
383	Electrical equipment	310,104	3	2.9	4	.....	.....	.....	.....	.....	.....
384	Transportation equipment	331,338	2	3.1	2	.....	.....	.....	.....	.....	.....
39	Other manufacturing industries	114,180	13	7.3	1	16,840	11	1,931	9	4.4	1

1. Compound annual growth rate for indicated years. Parentheses ( ) indicate decline.

2. Converted at 1993 rate of 3.1237 new pesos to the U.S. dollar.

Source: INEGI: Censos Economicos and Sistema de Cuentas Nacionales de Mexico with rate calculations and rankings by the editors.

industrial and commercial machinery, rubber and plastics, primary metals, and miscellaneous manufacturing had the highest rates of shipments growth during 1987-1995. In Canada, transportation equipment, industrial and commercial machinery, wood products, tobacco, and rubber and plastics had the fastest growth rates during 1987-1994. In Mexico, other manufacturing; metal products, machinery and equipment; food, beverages, and tobacco; basic metals; and paper and printing were the five fastest growing industries in 1988-1995.

U.S. GLOBAL TRADE

The largest U.S. worldwide manufactured exports in 1996 were industrial and commercial machinery (including computer equipment), transportation equipment, electronics, chemicals, and instruments (Table 4). The leading U.S. imports in 1996 were transportation equipment, electronics, industrial and commercial machinery, apparel, and chemicals. It is interesting that four of these product categories—transportation equipment, machinery, electronics, and chemicals—are leaders in both imports and exports. This reflects the many, diverse subindustries and products included within each group. For example, motor vehicles, major imports, are included with aircraft, major exports, in the transportation equipment industry. Additionally, the large imports and exports of computer equipment and semiconductors contribute to the prominent positions of industrial and commercial machinery and electronics, respectively, in both import and export trade.

TABLE 4

RANKINGS OF U.S. MANUFACTURING INDUSTRIES IN U.S. GLOBAL TRADE

(Values in millions of U.S. dollars)

SIC	INDUSTRY NAME	U.S. EXPORTS 1996 LEVEL	U.S. EXPORTS 1996 RANK	U.S. EXPORTS GROWTH RATE, 1989-1996[1] RATE	U.S. EXPORTS GROWTH RATE, 1989-1996[1] RANK	U.S. IMPORTS 1996 LEVEL	U.S. IMPORTS 1996 RANK	U.S. IMPORTS GROWTH RATE, 1989-1996[1] RATE	U.S. IMPORTS GROWTH RATE, 1989-1996[1] RANK	U.S. NET EXPORTS[2] 1996 LEVEL	U.S. NET EXPORTS[2] 1996 RANK
23	Apparel	8,104.4	11	19.14	1	43,074.5	4	7.77	9	(34,970.1)	19
28	Chemicals	58,502.7	4	7.19	15	42,825.7	5	11.32	2	15,677.0	1
36	Electronics	79,604.8	3	13.43	4	114,066.6	2	10.41	5	(34,461.8)	18
34	Fabricated metals	16,612.0	8	9.58	7	17,491.5	11	6.77	12	(879.5)	7
20	Food and beverages	27,041.3	6	8.64	11	20,947.0	9	5.53	18	6,094.3	2
25	Furniture	3,101.3	19	16.81	2	9,320.1	16	9.04	7	(6,218.8)	12
35	Industrial and commercial machinery	104,064.0	1	9.20	8	112,907.5	3	11.08	3	(8,843.5)	13
38	Instruments	32,760.0	5	9.11	9	28,746.6	8	9.37	6	4,013.4	4
31	Leather	1,725.0	20	6.70	16	14,187.1	14	5.98	15	(12,462.1)	15
24	Lumber	7,400.7	12	2.90	20	12,194.0	15	10.88	4	(4,793.3)	10
39	Miscellaneous	6,762.9	14	5.93	17	31,088.1	7	6.91	11	(24,325.2)	17
26	Paper	14,002.1	9	8.03	12	14,784.3	13	3.11	20	(782.2)	6
29	Petroleum and coal products	7,158.1	13	5.46	18	18,767.9	10	6.67	14	(11,609.8)	14
33	Primary metals	21,278.9	7	8.99	10	34,582.5	6	5.06	19	(13,303.6)	16
27	Printing and publishing	4,533.7	18	8.03	12	2,996.1	19	7.25	10	1,537.6	5
30	Rubber and plastics products	12,092.6	10	13.73	3	16,891.0	12	8.02	8	(4,798.4)	11
32	Stone, clay, and glass	5,097.0	17	10.53	6	9,088.4	17	6.74	13	(3,991.4)	9
22	Textiles	6,177.0	15	11.95	5	7,169.0	18	5.94	16	(992.0)	8
21	Tobacco	5,238.3	16	5.37	19	245.2	20	15.78	1	4,993.1	3
37	Transportation equipment	92,886.8	2	7.44	14	129,235.2	1	5.67	17	(36,348.4)	20

1. Compound annual growth rate.

2. Parentheses indicate negative values, i.e. excess of imports over exports.

Source: International Trade Administration; calculations by the editors.

Apparel, furniture, rubber and plastics, electronics, and textiles were the five fastest growing U.S. exports from 1989 to 1996 (Table 4). The fastest import growth was in tobacco, chemicals, industrial and commercial machinery, lumber, and electronics. Several of these industries are at relatively low levels in terms of total trade, however. For example, apparel is only the 11th largest export; textiles, 15th; and furniture, 19th. Moreover, sizable portions of the apparel and textile exports go to Mexico as semifinished products for processing and re-export to the United States.[7] Many firms classified in apparel manufacturing have few manufacturing facilities in the United States. Such firms may design and develop garments, purchase materials and fittings, and ultimately sell to retail outlets; however, they contract for the actual manufacturing with other companies or operate their own plants outside the country. The industries with the highest global *net* exports (excess of exports over imports) are chemicals, food, tobacco, instruments, and printing and publishing.

INTRA-NAFTA TRADE

The rankings of intra-NAFTA trade are by commodity groups and thus include, in addition to manufacturing goods, such major trade categories as agricultural products and crude petroleum.

The top five U.S. exports to Canada and Mexico in 1996 were transportation equipment, electronics, machinery, chemicals, and primary metals. These same product categories, with the exception of chemicals, are also in the top five imports, along with crude petroleum and natural gas (in third place). This remarkable symmetry suggests a substantial amount of integration in these industries. (See Tables 5, 6, and 7.)

Crude petroleum and natural gas ranked as the fastest growing U.S. export to Canada and Mexico during 1993-1996, followed by tobacco, apparel, forestry products, and agricultural products (Table 5). Here again, the results are somewhat misleading because of the very low levels of some of these exports. Agricultural products and apparel are substantial exports ($5.8 billion and $3.0 billion, respectively), but the others together accounted for less than $800 million in 1996. Crude oil, tobacco, and forestry exports were all at very low levels in 1993, so that small absolute increases caused them to have large percentage gains. Apparel exports may have been a fast grower because Mexican tariffs on apparel and textiles were reduced by 10.5 percentage points as a result of NAFTA. Also, as mentioned earlier, many U.S. firms classified as apparel manufacturers shipped materials to Mexico to be further processed and re-exported to the United States.

Intra-NAFTA trade in tobacco products is a special case. (See the tobacco products chapter in Part II of this book.) In the United States, tobacco products are under attack for health reasons. In Canada, imposition of a punitive tax caused a surge in Canadian tobacco exports to the United States, to a peak US$511 million in 1993, followed by a drop to one-tenth that level when the tax was rescinded. In Mexico, a reduction in tariffs on tobacco led to a small absolute increase, but a large percentage gain, in imports from the United States. Thus, an industry that ranks low in terms of imports and exports ranks high in terms of growth and change.

In the United States, industrial and commercial machinery; chemicals, and—not counting "manufactured commodities not identified"—electronics; fabricated metals; and instruments were the top five *net* exports to NAFTA in 1996 (Table 5).[8] Chemicals; machinery; scrap and waste; agricultural products; and tobacco products had the largest positive changes in *net* exports over the 1993 to 1996 period.

Canada's largest exports to the United States and Mexico were products of the transportation equipment; crude petroleum; primary metals; paper; and machinery industries (Table 6).

---

[7] See "The Maquiladora-9802 Program: A Forerunner to NAFTA" in this book.

[8] "Manufacturing commodities not identified" are products inadequately identified in export declaration documents to be classified by the Census Bureau.

Transportation equipment; crude petroleum; paper; lumber and wood products; and primary metals were the sources of the largest *net* exports. Canada's $12.6 billion in *net* exports of crude petroleum accounted for 71 percent of the total Canadian trade surplus on goods and services with the United States.

Mexico's top exports to the United States and Canada in 1996 were electrical and electronic equipment; transportation equipment; crude petroleum and natural gas; industrial and commercial machinery; and apparel (Table 7). The fastest growing exports from 1993 to 1996 were textiles; tobacco products; metallic ores and coal; industrial and commercial machinery; and printing and publishing. The largest *net* exports were transportation equipment; electrical and electronic equipment; crude petroleum and natural gas; apparel; and furniture and fixtures.

TABLE 5

RANKINGS OF U.S. COMMODITY GROUPS IN U.S.-NAFTA TRADE

(Values in millions of U.S. dollars)

		EXPORTS				IMPORTS				NET EXPORTS			
		1996		GROWTH RATE, 1993-1996[1]		1996		GROWTH RATE, 1993-1996[1]		1996		CHANGE, 1993-1996	
SIC	COMMODITIES BY INDUSTRY	Level	Rank	Rate	Rank	Level	Rank	Rate	Rank	Level[2]	Rank	Change[3]	Rank
1	Agricultural products	5,792	10	14.30	5	3,736	15	16.81	10	2,056	8	521.0	4
23	Apparel and related products	3,013	13	17.79	3	5,856	10	24.08	2	(2,843)	26	(1,375.0)	26
12	Bituminous coal and lignite	478	25	13.54	6	57	28	19.29	7	421	11	127.9	8
28	Chemicals & allied products	15,625	4	9.80	11	9,324	7	12.60	15	6,301	2	703.0	1
13	Crude petroleum and natural gas	656	22	22.10	1	19,515	3	13.00	21	(18,859)	30	(5,690.0)	30
36	Electrical & electronic equipment	29,968	2	13.38	7	26,573	2	18.25	9	3,395	4	(1,094.7)	22
34	Fabricated metal products	7,839	6	4.41	27	5,062	11	19.76	6	2,777	5	(1,163.8)	24
9	Fish, fresh or chilled; & other marine products	470	26	7.94	19	1,131	21	3.80	26	(661)	22	(23.5)	13
20	Food and beverages	6,298	9	4.89	26	6,065	9	13.73	20	233	13	(1,102.3)	23
8	Forestry products	79	30	16.64	4	38	29	1.86	27	40	16	27.0	10
25	Furniture and fixtures	2,046	19	1.40	28	4,241	13	20.94	5	(2,195)	25	(1,759.8)	27
35	Industrial and commercial machinery	29,219	3	11.20	14	15,626	4	20.95	4	13,594	1	1,177.3	2
38	Instruments	6,748	7	5.02	25	4,290	12	16.49	12	2,458	6	(653.3)	21
31	Leather and leather products	512	24	7.34	20	674	24	14.66	17	(162)	20	(128.8)	17
2	Livestock and livestock products	320	28	(0.36)	29	1,866	19	1.82	28	(1,545)	24	(101.8)	15
24	Lumber and wood products, ex. furniture	1,586	20	(1.28)	30	9,220	8	11.75	22	(7,635)	29	(2,676.3)	29
3X	Manufactured commodities not identified	4,612	12	(4.23)	31	.....	.....	.....	.....	4,612	3	(30.4)	14
10	Metallic ores and concentrates	514	23	10.19	15	568	25	19.23	8	(53)	18	(102.8)	16
39	Miscellaneous manufactured commodities	2,230	16	6.10	23	2,030	18	21.12	3	201	14	(524.6)	20
14	Nonmetallic minerals, except fuels	340	27	6.30	22	489	26	6.01	25	(148)	19	(21.5)	12
26	Paper and allied products	4,715	11	12.50	10	11,023	6	11.02	23	(6,308)	28	(1,564.4)	25
29	Petroleum refining and related products	2,156	18	11.70	12	3,236	16	10.23	24	(1,080)	23	(211.3)	18
33	Primary metal products	7,928	5	11.46	13	13,620	5	14.04	18	(5,693)	27	(2,234.1)	28
27	Printing, publishing, and allied products	2,389	15	5.20	24	947	23	16.60	11	1,442	9	(12.7)	11
30	Rubber and miscellaneous plastics products	6,430	8	12.59	9	4,115	14	15.95	16	2,314	7	449.7	6
91	Scrap and waste	1,403	21	9.64	16	1,105	22	16.47	13	298	12	707.0	3
32	Stone, clay, glass, and concrete products	2,180	17	6.78	21	2,378	17	16.44	14	(199)	21	(482.3)	19
22	Textile mill products	2,759	14	13.32	8	1,401	20	32.00	1	1,359	10	71.4	9
21	Tobacco manufactures	59	31	21.69	2	37	30	(58.41)	30	22	17	503.5	5
37	Transportation equipment	38,110	1	8.95	17	63,405	1	13.83	19	(25,295)	31	(11,781.9)	31
92	Used or second-hand merchandise	219	29	8.92	18	78	27	(4.05)	29	141	15	327.3	7

1. Compound annual growth rate. Parentheses indicate negative values.

2. Parentheses indicate excess of imports over exports.

3. Parentheses indicate decline in surplus/increase in deficit.

Source: U.S. Bureau of the Census, Foreign Trade Division. Calculation and ranking by the editors.

TABLE 6

RANKINGS OF CANADIAN COMMODITY GROUPS IN CANADA-NAFTA TRADE

(Values in millions of U.S. dollars)

U.S. SIC	COMMODITIES BY INDUSTRY	EXPORTS 1996 LEVEL	EXPORTS 1996 RANK	EXPORTS GROWTH RATE, 1993-1996[1] RATE	EXPORTS GROWTH RATE, 1993-1996[1] RANK	IMPORTS 1996 LEVEL	IMPORTS 1996 RANK	IMPORTS GROWTH RATE, 1993-1996[1] RATE	IMPORTS GROWTH RATE, 1993-1996[1] RANK	NET EXPORTS 1996 LEVEL[2]	NET EXPORTS 1996 RANK	NET EXPORTS CHANGE, 1993-1996 CHANGE[3]	NET EXPORTS CHANGE, 1993-1996 RANK
1, 2	Agriculture & livestock	3,304	12	12.80	17	2,900	11	3.01	27	404	8	755.19	8
23	Apparel and related products	1,189	17	24.49	2	1,075	19	15.90	5	114	11	188.27	13
28	Chemicals and allied products	7,967	8	15.41	8	11,126	4	11.63	9	(3,158)	26	(342.97)	24
13	Crude petroleum and natural gas	13,122	2	12.43	18	485	22	16.75	3	12,637	2	3,708.70	1
36	Electrical & electronic equipment	8,201	7	18.02	6	18,414	3	12.84	7	(10,212)	28	(2,383.67)	28
34	Fabricated metal products	3,394	11	18.95	5	5,017	7	0.61	28	(1,623)	24	1,286.50	6
9	Fish, fresh or chilled; and other marine products	702	21	(1.92)	25	434	23	9.66	15	269	10	(146.99)	23
20	Food and beverages	4,704	9	13.02	16	4,364	8	7.71	19	339	9	574.34	10
8	Forestry products	27	26	1.64	24	41	27	6.07	23	(14)	15	(5.33)	17
25	Furniture and fixtures	2,704	14	21.95	4	1,530	16	6.35	21	1,174	7	955.37	7
35	Industrial and commercial machinery	10,303	5	14.62	12	22,490	2	11.66	8	(12,187)	29	(2,874.81)	29
31	Leather and leather products	153	24	15.09	11	292	24	9.23	16	(138)	17	(15.19)	18
24	Lumber and wood products, except furniture	8,821	6	11.96	19	1,332	17	4.52	26	7,489	4	2,370.23	3
3X	Manufactured commodities not identified by kind					2,504	12	8.48	17	(2,504)	25	(542.50)	27
10, 12	Metallic ores and coal	575	22	29.54	1	919	21	18.88	2	(343)	19	(17.92)	19
38, 39	Miscellaneous manufactures and instruments	2,625	15	15.32	9	6,722	5	8.48	18	(4,096)	27	(542.27)	26
14	Nonmetallic minerals, except fuels	366	23	4.47	23	267	25	5.08	24	99	12	8.11	15
26	Paper and allied products	10,804	4	10.59	21	2,901	10	14.31	6	7,903	3	1,857.72	4
29	Petroleum refining and related products	2,830	13	15.71	7	1,019	20	11.02	11	1,811	6	729.02	9
33	Primary metal products	10,916	3	11.04	20	5,172	6	10.39	12	5,744	5	1,615.03	5
27	Printing, publishing, and allied products	760	20	13.19	15	2,049	13	4.62	25	(1,290)	23	(24.07)	20
30	Rubber and miscellaneous plastics products	3,426	10	14.54	13	3,836	9	9.96	14	(411)	21	194.77	12
91	Scrap and waste	824	19	14.29	14	1,085	18	6.47	20	(261)	18	86.01	14
32	Stone, clay, glass, and concrete products	1,411	16	15.29	10	1,757	15	6.09	22	(346)	20	204.68	11
22	Textile mill products	922	18	23.16	3	1,782	14	11.59	10	(860)	22	(70.90)	22
21	Tobacco manufactures	26	27	(62.80)	27	21	28	23.57	1	5	13	(494.08)	25
37	Transportation equipment	48,219	1	9.41	22	34,785	1	10.04	13	13,434	1	2,728.15	2
92	Used or second-hand merchandise	61	25	(3.35)	26	142	26	16.22	4	(80)	16	(58.00)	21

1. Compound annual growth rate. Parentheses indicate negative values.

2. Parentheses indicate excess of imports over exports.

3. Parentheses indicate decline in surplus/increase in deficit.

Source: U.S. trade: U.S. Bureau of the Census; Mexico-Canada trade: Statistics Canada, Foreign Trade Division, Special tabulation March 1997, converted to U.S. dollars by the editors. Calculation and ranking by the editors.

TABLE 7

RANKINGS OF MEXICAN COMMODITY GROUPS IN MEXICO-NAFTA TRADE

(Values in millions of U.S. dollars)

U.S. SIC	COMMODITIES BY INDUSTRY	EXPORTS				IMPORTS				NET EXPORTS			
		1996		GROWTH RATE, 1993-1996[1]		1996		GROWTH RATE, 1993-1996[1]		1996		CHANGE, 1993-1996	
		LEVEL	RANK	RATE	RANK	LEVEL	RANK	RATE	RANK	LEVEL[2]	RANK	CHANGE[3]	RANK
1,2	Agriculture & livestock	2,700	7	9.4	22	3,614	5	26.1	3	(914)	20	(1,174)	27
23	Apparel and related products	4,718	5	24.2	11	1,989	12	19.4	5	2,729	4	1,433	5
28	Chemicals and allied products	1,481	10	22.7	12	4,624	4	14.9	9	(3,143)	27	(897)	26
13	Crude petroleum and natural gas	6,521	3	13.5	20	299	19	11.0	15	6,222	3	1,981	3
36	Electrical & electronic equipment	19,441	1	18.8	15	12,624	1	15.2	8	6,817	2	3,478	2
34	Fabricated metal products	1,732	8	21.9	13	2,885	6	13.2	10	(1,154)	21	(123)	21
9	Fish, fresh or chilled; and other marine products	429	17	17.1	17	37	27	(6.6)	24	393	7	170	11
20	Food and beverages	1,480	11	16.5	18	2,052	11	0.3	22	(572)	18	528	8
8	Forestry products	12	25	2.4	24	38	25	34.8	2	(26)	12	(22)	20
25	Furniture and fixtures	1,549	9	19.2	14	528	16	(8.9)	25	1,021	5	804	6
35	Industrial and commercial machinery	5,497	4	37.0	4	6,903	2	9.6	16	(1,406)	22	1,697	4
31	Leather and leather products	543	14	15.3	19	243	21	7.1	20	300	8	144	13
24	Lumber and wood products, except furniture	402	18	7.5	23	256	20	(19.1)	26	146	9	306	9
3X	Manufactured commodities not identified by kind	.....	.....ʳ	.....	.....	2,108	10	11.1	14	(2,108)	25	(570)	24
10,12	Metallic ores and coal	132	21	40.3	3	156	22	93.7	1	(24)	11	(7)	18
38,39	Miscellaneous manufactures and instruments	118	23	24.4	10	2,398	9	(1.4)	23	(2,280)	26	157	12
14	Nonmetallic minerals, except fuels	122	22	11.1	21	73	24	11.2	13	49	10	13	16
26	Paper and allied products	246	19	29.2	8	1,842	13	9.1	18	(1,596)	23	(293)	22
29	Petroleum refining and related products	430	16	(10.5)	26	1,162	14	12.6	12	(732)	19	(518)	23
33	Primary metal products	2,763	6	29.4	7	2,814	7	13.1	11	(51)	14	619	7
27	Printing, publishing, and allied products	190	20	36.3	5	342	18	9.0	19	(152)	16	37	15
30	Rubber and miscellaneous plastics products	730	13	24.9	9	2,634	8	17.3	6	(1,904)	24	(644)	25
91	Scrap and waste	17	24	(6.4)	25	78	23	(21.3)	27	(61)	15	78	14
32	Stone, clay, glass, and concrete products	1,026	12	17.3	16	481	17	9.3	17	545	6	278	10
22	Textile mill products	540	15	54.0	1	1,039	15	17.1	7	(499)	17	(0)	17
21	Tobacco manufactures	11	26	43.7	2	38	25	20.9	4	(27)	13	(9)	19
37	Transportation equipment	17,767	2	30.1	6	5,906	3	4.0	21	11,861	1	9,054	1

1. Compound annual growth rate. Parentheses indicate negative values.

2. Parentheses indicate excess of imports over exports.

3. Parentheses indicate decline in surplus/increase in deficit.

Source: U.S. trade: U.S. Bureau of the Census; Mexico-Canada trade: Statistics Canada, Foreign Trade Division, Special tabulation March 1997, converted to U.S. dollars by the editors. Calculation and ranking by the editors.

U.S. CORPORATE PROFITS

In the United States, chemicals, instruments, petroleum, and electronics recorded the highest corporate profits as a percentage of sales in 1988-1996 (Table 8). Printing and publishing and food and beverages tied for 5th place. After-tax profit as a percentage of stockholder' equity was highest for food and beverages, chemicals, lumber, apparel, and miscellaneous manufacturing.

TABLE 8

RANKINGS OF U.S. MANUFACTURING INDUSTRIES BY CORPORATE PROFIT RATES

		PROFIT AFTER TAX					
		AS A PERCENT OF SALES			AS A PERCENT OF STOCKHOLDERS' EQUITY		
SIC	INDUSTRY	1996	AVERAGE, 1988-1996	RANK, BASED ON AVERAGE	1996	AVERAGE, 1988-1996	RANK, BASED ON AVERAGE
23	Apparel[1]	2.84	3.10	12	15.91	15.72	4
28	Chemicals	10.89	7.81	1	22.62	16.71	2
36	Electronics	7.17	5.06	4	15.19	11.57	9
34	Fabricated metals	5.52	3.50	10	18.50	12.16	7
20	Food and beverages[2]	5.61	4.74	5	19.15	16.92	1
25	Furniture[3]	4.2	3.23	11	15.49	12.12	8
35	Industrial and commercial machinery	5.58	2.42	15	14.67	5.50	18
38	Instruments	6.16	6.65	2	11.06	12.32	6
24	Lumber[3]	3.79	4.31	8	14.89	15.92	3
39	Miscellaneous[3]	4.86	4.42	7	14.18	13.15	5
26	Paper	4.04	3.92	9	10.63	10.32	13
29	Petroleum and coal products	8.25	5.57	3	18.22	11.41	10
33	Primary metals	3.61	2.39	16	10.74	8.39	14
27	Printing and publishing	6.25	4.74	5	13.64	11.27	11
30	Rubber & plastic products	3.98	2.97	13	13.86	11.19	12
32	Stone, clay, and glass	5.47	2.44	14	16.74	6.92	16
22	Textiles	2.67	2.14	17	9.57	7.81	15
37	Transportation equipment	4.96	1.84	18	17.83	5.75	17

1. Includes leather.
2. Includes tobacco.
3. Averages are for 1992-1996.

Source: U.S. Bureau of the Census, Quarterly Financial Report. Calculations and ranking by the editors.

NAFTA COUNTRIES AND THE EUROPEAN UNION: GEOGRAPHY, DEMOGRAPHY, AND ECONOMY

	CANADA	UNITED STATES	MEXICO	TOTAL NAFTA	EUROPEAN UNION[1]
GEOGRAPHY					
Land area, square kilometers	9,220,970	9,166,600	1,923,040	20,310,610	3,212,839
Percent of total NAFTA	45.4	45.1	9.5	100.0	15.8
Border with the United States, kilometers[2]	8,893	.....	3,326	.....	.....
Coastline, kilometers	243,791	19,924	9,330	273,045	.....
Land use, square kilometers:					
Arable land	892,887	1,833,320	230,765	2,956,972	.....
Meadows and pastures	276,629	2,383,316	749,986	3,409,931	.....
Forest and woodlands	4,149,437	2,658,314	461,530	7,269,281	.....
Irrigated land	8,400	181,020	51,500	240,920	.....
DEMOGRAPHY					
Population, thousands of persons, July 1996	28,820	266,476	95,772	391,068	371,300
Percent of total NAFTA	7.4	68.1	24.5	100.0	94.9
Gender ratio (males/females)	0.97	0.96	0.97	.....	.....
Age structure, percent:					
14 and younger	21	22	36	.....	.....
15 to 64	67	65	59	.....	.....
65 and older	12	13	5	.....	.....
Rates per thousand in population:					
Births	13.33	14.80	26.24	.....	.....
Deaths	7.17	8.80	4.58	.....	.....
Net migration	4.47	3.10	-2.97	.....	.....
Fertility rate, children born per woman	1.81	2.06	3.03		
Labor force, thousands of persons (1994)	14,832	131,056	33,354	179,242	165,924
Percent of total NAFTA	8.3	73.1	18.6	100.0	92.6
ECONOMY					
GDP, billions of U.S. dollars, current prices:					
Exchange rate basis, 1996	577.9	7,263.2	315.3	8,156.4	8,574
Exchange rate basis, 1995	560.0	6,954.8	279.3	7,794.1	8,417
Purchasing Power Parity basis, 1996	646.0	7,263.2	741.9	8,651.1	9,092
Purchasing Power Parity basis, 1995	624.9	6,954.8	703.1	8,282.7	9,051
Growth rate 95 - 96, PPP basis, percent	3.38	4.43	5.52	4.45	0.46
Percent of total NAFTA (1996, PPP)	7.5	84.0	8.6	100.0	105.1
GDP per capita 1996, U.S. dollars, current prices:					
Exchange rate basis	20,066	27,256	3,292	20,857	21,366
Purchasing Power Parity basis	22,431	27,256	7,746	22,122	22,658
Real growth, percent, 1996	1.5	2.4	5.1	.....	1.6
Unemployment rate, percent of labor force, 1996	9.7	5.4	5.5	.....	.....
Gini coefficient, 1992[3]	0.36	0.42	0.48	.....	.....
Distribution of GDP by sector, percent of total:					
Agriculture	2.1	2.0	8.5	.....	.....
Industry	25.7	23.0	28.4	.....	.....
Services	72.1	75.0	63.1	.....	.....

NAFTA COUNTRIES AND THE EUROPEAN UNION: GEOGRAPHY, DEMOGRAPHY, AND ECONOMY (CONTINUED)

	CANADA	UNITED STATES	MEXICO	TOTAL NAFTA	EUROPEAN UNION[1]
Distribution of employment by sector, percent of total:					
Agriculture	4.1	2.8	28.0	.....	.....
Industry	22.6	23.0	21.0	.....	.....
Services	73.3	74.2	51.0	.....	.....
Budget, FY 1994-1995, billions of U.S. dollars:					
Revenues	90.4	1,258.0	56.0	.....	.....
Expenditures	114.1	1,461.0	54.0	.....	.....
Exports (billions of U.S. dollars)	185.0	578.0	80.0	.....	512.0
Imports (billions of U.S. dollars)	166.7	751.0	72.0	.....	812.0
External debt (billions of U.S. dollars)	233.0	870.5	155.0	.....	.....

1. Belgium, Germany, France, Italy, Luxembourg, Netherlands, Denmark, Ireland, United Kingdom, Greece, Spain, Portugal, Austria, Sweden, and Finland.

2. Includes Alaska.

3. A measure of income distribution; 1.00 would be perfect inequality, 0.00 perfect equality. Based on income after taxes and government cash transfers. Income in most recent year for Canada and U.S., in most recent month for Mexico. Commission for Labor Cooperation, "North American Labor Markets," 1997, p. 102.

Source: CIA World Factbook, Statistical Abstract of the World, NAFTA Commission for Labor Cooperation, Department of State (Background Notes), OECD (National Product Tables, 9/97), *Survey of Current Business*, EUROSTAT.

NAFTA COUNTRIES: PHYSICAL AND HUMAN INFRASTRUCTURE

	CANADA	UNITED STATES	MEXICO
TRANSPORTATION & UTILITIES			
Electricity:			
Capacity, million kilowatts	108.1	695.1	28.8
Production, billion kilowatt hours	511	3,100	122
Consumption per capita, kilowatt hours	16,133	11,236	1,239
Transportation data, kilometers:			
Railroads	70,176	240,000	20,567
Highways	849,404	6,284,488	245,433
Paved	297,291	5,574,341	88,601
Expressways	15,983	85,267	4,286
Inland waterways	3,000	41,009	2,900
Pipelines:			
Oil & products	23,564	276,000	38,350
Natural gas	74,980	331,000	13,254
Petrochemicals			1,400
Merchant Marine:			
Number of ships 1000 gross register tons or over	62	322	51
Total gross register tonnage, thousands	573	10,716	875
Number of airports, permanent surface runways	1,138	13,387	1,411
COMMUNICATIONS			
Telephones, millions	15.3	182.6	11.9
Phones per capita	0.5	0.7	0.1
Radio broadcast stations:			
AM	900	4,987	679
FM	29	4,932	na
Radio sets, millions	na	541	23
Television broadcast stations[1]	70	1,092	238
Cable systems	na	9,000	na
Television sets, millions	11.5	215.0	13.1
HEALTH, 1995			
Health expenditures:			
Per capita, U.S. dollars, converted using Purchasing Power Parity	2,049	3,701	386
As a percentage of GDP	9.6	14.2	4.9
Public sector	6.9	6.6	2.8
Private sector	2.7	7.6	2.1
Health personnel:			
Doctors per 10,000 population	21.5	26.3	15.9
Nurse to doctor ratio	4.7	2.8	0.8
Hospital beds per 10,000 population	5.4	4.1	1.2
Average hospital stay, days	12.6	8.0	4.2
Percentage of children immunized:			
3rd dose of DPT	85	67	64
Measles	85	80	78
Percent of babies with low birth weight	6	7	15
Life expectancy at birth:			
male	75.3	72.5	69.5
female	81.3	79.2	76.0
Life expectancy at 40:			
male	37.5	35.5	35.0
female	42.5	40.7	39.7
Life expectancy at 60:			
male	19.9	18.9	18.9
female	24.3	22.9	22.4

NAFTA COUNTRIES: PHYSICAL AND HUMAN INFRASTRUCTURE (CONTINUED)

	CANADA	UNITED STATES	MEXICO
EDUCATION			
Total education expenditures:			
As percent of GDP, 1994	7.6	5.5	5.8
As percent of government expenditures	14.3	12.3	na
Literacy, percent of persons 15 and older with 5 or more years of schooling:			
Total	97.0	97.0	89.6
male	na	97.0	91.8
female	na	97.0	87.4
Percent of 25+ pop.w/post secondary education	21.4	46.5	9.2
Daily newspapers, number	106	1,586	292
Circulation (1,000's)	5,815	60,700	10,231
Research and development:			
Number of scientists & engineers engaged, thousands	65.4	962.7	8.6
Total expenditure, millions of U.S. dollars[2]	8,525	171,000	1,141

na = not available.

1. Canadian value excludes 1400 repeaters.

2. Converted to U.S. dollars using exchange rates.

Source: CIA World Factbook, OECD Health Data 97, Statistical Abstract of the World, NAFTA Commission for Labor Cooperation, Department of State (Background Notes), 1996 UNESCO Statistical Yearbook.

EXCHANGE RATES AND RATE INDEXES

(annual averages)

YEAR	CURRENCY UNITS PER U.S. DOLLAR[1]		INDEX OF CURRENCY UNITS PER U.S. DOLLAR, FIRST QUARTER 1985=100	
	CANADIAN DOLLARS	MEXICAN NEW PESOS	CANADIAN DOLLARS	MEXICAN NEW PESOS
1987	1.3259	.....	98.0	687.1
1988	1.2306	.....	90.9	1,133.3
1989	1.1843	.....	87.5	1,227.2
1990	1.1668	.....	86.2	1,402.3
1991	1.1460	.....	84.7	1,504.9
1992	1.2085	.....	89.3	1,543.1
1993	1.2902	3.1237	95.3	1,553.4
1994	1.3664	3.3853	100.9	1,682.8
1995	1.3725	6.4428	101.4	3,200.6
1996	1.3638	7.6004	100.7	3,789.7

1. Source: Federal Reserve Board.

2. Source: Federal Reserve Bank of Dallas. Peso Index is on a new peso basis, i.e. adjusted to eliminate distortion arising from conversion of 1000 old pesos to 1 new peso in November 1993.

PURCHASING POWER PARITIES AND COMPARATIVE PRICE LEVELS[1]

Purchasing power parities (PPPs) are the rates of currency conversion that eliminate the differences in price levels between countries. Per capita volume indices based on PPP converted data reflect only differences in the volume of goods and services produced.

Comparative price levels are defined as the ratios of PPPs to exchange rates. They provide measures of the differences in price levels between countries.

The PPPs are given in national currency units per US dollar. The price levels and volume indices derived using these PPPs have been rebased on the OECD average.

1990 and 1993: PPPs for all countries other than Korea and Mexico are triennial benchmark results calculated by Eurostat and the OECD. The PPPs for Korea and Mexico are OECD estimates obtained by a regression procedure.

1994 and 1995: PPPs for the European countries except Turkey are annual benchmark results calculated by Eurostat. PPPs for Turkey and the non-European countries are OECD estimates. These were obtained by extrapolating the 1993 benchmark PPPs using the relative rates of inflation between the countries and the United States as measured by their implicit price deflators for GDP.

1996: PPPs for all countries are OECD estimates obtained by extrapolating the 1995 PPPs.

	1990	1993	1994	1995	1996
PURCHASING POWER PARITIES FOR GDP					
Canada	1.30	1.26	1.25	1.24	1.23
Mexico	1.59	1.84	1.95	2.63	3.40
United States	1.00	1.00	1.00	1.00	1.00
COMPARATIVE PRICE LEVELS FOR GDP					
Canada	100	88	81	76	80
Mexico	50	53	51	35	39
United States	90	90	89	85	88
PER CAPITA VOLUME INDICES FOR GDP					
Canada	113	107	108	108	106
Mexico	34	41	41	38	38
United States	138	136	137	137	137

---

1 The data and the explanatory notes are from OECD Main Economic Indicators, August 1997.

PART II:

INDUSTRIES IN NORTH AMERICA

AGRICULTURE

THE UNITED STATES

Products and Processes. Agriculture is unchallenged in its gains in productivity over many decades.   Real output has increased steadily, sometimes radically, even as acreage, the number of farms, and the number of full-time farmers have declined (see Table 1 for the recent record.)[1] The mechanization of farming in the 1940s and 1950s released labor for other occupations, making possible the huge increase in manufacturing output during and after World War II. In the mid-1960s, one worker in 18 was in agriculture; in 1995, one in 31 was in farming and agricultural services combined, and only one in 50 was in farming.

TABLE 1

UNITED STATES: FARMS, LAND, INCOME, OUTPUT, INPUT, AND PRICES, 1986-1996

(Monetary values in U.S. dollars)

	1986	1987	1988	1989	1990	1991	1992	1993	1994	1995	1996
Number of farms (thousands)	2,250	2,213	2,201	2,175	2,146	2,117	2,108	2,083	2,065	2,072	2,063
Land in farms (thousand acres)	1,005,333	998,923	994,423	990,723	986,850	981,786	978,503	976,463	973,403	972,253	968,048
Average acres per farm	447	451	452	456	460	464	464	469	471	469	469
Gross farm income											
(Billions of dollars)	156	168	178	192	198	192	201	204	216	210	.....
Production expenses	125	131	140	147	153	153	152	161	167	176	.....
Net income	31	37	38	45	45	39	48	44	48	35	.....
GDP originating-farms (bill.$1992)[1]	....	63.7	56.6	64.8	72.8	71.1	80.5	70.9	83.9	.....	.....
FARM OUTPUT, INPUT, AND PRODUCTIVITY INDEXES, 1982=100											
Farm output	100	102	95	103	108	109	116	109	122	.....	.....
Farm input, total	90	88	88	87	89	90	88	89	89	.....	.....
Farm labor	84	84	86	87	85	88	83	80	80	.....	.....
Productivity (output per unit of total input)	111	115	109	118	122	121	131	123	136	.....	.....
HIRED FARMWORKERS:[2]											
Male (1,000)	.....	.....	.....	.....	735	.....	.....	680	653	704	.....
Median weekly earnings	.....	.....	.....	.....	216	.....	.....	225	248	250	.....
Female (1,000)	.....	.....	.....	.....	151	.....	.....	123	126	128	.....
Median weekly earnings	.....	.....	.....	.....	175	.....	.....	192	180	200	.....
Farm operators (1,000's)[3]	.....	2088	.....	.....	.....	.....	1925	.....	.....	.....	.....
Farm enterpreneurial population (1000's)[4]	.....	.....	.....	.....	.....	.....	4867	4862	5024	.....	.....
Producer prices, farm products, 1993=100[5]	104.8	89.2	97.9	103.5	104.8	98.7	96.7	100	99.3	100.3	114.3

1. U.S. Department of Commerce, Bureau of Economic Analysis, *Survey of Current Business*, August 1996.

2. 1990 data from *Statistical Abstract*, 1995, p. 682.

3. *Statistical Abstract*, 1996, p. 661.

4. All persons in households where at least one person was farm manager, operator, or reported self-employment farm income.

5. Prices received by domestic producers, Source: Bureau of Labor Statistics.

Source: US. Department of Agriculture, *Statistics of Agriculture*, 1997, expect as noted.

[1] Table 1 shows a slight increase in "farm entrepreneurial population" in 1994, but this may be misleading as it includes all families with any agricultural income, among them part-time and "hobby" farmers and their families.

Production techniques continue to change and improve; for example, "no till" and "low till" cropping. Plowing and cultivating used to be the principal occupation of farmers in the spring and summer; now, with herbicides and new planting techniques, many farmers do neither. The recent growth in the large-scale use of agricultural service contractors for soil preparation, and planting (in addition to harvesting) is changing farm operations. The successful cloning of the ewe "Dolly" may portend radical changes in animal husbandry. There seems to be no end to the productivity revolution in farming.

FIGURE 1

U.S. EMPLOYMENT ON FARMS

Percent distribution by region, 1995

As determined by employment—including self-employment—the largest concentration of farming activity is in the Southeast (26.3 percent in 1995), followed by the Plains (19.3 percent), the Great Lakes (15.4 percent), and the Pacific region (14.6 percent.) First place for the Southeast may seem counter-intuitive, but the region today produces a wide variety of farm products. These include labor-intensive tobacco and horticultural products, as well as grains, oilseeds, livestock, and dairy products. For example, North Carolina now is second in hog production next to Iowa, and Arkansas is the No. 1 poultry state.

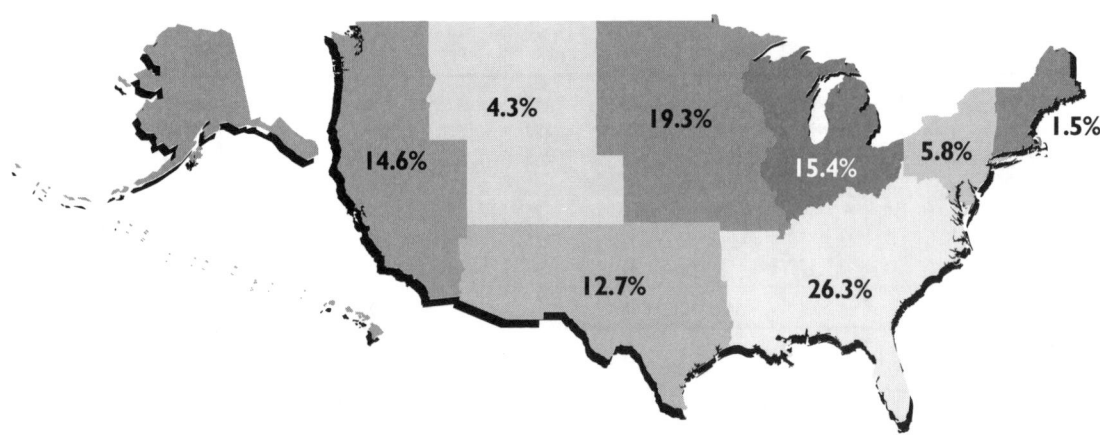

Source: U.S. Department of Commerce, Bureau of Economic Analysis.

What's New

Exports of feed and food grains were unusually high in the last several years as growing populations and economies, as well as a crop failure in China, led to increased demand and rising prices.[2] However, value of grain exports declined sharply in the first half of 1997, led by a 46 percent drop in wheat and 39 percent in coarse grains. China itself was an exporter of corn in 1997.

A recent decision by the Supreme Court in Glickman vs. Wileman Bros. upheld tax-supported advertising by farm industry groups to promote sales of farm commodities such as raisins, dairy products, and prunes. The practice had been challenged on the grounds that taxes on sales of such products violated the free speech rights of producers who did not want to participate yet were forced to pay taxes on their sales to pay for the advertising. As a result of the decision, advertising like "Beef—it's what's for dinner" will continue.

---

[2] *The Wall Street Journal*, June 26, 1997, A2.

Warmer than usual water temperatures off Peru have led many scientists to predict that the "El Niño"[3] phenomenon—erratic warming of currents off the west coast of South America—may be building to the record levels of 1982-1983 or beyond. Peru's anchovy catch has already dropped significantly, causing several Peruvian fishmeal plants to close; Australia has experienced drought, and Indonesia, forest fires. The significance to North America is that El Niño has been blamed in the past for drastic changes in the weather in the Northern Hemisphere, including droughts in the north and floods in the south. In addition, a low anchovy harvest often precipitates increased demand and higher prices for high protein animal feeds and oilseeds, such as soybeans.[4] The El Niño effect means that agriculture will almost certainly experience extremes of weather and that prices could be strongly affected in 1998.

Most U.S. agricultural organizations support NAFTA and free trade in general. The American Farm Bureau Federation has called for greater exports of farm products and supports fast track negotiating authority. Farm Bureau President Dean Kleckner said in October of 1997 that Congress had improved the legislation by addressing specific Bureau concerns. These concerns include the need to reduce foreign tariffs and subsidies, prevent barriers to biotechnology, reform state trading enterprises, eliminate unjustified sanitary and phytosanitary restrictions, and improve dispute settlement procedures, especially regarding perishable commodities.

Output. Real farm output, as measured by gross product originating (1992 prices), rose from $63.7 billion in 1987 to $83.9 billion in 1994—a 4 percent annual growth rate (Table 1). Farm sales increased steadily through the 1987-1995 period (Table 2). Cattle and calf sales, at $34 billion in 1995, remain the top revenue source; feed crops rank second, at $23 billion. Nonetheless, beef and other red meats have experienced a relative decline in the U.S. food budget. In addition, the ratio of beef to all other meats fell from 1.6 in 1987 to 1.2 in 1995. Current dollar revenues from beef, pork, and lamb have held their own, while those from chicken and turkey have more than doubled, perhaps reflecting a general trend toward health consciousness in food purchases.

Farm income has always been volatile, as its sharp drop in 1995 shows (Table 2). On the other hand, 1996 was probably a good year as exports and prices turned up. Moreover, the average of "net farm income" hides sharp differences in types of farming and in regions. For example, record flooding in the Midwest in the spring of 1997 and the consequent destruction of grain crops, particularly wheat, hurt farmers who were affected by the floods, while the resulting price increases helped those farmers who had ample grain to sell. Conversely, high prices for feedgrains and oilseeds and their products typically have a negative impact on livestock producers.

Government payments to farmers have declined in recent years, according to the U.S. Department of Agriculture (Table 2), from almost $17 billion in 1987 to somewhat more than $7 billion in 1995. They were 10.2 percent of gross cash income in 1987 but fell steadily in the following years to only 3.6 percent in 1995 (Table 2). Table 3 shows agricultural commodities supported by USDA's Commodity Credit Corporation in 1993; cotton and corn received the greatest support.

Investment. Farm investment, as suggested by real shipments of farm machinery, fell slightly in 1991-92, but then rebounded in 1995-96. It was expected to rise slightly in 1997. Higher grain prices have enabled some farmers to replace older equipment with that needed for the newer production techniques.

---

[3] Since the warmer waters are usually first detected by fishermen off the coast of Peru at Christmas time, the phenomenon is called "El Niño" after the Christ child.

[4] *The Wall Street Journal*, June 26, 1997, B12.

TABLE 2

U.S. FARM SALES, EXPENSES AND INCOME, 1987-1995

(Millions of U.S. dollars except as noted)

	1987	1988	1989	1990	1991	1992	1993	1994	1995
Total farm sales	141,797	151,243	160,810	169,571	167,864	171,346	177,617	180,775	185,750
Livestock and products	75,996	79,640	83,918	89,220	85,786	85,624	90,166	88,129	86,844
Cattle and calves	33,583	36,959	36,429	39,302	38,697	37,272	39,362	36,395	33,983
Hogs	10,337	9221	9,770	11,525	11,036	10,017	10,911	9,883	10,074
Sheep and lambs	558	522	487	414	399	460	552	507	557
Dairy products	17,727	17,632	19,357	20,153	18,007	19,736	19,243	19,935	19,924
Broilers	6,177	7435	8,778	8,365	8,383	9,177	10,415	11,370	11,761
Farm chickens	112	95	138	90	67	83	96	78	68
Chicken eggs	3,208	3,067	3,862	4,010	3,901	3,384	3,779	3,780	3,959
Turkeys	1,703	1,951	2,235	2,393	2,353	2,396	2,509	2,644	2,774
Ducks	11	9	9	8	8	9	8	9	10
Other poultry	304	311	356	422	441	474	516	563	549
Miscellaneous other livestock	2,276	2,439	2,497	2,537	2,494	2,615	2,775	2,966	3,183
Crops	65,800	71,603	76,892	80,297	82,077	85,722	87,451	92,646	98,906
Food grains	5,790	7,469	8,247	7,480	7,325	8,467	8,180	9,545	10,069
Feed crops	14,635	14,281	17,049	18,669	19,327	20,060	20,162	20,296	23,144
Cotton	4,189	4,525	5,025	5,488	5,236	5,196	5,250	6,738	7,567
Tobacco	1,816	2,069	2,410	2,733	2,881	2,958	2,948	2,645	2,594
Oil crops	11,283	13,501	11,867	12,258	12,698	13,282	13,220	14,657	14,829
Vegetables	9,891	9,792	11,562	11,464	11,625	11,896	13,466	13,740	14,773
Fruits/nuts	8,056	9,032	9,151	9,416	9,923	10,174	10,281	10,176	10,775
All other crops	10,141	10,935	11582	12,789	13,062	13,691	13,946	14,849	15,155
Government payments	16,747	14,480	10,887	9,298	8,214	9,169	13,402	7,879	7,252
Farm-related income	6,412	7,858	8,596	8,235	8,220	8,166	9,124	9,154	10,881
Gross cash income	164,955	173,581	180,292	187,050	184,298	188,680	200,143	197,808	203,883
Value of home consumption	743	732	672	706	620	590	519	481	495
Rental value of dwellings	5,041	7,695	7,182	7,181	7,156	7,142	8,030	9,327	9,397
Noncash income	5,784	8,427	7,854	7,887	7,775	7,732	8,549	9,808	9,892
Value of inventory adjustment	(2,319)	(4,095)	3,788	3,258	(207)	4,156	(4,512)	8,224	(3,376)
Gross farm income	168,420	177,913	191,934	196,196	191,867	200,567	204,180	215,840	210,399
Total production expenses	131,034	139,908	146,660	153,398	153,341	152,520	160,530	167,444	175,581
Net farm income	37,386	38,006	45,274	44,798	38,526	48,047	43,650	48,396	34,819
Percent change from previous year	21.0	1.7	19.1	-1.0	-14.0	24.7	-9.2	10.9	-28.1
Govt. as % of gross cash income	10.2	8.3	6.0	5.0	4.5	4.9	6.7	4.0	3.6

Note: Parentheses indicate negative value.

Source: USDA, Statistics of Agriculture, 1997.

TABLE 3

U.S. COMMODITY CREDIT CORPORATION: PRICE SUPPORT ON 1993 CROP, U.S. AND TERRITORIES[1]

| COMMODITY | UNIT | THROUGH SEPTEMBER 30, 1993 | |
		QUANTITY MILLIONS	VALUE IN MILLIONS OF U.S. DOLLARS
Cotton, upland	Bale	8	1,984
Cotton, extra long staple	Bale	*	67
Seed cotton, upland	Pound	4	2
Seed cotton, extra long staple	Pound	0	.....
Wheat	Bushel	258	628
Corn	Bushel	618	1,029
Honey	Pound	136	73
Milk and butterfat:			
Butter	Pound	0	.....
Cheese	Pound	0	.....
Dried milk	Pound	0	.....
Tobacco	Pound	361	862
Rice, rough	Cwt	31	197
Grain sorghum	Bushel	15	24
Peanuts, farmers', and stock	Pound	324	71
Oats	Bushel	2	2
Barley	Bushel	38	51
Beans, dry edible	Pound	0	.....
Rye	Bushel	*	*
Soybeans[2]	Bushel, cwt.	88	440
Sugar:			
Beets	Pound	2063	447
Cane	Pound	1709	299
Total			6,176

1. Represents loans made on the 1993 crop as reported through the FY1994 reporting year.

2. Includes flaxseed, sunflowerseed, canolaseed, safflowerseed, and mustardseed.

* Less than $500,000.

Source: USDA. Agricultural Statistics, 1997.

FIGURE 3

U.S. OCCUPATIONAL INJURY AND ILLNESS RATES: AGRICULTURE, FORESTRY, AND FISHING, 1995

Incidence of nonfatal injuries and illnesses per 100 full-time workers

The nonfatal injury and illness rate for agriculture, forestry, and fishing was 9.7 cases per 100 workers in 1995. This compares with 8.1 cases averaged for all private industry.

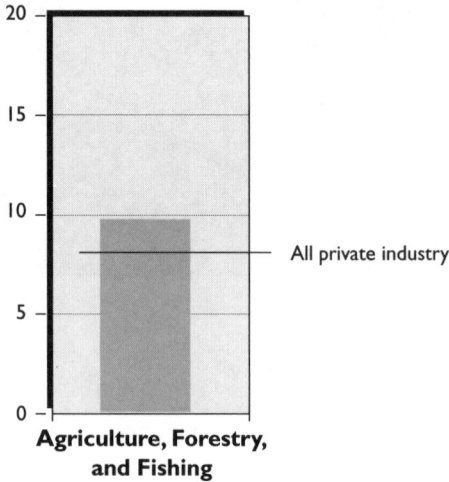

Source: U.S. Bureau of Labor Statistics.

CANADA

Total (current dollar) cash receipts (including government payments) of Canadian farms rose at a 3.2 percent rate from 1987 to 1996 (Table 4). Cash payments (excluding government payments) rose 2.1 percent after taking inflation into account. As in the United States, farmers' revenues from livestock exceeded their revenues from crops in 1987, but by 1996, revenues were about the same for each. Poultry sales rose sharply over the period, but sales of beef, pork, and lamb rose as well. Direct government payments to farmers were about 15 percent of total cash receipts in 1987. However, they fell sharply in the 1994-1996 period, to 3.8 percent by 1996, probably because of higher grain prices.

TABLE 4

CANADIAN AGRICULTURAL RECEIPTS, VALUES AND EARNINGS, 1987-1996

(Monetary values in thousands of Canadian dollars, except as noted)

	1987	1988	1989	1990	1991	1992	1993	1994	1995	1996
Total cash receipts: Farms	21,270,824	22,350,972	22,854,856	21,933,844	21,928,209	23,632,176	24,141,942	25,818,932	27,016,959	28,363,876
Livestock and products, total	10,618,888	10,697,839	10,843,186	11,210,310	10,854,358	11,329,858	12,276,641	12,494,641	12,670,244	13,697,379
In 1986 prices	10,309,600	10,740,802	10,704,034	10,717,314	10,599,959	11,162,422	11,070,010	11,389,828	11,975,656	12,682,758 e
Cattle	3,366,221	3,511,480	3,504,774	3,590,252	3,458,604	3,994,334	4,444,181	4,323,433	4,223,187	4,297,694
Calves	443,382	456,698	459,559	434,158	419,510	462,894	524,704	523,242	422,824	326,799
Hogs	2,121,787	1,788,452	1,803,154	2,030,117	1,841,623	1,776,385	2,040,121	2,036,367	2,254,766	2,908,190
Sheep	2,425	2,748	3,174	3,187	3,122	3,337	4,557	3,883	3,466	3,631
Lambs	36,631	34,421	34,161	34,489	33,956	40,284	54,975	56,352	62,763	73,048
Dairy products	2,889,857	3,087,950	3,102,428	3,154,774	3,162,712	3,089,477	3,129,885	3,355,341	3,464,087	3,515,176
Turkeys	191,825	202,043	219,248	230,493	222,293	212,841	210,047	221,061	237,891	270,059
Hens and chickens	798,362	835,250	918,822	970,988	935,397	922,803	1,006,808	1,060,948	1,050,977	1,247,062
Eggs	454,567	485,741	514,915	486,560	497,026	514,074	537,669	563,530	594,909	658,886
Wool	1,617	2,276	2,125	1,232	826	1,265	1,119	1,126	1,979	1,995
Honey	51,924	48,363	43,426	45,866	49,691	50,245	48,249	58,329	63,944	66,678
Furs	78,634	57,477	41,477	30,008	26,705	22,478	20,511	34,192	29,924	54,085
Crops, total	7,341,863	8,291,082	8,764,329	8,873,334	8,726,252	8,540,837	9,023,123	11,500,534	13,032,238	13,602,109
In 1986 prices	7,911,490	7,272,879	6,933,805	7,965,291	8,850,154	8,481,467	8,577,113	9,705,092	9,689,396	9,253,135 e
Wheat excluding durum	2,261,120	2,223,749	1,808,079	2,350,090	2,446,777	1,948,327	1,518,485	1,983,519	2,212,743	2,843,992
Durum wheat	289,928	349,699	359,592	343,993	297,146	284,471	233,880	453,488	603,955	642,216
Oats	48,200	117,617	145,025	81,083	53,801	97,900	144,940	145,716	225,510	315,959
Barley	491,518	514,206	685,954	545,047	472,485	386,377	401,878	518,461	721,529	982,566
Soybeans	262,007	328,541	257,544	256,221	284,671	323,840	438,870	508,494	663,896	631,005
Corn	443,132	543,443	503,873	516,967	505,096	507,665	419,428	505,540	703,093	803,960
Potatoes	336,156	324,384	410,545	399,198	365,733	349,118	425,291	540,558	517,883	487,991
Vegetables	614,684	651,983	707,660	697,407	708,219	760,861	807,753	845,128	897,327	844,903
Apples	109,476	114,131	114,511	131,895	148,866	143,092	136,570	143,881	186,210	167,748
Other tree fruits	46,294	47,562	49,943	56,585	52,094	49,180	45,180	64,549	65,959	49,284
Direct payments to farmers[1]	3,310,073	3,362,051	3,247,341	1,850,200	2,347,599	3,761,481	2,842,178	1,823,757	1,314,477	1,064,388
Percent of total cash income	15.6	15	14.2	8.4	10.7	15.9	11.8	7.1	4.9	3.8
ADDENDA, CANADIAN DOLLARS:										
Value/acre of farmland and buildings	456	464	518	555	560	538	537	556	594	665
AVERAGE HOURLY EARNINGS:										
General farm labor	.....	.....	.....	.....	.....	8.17	8.57	8.75	8.89	9.18
Average, all types of farm work	.....	.....	.....	.....	.....	8.14	8.29	8.69	8.76	8.94

e = Estimate.

1. Government insurance and subsidies.

Note. Products shown are selected, detail will not add to totals.

Source: Statistics Canada, Cansim Matrix 3571, July 1997, adapted.

MEXICO

Total agricultural employment, as measured by the number of paid employees, showed little change from 1988 to 1995 (Table 5.) Grain and oilseed production, on the other hand, fluctuated substantially during 1987-1995. Production of corn, by far the largest crop, rose 57 percent from 1987 to 1994 and then declined moderately in 1995. Mexican corn production is expected to decline substantially under NAFTA as tariffs on grain from the United States and Canada are eliminated. Wheat, barley, and grain sorghum crops in 1995 were below their 1987 levels, with a 54 percent drop in the latter. Soybean output in 1995 was almost two-thirds below the 1987 level. Beans and cottonseed were up slightly, but both showed extreme fluctuations during 1987-1995. In the livestock category, cattle, poultry, and sheep production increased between 1987 and 1994, while hogs declined. Milk and egg production also rose, but output of honey and wool declined. Production of bananas and citrus fruits rose during 1987-1995, with especially strong gains in the largest crop, oranges. Fruit in general may have benefited from the implementation of NAFTA, as U.S. tariffs were eliminated and exports increased.

TABLE 5

MEXICAN AGRICULTURAL PRODUCTION AND EMPLOYMENT, 1987-1995

	1987	1988	1989	1990	1991	1992	1993	1994p	1995e
Paid employees (thousands)	.....	6,077	5,942	6,043	6,029	5,973	6,061	6,136	6,017
ANIMALS SLAUGHTERED (1,000 HEAD):									
Cattle	1,273	1,217	1,163	1,114	1,189	1,247	1,257	1,365	
Hogs	915	861	727	757	812	820	822	873	.....
Goats	36	39	37	36	39	43	42	39	.....
Sheep	22	24	25	25	26	28	29	30	.....
Poultry	673	627	611	750	658	896	1,040	1,079	.....
ANIMAL PRODUCTS AND HONEY (METRIC TONS[1]):									
Milk	6,349,741	6,280,896	5,703,959	6,265,936	6,847,772	7,114,086	7,555,222	7,461,500	.....
Eggs	975,029	1,090,164	1,047,019	1,009,795	1,141,381	1,161,270	1,233,559	1,246,200	.....
Honey	62,931	57,803	61,757	66,493	69,495	63,886	62,000	56,400	.....
Wool	6,760	6,415	5,526	4,517	5,168	4,675	4,713	4,495	.....
GRAINS AND OILSEEDS (1,000 METRIC TONS[1]):									
Rice	390	301	348	260	229	260	197	251	.....
Beans	1,024	857	59	1,287	1,379	719	1,288	1,353	1,234
Corn	11,607	10,600	10,953	14,635	14,252	16,929	18,125	18,200	15,545
Wheat	4,415	3,665	4,375	3,931	4,061	3,621	3,582	4,171	3,559
Ajonjoli	51	34	46	60	37	23	23	9	20
Cottonseeds	414	491	257	293	307	50	42	191	453
Cartamo	219	247	142	159	86	41	64	64	114
Soybeans	828	226	992	575	725	594	496	525	298
Barley	617	350	435	492	580	550	541	308	552
Sorghum	6,298	5,895	5,002	5,978	4,308	5,353	2,581	3,708	2,909
FRUITS (1,000 METRIC TONS[1]):									
Avocados	523	540	473	686	780	725	709	773	774
Peaches —fresh	173	178	145	161	132	133	152	153	.....
Peaches — preserved	71	78	85	107	88	77	95	74	.....
Lemons	682	660	779	685	717	777	725	812	831
Mangos	1,007	998	1,111	1,074	1,118	1,076	1,151	1,087	1,088
Tangerine	90	89	90	80	88	90	118	105	.....
Apples	486	507	506	457	527	598	538	471	491
Melons (excluding watermelons)	339	425	496	523	645	496	394	438	404
Oranges	1,934	2,099	2,372	2,220	2,369	2,541	2,914	3,175	3,209
Nuts	28	28	30	40	41	44	47	45	.....
Pina	7	6	1	1	.....	1	1	2	.....
Peron	343	318	435	455	299	264	212	241	.....
Bananas	1,770	1,566	1,824	1,986	1,889	2,095	2,207	3,317	2,339
Grapes	556	563	502	429	530	522	467	538	550
Watermelons	581	400	504	404	393	494	388	357	402

p = Preliminary.

e = Estimate.

1. To convert metric tons to short tons multiply by 1.0989.

Source: INEGI, Anuario Estadistica 95.

INTERNATIONAL TRADE

United States. Trade in agricultural products, always important to the United States, has grown substantially in recent years.[5] Global U.S. exports of unprocessed agricultural products grew at an annual rate of 8.8 percent from 1992 to 1996, to $36.7 billion, while imports rose 9.1 percent annually, to $15.5 billion (Table 6). Despite the more rapid rate for imports, the positive agricultural trade balance during that period rose from $15.2 billion to $21.2 billion. The growth in trade appears to be due more to world market conditions than to the implementation of NAFTA.

Canada. The Canadian-U.S. Free Trade Agreement (CUSFTA) took effect in January of 1989, and Canadian exports to the United States in most years since have increased at a more rapid pace than U.S. exports to Canada. U.S. agricultural exports to Canada doubled between 1989 and 1990 but then rose only 28 percent between 1990 and 1996, to $2.7 billion (Table 6). Canadian exports to the United States gained 154 percent during 1989-1996, to $3.1 billion, with the largest increases in 1992 and 1996. This gave Canada a $342 million surplus in 1996 trade, compared with a small surplus in 1989 and a $792 million deficit in 1990. Grains and other crops account for most U.S. exports to Canada, while livestock and animal specialties account for more than half of all Canadian exports to the United States. Canadian trade with Mexico is quite small but growing rapidly. Canadian exports to Mexico grew at a 20 percent annual rate from 1989 to 1993 and then at a 16 percent rate from 1993 to 1996. The higher rate during the earlier period is due to the very small 1989 base ($69 million).

Mexico. Mexican exports to the United States grew at 4 percent rate from 1989 to 1993 and continued to grow from 1993 to 1995 before declining in 1996 (Table 6). U.S. exports to Mexico took a sharp upturn immediately following the implementation of NAFTA in 1994, owing to strong increases in grain shipments and prices. They then declined in 1995 and rose sharply again in 1996, pointing up the impact weather and related price changes have on agricultural production and trade.

NAFTA. All three NAFTA members have experienced both deficits and surpluses in their trade balances during the 1989-1996 period (Table 6). Canada ended up in 1996 with a favorable trade balance of $404 million following a $64 million deficit in 1995. The United States had a trade surplus of $511 million in 1996, compared with a 1995 deficit of $797 million. And Mexico had a $915 million deficit in 1996, after recording a record surplus of $861 million the previous year. These alternating results demonstrate the importance of weather and other unforeseen factors in agricultural trade.

It is probably too early to tell how NAFTA will affect trade in agricultural products in the long run. Total trade (exports plus imports) moved up sharply in 1993—the year before NAFTA's implementation—and again from 1994 to 1996. The total gain from 1993 to 1996 was an impressive 49 percent. It is widely anticipated that the agreement ultimately will bring greater integration of the three agricultural economies. One can observe a little of that in the numbers, but, as always, the effects of weather and world market conditions dominate short-run changes, and it will be several years before a definitive trend can be established.

---

[5] Trade figures in Table 6 differ substantially from those published by the USDA, which include trade in processed foods and other products (see the Food and Beverages chapter).

TABLE 6

INTERNATIONAL TRADE, AGRICULTURE

(Millions of U.S. dollars)

	1989	1990	1991	1992	1993	1994	1995	1996
GLOBAL TRADE IN UNPROCESSED AGRICULTURAL COMMODITIES, U.S.								
Imports	.....	.....	.....	10,928	11,337	12,005	14,119	15,507
Exports	.....	.....	.....	26,148	25,039	26,165	33,507	36,703
Trade balance	.....	.....	.....	15,219	13,702	14,160	19,388	21,196
Bilateral trade: NAFTA								
U.S. exports to Canada, total	1,097.8	2,134.0	2,114.9	2,147.1	2,547.1	2,504.5	2,698.7	2,730.2
Agricultural products[1]	986.8	1,955.2	1,939.8	1,977.8	2,344.0	2,275.3	2,485.2	2,509.2
Livestock and animal specialties[2]	111.0	178.8	175.1	169.3	203.1	229.2	213.5	221.0
Canadian exports to U.S., total	1,208.2	1,342.1	1,349.8	1,884.1	2,156.3	2,443.6	2,566.1	3,072.2
Agricultural products[1]	610.4	573.4	540.9	694.1	823.9	1,183.2	1,114.3	1,341.4
Livestock and animal specialties[2]	597.8	768.7	808.9	1,190.0	1,332.4	1,260.4	1,451.8	1,730.8
U.S. exports to Mexico, total	1,483.4	1,440.3	1,416.9	1,856.6	1,655.9	2,215.0	1,830.6	3,382.2
Agricultural products[1]	1,369.8	1,339.5	1,216.4	1,648.3	1,535.3	2,046.9	1,787.0	3,283.0
Livestock and animal specialties[2]	113.6	100.8	200.5	208.3	120.6	168.1	43.6	99.2
Mexican exports to U.S., total	1,661.8	1,896.0	1,790.7	1,588.2	1,955.1	2,010.4	2,759.8	2,529.5
Agricultural products[1]	1,373.6	1,469.1	1,426.3	1,242.6	1,520.2	1,654.9	2,204.2	2,394.7
Livestock and animal specialties[2]	288.2	426.9	364.4	345.6	434.9	355.5	555.6	134.8
Canadian exports to Mexico	69.2	21.9	44.7	125.0	145.6	223.1	216.8	231.9
Mexican exports to Canada	78.4	119.0	101.7	86.7	106.2	121.7	147.8	170.1
TRADE BALANCES WITHIN NAFTA[3]								
Canada	101.2	(889.0)	(822.1)	(224.7)	(351.4)	40.5	(63.6)	403.8
Mexico	187.6	552.8	430.8	(306.7)	259.8	(306.0)	860.2	(914.5)
U.S.	(288.8)	336.2	391.3	531.4	91.6	265.5	(796.6)	510.7

1. SIC 01 includes unprocessed grain and oilseeds; cotton; tobacco, potatoes, and other field crops; fruits and tree nuts; and horticultural specialties such as ornamental floriculture and nursery products and food crops grown under cover.

2. SIC 02 includes livestock (beef cattle, hogs, sheep and goats), dairy farms, poultry and eggs, fur-bearing animals and rabbits, horses and other equine, and animal specialties not elsewhere classified (e.g., alligator farms, apiaries, aviaries, earthworm hatcheries, honey production, and raw silk production).

3. Parentheses indicate an excess of imports over exports. Because of commodity coding and other data differences among the three countries, these trade balances are only rough estimates and should be used with caution.

Source for U.S. global trade; derived by editors from U.S. Department of Agriculture product data.

Source for U.S.-Canada and U.S.-Mexico bilateral trade: U.S. Bureau of the Census.

Source for Canada-Mexico and Mexico-Canada bilateral trade: Statistics Canada, Foreign Trade Division, Special tabulation, March 1997, converted to U.S. dollars by the editors.

FISHING

THE UNITED STATES

Overview. Water covers most of the earth's inhabitable surface and holds an infinite number and variety of food resources, many still largely untapped. For now, however, the greatest challenge is to improve management of these resources in ways that will provide both food for expanding populations and solutions to problems ranging from overfishing to pollution to "blooms" of fish-killing microbes. Many experts believe the latter two problems may be intertwined, as runoff containing nutrients such as nitrogen fertilizer appears to promote the toxic conditions. In addition to the negative impact of such incidents, commercial fishing has been affected by competition on several fronts, including foreign fleets and sport fishing. The good news is that awareness of the problems is growing, and concrete steps are being taken to protect marine resources.

Meanwhile, value of the U.S. fish catch recently has been stalled at levels of years past, and, according to the National Oceanic and Atmospheric Administration (NOAA), the fishing industry is largely overcapitalized with too many vessels and too much effort expended, to the detriment of both producers and consumers. Still, the United States ranks as the world's fifth largest seafood producer, accounting for almost 6 percent of the world catch volume. It is exceeded only by China (17 percent), Peru (8 percent), Japan (8 percent), and Chile (6 percent), according to NOAA.

What's New. The Pacific Northwest salmon wars continue. The problems are several-fold, according to articles in *The Seattle Times*. One bone of contention is that Washington State Native Americans are catching more salmon than the 50 percent originally designated for them (they caught 59 percent in 1994), at a time when the total catch is declining and non-tribal catches of "wild" salmon are largely prohibited. Since 1974, Native Americans have been permitted by law to catch half the wild salmon that pass by their traditional fishing grounds and to use nets or gaffs at the mouth of rivers as salmon return to spawn. This type of fishing makes it possible to count fish precisely and to adjust harvesting as needed to preserve adequate numbers of spawners. Also, at this stage, runs of threatened coho, chinook, and other wild salmon often are no longer mixed with hatchery salmon. Sport and commercial fishermen who work on the open ocean, on the other hand, have trouble differentiating between wild and hatchery fish and thus have to pass up many harvestable salmon. In 1994, nontribal commercial and sport fishermen who fish mainly in the Strait of Juan de Fuca caught only 56,000 Puget Sound coho because of the restrictions on harvesting of wild runs. This compares with 430,000 coho, mostly hatchery fish, caught by Native Americans.

Washington State fishermen also have protested Canadians' catching of salmon that would otherwise migrate to Washington State rivers, according to *The Seattle Times*. The 1986 U.S.-Canada Salmon Treaty allows Washington net fishermen to harvest part of British Columbia sockeye salmon headed for the Fraser River. In return, British Columbia fishermen are permitted to catch Washington coho and chinook migrating along the coast of Vancouver Island. These salmon runs have been declining, however, in part because of environmental factors and increased fishing off of Vancouver Island by sport fishermen and British Columbia trollers.

Arguments also continue over sport fishing versus commercial fishing, gill-netters and purse seiners versus hook-and-line trollers, efforts to hold Native American shares to 50 percent of the fish catch, and hatchery fish versus wild salmon—some say hatchery salmon are displacing the wild fish.

Also likely to affect Pacific Coast salmon is the return of the El Niño/Southern Oscillation, a periodic episode of abnormal temperature and precipitation patterns. In El Niño years (such as 1925-26, 1972-73, 1982-83, and 1991-92), changes in the distribution of tropical rainfall decrease the intensity of the easterly blowing trade winds, resulting in a warming of waters off the Pacific Coast of South America and a cooling of waters in the Western Pacific. This leads to weather changes around the world, ranging from drought in Indonesia and Australia to heavy rains and flooding in the southern United States and Peru. El Niño thus can have a dramatic effect on fishing and agriculture. Its impact on Peruvian anchovy catches has been widely publicized, but it also appears to have caused sharp reductions in Pacific Coast catches of coho salmon; for example, during the intense 1982-83 El Niño, less than 700,000 wild coho returned to spawn in Pacific Northwest rivers, compared with the 1.6 million expected. This occurred because the warmer water prevented the upwelling of colder water rich in nutrients on which coho normally feed. As a result, many salmon died prematurely, and many others were stunted and produced fewer eggs than normal. A recent research report by scientists at Oregon State University suggests that improved forecasting of El Niños can help prevent such drastic effects, saving some $250,000 to $900,000 a year by allowing better management of salmon fisheries.

Interestingly, catches of west coast coho salmon have changed inversely with those of Alaskan pink and sockeye salmon. In jeopardy 20 years ago while coho salmon were thriving, Alaskan salmon landings have returned to record levels in the 1990s. Some people believe the change reflects better fisheries management, while others attribute it to conditions relating largely to the intensity of the Aleutian Low pressure system present in the winter. A strong Low appears to favor Alaskan salmon while a weak Low may favor production of coho and other salmon of the lower west coast.

Environmental and economic concerns meet head on in cases of fish killers such as *Pfiesteria piscicida*, and red tide. Both are caused by sudden proliferation or "blooms" of toxic forms of single-celled organisms that form the base of the marine food chain. NOAA reports that such outbreaks have cost the U.S. economy over $1 billion during the past decade. They have killed billions of fish, as well as other marine life, and affected virtually all coastal areas at one time or another.

One of the most recent episodes was in the late summer of 1997, when high concentrations of the toxic microbe *Pfiesteria piscicida* caused major fish kills in the Pocomoke River and other tributaries of the Chesapeake Bay. *Pfiesteria* also was blamed for skin lesions, memory loss, and respiratory problems among watermen and others who came in contact with affected water. It probably was behind similar fish kills in Virginia's Rappahannock River in 1997, as well as the estuaries of North Carolina's Pamlico Sound and other waterways in previous years. An elusive 24-stage single-cell microorganism, *Pfiesteria* becomes a dangerous fish killer only when, in the dinoflagellate stage, it borrows chloroplasts from true algal cells and photosynthesizes, according to *Science News* (September 27, 1997). What triggers the change is not known, but some sources have blamed the Maryland outbreak on overenrichment of the water by runoff from fields fertilized with chicken manure, a byproduct of nearby poultry farms.

The economic implications of the problem and its solutions are enormous. For a time, many supermarkets stopped selling Chesapeake Bay fish, to the detriment of watermen and others who make a livelihood from fishing, while producers of poultry, Maryland's No.1 farm product, fear the high cost and red tape of mandatory regulation. In a move that may satisfy both concerns, federal and state officials have offered Maryland farmers as much as $250 million to leave 100,000 acres fallow as buffers against runoff from fertilized fields into the Chesapeake Bay and its tributaries, according to *The Washington Post* (October 19 and 20, 1997). The U.S. Department of Agriculture and state agencies will administer the voluntary program, which will be the largest environmental project of its kind if fully implemented. It could result in a buffer of trees and grasses along all year-round and most seasonal streams, equivalent to some 5,000 miles of shore, by 2002. *The Washington Post* also reported that

Virginia, Maryland, Delaware, and North Carolina have agreed to establish a single medical standard to evaluate illnesses possibly linked to *Pfiesteria*. The agreement will help make collection of data and test results consistent in the four states, which have voiced strong differences of opinion about the impact of *Pfiesteria* on humans. Meanwhile, the health of the Chesapeake Bay may actually be better than it was a decade ago, according to an October 27, 1997, article in *The Washington Post*. Improvements seen include a more than 50 percent drop in phosphorous emissions by sewage plants into the bay, a 14 percent decline since 1985 in nitrogen flows from point sources into the bay, more sea grass, and larger numbers of rockfish and other key fish species. It is also notable that *Pfiesteria* never was found in the bay itself.

Red tides—blooms of toxic single-celled algae called phytoplankton—are periodic phenomena that also can have devastating effects. In 1996, a prolonged red tide in the Gulf of Mexico off the coast of southern Florida killed 149 manatees, as well as fish of all species and sizes and may also have accounted for increased deaths of otters, sea turtles, dolphins, and water birds. Red tides get their name from the color the water takes on during a massive bloom of red-tinged algae; some species also can change the water color to brown or green, and others have no affect on water color. The toxins produced vary from species to species. According to an article in *Scientific American* (August 1994), some toxic phytoplankton produce polyunsaturated fatty acids and galactolipids that destroy blood cells, and others produce neurotoxins as well. Some nontoxic forms have barbed spines that lodge between gill tissues and cause excessive secretions of mucus, eventually exhausting the supply of mucus and mucous cells and causing death from reduced oxygen exchange. Airborne toxins from red tides can cause respiratory and allergy-like symptoms in humans. Shellfish such as clams, mussels, oysters, and scallops usually are not killed by the algae but may pass on the toxins to those who eat them.

Red tides have been recorded since the earliest times, but evidence is growing that there is a link to pollution; for example, red tides around Hong Kong's Tolo Harbor grew eightfold between 1976 and 1986, as population was increasing sixfold, according to *Scientific American*. Similarly, in the Inland Sea of Japan, visible red tides rose from 44 per year in 1965 to over 300 a year in 1975; subsequent effluent controls in the mid-1970s then led to a 50 percent reduction in the number of red tides. Currents such as the Gulf Stream and storms can carry red tides vast distances, as can the ballast water of ships, where algal species, including toxic dinoflagellate cysts, have been found.

Hypoxia, a low-oxygen condition caused by overenrichment of waters at the mouth of rivers and streams laden with nutrients, exists in pockets of the Gulf of Mexico, according to a report by the American Farm Bureau Federation. The nutrients promote growth of plankton and phytoplankton that subsequently die and consume large amounts of oxygen, killing fish and their food sources in the process. Some people have laid the blame on farms along the Mississippi River basin, although such farms have actually reduced their use of fertilizer during the past 15 years, according to the Farm Bureau. To research the problem, the Clinton administration has formed the Mississippi River/Gulf of Mexico Watershed Nutrient Task Force and has proposed spending some $322 million over the next five years in search of solutions.

The National Marine Fisheries Service of NOAA said in a report to Congress that 96 species of fish and shellfish targeted by commercial and recreational fishermen, or nearly one-third of the 279 species counted in federal waters, are overfished or nearing that point. The October 1997 report stated that species like Pacific salmon, bluefin tuna, and American lobster have been so reduced that they cannot reproduce enough to keep up with demand, according to *The Seattle Times*. Other species affected include several types of flounder, Atlantic sea scallops, and pink shrimp. The federal government will impose fishing restrictions to bring these species to sustainable levels, possibly within a year. The move is expected to have a negative effect on the $3.5 billion U.S. commercial fishing industry. The United States also has banned imports of bluefin tuna from Panama, Honduras, and Belize because their fishing activities have undermined efforts to manage and conserve the species.

Production and Employment. The value of U.S. finfish and shellfish landings in 1995 ($2.95 billion) was little changed from the 1988 level ($2.97 billion). The industry, however, regularly experiences sharp year-to-year fluctuations in volume and prices (Table 1). Value of the fish catch declined from $1.59 billion to $1.32 billion during 1988-1995, while value of the shellfish catch rose from $1.39 billion to $1.63 billion. Higher prices accounted for the value gains in shellfish, as volume in 1995 was below 1988. Conversely, volume of the Pacific salmon catch rose almost 50 percent during the period, but value dropped 42 percent as supply (including more "farmed" and imported fish) apparently greatly outpaced demand. Finfish landings recently have accounted for 80-90 percent of total volume, but only 48-58 percent of ex-vessel value, according to NOAA. These differences reflect the rapid growth in the low-unit-value groundfish catch in Alaska, along with declines in landings of higher val-ued finfish.   Crabs, shrimp, and salmon have the highest value by species groups, but Alaska pollock is first ranked in terms of individual species. Moreover, harvesting of Alaska pollock has soared since 1984, when it did not even rank within the top 15 species.

The U.S. fishing industry may be stagnant in terms of output, but the size of the fleet has been growing. NOAA reports that in 1987 (the latest year for which data are available), there were some 23,000 operating vessels, or 3 percent of the world total, compared with 17,545 estimated for 1977. The United Nations Food and Agriculture Organization (FAO) estimates that the U.S. fishing fleet in 1987 was the world's fourth largest in terms of its nearly one million gross registered tons, exceeded only by the then-USSR, China, and Japan. The number of commercial fishermen reportedly now totals about 170,000, compared with 181,000 in 1977. These high numbers do not appear economic when measured against over-all results. For example, NOAA reports that the number of full-time vessels in the Gulf of Mexico shrimp fishery more than doubled from 1966 to 1991, while annual net revenue per vessel plummeted 75 percent to about $25,000. Similarly, in the Bering Sea pollock fishery, the catching capacity of vessels is reportedly double the annual catch quota.

Dutch Harbor-Unalaska, Alaska, was the top U.S. fishing port in 1996, according to NOAA. The port's commercial catch of fish and shellfish in 1996 totaled 579 million pounds worth $118.7 million, the largest in both volume and dollar value. Dutch Harbor-Unalaska has ranked first in terms of value for nine years now, although its 1996 results were far below the port's 1994 record of $224 million. The second and third places for volume went to the Louisiana ports of Empire-Venice and Cameron, while New Bedford, Massachusetts, and Kodiak, Alaska, were second and third in value.

Regionally, the Pacific Coast states rank first in fish landings, which totaled 6.4 million pounds valued at $1.8 billion in 1995. The Gulf States were next with 1.5 million pounds worth $725 million, followed by New England with 593 million pounds at $581 million.

U.S. consumption of domestic and imported seafood in 1996 was slightly below that in past years at 3.9 billion pounds, or 14.8 pounds per person, according to NOAA. This compares with about 15 pounds per person in each previous year since 1960. A 0.2 pound drop in per capita consumption of canned seafood largely accounted for the decline. Of the 1996 per capita average, 10 pounds were fresh or frozen fish or shellfish, 4.5 pounds were canned, and 0.3 pound was cured.   Shrimp consumption remained steady at 2.5 pounds per person annually. Imports accounted for 57 percent of 1996 consumption, up 3 percent from 1995, while U.S. exports rose 4 percent.

TABLE 1

U.S. FISHERIES: QUANTITY AND VALUE OF PRINCIPAL SPECIES, 1988-1995

(Monetary values in U.S. dollars)

	1988	1989	1990	1991	1992	1993	1994	1995
QUANTITY (MILLIONS OF POUNDS)								
Total	5,824	6,957	7,703	7,758	7,702	8,312	8,202	7,585
FISH:								
Total	4,781	5,885	6,587	6,509	6,472	7,157	7,212	6,654
Cod, Atlantic	76	78	96	93	62	51	39	30
Flounder	229	202	255	405	646	599	427	423
Haddock	6	4	5	4	5	2	1	1
Halibut	82	75	70	66	67	63	58	45
Herring, sea	222	209	221	230	282	216	214	265
Jack mackerel	23	28	9	4	3	4	6	4
Menhaden	2,086	1,989	1,962	1,977	1,644	1,983	2,324	1,847
Ocean perch, Atlantic	14	1	1	1	2	2	1	1
Pollock	1,290	2,385	3,129	2,873	2,952	3,258	3,133	2,853
Salmon, Pacific	606	786	733	783	716	888	901	1,137
Tuna	111	89	62	36	57	55	72	14
Whiting	36	39	44	37	36	36	36	34
SHELLFISH:								
Total	1,043	1,072	1,116	1,249	1,230	1,155	990	931
Clams	132	138	139	134	142	148	131	134
Crabs	456	458	499	660	624	604	447	364
Lobsters, American	49	53	61	63	56	57	66	66
Oysters	32	30	29	32	36	34	38	40
Scallops	43	41	42	40	34	19	25	20
Shrimp	331	352	346	320	338	293	283	307
VALUE (MILLIONS OF U.S. DOLLARS)								
Total	2,977	2,665	2,930	2,615	2,921	2,670	3,042	2,954
FISH:								
Total	1,585	1,275	1,418	1,137	1,403	1,261	1,370	1,320
Cod, Atlantic	43	48	61	74	52	45	36	28
Flounder	140	120	113	145	144	136	127	150
Haddock	7	5	6	5	6	3	1	1
Halibut	73	85	97	100	54	62	85	67
Herring, sea	63	29	38	37	43	25	31	59
Jack mackerel	2	2	1	*	*	*	*	*
Menhaden	106	84	94	78	83	103	128	99
Ocean perch, Atlantic	4	1	1	1	1	1	1	5
Pollock	106	197	279	251	335	358	383	266
Salmon, Pacific	911	591	612	360	583	424	456	527
Tuna	121	104	105	75	91	91	108	103
Whiting	9	9	11	11	11	13	14	15
SHELLFISH:								
Total	1,392	1,390	1,512	1,478	1,518	1,409	1,672	1,634
Clams	135	135	130	125	127	138	122	140
Crabs	384	414	484	415	471	510	533	512
Lobsters, American	145	149	155	165	161	152	196	215
Oysters	78	84	94	98	115	87	133	102
Scallops	144	140	158	162	164	109	124	95
Shrimp	506	468	491	513	480	413	564	570

* Less than $500,000.

Source: U.S. Department of Agriculture, *Agricultural Statistics*, 1997.

CANADA

The value of Canada's fish catch in 1996 was below both the high 1995 level and the Can$1.64 billion of 1988 but above levels from 1989 to 1993 (data on the relatively small freshwater catch are not available for 1996, making exact comparisons impossible). During the 1988-1996 period, there were significant year-to-year variations in both value and quantity (Table 2). In 1995, when value reached Can$1.83 billion, high prices more than made up for an unusually low volume of about 891,000 metric tons. The largest volume was the 1.7 million tons for 1988. The smallest value was $1.47 billion in 1991.

Table 3 shows the 1996 ocean catch in volume and value terms. Total volume amounted to 841,522 tons (live weight), 208,766 of which were herring. Following at a distance were crab, shrimp, hake, scallop, redfish, lobster, and salmon, respectively. Atlantic Coast landings totaled 666,112 tons, and Pacific Coast landings (British Columbia) were 175,410.

Total value of the ocean catch was Can$1.46 billion (Table 3). The largest dollar returns, respectively, were for lobster, crab, shrimp, herring, scallop, and salmon. The largest producing province in dollar terms (Table 2) was Nova Scotia (Can $459 million), followed by British Columbia ($362 million), and Newfoundland (Can$270 million).

TABLE 2

CANADA: COMMERCIAL FISH CATCHES AND VALUES BY PROVINCE, 1988-1996

(Monetary values in thousands of Canadian dollars)

	1988	1989	1990	1991	1992	1993	1994	1995	1996
QUANTITY (METRIC TONS, LIVE WEIGHT)									
Total fisheries	1,703,387	1,656,286	1,690,656	1,558,212	1,362,452	1,201,636	1,071,549	890,843	.....
Seafisheries, total	1,651,084	1,605,087	1,645,938	1,509,032	1,319,816	1,163,185	1,035,215	852,636	841,522
Atlantic	1,385,137	1,317,902	1,342,428	1,192,445	1,020,426	872,288	719,330	633,301	666,112
Nova Scotia	520,431	491,485	493,382	517,335	492,930	402,416	340,154	268,860	278,325
New Brunswick	157,355	166,046	157,790	116,787	126,492	122,041	142,077	132,476	106,818
Prince Edward Island	57,912	56,931	71,504	59,644	47,372	43,370	47,630	46,079	51,740
Quebec	88,232	81,467	74,330	73,871	70,427	58,552	51,230	47,786	47,316
Newfoundland	561,207	521,973	545,422	424,808	283,205	245,909	138,239	138,100	181,913
Pacific	265,947	287,185	303,510	316,587	299,390	290,897	315,885	219,335	175,410
Freshwater fish	52,303	51,199	44,718	49,180	42,636	38,451	36,334	38,207	.....
VALUE (THOUSANDS OF CANADIAN DOLLARS)									
Total fisheries	1,643,869	1,496,078	1,500,161	1,467,353	1,478,147	1,484,073	1,770,874	1,831,830	.....
Seafisheries, total	1,550,036	1,413,388	1,433,748	1,393,950	1,400,267	1,422,343	1,701,042	1,755,240	1,463,158
Atlantic	1,016,478	959,775	953,930	1,013,769	984,140	957,547	1,125,948	1,344,240	1,101,001
Nova Scotia	437,504	438,204	444,970	498,544	511,572	478,092	502,876	504,896	459,427
New Brunswick	118,781	103,202	93,254	97,153	104,850	106,625	174,379	207,989	145,110
Prince Edward Island	68,955	69,813	62,092	70,612	79,715	73,708	93,327	114,383	95,171
Quebec	99,192	82,197	74,140	85,487	88,881	91,560	130,026	177,165	131,197
Newfoundland	292,046	266,359	279,474	261,973	199,122	207,562	225,340	339,807	270,096
Pacific	533,558	453,613	479,818	380,181	416,127	464,796	575,094	411,000	362,157
Freshwater fish	93,833	82,690	66,413	73,403	77,880	61,730	69,832	76,590	.....

Note: Seafisheries includes marine plants and miscellaneous.

Source: DFO, Ottawa, Ontario through Statistics Canada.

Table 3

Canada: Volume and Value of Atlantic and Pacific Coasts Commercial Fish and Shellfish Landings, by Species, 1996

	Quantity, metric tons, live weight			Value, thousands of Canadian dollars		
	Atlantic	Pacific	Total Canada	Atlantic	Pacific	Total Canada
Grand total	666,112	175,410	841,522	1,101,001	362,157	1,463,158
Subtotal, fish and shellfish	638,531	175,052	813,583	1,082,655	339,983	1,422,638
Groundfish, total	110,251	81,004	191,255	112,528	84,655	197,183
Cod	15,169	906	16,075	20,976	687	21,663
Haddock	10,217	0	10,217	16,213	0	16,213
Redfish	21,446	23,526	44,972	8,348	15,134	23,482
Halibut	1,053	5,466	6,519	6,964	32,526	39,490
Flatfishes	9,150	5,275	14,425	12,220	3,289	15,509
Greenland turbot	9,966	4,597	14,563	17,885	1,011	18,896
Pollock	9,528	2,156	11,684	7,133	670	7,803
Hake	29,106	33,034	62,140	19,071	3,303	22,374
Cusk	1,400	0	1,400	1,353	0	1,353
Catfish	422	0	422	167	0	167
Other	2,793	6,044	8,837	2,197	28,035	30,232
Pelagic and other finfish, total	251,263	64,592	315,855	85,326	135,987	221,313
Herring	186,619	22,147	208,766	41,510	54,969	96,479
Mackerel	19,687	363	20,050	9,234	1,159	10,393
Swordfish	724	0	724	6,296	0	6,296
Tuna	830	456	1,286	12,308	1,225	13,533
Alewife	5,082	0	5,082	1358	0	1,358
Eel	357	0	357	3,234	0	3,234
Salmon	57	34,194	34,251	337	74,442	74,779
Skate	3,777	802	4,579	1,311	205	1,516
Smelt	835	0	835	908	1	,909
Capelin	30,856	0	30,856	5,941	0	5,941
Other	2,439	6,630	9,069	2,889	3,986	6,875
Shellfish, total	277,017	29,456	306,473	884,801	119,341	1,004,142
Clams/quahaug	28,129	3,113	31,242	23,784	38,225	62,009
Oyster	2,106	5,274	7,380	3,966	6,071	10,037
Scallop	58,756	100	58,856	88,580	493	89,073
Squid	8,746	75	8,821	4,414	89	4,503
Mussel	7,891	0	7,891	9,676	0	9,676
Lobster	39,359	0	39,359	376,663	0	376,663
Shrimp	55,264	9,139	64,403	142,167	37,482	179,649
Crab, queen	65,673	0	65,673	221,404	0	221,404
Crab, other	5,043	4,942	9,985	4,156	23,395	27,551
Sea urchin	3,650	5,821	9,471	8,289	11,999	20,288
Other	2,400	992	3,392	1,702	1,587	3,289
Other marine products, total	27,581	358	27,939	18,346	22,174	40,520
Marine plants	24,260	0	24,260	2,347	0	2,347
Lumpfish roe	1,451	0	1,451	9,580	0	9,580
Miscellaneous	1,870	358	2,228	6,419	22,174	28,593

Source: DFO/MPO- Ottawa, Ontario, Canada.

MEXICO

Table 4 shows Mexican fish and shellfish catches from 1987 to 1994. The total catch declined from 1.46 million metric tons in 1987 to 1.26 million in 1994. However, fish and shellfish going for direct human consumption during that period rose from just under 900,000 tons to about one million. The primary difference was in anchovies, sardines, and other fish for indirect human consumption, which declined from nearly 520,000 tons in 1987 to some 217,000 in 1994. The largest catch was tuna, followed by mojarra, sardines, and shrimp. A significant amount of the total was caught but not registered (some 219,000 tons in 1994). The largest decline from 1987 to 1994 was in sardines, down 36 percent. The largest increase was in pulpo (octopus), which more than doubled to nearly 18,000 tons.

INTERNATIONAL TRADE

United States. Table 5 shows U.S. trade in fresh and processed fish and shellfish from 1992 to 1996 and NAFTA trade from 1989 to 1996. Table 6 gives a breakdown of U.S. trade by products and data for the first half of 1997 compared with the same period of 1996 (figures are unavailable on U.S. trade in fresh fish alone). U.S. exports in 1996 totaled $2.9 billion, down considerably from the recent high of $3.4 billion in 1992. Through the first half of 1997, they declined another 8.18 percent from the same period of 1996. Salmon (whole or eviscerated) was the largest single export, at $463 million in 1996, compared with $682 million in 1992 (Table 6).

U.S. imports of fish and seafood totaled $6.6 billion in 1996, compared with $6.7 billion the previous year and $5.6 billion in 1992. The resulting trade deficit reached a high for the period of $3.7 billion in 1996. Morever, imports through the first half of 1997 were up more than 12 percent from the first half of 1996, for a first-half trade deficit of $2.4 billion—more than the $2.3 billion deficit for all of 1992. Shrimp, at $2.5 billion in 1996, is by far the largest category and was the biggest import gainer in the first half of 1997, rising more than 16 percent. Tuna was the next largest import, at $630 million in 1996. The growth in imports of salmon to a new high in 1996 and a 7.8 percent gain in the first half of 1997 reflect increased quantities of inexpensive farmed salmon from suppliers like Chile (Table 6). The International Trade Commission was expected to hear a suit in November 1997 brought by eight U.S. salmon farmers who claim they are being unfairly priced out of the market by cheap Chilean-subsidized imports (*The Wall Street Journal*, October 13, 1997).

Canada. U.S. fish and seafood exports to Canada rose sevenfold between 1989 and 1996, to $434 million, while Canada's exports to the United States fell 37 percent to $702 million. The U.S. trade deficit with Canada thus fell from over $1 billion to $269 million during that period. Canadian exports to Mexico at their peak in 1996 were only $300,000 (Table 5).

Mexico. U.S. exports to Mexico are small. They rose 44 percent between 1989 and 1996, to $36 million but were well off their 1994 high of $53 million (Table 5). Mexican exports to the United States in 1996 were $429 million, up only slightly from their 1989 level but more than double the low of $205 million in 1992. Mexican exports to Canada are at about the same low level as Canadian exports to Mexico.

NAFTA. The United States has a sizable trade deficit with NAFTA, but it declined in 1996 to $661 million, slightly above the 1993 low and less than half the 1989 deficit of $1.4 billion (Table 5). All of the improvement came because of a reduction in the deficit with Canada, as that with Mexico rose substantially. Mexico's positive trade balance was $393 million in 1996, slightly above the $341 million of 1989 but more than double the 1992 low. Canada's surplus fell from $1.1 million in 1989 to $269 million in 1996.

TABLE 4

MEXICO: FISH AND SHELLFISH CATCH, PRINCIPAL SPECIES, 1987-1994

(Metric tons)

	1987	1988	1989	1990	1991	1992	1993	1994
Total	1,464,841	1,394,174	1,519,882	1,416,117	1,483,603	1,246,438	1,191,600	1,260,019
Human consumption, total	897,438	906,776	935,454	1,056,984	1,000,219	963,400	965,900	1,005,754
Abulon (abalone)	.....	.....	.....	.....	.....	.....	2,030	1,506
Almeja	13,661	20,684	27,583	30,073	29,798	12,818	12,419	15,961
Atun (tuna)	102,566	113,607	116,812	118,928	119,561	121,270	104,328	109,496
Bagre (catfish)	3,367	3,660	3,469	5,538	4,836	6,579	6,715	5,940
Bandera (shoal, flying fish)	5,896	6,409	.....	.....	.....	4,649	5,720	6,102
Baqueta (grouper)	.....	.....	.....	.....	.....	.....	2,154	1,791
Barriete	9,380	9,508	15,127	5,845	9,967	9,293	15,115	10,201
Bonito (type of tuna)	538	6,275	12,459	10,744	1,130	845	1,352	8,695
Camaron (shrimp)	83,882	73,200	74,804	62,747	70,580	66,210	74,361	76,324
Caracol (snail)	5,119	5,185	6,742	5,945	3,825	8,229	7,749	7,532
Carpa (carp)	26,170	27,056	22,504	27,214	28,079	22,407	25,173	23,726
Cazon	9,715	10,711	12,378	16,082	12,848	12,732	13,190	11,531
Charal	7,800	7,522	7,898	8,579	7,821	7,495	7,516	7,838
Corvina	4,422	4,074	3,822	3,909	3,033	3,440	3,448	3,168
Erizo (globefish)	4,145	3,512	.....	.....	.....	2,397	2,766	3,393
Guachinango	7,637	6,400	6,160	8,887	8,726	11,475	11,617	9,084
Jaiba (crayfish)	7,999	8,932	10,156	12,028	11,183	11,497	13,783	15,980
Jurel (horse mackerel)	3,934	4,346	3,700	3,125	2,580	2,837	3,563	3,913
Langosta (lobster)	2,451	2,351	.....	.....	.....	2,028	2,019	1,878
Langostino (king prawn)	3,224	3,667	.....	.....	.....	1,488	4,631	3,507
Lebrancha	3,285	2,829	2,206	3,050	2,885	3,604	5,464	6,626
Lisa	14,260	13,947	12,875	12,612	10,128	10,156	10,237	9,623
Lobina	.....	.....	.....	.....	.....	.....	1,407	1,598
Macarela (mackerel)	2,497	4,602	.....	.....	.....	20,162	20,617	12,106
Mero (grouper)	11,794	13,440	11,717	13,641	14,883	14,046	14,546	14,197
Mojarra	86,731	87,020	85,274	95,522	86,625	89,706	92,981	92,891
Ostion	50,715	56,118	56,599	52,614	38,799	32,145	25,847	36,699
Pargo	3,266	3,612	3,423	3,615	3,472	4,565	4,660	3,500
Peto	.....	.....	.....	.....	.....	.....	3,299	3,126
Pulpo (octopus)	8,417	8,346	13,436	16,387	16,809	17,125	16,995	17,801
Robalo	4,619	5,196	4,370	2,799	2,530	2,838	4,311	4,708
Ronco	2,932	2,934	2,324	1,404	1,105	1,928	2,661	2,610
Sardina (sardines)	123,772	107,521	110,335	115,236	95,246	74,076	66,481	79,315
Sierra (sawfish)	9,569	7,831	10,773	15,555	13,764	13,780	15,822	13,926
Tiburon (shark)	16,662	21,267	.....	.....	.....	21,932	23,119	23,824
Tortuga (turtle)	873	1,122	.....	.....	.....	.....	.....	.....
Trucha (trout)	.....	.....	.....	.....	.....	.....	5,300	4,721
Other	64,622	63,131	117,368	208,891	191,670	142,151	123,807	131,970
Caught but unregistered	191,518	190,761	181,140	196,014	208,336	207,497	208,697	218,947
Indirect human consumption, total	519,605	456,628	527,697	339,809	427,948	220,448	164,632	217,116
Industrial anchovies	159,132	113,386	104,748	1	11,026	3,406	1,717	1,117
Accompanying fauna	3,822	1,833	3,062	5,444	5,281	5,444	9,193	5,588
Unpackable fish	2,452	2,234	18,879	14,693	39,031	20,783	25,313	20,474
Industrial sardines	354,199	339,175	401,008	319,671	372,610	190,814	128,409	189,937
For industrial use, total	47,798	30,771	56,731	64,324	55,437	62,589	61,068	37,149
Seaweed and sargazo	46,309	29,120	54,744	62,602	53,826	61,590	60,416	36,706
Mosco (Bluebottle)	511	648	.....	.....	.....	.....	.....	.....
Other	978	1,003	1,987	1,722	1,611	998	652	443

Source: INEGI, *Anuario Estadístico*, 1995.

Despite the lack of improvement through 1996, the U.S. Department of Commerce expects that seafood exports to Mexico could grow in coming years because of a lowering of Mexican tariffs under NAFTA and improvements in transportation. Prior to implementation of NAFTA, U.S. seafood imports were generally duty-free, whereas Mexico had duties ranging from 0 to 20 percent. Under NAFTA, duties that were not immediately eliminated will be phased out over a 15-year period. U.S. fisheries in the Gulf of Mexico, in particular, should see some increase in exports to Mexico. For some time, resorts such as Acapulco and Cancun have been importing high-quality fresh and frozen products like spiny lobster, snapper, and swordfish by air from Miami and other southern cities. Other fish likely to find buyers in Mexico are mullet, Spanish mackerel, shark, squid, snow crab, and new-to-market products like farmed catfish. Mexican exports to the United States could be stimulated if U.S. seafood companies take advantage of liberalized regulations on U.S. and Canadian investment in Mexican companies; however, the impact of this change is expected to be minimal, according to NOAA.

TABLE 5

INTERNATIONAL TRADE, FISHERIES AND MARINE PRODUCTS

(MILLIONS OF U.S. DOLLARS)

	1989	1990	1991	1992	1993	1994	1995	1996
GLOBAL TRADE, U.S.								
IMPORTS								
Value	.....	.....	.....	5,619	5,765	6,553	6,702	6,621
EXPORTS								
Value	.....	.....	.....	3,354	2,959	3,002	3,138	2,897
Trade Balance[1]	.....	.....	.....	(2,265.0)	(2,806.0)	(3,551.0)	(3,564.0)	(3,724.0)
BILATERAL TRADE: NAFTA[2]								
U.S. exports to Canada	61.1	321.4	341.4	303.9	328.9	355.7	410.6	433.5
Canadian exports to U.S.	1,117.9	1,057.2	1,043.9	816.6	744.2	761.9	680.4	702.1
U.S. exports to Mexico	23.5	21.3	32.4	43.2	44.7	53.0	34.3	36.4
Mexican exports to U.S.	364.9	247.2	249.7	204.5	267.2	322.2	429.9	429.1
Canadian exports to Mexico[3]	0.7	0.0	0.0	0.0	0.2	0.3	0.1	0.2
Mexican exports to Canada[3]	0.1	0.0	0.0	0.1	0.0	0.1	0.2	0.3
TRADE BALANCES WITHIN NAFTA[1]								
Canada	1,057.4	735.8	702.5	512.6	415.5	406.4	269.7	268.5
Mexico	340.8	225.9	217.3	161.4	222.3	269.0	395.7	392.8
United States	(1,398.3)	(961.8)	(919.9)	(673.9)	(637.8)	(675.3)	(665.4)	(661.3)

1. Parentheses indicate an excess of imports over exports. Because of commodity coding and other data differences among the three countries, these trade balances are only rough estimates and should be used with caution.

2. Amounts less than U.S. $100,000 shown as zero.

3. Includes trapping.

Source for U.S. Global Trade: U.S. Department of Commerce, International Trade Administration.

Source for U.S. -Canada and U.S.-Mexico Bilateral Trade: U.S. Bureau of the Census.

Source for Canada-Mexico and Mexico-Canada Bilateral Trade: Statistics Canada, Foreign Trade Division, Special tabulation, March 1997, converted to U.S. dollars by the editors.

TABLE 6

U.S. GLOBAL TRADE IN EDIBLE FISH AND SEAFOOD PRODUCTS

(Thousands of U.S. dollars)

| | 1992 | 1993 | 1994 | 1995 | 1996 | JANUARY-JUNE | | |
						1996	1997	PERCENT CHANGE
Exports, total	3,354,070*	2,959,231	3,002,345	3,138,238	2,897,028	1,725,915	1,584,768	-8.18
Salmon, whole or eviscerated	681,663	583,060	518,413	545,283	462,982	317,001	183,661	-42.06
Salmon, canned	154,401	160,416	161,577	174,946*	152,809	72,446	71,183	-1.74
Crab and crabmeat	448,050*	417,660	349,136	209,070	168,711	99,186	82,790	-16.53
Surimi (fish paste)	367,627*	274,322	318,850	353,433	268,095	130,459	169,204	29.7
Roe and urchin (fish eggs)	421,396	415,319	408,963	505,873	461,618	323,012	270,126	-16.37
Other edible fish and seafood	1,280,934	1,108,454	1,245,405	1,349,633	1,382,813	783,811	807,805	3.06
Imports, total	5,618,659	5,764,729	6,552,875	6,702,469*	6,620,817	3,504,770	3,938,330	12.37
Shrimp	2,018,944	2,170,863	2,669,004*	2,582,185	2,458,431	1,149,783	1,335,876	16.19
Tuna	583,827	533,268	627,962	609,254	629,254	358,925	388,306	8.19
Lobster	483,603	416,030	497,656	548,061	505,096	290,379	280,283	-3.48
Groundfish, fillet/steak	591,535	516,977	487,359	510,725	497,827	284,161	310,675	9.33
Salmon, whole or eviscerated	233,889	246,838	252,966	280,781	304,612*	183,065	197,319	7.77
Other edible fish and seafood	1,706,862	1,880,753	2,017,928	2,171,462	2,225,597*	1,238,427	1,425,871	15.14

* Denotes highest levels since at least CY 1970.

Source: U.S Bureau of the Census trade data.

MINING

THE UNITED STATES

Products and Processes. The products of mining include ores containing metals such as iron, copper, lead, zinc, gold, silver, and platinum. They also include coal; oil and natural gas; and quarrying of stone, gravel, sand, phosphate rock, potash, chemical fertilizers, salt, and other nonmetallic minerals. The United States is the world's top consumer of most of these products, as well as a leading producer and exporter of several. It is the world's largest energy producer, ranking second to Saudi Arabia in crude oil production, to Russia in natural gas production, and to China in coal production.

It is second only to Australia in the export of coal and ranks first in world reserves of coal, sixth in natural gas, and ninth in oil. The United States also leads the world in production of beryllium, molybdenum, salt, and phosphate rock. And it is the second largest producer of copper (behind Chile), and gold (behind South Africa).

In the energy group, oil supplies about 40 percent of U.S. energy requirements, followed by 25 percent for natural gas and 22 percent for coal. About half of the crude oil used must be imported, and this dependence on imports is growing as U.S. reserves are drawn down and consumption increases. On the other hand, coal is in abundant supply, accounting for about 90 percent of U.S. energy reserves, versus 3 percent for crude oil and 4 percent for natural gas. The United States also produces all but about 13 percent of domestic natural gas needs (with most imports coming from Canada).

As shown in Table 1, oil and gas extraction is by far the largest subindustry, accounting for 69 percent of the value of industry shipments and 54 percent of employment in 1992. Coal mining is next in size (16.7 percent of 1992 industry shipment value and 21.1 percent of employment), followed by mining and quarrying of nonmetallic minerals (8.4 percent of shipments and 16.6 percent of employment), and metal mining (6.6 percent of shipments and 8.3 percent of employment). Within metal mining, the largest ore producers in terms of 1992 shipment value were gold/silver and gold mines, followed by producers of copper and iron ores. Surface and underground mining of bituminous coal and lignite (brown coal) accounted for 97 percent of the value of 1992 coal industry shipments. Crushed and broken stone was the largest single component under mining and quarrying, followed by sand and gravel and chemical and fertilizer mineral mining.

Employment in the mining industry has declined throughout the past decade and will continue on a downward track through 2005. The U.S. Bureau of Labor Statistics projects employment that year at only 439,100, compared with 610,000 in 1993 (Table 2). Most of the reduction will be in the oil and natural gas workforce, but employment in mining of coal, nonmetallic minerals, and metals also will decline.

TABLE 1

U.S. COMPONENT INDUSTRIES OF MINING SECTOR (SIC 10-14), 1992

(Monetary values in millions of U.S. dollars)

INDUSTRY	SIC	ESTABLISH-MENTS	VALUE OF SHIPMENTS	VALUE ADDED	CAPITAL EXPENDITURE	EMPLOY-MENT[1]	PAYROLL
MINING		30,790	162,994.2	114,453.9	17,142.6	637,300	24,178.0
METAL MINING	10	1,025	10,765.1	7,624.5	1,542.3	52,900	2,111.1
Iron ores	1011	40	1,714.8	985.4	53.0	8,700	348.2
Copper ores	1021	62	3,374.9	2,169.4	516.1	14,900	550.0
Lead and zinc ores	1031	44	471.9	287.1	22.4	2,800	113.3
Gold and silver ores	104	427	4,454.6	3,646.0	.....	19,200	825.3
Gold ores	1041	403	4,340.0	3,588.4	889.9	18,200	784.0
Silver ores	1044	24	114.6	57.6	.....	1,000	41.3
Metal mining services	1081	266	350.4	258.8	.....	3,300	117.0
Miscellaneous metal ores	109	186	398.5	277.8	60.9	4,000	157.3
Uranium-radium-vanadium ores	1094	78	86.3	69.4	28.7	1,200	49.6
Metal ores, n.e.c.	1099	108	312.2	208.4	32.2	2,800	107.7
COAL MINING	12	3,070	27,132.3	17,250.3	1,942.7	134,500	5,462.7
Bituminous coal and lignite mining	122	2,636	26,433.5	16,774.8	1,912.4	128,500	5,283.6
Bituminous coal and lignite surface mining	1221	1,503	13,824.4	8,025.9	901.2	55,500	2,272.1
Bituminous coal, underground	1222	1,133	12,609.1	8,748.9	1,011.2	73,000	3,011.5
Anthracite mining	1231	76	160.4	97.2	4.1	1,400	38.6
Coal mining services	1241	358	538.4	378.3	26.2	4,600	140.5
OIL AND GAS EXTRACTION	13	20,891	111,522.7	79,950.5	12,520.3	344,100	13,374.5
Crude petroleum and natural gas	1311	9,391	72,245.4	66,508.7	10,954.7	174,300	8,404.3
Natural gas liquids	1321	591	27,213.8	4,242.2	614.6	12,000	513.7
Oil and gas field services	138	10,909	12,063.5	9,199.6	951.0	157,800	4,456.5
Drilling oil and gas wells	1381	2,125	3,583.6	2,516.4	289.0	47,700	1,370.6
Oil and gas exploration services	1382	1,490	964.6	725.0	171.5	13,700	460.3
Oil and gas field services, n.e.c.	1389	7,294	7,515.3	5,958.2	490.5	96,400	2,625.6
NONMETALLIC MINING AND QUARRYING	14	5,804	13,574.1	9,628.6	1,137.3	105,800	3,229.7
Dimension stone	1411	166	98.9	76.7	4.5	1,400	30.5
Crushed and broken stone, including riprap	142	2,142	5,001.9	3,620.6	424.1	41,600	1,206.9
Crushed and broken limestone	1422	1,432	3,178.3	2,270.0	255.9	27,700	784.8
Crushed and broken granite	1423	264	895.3	659.6	69.6	6,100	184.6
Crushed and broken stone, n.e.c.	1429	446	928.3	691.0	98.6	7,800	237.5
Sand and gravel	144	2,677	3,160.5	2,318.0	258.7	30,300	887.9
Construction sand and gravel	1442	2,516	2,749.7	2,040.2	233.1	27,100	790.3
Industrial sand	1446	161	410.8	277.8	25.6	3,200	97.6
Clay, ceramic, and refractory minerals	145	200	1,400.2	936.5	83.9	10,000	317.8
Kaolin and ball clay	1455	45	780.4	506.3	53.0	5,000	180.4
Clay and related minerals, n.e.c.	1459	155	619.8	430.2	30.9	5,000	137.4
Chemical and fertilizer mineral mining	147	160	3,127.4	2,121.8	308.9	15,000	579.0
Potash, soda, and borate minerals	1474	33	1,515.7	1,154.8	64.0	5,500	225.4
Phosphate rock	1475	28	1,188.9	690.0	134.9	5,400	192.7
Chemical and fertilizer mining, n.e.c.	1479	99	422.8	277.0	110.0	4,100	160.9
Nonmetallic minerals services	1481	178	188.9	136.0	14.8	2,000	52.0
Miscellaneous nonmetallic minerals	1499	281	596.3	419.0	42.4	5,500	155.6

1. Employment numbers from the economic censuses differ in definition and classification from the Bureau of Labor Statistics estimates in Table 2. Year-to-year comparisons between Table 1 and Table 2 are not appropriate.

Source: U.S. Bureau of the Census, 1992 Census of Mining.

TABLE 2

U.S. EMPLOYMENT AND EARNINGS: MINING

INDUSTRY	SIC	1993			2005
		EMPLOYMENT[1]		AVERAGE HOURLY EARNINGS (U.S. DOLLARS)[2]	PROJECTED EMPLOYMENT[3]
		NUMBER OF PERSONS	PERCENT OF INDUSTRY TOTAL		
ALL MINING	10-14	610,000	100.0	14.60	439,100
Metal mining	10	49,800	8.2	15.29	41,500
Iron ores	101	8,500	1.4	16.67	.....
Copper ores	102	15,000	2.5	14.03	.....
Coal mining	12	108,600	17.8	17.27	69,500
Bituminous coal and lignite mining	122	100,900	16.5	17.46	.....
Oil and gas extraction	13	349,800	57.3	14.14	240,300
Crude petroleum and natural gas	131	171,200	28.1	17.14	104,600
Oil and gas field services	138	173,500	28.4	12.32	135,700
Nonmetallic minerals, except fuels	14	101,500	16.6	12.70	87,800
Crushed and broken stone	142	38,100	6.2	12.01	.....
Sand and gravel	144	32,400	5.3	.....	.....
Chemical and fertilizer minerals	147	13,600	2.2	.....	.....

1. Total payroll employment.

2. Earnings of production workers, including overtime.

3. Number of persons, moderate projection by the U.S. Bureau of Labor Statistics.

FIGURE 1

U.S. EMPLOYMENT IN MINING

Percent distribution by region, 1995

The Southwest, which includes the big oil and natural gas producing states of Texas and Oklahoma, accounted for 41 percent of all mining employment in 1995. The Southeast, with 22 percent of 1995 employment, was in second place, mainly because of the large offshore oil production in the Gulf of Mexico and coal production in West Virginia and Kentucky. The third largest employer was the Pacific region, with 9 percent of the total, reflecting large oil production in Alaska (26 percent of U.S. oil production) and California, as well as sizable metal and nonmetallic mineral mining.

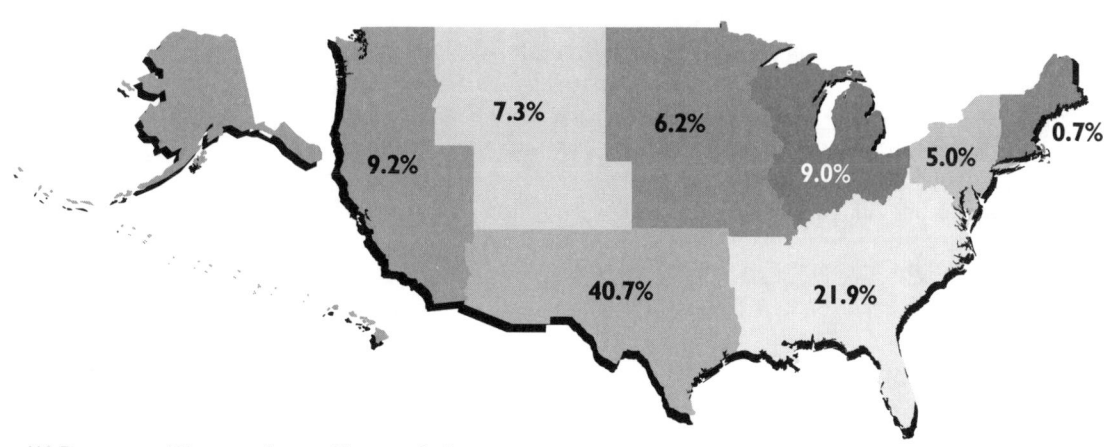

Source: U.S. Department of Commerce, Bureau of Economic Analysis.

What's New. In the **energy** group, strong prices in 1996 helped to stimulate oil exploration and development, which rose some 24 percent that year, according to an Arthur Andersen survey of Securities and Exchange Commission data. Crude oil prices declined during the first half of 1997 in response to increases in overseas supplies, but then rose some in the fall. Domestic crude oil production is in a downtrend, and refineries are operating at record levels. U.S. gasoline output in August 1997 rose to a new high for that month of just under eight million barrels a day, and gasoline prices rose sharply in August and again in September after having declined during the first half of 1997. Meanwhile, U.S. proven oil reserves have declined by more than four billion barrels since 1988, to some 22.5 billion barrels last year, and imports are accounting for half of U.S. consumption needs.

Energy use for transportation will rise one-third by 2015, according to projections by the Energy Information Administration (EIA) of the U.S. Department of Energy. Factors likely to keep consumption rising include low projected gasoline prices, a slowing of gains in fuel efficiency, and higher disposable incomes, which have stimulated sales of larger, more powerful vehicles. Consumption of gasoline, which accounts for more than half the energy demand from transportation, is expected to increase 0.8 percent a year up to 2015. However, environmental and energy legislation intended to reduce oil use will stimulate use of alternative fuels, which are projected to displace about 570,000 barrels of oil equivalent a day by 2015. Based on an economic growth rate of 1.9 percent a year, freight transport is projected to increase enough to boost diesel use by 1.5 percent a year. Jet fuel use is projected to rise by 2.3 percent a year, given continued economic growth and low jet fuel prices.

Sales of alternative-fuel vehicles (AFVs) resulting from federal and state requirements are projected to reach about 700,000 units in 2015, and total AFV sales may hit 1.6 million units, or 8.9 percent of all vehicle sales in 2015. The use of light-duty AFVs is seen displacing 389,000 barrels of oil per day in 2015, cutting carbon emissions from transportation by 5.2 million metric tons. These vehicles are fueled mainly by compressed natural gas or liquefied petroleum gas. Low Emission Vehicle Programs (LEVP) due to begin in New York in 1998 and California and Massachusetts in 2003 could boost electric and electric hybrid vehicles' share of the AFV market to about 33 percent by 2015.

U.S. demand for natural gas is expected to reach at least 29 quadrillion Btu (quads) by the year 2015, compared with 22.8 quadrillion in 1996, according to the American Gas Association's report *The Gas Energy Demand and Supply Outlook 1996-2015*. The study sees natural gas's share of electric generation rising to 22 percent by 2015 from 11 percent in 1995. Natural gas is expected to account for 46 percent of the commercial market in 2015, with demand growing at a relatively slow rate of 1 percent annually during the next two decades. Among the more dramatic growth areas, cooling equipment for residential and commercial markets will rise by some 10 million units and about 21 million residential heating customers will be added, bringing natural gas's share of the home heating market to 67 percent in 2015 from 58 percent in 1996. Demand in the industrial market is projected to increase 1.1 percent annually. U.S. proven reserves of natural gas amount to about a 55-year supply at current production levels, although most experts believe supplies will last several hundred years. During the past decade, annual additions of proven reserves have amounted to about 90 percent of natural gas production, and reserve replacement is expected to continue high as a result of new exploration and drilling technologies and consequent improvement in recovery rates.

Metal prices were weaker in 1997 than in 1996, with gold leading the decline. A gold mining scandal, increased production, rising stock prices, and gold sales by central bankers combined to diminish gold's sheen in 1997. These developments began in February with revelations that a reported gold discovery in Indonesia by Bre-X Mining contained virtually no gold and rock samples had been falsified. An improved inflation outlook, plus the need to raise cash, led a number of central banks to step up gold sales, which reached 220 metric tons in the first half of 1997, or only slightly under sales during all of 1996. The trend continued in the second half with a $2 billion gold sale by Australia followed by a round of selling in Europe. Some European Union members reportedly sold gold as a means of cutting deficits and improving balance sheets to meet European Monetary Union requirements. Moreover, Switzerland, the only developed country that still backs its currency with gold, moved to decouple the Swiss franc from gold.

After rising to over $400 a troy ounce in January 1996, gold prices fell to under $320 an ounce by early July 1997, their lowest level in more than a decade. In late 1997, gold plunged below $300 an ounce even as silver moved to its highest level in nine years.

On the other hand, demand for gold and gold jewelry has remained strong in the Middle East and India, and some producers recently have shut down high-cost operations, which could reduce future supply. According to the "Freemarket Gold & Money Report," central banks hold about 31 percent of the world supply as monetary gold reserves, while 31 percent is in monetary jewelry, 19 percent in fashion jewelry, 10 percent in industrial and dental uses, and 9 percent in private bar and coin.

Indian imports of silver rose to more than 100 million ounces in the first eight months of 1997. This was 50 percent more than in the same period of 1996 and just off the full-year 1996 record level of 105 million ounces, according to Goldfields Mineral Services LTD (GFMS) in a report for the Silver Institute. India's decision to deregulate silver imports was expected to give further impetus to 1997 imports. India accounted for 16 percent of world silver demand in 1996 and is the world's third largest fabricator of silver, with virtually all of its raw material coming from imports.

The 1997 recurrence of the El Niño weather pattern—a warming of the waters off the Pacific Coast of South America—threatened, in addition to Peruvian anchovies, some international mining operations. In Indonesia, drought attributed to El Niño caused PT International Nickel Indonesia (Inco) to reduce its production forecast to 75-80 million pounds of nickel in matte from a target of 92 million pounds. The drought led to a lowering of the level of the Soroako Reservoir on Sulawesi Island and thus limited the amount of hydroelectric power generated for mining by Inco, which is majority owned by Canada's Inco Ltd. In Papua-New Guinea, the Australian mining company BHP had to idle copper production at its OK Tedi mine because of drastically reduced water levels on the Fly River, its sole supply line from the mine.

FIGURE 2

U.S. EMPLOYMENT AND GROSS PRODUCT, MINING

Total payroll employment and inflation-adjusted gross product

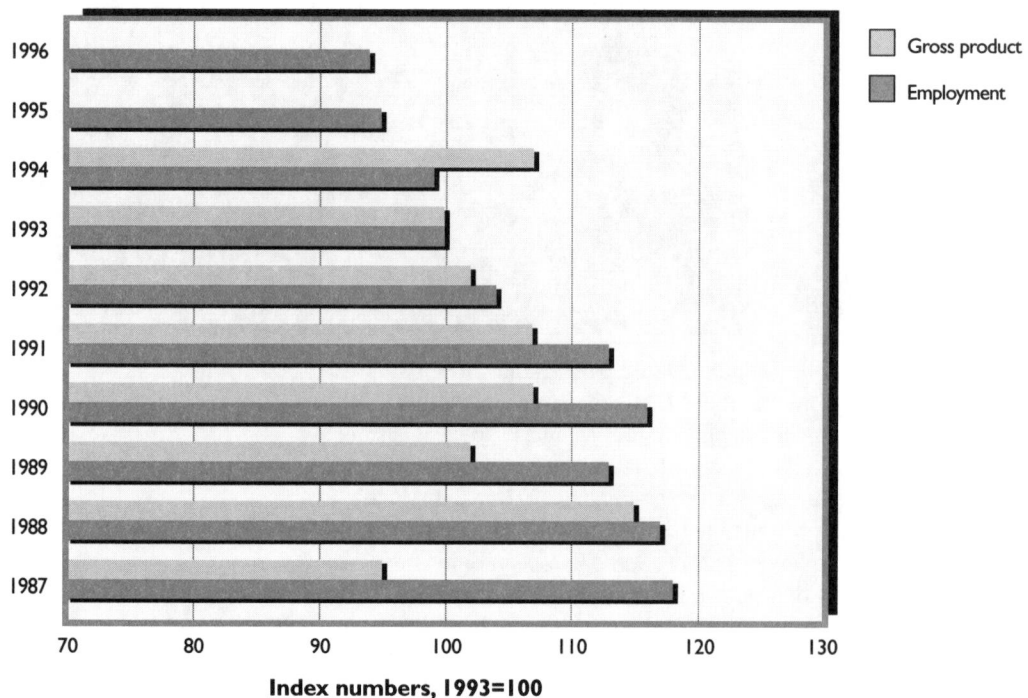

Index numbers, 1993=100

Source: U.S. Bureau of Labor Statistics, U.S. Department of Commerce, and estimates by the editors. Gross product data for 1995 and 1996 are not available.

Output. Employment in mining during the past decade declined in every year but 1990, while mining gross product fluctuated within a fairly narrow range through 1994 after peaking in 1988 and then pulling back sharply the following year (Figure 2).

Mining production in 1996, as measured by industrial production, was no higher than in 1988, as output during the intervening years declined to a low point in 1993 before heading gradually upward in the next three years (Table 3). During the 1987-1996 period, the fastest growth was in metal mining (up 5.7 percent annually). At the other extreme, crude oil production declined at an annual rate of 2.95 percent.

U.S. **crude oil** production has fallen from an average of just under nine million barrels per day in 1985 to 6.4 million estimated for 1997, according to the EIA. U.S. consumption, on the other hand, has risen from an annual average of 17.2 million barrels per day in 1993 to around 18.2 million currently. Prudhoe Bay, Alaska, is the largest U.S. oil field with about one million barrels per day of production. The next largest oil field also is in Alaska, followed in size by three in California. Alaskan oil production, however, declined in 1996 and 1997 as a result of reduced production from Prudhoe Bay and other North Slope fields.

The index of U.S. **natural gas** production rose at an annual rate of 1.58 percent from 1987 to 1996 (Table 3). Natural gas accounts for about 31 percent of U.S. energy production. In 1995, the United States produced 18.9 trillion cubic feet (Tcf) of natural gas and consumed 21.7 Tcf. From the mid-1970s to mid-1980s, production was depressed by weak demand and falling prices, but demand has grown about 37 percent since 1986, according to the American Gas Association. Restructuring of the natural gas pipeline industry, including a 60 percent increase in pipeline from Canada, has contributed to improvements in the industry. Production is expected to increase sharply in the future as a result of strong prices, abundant reserves, and improved recovery technology

U.S. production of **coal** rose at an annual rate of 1.52 percent from 1987 to 1996 (Table 3). Output hit a record of more than one billion short tons in 1990 but did not reach that level again until 1994. In 1995, output totaled 1.03 billion tons, of which 941 million went toward domestic consumption and 88.5 million were exported. Electric utilities account for most (87 percent) of U.S. coal consumption. Most of the rest goes to independent power producers and manufacturing industries.

Of 1995 coal output, 62 percent was bituminous coal, 29 percent sub-bituminous, and 9 percent lignite. Wyoming was the largest coal producer, followed by West Virginia and Kentucky. Production of low-sulfur coal in the West, particularly in Wyoming's Powder River Basin, has increased sharply since the 1995 implementation of Phase 1 of the Clean Air Act Amendments of 1990, which require lower sulfur emissions from coal combustion. The United States is estimated to have one-fourth of the 1.2 trillion short tons of recoverable coal reserves. This is about the same as reserves in all countries that made up the former Soviet Union and compares with 16 percent estimated for China, 9 percent for Australia, 7 percent for Germany, 5 percent for South Africa, and 9 percent for Poland.

According to the book *U.S. Gold Industry 1996,* **gold** production in 1995 totaled more than 10 million ounces for the fourth straight year. The price run up to over $400 a troy ounce in January 1996 prompted increases in mining and exploration and forecasts that production might rise another 20 percent over the next two years. Instead, prices crumpled to under $300 an ounce by late 1997. These problems notwithstanding, gold enjoys strong and growing demand in a number of industrial areas. Extremely fine, 99.999 percent pure gold bonding wire is used to connect computer circuits to the semiconductors, and gold paste is used in producing a printed circuit board. Gold is used in electrodes of the NASA-developed Heavy Ion Counter, as tiny transmitters in the diaphragms of telephone mouthpieces, in telephone wall jacks, in wiring for television and VCR circuits, and in the workings of telescopes and satellites.

U.S. **copper** mine production rose 2.7 percent in 1996 to an all-time high of 4.21 billion pounds, spurred by record domestic consumption of copper and copper alloy mill products, according to the Copper Development Association Inc. U.S. exports of mill products also were up by nearly 10 percent in 1996. The primary end-use market is building construction, which takes almost 43 percent of copper products. Another 24 percent goes for electrical and electronic products and about 12 percent each for transportation equipment and industrial machinery and equipment. The United States is virtually self-sufficient in copper and has been a net exporter for the past five years. Reserves will last hundreds of years and the high level of recycling of scrap—about 50 percent—will serve to extend these reserves and guarantee continued U.S. self-sufficiency in copper.

The following tabulation shows 1991 and 1996 production of coal and selected U.S. nonfuel minerals, as compiled by the U.S. Department of Interior, U.S. Geological Survey, *in thousands of metric tons (m.t.) unless otherwise noted:*

	1991	1996
Coal (millions of short tons)	996	1,063
Barite, sold or used	448	650
Beryllium, contained (m.t.)	174	217
Boron, production and marketable	626	622
Bromine, sold or used by producers	170	227
Clays (millions of m.t.)	9,550	9,530
Copper	1,630	1,900
Feldspar, marketable	580	990
Garnet, industrial, crude	51	54
Gold (m.t. of gold content)	294	325
Gypsum (millions of m.t.)	14	17
Iron ore (millions of m.t., usable)	57	60
Lead, concentrates	477	430
Lime (millions of m.t., sold or used by producers)	16	19
Molybdenum, moly content	53	57
Nickel (m.t. of nickel content)	5,520	—
alt (millions of m.t.)	36	40
Sand and gravel, construction (millions of m.t.)	708	963
Sand and gravel, industrial (millions of m.t.)	23	29
Silver (m.t. of silver content)	1,860	1,800
Stone, crushed (millions of m.t.)	997	1,300
Stone, dimension	1,100	1,300
Talc and pyrophyllite	1,040	976
Zinc, recoverable zinc content	518	620

Investment. Capacity utilization, an indication of past investment and future needs, amounted to 90.5 percent in 1996, the highest level in the 1987-1996 period (Table 3). In comparison, capacity utilization in 1987 was only 80.0 percent. Capacity utilization in 1996 was highest for stone and earth, which at 94.6 percent also was a record level for the decade ended in 1996, as was utilization by the oil and gas industry, at 91.6 percent in 1996. Metal mining had the fastest growth rate in capacity utilization (2.18 percent), but the high was reached in 1995. Utilization was virtually unchanged for coal between 1987 and 1996.

Prices. Producer prices rose at an annual rate of 1.33 percent from 1987 through 1996. A sharp rise in 1996 from the low 1995 average was the most dramatic price change in the past decade. In 1997, however, prices declined for a number of commodities.

During 1987-1996, stone and minerals showed the fastest price growth (2.13 percent annually). Oil and gas prices fluctuated widely from year to year, with 1996 the peak for the 10-year period.

TABLE 3

U.S. OUTPUT, INVESTMENT, AND PRICES: MINING

(Millions of U.S. dollars, except as noted)

	1987	1988	1989	1990	1991	1992	1993	1994	1995	1996	GROWTH RATE 1987-1996[1]
OUTPUT MEASURES:											
Industrial production, 1993=100, total mining	102.6	104.0	102.6	104.9	102.7	101.1	100.0	102.7	102.0	104.0	0.15
Metal mining	62.7	75.3	86.7	94.3	94.5	101.3	100.0	101.5	103.2	103.3	5.70
Coal mining	97.3	100.3	104.0	109.0	105.3	105.2	100.0	109.5	109.7	111.4	1.52
Oil and gas extraction	108.7	108.4	104.2	105.3	103.9	100.6	100.0	100.8	99.0	100.9	-0.82
Crude oil	122.4	119.6	111.9	108.1	109.0	105.0	100.0	97.3	95.2	93.5	-2.95
Natural gas	91.3	93.7	95.4	97.9	97.5	98.2	100.0	103.8	102.9	105.1	1.58
Stone and earth minerals	98.7	101.0	99.6	101.1	94.6	97.8	100.0	106.6	110.9	116.2	1.83
Gross domestic product:											
Current dollars	88,324	99,920	96,304	112,322	101,069	92,248	89,030	90,058	.....	.....	.....
Percent of total GDP	1.9	2.0	1.8	2.0	1.7	1.5	1.4	1.3	.....	.....	.....
Chained (1992) dollars	86,371	104,438	92,834	96,889	97,460	92,248	90,694	96,694	.....	.....	.....
INVESTMENT-RELATED MEASURES:											
Capacity utilization, percent, total mining	80.0	83.6	85.5	88.9	87.6	87.0	86.7	88.9	88.2	90.5	.....
Metal mining	70.9	80.5	85.4	85.7	82.9	86.9	83.9	85.4	87.3	86.1	.....
Coal mining	85.7	86.8	88.3	90.7	85.7	85.1	80.5	85.3	84.3	85.8	.....
Oil and gas extraction	78.9	82.8	85.0	89.1	89.2	87.7	88.6	90.1	88.8	91.6	.....
Stone and earth minerals	85.7	86.9	85.2	86.3	81.1	84.7	85.1	89.7	91.8	94.6	.....
Producer prices, 1993=100[2], total mining	98.2	92.4	100.0	107.2	102.7	100.7	100.0	96.0	93.0	110.6	1.33
Metal mining	143.6	144.5	143.9	134.0	117.9	109.9	100.0	116.8	145.5	132.1	-0.92
Coal mining	102.9	101.4	101.1	103.4	103.2	100.8	100.0	99.9	98.1	98.0	-0.54
Oil and gas extraction	97.5	89.9	99.3	108.5	102.2	100.4	100.0	93.3	87.0	111.3	1.48
Stone and earth minerals	88.5	90.9	93.6	95.7	97.9	98.9	100.0	101.4	104.2	107.0	2.13

1. Compound annual growth rate.

2. Prices received by domestic producers.

Source: Industrial production and capacity utilization: Federal Reserve Board of Governors; GDP: Bureau of Economic Analysis; Producer prices: Bureau of Labor Statistics.

Workforce and Employment. Employment in mining fell by 2.44 percent annually between 1987 and 1996, with declines in every year but 1990 (Table 4). Coal mining recorded the fastest rate of employment decline (off 5.59 percent annually for the period), while metal mining recorded the only gain (2.31 percent annually). Production worker employment declined at a slightly slower rate than that for all mining, so their share of the workforce rose to 74 percent in 1996 from 71-72 percent in most previous years. Employment of women also declined at a slightly slower rate than the total, but women still accounted for an extremely small share of employment (under 14 percent). Average hourly earnings of production workers during the past decade rose 2.46 annually in current dollars to $15.61, but fell at a 0.75 percent rate when adjusted for inflation. Hours worked per week in 1996 averaged 45.30, the highest level for the 10-year period.

TABLE 4

U.S. EMPLOYMENT, HOURS, AND EARNINGS: MINING

(Monetary values in U.S. dollars)

	1987	1988	1989	1990	1991	1992	1993	1994	1995	1996	CHANGE[1]
NUMBER OF EMPLOYEES, IN THOUSANDS:											
Total	717	713	692	709	689	635	610	601	581	574	-2.44
Metal mining	44	50	56	58	56	53	50	49	51	54	2.31
Coal mining	162	151	144	147	136	127	109	112	104	96	-5.59
Oil and gas extraction	402	400	381	395	393	353	350	337	320	317	-2.58
Stone and earth minerals extraction	110	112	111	110	105	102	102	104	105	106	-0.39
Production workers	511	512	493	509	489	448	431	427	424.0	426.0	-2.00
Percent of total	71.27	71.77	71.24	71.73	71.03	70.57	70.57	71.11	72.98	74.22	.....
Women	95	96	94	96	97	93	88	85	81	79	-2.03
Percent of total	13.25	13.44	13.61	13.48	14.12	14.65	14.48	14.19	13.94	13.76	.....
HOURS AND EARNINGS OF PRODUCTION WORKERS:											
AVERAGE HOURLY EARNINGS, U.S. DOLLARS[2]											
Current dollars	12.54	12.80	13.26	13.68	14.19	14.54	14.60	14.88	15.30	15.61	2.46
1992 dollars[3]	15.41	15.11	14.95	14.66	14.60	14.54	14.20	14.12	14.11	14.40	-0.75
Average weekly hours	.....	42.30	43.00	44.10	44.40	43.90	44.30	44.80	44.70	45.30	0.79
Average weekly earnings, current U.S. dollars	531.70	541.44	570.18	603.29	630.04	638.31	646.78	666.62	683.91	707.13	3.22

1. Compound annual growth rate, 1987-1996, except 1988-1996 for average weekly hours.

2. Including overtime.

3. Converted to 1992 dollars using Consumer Price Index for Urban Wage Earners and Clerical Workers.

Source: Bureau of Labor Statistics.

FIGURE 3

U.S. OCCUPATIONAL INJURY AND ILLNESS RATES: MINING, 1995

Incidence of nonfatal injuries and illnesses per 100 full-time workers

Nonfatal occupational illnesses and injuries in mining averaged 6.2 cases per 100 workers in 1995, compared with 8.1 percent for all private industry. The rate was highest for coal mining, at 9.1 percent, followed by 5.9 percent for oil and gas, 5.4 percent for nonmetallic minerals, and 5.2 percent for metals.

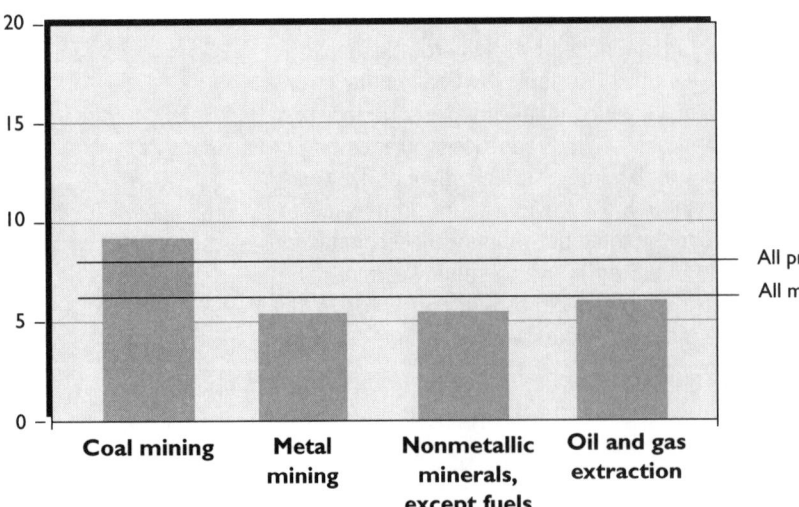

Source: U.S. Bureau of Labor Statistics.

TABLE 5

U.S. EMPLOYMENT PROJECTIONS BY MAJOR OCCUPATIONAL GROUP: MINING

OCCUPATION	1994 NUMBER OF EMPLOYEES	1994 PERCENT OF INDUSTRY TOTAL	PROJECTIONS, 2005 NUMBER OF EMPLOYEES LOW	MODERATE	HIGH	PERCENT OF INDUSTRY TOTAL, MODERATE PROJECTIONS
Total, all occupations	600,600	100.0	450,200	439,100	509,100	100.0
Executive, administrative, and managerial	69,837	11.6	56,018	50,885	59,761	11.6
Professional specialties	44,765	7.5	38,700	33,474	39,677	7.6
Technicians and related support	20,845	3.5	16,468	14,448	17,153	3.3
Marketing and sales	7,925	1.3	6,677	6,645	8,117	1.5
Administrative support including clerical	70,459	11.7	49,793	45,632	53,516	10.4
Service	4,822	0.8	3,254	3,168	3,672	0.7
Agriculture, forestry, and fisheries occupations	374	0.1	266	264	292	0.1
Precision production, craft, and repair	222,730	37.1	154,372	155,281	182,017	35.4
Operators, fabricators, assemblers	158,842	26.5	124,653	129,303	144,895	29.5

Source: Bureau of Labor Statistics, November 1995.

Employment in mining is projected to fall to 439,100 people by 2005, or 27 percent under that in 1994. Declines are seen for all occupational areas. Technicians, administrative support (including clerical), service occupations, and precision workers will account for smaller shares of the workforce in 2005.

FIGURE 4

U.S. CORPORATE INCOME AND WORKER EARNINGS: MINING, 1995

Corporate operating income and aggregate production worker earnings

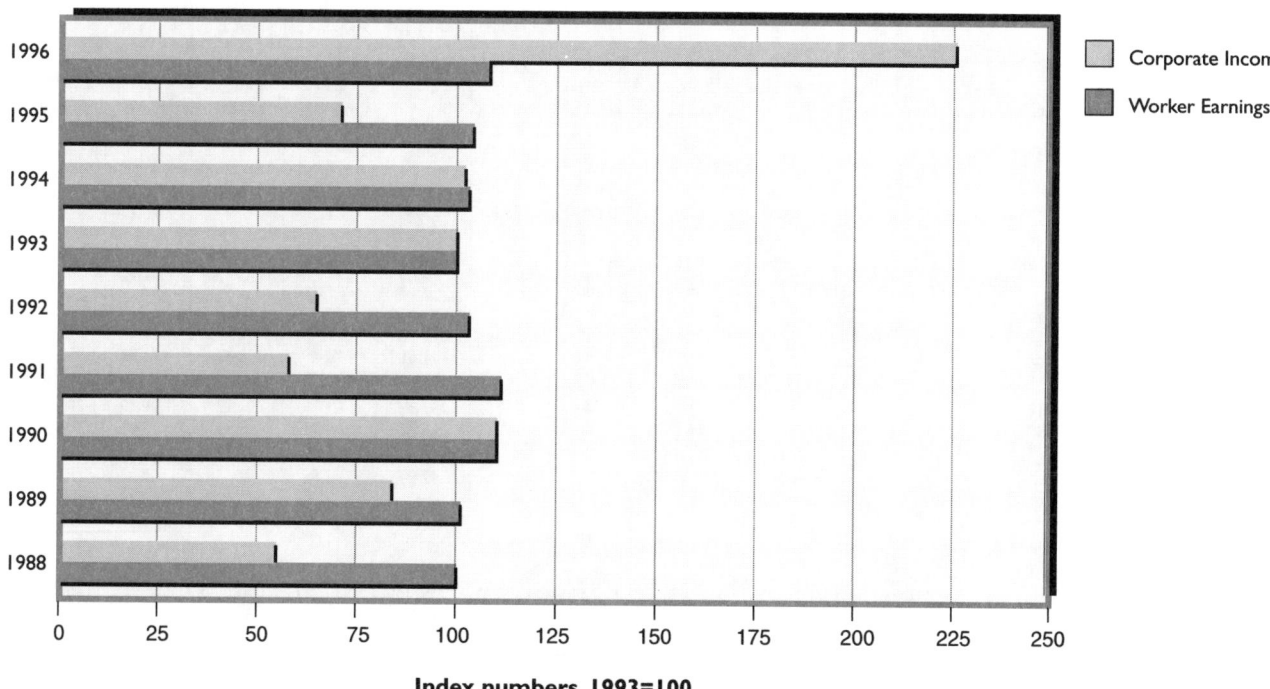

Index numbers, 1993=100

Source: U.S. Bureau of Labor Statistics, U.S. Bureau of the Census, and estimates by the editors.

Finance. While production worker earnings inched upward, corporate income showed some extreme fluctuations from 1988 to 1996, with the latest and most dramatic change being a tripling between 1995 and 1996 (Figure 4). Helped by high commodity prices, industry operating income soared to $7.4 billion in 1996 from $1.8 billion in 1988, for an annual growth rate of 19.4 percent (Table 6). Even faster was the 32.7 percent annual rate for after-tax income, which reached $5.6 billion in 1996, compared with a loss in 1992. In 1996, after-tax income amounted to 10.25 percent of sales (compared with a 3.41 percent average for 1988-1996) and 10.16 percent of stockholders' equity (3.97 percent). Inventories in 1996 were valued at $3.4 billion, and debt amounted to just under 28 percent of total assets, slightly below the average for 1988-1996.

TABLE 6

U.S. CORPORATE INCOME AND ASSETS: MINING[1]

(Millions of U.S. dollars)

	1988	1989	1990	1991	1992	1993	1994	1995	1996	CHANGE OR AVERAGE[2]
INCOME AND EXPENSES										
Sales and receipts	36,814	37,205	42,720	37,116	39,478	41,191	45,290	45,346	54,582	5.05
Depreciation and amortization	(4,726)	(5,079)	(5,544)	(5,734)	(6,252)	(6,519)	(7,111)	(7,556)	(8,503)	7.62
Other operating costs	(30,296)	(29,352)	(33,556)	(29,472)	(31,086)	(31,374)	(34,829)	(35,445)	(38,678)	3.10
Income from operations	1,792	2,775	3,620	1,911	2,139	3,297	3,348	2,344	7,402	19.40
Nonoperating income (expenditures)	(542)	(218)	(145)	(781)	(2,314)	(1,495)	(1,973)	(1,302)	(542)	.....
Income before taxes	1,250	2,558	3,475	1,130	(173)	1,802	1,377	1,044	6,858	23.71
Income after taxes	584	1,613	2,469	759	(240)	1,476	820	863	5,597	32.65
Cash dividends	1,095	2,264	1,544	1,000	1,079	880	1,023	2,405	1,516	4.15
Income retained in business	(511)	(652)	925	(241)	(1,320)	596	(201)	(1,542)	4,080	.....
Direct credits (charges)	(1,270)	(196)	(183)	(745)	170	271	(265)	(495)	(47)	.....
Ending retained earnings	6,293	6,175	6,440	2,593	418	5,689	5,933	5,869	10,342	6.41
ASSETS, END OF YEAR:										
Total	75,941	71,488	75,473	72,012	84,497	91,818	95,015	105,630	122,338	6.14
Accounts receivable	6,609	5,956	6,406	5,447	6,305	6,552	6,985	7,910	9,327	4.40
Inventories	3,099	2,437	2,516	2,392	2,637	2,669	2,973	3,404	3,381	1.09
Net property, plant and equipment	46,006	43,428	44,773	44,993	52,136	58,255	60,391	65,514	73,597	6.05
RATIOS, PERCENT:										
Income to sales:										
Before tax	3.40	6.88	8.13	3.04	-0.44	4.37	3.04	2.30	12.56	4.81
After tax	1.59	4.34	5.78	2.04	-0.61	3.58	1.81	1.90	10.25	3.41
Income to stockholders' equity:										
Before tax	4.47	9.05	11.43	3.94	-0.48	4.57	3.38	2.37	12.45	5.69
After tax	2.09	5.71	8.12	2.64	-0.66	3.74	2.01	1.96	10.16	3.97
Income to total assets:										
Before tax	1.65	3.58	4.60	1.57	-0.20	1.96	1.45	0.99	5.61	2.36
After tax	0.77	2.26	3.27	1.05	-0.28	1.61	0.86	0.82	4.58	1.66
As a percent of total assets:										
Property, plant and equipment	60.58	60.75	59.32	62.48	61.70	63.45	63.56	62.02	60.16	61.56
Short-term debt	0.69	1.19	1.81	1.24	0.73	0.72	0.98	0.75	0.61	0.97
Long-term debt	29.81	29.13	28.34	29.30	26.90	26.16	27.36	28.70	26.79	28.05
Stockholders' equity	36.83	39.54	40.27	39.85	42.72	42.99	42.86	41.73	45.03	41.31

1. Corporations with assets of $50 million and above.

2. For income and asset amounts: compound annual growth rate; for ratios, average of ratios for the years shown.

Source: U.S. Bureau of the Census, Quarterly Financial Report.

Notes: Parentheses ( ) indicate negative items, e.g., net expenses, charges, or losses. Net property, plant, and equipment is net of accumulated depreciation. Because the samples used to collect the data change, retained earnings at the end of a given year will not exactly equal the previous year's retained earnings plus the current year's retained income and credits.

CANADA

In 1993, Canada's extraction industries had 124,758 employees. About 41 percent of these were in mining, with metals accounting for 26.6 percent of all industry employees, non-metals for 7.8 percent, and coal for 6.2 percent. Some 26.6 percent of the employees were involved in extraction of crude petroleum and natural gas, 6.1 percent worked for quarries producing mainly stone and sand and gravel, and 26.6 percent were in services related to mining (Table 7).

TABLE 7

CANADA: COMPONENT INDUSTRIES OF MINING (CSIC 600-900), 1993

INDUSTRY	SIC	EMPLOYMENT[1]	
		NUMBER OF PERSONS	PERCENT OF INDUSTRY TOTAL
ALL MINING INDUSTRIES	600-900	124,758	100.0
Mining	600	50,736	40.7
Metal mining	610	33,231	26.6
Nonmetal mines	620	9,710	7.8
Coal mines	630	7,796	6.2
Crude petroleum and natural gas	700	33,193	26.6
Quarries	800	7,604	6.1
Stone quarries	810	2,114	1.7
Sand and gravel	820	5,490	4.4
Services related to minerals	900	33,225	26.6
Services related to petroleum	910	25,426	20.4
Services related to mining	920	7,799	6.3

Source: Adapted from Statistics Canada: CANSIM.

After a period of decline brought on by the price collapse in 1986, Canada's **oil** industry began a recovery in the early 1990s. Its output rose 21 percent between 1990 and 1995, to more than 1.8 million barrels a day, according to EIA. Improvements in exploration (such as seismic techniques), drilling (horizontal drilling), and production technology helped to bring about these gains. Drilling activity also rose sharply from about 2,000 wells in 1990 to more than 4,200 in 1994. Increased output in the early 1990s consisted largely of conventional heavy oil and synthetic oil. In addition, synthetic oil from bitumen in western Canadian oil sands accounts for about 21 percent of the country's crude oil supply. Offshore oil areas in eastern Canada also have grown in importance because of improved technology and their proximity to large markets in Canada and the northeastern United States. Western Canada (mainly Alberta) produces most of the country's oil, while most of the oil consumption is in central and eastern Canada and adjoining areas of the United States. As a result, the country has an extensive system of pipelines connecting the producing and consuming areas.

As with oil, Canada's **natural gas** industry is in an expansion phase, despite relatively low prices. The country produces about 5.3 trillion cubic feet (Tcf) of natural gas per year and is the world's second largest gas exporter. Much of this gas comes from the Western Canada Sedimentary Basin (WCSB), covering most of Alberta, Saskatchewan, British Columbia, and the Northwest Territories. Alberta alone accounts for most of Canada's 67 Tcf of natural gas reserves and along with other WCSB producers supplies almost 100 percent of the country's natural gas, as well as U.S. markets in California, the Pacific Northwest, the Midwest, and the Northeast. In addition to the traditional producing areas, the Yukon and Northwest Territories reportedly have up to 10.2 Tcf of undiscovered natural gas, although so far little exploration has been conducted there.

Canada is a major producer of **coal**, output of which totaled about 80 million short tons in 1994, according to the EIA. It also was the world's fourth largest coal exporter in 1994. Alberta accounts for about half the coal production, followed by British Columbia and Saskatchewan with 30 and 15 percent, respectively. About 90 percent of the coal goes for electric generation and the rest goes for steel production and other uses.

MEXICO

Mexico had 2,869 establishments and 94,251 employees involved in mining of metals, minerals, and fuel in 1993 (Table 9). Income (earnings plus benefits) of employees averaged 32,146 new pesos in 1993 ($10,291), with wages of the 58,261 miners averaging 21,554 ($6,900), compared with 51,111 ($16,362) for the 15,488 nonproduction employees. Nonmetallic minerals had the highest number of employees (34,412). Petroleum and natural gas had the highest average income for all employees, 57,670 new pesos ($18,462); the highest wages for production workers, 39,212 new pesos ($12,553); and the highest salaries for nonproduction employees, 84,954 new pesos ($27,197).

Mexican employment in mining declined at an annual rate of 5.46 percent from 1988 to 1995, with annual decreases ranging from 2.33 percent for extraction of carbon and graphite to 10.45 percent for nonmetallic minerals (Table 10). Industry gross domestic product originating totaled $5.2 billion in 1995, and the annual rate of gain for the 1988-1995 period was 1 percent. However, industry GDP was off slightly that year from 1994.

Despite these declines, Mexico has ambitious plans for its oil and natural gas industries. The country is a major non-OPEC **oil** producer and has the world's sixth largest oil company, PEMEX, which is state-owned and has a monopoly over exploration and extraction of all hydrocarbons. According to the EIA, Mexico has the second largest proven oil reserves in the Western Hemisphere after Venezuela. (Around 49.8 billion barrels were estimated at the beginning of 1997, although a study of reserves in the Bay of Campeche indicated they might be considerably lower than that.) Mexico's crude oil production in 1996 increased by more than 9 percent—the first major gain in more than 10 years and another 8 percent gain, to nearly 3.1 million barrels per day, is forecast for 1997. About 1.7 million barrels per day of the 1997 total is slated for export. Three-fourths of the production comes from offshore sites in the Bay of Campeche in the Gulf of Mexico.

Mexico only recently has begun to tap its **natural gas** reserves. The delay largely reflects a lack of past investment in pipeline for transporting gas from offshore and southern onshore locations to population centers inland and in the north. Currently, production is largely onshore in association with crude oil production, with only a third coming from offshore. Mexican plans include investing $2 billion in the northeastern gas field (Burgos) to double production there to 1 billion cubic feet by the year 2000. The government reportedly expects investment in Mexico's natural gas market to reach $1.4 billion by the year 2000, with some $900 million expected to be invested in natural gas distribution in Mexico City and $103 million in the central Bajio region. Legislation in 1995 opened natural gas transportation, storage, and distribution to private (including foreign) investment and allows private companies to import and export natural gas. Private investment in this sector is expected to total $3.5 billion during 1995-2000. Mexico's Energy Ministry expects production to increase by 10 percent annually during the 1996-2000 period, with domestic demand rising at an even faster 12 percent rate.

TABLE 9

MEXICO: COMPONENT INDUSTRIES OF MINING (CMAP 20), 1993

(Monetary values in 1993 Mexican New Pesos)

						ALL WORKERS								
						PAID WORKERS								
							PRODUCTION				NONPRODUCTION			
							MINERS		OTHERS					
INDUSTRY	CMAP	NUMBER OF UNITS	NUMBER	PERCENT OF INDUSTRY TOTAL	AVERAGE DAYS WORKED	REMUN-ERATION[1]	NUMBER	WAGES AND SALARIES	NUMBER	WAGES AND SALARIES	NUMBER	WAGES AND SALARIES	BENEFITS PER PAID EMPLOYEE	UNPAID WORKERS NUMBER
Mining	20	2,869	94,251	100	238	32,146	58,261	21,554	14,248	15,156.00	15,488	51,111	8,710	6,25
Carbon	21	35	7,099	8	275	24,375	5,497	6,090	722	8,046.00	857	39,965	14,062	2
Petroleum and natural gas	22	11	26,427	28	365	57,670	21,379	39,212	.....	.....	5,048	84,954	9,721	..
Extraction of metallic minerals	23	188	26,313	28	257	30,638	13,461	14,093	7080	19,072	5,656	38,400	10,087	11
Exploitation of nonmetallic minerals	29	2,635	34,412	37	236	15,300	17,924	10,837	6,446	11,652.00	3,927	28,348	5,154	6,11

1. Average annual remuneration including benefits.

2. Miners are those engaged in exploration or extraction—others are those engaged in benefication (processing).

Source: INEGI, Censos Economicos 1994.

TABLE 10

MEXICAN GROSS DOMESTIC PRODUCT AND EMPLOYMENT: MINING AND OIL-WELL INDUSTRIES, 1988-1995

	1988	1989	1990	1991	1992	1993	1994	1995	CHANGE[1]
GROSS DOMESTIC PRODUCT									
Millions of constant 1993 new pesos	15,134.33	15,090.35	15,602.48	15,765.20	15,963.08	16,257.50	16,669.70	16,223.03	1.00
Millions of constant 1993 U.S. dollars[2]	4,845.00	4,830.92	4,994.87	5,046.96	5,110.31	5,204.57	5,336.52	5,193.53	1.00
TOTAL EMPLOYMENT									
Mining	183,816	173,139	178,871	176,296	149,255	131,420	125,462	124,098	-5.46
Extraction of carbon and graphite	12,722	12,736	12,818	11,629	10,001	10,291	10,970	10,784	-2.33
Extraction of crude petroleum and natural gas	53,297	48,160	56,299	61,886	40,146	31,011	26,634	28,951	-8.35
Extraction of iron minerals	5,655	5,961	6,278	6,123	5,182	4,421	4,204	4,175	-4.24
Extraction of nonferrous metal minerals	44,291	38,113	35,040	29,583	28,260	26,086	24,795	23,589	-8.61
Quarry exploitation and extraction of clay and sand	50,790	50,658	51,065	51,188	51,663	51,014	50,601	48,723	-0.59
Extraction of other non-metallic minerals	17,061	17,511	17,371	15,887	14,003	8,597	8,258	7,876	-10.45

1. Compound annual growth rate.

2. Converted at 3.1237 new pesos to the U.S. dollar.

Source: Sistema se Cuentas Nacionales de Mexico, INEGI

INTERNATIONAL TRADE

United States. Value of U.S. mining product exports in 1996 totaled $7.3 billion, slightly above 1995's. In contrast, imports were $57.1 billion, up 12 percent from the previous year. The resulting trade deficit was $49.9 billion in 1996. Crude oil accounted for 95 percent of the 1996 imports and a similar share of the trade deficit.

One of the most dynamic trade areas has been in imports of crude oil, which have gained steadily in line with the extended growth in the U.S. economy. By 1996, U.S. net imports of oil and products had risen to 8.4 million barrels a day, or some 42 percent above those in 1987, according to the EIA. The American Petroleum Institute reports that petroleum imports (crude oil and products) in August 1997 reached 10.3 million barrels per day, compared with just under 10 million in August 1996. During January-June 1997, Venezuela supplied 17.4 percent of U.S. imports, Canada 14.7 percent, Saudi Arabia 14.0 percent, and Mexico 13.7 percent, according to API.

The U.S. Geological Survey estimates U.S. coal exports in 1995 at 88.5 million short tons, down from the 109.0 million shipped in 1991 but nearly one-fourth above the 1994 low of 71.4 million. About half of the exports went to Europe, one-quarter to Asia, and most of the rest to Canada and Brazil. Coal imports in 1995 totaled only 7.2 million tons.

U.S. imports of natural gas totaled 2.8 Tcf in 1995, with 2.7 Tcf coming from Canada, according to the EIA. That year, Canada accounted for about 12 percent of U.S. natural gas consumption.

U.S. gold exports normally account for around 36 percent of domestic production, which has totaled around 10 million ounces in recent years.

Canada. The value of U.S. mining product exports to Canada reached $1.5 billion in 1996, compared with $1.2 billion in 1989 (Table 11). In contrast, Canada's much larger exports to the United States more than doubled in that period to $14 billion, resulting in a 1996 U.S. trade deficit with Canada of $12.5 billion. Canadian exports to Mexico were extremely small in comparison, but they did rise by 77 percent between 1989 and 1996 to $70 million.

Mexico. U.S. exports to Mexico rose more than fourfold during the 1989-1996 period but, at $458 million in 1996, were dwarfed by the $6.6 billion in Mexican exports to the United States (Table 11). This left a U.S. trade deficit with Mexico of almost $6.2 billion in 1996. Excluding the exceptionally high 1989 figure, Mexican exports to Canada doubled between 1990 and 1996 to $139 million.

NAFTA. Both Canada and Mexico have large and growing NAFTA trade surpluses, reflecting their abundance of resources, particularly petroleum, and the close proximity of the world's largest petroleum consumer, the United States. Canada's trade surplus rose to $12.4 billion in 1996, 170 percent above the 1989 level, while Mexico's rose 41 percent during that period to $6.2 billion (Table 11). On the other hand, the U.S. trade deficit with its NAFTA partners reached $18.6 billion in 1996, compared with $9.0 billion in 1989.

TABLE 11

INTERNATIONAL TRADE: MINING

(Millions of U.S. dollars)

	1989	1990	1991	1992	1993	1994	1995	1996
GLOBAL TRADE, U.S.								
Value of imports, total	.....	.....	.....	.....	.....	.....	51,050.0	57,143.8
Metallic ores and concentrates	.....	.....	.....	.....	.....	.....	1,413.4	1,407.5
Coal	.....	.....	.....	.....	.....	.....	248.0	238.4
Crude petroleum and natural gas	.....	.....	.....	.....	.....	.....	48,494.7	54,462.6
Nonmetallic minerals, except fuels	.....	.....	.....	.....	.....	.....	893.9	1,035.3
Value of exports, total	.....	.....	.....	.....	.....	.....	7,159.0	7,283.6
Metallic ores and concentrates	.....	.....	.....	.....	.....	.....	1,561.9	1,091.4
Coal	.....	.....	.....	.....	.....	.....	3,572.1	3,693.8
Crude petroleum and natural gas	.....	.....	.....	.....	.....	.....	729.3	1,196.8
Nonmetallic minerals, except fuels	.....	.....	.....	.....	.....	.....	1,295.7	1,301.6
Trade balance	.....	.....	.....	.....	.....	.....	(43,891.0)	(49,860.2)
BILATERAL TRADE: NAFTA[1]								
U.S. exports to Canada	1,233.7	1,332.9	1,207.7	1,272.2	1,064.8	1,248.3	1,335.9	1,531.3
Canadian exports to U.S.	5,985.6	7,896.5	8,433.9	8,930.1	9,883.1	10,699.5	11,571.2	13,992.8
U.S. exports to Mexico	100.4	268.7	260.8	420.2	289.7	279.5	454.0	457.6
Mexican exports to U.S.	4,366.6	5,321.8	4,742.4	4,644.5	4,424.5	4,909.6	5,769.0	6,635.5
Canadian exports to Mexico	39.5	40.1	36.4	53.5	46.4	54.5	50.0	70.1
Mexican exports to Canada	205.8	67.6	92.3	158.5	171.2	107.6	93.9	139.2
TRADE BALANCES WITHIN NAFTA[1]								
Canada	4,585.6	6,536.1	7,170.3	7,552.9	8,693.5	9,398.1	10,191.4	12,392.4
Mexico	4,432.5	5,080.6	4,537.5	4,329.3	4,259.6	4,683.2	5,358.9	6,247.0
U.S.	(9,018.1)	(11,616.7)	(11,707.8)	(11,882.2)	(12,953.1)	(14,081.3)	(15,550.3)	(18,639.4)

1. Parentheses indicate an excess of imports over exports. Because of commodity coding and other data differences among the three countries, these trade balances are only rough estimates and should be used with caution.

Source for U.S. Global Trade: U.S. Bureau of the Census. Data before 1995 not available.

Source for U.S. -Canada and U.S.-Mexico Bilateral Trade: U.S. Bureau of the Census.

Source for Canada-Mexico and Mexico-Canada Bilateral Trade: Statistics Canada, Foreign Trade Division, Special tabulation, March 1997, converted to U.S. dollars by the editors.

CONSTRUCTION

THE UNITED STATES

Products and Processes. In 1996, the value of new construction put in place in the United States was $568.6 billion. The three main types of construction are private residential buildings (single-family homes, apartments, condominiums), private nonresidential buildings (industrial, office, hotels, motels, and other commercial), and public construction (schools, prisons, highways and streets, and other public buildings). Also included in private construction are construction of electric utilities and other public utility facilities, telecommunications facilities, farm buildings, and miscellaneous "nonbuilding" construction. The industry employed 5,400,000 people in 1996.

TABLE 1

U.S. COMPONENT INDUSTRIES OF CONSTRUCTION (SIC 15-17), 1992

(Monetary values in millions of U.S. dollars)

INDUSTRY	SIC	ESTABLISH-MENTS	NET VALUE OF CONSTRUCTION	VALUE ADDED	CAPITAL EXPENDITURE	EMPLOY-MENT[1]	PAYROLL
CONSTRUCTION	15-17	572,851	391,189.9	234,617.8	7,902.1	4,668,280	117,729.7
GENERAL BUILDING CONTRACTORS	15	168,407	114,722.2	63,116.8	1,442.7	1,096,859	27,077.6
Single-family housing construction	1521	107,495	33,660.2	17,183.0	461.8	403,754	7,277.9
Residential construction, n.e.c.	1522	6,490	4,337.9	2,453.7	51.7	48,803	1,160.6
Operative builders	1531	16,989	26,843.3	15,288.8	236.2	114,194	3,358.8
Industrial buildings and warehouses	1541	7,693	10,967.3	6,437.7	149.8	122,970	3,476.4
Nonresidential construction, n.e.c.	1542	29,739	38,913.4	21,753.6	543.3	407,138	11,804.0
HEAVY CONSTRUCTION CONTRACTORS	16	37,180	77,526.1	49,165.3	3,085.9	799,422	23,728.3
Highway and street construction	1611	10,090	27,863.0	15,710.7	1,281.5	257,356	7,357.7
Bridge, tunnel, and elevated highway construction	1622	1,041	5,316.0	3,078.3	155.2	43,701	1,485.5
Water, sewer, and utility lines	1623	10,233	17,587.4	11,734.1	765.5	194,252	5,624.4
Heavy construction, n.e.c.	1629	15,816	26,759.8	18,642.3	883.7	304,113	9,260.7
SPECIAL TRADE CONTRACTORS	17	367,263	198,941.6	122,335.7	3,373.6	2,771,999	66,923.8
Plumbing, heating, and air-conditioning	1711	75,395	50,755.7	29,431.5	754.2	612,516	16,613.2
Painting and paper hanging	1721	31,920	8,094.7	5,854.8	144.9	162,587	3,164.1
Electrical work	1731	54,022	38,541.0	23,548.3	508.2	487,072	13,623.8
Masonry, stone setting, and other stonework	1741	22,637	7,955.9	5,146.1	135.4	147,892	2,882.5
Plastering, dry wall, acoustical, and insulation work	1742	18,648	12,824.2	8,143.2	141.6	206,670	4,910.1
Terrazzo, tile, marble, and mosaic work	1743	6,499	2,322.6	1,358.0	27.4	34,012	774.8
Carpentry work	1751	38,210	11,334.5	6,759.7	155.1	177,601	3,488.8
Floor laying and other floor work, n.e.c.	1752	10,196	4,032.5	2,165.8	46.2	48,948	1,065.2
Roofing, siding, and sheet metal work	1761	27,569	15,589.8	8,906.0	232.7	215,545	4,622.5
Concrete work	1771	26,123	13,179.4	7,703.1	330.2	192,539	4,038.0
Water well drilling	1781	3,638	1,676.0	994.8	69.5	19,346	443.6
Structural steel erection	1791	3,792	4,486.7	3,021.0	77.3	57,986	1,628.9
Glass and glazing work	1793	4,590	2,634.1	1,423.9	23.6	32,067	795.9
Excavation work	1794	13,898	6,129.2	4,339.6	331.4	77,126	1,816.8
Wrecking and demolition work	1795	966	928.0	775.0	23.1	13,112	296.0
Installation or erection of building equipment, n.e.c.	1796	3,889	6,132.1	4,494.4	71.5	82,648	2,324.1
Special trade contractors, n.e.c.	1799	25,270	12,325.3	8,270.5	301.2	204,333	4,435.3

1. Employment numbers from the economic censuses differ in definition and classification from the Bureau of Labor Statistics estimates in Table 2. Year-to-year comparisons between Table 1 and Table 2 are not appropriate.

Source: U.S. Bureau of the Census, 1992 Census of Construction.

The industry is divided into three major subindustries: general building contractors, heavy construction contractors, and special trade contractors. Table 1 shows the net value of construction work for each subindustry in 1992 (the latest year for which economic census data are available). The largest subindustry was special trade contractors, responsible for slightly more than half of the total net value of construction work in 1992; general building contractors was the second largest, accounting for 29 percent of the total, followed by heavy construction contractors, with the remaining 20 percent.

Employment in the industry has been projected to grow substantially from its 1993 level of 4,668,000 to 5,500,000 by 2005, an increase of 17.8 percent. Growth is expected in all three subindustries, with special trade contractors accounting for most of the gain with an expected increase of more than 600,000 new workers.

TABLE 2

U.S. EMPLOYMENT AND EARNINGS: CONSTRUCTION

| | | 1993 | | | 2005 |
| | | EMPLOYMENT[1] | | AVERAGE HOURLY EARNINGS (U.S. DOLLARS)[2] | |
INDUSTRY	SIC	NUMBER OF PERSONS	PERCENT OF INDUSTRY TOTAL		PROJECTED EMPLOYMENT[3]
ALL CONSTRUCTION	15-17	4,668,000	100.0	14.38	5,500,000
General building contractors	15	1,119,500	24.0	13.64	1,233,600
Residential building construction	152	560,800	12.0	12.64	633,200
Operative builders	153	27,200	0.6	13.46	25,400
Nonresidential building construction	154	531,500	11.4	14.55	575,000
Heavy construction contractors	16	712,600	15.3	14.10	829,700
Highway and street construction	161	222,300	4.8	14.01	255,400
Heavy construction, except highway	162	490,200	10.5	14.14	574,300
Special trade contractors	17	2,835,600	60.7	14.73	3,436,700
Plumbing, heating, and air-conditioning	171	632,900	13.6	15.07	754,200
Painting and paper hanging	172	161,400	3.5	13.52	200,000
Electrical work	173	521,900	11.2	15.88	648,200
Masonry, stonework, and plastering	174	394,700	8.5	14.71	478,700
Carpentry and floor work	175	185,900	4.0	14.43	231,000
Roofing, siding, and sheet metal work	176	201,900	4.3	12.84	229,400
Concrete work	177	.....	.....	.....	271,800
All other special trade contractors	179	.....	.....	.....	623,400

1. Total payroll employment. Employment data from the economic censuses, shown in Table 1, differ in definition and classification from the Bureau of Labor Statistics estimates in this table. Year-to-year comparisons between Table 1 and Table 2 are not appropriate.

2. Earnings of nonsupervisory workers, including overtime.

3. Number of persons, moderate projection by the U.S. Bureau of Labor Statistics.

Source: Bureau of Labor Statistics.

FIGURE 1

U.S. EMPLOYMENT IN CONSTRUCTION

Percent distribution by region, 1995

In line with the distribution of total U.S. employment and population, employment in the construction industry is highest in the Southeast (26.7 percent of the total in 1995). It is lowest in the Rocky Mountain States (4.2 percent) and New England (5 percent).

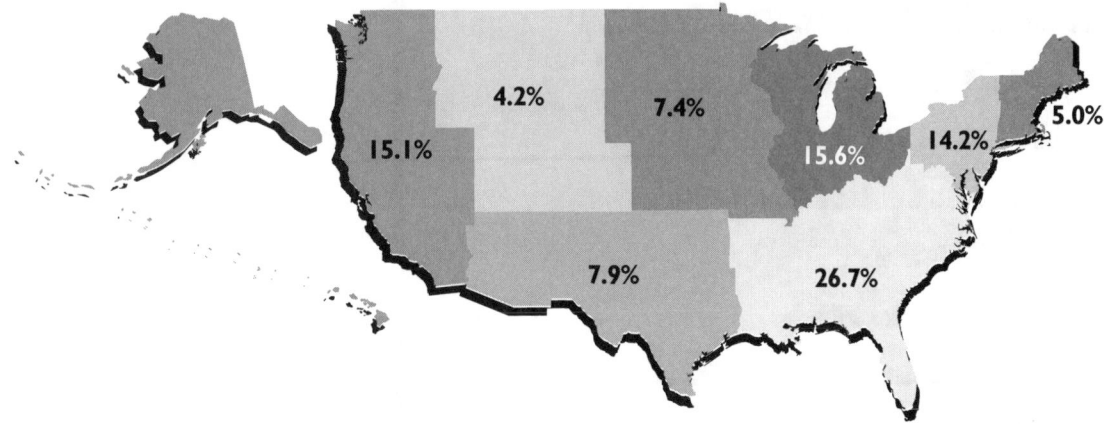

Source: U.S. Department of Commerce, Bureau of Economic Analysis.

What's New. According to the U.S. Bureau of the Census, the value of new construction put in place during July 1997 was estimated at a seasonally adjusted annual rate of $598.7 billion, a 6 percent increase over July 1996. Total new construction for the first seven months of 1997 was also 6 percent above the figure for the same time period in 1996.

New housing unit starts and building permits were down over the first nine months of 1997 when compared to the same time period for 1996. Relative to the 1,141,400 housing units started in the first nine months of 1996, the 1,116,000 started this year represent a 2 percent decline. Similarly, during the first nine months of 1997, 1,095,100 housing units were authorized by building permits compared with 1,102,000 units for the same period in 1996, a decrease of 1 percent.

A family earning the national median income of $43,500 could afford to buy 66.5 percent of the houses sold in the first quarter of 1997, according to the National Association of Home Builders' (NAHB) Housing Opportunity Index. This represents a slight increase over the fourth quarter of 1996 index of 63.4 percent. Kokomo, a small city in central Indiana, was the most affordable housing market, with a Housing Opportunity Index of 89.5 percent; San Francisco was the least affordable, with an index of 23 percent.

FIGURE 2

U.S. EMPLOYMENT IN CONSTRUCTION AND VALUE OF NEW CONSTRUCTION

Total payroll employment and inflation-adjusted value of new construction

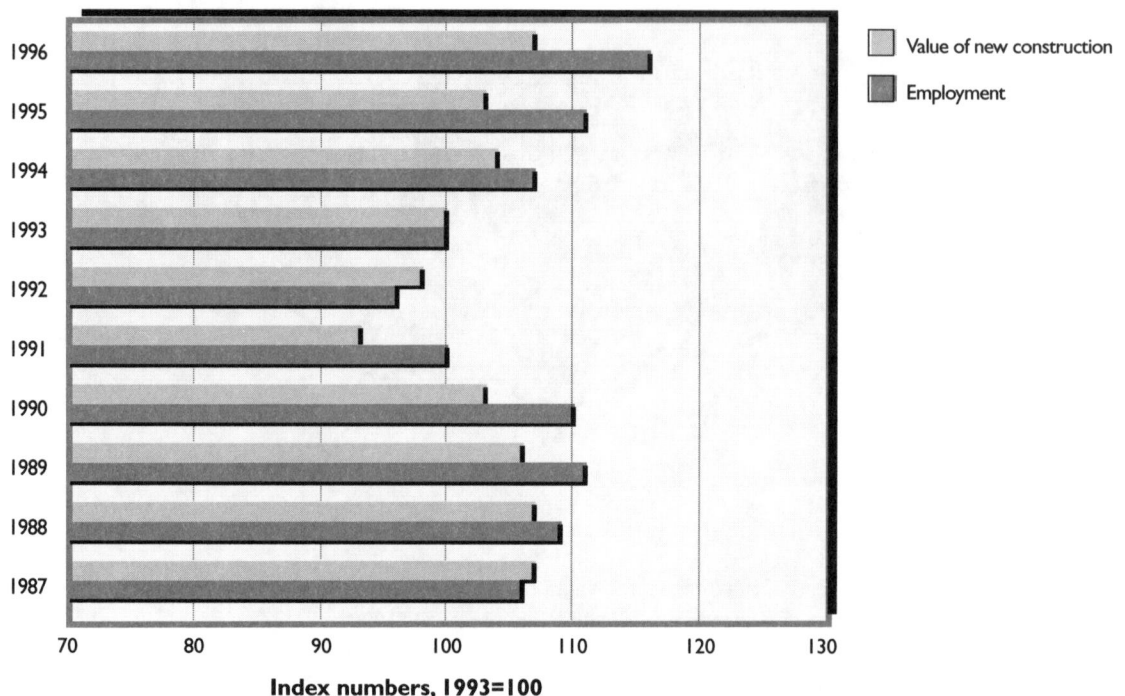

Source: U.S. Bureau of Labor Statistics, U.S. Bureau of the Census, and estimates by the editors.

Output. U.S. construction industry output, as measured by the value of new construction (in inflation-adjusted dollars), fell to a low for the 1987-1996 decade in 1991 before recovering nearly to its 1987 level in 1996. Employment in the industry followed a similar path, with its lowest point for the 1987-1996 period coming in 1992 (Figure 2). Since 1992, employment has expanded more rapidly than measured output.

In the residential sector, new housing starts fell over the period from 1,620,500 in 1987 to 1,474,700 in 1996. From a recessionary low of 1,013,900 in 1991, housing starts have risen 45 percent in the past five years, but they still had not regained their 1987 level by 1996.

In Table 3, the current dollar value of new construction is broken into three categories: private residential buildings, private nonresidential buildings, and total public construction. Of these three, total public construction grew the fastest from $90.7 billion in 1987 to $131.5 billion in 1996, at an annual rate of 4.21 percent. By 1996, public construction's share of total construction had risen from 20.5 percent in 1987 to 23 percent.

Investment. Information on new capital expenditures and research and development comparable to that elsewhere in the *Handbook* are unavailable for the construction industry. Some idea of the overall investment in construction can be obtained by looking at the shipments of the construction machinery and equipment industry (within the industrial and commercial equipment industry). In 1995, shipments of the construction machinery industry were $18.8 billion (1992 dollars), up from $13.1 billion in 1992.

Prices. Prices for construction, as measured by the implicit price deflator for new construction, have risen at an annual rate of 2.82 percent since 1987 (Table 3). The median price paid for a new single-family house in 1996 was $140,000, up from $133,900 in 1995, according to the U.S. Commerce Department's Bureau of the Census.

TABLE 3

U.S. OUTPUT, INVESTMENT, AND PRICES: CONSTRUCTION

(Millions of U.S. dollars, except as noted)

	1987	1988	1989	1990	1991	1992	1993	1994	1995	1996	GROWTH RATE 1987-1996[1]
Housing starts (thousands of units)	1,620.5	1,488.1	1,376.1	1,192.7	1,013.9	1,199.7	1,287.6	1,457.0	1,354.1	1,474.7	-1.04
Value of new construction (billions)											
Current dollars	441.7	455.6	469.8	468.5	424.2	452.1	478.6	519.9	534.1	568.6	2.85
Total private construction	351.0	360.9	371.6	361.1	314.1	336.2	362.7	399.4	406.8	437.1	2.47
Private residential buildings	194.7	198.1	196.6	182.9	157.8	187.8	210.5	238.9	230.6	247.2	2.69
Private nonresidential buildings	123.3	130.9	140.0	143.5	116.6	105.6	110.6	120.3	135.0	149.4	2.16
Total public construction	90.7	94.7	98.2	107.5	110.1	115.8	116.0	120.5	127.3	131.5	4.21
Chained (1992) dollars	495.2	492.5	489.4	475.2	427.2	452.0	461.1	481.0	474.4	493.6	-0.04
Output measures:											
Gross domestic product:											
Current dollars	216,976	233,365	242,232	245,232	228,766	229,657	243,601	269,232	.....	.....	.....
Percent of total GDP	4.6	4.6	4.5	4.3	3.9	3.7	3.7	3.9	.....	.....	.....
Chained (1992) dollars	239,601	248,790	251,915	247,503	229,036	229,657	236,079	253,056	.....	.....	.....
Implicit price deflator for new construction, 1993=100	86.0	89.2	92.6	95.1	95.8	96.4	100.0	104.2	108.4	110.5	2.82

1. Compound annual growth rate.

Source: Housing starts and new construction: Bureau of the Census, GDP: Bureau of Economic Analysis.

Workforce and Employment. Employment in the industry decreased from 4,958,000 in 1987 to a low of 4,492,000 in 1992 before climbing to a 1987-1996 high of 5,400,000 in 1996 (Table 4). The annual growth rate for the 1987-1996 time period was 0.95 percent; however, the growth rate was much higher, at 4.7 percent per year, from 1992 to 1996. Blue-collar construction workers' percent of total industry employment was down slightly over the period from 78.1 percent in 1987 to 77.5 percent in 1996. The number of women employed in the industry grew at an annual rate of 1.6 percent, faster than growth in overall employment.

Construction worker wages averaged $15.46 per hour in 1996, up slightly from $15.09 in 1995 (Table 4). In inflation-adjusted dollars (1992 dollars), wages actually fell at a rate of 1 percent per year from $15.61 per hour in 1987 to $14.26 in 1996. Average weekly hours worked increased over the period from 37.8 hours per week in 1987 to 39 hours per week in 1996.

TABLE 4

U.S. EMPLOYMENT, HOURS, AND EARNINGS: CONSTRUCTION

(Monetary values in U.S. dollars)

	1987	1988	1989	1990	1991	1992	1993	1994	1995	1996	CHANGE[1]
NUMBER OF EMPLOYEES, IN THOUSANDS:											
Total	4,958	5,098	5,171	5,120	4,650	4,492	4,668	4,986	5,160	5,400	0.95
Production workers	3,870	3,980	4,035	3,974	3,548	3,431	3,589	3,858	3,993	4,184	0.87
Percent of total	78.1	78.1	78.0	77.6	76.3	76.4	76.9	77.4	77.4	77.5	.....
Women	523	539	547	553	532	511	521	546	573	603	1.60
Percent of total	10.5	10.6	10.6	10.8	11.4	11.4	11.2	11.0	11.1	11.2	.....
HOURS AND EARNINGS OF PRODUCTION WORKERS:											
AVERAGE HOURLY EARNINGS, U.S. DOLLARS[2]											
Current dollars	12.71	13.08	13.54	13.77	14.00	14.15	14.38	14.73	15.09	15.46	2.20
1992 dollars[3]	15.61	15.44	15.26	14.76	14.40	14.15	13.99	13.98	13.92	14.26	-1.00
Average weekly hours	37.8	37.9	37.9	38.2	38.1	38.0	38.5	38.9	38.9	39.0	0.35
Average weekly earnings, current U.S. dollars	480.44	495.73	513.17	526.01	533.40	537.70	553.63	573.00	587.00	602.94	2.56

1. Compound annual growth rate, 1987-1996.

2. Including overtime.

3. Converted to 1992 dollars using Consumer Price Index for Urban Wage Earners and Clerical Workers.

Source: Bureau of Labor Statistics.

FIGURE 3

U.S. OCCUPATIONAL INJURY AND ILLNESS RATES: CONSTRUCTION, 1995

Incidence of nonfatal injuries and illnesses per 100 full-time workers

The 1995 incidence rate of illnesses and injuries in the construction industry, at 10.6 cases per 100 workers, was well above the average of 8.1 cases per 100 workers for all private industry. Special trades had the highest rate of incidence within the construction industry, at 11.1 cases per 100 workers.

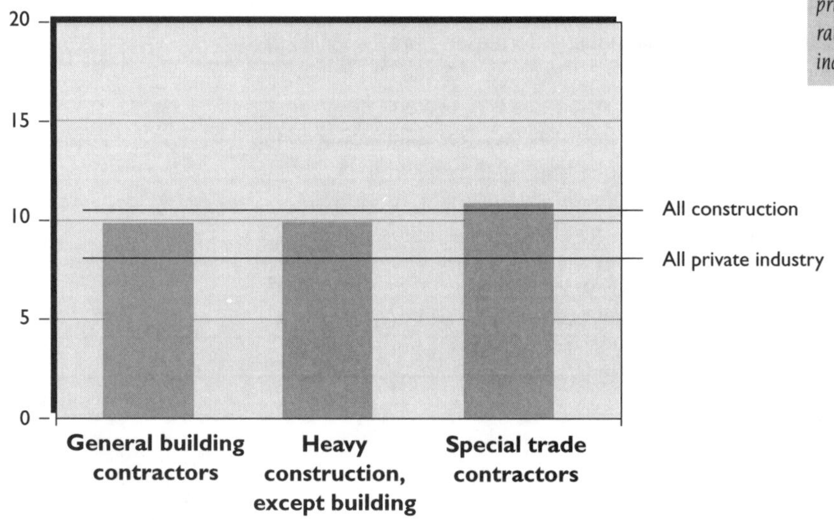

Source: U.S. Bureau of Labor Statistics.

TABLE 5

U.S. EMPLOYMENT PROJECTIONS BY MAJOR OCCUPATIONAL GROUP: CONSTRUCTION

OCCUPATION	1994		PROJECTIONS, 2005			
	NUMBER OF EMPLOYEES	PERCENT OF INDUSTRY TOTAL	NUMBER OF EMPLOYEES			PERCENT OF INDUSTRY TOTAL, MODERATE PROJECTIONS
			LOW	MODERATE	HIGH	
Total, all occupations	5,009,800	100.0	5,192,600	5,500,000	5,965,800	100.0
Executive, administrative, and managerial	592,327	11.8	657,278	696,189	755,150	12.7
Professional specialties	40,582	0.8	48,968	51,867	56,260	0.9
Technicians and related support	28,753	0.6	27,518	29,147	31,615	0.5
Marketing and sales	78,638	1.6	83,119	88,040	95,496	1.6
Administrative support including clerical	482,151	9.6	435,448	461,227	500,289	8.4
Service	17,563	0.4	16,912	17,913	19,431	0.3
Agriculture, forestry, and fisheries occupations	9,598	0.2	8,892	9,418	10,216	0.2
Precision production, craft, and repair	2,681,852	53.5	2,809,534	2,975,857	3,227,885	54.1
Operators, fabricators, assemblers	1,078,335	21.5	1,104,930	1,170,342	1,269,459	21.3

Source: Bureau of Labor Statistics, November 1995.

The construction industry is projected to employ almost 500,000 more people by the year 2005 (moderate assumptions), a substantial increase from the 5,009,800 employed in 1994. The bulk of the increase is in the skilled workers and laborers who account for most of industry employment, but the greatest percentage growth is projected to be among executives and professionals.

CANADA

Canada's construction industry had 440,322 employees in 1993, and new construction during that year was valued at Can$94.4 billion (Table 7). Construction in Canada is divided into four component industries: building, developing, and general contracting; industrial and heavy engineering construction; trade contracting; and services incidental to construction. Trade contracting, which is the rough equivalent of the U.S. category "special trade contractors" and includes construction specialties similar to those listed for the United States in Table 1, was the largest employer of the component industries with 59 percent of total industry employment. Building, developing, and contracting was second largest with 23.2 percent of employment.

The value of new construction put in place in Canada rose from Can$82 billion in 1987 to a 1987-1993 period peak of Can$102.4 billion in 1990. New construction fell substantially in 1991 to Can$94.2 billion and remained at approximately that level through 1993. Employment in the Canadian industry climbed from 529,918 in 1987 to 612,102 in 1989 before falling to 440,322 in 1993. By 1996, employment had recovered only modestly to 455,481. Current-dollar average weekly earnings increased over the period at an average annual rate of 2.8 percent to Can$693.50 in 1996.

The Canada Mortgage and Housing Corporation reports that new home building in Canada is expected to rise 20 percent in 1997 compared to 1996. Growth will continue into 1998 with an additional 6 percent increase over this year's figure. The provinces of Alberta and Ontario are expected to see the biggest gains in housing starts, resale volume, and prices.

TABLE 7

CANADA: COMPONENT INDUSTRIES OF CONSTRUCTION (CSIC 4000-4200, 4400), 1993

(Monetary values in Canadian dollars)

INDUSTRY	CSIC	EMPLOYMENT		VALUE OF NEW CONSTRUCTION (MILLIONS)
		NUMBER OF PERSONS	PERCENT OF INDUSTRY TOTAL	
CONSTRUCTION INDUSTRIES	4000-4400	440,322	100.0	Can $94,411.3
Building, developing, and general contracting	4000	102,327	23.2	.....
Residential building and development	4010	71,991	16.3	.....
Nonresidential building and development	4020	30,336	6.9	.....
Industrial and heavy (engineering) construction	4100	62,436	14.2	.....
Industrial construction (other than buildings)	4110	13,856	3.1	.....
Highway and heavy construction	4120	48,581	11.0	.....
Trade contracting	4200	259,914	59.0	.....
Services incidental to construction	4400	15,645	3.6	.....

Source: Adapted from Statistics Canada: CANSIM.

TABLE 8

CANADIAN EMPLOYMENT AND VALUE: CONSTRUCTION (CSIC 4000-4400), 1987-1996

(Monetary values in Canadian dollars)

	1987	1988	1989	1990	1991	1992	1993	1994	1995	1996	CHANGE[1]
All employees	529,918	557,618	612,102	602,729	502,953	458,162	440,322	450,879	455,021	455,481	-1.67
Production workers: Average weekly earnings	541.88	565.65	597.52	629.71	642.42	643.48	646.08	661.83	679.70	693.50	2.78
Value of new construction (millions)	81,971	90,871	100,412	102,367	94,155	91,861	94,411	.....	.....	.....	2.38

1. Compound annual growth rate for years shown.

Source: Adapted from Statistics Canada: CANSIM.

MEXICO

From 1988 to 1994, total employment in Mexico's construction industry increased from 1,939,971 employees to 3,053,734 employees and construction's inflation-adjusted gross product originating from the construction industry increased from 43.2 billion 1993 new pesos ($13.8 billion 1993 dollars) to 60 billion new pesos ($19.2 billion 1993 dollars). Employment and production in Mexican construction both fell substantially from 1994 to 1995 (employment, by 13.4 percent; production, by 23 percent) as part of the general economic downturn in Mexico in 1995.

TABLE 10

MEXICAN GROSS DOMESTIC PRODUCT AND EMPLOYMENT: CONSTRUCTION, 1988-1995

	1988	1989	1990	1991	1992	1993	1994	1995	CHANGE[1]
GROSS DOMESTIC PRODUCT:									
Millions of constant 1993 new pesos	43,240.3	43,995.3	48,040.2	50,385.4	53,753.5	55,379.0	60,047.7	45,958.4	0.87
Millions of constant 1993 U.S. dollars[2]	13,842.7	14,084.4	15,379.2	16,130.0	17,208.3	17,728.7	19,223.3	14,712.8	0.87
TOTAL EMPLOYMENT:									
Construction	1,939,971	2,179,170	2,528,703	2,666,818	2,734,161	2,837,982	3,053,734	2,645,841	4.53

1. Compound annual growth rate.

2. Converted at 3.1237 new pesos to the U.S. dollar.

Source: Sistema de Cuentas Nacionales de Mexico, INEGI.

MANUFACTURING OVERVIEW

In each of the three NAFTA countries, manufacturing output has increased in absolute terms (after adjustment for inflation) over the period since 1987, but has declined as a share of total GDP, as the trade and services share has grown. In the United States and Canada, productivity has increased and employment has declined; in Mexico, both productivity and employment have increased. The level and nature of manufacturing activity continue to be key factors in the vitality of the North American economy. Changes in manufacturing activity generate associated changes in trade and service activity; the large productivity gains achievable in manufacturing contribute to rising real incomes and higher standards of living; technological advances bring consumers affordable new products; and manufactured products constitute the predominant share of international trade. Each of the NAFTA countries has experienced important shifts in the composition of its manufacturing activity during the past decade, and each has greatly increased its manufactured exports to its NAFTA trading partners.

COMPARING MANUFACTURING IN NAFTA—A BRIEF LOOK AT THE METHODOLOGY

This section presents an overview of the manufacturing sectors in the United States, Canada, and Mexico, followed by chapters on each of the 20 major industry groups that constitute the U.S. manufacturing sector. For U.S. industries, the review for the most part covers the 10-year 1987-1996 period; it also includes more comprehensive industry profiles based on the 1992 U.S. economic census and employment profiles and projections for 1993, 1994, and 2005. Canadian data on employment and industry shipments generally are for 1987-1994, with more detailed industry profiles for 1993. Mexican data include a detailed breakdown of employment and earnings in 1993 and employment and gross domestic product (GDP) data for 1988-1995. International trade data are for 1989-1996.

Included are tables and charts showing the often quite different output and employment trends among the major industry groups within manufacturing. To the extent possible, the industries for all three countries are grouped in accordance with the U.S. Standard Industrial Classification (SIC) system. Since each NAFTA country currently uses its own classification system, this has involved some "regrouping" of Canadian and, particularly, Mexican industries to facilitate comparisons. An effort has been made to group the industries so as to achieve as meaningful comparisons as reasonably possible. It should also be noted that the official Mexican data used in these reports do not cover the export-oriented Maquiladora program, since its products never enter the domestic market. The Maquiladora program has attracted heavy investment from industries of the United States and other countries, including auto manufacturers, and is reported by some sources to account for about two-thirds of Mexico's recent trade surpluses (see "The Maquiladora-9802 Program: A Forerunner to NAFTA").

The NAFTA countries have recently agreed to adopt a common North American Industry Classification System (NAICS). This system, once it has come into full use, will greatly facilitate industry-by-industry comparisons among the three economies. More information about the industry classification systems and methodology used in this book may be found in "How to Use This Book."

THE UNITED STATES

Products and Processes. The U.S. manufacturing sector, which accounts for about 17 percent of GDP (compared to about 19 percent in the late 1980s) had industry shipments in 1996 worth some $3.7 trillion. The products of manufacturing range from the foods, clothing, household goods, and motor vehicles purchased directly by consumers to the metals, chemicals, lumber, concrete, computers, instruments, and heavy machinery used by other industries in their own production processes. The 20 industry groups that make up U.S. manufacturing vary widely in employment size and in contribution to total economic output.

Table 1 gives a profile of the manufacturing sector as it stood in 1992 (the latest year for which economic census data are available). The food and beverage industry ranked first in industry shipments in 1992, but a relatively high proportion of that value came from farm-grown materials. The chemical industry led in value added at the factory, followed closely by food and transportation equipment. The machinery industry was, and still is, the largest employer, while the high-paid transportation equipment industry had the largest payroll. Printing and publishing, where small companies still predominate, had the largest number of establishments.

Employment in manufacturing is expected to continue its long-term decline. Projections by the Bureau of Labor Statistics place employment in 2005 at just under 17 million (Table 2), compared with 18.1 million in 1993. Declines are foreseen for 14 industries. Those for which increases are expected include food and beverages, furniture and fixtures, paper and allied products, printing and publishing, rubber and plastic products, and miscellaneous manufacturing.

TABLE 1

UNITED STATES: COMPONENT INDUSTRIES OF MANUFACTURING SECTOR, 1992

(Monetary values in millions of U.S. dollars)

INDUSTRY	SIC	ESTABLISH-MENTS	VALUE OF SHIPMENTS	VALUE ADDED BY MANUFACTURE	NEW CAPITAL EXPENDI-TURES	EMPLOY-MENT[1]	PAYROLL
ALL MANUFACTURING		370,912	3,004,723	$1,426,699.8	$103,187.9	16,948,900	$494,108.8
Food and beverages	20	20,798	406,963	159,259.9	9,898.7	1,502,700	36,771.8
Tobacco products	21	114	35,198	27,206.6	389.3	38,000	1,524.4
Textile mill products	22	5,886	70,753	30,059.6	2,224.8	616,400	12,397.6
Apparel	23	23,093	71,658	36,422.6	945.0	985,300	15,325.1
Lumber and wood products	24	35,807	81,565	33,153.6	1,760.1	655,800	13,881.8
Furniture and fixtures	25	11,658	43,826	22,839.7	821.4	471,100	10,227.0
Paper and allied products	26	6,416	133,201	60,174.0	7,962.4	626,300	20,491.9
Printing and publishing	27	65,392	166,153	112,445.6	5,372.0	1,492,100	41,136.1
Chemicals and allied products	28	12,004	305,420	164,346.2	16,380.9	848,600	32,501.9
Petroleum and coal products	29	2,124	150,227	23,408.4	6,576.8	114,400	4,966.8
Rubber and plastic products	30	15,842	113,593	58,651.8	4,791.8	906,700	23,156.0
Leather and leather products	31	2,040	9,694	4,527.0	134.5	101,100	1,806.0
Stone, clay, and glass	32	16,254	62,521	34,641.2	2,457.6	468,800	13,113.1
Primary metals	33	6,501	138,287	52,027.2	5,294.0	662,100	22,202.4
Fabricated metals	34	36,429	166,532	83,761.4	4,437.5	1,362,300	38,961.8
Industrial and commercial machinery and computer equipment	35	53,956	258,661	132,922.7	8,056.8	1,738,900	57,230.9
Electronic and other electrical equipment	36	16,922	216,764	121,157.6	8,978.2	1,438,800	44,196.5
Transportation equipment	37	11,287	399,269	158,325.6	11,038.2	1,646,900	62,733.7
Instruments	38	11,354	134,940	89,393.8	4,617.9	907,100	33,067.0
Miscellaneous manufacturing	39	17,035	39,498	21,975.3	1,050.0	365,500	8,417.0

1. Employment numbers from the economic censuses differ in definition and classification from the Bureau of Labor Statistics estimates in Table 2. Year-to-year comparisons between Table 1 and Table 2 are not appropriate.

Source: U.S. Bureau of the Census, 1992 Census of Manufactures.

TABLE 2

U.S. EMPLOYMENT AND EARNINGS: ALL MANUFACTURING

| INDUSTRY | SIC | 1993 | | | 2005 |
| | | EMPLOYMENT[1] | | AVERAGE HOURLY EARNINGS (U.S. DOLLARS)[2] | PROJECTED EMPLOYMENT[3] |
		NUMBER OF PERSONS	PERCENT OF INDUSTRY TOTAL		
ALL MANUFACTURING		18,075,000	100.0	$ 11.74	16,990,500
Food and beverages	20	1,679,600	9.3	10.45	1,696,200
Tobacco products	21	43,700	0.2	16.89	26,300
Textile mill products	22	675,100	3.7	8.88	568,100
Apparel	23	989,100	5.5	7.09	771,600
Lumber and wood products	24	709,100	3.9	9.61	684,700
Furniture and fixtures	25	486,900	2.7	9.27	514,800
Paper and allied products	26	691,700	3.8	13.42	708,200
Printing and publishing	27	1,516,700	8.4	11.93	1,627,300
Chemicals and allied products	28	1,080,500	6.0	14.82	1,067,000
Petroleum and coal products	29	151,500	0.8	18.53	140,300
Rubber and plastic products	30	909,000	5.0	10.57	1,030,000
Leather and leather products	31	117,200	0.6	7.63	65,100
Stone, clay, and glass	32	517,000	2.9	11.85	433,900
Primary metals	33	683,100	3.8	13.99	531,600
Fabricated metals	34	1,338,500	7.4	11.69	1,180,500
Industrial and commercial machinery and computer equipment	35	1,930,600	10.7	12.73	1,768,900
Electronic and other electrical equipment	36	1,525,700	8.4	11.24	1,407,600
Transportation equipment	37	1,756,200	9.7	15.80	1,567,400
Instruments	38	895,500	5.0	12.23	797,500
Miscellaneous manufacturing	39	378,300	2.1	9.39	403,500

1. Total payroll employment. Employment data from the economic censuses, shown in Table 1, differ in definition and classification from the Bureau of Labor Statistics estimates in this table. Year-to-year comparisons between Table 1 and Table 2 are not appropriate.

2. Earnings of production workers, including overtime.

3. Number of persons, moderate projection by the U.S. Bureau of Labor Statistics.

Source: Bureau of Labor Statistics.

FIGURE 1

U.S. EMPLOYMENT IN ALL MANUFACTURING

Percent distribution by region, 1995

Manufacturing employment is highest in the Southeast, which had 26 percent of the U.S. manufacturing workforce in 1995. But it is in the Great Lakes region that the share of manufacturing employment (23 percent) notably exceeds the share of total employment (17 percent).

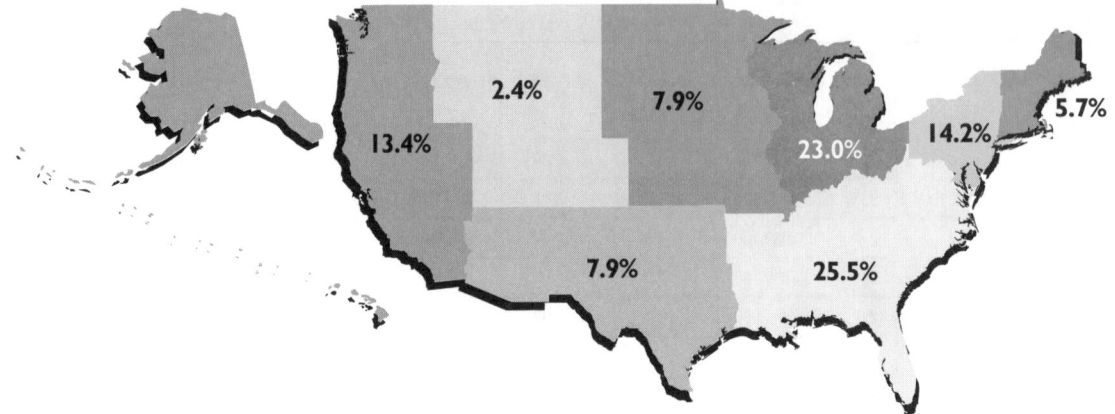

Source: U.S. Department of Commerce, Bureau of Economic Analysis.

What's New. The strength shown by the manufacturing sector in the last few years continued into 1997. Industrial production during the first eight months of 1997 averaged 4.9 percent above the 1996 period. Most of the strength was in durable goods, which make up 54 percent of total manufacturing production. Industrial production of durable goods was up 6.5 percent, while nondurable goods production rose 3.0 percent

Shipments data paint a similar picture: total current-dollar manufacturers' shipments were up 5.7 percent in the first half of 1997, compared to the year earlier period, with durable goods shipments up 7.2 percent and nondurables up only 3.9 percent. New orders and unfilled orders were at high levels at mid-year, and the factory inventory to sales ratio was at a historic low, indicating that manufacturing activity could continue at a brisk pace for the near future.

Along with its relatively rapid output growth, the manufacturing sector has been marked by virtually complete price stability during 1997, with the producer price index for manufacturing at mid-year slightly below the year earlier level.

Productivity gains also have continued during 1997, with manufacturing output per worker hour in the second quarter 3.5 percent above the year earlier period (4.0 percent for durable goods and 3.1 percent for nondurables). Hourly compensation was up 3.0 percent (0.6 percent after adjustment for inflation), and unit labor costs declined 0.5 percent.

The strong manufacturing performance in early 1997 was sufficient to interrupt temporarily the longer-term decline in manufacturing employment. Manufacturing employment during the first eight months was slightly (0.2 percent) above the year earlier period, a combination of a 1.1 percent gain in durable goods and a 1.1 percent decline in the smaller nondurable goods sector. During these eight months, the workweek averaged 41.9 hours and overtime averaged 4.8 hours per week. In both cases, these figures are in line with data for 1994 through 1996 and exceed the annual averages for all earlier years of the past three decades, suggesting a strong preference by employers for meeting production demands with the existing workforce before taking on new workers.

Exports of manufactured goods were up a strong 11.4 percent in the first half of 1997, compared to the same months of 1996. With imports also rising, however, the United States continued to experience a large deficit on trade in manufactures; the $62.7 billion deficit for the first half of 1997 was virtually unchanged from the year earlier period.

Exports of advanced technology products were especially strong, with the total for the first half up 16 percent from the corresponding months of 1996. In contrast to the deficit on total manufacturing, the United States has a large and growing trade surplus in advanced technology products, $20.7 billion in the first half of 1997, compared to $13.4 billion in the year earlier period.

FIGURE 2

U.S. EMPLOYMENT AND SHIPMENTS, ALL MANUFACTURING

Total payroll employment and manufacturers' inflation-adjusted shipments

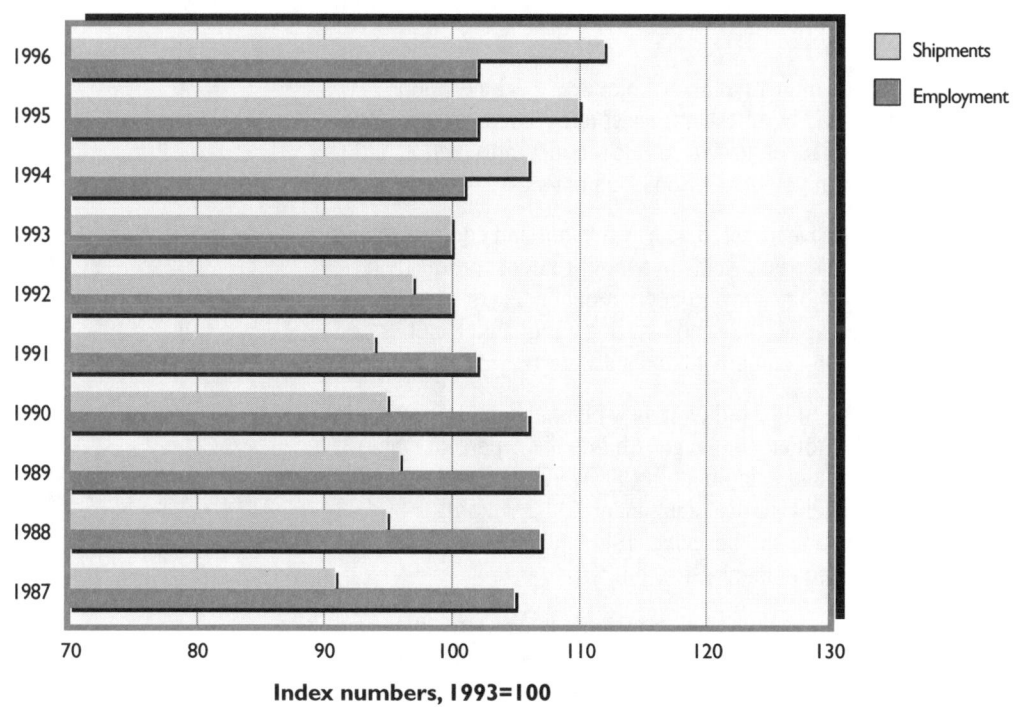

Index numbers, 1993=100

Source: U.S. Bureau of Labor Statistics, U.S. Department of Commerce, and estimates by the editors.

Output. Manufacturers' shipments, adjusted for inflation, dipped slightly during the 1990-1991 recession but then rose fairly steadily at a 3.7 percent annual rate from 1991 to 1996. Employment, however, fell 3.5 percent in 1991 and since has remained relatively flat (Figure 2).

Over the 1987-1996 period as a whole, manufacturers' shipments rose at an annual rate of 4.7 percent in current dollars and 2.4 percent in constant (inflation-adjusted) dollars (Table 3). However, manufacturing's share of the total economy has continued to decline, reflecting the ongoing shift in U.S. output to services, as well as lower price increases. The manufacturing sector's share of current-dollar GDP fell from 19.2 percent in 1988 to 17 percent in 1992 and 1993. In 1994 (the latest year for which data are available), the share rose slightly as shorter term business-cycle expansionary forces offset the longer term trend.

The five leading manufacturing industries in 1996 in terms of current-dollar industry shipments were:

	SHIPMENTS, BILLIONS CURRENT $	REAL RATE OF GROWTH 1987-1996[1]
Transportation equipment	472.0	1.4
Food and beverages	471.7	1.8
Industrial and commercial machinery and computer equipment	378.2	6.8
Chemicals and allied products	376.1	1.9
Electronic and other electrical equipment	323.4	6.8

1 Compound annual percent change, adjusted for inflation.

The two machinery and equipment groups (industrial and commercial machinery and electronic and other electric equipment) had by far the strongest rates of real growth. This impressive performance reflects the rapid rate of new electronic product introduction and the increasing affordability of computers and other electronic equipment.

Investment. Manufacturing industries have invested heavily in plant and equipment and research and development (R&D) during the past decade in a move to boost productivity and gain ground in the highly competitive domestic and international markets. Virtually all industries have participated in this drive, replacing or modernizing antiquated facilities and equipment and investing heavily in computer equipment and software.

All told, manufacturing industries invested $128.2 billion in new plant and equipment during 1995, compared with $78.6 billion in 1987, for an annual growth rate of 6.3 percent (Table 3). The five largest industry investors in plant and equipment in 1995 were chemicals and allied products ($17.6 billion), electronic and other electrical equipment ($17.2 billion), transportation equipment ($13.1 billion), food and beverages ($11.9 billion), and industrial and commercial machinery and computer equipment ($10.0 billion).

Investment in equipment increased far more rapidly than investment in new structures, and the rise in investment in computers was especially dramatic. Economy-wide inflation-adjusted investment in computers and peripherals in 1996 was more than seven times its 1987 level, and the manufacturing sector appears to have fully participated in this growth.

Manufacturing industries invested about $73 billion in R&D in 1994, compared to $56 billion in 1987. Individual industries making the largest R&D investments in 1994 were transportation equipment ($17.7 billion), chemicals ($16.6 billion), electronic and other electrical equipment ($13.5 billion), instruments ($8.1 billion), and industrial and commercial machinery and computer equipment ($8.0 billion). These five industries accounted for 87 percent of all manufacturers' investment in R&D, and their R&D spending rivaled or even exceeded their spending on physical capital.

Capacity utilization in manufacturing averaged 82.1 percent in 1996, off slightly from the previous two years. Apart from a recessionary dip in 1991, capacity utilization was relatively constant from 1987 through 1996, indicating that increases in productive capacity have kept pace with output growth.

Petroleum products had the highest level of capacity utilization, at 93.8 percent in 1996, followed by rubber and plastics (91.2 percent), primary metals (90.7 percent) and industrial and commercial machinery and computer equipment (89.9 percent). Capacity utilization in petroleum products remained above 90 percent from 1993 through 1996, but only in 1996 did prices of gasoline and other refined products increase sharply, suggesting that the 1996 product price rise was due more to higher prices for crude oil than to the high utilization level for petroleum refining. However, after falling during the first half of 1997, petroleum product prices took a new upward jump in mid-summer, a time when monthly data on capacity utilization in the industry was averaging 97 to 98 percent.

Prices. Producer prices in manufacturing rose at an annual rate of 2.6 percent from 1987 to 1996 (Table 3). The rate of gain accelerated in 1995, but then slowed as 1996 progressed, and, as mentioned earlier, prices actually declined in the first half of 1997 and by mid-1997 were slightly below year earlier levels.

TABLE 3

U.S. OUTPUT, INVESTMENT, AND PRICES: ALL MANUFACTURING

(Millions of U.S. dollars, except as noted)

	1987	1988	1989	1990	1991	1992	1993	1994	1995	1996	GROWTH RATE 1987-1996[1]
VALUE OF SHIPMENTS:											
BY INDUSTRY:											
Current dollars	2,476,023	2,695,432	2,840,375	2,912,228	2,878,164	3,004,723	3,127,621	3,348,019	3,589,158	3,734,936	4.67
Constant 1992 dollars	2,815,922	2,938,994	2,961,152	2,950,617	2,897,384	3,004,723	3,095,034	3,274,086	3,416,689	3,475,328	2.37
BY PRODUCT:											
Current dollars	2,349,410	2,544,963	2,654,112	2,731,175	2,680,296	2,846,460	2,969,828	3,176,548	3,404,307	3,542,577	4.67
Constant 1992 dollars	2,676,052	2,769,024	2,764,681	2,765,748	2,697,216	2,846,460	2,938,271	3,104,801	3,239,174	3,294,920	2.34
OTHER OUTPUT MEASURES:											
Industrial production, 1993=100	89.5	93.6	95.5	95.0	92.8	96.4	100.0	105.5	109.2	112.2	2.54
Gross domestic product:											
Current dollars	889,047	971,297	1,013,422	1,031,359	1,028,065	1,063,575	1,116,536	1,197,098	....	....	....
Percent of total GDP	18.9	19.2	18.6	18.0	17.4	17.0	17.0	17.3	....	....	....
Chained (1992) dollars	1,041,619	1,110,891	1,106,018	1,090,112	1,050,388	1,063,575	1,095,312	1,168,029	....	....	....
INVESTMENT-RELATED MEASURES:											
Capacity utilization, percent	81.3	83.8	83.6	81.4	78.0	79.5	80.8	83.1	83.1	82.1	....
New capital expenditures	78,649.9	81,593.1	98,737.6	105,018.1	103,002.9	103,188.0	103,132.9	112,783.6	128,234.7	....	....
Research and development spending	56,259.0	59,415.0	63,199.0	65,251.0	67,639.0	71,025.0	69,901.0	73,375.0	....	....	....
Producer prices, 1993=100[2]	84.7	87.7	92.0	96.1	97.30	98.6	100	101.3	104.3	106.7	2.60

1. Compound annual growth rate.

2. Prices received by domestic producers.

Sources: Shipments and new capital expenditures: U.S. Department of Commerce for 1987-1995, editor's estimates for constant dollar data for 1987-88 and all shipments data for 1996; Industrial production and capacity utilization: Federal Reserve Board of Governors; GDP: Bureau of Economic Analysis; Research and development spending: National Science Foundation; Producer prices: Bureau of Labor Statistics.

Workforce and Employment. Employment in manufacturing reached its recent peak in 1989 at 19.4 million workers, then experienced a recession-induced decline to a low of 18.1 million in 1992 and 1993. Employment has increased since 1993, but with industries downsizing, reorganizing, and merging in order to improve their competitiveness and profitability, 1989 employment levels have yet to be regained.

Production worker employment during the past decade declined more slowly than total employment, so that production workers made up a slightly larger percent of the manufacturing workforce in 1996 (69.1 percent) than in 1987 (68.2 percent). This trend suggests that the "downsizing" of manufacturing in recent years has affected production workers proportionately less than other workers, such as those in middle management, administrative, and clerical positions. The 0.6 percent annual decline in employment of women in 1987-1996 was faster than that for total employment, reflecting in part the decline in the apparel industry, which mainly employs women. From 1987 to 1993, employment of women moved in line with total employment, so that women remained a fairly constant percent of the manufacturing workforce. After 1993, their share declined, dipping to 32.2 percent in 1996 from 32.8 percent in 1993.

Average hourly earnings of production workers in 1996 were $12.78. Earnings during 1987-1996 rose at an annual rate of 2.87 percent, but fell by 0.67 percent annually when adjusted for inflation. As noted earlier, the average workweeks of 42 hours in 1994 and 41.6 hours in 1995 and 1996 were longer than in any previous year of the past three decades.

These employment figures measure number of workers on the payrolls of manufacturing companies and so do not capture industries' increased use of temporary employees obtained through help supply services or stepped-up outsourcing of noncore functions such as computer support and maintenance work. However, increased use of these staffing alternatives is evidenced by the rapid growth of help supply services and other business services.

TABLE 4

U.S. EMPLOYMENT, HOURS, AND EARNINGS: ALL MANUFACTURING

(Monetary values in U.S. dollars)

	1987	1988	1989	1990	1991	1992	1993	1994	1995	1996	CHANGE[1]
NUMBER OF EMPLOYEES, IN THOUSANDS:											
Total	18,999	19,314	19,391	19,076	18,406	18,104	18,075	18,321	18,524	18,457	-0.32
Production workers	12,952	13,193	13,230	12,947	12,434	12,287	12,341	12,632	12,826	12,749	-0.18
Percent of total	68.2	68.3	68.2	67.9	67.6	67.9	68.3	68.9	69.2	69.1	......
Women	6,242	6,352	6,399	6,285	6,067	5,964	5,933	5,987	6,010	5,934	-0.56
Percent of total	32.9	32.9	33.0	32.9	33.0	32.9	32.8	32.7	32.4	32.2	....
HOURS AND EARNINGS OF PRODUCTION WORKERS:											
Average hourly earnings, U.S. dollars[2]											
Current dollars	9.91	10.19	10.48	10.83	11.18	11.46	11.74	12.07	12.37	12.78	2.87
1992 dollars[3]	12.17	12.03	11.82	11.61	11.50	11.46	11.42	11.45	11.41	11.46	-0.67
Average weekly hours	41.0	41.1	41.0	40.8	40.7	41.0	41.4	42.0	41.6	41.6	0.16
Average weekly earnings, current U.S. dollars	406.31	418.81	429.68	441.86	455.03	469.86	486.04	506.94	514.59	531.65	3.03

1. Compound annual growth rate, 1987-1996.

2. Including overtime.

3. Converted to 1992 dollars using Consumer Price Index for Urban Wage Earners and Clerical Workers.

Source: Bureau of Labor Statistics.

FIGURE 3

U.S. OCCUPATIONAL INJURY AND ILLNESS RATES:
ALL MANUFACTURING, 1995

Incidence of nonfatal injuries and illnesses per 100 full-time workers

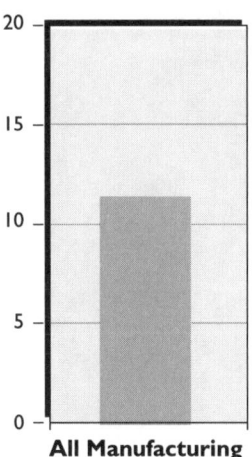

All Manufacturing

Nonfatal illnesses and injuries in manufacturing averaged 11.6 cases per 100 full-time workers in 1995. The range for the 20 industries was from 4.8 percent for petroleum and coal products to 18.6 percent for transportation equipment.

Source: U.S. Bureau of Labor Statistics.

TABLE 5

U.S. EMPLOYMENT PROJECTIONS BY MAJOR OCCUPATIONAL GROUP: MANUFACTURING

	1994		PROJECTIONS, 2005			
	NUMBER OF EMPLOYEES	PERCENT OF INDUSTRY TOTAL	NUMBER OF EMPLOYEES			PERCENT OF INDUSTRY TOTAL, MODERATE PROJECTIONS
OCCUPATION			LOW	MODERATE	HIGH	
Total, all occupations	18,303,800	100.0	16,217,500	16,990,500	18,000,200	100.0
Executive, administrative, and managerial	1,643,368	9.0	1,508,934	1,580,176	1,675,048	9.3
Professional specialties	1,165,406	6.4	1,231,041	1,292,088	1,375,516	7.6
Technicians and related support	539,662	3.0	448,118	469,804	500,916	2.8
Marketing and sales	613,234	3.4	586,185	609,919	638,819	3.6
Administrative support including clerical	2,028,960	11.1	1,658,626	1,734,478	1,830,046	10.2
Service	251,925	1.4	198,913	206,986	217,198	1.2
Agriculture, forestry, and fisheries occupations	90,951	0.5	83,165	84,942	86,464	0.5
Precision production, craft, and repair	3,795,450	20.7	3,354,498	3,511,624	3,727,722	20.7
Operators, fabricators, assemblers	8,174,844	44.7	7,148,019	7,500,484	7,948,471	44.2

Source: Bureau of Labor Statistics, November 1995.

Employment in manufacturing is projected to continue its long-term downtrend, falling to under 17 million workers by 2005, compared with 18.3 million in 1994. Declines are projected for all occupational areas except professional specialties, which even in 2005 will account for only about 7.6 percent of the workforce.

FIGURE 4

U.S. CORPORATE INCOME AND WORKER EARNINGS: ALL MANUFACTURING

Corporate operating income and aggregate production worker earnings

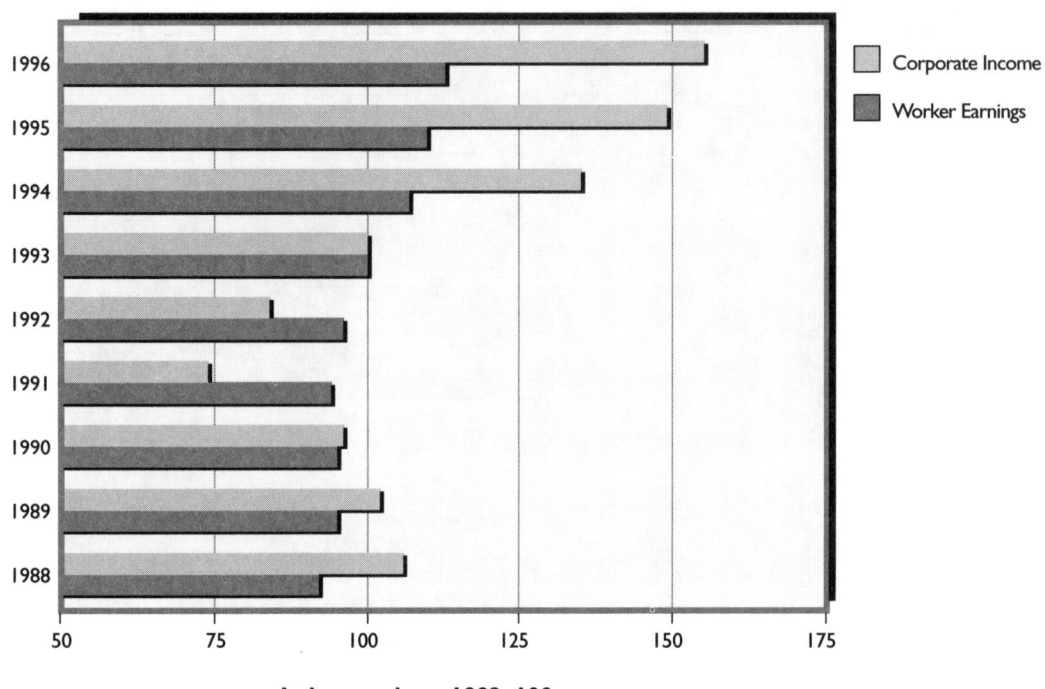

Index numbers, 1993=100

Source: U.S. Bureau of Labor Statistics, U.S. Bureau of the Census, and estimates by the editors.

Finance.   Aggregate earnings of production workers in manufacturing leveled off during the 1990-1991 recession, but have since grown steadily, though not rapidly. Corporate operating income declined sharply during the recession, and then staged a dramatic comeback, with particularly large gains in 1994 and 1995. (Figure 4).

The financial performance of the manufacturing sector was very strong from 1994 through 1996, with corporate profits (income before and after taxes) setting new records each year. Industries' extensive downsizing, investment in technology, consolidations, mergers, and acquisitions clearly were paying off financially. Operating incomes, profits, dividends, and assets all hit record levels in 1996 (Table 6). Returns on sales and stockholders' equity were the highest of the 1988 to 1996 period. Operating income from manufacturing in 1996 totaled $277.8 billion, more than double the 1991 low. The annual growth rate from 1988 to 1996 was 4.9 percent. After-tax income, after dropping to $23.2 billion in 1992, rebounded to a record $231.5 billion in 1996. Growth over the 1988-1996 period was at an annual rate of 5.2 percent.

After-tax returns on sales reached 6.2 percent in 1996, compared with an average of 4.2 percent for 1988-1996, and returns on stockholders' equity hit 16.6 percent, compared to a period average of 11.5 percent. The second best year for both these categories was 1988, when the after-tax return on sales was 6.0 percent and that on stockholders' equity was 15.8 percent. Debt, largely long-term, was under 24 percent of total assets in 1996, versus an average for 1988-1996 of 26.3 percent.

TABLE 6

U.S. CORPORATE INCOME AND ASSETS: ALL MANUFACTURING

(Monetary values in millions of U.S. dollars)

INCOME AND EXPENSES	1988	1989	1990	1991	1992	1993	1994	1995	1996	CHANGE OR AVERAGE[1]
Sales and receipts	2,596,199	2,745,067	2,810,736	2,761,071	2,890,238	3,015,095	3,255,838	3,528,349	3,753,394	4.72
Depreciation and amortization	(100,691)	(105,062)	(109,181)	(112,858)	(120,269)	(121,536)	(123,884)	(130,766)	(137,742)	3.99
Other operating costs	(2,305,384)	(2,457,505)	(2,528,847)	(2,515,115)	(2,618,818)	(2,713,988)	(2,889,501)	(3,129,757)	(3,337,815)	4.73
Income from operations	190,124	182,502	172,709	133,097	151,150	179,571	242,452	267,824	277,838	4.86
Nonoperating income (expenditures)	26,013	6,281	(13,146)	(33,270)	(118,645)	(60,956)	2,833	8,692	35,550	....
Income before taxes	216,135	188,781	159,563	99,827	32,505	118,616	245,284	276,517	313,387	4.75
Income after taxes	154,583	136,279	111,561	67,516	23,212	83,922	176,639	200,178	231,488	5.18
Cash dividends	57,064	65,243	62,201	60,231	63,061	66,756	69,977	80,866	94,718	6.54
Income retained in business	97,518	71,037	49,361	7,285	(39,847)	17,167	106,664	119,312	136,769	4.32
Direct credits (charges)	(35,405)	(40,368)	(20,810)	(19,181)	(26,652)	(13,279)	(17,575)	(9,562)	(45,205)	....
Ending retained earnings	717,685	729,012	750,288	741,278	674,448	668,796	742,484	829,472	908,280	2.99
ASSETS, END OF YEAR:										
Total	2,339,690	2,503,761	2,629,458	2,688,422	2,798,625	2,904,869	3,080,231	3,345,229	3,542,428	5.32
Accounts receivable	350,048	364,941	365,894	355,073	363,755	365,376	403,383	436,271	453,995	3.30
Inventories	358,012	369,910	375,516	369,374	370,974	376,016	390,284	423,528	424,591	2.15
Net property, plant and equipment	786,601	830,730	880,388	905,942	937,925	946,426	974,283	1,023,086	1,057,446	3.77
RATIOS, PERCENT:										
INCOME TO SALES:										
Before tax	8.33	6.88	5.68	3.62	1.12	3.93	7.53	7.84	8.35	5.92
After tax	5.95	4.96	3.97	2.45	0.80	2.78	5.43	5.67	6.17	4.24
INCOME TO STOCK HOLDERS' EQUITY:										
Before tax	22.06	18.62	15.13	9.25	3.15	11.22	21.27	21.63	22.43	16.08
After tax	15.77	13.44	10.58	6.25	2.25	7.94	15.32	15.66	16.57	11.53
INCOME TO TOTAL ASSETS:										
Before tax	9.24	7.54	6.07	3.71	1.16	4.08	7.96	8.27	8.85	6.32
After tax	6.61	5.44	4.24	2.51	0.83	2.89	5.73	5.98	6.53	4.53
AS A PERCENT OF TOTAL ASSETS:										
Property, plant and equipment	33.62	33.18	33.48	33.70	33.51	32.58	31.63	30.58	29.85	32.46
Short-term debt	3.80	4.10	4.35	3.90	4.20	3.76	3.84	3.82	3.84	3.96
Long-term debt	22.88	24.17	23.89	23.67	22.91	21.88	21.16	20.72	20.04	22.37
Stockholders' equity	41.88	40.50	40.10	40.15	36.85	36.40	37.43	38.22	39.44	39.00

1. For income and asset amounts, compound annual growth rate; for ratios, average of ratios for the years shown.

Source: U.S. Bureau of the Census, Quarterly Financial Report.

Notes: Parentheses ( ) indicate negative items, e.g., net expenses, charges, or losses. Net property, plant, and equipment is net of accumulated depreciation. Because the samples used to collect the data change, retained earnings at the end of a given year will not exactly equal the previous year's retained earnings plus the current year's retained income and credits.

CANADA

Canadian manufacturers had shipments of Can$310 billion in 1993 (US$240 billion at 1993 exchange rates). Manufacturing constituted 16 percent of Canadian GDP in 1993, compared to 17 percent in the United States.

The transportation equipment industry was the manufacturing industry with the highest 1993 value of shipments (Table 7). Autos are a major Canadian export, and their renaissance has led the exports of manufactured goods and had an appreciable affect on recovery from the 1990-1991 recession, according to the Conference Board of Canada. The industry with the second highest shipments value, and the largest industry in terms of employment, was food and beverages. Chemicals ranked third in shipments, although ninth in employment. Also of major importance to the Canadian economy are industries that perform basic processing of raw materials: Paper and allied products (fourth in shipment value); primary metals (fifth); and lumber and wood products (sixth).

TABLE 7

CANADA: COMPONENT INDUSTRIES OF MANUFACTURING SECTOR, 1993

(Monetary values in Canadian dollars)

INDUSTRY NAME	CSIC	ESTABLISH-MENTS (NUMBER)	EMPLOYMENT		VALUE OF SHIPMENTS (MILLIONS)	AVERAGE HOURLY EARNINGS[1]
			NUMBER	PERCENT OF INDUSTRY TOTAL		
ALL MANUFACTURING INDUSTRIES		32,943	1,644,260	100.0	CAN$309,675.0	CAN$15.43
Food and beverages	1000+1100	3,202	216,101	13.1	46,855.9	13.90
Tobacco products	1200	17	4,778	0.3	2,006.5	25.12
Textile mill products	1800+1900	928	46,022	2.8	5,609.0	11.65
Apparel	2400	1,921	82,737	5.0	5,933.3	8.71
Lumber and wood products	2500	2,894	109,961	6.7	19,082.9	15.48
Furniture and fixtures	2600	1,331	44,654	2.7	3,988.2	11.30
Paper and allied products	2700	664	101,926	6.2	21,232.6	20.08
Printing and publishing	2800	4,655	124,867	7.6	12,840.0	16.29
Chemicals and allied products	3700	1,248	87,453	5.3	22,609.5	17.66
Petroleum and coal products	3600	157	14,084	0.9	17,244.4	24.48
Rubber and plastic products	1500+1600	1,326	73,239	4.5	9,279.7	13.03
Leather and leather products	1700	230	12,818	0.8	930.5	9.76
Stone, clay, and glass	3500	1,519	42,661	2.6	6,226.7	15.68
Primary metals	2900	409	84,416	5.1	19,810.5	20.78
Fabricated metals	3000	5,117	132,606	8.1	15,404.1	14.41
Industrial and commercial machinery and computer equipment	3100+3360	2,037	89,806	5.5	13,744.9	14.96
Electronic and other electrical equipment	3300-3360	1,183	103,202	6.3	16,643.9	15.47
Transportation equipment	3200	1,349	209,879	12.8	64,112.8	18.08
Instruments	3910	533	19,911	1.2	2,252.2	13.61
Miscellaneous manufacturing	3900-3910	2,223	43,139	2.6	3,867.4	11.43

1. Including overtime.

Source: Statistics Canada, *Manufacturing Industries of Canada* (Cat. No. 31-203).

Average hourly earnings of production workers varied widely among manufacturing industries, with the relative rankings often similar to those in the United States. Tobacco industry workers were the highest paid in 1993, at Can$25.12 per hour, followed by those in petroleum and coal products at Can$24.48. These same two industries ranked second and first, respectively, in the United States. As in the United States, leather and leather products (Can$9.76) and apparel workers (Can$8.71) were the least well paid.

The 1990-1991 recession is evident in the statistics for Canadian shipments and employment. From 1989 to 1991, manufacturing shipments dropped 9 percent, and employment, 12 percent (Table 8). Shipments began rising again in 1992, but employment continued to decline into 1993, when it averaged almost 17 percent below 1989. Only in 1994 did employment begin a modest comeback.

TABLE 8

CANADIAN EMPLOYMENT AND SHIPMENTS: MANUFACTURING SECTOR, 1987-1994

(Monetary values in Canadian dollars)

	1987	1988	1989	1990	1991	1992	1993	1994	CHANGE[1]
All employees	1,864,545	1,946,702	1,969,325	1,868,983	1,737,606	1,674,444	1,644,260	1,669,654	-1.56
Establishments	36790	40262	39150	39864	36339	34511	32943	31974	-1.98
Employees per establishment	51	48	50	47	48	49	50	52	0.43
Production workers per establishment	.....	37	38	35	35	36	37	39	1.02
PRODUCTION WORKERS:									
Total	.....	1,473,102	1,493,302	1,393,324	1,288,206	1,234,208	1,218,777	1,243,026	-2.79
Percent of all employees	.....	76	76	75	74	74	74	74	.....
Male	.....	1,112,728	1,130,683	1,055,203	981,309	1,234,208	1,218,777	1,243,026	.....
Female	.....	360,374	362,619	338,121	306,897	.....	.....	.....	.....
Percent of all production workers	.....	24	24	24	24	.....	.....	.....	.....
Average hourly wage	.....	12.59	13.22	13.97	14.55	15.08	15.43	15.73	3.78
Average weekly earnings	.....	506.12	530.12	556.01	579.09	603.20	620.29	638.64	3.95
Average weekly hours	.....	40.2	40.1	39.8	39.8	40.0	40.2	40.6	0.17
Shipments (millions)	271,627	297,540	308,805	298,919	280,191	286,043	309,675	352,835	3.81

1. Compound annual growth rate.

Source: Adapted from Statistics Canada, *Manufacturing Industries of Canada* (Cat. No. 31-203).

MEXICO

Mexico's principal manufacturing industries are metal products; food and beverages; and textiles, garments, and leather. Metal products had 962,000 employees in 1993, or almost 30 percent of the manufacturing total (Table 9). This industry is more broadly defined than its U.S. and Canadian counterparts and includes fabricated metals; industrial and computer equipment; electronic equipment; transportation equipment; and instruments. Food and beverages employed 697,000 workers in 1993 and remains Mexico's second largest industry, as measured by employment. The third largest industry group is textiles, garments, and leather, which employs 547,000 workers, or 16.9 percent of the manufacturing total. As in Canada and the United States, average earnings vary widely by industry, with tobacco, chemicals and petroleum, and basic metals at the top of the scale and textiles, garments, and leather and wood and wood products at the bottom.

The Mexican manufacturing sector also is recovering from a recession, albeit a shorter, deeper, more recent one than that in Canada or the United States. The 1994-1995 peso crisis plunged the entire Mexican economy into a deep contraction with effects on every sector. This is evidenced by employment in manufacturing, which went down by more than 200,000, or about 7 percent, from 1993 to 1995 (Table 10). Constant-dollar gross product originating in manufacturing also experienced an abrupt decline of almost 5 percent from 1994 to 1995.

While the recession in Mexico was rapid and severe, reducing wages and prices across the board, the ensuing recovery also has been brisk. Reflecting in part strong gains in Mexican exports, the manufacturing sector has made an impressive recovery. In 1996, real gross product in manufacturing recovered to levels higher than before the recession, and employment in manufacturing increased slightly as well.

One sector that seems to have been aided by the devaluation of the peso is the Maquiladora manufacturing exports program, which is experiencing a boom of sorts following the crisis. Since the crisis in 1994, total remuneration per worker in the program has more than doubled (11,536 million constant new pesos in 1994 to 23,948 million in 1996), and the number of Maquiladora employees has increased by more than 170,000 to a total of 754,858 in 1996. Further, these trends appeared to be accelerating through the first six months of 1997, suggesting that the Maquiladora program, which produces exclusively for exportation and is not included in regular Mexican manufacturing numbers, is an important driving force in the Mexican recovery.

TABLE 9

MEXICO: COMPONENT INDUSTRIES OF MANUFACTURING SECTOR, 1993

(Monetary values in 1993 Mexican New Pesos)

INDUSTRY	CMAP	NUMBER OF UNITS	ALL WORKERS										UNPAID WORKERS, NUMBER
			NUMBER	PERCENT OF INDUSTRY TOTAL	AVERAGE DAYS WORKED	REMUN-ERATION[1]	PAID WORKERS						
							PRODUCTION WORKERS		NONPRODUCTION EMPLOYEES		BENEFITS PER PAID EMPLOYEE		
							NUMBER	WAGES AND SALARIES	NUMBER	WAGES AND SALARIES			
All manufacture		265,427	3,246,042	100.0	278	24,315	2,193,260	12,202	694,074	32,854	7,149		358,708
Food and beverages[2]	31-3140	91,894	696,539	21.5	299	21,951	403,926	11,491	160,385	25,825	6,385		132,228
Tobacco products	3140	38	7,778	0.2	279	48,763	5,489	11,722	2,261	62,472	22,234		28
Textiles, garments and leather	32	44,126	547,290	16.9	271	16,258	409,938	9,709	80,224	24,101	4,193		57,128
Wood and wood products	33	31,606	168,023	5.2	266	13,149	106,196	8,478	17,491	20,320	2,997		44,336
Paper and printing	34	15,049	197,371	6.1	275	26,324	112,704	14,139	66,665	28,863	6,712		18,002
Chemicals and petroleum	35	7,091	380,140	11.7	276	36,607	259,834	17,367	114,910	43,751	11,150		5,396
Non-metallic minerals	36	24,361	183,868	5.7	250	26,487	113,561	12,957	29,502	39,778	7,999		40,805
Basic metals	37	321	59,045	1.8	289	38,682	43,729	17,285	15,142	46,470	13,891		174
Metal products	38	46,246	962,060	29.6	266	25,236	708,788	12,083	199,409	36,638	7,761		53,863
Other manufacturing	39	4,695	43,928	1.4	270	16,840	29,095	9,579	8,085	22,178	4,521		6,748

1. Average annual remuneration including benefits.

2. Average annual remuneration, and wages, salaries, and benefits include tobacco industry.

Source: INEGI, Censos Economicos 1994.

TABLE 10

MEXICAN GROSS DOMESTIC PRODUCT AND EMPLOYMENT: MANUFACTURING SECTOR, 1988-1995

	1988	1989	1990	1991	1992	1993	1994	1995	CHANGE[1]
GROSS DOMESTIC PRODUCT:									
Millions of constant 1993 new pesos	178,416.1	192,500.9	205,524.5	212,578.0	221,427.4	219,934.1	228,891.6	217,839.2	2.89
Millions of constant 1993 U.S. dollars[2]	57,116.9	61,625.9	65,795.2	68,053.3	70,886.3	70,408.2	73,275.8	69,737.6	2.89
TOTAL EMPLOYMENT:									
Manufacturing sector	3,034,654	3,167,969	3,275,202	3,307,128	3,379,765	3,309,755	3,238,906	3,085,206	0.24
Food, beverages, and tobacco	609,757	630,202	641,193	655,022	672,345	679,253	667,973	650,911	0.94
Textiles, garments, and leather	522,032	527,761	527,607	531,034	518,280	515,872	497,454	481,961	-1.13
Wood products	169,382	168,034	164,274	163,450	165,263	154,367	151,584	137,231	-2.96
Paper and printing	167,577	176,532	187,261	192,492	196,017	192,612	185,327	172,399	0.41
Chemicals, derivatives of petroleum, et al	370,230	380,425	393,831	401,902	395,282	383,933	370,978	349,721	-0.81
Nonmetallic minerals	157,668	167,832	178,737	179,074	183,210	183,108	174,841	150,304	-0.68
Basic metals	103,516	97,038	88,467	81,812	70,279	59,441	56,143	52,724	-9.19
Metal products	864,602	932,137	988,820	998,935	1,062,024	1,025,021	1,018,573	975,775	1.74
Other manufacturing	69,890	88,008	105,012	103,427	117,065	116,148	116,033	114,180	7.26

1. Compound annual growth rate.

2. Converted at 3.1237 new pesos to the U.S. dollar.

Source: Sistema de Cuentas Nacionales de Mexico, INEGI.

INTERNATIONAL TRADE

United States. Total U.S. exports of manufactured goods rose 61 percent to $514 billion from 1990 to 1996. During the same period, global imports to the United States rose 67 percent to $681 billion, increasing the U.S. trade deficit on manufactured goods to $166.5 billion in 1996.

Canada. In total, U.S. manufactured goods exports to Canada rose 61.8 percent to $124.1 billion from 1990 to 1996, and Canadian exports to the United States rose 71.3 percent to $128.8 billion. Annual rates of increase were 8.4 and 9.4 percent, respectively. Trade with Mexico also increased, with imports from Mexico more than tripling and exports to Mexico rising 15 percent, although the trade totals were still tiny compared to U.S.-Canada levels.

Mexico. U.S.-Mexico trade increased dramatically between 1989 and 1996, with especially large gains in 1996. U.S. exports to Mexico have more than doubled since 1989, to $52.3 billion, while Mexican exports to the United States more than tripled to $60.3 billion. These represent annual rates of increase of 12.7 percent and 17.6 percent, respectively. Canada-Mexico trade also increased, as noted previously, but still is far below U.S.-Mexico trade (Table 11).

NAFTA. The U.S manufacturing trade balance within NAFTA has varied widely from year-to-year, from a surplus of $14 billion in 1992 to a deficit of almost $13 billion in 1996. In 1996, Canada achieved a modest surplus of $1.2 billion on trade within NAFTA, its first of the 1990s. Mexico's within-NAFTA trade balance has shown a dramatic change in the last few years, with a deficit in excess of $5 billion in 1994 turning into a surplus of $11.5 billion in 1996.

TABLE 11

INTERNATIONAL TRADE, MANUFACTURING

(Millions of U.S. dollars)

	1989[1]	1990	1991	1992	1993	1994	1995	1996
GLOBAL TRADE, U.S.								
IMPORTS								
Value	396,108.1	406,845.1	406,253.7	443,951.1	490,288.6	567,051.7	639,727.2	680,608.7
EXPORTS								
Value	279,391.9	320,236.9	348,759.7	371,785.5	388,986.8	428,388.6	481,435.0	514,143.6
TRADE BALANCE	(116,716.2)	(86,608.2)	(57,494.0)	(72,165.6)	(101,301.8)	(138,663.1)	(158,292.2)	(166,465.1)
BILATERAL TRADE: NAFTA								
U.S. exports to Canada	59,279.8	76,691.3	79,383.7	84,068.9	93,460.5	106,947.0	117,993.5	124,109.9
Canadian exports to U.S.	74,826.1	75,199.1	74,491.7	80,629.5	91,400.4	106,587.0	120,990.4	128,821.3
U.S. exports to Mexico	22,625.7	26,094.2	31,077.3	37,832.4	39,095.7	47,647.9	43,348.8	52,312.1
Mexican exports to U.S.	19,441.6	21,265.0	22,820.2	27,081.5	31,399.8	40,037.6	49,804.5	60,302.1
Canadian exports to Mexico	409.9	484.7	405.8	480.5	424.6	492.9	540.4	555.7
Mexican exports to Canada	1,136.3	1,300.4	2,045.1	2,039.5	2,589.6	3,072.1	3,639.5	4,082.9
TRADE BALANCES WITHIN NAFTA[2]								
Canada	14,819.9	(2,307.9)	(6,531.3)	(4,998.4)	(4,225.1)	(2,939.2)	(102.2)	1,184.2
Mexico	(2,457.7)	(4,013.5)	(6,617.8)	(9,191.9)	(5,530.9)	(5,031.1)	9,554.8	11,517.2
United States	(12,362.2)	6,321.4	13,149.1	14,190.3	9,756.0	7,970.3	(9,452.6)	(12,701.4)

1. 1989 and earlier data on U.S. exports to Canada for total manufacturing industries are not comparable with data for 1990 and later years because of a change in the reporting system. The NAFTA trade balances for the U.S. and Canada also are affected.

2. Parentheses indicate an excess of imports over exports. Because of commodity coding and other data differences among the three countries, these trade balances are only rough estimates and should be used with caution.

Source for U.S. Global Trade: U.S. Department of Commerce, International Trade Administration.

Source for U.S. -Canada and U.S.-Mexico Bilateral Trade: U.S. Bureau of the Census.

Source for Canada-Mexico and Mexico-Canada Bilateral Trade: Statistics Canada, Foreign Trade Division, Special tabulation, April 1997, converted to U.S. dollars by the editors.

APPAREL

THE UNITED STATES

Products and Processes. The apparel industry was the 14th or 15th largest U.S. manufacturing industry in terms of contribution to gross domestic product each year from 1987 to 1994 and was 16th in terms of industry shipments in 1996. Its products include garments of all

TABLE 1

UNITED STATES: COMPONENT INDUSTRIES OF APPAREL AND OTHER TEXTILE PRODUCTS (SIC 23), 1992

(Monetary values in millions of U.S. dollars)

INDUSTRY	SIC	ESTABLISH-MENTS	SHIPMENTS VALUE	SHIPMENTS PERCENT BY 4 LARGEST COMPANIES	VALUE ADDED BY MANUFACTURE	NEW CAPITAL EXPENDI-TURES	EMPLOY-MENT[1]	PAYROLL
APPAREL AND OTHER TEXTILE PRODUCTS	23	23,093	$71,657.9	....	$36,422.6	$945.0	985,300	$15,325.1
Men's and boys' suits, coats, and overcoats	231	303	2,430.1	....	1,375.1	21.9	44,000	722.5
Men's and boys' furnishings	232	2,288	17,866.6	....	9,864.2	248.1	261,000	3,648.7
Shirts, men's and boys'	2321	658	5,920.8	28	3,182.6	84.5	84,400	1,207.4
Men's and boys' underwear and nightwear	2322	86	820.1	52	441.4	7.7	14,200	192.3
Men's and boys' neckwear	2323	136	618.2	33	319.1	6.0	7,500	130.2
Men's and boys' trousers and slacks	2325	426	6,518.5	70	3,651.7	91.7	78,900	1,105.1
Men's and boys' work clothing	2326	282	1,503.3	36	818.3	23.5	30,400	386.8
Men's and boys' clothing, n.e.c.	2329	700	2,485.7	18	1,451.1	34.7	45,700	626.8
Women's and misses' outerwear	233	9,536	21,630.7	....	10,836.1	205.0	306,300	4,596.5
Women's and misses' blouses and waists	2331	1,474	3,969.8	12	1,952.8	38.2	56,100	831.6
Women's and misses' dresses	2335	4,000	5,366.1	11	2,823.9	42.5	83,200	1,204.9
Women's and misses' suits and coats	2337	1,038	4,396.7	24	2,034.0	31.7	48,300	848.2
Women's and misses' outerwear, n.e.c.	2339	3,024	7,898.2	12	4,025.5	92.7	118,600	1,711.7
Women's and children's undergarments	234	480	3,943.0	....	2,193.2	42.1	53,700	798.3
Women's and children's underwear	2341	357	2,368.1	29	1,308.1	29.2	41,600	579.3
Brassieres and allied garments	2342	123	1,574.9	56	885.1	12.9	12,100	219.0
Hats, caps, and millinery	235	369	976.0	....	572.1	21.5	18,600	279.8
Girls' and children's outerwear	236	755	3,144.5	....	1,667.1	23.9	53,400	774.7
Children's dresses and blouses	2361	394	1,619.3	18	821.9	13.2	23,900	363.5
Girls' and children's outerwear, n.e.c.	2369	361	1,525.2	26	845.2	10.7	29,400	411.2
Fur goods	237	210	171.9	....	68.4	1.8	900	20.6
Miscellaneous apparel and accessories	238	994	2,377.6	....	1,260.2	20.4	36,700	566.4
Fabric dress and work gloves	2381	71	282.7	64	151.8	2.8	4,000	59.3
Robes and dressing gowns	2384	81	373.5	37	182.8	2.2	6,800	85.9
Waterproof outer garments	2385	71	268.4	64	147.9	2.5	4,200	64.5
Leather and sheep lined clothing	2386	116	208.8	51	91.9	1.3	2,400	45.8
Apparel belts	2387	244	636.5	33	341.4	5.1	8,000	150.0
Apparel and accessories, n.e.c.	2389	411	607.7	23	344.4	6.5	11,200	160.8
Miscellaneous fabricated textile products	239	8,158	19,117.5	....	8,586.1	360.2	210,700	3,917.8
Curtains and draperies	2391	1,041	1,280.7	22	593.7	16.1	21,800	336.7
House furnishings, n.e.c.	2392	869	5,604.9	39	2,369.4	83.6	51,900	869.0
Textile bags	2393	310	772.6	17	333.6	11.9	11,800	184.4
Canvas and related products	2394	1,309	1,107.4	12	577.2	19.9	14,400	277.4
Pleating and stitching	2395	755	726.3	19	383.1	22.8	13,700	204.9
Automotive and apparel trimmings	2396	2,471	6,108.6	29	2,729.7	139.8	57,300	1,337.0
Schiffli machine embroideries	2397	221	310.6	24	186.8	6.7	5,500	100.2
Fabricated textile products, n.e.c.	2399	1,182	3,206.4	20	1,412.8	59.5	34,300	608.3

1. Employment numbers from the economic censuses differ in definition and classification from the Bureau of Labor Statistics estimates in Table 2. Year-to-year comparisons between Table 1 and Table 2 are not appropriate.

Source: U.S. Bureau of the Census, 1992 Census of Manufactures.

types for men, women, and children, as well as textile products such as curtains and draperies, canvas products, trimmings, and embroideries. The largest category is women's outerwear, with 30 percent of apparel shipments in 1992, the latest year for which economic census data are available (Table 1). Next in line are miscellaneous fabricated textile products, such as curtains, home furnishings, and canvas products (27 percent of 1992 shipments) and men's and boys' furnishings (25 percent).

Employment in the industry is declining and is expected to continue downward through 2005. Projections to the year 2005 indicate it will then be around 771,600, or about 22 percent below the 1993 level (Table 2). Average hourly earnings of production workers in 1993 were a low $7.09. Lowest earnings were $6.19 in women's and misses' blouses and shirts; the highest, $10.45 an hour, were in automotive and apparel trimmings.

TABLE 2

U.S. EMPLOYMENT AND EARNINGS: APPAREL AND OTHER TEXTILE PRODUCTS

| INDUSTRY | SIC | 1993 | | | 2005 |
| | | EMPLOYMENT[1] | | AVERAGE HOURLY EARNINGS (U.S. DOLLARS)[2] | PROJECTED EMPLOYMENT[3] |
		NUMBER OF PERSONS	PERCENT OF INDUSTRY TOTAL		
APPAREL AND OTHER TEXTILE PRODUCTS	23	989,100	100.0	$7.09	771,600
Apparel	231-8	784,500	79.3	.....	546,600
Men's and boys' suits and coats	231	42,000	4.2	7.76	.....
Men's and boys' furnishings	232	274,300	27.7	6.70	.....
Men's and boys' shirts	2321	65,100	6.6	6.66	.....
Men's and boys' trousers and slacks	2325	82,000	8.3	6.53	.....
Men's and boys' work clothing	2326	42,200	4.3	6.45	.....
Women's and misses' outerwear	233	302,800	30.6	6.71	.....
Women's and misses' blouses and shirts	2331	32,300	3.3	6.19	.....
Women's, juniors', and misses' dresses	2335	51,900	5.2	7.26	.....
Women's and misses' suits and coats	2337	35,600	3.6	7.15	.....
Women's and misses' outerwear, n.e.c.	2339	183,000	18.5	6.56	.....
Women's and children's undergarments	234	53,600	5.4	6.85	.....
Women's and children's underwear	2341	41,800	4.2	6.62	.....
Brassieres, girdles, and allied garments	2342	11,800	1.2	7.84	.....
Girls' and children's outerwear	236	48,500	4.9	6.38	.....
Girls' and children's dresses and blouses	2361	20,600	2.1	6.31	.....
Miscellaneous apparel and accessories	238	42,400	4.3	6.91	.....
Miscellaneous fabricated textile products	239	204,600	20.7	8.24	225,000
Curtains and draperies	2391	20,900	2.1	7.18	.....
House furnishings, n.e.c.	2392	52,700	5.3	7.30	.....
Automotive and apparel trimmings	2396	51,400	5.2	10.45	.....

1. Total payroll employment. Employment data from the economic censuses, shown in Table 1, differ in definition and classification from the Bureau of Labor Statistics estimates in this table. Year-to-year comparisons between Table 1 and Table 2 are not appropriate.

2. Earnings of production workers, including overtime.

3. Number of persons, moderate projection by the U.S. Bureau of Labor Statistics.

Source: Bureau of Labor Statistics.

FIGURE 1

U.S. EMPLOYMENT IN APPAREL
Percent distribution by region, 1995

The Southeast is by far the industry's dominant employer, with about 40 percent of total employment in 1995. The Mid-Atlantic and Pacific regions were next largest in 1995, with 18 percent each.

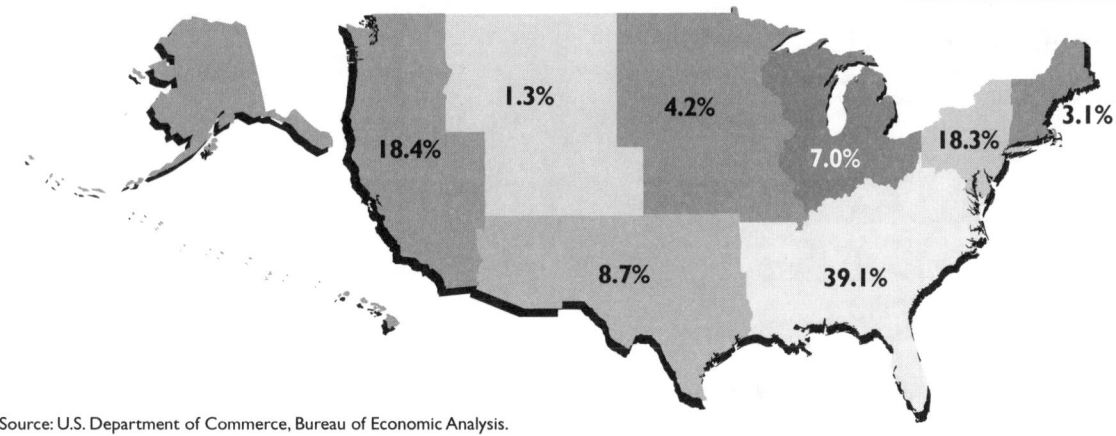

1.3%

4.2%

18.4%

3.1%

18.3%

7.0%

8.7%

39.1%

Source: U.S. Department of Commerce, Bureau of Economic Analysis.

What's New. The U.S. apparel industry continued to lose jobs through the first half of 1997. Preliminary figures for June were down 18,000 from January (seasonally adjusted). Strong growth in imports from Mexico so far has made apparel the U.S. manufacturing industry experiencing the largest NAFTA-induced job loss. Through June 18, 1997, the U.S. Department of Labor had certified 28,362 employees in the apparel industry as having lost their jobs because of NAFTA, largely because of shifts in production to Mexico. This was the highest number certified in any one manufacturing industry and was second highest in terms of share of employment (2.9 percent), exceeded only by 5 percent for the leather and leather products industry.

The rate of growth in the value of U.S. imports of apparel slowed in 1996 to 5 percent from 7 percent the year before. However, according to the International Trade Commission, imports of apparel and textiles still were a record 19.1 billion equivalent square meters as purchases from Mexico and Canada surged 42 and 15 percent, respectively. Sharp gains by Mexico and Canada since implementation of NAFTA and the Canadian-U.S. Free Trade Agreement have made them our top two suppliers in terms of quantity and second and sixth largest, respectively, in terms of value. For more information, see the International Trade Section.

Adapting computers to read four digits instead of just the last two will be a major challenge for the apparel industry as the millenium approaches. The online newsletter Eye on the Industry reports that most companies still are only assessing this problem, which is a large one for apparel and textile companies heavily dependent on computer-controlled equipment and on vendors who have similar computer worries of their own.

FIGURE 2

U.S. EMPLOYMENT AND SHIPMENTS, APPAREL

Total payroll employment and manufacturers' inflation-adjusted shipments

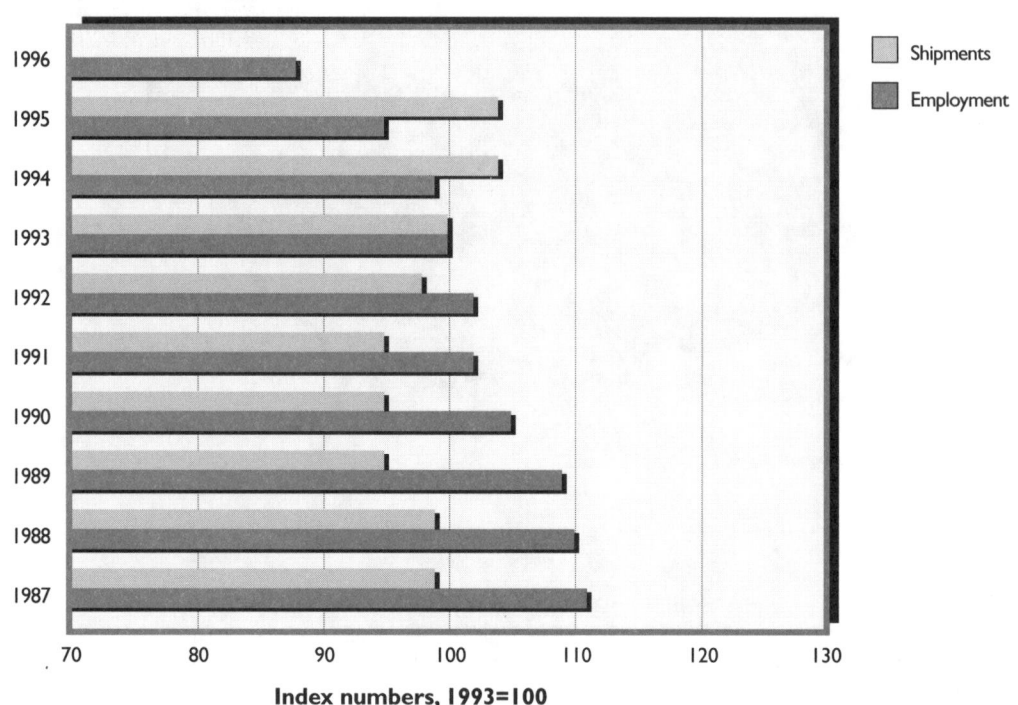

Index numbers, 1993=100

Source: U.S. Bureau of Labor Statistics, U.S. Department of Commerce, and estimates by the editors. Shipments data for 1996 are not available.

Output. Employment in the apparel industry has declined during most of the past 10 years, while industry shipments have grown slowly (Figure 2). Shipments through 1995 grew at an annual rate of 2.47 percent to $78.1 billion that year (Table 3). After adjustment for inflation, shipments grew at only a 0.62 percent rate.

Investment. Between 1987 and 1995, new capital expenditures by the industry rose in all but three years, reaching $1.2 billion in 1995, compared with $736 million in 1987 (Table 3). Capacity utilization amounted to 75.2 percent in 1996, down from 80.8 percent the year before and 85.2 percent in 1987. The decline may reflect new plants and equipment coming into production as a result of the increased investment.

Prices. Producer prices in the industry rose at a modest annual rate of 1.82 percent during 1987-1996; from 1992 to 1996, these prices rose at only a 0.9 percent rate

TABLE 3

U.S. OUTPUT, INVESTMENT, AND PRICES: APPAREL

(Millions of U.S. dollars, except as noted)

	1987	1988	1989	1990	1991	1992	1993	1994	1995	1996	GROWTH RATE 1987-1995[1]
VALUE OF SHIPMENTS:											
BY INDUSTRY:											
Current dollars	64,243	65,771	64,880	66,637	68,309	71,658	74,010	76,979	78,097	....	2.47
Constant 1992 dollars	72,854	72,371	69,404	69,371	69,578	71,658	73,323	76,010	76,546	....	0.62
BY PRODUCT:											
Current dollars	62,120	62,751	61,447	61,962	62,649	68,844	70,986	73,259	73,547	....	2.13
Constant 1992 dollars	66,524	65,203	65,733	64,468	63,780	68,844	70,329	72,331	72,077	....	1.01
OTHER OUTPUT MEASURES:											
Industrial production, 1993=100	103.0	101.2	97.9	94.9	95.5	97.7	100.0	104.0	100.9	95.9	-0.79
Gross domestic product:											
Current dollars	22,844	23,939	25,221	25,151	25,890	27,190	27,268	27,823	....	....	....
Percent of total GDP	0.5	0.5	0.5	0.4	0.4	0.4	0.4	0.4	....	....	....
Rank in manufacturing	14	15	14	14	14	14	14	15	....	....	....
Chained (1992) dollars	25,320	26,567	27,194	26,487	26,378	27,190	26,940	27,787	....	....	....
INVESTMENT-RELATED MEASURES:											
Capacity utilization, percent	85.2	83.6	80.9	78.3	78.7	80.3	82.0	84.9	80.8	75.2	....
New capital expenditures	736	692	868	857	801	945	962	1,091	1,194	....	....
Producer prices, 1993=100[2]	87.2	89.9	92.5	95.0	97.3	99.0	100.0	100.4	101.2	102.6	1.82

1. Compound annual growth rate.

2. Prices received by domestic producers.

Sources: Shipments and new capital expenditures: U.S. Department of Commerce for 1987-1995, editor's estimates for constant dollar data for 1987-88 and all shipments data for 1996; Industrial production and capacity utilization: Federal Reserve Board of Governors; GDP: Bureau of Economic Analysis; Research and development spending: National Science Foundation; Producer prices: Bureau of Labor Statistics.

Workforce and Employment. Employment in the apparel industry declined throughout the 1987-1996 period, dropping at an annual rate of 2.62 percent (Table 4). Employment of production workers declined at a slightly faster rate of 2.89 percent, which reduced their share of the workforce to 81.9 percent in 1996 from 84 percent in 1987. Women employees, with a 3.34 percent annual average decline, accounted for 74.5 percent of the workforce in 1996, compared with 79.7 percent in 1987. Earnings in the industry are the lowest in manufacturing, averaging only $7.96 an hour in 1996. After adjustment for inflation, average hourly earnings in 1996 were about two percent below 1987, but 3.5 percent above their 1993 low. The average workweek in 1996 was 37 hours, about the same as in past years.

TABLE 4

U.S. EMPLOYMENT, HOURS, AND EARNINGS: APPAREL

(Monetary values in U.S. dollars)

	1987	1988	1989	1990	1991	1992	1993	1994	1995	1996	CHANGE[1]
NUMBER OF EMPLOYEES, IN THOUSANDS:											
Total	1,097	1,085	1,076	1,036	1,006	1,007	989	974	936	864	-2.62
Production workers	922	912	907	869	841	844	829	815	776	708	-2.89
Percent of total	84.0	84.1	84.3	83.8	83.6	83.8	83.8	83.6	82.9	81.9	....
Women	875	864	856	818	791	787	765	744	706	644	-3.34
Percent of total	79.7	79.6	79.6	79.0	78.6	78.1	77.3	76.4	75.4	74.5	....
HOURS AND EARNINGS OF PRODUCTION WORKERS: AVERAGE HOURLY EARNINGS[2]											
Current dollars	5.94	6.12	6.35	6.57	6.77	6.95	7.09	7.34	7.64	7.96	3.31
1992 dollars[3]	7.30	7.23	7.16	7.04	6.97	6.95	6.90	6.96	7.05	7.14	-0.24
Average weekly hours	37.0	37.0	36.9	36.4	37.0	37.2	37.2	37.5	37.0	37.0	0.00
Average weekly earnings, current U.S. dollars	219.78	226.44	234.32	239.15	250.49	258.54	263.75	275.25	282.68	294.52	3.31

1. Compound annual growth rate, 1987-1996.

2. Including overtime.

3. Converted to 1992 dollars using Consumer Price Index for Urban Wage Earners and Clerical Workers.

Source: Bureau of Labor Statistics.

FIGURE 3

U.S. OCCUPATIONAL INJURY AND ILLNESS RATES: APPAREL, 1995

Incidence of nonfatal injuries and illnesses per 100 full-time workers

The incidence rate for occupational illnesses and injuries in the apparel industry was 8.2 cases per 100 workers in 1995, well below the 11.6 cases for all manufacturing.

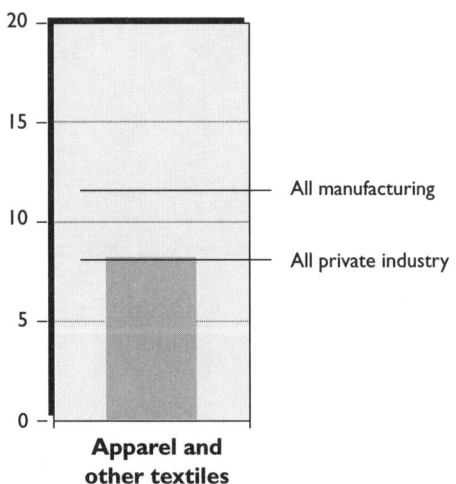

Source: U.S. Bureau of Labor Statistics.

Table 5

U.S. Employment Projections by Major Occupational Group: Apparel and Other Textile Products

Occupation	1994		Projections, 2005			
	Number of Employees	Percent of Industry Total	Number of Employees			Percent of Industry Total, Moderate Projections
			Low	Moderate	High	
Total, all occupations	969,400	100.0	723,200	771,600	814,900	100.0
Executive, administrative, and managerial	39,346	4.1	34,186	36,459	38,501	4.7
Professional specialties	9,833	1.0	9,907	10,565	11,157	1.4
Technicians and related support	2,618	0.3	2,067	2,204	2,327	0.3
Marketing and sales	18,990	2.0	16,710	17,821	18,820	2.3
Administrative support including clerical	85,459	8.8	65,507	69,880	73,799	9.1
Service	9,080	0.9	6,437	6,868	7,253	0.9
Agriculture, forestry, and fisheries occupations	....	....	....	....	....	....
Precision production, craft, and repair	105,025	10.8	93,183	99,426	105,007	12.9
Operators, fabricators, assemblers	699,030	72.1	495,189	528,361	558,019	68.5

Source: Bureau of Labor Statistics, November 1995.

Apparel industry employment is projected at 771,600 in 2005, compared with 969,400 in 1994. Among the occupational areas, only professional specialties are projected to show an increase. Operators, fabricators, and assemblers are expected to account for only 68.5 percent of all employment, compared with 72.1 percent in 1994.

Figure 4

U.S. Corporate Income and Worker Earnings: Apparel

Corporate operating income and aggregate production worker earnings

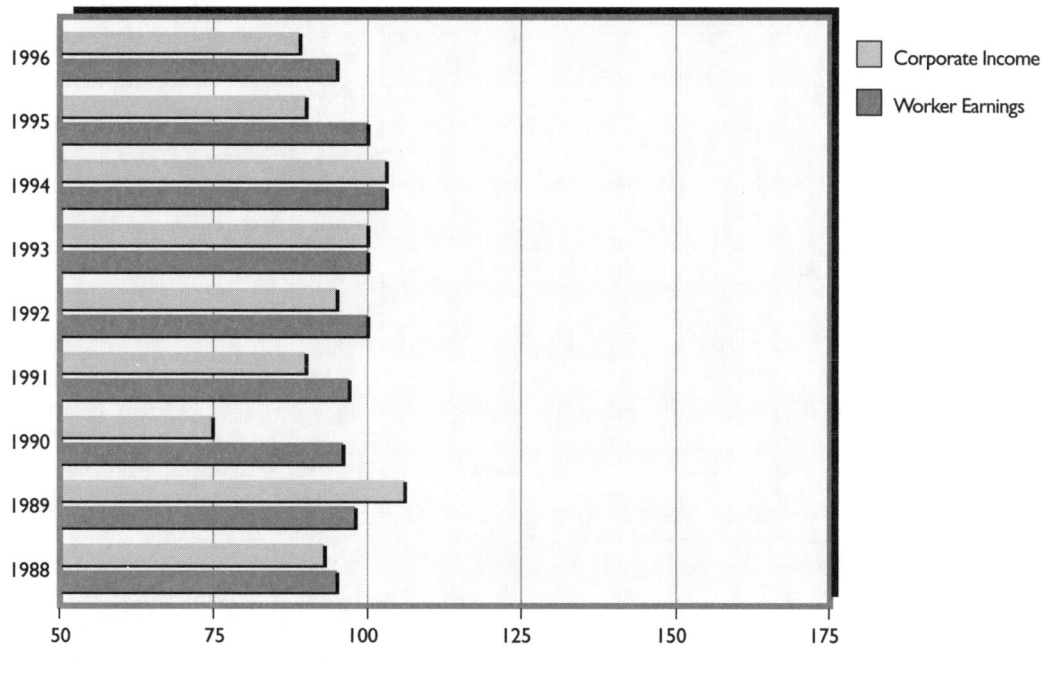

Index numbers, 1993=100

Source: U.S. Bureau of Labor Statistics, U.S. Bureau of the Census, and estimates by the editors. Corporate income includes leather industry.

Finance. Corporate income and production worker earnings in the apparel industry (including leather) fluctuated erratically between 1988 and 1996. The net outcome by 1996 was slightly lower corporate operating income than in 1988 and slightly higher production worker earnings (Figure 4). Corporate income from operations during the nine-year period declined at an annual rate of 0.58 percent to $3.3 billion in 1996 (Table 6). After-tax income, however, rose at a modest 0.73 percent rate to $1.97 billion in 1996. These averages for the period conceal a period of strong earnings from operations from 1991 to 1994, followed by considerably weaker performance in 1995 and 1996.

TABLE 6

U.S. CORPORATE INCOME AND ASSETS: APPAREL (INCLUDING LEATHER)

(Monetary values in millions of U.S. dollars)

INCOME AND EXPENSES	1988	1989	1990	1991	1992	1993	1994	1995	1996	CHANGE OR AVERAGE[1]
Sales and receipts	64,574	67,644	59,614	62,381	68,181	73,982	73,446	69,987	69,353	0.90
Depreciation and amortization	(901)	(852)	(858)	(911)	(953)	(1,007)	(1,088)	(1,092)	(1,040)	1.81
Other operating costs	(60,198)	(62,860)	(56,004)	(58,097)	(63,681)	(69,264)	(68,529)	(65,552)	(64,996)	0.96
Income from operations	3,476	3,932	2,753	3,374	3,548	3,712	3,830	3,343	3,317	-0.58
Nonoperating income (expenditures)	(677)	(886)	(888)	(575)	804	(187)	(852)	(449)	(597)	....
Income before taxes	2,798	3,047	1,866	2,798	4,351	3,521	2,978	2,894	2,720	-0.35
Income after taxes	1,862	2,080	1,276	1,906	3,483	2,444	1,972	1,962	1,973	0.73
Cash dividends	1,839	611	532	773	915	841	673	811	1,190	-5.30
Income retained in business	23	1,468	743	1,134	2,568	1,603	1,298	1,151	782	55.39
Direct credits (charges)	(1,332)	(807)	(538)	(814)	(826)	(310)	83	(236)	(4,114)	....
Ending retained earnings	8,410	9,876	8,713	8,906	8,547	10,003	11,263	10,746	7,426	-1.54
ASSETS, END OF YEAR:										
Total	33,031	32,439	31,672	31,495	35,684	38,005	40,005	40,053	38,412	1.90
Accounts receivable	8,584	7,894	7,873	8,151	8,875	9,463	9,207	8,782	9,327	1.04
Inventories	12,096	11,825	10,307	9,920	11,845	12,711	12,591	12,504	11,645	-0.47
Net property, plant and equipment	5,461	5,268	5,656	5,173	5,817	6,267	6,781	6,624	6,450	2.10
RATIOS, PERCENT:										
INCOME TO SALES:										
Before tax	4.33	4.50	3.13	4.49	6.38	4.76	4.05	4.14	3.92	4.41
After tax	2.88	3.07	2.14	3.06	5.11	3.30	2.68	2.80	2.84	3.10
INCOME TO STOCKHOLDERS' EQUITY:										
Before tax	24.80	23.57	15.73	22.52	34.05	22.37	18.05	17.85	21.93	22.32
After tax	16.51	16.09	10.76	15.34	27.25	15.53	11.95	12.10	15.91	15.72
INCOME TO TOTAL ASSETS:										
Before tax	8.47	9.39	5.89	8.88	12.19	9.26	7.44	7.23	7.08	8.43
After tax	5.64	6.41	4.03	6.05	9.76	6.43	4.93	4.90	5.14	5.92
AS A PERCENT OF TOTAL ASSETS:										
Property, plant and equipment	16.53	16.24	17.86	16.42	16.30	16.49	16.95	16.54	16.79	16.68
Short-term debt	11.34	9.48	9.50	8.69	9.19	9.28	7.90	6.88	7.19	8.83
Long-term debt	23.87	23.47	25.05	21.84	24.36	21.12	21.06	23.74	29.19	23.75
Stockholders' equity	34.15	39.86	37.46	39.44	35.81	41.41	41.25	40.47	32.29	38.02

1. For income and asset amounts, compound annual growth rate; for ratios, average of ratios for the years shown.

Source: U.S. Bureau of the Census, Quarterly Financial Report.

Notes: Parentheses ( ) indicate negative items, e.g., net expenses, charges, or losses. Net property, plant, and equipment is net of accumulated depreciation. Because the samples used to collect the data change, retained earnings at the end of a given year will not exactly equal the previous year's retained earnings plus the current year's retained income and credits.

CANADA

Canada's clothing industry in 1993 consisted of 1,921 establishments and 82,737 employees (Table 7). The industry has four major subindustries. The largest of these is women's clothing (accounting for 35 percent of total 1994 shipments). The others are men's and boys' clothing (33 percent of the total); other clothing and apparel, including sweaters, gloves, hosiery, occupational clothing, and foundation garments (24 percent), and children's clothing (8 percent).

Canadian clothing shipments and employment in 1994 were well below highs reached in the late 1980s and 1990 (Table 8). Shipments rebounded somewhat between 1992 and 1994, from $5.86 billion to $6.15 billion, but employment fell in 1994 for the sixth successive year, to 80,383. Production workers accounted for 83 percent of employment in 1994, compared with a high of 89 percent in 1988. Average hourly wages in 1994 were Can$8.92, and the average workweek was 39.7 hours.

TABLE 7

CANADA: COMPONENT INDUSTRIES OF CLOTHING (CSIC 24), 1993

(Monetary values in Canadian dollars)

| INDUSTRY NAME | CSIC | ESTABLISH-MENTS (NUMBER) | EMPLOYMENT | | VALUE OF SHIPMENTS (MILLIONS) | AVERAGE HOURLY EARNINGS[1] |
			NUMBER	PERCENT OF INDUSTRY TOTAL		
CLOTHING INDUSTRIES	24	1,921	82,737	100.0	CAN$5,933.3	CAN$8.71
Men's and boys' clothing	243	420	31,060	37.5	1,957.3	8.78
Men's and boys' coats	2431	57	2,936	3.5	161.8	8.34
Men's and boys' suits and jackets	2432	96	6,820	8.2	502.0	9.07
Men's and boys' pants	2433	46	6,481	7.8	535.7	10.01
Men's and boys' shirts and underwear	2434	82	9,067	11.0	594.2	8.46
Men's and boys' clothing contractors	2435	139	5,756	7.0	163.7	8.01
Women's clothing	244	839	24,901	30.1	2,066.4	8.68
Women's coats and jackets	2441	63	2,323	2.8	211.2	9.25
Women's sportswear	2442	227	10,070	12.2	1,181.1	9.14
Women's dresses	2443	71	1,918	2.3	280.4	11.58
Women's blouses and shirts	2444	23	947	1.1	80.9	10.10
Women's clothing contractors	2445	455	9,643	11.7	312.8	7.61
Children's clothing	245	113	4,762	5.8	457.3	8.37
Other clothing and apparel	249	549	22,014	26.6	1,452.4	8.71
Sweaters	2491	51	2,992	3.6	173.7	8.96
Occupational clothing	2492	78	2,840	3.4	181.7	8.20
Gloves	2493	29	795	1.0	46.4	8.37
Hosiery	2494	42	4,603	5.6	309.6	8.81
Fur goods	2495	138	759	0.9	80.5	10.00
Foundation garments	2496	19	2,881	3.5	167.2	9.53
Other clothing and apparel, n.e.c.	2499	192	7,144	8.6	493.3	8.34

1. Including overtime.

Source: Adapted from Statistics Canada, *Manufacturing Industries of Canada* (Cat. No. 31-203).

TABLE 8

CANADIAN EMPLOYMENT AND SHIPMENTS: CLOTHING INDUSTRIES, 1987-1994

(Monetary values in Canadian dollars)

	1987	1988	1989	1990	1991	1992	1993	1994	CHANGE[1]
All employees	112,002	115,485	112,177	103,431	93,464	83,927	82,737	80,383	-4.63
Establishments	2,390	2,819	2,686	2,785	2,390	2,137	1,921	1,760	-4.28
Employees per establishment	47	41	42	37	39	39	43	46	-0.37
Production workers per establishment	.....	37	36	32	33	33	36	38	0.70
PRODUCTION WORKERS:									
Total	.....	102,988	97,276	89,176	79,483	70,182	69,748	67,036	-6.91
Percent of all employees	.....	89.2	86.7	86.2	85.0	83.6	84.3	83.4	.....
Male	.....	22,374	20,282	18,876	16,710	.....	.....	.....	.....
Female	.....	80,614	76,994	70,300	62,773	.....	.....	.....	.....
Percent of total production workers	.....	78.3	79.2	78.8	79.0	.....	.....	.....	.....
Average hourly earnings	.....	7.36	7.96	9.05	9.25	8.61	8.71	8.92	3.26
Average weekly earnings	.....	292.62	304.98	350.05	356.51	338.05	341.87	353.68	3.21
Average weekly hours	.....	39.8	38.3	38.7	38.5	39.3	39.3	39.7	-0.05
Shipments (millions)	6,457	6,657	6,948	6,831	6,156	5,854	5,933	6,147	-0.70

1. Compound annual growth rate.

Source: Adapted from Statistics Canada, *Manufacturing Industries of Canada* (Cat. No. 31-203).

MEXICO

Apparel production in Mexico is included in the textiles, garments, and leather industry. In 1993, the garments subindustry (shown in Table 9) had 209,623 employees. The average yearly income (wages and benefits) of garment workers in 1993 was 11,720 new pesos (about $3,752). Production workers numbered 155,599 and earned on average 7,451 new pesos a year ($2,385), while there were 26,095 nonproduction employees whose average yearly earnings were 19,576 new pesos ($6,267). Employment of garment workers rose by 0.87 percent between 1988 and 1995 to 231,619 (Table 10).

TABLE 9

MEXICO: GARMENT INDUSTRY (CMAP 3220), 1993

(Monetary values in 1993 Mexican New Pesos)

			ALL WORKERS									
							PAID WORKERS					
							PRODUCTION WORKERS		NONPRODUCTION EMPLOYEES		BENEFITS	UNPAID
INDUSTRY	CMAP	NUMBER OF UNITS	NUMBER	PERCENT OF INDUSTRY TOTAL	AVERAGE DAYS WORKED	REMUN-ERATION[1]	NUMBER	WAGES AND SALARIES	NUMBER	WAGES AND SALARIES	PER PAID EMPLOYEE	WORKERS, NUMBER
Garments	3220	22,560	209,623	100	361	11,720	155,599	7,451	26,095	19,576	2,527	27,929

1. Average annual remuneration including benefits.

Source: INEGI, Censos Economicos, 1994.

TABLE 10

MEXICAN EMPLOYMENT: GARMENTS, 1988-1995

	1988	1989	1990	1991	1992	1993	1994	1995	CHANGE[1]
TOTAL EMPLOYMENT: Garments (Apparel)	217,984	217,746	219,949	221,290	220,586	230,609	231,336	231,619	0.87

1. Compound annual growth rate.

Source: Sistema de Cuentas Nacionales de Mexico, INEGI.

INTERNATIONAL TRADE

United States. Worldwide U.S. trade in apparel through 1996 has grown rapidly (Table 11). However, gains in imports between 1992 and 1995 were far greater than those in exports, resulting in a widening trade deficit. The deficit continued to widen in 1996, but at a slower pace. U.S. imports of apparel in 1996 totaled $43.1 billion in value, compared with $26.7 billion in 1990. Since 1992, imports have accounted for over one-third of apparent domestic consumption. Exports of apparel in 1996 amounted to $8.1 billion, against $2.9 billion in 1990. The resulting trade deficit for apparel was $35 billion in 1996, about 50 percent more than the 1990 deficit of $23.9 billion.

Canada. Apparel trade between the United States and Canada has skyrocketed so far in the 1990s, spurred by the implementation of the Canadian-U.S. Free Trade Agreement in 1989 and of NAFTA in January 1994. U.S. exports to Canada reached a record $1.03 billion in 1996, compared with $367 million in 1990 and $676 million in 1993. Canadian exports to the United States rose from $321 million in 1990 to $616 million in 1993 and a record $1.19 billion in 1996. (See Table 11.) In 1996, Canada was the second largest U.S. supplier of apparel and textiles in terms of quantity and the sixth largest in terms of value, according to the International Trade Commission (ITC).

Mexico. U.S. apparel trade with Mexico has grown even faster than that with Canada. U.S. exports to Mexico between 1990 and 1996 almost quadrupled to $1.99 billion, while Mexican exports to the United States soared 289 percent to $4.67 billion (Table 11). Since 1993, the year before implementation of NAFTA, U.S. exports to Mexico have risen 70 percent, and Mexican exports to the United States have gained 91 percent. The U.S. deficit in apparel trade with Mexico stood at $2.68 billion in 1996, compared with $677 million in 1990. The ITC reports that Mexico is now the largest U.S. supplier of textiles and apparel by quantity and the second largest by value, exceeded only by China.

NAFTA. Mexico has been the primary gainer in apparel trade in recent years (Table 11). Its positive trade balance surged from about $686 million in 1990 to $2.7 billion in 1996. Canada's positive trade balance in 1996 was considerably improved from deficits of most previous years. The United States, on the other hand, saw its deficit in apparel trade more than quadruple from $631 million in 1990 to $2.8 billion in 1996. Since 1993, the U.S. trade deficit has risen by $1.62 billion (or 133 percent). Mexico's trade surplus during that time has risen by $1.43 billion, and Canada has gone from a deficit of $74 million in 1993 to a $114-million surplus in 1996.

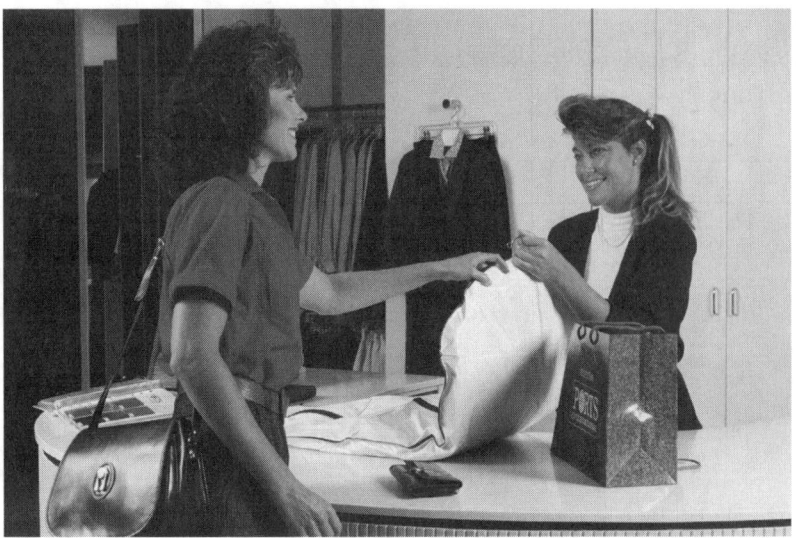

TABLE 11

INTERNATIONAL TRADE, APPAREL

(Millions of U.S. dollars)

	1989[1]	1990	1991	1992	1993	1994	1995	1996
GLOBAL TRADE, U.S.								
IMPORTS								
Value	25,509.3	26,746.7	27,376.9	32,644.5	35,474.7	38,560.8	41,208.1	43,074.5
Ratio to new supply[2]	29.3	30.2	30.5	32.1	33.1	34.2	.....	.....
Ratio to apparent consumption[3]	30.1	31.2	31.8	33.7	34.8	36.2	.....	.....
EXPORTS								
Value	2,378.9	2,887.3	3,746.2	4,659.2	5,432.7	6,144.5	7,190.1	8,104.4
Ratio to comparable domestic shipments	3.9	4.7	6.0	6.8	7.6	8.3	.....	.....
TRADE BALANCE	(23,130.4)	(23,859.4)	(23,630.7)	(27,985.3)	(30,042.0)	(32,416.3)	(34,018.0)	(34,970.1)
BILATERAL TRADE: NAFTA[4]								
U.S. exports to Canada	191.7	367.2	474.1	550.8	676.0	764.1	992.3	1,026.6
Canadian exports to U.S.	336.4	321.4	378.2	490.5	615.6	788.3	986.8	1,187.1
U.S. exports to Mexico	498.2	524.4	708.1	955.1	1,167.4	1,434.6	1,575.6	1,986.3
Mexican exports to U.S.	990.7	1,201.5	1,487.6	1,959.9	2,449.6	2,877.9	3,674.2	4,669.2
Canadian exports to Mexico	0.2	0.2	0.5	0.6	0.8	1.1	0.7	2.3
Mexican exports to Canada	7.5	8.8	10.8	11.9	14.8	18.4	28.4	48.9
TRADE BALANCES WITHIN NAFTA[5]								
Canada	137.4	(54.4)	(106.2)	(71.6)	(74.4)	6.9	(33.2)	113.9
Mexico	499.8	685.7	789.8	1,016.1	1,296.2	1,460.6	2,126.3	2,729.5
United States	(637.1)	(631.2)	(683.7)	(944.5)	(1,221.9)	(1,467.4)	(2,093.1)	(2,843.4)

1. 1989 and earlier data on U.S. exports to Canada for manufacturing total and manufacturing industries are not comparable with data for 1990 and later years because of a change in the reporting system. The NAFTA trade balances for the U.S. and Canada also are affected.

2. New supply equals comparable domestic shipments plus imports for consumption.

3. Apparent consumption equals comparable domestic shipments plus imports for consumption less exports.

4. Amounts less than U.S. $100,000 shown as zero.

5. Parentheses indicate an excess of imports over exports. Because of commodity coding and other data differences among the three countries, these trade balances are only rough estimates and should be used with caution.

Source for U.S. Global Trade: U.S. Department of Commerce, International Trade Administration.

Source for U.S. -Canada and U.S.-Mexico Bilateral Trade: U.S. Bureau of the Census.

Source for Canada-Mexico and Mexico-Canada Bilateral Trade: Statistics Canada, Foreign Trade Division, Special tabulation, March 1997, converted to U.S. dollars by the editors.

CHEMICALS AND ALLIED PRODUCTS

THE UNITED STATES

Products and Processes. The chemical industry, which in 1996 was the fourth largest U.S. manufacturing industry in terms of industry shipments, converts raw materials into more than 70,000 products that affect virtually every aspect of our lives. Much of this impact is indirect, as most chemicals go to other industries for use as raw and intermediate

TABLE 1

UNITED STATES: COMPONENT INDUSTRIES OF CHEMICALS AND ALLIED PRODUCTS (SIC 28), 1992

(Monetary values in millions of U.S. dollars)

INDUSTRY	SIC	ESTABLISH-MENTS	SHIPMENTS VALUE	SHIPMENTS PERCENT BY 4 LARGEST COMPANIES	VALUE ADDED BY MANUFACTURE	NEW CAPITAL EXPENDI-TURES	EMPLOY-MENT[1]	PAYROLL
CHEMICALS AND ALLIED PRODUCTS	28	12,004	$305,420.1	....	$164,346.2	$16,380.9	848,600	$32,501.9
Industrial inorganic chemicals	281	1,422	27,331.4	....	16,723.7	1,553.2	103,400	4,214.4
Alkalies and chlorine	2812	51	2,786.9	75	1,408.1	176.2	8,000	353.3
Industrial gases	2813	592	3,095.7	78	2,076.2	146.3	7,700	261.8
Inorganic pigments	2816	89	3,320.0	69	2,027.4	509.1	8,700	333.7
Industrial inorganic chemicals, n.e.c.	2819	690	18,128.9	39	11,212.0	721.6	78,900	3,265.7
Plastics materials and synthetics	282	628	48,697.6	....	20,979.3	2,846.5	128,500	5,137.3
Plastics materials and resins	2821	456	31,600.8	24	12,598.5	1,711.6	61,200	2,698.0
Synthetic rubber	2822	94	4,235.3	48	1,898.5	320.9	11,900	521.6
Cellulosic manmade fibers	2823	7	1,748.1	98	820.9	92.8	11,000	372.8
Manmade organic fibers, noncellulosic	2824	71	11,113.3	74	5,661.4	721.2	44,400	1,545.0
Drugs	283	1,426	67,791.5	....	48,602.2	3,887.3	194,400	7,840.3
Medicinal chemicals and botanical products	2833	227	6,526.3	76	3,405.2	553.7	13,100	590.9
Pharmaceutical preparations	2834	684	50,415.3	26	37,224.0	2,450.1	122,900	4,958.3
In vitro and in vivo diagnostic substances	2835	236	6,857.1	49	5,207.5	588.2	39,900	1,660.0
Biological products except diagnostic substances	2836	279	3,992.8	53	2,765.6	295.3	18,500	631.1
Soaps, cleaners, and toilet preparations	284	2,405	42,875.4	....	26,181.5	1,290.0	122,800	3,926.9
Soap and other detergents	2841	707	14,728.8	63	7,708.8	570.6	32,800	1,170.9
Polishes and sanitation goods	2842	744	6,658.5	52	4,218.9	121.4	22,000	661.9
Surface active agents	2843	204	2,859.0	37	1,169.5	92.2	8,200	319.8
Toilet preparations	2844	750	18,629.1	36	13,084.3	505.9	59,800	1,774.4
Paints and allied products	285	1,419	14,973.2	....	7,154.0	273.3	51,100	1,710.0
Paints and allied products	2851	1,419	14,973.2	29	7,154.0	273.3	51,100	1,710.0
Industrial organic chemicals	286	972	64,397.3	....	26,131.6	4,791.3	124,500	5,494.8
Gum and wood chemicals	2861	76	734.6	62	379.0	42.8	2,500	67.8
Cyclic crude and intermediates	2865	203	9,559.6	31	3,329.3	539.8	22,200	933.2
Industrial organic chemicals, n.e.c.	2869	693	54,103.1	29	22,423.4	4,208.7	99,800	4,493.8
Agricultural chemicals	287	890	18,841.4	....	8,659.0	988.1	40,300	1,451.2
Nitrogenous fertilizers	2873	153	3,177.4	48	1,264.8	208.8	7,000	257.8
Phosphatic fertilizers	2874	73	4,317.5	62	1,237.7	307.2	9,500	340.6
Fertilizers, mixing only	2875	403	2,204.3	19	642.4	44.2	7,000	183.5
Pesticides and agricultural chemicals, n.e.c.	2879	261	9,142.2	53	5,514.1	427.8	16,800	669.3
Miscellaneous chemical products	289	2,842	20,512.4	....	9,914.9	751.3	83,700	2,726.9
Adhesives and sealants	2891	691	5,657.1	25	2,634.7	188.3	21,100	675.4
Explosives	2892	122	1,222.9	57	787.7	39.6	11,300	337.4
Printing ink	2893	519	3,076.4	45	1,114.0	46.0	12,200	406.5
Carbon black	2895	24	628.8	77	330.2	33.4	2,000	74.5
Chemicals and chemical preparations, n.e.c.	2899	1,486	9,927.1	22	5,048.3	444.1	37,100	1,233.1

1. Employment numbers from the economic censuses differ in definition and classification from the Bureau of Labor Statistics estimates in Table 2. Year-to-year comparisons between Table 1 and Table 2 are not appropriate.

Source: U.S. Bureau of the Census, 1992 Census of Manufactures.

materials. The products of these industry customers include rubber and plastics, home furnishings, textiles, paper products, electrical and electronic equipment, motor vehicles, petroleum products, and adhesives. Consumer-ready items produced by chemical companies include fertilizer, soaps and detergents, pharmaceuticals, paints, and varnishes.

Raw materials used in the production of chemicals include oil, gas, and coal (organic chemicals) and the products of mining (inorganic chemicals).

Table 1 shows the major subgroups of the chemical industry in 1992 (latest year for which economic census data are available). The largest subindustry is drugs—primarily pharmaceutical products—with about 22 percent of total shipment value and 23 percent of employment. Producers of industrial organic chemicals account for about 21 percent of shipment value, followed by plastics materials and synthetics (almost 16 percent), and soaps, cleaners, and toilet preparations (14 percent).

Employment in the chemical industry is projected to decline slightly from the 1993 level to 1,067,000 (Table 2). Aside from growth in drug manufacturing (the largest subindustry) and in soap, cleaners, and toilet goods, most subindustries will decrease their employment. Production worker earnings in the industry averaged $14.82 per hour in 1993, with workers in industrial organic chemicals, not elsewhere classified, the highest paid at $17.88 an hour.

TABLE 2

U.S. EMPLOYMENT AND EARNINGS: CHEMICALS AND ALLIED PRODUCTS

INDUSTRY	SIC	1993			2005
		EMPLOYMENT[1]		AVERAGE HOURLY EARNINGS (U.S. DOLLARS)[2]	PROJECTED EMPLOYMENT[3]
		NUMBER OF PERSONS	PERCENT OF INDUSTRY TOTAL		
CHEMICALS AND ALLIED PRODUCTS	28	1,080,500	100.0	$14.82	1,067,000
Industrial inorganic chemicals	281	135,000	12.5	16.37	122,170
Industrial inorganic chemicals, n.e.c.	2819	87,000	8.1	16.83	....
Plastics materials and synthetics	282	166,700	15.4	15.22	142,500
Plastics materials and resins	2821	79,900	7.4	16.47	....
Organic fibers, noncellulosic	2824	56,900	5.3	13.98	....
Drugs	283	264,400	24.5	14.67	325,000
Pharmaceutical preparations	2834	215,800	20.0	14.72	....
Soap, cleaners, and toilet goods	284	156,800	14.5	12.39	165,200
Soap and other detergents	2841	44,800	4.1	15.96	....
Polishing, sanitation, and finishing preps	2842,3	42,700	4.0	11.54	....
Toilet preparations	2844	69,300	6.4	10.61	....
Paints and allied products	285	58,000	5.4	12.71	48,300
Industrial organic chemicals	286	151,100	14.0	17.68	136,330
Cyclic crudes and intermediates	2865	26,100	2.4	17.40	....
Industrial organic chemicals, n.e.c.	2869	122,100	11.3	17.88	....
Agricultural chemicals	287	55,800	5.2	15.09	42,500
Miscellaneous chemical products	289	92,700	8.6	13.50	85,000

1. Total payroll employment. Employment data from the economic censuses, shown in Table 1, differ in definition and classification from the Bureau of Labor Statistics estimates in this table. Year-to-year comparisons between Table 1 and Table 2 are not appropriate.

2. Earnings of production workers, including overtime.

3. Number of persons, moderate projection by the U.S. Bureau of Labor Statistics.

Source: Bureau of Labor Statistics.

FIGURE 1

U.S. EMPLOYMENT IN CHEMICALS
Percent distribution by region, 1995

Chemical industry employment is highest in the Southeast (26 percent in 1995), Mid-Atlantic region (25 percent), and Great Lakes region (21 percent) while the small shares for the Rocky Mountain states and New England are below their shares of total U.S. employment.

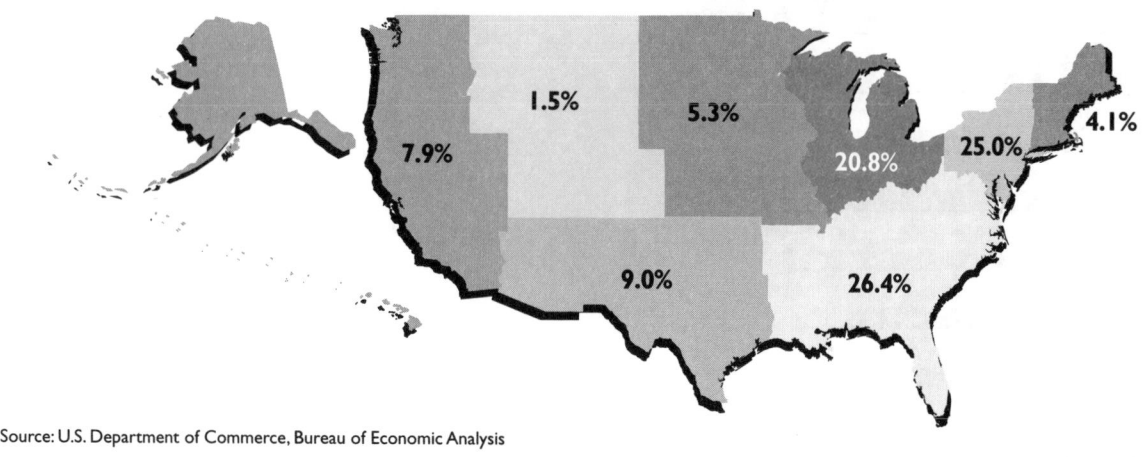

Source: U.S. Department of Commerce, Bureau of Economic Analysis

What's New. The outlook for chemicals and allied products continues bright for the near term as a result of expanding economic and industrial activity worldwide.[1] Production of chemicals is expected to rise more than 4.5 percent in 1997 and around 2.5 percent in 1998. Likely growth areas include pharmaceuticals, synthetic rubber, manmade fibers, organics, and plastic resins.

In the foreign market, demand is expanding in virtually all major outlets, including Canada and Mexico—respectively, the first and second largest markets for U.S. chemicals—Western Europe and Japan. U.S. import demand is burgeoning also, reflecting the vibrant U.S. economy and the strong dollar relative to other currencies. The trend to offshore production of chemicals for export will continue.

As in many other industries, growth in production and profits has been achieved despite declining employment. Downsizing, outsourcing, and increased investment in technology will tend to suppress employment growth over the short term, although a sharp increase in economic growth could reverse this trend.

The Chemical Manufacturers Association (CMA), in its 1996 survey of industry members, found chemical producers to be guardedly optimistic about the next two years. However, there were significant differences between expectations of large companies (sales over $1 billion) and small companies (sales under $150 million). Medium and large companies foresaw smaller gains in sales and profits in 1997 than in 1996, while small companies projected a near doubling of their sales growth and larger profits. Most small and medium-sized companies expected to increase their payrolls in 1997, while only about a third of the large companies anticipated gains. Virtually all respondents predicted higher wages in 1997.

---

1 *Information in this section is based on reports by the Chemical Manufacturers Association (CMA).*

FIGURE 2

U.S. EMPLOYMENT AND SHIPMENTS, CHEMICALS AND ALLIED PRODUCTS

Total payroll employment and manufacturers' inflation-adjusted shipments

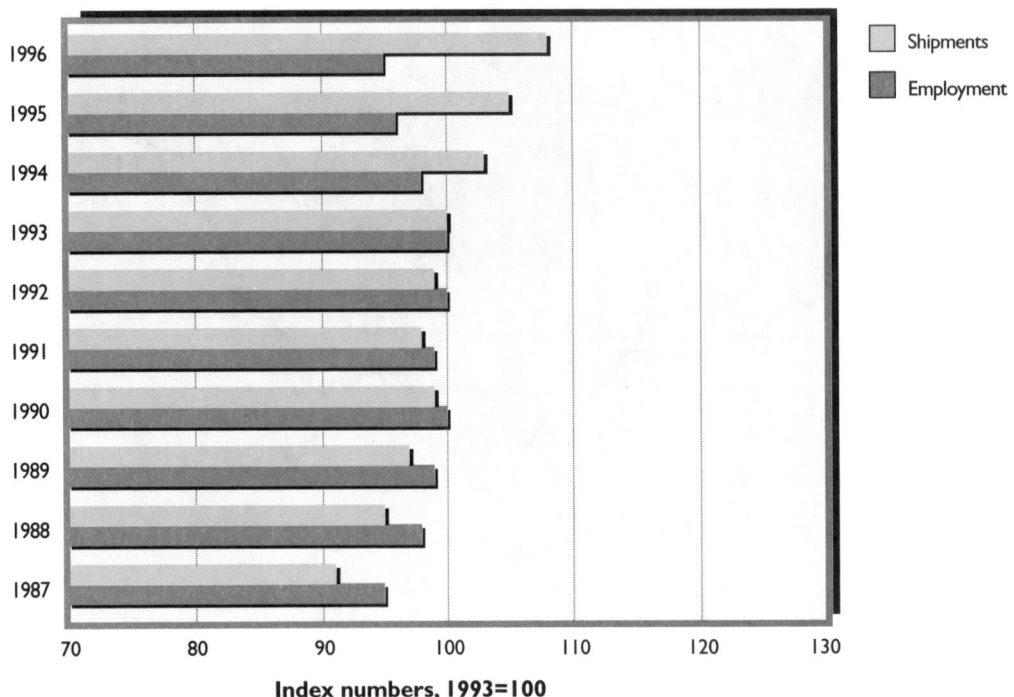

Index numbers, 1993=100

Source: U.S. Bureau of Labor Statistics, U.S. Department of Commerce, and estimates by the editors.

Output. The chemical industry is the fourth largest U.S. manufacturing industry, measured by value of shipments, following the transportation, food, and machinery industries. The chemical industry's well being is a good indicator of the economy as a whole, and vice versa, because so many other industries use chemicals as raw materials.

While employment by the chemical industry fluctuated within a narrow range between 1987 and 1996, industry shipments increased during most of that period (Figure 2). Shipments between 1987 and 1996 rose at an annual rate of 5.64 percent, to $376.1 billion, with the rate dropping to 1.88 percent when adjusted for inflation (Table 3). Partial-year results indicated that 1997 would be a growth year for chemicals, as second quarter shipments in current dollars were 6.6 percent ahead of those in the same period of 1996 while producer prices were up less than one percent from the previous year. Chemical sales were helped by increased production of appliances, textiles, paper and allied products, rubber and plastic products, primary metals, fabricated metal products, electronic components, and light vehicles.

Investment. New capital expenditures totaled $17.6 billion in 1995, more than double the $8.7 billion of 1987 and the highest level in the manufacturing sector (Table 3). Research and development (R&D) spending rose 75 percent between 1987 and 1994 to $16.6 billion, higher than for any other manufacturing industry except transportation equipment. Of the $16.6 billion, $9.6 billion was in the drug and medicine area. Record profits and strong cash flows are continuing to stimulate investment. The Chemical Manufacturers Association reports a 1.9 percent increase in R&D spending in 1996 and projects increases of 5 and 3.5 percent, respectively, for 1997 and 1998. Plant and equipment spending rose an estimated 10 percent in 1996, and CMA projections see it gaining 12.5 and 8.75 percent, respectively, in 1997 and 1998.

Prices. Prices for chemicals and allied products, as measured by producer prices, rose at an annual rate of 3.86 percent in the 10 years ended in 1996, with an especially strong 10-percent price rise in 1995 (Table 3). Costs to the industry for feedstock (hydrocarbons and other raw materials supplied to processing plants) were expected to rise only slightly in 1997, according to producers surveyed by CMA. Participants in the survey saw other energy costs (relating to fuel and power) decreasing 2.6 percent in 1997 following a 1996 increase of 17.8 percent.

TABLE 3

U.S. OUTPUT, INVESTMENT, AND PRICES: CHEMICALS AND ALLIED PRODUCTS

(Millions of U.S. dollars, except as noted)

	1987	1988	1989	1990	1991	1992	1993	1994	1995	1996	GROWTH RATE 1987-1996[1]
VALUE OF SHIPMENTS:											
BY INDUSTRY:											
Current dollars	229,546	261,238	283,196	292,803	298,544	305,420	314,907	333,905	362,127	376,104	5.64
Constant 1992 dollars	279,866	292,278	299,184	305,527	302,217	305,420	307,610	317,570	323,643	330,856	1.88
BY PRODUCT:											
Current dollars	214,618	244,515	260,649	268,505	268,935	282,242	292,416	309,592	338,065	351,113	5.62
Constant 1992 dollars	259,639	271,412	273,211	278,547	271,466	282,242	285,755	294,562	301,340	308,056	1.92
OTHER OUTPUT MEASURES:											
Industrial production, 1993=100	86.1	91.3	94.2	96.3	95.4	99.0	100.0	103.1	105.4	107.8	2.53
Gross domestic product:											
Current dollars	85,112	96,982	104,922	110,348	114,148	120,457	126,492	132,375	....	....	....
Percent of total GDP	1.8	1.9	1.9	1.9	1.9	1.9	1.9	1.9	....	....	....
Rank in manufacturing	3	3	3	2	1	1	1	1	....	....	....
Chained (1992) dollars	110,397	110,440	111,401	117,260	115,814	120,457	122,100	125,128	....	....	....
INVESTMENT-RELATED MEASURES:											
Capacity utilization, percent	81.3	84.0	83.7	83.0	80.1	80.3	78.8	79.1	79.1	78.6	....
New capital expenditures	8,711	11,006	13,775	15,645	16,599	16,381	15,690	15,411	17,627	....	....
Research and development spending	9,445	10,828	11,943	13,168	14,439	15,091	16,658	16,559	....	....	....
Producer prices, 1993=100[2]	81.5	88.8	94.1	95.2	97.8	98.9	100.0	102.2	112.8	114.6	3.86

1. Compound annual growth rate.

2. Prices received by domestic producers.

Sources: Shipments and new capital expenditures: U.S. Department of Commerce for 1987-1995, editor's estimates for constant dollar data for 1987-88 and all shipments data for 1996; Industrial production and capacity utilization: Federal Reserve Board of Governors; GDP: Bureau of Economic Analysis; Research and development spending: National Science Foundation; Producer prices: Bureau of Labor Statistics.

Workforce and Employment. Chemical industry employment rose moderately until 1992 but has since declined (Figure 2 and Table 4), even as shipments and production have grown. Employment totaled 1,032,000 in 1996, versus 1,084,000 in 1992. The average workweek has been almost steady since 1992, at 43.2 hours, so that productivity appears to have grown. Average hourly earnings of production workers totaled $16.17 in 1996. The annual growth rate for 1987-1996 was 3 percent, but represented a decline of 0.5 percent per year when adjusted for inflation. For 1997, CMA forecasts a fractional decline in industry employment as a result of cuts planned by large producers. Hourly wages, on the other hand, are expected to rise 3.5 percent.

TABLE 4

U.S. EMPLOYMENT, HOURS, AND EARNINGS: CHEMICALS AND ALLIED PRODUCTS

(Monetary values in U.S. dollars)

	1987	1988	1989	1990	1991	1992	1993	1994	1995	1996	CHANGE[1]
NUMBER OF EMPLOYEES, IN THOUSANDS:											
Total	1,025	1,057	1,074	1,086	1,076	1,084	1,081	1,057	1,038	1,032	0.08
Production workers	575	596	603	600	580	567	573	578	580	575	0.01
Percent of total	56.1	56.4	56.2	55.2	53.9	52.3	53.0	54.6	55.9	55.7	....
Women	294	308	318	328	327	335	339	334	330	327	1.19
Percent of total	28.7	29.1	29.6	30.2	30.4	30.9	31.4	31.6	31.8	31.7	....
HOURS AND EARNINGS OF PRODUCTION WORKERS:											
AVERAGE HOURLY EARNINGS[2]											
Current dollars	12.37	12.71	13.09	13.54	14.04	14.51	14.82	15.13	15.62	16.17	3.02
1992 dollars[3]	15.20	15.01	14.76	14.51	14.44	14.51	14.42	14.35	14.41	14.50	-0.52
Average weekly hours	42.3	42.2	42.4	42.6	42.9	43.1	43.1	43.2	43.2	43.2	0.23
Average weekly earnings, current U.S. dollars	523.25	536.36	555.02	576.80	602.32	625.38	638.74	653.62	674.78	698.54	3.26

1. Compound annual growth rate, 1987-1996.

2. Including overtime.

3. Converted to 1992 dollars using Consumer Price Index for Urban Wage Earners and Clerical Workers.

Source: Bureau of Labor Statistics.

FIGURE 3

U.S. OCCUPATIONAL INJURY AND ILLNESS RATES:

CHEMICALS AND ALLIED PRODUCTS, 1995

Incidence of nonfatal injuries and illnesses per 100 full-time workers

In 1995, the chemical industry averaged 5.5 cases of nonfatal occupational illnesses and injuries per 100 workers, one of the lowest levels in manufacturing.

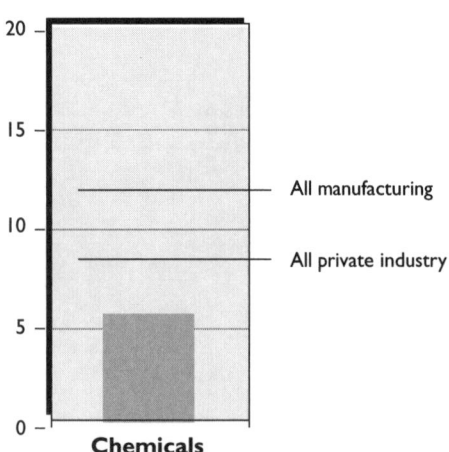

Source: U.S. Bureau of Labor Statistics.

TABLE 5

U.S. EMPLOYMENT PROJECTIONS BY MAJOR OCCUPATIONAL GROUP: CHEMICALS AND ALLIED PRODUCTS

| | 1994 | | PROJECTIONS, 2005 | | | |
| OCCUPATION | NUMBER OF EMPLOYEES | PERCENT OF INDUSTRY TOTAL | NUMBER OF EMPLOYEES | | | PERCENT OF INDUSTRY TOTAL, MODERATE PROJECTIONS |
			LOW	MODERATE	HIGH	
Total, all occupations	1,060,700	100.0	1,032,100	1,067,000	1,089,400	100.0
Executive, administrative, and managerial	138,875	13.1	141,161	145,955	149,123	13.7
Professional specialties	129,314	12.2	151,830	157,495	161,231	14.8
Technicians and related support	67,500	6.4	66,561	68,944	70,470	6.5
Marketing and sales	47,247	4.5	47,380	49,108	50,371	4.6
Administrative support including clerical	150,142	14.2	133,271	137,681	140,668	12.9
Service	18,883	1.8	17,070	17,673	18,071	1.7
Agriculture, forestry, and fisheries occupations	2,139	0.2	2,214	2,319	2,392	0.2
Precision production, craft, and repair	202,596	19.1	190,100	196,242	199,645	18.4
Operators, fabricators, assemblers	304,003	28.7	282,511	291,584	297,429	27.3

Source: Bureau of Labor Statistics, November 1995.

Projections by the Bureau of Labor Statistics indicate employment in 2005 may be slightly above the 1994 level of 1,060,700. Gains are seen for executives and managers, professional specialties, technicians, and marketing and sales, while declines will occur in most other areas, including employment of production workers.

FIGURE 4

U.S. CORPORATE INCOME AND WORKER EARNINGS: CHEMICALS AND ALLIED PRODUCTS

Corporate operating income and aggregate production worker earnings

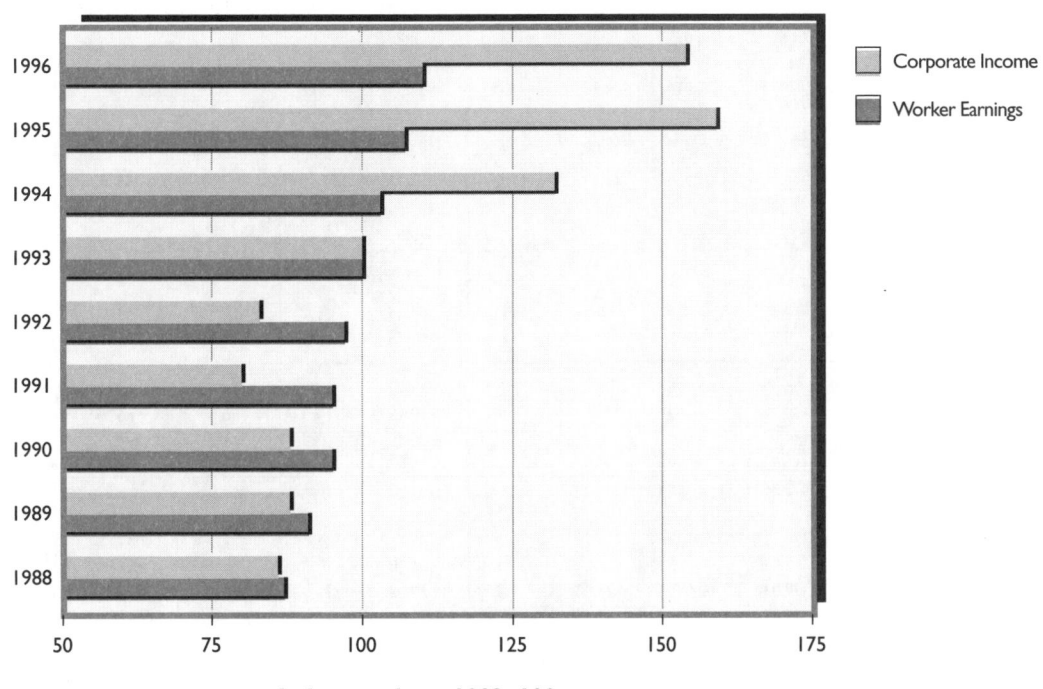

Index numbers, 1993=100

Source: U.S. Bureau of Labor Statistics, U.S. Bureau of the Census, and estimates by the editors.

Finance. Since 1992, corporate income of the chemical industry has risen at a much faster rate than the earnings of production workers (Figure 4). Industry sales and receipts grew at an annual rate of 5.96 percent during the 1988-96 period. Operating income rose 7.46 percent annually, to $44.9 billion in 1996, and after-tax income gained at an 8.46 percent rate, reaching $45.3 billion (Table 6). After-tax income to sales stood at 10.89 percent in 1996, compared with 9.27 percent the previous year and only 4.12 percent in 1992, the low point for the past 10 years. After-tax income to stockholders' equity reached 22.62 percent in 1996, compared with a low for the decade of 8.70 percent in 1992. CMA reports that profits may rise another 10 percent in 1997. Preliminary figures for the first quarter of 1997 show an 8 percent after-tax profit gain from the year-earlier period, with an extremely large (43 percent) increase in drug industry profits offsetting declines elsewhere.

Inventories have risen at an annual rate of 4.2 percent during the past 10 years, with gains in each of those years. The dollar value of inventories in 1996 was $48.2 billion, compared with $47.4 billion the previous year. Long-term debt has trended downward since its 1991 peak, standing at 20.79 percent of total assets in 1996.

TABLE 6

U.S. CORPORATE INCOME AND ASSETS: CHEMICALS AND ALLIED PRODUCTS

(Monetary values in millions of U.S. dollars)

INCOME AND EXPENSES	1988	1989	1990	1991	1992	1993	1994	1995	1996	CHANGE OR AVERAGE[1]
Sales and receipts	261,616	278,300	287,568	297,841	315,534	325,074	357,581	397,699	415,863	5.96
Depreciation and amortization	(11,027)	(12,104)	(12,947)	(13,689)	(14,783)	(15,300)	(16,155)	(17,107)	(17,733)	6.12
Other operating costs	(225,361)	(240,436)	(249,029)	(260,766)	(276,583)	(280,621)	(302,822)	(334,130)	(353,265)	5.78
Income from operations	25,229	25,759	25,591	23,386	24,166	29,152	38,602	46,462	44,867	7.46
Nonoperating income (expenditures)	8,321	8,130	7,236	4,575	(7,350)	(8,169)	2,537	3,868	13,057	....
Income before taxes	33,551	33,889	32,826	27,961	16,818	20,983	41,139	50,332	57,924	7.06
Income after taxes	23,651	24,523	23,393	19,997	12,996	15,550	30,447	36,878	45,300	8.46
Cash dividends	9,835	10,846	13,422	12,478	14,204	14,673	15,316	20,544	19,960	9.25
Income retained in business	13,816	13,677	9,972	7,520	(1,208)	877	15,131	16,334	25,341	7.88
Direct credits (charges)	(1,580)	(8,659)	(2,197)	(4,254)	(4,714)	(2,980)	(5,594)	(1,518)	(18,686)	....
Ending retained earnings	92,072	96,932	102,074	104,835	100,435	98,255	103,591	121,352	125,652	3.96
ASSETS, END OF YEAR:										
Total	277,582	293,317	325,370	357,665	385,374	418,285	462,321	516,968	537,221	8.60
Accounts receivable	37,614	39,103	41,260	41,421	42,361	44,254	49,635	53,547	55,353	4.95
Inventories	34,731	35,688	37,505	38,197	39,160	40,541	42,530	47,400	48,250	4.20
Net property, plant and equipment	92,835	100,219	114,586	129,785	141,857	147,292	156,416	164,849	163,108	7.30
RATIOS, PERCENT:										
INCOME TO SALES:										
Before tax	12.82	12.18	11.42	9.39	5.33	6.45	11.50	12.66	13.93	10.63
After tax	9.04	8.81	8.13	6.71	4.12	4.78	8.51	9.27	10.89	7.81
INCOME TO STOCKHOLDERS' EQUITY:										
Before tax	27.84	26.52	23.75	18.70	11.26	13.72	25.67	28.36	28.92	22.75
After tax	19.62	19.19	16.92	13.38	8.70	10.17	19.00	20.78	22.62	16.71
INCOME TO TOTAL ASSETS:										
Before tax	12.09	11.55	10.09	7.82	4.36	5.02	8.90	9.74	10.78	8.93
After tax	8.52	8.36	7.19	5.59	3.37	3.72	6.59	7.13	8.43	6.54
AS A PERCENT OF TOTAL ASSETS:										
Property, plant and equipment	33.44	34.17	35.22	36.29	36.81	35.21	33.83	31.89	30.36	34.14
Short-term debt	4.94	5.98	5.06	4.25	5.08	4.10	5.05	4.53	5.07	4.90
Long-term debt	21.21	22.03	23.05	23.48	21.35	20.92	21.83	21.76	20.79	21.82
Stockholders' equity	43.42	43.57	42.48	41.80	38.77	36.56	34.66	34.32	37.28	39.21

1. For income and asset amounts, compound annual growth rate; for ratios, average of ratios for the years shown.

Source: U.S. Bureau of the Census, Quarterly Financial Report.

Notes: Parentheses ( ) indicate negative items, e.g., net expenses, charges, or losses. Net property, plant, and equipment is net of accumulated depreciation. Because the samples used to collect the data change, retained earnings at the end of a given year will not exactly equal the previous year's retained earnings plus the current year's retained income and credits.

CANADA

Canada's chemical industry in 1993 included 1,248 establishments with 87,453 employees (Table 7). The largest subindustry, industrial chemical industries n.e.c., had 28.5 percent of 1993 industry shipments. Pharmaceutical and medicine accounted for 20.1 percent of 1993 shipments; plastic and synthetic resin, 14.7 percent; and soap and cleaning compounds, 7.1 percent. Average hourly earnings in 1993 were Can$17.66, with the highest (Can$26.44) in the chemical fertilizers industry.

Value of industry shipments rose to Can$25.6 billion in 1994 from $22.6 billion in 1993 and $20.3 billion in 1987 (Table 8). Employment, on the other hand, fell to 84,273, an eight-year low. Employment of production workers declined at a slower rate, so their share of the workforce rose slightly, to 56 percent in 1994. Average hourly wages of production workers totaled Can$18.27 in 1994, compared with Can$14.50 in 1988, and the average workweek was about 41 hours.

TABLE 7

CANADA: COMPONENT INDUSTRIES OF CHEMICALS AND CHEMICAL PRODUCTS (CSIC 37), 1993

(Monetary values in Canadian dollars)

| INDUSTRY NAME | CSIC | ESTABLISH-MENTS (NUMBER) | EMPLOYMENT | | VALUE OF SHIPMENTS (MILLIONS) | AVERAGE HOURLY EARNINGS[1] |
			NUMBER	PERCENT OF INDUSTRY TOTAL		
CHEMICAL AND CHEMICAL PRODUCTS INDUSTRIES	37	1,248	87,453	100.0	CAN$22,609.5	CAN$17.66
Industrial chemicals, n.e.c.	371	195	16,768	19.2	6,446.1	23.24
Industrial inorganic chemicals, n.e.c.	3711	135	9,035	10.3	2,494.6	21.45
Industrial organic chemicals	3712	60	7,733	8.8	3,951.5	25.06
Agricultural chemicals	372	150	4,164	4.8	1,532.4	19.15
Chemical fertilizers	3721	15	1,693	1.9	812.6	26.44
Mixed fertilizers	3722	124	1,905	2.2	423.8	13.21
Other agricultural chemicals	3729	11	566	0.6	296.0	13.83
Plastic and synthetic resins	373	91	8,819	10.1	3,319.5	20.94
Pharmaceuticals and medicines	374	119	20,584	23.5	4,544.0	16.47
Paint and varnish	375	127	7,314	8.4	1,482.6	14.28
Soap and cleaning compounds	376	118	8,014	9.2	1,601.6	15.70
Toilet preparations	377	74	7,208	8.2	967.2	12.07
Other chemical products	379	374	14,582	16.7	2,716.2	14.90
Printing ink	3791	62	1,686	1.9	291.8	14.92
Adhesives	3792	38	1,929	2.2	309.5	14.24
Other chemical products, n.e.c.	3799	274	10,967	12.5	2,114.9	15.01

1. Including overtime.

Source: Adapted from Statistics Canada, *Manufacturing Industries of Canada* (Cat. No. 31-203).

TABLE 8

CANADIAN EMPLOYMENT AND SHIPMENTS: CHEMICAL INDUSTRIES, 1987-1994

(Monetary values in Canadian dollars)

	1987	1988	1989	1990	1991	1992	1993	1994	CHANGE[1]
All employees	89,030	93,860	95,403	94,888	91,527	91,149	87,453	84,273	-0.78
Establishments	1,306	1,438	1,443	1,450	1,320	1,283	1,248	1,248	-0.65
Employees per establishment	68	65	66	65	69	71	70	68	-0.14
Production workers per establishment	.....	777	786	771	696	695	699	698	-1.77
PRODUCTION WORKERS:									
Total	.....	50,733	51,955	50,464	48,243	49,390	48,974	47,157	-1.21
Percent of all employees	.....	54.1	54.5	53.2	52.7	54.2	56.0	56.0	.....
Male	.....	38,985	40,087	39,345	38,013	49,390	48,974	47,157	.....
Female	.....	11,748	11,868	11,119	10,230	.....	.....	.....	.....
Percent of total production workers	.....	23.2	22.8	22.0	21.2	.....	.....	.....	.....
Average hourly earnings	.....	14.50	15.17	16.27	16.83	16.80	17.66	18.27	3.93
Average weekly earnings	.....	592.29	618.49	657.42	673.65	683.80	710.97	749.79	4.01
Average weekly hours	.....	40.9	40.8	40.4	40.0	40.7	40.3	41.1	0.08
Shipments (millions)	20,267	22,775	23,668	23,118	21,297	21,489	22,609	25,598	3.39

1. Compound annual growth rate.

Source: Adapted from Statistics Canada, *Manufacturing Industries of Canada* (Cat. No. 31-203).

MEXICO

Mexico's chemical industry is included in the chemicals, petroleum, rubber, and plastic industry. In 1993, the chemical industry components had over 2,800 production units and about 190,000 paid employees (Table 9). Average earnings of production workers ranged from 16,878 new pesos ($5,403) for the pharmaceutical industry to 29,069 new pesos ($9,305) in basic petrochemicals. In contrast, nonproduction employees of the pharmaceutical industry had average annual earnings of 54,378 new pesos ($17,408), and those in basic petrochemicals earned 63,049 new pesos ($20,184). Industry employment between 1988 and 1995 declined at an annual rate of 2.22 percent, to 167,750 people in 1995 (Table 10).

TABLE 9

MEXICO: COMPONENT INDUSTRIES OF CHEMICALS AND PETROLEUM (CMAP 35), 1993

(Monetary values in 1993 Mexican New Pesos)

INDUSTRY	CMAP	NUMBER OF UNITS	ALL WORKERS									UNPAID WORKERS, NUMBER
							PAID WORKERS					
							PRODUCTION WORKERS		NONPRODUCTION EMPLOYEES		BENEFITS PER PAID EMPLOYEE	
			NUMBER	PERCENT OF INDUSTRY TOTAL	AVERAGE DAYS WORKED	REMUN-ERATION[1]	NUMBER	WAGES AND SALARIES	NUMBER	WAGES AND SALARIES		
Chemicals and petroleum	35	7,091	380,140	100	276	36,607	259,834	17,367	114,910	43,751	11,150	5,396
Basic petrochemistry	3511	18	19,311	5	304	46,995	16,504	29,069	2,807	63,049	12,987	0
Manufacture of basic chemicals	3512	667	44,887	12	292	49,322	27,263	22,103	17,404	48,855	16,795	220
Artificial and synthetic fibers	3513	22	14,475	4	318	44,879	11,469	18,334	3,003	55,525	18,828	3
Pharmaceutical industry	3521	394	39,099	10	267	51,626	18,641	16,878	20,227	54,378	15,233	231
Other substances and chemicals	3522	1,738	74,153	20	266	39,915	40,957	17,730	31,696	41,874	11,652	1,500
Petroleum refining	3530	6	19,818	5	365	52,309	17,553	33,835	2,265	65,840	14,816	0
Coke, coal, and oil by-products	3540	205	10,114	3	278	36,636	6,933	15,926	3,094	43,158	12,307	87
Rubber industry	3550	792	33,265	9	276	34,936	25,700	19,607	6,919	37,345	11,566	646
Plastics products	3560	3,249	125,018	33	278	20,507	94,814	10,239	27,495	31,468	5,495	2,709

1. Average annual remuneration including benefits, excluding profit sharing.

Source: INEGI, Censos Economicos 1994.

TABLE 10

MEXICAN GROSS DOMESTIC PRODUCT AND EMPLOYMENT: CHEMICALS, DERIVATIVES OF PETROLEUM, RUBBER AND PLASTIC, 1988-1995

	1988	1989	1990	1991	1992	1993	1994	1995	CHANGE[1]
GROSS DOMESTIC PRODUCT:									
Millions of constant 1993 new pesos	30,417.9	33,279.1	34,724.7	35,060.4	35,684.2	35,075.2	36,270.1	35,953.9	2.42
Millions of constant 1993 U.S. dollars[2]	9,737.8	10,653.8	11,116.5	11,224.0	11,423.7	11,228.7	11,611.3	11,510.0	2.42
TOTAL EMPLOYMENT:									
Chemicals, derivatives of petroleum, et al	370,230	380,425	393,831	401,902	395,282	383,933	370,978	349,721	-0.81
Petroleum	53,548	49,861	50,944	46,858	41,015	35,528	32,703	32,691	-6.81
Chemicals and allied products	196,234	200,741	206,213	211,912	204,258	190,895	177,988	167,750	-2.22
Rubber and plastic	120,448	129,823	136,674	143,132	150,009	157,510	160,287	149,280	3.11

1. Compound annual growth rate.

2. Converted at 3.1237 new pesos to the U.S. dollar.

Source: Sistema de Cuentas Nacionales de Mexico, INEGI.

INTERNATIONAL TRADE

United States. Global U.S. exports of chemicals rose 54 percent to $58.5 billion between 1990 and 1996. Imports almost doubled to $42.8 billion (Table 11). The resulting trade surplus was $15.7 billion, down somewhat from 1990 and well under the high of $18.5 billion reached in 1991.

According to CMA, the five largest markets for U.S. chemical exports in 1995 were Canada (17.3 percent of all exports), Japan (9.9 percent), Mexico (6.9 percent), the Netherlands (4.8 percent), and the United Kingdom (3.9 percent). However, Mexico moved into second place in 1996, as demand from Japan stagnated. Demand from Western Europe also was flat in 1996, while the start-up of capacity in East Asia affected U.S. exports to that region. Leading exports in 1995 were organic chemicals (26.6 percent), plastics (24.4 percent), and pharmaceuticals (10.7 percent). Exports of primary plastics have been among the big gainers over the past decade while those of fertilizer and inorganic chemicals have lost ground.

The top five suppliers of U.S. chemical imports in 1995 were Canada (20.2 percent), Japan (12.6 percent), Germany (11.4 percent), France (6.1 percent), and the United Kingdom (8.6 percent). As with exports, this trade was led by organic chemicals (33.0 percent of imports), plastics (27.0 percent), and pharmaceuticals (13.7 percent).

Canada. Stimulated by the Canadian-U.S. Free Trade Agreement of 1989 and by NAFTA in 1994, chemical trade between Canada and the United States grew throughout the 1989-1996 period (Table 11). From 1990 to 1996, Canada's exports to the United States rose from $4.1 billion to $7.9 billion, and U.S. exports to Canada climbed from $5.7 billion to over $11 billion. In 1996, the United States had a favorable chemical trade balance with Canada of $3.1 billion, compared with $1.6 billion in 1990.

Mexico. U.S. chemical exports to Mexico gained by 112 percent between 1990 and 1996 to almost $4.6 billion, while Mexican exports to the United States rose 116 percent to $1.4 billion (Table 11). Mexico's small but rapidly growing exports to Canada rose 505 percent during 1990-1996 to $79 million, and Canadian exports to Mexico climbed 318 percent to $51 million.

NAFTA. In 1996, the United States had a surplus of $6.3 billion in chemical trade with its NAFTA partners, while Canada and Mexico each had deficits of over $3.1 billion (Table 11). Between 1990 and 1996, the U.S. trade surplus about doubled, while Canada's deficit grew 94 percent, and Mexico's climbed 108 percent. In the three years since NAFTA has been in effect (1994-1996), the U.S. trade surplus increased 24 percent, and Canada's and Mexico's trade deficits climbed 12 and 40 percent, respectively.

TABLE 11

INTERNATIONAL TRADE, CHEMICALS AND ALLIED PRODUCTS

(Millions of U.S. dollars)

	1989[1]	1990	1991	1992	1993	1994	1995	1996
GLOBAL TRADE, U.S.								
IMPORTS								
Value	20,215.4	21,732.0	23,138.4	26,006.2	27,258.9	31,696.9	38,079.0	42,825.7
Ratio to new supply[2]	7.4	7.7	8.1	8.7	8.8	9.6	.....	.....
Ratio to apparent consumption[3]	8.6	8.9	9.5	10.1	10.1	11.2	.....	.....
EXPORTS								
Value	35,993.1	38,056.3	41,669.0	42,129.0	42,741.9	48,950.1	57,896.6	58,502.7
Ratio to comparable domestic shipments	14.3	14.7	15.9	15.4	15.0	16.3	.....	.....
TRADE BALANCE	15,777.7	16,324.3	18,530.6	16,122.8	15,483.0	17,253.2	19,817.6	15,677.0
BILATERAL TRADE: NAFTA[4]								
U.S. exports to Canada	4,413.0	5,692.3	6,344.8	6,902.3	7,976.8	9,123.8	10,114.5	11,051.5
Canadian exports to U.S.	3,924.2	4,062.3	4,094.0	4,621.9	5,171.3	6,290.3	7,653.7	7,916.9
U.S. exports to Mexico	2,022.0	2,160.5	2,408.4	2,766.0	3,035.8	3,829.3	3,754.5	4,573.8
Mexican exports to U.S.	611.5	651.6	692.8	806.4	780.0	1,064.9	1,368.8	1,407.1
Canadian exports to Mexico	9.5	12.1	7.6	11.6	12.4	23.7	26.8	50.6
Mexican exports to Canada	14.9	13.0	13.7	14.8	22.3	36.1	76.9	78.7
TRADE BALANCES WITHIN NAFTA[5]								
Canada	(494.2)	(1,630.9)	(2,256.9)	(2,283.6)	(2,815.4)	(2,845.9)	(2,510.9)	(3,162.7)
Mexico	(1,405.1)	(1,508.0)	(1,709.5)	(1,956.4)	(2,245.9)	(2,752.0)	(2,335.6)	(3,138.6)
United States	1,899.3	3,138.9	3,966.3	4,240.1	5,061.3	5,597.9	4,846.5	6,301.3

1. 1989 and earlier data on U.S. exports to Canada for manufacturing total and manufacturing industries are not comparable with data for 1990 and later years because of a change in the reporting system. The NAFTA trade balances for the U.S. and Canada also are affected.

2. New supply equals comparable domestic shipments plus imports for consumption.

3. Apparent consumption equals comparable domestic shipments plus imports for consumption less exports.

4. Amounts less than U.S. $100,000 shown as zero.

5. Parentheses indicate an excess of imports over exports. Because of commodity coding and other data differences among the three countries, these trade balances are only rough estimates and should be used with caution.

Source for U.S. Global Trade: U.S. Department of Commerce, International Trade Administration.

Source for U.S. -Canada and U.S.-Mexico Bilateral Trade: U.S. Bureau of the Census.

Source for Canada-Mexico and Mexico-Canada Bilateral Trade: Statistics Canada, Foreign Trade Division, Special tabulation, March 1997, converted to U.S. dollars by the editors.

ELECTRONIC AND OTHER ELECTRICAL EQUIPMENT
(EXCEPT COMPUTERS)

THE UNITED STATES

Products and Processes. Electronic and other electrical equipment ranked as the fifth largest U.S. manufacturing industry in 1996 in terms of industry shipments. The industry also had one of the highest rates of growth in after-tax income, largely because of strong gains in electronic components for computers, telecommunications, scientific and medical instruments, and other high-tech areas.   In contrast, several subindustries, such as small appliances, have experienced slow growth and stiff competition in a virtually saturated marketplace.

Among the product categories included in this industry group are motors and generators, large and small household appliances, semiconductors, audio and video equipment, and communications equipment. (Note that computers per se are discussed in the Industrial and Commercial Machinery and Computer Equipment Chapter, and computer software is covered in the Business Services Chapter.)

In 1992 (the latest year for which economic census data are available), the industry had 16,922 establishments with a combined payroll of $44.2 billion (Table 1). The five largest subindustries in 1992 were electronic components and accessories (with 34.0 percent of the value of industry shipments), communications equipment (19.8 percent), miscellaneous electrical machinery and equipment such as batteries and engine electrical equipment (10.2 percent), electric lighting and wiring equipment (9.2 percent), and electrical industrial apparatus (8.8 percent).

Employment in the industry currently is below that of 10 years earlier and is likely to decline further as downsizing, mergers, and investment in labor-saving technology continue to hold down hiring. Projections to the year 2005 indicate that total industry employment may decline some 7.7 percent below the 1993 level to 1,407,600 (Table 2).   Declines are expected in most subindustries; a notable exception is electronic components and accessories, where employment is expected to account for over 39 percent of the industry total in 2005. Hourly earnings for production workers in 1993 averaged $11.24, with the highest earnings in semiconductors and related devices ($14.47 an hour) and the lowest in electric housewares and fans ($8.25).

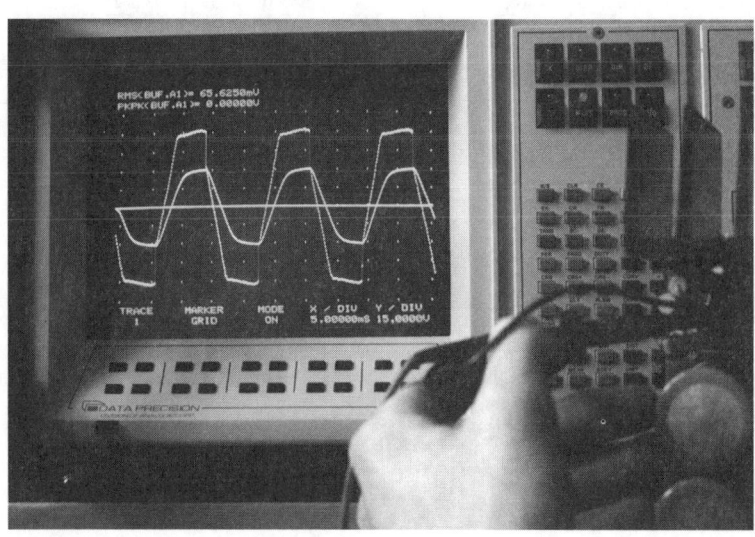

TABLE 1

UNITED STATES: COMPONENT INDUSTRIES OF ELECTRONIC AND OTHER ELECTRICAL EQUIPMENT (EXCEPT COMPUTERS) (SIC 36), 1992

(Monetary values in millions of U.S. dollars)

| INDUSTRY | SIC | ESTABLISH-MENTS | SHIPMENTS | | VALUE ADDED BY MANUFACTURE | NEW CAPITAL EXPENDI-TURES | EMPLOY-MENT[1] | PAYROLL |
			VALUE	PERCENT BY 4 LARGEST COMPANIES				
ELECTRONIC AND OTHER ELECTRICAL EQUIPMENT	36	16,922	$216,764.3	.....	$121,157.6	$8,978.20	1,438,800	$44,196.5
Electric transmission and distribution equipment	361	811	9,796.8	.....	5,436.8	197.5	68,100	1,946.2
Power, distribution, and specialty transformers	3612	278	4,118.2	51	2,026.7	85.3	29,000	779.6
Switchgear and switchboard apparatus	3613	533	5,678.5	46	3,410.1	112.2	39,100	1,166.6
Electrical industrial apparatus	362	2,173	19,266.4	.....	10,849.8	573.9	157,400	4,386.9
Motors and generators	3621	469	8,167.8	36	4,327.7	241.7	67,900	1,762.4
Carbon and graphite products	3624	109	1,325.2	46	741.6	43.0	9,400	288.7
Relays and industrial controls	3625	1,241	7,741.1	33	4,685.6	224.2	62,500	1,863.7
Electrical industrial apparatus, n.e.c.	3629	354	2,032.3	27	1,094.8	65.0	17,600	472.0
Household appliances	363	484	18,633.1	.....	7,963.8	556.3	102,800	2,571.0
Household cooking equipment	3631	89	2,950.0	60	1,141.4	82.9	18,800	437.0
Household refrigerators and freezers	3632	58	4,232.4	82	1,629.1	187.4	25,400	701.9
Household laundry equipment	3633	17	3,328.5	94	1,545.2	93.6	14,200	423.1
Electric housewares and fans	3634	209	2,896.7	30	1,381.1	46.3	20,400	400.6
Household vacuum cleaners	3635	43	1,905.3	59	1,054.6	66.8	11,300	278.7
Household appliances, n.e.c.	3639	68	3,320.2	70	1,212.3	79.2	12,700	329.7
Electric lighting and wiring equipment	364	2,049	19,843.9	.....	11,306.7	497.4	148,000	3,974.4
Electric lamp bulbs and tubes	3641	105	3,000.5	86	2,041.1	99.6	17,500	510.7
Current-carrying wiring devices	3643	473	4,584.5	28	2,822.9	122.3	40,400	1,050.2
Noncurrent-carrying wiring devices	3644	221	3,219.5	30	1,858.8	84.0	23,500	649.3
Residential electric lighting fixtures	3645	525	1,598.5	21	849.9	21.4	16,400	326.9
Commercial lighting fixtures	3646	337	3,046.5	50	1,486.7	58.1	21,100	540.7
Vehicular lighting equipment	3647	97	2,312.5	65	1,163.2	61.3	15,000	509.9
Lighting equipment, n.e.c.	3648	291	2,081.9	26	1,083.9	50.8	14,100	386.8
Household audio and video equipment and audio recs.	365	840	10,614.3	......	3,486.4	436.3	47,100	1,123.3
Household audio and video equipment	3651	.....	.....	.....	2,296.5	253.2	31,300	738.3
Prerecorded records, tapes, and discs	3652	421	1,820.6	40	1,189.9	183.1	15,800	384.9
Communications equipment	366	2,014	42,955.4	.....	26,521.5	1,382.0	238,600	9,110.5
Telephone and telegraph apparatus	3661	543	20,509.6	51	12,475.1	614.5	91,100	3,738.9
Radio and TV communications equipment	3663	954	19,521.1	41	12,278.9	702.4	124,900	4,721.3
Communications equipment, n.e.c.	3669	517	2,924.7	27	1,767.5	65.0	22,500	650.3
Electronic components and accessories	367	6,655	73,642.0	.....	44,305.4	4,482.9	529,800	16,752.0
Electron tubes	3671	189	3,144.9	58	1,280.4	61.7	22,200	677.4
Printed circuit boards	3672	1,327	7,319.9	27	4,353.9	317.5	76,000	2,114.2
Semiconductors and related devices	3674	920	32,191.4	41	22,342.9	3,120.7	172,000	6,883.7
Electronic capacitors	3675	117	1,581.3	55	881.2	64.0	17,900	415.7
Electronic resistors	3676	105	827.2	44	562.6	21.3	11,700	258.7
Electronic coils and transformers	3677	423	1,133.8	13	680.6	20.1	19,200	374.0
Electronic connectors	3678	285	3,773.5	40	2,385.9	144.3	30,700	909.2
Electronic components, n.e.c.	3679	3,289	23,670.0	28	11,817.9	733.4	180,200	5,119.1
Miscellaneous electrical equipment and supplies	369	1,896	22,012.5	.....	11,287.2	852.1	147,100	4,332.2
Storage batteries	3691	153	3,325.7	60	1,751.4	116.2	20,800	586.0
Primary batteries, dry and wet	3692	69	1,907.5	87	893.6	56.2	10,700	279.7
Engine electrical equipment	3694	521	7,240.4	57	3,755.4	167.0	49,900	1,405.7
Magnetic and optical recording media	3695	261	4,641.3	47	2,091.5	394.2	22,600	695.0
Electrical equipment and supplies, n.e.c.	3699	892	4,897.6	22	2,795.4	118.3	43,200	1,365.7

1. Employment numbers from the economic censuses differ in definition and classification from the Bureau of Labor Statistics estimates in Table 2. Year-to-year comparisons between Table 1 and Table 2 are not appropriate.

Source: U.S. Bureau of the Census, 1992 Census of Manufactures.

TABLE 2

U.S. EMPLOYMENT AND EARNINGS: ELECTRONIC AND OTHER ELECTRICAL EQUIPMENT

| INDUSTRY | SIC | 1993 | | | 2005 |
| | | EMPLOYMENT[1] | | AVERAGE HOURLY EARNINGS (U.S. DOLLARS)[2] | PROJECTED EMPLOYMENT[3] |
		NUMBER OF PERSONS	PERCENT OF INDUSTRY TOTAL		
ELECTRONIC AND OTHER ELECTRICAL EQUIPMENT	36	1,525,700	100.0	$11.24	1,407,600
Electric distribution equipment	361	81,400	5.3	10.98	70,000
Transformers, except electronic	3612	41,100	2.7	10.42	.....
Switchgear and switchboard apparatus	3613	40,300	2.6	11.57	.....
Electrical industrial apparatus	362	152,800	10.0	10.67	115,900
Motors and generators	3621	75,300	4.9	9.95	.....
Relays and industrial controls	3625	58,900	3.9	11.96	.....
Household appliances	363	118,700	7.8	10.47	97,500
Household refrigerators and freezers	3632	29,100	1.9	11.55	.....
Household laundry equipment	3633	15,800	1.0	12.77	.....
Electric housewares and fans	3634	28,000	1.8	8.25	.....
Electric lighting and wiring equipment	364	171,400	11.2	10.99	155,100
Electric lamps	3641	21,600	1.4	11.61	.....
Current-carrying wiring devices	3643	61,100	4.0	10.85	.....
Noncurrent-carrying wiring devices	3644	19,000	1.2	10.49	.....
Residential lighting fixtures	3645	19,500	1.3	8.33	.....
Household audio and video equipment & audio recordings	365	83,200	5.5	11.00	55,000
Household audio and video equipment	3651	59,500	3.9	11.38	.....
Communications equipment	366	239,000	15.7	11.75	210,000
Telephone and telegraph apparatus	3661	110,000	7.2	12.64	.....
Electronic components and accessories	367	527,700	34.6	11.20	552,800
Electron tubes	3671	24,800	1.6	13.13	.....
Semiconductors and related devices	3674	213,800	14.0	14.47	.....
Electronic components, n.e.c.	3679	127,500	8.4	9.52	.....
Miscellaneous electrical equipment and supplies	369	151,500	9.9	12.59	151,300
Storage batteries	3691	25,500	1.7	13.73	.....
Engine electrical equipment	3694	65,100	4.3	13.30	.....

1. Total payroll employment. Employment data from the economic censuses, shown in Table 1, differ in definition and classification from the Bureau of Labor Statistics estimates in this table. Year-to-year comparisons between Table 1 and Table 2 are not appropriate.

2. Earnings of production workers, including overtime.

3. Number of persons, moderate projection by the U.S. Bureau of Labor Statistics.

Source: Bureau of Labor Statistics.

FIGURE 1

U.S. EMPLOYMENT IN ELECTRONIC AND OTHER ELECTRICAL EQUIPMENT

Percent distribution by region, 1995

The Southeast and the Great Lakes region respectively accounted for 22 and 21 percent of 1995 employment in the industry. Next in line were the Pacific region, with 17 percent, and the Mid-Atlantic States, with 13 percent.

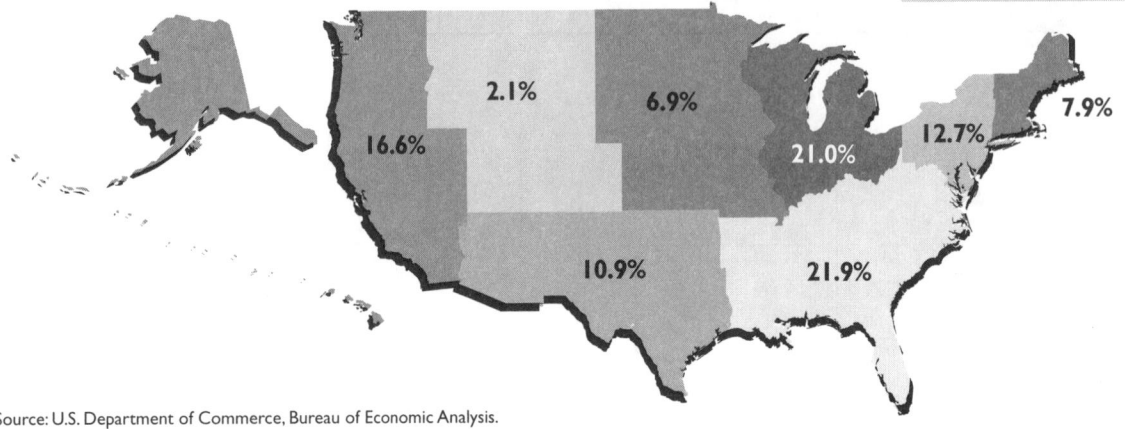

Source: U.S. Department of Commerce, Bureau of Economic Analysis.

What's New. The Information Technology Agreement signed March 26, 1997, in Geneva, Switzerland, is expected to increase consumer access to information technology and open doors to U.S. products in markets like the European Union (EU). Under the Agreement, the EU began reducing tariffs on semiconductors by 50 percent beginning in July 1997 and will eliminate all tariffs on chips by January 1, 1999. The United States eliminated all duties on chips in 1985.

The Semiconductor Industry Association forecasts a 4.6 percent increase in the global semiconductor market during 1997, followed by gains of more than 20 percent annually over the next three years. Revenues are expected to hit $245.7 billion by the year 2000, compared with $138 billion forecast for 1997. Sales of microprocessors—the brains of computers—are forecast to rise some 33 percent in 1997 and to exceed those of DRAMs (dynamic random access memories) for the first time. This growth and another 26 percent advance forecast for 1998 will help to offset continued sluggishness in the DRAM market. Leading markets for chips in 1997 will be North and South America (expected to account for 33 percent of the global market); Japan (almost 24 percent); the Asia-Pacific market excluding Japan (22 percent); and Europe (21 percent).

The Electronic Industries Association (EIA) reports that factory sales of electronics equipment, components, and related products are continuing to set records. Total sales of electronics equipment (including computers and peripherals, discussed in the Industrial and Commercial Machinery and Computer Equipment Chapter) rose another 9 percent in the first half of 1997 to nearly $219 billion, following a 9 percent gain in calendar year 1996 to $409 billion. Sales of electronic components also rose 9 percent in both the first half of 1997 and all of 1996, hitting records of $70.5 billion and $113 billion, respectively. Telecommunications equipment sales shot up 15 percent in both the first half of 1997 and calendar 1996, to $29.6 billion and $63.5 billion. Industrial electronics climbed a modest 4 percent in the first half of 1997 and 6 percent in 1996 to $16.7 billion and $36.3 billion. Consumer electronics rose 8 percent in the first half of 1997 to $4.9 billion after a 6 percent increase to $11.3 billion for all of 1996.

On the other hand, many appliance manufacturers are beset by intense competition in a highly saturated and retailer-dictated market. This had led to downsizing and price wars. For example, "Chainsaw Al" Dunlap has been closing plants, slashing employment, and reducing product lines at Sunbeam in an effort to shore up profits and attract investors. According to the *Wall Street Journal*, General Electric has introduced a new washer with a plastic basket, developed at a cost of $100 million, in a move to dislodge Whirlpool from its No. 1 slot in the clothes washer market. And both companies are using price discounts and factory rebates to lure consumers of large appliances.

FIGURE 2

U.S. EMPLOYMENT AND SHIPMENTS IN ELECTRONIC AND OTHER ELECTRICAL EQUIPMENT
Total payroll employment and manufacturers' inflation-adjusted shipments

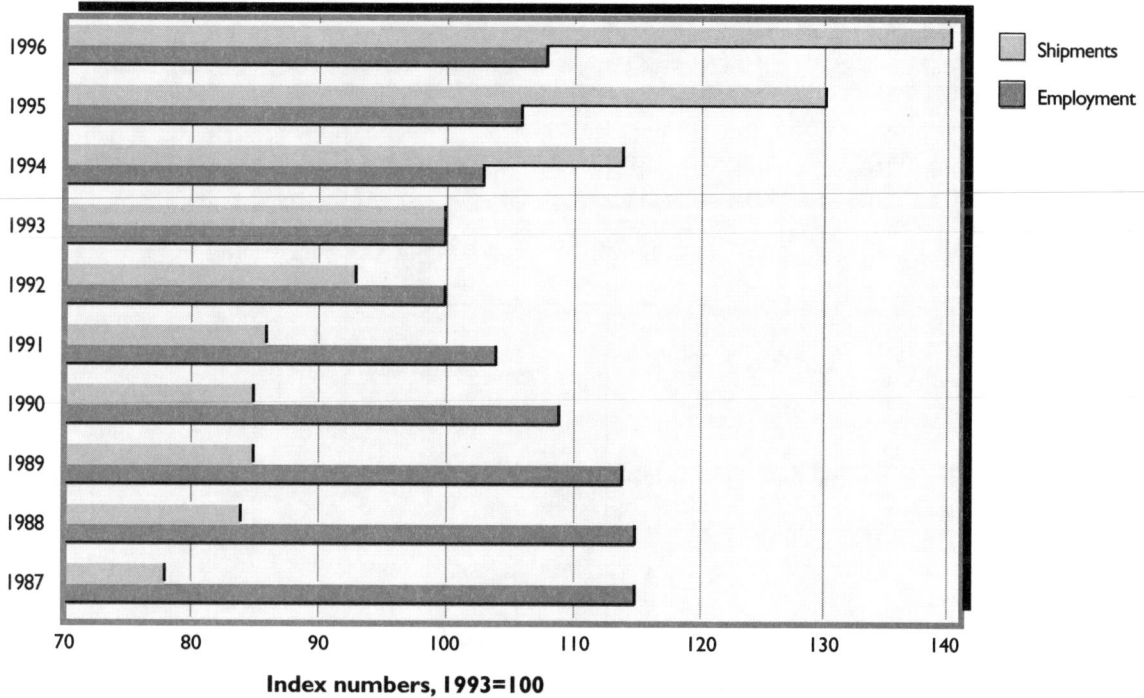

Index numbers, 1993=100

Source: U.S. Bureau of Labor Statistics, U.S. Department of Commerce, and estimates by the editors.

Output. During the past 10 years, manufacturers of electronic and other electrical equipment steadily increased their product shipments, with most of the growth taking place between 1992 and 1996. At the same time, they reduced employment through 1992 and then increased it only marginally even as shipments were skyrocketing (Figure 2). Industry shipments in 1996 totaled $323.4 billion, up from $299.8 billion the previous year and $171.3 billion in 1987 (Table 3). The annual growth rate for 1989-1996 was 7.32 percent in current dollars and 6.81 percent in inflation-adjusted dollars.

Investment. Not surprisingly for a technology-dominated industry, investments in plants and equipment and research soared during the past decade. New capital expenditures by the industry reached $17.2 billion in 1995 (Table 3). This represented a 36 percent gain from the previous year and was more than 2.5 times the 1987 level. It also was the second highest level for all manufacturing, exceeded only by chemical industry expenditures. Research and development (R&D) spending totaled $13.5 billion in 1994 (latest year for which data are available), compared with $11.7 billion the previous year. The 1994 showing was the third highest level in manufacturing next to R&D investment by the transportation equipment and chemical industries. Capacity utilization in 1996 declined to 82.9 percent from 87.8 percent the previous year, probably reflecting additional capacity coming on stream as a result of the growth in capital investment.

Prices. The rate of growth in producer prices between 1987 and 1996 was only 1.03 percent a year, with the highest rates of gain between 1987 and 1990 (Table 3). Competition and the rapid introduction and acceptance of new products have helped to keep prices in check.

TABLE 3

U.S. OUTPUT, INVESTMENT, AND PRICES: ELECTRONIC AND OTHER ELECTRICAL EQUIPMENT

(Millions of U.S. dollars, except as noted)

	1987	1988	1989	1990	1991	1992	1993	1994	1995	1996	GROWTH RATE 1987-1996[1]
VALUE OF SHIPMENTS:											
BY INDUSTRY:											
Current dollars	171,286	187,301	194,599	195,898	199,280	216,764	233,621	266,405	299,837	323,383	7.32
Constant 1992 dollars	180,396	194,760	197,535	197,278	199,123	216,764	232,396	264,809	302,252	326,310	6.81
BY PRODUCT:											
Current dollars	162,931	176,397	182,609	187,025	187,046	204,511	219,332	250,409	281,650	303,768	7.17
Constant 1992 dollars	171,669	183,498	185,438	188,437	186,992	204,511	218,181	248,821	283,639	306,215	6.64
OTHER OUTPUT MEASURES:											
Industrial production, 1993=100	68.7	75.0	78.0	79.7	81.5	90.9	100.0	114.8	134.7	148.5	8.94
Gross domestic product:											
Current dollars	83,281	88,412	96,707	94,926	98,191	98,601	111,774	129,990	.....	.....	.....
Percent of total GDP	2	2	2	2	2	2	2	2	.....	.....	.....
Rank in manufacturing	4	4	4	4	5	5	4	3	.....	.....	.....
Chained (1992) dollars	78,115	85,331	92,821	92,559	95,983	98,601	113,638	138,430	.....	.....	.....
INVESTMENT-RELATED MEASURES:											
Capacity utilization, percent	78.7	82.3	81.3	78.9	76.4	80.5	82.5	85.8	87.8	82.9	.....
New capital expenditures	6,875	8,058	9,029	9,495	8,465	8,978	9,988	12,671	17,247	.....	.....
Research and development spending	10,449	9,975	9,575	9,267	8,865	9,516	11,682	13,537	.....	.....	.....
Producer prices, 1993=100[2]	92.2	93.4	95.6	97.2	98.3	98.9	100.0	100.6	101.2	101.1	1.03

1. Compound annual growth rate.

2. Prices received by domestic producers.

Sources: Shipments and new capital expenditures: U.S. Department of Commerce for 1987-1995, editor's estimates for constant dollar data for 1987-88 and all shipments data for 1996; Industrial production and capacity utilization: Federal Reserve Board of Governors; GDP: Bureau of Economic Analysis; Research and development spending: National Science Foundation; Producer prices: Bureau of Labor Statistics.

Workforce and Employment. Employment in the electronic and electrical equipment industry declined at the rate of 0.64 percent annually during 1987-1996 (Table 4). All of the reduction took place between 1987 and 1993. Recovery since then has been steady but slow. Employment of production workers declined at a slightly faster rate during the 1988-1996 period; but their share of the workforce, at 63.7 percent in 1996, showed little change. Employment of women declined at an annual rate of 1.23 percent between 1988 and 1996, and their share of the workforce fell slightly to 41.4 percent in 1996. Hourly earnings of production workers averaged $12.18 in 1996. The rate of growth in earnings between 1988 and 1996 was 2.77 percent annually, which falls to a minus 0.70 percent when adjusted for inflation.

As of June 18, 1997, the industry had the second highest number, and third highest percentage share, of manufacturing-sector workers certified by the U.S. Department of Labor as having lost their jobs because of NAFTA. The total number certified was 21,029, including 18,108 affected by the movement of jobs to Mexico, 1,296 to Canada, and 1,625 where the country was not identified. This amounted to about 1.4 percent of the U.S. industry's workforce.

TABLE 4

U.S. EMPLOYMENT, HOURS, AND EARNINGS: ELECTRONIC AND OTHER ELECTRICAL EQUIPMENT

(Monetary values in U.S. dollars)

	1987	1988	1989	1990	1991	1992	1993	1994	1995	1996	CHANGE[1]
NUMBER OF EMPLOYEES, IN THOUSANDS:											
Total	1,750	1,764	1,744	1,673	1,591	1,528	1,526	1,571	1,625	1,651	-0.64
Production workers	.....	1,112	1,102	1,055	999	971	975	1,010	1,045	1,051	-0.71
Percent of total	.....	63.1	63.2	63.0	62.8	63.5	63.9	64.3	64.3	63.7	.....
Women	.....	755	748	714	675	648	645	661	679	684	-1.23
Percent of total	.....	42.8	42.9	42.7	42.4	42.4	42.2	42.1	41.8	41.4	.....
Hours and earnings of production workers:											
AVERAGE HOURLY EARNINGS[2]											
Current dollars	.....	9.79	10.05	10.30	10.70	11.00	11.24	11.50	11.69	12.18	2.77
1992 dollars[3]	.....	11.56	11.33	11.04	11.01	11.00	10.93	10.91	10.78	10.92	-0.70
Average weekly hours	.....	41.0	40.8	40.8	40.7	41.2	41.8	42.2	41.6	41.5	0.15
Average weekly earnings, current U.S. dollars	406.31	401.39	410.04	420.24	435.49	453.20	469.83	485.30	486.30	505.47	2.92

1. Compound annual growth rate, 1987-1996 for total workers and weekly earnings, 1988-1996 for all other categories.

2. Including overtime.

3. Converted to 1992 dollars using Consumer Price Index for Urban Wage Earners and Clerical Workers.

Source: Bureau of Labor Statistics.

FIGURE 3

U.S. OCCUPATIONAL INJURY AND ILLNESS RATES: ELECTRONIC AND OTHER ELECTRICAL EQUIPMENT, 1995

Incidence of nonfatal injuries and illnesses per 100 full-time workers

Nonfatal occupational illnesses and injuries in the industry are on the low side for the manufacturing sector. They averaged 7.6 cases per 100 workers in 1995, compared with 11.6 for all manufacturing.

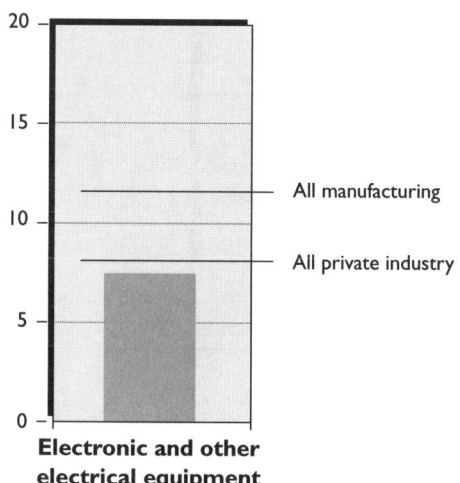

All manufacturing

All private industry

Electronic and other electrical equipment

Source: U.S. Bureau of Labor Statistics.

TABLE 5

U.S. EMPLOYMENT PROJECTIONS BY MAJOR OCCUPATIONAL GROUP: ELECTRONIC AND OTHER ELECTRICAL EQUIPMENT

OCCUPATION	1994		PROJECTIONS, 2005			
	NUMBER OF EMPLOYEES	PERCENT OF INDUSTRY TOTAL	NUMBER OF EMPLOYEES			PERCENT OF INDUSTRY TOTAL, MODERATE PROJECTIONS
			LOW	MODERATE	HIGH	
Total, all occupations	1,570,700	100.0	1,347,000	1,407,600	1,524,200	100.0
Executive, administrative, and managerial	162,458	10.3	143,359	149,885	162,352	10.7
Professional specialties	161,117	10.3	182,287	190,955	207,653	13.6
Technicians and related support	99,930	6.4	90,736	95,188	104,042	6.8
Marketing and sales	39,609	2.5	34,687	36,271	39,301	2.6
Administrative support including clerical	165,342	10.5	127,362	133,040	143,865	9.5
Service	15,416	1.0	11,413	11,934	12,939	0.9
Agriculture, forestry, and fisheries occupations	141	0.0	124	130	142	0.0
Precision production, craft, and repair	326,702	20.8	268,658	280,561	303,429	19.9
Operators, fabricators, assemblers	599,984	38.2	488,376	509,635	550,477	36.2

Source: Bureau of Labor Statistics, November 1995.

Employment in the industry is projected to decline to 1,407,600 by the year 2005 (moderate assumptions), compared with 1,570,700 in 1994. With the exception of professional specialties, all occupational areas are expected to show declines.

FIGURE 4

U.S. CORPORATE INCOME AND WORKER EARNINGS: ELECTRONIC AND OTHER ELECTRICAL EQUIPMENT

Corporate operating income and aggregate production worker earnings

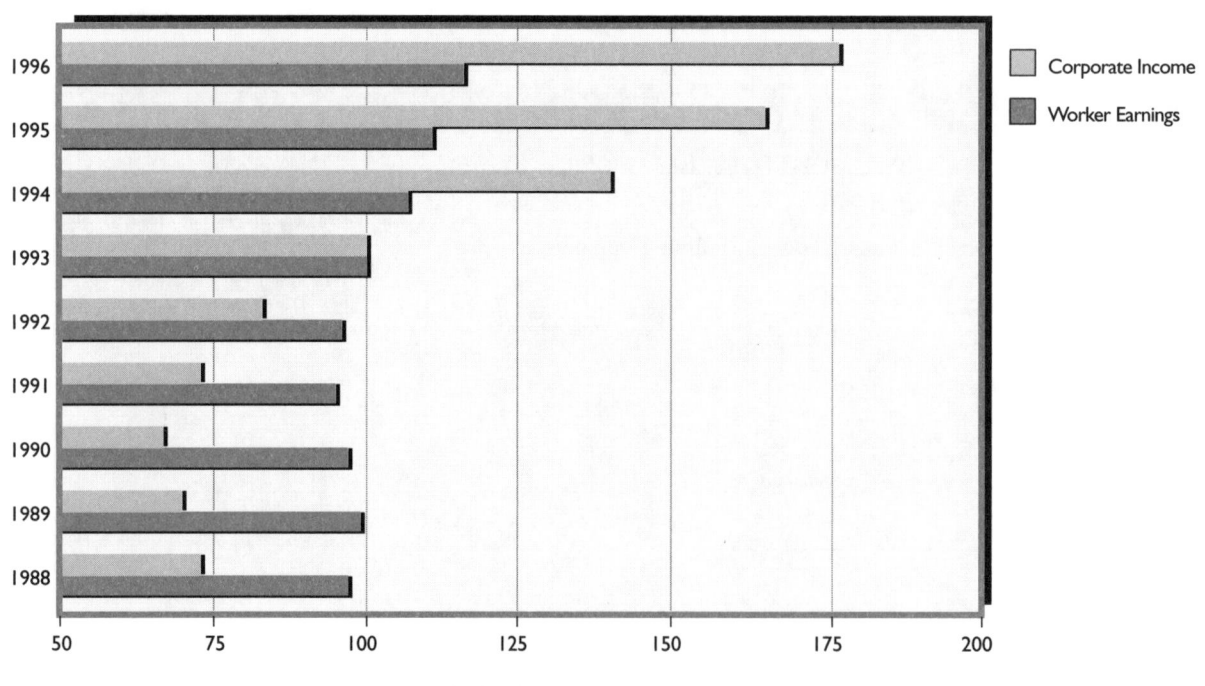

Index numbers, 1993=100

Source: U.S. Bureau of Labor Statistics, U.S. Bureau of the Census, and estimates by the editors.

Finance. After declining from 1988 through 1990, corporate income headed sharply higher. By 1996, it was more than 2.5 times the 1990 level, largely because of huge gains in 1994 and 1995. Production worker earnings held up well when corporate income was faltering but have not gained significantly over the past nine years. (See Figure 4.)

The sales spurt since 1993 is reflected in an 11.78 percent annual rate of growth in the industry's operating income for 1988-1996 (Table 6). In 1996, income from operations totaled $32.5 billion. After-tax income reached $26.6 billion in 1996 and had an 11.48 percent rate of gain for the nine-year period. The ratio of after-tax income to sales hit a high 8.32 percent in 1995 and then declined slightly to 7.17 percent in 1996. After-tax income in relation to stockholders' equity was 17.57 and 15.19 percent, respectively, in 1995 and 1996. Value of industry inventories has increased during the past nine years, reaching its highest level of $48.97 billion in 1996. Debt has declined in most years since 1991.

TABLE 6

U.S. CORPORATE INCOME AND ASSETS: ELECTRONIC AND OTHER ELECTRICAL EQUIPMENT

(Monetary values in millions of U.S. dollars)

INCOME AND EXPENSES	1988	1989	1990	1991	1992	1993	1994	1995	1996	CHANGE OR AVERAGE[1]
Sales and receipts	209,866	221,549	216,031	220,145	232,185	250,986	272,647	317,649	370,844	7.38
Depreciation and amortization	(7,582)	(8,178)	(8,073)	(8,234)	(8,836)	(9,472)	(10,014)	(11,7110)	(14,354)	8.31
Other operating costs	(188,968)	(200,384)	(195,626	(198,607)	(207,973)	(223,046)	(236,859)	(275,418)	(324,034)	6.97
Income from operations	13,317	12,987	12,330	13,304	15,377	18,470	25,775	30,518	32,456	11.78
Nonoperating income (expenditures)	1,677	807	(1,506)	(5,167)	(3,173)	(876)	836	5,598	5,105	.....
Income before taxes	14,994	13,794	10,825	8,137	12,203	17,595	26,612	36,118	37,561	12.16
Income after taxes	11,143	9,663	6,400	4,695	8,354	12,508	18,344	26,428	26,589	11.48
Cash dividends	3,763	4,602	4,371	4,300	4,273	4,941	5,473	6,273	7,585	9.16
Income retained in business	7,380	5,062	2,027	395	4,080	7,566	12,871	20,154	19,003	12.55
Direct credits (charges)	(1,610)	(2,259)	13	244	(2,160)	(2,094)	(2,164)	(2,267)	(2,345)	.....
Ending retained earnings	55,201	56,363	57,030	58,092	55,921	59,072	74,465	92,926	109,192	8.90
ASSETS, END OF YEAR:										
Total	186,945	203,738	204,294	211,567	224,113	239,046	255,026	317,455	356,101	8.39
Accounts receivable	35,732	37,811	35,235	33,870	37,057	38,116	41,830	51,418	56,779	5.96
Inventories	37,791	39,766	38,843	37,218	38,148	38,787	41,066	48,497	48,973	3.29
Net property, plant and equipment	43,433	46,046	45,050	47,392	49,546	51,087	55,716	70,041	78,464	7.67
RATIOS, PERCENT:										
INCOME TO SALES:										
Before tax	7.14	6.23	5.01	3.70	5.26	7.01	9.76	11.37	10.13	7.29
After tax	5.31	4.36	2.96	2.13	3.60	4.98	6.73	8.32	7.17	5.06
INCOME TO STOCKHOLDERS' EQUITY:										
Before tax	17.85	15.33	12.41	8.78	12.24	16.33	21.73	24.01	21.46	16.68
After tax	13.27	10.74	7.34	5.07	8.38	11.61	14.98	17.57	15.19	11.57
INCOME TO TOTAL ASSETS:										
Before tax	8.02	6.77	5.30	3.85	5.45	7.36	10.44	11.38	10.55	7.68
After tax	5.96	4.74	3.13	2.22	3.73	5.23	7.19	8.32	7.47	5.33
AS A PERCENT OF TOTAL ASSETS:										
Property, plant and equipment	23.23	22.60	22.05	22.40	22.11	21.37	21.85	22.06	22.03	22.19
Short-term debt	4.62	7.21	8.54	7.50	6.65	5.56	5.08	5.07	5.50	6.19
Long-term debt	16.25	16.32	15.52	16.51	15.63	14.68	13.47	12.89	12.65	14.88
Stockholders' equity	44.92	44.16	42.69	43.79	44.47	45.07	48.02	47.39	49.15	45.52

1. For income and asset amounts, compound annual growth rate; for ratios, average of ratios for the years shown.

Source: U.S. Bureau of the Census, Quarterly Financial Report.

Notes: Parentheses ( ) indicate negative items, e.g., net expenses, charges, or losses. Net property, plant, and equipment is net of accumulated depreciation. Because the samples used to collect the data change, retained earnings at the end of a given year will not exactly equal the previous year's retained earnings plus the current year's retained income and credits.

CANADA

In 1993, Canada's electrical and electronic products industry (excluding computers and office machines) consisted of 1,183 establishments with 103,202 employees (Table 7). The largest subindustry is electronic equipment, with 59 percent of industry shipments in 1993. Electrical industrial equipment accounted for 13 percent, and communications, energy wire, and cable had 9 percent. Hourly earnings in the industry (including computers and office machines) averaged Can$15.47 in 1993. Workers in the telecommunications equipment industry were the highest paid, averaging Can$18.98 per hour.

Shipments by the industry totaled Can$18.4 billion in 1994, or more than a third above those in 1987 (Table 8). This growth was achieved despite uninterrupted declines in the workforce from 1988 through 1994, to 101,230 employees. Production worker employment declined also, but their share of the workforce in 1984, at 71 percent, was up slightly from all previous years except 1988. Average hourly wages of production workers in 1994 were Can$15.58, compared with Can$12.44 in 1988, for an annual growth rate of 3.82 percent. After adjustment for inflation, that rate was only 0.67 percent.

TABLE 7

CANADA: COMPONENT INDUSTRIES OF ELECTRONIC AND OTHER ELECTRICAL EQUIPMENT (CSIC 33 EXCEPT 336), 1993

(Monetary values in Canadian dollars)

INDUSTRY NAME	CSIC	ESTABLISH-MENTS (NUMBER)	EMPLOYMENT		VALUE OF SHIPMENTS (MILLIONS)	AVERAGE HOURLY EARNINGS[1]
			NUMBER	PERCENT OF INDUSTRY TOTAL		
ELECTRICAL AND ELECTRONIC PRODUCTS[2]	33, exc. 336	1,183	103,202	100.0	CAN$16,643.9	CAN$15.47
Small appliances	331	48	2,785	2.7	364.0	12.87
Major appliances (electric and non-electric)	332	24	6,266	6.1	917.3	14.38
Electric lightings	333	165	5,767	5.6	655.7	11.36
Lighting fixtures	3331	105	3,701	3.6	434.0	10.89
Electric lamps and shades	3332	50	1,013	1.0	74.0	8.68
Electric lamp (bulbs and tubes)	3333	10	1,053	1.0	147.8	15.31
Record players, radio and TV receivers	334	15	1,433	1.4	272.8	11.33
Electronic equipment	335	467	53,333	51.7	9,840.1	16.77
Telecommunications equipment	3351	62	18,704	18.1	3,811.2	18.98
Electronic parts and components	3352	208	13,065	12.7	3,568.1	12.50
Other office and business machines	3359	197	21,564	20.9	2,460.7	18.11
Electrical industrial equipment	337	291	19,187	18.6	2,164.6	14.67
Electrical transformers	3371	49	4,779	4.6	618.6	15.68
Electrical switchgear, protective equipment	3372	104	7,117	6.9	755.1	14.26
Other electrical industrial equipment	3379	138	7,291	7.1	790.9	14.35
Communications and energy wire and cable	338	58	7,361	7.1	1,512.5	16.80
Other electrical products	339	115	7,070	6.9	916.9	13.42
Batteries	3391	16	1,441	1.4	267.9	15.00
Noncurrent carrying wiring devices	3392	26	1,293	1.3	149.7	14.21
Other electrical products, n.e.c.	3399	73	4,336	4.2	499.3	12.74

1. Including overtime.

2. Figures except hourly earnings do not include CSIC 336, computers and office equipment, for easier comparison to the U.S. industry.

Source: Adapted from Statistics Canada, *Manufacturing Industries of Canada* (Cat. No. 31-203).

TABLE 8

CANADIAN EMPLOYMENT AND SHIPMENTS: ELECTRONIC AND OTHER ELECTRICAL EQUIPMENT (EXCEPT COMPUTERS), 1987-1994

(Monetary values in Canadian dollars)

	1987	1988	1989	1990	1991	1992	1993	1994	CHANGE[1]
All employees	126,521	132,946	132,365	125,222	115,353	112,000	103,202	101,230	-3.14
Establishments	1,252	1,384	1,395	1,393	1,294	1,234	1,183	1,140	-1.33
Employees per establishment	101	96	95	90	89	91	87	89	-1.83
Production workers per establishment	.....	69	67	62	61	64	61	63	-1.41
PRODUCTION WORKERS:									
Total	.....	95,099	92,898	85,940	78,746	79,304	72,358	71,946	-4.54
Percent of all employees	.....	71.5	70.2	68.6	68.3	70.8	70.1	71.1	.....
Male	.....	61,535	59,827	55,178	50,888	.....	.....	.....	.....
Female	.....	33,564	33,071	30,762	27,858	.....	.....	.....	.....
Percent of all production workers	.....	35.3	35.6	35.8	35.4	.....	.....	.....	.....
Average hourly earnings	.....	12.44	12.90	13.71	14.28	15.19	15.47	15.58	3.82
Average weekly earnings	.....	490.63	511.61	546.89	571.34	606.54	621.74	639.25	4.51
Average weekly hours	.....	39.4	39.7	39.9	40.0	39.9	40.2	41.0	0.66
Shipments (millions)	13,615	15,121	16,349	15,267	16,197	16,789	16,644	18,366	4.37

1. Compound annual growth rate.

Note: Excludes computers and office equipment for easier comparison to U.S. industry.

Source: Adapted from Statistics Canada, *Manufacturing Industries of Canada* (Cat. No. 31-203).

MEXICO

Mexico's electronic and other electrical equipment industry is part of the huge metal products and machinery equipment industry, whose subindustries in some cases are not comparable to similar U.S. industries. Table 9 shows total employment for subindustries that correspond to those in the U.S. electronic and other electrical equipment industry,

TABLE 9

MEXICO: COMPONENT INDUSTRIES OF ELECTRICAL AND ELECTRONIC EQUIPMENT (CMAP 3831, 3832, 3833), 1993

(Monetary values in 1993 Mexican New Pesos)

			ALL WORKERS									
							PAID WORKERS					
							PRODUCTION WORKERS		NONPRODUCTION EMPLOYEES		BENEFITS	UNPAID
INDUSTRY	CMAP	NUMBER OF UNITS	NUMBER	PERCENT OF INDUSTRY TOTAL	AVERAGE DAYS WORKED	REMUN- ERATION[1]	NUMBER	WAGES AND SALARIES	NUMBER	WAGES AND SALARIES	PER PAID EMPLOYEE	WORKERS, NUMBER
Machinery, equipment and electrical accessories	3831	1,409	211,559	56	273	21,044	171,486	9,957	38,679	35,183	6,445	1,157
Electronic communications and medical equipment	3832	535	130,054	35	272	22,062	102,852	10,188	26,961	33,326	7,068	241
Home appliances excluding electronics	3833	247	34,906	9	271	24,461	27,908	11,468	6,799	39,970	7,997	199

1. Average annual remuneration including benefits.

Source: INEGI, Censos Economicos 1994.

broken down into that of production workers, nonproduction employees (including supervisory), and unpaid workers, as well as average days worked and yearly remuneration for the first three categories. Electrical machines, the largest component of this subindustry, had 211,559 employees in 1993 who worked an average of 273 days a year and had incomes (earnings plus benefits) of about 21,044 new pesos ($6,737) a year. The electronic machinery component had 130,054 employees, with average incomes of 22,062 new pesos ($7,063) a year. Employment in the electrical and electronic equipment industry rose at the annual rate of 2.92 percent between 1988 and 1995 to 310,104 people (Table 10).

TABLE 10

MEXICAN EMPLOYMENT: ELECTRIC AND ELECTRONIC EQUIPMENT, 1988-1995

	1988	1989	1990	1991	1992	1993	1994	1995	CHANGE[1]
TOTAL EMPLOYMENT: Electrical and electronic equipment	253,543	260,756	269,938	277,555	282,289	292,379	304,284	310,104	2.92

1. Compound annual growth rate.

Source: Sistema de Cuentas Nacionales de Mexico, INEGI.

INTERNATIONAL TRADE

United States. Global U.S. exports of electronic and other electrical equipment almost doubled, to $79.6 billion, between 1990 and 1996. This was not enough, however, to keep pace with growth in imports, which also about doubled during that time period, to $114.1 billion in 1996 (Table 11). The resulting U.S. trade deficit was $34.5 billion in 1996, compared with about $24 billion in 1993 and $17.7 billion 1990. The widening trade gap reflects stronger economic growth in the United States than in other developed countries and stiff competition from low-cost developing country producers. Canada accounted for about 22 percent of U.S. exports and 7 percent of U.S. imports in 1996. Mexico accounted for about 16 percent of both U.S. exports and imports that year.

Electronic components and accessories and semiconductors and related devices are the top trade items, and imports of them exceed exports. Canada is the largest market for both categories, and Mexico is a leading buying of electronic components and accessories. Other leading markets, and important sources, are the European Union, Japan, and East Asian countries such as South Korea, Taiwan, and Malaysia.

Canada. Exports to the United States rose from $4.4 billion in 1990 to $8.1 billion in 1996—a gain of 83 percent (Table 11). U.S. shipments to Canada between 1990 and 1996 almost doubled, to $17.4 billion. The resulting U.S. trade surplus with Canada was $9.3 billion in 1996, versus $4.8 billion in 1990. (See footnote on 1989 Canadian-U.S. trade figures.) Canada's exports to Mexico rose 80 percent to $102 million during 1990-1996, but Mexico's much larger exports to Canada almost tripled, to $968 million.

Mexico. Mexican exports to the United States, almost tripled between 1990 and 1996, to $18.5 billion, while U.S. exports to Mexico climbed 150 percent, to $12.5 billion (Table 11). This gave Mexico a 1996 trade surplus of almost $6 billion, compared with about $1.2 billion in 1990.

NAFTA. The United States had a trade surplus with NAFTA throughout the 1990-1996 period, due entirely to fast growth in U.S. exports to Canada (Table 11). The U.S. surplus reached a high of $4.9 billion in 1992 and declined thereafter to $3.4 billion in 1996. Mexico's trade surplus shot from $1.5 billion in 1990 to $6.8 billion in 1996, with virtually all of that growth occurring between 1992 and 1996. Canada's trade deficit climbed from $5.1 billion in 1990, to $7.8 billion in 1993, to $10.2 billion in 1996. (See the "Workforce and Employment" section for information about NAFTA's effect on employment in the U.S. industry.)

TABLE 11

INTERNATIONAL TRADE, ELECTRONIC AND OTHER ELECTRICAL EQUIPMENT
(Millions of U.S. dollars)

	1989[1]	1990	1991	1992	1993	1994	1995	1996
GLOBAL TRADE, U.S.								
IMPORTS								
Value	57,027.6	57,620.3	60,393.4	67,701.5	76,868.5	94,331.5	114,911.1	114,066.6
Ratio to new supply[2]	23.6	23.3	24.2	24.6	25.7	27.8	.....	.....
Ratio to apparent consumption[3]	27.3	27.8	29.1	29.6	31.2	34.2	.....	.....
EXPORTS								
Value	32,939.3	39,887.5	42,351.1	46,220.2	52,947.3	63,839.1	76,235.2	79,604.8
Ratio to comparable domestic shipments	17.8	21.0	22.3	22.3	23.8	26.0	.....	.....
TRADE BALANCE	(24,088.3)	(17,732.8)	(18,042.3)	(21,481.3)	(23,921.2)	(30,492.4)	(38,675.9)	(34,461.8)
BILATERAL TRADE: NAFTA[4]								
U.S. exports to Canada	5,850.0	9,260.1	10,006.7	10,847.1	12,368.9	14,511.5	17,165.6	17,445.7
Canadian exports to U.S.	3,408.3	4,419.9	4,759.8	4,902.2	4,918.7	5,734.8	6,920.8	8,100.0
U.S. exports to Mexico	4,934.6	5,017.7	5,762.9	6,902.8	8,190.8	9,917.5	10,388.7	12,522.5
Mexican exports to U.S.	5,829.3	6,238.3	6,763.5	7,991.1	11,151.1	14,465.0	16,412.8	18,473.0
Canadian exports to Mexico[5]	34.8	56.3	32.6	61.2	70.2	45.9	63.8	101.5
Mexican exports to Canada[5]	320.0	334.1	341.5	371.8	448.4	600.5	790.4	967.8
TRADE BALANCES WITHIN NAFTA[6]								
Canada	(2,726.9)	(5,118.0)	(5,555.8)	(6,255.5)	(7,828.4)	(9,331.3)	(10,971.4)	(10,212.0)
Mexico	1,179.9	1,498.4	1,309.5	1,398.9	3,338.5	5,102.1	6,750.7	6,816.8
United States	1,547.0	3,619.6	4,246.3	4,856.6	4,489.9	4,229.2	4,220.8	3,395.2

1. 1989 and earlier data on U.S. exports to Canada for manufacturing total and manufacturing industries are not comparable with data for 1990 and later years because of a change in the reporting system. The NAFTA trade balances for the U.S. and Canada also are affected.
2. New supply equals comparable domestic shipments plus imports for consumption.
3. Apparent consumption equals comparable domestic shipments plus imports for consumption less exports.
4. Amounts less than U.S. $100,000 shown as zero.
5. Includes computer equipment.
6. Parentheses indicate an excess of imports over exports. Because of commodity coding and other data differences among the three countries, these trade balances are only rough estimates and should be used with caution.
Source for U.S. Global Trade: U.S. Department of Commerce, International Trade Administration.
Source for U.S. -Canada and U.S.-Mexico Bilateral Trade: U.S. Bureau of the Census.
Source for Canada-Mexico and Mexico-Canada Bilateral Trade: Statistics Canada, Foreign Trade Division, Special tabulation, March 1997, converted to U.S. dollars by the editors.

FABRICATED METAL PRODUCTS

THE UNITED STATES

Products and Processes.   The fabricated metal products industry ranked sixth among U.S. manufacturing industries in 1996 in terms of industry shipments and employment. Because of the innumerable uses for metals, this industry has a wide diversity of products and markets. The products include metal building systems, forgings and stampings, plumbing and heating fixtures, tools of all types, metal cans and containers, nuts and bolts, small arms and ammunition, valves and pipefittings, coatings and engraving, electroplating, and metal cutlery.

Table 1 gives a breakdown of the industry as of 1992 (the latest year for which economic census data are available). That year, 36,429 establishments with a combined payroll of $38.96 billion were in the fabricated metals business. Fabricated structural metal products (i.e., doors, frames, sheet metal, architectural and ornamental metal, and prefabricated buildings) accounted for 26.9 percent of industry shipments in 1992. Next in order were miscellaneous fabricated metal products (valves, steel and wire springs, metal foil and leaf, and fabricated pipe and pipe fittings), with 18.4 percent; metal forgings and stampings, 18.3 percent; cutlery, handtools, and general hardware, 9.3 percent; and metal cans and shipping containers, almost 8 percent.

The industry employed 1,339,000 people in 1993 (Table 2). The largest employers were manufacturers of fabricated structural metal products (29.5 percent of the total), miscellaneous fabricated metal products (17.3 percent), and metal forging and stamping (16.6 percent). Total industry employment is projected to decline about 11.8 percent, to 1,180,500, by the year 2005. Among the subindustries, only coating, engraving, and allied services and miscellaneous fabricated metal products are expected to gain from their 1993 levels.

TABLE 1

UNITED STATES: COMPONENT INDUSTRIES OF FABRICATED METAL PRODUCTS (SIC 34), 1992

(Monetary values in millions of U.S. dollars)

INDUSTRY	SIC	ESTABLISH-MENTS	SHIPMENTS		VALUE ADDED BY MANUFACTURE	NEW CAPITAL EXPENDI-TURES	EMPLOY-MENT[1]	PAYROLL
			VALUE	PERCENT BY 4 LARGEST COMPANIES				
FABRICATED METAL PRODUCTS	34	36,429	$166,532.0	.....	$83,761.4	$4,437.5	1,362,300	$38,961.8
Metal cans and shipping containers	341	481	13,262.7	.....	3,736.0	372.8	39,600	1,464.7
Metal cans	3411	324	12,112.2	56	3,290.1	350.6	32,300	1,261.9
Metal shipping barrels, drums, kegs, and pails	3412	157	1,150.5	36	445.9	22.3	7,300	202.7
Cutlery, handtools, and general hardware	342	2,475	15,447.7	.....	9,043.7	460.3	134,400	3,648.1
Cutlery	3421	134	1,563.0	56	1,114.9	58.1	11,500	301.3
Hand and edge tools, n.e.c.	3423	917	4,227.9	27	2,595.7	124.0	39,900	1,064.4
Handsaws and saw blades	3425	140	850.3	45	509.1	34.3	7,700	219.6
Hardware, n.e.c.	3429	1,284	8,806.4	24	4,824.0	244.0	75,400	2,062.7
Plumbing and heating, except electric and warm air	343	688	5,825.2	.....	3,105.2	129.5	41,900	1,152.3
Enameled iron and metal sanitary ware	3431	81	792.2	60	483.3	17.4	6,400	198.5
Plumbing fixture fittings and trim	3432	184	2,723.1	45	1,370.9	74.5	17,400	444.2
Heating equipment, except electric and warm air	3433	423	2,309.9	16	1,251.1	37.5	18,100	509.6
Fabricated structural metal products	344	13,255	44,875.6	.....	21,255.5	789.5	388,900	10,362.2
Fabricated structural metal	3441	2,547	8,918.7	10	3,947.0	133.3	72,000	1,963.5
Metal doors, sash, frames, molding and trim	3442	1,416	7,182.8	14	3,245.2	110.8	67,900	1,536.6
Fabricated plate work (boiler shops)	3443	1,937	8,974.9	9	4,789.0	201.6	78,400	2,311.9
Sheet metal work	3444	4,685	11,298.8	9	5,714.8	222.5	103,900	2,833.9
Architectural and ornamental metal work	3446	1,473	2,372.7	14	1,270.6	32.8	24,900	621.8
Prefabricated metal buildings and components	3448	538	2,788.6	31	1,150.3	28.9	20,300	511.8
Miscellaneous structural metal work	3449	659	3,339.1	26	1,138.6	59.7	21,400	582.5
Screw machine products, bolts, etc.	345	2,642	9,025.5	.....	5,268.7	286.6	90,500	2,624.2
Screw machine products	3451	1,707	3,830.6	5	2,394.0	135.3	46,400	1,271.0
Bolts, nuts, screws, rivets, and washers	3452	935	5,194.9	17	2,874.7	151.3	44,100	1,353.2
Metal forgings and stampings	346	3,979	30,621.3	.....	14,913.4	1,000.2	233,700	7,748.6
Iron and steel forgings	3462	402	3,186.0	20	1,568.6	109.8	24,000	757.7
Nonferrous forgings	3463	80	1,240.5	59	605.4	57.4	8,000	283.6
Automotive stampings	3465	699	15,802.5	51	7,231.3	519.4	105,100	4,093.8
Crowns and closures	3466	51	832.9	57	407.6	18.4	4,800	143.4
Metal stampings, n.e.c.	3469	2,747	9,559.4	8	5,100.4	295.3	91,800	2,470.1
Coating, engraving, and allied services	347	5,247	9,952.5	.....	5,678.8	364.1	108,200	2,652.4
Plating and polishing	3471	3,294	4,625.3	10	3,126.6	205.2	64,100	1,538.1
Coating, engraving, and allied services, n.e.c.	3479	1,953	5,327.3	15	2,552.1	158.8	44,100	1,114.3
Ordnance, except vehicles and guided missiles	348	427	6,855.0	.....	4,536.1	115.0	62,200	2,124.3
Small arms ammunition	3482	102	1,023.1	84	572.1	30.0	7,900	250.4
Ammunition, except for small arms	3483	69	3,083.6	57	1,884.4	36.3	23,100	715.1
Small arms	3484	184	1,384.0	43	939.8	32.0	11,800	334.9
Ordnance and accessories, n.e.c.	3489	72	1,364.3	83	1,139.8	16.7	19,500	823.9
Miscellaneous fabricated metal products	349	7,235	30,666.5	.....	16,224.1	919.5	262,900	7,185.0
Industrial valves	3491	496	6,810.7	24	4,084.2	213.1	51,800	1,611.2
Fluid power valves and hose fittings	3492	368	3,328.4	40	1,782.4	115.9	28,500	862.3
Steel springs, except wire	3493	114	495.8	42	247.3	17.5	4,400	118.9
Valves and pipe fittings, n.e.c.	3494	247	1,912.7	24	985.3	51.8	16,200	459.2
Wire springs	3495	399	1,743.5	36	953.1	61.5	18,000	443.4
Miscellaneous fabricated wire products	3496	1,165	3,526.1	9	1,835.7	99.9	38,400	870.7
Metal foil and leaf	3497	123	3,161.8	46	1,288.2	92.4	12,200	414.2
Fabricated pipe and pipe fittings	3498	863	2,861.4	10	1,383.1	61.6	25,200	661.0
Fabricated metal products, n.e.c.	3499	3,460	6,826.0	10	3,664.7	205.8	68,400	1,744.2

1. Employment numbers from the economic censuses differ in definition and classification from the Bureau of Labor Statistics estimates in Table 2. Year-to-year comparisons between Table 1 and Table 2 are not appropriate.

Source: U.S. Bureau of the Census, 1992 Census of Manufactures.

TABLE 2

U.S. EMPLOYMENT AND EARNINGS: FABRICATED METAL PRODUCTS

		1993			2005
		EMPLOYMENT[1]		AVERAGE	
INDUSTRY	SIC	NUMBER OF PERSONS	PERCENT OF INDUSTRY TOTAL	HOURLY EARNINGS (U.S. DOLLARS)[2]	PROJECTED EMPLOYMENT[3]
FABRICATED METAL PRODUCTS	34	1,338,500	100.0	$11.69	1,180,500
Metal cans and shipping containers	341	42,100	3.1	15.18	26,900
Metal cans	3411	34,000	2.5	16.23	.....
Cutlery, handtools, and hardware	342	124,000	9.3	11.60	89,900
Hand and edge tools, blades, and handsaws	3423,5	42,400	3.2	10.97	.....
Hardware, n.e.c.	3429	69,900	5.2	11.63	.....
Plumbing and heating, except electric	343	56,500	4.2	10.49	48,000
Plumbing fixture fittings and trim	3432	24,300	1.8	9.89	.....
Heating equipment, except electric	3433	19,000	1.4	10.63	.....
Fabricated structural metal products	344	395,100	29.5	10.89	315,300
Fabricated structural metal	3441	67,400	5.0	10.77	.....
Metal doors, sash, and trim	3442	71,100	5.3	9.18	.....
Fabricated plate work (boiler shops)	3443	98,200	7.3	12.31	.....
Sheet metal work	3444	97,000	7.2	11.09	.....
Architectural metal work	3446	25,900	1.9	10.06	.....
Screw machine products, bolts, etc.	345	91,500	6.8	11.55	77,900
Screw machine products	3451	45,700	3.4	10.76	.....
Bolts, nuts, rivets, and washers	3452	45,800	3.4	12.42	.....
Metal forgings and stampings	346	221,600	16.6	14.01	194,100
Iron and steel forgings	3462	28,900	2.2	13.59	.....
Automotive stampings	3465	101,000	7.5	16.08	.....
Metal stampings, n.e.c.	3469	80,500	6.0	11.10	.....
Coating, engraving, and allied services	347	117,500	8.8	9.64	140,000
Plating and polishing	3471	73,100	5.5	9.68	.....
Metal coating and allied services	3479	44,400	3.3	9.58	.....
Ordnance and accessories, n.e.c.	348	58,800	4.4	13.31	50,700
Ammunition, except for small arms, n.e.c.	3483	35,000	2.6	13.41	.....
Miscellaneous fabricated metal products	349	231,400	17.3	10.86	237,700
Valves and pipe fittings, n.e.c.	3494	24,800	1.9	11.31	.....
Miscellaneous fabricated wire products	3496	53,800	4.0	9.68	.....

1. Total payroll employment. Employment data from the economic censuses, shown in Table 1, differ in definition and classification from the Bureau of Labor Statistics estimates in this table. Year-to-year comparisons between Table 1 and Table 2 are not appropriate.

2. Earnings of production workers, including overtime.

3. Number of persons, moderate projection by the U.S. Bureau of Labor Statistics.

Source: Bureau of Labor Statistics.

FIGURE 1

U.S. EMPLOYMENT IN FABRICATED METALS

Percent distribution by region, 1995

Employment in the industry is highest in the Great Lakes region, which had 34 percent of the total in 1995. Next largest employer is the Southeast (18 percent of the 1995 total), but this figure is well below the Southeast's share of total employment.

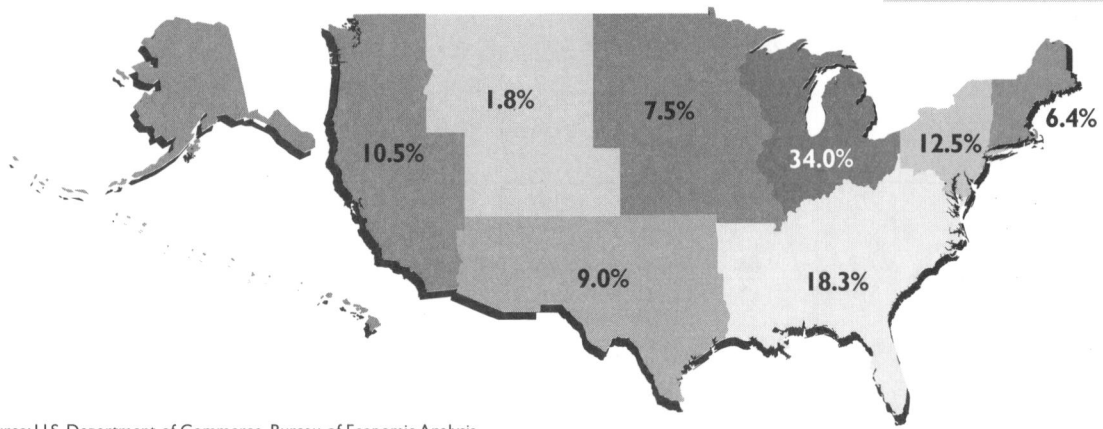

Source: U.S. Department of Commerce, Bureau of Economic Analysis.

What's New.   New orders for fabricated metal products grew steadily from 1996 to 1997, resulting in an overall increase of 5.9 percent in the first half of 1997 over the same period of 1996.

Metal standing seam roofing for new and retrofit applications is the fastest-growing segment of the metal buildings systems industry, according to the Metal Building Manufacturers Association. The sloped standing seam roofs are coated with long-lasting materials that require little maintenance, are light weight and easily installed over traditional flat roofs, and can be used with all types of insulation to meet today's code requirements. The association expects sales of metal reroofing systems to reach a billion square feet a year in the near future; popular uses include schools, large warehouses, and manufacturing plants.

FIGURE 2

U.S. EMPLOYMENT AND SHIPMENTS IN FABRICATED METALS

Total payroll employment and manufacturers' inflation-adjusted shipments

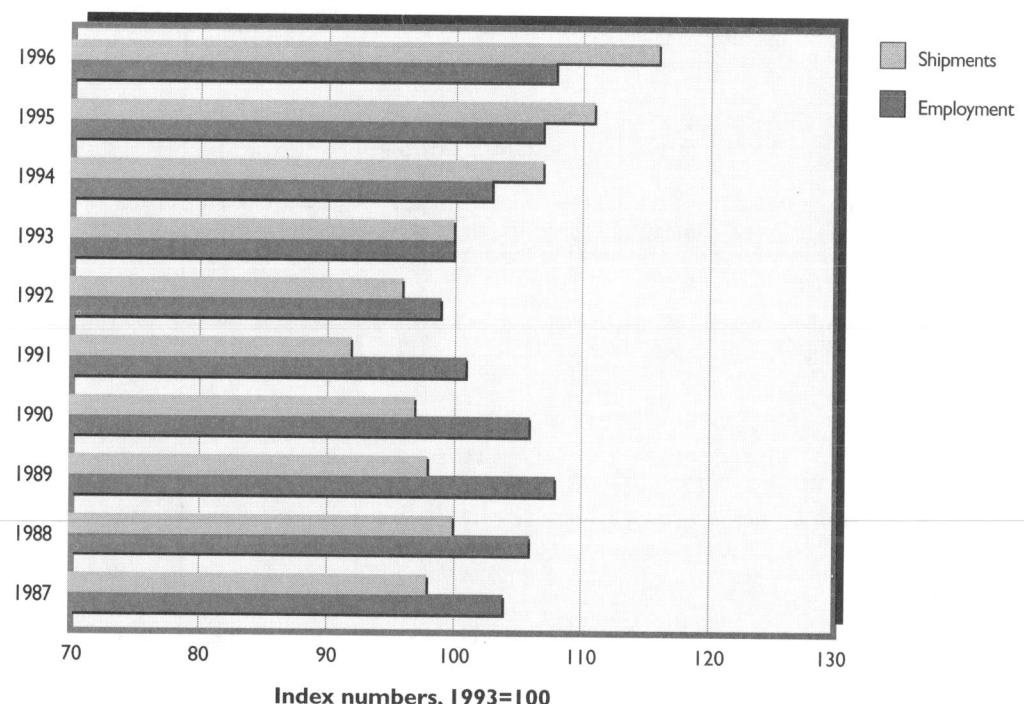

Index numbers, 1993=100

Source: U.S. Bureau of Labor Statistics, U.S. Department of Commerce, and estimates by the editors.

Output.   After turning down in 1989, constant-dollar industry shipments declined through 1991 and then rebounded to new highs in succeeding years. Employment followed a similar trend, delayed by a year, but had a less vigorous recovery than shipments as industry restructuring and modernization led to gains in productivity (Figure 2). Industry shipments in 1996 were a record $215.2 billion, compared with $204.8 billion the year before and $147.4 billion in 1987 (Table 3). The annual rate of growth in shipments during the 1987-1996 period was 4.29 percent (1.89 percent when adjusted for inflation).

Investment.   Producers of fabricated metals have invested heavily in plants and equipment during the past 10 years, with the largest gains occurring between 1992 and 1995 (Table 3). By 1995, new capital expenditures had reached $7.1 billion, compared with $5.8 billion in 1994 and $4.8 billion in 1987. Data through 1994 show research and development spending hitting a peak of $936 million in 1993 and then slipping to $868 million in 1994. Capacity utilization appears to have risen in step with expansion of facilities, reaching a peak of 84.8 percent in 1994 and then dipping to 84.5 percent in 1996.

Prices.   Producer prices for fabricated metal products rose at an annual rate of 2.39 percent between 1987 and 1996 (Table 3). Most of the gains occurred between 1987 and 1989 and 1993 and 1995.

TABLE 3

U.S. OUTPUT, INVESTMENT, AND PRICES: FABRICATED METALS

(Millions of U.S. dollars, except as noted)

	1987	1988	1989	1990	1991	1992	1993	1994	1995	1996	GROWTH RATE 1987-1996[1]
VALUE OF SHIPMENTS:											
BY INDUSTRY:											
Current dollars	147,438	159,504	164,073	165,065	159,759	166,532	175,118	190,545	204,819	215,163	4.29
Constant 1992 dollars	169,840	174,703	171,293	168,369	160,529	166,532	173,940	186,310	193,322	200,991	1.89
BY PRODUCT:											
Current dollars	138,737	149,553	153,969	156,288	151,399	156,945	166,223	180,474	193,871	203,661	4.36
Constant 1992 dollars	159,743	163,732	160,675	159,358	152,075	156,945	165,185	176,519	183,087	190,350	1.97
OTHER OUTPUT MEASURES:											
Industrial production, 1993=100	97.6	101.6	100.4	96.9	92.1	95.8	100.0	107.3	110.8	113.6	1.70
Gross domestic product:									.....	.....	.....
Current dollars	61,577	66,193	68,264	69,383	67,590	70,055	74,474	82,465	.....	.....	.....
Percent of total GDP	1.3	1.3	1.3	1.2	1.1	1.1	1.1	1.2	.....	.....	.....
Rank in manufacturing	7	7	7	7	7	7	7	7	.....	.....	.....
Chained (1992) dollars	72,262	77,134	75,211	72,567	68,210	70,055	74,231	82,911	.....	.....	.....
INVESTMENT-RELATED MEASURES:											
Capacity utilization, percent	78.1	81.1	80.0	77.4	73.7	76.7	79.4	83.9	84.8	84.5	.....
New capital expenditures	4,817	4,195	4,636	4,825	4,178	4,438	5,774	5,806	7,106	.....	.....
Research and development spending	633	718	726	736	748	723	936	868	.....	.....	.....
Producer prices, 1993=100[2]	86.3	90.8	95.2	97.3	98.6	99.1	100.0	101.7	105.6	106.7	2.39

1. Compound annual growth rate.

2. Prices received by domestic producers.

Sources: Shipments and new capital expenditures: U.S. Department of Commerce for 1987-1995, editor's estimates for constant dollar data for 1987-88 and all shipments data for 1996; Industrial production and capacity utilization: Federal Reserve Board of Governors; GDP: Bureau of Economic Analysis; Research and development spending: National Science Foundation; Producer prices: Bureau of Labor Statistics.

Workforce and Employment. Industry employment has risen slowly since its low point in 1992, reaching 1.45 million in 1996 (Table 4). However, the rate of gain since 1987 has been only 0.38 percent a year, and employment did not surpass the 1989 level until 1996. Employment of production workers has grown at a slightly faster pace of 0.53 percent a year to 1.09 million in 1996, or 75.1 percent of total employment. Employment of women in 1996 was little changed from the 1987 level, and their share of total employment has declined slightly to 22 percent in 1996. Average hourly earnings of production workers stood at $12.52 in 1996. The rate of growth in earnings over the 10-year period was 2.52 percent annually, but in inflation-adjusted dollars, earnings declined by 1.0 percent a year. The average workweek in 1996, at 42.4 hours, was a little longer than in 1987.

TABLE 4

U.S. EMPLOYMENT, HOURS, AND EARNINGS: FABRICATED METALS

(Monetary values in U.S. dollars)

	1987	1988	1989	1990	1991	1992	1993	1994	1995	1996	CHANGE[1]
NUMBER OF EMPLOYEES, IN THOUSANDS:											
Total	1,399	1,428	1,445	1,419	1,355	1,329	1,339	1,388	1,437	1,448	0.38
Production workers	1,038	1,062	1,070	1,045	991	975	988	1,037	1,080	1,088	0.53
Percent of total	74.2	74.3	74.1	73.6	73.1	73.4	73.8	74.7	75.2	75.1	.....
Women	317	322	324	316	300	294	295	306	316	318	0.04
Percent of total	22.7	22.5	22.4	22.2	22.1	22.1	22.0	22.1	22.0	22.0	.....
HOURS AND EARNINGS OF PRODUCTION WORKERS:											
AVERAGE HOURLY EARNINGS[2]											
Current dollars	10.01	10.29	10.57	10.83	11.19	11.42	11.69	11.93	12.13	12.52	2.52
1992 dollars[3]	12.30	12.15	11.92	11.61	11.51	11.42	11.37	11.32	11.19	11.23	-1.00
Average weekly hours	41.6	41.9	41.6	41.3	41.2	41.6	42.1	42.9	42.4	42.4	0.21
Average weekly earnings, current U.S. dollars	416.42	431.15	439.71	447.28	461.03	475.07	492.15	511.8	514.31	530.85	2.73

1. Compound annual growth rate, 1987-1996.

2. Including overtime.

3. Converted to 1992 dollars using Consumer Price Index for Urban Wage Earners and Clerical Workers.

Source: Bureau of Labor Statistics.

FIGURE 3

U.S. OCCUPATIONAL INJURY AND ILLNESS RATES: FABRICATED METALS, 1995
Incidence of nonfatal injuries and illnesses per 100 full-time workers

Nonfatal occupational illnesses and injuries in the industry averaged 15.8 cases per 100 workers in 1995. This was the fourth highest rank among the manufacturing industries.

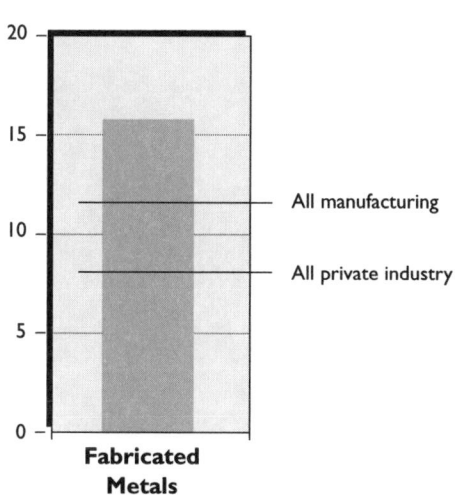

All manufacturing

All private industry

Fabricated Metals

Source: U.S. Bureau of Labor Statistics.

TABLE 5

U.S. EMPLOYMENT PROJECTIONS BY MAJOR OCCUPATIONAL GROUP: FABRICATED METALS

Projections to the year 2005 (moderate assumptions) show a decline in total industry employment to 1,180,500 million from 1,387,200 million in 1994, with declines occurring in all occupational areas except professional specialties.

Occupation	1994		Projections, 2005			
	Number of Employees	Percent of Industry Total	Number of Employees			Percent of Industry Total, Moderate Projections
			Low	Moderate	High	
Total, all occupations	1,387,200	100	1,113,900	1,180,500	1,271,000	100.0
Executive, administrative, and managerial	125,710	9.1	105,858	112,174	120,770	9.5
Professional specialties	32,070	2.3	31,806	33,638	35,863	2.8
Technicians and related support	28,087	2.0	19,985	21,161	22,648	1.8
Marketing and sales	35,215	2.5	29,530	31,383	33,883	2.7
Administrative support including clerical	137,976	9.9	103,132	109,380	117,793	9.3
Service	16,291	1.2	11,558	12,223	13,074	1.0
Agriculture, forestry, and fisheries occupations	134	0.0	115	121	130	0.0
Precision production, craft, and repair	311,413	22.4	239,481	253,674	273,021	21.5
Operators, fabricators, assemblers	700,304	50.5	572,434	606,747	653,819	51.4

Source: Bureau of Labor Statistics, November 1995.

FIGURE 4

U.S. CORPORATE INCOME AND WORKER EARNINGS: FABRICATED METALS

Corporate operating income and aggregate production worker earnings

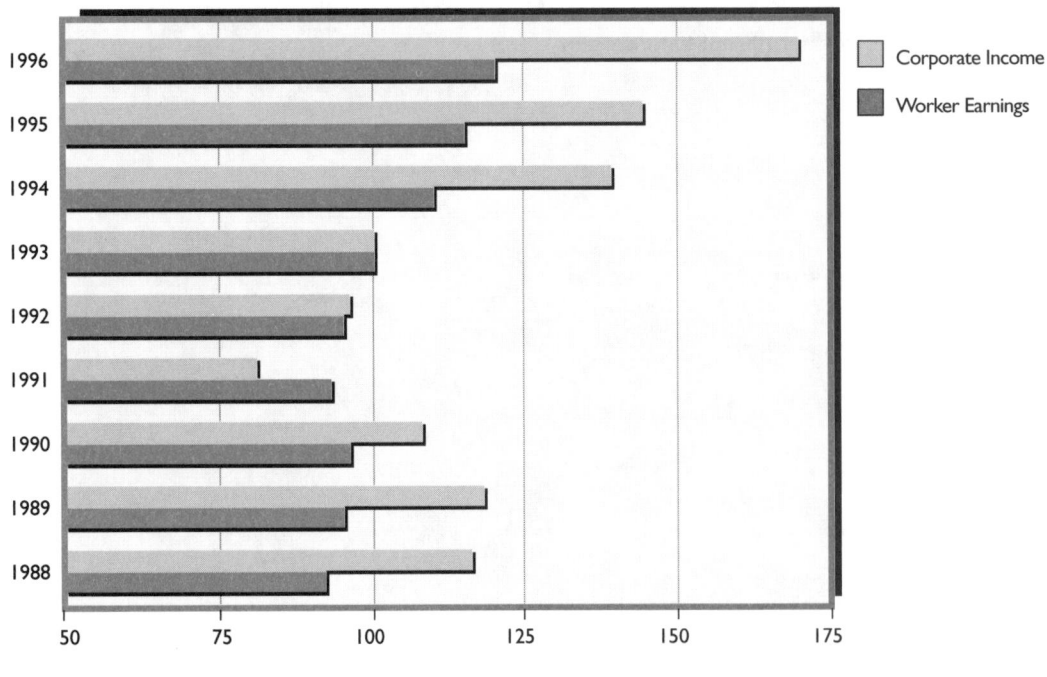

Index numbers, 1993=100

Source: U.S. Bureau of Labor Statistics, U.S. Bureau of the Census, and estimates by the editors.

Finance. Corporate earnings by the fabricated metals industry have rebounded strongly from the 1991 recession, with the fastest growth in 1994 and 1996. Production worker earning trended upward in those years also, but at a much slower rate (Figure 4).

Industry income from operations reached $13.4 billion in 1996, up significantly from the $11.5 billion of 1995 and more than double the low 1991 level of $6.4 billion (Table 6). The annual growth rate between 1988 and 1996 was 4.73 percent. After-tax income showed even better growth in 1996 as it soared 68 percent above the 1995 level to $9.3 billion; this resulted in an impressive annual growth rate of 7.16 percent for the 1988-1996 period. After-tax income amounted to 5.52 percent of sales in 1996 (compared with 3.48 percent in 1995) and 18.5 percent of stockholders' equity (13.15 percent). Inventories in 1996 were down slightly from the previous year's to $19.8 billion, the lowest level in nine years. Debt, mainly long-term, amounted to 37.3 percent of total assets, the highest level in nine years.

TABLE 6

U.S. CORPORATE INCOME AND ASSETS: FABRICATED METALS

(Monetary values in millions of U.S. dollars)

INCOME AND EXPENSES	1988	1989	1990	1991	1992	1993	1994	1995	1996	CHANGE OR AVERAGE[1]
Sales and receipts	140,003	145,057	135,935	127,223	131,643	133,798	149,751	158,698	168,186	2.32
Depreciation and amortization	(4,030)	(3,983)	(3,673)	(3,761)	(3,846)	(4,122)	(4,281)	(4,388)	(4,745)	2.06
Other operating costs	(126,692)	(131,643)	(123,703)	(117,063)	(120,149)	(121,682)	(134,402)	(142,814)	(150,009)	2.13
Income from operations	9,282	9,431	8,561	6,398	7,648	7,991	11,067	11,497	13,431	4.73
Nonoperating income (expenditures)	(1,385)	(1,597)	(1,899)	(1,433)	(2,079)	(3,871)	(2,928)	(3,574)	(1,285)	.....
Income before taxes	7,895	7,834	6,662	4,964	5,568	4,121	8,139	7,922	12,147	5.53
Income after taxes	5,335	5,514	4,610	3,361	4,058	2,788	5,529	5,519	9,277	7.16
Cash dividends	1,883	1,616	1,307	1,205	1,396	1,367	1,311	2,111	3,205	6.87
Income retained in business	3,452	3,897	3,301	2,156	2,662	1,421	4,218	3,406	6,072	7.31
Direct credits (charges)	(2,027)	(728)	(1,058)	(1,436)	(1,189)	(1,364)	(1,546)	(906)	874	.....
Ending retained earnings	31,483	29,685	28,380	28,635	26,749	24,275	26,512	27,738	32,563	0.42
ASSETS, END OF YEAR:										
Total	98,770	102,564	99,116	99,217	98,287	96,375	96,063	95,795	94,213	(0.59)
Accounts receivable	20,957	21,480	21,590	21,598	19,745	20,006	20,330	20,231	18,721	(1.40)
Inventories	21,159	22,573	22,847	22,487	21,835	21,159	20,769	20,197	19,806	(0.82)
Net property, plant and equipment	26,802	27,279	26,747	26,827	26,738	26,461	26,353	26,552	27,201	0.18
RATIOS, PERCENT:										
INCOME TO SALES:										
Before tax	5.64	5.40	4.90	3.90	4.23	3.08	5.44	4.99	7.22	4.98
After tax	3.81	3.80	3.39	2.64	3.08	2.08	3.69	3.48	5.52	3.50
INCOME TO STOCKHOLDERS' EQUITY:										
Before tax	19.23	19.63	17.28	12.32	14.45	10.67	18.99	18.87	24.22	17.30
After tax	13.00	13.82	11.96	8.34	10.53	7.22	12.90	13.15	18.50	12.16
INCOME TO TOTAL ASSETS:										
Before tax	7.99	7.64	6.72	5.00	5.67	4.28	8.47	8.27	12.89	7.44
After tax	5.40	5.38	4.65	3.39	4.13	2.89	5.76	5.76	9.85	5.24
AS A PERCENT OF TOTAL ASSETS:										
Property, plant and equipment	27.14	26.60	26.99	27.04	27.20	27.46	27.43	27.72	28.87	27.38
Short-term debt	4.40	4.16	4.28	3.64	4.54	5.19	6.32	7.09	7.10	5.19
Long-term debt	24.81	23.25	24.20	23.52	23.99	24.68	26.44	25.84	30.20	25.22
Stockholders' equity	41.56	38.91	38.90	40.62	39.19	40.06	44.61	43.83	53.23	42.32

1. For income and asset amounts, compound annual growth rate; for ratios, average of ratios for the years shown.

Source: U.S. Bureau of the Census, Quarterly Financial Report.

Notes: Parentheses ( ) indicate negative items, e.g., net expenses, charges, or losses. Net property, plant, and equipment is net of accumulated depreciation. Because the samples used to collect the data change, retained earnings at the end of a given year will not exactly equal the previous year's retained earnings plus the current year's retained income and credits.

CANADA

Canada's fabricated metal products industry in 1993 consisted of 5,117 establishments and 132,606 employees (Table 7). The largest subindustry in 1993 was stamped, pressed, and coated metals, with 26.9 percent of total shipments. Other large components are hardware, tools and cutlery industries (12 percent), wire and wire products (10.7 percent), fabricated structural metal products (10.7 percent) and ornamental and architect metal products (10.2 percent). Hourly earnings averaged Can$14.41, with the highest being Can$17.48 for wire and wire rope production.

TABLE 7

CANADA: COMPONENT INDUSTRIES OF FABRICATED METAL PRODUCTS (CSIC 30), 1993

(Monetary values in Canadian dollars)

INDUSTRY NAME	CSIC	ESTABLISH-MENTS (NUMBER)	EMPLOYMENT		VALUE OF SHIPMENTS (MILLIONS)	AVERAGE HOURLY EARNINGS[1]
			NUMBER	PERCENT OF INDUSTRY TOTAL		
FABRICATED METAL PRODUCTS	30	5,117	132,606	100.0	CAN$15,404.1	CAN$14.41
Power boilers and heat exchangers	301	45	5,277	4.0	786.4	16.42
Fabricated structural metal products	302	429	14,769	11.1	1,640.7	15.37
Metal tanks (heavy gauge)	3021	87	3,549	2.7	347.8	14.80
Plate work	3022	48	1,599	1.2	171.0	15.81
Pre-engineered metal buildings (except portables)	3023	48	1,545	1.2	178.6	14.23
Other fabricated structural metal	3029	246	8,076	6.1	943.4	15.74
Ornamental and architect metal products	303	711	14,554	11.0	1,576.9	12.81
Metal doors and windows	3031	303	8,549	6.4	921.6	12.27
Prefabricated portable metal products	3032	26	583	0.4	73.6	11.83
Other architectural metal products	3039	382	5,422	4.1	581.7	13.80
Stamped, pressed and coated metals	304	879	28,396	21.4	4,140.2	14.17
Custom coating of metal products	3041	265	8,868	6.7	922.9	13.26
Metal closures and containers	3042	75	5,791	4.4	1,278.0	16.21
Other stamped and pressed metal products	3049	539	13,737	10.4	1,939.3	13.88
Wire and wire products	305	257	11,814	8.9	1,652.3	14.92
Upholstery and coil springs	3051	15	369	0.3	34.1	13.04
Wire and wire rope	3052	34	3,159	2.4	613.4	17.48
Industrial fasteners	3053	80	4,021	3.0	521.7	14.77
Other wire products	3059	128	4,265	3.2	483.1	13.35
Hardware, tools and cutlery	306	744	20,051	15.1	1,855.6	15.26
Basic hardware	3061	64	3,833	2.9	408.3	13.88
Metal dies, moulds and patterns	3062	472	11,571	8.7	1,031.7	16.35
Hand tools and implements	3063	61	1,228	0.9	108.2	12.71
Other hardware and cutlery	3069	147	3,419	2.6	307.4	13.54
Heating equipment	3071	116	4,463	3.4	502.1	11.88
Machine shops	3081	1418	18,840	14.2	1,490.2	14.23
Other metal fabricating	309	518	14,442	10.9	1,759.6	14.07
Metal plumbing fixtures and fittings	3091	30	1,867	1.4	215.4	12.71
Metal valves	3092	49	2,484	1.9	337.6	13.45
Other metal fabricating, n.e.c.	3099	439	10,091	7.6	1,206.6	14.45

1. Including overtime.

Source: Adapted from Statistics Canada, *Manufacturing Industries of Canada* (Cat. No. 31-203).

Canadian shipments of fabricated metal products totaled Can$17.8 billion in 1994, up considerably from Can$15.4 billion the previous year but below the eight-year high of Can$19.2 billion in 1989 (Table 8). Industry employment rose to 140,452 in 1994 after declining for four successive years from the 1989 high of 180,228. Production workers' share of the workforce stabilized at about 80 percent of the workforce in 1994. Production workers, on average, worked just over 40 hours each week and earned Can$14.76 per hour in 1994, compared with Can$11.82 in 1988, an annual growth rate of 3.77 percent. However, when adjusted for inflation, that rate is only 0.62 percent.

TABLE 8

CANADIAN EMPLOYMENT AND SHIPMENTS: FABRICATED METALS, 1987-1994

(Monetary values in Canadian dollars)

	1987	1988	1989	1990	1991	1992	1993	1994	CHANGE[1]
All employees	157,478	168,796	180,228	166,822	153,370	134,285	132,606	140,452	-1.62
Establishments	5,498	6,004	5,926	6,030	5,649	5,359	5,117	5,003	-1.34
Employees per establishment	29	28	30	28	27	25	26	28	-0.29
Production workers per establishment	.....	24	26	23	22	20	21	22	-0.79
PRODUCTION WORKERS:									
Total	.....	141,228	153,392	137,418	126,869	106,465	106,043	112,233	-3.76
Percent of all employees	.....	83.7	85.1	82.4	82.7	79.3	80.0	79.9	.....
Male	.....	125,080	136,421	122,710	114,718	.....	.....	.....	.....
Female	.....	16,148	16,971	14,708	12,151	.....	.....	.....	.....
Percent of all production workers	.....	11.4	11.1	10.7	9.6	.....	.....	.....	.....
Average hourly earnings	.....	11.82	12.53	13.34	13.90	14.36	14.41	14.76	3.77
Average weekly earnings	.....	473.89	501.10	532.77	556.32	572.95	577.08	591.65	3.77
Average weekly hours	.....	40.1	40.0	40.0	40.0	39.9	40.1	40.1	.....
Shipments (millions)	16,750	17,946	19,154	17,877	15,924	14,961	15,404	17,815	0.88

1. Compound annual growth rate.

Source: Adapted from Statistics Canada, *Manufacturing Industries of Canada* (Cat. No. 31-203).

MEXICO

Fabricated metal products are classified under Mexico's huge metal products and machinery industry (Table 9), in which fabricated metal components are difficult to compare directly with the U.S. industry. The largest component of the Mexican industry that would be comparable in part is "other metal products," with 117,331 employees and incomes (earnings plus benefits) averaging 24,866 new pesos ($7,960) in 1993. Other categories are metal structures, industrial boilers, and tanks, with 100,922 employees and incomes averaging 17,517 new pesos ($5,608) in 1993, and smelting and molding of casting, with 16,577 employees and incomes averaging 22,308 new pesos ($7,142).

Employment in the other metal products industry (Table 10) increased at an annual rate of only 0.16 between 1988 and 1995, to 168,520 workers. This growth rate masks the fact that employment actually has declined significantly since reaching its 1993 high of 201,528.

TABLE 9

MEXICO: COMPONENT INDUSTRIES OF FABRICATED METAL PRODUCTS (CMAP 38), 1993

(Monetary values in 1993 Mexican New Pesos)

INDUSTRY	CMAP	NUMBER OF UNITS	ALL WORKERS									
							PAID WORKERS					
							PRODUCTION WORKERS		NONPRODUCTION EMPLOYEES		BENEFITS PER PAID EMPLOYEE	UNPAID WORKERS, NUMBER
			NUMBER	PERCENT OF INDUSTRY TOTAL	AVERAGE DAYS WORKED	REMUN- ERATION[1]	NUMBER	WAGES AND SALARIES	NUMBER	WAGES AND SALARIES		
Metal products	38	46,246	962,060	100	266	25,236	708,788	12,083	199,409	36,638	7,761	53,863
Smelting and molding of castings	3811	1,049	16,577	2	267	22,308	11,985	11,839	3,460	30,638	6,258	1,132
Metal structure, industrial boilers, and tanks	3812	29,347	100,922	10	261	17,517	51,337	10,696	11,598	25,873	4,023	37,987
Metal furniture	3813	1,031	25,052	3	273	17,470	19,525	10,555	4,630	25,239	4,100	897
Other metal products	3814	4,225	117,331	12	274	24,866	86,882	12,018	25,951	37,383	7,014	4,498
Machinery and equipment, special	3821	823	30,058	3	276	32,299	20,205	15,310	9,511	39,258	9,324	579
Machinery and equipment, general (incl. weaponry)	3822	5,145	67,338	7	279	24,661	45,675	12,398	16,497	32,717	6,872	5,166
Office calculator, and data processing machines	3823	87	16,718	2	263	28,072	11,564	11,319	5,034	41,676	7,546	120
Machinery, equipment, and electrical accessories	3831	1,409	211,559	22	273	21,044	171,486	9,957	38,679	35,183	6,445	1,157
Electronic communications and medical equipment	3832	535	130,054	14	272	22,062	102,852	10,188	26,961	33,326	7,068	241
Home appliances excluding electronics	3833	247	34,906	4	271	24,461	27,908	11,468	6,799	39,970	7,997	199
Automobile industry	3841	1,401	167,221	17	281	37,377	125,301	17,478	40,880	45,561	12,991	1,040
Aircraft and other	3842	171	14,151	1	277	22,322	11,023	11,482	3,030	36,520	5,442	98
Instruments	3850	776	30,173	3	276	21,242	23,045	9,756	6,379	32,304	6,598	749

1. Average annual remuneration including benefits.

Source: INEGI, Censos Economicos 1994.

TABLE 10

MEXICAN GROSS DOMESTIC PRODUCT AND EMPLOYMENT: FABRICATED METAL PRODUCTS, MACHINERY AND EQUIPMENT, 1988-1995

	1988	1989	1990	1991	1992	1993	1994	1995	CHANGE[1]
GROSS DOMESTIC PRODUCT:									
Millions of constant 1993 new pesos	39,732.7	44,107.4	49,037.5	53,022.1	56,333.0	54,000.8	57,610.8	51,940.8	3.90
Millions of constant 1993 U.S. dollars[2]	12,719.7	14,120.2	15,698.5	16,974.1	18,034.1	17,287.4	18,443.1	16,628.0	3.90
TOTAL EMPLOYMENT:									
Metal products	864,602	932,137	988,820	998,935	1,062,024	1,025,021	1,018,573	975,775	1.74
Transportation equipment	267,742	313,448	342,837	335,396	386,370	348,058	338,755	331,338	3.09
Machinery	176,670	180,461	187,243	189,374	195,947	183,056	177,822	165,813	-0.90
Electrical and electronic equipment	253,543	260,756	269,938	277,555	282,289	292,379	304,284	310,104	2.92
Other metal products	166,647	177,472	188,802	196,610	197,418	201,528	197,712	168,520	0.16

1. Compound annual growth rate.

2. Converted at 3.1237 new pesos to the U.S. dollar.

Source: Sistema de Cuentas Nacionales de Mexico, INEGI.

INTERNATIONAL TRADE

United States. Global U.S. exports of fabricated metal products picked up in 1995 and 1996, following slow growth in the previous three years. They ended up at $16.6 billion in 1996, compared with $13.5 billion in 1993 and $10.8 billion in 1990. Imports also have accelerated in recent years, reaching $17.5 billion in 1996, versus $12.9 billion in 1993 and $11.0 billion in 1990. The U.S. trade balance has fluctuated between deficits and surpluses during the past seven years, ending up at a negative $880 million in 1996. In 1996, Canada received 30 percent of U.S. exports and supplied 19 percent of U.S. imports. Mexico took about 17 percent of U.S. exports that year and accounted for more than 10 percent of the imports (compared with only 7 percent in 1993).

Canada. U.S. exports to Canada rose from $4.3 billion in 1990 to $5.0 billion in 1996 (Table 11). Canadian exports to the United States during 1990-1996 rose 82 percent, to $3.4 billion, with all of that growth taking place after 1993. Canada's small export trade with Mexico declined from $25 million in 1990 to $11 million in 1996, while Mexican shipments to Canada rose almost fivefold, to $52 million.

Mexico. U.S. exports to Mexico climbed more than 139 percent between 1990 and 1996, to $2.9 billion, while Mexican exports to the United States soared 152 percent, to $1.7 billion (Table 11). This resulted in a 1996 U.S. trade surplus with Mexico of $1.2 billion, compared with a $536 million surplus in 1990.

NAFTA. Trade balances for fabricated metal products were in the United States favor throughout the 1990-1996 period, although the U.S. surplus declined from a high of $3.9 billion in 1993 to $2.8 billion in 1996 (Table 11). Canada's trade deficit widened between 1990 and 1993 and then decreased to $1.6 billion in 1996. Mexico's deficit rose to a high of $1.4 billion in 1994 before settling back to $1.2 billion in 1996.

TABLE 11

INTERNATIONAL TRADE, FABRICATED METALS

(Millions of U.S. dollars)

	1989[1]	1990	1991	1992	1993	1994	1995	1996
GLOBAL TRADE, U.S.								
IMPORTS								
Value	11,057.4	11,023.6	10,864.9	11,878.5	12,941.2	14,664.2	16,213.0	17,491.5
Ratio to new supply[2]	6.9	6.8	6.9	7.3	7.5	7.8	.....	.....
Ratio to apparent consumption[3]	7.3	7.3	7.4	7.9	8.1	8.4	.....	.....
EXPORTS								
Value	8,757.4	10,811.8	11,563.7	12,794.8	13,496.4	13,395.2	15,161.0	16,612.0
Ratio to comparable domestic shipments	5.8	7.1	7.9	8.4	8.4	7.8	.....	.....
TRADE BALANCE	(2,300.0)	(211.8)	698.8	916.3	555.2	(1,269.0)	(1,052.0)	(879.5)
BILATERAL TRADE: NAFTA[4]								
U.S. exports to Canada	3,044.1	4,261.5	4,430.5	4,643.7	4,910.6	4,236.8	4,569.1	4,964.8
Canadian exports to U.S.	1,949.7	1,854.4	1,802.0	1,867.7	2,005.2	2,440.6	2,884.6	3,382.9
U.S. exports to Mexico	1,021.0	1,201.9	1,431.1	1,871.2	1,976.7	2,522.2	2,245.4	2,874.0
Mexican exports to U.S.	619.6	666.0	714.3	830.9	941.6	1,127.0	1,277.2	1,679.2
Canadian exports to Mexico	14.1	25.2	3.2	3.9	11.3	16.0	27.8	11.2
Mexican exports to Canada	9.8	11.4	12.1	15.2	15.5	30.9	32.0	52.4
TRADE BALANCES WITHIN NAFTA[5]								
Canada	(1,090.1)	(2,393.3)	(2,637.4)	(2,787.3)	(2,909.6)	(1,811.1)	(1,688.7)	(1,623.1)
Mexico	(405.7)	(549.7)	(707.9)	(1,029.0)	(1,030.9)	(1,380.3)	(964.0)	(1,153.6)
United States	1,495.9	2,942.9	3,345.4	3,816.3	3,940.5	3,191.4	2,652.7	2,776.7

1. 1989 and earlier data on U.S. exports to Canada for manufacturing total and manufacturing industries are not comparable with data for 1990 and later years because of a change in the reporting system. The NAFTA trade balances for the U.S. and Canada also are affected.

2. New supply equals comparable domestic shipments plus imports for consumption.

3. Apparent consumption equals comparable domestic shipments plus imports for consumption less exports.

4. Amounts less than U.S. $100,000 shown as zero.

5. Parentheses indicate an excess of imports over exports. Because of commodity coding and other data differences among the three countries, these trade balances are only rough estimates and should be used with caution.

Source for U.S. Global Trade: U.S. Department of Commerce, International Trade Administration.

Source for U.S. -Canada and U.S.-Mexico Bilateral Trade: U.S. Bureau of the Census.

Source for Canada-Mexico and Mexico-Canada Bilateral Trade: Statistics Canada, Foreign Trade Division, Special tabulation, March 1997, converted to U.S. dollars by the editors.

FOOD AND BEVERAGES

THE UNITED STATES

Products and Processes. Virtually everything that humans (and domestic animals) put in their mouths comes from the food and beverage industry. The exceptions are drugs, artificial sweeteners, and unprocessed food and animal feed direct from the field, garden, sea, or forest. Processes and technologies employed cover the spectrum from the ancient processes of brewing and bread making to genetically altered fruits and vegetables and irradiation for preservation. Domestic animals get meat- and grain-based rations from the industry, as well. (Unprocessed livestock feed is included with agricultural production data; see the Agriculture chapter).

Not surprisingly, the food and beverage industry is a leader in the manufacturing sector. In 1996, the value of its manufacturers' shipments was exceeded only by that for transportation equipment. The industry also was the manufacturing sector's third largest employer next to the commercial and industrial machinery and transportation-equipment industries.

Table 1 lists the many food and beverage subindustries. The largest subindustry in 1992 was meat products, with 23.1 percent ($94 billion) of the $406.9 billion worth of industry shipments that year. Next in line were beverages (14.2 percent of the total), dairy products (13.0 percent), grain mill products (12.3 percent), and preserved fruits and vegetables (11.7 percent). Establishments tend to be small; there were 20,798 of them in 1992, and 55 percent had less than 20 employees.

Employment in the industry has changed little over the past decade and is projected to increase only slightly through the year 2005 to 1,696,200 employees, compared with 1,679,600 in 1993 (moderate projections—see Table 2). Most of the employment growth will be in production of meat products and preserved fruits and vegetables, while declines are seen for beverages, bakery products, dairy products, and sugar and confectionery products. Earnings of the industry's production workers averaged $10.45 an hour in 1993 and ranged from $7.47 an hour for workers involved in poultry processing to $20 an hour for those employed by breweries.

TABLE 1

UNITED STATES: COMPONENT INDUSTRIES OF FOOD AND BEVERAGES (SIC 20), 1992

(Monetary values in millions of U.S. dollars)

| INDUSTRY | SIC | ESTABLISH-MENTS | SHIPMENTS | | VALUE ADDED BY MANUFACTURE | NEW CAPITAL EXPENDI-TURES | EMPLOY-MENT[1] | PAYROLL |
			VALUE	PERCENT BY 4 LARGEST COMPANIES				
FOOD AND BEVERAGES	20	20,798	$406,962.8	.....	$159,259.9	$9,898.7	1,502,700	$36,771.8
Meat products	201	3,240	94,072.1	.....	19,140.6	1,188.2	400,400	7,564.2
Meat packing plants	2011	1,383	50,167.2	50	6,958.2	341.4	121,200	2,440.9
Sausages and other prepared meats	2013	1,264	19,940.2	25	5,479.6	377.5	85,400	2,023.0
Poultry slaughtering and processing	2015	593	23,964.8	34	6,702.8	469.3	193,800	3,100.2
Dairy products	202	2,020	52,719.6	.....	15,257.7	990.0	135,400	3,720.0
Creamery butter	2021	31	1,029.4	49	147.5	9.1	1,500	42.3
Cheese, natural and processed	2022	573	16,932.9	42	33,668.4	241.9	34,500	827.5
Condensed and evaporated milk	2023	214	7,541.0	43	3,380.5	188.5	15,200	451.6
Ice cream and frozen desserts	2024	456	5,290.6	24	2,096.5	188.1	20,900	558.2
Fluid milk	2026	746	21,925.7	22	5,964.8	362.5	63,400	1,840.4
Preserved fruits and vegetables	203	2,052	47,805.5	.....	23,643.6	1,494.5	215,800	4,825.1
Canned specialties	2032	219	6,660.9	69	3,616.6	274.6	21,000	564.9
Canned fruits and vegetables	2033	683	15,071.3	27	6,975.6	445.1	63,600	1,465.3
Dehydrated fruits, vegetables, and soups	2034	155	2,853.1	39	1,515.0	91.7	13,500	321.2
Pickles, sauces, and salad dressings	2035	377	7,807.0	41	4,549.2	178.6	23,200	586.3
Frozen fruits and vegetables	2037	255	7,527.5	28	2,911.5	254.8	47,800	916.0
Frozen specialties, n.e.c.	2038	363	7,885.7	40	4,075.8	249.7	46,700	971.5
Grain mill products	204	2,616	49,957.1	.....	21,000.0	1,606.6	107,200	3,374.8
Flour and other grain mill products	2041	365	6,294.4	56	1,624.5	253.5	13,100	408.9
Cereal breakfast foods	2043	65	9,736.8	85	7,258.6	396.6	16,100	745.3
Rice milling	2044	53	1,650.7	50	437.0	23.5	3,900	94.4
Blended and prepared flour	2045	209	3,865.7	39	1,821.7	160.6	15,800	429.2
Wet corn milling	2046	51	7,045.2	73	3,257.5	409.2	9,300	371.3
Dog and cat food	2047	161	7,023.9	58	3,729.9	179.8	13,700	452.7
Prepared feeds, n.e.c.	2048	1,712	14,340.4	23	2,870.7	183.4	35,400	873.0
Bakery products	205	3,150	28,494.2	.....	17,904.8	861.4	215,000	5,599.1
Bread, cake, and related products	2051	2,535	18,129.8	34	11,453.1	513.8	154,900	4,058.8
Cookies and crackers	2052	440	8,668.4	56	5,512.8	309.7	47,000	1,246.5
Frozen bakery products, except bread	2053	175	1,696.0	45	938.9	37.8	13,100	293.9
Sugar and confectionery products	206	1,129	22,709.7	.....	10,949.8	897.3	91,300	2,401.9
Raw cane sugar	2061	45	1,459.8	52	561.9	59.3	7,000	175.8
Cane sugar refining	2062	17	2,822.9	85	737.2	56.3	4,800	187.5
Beet sugar	2063	40	2,282.0	71	799.7	96.5	7,600	220.2
Candy and other confectionery products	2064	758	10,201.7	45	6,346.5	378.4	51,500	1,261.4
Chocolate and cocoa products	2066	156	3,106.4	75	1,475.3	261.9	9,900	323.3
Salted and roasted nuts and seeds	2068	113	2,836.8	42	1,029.2	44.9	10,500	233.8
Fats and oils	207	541	18,724.4	.....	3,770.0	323.2	27,800	778.2
Cottonseed oil mills	2074	44	730.1	62	210.6	12.0	2,300	48.8
Soybean oil mills	2075	99	10,650.6	71	1,273.8	123.2	7,400	225.3
Vegetable oil mills, n.e.c.	2076	26	666.2	89	133.8	10.4	900	26.2
Animal and marine fats and oil	2077	270	1,865.2	37	760.5	70.5	8,500	220.8
Shortening and cooking oils	2079	102	4,812.4	35	1,391.2	107.0	8,700	257.1
Beverages	208	2,065	57,957.0	.....	29,260.0	1,538.2	144,300	4,785.6
Malt beverages	2082	194	17,340.2	90	10,189.3	565.0	34,500	1,566.7
Malt	2083	26	575.8	65	175.9	27.1	1,300	44.4
Wines, brandy, and brandy spirits	2084	553	4,301.0	54	2,082.2	114.7	14,000	425.9
Distilled liquor, except brandy	2085	65	3,394.1	62	1,945.6	56.3	7,100	243.9
Bottled and canned soft drinks	2086	926	25,422.5	37	9,591.9	6,985.0	77,100	2,162.8
Flavoring extracts and syrups, n.e.c.	2087	301	6,923.4	69	5,275.1	76.5	10,300	341.8
Miscellaneous food and kindred products	209	3,985	34,523.1	.....	16,333.5	999.3	165,600	3,722.9
Canned and cured seafood	2091	159	969.2	29	362.0	20.2	7,000	133.0
Fresh or frozen packaged fish	2092	685	7,039.2	19	2,351.2	150.4	41,400	771.2
Roasted coffee	2095	172	5,294.6	66	2,754.3	149.1	10,500	340.0
Potato chips and similar snacks	2096	408	7,309.1	70	3,901.2	258.8	34,800	826.4
Manufactured ice	2097	560	356.4	24	253.4	13.2	4,600	92.5
Macaroni and spaghetti	2098	199	1,389.6	78	830.9	74.7	5,900	146.8
Food preparations, n.e.c.	2099	1,802	12,165.1	22	5,880.5	332.8	61,400	1,412.9

1. Employment numbers from the economic censuses differ in definition and classification from the Bureau of Labor Statistics estimates in Table 2. Year-to-year comparisons between Table 1 and Table 2 are not appropriate.

Source: U.S. Bureau of the Census, 1992 Census of Manufactures.

TABLE 2

U.S. EMPLOYMENT AND EARNINGS: FOOD AND BEVERAGES

INDUSTRY	SIC	1993			2005
		EMPLOYMENT[1]		AVERAGE HOURLY EARNINGS (U.S. DOLLARS)[2]	PROJECTED EMPLOYMENT[3]
		NUMBER OF PERSONS	PERCENT OF INDUSTRY TOTAL		
FOOD AND BEVERAGES	20	1,679,600	100.0	$10.45	1,696,200
Meat products	201	443,500	26.4	8.49	515,000
Meat packing plants	2011	138,100	8.2	9.26	.....
Sausages and other prepared meats	2013	88,800	5.3	9.89	.....
Poultry slaughtering and processing	2015	216,700	12.9	7.47	.....
Dairy products	202	152,800	9.1	11.66	132,500
Cheese, natural and processed	2022	40,500	2.4	10.44	.....
Fluid milk	2026	68,800	4.1	12.37	.....
Preserved fruits and vegetables	203	245,700	14.6	10.05	260,000
Canned specialties	2032	22,600	1.3	13.12	.....
Canned fruits and vegetables	2033	82,200	4.9	10.37	.....
Frozen fruits and vegetables	2037	50,000	3.0	9.00	.....
Grain mill products	204	128,500	7.7	12.66	.....
Flour and other grain mill products	2041	20,100	1.2	10.66	.....
Prepared feeds, n.e.c.	2048	42,200	2.5	10.17	.....
Bakery products	205	210,600	12.5	11.71	195,000
Bread, cake, and related products	2051	151,100	9.0	11.63	.....
Cookies, crackers, and frozen bakery products	2052,3	59,500	3.5	11.87	.....
Sugar and confectionery products	206	102,600	6.1	11.24	90,000
Raw cane sugar	2061	6,300	0.4	10.67	.....
Cane sugar refining	2062	4,900	0.3	15.82	.....
Beet sugar	2063	9,900	0.6	11.81	.....
Candy and other confectionery products	2064	52,400	3.1	10.27	.....
Fats and oils	207	32,000	1.9	10.96	.....
Beverages	208	178,400	10.6	14.63	132,200
Malt beverages	2082	39,500	2.4	20.00	.....
Bottled and canned soft drinks	2086	94,200	5.6	11.97	.....
Miscellaneous food and kindred products	209	185,500	11.0	9.51	211,000
Grain mill products and fats and oils	204,7	160,500	9.6	.....	160,500

1. Total payroll employment. Employment data from the economic censuses, shown in Table 1, differ in definition and classification from the Bureau of Labor Statistics estimates in this table. Year-to-year comparisons between Table 1 and Table 2 are not appropriate.

2. Earnings of production workers, including overtime.

3. Number of persons, moderate projection by the U.S. Bureau of Labor Statistics.

Source: Bureau of Labor Statistics.

FIGURE 1

U.S. EMPLOYMENT IN FOOD AND BEVERAGES
Percent distribution by region, 1995

The food industry is distributed widely throughout the United States. The largest concentration is in the Southeast (26 percent in 1995). The 14 percent located in the Plains states substantially exceeds that region's 8 percent share of total U.S. employment.

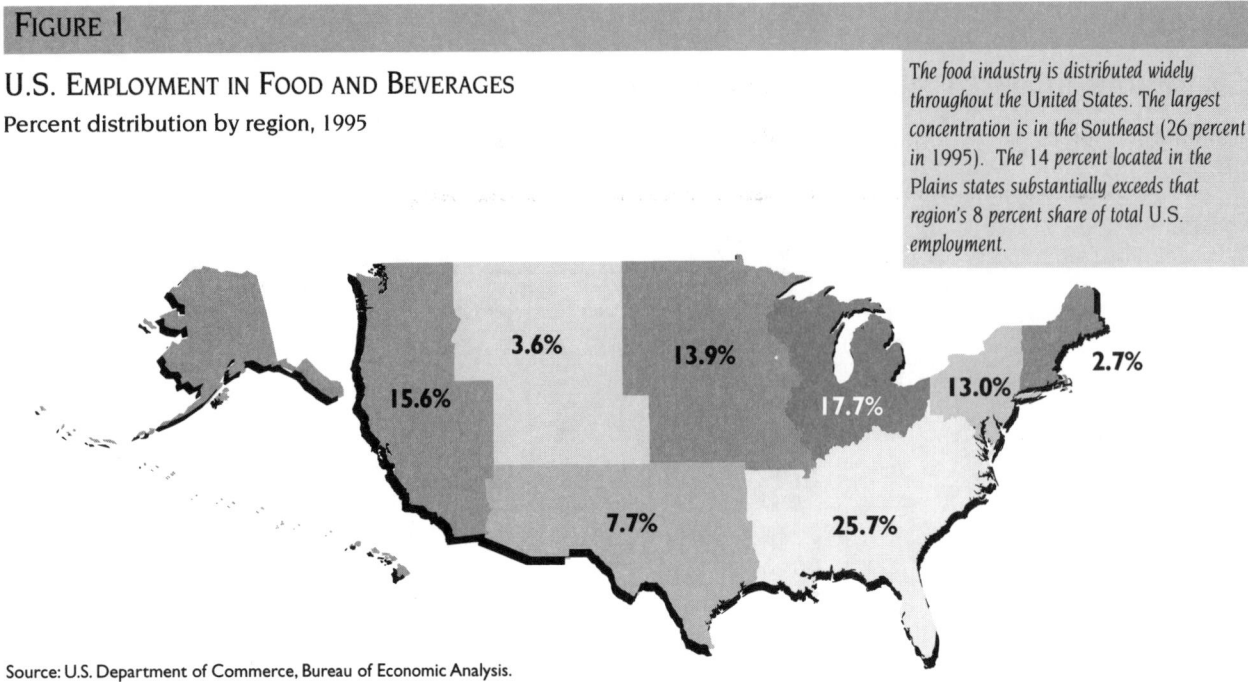

Source: U.S. Department of Commerce, Bureau of Economic Analysis.

What's New. Several changes in U.S. food safety regulations took place in 1996, and more may lie ahead if Congress approves proposals in the Administration's budget for Fiscal Year 1998.

In July 1996, new regulations to modernize the U.S. meat and poultry inspection system were announced. The new regulations require the following: written sanitation procedures in each processing establishment, regular microbial testing by slaughter establishments, pathogen reduction standards for salmonella, and development by all meat and poultry establishments of a risk-based system of preventive controls known as Hazard Analysis and Critical Control Point (HACCP). The meat and poultry industry already had been converting its operations to HACCP for several years, and, according to industry sources, the system is already in use by substantially more than half of all meat and poultry packers and processors.

In August 1996, the Food Quality Protection Act—a comprehensive overhaul of U.S. laws that regulate pesticides in food—and a new safe drinking water act were signed into law.

Actions planned by the Administration in its latest food safety initiative include hiring additional inspectors for seafood plants, increasing research on detecting food-borne pathogens (such as Hepatitis A), and expanding the use of the HACCP approach to fruit and vegetable juices and eggs as well as meats. The Administration also has proposed imposing fees on meat and poultry processors to help cover inspection costs, a proposal that has met with industry opposition.

FIGURE 2

U.S. EMPLOYMENT AND SHIPMENTS IN FOOD AND BEVERAGES

Total payroll employment and manufacturers' inflation-adjusted shipments

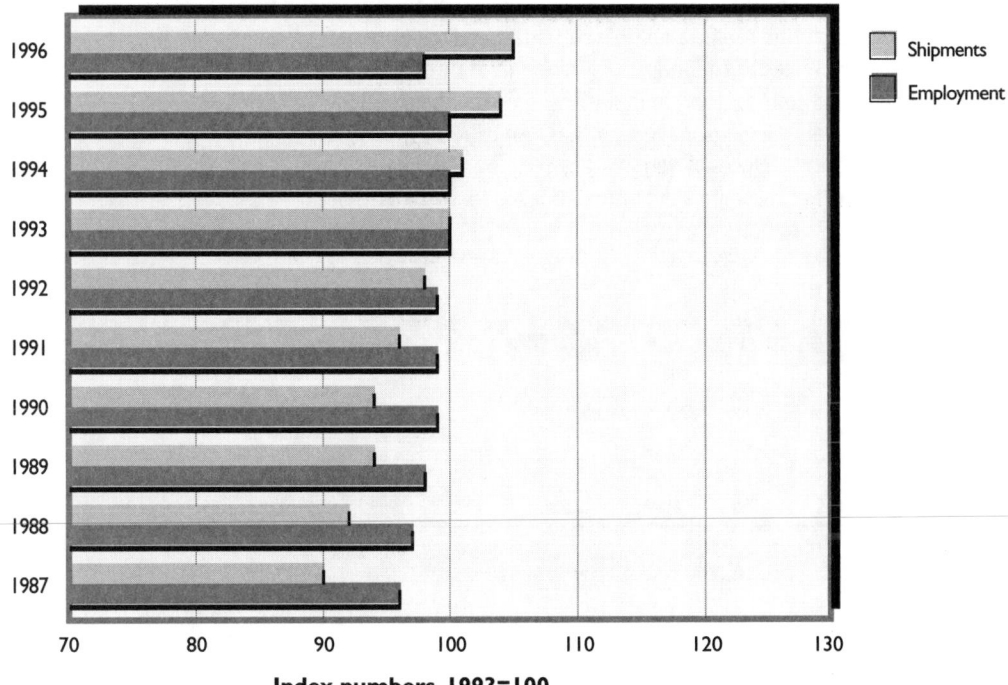

Source: U.S. Bureau of Labor Statistics, U.S. Department of Commerce, and estimates by the editors.

Output. The value of industry shipments (adjusted for inflation) rose in most years of the past decade, while employment has grown by less than one percent annually (Figure 2). Industry shipments in current-dollar terms rose at an annual rate of 4.06 percent during the past 10 years, reaching $471.7 billion in 1996. The inflation-adjusted rate of growth was just under 2 percent per year (Table 3). The most rapid growth appears to have been in the "higher valued" food items, as consumers turned to more highly processed foods, moved up the "quality" scale, or attempted to improve their health through special diets.

Investment. New capital expenditures, after rising from 1987 through 1991, were virtually level (after adjustment for inflation) in the early 1990s, but turned up noticeably in 1995. Capacity utilization—one gauge of the need for net new investment—was above 84 percent in the late 1980s, but had fallen to just over 81 percent by 1996 (Table 3).

Prices. Consumer prices, as measured by the consumer price index for food at home, rose at a compound annual rate of 3.7 percent from 1986 to 1996. This average consists of a more rapid rate of increase (4.8 percent) during the first half of the period and a slowing to only a 2.6 percent rate during 1991-1996. Prices to the industry, as measured by either the producer price index for intermediate materials for food manufacturing or the index for crude foodstuffs and feedstuffs, tend to vary widely from year to year. An especially sharp increase in 1996 reflected in part perceptions (since proved mistaken) of looming grain shortages. On the average, however, each of these producer price indexes rose at a rate of about 2.5 percent per year over the 10-year period.

TABLE 3

U.S. OUTPUT, INVESTMENT, AND PRICES: FOOD AND BEVERAGES

(Millions of U.S. dollars, except as noted)

	1987	1988	1989	1990	1991	1992	1993	1994	1995	1996	GROWTH RATE 1987-1996[1]
VALUE OF SHIPMENTS:											
BY INDUSTRY:											
Current dollars	329,725	354,085	380,161	391,728	397,892	406,963	422,220	430,963	448406	471,741	4.06
Constant 1992 dollars	371,982	382,877	392,233	390,859	398,551	406,963	415,104	419,167	433666	437,065	1.81
BY PRODUCT:											
Current dollars	305,761	326,728	340,733	359,713	363,943	382,889	397,633	405,490	421329	443,255	4.21
Constant 1992 dollars	344,636	352,990	351,223	358,812	364,419	382,889	391,063	394,415	407159	410,351	1.96
OTHER OUTPUT MEASURES:											
Industrial production, 1993=100	91.6	92.9	93.9	95.0	96.4	97.9	100.0	101.6	103.5	104.1	1.43
Gross domestic product:											
Current dollars	78,020	81,726	87,662	94,160	99,148	102,094	103,673	108,076	.....	.....	.....
Percent of total GDP	1.7	1.6	1.6	1.6	1.7	1.6	1.6	1.6	.....	.....	.....
Rank in manufacturing	5	5	5	5	4	4	5	5	.....	.....	.....
Chained (1992) dollars	95,884	104,566	102,534	103,082	102,264	102,094	102,204	104,849	.....	.....	.....
INVESTMENT-RELATED MEASURES:											
Capacity utilization, percent	84.1	84.4	84.3	83.9	83.4	82.8	82.7	82.4	82.4	81.2	.....
New capital expenditures	7,198	7651	8,710	9,332	9,994	9,898	9,389	10,093	11,929	.....	.....
Research & development spending[2]	1,204	1,173	1,244	1,248	1,277	1,386	1,345	1,476	.....	.....	.....
Producer prices, 1993=100[3]	86.5	90.2	94.6	97.9	98.2	98.5	100.0	101.2	102.6	107.1	2.40

1. Compound annual growth rate.

2. Also includes tobacco.

3. Prices received by domestic producers.

Sources: Shipments and new capital expenditures: U.S. Department of Commerce for 1987-1995, editor's estimates for constant dollar data for 1987-88 and all shipments data for 1996; Industrial production and capacity utilization: Federal Reserve Board of Governors; GDP: Bureau of Economic Analysis; Research and development spending: National Science Foundation; Producer prices: Bureau of Labor Statistics.

Workforce and Employment. Total industry employment rose in most years shown in Table 4, but there were exceptions; in 1992 and again in 1994 employment fell, and it was virtually unchanged from 1995 to 1996. This resulted in a slow annual rate of growth (only 0.51 percent) for the decade. The number of production workers increased in every year. As a percent of total workers, their numbers grew from 71 percent in 1987 to 74 percent in 1996—a significant change suggesting a reduction in middle management and technical jobs.

Within these total employment numbers are markedly different patterns for food and for beverages from 1987 to 1992, a period during which employment in the beverage industries fell 14 percent, while employment in food industries grew 5 percent. From 1992 to 1996, employment in beverages was little changed; employment in food grew slowly through 1995 and then fell slightly in 1996.

Productivity apparently increased over the 1987-1996 period. The number of production workers increased at only a 1 percent compound annual average rate, while real shipments rose at almost a 2 percent rate. (See Figure 2 and Table 3.)

TABLE 4

U.S. EMPLOYMENT, HOURS, AND EARNINGS: FOOD AND BEVERAGES

(Monetary values in U.S. dollars)

	1987	1988	1989	1990	1991	1992	1993	1994	1995	1996	CHANGE[1]
NUMBER OF EMPLOYEES, IN THOUSANDS:											
Total	1,617	1,626	1,644	1,661	1,667	1,663	1,680	1,678	1,692	1,693	0.51
Production workers	1,145	1,155	1,176	1,194	1,205	1,212	1,228	1,231	1,248	1,254	1.02
Percent of total	70.8	71.0	71.5	71.9	72.3	72.9	73.1	73.4	73.7	74.1	.....
Women	514	524	537	540	540	540	543	547	558	556	0.87
Percent of total	31.8	32.2	32.7	32.5	32.4	32.5	32.3	32.6	33.0	32.8	.....
HOURS AND EARNINGS OF PRODUCTION WORKERS:											
AVERAGE HOURLY EARNINGS[2]											
Current dollars	8.93	9.12	9.38	9.62	9.90	10.20	10.45	10.66	10.93	11.20	2.55
1992 dollars[3]	10.97	10.77	10.57	10.31	10.19	10.20	10.17	10.11	10.08	10.04	-0.97
Average weekly hours	40.2	40.3	40.7	40.8	40.6	40.6	40.7	41.3	41.1	41.0	0.22
Average weekly earnings, current U.S. dollars	358.99	367.54	381.77	392.50	401.94	414.12	425.32	440.26	449.22	459.20	2.77

1. Compound annual growth rate, 1987-1996.

2. Including overtime.

3. Converted to 1992 dollars using Consumer Price Index for Urban Wage Earners and Clerical Workers.

Source: Bureau of Labor Statistics.

U.S. OCCUPATIONAL INJURY AND ILLNESS RATES: FOOD AND BEVERAGES, 1995

Incidence of nonfatal injuries and illnesses per 100 full-time workers

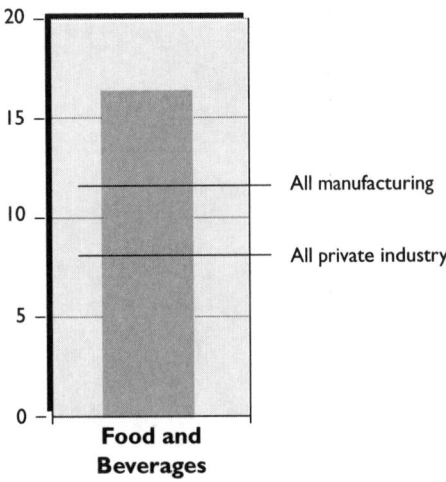

Source: U.S. Bureau of Labor Statistics.

U.S. EMPLOYMENT PROJECTIONS BY MAJOR OCCUPATIONAL GROUP: FOOD AND BEVERAGES

OCCUPATION	1994		PROJECTIONS, 2005			
	NUMBER OF EMPLOYEES	PERCENT OF INDUSTRY TOTAL	NUMBER OF EMPLOYEES			PERCENT OF INDUSTRY TOTAL, MODERATE PROJECTIONS
			LOW	MODERATE	HIGH	
Total, all occupations	1,679,600	100.0	1,692,600	1,696,200	1,695,500	100.0
Executive, administrative, and managerial	106,801	6.4	106,846	106,918	106,864	6.3
Professional specialties	19,562	1.2	22,614	22,626	22,625	1.3
Technicians and related support	19,376	1.2	18,569	18,598	18,604	1.1
Marketing and sales	64,518	3.8	61,694	61,737	61,716	3.6
Administrative support including clerical	145,080	8.6	125,887	126,035	125,993	7.4
Service	54,472	3.2	48,073	48,202	48,186	2.8
Agriculture, forestry, and fisheries occupations	21,225	1.3	21,845	22,005	22,070	1.3
Precision production, craft, and repair	346,996	20.7	354,740	355,376	355,105	21.0
Operators, fabricators, assemblers	901,571	53.7	932,331	934,703	934,337	55.1

Source: Bureau of Labor Statistics, November 1995.

Total employment in the food and beverage industry is not expected to change very much by 2005, according to projections prepared by the Bureau of Labor Statistics. The trend to increasing production workers as a percent of the total is expected to continue, although at a slower pace.

FIGURE 4

U.S. CORPORATE INCOME AND WORKER EARNINGS: FOOD AND BEVERAGES

Corporate operating income and aggregate production worker earnings

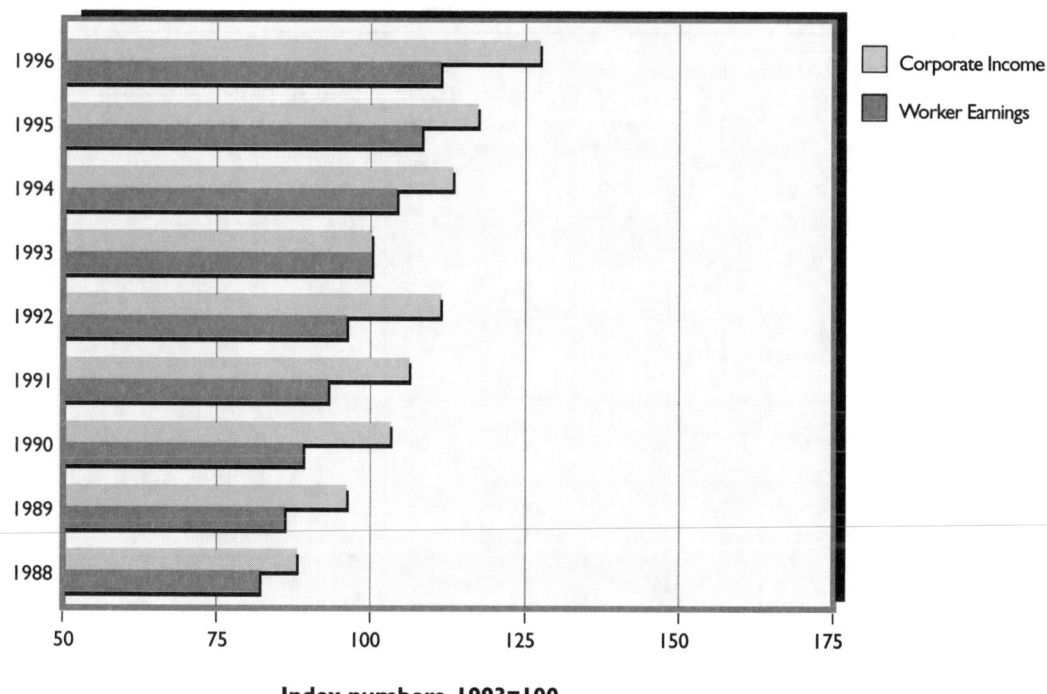

Index numbers, 1993=100

Source: U.S. Bureau of Labor Statistics, U.S. Bureau of the Census, and estimates by the editors. Corporate income includes tobacco industry.

Finance.[1] Production worker earnings in the food and beverage industry rose throughout the 1988-1996 period. Corporate income, increasing in every year but 1993, gained at an even faster rate (Figure 4).

Corporate operating income rose at an annual rate of 4.6 percent during the 1988-1996 period, to $41.1 billion by 1996 (Table 6). After-tax income varied significantly, however, falling from $20.7 billion in 1988 to a low of $15.9 billion in 1993 and then rising to $27.0 billion in 1996. The 1991-1992 recession does not seem to have been the dominant factor. Sales rose at a fairly steady pace throughout, as did income from operations, but before- and, especially, after-tax income was reduced by substantial nonoperating expenditures that reached a high of $8.9 billion in 1993. Steadily increasing output and low employment growth (implying productivity gains) clearly helped improve profits; the reduction in the proportion of managerial, administrative, and clerical (nonoperating) workers on the payrolls may have helped as well. After-tax income averaged 4.7 percent of sales and 16.9 percent of stockholders' equity over the period. Food and beverages carried a higher percentage of total assets in both long- and short-term debt and a lower percentage of stockholders' equity than manufacturing as a whole.

---

1 Financial data are based on company data, whereas most other statistics here are based on establishment data (see the section, "How To Use This Book").

TABLE 6

U.S. CORPORATE INCOME AND ASSETS: FOOD AND BEVERAGES (INCLUDING TOBACCO)

(Monetary values in millions of U.S. dollars)

INCOME AND EXPENSES	1988	1989	1990	1991	1992	1993	1994	1995	1996	CHANGE OR AVERAGE[1]
Sales and receipts	376,984	393,493	397,452	408,858	411,586	424,760	439,375	456,264	482,366	3.13
Depreciation and amortization	(9,170)	(9,681)	(9,990)	(10,565)	(10,605)	(11,429)	(11,431)	(12,167)	(12,669)	4.12
Other operating costs	(339,128)	(352,754)	(353,665)	(364,022)	(364,798)	(380,704)	(391,040)	(406,266)	(428,580)	2.97
Income from operations	28,686	31,057	33,796	34,271	36,179	32,630	36,905	37,834	41,117	4.60
Nonoperating income (expenditures)	1,566	(6,250)	(8,658)	(4,918)	(8,620)	(8,923)	(4,017)	(1,107)	(2,488)	.....
Income before taxes	30,250	24,807	25,138	29,353	27,559	23,706	32,889	36,726	38,631	3.10
Income after taxes	20,671	16,545	16,073	19,632	17,576	15,870	22,004	24,967	27,041	3.41
Cash dividends	7,560	6,662	6,600	7,814	7,804	9,118	9,575	11,182	13,796	7.81
Income retained in business	13,112	9,882	9,471	11,817	9,773	6,751	12,432	13,785	13,245	0.13
Direct credits (charges)	(5,871)	(9,037)	(10,298)	(5,633)	(5,079)	(2,778)	(5,119)	2,146	(3,042)	.....
Ending retained earnings	82,114	79,459	78,228	88,246	92,701	95,808	99,381	116,504	127,533	5.66
ASSETS, END OF YEAR:										
Total	284,253	307,632	314,925	319,782	338,344	345,002	362,769	392,551	402,114	4.43
Accounts receivable	28,409	30,526	28,550	28,826	30,556	31,867	33,335	36,927	37,132	3.40
Inventories	39,534	40,072	41,328	43,070	46,141	45,949	46,427	49,263	50,203	3.03
Net property, plant and equipment	90,067	92,713	94,328	88,731	97,811	97,903	99,617	103,726	108,174	2.32
RATIOS, PERCENT:										
INCOME TO SALES:										
Before tax	8.02	6.30	6.32	7.18	6.70	5.58	7.49	8.05	8.01	7.07
After tax	5.48	4.20	4.04	4.80	4.27	3.74	5.01	5.47	5.61	4.74
INCOME TO STOCKHOLDERS' EQUITY:										
Before tax	28.47	25.41	24.66	25.43	23.40	19.93	26.55	26.42	27.35	25.29
After tax	19.46	16.95	15.77	17.01	14.92	13.34	17.76	17.96	19.15	16.92
INCOME TO TOTAL ASSETS:										
Before tax	10.64	8.06	7.98	9.18	8.15	6.87	9.07	9.36	9.61	8.77
After tax	7.27	5.38	5.10	6.14	5.19	4.60	6.07	6.36	6.72	5.87
AS A PERCENT OF TOTAL ASSETS:										
Property, plant and equipment	31.69	30.14	29.95	27.75	28.91	28.38	27.46	26.42	26.90	28.62
Short-term debt	4.52	4.22	4.99	4.50	5.22	4.89	5.64	5.52	5.41	4.99
Long-term debt	32.08	34.78	33.79	30.93	30.62	30.12	29.32	28.96	28.03	30.96
Stockholders' equity	37.38	31.74	32.37	36.10	34.81	34.47	34.15	35.41	35.12	34.62

1. For income and asset amounts, compound annual growth rate; for ratios, average of ratios for the years shown.

Source: U.S. Bureau of the Census, Quarterly Financial Report.

Notes: Parentheses ( ) indicate negative items, e.g., net expenses, charges, or losses. Net property, plant, and equipment is net of accumulated depreciation. Because the samples used to collect the data change, retained earnings at the end of a given year will not exactly equal the previous year's retained earnings plus the current year's retained income and credits.

CANADA

The Canadian food and beverage industry is comprised of the subindustries shown in Table 7. The distribution of employment within the industry is generally similar to that of the United States. Meat products is the largest group, followed by bakery products, the beverage industries, other food products, and dairy products. However, meat products accounted for

TABLE 7

CANADA: COMPONENT INDUSTRIES OF FOOD AND BEVERAGES (CSIC 10 AND 11), 1993

(Monetary values in Canadian dollars)

| INDUSTRY NAME | CSIC | ESTABLISH-MENTS (NUMBER) | EMPLOYMENT | | VALUE OF SHIPMENTS (MILLIONS) | AVERAGE HOURLY EARNINGS[1] |
			NUMBER	PERCENT OF INDUSTRY TOTAL		
FOOD AND BEVERAGES[2]	10+11	3,202	216,101	100.0	CAN$46,855.9	CAN$13.90
FOOD INDUSTRIES	100	3,008	189,499	87.7	40,292.1	13.40
Meat and poultry products	101	567	46,167	21.4	11,672.8	13.40
Meat and meat products (except poultry)	1011	467	31,897	14.8	9,215.5	13.60
Poultry products	1012	100	14,270	6.6	2,457.2	12.99
Fish products	1021	428	21,839	10.1	2,564.5	9.98
Fruit and vegetables	103	199	17,844	8.3	3,513.3	12.16
Canned and preserved fruit and vegetables	1031	161	13,064	6.0	2,476.9	12.63
Frozen fruit and vegetables	1032	38	4,780	2.2	1,036.4	10.95
Dairy products	104	291	23,318	10.8	7,319.0	16.21
Fluid milk	1041	133	12,346	5.7	3,478.2	17.25
Other dairy products	1049	158	10,972	5.1	3,840.7	15.40
Flour, cereal food and feed	105	535	14,399	6.7	4,384.0	15.63
Cereals, grains, and flour	1051	37	2,346	1.1	715.6	17.35
Prepared flour mixes and cereal foods	1052	23	3,102	1.4	787.6	19.69
Feeds	1053	475	8,951	4.1	2,880.8	13.90
Vegetable oil mils (except corn oil)	106	10	909	0.4	1,065.7	18.22
Bakery products	107	511	27,953	12.9	2,598.4	13.30
Biscuits	1071	30	6,270	2.9	569.6	14.22
Bread and other bakery products	1072	481	21,683	10.0	2,028.8	13.03
Sugar and sugar confectionery	108	95	11,353	5.3	2,103.6	14.80
Cane and beet sugar	1081	7	1,607	0.7	628.5	20.01
Chewing gum	1082	5	2,120	1.0	329.9	15.40
Sugar and chocolate confections	1083	83	7,626	3.5	1,145.3	13.72
Other food products	109	372	25,717	11.9	5,071.0	13.57
Tea and coffee	1091	31	2,928	1.4	675.5	16.27
Dry pasta products	1092	29	1,496	0.7	180.7	11.73
Potato chip, pretzel and popcorn	1093	30	5,515	2.6	751.3	11.97
Malt and malt flour	1094	7	401	0.2	201.5	21.72
Other food products, n.e.c.	1099	275	15,377	7.1	32,622.1	13.54
BEVERAGE INDUSTRIES	11	194	26,602	12.3	6,563.7	18.97
Soft drinks	111	96	10,861	5.0	2,361.0	17.16
Distillery products	112	20	2,673	1.2	794.6	20.72
Brewery products	113	44	11,799	5.5	3,105.7	20.00
Wine	114	34	1,269	0.6	302.5	16.25

1. Including overtime.

2. The food and beverage industries are combined for easier comparison to the U.S. industry.

Source: Adapted from Statistics Canada, *Manufacturing Industries of Canada* (Cat. No. 31-203).

only 21.4 percent of total food and beverage employment in 1993, compared to 26.6 percent in the United States. In 1993, average hourly earnings ranged from Can$20.72 (US$19.75) in distilled beverages to only Can$9.98 (US$9.51) in fish products.

Value of shipments by the Canadian industry rose from Can$41.4 billion in 1987 to Can$49.5 billion in 1994, with the fastest growth between 1991 and 1994 (Table 8). Industry employment rose between 1987 and 1988, but then fell substantially in the 1988 to 1994 period. Employment in foods declined by 5.1 percent and that in beverages, by 19.5 percent. In the foods industry, the biggest employment declines were in fish products, which lost more than 9,000 employees, and dairy products, down almost 2,700 employees. Meat and poultry gained 2,000 employees. The beverage industry lost employees across the board: Soft drinks (off by more than 1,000), distillery products (about 1,500), brewery products (more than 3,000), and the smaller winery products category (almost 400). The employment losses do not, in general, seem to be attributable to NAFTA or the Canadian-U.S. Free Trade Agreement (CUSFTA), but to factors such as restructuring of domestic industries. For example, in the brewery industry, the major companies consolidated brewing operations—establishments fell from 51 in 1988 to 47 in 1994—while physical production remained virtually unchanged.

The increase in average hourly earnings by production workers from Can$11.86 in 1988 to Can$14.07 in 1994 (Table 8) did not quite keep pace with inflation. Adjusted by the Canadian consumer price index, earnings in the food industries fell 1.4 percent over the period; for beverages, there was an inflation-adjusted gain of 6.4 percent. However, with the large employment declines in the high-wage brewery and distillery industries, the industry mix of employment shifted toward lower wage workers. This shift contributed to a drop of 1.5 percent in average hourly earnings for food and beverages combined. The shifting industry mix also explains the relatively small rise in the proportion of production workers to total employment, from 69.3 percent in 1988 to 71.1 percent in 1994. In the food industries, production workers rose from 71.5 percent of the total in 1988 to 79.8 percent in 1994; in beverages, the proportion is lower and declining, from 55.2 percent in 1988 to 50.7 percent in 1994.

TABLE 8

CANADIAN EMPLOYMENT AND SHIPMENTS: FOOD AND BEVERAGES, 1987-1994

(Monetary values in Canadian dollars)

	1987	1988	1989	1990	1991	1992	1993	1994	CHANGE[1]
All employees	228,528	231,776	229,834	221,704	214,929	220,660	216,101	215,487	-0.84
Establishments	3,440	3,600	3,659	3,657	3,410	3,282	3,202	3,146	-1.27
Employees per establishment	66	64	63	61	63	67	67	68	0.44
Production workers per establishment	.....	45	44	42	44	47	48	49	1.46
PRODUCTION WORKERS:									
Total	.....	160,664	161,632	155,318	149,827	155,690	152,770	153,173	-0.79
Percent of all employees	.....	69.3	70.3	70.3	69.7	70.6	70.7	71.1	.....
Male	.....	111,983	112,615	107,812	103,746	.....	.....	.....	.....
Female	.....	48,681	49,017	47,506	46,081	.....	.....	.....	.....
Percent of all production workers	.....	30.3	30.3	30.6	30.8	.....	.....	.....	.....
Average hourly earnings	.....	11.86	12.31	12.75	13.32	13.75	13.90	14.07	2.89
Average weekly earnings	.....	466.10	482.06	502.86	525.61	540.93	542.93	548.45	2.75
Average weekly hours	.....	39.3	39.2	39.4	39.5	39.3	39.1	39.0	-0.14
Shipments (millions)	41,366	42,982	43,795	44,203	44,015	45,242	46,856	49,523	2.60

1. Compound annual growth rate.

Source: Adapted from Statistics Canada, *Manufacturing Industries of Canada* (Cat. No. 31-203).

MEXICO

The Mexican food and beverage industry is comprised of the subindustries shown in Table 9. The distribution of employment is strikingly different than in Canada or the United States.[2] The major subindustry is beverages, followed closely by bread products and tortillas. In both the United States and Canada, the bread products and tortilla industries would be combined into bakery products. Thus, bakery products constitute more than one-third of food and beverage employment in Mexico, compared to around 12.5 percent in both Canada and the United States. In Mexico, the food and beverage industry accounts for 21.4 percent of total manufacturing employment; in the United States and Canada, respectively, the industry accounts for 8.9 and 13.6 percent.

Table 10 shows growth in the industry in terms of gross domestic product originating and employment. Real gross product originating grew at a 3.7 percent annual rate from 1988 to 1995. Employment in food products grew at a 1.2 percent annual rate and beverages at a 1.1 percent rate. Employment in tobacco (discussed in the Tobacco Products Chapter) in 1995 was only a bit over one-half of its 1988 level.

TABLE 9

MEXICO: COMPONENT INDUSTRIES OF FOOD AND BEVERAGES (CMAP 31), 1993

(Monetary values in 1993 Mexican New Pesos)

INDUSTRY	CMAP	NUMBER OF UNITS	ALL WORKERS									
			NUMBER	PERCENT OF INDUSTRY TOTAL	AVERAGE DAYS WORKED	PAID WORKERS					BENEFITS PER PAID EMPLOYEE	UNPAID WORKERS, NUMBER
						REMUN-ERATION[1]	PRODUCTION WORKERS		NONPRODUCTION EMPLOYEES			
							NUMBER	WAGES AND SALARIES	NUMBER	WAGES AND SALARIES		
Food and beverages[2]	31	91,894	696,539	101	299	21,951	403,926	11,491	160,385	25,825	6,385	132,228
Meat industry	3111	4,736	40,103	6	252	18,701	25,257	10,252	8,271	25,234	4,753	6,575
Dairy products	3112	11,350	57,281	8	293	22,651	26,436	11,756	13,944	21,805	7,425	16,901
Canned and preserved goods	3113	923	60,985	9	229	15,340	49,610	7,599	9,640	31,201	3,901	1,735
Cereals and other agricultural products	3114	1,734	27,083	4	278	21,311	17,082	10,213	8,028	27,009	5,728	1,973
Bread products	3115	22,702	131,895	19	283	16,753	67,227	10,708	26,739	18,428	3,848	37,929
Tortilla industry	3116	41,313	100,858	15	321	7,176	35,240	6,347	9,605	6,788	734	56,013
Kitchen oil and grease industry	3117	137	12,966	2	288	29,031	7,867	14,780	5,026	31,620	7,686	73
Sugar industry	3118	66	37,153	5	309	29,546	30,035	15,654	7,066	36,411	9,939	52
Cocoa, chocolate, & sweets industry	3119	1,057	27,752	4	252	26,978	20,108	11,457	5,948	32,193	10,788	1,696
Other food products	3121	4,980	51,203	7	276	26,045	30,637	13,567	14,068	31,670	6,780	6,498
Beverage industry	3130	2,432	134,444	19	288	27,520	84,423	14,565	47,493	27,024	8,469	2,528

1. Average annual remuneration including benefits.
2. Average annual remuneration, and wages, salaries, and benefits include tobacco industry.

Source: INEGI, Censos Economicos 1994.

2 Unpaid family members constitute a significant part of all employment (18%) and are included in total employment.

TABLE 10

MEXICAN GROSS DOMESTIC PRODUCT AND EMPLOYMENT: FOOD, BEVERAGES AND TOBACCO, 1988-1995

	1988	1989	1990	1991	1992	1993	1994	1995	CHANGE[1]
GROSS DOMESTIC PRODUCT:									
Millions of constant 1993 new pesos	47,428.9	51,187.8	53,509.2	55,234.2	57,489.1	59,297.1	61,240.5	61,261.3	3.72
Millions of constant 1993 U.S. dollars[2]	15,183.6	16,386.9	17,130.1	17,682.3	18,404.2	18,983.0	19,605.1	19,611.8	3.72
TOTAL EMPLOYMENT:									
Food, beverages, and tobacco	609,757	630,202	641,193	655,022	672,345	679,253	667,973	650,911	0.94
Food products	468,823	487,607	496,055	506,860	521,761	525,123	517,454	510,042	1.21
Beverages	120,208	125,369	132,547	135,359	138,569	138,411	138,046	129,891	1.11
Tobacco	20,726	17,226	12,591	12,803	12,015	15,719	12,473	10,978	-8.68

1. Compound annual growth rate.

2. Converted at 3.1237 new pesos to the U.S. dollar.

Source: Sistema de Cuentas Nacionales de Mexico, INEGI.

INTERNATIONAL TRADE

United States. Total U.S. food and beverage industry exports have consistently exceeded imports, and exports grew more than twice as fast as imports during the 1989-1996 period (Table 11). They rose to $27.0 billion in 1996 from $16.0 billion in 1990, while imports increased to $20.9 billion from $15.6 billion. As a result, the U.S. trade surplus in food and beverages rose to $6.1 billion in 1996, versus $397 million in 1990. As in the domestic market, higher valued foods led the export increase. Exports of lower valued foods also rose, but at a lower rate.

Canada. U.S.-Canadian trade in food and beverage products has grown rapidly since the CUSFTA took effect in 1989, but after 1990, the growth was faster for Canada than for the United States. Between 1990 and 1996, U.S. exports to Canada rose 56 percent to $4.3 billion, and Canada's exports to the United States doubled to $4.7 billion. The United States had a trade surplus with Canada from 1990 through 1995, but ended up with a $352 million deficit in 1996.

Mexico. Food and beverage industry trade between the United States and Mexico grew rapidly from the late 1980s until the Mexican peso crisis in 1995 (see feature article). By 1994, U.S. exports to Mexico had reached $2.4 billion, and the surplus with Mexico was $1.3 billion. In 1995, the sharp Mexican recession, brought on by the peso crisis, reduced consumer demand for processed foods and higher valued food products from the United States. U.S. exports to Mexico dropped sharply (about $735 million), but almost one-half of this lost ground was regained in 1996.

NAFTA. Exports to NAFTA partners have increased for all three countries over the short life of the agreement. Canada-Mexico bilateral trade was, and has remained, very small, but Mexican exports to Canada more than doubled during NAFTA's first three years. U.S. exports to Canada have increased substantially, while those to Mexico rose briskly in 1994, dropped 31 percent in 1995 after the peso crisis, but regained their 1993 level in 1996.

The United States maintained a favorable balance in NAFTA trade throughout the agreement's first three years. However, this trade surplus shrank considerably, in contrast to a growing surplus in global U.S. food and beverage trade. The U.S. trade surplus with NAFTA was $1.6 billion in 1994, but fell to $484 million in 1995, in part because of the Mexican peso crisis. In 1996, it fell further, to $233 million, primarily due to a large increase in imports from Canada.

TABLE 11

INTERNATIONAL TRADE, FOOD AND BEVERAGES

(Millions of U.S. dollars)

	1989[1]	1990	1991	1992	1993	1994	1995	1996
GLOBAL TRADE, U.S.								
IMPORTS								
Value	14,373.1	15,632.3	15,259.8	16,290.2	16,090.0	17,342.0	18,325.9	20,947.4
Ratio to new supply[2]	4.1	4.2	4.1	4.2	4.0	4.2	.....	.....
Ratio to apparent consumption[3]	4.3	4.4	4.3	4.4	4.2	4.4	.....	.....
EXPORTS								
Value	15,141.1	16,029.7	17,406.2	19,662.4	20,508.8	23,094.7	26,020.8	27,041.3
Ratio to comparable domestic shipments	4.5	4.5	4.9	5.2	5.2	5.8	.....	.....
TRADE BALANCE	768.0	397.4	2,146.4	3,372.2	4,418.8	5,752.7	7,694.9	6,093.9
BILATERAL TRADE: NAFTA[4]								
U.S. exports to Canada	1,576.3	2,753.3	3,207.2	3,466.2	3,462.0	3,842.6	3,957.4	4,298.4
Canadian exports to U.S.	2,169.1	2,335.1	2,571.9	2,954.4	3,218.3	3,618.9	3,890.2	4,650.8
U.S. exports to Mexico	1,277.2	1,105.9	1,596.7	1,949.6	1,996.1	2,370.8	1,635.5	1,999.5
Mexican exports to U.S.	718.7	857.0	852.7	944.1	904.6	1,035.0	1,218.2	1,414.2
Canadian exports to Mexico	64.6	76.6	28.5	55.9	39.3	47.1	47.4	52.8
Mexican exports to Canada	30.9	33.7	28.2	29.2	30.9	40.3	68.2	66.1
TRADE BALANCES WITHIN NAFTA[5]								
Canada	626.5	(375.3)	(635.0)	(485.1)	(235.3)	(216.9)	(88.0)	339.1 .
Mexico	(592.2)	(291.8)	(744.3)	(1,032.2)	(1,099.9)	(1,342.6)	(396.5)	(572.0)
United States	(34.3)	667.0	1,379.3	1,517.3	1,335.2	1,559.5	484.5	232.9

1. 1989 and earlier data on U.S. exports to Canada for manufacturing total and manufacturing industries are not comparable with data for 1990 and later years because of a change in the reporting system. The NAFTA trade balances for the U.S. and Canada also are affected.

2. New supply equals comparable domestic shipments plus imports for consumption.

3. Apparent consumption equals comparable domestic shipments plus imports for consumption less exports.

4. Amounts less than U.S. $100,000 shown as zero.

5. Parentheses indicate an excess of imports over exports. Because of commodity coding and other data differences among the three countries, these trade balances are only rough estimates and should be used with caution.

Source for U.S. Global Trade: U.S. Department of Commerce, International Trade Administration.

Source for U.S. -Canada and U.S.-Mexico Bilateral Trade: U.S. Bureau of the Census.

Source for Canada-Mexico and Mexico-Canada Bilateral Trade: Statistics Canada, Foreign Trade Division, Special tabulation, March 1997, converted to U.S. dollars by the editors.

FURNITURE AND FIXTURES

THE UNITED STATES

Products and Processes.   The furniture and fixtures industry is one of the smaller U.S. manufacturing industries, ranking 17th out of 20 in terms of industry shipments. However, it has enjoyed strong growth since its recession low in 1991, a result of a fortunate combination of low interest rates, low inflation, rising housing starts, and gains in consumer purchasing power. Household furniture accounts for almost half of all output by the industry, with the three largest subcategories being wood furniture, upholstered furniture, and mattresses and bedsprings. Office furniture makes up another 18 percent, followed in importance by partitions and fixtures (15 percent). See Table 1 for a comprehensive profile of the industry as it stood in 1992 (the latest year for which economic census data are available).

Employment in the industry totaled 486,900 in 1993 and is projected to gain modestly to 514,800 in 2005 (Table 2). Growth is projected for all major industry subdivisions, including household furniture (the largest employer with 57 percent of the 1993 total), office and miscellaneous furniture, and partitions and fixtures.

TABLE 1

UNITED STATES: COMPONENT INDUSTRIES OF FURNITURE AND FIXTURES (SIC 25), 1992

(Monetary values in millions of U.S. dollars)

INDUSTRY	SIC	ESTABLISH-MENTS	SHIPMENTS VALUE	SHIPMENTS PERCENT BY 4 LARGEST COMPANIES	VALUE ADDED BY MANUFACTURE	NEW CAPITAL EXPENDI-TURES	EMPLOY-MENT[1]	PAYROLL
FURNITURE AND FIXTURES	25	11,658	$43,825.9	.....	$22,839.7	$821.4	471,100	$10,227.0
Household furniture	251	5,412	20,507.5	.....	10,492.4	345.7	253,300	4,803.8
Wood household furniture	2511	2,785	8,730.4	20	4,726.1	197.3	121,100	2,174.0
Upholstered household furniture	2512	1,184	6,231.4	25	3,012.6	73.9	79,200	1,535.1
Metal household furniture	2514	351	1,954.8	22	998.1	29.2	20,700	416.3
Mattresses, foundations and convertible beds	2515	788	2,820.7		1,394.2	30.9	22,300	483.8
Wood TV and radio cabinets	2517	104	318.9	55	167.3	3.7	4,400	81.6
Household furniture, n.e.c.	2519	200	451.2	48	194.1	10.8	5,600	113.0
Office furniture	252	1,025	7,978.6	.....	4,625.7	200.1	68,000	1,868.4
Wood office furniture	2521	636	1,918.7	26	1,083.8	35.6	23,300	527.5
Metal office furniture	2522	389	6,060.0	56	3,541.9	164.5	44,700	1,340.9
Public building and related furniture	253	520	4,483.1	.....	1,735.8	85.6	30,300	732.3
Public building and related furniture	2531	520	4,483.1	45	1,735.8	85.6	30,300	732.3
Partitions and fixtures	254	2,734	6,580.4	.....	3,632.6	114.9	74,500	1,817.8
Wood office and store fixtures	2541	1,945	3,114.7	6	1,734.8	48.8	39,500	948.1
Metal partitions and fixtures	2542	789	3,465.7	18	1,897.7	66.1	35,100	869.7
Miscellaneous furniture and fixtures	259	1,967	4,276.3	.....	2,353.2	75.2	45,000	1,004.7
Drapery hardware, blinds, and shades	2591	556	1,915.6	40	959.9	27.6	19,400	395.5
Furniture and fixtures, n.e.c.	2599	1,411	2,360.6	24	1,393.3	47.6	25,600	609.2

1. Employment numbers from the economic censuses differ in definition and classification from the Bureau of Labor Statistics estimates in Table 2. Year-to-year comparisons between Table 1 and Table 2 are not appropriate.

Source: U.S. Bureau of the Census, 1992 Census of Manufactures.

TABLE 2

U.S. EMPLOYMENT AND EARNINGS: FURNITURE AND FIXTURES

INDUSTRY	SIC	1993			2005
		EMPLOYMENT[1]		AVERAGE HOURLY EARNINGS (U.S. DOLLARS)[2]	PROJECTED EMPLOYMENT[3]
		NUMBER OF PERSONS	PERCENT OF INDUSTRY TOTAL		
FURNITURE AND FIXTURES	25	486,900	100.0	$9.27	514,800
Household furniture	251	278,100	57.1	8.72	280,200
Wood household furniture	2511	123,600	25.4	8.15	....
Upholstered household furniture	2512	91,000	18.7	9.48	....
Metal household furniture	2514	21,500	4.4	8.69	....
Mattresses and bedsprings	2515	29,000	6.0	9.19	....
Office furniture	252	60,700	12.5	10.03	....
Public building and related furniture	253	37,200	7.6	9.61	....
Partitions and fixtures	254	75,600	15.5	10.58	88,300
Miscellaneous furniture and fixtures	259	35,300	7.2	9.57	....
Office and miscellaneous furniture and fixtures	252,3,9	133,200	27.4	....	146,300

1. Total payroll employment. Employment data from the economic censuses, shown in Table 1, differ in definition and classification from the Bureau of Labor Statistics estimates in this table. Year-to-year comparisons between Table 1 and Table 2 are not appropriate.

2. Earnings of production workers, including overtime.

3. Number of persons, moderate projection by the U.S. Bureau of Labor Statistics.

Source: Bureau of Labor Statistics.

FIGURE 1

U.S. EMPLOYMENT IN FURNITURE AND FIXTURES

Percent distribution by region, 1995

By far the largest share (almost 41 percent in 1995) of furniture production is in the Southeast, where North Carolina and Virginia dominate. The Great Lakes region is second, with 22 percent of the 1995 total, followed by the Pacific region with 12 percent.

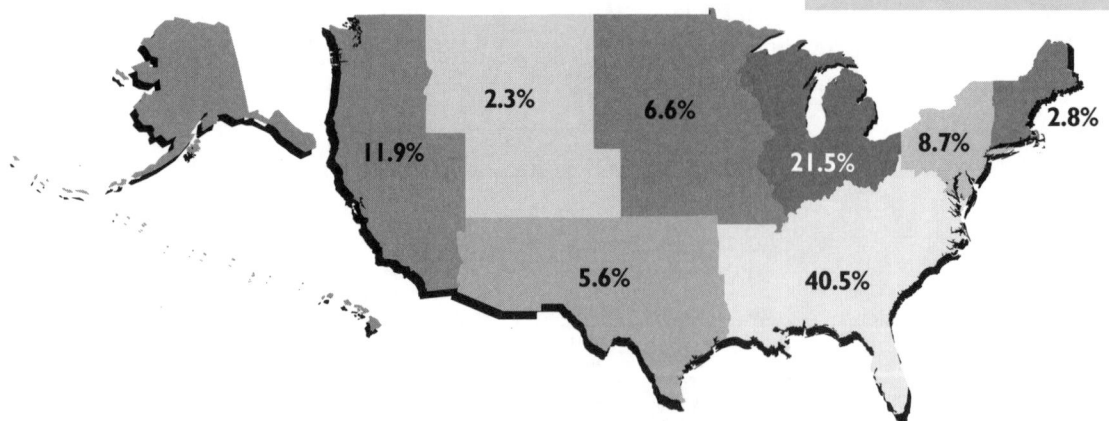

Source: U.S. Department of Commerce, Bureau of Economic Analysis.

What's New. The 25 leading residential furniture manufacturers expected generally good sales results in 1997, according to the Wood & Wood Products' Ninth Annual Survey of the Top 25 Residential Furniture Manufacturers. Half of the respondents expected an "okay" year, 39 percent predicted it would be "very good," and 11 percent said it would be their "best ever." Some of the industry concerns reported in the survey included price-cutting, the impact of government regulations regarding wood dust and clean air provisions, and the level of employee skills. The American Furniture Manufacturers Association (AFMA) expects 1997 shipments to gain some 5.7 percent from the 1996 level, or 2.8 percent when adjusted for inflation. AFMA sees wood furniture shipments surpassing $10 billion for the first time, with shipments of upholstered furniture rising to $8.3 billion, and those of metal furniture hitting $2.5 billion.

Sustained economic growth, with accompanying expansion and modernization of U.S. companies, is bolstering demand for office furniture. U.S. office furniture shipments are expected to rise 8.5 percent in 1997, 5 percent in 1998, and 4.5 percent by 1999, according to an industry source. Shipments in the first quarter of 1997 rose some 13 percent, led by a 19 percent surge in those by large manufacturers (sales over $150 million annually). Among the product categories, systems furniture was the big gainer—23 percent. Sales of nonwood furniture rose 16 percent, and wood furniture, 10 percent.

FIGURE 2

U.S. EMPLOYMENT AND SHIPMENTS, FURNITURE AND FIXTURES

Total payroll employment and manufacturers' inflation-adjusted shipments

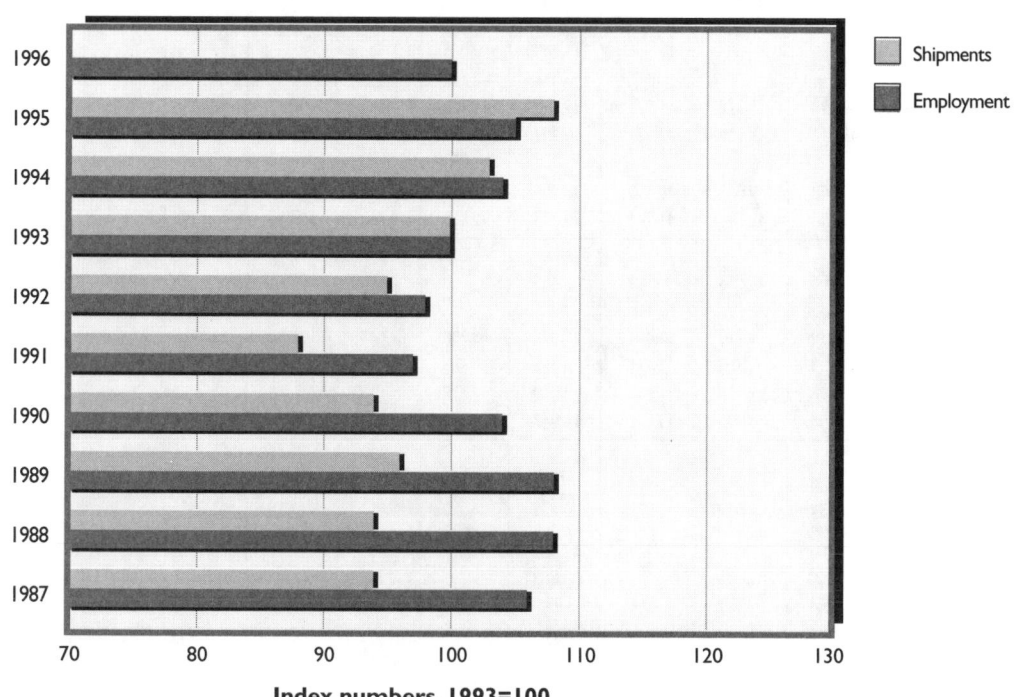

Index numbers, 1993=100

Source: U.S. Bureau of Labor Statistics, U.S. Department of Commerce, and estimates by the editors. Shipments data for 1996 are not available.

Output. Constant-dollar shipments of furniture and fixtures between 1988 and 1995 rose in every year but 1990 and 1991, when the U.S. economy was in the grip of recession. Employment in 1995, although below the high levels of 1987-1989, continued the recovery that began after the 1991 recession (Figure 2). Industry restructuring and investment in labor-saving technology has helped to improve productivity and efficiency, so that fewer workers are needed than in the past, even though production is on the rise. The value of industry shipments, in current dollars, rose to $53.6 billion in 1995, compared with $50.1 billion in 1994 and $37.5 billion in 1987 (Table 3). The annual growth rate in 1987-1995 was 4.57 percent (1.64 percent when adjusted for inflation).

Investment. After the 1991 recession, new capital expenditures rose steadily to $1.23 billion by 1995—a record for the nine-year period (Table 3). A decline in capacity utilization since 1994, to a relatively low 81.0 percent estimated for 1996, reflected in part, the increased capacity coming on stream.

Prices. Producer prices for furniture and fixtures rose at an average annual rate of 2.77 percent between 1987 and 1996 (Table 3). Prices and industry costs are strongly affected by prices for lumber—the single most important raw material used by the industry. During the 1987-1996 period, prices for lumber and wood products rose more rapidly (4.29 percent a year) than did those for furniture, with especially rapid increases between 1992 and 1994.

TABLE 3

U.S. OUTPUT, INVESTMENT, AND PRICES: FURNITURE AND FIXTURES

(Millions of U.S. dollars, except as noted)

	1987	1988	1989	1990	1991	1992	1993	1994	1995	1996	GROWTH RATE 1987-1995[1]
VALUE OF SHIPMENTS:											
BY INDUSTRY:											
Current dollars	37,462	39,173	41,317	41,523	39,815	43,826	46,817	50,077	53,571	.....	4.57
Constant 1992 dollars	43,334	43,314	43,985	42,921	40,297	43,826	45,891	47,401	49,358	.....	1.64
BY PRODUCT:											
Current dollars	35,856	37,703	39,649	40,395	38,753	41,878	44,658	48,311	51,657	.....	4.67
Constant 1992 dollars	41,457	41,670	42,190	41,746	39,223	41,878	43,782	45,736	47,619	.....	1.75
OTHER OUTPUT MEASURES:											
Industrial production, 1993=100	96.4	96.6	97.8	96.4	90.5	95.5	100.0	103.1	103.7	103.9	0.84
Gross domestic product:											
Current dollars	14,602	15,019	15,710	15,404	15,056	16,208	17,644	18,952	.....	.....	.....
Percent of total GDP	0.3	0.3	0.3	0.3	0.3	0.3	0.3	0.3	.....	.....	.....
Rank in manufacturing	18	18	18	19	19	19	18	18	.....	.....	.....
Chained (1992) dollars	16,912	16,858	16,900	15,842	14,947	16,208	17,845	18,448	.....	.....	.....
INVESTMENT-RELATED MEASURES:											
Capacity utilization, percent	86.0	84.0	83.1	80.1	74.7	78.7	81.6	82.9	82.4	81.0	.....
New capital expenditures	895	934	1,039	912	723	822	974	1,018	1,232	.....	.....
Research and development spending[2]	.....	.....	.....	.....	.....	.....	.....	.....	.....	.....	.....
Producer prices, 1993=100[3]	84.9	88.8	92.3	95.0	97.0	98.0	100.0	103.4	106.4	108.6	2.77

1. Compound annual growth rate.

2. Included with lumber and wood products.

3. Prices received by domestic producers.

Sources: Shipments and new capital expenditures: U.S. Department of Commerce for 1987-1995, editor's estimates for constant dollar data for 1987-88 and all shipments data for 1996; Industrial production and capacity utilization: Federal Reserve Board of Governors; GDP: Bureau of Economic Analysis; Research and development spending: National Science Foundation; Producer prices: Bureau of Labor Statistics.

Workforce and Employment. After declining from 1988 through 1991, employment gained for four years in a row and then dipped again in 1996 (Table 4). At 504,000, 1996 employment was above the low of 475,000 in 1991 but under 1987's 515,000. The overall result was an annual decline of 0.24 percent for the 10-year period. Employment of production workers declined at a rate of 0.38 percent; their share of the workforce dipped to 79 percent in 1996 from 80 percent in 1987. Employment of women, at 31.2 percent of the workforce, was little changed from the 1987 proportion. Average hourly earnings of production workers were $10.15 in 1996, with the yearly growth rate for 1987-1996 at 3.16 percent in current dollars, but this represented a decline of 0.38 percent when adjusted for inflation. The average workweek declined fractionally to 39.4 hours in 1996.

TABLE 4

U.S. EMPLOYMENT, HOURS, AND EARNINGS: FURNITURE AND FIXTURES

(Monetary values in U.S. dollars)

	1987	1988	1989	1990	1991	1992	1993	1994	1995	1996	CHANGE[1]
NUMBER OF EMPLOYEES, IN THOUSANDS:											
Total	515	527	524	506	475	478	487	505	510	504	-0.24
Production workers	412	420	418	400	373	377	385	400	403	398	-0.38
Percent of total	80.0	79.7	79.7	79.0	78.4	78.8	79.0	79.1	79.0	79.0	.....
Women	161	163	163	158	146	145	148	155	158	157	-0.29
Percent of total	31.3	30.9	31.1	31.2	30.7	30.3	30.3	30.7	31.0	31.2	.....
HOURS AND EARNINGS OF PRODUCTION WORKERS:											
Average hourly earnings, U.S. dollars[2]											
Current dollars	7.67	7.95	8.25	8.52	8.76	9.01	9.27	9.55	9.82	10.15	3.16
1992 dollars[3]	9.42	9.39	9.30	9.13	9.01	9.01	9.02	9.06	9.06	9.10	-0.38
Average weekly hours	40.0	39.4	39.5	39.1	38.9	39.7	40.1	40.4	39.6	39.4	-0.17
Average weekly earnings, current U.S. dollars	306.80	313.23	325.88	333.13	340.76	357.70	371.73	385.82	388.87	399.91	2.99

1. Compound annual growth rate, 1987-1996.

2. Including overtime.

3. Converted to 1992 dollars using Consumer Price Index for Urban Wage Earners and Clerical Workers.

Source: Bureau of Labor Statistics.

FIGURE 3

U.S. OCCUPATIONAL INJURY AND ILLNESS RATES: FURNITURE AND FIXTURES, 1995

In 1995, the furniture and fixtures industry averaged 13.9 cases of nonfatal occupational illnesses and injuries per 100 workers—above the average for all manufacturing.

Incidence of nonfatal injuries and illnesses per 100 full-time workers

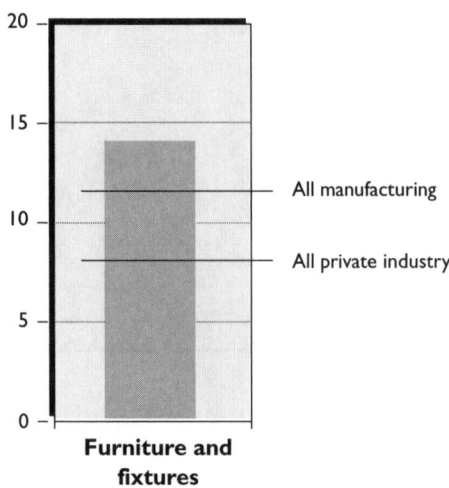

Source: U.S. Bureau of Labor Statistics.

TABLE 5

U.S. EMPLOYMENT PROJECTIONS BY MAJOR OCCUPATIONAL GROUP: FURNITURE AND FIXTURES

Employment in the furniture and fixtures industry is projected to reach 514,800 in the year 2005 (moderate assumptions), 12,900 above the 1994 level. Most of the growth will take place in professional specialties and precision workers, reflecting continuing strong demand for skilled workers.

| | 1994 | | PROJECTIONS, 2005 | | | |
| | NUMBER OF EMPLOYEES | PERCENT OF INDUSTRY TOTAL | NUMBER OF EMPLOYEES | | | PERCENT OF INDUSTRY TOTAL, MODERATE PROJECTIONS |
OCCUPATION			LOW	MODERATE	HIGH	
Total, all occupations	501,900	100.0	485,700	514,800	580,900	100.0
Executive, administrative, and managerial	32,130	6.4	31,089	32,934	36,757	6.4
Professional specialties	5,138	1.0	6,074	6,432	7,129	1.3
Technicians and related support	5,705	1.1	4,752	5,031	5,551	1.0
Marketing and sales	11,778	2.4	11,382	12,057	13,469	2.3
Administrative support including clerical	46,594	9.3	39,842	42,217	47,404	8.2
Service	4,918	1.0	3,948	4,185	4,722	0.8
Agriculture, forestry, and fisheries occupations	102	0.0	87	93	107	0.0
Precision production, craft, and repair	143,842	28.7	159,893	169,520	192,111	32.9
Operators, fabricators, assemblers	251,694	50.2	228,633	242,331	273,650	47.1

Source: Bureau of Labor Statistics, November 1995.

FIGURE 4

U.S. CORPORATE INCOME AND WORKER EARNINGS: FURNITURE AND FIXTURES

Corporate operating income and aggregate production worker earnings

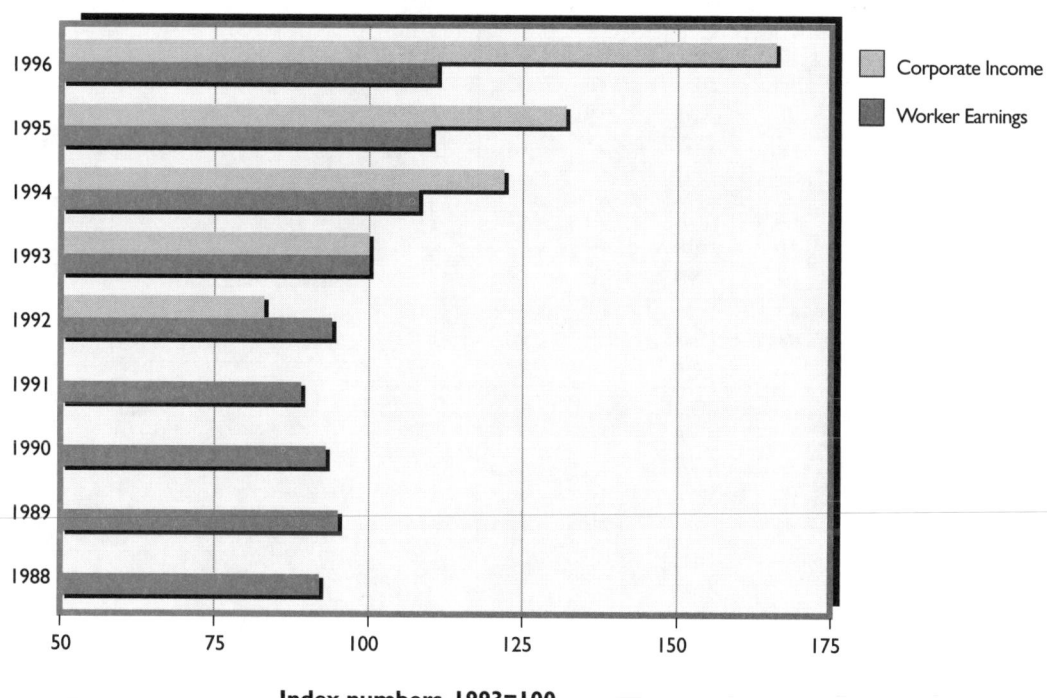

Index numbers, 1993=100

Source: U.S. Bureau of Labor Statistics, U.S. Bureau of the Census, and estimates by the editors. Corporate earnings data prior to 1992 are not available.

Finance. Corporate income in the furniture industry has grown significantly since 1992, whereas earnings of production workers have shown steady but slow growth (Figure 4). The industry had an especially good year in 1996, as sales, operating income, and profits all hit five-year highs, in contrast to their unspectacular showing of 1995. During the economic recovery period 1992-1996, income from operations grew at an annual rate of 18.80 percent, totaling $3.87 billion in 1996 (Table 6). It should be noted, however, that these data are not comparable to those in other chapters covering 9- or 10-year periods that include the recession of 1991. After-tax income rose at an even more spectacular annual rate of 24.58 percent, reaching $2.3 billion in 1996; it amounted to 4.20 percent of sales in 1996 (compared with 2.24 percent in 1995) and 15.49 percent of stockholders' equity (compared to 8.11 percent). Industry inventories in 1996 stood at $5.9 billion, about equal to $6.0 billion the year before but well above the $3.9 billion in 1992. Debt as a percentage of assets decreased slightly from 1995 as long-term debt declined and short-term debt increased.

TABLE 6

U.S. CORPORATE INCOME AND ASSETS: FURNITURE AND FIXTURES

(Monetary values in millions of U.S. dollars)

INCOME AND EXPENSES	1992	1993	1994	1995	1996	CHANGE OR AVERAGE[1]
Sales and receipts	35,079	39,326	44,969	48,731	54,784	11.79
Depreciation and amortization	(847)	(916)	(959)	(1,012)	(1,198)	9.05
Other operating costs	(32,291)	(36,089)	(41,170)	(44,655)	(49,719)	11.39
Income from operations	1,942	2,321	2,839	3,062	3,868	18.80
Nonoperating income (expenditures)	(403)	(390)	(501)	(1,218)	(492)	....
Income before taxes	1,539	1,932	2,337	1,844	3,376	21.70
Income after taxes	955	1,339	1,615	1,091	2,300	24.58
Cash dividends	305	522	586	637	744	24.97
Income retained in business	649	817	1,029	454	1,556	24.43
Direct credits (charges)	1,199	(278)	(334)	(347)	(602)	....
Ending retained earnings	7,011	7,611	8,397	9,681	9,720	8.51
ASSETS, END OF YEAR:						
Total	20,027	22,854	23,887	31,561	33,295	13.55
Accounts receivable	4,714	5,445	5,840	7,114	6,929	10.11
Inventories	3,867	4,126	5,011	6,008	5,916	11.22
Net property, plant and equipment	5,546	6,368	6,332	8,278	8,735	12.03
RATIOS, PERCENT:						
INCOME TO SALES:						
Before tax	4.39	4.91	5.20	3.78	6.16	4.89
After tax	2.72	3.40	3.59	2.24	4.20	3.23
INCOME TO STOCKHOLDERS' EQUITY:						
Before tax	16.48	18.15	20.55	13.71	22.74	18.33
After tax	10.23	12.58	14.20	8.11	15.49	12.12
INCOME TO TOTAL ASSETS:						
Before tax	7.68	8.45	9.78	5.84	10.14	8.38
After tax	4.77	5.86	6.76	3.46	6.91	5.55
AS A PERCENT OF TOTAL ASSETS:						
Property, plant and equipment	27.69	27.86	26.51	26.23	26.24	26.91
Short-term debt	3.26	3.75	4.93	4.12	6.44	4.50
Long-term debt	23.85	21.54	19.69	23.87	19.80	21.75
Stockholders' equity	46.62	46.59	47.62	42.62	44.58	45.61

1. For income and asset amounts, compound annual growth rate; for ratios, average of ratios for the years shown.

Source: U.S. Bureau of the Census, Quarterly Financial Report.

Notes: Parentheses ( ) indicate negative items, e.g., net expenses, charges, or losses. Net property, plant, and equipment is net of accumulated depreciation. Because the samples used to collect the data change, retained earnings at the end of a given year will not exactly equal the previous year's retained earnings plus the current year's retained income and credits.

CANADA

Canada's furniture and fixtures industry consisted of 1,331 establishments with 44,654 employees in 1993 (Table 7). Major subindustries include household furniture (with 40 percent of total industry shipments and 43 percent of employees in 1993) and office furniture (22 percent of shipments). Within the large "other furniture and fixture" category, hotel and restaurant furniture had 17 percent of industry shipments.

Canada's furniture shipments in 1994 totaled Can$4.5 billion, only 3 percent above the 1987 level despite some wide fluctuations in the intervening years (Table 8). Industry employment reached its recent peak of 63,379 in 1989 and then declined through 1992 before edging up to 46,960 in 1994. Employment of production workers fell even faster; they accounted for 83 percent of the workforce in 1994, compared with 87 percent in 1988. The number of establishments declined to 1,238 in 1994 from 1,822 in 1987. Production workers' wages averaged Can$11.38 per hour in 1994, and the average workweek was 40 hours.

TABLE 7

CANADA: COMPONENT INDUSTRIES OF FURNITURE AND FIXTURES (CSIC 26), 1993

(Monetary values in Canadian dollars)

INDUSTRY NAME	CSIC	ESTABLISH-MENTS (NUMBER)	EMPLOYMENT		VALUE OF SHIPMENTS (MILLIONS)	AVERAGE HOURLY EARNINGS[1]
			NUMBER	PERCENT OF INDUSTRY TOTAL		
FURNITURE AND FIXTURE INDUSTRIES	26	1,331	44,654	100.0	CAN$3,988.2	CAN$11.30
Household furniture	261	620	19,258	43.1	1,591.4	10.50
Wooden household furniture	2611	450	11,699	26.2	951.9	10.37
Upholstered household furniture	2612	124	5,900	13.2	486.8	10.76
Other household furniture	2619	46	1,659	3.7	152.8	10.47
Office furniture	264	179	9,215	20.6	889.0	12.12
Metal office furniture	2641	59	4,531	10.1	501.7	12.57
Other office furniture	2649	120	4,684	10.5	387.3	11.70
Other furniture and fixtures	269	532	16,181	36.2	1,507.7	11.83
Bed springs and mattresses	2691	90	3,212	7.2	391.2	11.94
Hotel and restaurant furniture, n.e.c.	2692	268	7,943	17.8	681.9	12.47
Other furniture and fixtures, n.e.c.	2699	174	5,026	11.3	434.7	10.81

1. Including overtime.

Source: Adapted from Statistics Canada, *Manufacturing Industries of Canada* (Cat. No. 31-203).

TABLE 8

CANADIAN EMPLOYMENT AND SHIPMENTS: FURNITURE AND FIXTURES, 1987-1994

(Monetary values in Canadian dollars)

	1987	1988	1989	1990	1991	1992	1993	1994	CHANGE[1]
All employees	61,584	62,373	63,379	59,110	50,686	43,938	44,654	46,960	-3.80
Establishments	1,822	1,947	1,845	1,939	1,575	1,409	1,331	1,238	-5.37
Employees per establishment	34	32	34	30	32	31	34	38	1.66
Production workers per establishment	.....	28	30	26	28	26	28	32	2.07
PRODUCTION WORKERS:									
Total	.....	54,372	55,784	51,379	43,390	36,002	36,992	39,104	-5.35
Percent of all employees	.....	87.2	88.0	86.9	85.6	81.9	82.8	83.3	.....
Male	.....	43,514	44,128	40,843	34,536	.....	.....	.....	.....
Female	.....	10,858	11,656	10,536	8,854	.....	.....	.....	.....
Percent of all production workers	.....	20.0	20.9	20.5	20.4	.....	.....	.....	.....
Average hourly earnings	.....	9.44	9.86	10.47	10.69	11.21	11.30	11.38	3.17
Average weekly earnings	.....	380.91	396.48	416.81	427.55	447.00	450.14	455.36	3.02
Average weekly hours	.....	40.4	40.2	39.8	40.0	39.9	39.8	40.0	-0.14
Shipments (millions)	4,389	4,620	4,903	4,662	3,939	3,771	3,988	4,523	0.43

1. Compound annual growth rate.

Source: Adapted from Statistics Canada, *Manufacturing Industries of Canada* (Cat. No. 31-203).

MEXICO

Mexico classifies wood furniture as a subindustry within its wood and wood products industry, and metal furniture within the metal products industry but they have been separated out here to facilitate comparisons. In 1993, the wood furniture and mattress subindustry had 18,616 production units and 94,729 employees (Table 9). Annual earnings plus benefits of all workers averaged 14,210 new pesos ($4,549) a year. Production workers earnings (not including benefits) averaged 9,087 new pesos ($2,909) a year, and those for nonproduction employees averaged 22,195 new pesos ($7,105). The metal furniture category had 1,031 production units in 1993 and employed 25,052 workers. At 17,470 new pesos, remuneration was about 23 percent above that in the wood furniture category.

TABLE 9

MEXICO: COMPONENT INDUSTRIES OF FURNITURE AND FIXTURES (CMAP 3220 AND 3813), 1993

(Monetary values in 1993 Mexican New Pesos)

			ALL WORKERS									
							PAID WORKERS					
							PRODUCTION WORKERS		NONPRODUCTION EMPLOYEES		BENEFITS	UNPAID
INDUSTRY	CMAP	NUMBER OF UNITS	NUMBER	PERCENT OF INDUSTRY TOTAL	AVERAGE DAYS WORKED	REMUN-ERATION[1]	NUMBER	WAGES AND SALARIES	NUMBER	WAGES AND SALARIES	PER PAID EMPLOYEE	WORKERS, NUMBER
Wood furniture, and mattresses	3320	18,616	94,729	79	261	14,210	59,572	9,087	10,358	22,195	3,181	24,799
Metal furniture	3813	1,031	25,052	21	273	17,470	19,525	10,555	4,630	25,239	4,100	897

1. Average annual remuneration including benefits.

Source: INEGI, Censos Economicos 1994.

INTERNATIONAL TRADE

United States. Worldwide U.S. exports of furniture almost doubled between 1990 and 1996 to $3.1 billion. The much larger import trade climbed 80 percent during the period to $7.5 billion (Table 11). The U.S. trade deficit fell early in that period but then rose to $6.2 billion by 1996, reflecting stronger growth in the U.S. economy than in the major U.S. markets and a strengthening of the U.S. dollar. Wood furniture accounts for about half of U.S. exports and 60 percent of imports. Canada now receives around half the U.S. exports. Imports come mainly from Taiwan, China, Canada, Mexico, and Italy.

Canada. Canadian furniture exports to the United States rose from $1.2 billion in 1990 to $2.7 billion in 1996, and U.S. exports to Canada climbed from $743 million to $1.5 billion (Table 11). As a result, the U.S. furniture trade deficit with Canada was considerably higher in 1996 than in 1990 ($1.2 billion versus $467 million).

Mexico. Mexican furniture exports to the United States totaled $1.5 billion in 1996, almost 160 percent higher than in 1990 (Table 11). The much smaller U.S. exports to Mexico rose 59 percent during that period to $527 million. As a result, the U.S. deficit in furniture trade with Mexico shot from $260 million in 1990 to just over $1 billion in 1996.

NAFTA. Since 1991, Canada and Mexico have had favorable, and roughly equal, NAFTA trade balances (Table 11). The United States, on the other hand, has had a persistent trade deficit that grew to $2.2 billion in 1996. The most dramatic changes have taken place since 1993.

TABLE 11

INTERNATIONAL TRADE, FURNITURE AND FIXTURES

(Millions of U.S. dollars)

	1989[1]	1990	1991	1992	1993	1994	1995	1996
GLOBAL TRADE, U.S.								
IMPORTS								
Value	5,085.9	5,168.8	5,063.4	5,561.7	6,241.5	7,521.5	8,303.0	9,320.1
Ratio to new supply[2]	11.4'	11.3	11.6	11.7	12.3	13.5	.....	.....
Ratio to apparent consumption[3]	11.6	11.8	12.2	12.4	13.0	14.3	.....	.....
EXPORTS								
Value	1,045.2	1,627.7	2,152.8	2,582.1	2,817.6	3,030.4	2,952.6	3,101.3
Ratio to comparable domestic shipments	2.6	4.0	5.6	6.2	6.3	6.3	.....	.....
TRADE BALANCE	(4,040.7)	(3,541.1)	(2,910.6)	(2,979.6)	(3,423.9)	(4,491.1)	(5,350.4)	(6,218.8)
BILATERAL TRADE: NAFTA[4]								
U.S. exports to Canada	286.9	743.1	942.5	1,117.6	1,266.4	1,500.4	1,531.7	1,519.3
Canadian exports to U.S.	1,179.7	1,210.1	1,069.7	1,264.2	1,488.8	1,910.5	2,275.6	2,703.0
U.S. exports to Mexico	219.4	332.4	541.1	639.5	696.0	677.6	531.1	526.9
Mexican exports to U.S.	541.5	592.1	664.7	794.2	908.8	1,141.4	1,217.6	1,538.2
Canadian exports to Mexico	0.3	0.2	1.9	2.9	1.9	1.2	0.9	1.0
Mexican exports to Canada	7.8	1.5	3.2	4.7	5.6	6.2	9.3	10.5
TRADE BALANCES WITHIN NAFTA[5]								
Canada	885.3	465.7	125.9	144.8	218.7	405.1	735.5	1,174.2
Mexico	329.6	261.0	124.9	156.5	216.5	468.8	694.9	1,020.8
United States	(1,214.8)	(726.7)	(250.9)	(301.3)	(435.2)	(874.0)	(1,430.3)	(2,195.0)

1. 1989 and earlier data on U.S. exports to Canada for manufacturing totals and manufacturing industries are not comparable with data for 1990 and later years because of a change in the reporting system. The NAFTA trade balances for the U.S. and Canada also are affected.

2. New supply equals comparable domestic shipments plus imports for consumption.

3. Apparent consumption equals comparable domestic shipments plus imports for consumption less exports.

4. Amounts less than U.S. $100,000 shown as zero.

5. Parentheses indicate an excess of imports over exports. Because of commodity coding and other data differences among the three countries, these trade balances are only rough estimates and should be used with caution.

Source for U.S. Global Trade: U.S. Department of Commerce, International Trade Administration.

Source for U.S. -Canada and U.S.-Mexico Bilateral Trade: U.S. Bureau of the Census.

Source for Canada-Mexico and Mexico-Canada Bilateral Trade: Statistics Canada, Foreign Trade Division, Special tabulation, March 1997, converted to U.S. dollars by the editors.

INDUSTRIAL AND COMMERCIAL MACHINERY AND COMPUTER EQUIPMENT

THE UNITED STATES

Products and Processes. The huge machinery and computer equipment industry was the top U.S employer in manufacturing last year. It ranked third in manufacturing in terms of industry shipments, surpassed only by the food and transportation-equipment sectors. The industry produces machinery for virtually all manufacturing areas of the economy and thus has benefited from the sustained economic growth of recent years. Computer equipment manufacturing is the largest subindustry, with 1996 shipments more than two-thirds larger than those in 1991. Other important subindustries are air conditioning, heating, and refrigeration; construction; metalworking; engines and turbines; and general industrial equipment such as compressors, pumps, and packaging machinery.

Table 1 shows the composition of the industry in 1992 (the latest year for which economic census data are available). That year, there were 53,956 establishments in the industry with a combined payroll of $57.2 billion and shipments of $258.7 billion. The five largest subindustries were computers and office equipment (with 25.8 percent of total shipments), general industrial machinery and equipment (12.2 percent), refrigeration and service industry machinery (10.6 percent), construction and related equipment (10.5 percent), and metalworking machinery and equipment (10.2 percent).

Pressed by stiff competition from both domestic and foreign producers, many of the subindustries are cutting payrolls, eliminating nonproductive units, modernizing through investment in new technology and plants, and merging with other companies. As a result, growth in industry employment has been suppressed in recent years and is seen declining by the year 2005 to 1.77 million people from the 1.93 million employed in 1993 (Table 2). Most of the decline will occur in the highly competitive computer equipment industry, where employment is projected to fall from 363,400 in 1993 to 263,000 in 2005 (moderate assumptions). Production workers in the industry generally are in the middle pay range for manufacturing, with hourly earnings in 1993 averaging $12.73 and ranging from $10.46 for producers of blowers and fans to $16.74 for turbines and turbine generator sets.

TABLE 1

UNITED STATES: COMPONENT INDUSTRIES OF INDUSTRIAL AND COMMERCIAL EQUIPMENT (SIC 35), 1992

(Monetary values in millions of U.S. dollars)

INDUSTRY	SIC	ESTABLISH-MENTS	SHIPMENTS VALUE	SHIPMENTS PERCENT BY 4 LARGEST COMPANIES	VALUE ADDED BY MANUFACTURE	NEW CAPITAL EXPENDI-TURES	EMPLOY-MENT[1]	PAYROLL
INDUSTRIAL AND COMMERCIAL EQUIPMENT	35	53,956	$258,661.4	....	$132,922.7	$8,056.8	1,738,900	$57,230.9
Engines and turbines	351	370	17,549.3	....	7,738.1	756.5	82,600	3,135.4
Turbines and turbine generator sets	3511	79	5,842.6	79	2,952.2	312.0	27,100	1,106.5
Internal combustion engines, n.e.c.	3519	291	11,706.7	56	4,785.8	444.5	55,500	2,029.0
Farm and garden machinery and equipment	352	1,774	14,784.1	....	7,318.1	321.2	86,400	2,354.1
Farm machinery and equipment	3523	1,633	9,620.1	47	5,166.5	196.2	61,500	1,785.7
Lawn and garden equipment	3524	141	5,164.1	62	2,151.6	125.0	24,900	568.4
Construction and related machinery	353	3,341	27,193.4	....	12,488.7	677.0	176,200	5,663.5
Construction machinery and equipment	3531	945	13,138.5	42	5,683.2	394.5	74,600	2,457.5
Mining machinery and equipment	3532	295	1,547.5	30	728.8	33.0	12,600	394.0
Oil and gas field machinery and equipment	3533	539	3,921.1	37	2,105.3	104.6	26,300	877.4
Elevators and moving stairways	3534	178	971.7	57	384.2	20.2	7,700	232.6
Conveyors and conveying equipment	3535	751	3,926.7	14	2,041.2	55.4	30,400	994.6
Hoists, cranes, and monorails	3536	181	913.4	29	490.6	11.6	7,000	206.1
Industrial trucks, tractors, trailers, stackers	3537	452	2,774.4	40	1,055.3	57.7	17,600	501.1
Metalworking machinery and equipment	354	11,506	26,473.5	....	16,541.7	826.9	254,900	8,571.3
Machine tools, metal cutting types	3541	426	3,618.2	35	1,877.9	82.8	27,400	996.6
Machine tools, metal forming types	3542	219	1,484.2	21	745.5	40.7	12,500	424.9
Industrial patterns	3543	710	538.0	10	415.6	15.0	7,900	258.1
Special dies, tools, jigs, and fixtures	3544	7,337	9,265.1	3	6,616.8	369.4	110,800	3,883.3
Machine tool accessories	3545	1,862	3,844.4	17	2,689.1	143.5	43,300	1,263.1
Power-driven handtools	3546	226	2,872.5	50	1,506.8	72.3	16,100	440.6
Rolling mill machinery and equipment	3547	87	476.6	42	250.2	9.7	4,000	148.5
Electric and gas welding and soldering equipment	3548	239	2,737.6	43	1,485.7	65.3	19,600	658.8
Metalworking machinery, n.e.c.	3549	400	1,636.9	18	954.2	28.1	13,400	497.5
Special industry machinery, except metalworking	355	4,739	21,522.4	....	11,666.7	587.2	162,000	5,515.3
Textile machinery	3552	509	1,571.2	21	912.9	39.5	15,000	426.5
Woodworking machinery	3553	291	896.2	32	461.1	19.5	7,200	206.7
Paper industries machinery	3554	333	2,524.3	27	1,273.8	65.4	18,200	651.8
Printing trades machinery and equipment	3555	510	2,635.4	27	1,295.2	62.7	19,200	672.2
Food products machinery	3556	522	2,416.5	19	1,392.7	46.8	18,900	611.6
Special industry machinery, n.e.c.	3559	2,574	11,478.8	13	6,331.1	353.3	83,300	2,946.5
General industrial machinery and equipment	356	4,132	31,442.8	....	17,817.4	983.1	244,000	7,742.0
Pumps and pumping equipment	3561	430	5,300.7	24	2,757.3	156.5	37,200	1,234.3
Ball and roller bearings	3562	184	4,289.5	51	2,548.0	206.5	35,000	1,092.5
Air and gas compressors	3563	259	4,176.8	41	2,073.0	138.3	23,500	778.7
Blowers, fans, and air purification equipment	3564	590	3,016.0	14	1,660.4	60.7	26,100	727.7
Packaging machinery	3565	632	3,149.8	16	1,928.9	70.6	26,400	902.2
Speed changers, drives, and gears	3566	288	1,827.3	28	1,162.9	69.9	15,700	496.8
Industrial process furnaces and ovens	3567	409	1,757.7	19	982.1	27.6	17,000	529.4
Mechanical power transmission equipment, n.e.c.	3568	311	2,401.6	31	1,486.7	72.3	21,700	675.6
General industrial machinery, n.e.c.	3569	1,029	5,523.5	15	3,218.0	180.7	41,400	1,304.9
Computer and office equipment	357	2,227	66,709.1	....	29,228.5	2,277.9	250,500	10,142.8
Electronic computers	3571	834	38,202.3	45	16,128.7	1,242.6	110,600	4,849.0
Computer storage devices	3572	179	9,544.3	55	4,658.8	455.6	41,300	1,808.3
Computer terminals	3575	190	2,070.7	49	800.2	44.4	9,300	344.1
Computer peripheral equipment, n.e.c.	3577	773	12,152.0	44	5,039.2	394.7	59,300	2,173.0
Calculating and accounting equipment	3578	94	1,177.0	62	756.9	25.2	6,200	187.2
Office machines, n.e.c.	3579	157	3,562.8	45	1,844.8	115.4	23,800	781.1

TABLE 1 (CONTINUED)

UNITED STATES: COMPONENT INDUSTRIES OF INDUSTRIAL AND COMMERCIAL EQUIPMENT (SIC 35), 1992

(Monetary values in millions of U.S. dollars)

INDUSTRY	SIC	ESTABLISH-MENTS	SHIPMENTS		VALUE ADDED BY MANUFACTURE	NEW CAPITAL EXPENDI-TURES	EMPLOY-MENT[1]	PAYROLL
			VALUE	PERCENT BY 4 LARGEST COMPANIES				
Refrigeration and service industry machinery	358	2,306	$27,544.1	....	$13,596.8	$721.1	178,700	$5,263.5
Automatic vending machines	3581	108	845.1	52	396.4	13.7	7,500	185.2
Commercial laundry equipment	3582	78	630.1	41	308.7	10.9	5,100	136.6
Refrigeration and heating equipment	3585	918	19,739.0	35	9,449.5	557.0	120,700	3,593.8
Measuring and dispensing pumps	3586	78	899.6	51	423.6	27.2	6,500	196.9
Service industry machinery, n.e.c.	3589	1,124	5,430.3	14	3,018.6	112.3	38,900	1,151.0
Industrial and commercial machinery and equipment	359	23,561	25,442.7	....	16,526.7	905.9	303,700	8,842.9
Carburetors, pistons, piston rings, and valves	3592	137	2,101.2	50	1,121.6	75.9	18,100	581.4
Fluid power cylinders and actuators	3593	346	2,114.7	40	1,274.6	82.4	19,000	646.3
Fluid power pumps and motors	3594	177	1,488.1	48	910.4	47.2	12,200	422.0
Scales and balances, except laboratory	3596	128	621.2	51	338.4	15.3	5,500	153.7
Industrial machinery, n.e.c.	3599	22,773	19,117.4	1	12,881.8	685.2	248,900	7,039.5

1. Employment numbers from the economic censuses differ in definition and classification from the Bureau of Labor Statistics estimates in Table 2. Year-to-year comparisons between Table 1 and Table 2 are not appropriate.

Source: U.S. Bureau of the Census, 1992 Census of Manufactures.

TABLE 2

U.S. EMPLOYMENT AND EARNINGS: INDUSTRIAL MACHINERY AND EQUIPMENT

| INDUSTRY | SIC | 1993 | | | 2005 |
| | | EMPLOYMENT[1] | | AVERAGE HOURLY EARNINGS (U.S. DOLLARS)[2] | PROJECTED EMPLOYMENT[3] |
		NUMBER OF PERSONS	PERCENT OF INDUSTRY TOTAL		
INDUSTRIAL MACHINERY AND EQUIPMENT	35	1,930,600	100.0	$12.73	1,768,900
Engines and turbines	351	87,600	4.5	16.11	70,400
Turbines and turbine generator sets	3511	28,400	1.5	16.74	....
Internal combustion engines, n.e.c.	3519	59,200	3.1	15.84	....
Farm and garden machinery	352	98,400	5.1	12.07	87,000
Farm machinery and equipment	3523	73,000	3.8	13.04	....
Construction and related machinery	353	209,000	10.8	12.94	188,400
Construction machinery	3531	77,700	4.0	14.47	....
Mining machinery	3532	15,300	0.8	13.09	....
Oil and gas field machinery	3533	37,900	2.0	11.82	....
Conveyors and conveying equipment	3535	35,200	1.8	11.86	....
Industrial trucks and tractors	3537	26,000	1.3	11.22	....
Metalworking machinery	354	308,700	16.0	13.34	290,900
Machine tools, metal cutting types	3541	36,700	1.9	13.58	....
Machine tools, metal forming types	3542	15,500	0.8	13.50	....
Special dies, tools, jigs, and fixtures	3544	144,800	7.5	13.93	....
Machine tool accessories	3545	48,400	2.5	11.75	....
Power driven handtools	3546	23,900	1.2	10.98	....
Special industry machinery	355	149,100	7.7	13.15	150,000
Textile machinery	3552	15,500	0.8	11.27	....
Printing trades machinery	3555	21,400	1.1	14.85	....
Food products machinery	3556	23,000	1.2	12.85	....
General industrial machinery	356	236,400	12.2	12.45	235,000
Pumps and pumping equipment	3561	30,800	1.6	13.30	....
Ball and roller bearings	3562	37,300	1.9	13.59	....
Air and gas compressors	3563	25,000	1.3	12.51	....
Blowers and fans	3564	32,000	1.7	10.46	....
Speed changers, drives, and gears	3566	15,400	0.8	13.33	....
Power transmission equipment, n.e.c.	3568	19,100	1.0	12.33	....
Computer and office equipment	357	363,400	18.8	12.54	263,000
Electronic computers	3571	216,100	11.2	13.58	....
Computer terminals, calculators, office machinery	3575,8,9	54,100	2.8	12.50	....
Refrigeration and service industry machinery	358	177,000	9.2	11.51	192,100
Refrigeration and heating equipment	3585	120,400	6.2	11.67	....
Miscellaneous industrial and commercial machinery	359	300,900	15.6	12.17	292,000
Carburetors, pistons, rings, valves	3592	20,500	1.1	13.28	....
Scales, balances, and industrial machinery	3596,9	238,000	12.3	11.85	....

1. Total payroll employment. Employment data from the economic censuses, shown in Table 1, differ in definition and classification from the Bureau of Labor Statistics estimates in this table. Year-to-year comparisons between Table 1 and Table 2 are not appropriate.

2. Earnings of production workers, including overtime.

3. Number of persons, moderate projection by the U.S. Bureau of Labor Statistics.

Source: Bureau of Labor Statistics.

FIGURE 1

U.S. EMPLOYMENT IN INDUSTRIAL AND COMMERCIAL MACHINERY

Percent distribution by region, 1995

Employment in the industrial and commercial machinery industry is highest in the Great Lakes region, which had about 30 percent of the total in 1995. The Southeast was next with 18 percent of the total, followed by the Pacific and Mid-Atlantic regions with 12 percent each.

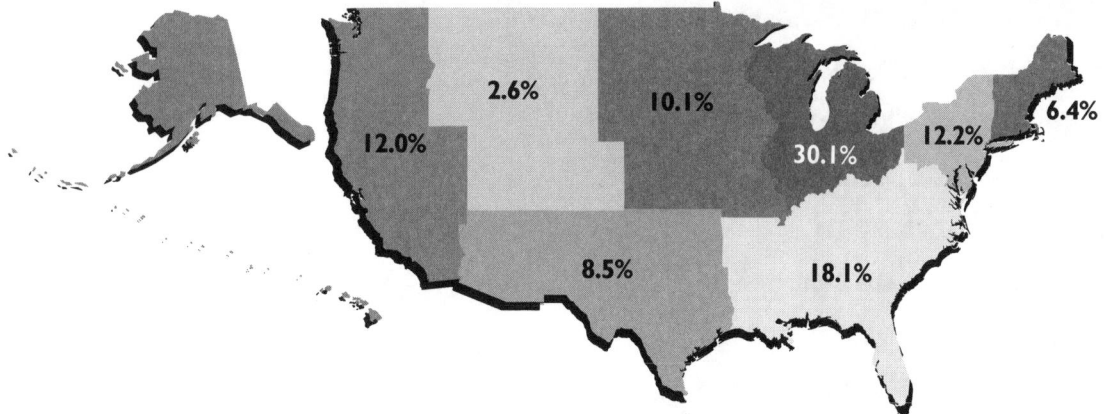

Source: U.S. Department of Commerce, Bureau of Economic Analysis.

What's New. China is the fastest growing computer market in the world, according to the Department of Commerce's International Trade Administration. Chinese demand for computer hardware, software, networking equipment, and information services recently has risen by more than 54 percent annually, from $848 million in 1990 to $7.4 billion in 1995. Forecasts by the Chinese Ministry of Electronics Industry predict that the market will exceed $24 billion by the year 2000. Sales of personal computers in China topped $2 billion in 1995 and $3.4 billion in 1996. American brands with Pentiums are hot sellers in the market, which includes more individual consumers in addition to the business and government sectors.

The Electronic Industries Association (EIA) reports continued record-breaking growth in U.S. factory sales of computers and peripherals, which rose 6 percent in the first half of 1997 to $42.2 billion. This follows a gain of 13 percent in calendar year 1996 to $84.3 billion.

The Information Technology Agreement, signed in December 1996 by the United States and 27 other countries, calls for elimination of tariffs on more than 200 information technology products, including computers and peripherals, by the year 2000. The agreement will affect about $500 billion of annual trade in information technology among participating countries and save $5 billion in tariffs on U.S. exports each year, according to the American Electronics Association's online publication *Impact*.

The Association for Manufacturing Technology reports that orders for machine tools have risen in each of the past four years, with especially strong gains of 33 and 42 percent, respectively, in 1993 and 1994. Increasingly, these products are moving into the export market, which has grown in 11 of the last 13 years and now accounts for about 30 percent of machine-tool sales. Production areas in which the United States excels include metrology, composite tape-laying machines, spar and skin mills for aircraft components, assembly systems, grinding machines, spiral bevel and parallel axis gear-making machinery, and waterjet cutting and laser processing machines. U.S. manufacturers also are leaders in the application of linear drive motors that provide high acceleration, which allows for short, quick moves and reduced part processing time.

FIGURE 2

U.S. EMPLOYMENT AND SHIPMENTS, INDUSTRIAL AND COMMERCIAL MACHINERY

Total payroll employment and manufacturers' inflation-adjusted shipments

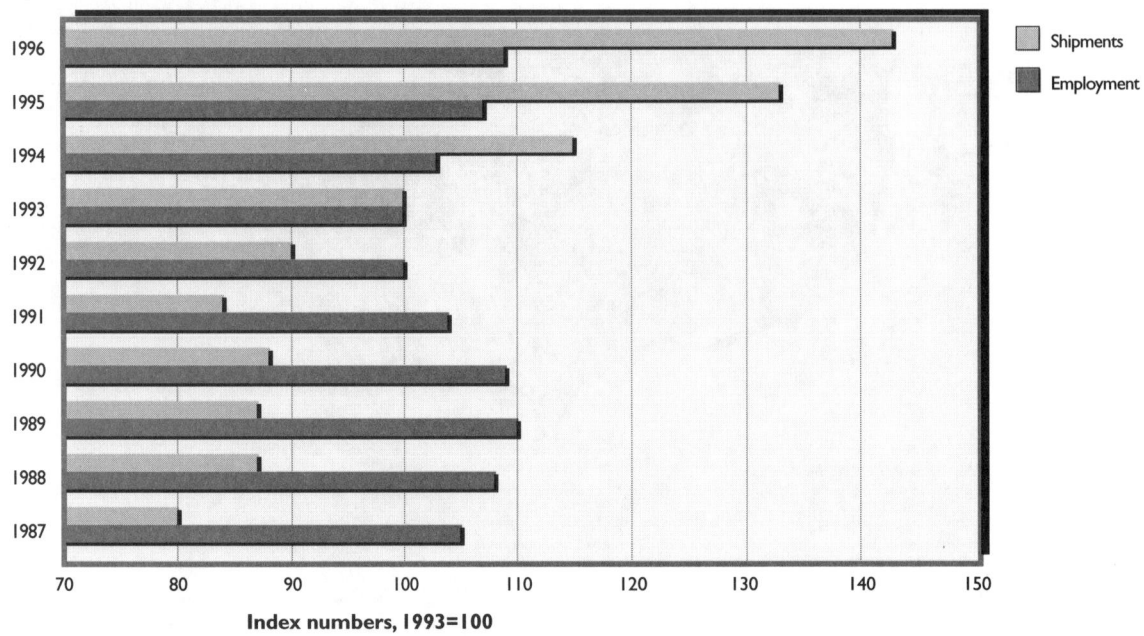

Index numbers, 1993=100

Source: U.S. Bureau of Labor Statistics, U.S. Department of Commerce, and estimates by the editors.

FIGURE 2A

U.S. EMPLOYMENT AND SHIPMENTS, COMPUTERS AND OFFICE EQUIPMENT

Total payroll employment and manufacturers' inflation-adjusted shipments

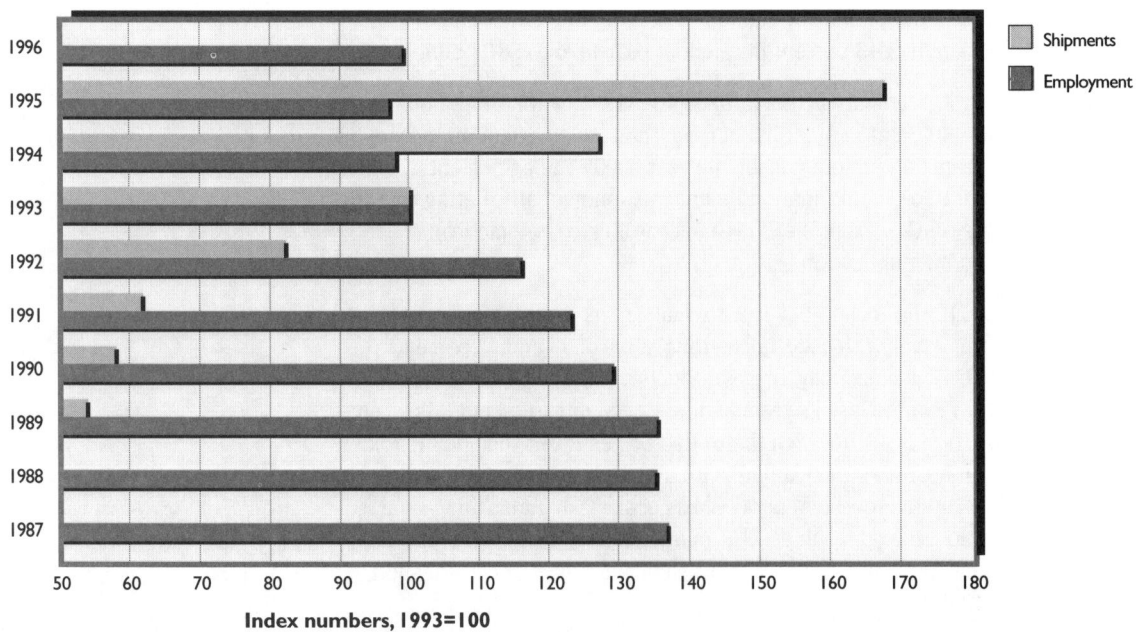

Index numbers, 1993=100

Source: U.S. Bureau of Labor Statistics, U.S. Department of Commerce, and estimates by the editors. Shipments data for 1987, 1988, and 1996 are not available.

Output. While its employment has exceeded the 1987 level only in the last two years, shipments by the machinery and computer equipment industry have increased in each of the past 10 years, except for the recession year of 1991 (Figure 2). The divergent trends are even more striking for the computer and office equipment industry, where employment has fallen dramatically since 1989 while industry shipments have expanded sharply, especially since 1993 (Figure 2A).

Industry shipments of machinery and computer equipment rose at an annual rate of 6.33 percent between 1987 and 1996 to a record $378.2 billion in 1996 (Table 3). This compares with $217.7 billion in 1987. Shipments of computer and office equipment alone rose at an annual rate of 5.84 percent during the 10-year period to $101.1 billion in 1996. Shipments slumped between 1988 and 1991 but recovered strongly in the following five years as U.S. industries and consumers went on a technology spending spree.

Investment. New capital expenditures by the industrial and commercial machinery and computer equipment industry totaled almost $10 billion in 1995, or 43 percent more than the $7 billion spent in 1987 (Table 3). Research and development (R&D) spending, on the other hand, declined 24 percent between 1987 and 1994 (latest year for which data are available) to $8.0 billion. New capital expenditures by the computer and office equipment industry totaled around $2.1 billion in 1995, slightly less than in 1987. R&D spending by the industry in 1994 was $4.1 billion, or only half the $8.2 billion for 1987.

Prices. Price gains in the machinery and computer equipment industry have amounted to only 1.62 percent a year since 1987, one of the slowest rates in the manufacturing sector (Table 3). Computer prices have actually fallen during the past decade as a result of intense competition within the industry, rapid sales growth, and declining costs associated with mass production of high-tech equipment.

TABLE 3

U.S. OUTPUT, INVESTMENT, AND PRICES: INDUSTRIAL AND COMMERCIAL MACHINERY AND COMPUTER EQUIPMENT

(Millions of U.S. dollars, except as noted)

	1987	1988	1989	1990	1991	1992	1993	1994	1995	1996	GROWTH RATE 1987-1996[1]
TOTAL INDUSTRIAL AND COMMERCIAL MACHINERY AND OFFICE EQUIPMENT											
VALUE OF SHIPMENTS:											
BY INDUSTRY:											
Current dollars	217,656	244,365	256,214	259,366	247,509	258,661	278,063	313,047	351,113	378,236	6.33
Constant 1992 dollars	228,390	248,540	250,438	251,164	241,090	258,661	286,926	330,380	382,339	411,470	6.76
BY PRODUCT:											
Current dollars	199,791	221,689	235,818	237,175	225,986	238,091	258,366	290,464	329,312	354,751	6.59
Constant 1992 dollars	210,240	226,121	231,163	230,563	220,579	238,091	266,136	305,403	359,194	386,562	7.00
OTHER OUTPUT MEASURES:											
Industrial production, 1993=100	78.3	88.4	93.7	91.1	86.8	91.0	100.0	114.0	128.7	142.3	6.86
Gross domestic product:											
Current dollars	94,595	106,379	113,826	114,831	105,739	108,640	111,871	119,341	.....	.....	.....
Percent of total GDP	2.0	2.1	2.1	2.0	1.8	1.7	1.7	1.7	.....	.....	.....
Rank in manufacturing	2	2	1	1	2	3	3	4	.....	.....	.....
Chained (1992) dollars	91,340	106,174	112,367	113,363	103,653	108,640	115,781	127,573	.....	.....	.....
INVESTMENT-RELATED MEASURES:											
Capacity utilization, percent	72.1	79.6	83.4	79.4	74.3	75.6	79.6	85.8	89.8	89.9	.....
New capital expenditures	6,955	6,893	8,148	8,395	7,468	8,057	7,909	9,196	9,998	.....	.....
Research and development spending	10,577	11,929	13,342	13,575	13,720	13,903	8,295	8,011	.....	.....	.....
Producer prices, 1993=100[2]	88.3	91.1	94.8	97.5	99.6	99.9	100.0	100.6	101.9	102.0	1.62
COMPUTER AND OFFICE EQUIPMENT											
VALUE OF SHIPMENTS:											
BY INDUSTRY:											
Current dollars	60,627	68,056	66,249	65,309	60,403	66,709	69,249	78,230	90,249	101,083	5.84
Constant 1992 dollars	.....	.....	43,880	47,603	50,631	66,709	81,803	103,653	136,371	.....	.....
BY PRODUCT:											
Current dollars	53,262	57,237	59,111	56,484	52,694	59,007	62,427	70,107	85,534	95,802	6.74
Constant 1992 dollars	.....	.....	38,919	40,955	44,162	59,007	73,672	92,672	129,360	.....	.....
OTHER OUTPUT MEASURES:											
Industrial production, 1993=100	51.2	61.4	68.3	67.0	67.7	82.3	100.0	125.2	175.8	244.4	18.97
INVESTMENT-RELATED MEASURES:											
Capacity utilization, percent	74.6	79.5	81.2	73.7	68.8	74.6	77.2	79.5	88.2	91.9	.....
New capital expenditures	2,185	2,386	2,349	2,249	1,944	2,278	2,189	2,059	2,127	.....	.....
Research and development spending	8,193	9,347	10,725	10,988	10,419	10,614	4,917	4,078	.....	.....	.....

1. Compound annual growth rate.

2. Prices received by domestic producers.

Sources: Shipments and new capital expenditures: U.S. Department of Commerce for 1987-1995, editor's estimates for constant dollar data for 1987-88 and all shipments data for 1996; Industrial production and capacity utilization: Federal Reserve Board of Governors; GDP: Bureau of Economic Analysis; Research and development spending: National Science Foundation; Producer prices: Bureau of Labor Statistics.

Workforce and Employment. Employment in the machinery and computer equipment industry has shown little change in the past 10 years, totaling 2,112,000 in 1996 compared with 2,028,000 in 1987 (Table 4). The annual growth rate for the period was 0.45 percent. Production worker numbers rose by 1.02 percent a year to 1,319,000 employees, or 62.5 percent of the workforce, in 1996. Employment of women declined fractionally, and their share of the workforce was only 21.6 percent in 1996. Hourly earnings averaged $13.59 in 1996, for an annual growth rate of 2.7 percent in current dollars but a loss of 87 cents in inflation-adjusted dollars. The average workweek was 43.1 hours.

Employment in the computer and office equipment industry has declined at an annual rate of 2.76 percent since 1987, to 359,000 employees in 1996 (Table 4). Production worker numbers declined by 2.32 percent a year and accounted for only 34.9 percent of the workforce in 1996. Women employees, off by 2.49 percent a year, accounted for 36.5 percent of the workforce. Average hourly earnings in the industry totaled $13.86 in 1996, for a yearly growth rate of 3.38 percent in current dollars but a loss of 0.18 percent in inflation-adjusted dollars. The average workweek in 1996 was 42.2 hours.

TABLE 4

U.S. EMPLOYMENT, HOURS, AND EARNINGS: INDUSTRIAL AND COMMERCIAL MACHINERY AND COMPUTER EQUIPMENT

(Monetary values in U.S. dollars)

	1987	1988	1989	1990	1991	1992	1993	1994	1995	1996	CHANGE[1]
TOTAL INDUSTRIAL AND COMMERCIAL MACHINERY AND COMPUTER EQUIPMENT											
NUMBER OF EMPLOYEES, IN THOUSANDS:											
Total	2,028	2,089	2,125	2,095	2,000	1,929	1,931	1,990	2,067	2,112	0.45
Production workers	1,203	1,256	1,282	1,260	1,193	1,152	1,170	1,233	1,295	1,319	1.02
Percent of total	59.3	60.1	60.3	60.1	59.7	59.7	60.6	62.0	62.7	62.5	.....
Women	454	458	465	454	435	421	420	432	445	456	0.05
Percent of total	22.4	21.9	21.9	21.7	21.8	21.8	21.7	21.7	21.5	21.6	.....
HOURS AND EARNINGS OF PRODUCTION WORKERS:											
Average hourly earnings, U.S. dollars[2]											
Current dollars	10.73	11.08	11.40	11.77	12.15	12.41	12.73	13.00	13.24	13.59	2.66
1992 dollars[3]	13.18	13.08	12.85	12.62	12.50	12.41	12.38	12.33	12.21	12.19	-0.87
Average weekly hours	42.2	42.7	42.4	41.9	41.7	42.2	43.0	43.7	43.4	43.1	0.35
Average weekly earnings, current U.S. dollars	452.81	473.12	483.36	493.16	506.66	523.7	547.39	568.10	574.62	585.73	2.90
COMPUTERS AND OFFICE EQUIPMENT											
NUMBER OF EMPLOYEES, IN THOUSANDS:											
Total	461	459	459	438	415	391	363	354	351	359	-2.76
Production workers	155	148	145	137	135	128	121	123	122	125	-2.32
Percent of total	33.5	32.2	31.6	31.3	32.6	32.8	33.2	34.6	34.6	34.9	.....
Women	164	162	161	150	141	135	130	129	128	131	-2.49
Percent of total	35.6	35.3	35.0	34.2	33.9	34.5	35.8	36.3	36.4	36.5	.....
HOURS AND EARNINGS OF PRODUCTION WORKERS:											
Average hourly earnings, U.S. dollars[2]											
Current dollars	10.28	10.65	10.99	11.51	12.13	12.33	12.54	13.08	13.59	13.86	3.38
1992 dollars[3]	12.63	12.57	12.39	12.34	12.48	12.33	12.20	12.41	12.54	12.43	-0.18
Average weekly hours	42.6	41.7	42.3	42.0	41.5	42.0	41.9	42.7	43.0	42.2	-0.1
Average weekly earnings, current U.S. dollars	437.93	444.11	464.88	483.42	503.40	517.86	525.43	558.52	584.37	584.89	3.27

1. Compound annual growth rate, 1987-1996.

2. Including overtime.

3. Converted to 1992 dollars using Consumer Price Index for Urban Wage Earners and Clerical Workers.

Source: Bureau of Labor Statistics.

FIGURE 3

U.S. OCCUPATIONAL INJURY AND ILLNESS RATES: INDUSTRIAL AND COMMERCIAL MACHINERY AND COMPUTER EQUIPMENT, 1995

Incidence of nonfatal injuries and illnesses per 100 full-time workers

Nonfatal occupational illnesses and injuries in the machinery and computer equipment industry averaged 11.2 cases per 100 workers in 1995, just below the 11.6 cases for all manufacturing.

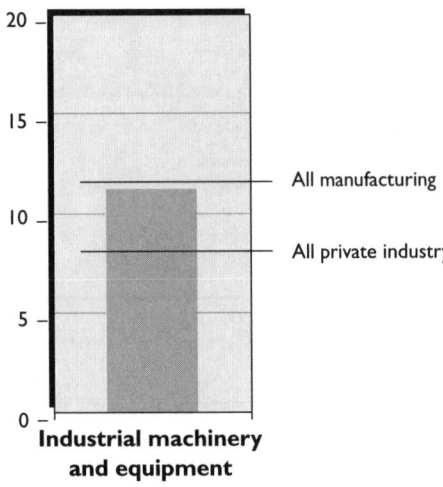

Source: U.S. Bureau of Labor Statistics.

FIGURE 4

U.S. CORPORATE INCOME AND WORKER EARNINGS: INDUSTRIAL AND COMMERCIAL MACHINERY AND COMPUTER EQUIPMENT

Corporate operating income and aggregate production worker earnings

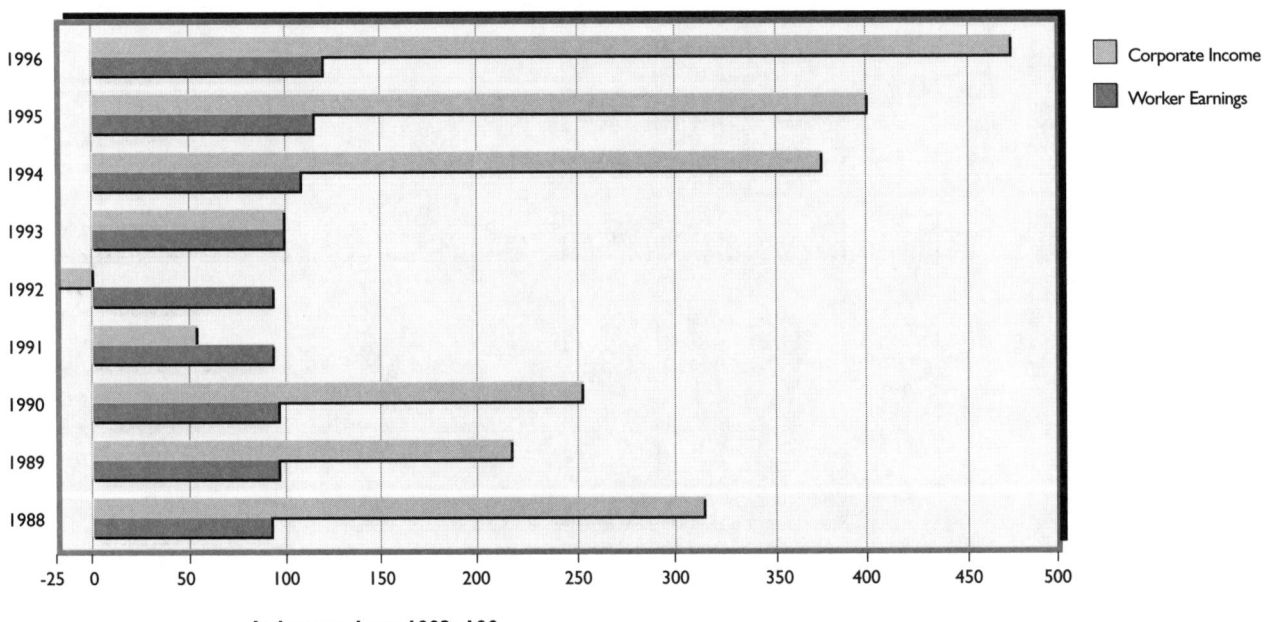

Source: U.S. Bureau of Labor Statistics, U.S. Bureau of the Census, and estimates by the editors.

TABLE 5

U.S. EMPLOYMENT PROJECTIONS BY MAJOR OCCUPATIONAL GROUP: INDUSTRIAL AND COMMERCIAL MACHINERY AND COMPUTER EQUIPMENT

OCCUPATION	1994		PROJECTIONS, 2005			
	NUMBER OF EMPLOYEES	PERCENT OF INDUSTRY TOTAL	NUMBER OF EMPLOYEES			PERCENT OF INDUSTRY TOTAL, MODERATE PROJECTIONS
			LOW	MODERATE	HIGH	
INDUSTRIAL AND COMMERCIAL MACHINERY AND COMPUTER EQUIPMENT, TOTAL						
Total, all occupations	1,984,800	100.0	1,687,300	1,768,900	1,904,300	100.0
Executive, administrative, and managerial	239,182	12.1	201,713	212,375	229,422	12.0
Professional specialties	171,395	8.6	163,333	173,387	188,062	9.8
Technicians and related support	97,423	4.9	69,531	73,455	79,359	4.2
Marketing and sales	69,261	3.5	58,519	61,272	65,752	3.5
Administrative support including clerical	242,429	12.2	180,594	189,590	204,270	10.7
Service	21,680	1.1	15,711	16,441	17,671	0.9
Agriculture, forestry, and fisheries occupations	192	0.0	168	174	183	0.0
Precision production, craft, and repair	508,931	25.6	436,039	455,059	488,331	25.7
Operators, fabricators, assemblers	634,308	32.0	561,694	587,146	631,250	33.2
COMPUTER AND OFFICE EQUIPMENT						
Total, all occupations	351,000	100.0	239,600	263,000	292,900	100.0
Executive, administrative, and managerial	68,542	19.5	46,474	51,013	56,813	19.4
Professional specialties	82,077	23.4	70,707	77,613	86,436	29.5
Technicians and related support	40,010	11.4	23,625	25,932	28,881	9.9
Marketing and sales	16,166	4.6	10,348	11,358	12,650	4.3
Administrative support including clerical	56,852	16.2	32,633	35,820	39,892	13.6
Service	3,078	0.9	1,753	1,924	2,143	0.7
Agriculture, forestry, and fisheries occupations	......	......	......	......	......	......
Precision production, craft, and repair	48,719	13.9	27,645	30,345	33,795	11.5
Operators, fabricators, assemblers	35,543	10.1	26,406	28,985	32,281	11.0

Source: Bureau of Labor Statistics, November 1995.

Employment in the machinery and computer equipment industry is projected to decline to 1,768,900 in 2005, compared with 1,984,800 in 1994 (moderate assumptions). Declines are anticipated for all but one occupational area in the machinery and computer equipment industry. Bucking the trend, professional specialties are expected to gain about 2,000 employees. The computer and office equipment industry is projected to have 25 percent fewer employees in 2005 than the 351,000 of 1994 (moderate assumptions). All occupational areas are likely to show declines.

Finance. While growth in production worker earnings for the industry was remarkably stable between 1988 and 1996, corporate income showed wild swings, losing ground in all but one of the first five years and then heading sharply higher (Figure 4). Industry income from operations soared to a record $19.5 billion in 1996, after having posted a $1.06-billion deficit just four years earlier (Table 6). After-tax income rose by 6.45 percent a year to $22.7 billion in 1996, in contrast to successive deficits totaling $18.7 billion in 1991-1993. After-tax income amounted to 5.58 percent of sales in 1996 and 14.67 percent of stockholders' equity. Inventories in 1996 were valued at $51.6 billion, down slightly from 1995 but the second highest level for the nine-year period. Debt, at 19.4 percent of assets, was down somewhat from previous years.

TABLE 6

U.S. CORPORATE INCOME AND ASSETS: INDUSTRIAL AND COMMERCIAL MACHINERY AND COMPUTER EQUIPMENT

(Monetary values in millions of U.S. dollars)

INCOME AND EXPENSES	1988	1989	1990	1991	1992	1993	1994	1995	1996	CHANGE OR AVERAGE[1]
Sales and receipts	234,942	255,125	255,453	249,480	266,357	295,075	334,965	376,710	406,735	7.10
Depreciation and amortization	(9,616)	(10,524)	(11,000)	(12,078)	(14,805)	(13,035)	(12,106)	(12,239)	(12,621)	3.46
Other operating costs	(212,267)	(235,667)	(233,996)	(235,284)	(252,609)	(278,018)	(307,292)	(348,263)	(374,616)	7.36
Income from operations	13,057	8,934	10,457	2,119	(1,057)	4,022	15,567	16,208	19,500	5.14
Nonoperating income (expenditures)	5,615	3,639	4,386	(4,336)	(11,581)	(9,566)	5,593	6,946	11,875	....
Income before taxes	18,675	17,286	14,844	(2,218)	(12,637)	(5,543)	21,160	23,154	31,375	6.70
Income after taxes	13,778	9,694	11,153	(2,737)	(9,228)	(6,725)	15,766	16,294	22,711	6.45
Cash dividends	5,123	5,648	5,236	5,383	5,462	4,421	4,771	4,490	4,811	-0.78
Income retained in business	8,655	4,048	5,916	(8,120)	(14,689)	(11,147)	10,995	11,803	17,902	9.51
Direct credits (charges)	(2,534)	(3,634)	637	(1,776)	(3,753)	(973)	1,675	(5,541)	(6,889)	....
Ending retained earnings	79,686	81,485	85,914	76,000	57,320	47,518	55,121	61,372	75,472	-0.68
ASSETS, END OF YEAR:										
Total	233,080	260,571	267,534	268,912	271,780	277,967	304,263	343,605	353,093	5.33
Accounts receivable	43,252	44,084	44,543	43,916	46,575	47,919	56,347	63,790	64,731	5.17
Inventories	42,014	44,407	42,619	41,340	41,292	43,411	46,427	53,796	51,584	2.60
Net property, plant and equipment	53,720	61,939	63,697	66,125	63,069	61,482	62,696	66,375	67,107	2.82
RATIOS, PERCENT:										
INCOME TO SALES:										
Before tax	7.95	6.78	5.81	-0.89	-4.74	-1.88	6.32	6.15	7.71	3.69
After tax	5.86	3.80	4.37	-1.10	-3.46	-2.28	4.71	4.33	5.58	2.42
INCOME TO STOCKHOLDERS' EQUITY:										
Before tax	15.59	13.04	10.66	-1.68	-10.95	-4.99	16.69	16.67	20.27	8.36
After tax	11.50	7.31	8.01	-2.08	-8.00	-6.05	12.43	11.73	14.67	5.50
INCOME TO TOTAL ASSETS:										
Before tax	8.01	6.63	5.55	-0.82	-4.65	-1.99	6.95	6.74	8.89	3.92
After tax	5.91	3.72	4.17	-1.02	-3.40	-2.42	5.18	4.74	6.43	2.59
AS A PERCENT OF TOTAL ASSETS:										
Property, plant and equipment	23.05	23.77	23.81	24.59	23.21	22.12	20.61	19.32	19.01	22.16
Short-term debt	3.34	2.77	3.40	2.79	4.64	3.86	3.90	4.56	4.08	3.71
Long-term debt	18.62	19.70	18.07	19.13	18.88	19.38	18.00	17.89	15.36	18.34
Stockholders' equity	51.41	50.86	52.07	48.98	42.45	39.97	41.67	40.43	43.84	45.74

1. For income and asset amounts, compound annual growth rate; for ratios, average of ratios for the years shown.

Source: U.S. Bureau of the Census, Quarterly Financial Report.

Notes: Parentheses ( ) indicate negative items, e.g., net expenses, charges, or losses. Net property, plant, and equipment is net of accumulated depreciation. Because the samples used to collect the data change, retained earnings at the end of a given year will not exactly equal the previous year's retained earnings plus the current year's retained income and credits.

CANADA

Table 7 gives a breakdown of Canada's machinery and office and business machine industries for 1993. That year, the combined industries had 2,037 establishments and 89,806 employees. Computers and office equipment accounted for 26.6 percent of total industry shipments that year, with computers and peripherals making up most of that share. Agricultural machinery and equipment accounted for 8 percent of the total. Within the broad "other machinery and equipment category," construction and mining machinery accounted for 19.3 percent of industry shipments, and turbine and power transmission equipment, for 10.1 percent.

Canada's machinery and computer industries, like many U.S. industries, have achieved big gains in sales and shipments while reducing employment. Combined shipments by the machinery and computer industries rose to a record Can$17.9 billion in 1994, up 30 percent from the previous year and 70 percent from the 1987 level (Table 8). Employment fell from 99,738 people in 1987 to a low of 89,806 in 1993 before partially recovering to 95,485 in 1994. The number of establishment declined from 2,095 to 1,971 during 1987-1994. Production workers accounted for about 72 percent of the workforce in most years. The average hourly wage in 1994 was Can$15.82, compared with Can$11.78 in 1988, and the workweek averaged 40.3 hours (Table 8).

TABLE 7

CANADA: COMPONENT INDUSTRIES OF MACHINERY AND COMPUTERS (CSIC 31 AND 336), 1993

(Monetary values in Canadian dollars)

INDUSTRY NAME	CSIC	ESTABLISH-MENTS (NUMBER)	EMPLOYMENT		VALUE OF SHIPMENTS (MILLIONS)	AVERAGE HOURLY EARNINGS[1]
			NUMBER	PERCENT OF INDUSTRY TOTAL		
MACHINERY INDUSTRIES[2]	31+336	2,037	89,806	100.0	CAN$13,744.9	CAN$14.96
Agricultural implement industry	311	196	8,549	9.5	1,104.8	13.86
Commercial refrigeration equipment	312	73	2,929	3.3	342.3	13.09
Other machinery and equipment	319	1586	62,901	70.0	8,642.5	15.59
Compressors, pumps, and industrial fans	3191	130	5,932	6.6	801.6	16.22
Constuction and mining machinery	3192	521	19,845	22.1	2,647.2	15.17
Sawmill and woodworking machinery	3193	54	2,193	2.4	263.2	17.87
Turbine and power transmission equipment	3194	131	8,559	9.5	1,391.2	17.20
Other machinery and equipment, n.e.c.	3199	750	27,072	30.1	3,539.4	15.13
Computers and office equipment	336	182	15,427	17.2	3,655.3	12.96
Electronic computers and peripherals	3361	142	10,983	12.2	3,241.7	12.74
Electronic business machines	3362	11	3,037	3.4	309.8	15.67
Other office and business machines	3369	29	1,407	1.6	103.8	12.18

1. Including overtime.

2. Figures except hourly earnings include CSIC 3360, computers and office equipment, for easier comparison to the U.S. industry.

Source: Adapted from Statistics Canada, *Manufacturing Industries of Canada* (Cat. No. 31-203).

Canada's computers and equipment industry also experienced large gains in shipments during a period of declining employment (Table 8). Industry shipments rose at an annual rate of 13.86 percent from 1987 to 1994, when they reached $5.5 billion or 148 percent more than in 1987 and 50 percent more than in 1993. Yet employment declined at an annual rate of 1.3 percent from 1987 to 1994. The 1994 total of 15,852 employees was only 3 percent above 1993 employment and the third lowest level in the eight-year period, despite the huge jump in 1994 shipments. Production workers' share of the workforce rose to 56.6 percent in 1994 from 49.6 percent in 1988 as a result of a slower rate of decline (0.56 percent) than in total employment. Hourly earnings in the computer industry averaged Can$13.69 in 1994, compared with Can$10.32 in 1988, a 4.82 rate of gain in current dollars. The average workweek, at 41.2 hours, was about the same as in 1988.

TABLE 8

CANADIAN EMPLOYMENT AND SHIPMENTS: MACHINERY AND COMPUTER INDUSTRIES, 1987-1994

(Monetary values in Canadian dollars)

	1987	1988	1989	1990	1991	1992	1993	1994	CHANGE[1]
TOTAL MACHINERY AND COMPUTERS[2]									
All employees	99,738	108,769	112,706	101,496	92,756	90,070	89,806	95,485	-0.62
Establishments	2,095	2,429	2,405	2,414	2,199	2,124	2,037	1,971	-0.87
Employees per establishment	48	45	47	42	42	42	44	48	0.25
Production workers per establishment	.....	28	29	26	26	30	32	35	3.93
PRODUCTION WORKERS:									
Total	.....	78,273	81,245	72,259	66,094	63,726	64,833	68,522	-2.19
Percent of all employees	.....	72.0	72.1	71.2	71.3	70.8	72.2	71.8	.....
Male	.....	67,026	69,287	62,417	56,504	.....	.....	.....	.....
Female	.....	11,247	11,958	9,842	9,590	.....	.....	.....	.....
Percent of all production workers	.....	16.8	17.3	15.8	17.0	.....	.....	.....	.....
Average hourly earnings	.....	11.78	12.28	13.79	14.28	14.60	14.95	15.82	5.04
Average weekly earnings	.....	474.97	496.60	550.63	574.34	583.42	602.49	636.91	5.01
Average weekly hours	.....	40.3	40.4	39.9	40.2	40.0	40.3	40.3	-0.02
Shipments (millions)	10,491	13,083	14,135	13,604	12,201	12,109	13,745	17,871	7.91
COMPUTERS AND EQUIPMENT									
All employees	17,316	17,514	18,021	16,196	15,680	16,735	15,427	15,852	-1.25
Establishments	187	247	232	225	189	190	182	173	-1.11
Employees per establishment	93	71	78	72	83	88	85	92	-0.15
Production workers per establishment	.....	35	38	37	42	46	48	52	6.71
PRODUCTION WORKERS:									
Total	.....	8,680	8,726	8,340	7,886	8,826	8,743	8,974	0.56
Percent of all employees	.....	49.6	48.4	51.5	50.3	52.7	56.7	56.6	.....
Male	.....	5221	4933	4868	4802	.....	.....	.....	.....
Female	.....	3459	3793	3472	3084	.....	.....	.....	.....
Percent of all production workers	.....	39.9	43.5	41.6	39.1	.....	.....	.....	.....
Average hourly earnings	.....	10.32	10.92	12.06	12.94	12.75	12.96	13.69	4.82
Average weekly earnings	.....	423.74	436.80	487.34	530.67	507.83	541.99	563.34	4.86
Average weekly hours	.....	41.1	40.0	40.4	41.0	39.8	41.8	41.2	0.04
Shipments (millions)	2,216	3,071	3,140	3,208	3,297	3,353	3,655	5,496	13.86

1. Compound annual growth rate.

2. Includes computers and office equipment for easier comparison to U.S. industry.

Source: Adapted from Statistics Canada, *Manufacturing Industries of Canada* (Cat. No. 31-203).

MEXICO

Mexico's machinery industries are part of the larger metal products and machinery equipment industry. The machinery industries (shown in Table 9) may not be comparable to the U.S. industrial and commercial machinery and computer equipment industry. They include special machinery and equipment (with 30,058 employees in 1993), general machinery and equipment (67,338), and office calculator and data processing machinery (16,718). Average yearly incomes (earnings plus benefits) range from 24,661 new pesos ($7,894) for general machinery and equipment to 32,299 new pesos ($10,340) for special machinery and equipment. Employment in the machinery industry declined by 0.90 percent a year between 1988 and 1995, to 165,813 (Table 10).

TABLE 9

MEXICO: COMPONENT INDUSTRIES OF INDUSTRIAL, COMMERCIAL AND OFFICE MACHINERY (CMAP 3821, 3822, 3823), 1993

(Monetary values in 1993 Mexican New Pesos)

			ALL WORKERS									
							PAID WORKERS					
							PRODUCTION WORKERS		NONPRODUCTION EMPLOYEES		BENEFITS	UNPAID
INDUSTRY	CMAP	NUMBER OF UNITS	NUMBER	PERCENT OF INDUSTRY TOTAL	AVERAGE DAYS WORKED	REMUN-ERATION[1]	NUMBER	WAGES AND SALARIES	NUMBER	WAGES AND SALARIES	PER PAID EMPLOYEE	WORKERS, NUMBER
Machinery and equipment, special	3821	823	30,058	26	276	32,299	20,205	15,310	9,511	39,258	9,324	579
Machinery and equipment, general (incl. weaponry)	3822	5,145	67,338	59	279	24,661	45,675	12,398	16,497	32,717	6,872	5,166
Office calculator, and data proc. machinery	3823	87	16,718	15	263	28,072	11,564	11,319	5,034	41,676	7,546	120

1. Average annual remuneration including benefits.

Source: INEGI, Censos Economicos 1994.

TABLE 10

MEXICAN EMPLOYMENT: MACHINERY, 1988-1995

	1988	1989	1990	1991	1992	1993	1994	1995	CHANGE[1]
TOTAL EMPLOYMENT: Machinery	176,670	180,461	187,243	189,374	195,947	183,056	177,822	165,813	-0.90

1. Compound annual growth rate.

Source: Sistema de Cuentas Nacionales de Mexico, INEGI.

INTERNATIONAL TRADE

United States. Global U.S. trade in machinery and computer equipment has gained dramatically since 1989, but faster growth in imports than in exports led to trade deficits by 1993. Export value totaled $104.1 billion in 1996, or 68 percent above the 1990 figure. Value of imports during the same period rose 105 percent, to $112.9 billion. The United States thus had a 1996 deficit of $8.8 billion in its trade, contrasted with a 1990 surplus of $6.9 billion. (Table 11). There would have been a favorable trade balance had it not been for the growing imbalance in computer and computer equipment trade (discussed in the following paragraphs).

U.S. Department of Commerce and Bureau of the Census data for 1996 show that U.S. computer equipment trade increased once again, but at a slower rate than in 1995, and the U.S. trade deficit widened further. Exports of computers, peripherals, and parts rose 9.7 percent in 1996 to $37.6 billion, compared with an 18.5 percent gain to $34.3 billion the previous year. Peripherals and parts (up 28.3 and 10.5 percent, respectively) accounted for all of the gain while computer exports fell 8.2 percent. Computer-equipment imports rose 9.2 percent to $60.2 billion following a 22 percent gain in 1995, with computers (up 26 percent) leading the advance.

The resulting trade deficit in computers and computer equipment—the sixth in a row—was $22.6 billion, compared with $20.9 billion the year before. All of the deficit was in computer peripherals (-$20.9 billion) and parts (-$4.7 billion), while there was a $3.1 billion U.S. trade surplus in computers. Most of the deficit was in trade with Asia, as a smaller deficit with Japan was offset by larger ones with Singapore, Taiwan, Malaysia, and China.

Canada was the largest country market for U.S. computer equipment exports in 1996, taking $5 billion worth, followed by Japan ($4.9 billion) and the United Kingdom ($3.3 billion). The largest regional markets were Europe ($14.4 billion) and Asia ($11.7 billion), but the biggest gain was in shipments to Latin America, up 32 percent to $5.2 billion. Exports to the "Big Emerging Markets"—Argentina, Brazil, China, India, Mexico, Poland, South Africa, South Korea, Turkey, and Asean countries—rose 20 percent to $10.3 billion.

Canada. U.S. machinery and special equipment trade with this top market rose again in 1996, but at a considerably slower rate than in past years. U.S. exports to Canada totaled $22.4 billion in 1996, up about 5 percent from 1995 and 61 percent from 1990 (Table 11). Canadian exports to the United States totaled $10.3 billion in 1996, off slightly from the previous year but double the 1990 level. The resulting U.S. trade surplus was $12.1 billion in 1996, compared with $8.8 billion in 1990. Canadian machinery and computer equipment exports to Mexico totaled only $43.6 million in 1996, compared with $65.8 million the year before.

Mexico. U.S. exports of machinery and computer equipment to Mexico rose 22 percent in 1996, to $6.9 billion, and were up 81 percent from the 1990 level (Table 11). Mexican exports to the United States rose 37 percent over 1995's, to $5.4 billion, almost four times 1990 shipments. The U.S. trade surplus with Mexico was $1.5 billion in 1996, compared with $1.7 billion the year before. Mexican machinery and equipment exports to Canada are small but growing, totaling $81.5 million and $130.6 million in 1995 and 1996, respectively.

NAFTA. The U.S. trade surplus with Canada and Mexico totaled $13.6 billion in 1996, compared with $12.4 billion in 1993, the year before NAFTA went into effect, and $11.2 billion in 1990, the year after the Canadian-U.S. Free Trade Agreement was signed (Table 11). Canada's trade deficit with the United States and Mexico rose to $12.2 billion in 1996 from $10.7 billion the year before and $8.8 billion in 1990. Mexico's deficit was $1.4 billion in 1996, less than half the high levels during 1992-1994.

TABLE 11

INTERNATIONAL TRADE, INDUSTRIAL AND COMMERCIAL MACHINERY AND COMPUTER EQUIPMENT

(Millions of U.S. dollars)

	1989[1]	1990	1991	1992	1993	1994	1995	1996
GLOBAL TRADE, U.S.								
IMPORTS								
Value	54,122.7	55,013.7	55,710.1	62,580.0	73,376.8	89,711.0	106,390.0	112,907.5
Ratio to new supply[2]	19.8	20.0	21.0	22.4	23.7	25.3	.....	.....
Ratio to apparent consumption[3]	24.9	25.8	28.0	29.7	31.0	32.9	.....	.....
EXPORTS								
Value	56,204.3	61,954.7	65,971.4	68,977.9	72,293.0	82,132.3	95,927.2	104,064.0
Ratio to comparable domestic shipments	25.6	28.1	31.5	31.8	30.7	31.0		
TRADE BALANCE	2,081.6	6,941.0	10,261.3	6,397.9	(1,083.8)	(7,578.7)	(10,462.8)	(8,843.5)
BILATERAL TRADE: NAFTA[4]								
U.S. exports to Canada	9,988.6	13,892.7	13,726.9	14,594.4	16,038.2	19,563.6	21,295.7	22,359.9
Canadian exports to U.S.	5,211.1	5,121.4	5,354.7	5,770.5	6,812.1	8,931.9	10,616.4	10,259.5
U.S. exports to Mexico	3,078.3	3,782.9	4,510.9	5,409.6	5,209.7	6,636.3	5,629.6	6,859.5
Mexican exports to U.S.	1,505.3	1,398.4	1,456.8	1,774.0	2,019.5	3,249.3	3,931.7	5,366.3
Canadian exports to Mexico[5]	27.7	38.2	21.6	29.4	30.3	36.3	65.8	43.6
Mexican exports to Canada[5]	60.6	71.8	79.6	123.8	116.8	95.1	81.5	130.6
TRADE BALANCES WITHIN NAFTA[6]								
Canada	(4,810.4)	(8,804.9)	(8,430.2)	(8,918.3)	(9,312.6)	(10,690.5)	(10,695.0)	(12,187.4)
Mexico	(1,540.1)	(2,350.9)	(2,996.1)	(3,541.2)	(3,103.7)	(3,328.2)	(1,682.2)	(1,406.2)
United States	6,350.5	11,155.9	11,426.3	12,459.5	12,416.3	14,018.8	12,377.2	13,593.6

1. 1989 and earlier data on U.S. exports to Canada for manufacturing total and manufacturing industries are not comparable with data for 1990 and later years because of a change in the reporting system. The NAFTA trade balances of the U.S. and Canada also are affected.

2. New supply equals comparable domestic shipments plus imports for consumption.

3. Apparent consumption equals comparable domestic shipments plus imports for consumption less exports.

4. Amounts less than U.S. $100,000 shown as zero.

5. Does not includes computer equipment.

6. Parentheses indicate an excess of imports over exports. Because of commodity coding and other data differences among the three countries, these trade balances are only rough estimates and should be used with caution.

Source for U.S. Global Trade: U.S. Department of Commerce, International Trade Administration.

Source for U.S. -Canada and U.S.-Mexico Bilateral Trade: U.S. Bureau of the Census.

Source for Canada-Mexico and Mexico-Canada Bilateral Trade: Statistics Canada, Foreign Trade Division, Special tabulation, March 1997, converted to U.S. dollars by the editors.

INSTRUMENTS

THE UNITED STATES

Products and Processes. The instruments industry, 11th largest U.S. manufacturing industry in 1996, produces measuring, controlling, detecting, analyzing, and operating devises used, in one form or another, by almost all businesses, institutions, and individuals. The product categories include laboratory apparatus and analytical equipment; environmental and appliance controls; optical instruments and lenses; aircraft engine instruments; instruments for measuring temperature, liquid levels, pressure, and electricity; photographic equipment; medical and dental instruments and supplies; search and navigation equipment; X-ray apparatus; and watches and clocks.

Table 1 gives a comprehensive breakdown of the industry and its components as of 1992 (latest year for which economic census data are available), which at that time included 11,354 establishments with a combined payroll of $33 billion. The largest subindustries

TABLE 1

UNITED STATES: COMPONENT INDUSTRIES OF INSTRUMENTS (SIC 38), 1992

(Monetary values in millions of U.S. dollars)

| INDUSTRY | SIC | ESTABLISH-MENTS | SHIPMENTS | | VALUE ADDED BY MANUFACTURE | NEW CAPITAL EXPENDI-TURES | EMPLOY-MENT[1] | PAYROLL |
			VALUE	PERCENT BY 4 LARGEST COMPANIES				
INSTRUMENTS	38	11,354	$134,940.4	.....	$89,393.8	$4,617.9	907,100	$33,067.0
Search and navigation equipment	381	762	35,039.2	.....	24,299.2	849.1	253,000	10,961.5
Search and navigation equipment	3812	762	35,039.2	27	24,299.2	849.1	253,000	10,961.5
Measuring and controlling devices	382	4,737	34,729.5	.....	21,774.9	1,180.3	275,500	9,631.6
Laboratory apparatus and furniture	3821	345	2,111.4	34	1,315.8	55.8	17,800	574.8
Environmental and appliance controls	3822	315	2,594.1	54	1,625.6	80.6	24,700	676.7
Process control instruments	3823	890	6,470.1	27	4,268.7	165.4	50,500	1,774.5
Totalizing fluid meters and counting devices	3824	194	2,600.5	56	1,468.1	74.1	16,200	533.8
Instruments to measure and test electricity	3825	960	8,825.8	33	5,684.5	324.4	68,500	2,544.3
Laboratory analytical instruments	3826	595	5,222.5	25	3,029.3	227.7	40,100	1,489.9
Optical instruments and lenses	3827	430	2,489.3	30	1,573.2	71.4	20,300	738.7
Measuring and controlling devices, n.e.c.	3829	1,008	4,415.8	19	2,809.8	181.0	37,600	1,298.9
Medical instruments and supplies	384	4,204	39,534.7	.....	26,081.8	1,559.8	264,100	8,522.0
Surgical and medical instruments and apparatus	3841	1,340	13,396.0	25	9,400.0	689.4	98,200	3,099.4
Orthopedic, prosthetic, and surgical appliances	3842	1,764	13,801.0	20	8,900.9	503.5	96,400	2,846.1
Dental equipment and supplies	3843	611	1,914.1	31	1,205.6	48.6	15,100	458.1
X-Ray apparatus and tubes	3844	128	3,235.0	70	1,871.4	63.6	14,300	562.7
Electromedical and electrotherapeutic apparatus	3845	361	7,188.6	29	4,703.8	254.7	40,100	1,555.7
Ophthalmic goods	385	568	2,675.3	.....	1,938.4	201.5	29,400	714.0
Opthalmic goods	3851	568	2,675.3	46	1,938.4	201.5	29,400	714.0
Photographic equipment and supplies	386	902	22,118.8	78	14,862.0	804.7	77,300	3,061.2
Watches, clocks, watchcases, and parts	387	181	843.0	40	437.5	22.5	7,700	176.7

1. Employment numbers from the economic censuses differ in definition and classification from the Bureau of Labor Statistics estimates in Table 2. Year-to-year comparisons between Table 1 and Table 2 are not appropriate.

Source: U.S. Bureau of the Census, 1992 Census of Manufactures.

within the group then were medical instruments and supplies (29.3 percent of the value of industry shipments), search and navigation equipment (26.0 percent), measuring and controlling devices (25.7 percent), and photographic equipment and supplies (16.4 percent).

Table 2 gives a profile of industry employment in 1993, along with projections to 2005. Employment, which totaled 895,500 in 1993, is projected to shrink by almost 100,000 workers by 2005. Much of the decline is expected in companies producing search and navigation equipment, reflecting in part recent and prospective cuts in military spending. In 1993, production workers in that sector had the highest average earnings ($16.12 per hour, compared with $12.23 for the industry as a whole). Makers of watches and clocks had the lowest average earnings ($8.22 an hour).

TABLE 2

U.S. EMPLOYMENT AND EARNINGS: INSTRUMENTS

| INDUSTRY | SIC | 1993 | | | 2005 |
| | | EMPLOYMENT[1] | | AVERAGE HOURLY EARNINGS (U.S. DOLLARS)[2] | PROJECTED EMPLOYMENT[3] |
		NUMBER OF PERSONS	PERCENT OF INDUSTRY TOTAL		
INSTRUMENTS	38	895,500	100.0	$12.23	797,500
Search and navigation equipment	381	204,200	22.8	16.12	132,000
Measuring and controlling devices	382	283,900	31.7	12.07	248,300
Environmental controls	3822	42,800	4.8	10.75	....
Process control instruments	3823	60,500	6.8	11.70	....
Instruments to measure electricity	3825	72,800	8.1	13.12	....
Medical instruments and supplies	384	269,000	30.0	10.88	305,700
Surgical and medical instruments	3841	108,100	12.1	10.78	....
Surgical appliances and supplies	3842	96,800	10.8	10.19	....
Ophthalmic goods	385	38,600	4.3	8.76	37,000
Photographic equipment and supplies	386	91,400	10.2	14.66	69,900
Watches, clocks, watchcases, and parts	387	8,400	0.9	8.22	5,000

1. Total payroll employment. Employment data from the economic censuses, shown in Table 1, differ in definition and classification from the Bureau of Labor Statistics estimates in this table. Year-to-year comparisons between Table 1 and Table 2 are not appropriate.

2. Earnings of production workers, including overtime.

3. Number of persons, moderate projection by the U.S. Bureau of Labor Statistics.

Source: Bureau of Labor Statistics.

FIGURE 1

U.S. EMPLOYMENT IN INSTRUMENTS

Percent distribution by region, 1995

Employment in the instruments industry is highest in the Pacific and Middle Atlantic regions, with about 23 and 22 percent of the 1995 total, respectively. The Southeast has 24 percent of total U.S. employment but only 12 percent of employment in this industry.

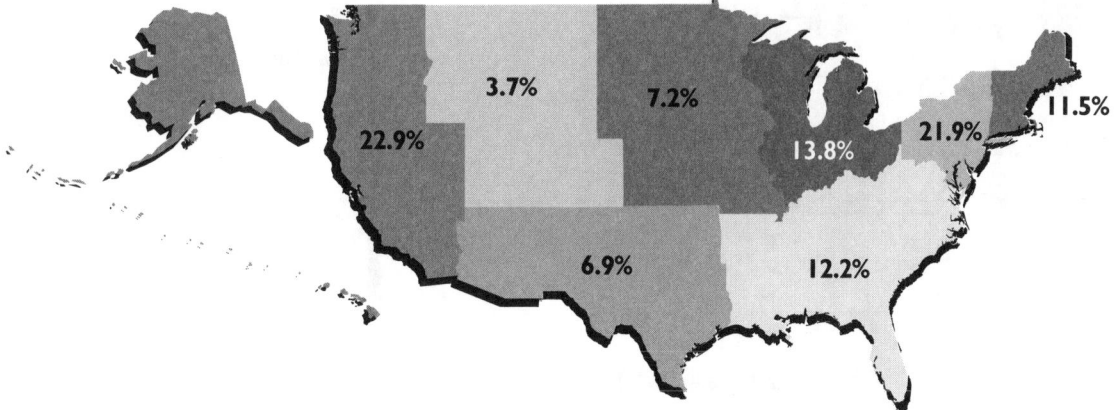

Source: U.S. Department of Commerce, Bureau of Economic Analysis.

What's New. Shipments of instruments and related products rose 6.2 percent in the first half of 1997, versus the same period of 1996. This growth was in line with the continued increase of overall U.S. business investment, which increased 8.4 percent from the first half of 1996 to the first half of 1997. Growth of business investment continued at the same strong pace in the third quarter, according to preliminary data, and shipments of instruments were more than 8 percent above year earlier levels. Future shipments growth for instruments will be heavily dependent on patterns of capital expenditure by industries that purchase measuring and controlling instruments. Chemical process industries, for example, account for over 70 percent of the demand for process control products, and some industry observers expect capital spending in the chemical process industry to level off or decline over the next few years.

Outsourcing is on the rise in the instruments industry, as in most other U.S. industries involved in downsizing and restructuring. It is one way such industries can keep production and profits growing while also avoiding costly employee benefits. Areas most often targeted for outsourcing are noncore functions such as accounting, computer support, purchasing, maintenance, and construction. One large instruments manufacturer, for example, recently signed a five-year $23 million outsourcing agreement with a systems management firm.

FIGURE 2

U.S. EMPLOYMENT AND SHIPMENTS, INSTRUMENTS

Total payroll employment and manufacturers' inflation-adjusted shipments

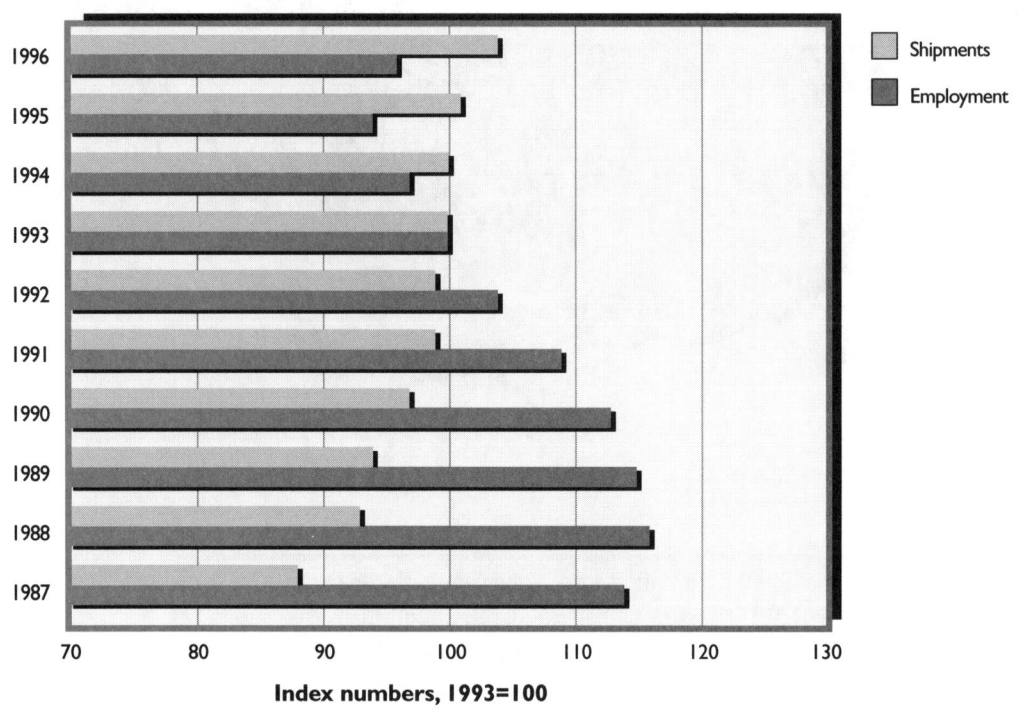

Index numbers, 1993=100

Source: U.S. Bureau of Labor Statistics, U.S. Department of Commerce, and estimates by the editors.

Output. Employment and shipments by the instruments industry moved in opposite directions between 1987 and 1996, suggesting increased productivity but also probably reflecting growth in outsourcing. Employment declined in every year except 1988 and 1996, and value of industry shipments rose during most of the 10-year period (Figure 2). Value of industry shipments reached $146.2 billion in 1996, compared with $107.3 billion in 1987, for an annual growth rate of 3.49 percent. Growth in inflation-adjusted dollars was 1.88 percent (Table 3).

Investment. New capital expenditures by the industry in 1995, at $4.37 billion, were above levels for 1994, 1987, and 1988, but below those for other recent years (Table 3). In contrast, sharp gains occurred in spending on research and development (R&D), which reached $8.06 billion in 1994, compared with $4.95 billion in 1987. These large gains in R&D spending apparently paid off in greater productivity per worker. Capacity utilization in 1996 was 79.2 percent, little changed from past years.

Prices. Producer prices in the industry rose at a relatively slow annual rate of 1.96 percent from 1987 through 1996, with only a moderate gain between 1995 and 1996 (Table 3).

TABLE 3

U.S. OUTPUT, INVESTMENT, AND PRICES: INSTRUMENTS

(Millions of U.S. dollars, except as noted)

	1987	1988	1989	1990	1991	1992	1993	1994	1995	1996	GROWTH RATE 1987-1996[1]
VALUE OF SHIPMENTS:											
BY INDUSTRY:											
Current dollars	107,325	116,009	121,523	127,977	132,836	134,941	137,387	138,399	140,911	146,181	3.49
Constant 1992 dollars	119,502	126,883	128,350	131,379	135,071	134,941	135,946	136,317	137,256	141,289	1.88
BY PRODUCT:											
Current dollars	98,758	105,325	108,307	114,625	116,753	124,995	126,882	127,672	129,029	.....	.....
Constant 1992 dollars	110,307	115,551	114,753	117,833	118,740	124,995	125,516	125,638	125,640	.....	.....
OTHER OUTPUT MEASURES:											
Industrial production, 1993=100	93.2	96.6	97.6	97.8	99.2	99.4	100.0	99.3	99.8	102.2	1.03
Gross domestic product:											
Current dollars	39,061	47,096	46,632	52,212	54,625	54,246	53,638	54,507	.....	.....	.....
Percent of total GDP	0.8	0.9	0.9	0.9	0.9	0.9	0.8	0.8	.....	.....	.....
Rank in manufacturing	8	8	8	8	8	8	8	8	.....	.....	.....
Chained (1992) dollars	48,804	59,551	56,239	58,622	58,065	54,246	51,346	50,887	.....	.....	.....
INVESTMENT-RELATED MEASURES:											
Capacity utilization, percent	80.2	80.8	79.8	78.5	78.7	77.9	77.7	77.0	77.3	79.2	.....
New capital expenditures	3,872	4,014	4,596	4,450	4,700	4,618	4,469	4,248	4,367	.....	.....
Research and development spending	4,950	5,339	5,729	6,318	6,840	7,321	7,542	8,058	.....	.....	.....
Producer prices, 1993=100[2]	86.9	88.5	91.7	94.8	96.7	98.2	100.0	101.1	102.7	103.5	1.96

1. Compound annual growth rate.

2. Prices received by domestic producers.

Sources: Shipments and new capital expenditures: U.S. Department of Commerce for 1987-1995, editor's estimates for constant dollar data for 1987-88 and all shipments data for 1996; Industrial production and capacity utilization: Federal Reserve Board of Governors; GDP: Bureau of Economic Analysis; Research and development spending: National Science Foundation; Producer prices: Bureau of Labor Statistics.

Workforce and Employment. Employment in the industry declined at an annual rate of 1.86 percent between 1987 and 1996, despite a slight upturn in 1996 to 854,000 workers (Table 4). Employment of production workers in 1996, at 422,000 or 49.4 percent of the total, was low compared to other industries. Women employees accounted for 40.9 percent of total employment, not much different than in past years. Average hourly earnings of production workers were $13.14 in 1996; the annual rate of gain during 1988-1996 was 2.72 percent in current dollars but minus 0.75 percent yearly in inflation-adjusted dollars.

As of June 18, 1997, the U.S. Department of Labor had certified that 4,823 workers in the instruments industry lost their jobs because of NAFTA. This total included 3,121 employees certified to have lost jobs to Mexico and 293 who lost jobs to Canada. For more details, see "NAFTA—The First Four Years."

TABLE 4

U.S. EMPLOYMENT, HOURS, AND EARNINGS: INSTRUMENTS

(Monetary values in U.S. dollars)

	1987	1988	1989	1990	1991	1992	1993	1994	1995	1996	CHANGE[1]
NUMBER OF EMPLOYEES, IN THOUSANDS:											
Total	1,011	1,031	1,026	1,006	974	929	896	861	843	854	-1.86
Production workers	.....	508	509	499	479	457	438	422	417	422	-2.29
Percent of total	.....	49.3	49.6	49.6	49.2	49.1	48.9	49.0	49.5	49.4	.....
Women	.....	425	424	417	403	383	366	352	346	349	-2.43
Percent of total	.....	41.2	41.4	41.4	41.4	41.3	40.9	40.9	41.0	40.9	.....
HOURS AND EARNINGS OF PRODUCTION WORKERS:											
Average hourly earnings, U.S. dollars[2]											
Current dollars	.....	10.60	10.83	11.29	11.64	11.89	12.23	12.47	12.71	13.14	2.72
1992 dollars[3]	.....	12.51	12.21	12.10	11.98	11.89	11.90	11.83	11.73	11.78	-0.75
Average weekly hours	.....	41.4	41.1	41.1	41.0	41.1	41.1	41.7	41.4	41.7	0.09
Average weekly earnings, current U.S. dollars	406.31	438.84	445.11	464.02	477.24	488.68	502.65	520.00	526.19	547.94	3.38

1. Compound annual growth rate, 1987-1996.

2. Including overtime.

3. Converted to 1992 dollars using Consumer Price Index for Urban Wage Earners and Clerical Workers.

Source: Bureau of Labor Statistics.

FIGURE 3

U.S. OCCUPATIONAL INJURY AND ILLNESS RATES: INSTRUMENTS AND RELATED PRODUCTS, 1995

In 1995, nonfatal occupational illnesses and injuries among employees of the instruments industry averaged only 5.3 cases per 100 workers—the second lowest level for all manufacturing.

Incidence of nonfatal injuries and illnesses per 100 full-time workers

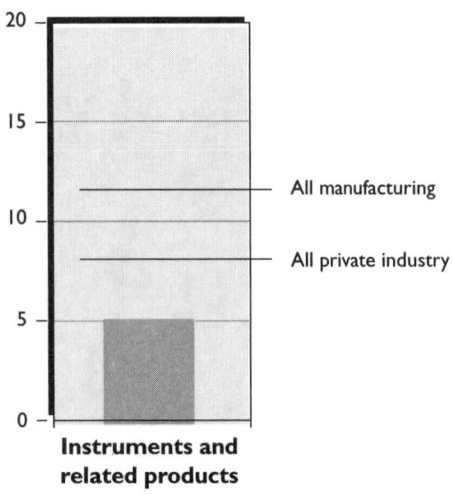

Source: U.S. Bureau of Labor Statistics.

TABLE 5

U.S. EMPLOYMENT PROJECTIONS BY MAJOR OCCUPATIONAL GROUP: INSTRUMENTS

| | 1994 | | PROJECTIONS, 2005 | | | |
| OCCUPATION | NUMBER OF EMPLOYEES | PERCENT OF INDUSTRY TOTAL | NUMBER OF EMPLOYEES | | | PERCENT OF INDUSTRY TOTAL, MODERATE PROJECTIONS |
			LOW	MODERATE	HIGH	
Total, all occupations	863,200	100.0	771,000	797,500	836,400	100.0
Executive, administrative, and managerial	122,354	14.2	108,624	112,693	118,622	14.1
Professional specialties	125,533	14.5	126,593	131,960	139,917	16.6
Technicians and related support	66,200	7.7	54,024	56,194	59,323	7.1
Marketing and sales	35,161	4.1	34,517	35,480	36,980	4.5
Administrative support including clerical	126,952	14.7	102,065	105,544	110,590	13.2
Service	10,461	1.2	8,020	8,301	8,711	1.0
Agriculture, forestry, and fisheries occupations	176	0.0	160	164	170	0.0
Precision production, craft, and repair	178,213	20.7	152,709	158,147	166,220	19.8
Operators, fabricators, assemblers	198,151	23.0	184,289	189,019	195,867	23.7

Source: Bureau of Labor Statistics, November 1995.

Employment in the instruments industry is projected at 797,500 for 2005 (moderate assumptions), well below the 863,200 employees of 1994. Declines are seen for all occupational areas except professional specialties and marketing and sales.

FIGURE 4

U.S. CORPORATE INCOME AND WORKER EARNINGS: INSTRUMENTS

Corporate operating income and aggregate production worker earnings

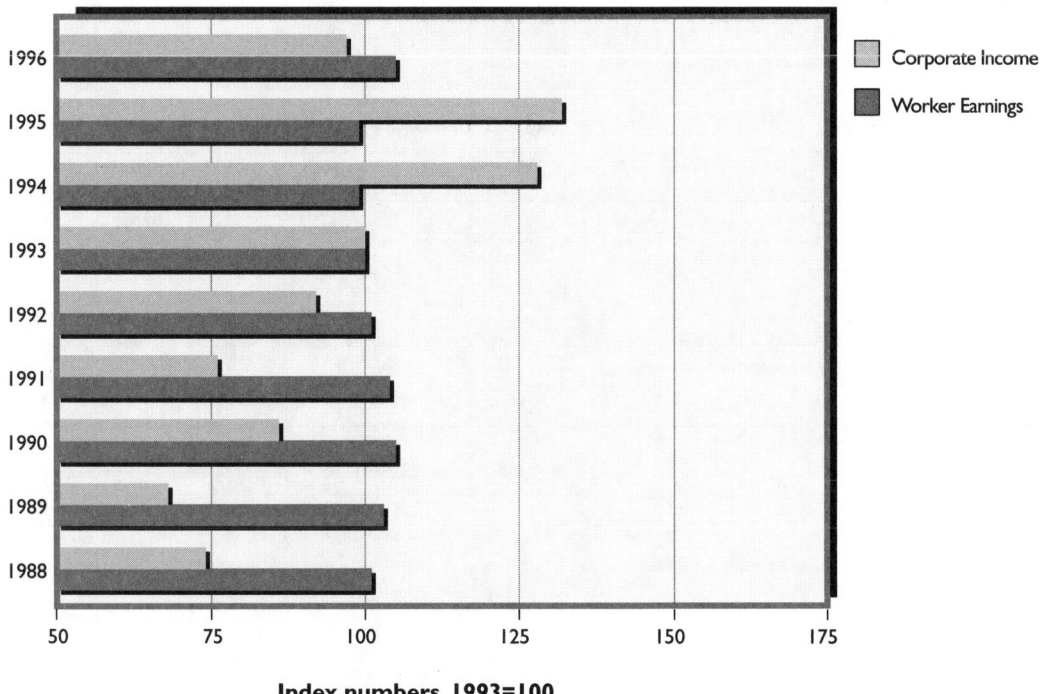

Index numbers, 1993=100

Source: U.S. Bureau of Labor Statistics, U.S. Bureau of the Census, and estimates by the editors.

Finance. Production worker earnings increased in only three of the nine years under review—1989, 1990, and 1996. Corporate income, on the other hand, rose in each year but 1989, 1991, and 1996 (Figure 4). In 1996, income from operations fell to $8.7 billion, losing all the ground gained in the sales surge of the previous two years and slowing average growth for the nine-year period to 3.47 percent annually (Table 6). After-tax income in 1996 was $7.3 billion, with a steep decline from 1995 and 1994 levels resulting in an annual loss of 0.74 percent during the nine-year period. The ratio of after-tax income to sales was 6.16 percent in 1996, compared with 7.65 and 9.20 percent, respectively, in the two previous years. After-tax income in 1996 amounted to 11.06 percent of stockholders' equity, compared with 15.24 and 16.70 percent in 1995 and 1994. The value of inventories, at $17.6 billion in 1996, was little changed from previous years. Long-term debt relative to assets has declined in most of the past nine years and in 1996 stood at 15.79 percent of assets.

TABLE 6

U.S. CORPORATE INCOME AND ASSETS: INSTRUMENTS

(Monetary values in millions of U.S. dollars)

INCOME AND EXPENSES	1988	1989	1990	1991	1992	1993	1994	1995	1996	CHANGE OR AVERAGE[1]
Sales and receipts	90,708	99,088	102,755	102,167	109,827	114,897	125,269	123,004	118,631	3.41
Depreciation and amortization	(4,023)	(4,396)	(4,502)	(4,295)	(4,776)	(5,101)	(5,226)	(4,670)	(4,571)	1.61
Other operating costs	(80,052)	(88,577)	(90,483)	(91,051)	(96,818)	(100,854)	(108,596)	(106,442)	(105,345)	3.49
Income from operations	6,633	6,115	7,770	6,822	8,233	8,943	11,448	11,890	8,714	3.47
Nonoperating income (expenditures)	3,288	1,678	1,149	1,820	(1,882)	(2,326)	3,580	1,436	1,902	....
Income before taxes	9,921	7,792	8,920	8,643	6,350	6,618	15,028	13,326	10,616	0.85
Income after taxes	7,751	6,098	6,739	6,754	4,317	5,798	11,521	9,414	7,302	-0.74
Cash dividends	2,591	2,816	3,007	3,425	3,367	3,579	4,197	3,515	2,939	1.59
Income retained in business	5,160	3,282	3,730	3,328	951	2,219	7,321	5,898	4,362	-2.08
Direct credits (charges)	(1,699)	(2,509)	(356)	(288)	(2,671)	(1,670)	(5,181)	712	(1,310)	....
Ending retained earnings	36,640	36,369	38,669	43,513	49,209	50,346	54,091	40,588	40,618	1.30
ASSETS, END OF YEAR: Total	106,041	111,085	114,718	117,939	131,347	143,077	143,316	132,163	136,985	3.25
Accounts receivable	16,717	17,360	16,744	16,321	18,526	19,801	21,389	18,930	19,028	1.63
Inventories	17,223	17,088	16,815	16,679	17,983	18,733	18,419	17,865	17,608	0.28
Net property, plant and equipment	25,811	28,441	28,607	30,038	32,084	33,911	31,009	26,819	27,918	0.99
RATIOS, PERCENT: INCOME TO SALES:										
Before tax	10.94	7.86	8.68	8.46	5.78	5.76	12.00	10.83	8.95	8.81
After tax	8.55	6.15	6.56	6.61	3.93	5.05	9.20	7.65	6.16	6.65
INCOME TO STOCKHOLDERS' EQUITY:										
Before tax	20.04	15.20	16.58	15.23	10.43	10.09	21.78	21.57	16.07	16.33
After tax	15.66	11.89	12.52	11.90	7.09	8.84	16.70	15.24	11.06	12.32
INCOME TO TOTAL ASSETS:										
Before tax	9.36	7.01	7.78	7.33	4.83	4.63	10.49	10.08	7.75	7.69
After tax	7.31	5.49	5.87	5.73	3.29	4.05	8.04	7.12	5.33	5.80
AS A PERCENT OF TOTAL ASSETS:										
Property, plant and equipment	24.34	25.60	24.94	25.47	24.43	23.70	21.64	20.29	20.38	23.42
Short-term debt	4.56	5.41	4.78	3.36	3.34	2.30	3.60	2.60	3.20	3.68
Long-term debt	22.67	23.62	21.29	21.54	19.80	19.66	15.45	16.02	15.79	19.54
Stockholders' equity	46.69	46.15	46.90	48.12	46.35	45.84	48.15	46.75	48.22	47.02

1. For income and asset amounts, compound annual growth rate; for ratios, average of ratios for the years shown.

Source: U.S. Bureau of the Census, Quarterly Financial Report.

Notes: Parentheses ( ) indicate negative items, e.g., net expenses, charges, or losses. Net property, plant, and equipment is net of accumulated depreciation. Because the samples used to collect the data change, retained earnings at the end of a given year will not exactly equal the previous year's retained earnings plus the current year's retained income and credits.

CANADA

Canada's instruments industry (usually included under "other manufacturing") had 533 establishments and 19,911 employees in 1993 (Table 7). Indicating and recording instruments accounted for almost half of all shipments in 1993. Hourly earnings averaged Can$13.61.

Shipments by the industry in 1994 rose slightly to Can$2.48 billion, compared with Can$2.25 billion in 1993 and Can$1.95 billion in 1987 (Table 8). Employment in 1994, at 20,393, was above the previous year's but below levels for 1987 through 1992. Production worker employment declined to 13,326, or 65 percent of the workforce, in 1994. Average hourly earnings by production workers totaled Can$13.79 in 1994, compared with Can$11.90 in 1988.

TABLE 7

CANADA: COMPONENT INDUSTRIES OF SCIENTIFIC AND PROFESSIONAL EQUIPMENT (CSIC 391), 1993

(Monetary values in Canadian dollars)

INDUSTRY NAME	CSIC	ESTABLISH-MENTS (NUMBER)	EMPLOYMENT		VALUE OF SHIPMENTS (MILLIONS)	AVERAGE HOURLY EARNINGS[1]
			NUMBER	PERCENT OF INDUSTRY TOTAL		
SCIENTIFIC AND PROFESSIONAL EQUIPMENT	391	533	19,911	100.0	CAN$2,252.2	CAN$13.61
Indicating and recordings instrument	3911	221	9,678	48.6	1,031.8	14.09
Other instrument, related products	3912	148	7,496	37.6	939.3	14.25
Clocks and watches	3913	17	259	1.3	34.3	10.03
Ophthalmic goods	3914	147	2,478	12.4	246.8	11.34

1. Including overtime.

Source: Adapted from Statistics Canada, *Manufacturing Industries of Canada* (Cat. No. 31-203).

TABLE 8

CANADIAN EMPLOYMENT AND SHIPMENTS: SCIENTIFIC AND PROFESSIONAL EQUIPMENT, 1987-1994

(Monetary values in Canadian dollars)

	1987	1988	1989	1990	1991	1992	1993	1994	CHANGE[1]
All employees	21,512	23,290	22,106	21,562	21,622	20,813	19,911	20,393	-0.76
Establishments	603	701	684	686	610	590	533	527	-1.91
Employees per establishment	36	33	32	31	35	35	37	39	1.17
Production workers per establishment	.....	22	22	21	23	24	25	25	2.14
PRODUCTION WORKERS:									
Total	.....	15,614	15,286	14,070	14,091	14,040	13,348	13,326	-2.61
Percent of all employees	.....	67.0	69.1	65.3	65.2	67.5	67.0	65.3	.....
Male	.....	8,846	8,495	7,795	8,141	.....	.....	.....	.....
Female	.....	6,768	6,791	6,275	5,950	.....	.....	.....	.....
Percent of all production workers	.....	43.3	44.4	44.6	42.2	.....	.....	.....	.....
Average hourly earnings	.....	11.90	12.56	12.88	13.17	13.59	13.61	13.79	2.49
Average weekly earnings	.....	464.46	492.17	508.00	521.27	537.70	540.53	549.47	2.84
Average weekly hours	.....	39.0	39.2	39.4	39.6	39.6	39.7	39.8	0.34
Shipments (millions)	1,953	2,135	2,205	2,155	2,190	2,218	2,252	2,480	3.47

1. Compound annual growth rate.

Source: Adapted from Statistics Canada, *Manufacturing Industries of Canada* (Cat. No. 31-203).

Mexico

Mexico's instrument industry had about 30,173 employees in 1993 (Table 9). Average yearly earnings plus benefits in the industry were 21,242 new pesos ($6,800) in 1993. The 23,045 production workers had average yearly earnings of 9,756 new pesos ($3,123), and the 6,379 nonproduction employees earned about 32,304 ($10,341).

Table 9

Mexico: Instrument Industry (CMAP 3850), 1993

(Monetary values in 1993 Mexican New Pesos)

			All workers									
						Paid workers						
							Production workers		Nonproduction employees		Benefits	Unpaid
INDUSTRY	CMAP	Number of units	Number	Percent of industry total	Average days worked	Remuneration[1]	Number	Wages and salaries	Number	Wages and salaries	per paid employee	workers, number
Instruments	3850	776	30,173	100	276	21,242	23,045	9,756	6,379	32,304	6,598	749

1. Average annual remuneration including benefits.

Source: INEGI, Censos Economicos 1994.

International Trade

United States. Exports of U.S. instruments exceeded imports through 1996, with the U.S. trade surplus reaching its highest level that year (Table 11). Exports totaled $32.8 billion in 1996, compared with $20.0 billion in 1990, and imports were $28.7 billion, versus $16.9 billion in 1990. The resulting U.S. trade surplus in 1996 was $4.0 billion, compared with $2.1 billion in 1995 and the previous high of $3.5 billion in 1991. Canada received over 15 percent of U.S. exports and supplied about 6 percent of U.S. imports in 1996. Mexico took about 5.5 percent of U.S. exports and supplied 8.9 percent of U.S. imports that year.

Industry reports for 1996 show good export growth for measuring, testing, and control instruments, which rose 8.4 percent above the 1995 level to an estimated $9.77 billion. A similar increase is forecast for 1997. Imports amounted to $5.96 billion in 1996, or almost $4 billion less than exports.

Canada. U.S. exports of instruments to Canada in 1996 were almost $5 billion, or 59 percent above the $3.1 billion for 1990 (Table 11). Canadian exports to the United States totaled $1.7 billion in 1996, almost double the 1990 level. This left a U.S. trade surplus of $3.2 billion in 1996, versus $2.2 billion in 1990.

Mexico. U.S. exports of instruments to Mexico rose to $1.8 billion in 1996 from just under $1 billion in 1990, but this growth was vastly outpaced by a more than tripling of Mexico's exports to the United States, to $2.6 billion in 1996 (Table 11). Consequently, Mexico had a $763-million surplus in 1996 instrument trade with the United States, compared with a deficit of $168 million in 1990. Optical and photographic devices and photographic goods accounted for most of the growth in Mexican exports to the United States.

NAFTA. The positive U.S. trade balance with NAFTA totaled nearly $2.5 billion in 1996. Except for surpluses of over $3 billion in 1993 and 1994, this was not much changed from previous levels since 1990. (Table 11). Data on Canada-Mexico trade and their NAFTA trade balances are unavailable.

(For information on U.S. job losses to NAFTA, see the "Workforce and Employment" section and "NAFTA—The First Four Years.")

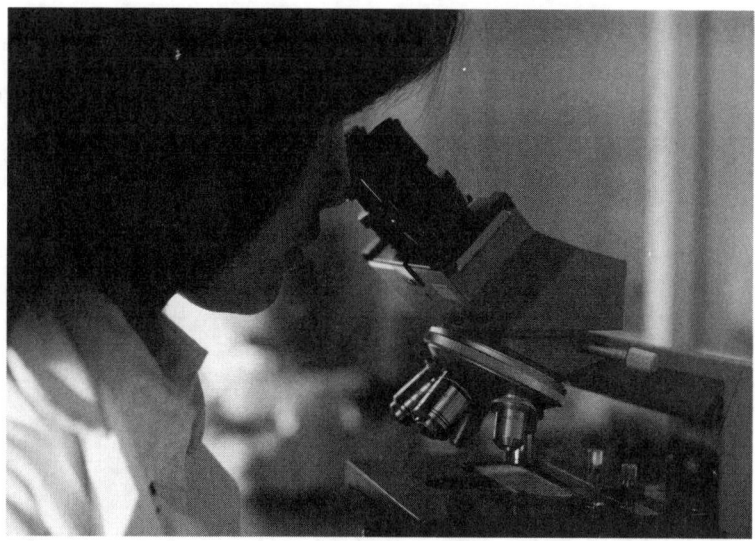

TABLE 11

INTERNATIONAL TRADE, INSTRUMENTS

(Millions of U.S. dollars)

	1989[1]	1990	1991	1992	1993	1994	1995	1996
GLOBAL TRADE, U.S.								
IMPORTS								
Value	15,359.0	16,908.4	18,755.2	20,406.8	22,073.1	24,404.1	27,472.7	28,746.6
Ratio to new supply[2]	12.4	12.9	13.8	14.0	14.8	16.1	.....	.....
Ratio to apparent consumption[3]	14.5	15.2	16.6	16.8	17.8	19.5	.....	.....
EXPORTS								
Value	17,790.9	19,998.4	22,291.7	23,543.5	24,683.8	26,547.4	29,562.4	32,760.0
Ratio to comparable domestic shipments	16.4	17.5	19.1	18.9	19.5	20.8	.....	.....
TRADE BALANCE	2,431.9	3,090.0	3,536.5	3,136.7	2,610.7	2,143.3	2,089.7	4,013.4
BILATERAL TRADE: NAFTA[4]								
U.S. exports to Canada	2,117.9	3,123.3	3,205.8	3,352.0	3,883.5	4,439.9	4,692.3	4,950.6
Canadian exports to U.S.	845.4	889.0	1,049.4	1,170.8	1,217.7	1,451.2	1,574.7	1,730.0
U.S. exports to Mexico	1,000.9	975.4	1,199.2	1,385.4	1,941.3	2,067.1	1,619.4	1,797.0
Mexican exports to U.S.	645.0	807.5	965.7	1,230.7	1,496.2	2,011.2	2,347.2	2,559.9
Canadian exports to Mexico	.....	.....	.....	.....	.....	.....	.....	.....
Mexican exports to Canada	.....	.....	.....	.....	.....	.....	.....	.....
TRADE BALANCES WITHIN NAFTA[5]								
Canada	.....	.....	.....	.....	.....	.....	.....	.....
Mexico	.....	.....	.....	.....	.....	.....	.....	.....
United States	1,628.4	2,402.2	2,389.8	2,335.9	3,111.0	3,044.6	2,389.9	2,457.7

1. 1989 and earlier data on U.S. exports to Canada for manufacturing total and manufacturing industries are not comparable with data for 1990 and later years because of a change in the reporting system. The NAFTA trade balances of the U.S. and Canada also are affected.

2. New supply equals comparable domestic shipments plus imports for consumption.

3. Apparent consumption equals comparable domestic shipments plus imports for consumption less exports.

4. Amounts less than U.S. $100,000 shown as zero. Canada- Mexico data not available for instruments, which are included in "miscellaneous manufacturing" in Canadian trade statistics.

5. Parentheses indicate an excess of imports over exports. Because of commodity coding and other data differences among the three countries, these trade balances are only rough estimates and should be used with caution.

Source for U.S. Global Trade: U.S. Department of Commerce, International Trade Administration.

Source for U.S. -Canada and U.S.-Mexico Bilateral Trade: U.S. Bureau of the Census.

LEATHER AND LEATHER PRODUCTS

THE UNITED STATES

Products and Processes. The leather and leather products industry is the smallest of the U.S. manufacturing industries. It includes both tanning and finishing establishments and the producers of ready-made leather products such as footwear, gloves and mittens, luggage, handbags and purses, and personal leather goods. The leading production category in the group in 1992 (latest year for which economic census data are available) was footwear, except rubber, with 40 percent of all industry shipments that year (Table 1). The next largest category was leather tanning and finishing (with about 30 percent of the total).

Employment in the industry totaled only 117,200 people in 1993 and is projected to decline some 44 percent below that level by the year 2005 (Table 2). In 1993, over half of these employees worked for footwear producers. Leather tanning and finishing accounted for another 13 percent, and luggage, for 9 percent. Average hourly earnings of production workers were the lowest in manufacturing, at $7.63, with tanning and finishing the highest paying subindustry ($9.94 per hour).

TABLE 1

UNITED STATES: COMPONENT INDUSTRIES OF LEATHER AND LEATHER PRODUCTS (SIC 31), 1992

(Monetary values in millions of U.S. dollars)

| INDUSTRY | SIC | ESTABLISH- MENTS | SHIPMENTS | | VALUE ADDED BY MANUFACTURE | NEW CAPITAL EXPENDI- TURES | EMPLOY- MENT[1] | PAYROLL |
			VALUE	PERCENT BY 4 LARGEST COMPANIES				
LEATHER AND LEATHER PRODUCTS	31	2,040	$9,693.8	.....	$4,527.0	$134.5	101,100	$1,806.0
Leather tanning and finishing	311	332	2,905.2	36	890.7	48.5	16,600	420.3
Boot and shoe cut stock and findings	313	100	316.9	42	148.6	3.3	3,700	63.3
Footwear, except rubber	314	392	3,898.4	.....	2,059.8	51.2	48,900	761.9
House slippers	3142	31	285.1	68	176.3	2.1	3,800	59.2
Men's footwear, except athletic	3143	140	2,209.5	36	1,087.7	32.8	24,000	398.9
Women's footwear, except athletic	3144	127	1,095.1	61	636.9	10.5	15,000	219.5
Footwear, except rubber, n.e.c.	3149	94	308.6	38	159.0	5.8	6,000	84.4
Leather gloves and mittens	315	70	139.5	50	68.8	0.5	2,700	34.9
Luggage	316	294	968.2	43	508.5	15.9	10,200	190.7
Handbags and personal leather goods	317	409	890.3	.....	546.1	10.2	11,100	201.6
Women's handbags and purses	3171	213	462.8	55	274.3	3.4	5,000	95.2
Personal leather goods, except women's handbags	3172	196	427.5	42	271.8	6.8	6,100	106.4
Leather goods, n.e.c.	319	443	575.2	21	304.4	5.0	7,900	133.4

1. Employment numbers from the economic censuses differ in definition and classification from the Bureau of Labor Statistics estimates in Table 2. Year-to-year comparisons between Table 1 and Table 2 are not appropriate.

Source: U.S. Bureau of the Census, 1992 Census of Manufactures.

TABLE 2

U.S. EMPLOYMENT AND EARNINGS: LEATHER AND LEATHER PRODUCTS

| INDUSTRY | SIC | 1993 | | | 2005 |
| | | EMPLOYMENT[1] | | AVERAGE HOURLY EARNINGS (U.S. DOLLARS)[2] | PROJECTED EMPLOYMENT[3] |
		NUMBER OF PERSONS	PERCENT OF INDUSTRY TOTAL		
LEATHER AND LEATHER PRODUCTS	31	117,200	100.0	$7.63	65,100
Leather tanning and finishing	311	15,500	13.2	9.94	....
Footwear, except rubber	314	62,100	53.0	7.20	....
Men's footwear, except athletic	3143	30,400	25.9	7.74	....
Women's footwear, except athletic	3144	21,400	18.3	6.62	....
Luggage	316	10,700	9.1	7.82	....
Handbags and personal leather goods	317	12,300	10.5	6.85	....
Footwear, except rubber and plastic	313,4	....	....	....	28,600
Luggage, handbags, and leather products, n.e.c.	311,5-7,9	....	....	....	36,500

1. Total payroll employment. Employment data from the economic censuses, shown in Table 1, differ in definition and classification from the Bureau of Labor Statistics estimates in this table. Year-to-year comparisons between Table 1 and Table 2 are not appropriate.

2. Earnings of production workers, including overtime.

3. Number of persons, moderate projection by the U.S. Bureau of Labor Statistics.

Source: Bureau of Labor Statistics.

FIGURE 1

U.S. EMPLOYMENT IN LEATHER AND LEATHER PRODUCTS

Percent distribution by region, 1995

Employment in the leather and leather products industry is highest in the Southeast region, which had 20 percent of total industry employment in 1995. New England's 17 percent is about three times its share of total U.S. employment. The Great Lakes and Mid-Atlantic regions also had about 17 percent each of leather industry employment.

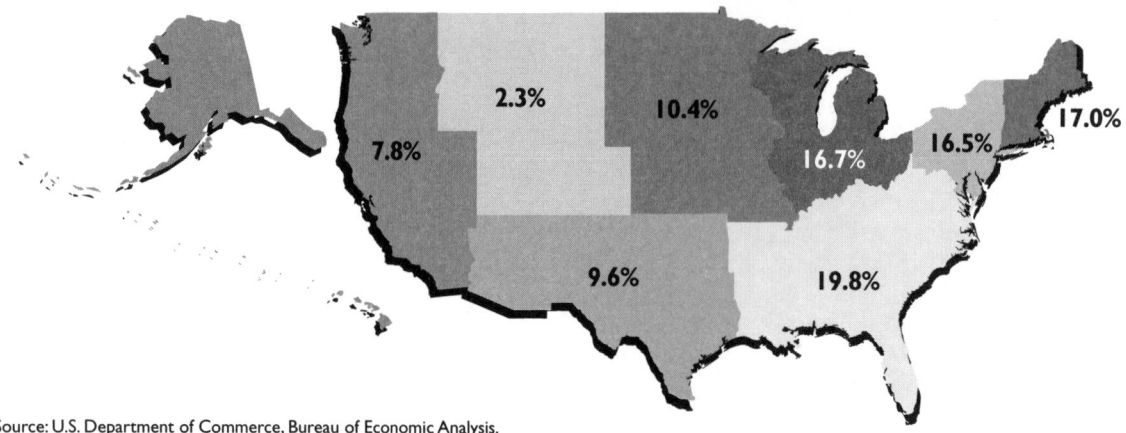

Source: U.S. Department of Commerce, Bureau of Economic Analysis.

What's New. Footwear Industries of America (FIA) is developing a hangtag that U.S. firms can use to meet European Union (EU) requirements for labeling of footwear sold in the EU. Effective since March 23, 1996, the new requirements call for U.S. manufacturers' labels to indicate with pictographs either the principal materials or the two principal materials used in the upper, lining, and outersole. One side of the FIA label would have a common logo or designation, while the reverse side would be reserved for information specific to each company using the label.

Among the manufacturing industries, leather had the highest percentage of its pre-NAFTA workforce (five percent) certified by the Department of Labor as being displaced by NAFTA and the sixth largest absolute number of workers certified through June 18, 1997. Of the 5,873 leather industry employees certified, 1,617 were found to have lost their jobs to Mexican imports or production shifts and 2,619 to Canada (2,400 from one case alone, the Brown Group); another 1,637 were certified without the country being identified. For additional information, see "NAFTA—The First Four Years."

FIGURE 2

U.S. EMPLOYMENT AND SHIPMENTS, LEATHER AND LEATHER PRODUCTS

Total payroll employment and manufacturers' inflation-adjusted shipments

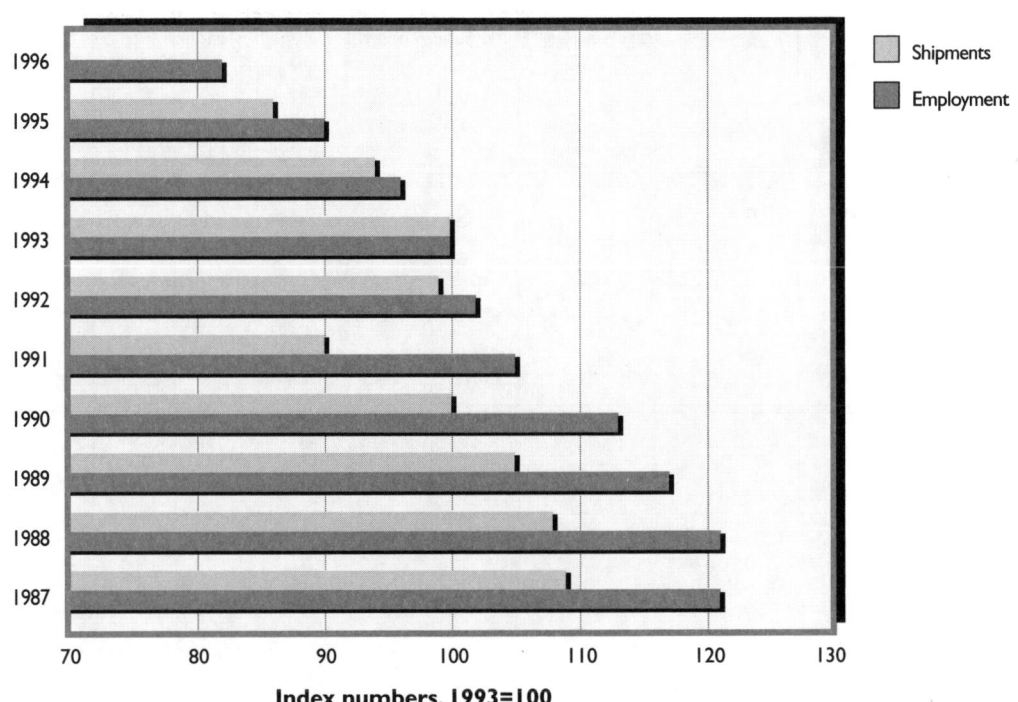

Index numbers, 1993=100

Source: U.S. Bureau of Labor Statistics, U.S. Department of Commerce, and estimates by the editors. Shipments data for 1996 are not available.

Output. Employment in the leather and leather products industry fell sharply between 1987 and 1995; industry shipments (in constant dollars) also declined during most of that period, but at a slower rate than employment (Figure 2). For the 1987-1995 period, shipments declined at annual rates of 0.03 percent in current dollars and 3.01 percent when adjusted for inflation (Table 3). The decline came as current-dollar value of shipments in the final two years pulled back from the 1993 high to $9.06 billion in 1995.

Investment. New capital expenditures by the industry totaled $126 million in 1995, off slightly from levels of the previous three years (Table 3). Capacity utilization has been declining since its 1993 peak and in 1996 hit a 10-year low of 71.5 percent.

Prices. Producer prices in the industry have risen at the annual rate of 2.64 percent since 1987 (Table 3), but gained only fractionally in 1996.

TABLE 3

U.S. OUTPUT, INVESTMENT, AND PRICES: LEATHER AND LEATHER PRODUCTS

(Millions of U.S. dollars, except as noted)

	1987	1988	1989	1990	1991	1992	1993	1994	1995	1996	GROWTH RATE 1987-1995[1]
VALUE OF SHIPMENTS:											
BY INDUSTRY:											
Current dollars	9,082	9,550	9,626	9,548	8,689	9,694	10,007	9,551	9,064	.....	-0.03
Constant 1992 dollars	10,726	10,597	10,267	9,793	8,824	9,694	9,811	9,175	8,401	.....	-3.01
BY PRODUCT:											
Current dollars	8,634	9,170	9,220	9,154	8,540	9,283	9,620	9,506	8,932	.....	0.42
Constant 1992 dollars	10,182	10,160	9,819	9,368	8,669	9,283	9,426	9,136	8,284	.....	-2.55
OTHER OUTPUT MEASURES:											
Industrial production, 1993=100	111.3	110.9	110.8	106.7	97.4	99.0	100.0	92.7	84.9	79.0	-3.74
Gross domestic product:											
Current dollars	3,906	4,277	4,545	4,594	4,427	4,771	4,642	4,131	.....	.....	.....
Percent of total GDP	0.1	0.1	0.1	0.1	0.1	0.1	0.1	0.1	.....	.....	.....
Rank in manufacturing	20	20	20	20	20	20	20	20	.....	.....	.....
Chained (1992) dollars	4,675	4,708	4,896	4,767	4,527	4,771	4,567	3,899	.....	.....	.....
INVESTMENT-RELATED MEASURES:											
Capacity utilization, percent	74.7	78.7	82.5	82.7	78.8	82.8	85.5	80.8	75.3	71.5	.....
New capital expenditures	101	97	117	107	89	135	131	135	126	.....	.....
Producer prices, 1993=100[2]	82.6	87.9	91.4	95.0	96.8	98.4	100.0	101.2	103.9	104.4	2.64

1. Compound annual growth rate.

2. Prices received by domestic producers.

Sources: Shipments and new capital expenditures: U.S. Department of Commerce for 1987-1995, editor's estimates for constant dollar data for 1987-88 and all shipments data for 1996; Industrial production and capacity utilization: Federal Reserve Board of Governors; GDP: Bureau of Economic Analysis; Research and development spending: National Science Foundation; Producer prices: Bureau of Labor Statistics.

Workforce and Employment. Industry employment declined at an annual rate of 4.33 percent during 1987-1996 (Table 4). In 1996, it stood at only 96,000, down by almost a third from 1987 employment. Production worker employment fell by 5.19 percent annually to 74,000, or 77.2 percent of the workforce. Employment of women declined by 5.15 percent a year to 53,000, or 55 percent of the total. Hourly earnings of production workers averaged only $8.56 in 1996, and the average workweek was 38.1 hours.

TABLE 4

U.S. EMPLOYMENT, HOURS, AND EARNINGS: LEATHER

(Monetary values in U.S. dollars)

	1987	1988	1989	1990	1991	1992	1993	1994	1995	1996	CHANGE[1]
NUMBER OF EMPLOYEES, IN THOUSANDS:											
Total	143	143	138	133	124	120	117	113	106	96	-4.33
Production workers	120	118	114	109	100	97	94	90	83	74	-5.19
Percent of total	83.7	82.4	82.7	82.3	80.8	80.8	80.1	79.3	78.1	77.2	.....
Women	85	84	81	78	71	67	65	63	59	53	-5.15
Percent of total	59.4	58.9	58.4	58.4	57.4	55.8	55.5	55.8	55.6	55.0	.....
HOURS AND EARNINGS OF PRODUCTION WORKERS:											
Average hourly earnings, U.S. dollars[2]											
Current dollars	6.08	6.28	6.59	6.91	7.18	7.42	7.63	7.97	8.17	8.56	3.87
1992 dollars[3]	7.47	7.41	7.43	7.41	7.39	7.42	7.42	7.56	7.54	7.68	0.31
Average weekly hours	38.2	37.5	37.9	37.4	37.5	38.0	38.6	38.5	38.0	38.1	-0.03
Average weekly earnings, current U.S. dollars	232.26	235.50	249.76	258.43	269.25	281.96	294.52	306.85	310.46	326.14	3.84

1. Compound annual growth rate, 1987-1996.

2. Including overtime.

3. Converted to 1992 dollars using Consumer Price Index for Urban Wage Earners and Clerical Workers.

Source: Bureau of Labor Statistics.

FIGURE 3

U.S. OCCUPATIONAL INJURY AND ILLNESS RATES:
LEATHER AND LEATHER PRODUCTS, 1995

Incidence of nonfatal injuries and illnesses per 100 full-time workers

Occupational illnesses and injuries in the leather and leather products industry averaged 11.4 cases per 100 workers in 1995, about equal to the 11.6 percent average for all manufacturing.

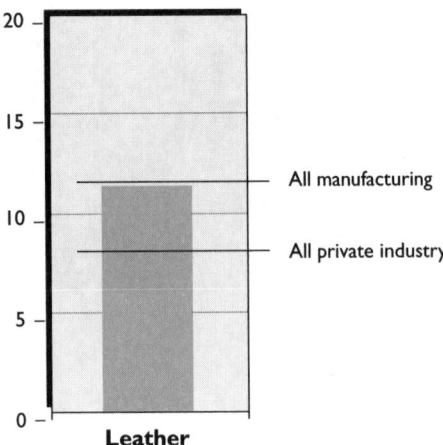

Source: U.S. Bureau of Labor Statistics.

TABLE 5

U.S. EMPLOYMENT PROJECTIONS BY MAJOR OCCUPATIONAL GROUP:
LEATHER AND LEATHER PRODUCTS

Industry employment by 2005 will be barely over half that of 1994 if the steeply declining trend continues, according to projections by the Bureau of Labor Statistics. Reductions are seen for all occupational areas, with the steepest decline (46 percent) projected for operators, fabricators, and laborers.

OCCUPATION	1994		PROJECTIONS, 2005			
	NUMBER OF EMPLOYEES	PERCENT OF INDUSTRY TOTAL	NUMBER OF EMPLOYEES			PERCENT OF INDUSTRY TOTAL, MODERATE PROJECTIONS
			LOW	MODERATE	HIGH	
Total, all occupations	113,600	100.0	54,100	65,100	79,000	100.0
Executive, administrative, and managerial	6,115	5.4	3,547	4,166	4,924	6.4
Professional specialties	1,160	1.0	777	925	1,108	1.4
Technicians and related support	563	0.5	308	358	418	0.6
Marketing and sales	2,662	2.3	1,548	1,821	2,155	2.8
Administrative support including clerical	11,343	10.0	5,664	6,772	8,161	10.4
Service	1,210	1.1	554	678	837	1.0
Agriculture, forestry, and fisheries occupations	.....	......	.....	.....	.....	......
Precision production, craft, and repair	22,753	20.0	11,519	14,088	17,386	21.6
Operators, fabricators, assemblers	67,788	59.7	30,179	36,290	44,006	55.7

Source: Bureau of Labor Statistics, November 1995.

Finance. Financial data for the leather and leather products industry are not broken out separately but are included with those for apparel (see the Apparel Chapter)

CANADA

The Canadian leather industry in 1993 consisted of 230 establishments and 12,818 employees (Table 7). The largest subindustry was footwear, with 68 percent of industry shipments in 1993. Leather tanneries accounted for 16 percent of the total, and luggage and purses, for 8 percent. Earnings averaged Can$9.76, with the highest (Can$11.96) in leather tanning.

Shipments by the industry amounted to just over Can$1 billion in 1994, up from the previous three years, but below levels for 1987-1990 (Table 8). Employment in 1994 totaled only 13,010, or 40 percent less than in 1987; over the eight-year period, employment declined at an annual rate of 7.10 percent. An even faster decline in employment of production workers reduced their share of the workforce to 85 percent from 88 percent in 1988. Hourly wages of production workers averaged only Can$9.87 in 1994, compared with Can$7.86 in 1988. The average workweek was 38.7 hours in 1994.

TABLE 7

CANADA: COMPONENT INDUSTRIES OF LEATHER AND LEATHER PRODUCTS (CSIC 17), 1993

(Monetary values in Canadian dollars)

INDUSTRY NAME	CSIC	ESTABLISH-MENTS (NUMBER)	EMPLOYMENT		VALUE OF SHIPMENTS (MILLIONS)	AVERAGE HOURLY EARNINGS[1]
			NUMBER	PERCENT OF INDUSTRY TOTAL		
LEATHER AND LEATHER PRODUCTS INDUSTRIES	17	230	12,818	100.0	CAN$930.5	CAN$9.76
Leather tanneries	1711	22	899	7.0	149.9	11.96
Footwear industries	1712	95	9,501	74.1	631.3	9.77
Luggage, purses, and handbags	1713	58	1,378	10.8	70.5	8.41
Other leather and allied products	1719	55	1,040	8.1	78.7	9.42

1. Including overtime.

Source: Statistics Canada, *Manufacturing Industries of Canada* (Cat. No. 31-203).

TABLE 8

CANADIAN EMPLOYMENT AND SHIPMENTS: LEATHER INDUSTRY, 1987-1994

(Monetary values in Canadian dollars)

	1987	1988	1989	1990	1991	1992	1993	1994	CHANGE[1]
All employees	21,782	20,298	18,607	16,709	13,948	12,382	12,818	13,010	-7.10
Establishments	384	369	353	338	272	250	230	216	-7.89
Employees per establishment	57	55	53	49	51	50	56	60	0.86
Production workers per establishment	.....	48	46	43	44	42	47	51	0.98
PRODUCTION WORKERS:									
Total	.....	17,767	16,353	14,389	11,973	10,452	10,847	11,025	-7.64
Percent of all employees	.....	87.5	87.9	86.1	85.8	84.4	84.6	84.7	.....
Male	.....	7,763	7,049	6,194	5,271	.....	.....	.....	.....
Female	.....	10,004	9,304	8,195	6,702	.....	.....	.....	.....
Percent of all production workers	.....	56.3	56.9	57.0	56.0	.....	.....	.....	.....
Average hourly earnings	.....	7.86	8.16	9.08	9.13	9.69	9.76	9.87	3.87
Average weekly earnings	.....	308.44	319.26	348.71	348.14	372.87	370.49	381.67	3.61
Average weekly hours	.....	39.3	39.1	38.4	38.1	38.5	38.0	38.7	-0.25
Shipments (millions)	1,316	1,293	1,289	1,162	941	889	930	1,006	-4.10

1. Compound annual growth rate.

Source: Adapted from Statistics Canada, *Manufacturing Industries of Canada* (Cat. No. 31-203).

MEXICO

Mexican leather industry statistics are included under textiles, garments, and leather but are shown here separately in Tables 9 and 10. Manufacturers of footwear and other leather products had 109,885 employees and 7,334 production units in 1993 (Table 9). The 83,030 workers in footwear manufacturing had average annual incomes (earnings plus benefits) of 16,173 new pesos ($5,178) a year in 1993, with earnings of the 66,189 production workers averaging 10,782 new pesos ($3,452) a year and the 10,300 nonproduction employees earning 23,273 new pesos ($7,450). Earnings were slightly higher for the 26,855 workers producing leather products other than footwear (Table 9).

Employment in the Mexican leather industry fell at an annual rate of 4.12 percent between 1988 and 1995, to 83,519 (Table 10).

TABLE 9

MEXICO: COMPONENT INDUSTRIES OF LEATHER AND FOOTWEAR INDUSTRIES (CMAP 3230, 3240), 1993

(Monetary values in 1993 Mexican New Pesos)

			ALL WORKERS									
							PAID WORKERS					
							PRODUCTION WORKERS		NONPRODUCTION EMPLOYEES		BENEFITS	UNPAID
INDUSTRY	CMAP	NUMBER OF UNITS	NUMBER	PERCENT OF INDUSTRY TOTAL	AVERAGE DAYS WORKED	REMUN-ERATION[1]	NUMBER	WAGES AND SALARIES	NUMBER	WAGES AND SALARIES	PER PAID EMPLOYEE	WORKERS, NUMBER
Leather (excluding footwear)	3230	2,348	26,855	24	275	16,345	20,041	10,424	3,889	23,823	3,744	2,925
Footwear	3240	4,986	83,030	76	260	16,173	66,189	10,782	10,300	23,273	3,709	6,541

1. Average annual remuneration including benefits.

Source: INEGI, Census Economics 1994.

TABLE 10

MEXICAN EMPLOYMENT: LEATHER INDUSTRY, 1988-1995

	1988	1989	1990	1991	1992	1993	1994	1995	CHANGE[1]
TOTAL EMPLOYMENT: Leather	112,148	111,300	108,353	112,292	107,886	101,163	92,557	83,519	-4.12

1. Compound annual growth rate.

Source: Sistema de Cuentas Nacionales de Mexico, INEGI.

INTERNATIONAL TRADE

United States. U.S. imports of leather and leather products rose by slightly more than a third between 1990 and 1996 to $14.2 billion. Although this growth seems moderate compared with that in other industries, leather imports have taken over most of the domestic market (accounting for 62.4 percent of apparent consumption in 1994). Exports during 1990-1996 gained 31 percent, to $1.7 billion in 1996 and amounted to only about 12 percent of the 1996 import value. This left a trade deficit of $12.5 billion in 1996, the highest so far in the 1990s (Table 11). Developing countries, particularly China, supply most of the imports, reflecting their competitive advantage over U.S. producers in this labor-intensive industry. Footwear is by far the largest import category.

Canada. About 16 percent of U.S. exports went to Canada in 1996, while Canada accounted for only about one percent of U.S. imports (Table 11). U.S. leather exports to Canada in 1996 totaled $270 million (versus $188 million in 1990), and Canadian exports to the United States were $153 million ($99 million). Canada had almost no exports to Mexico in 1996.

Mexico. Leather products trade between the United States and Mexico is small, but about two to one in favor of Mexico (Table 11). U.S. leather products exports to Mexico almost doubled between 1990 and 1996 to $243 million, while Mexican shipments to the United States more than doubled to $521 million. Mexican exports to Canada rose to $22 million in 1996 from $5 million in 1990.

NAFTA. Mexico's trade surplus with Canada and the United States rose 127 percent during 1990-1996 to $300 million (Table 11). After declining to a low of $5 million in 1991, the U.S. trade deficit with NAFTA rose steadily to $162 million in 1996. Canada's deficit rose 38 percent between 1990 and 1992 to $131 million and, after dipping below that level for three years, edged up to $139 million in 1996. (Among the manufacturing industries, the U.S. leather industry had the highest percentage of workers displaced by NAFTA. See the What's New section and "NAFTA—The First Four Years" for more information.)

TABLE 11

INTERNATIONAL TRADE, LEATHER AND LEATHER PRODUCTS

(Millions of U.S. dollars)

	1989[1]	1990	1991	1992	1993	1994	1995	1996
GLOBAL TRADE, U.S.								
IMPORTS								
Value	9,450.3	10,558.2	10,258.2	10,793.4	11,692.4	12,977.5	13,627.5	14,187.1
Ratio to new supply[2]	51.0	53.6	54.7	54.2	55.2	58.1	.....	.....
Ratio to apparent consumption[3]	54.2	57.5	58.8	58.5	59.5	62.4	.....	.....
EXPORTS								
Value	1,095.6	1,321.2	1,329.6	1,453.7	1,536.4	1,538.5	1,564.5	1,725.0
Ratio to comparable domestic shipments	12.1	14.5	15.6	16.0	16.2	16.4	.....	.....
TRADE BALANCE	(8,354.7)	(9,237.0)	(8,928.6)	(9,339.7)	(10,156.0)	(11,439.0)	(12,063.0)	(12,462.1)
BILATERAL TRADE: NAFTA[4]								
U.S. exports to Canada	126.3	188.3	193.4	203.9	216.8	246.4	255.5	269.7
Canadian exports to U.S.	88.6	98.7	72.8	79.6	100.3	134.8	141.3	153.1
U.S. exports to Mexico	128.6	123.0	127.9	186.5	197.4	199.9	216.0	242.6
Mexican exports to U.S.	253.9	249.8	253.7	321.1	346.7	370.9	433.5	520.8
Canadian exports to Mexico	0.3	0.1	0.2	0.4	0.1	0.5	0.0	0.0
Mexican exports to Canada	5.5	5.3	5.0	6.7	6.9	6.9	12.8	21.9
TRADE BALANCES WITHIN NAFTA[5]								
Canada	(42.9)	(94.8)	(125.4)	(130.6)	(123.3)	(118.0)	(127.0)	(138.5)
Mexico	130.5	132.0	130.6	140.9	156.1	177.4	230.3	300.1
United States	(87.6)	(37.2)	(5.2)	(10.3)	(32.8)	(59.4)	(103.3)	(161.6)

1. 1989 and earlier data on U.S. exports to Canada for manufacturing total and manufacturing industries are not comparable with data for 1990 and later years because of a change in the reporting system. The NAFTA trade balances for the U.S. and Canada also are affected.

2. New supply equals comparable domestic shipments plus imports for consumption.

3. Apparent consumption equals comparable domestic shipments plus imports for consumption less exports.

4. Amounts less than U.S. $100,000 shown as zero.

5. Parentheses indicate an excess of imports over exports. Because of commodity coding and other data differences among the three countries, these trade balances are only rough estimates and should be used with caution.

Source for U.S. Global Trade: U.S. Department of Commerce, International Trade Administration.

Source for U.S.-Canada and U.S.-Mexico Bilateral Trade: U.S. Bureau of the Census.

Source for Canada-Mexico and Mexico-Canada Bilateral Trade: Statistics Canada, Foreign Trade Division, Special tabulation, March 1997, converted to U.S. dollars by the editors.

LUMBER AND WOOD PRODUCTS

THE UNITED STATES

Products and Processes. The lumber and wood products industry ranked as the 13th largest U.S. manufacturing industry in value of 1995 shipments. The industry encompasses all stages of wood production, from logging to manufacturing of panels for mobile homes. It does not, however, include production of pulpwood for paper (a separate industry, discussed in the Paper and Allied Products Chapter).

The lumber and wood products industry provides the bulk of raw materials used in residential construction, home repair and remodeling, and furniture manufacturing. Those industries, in turn, drive demand for wood products—construction alone takes more than 80 percent of the softwood lumber produced, most of the millwork, and almost two-thirds of the structural panels.

Table 1 shows the major components of the industry and their production, employment, and expenditures in 1992 (latest year for which economic census data are available). That

TABLE 1

UNITED STATES: COMPONENT INDUSTRIES OF LUMBER AND WOOD PRODUCTS (SIC 24), 1992

(Monetary values in millions of U.S. dollars)

INDUSTRY	SIC	ESTABLISH- MENTS	SHIPMENTS		VALUE ADDED BY MANUFACTURE	NEW CAPITAL EXPENDI- TURES	EMPLOY- MENT[1]	PAYROLL
			VALUE	PERCENT BY 4 LARGEST COMPANIES				
LUMBER AND WOOD PRODUCTS	24	35,807	$81,564.8	....	$33,153.6	$1,760.1	655,800	$13,881.8
Logging	241	13,063	13,591.7	....	5,016.7	373.8	83,200	1,688.9
Logging camps and logging contractors	2411	13,063	13,591.7	19	5,016.7	373.8	83,200	1,688.9
Sawmills and planning mills	242	6,845	23,294.3	....	8,848.0	512.0	168,400	3,584.8
Sawmills and planning mills, general	2421	5,815	21,060.6	14	7,754.5	458.7	137,600	3,039.8
Hardwood dimension and flooring mills	2426	833	2,084.6	17	1,028.3	48.5	28,900	510.0
Special product sawmills, n.e.c.	2429	197	149.1	23	65.2	4.8	1,900	34.9
Millwork, plywood, and structural members	243	8,947	24,744.1	....	10,843.8	466.0	224,100	5,004.5
Millwork	2431	3,176	9,649.3	20	4,057.7	190.5	85,800	1,967.5
Wood kitchen cabinets	2434	4,355	4,968.2	19	2,733.6	91.1	63,200	1,314.7
Hardwood veneer and plywood	2435	316	2,238.0	27	855.9	45.1	19,900	391.7
Softwood veneer and plywood	2436	203	5,350.1	47	2,158.3	94.5	30,900	814.9
Structural wood members, n.e.c.	2439	897	2,538.6	19	1,038.3	44.9	24,300	515.7
Wood containers	244	2,466	2,942.0	....	1,320.9	67.4	40,100	645.1
Nailed and lock corner wood boxes and shook	2441	308	439.0	18	185.5	8.1	5,900	101.3
Wood pallets and skids	2448	1,929	2,146.9	5	964.9	52.8	28,700	450.8
Wood containers, n.e.c.	2449	229	356.2	34	170.5	6.5	5,500	92.9
Wood buildings and mobile homes	245	950	6,644.9	....	2,530.8	75.7	56,000	1,233.6
Mobile homes	2451	287	4,483.8	35	1,654.2	50.4	36,800	809.4
Prefabricated wood buildings	2452	663	2,161.1	14	876.5	25.2	19,200	424.2
Miscellaneous wood products	249	3,536	10,347.8	....	4,593.3	265.3	84,000	1,725.0
Wood preserving	2491	488	2,701.1	17	666.8	55.7	10,800	231.9
Reconstituted wood products	2493	288	3,986.4	50	1,934.8	143.0	22,800	615.5
Wood products, n.e.c.	2499	2,760	3,660.3	13	1,991.8	66.6	50,400	877.6

1. Employment numbers from the economic censuses differ in definition and classification from the Bureau of Labor Statistics estimates in Table 2. Year-to-year comparisons between Table 1 and Table 2 are not appropriate.

Source: U.S. Bureau of the Census, 1992 Census of Manufactures.

year, the industry had 35,807 establishments, more than a third of which were the mostly small-scale logging camps and contractors. The largest categories in terms of shipment value were millwork, plywood, and structural members ($24.7 billion in shipments), sawmills and planing mills ($23.3 billion), and logging ($13.6 billion). Among the subcategories, reconstituted wood products such as particleboard, hardboard, medium-density fiberboard (MDF), and oriented strand board (OSB) are finding increased use in construction and furniture making.

Recent strong growth in the industry has pushed up employment in the last five years, but projections to 2005 foresee a decline to about 684,700, compared with 709,100 in 1993 (Table 2). Virtually all of the decline will be in employment by sawmills and planing mills. Employment in millwork, plywood, and structural members—the largest employer—is projected to decrease only slightly. Hourly earnings in 1993 averaged $9.61 for the industry as a whole, with the highest earnings in softwood veneer and plywood manufacturing ($11.47) and logging ($11.37).

TABLE 2

U.S. EMPLOYMENT AND EARNINGS: LUMBER AND WOOD PRODUCTS

		1993			2005
		EMPLOYMENT[1]		AVERAGE	
INDUSTRY	SIC	NUMBER OF PERSONS	PERCENT OF INDUSTRY TOTAL	HOURLY EARNINGS (U.S. DOLLARS)[2]	PROJECTED EMPLOYMENT[3]
LUMBER AND WOOD PRODUCTS	24	709,100	100.0	$9.61	684,700
Logging	241	81,100	11.4	11.37	74,400
Sawmills and planning mills	242	181,900	25.7	9.78	150,000
Sawmills and planning mills, general	2421	145,200	20.5	10.15	....
Hardwood dimension and flooring mills	2426	34,800	4.9	8.21	....
Millwork, plywood, and structural members	243	252,100	35.6	9.65	250,200
Millwork	2431	103,300	14.6	9.87	....
Wood kitchen cabinets	2434	68,800	9.7	9.02	....
Hardwood veneer and plywood	2435	23,600	3.3	8.37	....
Softwood veneer and plywood	2436	28,400	4.0	11.47	....
Wood containers	244	45,900	6.5	7.04	....
Wood buildings and mobile homes	245	64,200	9.1	9.34	71,600
Mobile homes	2451	48,000	6.8	9.39	....
Miscellaneous wood products	249	83,800	11.8	9.02	....
Wood containers and miscellaneous wood products	244,9	129,700	18.3	....	138,500

1. Total payroll employment. Employment data from the economic censuses, shown in Table 1, differ in definition and classification from the Bureau of Labor Statistics estimates in this table. Year-to-year comparisons between Table 1 and Table 2 are not appropriate.

2. Earnings of production workers, including overtime.

3. Number of persons, moderate projection by the U.S. Bureau of Labor Statistics.

Source: Bureau of Labor Statistics.

FIGURE 1

U.S. EMPLOYMENT IN LUMBER

Percent distribution by region, 1995

The Southeast is now the largest single industry employer, with 37 percent of the total workforce in 1995. The relative importance of the Pacific region (18 percent of employment) has fallen in recent years, reflecting sharply curtailed logging on government lands because of environmental concerns such as the diminishing habitat of the northern spotted owl.

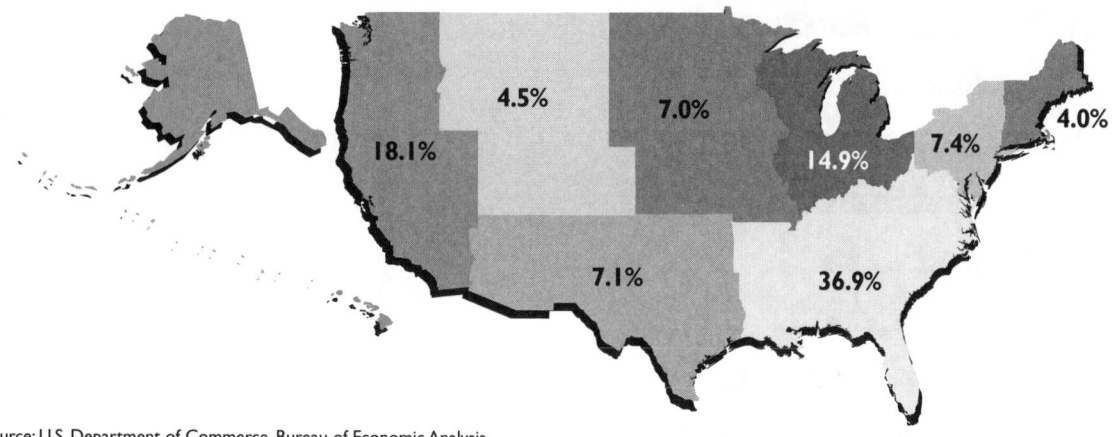

Source: U.S. Department of Commerce, Bureau of Economic Analysis.

What's New. Employment growth in the industry continued in the early months of 1997, but leveled off in the April to July period (seasonally adjusted). None of the growth was in logging, where each month's employment was slightly below year-ago levels, but was spread among the other components of the industry.

North American particleboard capacity rose an estimated 5 percent during 1996, in part because of a 32 percent gain in the relatively small Mexican particleboard industry, according to the Composite Panel Association. MDF capacity in North America grew by 26 percent in 1996. Further gains probably took place in 1997 particleboard and MDF capacity if new plants and expansion took place as planned.

The lumber industry and environmentalists have continued to battle over issues involving threatened species such as the northern spotted owl and the murrelet. The northern spotted owl, whose habitat includes around 5 million acres of Pacific Northwest forests, was listed as a threatened species in June 1990. As a result, the U.S. government prohibited timber harvesting on 7 million acres of federal and state timberlands, and by 1992 had cut its sales of Pacific Northwest timber by about 75 percent. Because of the devastating impact that action had on logging communities, and reported smaller timber sales than agreed to by the U.S. Forest Service, the U.S. Congress in the summer of 1995 passed the Emergency Salvage Timber Sale Program. The program allowed logging in 1996 of dead and dying timber damaged by fire, insects, or wind, as well as temporary resumption of logging on 350 acres of old-growth timber in the Olympic National Forest and certain other areas. However, the program raised the ire of environmentalists by permitting clear-cutting and other old-style practices that have a more damaging impact on the environment then do more modern forestry practices.

FIGURE 2

U.S. EMPLOYMENT AND SHIPMENTS, LUMBER

Total payroll employment and manufacturers' inflation-adjusted shipments

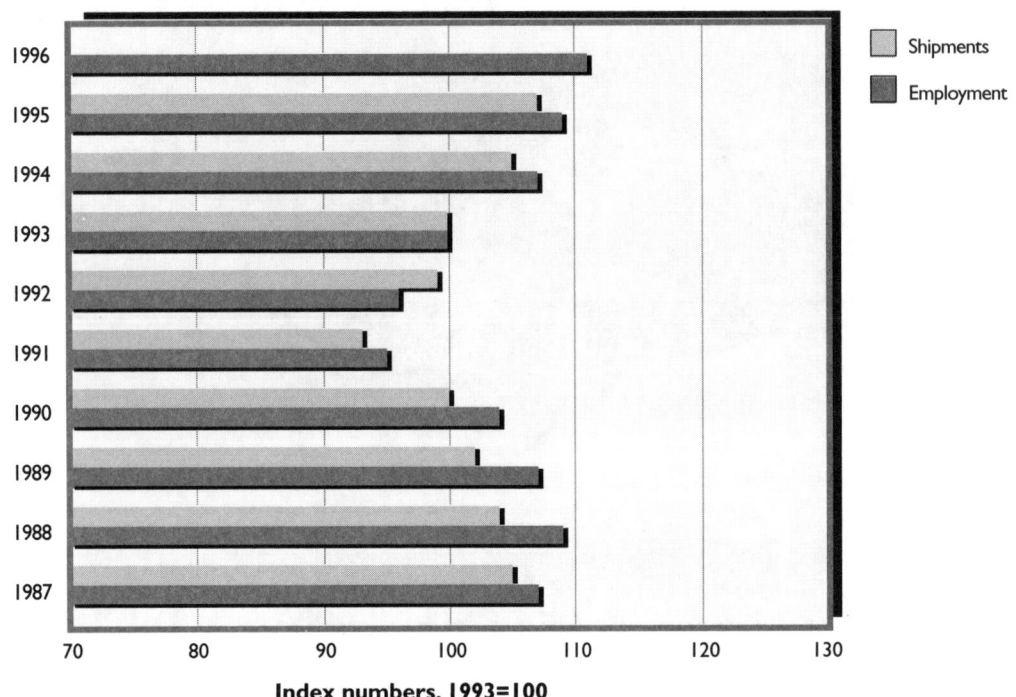

Index numbers, 1993=100

Source: U.S. Bureau of Labor Statistics, U.S. Department of Commerce, and estimates by the editors. Shipments data for 1996 are not available.

Output. U.S. economic improvement after the 1991 recession and strength in the construction and furniture sectors sparked a rebound in the lumber and wood products industry. This recovery has been reflected in both employment and shipments during the last five years (Figure 2). Industry shipments by the lumber and wood products industry hit a nine-year high of $104.9 billion in 1995 (latest year for which complete data are available), compared with $69.7 billion in 1987 (Table 3). Annual growth during the nine-year period averaged 5.24 percent, but only 0.26 percent when adjusted for inflation. Industrial production continued to rise in 1996, bringing the annual index to an all-time high. None of the gain was in logging, however, where the index fell to the lowest annual average since 1982. Millwork and plywood gained 4.1 percent, and manufactured home production rose a strong 8.6 percent. (See Table 3A for data on production and consumption of and trade in roundwood and its end products, including pulp products, during the 1987-1993 period.)

Investment. New capital expenditures by the industry in 1995 rose to $2.97 billion from $2.66 billion the previous year and a low $1.73 billion in 1991, indicating considerable modernization of plants and equipment (Table 3). Research and development expenditures grew erratically between 1987 and 1994, from $137 million to $201 million. Reflecting plant modernization and expansion, capacity utilization in 1996 stood at 85.2 percent, up slightly from that in 1995 but below high levels of the late 1980s.

Prices. Producer prices (Table 3) hit their highest level in 1994 and have since hovered slightly below that level. Price gains averaged 4.29 percent a year between 1987 and 1996, with the largest gains occurring in 1992 and 1993.

TABLE 3

U.S. OUTPUT, INVESTMENT, AND PRICES: LUMBER AND WOOD PRODUCTS

(Millions of U.S. dollars, except as noted)

	1987	1988	1989	1990	1991	1992	1993	1994	1995	1996	GROWTH RATE 1987-1995[1]
VALUE OF SHIPMENTS:											
BY INDUSTRY:											
Current dollars	69,747	72,046	74,410	74,229	70,491	81,565	94,272	103,501	104,923	.....	5.24
Constant 1992 dollars	86,214	85,882	84,006	82,073	76,541	81,565	82,230	86,465	88,002	.....	0.26
BY PRODUCT:											
Current dollars	67,080	69,606	71,673	71,404	67,717	78,061	90,329	98,798	99,858	.....	5.10
Constant 1992 dollars	82,907	82,963	80,911	78,982	73,562	78,061	78,759	82,498	83,721	.....	0.12
OTHER OUTPUT MEASURES:											
Industrial production, 1993=100	104.0	104.2	103.4	100.7	93.7	99.1	100.0	105.0	105.3	108.7	0.49
Gross domestic product:											
Current dollars	31,884	32,665	33,579	31,799	29,972	32,016	35,283	40,952	.....	.....	.....
Percent of total GDP	0.7	0.6	0.6	0.6	0.5	0.5	0.5	0.6	.....	.....	.....
Rank in manufacturing	11	11	11	13	12	12	12	12	.....	.....	.....
Chained (1992) dollars	40,047	39,928	38,736	36,972	34,127	32,016	28,729	31,546	.....	.....	.....
INVESTMENT-RELATED MEASURES:											
Capacity utilization, percent	92.1	91.1	88.7	85.0	78.5	83.0	83.6	86.3	84.6	85.2	.....
New capital expenditures	1,825	1,772	2,024	1,994	1,732	1,760	1,949	2,657	2,974	.....	.....
Research and development spending[2]	137	165	192	216	200	234	196	201	.....	.....	.....
Producer prices, 1993=100[3]	71.0	73.7	77.8	78.9	80.6	87.5	100.0	104.1	103.9	103.6	4.29

1. Compound annual growth rate.
2. Also includes furniture.
3. Prices received by domestic producers.

Sources: Shipments and new capital expenditures: U.S. Department of Commerce for 1987-1995, editor's estimates for constant dollar data for 1987-88 and all shipments data for 1996; Industrial production and capacity utilization: Federal Reserve Board of Governors; GDP: Bureau of Economic Analysis; Research and development spending: National Science Foundation; Producer prices: Bureau of Labor Statistics.

TABLE 3A

U.S. PRODUCTION, IMPORTS, AND CONSUMPTION: TIMBER PRODUCTS

(Thousands of Cubic Meters)

	INDUSTRIAL ROUNDWOOD USED FOR...											
	LUMBER				PLYWOOD AND VENEER				PULP PRODUCTS			
YEAR	PRODUCTION	IMPORTS	EXPORTS	CONSUMPTION	PRODUCTION	IMPORTS	EXPORTS	CONSUMPTION	PRODUCTION	IMPORTS	EXPORTS	CONSUMPTION
1987	197,935	67,394	14,442	250,887	46,723	5,380	2,265	50,404	132,240	56,209	33,839	154,752
1988	195,953	63,005	20,388	238,569	46,156	4,672	2,832	47,997	138,328	57,908	38,086	158,150
1989	204,051	62,467	17,783	248,764	39,813	3,256	2,775	40,295	138,045	28,798	18,094	148,748
1990	195,160	53,519	15,971	147,786	38,737	2,718	3,115	38,341	131,532	26,873	18,349	140,650
1991	182,474	47,997	16,792	213,679	34,433	2,350	2,690	34,093	137,167	26,306	20,983	142,490
1992	192,356	55,048	15,206	232,198	35,821	2,832	3,030	33,074	141,018	26,335	22,710	144,642
1993	187,911	62,948	14,328	236,531	35,594	2,860	2,860	35,594	138,724	28,175	20,841	146,030
1994	207,364	68,527	13,649	262,242	37,095	2,662	2,464	37,293	153,421	32,593	22,144	163,870
1995	199,181	72,378	13,054	258,504	36,727	3,058	2,577	37,208	156,762	34,886	25,400	166,220

	INDUSTRIAL ROUNDWOOD (CON'T)										
	OTHER INDUSTRIAL PRODUCTS, PRODUCTION AND CONSUMPTION	LOGS		PULPWOOD CHIP EXPORTS	TOTAL				FUELWOOD PRODUCTION AND CONSUMPTION	PRODUCTION, ALL PRODUCTS	CONSUMPTION, ALL PRODUCTS
YEAR		IMPORTS	EXPORTS		PRODUCTION	IMPORTS	EXPORTS	CONSUMPTION			
1987	14,017	425	19,963	4,531	415,408	129,550	75,040	469,918	89,198	504,606	559,116
1988	14,442	425	23,361	6,088	424,328	125,868	90,614	459,582	95,145	519,473	554,727
1989	14,442	170	21,323	3,483	415,238	97,835	63,543	472,721	86,112	526,127	558,833
1990	14,611	113	19,086	3,483	399,947	86,480	59,550	448,114	85,489	508,033	533,603
1991	14,498	57	17,018	5,069	389,102	79,485	62,807	426,565	85,772	496,961	512,308
1992	14,895	198	14,866	6,230	407,310	87,641	62,184	452,701	86,168	514,545	538,898
1993	14,866	425	13,026	5,522	401,788	98,259	56,775	460,658	87,301	507,664	547,988
1994	15,744	510	12,148	6,003	413,624	105,056	56,407	479,178	88,745	520,492	567,923
1995	16,056	368	12,771	7,051	408,725	112,276	60,851	478,017	90,444	518,963	568,432

Note: Converted to cubic meters by the editors.

Source: FSA, *Agricultural Conservation and Forestry Statistics*, 1997.

Workforce and Employment. After declining in each year from 1988 to 1991, employment in the industry gained steadily to 780,000 in 1996 (Table 4). Annual growth was at a 0.37 percent rate for the 10-year period. The number of production workers grew at a slightly slower rate of 0.23 percent to 641,000 and accounted for 82.2 percent of the workforce in 1996, compared with 83.3 percent in 1987. Employment of women gained slightly, reaching about 17.2 percent of the workforce in 1996. Average hourly earnings were $10.44 in 1996, and the annual growth rate since 1987 was 2.4 percent. This was insufficient to keep pace with inflation, however, as earnings in constant dollars fell at an annual rate of 1.11 percent.

Of the manufacturing industries, the lumber and wood products industry had the sixth highest number of workers certified by the Department of Labor as having lost their jobs because of NAFTA. As of June 18, 1997, 5,517 workers in the industry were so certified, with intensified competition from Canada accounting for most of the job losses. (See "NAFTA—The First Four Years" for more details.)

TABLE 4

U.S. EMPLOYMENT, HOURS, AND EARNINGS: LUMBER AND WOOD PRODUCTS

(Monetary values in U.S. dollars)

	1987	1988	1989	1990	1991	1992	1993	1994	1995	1996	CHANGE[1]
NUMBER OF EMPLOYEES, IN THOUSANDS:											
Total	754	767	756	733	675	680	709	754	769	780	0.37
Production workers	628	639	626	603	553	558	584	623	632	641	0.23
Percent of total	83.3	83.3	82.8	82.3	81.9	82.1	82.3	82.6	82.2	82.2	.....
Women	121	124	122	118	108	110	115	124	129	134	1.17
Percent of total	16.0	16.2	16.1	16.1	16.0	16.1	16.2	16.5	16.8	17.2	.....
HOURS AND EARNINGS OF PRODUCTION WORKERS:											
Average hourly earnings, U.S. dollars[2]											
Current dollars	8.43	8.59	8.84	9.08	9.24	9.44	9.61	9.84	10.12	10.44	2.40
1992 dollars[3]	10.36	10.14	9.97	9.73	9.51	9.44	9.35	9.34	9.34	9.36	-1.11
Average weekly hours	40.6	40.1	40.1	40.2	40.0	40.6	40.8	41.2	40.6	40.8	0.05
Average weekly earnings, current U.S. dollars	342.26	344.46	354.48	365.02	369.6	383.26	392.09	405.41	410.87	425.95	2.46

1. Compound annual growth rate, 1987-1996.

2. Including overtime.

3. Converted to 1992 dollars using Consumer Price Index for Urban Wage Earners and Clerical Workers.

Source: Bureau of Labor Statistics.

FIGURE 3

U.S. OCCUPATIONAL INJURY AND ILLNESS RATES: LUMBER AND WOOD PRODUCTS, 1995

Nonfatal occupational illnesses and injuries in the industry during 1995 averaged 14.9 cases per 100 workers, which is high compared to the average of 11.6 cases for all manufacturing.

Incidence of nonfatal injuries and illnesses per 100 full-time workers

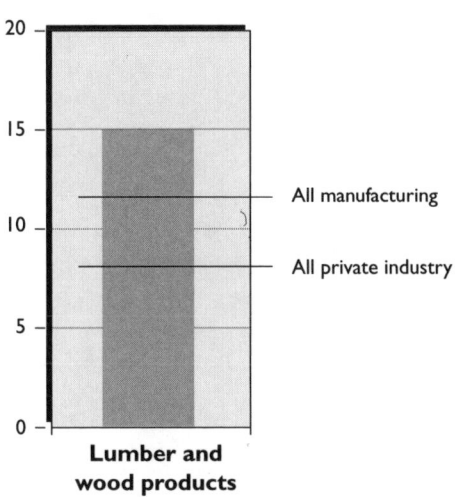

All manufacturing

All private industry

Lumber and wood products

Source: U.S. Bureau of Labor Statistics.

TABLE 5

U.S. EMPLOYMENT PROJECTIONS BY MAJOR OCCUPATIONAL GROUP: LUMBER AND WOOD PRODUCTS

| OCCUPATION | 1994 | | PROJECTIONS, 2005 | | | |
| | NUMBER OF EMPLOYEES | PERCENT OF INDUSTRY TOTAL | NUMBER OF EMPLOYEES | | | PERCENT OF INDUSTRY TOTAL, MODERATE PROJECTIONS |
			LOW	MODERATE	HIGH	
Total, all occupations	752,300	100.0	649,000	684,700	728,700	100.0
Executive, administrative, and managerial	49,682	6.6	44,926	47,442	50,590	6.9
Professional specialties	5,361	0.7	5,439	5,741	6,102	0.8
Technicians and related support	6,555	0.9	5,012	5,325	5,725	0.8
Marketing and sales	15,019	2.0	14,041	14,882	15,958	2.2
Administrative support including clerical	51,726	6.9	41,116	43,396	46,244	6.3
Service	9,251	1.2	7,124	7,526	8,021	1.1
Agriculture, forestry, and fisheries occupations	62,321	8.3	54,390	55,717	56,921	8.1
Precision production, craft, and repair	172,756	23.0	157,618	167,130	179,030	24.4
Operators, fabricators, assemblers	379,629	50.5	319,334	337,539	360,109	49.3

Source: Bureau of Labor Statistics, November 1995.

Projections to the year 2005 show employment in the industry declining to 684,700 (moderate assumption) with reductions in all occupational groups except professional specialties.

Finance. From 1992 to 1995, production worker earnings showed steady, if slow, growth, while corporate income grew faster but more erratically. Corporate earnings from operations hit their highest level in 1994, pulled back significantly in 1995, and then rose again in 1996 (Figure 4).

Total sales and receipts by the industry rose from $45.6 billion in 1992 to $71.4 billion in 1996, for an annual growth rate of 11.87 percent. Income from operations totaled $4.3 billion in 1996, compared with $2.9 billion in 1992, and the annual growth rate was 10.68 percent. After-tax income rose sharply from $1.7 billion to a peak $3.3 billion in 1994, settling back to $2.7 billion in 1996. After-tax income amounted to 3.79 percent of sales and 14.89 percent of stockholders' equity in 1996. Inventories ended at a relatively high level of $7.9 billion in 1996. Debt as a percentage of total assets was slightly above the 1995 level but below that of 1992. (See Table 6.)

FIGURE 4

U.S. CORPORATE INCOME AND WORKER EARNINGS: LUMBER AND WOOD PRODUCTS

Corporate operating income and aggregate production worker earnings

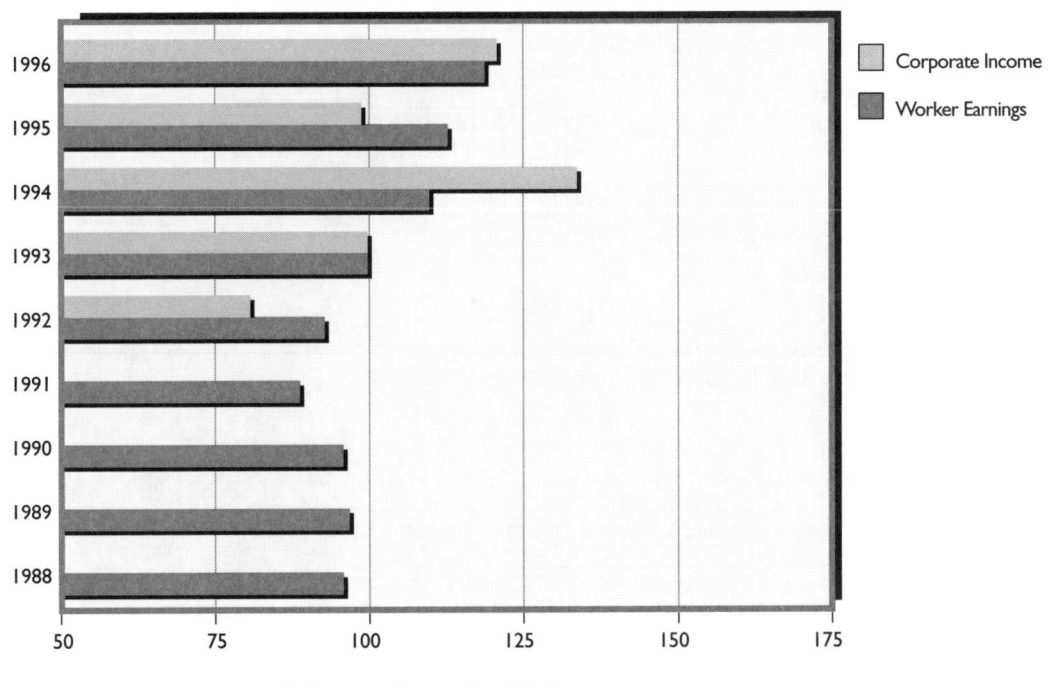

Index numbers, 1993=100

Source: U.S. Bureau of Labor Statistics, U.S. Bureau of the Census, and estimates by the editors. Corporate earnings data prior to 1992 are not available.

TABLE 6

U.S. CORPORATE INCOME AND ASSETS: LUMBER AND WOOD PRODUCTS

(Monetary values in millions of U.S. dollars)

INCOME AND EXPENSES	1992	1993	1994	1995	1996	CHANGE OR AVERAGE[1]
Sales and receipts	45,567	49,896	58,088	60,774	71,379	11.87
Depreciation and amortization	(1,260)	(1,330)	(1,551)	(1,725)	(1,840)	9.93
Other operating costs	(41,432)	(44,989)	(51,766)	(55,524)	(65,221)	12.01
Income from operations	2,875	3,577	4,771	3,523	4,315	10.68
Nonoperating income (expenditures)	(407)	(268)	(233)	(548)	(889)	.....
Income before taxes	2,469	3,309	4,538	2,977	3,428	8.55
Income after taxes	1,747	2,367	3,300	2,115	2,705	11.55
Cash dividends	498	461	592	610	1,446	30.54
Income retained in business	1,249	1,905	2,708	1,505	1,259	0.20
Direct credits (charges)	(31)	(304)	(748)	(445)	(473)	.....
Ending retained earnings	9,629	10,585	12,123	13,855	14,935	11.60
ASSETS, END OF YEAR:						
Total	24,878	27,309	31,818	33,479	35,455	9.26
Accounts receivable	3,386	3,990	4,911	4,774	5,555	13.17
Inventories	5,174	6,333	6,472	7,422	7,872	11.06
Net property, plant and equipment	9,628	10,295	12,391	13,190	14,137	10.08
RATIOS, PERCENT:						
INCOME TO SALES:						
Before tax	5.42	6.63	7.81	4.90	4.80	5.91
After tax	3.83	4.74	5.68	3.48	3.79	4.31
INCOME TO STOCKHOLDERS' EQUITY:						
Before tax	20.88	23.97	28.41	17.07	18.87	21.84
After tax	14.78	17.14	20.66	12.13	14.89	15.92
INCOME TO TOTAL ASSETS:						
Before tax	9.92	12.12	14.26	8.89	9.67	10.97
After tax	7.02	8.67	10.37	6.32	7.63	8.00
AS A PERCENT OF TOTAL ASSETS:						
Property, plant and equipment	38.70	37.70	38.94	39.40	39.87	38.92
Short-term debt	5.10	5.27	5.12	7.00	5.96	5.69
Long-term debt	24.07	19.66	19.53	18.82	20.21	20.46
Stockholders' equity	47.52	50.55	50.21	52.10	51.25	50.33

1. For income and asset amounts, compound annual growth rate; for ratios, average of ratios for the years shown.
Source: U.S. Bureau of the Census, Quarterly Financial Report.

Notes: Parentheses ( ) indicate negative items, e.g., net expenses, charges, or losses. Net property, plant, and equipment is net of accumulated depreciation. Because the samples used to collect the data change, retained earnings at the end of a given year will not exactly equal the previous year's retained earnings plus the current year's retained income and credits.

CANADA

The wood products industry is hugely important to Canada, where 90 percent of the timberland is publicly owned. The industry reportedly accounts for 50 cents out of every $1 earned in British Columbia, which has about half of Canada's lumber production. In Quebec, 250 towns and cities depend on wood processing and there are 225 sawmills and 19,000 direct jobs in the industry.

Canada's lumber and wood industry includes everything from the cutting and planing of lumber to production of prefabricated wood buildings, coffins, and caskets to wood preservation. The largest subindustry is sawmill, planing, and shingle mills, with almost two-thirds of total industry shipments in 1993 (Table 7). Other areas of note are sash, door, and other millwork (17 percent of shipments in 1993) and veneer and plywood (7 percent). In 1993, the highest paying subindustry in this group was softwood veneer and plywood (Can$19.84 an hour).

Shipments by the wood products industry rose 57 percent between 1987 and 1994 to Can$22.9 billion (Table 8). Employment during the same period declined 3 percent to 117,982, which, however, was the highest level since 1989 and 17 percent above the 1991 low. Number of establishments fell from 3,424 in 1987 to 2,861, reflecting consolidation and modernization of the industry. Production worker numbers declined at a slightly faster rate than total employment, and they accounted for 84 percent of the workforce in 1994, compared with 86 percent in 1988. Average hourly earnings of production workers in 1994 were Can$15.77, up from Can$12.58 in 1988, and the workweek averaged 40 hours. (See Table 8A for additional data on employment and production in Canada's forest products industry.)

TABLE 7

CANADA: COMPONENT INDUSTRIES OF WOOD INDUSTRIES (CSIC 25), 1993

(Monetary values in Canadian dollars)

| INDUSTRY NAME | CSIC | ESTABLISH-MENTS (NUMBER) | EMPLOYMENT | | VALUE OF SHIPMENTS (MILLIONS) | AVERAGE HOURLY EARNINGS[1] |
			NUMBER	PERCENT OF INDUSTRY TOTAL		
WOOD INDUSTRIES	25	2,894	109,961	100.0	CAN$19,082.9	CAN$15.48
Sawmill, planing, and shingle mills	251	876	58,045	52.8	12,530.2	17.51
Shingles and shakes	2511	70	1,954	1.8	283.7	15.21
Sawmill and planing mill products	2512	806	56,091	51.0	12,246.5	17.60
Veneer and plywood	252	67	8,099	7.4	1,255.4	16.41
Hardwood veneer and plywood	2521	43	3,593	3.3	395.8	12.12
Softwood veneer and plywood	2522	24	4,506	4.1	859.6	19.84
Sash, door, and other millwork	254	1,475	32,545	29.6	3,255.0	11.85
Prefabricated wooden buildings	2541	88	2,552	2.3	340.5	12.52
Kitchen cabinets, bathroom vanities	2542	693	9,977	9.1	862.2	11.76
Wooden door and window	2543	326	10,842	9.9	1,067.4	11.89
Other millwork	2549	368	9,174	8.3	984.9	11.73
Wooden boxes and pallets	256	162	2,390	2.2	243.6	10.28
Coffins and caskets	258	26	725	0.7	54.9	11.75
Other wood industries	259	288	8,157	7.4	1,743.8	14.72
Wood preservation	2591	57	1,201	1.1	371.1	14.12
Particle board	2592	24	1,867	1.7	423.1	16.30
Wafer board	2593	12	2,092	1.9	669.2	18.93
Other wood, n.e.c.	2599	195	2,997	2.7	280.2	11.16

1. Including overtime.

Source: Adapted from Statistics Canada, *Manufacturing Industries of Canada* (Cat. No. 31-203).

TABLE 8

CANADIAN EMPLOYMENT AND SHIPMENTS: WOOD INDUSTRIES, 1987-1994

(Monetary values in Canadian dollars)

	1987	1988	1989	1990	1991	1992	1993	1994	CHANGE[1]
All employees	121,655	123,934	123,609	115,490	100,656	103,586	109,961	117,982	-0.44
Establishments	3,424	3,639	3,380	3,409	3,173	3,014	2,894	2,861	-2.53
Employees per establishment	36	34	37	34	32	34	38	41	2.15
Production workers per establishment	.....	29	32	29	27	29	32	35	2.79
PRODUCTION WORKERS:									
Total	.....	106,992	106,682	98,688	85,212	87,213	92,000	99,201	-1.25
Percent of all employees	.....	86.3	86.3	85.5	84.7	84.2	83.7	84.1	.....
Male	.....	99,665	99,289	92,031	80,090	.....	.....	.....	.....
Female	.....	7,327	7,393	6,657	5,122	.....	.....	.....	.....
Percent of all production workers	.....	6.8	6.9	6.7	6.0	.....	.....	.....	.....
Average hourly earnings	.....	12.58	13.18	13.97	14.43	14.97	15.48	15.77	3.84
Average weekly earnings	.....	511.01	530.37	555.85	578.90	596.08	613.59	631.00	3.58
Average weekly hours	.....	40.6	40.2	39.8	40.1	39.8	39.7	40.0	-0.25
Shipments (millions)	14,611	15,322	15,843	14,806	13,166	15,060	19,083	22,907	6.63

1. Compound annual growth rate.

Source: Adapted from Statistics Canada, *Manufacturing Industries of Canada* (Cat. No. 31-203).

TABLE 8A

CANADIAN FOREST PRODUCTS: EMPLOYMENT AND PRODUCTION, 1987-1996

(Monetary values in Canadian dollars)

	1987	1988	1989	1990	1991	1992	1993	1994	1995	1996
EMPLOYMENT	68,087	67,035	68,830	62,854	62,196	60,879	64,664	65,621	68,273	65,792
ROUNDWOOD PRODUCTION (THOUSANDS OF CUBIC METERS):										
Total	191,685	190,616	188,254	162,127	160,168	169,895	176,193	183,224	188,433	.....
Softwood	174,566	172,770	170,095	141,090	138,379	146,700	150,494	154,134	157,243	.....
Hardwood	10,490	11,557	12,009	14,869	15,109	16,807	19,276	23,211	25,871	.....
Fuel and firewood	6,629	6,289	6,150	6,169	6,681	6,388	6,423	5,879	5,319	.....

Source: Statistics Canada, CANSIM, adapted.

MEXICO

Mexico's wood and wood products industry includes lumbering as well as furniture production (Tables 9 and 10). In 1993, the sawing and carpentry component of that industry had 5,510 production units and 47,897 employees. There were 35,102 production workers with average annual earnings of 7,712 new pesos ($2,469) and 5,254 nonproduction employees with annual earnings of 18,383 new pesos ($5,885).

The gross domestic product originating of the lumber and wood products industry amounted to the equivalent of $2.15 billion in 1995 (in constant 1993 dollars), compared with $2.27 billion in 1988, resulting in a negative 0.79-percent annual rate of change. Employment by the wood products industry declined at an annual rate of 2.96 percent between 1988 and 1995, from 169,382 employees to 137,231 (Table 10). Numbers for lumber production decreased at an even faster rate of 6.12 percent, from 74,591 in 1988 to 47,944 in 1995. (See Table 10A for additional data on employment and production by Mexico's forest products industry.)

TABLE 9

MEXICO: COMPONENT INDUSTRIES OF WOOD AND WOOD PRODUCTS (CMAP 33), 1993

(Monetary values in 1993 Mexican New Pesos)

			ALL WORKERS									
							PAID WORKERS					
							PRODUCTION WORKERS		NONPRODUCTION EMPLOYEES		BENEFITS	UNPAID
INDUSTRY	CMAP	NUMBER OF UNITS	NUMBER	PERCENT OF INDUSTRY TOTAL	AVERAGE DAYS WORKED	REMUN-ERATION[1]	NUMBER	WAGES AND SALARIES	NUMBER	WAGES AND SALARIES	PER PAID EMPLOYEE	WORKERS, NUMBER
Wood and wood products	33	31,606	168,023	100	266	13,149	106,196	8,478	17,491	20,320	2,997	44,336
Sawmill and carpentry products	3311	5,510	47,897	29	252	11,903	35,102	7,712	5,254	18,383	2,801	7,541
Fabrication of containers and other	3312	7,480	25,397	15	288	11,370	11,522	7,662	1,879	15,398	2,623	11,996
Wood furniture and mattresses	3320	18,616	94,729	56	261	14,210	59,572	9,087	10,358	22,195	3,181	24,799

1. Average annual remuneration including benefits.

Source: INEGI, Census Economics 1994.

TABLE 10

MEXICAN GROSS DOMESTIC PRODUCT AND EMPLOYMENT: LUMBER AND WOOD PRODUCTS, 1988-1995

	1988	1989	1990	1991	1992	1993	1994	1995	CHANGE[1]
GROSS DOMESTIC PRODUCT:									
Millions of constant 1993 new pesos	7,104.0	7,110.5	7,083.4	7,131.7	7,331.4	7,145.0	7,278.8	6,718.5	-0.79
Millions of constant 1993 U.S. dollars[2]	2,274.2	2,276.3	2,267.6	2,283.1	2,347.0	2,287.3	2,330.2	2,150.8	-0.79
TOTAL EMPLOYMENT:									
Wood products	169,382	168,034	164,274	163,450	165,263	154,367	151,584	137,231	-2.96
Lumber	74,591	70,452	64,485	60,631	59,629	49,518	49,485	47,944	-6.12
Other wood products	94,791	97,582	99,789	102,819	105,634	104,849	102,099	89,287	-0.85

1. Compound annual growth rate.
2. Converted at 3.1237 new pesos to the U.S. dollar.

Source: Sistema de Cuentas Nacionales de Mexico, INEGI.

TABLE 10A

MEXICAN FOREST PRODUCTS: EMPLOYMENT AND OUTPUT, 1987-1995

	1987	1988	1989	1990	1991	1992	1993	1994	1995
Paid employees		94,112	94,206	91,191	90,097	90,838	85,582	87,273	80,727
OUTPUT									
Total quantity (thousands of cubic meters)	9,791	9,314	8,888	8,158	7,688	7,681	6,350	5,956	....
Pine	7,873	7,561	7,462	6,862	6,455	6,441	5,066	4,837	....
Oyamel	453	369	238	233	220	222	217	196	....
Other conifers	101	69	73	62	68	57	41	36	....
Oak	394	469	438	409	385	417	526	434	....
Other broadleaf	203	179	170	173	145	136	165	165	....
Precious	104	79	74	47	42	29	31	15	....
Common tropicals	663	588	433	372	373	379	304	273	....
Total value (thousands of new pesos)	393,359	668,265	895,506	923,085	1,027,878	1,143,947	970,521	979,259	....
Pine	295,052	518,227	776,233	806,117	883,807	989,496	794,563	819,053	....
Oyamel	9,082	11,380	14,592	15,398	24,840	24,272	27,747	26,794	....
Other conifers	4,737	3,725	5,999	5,787	7,506	7,003	5,003	4,742	....
Oak	30,749	48,776	24,407	25,066	31,879	38,866	59,575	53,559	....
Other broadleaf	6,662	11,849	10,602	12,993	11,850	12,849	16,570	17,892	....
Precious	8,840	15,940	16,699	14,303	18,775	15,615	16,982	9,484	....
Common tropicals	38,237	58,368	46,707	40,442	49,221	55,846	50,081	47,735	....

Source: INEGI: Anuario Estadística 95.

INTERNATIONAL TRADE

United States. U.S. worldwide exports of lumber totaled $7.4 billion in 1996, up only 13 percent from 1990 (Table 11). In contrast, imports during 1990-1996 rose 121 percent to $12.2 billion, with most of the growth occurring after 1992. By 1996, the United States had a trade deficit of $4.8 billion, compared with a surplus of over $1 billion in 1990 and 1991. The U.S. export growth reflected higher prices, rather than volume, which declined during 1989-1994 as lumbering was restricted because of environmental concerns such as its threat to the northern spotted owl. Exports include sawlogs, veneer logs, and pulpwood; softwood and hardwood lumber, veneer, and plywood; and reconstituted panel products. Japan, Canada, and Mexico are the major markets, and Canada is by far the leading source for imports.

Canada. U.S. lumber and wood products exports to Canada totaled $1.3 billion in 1996, about 38 percent above those in 1990, but Canada's much larger exports to the United States grew 153 percent to $8.8 billion during that period (Table 11). The resulting U.S. trade deficit was $7.5 billion in 1996, compared with $2.5 billion in 1990. The United States takes about 60 percent of Canada's lumber exports, but Canada reportedly is eyeing Japan (which now receives about 7 percent of its exports) and China as markets of the future.

Mexico. Trade by Mexico is almost entirely with the United States (Table 11), as that with Canada is still extremely small. U.S. exports to Mexico in 1996 totaled $256 million, only about half the 1992 level and the smallest so far in the 1990s. Mexican exports to the United States rose from $213 million in 1990 to almost $400 million in 1996. This faster growth for Mexico wiped out its trade deficit with the United States by 1995 and gave it a $146 million trade surplus in 1996.

NAFTA. Canada has a large and growing surplus in lumber and wood products trade, while the United States has a ballooning trade deficit (Table 11). These trends largely reflect restrictions on lumbering during a time of economic growth in the United States. Canada's trade surplus totaled $7.5 billion in 1996, compared with $2.5 billion in 1990, just after the Canadian-U.S. Free Trade Agreement went into effect. Mexico moved from persistent trade deficits until 1994 to a 1996 surplus of $146 million.

TABLE 11

INTERNATIONAL TRADE, LUMBER AND WOOD PRODUCTS

(Millions of U.S. dollars)

	1989[1]	1990	1991	1992	1993	1994	1995	1996
Global trade, U.S.								
Imports								
Value	5,919.4	5,524.8	5,296.6	6,748.7	8,900.9	10,527.8	10,405.7	12,194.0
Ratio to new supply[2]	7.9	7.5	7.6	8.3	9.3	10.0	.....	.....
Ratio to apparent consumption[3]	8.6	8.2	8.4	9.1	10.1	10.7	.....	.....
Exports								
Value	6,060.2	6,549.6	6,589.4	6,821.5	7,360.7	7,252.2	7,423.5	7,400.7
Ratio to comparable domestic shipments	8.8	9.6	10.2	9.2	8.5	7.6	.....	.....
TRADE BALANCE	140.8	1,024.8	1,292.8	72.8	(1,540.2)	(3,275.6)	(2,982.2)	(4,793.3)
BILATERAL TRADE: NAFTA[4]								
U.S. exports to Canada	670.0	966.8	1,005.4	1,066.8	1,164.8	1,247.8	1,350.4	1,330.0
Canadian exports to U.S.	3,890.1	3,490.4	3,385.0	4,487.1	6,285.1	7,570.9	7,233.0	8,820.8
U.S. exports to Mexico	237.0	278.0	394.1	518.2	483.6	423.3	261.9	255.8
Mexican exports to U.S.	221.0	213.1	246.7	293.9	321.6	303.4	307.8	399.5
Canadian exports to Mexico	0.3	0.2	3.5	0.6	0.3	2.9	0.2	0.2
Mexican exports to Canada	0.4	0.5	0.8	1.3	1.9	1.6	1.4	2.1
TRADE BALANCES WITHIN NAFTA[5]								
Canada	3,220.0	2,523.3	2,382.3	3,419.6	5,118.7	6,324.4	5,881.4	7,488.9
Mexico	(15.9)	(64.6)	(150.1)	(223.6)	(160.4)	(121.2)	47.1	145.6
United States	(3,204.1)	(2,458.7)	(2,232.2)	(3,196.1)	(4,958.2)	(6,203.3)	(5,928.5)	(7,634.5)

1. 1989 and earlier data on U.S. exports to Canada for manufacturing total and manufacturing industries are not comparable with data for 1990 and later years because of a change in the reporting system. The NAFTA trade balances for the U.S. and Canada also are affected.

2. New supply equals comparable domestic shipments plus imports for consumption.

3. Apparent consumption equals comparable domestic shipments plus imports for consumption less exports.

4. Amounts less than U.S. $100,000 shown as zero.

5. Parentheses indicate an excess of imports over exports. Because of commodity coding and other data differences among the three countries, these trade balances are only rough estimates and should be used with caution.

Source for U.S. Global Trade: U.S. Department of Commerce, International Trade Administration.

Source for U.S. -Canada and U.S.-Mexico Bilateral Trade: U.S. Bureau of the Census.

Source for Canada-Mexico and Mexico-Canada Bilateral Trade: Statistics Canada, Foreign Trade Division, Special tabulation, March 1997, converted to U.S. dollars by the editors.

MISCELLANEOUS MANUFACTURING

THE UNITED STATES

Products and Processes. Miscellaneous manufacturing includes some relatively small but hardly insignificant industries such as jewelry and silverware; musical instruments; dolls, toys, games, and athletic equipment; fasteners, buttons, needles and pins; brooms and brushes; and burial caskets. The group as a whole ranks 18th among the 20 U.S. manufacturing industries in terms of industry shipments.

Table 1 shows the various industries included in this category in 1992 (the latest year for which economic census data are available). The largest four-digit product category in 1992 was sporting and athletic equipment not elsewhere included (19 percent of total industry shipments). Next in size were signs and advertising displays (13.8 percent of the total); games, toys, and children's vehicles (10.8 percent); and precious metal jewelry (10.9 percent).

TABLE 1

UNITED STATES: COMPONENT INDUSTRIES OF MISCELLANEOUS MANUFACTURING (SIC 39), 1992

(Monetary values in millions of U.S. dollars)

| INDUSTRY | SIC | ESTABLISH-MENTS | SHIPMENTS | | VALUE ADDED BY MANUFACTURE | NEW CAPITAL EXPENDI-TURES | EMPLOY-MENT[1] | PAYROLL |
			VALUE	PERCENT BY 4 LARGEST COMPANIES				
MISCELLANEOUS MANUFACTURING INDUSTRIES	39	17,035	$39,498.3	.....	$21,975.3	$1,050.0	365,500	$8,417.0
Jewelry, silverware, and plated ware	391	2,838	5,730.9	.....	2,500.7	66.4	45,500	1,068.4
Jewelry, precious metal	3911	2,204	4,190.1	16	1,768.3	36.8	32,500	758.0
Silverware, plated ware, stainless steel ware	3914	213	685.5	66	407.0	17.0	6,700	157.3
Jewelers' materials and lapidary work	3915	421	855.3	34	325.3	12.6	6,300	153.1
Musical instruments	393	461	982.1	25	589.2	13.8	12,200	272.7
Toys and sporting goods	394	3,242	12,122.6	.....	6,815.8	323.0	97,500	2,133.0
Dolls and stuffed toys	3942	209	251.0	34	156.5	3.0	3,600	64.1
Games, toys, and children's vehicles	3944	919	4,291.0	44	2,451.8	142.6	31,900	702.9
Sporting and athletic goods, n.e.c.	3949	2,114	7,580.7	14	4,207.5	89.1	62,000	1,366.0
Pens, pencils, office and art supplies	395	1,055	3,515.2	.....	2,029.6	95.9	30,300	684.2
Pens, mechanical pencils and parts	3951	107	1,148.5	49	694.9	51.7	8,100	208.6
Lead pencils, crayons, and artists' materials	3952	164	975.9	62	576.8	23.0	7,300	152.9
Marking devices	3953	650	545.4	22	349.9	9.4	7,600	161.1
Carbon paper and inked ribbons	3955	134	845.5	36	408.1	11.8	7,300	161.6
Costume jewelry and notions, except precious metal	396	1,132	2,315.7	.....	1,365.6	132.0	27,400	556.5
Costume jewelry	3961	893	1,444.0	27	871.7	12.8	17,400	328.8
Fasteners, buttons, needles, and pins	3965	239	871.7	41	494.0	119.3	10,100	227.7
Miscellaneous manufacturing industries	399	8,307	14,831.9	.....	8,674.4	418.9	152,500	3,702.2
Brooms and brushes	3991	281	1,291.3	23	751,800.0	35.8	12,700	293.6
Signs and advertising displays	3993	4,584	5,444.7	6	3,179.2	97.6	67,800	1,686.8
Burial caskets	3995	210	1,052.9	64	660.5	28.5	7,800	196.1
Hard surface floor coverings, n.e.c.	3996	28	1,521.1	83	902.7	65.7	6,700	240.2
Manufacturing industries, n.e.c.	3999	3,204	5,521.8	12	3,180.3	191.3	57,500	1,285.6

1. Employment numbers from the economic censuses differ in definition and classification from the Bureau of Labor Statistics estimates in Table 2. Year-to-year comparisons between Table 1 and Table 2 are not appropriate.

Source: U.S. Bureau of the Census, 1992 Census of Manufactures.

Employment in miscellaneous manufacturing totaled 378,300 in 1993 and is projected to rise slightly, to 403,500 by the year 2005 (Table 2). Among the larger employment areas in 1993 were sporting and athletic goods not elsewhere included (67,600 employees); signs and advertising displays (57,600); precious metal jewelry (37,800); and pens, pencils, and office and art supplies (33,500). Hourly earnings of production workers in these industries averaged $9.39 in 1993.

TABLE 2

U.S. EMPLOYMENT AND EARNINGS: MISCELLANEOUS MANUFACTURING

| | | 1993 | | | 2005 |
| | | EMPLOYMENT[1] | | AVERAGE HOURLY | |
INDUSTRY	SIC	NUMBER OF PERSONS	PERCENT OF INDUSTRY TOTAL	EARNINGS (U.S. DOLLARS)[2]	PROJECTED EMPLOYMENT[3]
MISCELLANEOUS MANUFACTURING INDUSTRIES	39	378,300	100.0	$9.39	403,500
Jewelry, silverware, and plated ware	391	51,000	13.5	9.67	43,500
Jewelry, precious metal	3911	37,800	10.0	9.58	....
Musical instruments	393	13,000	3.4	9.19	....
Toys and sporting goods	394	110,800	29.3	8.81	135,000
Dolls, games, toys, and children's vehicles	3942,4	43,300	11.4	8.51	....
Sporting and athletic goods, n.e.c.	3949	67,600	17.9	8.98	....
Pens, pencils, office, and art supplies	395	33,500	8.9	10.32	....
Costume jewelry and notions	396	29,500	7.8	8.07	....
Costume jewelry	3961	18,200	4.8	7.12	....
Miscellaneous manufactures	399	140,400	37.1	9.86	....
Signs and advertising specialties	3993	57,600	15.2	10.15	....
Manufactured products, n.e.c.	393,5,6,9	....	....	....	225,000

1. Total payroll employment. Employment data from the economic censuses, shown in Table 1, differ in definition and classification from the Bureau of Labor Statistics estimates in this table. Year-to-year comparisons between Table 1 and Table 2 are not appropriate.

2. Earnings of production workers, including overtime.

3. Number of persons, moderate projection by the U.S. Bureau of Labor Statistics.

Source: Bureau of Labor Statistics.

FIGURE 1

U.S. EMPLOYMENT IN MISCELLANEOUS MANUFACTURING

Percent distribution by region, 1995

Employment in miscellaneous manufacturing is highest in the Mid-Atlantic States (with about 18 percent of the total in 1995). Close behind are the Great Lakes region (about 17 percent), the Pacific region (17 percent), and the Southeast (16 percent).

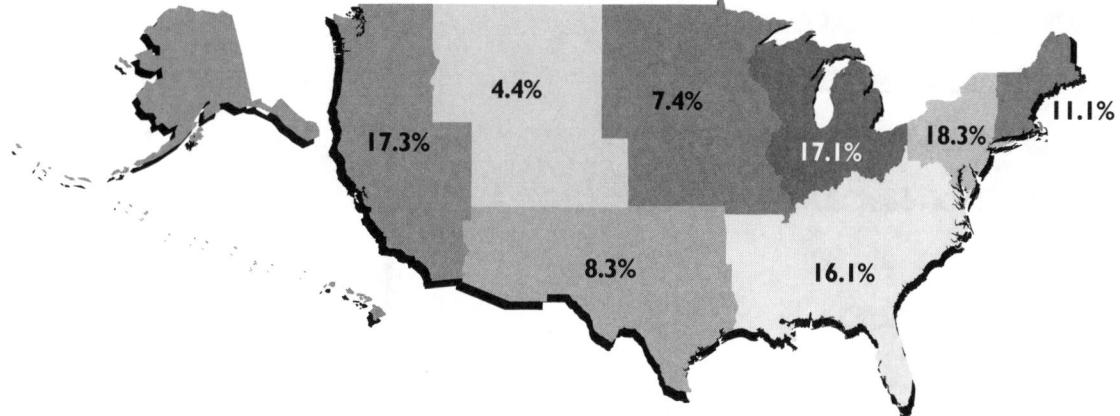

Source: U.S. Department of Commerce, Bureau of Economic Analysis.

What's New. Attendance at the 1997 American International Toy Fair in New York City's Javits Center was up 13 percent from the previous year, according to trade press reports. The fair attracted nearly 11,500 buyers and 1,174 exhibitors from the United States and 24 foreign countries during its February 14-17 run. New items displayed included the Beanie Babies and other plush toys, the Beatrix Potter line, a weight-loss game featuring food trivia and dieting dilemmas; new types of construction toys, including solar-powered building sets; and cutting-edge CD-ROM games. Exhibit space for the annual event is to be increased 30 percent in the next two years, according to an industry spokesperson.

The most popular outdoor sport today is freshwater fishing (with an estimated 45.9 million participants in 1996), according to the Sporting Goods Manufacturers Association and *American Sports Data, Inc.* Next in line are tent camping (38.0 million), tenting/backpacking (19.9 million), and hunting (17.8 million).

Sales of gifts and decorative accessories totaled almost $36 billion in 1996, compared with $21.5 billion in 1991, a compound annual growth rate of 10.8 percent, according to *Gifts & Decorative Accessories* magazine. Gifts not only are being sold in more stores, but also through more alternative outlets such as electronic and TV retailing and catalogs.

Collecting, cross retailing in restaurants and other establishments, and cocooning (people spending more quality time at home with family and friends) have contributed to this growth.

FIGURE 2

U.S. EMPLOYMENT AND SHIPMENTS, MISCELLANEOUS MANUFACTURING

Total payroll employment and manufacturers' inflation-adjusted shipments

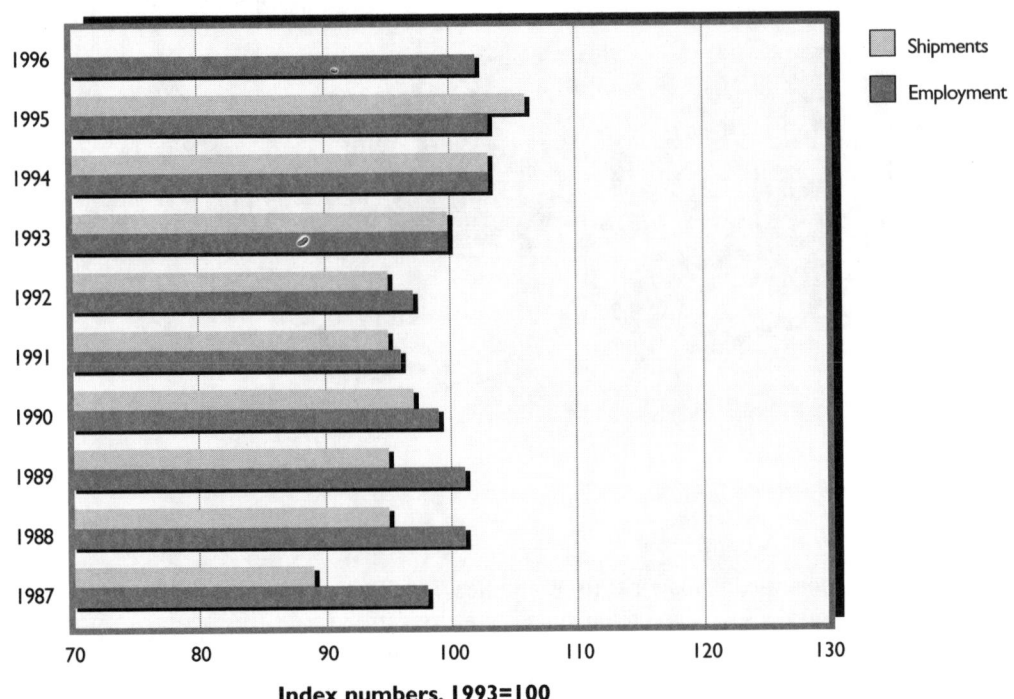

Index numbers, 1993=100

Source: U.S. Bureau of Labor Statistics, U.S. Department of Commerce, and estimates by the editors. Shipments data for 1996 are not available.

Output. After erratic performances during 1987-1991, both shipments and employment by the miscellaneous manufacturing industries trended upward, with shipments registering the stronger growth (Figure 2). Industry shipments in 1995 were valued at $46.9 billion, compared with $44.4 billion the previous year and $32.0 billion in 1987 (Table 3). The annual rate of growth was 4.89 percent in current dollars and 2.23 when adjusted for inflation.

Investment. New capital expenditures rose from $712 million in 1987 to $1.25 billion in 1995. Capacity utilization also has trended upward, hitting 78.3 percent in 1996, compared with 74 percent in 1987 (Table 3).

Prices. Producer prices rose at an annual rate of 2.34 percent during 1987-1996 (Table 3).

Workforce and Employment. After reaching a low point in the recession year of 1991, employment in miscellaneous manufacturing rose steadily through 1995 and then dipped to 387,000 in 1996 (Table 4). The annual growth rate for the 1987-1996 period was 0.50 percent. The rate of growth in employment of production workers was only 0.15 percent a year, so their share of the workforce slipped to 70.5 percent in 1996 from 72.8 percent in 1987. Employment of women rose at an even slower annual rate of 0.14 percent, which was reflected in a decline in their share of employment to 44.3 percent in 1996 from 45.8 percent in 1987.

Average hourly earnings of production workers totaled $10.38 in 1996 (Table 4). The annual rate of growth in their earnings from 1987 to 1996 was 3.29 percent in current dollars but fell to a negative 0.26 percent when adjusted for inflation. The average workweek (39.7 hours in 1996) has not changed much since 1987.

TABLE 3

U.S. OUTPUT, INVESTMENT, AND PRICES: MISCELLANEOUS MANUFACTURING

(Millions of U.S. dollars, except as noted)

	1987	1988	1989	1990	1991	1992	1993	1994	1995	1996	GROWTH RATE 1987-1995[1]
VALUE OF SHIPMENTS:											
BY INDUSTRY:											
Current dollars	32,012	35,272	36,646	38,411	38,739	39,499	42,366	44,373	46,891	.....	4.89
Constant 1992 dollars	37,114	39,462	39,439	40,215	39,557	39,499	41,591	42,788	44,274	.....	2.23
BY PRODUCT:											
Current dollars	29,501	31,983	33,324	34,665	34,657	36,399	38,558	40,678	42,747	.....	4.75
Constant 1992 dollars	34,182	35,760	35,842	36,272	35,372	36,399	37,860	39,229	40,382	.....	2.11
OTHER OUTPUT MEASURES:											
Industrial production, 1993=100	88.5	94.5	95.0	94.7	93.2	94.7	100.0	103.3	104.5	106.9	2.12
Gross domestic product:											
Current dollars	15,840	18,110	19,494	20,237	20,279	20,149	21,762	23,147	.....	.....	.....
Percent of total GDP	0.3	0.4	0.4	0.4	0.3	0.3	0.3	0.3	.....	.....	.....
Rank in manufacturing	17	17	17	17	17	17	17	17	.....	.....	.....
Chained (1992) dollars	18,737	21,367	22,178	22,154	21,068	20,149	21,123	22,372	.....	.....	.....
INVESTMENT-RELATED MEASURES:											
Capacity utilization, percent	74.0	78.2	77.4	75.6	73.1	73.4	76.4	77.8	77.6	78.3	.....
New capital expenditures	712	722	840	828	852	1,050	939	1,000	1,253	.....	.....
Producer prices, 1993=100[2]	85.4	88.5	92.0	94.6	96.7	98.4	100.0	101.5	103.6	105.2	2.34

1. Compound annual growth rate.

2. Prices received by domestic producers.

Sources: Shipments and new capital expenditures: U.S. Department of Commerce for 1987-1995, editor's estimates for constant dollar data for 1987-88 and all shipments data for 1996; Industrial production and capacity utilization: Federal Reserve Board of Governors; GDP: Bureau of Economic Analysis; Research and development spending: National Science Foundation; Producer prices: Bureau of Labor Statistics.

TABLE 4

U.S. EMPLOYMENT, HOURS, AND EARNINGS: MISCELLANEOUS MANUFACTURING

(Monetary values in U.S. dollars)

	1987	1988	1989	1990	1991	1992	1993	1994	1995	1996	CHANGE[1]
NUMBER OF EMPLOYEES, IN THOUSANDS:											
Total	370	383	381	375	366	368	378	389	390	387	0.50
Production workers	269	280	278	272	263	265	271	277	276	273	0.15
Percent of total	72.8	73.2	72.9	72.6	71.8	71.9	71.7	71.2	70.8	70.5	.....
Women	170	178	178	174	169	168	172	174	174	172	0.14
Percent of total	45.8	46.4	46.8	46.5	46.2	45.8	45.5	44.7	44.6	44.3	.....
HOURS AND EARNINGS OF PRODUCTION WORKERS:											
Average hourly earnings, U.S. dollars[2]											
Current dollars	7.76	8.00	8.29	8.61	8.85	9.15	9.39	9.67	10.05	10.38	3.29
1992 dollars[3]	9.53	9.45	9.35	9.23	9.10	9.15	9.13	9.17	9.27	9.31	-0.26
Average weekly hours	39.4	39.2	39.4	39.5	39.7	39.9	39.8	40.0	39.9	39.7	0.08
Average weekly earnings, current U.S. dollars	305.74	313.60	326.63	340.10	351.35	365.09	373.72	386.80	401.00	412.09	3.37

1. Compound annual growth rate, 1987-1996.

2. Including overtime.

3. Converted to 1992 dollars using Consumer Price Index for Urban Wage Earners and Clerical Workers.

Source: Bureau of Labor Statistics.

FIGURE 3

U.S. OCCUPATIONAL INJURY AND ILLNESS RATES: MISCELLANEOUS MANUFACTURING, 1995

Incidence of nonfatal injuries and illnesses per 100 full-time workers

Nonfatal occupational injuries and illnesses in miscellaneous manufacturing amounted to 9.1 cases per 100 workers in 1995, compared with an average of 11.6 for all manufacturing.

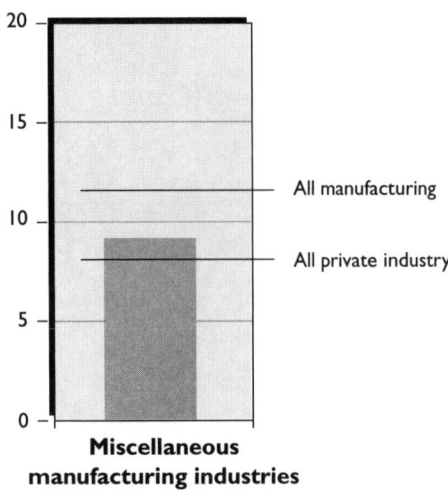

Miscellaneous manufacturing industries

Source: U.S. Bureau of Labor Statistics.

TABLE 5

U.S. EMPLOYMENT PROJECTIONS BY MAJOR OCCUPATIONAL GROUP: MISCELLANEOUS MANUFACTURING

Employment in miscellaneous manufacturing is projected at 403,500 by the year 2005 (moderate assumption), up slightly from the 390,500 estimated for 1994. Employment is expected to grow in all occupational areas except for technicians, administrative support, and service occupations.

| | 1994 | | PROJECTIONS, 2005 | | | |
| | NUMBER OF EMPLOYEES | PERCENT OF INDUSTRY TOTAL | NUMBER OF EMPLOYEES | | | PERCENT OF INDUSTRY TOTAL, MODERATE PROJECTIONS |
OCCUPATION			LOW	MODERATE	HIGH	
Total, all occupations	390,500	100.0	373,600	403,500	427,500	100.0
Executive, administrative, and managerial	35,340	9.1	35,108	37,870	40,125	9.4
Professional specialties	10,155	2.6	11,726	12,689	13,466	3.1
Technicians and related support	5,326	1.4	4,646	5,032	5,343	1.3
Marketing and sales	16,719	4.3	16,437	17,628	18,665	4.4
Administrative support including clerical	55,735	14.3	48,786	52,594	55,631	13.0
Service	4,302	1.1	3,600	3,868	4,091	1.0
Agriculture, forestry, and fisheries occupations	84	0.0	86	93	99	0.0
Precision production, craft, and repair	73,794	18.9	71,883	76,793	81,081	19.0
Operators, fabricators, assemblers	189,045	48.4	181,330	196,933	208,999	48.8

Source: Bureau of Labor Statistics, November 1995.

FIGURE 4

U.S. CORPORATE INCOME AND WORKER EARNINGS: MISCELLANEOUS MANUFACTURING

Corporate operating income and aggregate production worker earnings

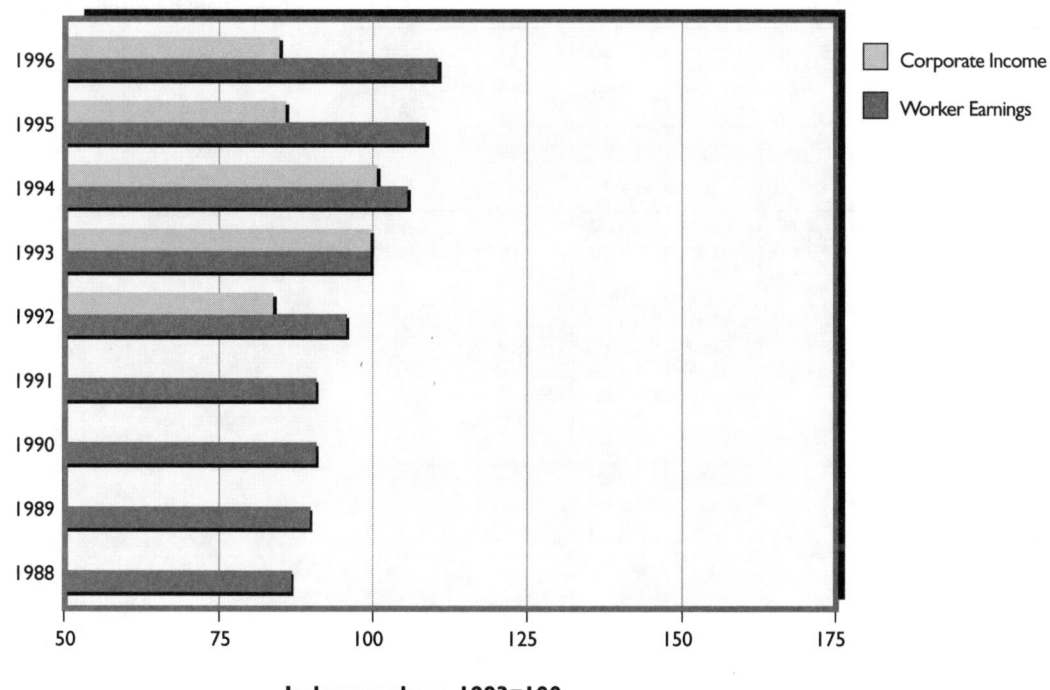

Index numbers, 1993=100

Source: U.S. Bureau of Labor Statistics, U.S. Bureau of the Census, and estimates by the editors. Corporate earnings data prior to 1992 are not available.

Finance. Corporate income in miscellaneous manufacturing reached its peak in 1994 and then declined in the following two years (Figure 4, Table 6). Production worker earnings, in contrast, trended upward throughout that period, albeit at a relatively slow rate (Figure 4 and Table 4).

Corporate income from operations in miscellaneous manufacturing hit a five-year high of $2.9 billion in 1994 before dropping to about $2.4 billion in each of the following two years (Table 6). That downturn reduced annual growth in 1992-1996 to a slow 0.22 percent. After-tax income amounted to $1.7 billion in 1996, compared with the five-year high of $1.9 billion in 1994. The ratio of after-tax income to sales was 4.86 percent in 1996, and that of after-tax income to stockholders' equity was 14.18 percent. Inventories have fluctuated in a narrow range since 1992, totaling $5.6 billion in 1996. Debt also has shown little change since 1992.

TABLE 6

U.S. CORPORATE INCOME AND ASSETS: MISCELLANEOUS MANUFACTURING

(Monetary values in millions of U.S. dollars)

INCOME AND EXPENSES	1992	1993	1994	1995	1996	CHANGE OR AVERAGE[1]
Sales and receipts	32,034	35,775	34,410	34,529	34,174	1.63
Depreciation and amortization	(838)	(964)	(855)	(913)	(860)	0.65
Other operating costs	(28,780)	(31,942)	(30,654)	(31,152)	(30,875)	1.77
Income from operations	2,417	2,870	2,899	2,465	2,438	0.22
Nonoperating income (expenditures)	(575)	(573)	(238)	(437)	(114)	-33.27
Income before taxes	1,842	2,297	2,661	2,029	2,325	5.99
Income after taxes	1,214	1,403	1,874	1,416	1,660	8.14
Cash dividends	392	392	464	354	490	5.74
Income retained in business	823	1,009	1,411	1,062	1,170	9.19
Direct credits (charges)	(206)	(329)	(607)	(165)	(802)	....
Ending retained earnings	7,278	8,608	8,284	8,249	8,118	2.77
ASSETS, END OF YEAR:						
Total	23,830	25,691	23,964	24,721	26,586	2.77
Accounts receivable	5,669	6,098	5,816	5,817	6,028	1.55
Inventories	5,404	5,839	5,220	5,436	5,635	1.05
Net property, plant and equipment	5,317	5,683	5,382	5,024	5,718	1.83
RATIOS, PERCENT:						
INCOME TO SALES:						
Before tax	5.75	6.42	7.73	5.88	6.80	6.52
After tax	3.79	3.92	5.45	4.10	4.86	4.42
INCOME TO STOCKHOLDERS' EQUITY:						
Before tax	16.73	18.06	23.05	19.05	19.85	19.35
After tax	11.02	11.03	16.23	13.29	14.18	13.15
INCOME TO TOTAL ASSETS:						
Before tax	7.73	8.94	11.10	8.21	8.75	8.95
After tax	5.09	5.46	7.82	5.73	6.24	6.07
AS A PERCENT OF TOTAL ASSETS:						
Property, plant and equipment	22.31	22.12	22.46	20.32	21.51	21.74
Short-term debt	6.98	8.36	7.64	6.72	6.91	7.32
Long-term debt	20.34	16.08	16.58	19.76	20.77	18.71
Stockholders' equity	46.21	49.51	48.17	43.09	44.05	46.21

1. For income and asset amounts, compound annual growth rate; for ratios, average of ratios for the years shown.

Source: U.S. Bureau of the Census, Quarterly Financial Report.

Notes: Parentheses ( ) indicate negative items, e.g., net expenses, charges, or losses. Net property, plant, and equipment is net of accumulated depreciation. Because the samples used to collect the data change, retained earnings at the end of a given year will not exactly equal the previous year's retained earnings plus the current year's retained income and credits.

CANADA

Canada's miscellaneous manufacturing industries comparable to those in the United States had 2,223 establishments and 43,139 employees in 1993 (Table 7). Hourly earnings averaged Can$11.43, with the highest (Can$14.62) in floor tile, linoleum, and coated fabric.

Industry shipments in 1994 rose 14 percent above 1993's to an eight-year high of Can$4.4 billion, (Table 8). Employment in 1994 totaled 44,691, up slightly from 1993 but below the 1987-91 levels. Production workers in 1994 accounted for 77.4 percent of the workforce, down from a high of 85.4 percent in 1990. Hourly earnings of production workers averaged Can$11.47 in 1994, and the average workweek was 39.5 hours.

TABLE 7

CANADA: COMPONENT INDUSTRIES OF MISCELLANEOUS MANUFACTURING (CSIC 39 EXCEPT 391), 1993

(Monetary values in Canadian dollars)

INDUSTRY NAME	CSIC	ESTABLISH-MENTS (NUMBER)	EMPLOYMENT		VALUE OF SHIPMENTS (MILLIONS)	AVERAGE HOURLY EARNINGS[1]
			NUMBER	PERCENT OF INDUSTRY TOTAL		
MISCELLANEOUS MANUFACTURING INDUSTRIES[2]	39 exc. 391	2223	43,139	100.0	CAN$3,867.4	CAN$11.43
Jewelry and precious metals	392	312	5,021	11.6	450.4	10.75
Sporting goods and toys	393	241	9,178	21.3	949.4	10.51
Sporting goods	3931	198	8,139	18.9	847.2	10.61
Toys and games	3932	43	1,039	2.4	102.2	9.66
Signs and displays	397	524	7,805	18.1	568.0	12.54
Other manufactured products	399	1146	21,135	49.0	1,899.7	11.65
Brooms, brushes, and mops	3991	27	1,028	2.4	104.5	10.37
Buttons, buckles, and clothes fasteners	3992	19	861	2.0	80.9	11.54
Floor tile, linoleum, coated fabric	3993	17	1,791	4.2	280.7	14.62
Musical instrument, sound recording	3994	41	2,734	6.3	425.8	11.86
Other manufactured products, n.e.c.	3999	1042	14,721	34.1	1,007.6	11.37

1. Including overtime.

2. Figures, except hourly earnings, do not include CSIC 391, scientific and professional equipment, for easier comparison to U.S. industries.

Note: The jewelry and precious metal industry includes secondary refining of precious metals, included in nonferrous metals in the U.S.

Source: Adapted from Statistics Canada, *Manufacturing Industries of Canada* (Cat. No. 31-203).

TABLE 8

CANADIAN EMPLOYMENT AND SHIPMENTS: MISCELLANEOUS MANUFACTURING, 1987-1994

(Monetary values in Canadian dollars)

	1987	1988	1989	1990	1991	1992	1993	1994	CHANGE[1]
All employees	47,860	51,373	54,342	53,875	49,826	44,626	43,139	44,691	-0.97
Establishments	2,599	2,959	2,743	2,935	2,598	2,406	2,223	2,112	-2.92
Employees per establishment	18	17	20	18	19	19	19	21	2.01
Production workers per establishment	.....	14	16	16	16	14	15	16	2.26
PRODUCTION WORKERS:									
Total	.....	42,369	45,206	46,009	41,630	34,151	32,836	34,585	-3.33
Percent of all employees	.....	82.5	83.2	85.4	83.6	76.5	76.1	77.4	.....
Male	.....	27,186	29,362	30,737	28,172	.....	.....	.....	.....
Female	.....	15,183	15,844	15,272	13,458	.....	.....	.....	.....
Percent of all production workers	.....	55.8	54.0	49.7	47.8	.....	.....	.....	.....
Average hourly earnings	.....	9.55	10.15	10.73	11.09	11.24	11.43	11.47	3.09
Average weekly earnings	.....	364.19	383.55	403.95	418.14	433.76	447.58	452.97	3.70
Average weekly hours	.....	38.1	37.8	37.6	37.7	38.6	39.2	39.5	0.59
Shipments (millions)	3,682	3,957	4,119	4,063	3,876	3,737	3,867	4,420	2.64

1. Compound annual growth rate.

Note: Includes secondary refining of precious metals, included in Nonferrous Metals in U.S.

Source: Adapted from Statistics Canada, *Manufacturing Industries of Canada* (Cat. No. 31-203).

MEXICO

Mexico's "other manufacturing" industry includes precious metal and costume jewelry, gold, silver, musical instruments, sporting goods, arts and crafts, toys, brushes, coinage, scales, and a number of other products. The industry had 43,928 employees in 1993 (Table 9). Their annual incomes (earnings plus benefits) averaged 16,840 new pesos ($5,391), with the 29,095 production workers earning 9,579 new pesos ($3,066) and the 8,085 nonproduction employees earning 22,178 new pesos ($7,099). Table 10 includes a more comprehensive listing of other manufacturing industries, in which combined employment amounted to 114,180 workers in 1995. The annual growth for employment between 1988 and 1995 was 7.26 percent. Industry gross domestic product rose at an annual rate of 4.4 percent during that period, to the equivalent of $1.9 billion in 1995.

TABLE 9

MEXICO: OTHER MANUFACTURING INDUSTRY (CMAP 39), 1993

(Monetary values in 1993 Mexican New Pesos)

						ALL WORKERS						
							PAID WORKERS					
							PRODUCTION WORKERS		NONPRODUCTION EMPLOYEES		BENEFITS	UNPAID
INDUSTRY	CMAP	NUMBER OF UNITS	NUMBER	PERCENT OF INDUSTRY TOTAL	AVERAGE DAYS WORKED	REMUN-ERATION[1]	NUMBER	WAGES AND SALARIES	NUMBER	WAGES AND SALARIES	PER PAID EMPLOYEE	WORKERS, NUMBER
Other manufacturing	39	4,695	43,928	100.0	270	16,840	29,095	9,579	8,085	22,178	4,521	6,748

1. Average annual remuneration including benefits.

Source: INEGI, Census Economics 1994.

TABLE 10

MEXICAN GROSS DOMESTIC PRODUCT AND EMPLOYMENT: OTHER MANUFACTURING, 1988-1995

	1988	1989	1990	1991	1992	1993	1994	1995	CHANGE[1]
GROSS DOMESTIC PRODUCT:									
Millions of constant 1993 new pesos	4,464.2	4,947.1	5,844.9	5,799.6	6,732.8	6,565.3	6,710.9	6,032.8	4.40
Millions of constant 1993 U.S. dollars[2]	1,429.1	1,583.7	1,871.1	1,856.6	2,155.4	2,101.8	2,148.4	1,931.3	4.40
TOTAL EMPLOYMENT:									
Other manufacturing	69,890	88,008	105,012	103,427	117,065	116,148	116,033	114,180	7.26

1. Compound annual growth rate.

2. Converted at 3.1237 new pesos to the U.S. dollar.

Source: Sistema de Cuentas Nacionales de Mexico, INEGI.

International Trade

United States. Global U.S. imports of products in the miscellaneous manufacturing category far exceed exports, reflecting the labor-intensive nature of subindustries such as toys and games, musical instruments, and sporting goods and the recent strength in the U.S. dollar vis-á-vis other currencies. Imports, which in 1994 amounted to 45 percent of apparent consumption, rose 57 percent between 1990 and 1996, to $31.1 billion (Table 11). U.S. exports during that period rose 59 percent, to almost $6.8 billion. The resulting U.S. trade deficit was $24.3 billion in 1996, compared with $15.5 billion in 1990. East Asian countries are growing suppliers of imports. Canada and Mexico received 24 and 8.5 percent of U.S. exports, respectively, but each supplied less than 4 percent of U.S. imports.

Canada. U.S. exports to Canada climbed 180 percent between 1990 and 1996, to $1.65 billion, while Canadian exports to the United States rose 182 percent to $872 million (Table 11). The U.S. trade surplus with Canada was $781 million in 1996, compared with $558 million in 1990. Canada's small export trade with Mexico rose 154 percent between 1990 and 1996 to $23 million.

Mexico. U.S. exports to Mexico rose from $430.7 million in 1990 to $577.5 million in 1996, an increase of 34 percent, while Mexican exports to the United States gained 162 percent, to $1.16 billion (Table 11). The 1996 U.S. trade deficit with Mexico was about $580 million, compared with only $11 million in 1990. Mexican exports to Canada rose 305 percent, to $118 million, between 1990 and 1996.

NAFTA. Between 1990 and 1993, the year before NAFTA went into effect, the U.S. trade surplus with NAFTA rose 33 percent, to $725 million; it then declined sharply, to $201 million in 1996 (Table 11). All of the U.S. surplus was with Canada, whose trade deficit reached a peak $913 million in 1994 before dipping below that level in 1995 and 1996. Mexico had a trade surplus in every year except 1992, and the 1996 surplus of $675 million was a new high.

TABLE 11

INTERNATIONAL TRADE, MISCELLANEOUS MANUFACTURING

(Millions of U.S. dollars)

	1989[1]	1990	1991	1992	1993	1994	1995	1996
GLOBAL TRADE, U.S.								
IMPORTS								
Value	19,470.3	19,773.4	19,696.0	22,674.3	25,219.1	26,830.2	28,693.9	31,088.1
Ratio to new supply[2]	38.0	37.5	37.5	39.7	40.9	41.2	.....	.....
Ratio to apparent consumption[3]	41.7	40.8	41.0	43.9	44.8	45.2	.....	.....
EXPORTS								
Value	4,518.1	4,252.2	4,579.6	5,386.2	5,287.8	5,812.4	6,444.9	6,762.9
Ratio to comparable domestic shipments	14.2	12.9	13.9	15.7	14.5	15.2	.....	.....
TRADE BALANCE	(14,952.2)	(15,521.2)	(15,116.4)	(17,288.1)	(19,931.3)	(21,017.8)	(22,249.0)	(24,325.2)
BILATERAL TRADE: NAFTA[4]								
U.S. exports to Canada	563.1	867.8	1,069.9	1,211.7	1,321.0	1,515.5	1,559.3	1,652.9
Canadian exports to U.S.	322.4	309.5	329.4	415.3	484.4	652.5	772.9	872.1
U.S. exports to Mexico	394.8	430.7	490.2	633.8	546.6	670.3	493.1	577.5
Mexican exports to U.S.	418.2	442.0	512.3	580.6	657.9	850.6	1,048.2	1,157.6
Canadian exports to Mexico[5]	6.3	9.2	8.6	7.3	9.8	30.3	21.2	23.4
Mexican exports to Canada[5]	34.5	29.2	37.9	46.1	61.4	80.7	94.4	118.3
TRADE BALANCES WITHIN NAFTA[6]								
Canada	(268.9)	(578.3)	(769.8)	(835.2)	(888.2)	(913.4)	(859.6)	(875.7)
Mexico	51.6	31.3	51.4	(14.4)	162.9	230.7	628.3	675.0
United States	217.3	547.0	718.4	849.6	725.3	682.7	231.3	200.7

1. 1989 and earlier data on U.S. exports to Canada for manufacturing total and manufacturing industries are not comparable with data for 1990 and later years because of a change in the reporting system. The NAFTA trade balances for the U.S. and Canada also are affected.

2. New supply equals comparable domestic shipments plus imports for consumption.

3. Apparent consumption equals comparable domestic shipments plus imports for consumption less exports.

4. Amounts less than U.S. $100,000 shown as zero.

5. Includes instruments.

6. Parentheses indicate an excess of imports over exports. Because of commodity coding and other data differences among the three countries, these trade balances are only rough estimates and should be used with caution.

Source for U.S. Global Trade: U.S. Department of Commerce, International Trade Administration.

Source for U.S. -Canada and U.S.-Mexico Bilateral Trade: U.S. Bureau of the Census.

Source for Canada-Mexico and Mexico-Canada Bilateral Trade: Statistics Canada, Foreign Trade Division, Special tabulation, March 1997, converted to U.S. dollars by the editors.

PAPER AND ALLIED PRODUCTS

THE UNITED STATES

Products and Processes. The United States is the world's largest producer of paper and paper products, as well as one of the most efficient and technologically advanced. The paper industry, in turn, is an important contributor to economic growth, ranking 10th among the U.S. manufacturing industries in value of 1996 shipments.

Components of the industry include pulp mills, paper mills, paperboard mills, paperboard containers and boxes, and miscellaneous converted paper products. Table 1 shows the value of their shipments in 1992 (latest year for which economic census data are available). The largest subindustry is miscellaneous converted paper products, with more than a third of the value of all paper industry shipments in 1992; it includes coated and laminated paper and packaging, bags, die-cut paper and paperboard and cardboard, sanitary products, envelopes, and stationery. Pulp mills, on the other hand, had just over four percent of the total.

Employment in the industry is projected to increase slightly by the year 2005 to 708,200 (moderate assumptions), compared with 691,700 people in 1993 (Table 2). Growth is expected in the two leading subindustries—converted paper products except containers (which had 35.2 percent of 1993 industry employment) and paperboard containers and boxes (30.6 percent).

TABLE 1

UNITED STATES: COMPONENT INDUSTRIES OF PAPER AND ALLIED PRODUCTS (SIC 26), 1992

(Monetary values in millions of U.S. dollars)

INDUSTRY	SIC	ESTABLISH-MENTS	SHIPMENTS VALUE	SHIPMENTS PERCENT BY 4 LARGEST COMPANIES	VALUE ADDED BY MANUFACTURE	NEW CAPITAL EXPENDI-TURES	EMPLOY-MENT[1]	PAYROLL
PAPER AND ALLIED PRODUCTS	26	6,416	$133,200.7	....	$60,174.0	$7,962.4	626,300	$20,491.9
Pulp mills	2611	45	5,465.6	48	2,554.2	772.3	15,900	689.1
Paper mills	2621	280	32,786.4	29	14,847.7	2,911.5	130,600	5,420.5
Paperboard mills	2631	204	16,140.0	31	8,195.3	2,040.7	51,500	2,136.4
Paperboard containers and boxes	265	2,787	32,654.8	....	12,406.0	887.1	199,400	5,722.4
Set-Up paperboard boxes	2652	155	435.8	14	240.4	10.0	6,600	129.2
Corrugated and solid fiber boxes	2653	1,651	19,833.8	28	6,759.9	464.6	112,300	3,275.8
Fiber cans, drums, and similar products	2655	300	1,922.1	63	783.1	46.7	12,400	337.1
Sanitary food containers, except folding	2656	91	2,533.9	59	1,062.2	70.0	15,600	388.9
Folding paperboard boxes, including sanitary	2657	590	7,929.2	23	3,560.3	295.8	52,600	1,591.5
Miscellaneous converted paper products	267	3,100	46,154.0	....	22,170.9	1,350.9	229,000	6,523.5
Paper, coated and laminated: packaging	2671	205	3,532.4	39	1,437.9	130.2	17,200	537.1
Paper, coated and laminated: n.e.c.	2672	449	7,670.8	46	3,542.0	268.3	32,400	1,041.2
Bags: plastics, foil, and coated	2673	523	5,729.4	23	2,857.2	186.2	38,800	992.7
Bags, uncoated paper and multiwall	2674	143	2,844.6	50	1,023.1	55.1	18,700	440.4
Die-Cut paper and paperboard and cardboard	2675	380	1,999.5	35	840.3	52.5	15,500	373.4
Sanitary paper products	2676	150	15,646.7	68	8,226.0	429.8	40,600	1,454.3
Envelopes	2677	281	2,816.0	30	1,343.6	55.3	24,700	664.9
Stationery, tablets, and related products	2678	176	1,413.7	50	689.7	28.0	9,300	217.9
Converted paper and paperboard products, n.e.c.	2679	793	4,500.9	16	2,211.1	145.5	31,800	801.7

1. Employment numbers from the economic censuses differ in definition and classification from the Bureau of Labor Statistics estimates in Table 2. Year-to-year comparisons between Table 1 and Table 2 are not appropriate.

Source: U.S. Bureau of the Census, 1992 Census of Manufactures.

TABLE 2

U.S. EMPLOYMENT AND EARNINGS: PAPER AND ALLIED PRODUCTS

| INDUSTRY | SIC | 1993 | | | 2005 |
| | | EMPLOYMENT[1] | | AVERAGE HOURLY EARNINGS (U.S. DOLLARS)[2] | PROJECTED EMPLOYMENT[3] |
		NUMBER OF PERSONS	PERCENT OF INDUSTRY TOTAL		
PAPER AND ALLIED PRODUCTS	26	691,700	100.0	$13.42	708,200
Pulp, paper, and paperboard mills	261,2,3	....	....	....	218,200
Paper mills	262	171,700	24.8	16.58	....
Paperboard mills	263	51,300	7.4	16.77	....
Paperboard containers and boxes	265	211,900	30.6	11.33	230,000
Corrugated and solid fiber boxes	2653	122,800	17.8	11.39	....
Sanitary food containers	2656	16,700	2.4	11.24	....
Folding paperboard boxes	2657	48,900	7.1	11.90	....
Converted paper products except containers	267	243,500	35.2	11.79	260,000
Paper, coated and laminated, n.e.c.	2672	46,400	6.7	13.50	....
Bags: plastics, laminated, and coated	2673	38,200	5.5	11.16	....
Envelopes	2677	23,900	3.5	10.89	....

1. Total payroll employment. Employment data from the economic censuses, shown in Table 1, differ in definition and classification from the Bureau of Labor Statistics estimates in this table. Year-to-year comparisons between Table 1 and Table 2 are not appropriate.

2. Earnings of production workers, including overtime.

3. Number of persons, moderate projection by the U.S. Bureau of Labor Statistics.

Source: Bureau of Labor Statistics.

FIGURE 1

U.S. EMPLOYMENT IN PAPER AND ALLIED PRODUCTS

Percent distribution by region, 1995

Employment in the paper industry is highest in the Southeast (29 percent of the total in 1995) and the Great Lakes region (24 percent). It is lowest in the Rocky Mountain states (only about one percent).

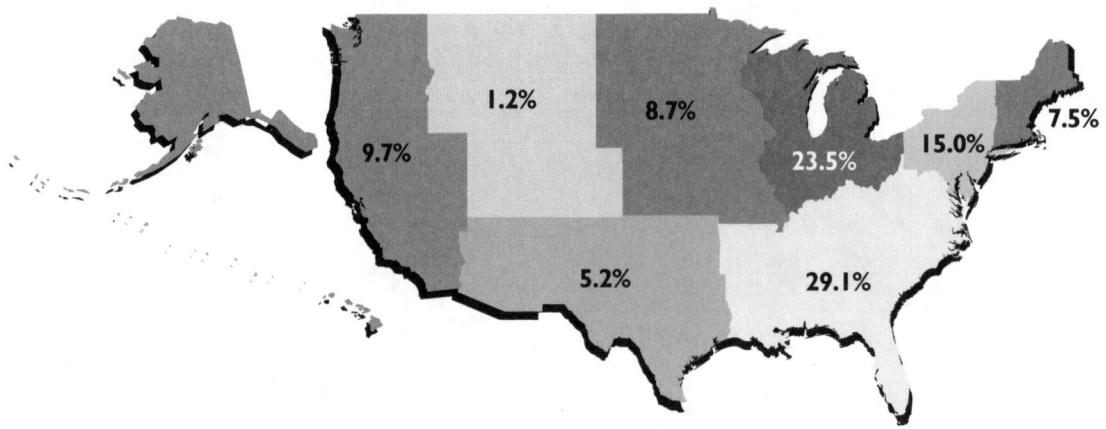

Source: U.S. Department of Commerce, Bureau of Economic Analysis.

What's New. U.S. production of paperboard and paper accelerated in the last quarter of 1996 compared with the year-ago level, according to the American Forest and Paper Association (AF&PA). Paperboard production in 1996 rose an estimated 2.3 percent from 1995, while that of paper declined 1 percent, despite strong fourth-quarter growth.

Exports of paper and paperboard recently have outpaced imports and amounted to nearly half of total U.S. production growth during the past six years, according to government and trade reports. Trade with Canada, the leading U.S. trading partner in this sector, has been stimulated by the elimination of tariffs since 1993 under the Canadian-U.S. Free Trade Agreement and, since 1994, under NAFTA. However, the United States continues to show a large deficit in this trade. Exports to Mexico, the third largest U.S. market, have risen sharply over the past decade; growth was unusually strong in the first year after signing of NAFTA, but slowed considerably in the following two years (see Table 11).

Recycling has become a way of life for many Americans, who on average recycle 0.9 pounds of paper per person daily. This trend has had a major impact on the paper industry: it has created new demand for recycled paper products while helping to preserve our forests but also has suppressed growth in production and sales of paper-grade pulp. AF&PA reports that paper and paperboard mills increased their use of recovered paper by 9 percent in 1996, pushing the paper recovery rate up to 45 percent. (The recovery rate is the combined volume of paper recycled—and used domestically or exported—divided by the total amount of paper used during the year.) Domestic mill use of recycled paper rose 2.9 million tons to 34.3 million tons in 1996—the largest increase on record. Exports, on the other hand, fell sharply in 1996. The goal of the paper industry is to recover half of all paper used by Americans by the year 2000.

FIGURE 2

U.S. EMPLOYMENT AND SHIPMENTS, PAPER AND ALLIED PRODUCTS

Total payroll employment and manufacturers' inflation-adjusted shipments

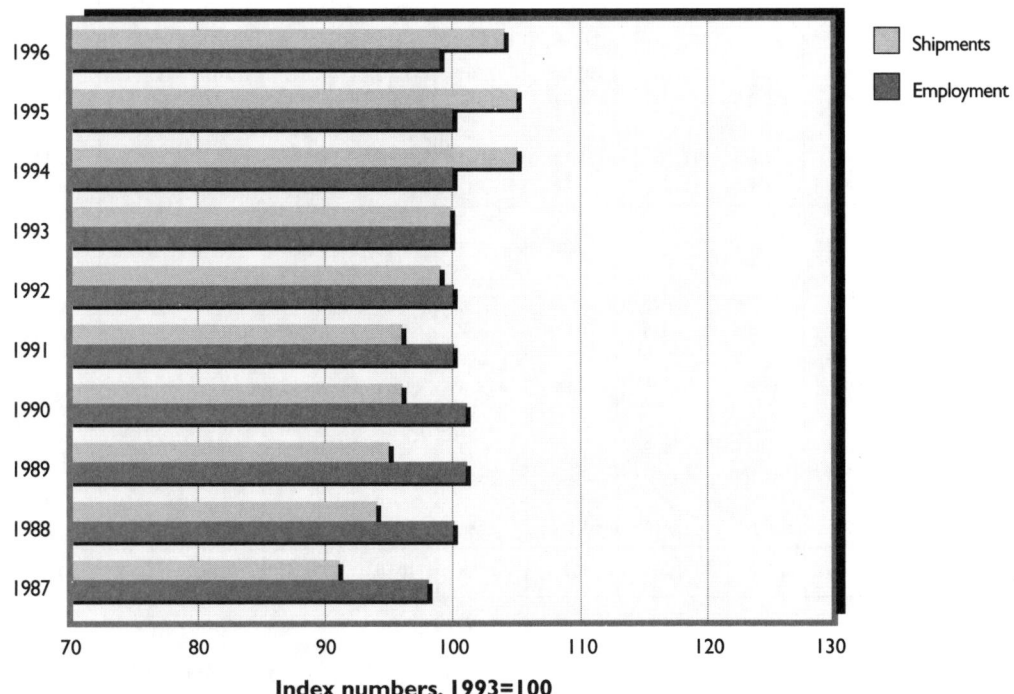

Index numbers, 1993=100

Source: U.S. Bureau of Labor Statistics, U.S. Department of Commerce, and estimates by the editors.

Output. Most growth in constant-dollar industry shipments occurred in 1987-1990 and 1994. The latest surge (in current dollars) came in 1994-1995 as prices for paper and paper products soared. Industry employment, on the other hand, barely changed during the 1987-1996 period (Figure 2 and Tables 3 and 4). For 1987-1996 as a whole, value of industry shipments rose at an annual rate of 4.5 percent, which drops to 1.53 percent when adjusted for inflation (Table 3). Value of shipments (current dollars) totaled $162 billion in 1996, compared with $109 billion in 1987.

The industry trade association, AF&PA, reports that shipments of containerboard rose 3.9 percent in 1996 as exports surged, and shipments of tissue paper gained 0.9 percent. Shipments of printing and writing paper declined 2.1 percent in 1996 after rising 3.6 percent yearly during 1985-1995. Declines also occurred in newsprint (-0.8 percent), kraft paper (-3.5 percent), box board (-1.1 percent), and chemical paper-grade market pulp (-8.2 percent).

Investment. New capital expenditures by the industry reached a peak of almost $11 billion in 1990 (Table 3). After then declining steadily through 1994, they rose slightly to $8.2 billion in 1995—the sixth highest level for all manufacturing that year. Research and development spending rose steadily from 1987 to 1994 (the latest year for which data are available), when it totaled about $1.3 billion.

The industry operated at 88.1 percent of capacity in 1996, slightly below levels in most of the past 10 years. AF&PA reports that industry capacity grew by 3.5 percent in 1996 and is slated to rise 1.5 percent annually during the next three years, largely because of efficiency improvements from existing machinery and equipment.

TABLE 3

U.S. OUTPUT, INVESTMENT, AND PRICES: PAPER AND ALLIED PRODUCTS

(Millions of U.S. dollars, except as noted)

	1987	1988	1989	1990	1991	1992	1993	1994	1995	1996	GROWTH RATE 1987-1996[1]
VALUE OF SHIPMENTS:											
BY INDUSTRY:											
Current dollars	108,989	122,883	131,895	132,424	130,131	133,201	133,262	143,649	172,638	162,033	4.50
Constant 1992 dollars	122,515	127,525	128,783	129,041	129,289	133,201	135,076	141,329	141,416	140,442	1.53
BY PRODUCT:											
Current dollars	105,399	118,725	127,266	127,528	124,658	128,941	128,695	138,540	166,827	156,579	4.50
Constant 1992 dollars	118,121	122,840	123,886	124,086	123,908	128,941	130,568	136,386	136,292	135,354	1.52
OTHER OUTPUT MEASURES:											
Industrial production, 1993=100	87.4	90.2	91.7	92.3	93.1	96.2	100.0	104.2	105.7	103.8	1.93
Gross domestic product:											
Current dollars	38,073	44,036	45,818	45,323	44,849	45,828	47,610	49,048	....	....	....
Percent of total GDP	0.8	0.9	0.8	0.8	0.8	0.7	0.7	0.7	....	....	....
Rank in manufacturing	9	9	9	9	9	9	9	9	....	....	....
Chained (1992) dollars	42,998	45,066	43,763	44,146	44,622	45,828	49,914	49,658	....	....	....
INVESTMENT-RELATED MEASURES:											
Capacity utilization, percent	90.8	92.2	91.1	88.9	86.7	87.8	89.4	91.5	91.3	88.1	....
New capital expenditures	5,752	7,260	9,579	10,957	9,206	7,963	7,370	7,731	8,219	....	....
Research and development spending	604	752	879	1,059	1,174	1,182	1,191	1,263	....	....	....
Producer prices, 1993=100[2]	87.3	94.6	100.5	101.4	100.7	100.8	100.0	102.9	122.0	115.3	3.14

1. Compound annual growth rate.

2. Prices received by domestic producers.

Sources: Shipments and new capital expenditures: U.S. Department of Commerce for 1987-1995, editor's estimates for constant dollar data for 1987-88 and all shipments data for 1996; Industrial production and capacity utilization: Federal Reserve Board of Governors; GDP: Bureau of Economic Analysis; Research and development spending: National Science Foundation; Producer prices: Bureau of Labor Statistics.

Prices. Producer prices for paper and allied products have risen at an annual rate of 3.14 percent since 1987. Much of that growth occurred during the price surge of 1995 (Table 3). Prices in 1996 dipped below the previous year's but still remained above historical levels.

Workforce and employment. Employment in the industry was level from 1991 to 1995, but declined 1.7 percent in 1996 to 681,000 workers—the lowest level since 1987 (Table 4). Production workers accounted for 75.9 percent of the total in 1996.

Production worker wages averaged $14.67 per hour in 1996, compared with $14.23 in 1995 (Table 4). In inflation-adjusted dollars, earnings declined from 1987 to 1993 and, despite small gains in 1995 and 1996, constant-dollar earnings remained below the 1987-1990 levels.

TABLE 4

U.S. EMPLOYMENT, HOURS, AND EARNINGS: PAPER AND ALLIED PRODUCTS

(Monetary values in U.S. dollars)

	1987	1988	1989	1990	1991	1992	1993	1994	1995	1996	CHANGE[1]
NUMBER OF EMPLOYEES, IN THOUSANDS:											
Total	674	689	696	697	688	690	692	692	693	681	0.11
Production workers	512	516	521	522	517	520	522	524	525	517	0.10
Percent of total	76.0	74.9	74.8	74.9	75.2	75.3	75.4	75.8	75.7	75.9	.....
Women	163	169	171	172	169	168	169	167	166	165	0.13
Percent of total	24.2	24.5	24.6	24.6	24.5	24.4	24.4	24.2	23.9	24.2	.....
HOURS AND EARNINGS OF PRODUCTION WORKERS:											
Average hourly earnings, U.S. dollars[2]											
Current dollars	11.43	11.69	11.96	12.31	12.72	13.07	13.42	13.77	14.23	14.67	2.81
1992 dollars[3]	14.04	13.80	13.48	13.19	13.09	13.07	13.05	13.06	13.13	13.16	-0.72
Average weekly hours	43.4	43.3	43.3	43.3	43.3	43.6	43.6	43.9	43.1	43.3	-0.09
Average weekly earnings, current U.S. dollars	496.06	506.18	517.87	533.02	550.78	569.85	585.11	604.5	613.31	635.21	2.79

1. Compound annual growth rate, 1987-1996.

2. Including overtime.

3. Converted to 1992 dollars using Consumer Price Index for Urban Wage Earners and Clerical Workers.

Source: Bureau of Labor Statistics.

FIGURE 3

U.S. OCCUPATIONAL INJURY AND ILLNESS RATES:
PAPER AND ALLIED PRODUCTS, 1995

Incidence of nonfatal injuries and illnesses per 100 full-time workers

The 1995 incidence rate of nonfatal illnesses and injuries in the paper industry, at 8.5 cases per 100 workers, was well below the average of 11.6 cases for all manufacturing.

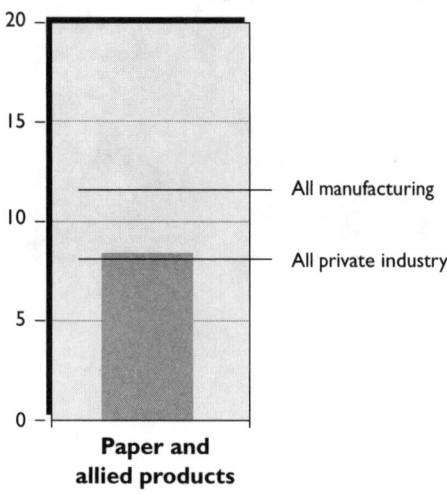

Source: U.S. Bureau of Labor Statistics.

TABLE 5

U.S. EMPLOYMENT PROJECTIONS BY MAJOR OCCUPATIONAL GROUP:
PAPER AND ALLIED PRODUCTS

Employment in the paper and allied products industry is projected to gain slightly by the year 2005 (moderate assumptions) from the 691,300 employed in 1994. Gains are seen for executive and managerial positions, professional specialties, marketing and sales, and production workers.

| | 1994 | | PROJECTIONS, 2005 | | | |
| | NUMBER OF EMPLOYEES | PERCENT OF INDUSTRY TOTAL | NUMBER OF EMPLOYEES | | | PERCENT OF INDUSTRY TOTAL, MODERATE PROJECTIONS |
OCCUPATION			LOW	MODERATE	HIGH	
Total, all occupations	691,300	100.0	674,300	708,200	729,600	100.0
Executive, administrative, and managerial	51,353	7.4	50,295	52,829	54,409	7.5
Professional specialties	25,025	3.6	28,853	30,236	31,047	4.3
Technicians and related support	8,904	1.3	8,034	8,402	8,618	1.2
Marketing and sales	20,494	3.0	20,568	21,718	22,476	3.1
Administrative support including clerical	65,311	9.5	57,689	60,659	62,529	8.6
Service	7,403	1.1	6,053	6,343	6,520	0.9
Agriculture, forestry, and fisheries occupations	2,940	0.4	2,635	2,729	2,783	0.4
Precision production, craft, and repair	122,544	17.7	118,931	124,433	127,854	17.6
Operators, fabricators, assemblers	387,325	56.0	381,244	400,851	413,365	56.6

Source: Bureau of Labor Statistics, November 1995.

FIGURE 4

U.S. CORPORATE INCOME AND WORKER EARNINGS: PAPER AND ALLIED PRODUCTS

Corporate operating income and aggregate production worker earnings

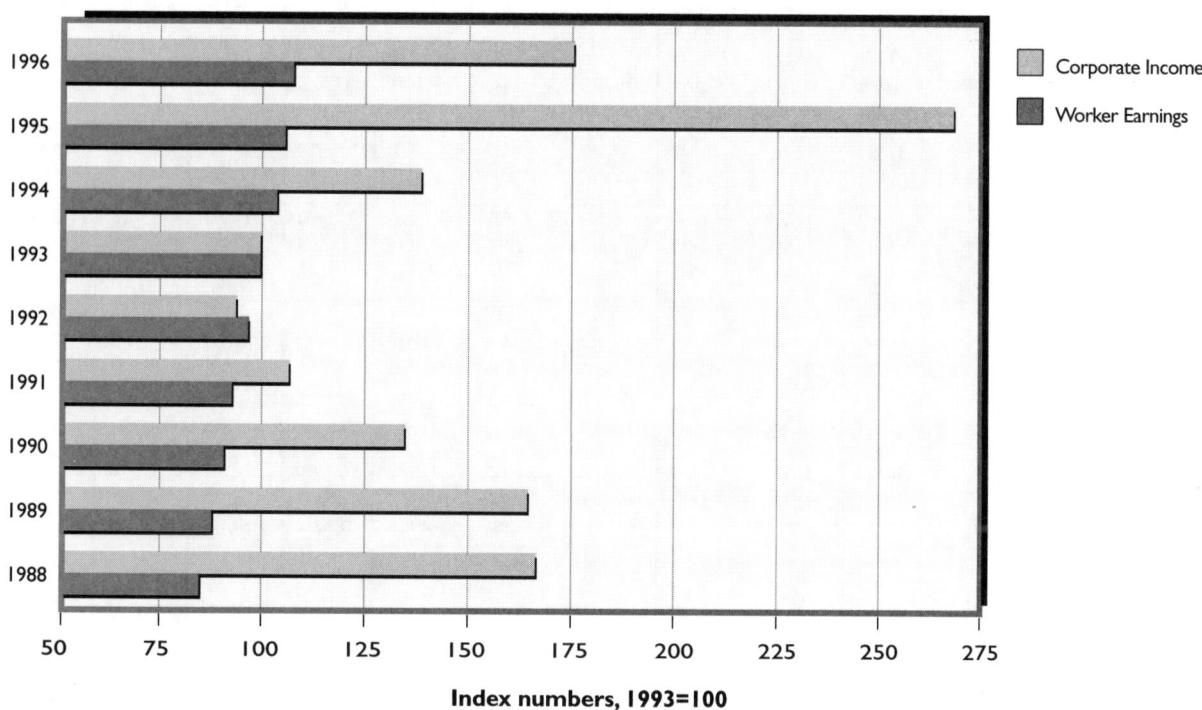

Index numbers, 1993=100

Source: U.S. Bureau of Labor Statistics, U.S. Bureau of the Census, and estimates by the editors.

Finance. Following successive declines through 1992, corporate operating income staged a dramatic reversal, soaring to a new high in 1995 as short supplies and high prices pushed up revenues. Earnings of production workers, on the other hand, showed slow but steady gains during 1988-1996 (Figure 4). Sales and receipts by the industry grew by 5.14 percent annually between 1988 and 1996 to stand at $160 billion in 1996; however, this was some $10.2 billion below the 1995 record (Table 6). Income from operations fell to $13.7 billion in 1996 from $20.8 billion the year before and posted average annual growth of only 0.68 percent during 1988-1996. Moreover, after-tax income during that period declined at a 2.75 percent rate, ending at $6.5 billion in 1996 compared with $8.1 billion in 1988.

After-tax income was 4.04 percent of sales and 10.63 percent of stockholders' equity in 1996, compared with 7.54 and 18.82 percent, respectively, in 1988. Debt, largely long-term, amounted to about 37 percent of total assets in 1996, little changed from the previous year but well above the average of 26.3 percent for manufacturing as a whole.

TABLE 6

U.S. CORPORATE INCOME AND ASSETS: PAPER AND ALLIED PRODUCTS

(Monetary values in millions of U.S. dollars)

INCOME AND EXPENSES	1988	1989	1990	1991	1992	1993	1994	1995	1996	CHANGE OR AVERAGE[1]
Sales and receipts	107,221	113,573	115,523	122,969	127,562	131,232	142,832	170,329	160,134	5.14
Depreciation and amortization	(4,625)	(5,010)	(5,578)	(6,504)	(6,974)	(7,345)	(7,653)	(8,193)	(8,571)	8.02
Other operating costs	(89,657)	(95,786)	(99,514)	(108,172)	(113,280)	(116,158)	(124,419)	(141,314)	(137,903)	5.53
Income from operations	12,939	12,777	10,432	8,292	7,307	7,727	10,759	20,820	13,661	0.68
Nonoperating income (expenditures)	(729)	(1,912)	(3,197)	(4,721)	(5,379)	(6,511)	(2,800)	(3,236)	(4,102)	....
Income before taxes	12,210	10,865	7,236	3,573	1,929	1,217	7,960	17,584	9,558	-3.01
Income after taxes	8,081	7,047	4,882	2,164	1,196	(201)	5,269	11,929	6,465	-2.75
Cash dividends	1,700	3,183	2,351	2,450	2,391	2,192	2,518	3,096	3,288	8.60
Income retained in business	6,381	3,864	2,530	(286)	(1,195)	(2,394)	2,752	8,833	3,176	-8.35
Direct credits (charges)	(2,084)	(942)	(184)	63	(403)	(451)	(404)	(1,493)	(737)	....
Ending retained earnings	30,539	32,684	33,193	33,977	30,231	26,460	30,009	37,550	38,235	2.85
ASSETS, END OF YEAR:										
Total	95,444	109,038	117,335	130,748	138,246	141,052	150,366	161,450	168,092	7.33
Accounts receivable	10,913	11,715	11,389	11,523	11,795	12,472	14,930	16,786	15,478	4.47
Inventories	10,214	11,136	11,657	12,576	13,018	13,662	13,932	16,312	15,372	5.24
Net property, plant and equipment	55,520	62,804	68,726	77,432	81,834	84,111	85,817	89,412	94,729	6.91
RATIOS, PERCENT:										
INCOME TO SALES:										
Before tax	11.39	9.57	6.26	2.91	1.51	0.93	5.57	10.32	5.97	6.05
After tax	7.54	6.20	4.23	1.76	0.94	-0.15	3.69	7.00	4.04	3.92
INCOME TO STOCK HOLDERS' EQUITY:										
Before tax	28.44	23.80	15.75	7.35	4.06	2.72	15.92	29.97	15.71	15.97
After tax	18.82	15.44	10.62	4.45	2.52	-0.45	10.54	20.33	10.63	10.32
INCOME TO TOTAL ASSETS:										
Before tax	12.79	9.96	6.17	2.73	1.40	0.86	5.29	10.89	5.69	6.20
After tax	8.47	6.46	4.16	1.66	0.87	-0.14	3.50	7.39	3.85	4.02
AS A PERCENT OF TOTAL ASSETS:										
Property, plant and equipment	58.17	57.60	58.57	59.22	59.19	59.63	57.07	55.38	56.36	57.91
Short-term debt	1.58	1.24	1.56	2.34	2.81	3.21	3.28	3.29	3.45	2.53
Long-term debt	28.48	31.68	34.70	36.28	36.68	37.34	35.37	33.61	33.63	34.20
Stockholders' equity	44.99	41.86	39.16	37.20	34.36	31.68	33.26	36.34	36.19	37.23

1. For income and asset amounts, compound annual growth rate; for ratios, average of ratios for the years shown.

Source: U.S. Bureau of the Census, Quarterly Financial Report.

Notes: Parentheses ( ) indicate negative items, e.g., net expenses, charges, or losses. Net property, plant, and equipment is net of accumulated depreciation. Because the samples used to collect the data change, retained earnings at the end of a given year will not exactly equal the previous year's retained earnings plus the current year's retained income and credits.

CANADA

Canada's paper and allied products industry in 1993 had 664 establishments and 101,926 employees (Table 7). Pulp and paper accounted for 74 percent of the Can$21 billion in industry shipments that year, with newsprint and pulp the largest categories here. Paper boxes and bags accounted for 13 percent of industry shipments in 1993, and other converted paper products, for 11 percent.

Canadian shipments of paper and allied products fell almost 20 percent from the 1989 cyclical peak to the 1992 low but had almost regained 1989 levels in 1994 (Table 8). However, employment continued to decline through 1994. Shipments totaled Can$25.6 billion in 1994, compared with Can$23.1 billion in 1987. Employment declined to 101,834 in 1994 from 119,346 in 1987. The decline in employment of production workers has been slower, and they accounted for 77 percent of the workforce in 1994, compared with 75 percent in 1988. Average hourly wages of production workers in 1994 were Can$20.48, up from Can$16.45 in 1988. The average workweek in 1994 was slightly over 41 hours.

TABLE 7

CANADA: COMPONENT INDUSTRIES OF PAPER AND ALLIED PRODUCTS (CSIC 27), 1993

(Monetary values in Canadian dollars)

INDUSTRY NAME	CSIC	ESTABLISH-MENTS (NUMBER)	EMPLOYMENT Number	EMPLOYMENT Percent of Industry Total	VALUE OF SHIPMENTS (MILLIONS)	AVERAGE HOURLY EARNINGS[1]
PAPER AND ALLIED PRODUCTS	27	664	101,926	100.0	CAN$21,232.6	CAN$20.08
Pulp and paper	271	158	68,053	66.8	15,630.6	22.43
Pulp	2711	42	17,599	17.3	4,492.6	23.24
Newprint	2712	42	30,264	29.7	6,545.3	23.38
Paperboard	2713	32	6,681	6.6	1,529.7	20.74
Building board	2714	7	948	0.9	159.3	17.11
Other paper	2719	35	12,561	12.3	2,903.7	20.47
Asphalt roofing	272	13	1,223	1.2	380.6	16.04
Paper boxes and bags	273	249	18,107	17.8	2,824.3	15.92
Folding cartons and set-up boxes	2731	99	6,472	6.3	990.3	15.26
Corrugated boxes	2732	126	10,010	9.8	1,583.1	16.46
Paper bags	2733	24	1,625	1.6	250.9	15.50
Other converted paper products	279	244	14,543	14.3	2,397.0	14.46
Coated and treated paper	2791	52	3,851	3.8	674.9	13.19
Stationery paper products	2792	60	3,153	3.1	381.9	14.22
Paper consumer products	2793	18	2,811	2.8	627.9	18.28
Other converted paper products, n.e.c.	2799	114	4,728	4.6	712.3	13.61

1. Including overtime.

Source: Adapted from Statistics Canada, *Manufacturing Industries of Canada* (Cat. No. 31-203).

TABLE 8

CANADIAN EMPLOYMENT AND SHIPMENTS: PAPER AND ALLIED PRODUCTS, 1987-1994

(Monetary values in Canadian dollars)

	1987	1988	1989	1990	1991	1992	1993	1994	CHANGE[1]
All employees	119,346	121,075	120,106	115,176	110,086	105,008	101,926	101,834	-2.24
Establishments	694	718	746	731	681	681	664	668	-0.54
Employees per establishment	172	169	161	158	162	154	154	152	-1.71
Production workers per establishment	.....	127	122	119	123	117	117	117	-1.36
PRODUCTION WORKERS:									
Total	.....	90,976	90,781	87,012	83,550	79,911	77,590	77,979	-2.54
Percent of all employees	.....	75.1	75.6	75.5	75.9	76.1	76.1	76.6	.....
Male	.....	83,225	82,985	79,558	76,802	.....	.....	.....	.....
Female	.....	7,751	7,796	7,454	6,748	.....	.....	.....	.....
Percent of all production workers	.....	8.5	8.6	8.6	8.1	.....	.....	.....	.....
Average hourly earnings	.....	16.45	17.06	18.14	19.18	19.50	20.08	20.48	3.72
Average weekly earnings	.....	671.19	531.56	553.10	582.74	601.99	622.70	644.16	-0.68
Average weekly hours	.....	40.8	41.2	40.4	40.0	40.6	40.7	41.1	0.11
Shipments (millions)	23,073	25,661	25,848	24,026	21,003	20,825	21,233	25,648	1.52

1. Compound annual growth rate.

Source: Adapted from Statistics Canada, *Manufacturing Industries of Canada* (Cat. No. 31-203).

MEXICO

Mexico's paper industry is included in the paper and printing group (Table 9). In 1993, the pulp and paper industry had 63,787 employees, and its 46,400 production workers had average yearly earnings of 13,946 new pesos ($4,465). Its 15,451 nonproduction employees had average earnings of 38,931 new pesos ($12,463) in 1993. Total employment in the paper industry rose from 1988 to 1991, reaching 61,974, but by 1995 had declined to 54,756, just about equal to 1988 (Table 10).

TABLE 9

MEXICO: COMPONENT INDUSTRIES OF PAPER AND PRINTING (CMAP 34), 1993

(Monetary values in 1993 Mexican New Pesos)

			ALL WORKERS									
						PAID WORKERS						
							PRODUCTION WORKERS		NONPRODUCTION EMPLOYEES		BENEFITS	UNPAID
INDUSTRY	CMAP	NUMBER OF UNITS	NUMBER	PERCENT OF INDUSTRY TOTAL	AVERAGE DAYS WORKED	REMUN- ERATION[1]	NUMBER	WAGES AND SALARIES	NUMBER	WAGES AND SALARIES	PER PAID EMPLOYEE	WORKERS, NUMBER
Paper and printing	34	15,049	19,737[1]	100.0	275	26,324	112,704	14,139	66,665	28,863	6,712	18,002
Pulp and paper production	3410	1,491	63,787	32.3	261	30,438	46,400	13,946	15,451	38,931	10,250	1,936
Printing, publishing, and allied industries	3420	13,558	133,584	67.7	277	24,159	66,304	14,274	51,214	25,826	4,850	16,066

1. Average annual remuneration including benefits.

Source: INEGI, Censos Economicos 1994.

TABLE 10

MEXICAN GROSS DOMESTIC PRODUCT AND EMPLOYMENT: PAPER AND PRINTING, 1988-1995

	1988	1989	1990	1991	1992	1993	1994	1995	CHANGE[1]
GROSS DOMESTIC PRODUCT:									
Millions of constant 1993 new pesos	9,077.2	9,959.5	10,760.3	11,173.8	11,559.9	11,329.8	11,657.6	10,769.8	2.47
Millions of constant 1993 U.S. dollars[2]	2,905.9	3,188.4	3,444.7	3,577.1	3,700.7	3,627.0	3,732.0	3,447.8	2.47
TOTAL EMPLOYMENT:									
Paper and printing	167,577	176,532	187,261	192,492	196,017	192,612	185,327	172,399	0.41
Paper	54,543	59,102	61,953	61,974	61,638	58,984	56,963	54,756	0.06
Printing	113,034	117,430	125,308	130,518	134,379	133,628	128,364	117,643	0.57

1. Compound annual growth rate.

2. Converted at 3.1237 new pesos to the U.S. dollar.

Source: Sistema de Cuentas Nacionales de Mexico, INEGI.

INTERNATIONAL TRADE

United States. U.S. worldwide paper exports rose at a faster pace than imports between 1990 and 1996, resulting in a sharp decline in the global U.S. trade deficit. Exports rose from $8.7 billion to $14 billion during the period, while imports climbed from $11.7 billion to $14.8 billion (Table 11). Both imports and exports showed large value increases in 1995, reflecting the price surge that year. With prices moderating in 1996, trade values fell, and the 1996 deficit roughly equaled that in 1994. Canada and Mexico together received only about one-third of 1996 U.S. exports, whereas Canada supplied 73 percent of the U.S. imports.

Volume measures give a somewhat different picture than the monetary values in Table 11. AF&PA estimates 1996 exports of paper and paperboard at 12.0 million tons, 10.2 percent above that in the previous year. Imports, on the other hand, are estimated to have fallen 8.4 percent to 14.2 million tons. Between 1990 and 1996, volume of exports rose 4.5 times that of imports, according to the trade association.

Canada. Canadian exports to the United States totaled $10.8 billion in 1996, below the $12.3 billion shipped in 1995 but up considerably from the $7.9-$8.9 billion range for the previous years (Table 11). U.S. exports to Canada in 1996 were $2.9 billion, up significantly from the $1.5 billion shipped in 1990. The U.S. trade deficit with Canada in 1996 was $7.9 billion, up only slightly from the 1990 level but well above the $6 billion of 1993, before the advent of NAFTA. Two-way trade between Canada and Mexico continued small through 1996.

Mexico. U.S. paper exports to Mexico totaled $1.8 billion in 1996, more than double shipments in 1990 (Table 11). Mexican exports to the United States were $240 million, compared with $188 million in 1990. The resulting U.S. trade surplus with Mexico was $1.58 billion in 1996, compared with $709 million in 1990.

NAFTA. North American trade balances favor Canada, which had a surplus of $7.9 billion in 1996, slightly above the $7.5 billion of 1990 (Table 11). The U.S. deficit declined slightly to $6.3 billion in 1996 from $6.7 billion in 1990, while Mexico's deficit rose to $1.6 billion from $759 million. Between 1993 (immediately prior to NAFTA's implementation) and 1996, the U.S. trade deficit with Canada and Mexico rose 33 percent, Mexico's deficit rose about 23 percent, and Canada's surplus climbed 31 percent.

TABLE 11

INTERNATIONAL TRADE, PAPER AND ALLIED PRODUCTS

(Millions of U.S. dollars)

	1989[1]	1990	1991	1992	1993	1994	1995	1996
GLOBAL TRADE, U.S.								
IMPORTS								
Value	11,935.2	11,736.7	10,511.5	10,460.7	10,891.0	11,771.9	16,757.4	14,784.3
Ratio to new supply[2]	8.6	8.4	7.8	7.5	7.8	7.8	.....	.....
Ratio to apparent consumption[3]	9.1	9.0	8.4	8.1	8.4	8.5	.....	.....
EXPORTS								
Value	8,154.2	8,671.1	9,263.0	10,042.3	9,456.5	11,000.4	14,943.2	14,002.1
Ratio to comparable domestic shipments	6.4	6.8	7.4	7.8	7.4	8.0	.....	.....
TRADE BALANCE	(3,781.0)	(3,065.6)	(1,248.5)	(418.4)	(1,434.5)	(771.5)	(1,814.2)	(782.2)
BILATERAL TRADE: NAFTA[4]								
U.S. exports to Canada	957.8	1,518.1	1,689.0	1,819.4	1,936.2	2,212.6	2,797.9	2,894.3
Canadian exports to U.S.	8,969.5	8,931.1	8,054.6	7,827.9	7,947.4	8,530.2	12,251.0	10,783.5
U.S. exports to Mexico	896.0	897.8	1,027.6	1,270.3	1,376.0	1,712.1	1,776.3	1,821.1
Mexican exports to U.S.	375.2	188.4	111.2	116.3	108.0	138.7	305.9	239.5
Canadian exports to Mexico	30.9	54.7	78.6	52.6	40.5	64.6	46.1	20.7
Mexican exports to Canada	4.5	5.2	0.8	2.3	6.0	6.6	7.4	6.5
TRADE BALANCES WITHIN NAFTA[5]								
Canada	8,038.1	7,462.5	6,443.4	6,058.8	6,045.7	6,375.6	9,491.8	7,903.4
Mexico	(547.2)	(758.9)	(994.2)	(1,204.3)	(1,302.5)	(1,631.4)	(1,509.1)	(1,595.8)
United States	(7,490.9)	(6,703.6)	(5,449.2)	(4,854.5)	(4,743.2)	(4,744.2)	(7,982.7)	(6,307.6)

1. 1989 and earlier data on U.S. exports to Canada for manufacturing total and manufacturing industries are not comparable with data for 1990 and later years because of a change in the reporting system. The NAFTA trade balances for the U.S. and Canada also are affected.

2. New supply equals comparable domestic shipments plus imports for consumption.

3. Apparent consumption equals comparable domestic shipments plus imports for consumption less exports.

4. Amounts less than U.S. $100,000 shown as zero.

5. Parentheses indicate an excess of imports over exports. Because of commodity coding and other data differences among the three countries, theses trade balances are only rough estimates and should be used with caution.

Source for U.S. Global Trade: U.S. Department of Commerce, International Trade Administration.

Source for U.S. -Canada and U.S.-Mexico Bilateral Trade: U.S. Bureau of the Census.

Source for Canada-Mexico and Mexico-Canada Bilateral Trade: Statistics Canada, Foreign Trade Division, Special tabulation, March 1997, converted to U.S. dollars by the editors.

PETROLEUM REFINING AND COAL PRODUCTS

THE UNITED STATES

Products and Processes. Petroleum refining and related industries ranked eighth among U.S. manufacturing industries in 1996 in terms of industry shipments and was third in after-tax income, exceeded only by the chemical and food industries. Petroleum refining accounts for over 90 percent of industry shipments, with asphalt industries and production of miscellaneous products making up the remainder.

Table 1 gives a profile of the industry as it stood in 1992 (the latest year for which economic census data are available). The industry that year consisted of 2,124 establishments with 114,400 employees and a total payroll of almost $5 billion. Refined petroleum accounted for $136.6 billion of the $150.2 billion in shipments that year, followed at a distance by $7.7 billion for asphalt paving and roofing materials.

Like many other industries today, petroleum refining is in a merger and consolidation phase, which is likely to hold down employment for some time. Projections to the year 2005 indicate that industry employment will fall to 140,300, compared with 151,500 in 1993 (Table 2). Employment in petroleum refining is projected to be 102,500 by 2005, and that in all other areas (asphalt paving and roofing materials and miscellaneous petroleum and coal products) will total about 37,800. Average earnings of production workers in 1993 were $18.53 per hour, including $20.36 averaged for petroleum refining and $13.76 for other areas.

TABLE 1

UNITED STATES: COMPONENT INDUSTRIES OF PETROLEUM AND COAL PRODUCTS (SIC 29), 1992

(Monetary values in millions of U.S. dollars)

INDUSTRY	SIC	ESTABLISH-MENTS	SHIPMENTS		VALUE ADDED BY MANUFACTURE	NEW CAPITAL EXPENDI-TURES	EMPLOY-MENT[1]	PAYROLL
			VALUE	PERCENT BY 4 LARGEST COMPANIES				
PETROLEUM AND COAL PRODUCTS	29	2,124	$150,226.9	.....	$23,408.4	$6,576.8	114,400	$4,966.8
Petroleum refining	291	231	136,551.0	30	18,606.7	6,181.8	74,900	3,639.9
Asphalt paving and roofing materials	295	1,393	7,748.6	.....	3,006.0	179.9	25,600	845.7
Asphalt paving mixtures and blocks	2951	1,150	3,835.0	15	1,451.9	111.1	13,200	433.0
Asphalt felts and coatings	2952	243	3,913.6	47	1,554.1	68.8	12,400	412.7
Miscellaneous petroleum and coal products	299	500	5,927.3	.....	1,795.7	215.1	13,900	481.2
Lubricating oils and greases	2992	420	5,084.1	35	1,479.4	191.7	11,900	412.7
Petroleum and coal products, n.e.c.	2999	80	843.1	43	316.3	23.3	2,000	68.5

1. Employment numbers from the economic censuses differ in definition and classification from the Bureau of Labor Statistics estimates in Table 2. Year-to-year comparisons between Table 1 and Table 2 are not appropriate.

Source: U.S. Bureau of the Census, 1992 Census of Manufactures.

TABLE 2

U.S. EMPLOYMENT AND EARNINGS: PETROLEUM AND COAL PRODUCTS

INDUSTRY	SIC	1993			2005
		EMPLOYMENT[1]		AVERAGE HOURLY EARNINGS (U.S. DOLLARS)[2]	PROJECTED EMPLOYMENT[3]
		NUMBER OF PERSONS	PERCENT OF INDUSTRY TOTAL		
PETROLEUM AND COAL PRODUCTS	29	151,500	100.0	$18.53	140,300
Petroleum refining	291	112,200	74.1	20.36	102,500
Asphalt paving and roofing materials	295	26,800	17.7	13.76	....
Asphalt paving and roofing materials and miscellaneous petroleum and coal products	295,9	....	....	....	37,800

1. Total payroll employment. Employment data from the economic censuses, shown in Table 1, differ in definition and classification from the Bureau of Labor Statistics estimates in this table. Year-to-year comparisons between Table 1 and Table 2 are not appropriate.
2. Earnings of production workers, including overtime.
3. Number of persons, moderate projection by the U.S. Bureau of Labor Statistics.
Source: Bureau of Labor Statistics.

FIGURE 1

U.S. EMPLOYMENT IN PETROLEUM AND COAL PRODUCTS

Percent distribution by region, 1995

The Southwest region accounted for about 24 percent of U.S. petroleum refining and related employment in 1995, followed by the Southeast (18 percent), the Pacific region (17 percent), and the Mid-Atlantic states and the Great Lakes region (16 percent each).

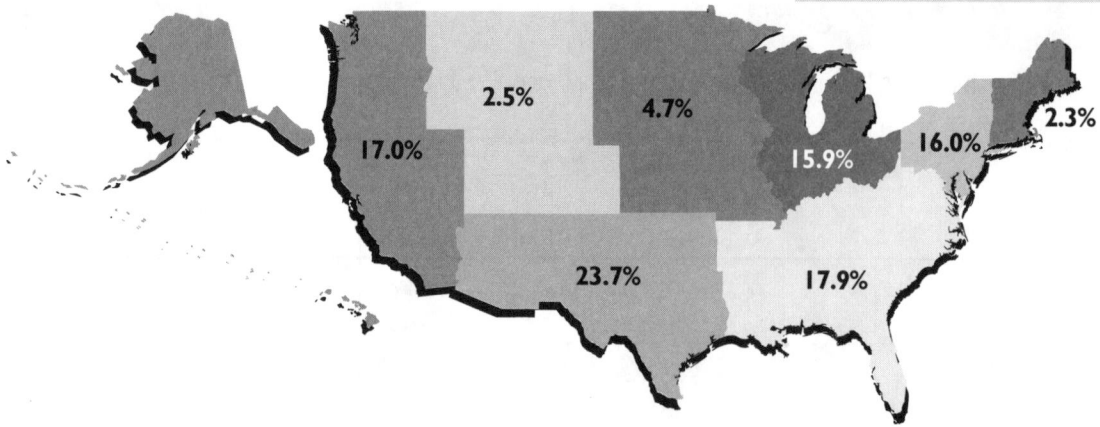

Source: U.S. Department of Commerce, Bureau of Economic Analysis.

What's New.[1] U.S. oil companies had a good year in 1996, as oil prices surged to their highest levels in five years, gasoline prices rose an average of five cents per gallon for the year, and strong margins in refining and marketing boosted profits. Major refiners had profit gains of as much as 337 percent in the second quarter from the same period of 1995 as gasoline prices jumped by about 20 cents per gallon on average between February and May. Prices weakened in the first half of 1997 (producer prices for the petroleum refining and coal products industry in May 1997 were about 8 percent below the year-earlier level) and then rose again in August as demand increased and the Labor Day holiday approached. Crude oil prices in the summer of 1997 were at a relatively modest level of $19-$21, but refiners had been running at almost full capacity, with utilization surpassing 99 percent in May and June.

Mergers and acquisitions in the U.S. oil and gas sector amounted to $14.5 billion in the first half of 1996, compared with $11.5 billion in all of 1995. In 1997, Shell Oil Company and Texaco, Inc. agreed to form a new company, with $9 billion in assets, from their West Coast and Midwestern operations. They were considering a similar merger for the East Coast involving Shell and Star Enterprise (owned jointly by Texaco and Saudi Refining Inc.). Other merger talks have involved Mobil Corp. and Amoco Corp., the sale by Unocal Corp. of its refining and marketing assets to Tosco Corp., and plans by Marathon Oil Co. and Ashland, Inc., to combine their refining and marketing operations.

The mergers are intended to reduce expenses in an industry where new equipment and maintenance costs are high and returns are much lower than those from oil exploration and production. Consumer advocates worry, however, that such mergers may result in higher gasoline prices by giving too much power to refiners and may accelerate the long-term decline in numbers of gas stations, down about 17 percent since the 1970s. Refining capacity also has been in a long-term downtrend, with the number of refineries falling by 154 since 1981 and capacity utilization rising to almost 95 percent.

Another, possibly offsetting, trend is the growth in joint ventures with foreign companies. Venezuela's state oil company PDVSA acquired a 50 percent interest in Citgo's U.S. refining operation in 1986, in 1989 formed Uno-Ven Co. with Unocal, and in 1993 joined its Citgo subsidiary with Lyondell Petrochemical to form Lyondell-Citgo Refining Co. Texaco and Saudi Aramco in 1988 created Star Enterprise, a refining/marketing operation with three refineries and a network of Texaco gasoline stations. In 1992, Shell and Pemex, the Mexican state oil company, formed Deer Park Refining, with a refinery in Deer Park, Texas, that was recently upgraded to process heavy Mexican Mayan crude oil. In July 1997, the Russian oil company, Lukoil, in a joint undertaking with Nexus Fuels, Inc., opened a gasoline station in a supermarket parking lot in Altavista, Virginia, according to *The Washington Post*. This is Lukoil's first venture into the U.S. market, where it plans to build 100 fueling centers in parking lots of supermarkets next year. Initially, Nexus-Lukoil will buy domestic unbranded gasoline for its stations but eventually will trade its own oil to U.S. refiners.

---

[1] Information in this section is based on reports by the U.S. Department of Energy and the American Petroleum Institute and on articles in *The Washington Post*.

FIGURE 2

U.S. EMPLOYMENT AND SHIPMENTS, PETROLEUM AND COAL PRODUCTS

Total payroll employment and manufacturers' inflation-adjusted shipments

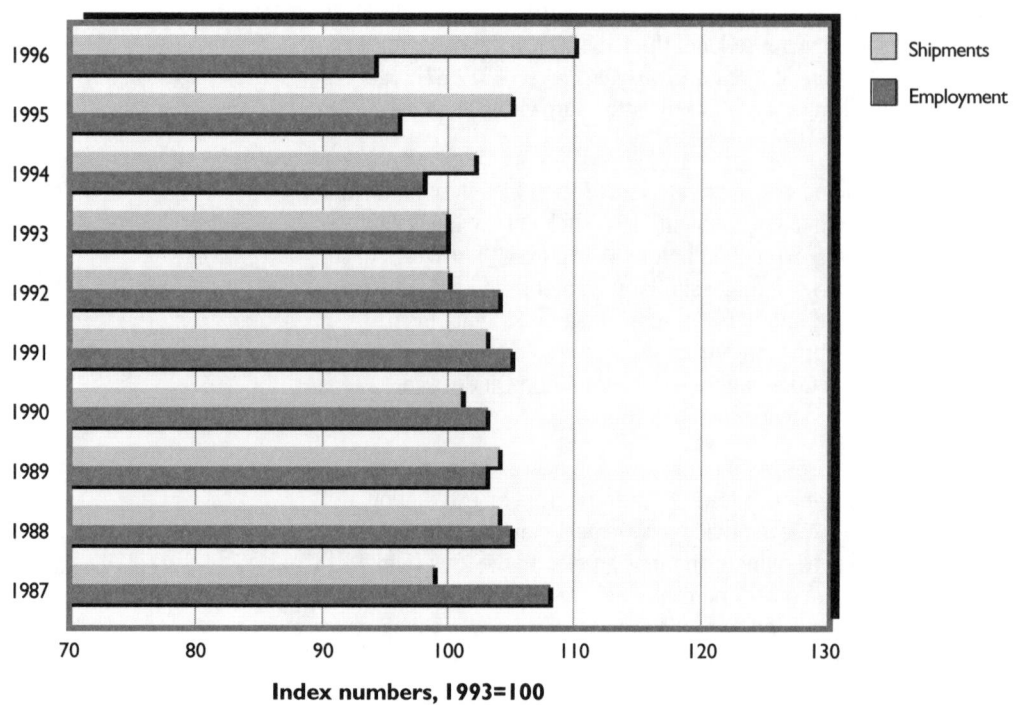

Index numbers, 1993=100

Source: U.S. Bureau of Labor Statistics, U.S. Department of Commerce, and estimates by the editors.

Output. While industry employment declined at an annual rate of 1.59 percent during 1987-1996, constant-dollar shipments of petroleum and coal products rose by 1.22 percent a year (Figure 2). Much of the increase took place in 1996 as constant-dollar shipments rose more than 5 percent and soaring prices caused a spike in the current-dollar value of shipments that year to $180.1 billion (Table 3). This compares with $151.3 billion in 1995 and $130.4 billion in 1987.

Investment. New capital expenditures by the industry totaled $6.2 billion in 1995, up from $5.8 billion in 1994 and $2.3 billion in 1987. Capacity utilization in 1996 reached 93.8 percent as refiners stepped up activity to capitalize on rising prices (Table 3).

Prices. Producer prices rose at a 2.41 annual rate between 1987 and 1996. Most of that increase took place in 1996, when the index shot to 112.6 from 99.5 in 1995 (Table 3). As noted, prices were declining during the early months of 1997 but rose again in August and September.

TABLE 3

U.S. OUTPUT, INVESTMENT, AND PRICES: PETROLEUM AND COAL PRODUCTS

(Millions of U.S. dollars, except as noted)

	1987	1988	1989	1990	1991	1992	1993	1994	1995	1996	GROWTH RATE 1987-1995[1]
VALUE OF SHIPMENTS:											
BY INDUSTRY:											
Current dollars	130,414	131,681	146,487	173,389	159,144	150,227	144,833	143,329	151,261	180,147	3.65
Constant 1992 dollars	148,586	156,261	155,396	152,286	153,872	150,227	150,076	153,676	157,489	165,743	1.22
BY PRODUCT:											
Current dollars	125,811	124,741	136,104	163,783	150,406	144,641	139,686	137,984	145,248	172,985	3.60
Constant 1992 dollars	143,374	148,043	144,406	143,809	145,420	144,641	144,749	147,938	151,217	159,142	1.17
OTHER OUTPUT MEASURES:											
Industrial production, 1993=100	94.3	96.0	96.5	97.5	96.3	97.2	100.0	100.1	101.6	103.5	1.04
Gross domestic product:											
Current dollars	22,719	31,940	28,826	32,985	29,702	28,225	29,771	29,708	....	....	....
Percent of total GDP	0.5	0.6	0.5	0.6	0.5	0.5	0.5	0.4	....	....	....
Rank in manufacturing	15	12	13	12	13	13	13	13	....	....	....
Chained (1992) dollars	36,260	37,128	33,397	28,434	28,281	28,225	27,081	26,782	....	....	....
INVESTMENT-RELATED MEASURES:											
Capacity utilization, percent	83.5	85.3	87.0	87.6	86.6	88.6	92.1	91.3	92.0	93.8	....
New capital expenditures	2,341	2,626	3,394	4,193	5,942	6,577	6,303	5,839	6,213	....	....
Producer prices, 1993=100[2]	90.9	87.3	97.6	117.8	107.1	103.5	100.0	96.5	99.5	112.6	2.41

1. Compound annual growth rate.

2. Prices received by domestic producers.

Sources: Shipments and new capital expenditures: U.S. Department of Commerce for 1987-1995, editor's estimates for constant dollar data for 1987-88 and all shipments data for 1996; Industrial production and capacity utilization: Federal Reserve Board of Governors; GDP: Bureau of Economic Analysis; Research and development spending: National Science Foundation; Producer prices: Bureau of Labor Statistics.

Workforce and Employment. The petroleum refining industry had 142,000 employees in 1996, the lowest level in the 1987-1996 period for an annual decline of 1.59 percent during that period (Table 4). Employment of production workers fell even faster, by 1.64 percent a year to 92,000; they accounted for 64.8 percent of the workforce in 1996, compared with 65.1 percent in 1987. Employment of women changed little during the decade, so their share of the workforce rose to 16.8 percent in 1996 from 14.5 percent in 1987. Hourly earnings of production workers averaged $19.32 in 1996, compared with $14.58 in 1987, for an annual growth rate of 3.18 percent in current dollars. This represented a decline of 0.37 percent a year when adjusted for inflation. These earnings were the second highest in manufacturing, barely edged out by the $19.34 average in the tobacco industry.

TABLE 4

U.S. EMPLOYMENT, HOURS, AND EARNINGS: PETROLEUM AND COAL PRODUCTS

(Monetary values in U.S. dollars)

	1987	1988	1989	1990	1991	1992	1993	1994	1995	1996	CHANGE[1]
NUMBER OF EMPLOYEES, IN THOUSANDS:											
Total	164	160	156	157	160	158	152	149	145	142	-1.59
Production workers	107	104	102	103	103	103	99	97	94	92	-1.64
Percent of total	65.1	65.2	65.3	65.5	64.6	65.4	65.1	64.8	64.8	64.8	.....
Women	24	24	25	26	27	26	24	25	25	24	0.05
Percent of total	14.5	15.0	16.1	16.4	16.6	16.4	15.9	16.6	16.9	16.8	.....
HOURS AND EARNINGS OF PRODUCTION WORKERS:											
Average hourly earnings, U.S. dollars[2]											
Current dollars	14.58	14.97	15.41	16.24	17.04	17.90	18.53	19.07	19.36	19.32	3.18
1992 dollars[3]	17.91	17.67	17.37	17.41	17.53	17.90	18.03	18.09	17.86	17.33	-0.37
Average weekly hours	44.0	44.4	44.3	44.6	44.1	43.8	44.2	44.4	43.7	43.6	-0.10
Average weekly earnings, current U.S. dollars	641.52	664.67	682.66	724.3	751.46	784.02	819.03	846.71	846.03	842.35	3.07

1. Compound annual growth rate, 1987-1996.

2. Including overtime.

3. Converted to 1992 dollars using Consumer Price Index for Urban Wage Earners and Clerical Workers.

Source: Bureau of Labor Statistics.

FIGURE 3

U.S. OCCUPATIONAL INJURY AND ILLNESS RATES: PETROLEUM AND COAL PRODUCTS, 1995

Incidence of nonfatal injuries and illnesses per 100 full-time workers

Nonfatal occupational illnesses and injuries in the petroleum refining and coal products industry averaged only 4.8 cases per 100 workers in 1995, the lowest level in manufacturing.

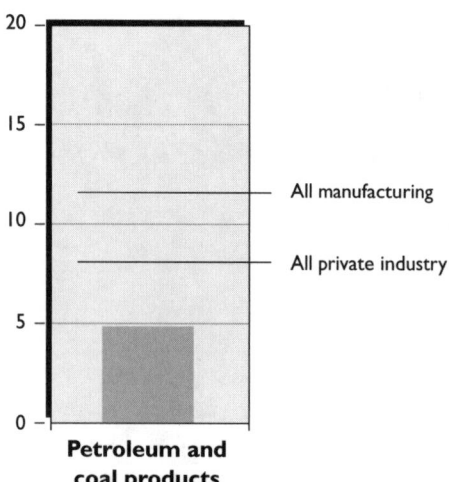

All manufacturing

All private industry

Petroleum and coal products

Source: U.S. Bureau of Labor Statistics.

TABLE 5

U.S. EMPLOYMENT PROJECTIONS BY MAJOR OCCUPATIONAL GROUP: PETROLEUM AND COAL PRODUCTS

OCCUPATION	1994		PROJECTIONS, 2005			
	NUMBER OF EMPLOYEES	PERCENT OF INDUSTRY TOTAL	NUMBER OF EMPLOYEES			PERCENT OF INDUSTRY TOTAL, MODERATE PROJECTIONS
			LOW	MODERATE	HIGH	
Total, all occupations	148,900	100.0	142,400	140,300	136,700	100.0
Executive, administrative, and managerial	15,519	10.4	15,039	14,821	14,446	10.6
Professional specialties	14,086	9.5	15,509	15,137	14,546	10.8
Technicians and related support	7,704	5.2	7,124	6,968	6,716	5.0
Marketing and sales	3,141	2.1	2,996	3,009	3,012	2.1
Administrative support including clerical	16,043	10.8	13,165	13,015	12,744	9.3
Service	1,588	1.1	1,402	1,380	1,342	1.0
Agriculture, forestry, and fisheries occupations	......	......	......	......	......	......
Precision production, craft, and repair	55,974	37.6	54,694	53,579	51,766	38.2
Operators, fabricators, assemblers	34,838	23.4	32,464	32,385	32,122	23.1

Source: Bureau of Labor Statistics, November 1995.

Employment in the petroleum refining industry is projected at 140,300 for 2005 (moderate assumptions), compared with 148,900 in 1994. Declines are seen for all occupational areas except professional specialties, with the largest decrease (almost 3,000 employees) in administrative support positions.

FIGURE 4

U.S. CORPORATE INCOME AND WORKER EARNINGS: PETROLEUM AND COAL PRODUCTS

Corporate operating income and aggregate production worker earnings

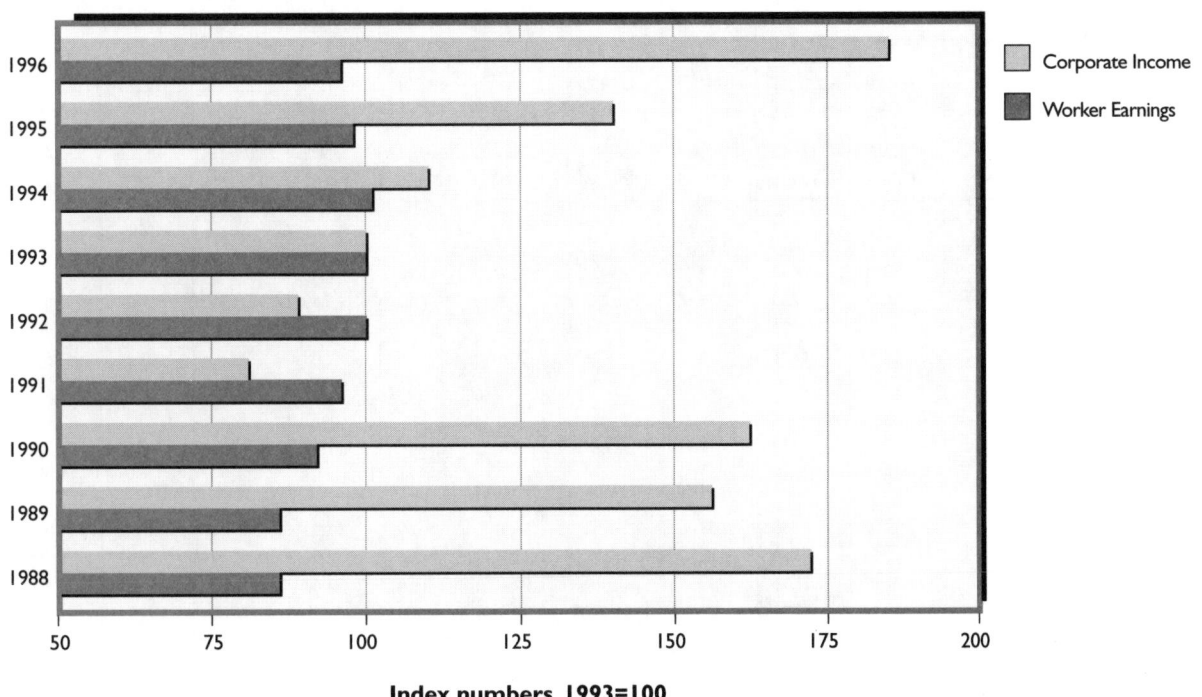

Index numbers, 1993=100

Source: U.S. Bureau of Labor Statistics, U.S. Bureau of the Census, and estimates by the editors.

Finance. While production worker earnings increased slightly between 1988 and 1996, corporate income fell sharply in 1991 from high levels of the previous three years and did not completely recover until 1996 (Figure 4). Operating income in 1996 shot to $23.1 billion from $17.5 billion the year before, resulting in an 0.84 percent yearly rate of gain for 1988-1996 (Table 6). After-tax income, aided by a big jump in nonoperating income, almost doubled between 1995 and 1996 to $27 billion, for an annual growth rate of 3.07 percent from 1988 through 1996. After-tax income in relation to sales was 8.25 percent in 1996 (versus 4.99 percent in 1995), and it was 18.22 percent of stockholders' equity (10.67 percent in 1995). Inventories totaled $15.8 billion in 1996, about the same as in 1995 but below levels for 1988-1994. Debt, at just over 18 percent of total assets, was at its lowest level for the nine-year period.

TABLE 6

U.S. CORPORATE INCOME AND ASSETS: PETROLEUM AND COAL PRODUCTS

(Monetary values in millions of U.S. dollars)

INCOME AND EXPENSES	1988	1989	1990	1991	1992	1993	1994	1995	1996	CHANGE OR AVERAGE[1]
Sales and receipts	252,246	265,346	318,490	282,244	278,034	266,128	268,224	283,146	327,831	3.33
Depreciation and amortization	(19,973)	(18,480)	(18,643)	(17,998)	(18,264)	(17,368)	(17,062)	(16,741)	(16,101)	-2.66
Other operating costs	(210,720)	(227,298)	(279,514)	(254,039)	(248,605)	(236,292)	(237,435)	(248,898)	(288,674)	4.01
Income from operations	21,554	19,568	20,333	10,209	11,163	12,467	13,728	17,507	23,054	0.84
Nonoperating income (expenditures)	5,707	4,109	2,961	2,004	(9,116)	2,522	3,551	(809)	10,134	....
Income before taxes	27,261	23,676	23,295	12,214	2,047	14,989	17,279	16,699	33,187	2.49
Income after taxes	21,225	19,512	18,012	10,872	3,209	13,067	15,004	14,123	27,034	3.07
Cash dividends	9,888	14,618	11,151	11,288	10,983	11,193	11,908	12,472	13,607	4.07
Income retained in business	11,337	4,894	6,861	(415)	(7,775)	1,873	3,097	1,649	13,427	2.14
Direct credits (charges)	(6,282)	(4,532)	(1,209)	(1,447)	119	(1)	944	(364)	(1,119)	....
Ending retained earnings	111,713	111,653	119,461	115,884	109,662	110,245	114,710	112,306	124,610	1.38
ASSETS, END OF YEAR:										
Total	328,431	320,017	339,451	327,961	319,968	313,721	321,234	312,790	334,282	0.22
Accounts receivable	25,253	27,298	34,524	28,763	26,263	24,385	26,842	27,291	31,984	3.00
Inventories	17,937	17,505	19,411	18,459	17,867	16,031	16,212	15,486	15,766	-1.60
Net property, plant and equipment	178,986	172,050	179,352	179,146	180,975	177,856	175,063	164,935	168,496	-0.75
RATIOS, PERCENT:										
INCOME TO SALES:										
Before tax	10.81	8.92	7.31	4.33	0.74	5.63	6.44	5.90	10.12	6.69
After tax	8.41	7.35	5.66	3.85	1.15	4.91	5.59	4.99	8.25	5.57
INCOME TO STOCKHOLDERS' EQUITY:										
Before tax	19.24	17.38	16.36	8.71	1.64	11.65	13.08	12.62	22.36	13.67
After tax	14.98	14.32	12.65	7.75	2.57	10.16	11.36	10.67	18.22	11.41
INCOME TO TOTAL ASSETS:										
Before tax	8.30	7.40	6.86	3.72	0.64	4.78	5.38	5.34	9.93	5.82
After tax	6.46	6.10	5.31	3.32	1.00	4.17	4.67	4.52	8.09	4.85
AS A PERCENT OF TOTAL ASSETS:										
Property, plant and equipment	54.50	53.76	52.84	54.62	56.56	56.69	54.50	52.73	50.41	54.07
Short-term debt	2.70	3.01	2.80	3.77	3.50	2.65	2.50	1.92	1.51	2.71
Long-term debt	21.39	21.71	20.57	22.10	22.35	21.36	21.60	19.60	16.76	20.83
Stockholders' equity	43.13	42.57	41.94	42.77	39.09	41.00	41.13	42.30	44.39	42.04

1. For income and asset amounts, compound annual growth rate; for ratios, average of ratios for the years shown.

Source: U.S. Bureau of the Census, Quarterly Financial Report.

Notes: Parentheses ( ) indicate negative items, e.g., net expenses, charges, or losses. Net property, plant, and equipment is net of accumulated depreciation. Because the samples used to collect the data change, retained earnings at the end of a given year will not exactly equal the previous year's retained earnings plus the current year's retained income and credits.

CANADA

Canada's petroleum refining and related industries had 157 establishments and 14,084 employees in 1993. Petroleum refining accounted for 90 percent of employment and 98 percent of shipments that year (Table 7). Ontario, Alberta, and Quebec together have nearly two-thirds of Canada's refining capacity of 1.9 million barrels per day. Domestic demand for refined petroleum averaged about 1.4 million barrels a day in 1994. Refiners in Canada face stiff competition from U.S. exporters, as well as investment cost increases of Can$1-$3 billion over the next few years to meet federal and provincial requirements for cleaner fuels.[2]

Shipments by the industry in 1994 amounted to Can$17.5 billion, up slightly from the previous year but below the 1990 high of Can$18.6 billion (Table 8). Employment in the industry declined from 15,148 people in 1987 to 13,554 in 1994. Production worker employment in 1994 was slightly above that in 1988, and their share of the workforce was up to 51 percent from 44 percent in 1988. Earnings of production workers averaged Can$24.00 in 1994, versus Can$20.80 in 1988. The average workweek was 39.8 hours, down from 43.0 in 1988.

TABLE 7

CANADA: COMPONENT INDUSTRIES OF REFINED PETROLEUM AND COAL PRODUCTS (CSIC 36), 1993

(Monetary values in Canadian dollars)

INDUSTRY NAME	CSIC	ESTABLISH-MENTS (NUMBER)	EMPLOYMENT		VALUE OF SHIPMENTS (MILLIONS)	AVERAGE HOURLY EARNINGS[1]
			NUMBER	PERCENT OF INDUSTRY TOTAL		
REFINED PETROLEUM AND COAL PRODUCTS	36	157	14,084	100.0	CAN$17,244.4	CAN$24.48
Refined petroleum	361	62	12,683	90.1	16,956.9	25.88
Petroleum products (except lubricating oil, grease)	3611	34	10,819	76.8	16,388.1	27.29
Lubricating oil and grease	3612	28	1,864	13.2	568.8	18.46
Other petroleum and coal products	369	95	1,401	9.9	287.5	15.74

1. Including overtime.

Source: Adapted from Statistics Canada, *Manufacturing Industries of Canada* (Cat. No. 31-203).

---

[2] *Based on reports from the U.S. Department of Energy's Energy Information Administration.*

TABLE 8

CANADIAN EMPLOYMENT AND SHIPMENTS: REFINED PETROLEUM AND COAL PRODUCTS, 1987-1994

(Monetary values in Canadian dollars)

	1987	1988	1989	1990	1991	1992	1993	1994	CHANGE[1]
All employees	15,148	15,610	16,045	15,868	14,643	14,119	14,084	13,554	-1.58
Establishments	126	141	163	138	140	148	157	168	4.20
Employees per establishment	120	111	98	115	105	95	90	81	-5.54
Production workers per establishment	.....	48	43	49	50	45	44	41	-2.82
PRODUCTION WORKERS:									
Total	.....	6,837	6,973	6,781	7,020	6,633	6,883	6,862	0.06
Percent of all employees	.....	43.8	43.5	42.7	47.9	47.0	48.9	50.6	.....
Male	.....	6,647	6,755	6,557	6,789	.....	.....	.....	.....
Female	.....	190	218	224	231	.....	.....	.....	.....
Percent of all production workers	.....	2.8	3.1	3.3	3.3	.....	.....	.....	.....
Average hourly earnings	.....	20.80	22.79	23.24	23.62	23.83	24.48	24.00	2.41
Average weekly earnings	.....	893.67	907.55	945.79	956.05	966.21	987.52	956.00	1.13
Average weekly hours	.....	43.0	39.8	40.7	40.5	40.5	40.3	39.8	-1.25
Shipments (millions)	16,439	14,274	14,959	18,569	18,066	17,450	17,244	17,536	0.93

1. Compound annual growth rate.

Source: Adapted from Statistics Canada, *Manufacturing Industries of Canada* (Cat. No. 31-203).

MEXICO

PEMEX, the state-owned oil company of Mexico, ranks as the world's sixth largest oil company and the single most important component of the Mexican economy. It has a monopoly over exploration and extraction of all hydrocarbons. The country's domestic refineries need upgrading to produce cleaner burning transportation fuel, but the only major project so far involves a $1.2 billion investment to reconfigure the Cadereyta refinery. The Deer Park refinery in Texas, a joint venture with Shell Oil Co., is an important source of unleaded gasoline (see the What's New section).[3]

In 1993, the government-owned petroleum refining industry had only six units (establishments), while the coke industry had 205 (Table 9). Employment totaled 19,818 for petroleum refining and 10,114 for the coke industry. Petroleum industry employees had an average income (earnings plus benefits) of 52,309 new pesos ($16,746) a year, which is high compared with other industries. Earnings of production workers averaged 33,835 new pesos ($10,832), only about half the average of 65,840 ($21,078) for nonproduction employees. Annual income in the coke industry averaged 36,636 new pesos ($11,728); production worker earnings averaged 15,926 ($5,098) a year, contrasted with the 43,158 ($13,816) for nonproduction employees. Employment in petroleum refining and related industries declined at an annual rate of 6.81 percent a year between 1988 and 1995 (Table 10).

---

[3] *Ibid.*

Table 9

Mexico: Component Industries of Petroleum and Coke (CMAP 3530 and 3540), 1993

(Monetary values in 1993 Mexican New Pesos)

			All workers									
							Paid workers					
							Production workers		Nonproduction employees		Benefits	Unpaid
Industry	CMAP	Number of units	Number	Percent of industry total	Average days worked	Remun-eration[1]	Number	Wages and salaries	Number	Wages and salaries	Per paid employee	Workers, number
Petroleum refining	3530	6	19,818	100	365	52,309	17,553	33,835	2,265	65,840	14,816	0
Coke, coal and oil by-products	3540	205	10,114	100	278	36,636	6,933	15,926	3,094	43,158	12,307	87

1. Average annual remuneration including benefits and excluding profit sharing.

Source: INEGI, Censos Economicos 1994.

Table 10

Mexican Employment: Derivatives of Petroleum, 1988-1995

	1988	1989	1990	1991	1992	1993	1994	1995	Change[1]
Total employment: Petroleum	53,548	49,861	50,944	46,858	41,015	35,528	32,703	32,691	-6.81

1. Compound annual growth rate.

Source: Sistema de Cuentas Nacionales de Mexico, INEGI.

International Trade

United States. U.S. global exports of refined petroleum and coal products in 1996 rose for the second successive year, to an eight-year high of almost $7.2 billion (Table 11). Imports declined from 1990 through 1995 but then suddenly more than doubled in 1996, reaching nearly $18.8 billion. As a result, the U.S. trade deficit in this group soared to $11.6 billion in 1996 from the relatively low deficit of $3 billion in 1995. Higher prices in 1996 contributed to the sharp value gains in both imports and exports. Canada took 13.9 percent of U.S. exports and supplied 15.1 percent of U.S. imports in 1996. Mexico accounted for 16.2 percent of U.S. exports and 2.2 percent of the imports that year.

Canada. U.S. exports to Canada in 1996, at just under $1 billion, were not much changed from 1990, although improved over those in the intervening years (Table 11). Canadian shipments to the United States rose to $2.8 billion in 1996 from $2.4 billion in 1990. Canada's trade surplus with the United States thus totaled over $1.8 billion in 1996, versus $1.4 billion in 1990. Canadian exports to Mexico are nil.

Mexico. U.S. petroleum product exports to Mexico rose to $1.16 billion in 1996, almost double the $610 million total for 1990 (Table 11). Mexico's sales to the United States increased to $406 million from $313 million during the same period. This gave the United States a $756 million trade surplus with Mexico in 1996, compared with a surplus of $298 million in 1990. Mexican exports to Canada have grown from virtually none in 1989 to $24 million in 1996.

NAFTA. After fluctuating in a fairly narrow range for six years, Canada's trade surplus within NAFTA rose 58 percent between 1995 and 1996 as shipments to the United States increased dramatically. The U.S. trade deficit jumped 81 percent between 1995 and 1996 to $1.08 billion, and Mexico's rose 33 percent to $732 million (Table 11).

TABLE 11

INTERNATIONAL TRADE, PETROLEUM AND COAL PRODUCTS

(Millions of U.S. dollars)

	1989[1]	1990	1991	1992	1993	1994	1995	1996
GLOBAL TRADE, U.S.								
IMPORTS								
Value	11,940.4	14,422.7	11,037.9	10,344.1	9,906.0	9,503.5	8,971.1	18,767.9
Ratio to new supply[2]	7.6	7.7	6.5	6.3	6.2	6.0	.....	.....
Ratio to apparent consumption[3]	7.8	7.9	6.8	6.5	6.5	6.2	.....	.....
EXPORTS								
Value	4,933.5	6,694.7	6,969.4	6,365.8	6,163.4	5,510.1	6,013.6	7,158.1
Ratio to comparable domestic shipments	3.4	3.9	4.4	4.1	4.1	3.7	.....	.....
TRADE BALANCE	(7,006.9)	(7,728.0)	(4,068.5)	(3,978.3)	(3,742.6)	(3,993.4)	(2,957.5)	(11,609.8)
BILATERAL TRADE: NAFTA[4]								
U.S. exports to Canada	672.6	1,000.6	769.9	671.7	734.1	739.0	836.5	994.8
Canadian exports to U.S.	1,886.5	2,356.7	2,173.7	1,857.1	1,827.0	1,751.6	1,978.2	2,830.4
U.S. exports to Mexico	715.0	610.6	755.5	923.0	813.2	802.1	900.7	1,161.5
Mexican exports to U.S.	185.5	312.6	230.2	325.6	588.9	389.1	355.5	405.8
Canadian exports to Mexico	0.0	4.4	14.1	5.8	0.1	0.2	9.8	0.0
Mexican exports to Canada	0.0	0.0	6.4	6.6	10.6	8.7	6.7	24.2
TRADE BALANCES WITHIN NAFTA[5]								
Canada	1,213.9	1,360.5	1,411.5	1,184.6	1,082.4	1,004.1	1,144.8	1,811.4
Mexico	(529.6)	(302.4)	(533.0)	(596.6)	(213.8)	(404.5)	(548.3)	(731.5)
United States	(684.3)	(1,058.1)	(878.5)	(588.0)	(868.6)	(599.6)	(596.5)	(1,079.9)

1. 1989 and earlier data on U.S. exports to Canada for manufacturing total and manufacturing industries are not comparable with data for 1990 and later years because of a change in the reporting system. The NAFTA trade balances for the U.S. and Canada also are affected.

2. New supply equals comparable domestic shipments plus imports for consumption.

3. Apparent consumption equals comparable domestic shipments plus imports for consumption less exports.

4. Amounts less than U.S. $100,000 shown as zero.

5. Parentheses indicate an excess of imports over exports. Because of commodity coding and other data differences among the three countries, these trade balances are only rough estimates and should be used with caution.

Source for U.S. Global Trade: U.S. Department of Commerce, International Trade Administration.

Source for U.S. -Canada and U.S.-Mexico Bilateral Trade: U.S. Bureau of the Census.

Source for Canada-Mexico and Mexico-Canada Bilateral Trade: Statistics Canada, Foreign Trade Division, Special tabulation, March 1997, converted to U.S. dollars by the editors.

PRIMARY METALS

THE UNITED STATES

Products and Processes. The primary metals industries, combined, ranked ninth among U.S. manufacturing industries in 1996 in terms of manufacturers' shipments. Their products include ferrous metals (iron and steel) and nonferrous metals (including aluminum, copper, lead, titanium, and zinc). Cyclical in nature, this industry group is highly responsive to U.S. and world economic activity since so many other industries use metals. Among these outlets are motor vehicle manufacturing (steel, aluminum, and other metals); the aerospace industry (titanium, steel, aluminum); building materials and construction (steel, aluminum, copper, zinc); container manufacturers (aluminum, steel); and battery manufacturers (lead).

Iron and steel together accounted for slightly over half of the $138.3 billion worth of metals industries shipments in 1992, the latest year for which economic census data are available (Table 1). Among the nonferrous metals, the largest two categories in 1992 were rolling and drawing, ($37.1 billion in shipments) and primary smelting and refining ($13.9 billion).

Employment in the primary metals industries is in a long-term downtrend as a result of extensive cost cutting and restructuring—a trend expected to continue given the intense competition in this sector. Projections to the year 2005 (Table 2) show employment sliding to 531,600 (moderate assumptions) in 2005, or some 22 percent less than in 1993. Much of this decline will be in iron and steel production, which accounts for about half of total employment. A sizable decrease also is projected for nonferrous rolling and drawing, the second largest production area with 161,700 employees in 1993.

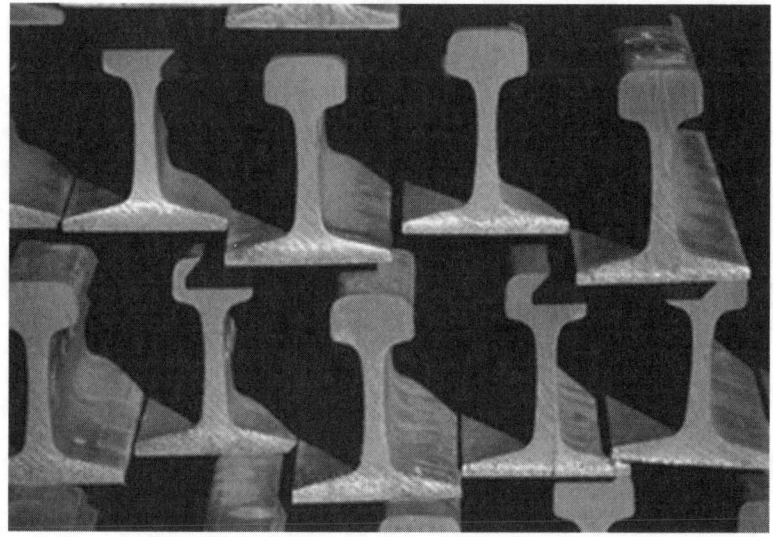

TABLE 1

UNITED STATES: COMPONENT INDUSTRIES OF PRIMARY METAL INDUSTRIES (SIC 33), 1992

(Monetary values in millions of U.S. dollars)

INDUSTRY	SIC	ESTABLISH-MENTS	SHIPMENTS		VALUE ADDED BY MANUFACTURE	NEW CAPITAL EXPENDI-TURES	EMPLOY-MENT[1]	PAYROLL
			VALUE	PERCENT BY 4 LARGEST COMPANIES				
PRIMARY METAL INDUSTRIES	33	6,501	$138,287.0	.....	$52,027.2	$5,294.0	662,100	$22,202.4
Blast furnaces and basic steel products	331	1,012	58,449.1	.....	22,173.4	2,605.2	238,700	9,179.2
Blast furnaces and steel mills	3312	213	42,154.0	37	16,541.4	2,210.5	170,100	7,021.7
Electrometallurgical products, except steel	3313	36	1,261.9	56	413.6	36.8	4,900	170.9
Steel wiredrawing and steel nails and spikes	3315	349	4,298.5	19	1,785.2	135.7	25,200	708.8
Cold-rolled steel sheet, strip, and bars	3316	183	5,492.9	43	1,717.1	109.6	15,100	547.6
Steel pipe and tubes	3317	231	5,241.9	19	1,716.0	112.6	23,400	730.2
Iron and steel foundries	332	1,172	11,860.2	.....	6,872.8	465.3	122,100	3,739.2
Gray and ductile iron foundries	3321	709	7,775.7	24	4,322.4	338.9	76,700	2,462.2
Malleable iron foundries	3322	24	247.7	80	144.3	3.8	2,800	100.9
Steel investment foundries	3324	152	1,737.7	50	1,136.2	51.0	20,200	557.3
Steel foundries, n.e.c.	3325	287	2,099.1	21	1,270.0	71.7	22,400	618.7
Primary smelting and refining of nonferrous metals	333	176	13,905.2	.....	3,390.5	557.0	34,700	1,334.0
Primary smelting and refining of copper	3331	20	5,565.3	98	948.8	194.4	5,500	186.8
Primary production of aluminum	3334	42	5,856.1	59	1,612.8	215.1	20,400	806.9
Primary nonferrous metals, n.e.c.	3339	114	2,483.9	43	828.8	147.6	8,700	340.2
Secondary nonferrous metals	334	385	6,131.4	28	1,232.6	153.6	13,400	406.7
Nonferrous rolling and drawing	335	1,117	37,101.3	....	12,334.8	1,110.9	147,400	4,635.4
Copper rolling, drawing, and extruding	3351	115	6,004.0	45	1,455.1	125.2	18,900	606.5
Aluminum sheet, plate, and foil	3353	64	10,701.5	68	3,276.0	364.7	24,500	1,016.5
Aluminum extruded products	3354	195	3,788.3	35	1,425.2	150.5	25,700	689.4
Aluminum rolling and drawing, n.e.c.	3355	28	761.8	86	125.6	12.7	1,500	50.2
Nonferrous rolling and drawing, n.e.c.	3356	184	2,802.1	32	1,211.8	92.3	16,100	548.8
Nonferrous wire drawing and insulating	3357	531	13,043.6	28	4,841.1	365.5	60,600	1,724.0
Nonferrous foundries (castings)	336	1,635	7,002.4	....	3,926.5	254.2	74,500	1,942.4
Aluminum die-castings	3363	333	2,817.6	21	1,536.1	122.5	27,100	744.5
Nonferrous die-castings, except aluminum	3364	263	1,023.5	16	545.6	33.8	11,200	273.5
Aluminum foundries	3365	591	1,959.2		1,153.5	65.4	22,900	580.7
Copper foundries	3366	329	744.3	13	413.3	19.8	8,700	205.1
Nonferrous foundries, except aluminum and copper	3369	119	458.0	70	278.1	12.7	4,800	138.6
Miscellaneous primary metal products	339	1,004	3,837.3	....	2,096.7	147.8	31,200	965.5
Metal heat treating	3398	733	1,956.9	25	1,198.2	67.1	17,500	516.2
Primary metal products, n.e.c.	3399	271	1,880.4	34	898.6	80,700	13,800	449.3

1. Employment numbers from the economic censuses differ in definition and classification from the Bureau of Labor Statistics estimates in Table 2. Year-to-year comparisons between Table 1 and Table 2 are not appropriate.

Source: U.S. Bureau of the Census, 1992 Census of Manufactures.

TABLE 2

U.S. EMPLOYMENT AND EARNINGS: PRIMARY METALS

INDUSTRY	SIC	1993 EMPLOYMENT[1] NUMBER OF PERSONS	1993 EMPLOYMENT[1] PERCENT OF INDUSTRY TOTAL	1993 AVERAGE HOURLY EARNINGS (U.S. DOLLARS)[2]	2005 PROJECTED EMPLOYMENT[3]
PRIMARY METAL INDUSTRIES	33	683,100	100.0	$13.99	531,600
Blast furnaces and basic steel products	331	240,300	35.2	16.36	154,900
Blast furnaces and steel mills	3312	175,400	25.7	17.52	....
Steel pipe and tubes	3317	25,800	3.8	12.71	....
Iron and steel foundries	332	119,000	17.4	12.52	92,400
Gray and ductile iron foundries	3321	75,600	11.1	13.08	....
Malleable iron foundries	3322	5,100	0.7	13.72	....
Steel foundries, n.e.c.	3325	24,400	3.6	11.65	....
Primary nonferrous smelting and refining	333	42,000	6.1	15.19	36,000
Primary aluminum	3334	24,000	3.5	15.37	....
Nonferrous rolling and drawing	335	161,700	23.7	13.20	135,000
Copper rolling and drawing	3351	22,200	3.2	12.82	....
Aluminum sheet, plate, and foil	3353	24,400	3.6	15.70	....
Nonferrous wire drawing and insulating	3357	69,000	10.1	13.21	....
Nonferrous foundries (castings)	336	78,500	11.5	11.20	73,700
Aluminum foundries	3365	22,400	3.3	10.69	....
All other primary metals	334,9	....	....	....	40,000

1. Total payroll employment. Employment data from the economic censuses, shown from Table 1, differ in definition and classification from the Bureau of Labor Statistics estimates in this table. Year-to-year comparisons between Table 1 and Table 2 are not appropriate.

2. Earnings of production workers, including overtime.

3. Number of persons, moderate projection by the U.S. Bureau of Labor Statistics.

Source: Bureau of Labor Statistics.

FIGURE 1

U.S. EMPLOYMENT IN PRIMARY METAL INDUSTRIES

Percent distribution by region, 1995

Employment in the primary metals industries is highest in the Great Lakes region, with about 38 percent of total 1995 employment, followed by the Southeast, with 20 percent. Employment in the Rocky Mountain states, on the other hand, is only about 2 percent of the total.

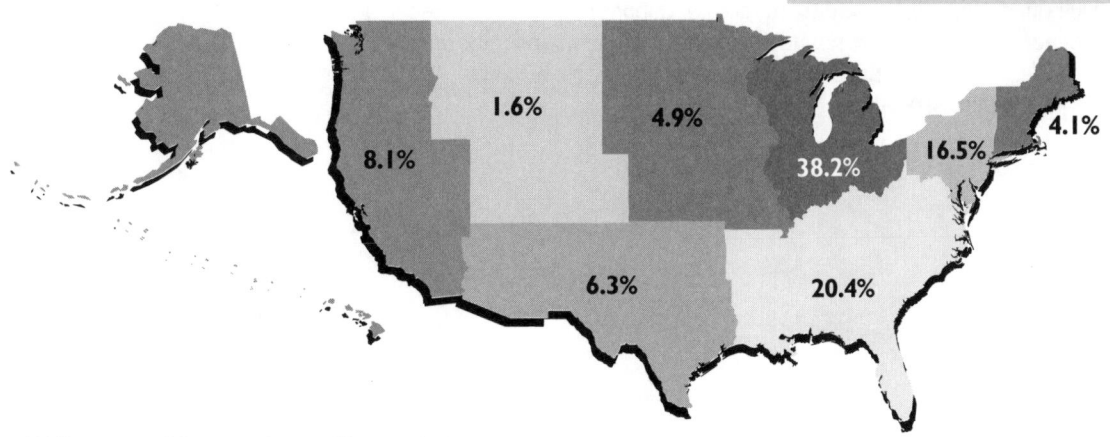

Source: U.S. Department of Commerce, Bureau of Economic Analysis.

What's New. The U.S. steel industry continues to benefit from a relatively strong U.S. economy and from its improved competitive position gained through extensive restructuring and consolidation. By modernizing, reducing capacity, and cutting employment, the industry produced a turnaround in efficiency during the 1980s and early 1990s. According to industry sources, the North American steel industry invested some $50 billion in new technologies and facilities over this period and by 1995 had transformed itself from a laggard by world standards to an efficient industry highly competitive in world markets. Worker hours required to produce a ton of finished steel fell from 10.1 hours in 1982 to 3.9 in 1995, and a number of mills have cut the time to under two worker hours. Production costs in 1995 were below those of world-class mills in Germany and Japan. As a result, U.S. producers have been able to hold down steel prices, even as prices for other materials have risen, and thus have improved their ability to compete.

Currently, the industry is working to develop Advanced Process Control. This five-year research and development program consists of several projects intended to lower product costs while producing superior-quality steel products. Examples are optical sensors and controls for improved basic oxygen furnace operation.

The U.S. steel industry is generally supportive of NAFTA, and the American Iron and Steel Institute has created the North American Steel Council to address NAFTA-related issues. NAFTA preserves two special trade provisions of importance to U.S. steel: (1) it leaves U.S. antidumping and countervailing duty laws essentially intact; and (2) it preserves Buy American preferences under the Highway Act.

Ford Motor Company is using aluminum-head engines and other aluminum components to help hold the curb weight of its new super-SUV sports utility vehicle under 5,500 pounds, according to AMM Online. Aluminum's use in vehicles has risen more than 65 percent during the past decade, mainly because of the need for lighter weight, fuel-efficient vehicles. The largest domestic outlet for aluminum, the transportation sector in 1996 took 5.8 billion pounds, with 3.6 billion going into passenger cars and light trucks.

Phillip Townsend Associates reports that instrument panels in cars and trucks are the second biggest interior market (next to seats) for materials such as steel, aluminum, magnesium, and plastics, consuming more than 500 million pounds of materials in 1996.

General Motors Corporation reportedly plans to use powder stainless steel exhaust system flanges in high volumes for the first time in its next generation of standard-size pickup trucks and spots utility vehicles.

Many small markets can make a big difference for a product like copper. Use of the metal in cars reportedly has picked up because of increased buying of cars loaded with options, some containing copper. IBM in September 1997 announced development of a new semiconductor chip that uses copper circuitry, rather than aluminum, which could boost copper consumption by some 17,000 pounds annually, according to the U.S. Copper Development Association. While only a fraction of the 7.6 billion pounds of copper consumed annually, this new use indicates that copper "remains on the cutting edge of technological advances," according to a spokesperson for the trade association.

Zinc, which has seen some wide price swings in the past two years, is finding increased uses in products ranging from roofing to batteries to water purification systems, says the American Zinc Association. Zinc roofing is becoming popular in North America because it is long-lived, requires little maintenance, is easily worked and formed, and has a subtle color that becomes richer over time. Zinc-air batteries used in lap-top computers reportedly provide more than 12 hours of usage on a single charge, or almost 10 times the level for regular batteries. The batteries use oxygen from the air to support reactions that generate electricity. A high-purity alloy of zinc and copper, patented by KDF Fluid Treatment, Inc., is a cost-effective way of removing chlorine, heavy metals, and bacteria from water. Water passes through a filtration unit in which zinc/copper granules exchange electrons with the contaminants, changing them into compounds that are harmless or filterable.

FIGURE 2

U.S. EMPLOYMENT AND SHIPMENTS, PRIMARY METAL INDUSTRIES

Total payroll employment and manufacturers' inflation-adjusted shipments

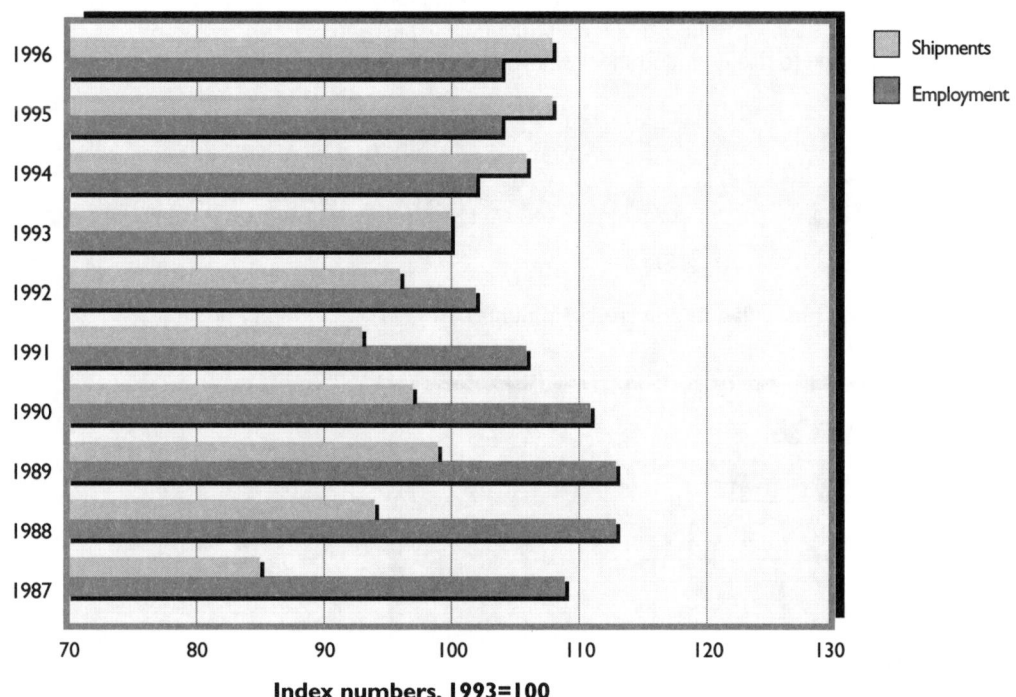

Index numbers, 1993=100

Source: U.S. Bureau of Labor Statistics, U.S. Department of Commerce, and estimates by the editors. Shipments data for 1996 are not available.

Output. Recent shipments of primary metals have rebounded strongly from the recession-reduced levels of 1990-1991, while employment has edged up only slightly from 1993 and is considerably below that of 1987 (Figure 2).

Total shipments by the **primary metals industries** in 1996 were valued at $174.8 billion, down slightly from the previous year but far above the $136.4 billion of 1991 and the $120.3 billion of 1987 (Table 3). Annual growth from 1987 to 1996 averaged 4.23 percent in current dollars and 2.73 percent when adjusted for inflation.

Shipments of **iron and steel** stairstepped downward from 1989 to 1991. They then reversed course, climbing steadily through 1995, while employment declined during most of the 1989-1995 period (Figure 2A). Value of industry shipments in 1996 totaled $89.4 billion, compared with $89.8 billion in 1995 and $62.4 billion in 1987 (Table 3). The average growth rate from 1987 to 1996 was 4.06 percent in current-dollar terms.

For **nonferrous metals**, shipments declined from 1989 through 1991 before heading sharply higher in 1994 and 1995. Employment reached its low point in 1992-1993 before partly recovering in the next three years (Figure 2B). Value of shipments in 1996 totaled $85.4 billion, compared with a high for the period of $90.6 billion in 1995 and a low of $57.8 billion in 1987. The annual growth rate for 1987-1996 was 4.44 percent (Table 3). Industry reports indicate that volume of shipments in 1996 rose by 3.1 percent to 100.5 million tons. Largest gainers were construction products such as reinforcing bars, structural shapes, and merchant bars; sheet products are expected to rise in importance as new mini-mills come on stream.

FIGURE 2A

U.S. EMPLOYMENT AND SHIPMENTS, IRON AND STEEL

Total payroll employment and manufacturers' inflation-adjusted shipments

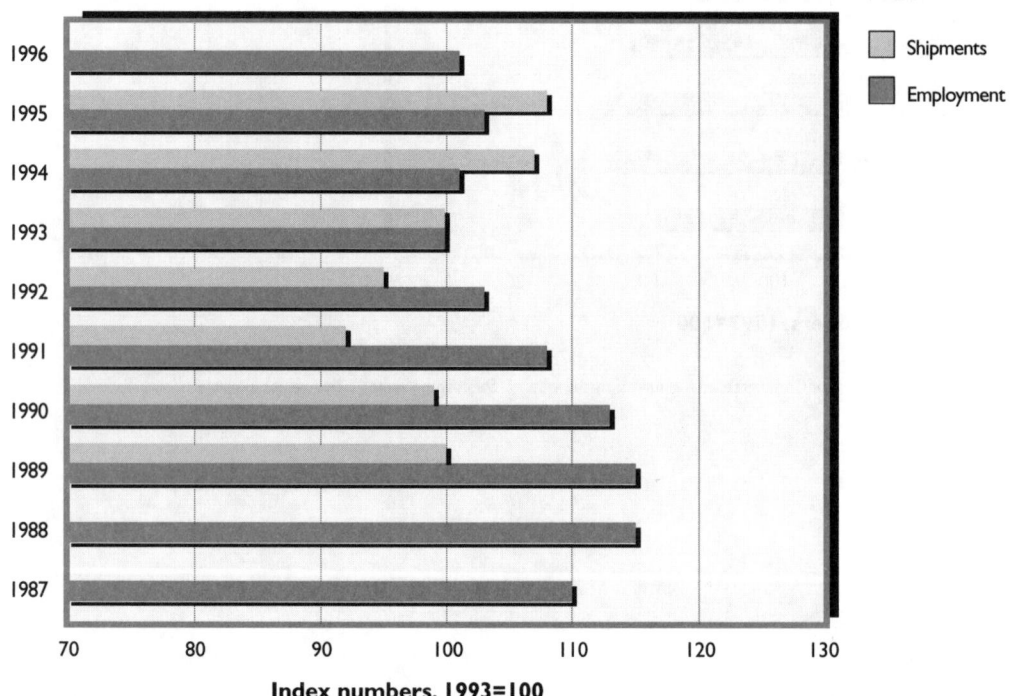

Index numbers, 1993=100

Source: U.S. Bureau of Labor Statistics, U.S. Department of Commerce, and estimates by the editors. Shipments data for 1987, 1988, and 1996 are not available.

FIGURE 2B

U.S. EMPLOYMENT AND SHIPMENTS, NONFERROUS METALS

Total payroll employment and manufacturers' inflation-adjusted shipments

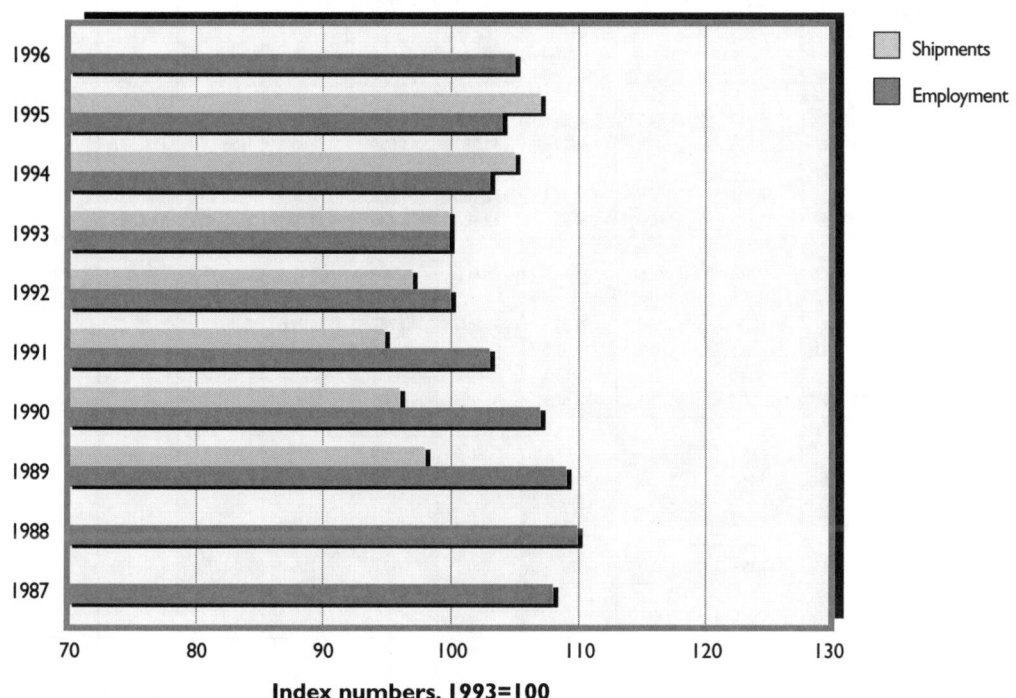

Index numbers, 1993=100

Source: U.S. Bureau of Labor Statistics, U.S. Department of Commerce, and estimates by the editors. Shipments data for 1987, 1988, and 1996 are not available.

Investment. New capital expenditures by the primary metals industry totaled $6.7 billion in 1995, almost 75 percent above those in 1987 (Table 3). Research and development (R&D) spending totaled $672 million in 1994, not much changed from 1987. Capacity utilization—one indicator of the need for new investment— was 90.7 percent in 1996, down slightly from that in the previous two years but above levels for 1987-1993.

The **iron and steel** industry spent $3.9 billion on new plant and equipment in 1995, compared with $2.1 billion in 1987. R&D spending was $241 million in 1994. Much of this spending went toward transforming largely obsolete mills into streamlined, technology-intensive plants. Capacity utilization totaled 88.8 percent in 1996, off slightly from that in the previous two years.

New capital expenditures by the **nonferrous metals industries** rose from $1.7 billion in 1987 to a high of $2.8 billion in 1994 and then declined slightly in 1995. R&D spending in 1994 was $431 million. Capacity utilization rose to a peak of 93.1 percent in 1996, compared with 92.3 percent in the previous year and 84.1 percent in 1987.

Prices. Primary metals prices rose at an annual rate of 2.27 percent from 1987 to 1996. They actually declined some in 1996 after a steep increase in 1995 (Table 3).

TABLE 3

U.S. OUTPUT, INVESTMENT, AND PRICES: PRIMARY METALS

(Millions of U.S. dollars, except as noted)

	1987	1988	1989	1990	1991	1992	1993	1994	1995	1996	GROWTH RATE 1987-1995[1]
TOTAL PRIMARY METALS											
VALUE OF SHIPMENTS:											
BY INDUSTRY:											
Current dollars	120,343	149,837	155,717	148,787	136,378	138,287	142,685	161,189	180,303	174,762	4.23
Constant 1992 dollars	122,661	136,464	142,875	140,478	134,144	138,287	144,559	153,486	155,576	156,281	2.73
BY PRODUCT:											
Current dollars	115,958	143,311	147,001	140,225	126,349	132,106	136,806	154,709	172,167	166,877	4.13
Constant 1992 dollars	128,814	130,758	135,127	132,631	124,321	132,106	138,446	147,285	148,963	149,638	1.68
OTHER OUTPUT MEASURES:											
Industrial production, 1993=100	92.7	100.7	99.4	98.6	91.7	94.8	100.0	107.1	109.7	111.1	2.03
Gross domestic product:											
Current dollars	35,214	43,504	45,056	42,638	39,571	38,999	40,783	44,166	.....	.....	.....
Percent of total GDP	0.8	0.9	0.8	0.7	0.7	0.6	0.6	0.6	.....	.....	.....
Rank in manufacturing	10	10	10	10	10	10	11	11	.....	.....	.....
Chained (1992) dollars	38,572	41,105	39,397	38,983	38,638	38,999	41,908	42,853	.....	.....	.....
INVESTMENT-RELATED MEASURES:											
Capacity utilization, percent	79.2	87.4	85.2	83.4	77.6	80.9	85.9	91.2	91.9	90.7	.....
New capital expenditures	3,851	4,721	5,594	5,941	6,082	5,294	4,744	6,525	6,718	.....	.....
Research and development spending	711	620	666	717	706	514	646	672	.....	.....	.....
Producer prices, 1993=100[2]	90.7	101.4	106.6	104.6	101.5	100.3	100.0	105.0	115.1	111.0	2.27
IRON AND STEEL											
VALUE OF SHIPMENTS:											
BY INDUSTRY:											
Current dollars	62,443	76,491	77,374	75,287	68,981	70,309	75,312	84,121	89,784	89,373	4.06
Constant 1992 dollars	....	....	74,232	73,191	67,941	70,309	74,195	79,577	80,336	.....	.....
BY PRODUCT:											
Current dollars	61,012	74,268	74,975	72,558	65,577	68,551	73,470	82,373	87,859	87,456	4.08
Constant 1992 dollars	....	....	71,951	70,502	64,576	68,551	72,387	77,917	78,625	.....	.....
Other output measures:											
Industrial production, 1993=100	89.1	100.5	99.2	99.3	89.6	93.4	100.0	105.7	108.6	108.7	2.23
INVESTMENT-RELATED MEASURES:											
Capacity utilization, percent	76.2	87.4	84.7	83.6	75.7	80.5	87.6	91.4	91.6	88.8	.....
New capital expenditures	2,103	2,749	3,410	3,603	3,903	3,071	2,707	3,704	3,928	.....	.....
Research and development spending	249	252	244	231	225	221	272	241	.....	.....	.....
NONFERROUS METALS											
VALUE OF SHIPMENTS:											
BY INDUSTRY:											
Current dollars	57,805	73,344	78,342	73,499	67,397	67,978	67,373	77,067	90,519	85,440	4.44
Constant 1992 dollars	....	....	68,643	67,288	66,203	67,978	70,364	73,909	75,240	.....	.....
BY PRODUCT:											
Current dollars	54,947	69,043	72,026	67,667	60,772	63,555	63,336	72,336	84,309	79,578	4.20
Constant 1992 dollars	....	....	63,176	62,129	59,745	63,555	66,058	69,368	70,338	.....	.....
OTHER OUTPUT MEASURES:											
Industrial production, 1993=100	97.8	101.1	99.7	97.5	94.4	96.6	100.0	108.8	111.1	114.1	1.73
INVESTMENT-RELATED MEASURES:											
Capacity utilization, percent	84.1	87.5	85.9	83.1	80.1	81.7	83.8	91.1	92.3	93.1	.....
New capital expenditures	1,748	1,971	2,182	2,337	2,178	2,224	2,038	2,822	2,789	.....	.....
Research and development spending	462	368	422	486	481	293	374	431	.....	.....	.....

1. Compound annual growth rate.

2. Prices received by domestic producers.

Sources: Shipments and new capital expenditures: U.S. Department of Commerce for 1987-1995, editor's estimates for constant dollar data for 1987-88 and all shipments data for 1996; Industrial production and capacity utilization: Federal Reserve Board of Governors; GDP: Bureau of Economic Analysis; Research and development spending: National Science Foundation; Producer prices: Bureau of Labor Statistics.

Workforce and Employment. Employment in the **primary metals** industries declined at an annual rate of 0.53 percent between 1987 and 1996, to 711,000, reflecting steady decreases from 1989 to 1993 (Table 4). Subsequent gains were not enough to reverse the long-term downtrend. Employment of production workers declined at a slower rate over the 10 years (-0.16 percent annually) as supervisors and administrative/sales personnel apparently took the brunt of the contraction. In 1996, production workers accounted for 77.9 percent of the workforce, compared with 75.4 percent in 1987. Overall employment of women was unchanged in 1996 from the 1987 level, and their share of the workforce was up slightly to 14.2 percent. Production workers earned, on average, $14.97 an hour in 1996, compared with $11.94 in 1987, for a 2.54 percent rate of gain during the 10-year period. In inflation-adjusted dollars, however, the rate was a negative 0.98 percent.

Employment in **iron and steel** industries rose between 1987 and 1989, but declined in most subsequent years, to 364,000 by 1996. The result was an annual decline of 0.98 percent for the 1987-1996 period (Table 4). Employment of production workers declined at a slightly slower rate, so that their share of the workforce rose to 78.6 percent in 1996 from 76.7 percent in 1987. Employment of women, at 10.2 percent in 1996, was up slightly. Average hourly earnings during the 10-year period rose 2.92 percent a year in current dollars but fell 0.62 percent in inflation-adjusted dollars. Still, at $17.84 an hour, earnings were among the highest in manufacturing.

Employment in **nonferrous metals** industries declined at an annual rate of 0.34 percent between 1987 and 1996, to 297,000 employees, as growth in recent years failed to offset reductions made through 1993. Production worker employment followed a similar pattern of decline followed by growth but showed a positive growth rate of 0.24 percent annually for the 1987-1996 period. In 1996, employment of production workers stood at 231,000 or 77.8 percent of the workforce, compared with 73.9 percent in 1987. Women made up 19.4 percent of the workforce in 1996, compared with 18.7 percent in 1987.

TABLE 4

U.S. EMPLOYMENT, HOURS, AND EARNINGS: PRIMARY METALS

(Monetary values in U.S. dollars)

	1987	1988	1989	1990	1991	1992	1993	1994	1995	1996	CHANGE[1]
ALL PRIMARY METALS											
NUMBER OF EMPLOYEES, IN THOUSANDS:											
Total	746	770	772	756	723	695	683	698	712	711	-0.53
Production workers	562	589	589	574	545	525	520	537	553	554	-0.16
Percent of total	75.4	76.5	76.3	75.9	75.4	75.6	76.2	76.9	77.7	77.9	.....
Women	101	104	105	103	98	93	92	97	100	101	0.00
Percent of total	13.5	13.5	13.5	13.6	13.6	13.4	13.5	13.9	14.1	14.2	.....
HOURS AND EARNINGS OF PRODUCTION WORKERS:											
Average hourly earnings, U.S. dollars[2]											
Current dollars	11.94	12.16	12.43	12.92	13.33	13.66	13.99	14.34	14.62	14.97	2.54
1992 dollars[3]	14.67	14.36	14.01	13.85	13.71	13.66	13.61	13.61	13.49	13.43	-0.98
Average weekly hours	43.1	43.5	43.0	42.7	42.2	43.0	43.7	44.7	44.0	44.2	0.28
Average weekly earnings, current U.S. dollars	514.61	528.96	534.49	551.68	562.53	587.38	611.36	641	643.28	661.67	2.83
IRON AND STEEL											
NUMBER OF EMPLOYEES, IN THOUSANDS:											
Total	398	415	416	409	389	371	359	364	371	364	-0.98
Production workers	305	325	325	317	299	285	278	284	290	286	-0.72
Percent of total	76.7	78.3	78.0	77.6	77.0	76.9	77.4	77.8	78.3	78.6	.....
Women	39	41	42	41	39	36	35	36	37	37	-0.41
Percent of total	9.7	9.9	10.0	10.1	10.0	9.8	9.7	10.0	10.1	10.2	.....
HOURS AND EARNINGS OF PRODUCTION WORKERS:											
Average hourly earnings, U.S. dollars[2]											
Current dollars	13.77	13.98	14.25	14.82	15.36	15.87	16.36	16.85	17.35	17.84	2.92
1992 dollars[3]	16.92	16.51	16.07	15.88	15.80	15.87	15.91	15.99	16.01	16.00	-0.62
Average weekly hours	43.4	44.0	43.4	43.4	42.7	43.5	44.1	44.9	44.4	.....	0.29
Average weekly earnings, current U.S. dollars	587.62	615.12	618.45	643.19	655.87	690.35	721.48	756.57	770.34	793.88	3.40
NONFERROUS METALS											
NUMBER OF EMPLOYEES, IN THOUSANDS:											
Total	306	311	310	302	291	283	282	290	295	297	-0.34
Production workers	226	231	230	223	214	211	212	222	229	231	0.24
Percent of total	73.9	74.4	74.3	74.0	73.8	74.4	75.2	76.5	77.5	77.8	.....
Women	57	57	57	55	54	51	52	55	57	58	0.08
Percent of total	18.7	18.4	18.2	18.3	18.5	18.1	18.4	19.0	19.3	19.4	.....

1. Compound annual growth rate, 1987-1996.

2. Including overtime.

3. Converted to 1992 dollars using Consumer Price Index for Urban Wage Earners and Clerical Workers.

Source: Bureau of Labor Statistics.

FIGURE 3

U.S. OCCUPATIONAL INJURY AND ILLNESS RATES:

PRIMARY METALS, 1995

Incidence of nonfatal injuries and illnesses per 100 full-time workers

The 1995 incidence rate for nonfatal occupational illnesses and injuries in the primary metals industries was 16.5 cases per 100 employees. This was the second highest rate in manufacturing.

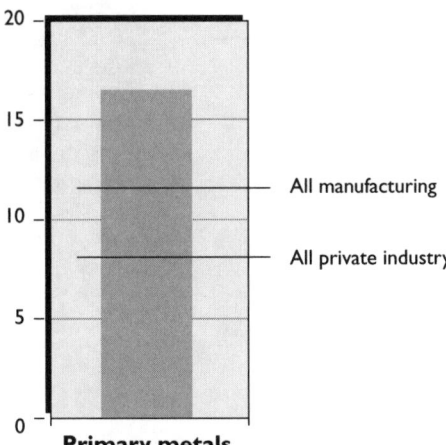

Primary metals

All manufacturing

All private industry

Source: U.S. Bureau of Labor Statistics.

TABLE 5

U.S. EMPLOYMENT PROJECTIONS BY MAJOR OCCUPATIONAL GROUP: PRIMARY METALS

| OCCUPATION | 1994 | | PROJECTIONS, 2005 | | | |
| | NUMBER OF EMPLOYEES | PERCENT OF INDUSTRY TOTAL | NUMBER OF EMPLOYEES | | | PERCENT OF INDUSTRY TOTAL, MODERATE PROJECTIONS |
			LOW	MODERATE	HIGH	
TOTAL PRIMARY METALS						
Total, all occupations	699,100	100.0	507,900	531,600	564,800	100.0
Executive, administrative, and managerial	47,552	6.8	34,596	36,150	38,317	6.8
Professional specialties	23,834	3.4	19,956	20,869	22,072	3.9
Technicians and related support	14,370	2.1	9,680	10,125	10,711	1.9
Marketing and sales	11,328	1.6	8,141	8,476	8,948	1.6
Administrative support including clerical	54,189	7.8	33,780	35,258	37,329	6.6
Service	10,468	1.5	6,312	6,612	7,029	1.2
Agriculture, forestry, and fisheries occupations	62	0.0	42	44	47	0.0
Precision production, craft, and repair	187,235	26.8	131,843	138,192	147,089	26.0
Operators, fabricators, assemblers	350,063	50.1	263,550	275,874	293,257	51.9
IRON AND STEEL						
Total, all occupations	363,700	100.0	238,000	247,300	262,100	100.0
Executive, administrative, and managerial	22,518	6.2	14,208	14,758	15,627	6.0
Professional specialties	11,892	3.3	8,877	9,213	9,736	3.7
Technicians and related support	7,043	1.9	4,172	4,331	4,580	1.8
Marketing and sales	5,458	1.5	3,410	3,541	3,749	1.4
Administrative support including clerical	27,860	7.7	15,126	15,703	16,608	6.3
Service	5,847	1.6	3,122	3,244	3,437	1.3
Agriculture, forestry, and fisheries occupations	......	......	......	......	......	......
Precision production, craft, and repair	106,775	29.4	69,583	72,283	76,558	29.2
Operators, fabricators, assemblers	176,266	48.5	119,476	124,198	131,776	50.2
NONFERROUS METALS						
Total, all occupations	335,400	100.0	269,900	284,300	302,700	100.0
Executive, administrative, and managerial	25,034	7.5	20,388	21,392	22,690	7.5
Professional specialties	11,942	3.6	11,079	11,656	12,336	4.1
Technicians and related support	7,327	2.2	5,508	5,794	6,131	2.0
Marketing and sales	5,870	1.8	4,731	4,935	5,199	1.7
Administrative support including clerical	26,329	7.9	18,654	19,555	20,721	6.9
Service	4,621	1.4	3,190	3,368	3,592	1.2
Agriculture, forestry, and fisheries occupations	62	0.0	42	44	47	0.0
Precision production, craft, and repair	80,460	24.0	62,260	65,909	70,531	23.2
Operators, fabricators, assemblers	173,797	51.8	144,074	151,676	161,481	53.4

Source: Bureau of Labor Statistics, November 1995.

Projections for employment in the primary metals industries foresee a decline by the year 2005, to 531,600 employees (moderate assumptions) from the 699,100 on the payroll in 1994. Numerical declines are likely for all major occupational categories. The largest declines will take place in the iron and steel industries, where, under moderate assumptions, employment will fall some 32 percent by 2005. For nonferrous industries, a reduction of 15 percent is projected.

FIGURE 4

U.S. CORPORATE INCOME AND WORKER EARNINGS: PRIMARY METALS

Corporate operating income and aggregate production worker earnings

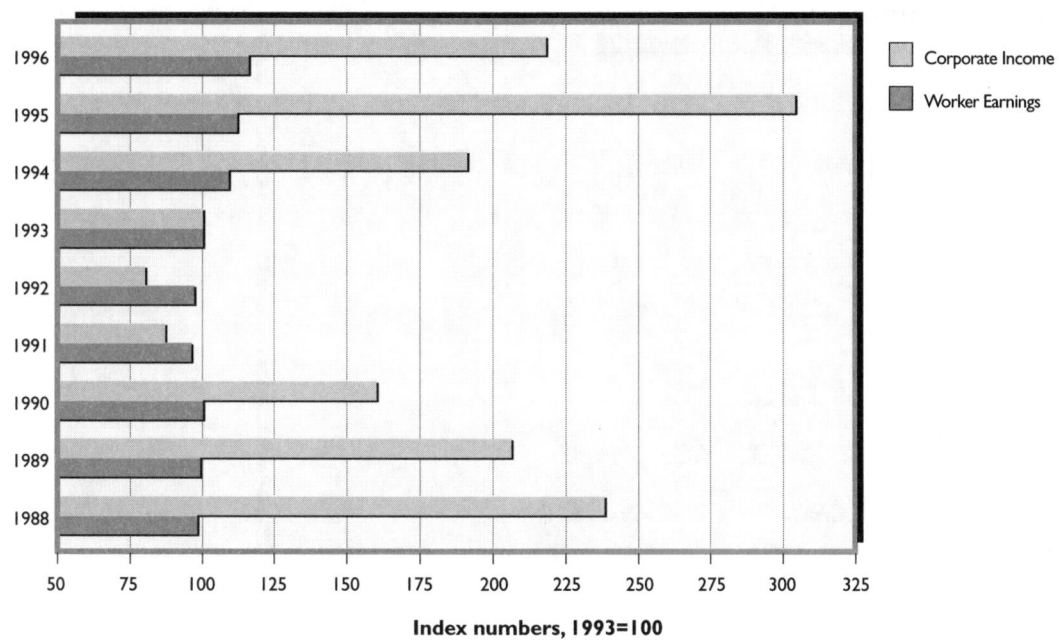

Index numbers, 1993=100

Source: U.S. Bureau of Labor Statistics, U.S. Bureau of the Census, and estimates by the editors.

FIGURE 4A

U.S. CORPORATE INCOME AND WORKER EARNINGS: IRON AND STEEL

Corporate operating income and aggregate production worker earnings

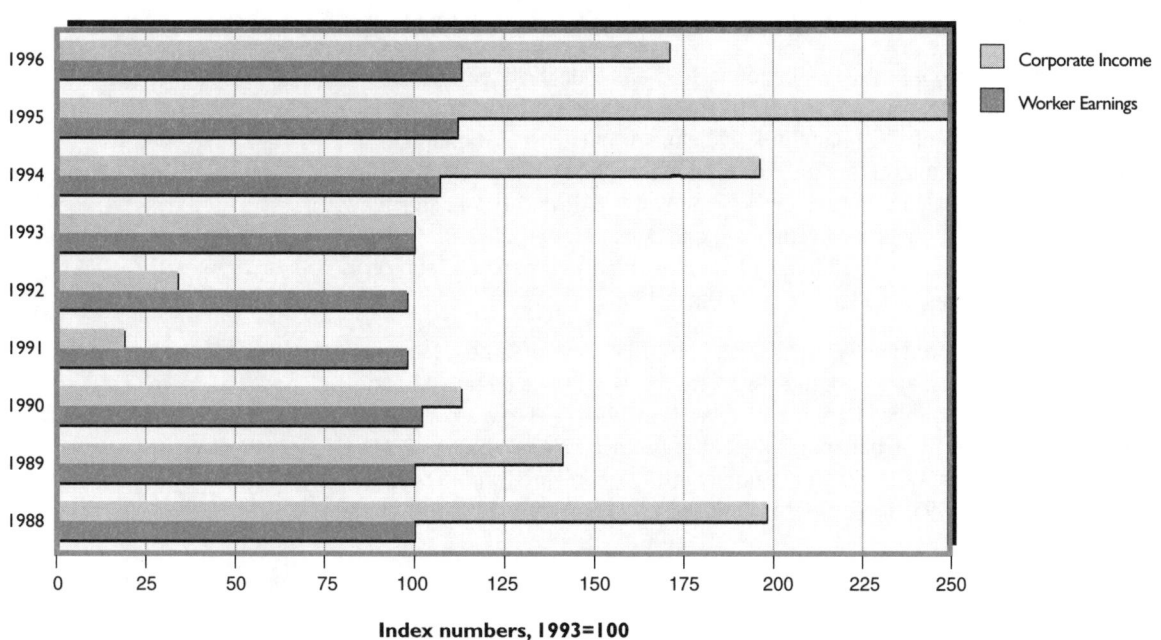

Index numbers, 1993=100

Source: U.S. Bureau of Labor Statistics, U.S. Bureau of the Census, and estimates by the editors.

FIGURE 4B

U.S. CORPORATE INCOME AND WORKER EARNINGS: NONFERROUS METALS

Corporate operating income and aggregate production worker earnings

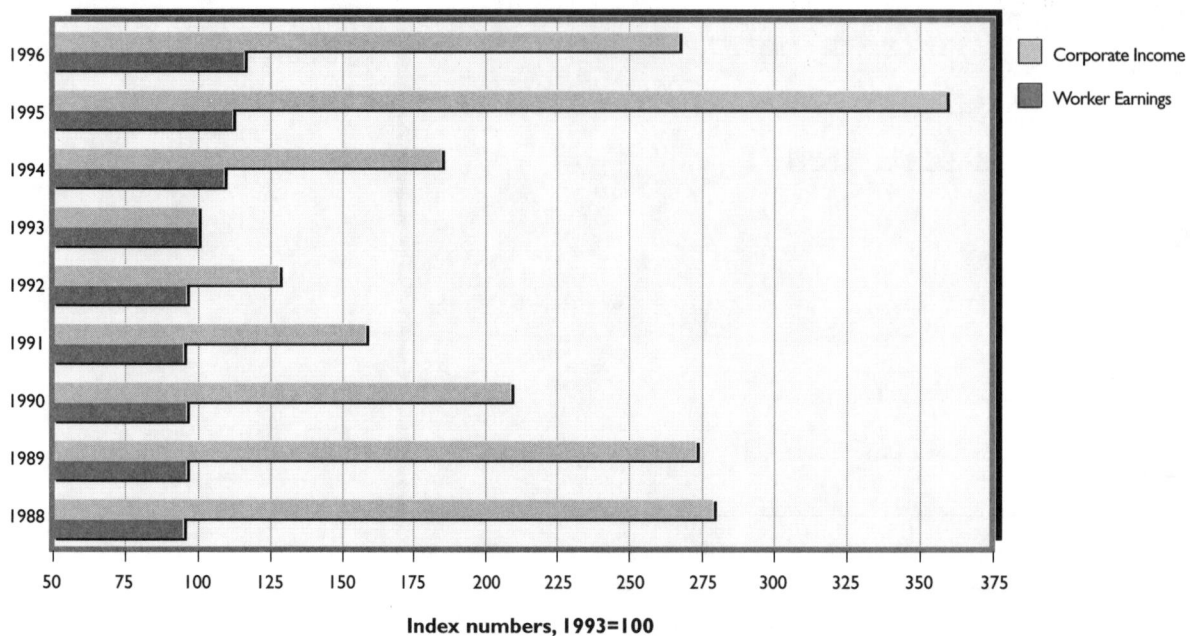

Index numbers, 1993=100

Source: U.S. Bureau of Labor Statistics, U.S. Bureau of the Census, and estimates by the editors.

Finance. While production worker earnings in the **primary metals** industries rose modestly in most years, corporate income during 1988-1996 showed some extreme fluctuations. The best year in terms of operating income was 1995, followed by 1988 and then 1996. The worst years were 1992, 1991, and 1993, respectively (Figure 4 and Table 6).

Income from operations reached a peak $11.9 billion in 1995 and then declined to $8.5 billion in 1996, resulting in a negative annual growth rate of 1.08 percent for 1988-1996. After-tax income reached a high of $8.1 billion in 1995 before dropping to $5.3 billion in 1996. This contrasts with a cumulative loss of $3.63 billion from 1991 through 1993. After-tax income as a percentage of sales and stockholders' equity was 3.61 and 10.74 percent, respectively, in 1996; here again, there were extreme fluctuations between 1988 and 1996. Inventories in 1996 were valued at $19.8 billion, a high for the nine-year period. Debt, on the other hand, reached its lowest level relative to assets in 1996.

The **iron and steel** industry showed similar trends: 1995 and 1988 were their best years in terms of income from operations, and 1991 and 1992 were the worst years (Figure 4A and Table 6A). After-tax income rebounded from negative levels in 1991-1993 to a record $2.69 billion in 1995 before easing to $1.56 billion in 1996. After-tax income amounted to 2.24 percent of sales and 7.16 percent of stockholders' equity in 1996, compared with 3.86 and 13.82 percent, respectively, in 1995. Inventories in 1996 were at a peak ($11.5 billion) for the nine-year period, while the debt ratio was lower than in any year but 1995.

Income from operations in the **nonferrous metals** industry declined steadily from 1988 through 1993 and then rebounded strongly to a record $6.89 billion in 1995 (Figure 4B and Table 6B). After-tax income declined through 1992, with a $1.2 billion loss that year and then surged to a high of $5.5 billion in 1995 before settling back to $3.7 billion in 1996. After-tax income in relation to sales was 6.74 and 4.85 percent, respectively, in 1995 and 1996, and the ratio of income to stockholders' equity was 20.30 and 13.57 percent, respectively, in the two years. Inventories of nonferrous metals hit a high of $8.7 billion in 1995 before declining slightly in 1996. Debt as a percentage of assets reached a 10-year low of 22.1 percent in 1996.

TABLE 6

U.S. CORPORATE INCOME AND ASSETS: PRIMARY METALS

(Monetary values in millions of U.S. dollars)

INCOME AND EXPENSES	1988	1989	1990	1991	1992	1993	1994	1995	1996	CHANGE OR AVERAGE[1]
Sales and receipts	110,032	113,861	120,547	114,834	114,565	116,369	134,506	150,532	146,501	3.64
Depreciation and amortization	(3,721)	(3,906)	(4,255)	(4,650)	(4,781)	(4,869)	(4,993)	(5,197)	(5,329)	4.59
Other operating costs	(96,995)	(101,900)	(110,028)	(106,770)	(106,652)	(107,584)	(122,037)	(133,449)	(132,630)	3.99
Income from operations	9,316	8,056	6,265	3,412	3,132	3,915	7,474	11,889	8,541	-1.08
Nonoperating income (expenditures)	(1,792)	(731)	(1,608)	(3,601)	(6,896)	(5,068)	(825)	(712)	(822)	....
Income before taxes	7,523	7,324	4,656	(187)	(3,763)	(1,153)	6,650	11,175	7,720	0.32
Income after taxes	5,249	5,298	3,183	(452)	(2,382)	(794)	4,826	8,144	5,284	0.08
Cash dividends	936	2,278	1,490	1,334	1,311	1,215	1,462	1,813	1,801	8.52
Income retained in business	4,315	3,020	1,693	(1,786)	(3,693)	(2,008)	3,362	6,334	3,482	-2.65
Direct credits (charges)	(1,445)	(1,129)	(2,286)	(455)	(838)	5,327	(109)	(529)	(470)	....
Ending retained earnings	9,929	12,498	16,037	13,718	8,423	12,674	14,518	19,401	21,199	9.95
ASSETS, END OF YEAR:										
Total	88,182	90,767	101,707	105,558	105,251	108,180	117,085	125,119	130,153	4.99
Accounts receivable	14,002	13,332	14,714	14,629	13,903	14,987	17,603	17,278	17,520	2.84
Inventories	15,377	15,471	17,902	17,292	15,705	16,467	17,814	19,126	19,769	3.19
Net property, plant and equipment	36,979	38,393	42,580	47,452	47,351	46,330	49,318	52,996	56,073	5.34
RATIOS, PERCENT:										
INCOME TO SALES:										
Before tax	6.84	6.43	3.86	-0.16	-3.28	-0.99	4.94	7.42	5.27	3.37
After tax	4.77	4.65	2.64	-0.39	-2.08	-0.68	3.59	5.41	3.61	2.39
INCOME TO STOCKHOLDERS' EQUITY:										
Before tax	27.34	25.18	13.65	-0.57	-13.16	-3.53	17.55	24.12	15.69	11.81
After tax	19.07	18.22	9.33	-1.38	-8.33	-2.43	12.74	17.58	10.74	8.39
INCOME TO TOTAL ASSETS:										
Before tax	8.53	8.07	4.58	-0.18	-3.58	-1.07	5.68	8.93	5.93	4.10
After tax	5.95	5.84	3.13	-0.43	-2.26	-0.73	4.12	6.51	4.06	2.91
AS A PERCENT OF TOTAL ASSETS:										
Property, plant and equipment	41.93	42.30	41.87	44.95	44.99	42.83	42.12	42.36	43.08	42.94
Short-term debt	3.02	2.92	3.11	2.72	3.38	3.25	2.17	1.73	2.35	2.74
Long-term debt	25.90	26.01	25.59	27.04	25.59	24.04	23.04	22.05	20.17	24.38
Stockholders' equity	31.21	32.04	33.53	31.08	27.16	30.18	32.36	37.03	37.81	32.49

1. For income and asset amounts, compound annual growth rate; for ratios, average of ratios for the years shown.

Source: U.S. Bureau of the Census, Quarterly Financial Report.

Notes: Parentheses ( ) indicate negative items, e.g., net expenses, charges, or losses. Net property, plant, and equipment is net of accumulated depreciation. Because the samples used to collect the data change, retained earnings at the end of a given year will not exactly equal the previous year's retained earnings plus the current year's retained income and credits.

TABLE 6A

U.S. CORPORATE INCOME AND ASSETS: IRON AND STEEL

(Monetary values in millions of U.S. dollars)

INCOME AND EXPENSES	1988	1989	1990	1991	1992	1993	1994	1995	1996	CHANGE OR AVERAGE[1]
Sales and receipts	54,498	55,153	56,022	50,879	50,212	54,652	65,087	69,560	69,578	3.10
Depreciation and amortization	(1,853)	(1,868)	(1,937)	(1,924)	(1,997)	(2,176)	(2,449)	(2,606)	(2,665)	4.65
Other operating costs	(48,679)	(50,470)	(51,822)	(48,568)	(47,540)	(50,477)	(58,712)	(61,956)	(63,487)	3.38
Income from operations	3,967	2,815	2,265	386	674	1,999	3,926	4,998	3,425	-1.82
Nonoperating income (expenditures)	(2,124)	(579)	(1,068)	(1,795)	(2,317)	(2,204)	(512)	(1,222)	(1,020)	....
Income before taxes	1,842	2,238	1,197	(1,410)	(1,642)	(205)	3,414	3,777	2,405	3.39
Income after taxes	993	1,512	586	(1,438)	(1,211)	(207)	2,501	2,686	1,556	5.77
Cash dividends	446	1,027	503	335	424	432	701	786	688	5.57
Income retained in business	548	483	83	(1,773)	(1,635)	(638)	1,799	1,900	868	5.92
Direct credits (charges)	(2,366)	(181)	(540)	(6)	(301)	5,764	(78)	(163)	(64)	....
Ending retained earnings	(1,514)	(821)	(861)	(2,024)	(3,929)	2,258	4,047	4,694	5,397	....
ASSETS, END OF YEAR:										
Total	41,439	43,404	45,390	44,766	45,236	49,868	55,666	57,549	63,019	5.38
Accounts receivable	6,322	6,278	6,291	5,999	5,967	7,111	8,339	7,356	8,113	3.17
Inventories	8,267	8,514	9,344	8,857	7,734	8,639	9,798	10,442	11,513	4.23
Net property, plant and equipment	18,043	18,532	20,084	20,951	20,776	22,240	24,970	26,203	29,003	6.11
RATIOS, PERCENT:										
INCOME TO SALES:										
Before tax	3.38	4.06	2.14	-2.77	-3.27	-0.38	5.25	5.43	3.46	1.92
After tax	1.82	2.74	1.05	-2.83	-2.41	-0.38	3.84	3.86	2.24	1.10
INCOME TO STOCKHOLDERS' EQUITY:										
Before tax	27.54	29.31	14.66	-19.75	-27.37	-1.61	20.67	19.43	11.06	8.22
After tax	14.85	19.80	7.18	-20.14	-20.19	-1.63	15.14	13.82	7.16	4.00
INCOME TO TOTAL ASSETS:										
Before tax	4.45	5.16	2.64	-3.15	-3.63	-0.41	6.13	6.56	3.82	2.40
After tax	2.40	3.48	1.29	-3.21	-2.68	-0.42	4.49	4.67	2.47	1.39
AS A PERCENT OF TOTAL ASSETS:										
Property, plant and equipment	43.54	42.70	44.25	46.80	45.93	44.60	44.86	45.53	46.02	44.91
Short-term debt	1.98	2.58	2.33	2.44	2.65	2.06	1.90	1.72	2.01	2.19
Long-term debt	26.88	27.57	27.80	27.33	26.28	21.29	21.09	20.76	20.94	24.44
Stockholders' equity	16.14	17.59	17.99	15.95	13.26	25.48	29.67	33.78	34.50	22.71

1. For income and asset amounts, compound annual growth rate; for ratios, average of ratios for the years shown.

Source: U.S. Bureau of the Census, Quarterly Financial Report.

Notes: Parentheses ( ) indicate negative items, e.g., net expenses, charges, or losses. Net property, plant, and equipment is net of accumulated depreciation. Because the samples used to collect the data change, retained earnings at the end of a given year will not exactly equal the previous year's retained earnings plus the current year's retained income and credits.

TABLE 6B

U.S. CORPORATE INCOME AND ASSETS: NONFERROUS METALS

(Monetary values in millions of U.S. dollars)

INCOME AND EXPENSES	1988	1989	1990	1991	1992	1993	1994	1995	1996	CHANGE OR AVERAGE[1]
Sales and receipts	55,534	58,709	64,525	63,954	64,354	61,717	69,417	80,972	76,923	4.16
Depreciation and amortization	(1,868)	(2,038)	(2,319)	(2,727)	(2,784)	(2,693)	(2,543)	(2,591)	(2,663)	4.53
Other operating costs	(48,317)	(51,431)	(58,206)	(58,200)	(59,113)	(57,106)	(63,325)	(71,493)	(69,142)	4.58
Income from operations	5,349	5,239	3,999	3,027	2,458	1,917	3,550	6,888	5,116	-0.56
Nonoperating income (expenditures)	333	(153)	(540)	(1,806)	(4,579)	(2,865)	(314)	510	199	....
Income before taxes	5,683	5,087	3,460	1,223	(2,122)	(947)	3,235	7,398	5,315	-0.83
Income after taxes	4,256	3,785	2,598	986	(1,171)	(585)	2,323	5,459	3,727	-1.65
Cash dividends	489	1,250	990	998	886	784	762	1,027	1,113	10.83
Income retained in business	3,767	2,537	1,609	(13)	(2,057)	(1,370)	1,562	4,432	2,615	-4.46
Direct credits (charges)	921	(947)	(1,747)	(449)	(537)	(438)	(32)	(364)	(405)	....
Ending retained earnings	11,443	13,318	16,898	15,751	12,352	10,416	10,471	14,707	15,802	4.12
ASSETS, END OF YEAR: Total	46,742	47,363	56,317	60,792	60,015	58,312	61,419	67,570	67,133	4.63
Accounts receivable	7,680	7,054	8,423	8,630	7,936	7,877	9,263	9,922	9,407	2.57
Inventories	7,110	6,958	8,557	8,434	7,971	7,828	8,016	8,684	8,255	1.88
Net property, plant and equipment	18,935	19,860	22,496	26,501	26,575	24,090	24,348	26,792	27,070	4.57
RATIOS, PERCENT: INCOME TO SALES:										
Before tax	10.23	8.66	5.36	1.91	-3.30	-1.53	4.66	9.14	6.91	4.67
After tax	7.66	6.45	4.03	1.54	-1.82	-0.95	3.35	6.74	4.85	3.54
INCOME TO STOCKHOLDERS' EQUITY:										
Before tax	27.28	23.72	13.34	4.76	-9.39	-4.75	15.14	27.52	19.35	13.00
After tax	20.43	17.65	10.02	3.84	-5.18	-2.93	10.87	20.30	13.57	9.84
INCOME TO TOTAL ASSETS:										
Before tax	12.16	10.74	6.14	2.01	-3.54	-1.62	5.27	10.95	7.92	5.56
After tax	9.11	7.99	4.61	1.62	-1.95	-1.00	3.78	8.08	5.55	4.20
AS A PERCENT OF TOTAL ASSETS:										
Property, plant and equipment	40.51	41.93	39.95	43.59	44.28	41.31	39.64	39.65	40.32	41.24
Short-term debt	3.94	3.24	3.74	2.93	3.94	4.26	2.40	1.73	2.67	3.21
Long-term debt	25.02	24.57	23.81	26.84	25.06	26.39	24.82	23.14	19.43	24.34
Stockholders' equity	44.57	45.29	46.06	42.22	37.64	34.21	34.79	39.79	40.91	40.61

1. For income and asset amounts, compound annual growth rate; for ratios, average of ratios for the years shown.

Source: U.S. Bureau of the Census, Quarterly Financial Report.

Notes: Parentheses ( ) indicate negative items, e.g., net expenses, charges, or losses. Net property, plant, and equipment is net of accumulated depreciation. Because the samples used to collect the data change, retained earnings at the end of a given year will not exactly equal the previous year's retained earnings plus the current year's retained income and credits.

CANADA

Canada's primary metal industries in 1993 consisted of 409 establishments with 84,416 employees (Table 7). The primary steel industry accounted for 42 percent of industry shipments that year, followed by nonferrous smelting and refining with 30 percent. Aluminum rolling, casting, and extruding accounted for 9 percent of the total. Hourly earnings in 1993 averaged Can$20.78, with the highest in primary production of aluminum (Can$24.23).

Shipments by the **primary metals industry** totaled Can$23.4 billion in 1994, compared with Can$19.8 billion the year before (Table 8). Industry employment rose in 1988 and then declined steadily to 83,915 in 1994. Employment of production workers also declined, but their share of the workforce rose slightly to 79 percent in 1994. Earnings of production workers averaged Can$20.67 an hour in 1994, compared with Can$17.24 in 1988. The average workweek in 1994 was 43.1 hours.

Iron and steel shipments by Canada in 1994 were valued at Can$12.8 billion, compared with Can$10.9 billion the year before (Table 8). Employment declined steadily from 1988 to 1993 and then rose slightly to 46,398 in 1994. Production workers accounted for about 80 percent of the workforce in 1994, the highest level for the eight-year period, and averaged Can$20.67 an hour in earnings. The average workweek was 43.9 hours.

Nonferrous metals shipments in 1994 were valued at $10.7 billion, the highest level since 1988 and 1989 (Table 8). Employment continued a decline that began in 1990, dropping to 37,517 employees in 1994. Employment of production workers inched up in 1994, and their share of the workforce rose to almost 77 percent from 75 percent in 1993.

TABLE 7

CANADA: COMPONENT INDUSTRIES OF PRIMARY METALS (CSIC 29), 1993[1]

(Monetary values in Canadian dollars)

| INDUSTRY NAME | CSIC | ESTABLISH- MENTS (NUMBER) | EMPLOYMENT | | VALUE OF SHIPMENTS (MILLIONS) | AVERAGE HOURLY EARNINGS[2] |
			NUMBER	PERCENT OF INDUSTRY TOTAL		
PRIMARY METAL INDUSTRIES	29	409	84,416	100.0	CAN$19,810.5	CAN$20.78
Primary steel	291	61	33,327	39.5	8,306.0	21.80
Ferro-alloys	2911	3	320	0.4	109.4	20.27
Steel foundries	2912	28	2,577	3.1	216.0	14.18
Other primary steel	2919	30	30,430	36.0	7,980.5	22.46
Steel pipe and tube	292	51	5,555	6.6	1,563.1	18.17
Iron foundries	294	75	7,174	8.5	1,026.0	19.43
Nonferrous smelting and refining	295	34	26,175	31.0	5,882.4	22.66
Primary production of aluminum	2951	13	12,220	14.5	3,418.3	24.23
Other nonferrous smelting, refining	2959	21	13,955	16.5	2,464.1	21.28
Aluminum rolling, casting, and extruding	296	65	5,128	6.1	1,777.2	17.11
Copper rolling, casting, and extruding	297	36	2,111	2.5	477.1	16.58
Other nonferrous rolling, casting, extruding	299	87	4,946	5.9	778.7	15.99

1. Does not include secondary refining of precious metals, classified under Miscellaneous Manufacturing in Canada.
2. Including overtime.

Source: Statistics Canada, *Manufacturing Industries of Canada* (Cat. No. 31-203).

TABLE 8

CANADIAN EMPLOYMENT AND SHIPMENTS: PRIMARY METAL INDUSTRIES, 1987-1994

(Monetary values in Canadian dollars)

	1987	1988	1989	1990	1991	1992	1993	1994	CHANGE[1]
TOTAL PRIMARY METALS									
All employees	104,088	108,674	106,414	96,667	92,331	87,471	84,416	83,915	-3.03
Establishments	427	501	523	474	438	425	409	406	-0.72
Employees per establishment	244	217	203	204	211	206	206	207	-2.33
Production workers per establishment	.....	168	157	154	160	158	160	162	-0.51
PRODUCTION WORKERS:									
Total	.....	83,926	82,110	73,012	70,138	67,053	65,471	65,973	-3.93
Percent of all employees	.....	77.2	77.2	75.5	76.0	76.7	77.6	78.6	.....
Male	.....	80,733	78,784	70,388	67,704	.....	.....	.....	.....
Female	.....	3,193	3,326	2,624	2,434	.....	.....	.....	.....
Percent of all production workers	.....	3.8	4.1	3.6	3.5	.....	.....	.....	.....
Average hourly earnings	.....	17.24	18.32	19.06	19.98	20.64	20.78	20.67	3.07
Average weekly earnings	.....	699.67	742.84	782.92	817.76	863.86	884.28	890.29	4.10
Average weekly hours	.....	40.6	40.5	41.1	40.9	41.9	42.6	43.1	1.00
Shipments (millions)	19,154	22,715	22,885	19,244	17,851	18,045	19,811	23,442	2.93
IRON AND STEEL									
All employees	59,317	62,362	59,714	52,836	51,424	47,470	46,056	46,398	-3.45
Establishments	187	211	229	214	195	192	187	185	-0.15
Employees per establishment	317	296	261	247	264	247	246	251	-3.30
Production workers per establishment	.....	234	207	190	207	194	196	201	-2.48
PRODUCTION WORKERS:									
Total	.....	49,354	47,360	40,730	40,277	37,290	36,730	37,210	-4.60
Percent of all employees	.....	79.1	79.3	77.1	78.3	78.6	79.8	80.2	.....
Male	.....	47,797	45,760	39,450	39,215	.....	.....	.....	.....
Female	.....	1557	1600	1280	1062	.....	.....	.....	.....
Percent of all production workers	.....	3.2	3.4	3.1	2.6	.....	.....	.....	.....
Average hourly earnings	.....	17.24	18.33	19.20	20.05	20.70	20.96	20.67	3.07
Average weekly earnings	.....	708.74	745.48	786.62	809.62	852.63	880.11	906.79	4.19
Average weekly hours	.....	41.1	40.7	41.0	40.4	41.2	42.0	43.9	1.09
Shipments (millions)	10,281	11,669	12,045	10,101	9,314	9,393	10,895	12,781	3.16
NONFERROUS METALS									
All employees	44,771	46,312	46,700	43,831	40,907	40,001	38,360	37,517	-2.49
Establishments	240	290	294	260	243	233	222	221	-1.17
Employees per establishment	187	160	159	169	168	172	173	170	-1.34
Production workers per establishment	.....	216	219	191	177	173	166	169	-4.00
PRODUCTION WORKERS:									
Total	.....	34,572	34,750	32,282	29,861	29,763	28,741	28,763	-3.02
Percent of all employees	.....	74.7	74.4	73.7	73.0	74.4	74.9	76.7	.....
Male	.....	32,936	33,024	30,938	28,489	.....	.....	.....	.....
Female	.....	1,636	1,726	1,344	1,372	.....	.....	.....	.....
Percent of all production workers	.....	4.7	5.0	4.2	4.6	.....	.....	.....	.....
Average hourly earnings	.....	12.88	13.63	13.91	14.53	15.31	15.40	15.84	3.51
Average weekly earnings	.....	515.91	550.27	573.18	604.98	653.31	666.86	666.37	4.36
Average weekly hours	.....	40.1	40.4	41.2	41.6	42.7	43.3	42.1	0.82
Shipments (millions)	8,873	11,046	10,839	9,142	8,537	8,652	8,915	10,661	2.66

1. Compound annual growth rate.

Source: Adapted from Statistics Canada, *Manufacturing Industries of Canada* (Cat. No. 31-203).

MEXICO

Mexico's basic metals industry had 321 units and 59,045 employees in 1993. The workforce included 43,729 production workers and 15,142 nonproduction employees (Table 9). Yearly income (earnings plus benefits) averaged 38,682 new pesos ($12,383 at the 1993 exchange rate). Annual earnings of production workers averaged 17,285 new pesos ($5,534), while nonproduction employees (including supervisors) averaged a considerably higher 46,470 new pesos ($14,766). Iron and steel accounted for 57 percent of the 1993 employment, and nonferrous metals, for the remainder.

Total employment in the basic metals industry declined at an annual rate of 9.19 percent between 1988 and 1995, to 52,724 (Table 10). Most of the decline was in iron and steel employment, down by 12.19 percent a year to 32,887. The industry's real gross domestic product rose at the rate of 2.73 percent a year during that period, to the equivalent of $3.4 billion.

TABLE 9

MEXICO: COMPONENT INDUSTRIES OF BASIC METALS (CMAP 37), 1993

(Monetary values in 1993 Mexican New Pesos)

			ALL WORKERS									
							PAID WORKERS					
							PRODUCTION WORKERS		NONPRODUCTION EMPLOYEES		BENEFITS	UNPAID
INDUSTRY	CMAP	NUMBER OF UNITS	NUMBER	PERCENT OF INDUSTRY TOTAL	AVERAGE DAYS WORKED	REMUN-ERATION[1]	NUMBER	WAGES AND SALARIES	NUMBER	WAGES AND SALARIES	PER PAID EMPLOYEE	WORKERS, NUMBER
Basic metals	37	321	59,045	100	289	38,682	43,729	17,285	15,142	46,470	13,891	174
Iron and steel	3710	191	33,410	57	291	47,958	24,384	20,235	8,957	57,011	17,844	69
Nonferrous metals	3720	130	25,635	43	287	26,568	19,345	13,567	6,185	31,204	8,728	105

1. Average annual remuneration including benefits.

Source: INEGI, Censos Economicos 1994.

TABLE 10

MEXICAN GROSS DOMESTIC PRODUCT AND EMPLOYMENT: BASIC METALS INDUSTRIES, 1988-1995

	1988	1989	1990	1991	1992	1993	1994	1995	CHANGE[1]
GROSS DOMESTIC PRODUCT:									
Millions of constant 1993 new pesos	8,863.0	9,076.9	9,731.9	9,267.1	9,410.5	9,707.1	10,304.9	10,698.5	2.73
Millions of constant 1993 U.S. dollars[2]	2,837.3	2,905.8	3,115.5	2,966.7	3,012.6	3,107.6	3,298.9	3,424.9	2.73
TOTAL EMPLOYMENT:									
Basic metals	103,516	97,038	88,467	81,812	70,279	59,441	56,143	52,724	-9.19
Iron and steel	81,731	74,732	63,909	55,546	45,265	35,921	34,103	32,887	-12.19
Nonferrous metals	21,785	22,306	24,558	26,266	25,014	23,520	22,040	19,837	-1.33

1. Compound annual growth rate.

2. Converted at 3.1237 new pesos to the U.S. dollar.

Source: Sistema de Cuentas Nacionales de Mexico, INEGI.

International Trade

United States. Global U.S. exports of primary metals in 1996 totaled $21.3 billion, compared with $20.2 billion the previous year and $12.7 billion in 1990. Imports, however, were considerably higher, at $34.6 billion. The resulting 1996 trade deficit was $13.3 billion—about the same as in the two previous years but more than triple the 1993 low of $4.1 billion (Table 11). Canada took 24 percent of U.S. exports and supplied 32 percent of U.S. imports in 1996. Mexico accounted for 13 percent of U.S. exports and 8 percent of U.S. imports that year.

The European Union, Japan, and China are other major export markets for U.S. steel, while Japan, the European Union, and South Korea are important sources of imports. The European Union and Japan are major U.S. markets for aluminum semifabricated products. Russia is a major supplier of aluminum ingot and of unwrought titanium products. The Republic of South Africa, Australia, Sierra Leone, Norway, and Canada supply titanium raw materials; the United States, in turn, is a major exporter of titanium mill products. U.S. slab zinc imports come primarily from Canada and Mexico. The United States exports refined copper to Europe and Asia and wire mill products to Mexico, Canada, Saudi Arabia, the United Kingdom, and the Philippines; imports come primarily from South America.

Canada. U.S. exports of primary metals to Canada rose from $3.8 billion in 1990 to $5.1 billion in 1996, as Canadian exports to the United States climbed from $6.2 billion to $10.9 billion (Table 11). This gave Canada a $5.8 billion trade surplus with the United States in 1996, in contrast to a surplus of only $2.4 billion in 1990. Canada's metal exports to Mexico declined some 72 percent between 1990 and 1996, to $18 million, while Mexican exports to Canada rose more than fourfold to $40 million.

Mexico. U.S. exports of primary metals to Mexico rose 55 percent between 1990 and 1996 to $2.8 billion, while Mexican exports to the United States rose only about 9 percent to $2.7 billion (Table 11). As a result, Mexico had a slight deficit in its 1996 trade with the United States, compared with a surplus of $691 million in 1990.

NAFTA. The U.S. trade deficit with NAFTA has risen sharply since 1990, reaching $5.7 billion in 1996, or almost double the 1990 deficit (Table 11). Canada's trade surplus followed a similar pattern, rising from $2.4 billion in 1990 to $5.7 billion in 1996. Mexico started the 1990-1996 period with a sizable trade surplus and ended with a deficit of $51 million, reflecting increased production by the country's motor vehicle industry and by other users of primary metals.

TABLE 11

INTERNATIONAL TRADE, PRIMARY METALS

(Millions of U.S. dollars)

	1989[1]	1990	1991	1992	1993	1994	1995	1996
GLOBAL TRADE, U.S.								
IMPORTS								
Value	24,477.2	22,132.0	21,074.2	21,325.4	22,772.2	30,106.2	33,519.5	34,582.5
Ratio to new supply[2]	14.8	14.2	14.9	14.5	14.9	16.9	.....	.....
Ratio to apparent consumption[3]	16.0	15.4	16.6	16.0	16.9	18.6	.....	.....
EXPORTS								
Value	11,649.7	12,660.6	14,698.4	14,284.1	18,668.6	16,327.4	20,190.9	21,278.9
Ratio to comparable domestic shipments	8.3	9.5	12.2	11.3	14.3	11.1	.....	.....
TRADE BALANCE	(12,827.5)	(9,471.4)	(6,375.8)	(7,041.3)	(4,103.6)	(13,778.8)	(13,328.6)	(13,303.6)
BILATERAL TRADE: NAFTA[4]								
U.S. exports to Canada	2,191.8	3,832.7	3,629.1	3,706.4	3,832.6	4,240.0	5,049.9	5,131.5
Canadian exports to U.S.	7,678.8	6,213.6	6,571.5	7,165.5	7,918.7	9,122.3	10,595.5	10,897.4
U.S. exports to Mexico	1,221.2	1,809.6	2,349.9	2,836.4	1,891.7	2,196.9	2,198.4	2,796.0
Mexican exports to U.S.	2,653.7	2,501.0	2,326.6	2,690.0	1,264.3	1,613.7	2,455.1	2,722.9
Canadian exports to Mexico	87.3	66.4	44.8	83.7	54.7	54.2	29.0	18.3
Mexican exports to Canada	16.2	9.8	7.6	3.2	11.8	18.3	75.9	40.1
TRADE BALANCES WITHIN NAFTA[5]								
Canada	5,558.1	2,437.5	2,979.6	3,539.6	4,129.0	4,918.2	5,498.7	5,744.1
Mexico	1,361.4	634.8	(60.5)	(226.9)	(670.3)	(619.1)	303.6	(51.3)
United States	(6,919.5)	(3,072.2)	(2,919.1)	(3,312.6)	(3,458.7)	(4,299.0)	(5,802.4)	(5,692.8)

1. 1989 and earlier data on U.S. exports to Canada for manufacturing total and manufacturing industries are not comparable with data for 1990 and later years because of a change in the reporting system. The NAFTA trade balances for the U.S. and Canada also are affected.

2. New supply equals comparable domestic shipments plus imports for consumption.

3. Apparent consumption equals comparable domestic shipments plus imports for consumption less exports.

4. Amounts less than U.S. $100,000 shown as zero.

5. Parentheses indicate an excess of imports over exports. Because of commodity coding and other data differences among the three countries, these trade balances are only rough estimates and should be used with caution.

Source for U.S. Global Trade: U.S. Department of Commerce, International Trade Administration.

Source for U.S. -Canada and U.S.-Mexico Bilateral Trade: U.S. Bureau of the Census.

Source for Canada-Mexico and Mexico-Canada Bilateral Trade: Statistics Canada, Foreign Trade Division, Special tabulation, March 1997, converted to U.S. dollars by the editors.

PRINTING AND PUBLISHING

THE UNITED STATES

Products and Processes. Printing and publishing, which together ranked as the seventh largest manufacturing sector in 1995, measured by shipments, are both interdependent and distinctive industries. Publishing is the broadest in scope since it encompasses writing, editing, and design, as well as advertising and sale of the final printed products. Printing can be one stage of the publishing process—as in magazine and book publishing—or it can involve an entirely separate activity such as printing of lottery tickets, coupons, labels, and wrappers. The performance of both, however, depends on overall economic growth; consumer demand for books, magazines, and newspapers; advertising requirements; and their own ability to adapt to changes in technology and customer needs.

Printing, publishing, and allied industries in 1992 (the latest year for which economic census data are available), consisted of 65,392 establishments and 1,492,100 employees, or an average of fewer than 23 employees per establishment (Table 1). This preponderance of small firms, particularly in printing, is changing, however, as mergers and acquisitions increase. Shipments by the industry in 1992 were valued at $166.2 billion. Leading industry

TABLE 1

UNITED STATES: COMPONENT INDUSTRIES OF PRINTING, PUBLISHING, AND ALLIED INDUSTRIES (SIC 27), 1992

(Monetary values in millions of U.S. dollars)

INDUSTRY	SIC	ESTABLISH-MENTS	SHIPMENTS		VALUE ADDED BY MANUFACTURE	NEW CAPITAL EXPENDI-TURES	EMPLOY-MENT[1]	PAYROLL
			VALUE	PERCENT BY 4 LARGEST COMPANIES				
PRINTING, PUBLISHING AND ALLIED INDUSTRIES	27	65,392	$166,153.1	....	$112,445.6	$5,372.0	1,492,100	$41,136.1
Newspapers: publishing, or publishing and printing	271	8,668	33,781.5	25	26,919.5	1,664.5	413,900	10,436.5
Periodicals: publishing, or publishing and printing	272	4,700	22,104.4	20	15,879.6	234.5	115,100	4,077.1
Books	273	3,265	21,378.2	....	14,325.3	522.3	129,500	4,037.0
Books: publishing, or publishing and printing	2731	2,640	16,697.5	23	11,493.8	326.8	79,000	2,675.9
Book printing	2732	625	4,680.7	32	2,831.5	195.4	50,500	1,361.1
Miscellaneous publishing	274	3,385	10,907.6	32	8,472.8	189.0	65,100	1,720.4
Commercial printing	275	38,441	56,228.6	....	31,897.8	2,143.6	567,200	15,337.1
Commercial printing, lithographic	2752	29,330	43,352.1	7	24,703.8	1,628.5	438,200	12,016.4
Commercial printing, gravure	2754	434	3,611.4	70	1,710.4	171.3	21,600	733.2
Commercial printing, n.e.c.	2759	8,677	9,265.1	6	5,483.6	343.7	107,400	2,587.5
Manifold business forms	276	921	7,428.6	30	3,922.3	160.8	47,900	1,341.2
Greeting cards	277	172	4,189.8	....	3,388.9	85.7	22,800	584.4
Blankbooks and bookbinding	278	1,649	5,049.0	....	3,640.3	142.0	65,600	1,460.6
Blankbooks, looseleaf binders and devices	2782	551	3,758.0	55	2,639.0	100.9	38,700	923.9
Bookbinding and related work	2789	1,098	1,291.0	12	1,001.3	41.1	26,900	536.7
Service industries for the printing trade	279	4,191	5,085.5	....	3,999.0	229.7	65,000	2,141.8
Typesetting	2791	2,513	1,609.1	16	1,320.6	60.8	26,100	686.4
Platemaking and related services	2796	1,678	3,476.3	10	2,678.3	168.8	38,900	1,455.4

1. Employment numbers from the economic censuses differ in definition and classification from the Bureau of Labor Statistics estimates in Table 2. Year-to-year comparisons between Table 1 and Table 2 are not appropriate.

Source: U.S. Bureau of the Census, 1992 Census of Manufactures.

areas were commercial printing (33.8 percent of the total), newspaper publishing and printing (20.3 percent), periodicals printing and publishing (13.3 percent), and book publishing (12.9 percent).

Projections to the year 2005 show employment in printing and publishing rising from the 1993 level of 1,516,700 (Table 2). Most of the growth will be in commercial printing, periodicals, and books, while newspaper publishing and printing will experience a decline. Hourly earnings of production workers in 1993 averaged $11.93; the highest earnings were in the printing trade services ($14.64) and periodicals publishing ($13.23).

TABLE 2

U.S. EMPLOYMENT AND EARNINGS: PRINTING AND PUBLISHING

INDUSTRY	SIC	1993			2005
		EMPLOYMENT[1]		AVERAGE HOURLY EARNINGS (U.S. DOLLARS)[2]	PROJECTED EMPLOYMENT[3]
		NUMBER OF PERSONS	PERCENT OF INDUSTRY TOTAL		
PRINTING AND PUBLISHING	27	1,516,700	100.0	$11.93	1,627,300
Newspapers	271	450,500	29.7	11.83	412,500
Periodicals	272	129,100	8.5	13.23	163,200
Books	273	118,400	7.8	10.99	130,000
Book publishing	2731	82,000	5.4	10.64	....
Book printing	2732	36,400	2.4	11.37	....
Miscellaneous publishing	274	81,400	5.4	11.24	85,000
Commercial printing and business forms	275,6	583,900	38.5	....	675,000
Commercial printing	275	537,100	35.4	12.11	....
Commercial printing, lithographic	2752	350,400	23.1	12.20	....
Commercial printing, n.e.c.	2759	166,700	11.0	11.74	....
Business forms	276	46,800	3.1	12.58	....
Greeting cards	277	....	....	....	32,000
Blankbooks and bookbinding	278	69,100	4.6	9.33	77,100
Printing trade services	279	56,900	3.8	14.64	53,000

1. Total payroll employment. Employment data from the economic censuses, shown in Table 1, differ in definition and classification from the Bureau of Labor Statistics estimates in this table. Year-to-year comparisons between Table 1 and Table 2 are not appropriate.

2. Earnings of production workers, including overtime.

3. Number of persons, moderate projection by the U.S. Bureau of Labor Statistics.

Source: Bureau of Labor Statistics.

FIGURE 1

U.S. EMPLOYMENT IN PRINTING AND PUBLISHING

Percent distribution by region, 1995

The Mid-Atlantic states accounted for nearly 21 percent of all printing and publishing in the United States in 1995, followed closely by the Great Lakes region with 20 percent and the Southeast with 19 percent.

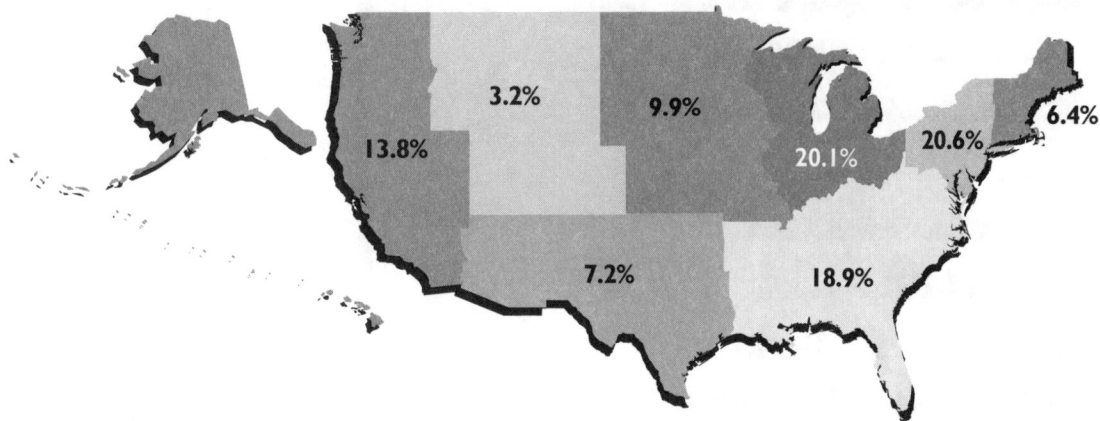

Source: U.S. Department of Commerce, Bureau of Economic Analysis.

What's New. Printing Industries of America, Inc. reports year-end 1996 sales 9.3 percent above year earlier levels among printers who participated in its quarterly print market survey—the fastest rate since 1992. Survey participants predicted that 1997 would be their best year ever, with sales gaining 10.5 percent during the year. Fast-growing areas include electronic prepress service (up 14.6 percent in 1996), marketing and promotional printing, and direct mail printing. Among the laggards are traditional prepress services and printing of business forms and annual reports. Finding skilled employees in this booming environment has become more of a problem lately, with sales and skilled technical positions the hardest to fill. Declines in paper costs, on the other hand, helped to hold down industry costs in 1996.

Industry mergers and acquisitions also are rising, although the average printing plant in 1995 still employed only about 25 employees. Firms with 100 or more employees already dominate printing of magazines/periodicals, books, financial and legal documents, business forms, and labels and wrappers; but they have only about 40 percent of the large general commercial market.

Publishing is continuing its growth pattern, helped by ongoing economic expansion. The cyclical newspaper business has been helped recently by lower newsprint costs and rising advertising revenues. However, circulation is on the decline, and some papers are trying to boost readership by adding color and new sections (The New York Times) or lowering prices (the L.A. Times). Periodical and book publishing is on the rise. Niche magazines directed to specific age, ethnic, and special-interest groups are doing well and are attractive to advertisers because potential customers can be more easily identified. For books, large-store retailing is driving sales, but threatening the survival of small bookstores, and increased demand from libraries has boosted textbook sales.

Printing and publishing have been dramatically affected by the ongoing changeover in technology from analog to digital, and by the many new products and services being introduced. Products and services on the rise include electronic publishing of newspapers and magazines, customized bookbinding, special packaging, technology printing, creating of web pages for customers, on-demand printing, customized magazines/catalogs (a magazine or catalog with half advertising and half editorial content), and customized direct-mail advertising.

FIGURE 2

U.S. EMPLOYMENT AND SHIPMENTS, PRINTING AND PUBLISHING

Total payroll employment and manufacturers' inflation-adjusted shipments

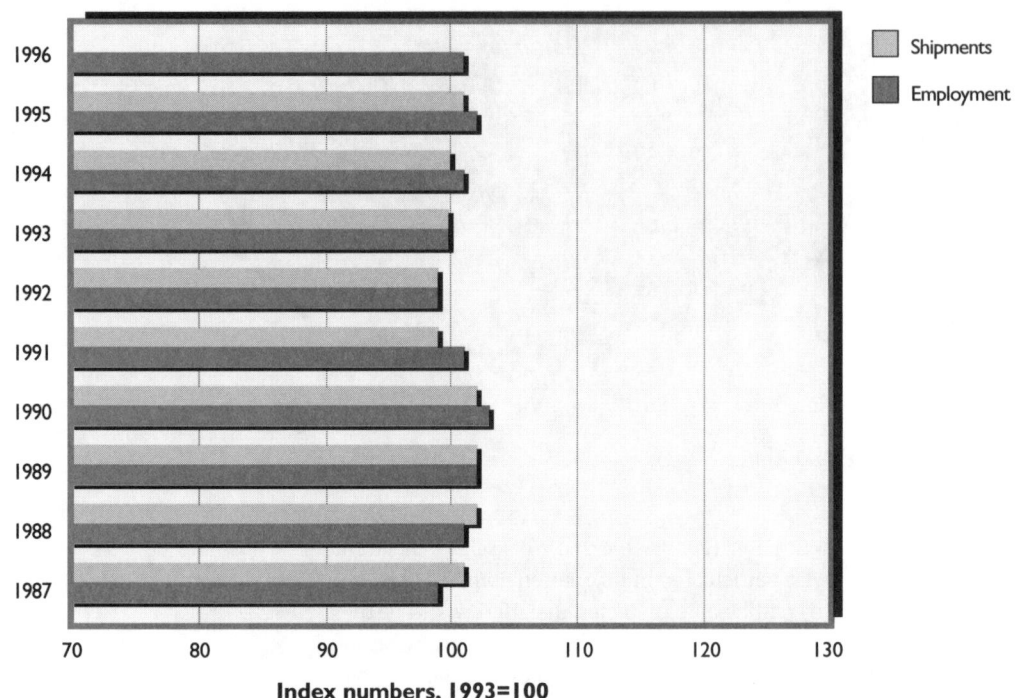

Index numbers, 1993=100

Source: U.S. Bureau of Labor Statistics, U.S. Department of Commerce, and estimates by the editors. Shipments data for 1996 are not available.

Output. Constant-dollar value of shipments by the printing and publishing industry in 1995 ended up unchanged from the 1987 level (Figure 2), while employment in 1995 was above the 1987 level but below the 1990 peak. Industry shipments in 1995 were valued at $188.4 billion (current dollars), compared with $176.9 billion the year before and $136.2 billion in 1987. Growth during 1987-1995 was at a 4.1 percent annual rate in current dollars, but in inflation-adjusted dollars, 1995 shipments were slightly below those in 1987.

Investment. New capital expenditures by the industry totaled $5.62 billion in 1995 (Table 3). This was slightly below the previous year but above 1993. Capacity utilization in 1996, at 80.8 percent, was lower than in all of the past nine years except for the recession year of 1991. This lower use of capacity than in the past suggests that growth in capital spending has outpaced requirements and may slow over the near term.

Prices. Producer prices for the industry have risen by an average of 4.41 percent per year during the past 10 years, one of the most rapid rates in manufacturing (Table 3).

TABLE 3

U.S. OUTPUT, INVESTMENT, AND PRICES: PRINTING AND PUBLISHING

(Millions of U.S. dollars, except as noted)

	1987	1988	1989	1990	1991	1992	1993	1994	1995	1996	GROWTH RATE 1987-1995[1]
VALUE OF SHIPMENTS:											
BY INDUSTRY:											
Current dollars	136,196	144,803	151,854	159,749	160,271	166,153	172,634	176,876	188,439	....	4.14
Constant 1992 dollars	169,736	171,425	170,245	171,458	165,225	166,153	167,488	167,296	168,855	....	-0.07
BY PRODUCT:											
Current dollars	131,197	138,534	144,637	151,699	151,176	158,729	165,793	169,893	180,195	....	4.05
Constant 1992 dollars	163,363	163,868	162,006	162,717	155,804	158,729	160,885	160,812	161,679	....	-0.13
OTHER OUTPUT MEASURES:											
Industrial production, 1993=100	101.7	102.6	102.7	102.3	98.3	99.2	100.0	99.7	99.0	97.6	-0.46
Gross domestic product:											
Current dollars	62,438	66,822	72,243	73,875	75,870	79,743	81,684	85,711	....	....	....
Percent of total GDP	1.3	1.3	1.3	1.3	1.3	1.3	1.2	1.2	....	....	....
Rank in manufacturing	6	6	6	6	6	6	6	6	....	....	....
Chained (1992) dollars	84,136	86,846	87,893	84,498	80,822	79,743	77,329	78,183	....	....	....
INVESTMENT-RELATED MEASURES:											
Capacity utilization, percent	91.0	89.5	87.7	85.2	80.8	81.1	81.9	82.1	81.6	80.8	....
New capital expenditures	4,908	5,109	5,962	6,116	5,447	5,372	4,874	5,637	5,617	....	....
Producer prices, 1993=100[2]	77.1	81.1	85.7	89.7	93.7	96.7	100.0	102.8	109.2	113.7	4.41

1. Compound annual growth rate.

2. Prices received by domestic producers.

Sources: Shipments and new capital expenditures: U.S. Department of Commerce for 1987-1995, editor's estimates for constant dollar data for 1987-88 and all shipments data for 1996; Industrial production and capacity utilization: Federal Reserve Board of Governors; GDP: Bureau of Economic Analysis; Research and development spending: National Science Foundation; Producer prices: Bureau of Labor Statistics.

Workforce and Employment. Employment in the printing and publishing industry grew slowly during 1987-1996 (at an annual rate of 0.26 a year) and actually dipped slightly in 1996 (Table 4). The number of production workers showed a slight declining trend during this period, totaling 839,000, or 54.6 percent of the total workforce, in 1996. Employment of women rose by 0.81 percent a year, and women accounted for 45.1 percent of the workforce in 1996, a bit higher than in earlier years.

Average hourly earnings of production workers were $12.65 in 1996, and the annual growth rate since 1987 was 2.33 percent. However, when adjusted for inflation, earnings fell during the period at a rate of 1.18 percent per year, to $11.35.

TABLE 4

U.S. EMPLOYMENT, HOURS, AND EARNINGS: PRINTING AND PUBLISHING

(Monetary values in U.S. dollars)

	1987	1988	1989	1990	1991	1992	1993	1994	1995	1996	CHANGE[1]
NUMBER OF EMPLOYEES, IN THOUSANDS:											
Total	1,503	1,543	1,556	1,569	1,536	1,507	1,517	1,537	1,546	1,538	0.26
Production workers	839	864	863	871	847	833	839	846	848	839	-0.01
Percent of total	55.8	56.0	55.5	55.5	55.1	55.3	55.3	55.0	54.9	54.6	.....
Women	644	670	683	691	678	664	673	686	694	693	0.81
Percent of total	42.9	43.4	43.9	44.0	44.1	44.1	44.4	44.6	44.9	45.1	.....
HOURS AND EARNINGS OF PRODUCTION WORKERS:											
Average hourly earnings, U.S. dollars[2]											
Current dollars	10.28	10.53	10.88	11.24	11.48	11.74	11.93	12.14	12.33	12.65	2.33
1992 dollars[3]	12.63	12.43	12.27	12.05	11.81	11.74	11.61	11.52	11.37	11.35	-1.18
Average weekly hours	38.0	38.0	37.9	37.9	37.7	38.1	38.3	38.6	38.2	38.2	0.06
Average weekly earnings, current U.S. dollars	390.64	400.14	412.35	426.00	432.80	447.29	456.92	468.60	471.01	483.23	2.39

1. Compound annual growth rate, 1987-1996.

2. Including overtime.

3. Converted to 1992 dollars using Consumer Price Index for Urban Wage Earners and Clerical Workers.

Source: Bureau of Labor Statistics.

FIGURE 3

U.S. OCCUPATIONAL INJURY AND ILLNESS RATES:
PRINTING AND PUBLISHING, 1995

Incidence of nonfatal injuries and illnesses per 100 full-time workers

Nonfatal occupational illnesses and injuries in the printing and publishing industry averaged only 6.4 cases per 100 workers in 1995, in contrast to 11.6 cases for all manufacturing.

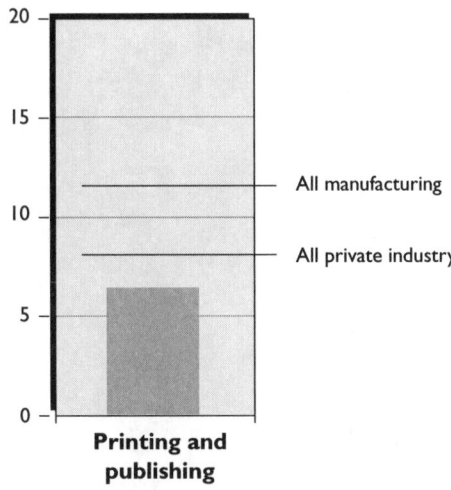

All manufacturing

All private industry

Printing and publishing

Source: U.S. Bureau of Labor Statistics.

TABLE 5

U.S. EMPLOYMENT PROJECTIONS BY MAJOR OCCUPATIONAL GROUP:
PRINTING AND PUBLISHING

Employment in the printing and publishing industries is expected to gain about 5.6 percent by the year 2005 from the 1,541,700 employees of 1994 (moderate projections). Executive, administrative, and managerial staff will account for a slightly larger share (10.8 percent) than in 1994. Gains also are seen for marketing and sales (to 10.6 percent of the workforce), professional specialties (12.2 percent), and skilled workers (14.0 percent).

	1994		PROJECTIONS, 2005			
	NUMBER OF EMPLOYEES	PERCENT OF INDUSTRY TOTAL	NUMBER OF EMPLOYEES			PERCENT OF INDUSTRY TOTAL, MODERATE PROJECTIONS
OCCUPATION			LOW	MODERATE	HIGH	
Total, all occupations	1,541,700	100.0	1,575,600	1,627,300	1,675,500	100.0
Executive, administrative, and managerial	152,079	9.9	169,278	174,911	180,102	10.8
Professional specialties	174,360	11.3	191,351	197,863	203,349	12.2
Technicians and related support	11,150	0.7	10,561	10,902	11,202	0.7
Marketing and sales	154,025	10.0	167,373	172,819	177,763	10.6
Administrative support including clerical	330,203	21.4	312,079	322,352	331,726	19.8
Service	16,971	1.1	15,678	16,187	16,654	1.0
Agriculture, forestry, and fisheries occupations	663	0.0	675	697	717	0.0
Precision production, craft, and repair	212,268	13.8	221,415	228,528	235,472	14.0
Operators, fabricators, assemblers	489,981	31.8	487,190	503,039	518,515	30.9

Source: Bureau of Labor Statistics, November 1995.

FIGURE 4

U.S. CORPORATE INCOME AND WORKER EARNINGS: PRINTING AND PUBLISHING

Corporate operating income and aggregate production worker earnings

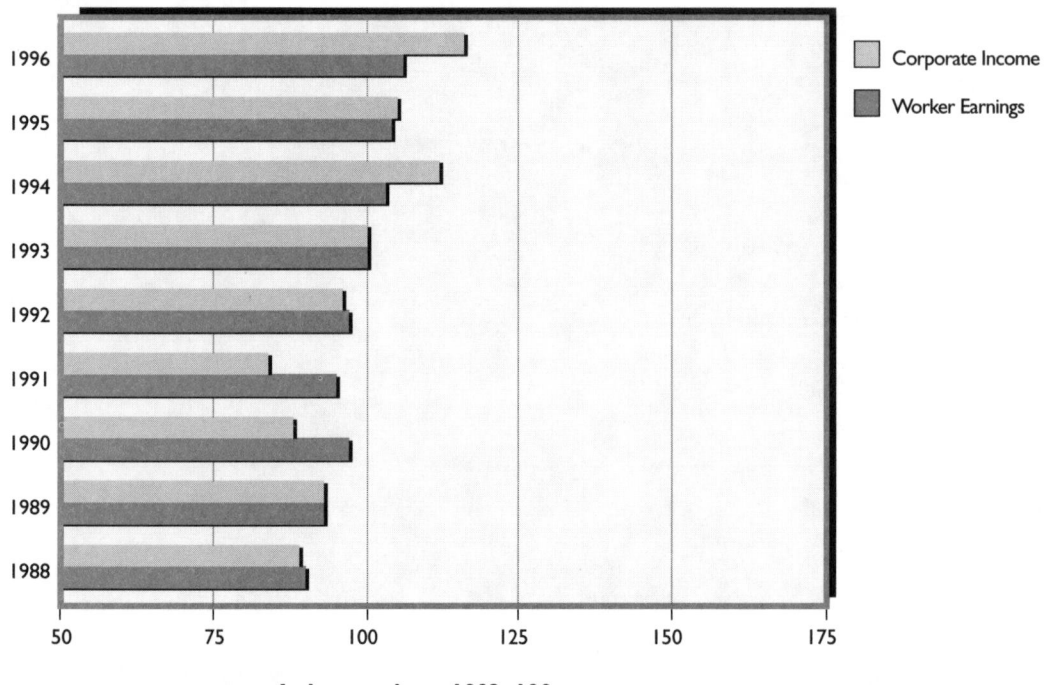

Index numbers, 1993=100

Source: U.S. Bureau of Labor Statistics, U.S. Bureau of the Census, and estimates by the editors.

Finance. Production workers' earnings have risen slowly but steadily since 1988 (Figure 3). Corporate income, on the other hand, declined, although less steeply than for manufacturing overall, when the United States slipped into the 1990-91 recession and then rebounded in line with subsequent economic growth. Sales and receipts of the industry rose at an annual rate of 4.3 percent a year for the 1988-96 period, to $175.9 billion (Table 6). Income from operations rose by 3.4 percent a year to a high of $16 billion in 1996. After-tax income grew by 4.9 percent annually, to $11 billion—almost triple the $4 billion earned in 1991; it amounted to 6.25 percent of sales and 13.64 percent of stockholders' equity in 1996, not significantly changed from 1995 but markedly above the 1991 lows. Long-term debt was up slightly from the previous year to $27.7 billion, while short-term debt eased to $2.07 billion.

TABLE 6

U.S. CORPORATE INCOME AND ASSETS: PRINTING AND PUBLISHING

(Monetary values in millions of U.S. dollars)

INCOME AND EXPENSES	1988	1989	1990	1991	1992	1993	1994	1995	1996	CHANGE OR AVERAGE[1]
Sales and receipts	125,700	136,449	143,484	145,745	150,499	154,675	155,452	164,619	175,890	4.29
Depreciation and amortization	(4,641)	(5,187)	(5,585)	(5,848)	(6,073)	(6,398)	(6,246)	(6,941)	(7,618)	6.39
Other operating costs	(108,809)	(118,447)	(125,724)	(128,395)	(131,259)	(134,619)	(133,974)	(143,379)	(152,272)	4.29
Income from operations	12,249	12,813	12,174	11,503	13,166	13,658	15,231	14,297	15,996	3.39
Nonoperating income (expenditures)	(384)	(185)	(3,589)	(4,711)	(5,009)	(4,177)	(2,250)	(692)	154	....
Income before taxes	11,865	12,628	8,587	6,792	8,156	9,481	12,980	13,604	16,151	3.93
Income after taxes	7,490	7,860	5,180	3,993	4,855	5,548	8,395	10,043	10,997	4.92
Cash dividends	2,175	2,569	3,093	2,767	2,752	3,153	3,387	3,677	3,982	7.85
Income retained in business	5,316	5,291	2,087	1,223	2,103	2,395	5,007	6,365	7,016	3.53
Direct credits (charges)	(738)	(1,380)	(1,609)	(105)	(614)	(1,905)	158	1,005	(711)	....
Ending retained earnings	38,263	40,881	43,583	44,842	44,052	44,833	44,330	51,428	56,999	5.11
ASSETS, END OF YEAR:										
Total	115,454	144,467	155,635	159,752	164,060	159,407	159,582	183,795	205,168	7.45
Accounts receivable	19,749	21,982	22,756	23,123	24,105	23,749	24,438	26,970	27,398	4.18
Inventories	8,768	8,742	10,281	9,707	9,595	9,482	9,388	10,723	10,149	1.85
Net property, plant and equipment	32,046	34,346	36,567	37,837	39,215	38,366	37,329	38,676	40,626	3.01
RATIOS, PERCENT:										
INCOME TO SALES:										
Before tax	9.44	9.25	5.98	4.66	5.42	6.13	8.35	8.26	9.18	7.41
After tax	5.96	5.76	3.61	2.74	3.23	3.59	5.40	6.10	6.25	4.74
INCOME TO STOCKHOLDERS' EQUITY:										
Before tax	25.07	22.66	13.59	10.05	12.08	15.35	21.20	18.78	20.03	17.65
After tax	15.82	14.10	8.20	5.91	7.19	8.98	13.71	13.87	13.64	11.27
INCOME TO TOTAL ASSETS:										
Before tax	10.28	8.74	5.52	4.25	4.97	5.95	8.13	7.40	7.87	7.01
After tax	6.49	5.44	3.33	2.50	2.96	3.48	5.26	5.46	5.36	4.48
AS A PERCENT OF TOTAL ASSETS:										
Property, plant and equipment	27.76	23.77	23.50	23.68	23.90	24.07	23.39	21.04	19.80	23.44
Short-term debt	2.65	1.83	2.18	2.26	2.00	2.33	2.59	2.74	2.07	2.29
Long-term debt	28.65	33.00	31.43	29.20	29.18	29.67	26.12	25.48	27.66	28.93
Stockholders' equity	41.00	38.58	40.59	42.29	41.16	38.74	38.36	39.41	39.30	39.94

1. For income and asset amounts, compound annual growth rate; for ratios, average of ratios for the years shown.

Source: U.S. Bureau of the Census, Quarterly Financial Report.

Notes: Parentheses ( ) indicate negative items, e.g., net expenses, charges, or losses. Net property, plant, and equipment is net of accumulated depreciation. Because the samples used to collect the data change, retained earnings at the end of a given year will not exactly equal the previous year's retained earnings plus the current year's retained income and credits.

CANADA

Canada's printing, publishing, and allied industries had 4,655 establishments and 124,867 employees in 1993 (Table 7). Hourly earnings in the industry were Can$16.29, with the highest average earnings (Can$20.00) in publishing of newspapers, magazines, and periodicals. Commercial printing industries accounted for 47.8 percent of industry shipments in 1993, followed by combined publishing and printing (i.e., newspapers, magazines, and periodicals) with 22.2 percent. The other two subindustries were publishing (21.4 percent) and platemaking, typesetting, and bindery (8.6 percent).

Shipments by Canada's printing and publishing industry totaled Can$13.5 billion in 1994, up from Can$12.8 billion the previous year and Can$11.2 billion in 1987 (Table 8). Yet employment in 1994, at 122,594 people, was below both the 1990 peak of 141,970 and the 1987 level of 127,543. The number of establishments showed a similar declining trend, to 4,472 in 1994 from 5,276 in 1987. Production worker numbers fell even faster than total employment, and production workers accounted for 56 percent of the workforce in 1994, compared with 62 percent in 1988. Average hourly earnings of production workers in 1994 were Can$16.40, and the average workweek was 39 hours.

TABLE 7

CANADA: COMPONENT INDUSTRIES OF PRINTING AND PUBLISHING (CSIC 28), 1993

(Monetary values in Canadian dollars)

INDUSTRY NAME	CSIC	ESTABLISH-MENTS (NUMBER)	EMPLOYMENT NUMBER	EMPLOYMENT PERCENT OF INDUSTRY TOTAL	VALUE OF SHIPMENTS (MILLIONS)	AVERAGE HOURLY EARNINGS[1]
PRINTING, PUBLISHING, AND ALLIED INDUSTRIES	28	4,655	124,867	100.0	CAN$12,840.0	CAN$16.29
Commercial printing	281	2,566	58,938	47.2	6,130.6	15.51
Business forms printing	2811	175	8,299	6.6	888.4	15.73
Other commercial printing	2819	2,391	50,639	40.6	5,242.2	15.48
Platemaking, typesetting, and bindery	282	777	14,847	11.9	1,100.3	14.85
Publishing	283	882	20,412	16.3	2,752.4	....
Book publishing and printing	2831	186	6,308	5.1	1,054.0	....
Other publishing industries	2839	696	14,104	11.3	1,698.3	....
Combined publishing and printing	284	430	30,670	24.6	2,856.8	19.59
Newpapers, magazines, and periodicals	2841	380	29,175	23.4	2,713.5	20.00
Other combined publishing and printing	2849	50	1,495	1.2	143.3	13.94

1. Including overtime.

Source: Adapted from Statistics Canada, *Manufacturing Industries of Canada* (Cat. No. 31-203).

TABLE 8

CANADIAN EMPLOYMENT AND SHIPMENTS: PRINTING AND PUBLISHING, 1987-1994

(Monetary values in Canadian dollars)

	1987	1988	1989	1990	1991	1992	1993	1994	CHANGE[1]
All employees	127,543	133,763	140,698	141,970	133,532	128,721	124,867	122,594	-0.56
Establishments	5,276	5,618	5,207	5,522	5,067	4,894	4,655	4,472	-2.33
Employees per establishment	24	24	27	26	26	26	27	27	1.81
Production workers per establishment	.....	15	17	15	16	15	15	15	0.69
PRODUCTION WORKERS:									
Total	.....	83,347	87,002	85,319	78,931	74,397	71,165	69,138	-3.07
Percent of all employees	.....	62.3	61.8	60.1	59.1	57.8	57.0	56.4	.....
Male	.....	55,893	58,220	56,677	52,523	74,397	71,165	69,138	.....
Female	.....	27,454	28,782	28,642	26,408	.....	.....	.....	.....
Percent of all production workers	.....	32.9	33.1	33.6	33.5	.....	.....	.....	.....
Average hourly earnings	.....	14.19	15.03	15.49	15.67	15.93	16.29	16.40	2.44
Average weekly earnings	.....	541.62	573.72	593.73	614.13	622.28	634.56	638.63	2.78
Average weekly hours	.....	38.2	38.2	38.3	39.2	39.1	39.0	39.0	0.33
Shipments (millions)	11,180	12,526	13,531	13,704	13,046	12,875	12,840	13,496	2.73

1. Compound annual growth rate.

Source: Adapted from Statistics Canada, *Manufacturing Industries of Canada* (Cat. No. 31-203).

MEXICO

Printing is included in Mexico's printing and paper industry. The printing component of the industry (broken out here) had 13,558 production units and 133,584 employees in 1993 (Table 9). Employee earnings and benefits averaged 24,159 new pesos ($7,734) in 1993 for 277 days worked (Table 9). There were 66,304 production workers in 1993 earning 14,274 new pesos ($4,550) and 51,214 nonproduction employees earning 25,826 new pesos ($8,268). Total employment in printing rose at the annual rate of 0.57 percent between 1988 and 1995, to 117,643 (Table 10).

TABLE 9

MEXICO: PRINTING INDUSTRY (CMAP 3420), 1993

(Monetary values in 1993 Mexican New Pesos)

			ALL WORKERS									
							PAID WORKERS					
							PRODUCTION WORKERS		NONPRODUCTION EMPLOYEES		BENEFITS	UNPAID
INDUSTRY	CMAP	NUMBER OF UNITS	NUMBER	PERCENT OF INDUSTRY TOTAL	AVERAGE DAYS WORKED	REMUN-ERATION[1]	NUMBER	WAGES AND SALARIES	NUMBER	WAGES AND SALARIES	PER PAID EMPLOYEE	WORKERS, NUMBER
Printing	3420	13,558	133,584	100	277	24,159	66,304	14,274	51,214	25,826	4,850	16,066

1. Average annual remuneration including benefits.

Source: INEGI, Censos Economicos 1994.

TABLE 10

MEXICAN EMPLOYMENT: PRINTING, 1988-1995

	1988	1989	1990	1991	1992	1993	1994	1995	CHANGE[1]
TOTAL EMPLOYMENT:									
Printing	113,034	117,430	125,308	130,518	134,379	133,628	128,364	117,643	0.57

1. Compound annual growth rate.

Source: Sistema de Cuentas Nacionales de Mexico, INEGI.

INTERNATIONAL TRADE

United States. Through 1996, the United States continued to have a positive balance in its global printing and publishing trade, although the $1.5-billion trade surplus in 1996 was below levels in 1991-1995. The value of U.S. exports from 1990 to 1996 rose 42 percent to $4.5 billion, while imports climbed 60 percent to $3.0 billion (Table 11). The United States is the world's leading market for printed products and the second largest exporter, exceeded only by Germany. Imports come largely from Canada, the United Kingdom, Germany, and Hong Kong, with books being the largest single import item.   Exports, 60 percent of which are books and periodicals, go mainly to Canada, Mexico, the United Kingdom, and Japan.

Canada.   Canada received 45 percent of all U.S. exports in 1996: $2 billion, as compared with $1.5 billion in 1990 (Table 11). Canadian exports to the United States totaled $759 million in 1996 and accounted for about 25 percent of U.S. imports. They were 131 percent above the 1990 level. Canadian-Mexican trade in printing and publishing has grown during the past seven years, but is still minimal.

Mexico. U.S. exports to Mexico almost tripled between 1990 and 1996 to $341 million. Starting from a much smaller base, Mexican exports to the United States during that period more than quadrupled to $188 million (Table 11).

NAFTA. The United States has a sizable surplus in printing and publishing trade with its North American neighbors (Table 11). This surplus totaled $1.44 billion in 1996, compared with the record surplus of $1.58 billion in 1994. Canada and Mexico had deficits of $1.29 billion and $152 million, respectively, in 1996.

TABLE 11

INTERNATIONAL TRADE, PRINTING AND PUBLISHING

(Millions of U.S. dollars)

	1989[1]	1990	1991	1992	1993	1994	1995	1996
GLOBAL TRADE, U.S.								
IMPORTS								
Value	1,836.0	1,881.6	1,888.8	2,053.3	2,211.2	2,421.5	2,902.0	2,996.1
Ratio to new supply[2]	1.8	1.7	1.7	1.8	1.8	1.9	.....	.....
Ratio to apparent consumption[3]	1.8	1.8	1.8	1.8	1.9	2.0	.....	.....
EXPORTS								
Value	2,639.9	3,199.0	3,644.1	3,866.1	4,057.0	4,069.8	4,470.7	4,533.7
Ratio to comparable domestic shipments	2.6	3.0	3.4	3.4	3.4	3.3	.....	.....
TRADE BALANCE	803.9	1,317.4	1,755.3	1,812.8	1,845.8	1,648.3	1,568.7	1,537.6
BILATERAL TRADE: NAFTA[4]								
U.S. exports to Canada	919.7	1,518.0	1,679.0	1,747.1	1,789.0	1,879.6	2,065.4	2,047.8
Canadian exports to U.S.	404.7	328.3	343.9	394.0	523.0	548.0	680.6	758.8
U.S. exports to Mexico	90.8	115.0	164.9	219.8	262.8	347.6	275.8	340.8
Mexican exports to U.S.	35.3	45.2	66.0	80.9	74.2	100.5	144.9	187.9
Canadian exports to Mexico	0.3	0.4	0.4	1.1	0.9	1.8	0.8	0.8
Mexican exports to Canada	0.2	0.3	0.3	1.7	0.6	0.8	2.2	1.7
TRADE BALANCES WITHIN NAFTA[5]								
Canada	(514.9)	(1,189.6)	(1,335.0)	(1,353.7)	(1,265.7)	(1,330.6)	(1,386.2)	(1,289.9)
Mexico	(55.6)	(69.9)	(99.0)	(138.3)	(188.9)	(248.1)	(129.5)	(152.0)
United States	570.5	1,259.5	1,433.9	1,492.0	1,454.6	1,578.7	1,515.7	1,441.9

1. 1989 and earlier data on U.S. exports to Canada for manufacturing total and manufacturing industries are not comparable with data for 1990 and later years because of a change in the reporting system. The NAFTA trade balances for the U.S. and Canada also are affected.

2. New supply equals comparable domestic shipments plus imports for consumption.

3. Apparent consumption equals comparable domestic shipments plus imports for consumption less exports.

4. Amounts less than U.S. $100,000 shown as zero.

5. Parentheses indicate an excess of imports over exports. Because of commodity coding and other data differences among the three countries, these trade balances are only rough estimates and should be used with caution.

Source for U.S. Global Trade: U.S. Department of Commerce, International Trade Administration.

Source for U.S. -Canada and U.S.-Mexico Bilateral Trade: U.S. Bureau of the Census.

Source for Canada-Mexico and Mexico-Canada Bilateral Trade: Statistics Canada, Foreign Trade Division, Special tabulation, March 1997, converted to U.S. dollars by the editors.

RUBBER AND PLASTIC PRODUCTS

THE UNITED STATES

Products and Processes. The rubber and plastic products industry ranked 12th among U.S. manufacturing industries in 1996 in terms of industry shipments. Its products range from rubber tires, inner tubes, and hose and belting to plastic film and sheet, bottles, foam products, resins, and plumbing fixtures.

Table 1 gives a profile of the industry as of 1992 (the latest year for which economic census data are available). That year, 15,842 establishments, with a combined payroll of $23.2 billion, manufactured rubber and plastic products. Some of their leading product categories were tires and inner tubes ($11.8 billion of sales in 1992); gaskets, packing, hose, and belting ($6.0 billion); mechanical rubber goods ($4.5 billion); unsupported plastic film and sheet ($10.6 billion); plastic foam products ($9.4 billion); custom compound plastic resins ($4.6 billion) and plastic bottles ($4.5 billion).

TABLE 1

UNITED STATES: COMPONENT INDUSTRIES OF RUBBER AND MISCELLANEOUS PLASTIC PRODUCTS (SIC 30), 1992

(Monetary values in millions of U.S. dollars)

INDUSTRY	SIC	ESTABLISH-MENTS	SHIPMENTS		VALUE ADDED BY MANUFACTURE	NEW CAPITAL EXPENDI-TURES	EMPLOY-MENT[1]	PAYROLL
			VALUE	PERCENT BY 4 LARGEST COMPANIES				
RUBBER AND MISCELLANEOUS PLASTIC PRODUCTS	30	15,842	$113,592.8	....	$58,651.8	$4,791.8	906,700	$23,156.0
Tires and inner tubes	301	152	11,814.2	70	6,503.7	506.4	64,600	2,499.3
Rubber and plastic footwear	302	67	867.5	38	463.7	12.9	13,600	215.5
Hose and belting and gaskets and packing	305	755	5,950.1	....	3,290.0	164.9	52,400	1,411.1
Rubber and plastics hose and belting	3052	203	2,609.6	53	1,334.6	74.4	19,900	533.2
Gaskets, packing, and sealing devices	3053	552	3,340.5	26	1,955.4	90.5	32,400	878.0
Fabricated rubber products, n.e.c.	306	1,783	11,474.0	....	6,024.2	359.2	105,100	2,616.9
Mechanical rubber goods	3061	651	4,541.5	20	2,555.7	154.7	48,600	1,200.3
Fabricated rubber products, n.e.c.	3069	1,132	6,932.5	18	3,468.5	204.5	56,500	1,416.6
Miscellaneous plastics products	308	13,085	83,486.9	....	42,370.2	3,748.5	671,100	16,413.2
Unsupported plastics film and sheet	3081	757	10,618.9	18	5,267.9	593.7	54,700	1,680.2
Unsupported plastics profile shapes	3082	671	3,243.5	23	1,743.7	208.0	26,100	691.7
Laminated plastics plate, sheet, and profile shapes	3083	300	2,167.1	41	1,086.2	56.2	15,500	431.6
Plastics pipe	3084	286	2,477.2	23	873.3	106.9	12,800	320.9
Plastics bottles	3085	415	4,507.1	39	2,198.8	267.9	33,300	795.5
Plastics foam products	3086	1,212	9,410.2	22	4,312.9	369.0	66,500	1,576.9
Custom compound purchased plastics resins	3087	666	4,597.9	20	1,858.3	148.0	23,600	687.7
Plastics plumbing fixtures	3088	344	1,089.2	38	630.8	31.2	10,900	230.7
Plastics products, n.e.c.	3089	8,434	45,375.8	5	24,398.4	1,967.6	427,800	9,998.0

1. Employment numbers from the economic censuses differ in definition and classification from the Bureau of Labor Statistics estimates in Table 2. Year-to-year comparisons between Table 1 and Table 2 are not appropriate.

Source: U.S. Bureau of the Census, 1992 Census of Manufactures.

Employment in the industry is projected to reach 1,030,000 in 2005, compared with 909,000 in 1993 (Table 2). Miscellaneous plastic products, the primary employment area, will account for virtually all of the growth, whereas employment in tire and inner tube manufacturing will decline significantly. Hourly wages of production workers averaged $10.57 per hour in 1993 and ranged from $7.59 for rubber and plastic footwear to $17.57 for tires and inner tubes.

TABLE 2

U.S. EMPLOYMENT AND EARNINGS: RUBBER AND MISCELLANEOUS PLASTIC PRODUCTS

| INDUSTRY | SIC | 1993 | | | 2005 |
| | | EMPLOYMENT[1] | | AVERAGE HOURLY EARNINGS (U.S. DOLLARS)[2] | PROJECTED EMPLOYMENT[3] |
		NUMBER OF PERSONS	PERCENT OF INDUSTRY TOTAL		
RUBBER AND MISCELLANEOUS PLASTIC PRODUCTS	30	909,000	100.0	$10.57	1,030,000
Tires and inner tubes	301	81,500	9.0	17.57	60,000
Rubber products and plastic hose and footwear	302,5,6	174,500	19.2	....	170,000
Rubber and plastic footwear	302	10,700	1.2	7.59	....
Hose, belting, gaskets, and packing	305	60,200	6.6	10.53	....
Rubber and plastics hose and belting	3052	23,800	2.6	10.71	....
Fabricated rubber products, n.e.c.	306	103,600	11.4	9.98	....
Miscellaneous plastics products, n.e.c.	308	652,900	71.8	9.85	800,000

1. Total payroll employment. Employment data from the economic censuses, shown in Table 1, differ in definition and classification from the Bureau of Labor Statistics estimates in this table. Year-to-year comparisons between Table 1 and Table 2 are not appropriate.

2. Earnings of production workers, including overtime.

3. Number of persons, moderate projection by the U.S. Bureau of Labor Statistics.

Source: Bureau of Labor Statistics.

FIGURE 1

U.S. EMPLOYMENT IN RUBBER AND MISCELLANEOUS PLASTIC PRODUCTS

Percent distribution by region, 1995

Two regions dominate employment in the rubber and plastics products industry—the Great Lakes, with over 32 percent of the total in 1995, and the Southeast, with 24 percent of the total.

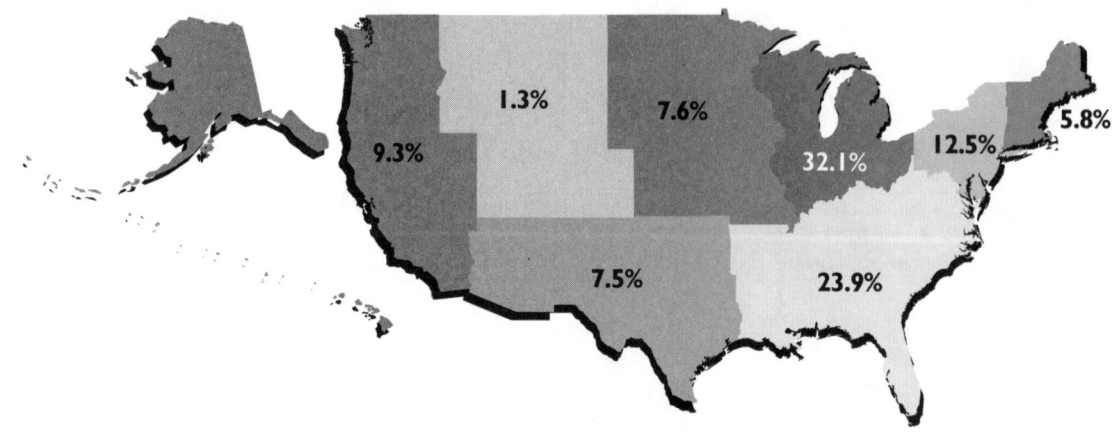

Source: U.S. Department of Commerce, Bureau of Economic Analysis.

What's New. North American tire shipments are likely to rise slowly through 1997 and 1998, according to an August 25, 1997, report in *Rubber & Plastics News*. The growth is expected to come from shipments of replacement tires and from original-equipment medium truck tires.

The Rubber Manufacturers Association (RMA) forecasts that U.S. shipments of replacement passenger and light truck tires will rise slightly to a record 177 million units in 1997, following a 5 percent gain to 175.3 million tires in 1996. Shipments of original-equipment passenger tires are expected to reach 60.3 million in 1997, compared with 57.1 million in 1996, largely because of increased production of light trucks fitted with passenger tires. This trend will depress demand for original-equipment light truck tires, shipments of which are forecast at 5.7 million units in 1997, versus 5.8 million and 6.0 million in 1996 and 1995, respectively. Yearly increases of 1 or 2 percent are seen for medium- and wide-base original-equipment truck tire shipments over the near term as a result of gradual increases expected in truck and trailer production. Replacement shipments of truck tires are seen growing at an even slower rate. Regarding trade, RMA forecasts that exports of passenger tires, which totaled 23.7 million units in 1996, will rise by less than 1 percent a year through the turn of the century. It further reports that imports recently have leveled off at about 43 million tires per year.

First-quarter 1997 bookings by the rubber and plastics industry to manufacturing end-market industries rose 22.3 percent from the fourth quarter of 1996 and 100 percent from the first quarter of 1996, according to a survey by the Measurement, Control & Automation Association.

FIGURE 2

U.S. EMPLOYMENT AND SHIPMENTS, RUBBER AND MISCELLANEOUS PLASTIC PRODUCTS

Total payroll employment and manufacturers' inflation-adjusted shipments

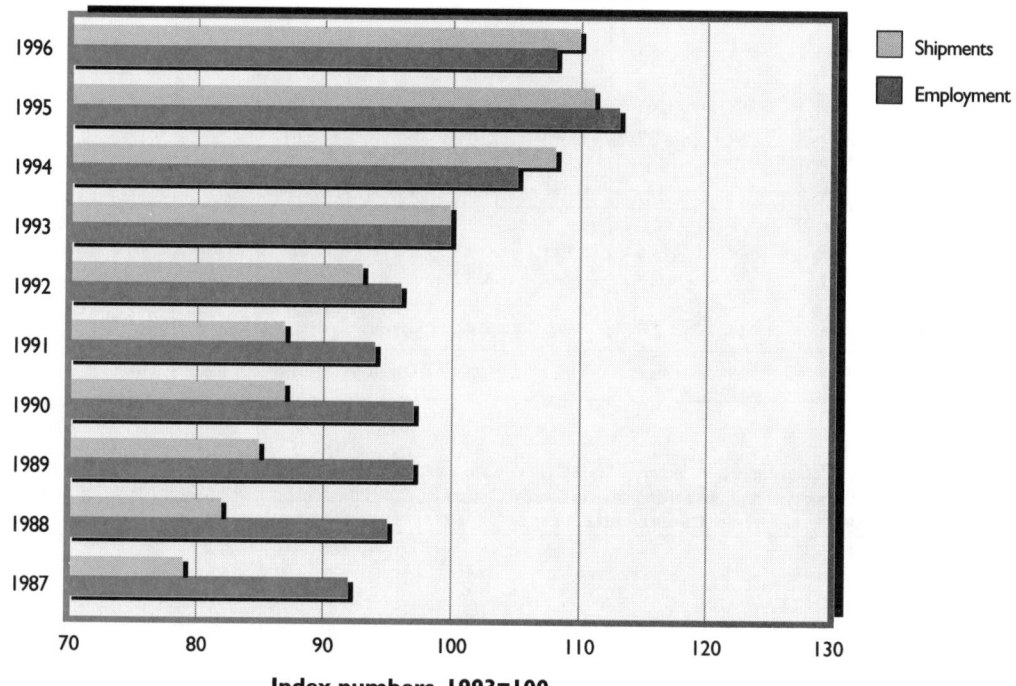

Index numbers, 1993=100

Source: U.S. Bureau of Labor Statistics, U.S. Department of Commerce, and estimates by the editors.

Output. Shipments and employment by the rubber and plastic products industry leveled off in 1996 following a nine-year growth trend in shipments and four years of employment gains (Figure 2). Despite the 1996 slowdown, shipments between 1987 and 1996 rose at an annual rate of 5.8 percent (3.8 percent when adjusted for inflation). The current-dollar value of shipments in 1996 was $143.9 billion, compared with $145.4 billion in 1995 and $86.6 billion in 1987 (Table 3). Shipments began to grow again in early 1997 and for the first six months, averaged 3.3 percent above those in the year-earlier period. Because producer prices during these months were actually below year-earlier levels, the inflation-adjusted shipment growth was at least as rapid as the current-dollar gain.

Investment. New capital expenditures by the industry hit a high of $6.7 billion in 1995, almost double those in 1987 (Table 3). Research and development spending in 1994 totaled $1.4 billion, or 140 percent more than in 1987. Capacity utilization reached its peak of 92.3 percent in 1994 and then declined slightly in the following two years.

Prices. Industry prices rose by at an annual rate of 2.2 percent between 1987 and 1996. Prices declined slightly in 1996 after a sharp gain in 1995 (Table 3).

TABLE 3

U.S. OUTPUT, INVESTMENT, AND PRICES: RUBBER AND PLASTIC PRODUCTS

(Millions of U.S. dollars, except as noted)

	1987	1988	1989	1990	1991	1992	1993	1994	1995	1996	GROWTH RATE 1987-1996[1]
VALUE OF SHIPMENTS:											
BY INDUSTRY:											
Current dollars	86,603	95,484	101,236	105,250	105,804	113,593	122,777	135,145	145,426	143,889	5.80
Constant 1992 dollars	96,097	100,288	102,911	105,947	105,620	113,593	121,724	132,070	135,238	134,060	3.77
BY PRODUCT:											
Current dollars	85,404	92,833	96,752	99,785	99,008	110,237	119,158	130,941	140,420	138,936	5.56
Constant 1992 dollars	94,767	97,503	98,353	100,487	98,857	110,237	118,135	127,978	130,556	129,419	3.52
OTHER OUTPUT MEASURES:											
Industrial production, 1993=100	80.5	82.6	85.4	86.3	84.9	93.6	100.0	108.7	111.3	112.8	3.82
Gross domestic product:											
Current dollars	29,369	30,192	33,498	33,963	35,650	38,095	41,076	44,952	.....	.....	.....
Percent of total GDP	0.6	0.6	0.6	0.6	0.6	0.6	0.6	0.6	.....	.....	.....
Rank in manufacturing	12	13	12	11	11	11	10	10	.....	.....	.....
Chained (1992) dollars	29,280	30,944	34,523	34,436	35,337	38,095	40,872	45,746			
INVESTMENT-RELATED MEASURES:											
Capacity utilization, percent	89.0	87.8	87.4	84.6	80.3	85.3	88.0	92.3	91.5	91.2	.....
New capital expenditures	3,410	3,663	4,776	4,658	4,633	4,792	5,001	5,795	6,651	.....	.....
Research and development spending	596	718	867	1,056	.....	1,256	1,059	1,432	.....	.....	.....
Producer prices, 1993=100[2]	87.4	92.4	95.5	96.4	98.5	98.9	100.0	101.4	106.8	106.6	2.23

1. Compound annual growth rate.

2. Prices received by domestic producers.

Sources: Shipments and new capital expenditures: U.S. Department of Commerce for 1987-1995, editor's estimates for constant dollar data for 1987-88 and all shipments data for 1996; Industrial production and capacity utilization: Federal Reserve Board of Governors; GDP: Bureau of Economic Analysis; Research and development spending: National Science Foundation; Producer prices: Bureau of Labor Statistics.

Workforce and Employment. Employment in the rubber and plastic products industry increased at an annual rate of 1.71 percent between 1987 and 1996, when it reached 981,000 (Table 4). Production worker employment rose at about the same yearly rate and in 1996 totaled 761,000, or 77.6 percent of the workforce. Employment of women in 1996 was 334,000, or 34 percent of the workforce. Production worker earnings during 1987-1996 rose at an annual rate of 2.53 percent (but fell by 1 percent a year when adjusted for inflation). In 1996, the average hourly wage was $11.24, compared with $8.98 in 1987. The average workweek in 1996 was 41.5 hours, not much changed from years past.

TABLE 4

U.S. EMPLOYMENT, HOURS, AND EARNINGS: RUBBER AND PLASTIC PRODUCTS

(Monetary values in U.S. dollars)

	1987	1988	1989	1990	1991	1992	1993	1994	1995	1996	CHANGE[1]
NUMBER OF EMPLOYEES, IN THOUSANDS:											
Total	842	866	888	888	862	878	909	953	980	981	1.71
Production workers	653	674	692	687	662	677	703	742	763	761	1.72
Percent of total	77.5	77.8	77.9	77.4	76.8	77.1	77.4	77.8	77.9	77.6	.....
Women	286	307	313	312	299	301	309	326	334	334	1.73
Percent of total	34.0	35.4	35.3	35.1	34.7	34.3	34.0	34.2	34.1	34.0	.....
HOURS AND EARNINGS OF PRODUCTION WORKERS:											
Average hourly earnings, U.S. dollars[2]											
Current dollars	8.98	9.19	9.46	9.76	10.07	10.36	10.57	10.70	10.91	11.24	2.53
1992 dollars[3]	11.03	10.85	10.67	10.46	10.36	10.36	10.28	10.15	10.06	10.08	-1.00
Average weekly hours	41.6	41.7	41.4	41.1	41.1	41.7	41.8	42.2	41.5	41.5	-0.03
Average weekly earnings, current U.S. dollars	373.57	383.22	391.64	401.14	413.88	432.01	441.83	451.54	452.77	466.46	2.50

1. Compound annual growth rate, 1987-1996.

2. Including overtime.

3. Converted to 1992 dollars using Consumer Price Index for Urban Wage Earners and Clerical Workers.

Source: Bureau of Labor Statistics.

FIGURE 3

U.S. OCCUPATIONAL INJURY AND ILLNESS RATES:
RUBBER AND PLASTIC PRODUCTS , 1995

Incidence of nonfatal injuries and illnesses per 100 full-time workers

Nonfatal occupational illnesses and injuries in the rubber and plastic products industry during 1995 averaged 12.9 cases per 100 workers, slightly higher than the 11.6 percent for all manufacturing.

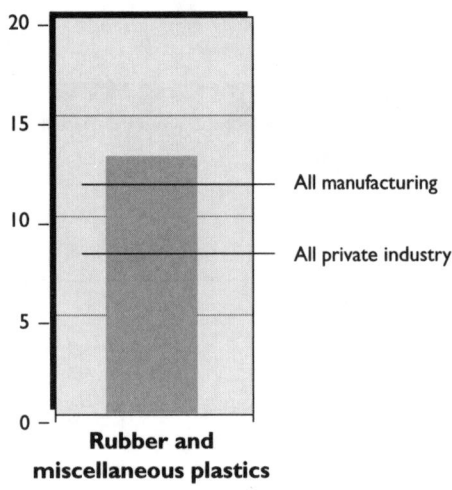

Source: U.S. Bureau of Labor Statistics.

TABLE 5

U.S. EMPLOYMENT PROJECTIONS BY MAJOR OCCUPATIONAL GROUP:
RUBBER AND PLASTIC PRODUCTS

Employment in the rubber and plastic products industry is projected to rise to 1,030,000 people by the year 2005 (moderate assumptions), compared with 951,900 in 1994. Gains are seen for all occupational areas except technicians and related support (projected to hold steady at the 1994 level) and service occupations (likely to decline slightly).

	1994		PROJECTIONS, 2005			
	NUMBER OF EMPLOYEES	PERCENT OF INDUSTRY TOTAL	NUMBER OF EMPLOYEES			PERCENT OF INDUSTRY TOTAL, MODERATE PROJECTIONS
OCCUPATION			LOW	MODERATE	HIGH	
Total, all occupations	951,900	100.0	971,500	1,030,000	1,100,400	100.0
Executive, administrative, and managerial	68,644	7.2	72,617	77,075	82,396	7.5
Professional specialties	18,952	2.0	22,175	23,530	25,169	2.3
Technicians and related support	13,592	1.4	12,816	13,592	14,533	1.3
Marketing and sales	20,829	2.2	21,862	23,215	24,835	2.3
Administrative support including clerical	85,004	8.9	81,291	86,310	92,292	8.4
Service	9,907	1.0	8,412	8,914	9,526	0.9
Agriculture, forestry, and fisheries occupations	65	0.0	67	71	76	0.0
Precision production, craft, and repair	155,477	16.3	159,735	169,345	180,903	16.4
Operators, fabricators, assemblers	579,430	60.9	592,526	627,949	670,669	61.0

Source: Bureau of Labor Statistics, November 1995.

FIGURE 4

U.S. CORPORATE INCOME AND WORKER EARNINGS: RUBBER AND PLASTIC PRODUCTS

Corporate operating income and aggregate production worker earnings

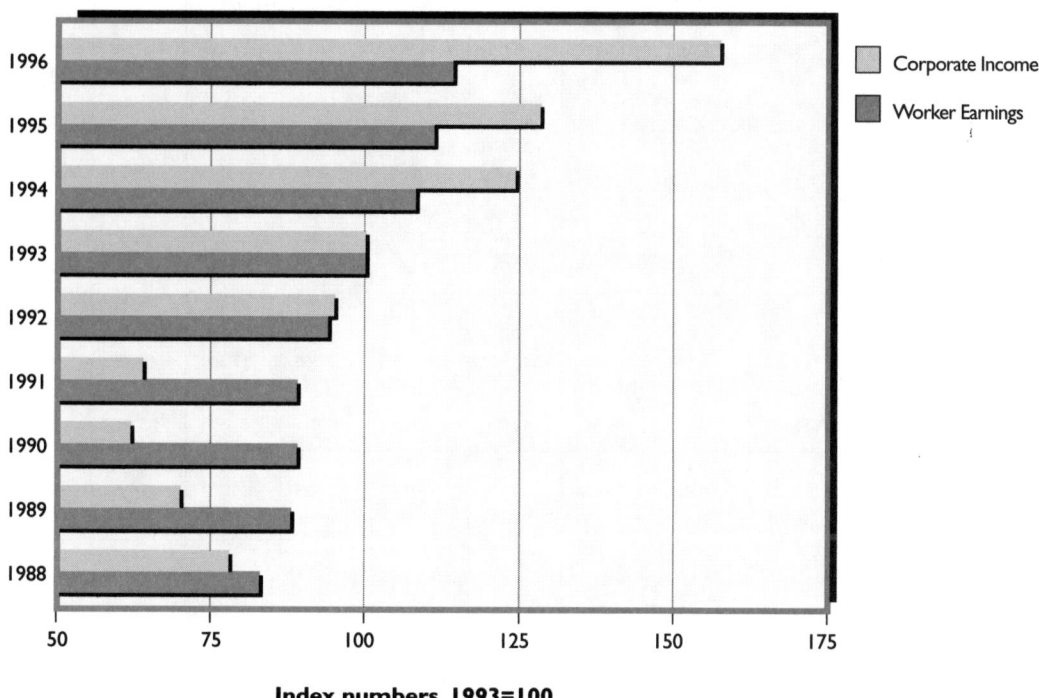

Index numbers, 1993=100

Source: U.S. Bureau of Labor Statistics, U.S. Bureau of the Census, and estimates by the editors.

Finance. After declining from 1988 to 1990, corporate operating income in the rubber and plastic products industry headed sharply higher. Production worker earnings trended upward throughout the nine years, but at a much slower pace (Figure 4).

Industry income from operations in 1996 totaled nearly $8.9 billion, or more than double the $4.4 billion recorded in 1988 (Table 6). The annual growth rate for the nine-year period was a healthy 9.19 percent. After-tax income rose at a more subdued annual rate of 6.2 percent, reaching a record $4.7 billion in 1996. After-tax income in relation to sales was 3.98 percent in 1996, compared with an average of 2.97 percent for the 1988-1996 period. After-tax income to stockholders' equity was 13.86 percent in 1996, compared with the 1988-1996 average of 11.19 percent. Inventories in 1996 reached $13.7 billion in value, the highest level for the nine-year period. Debt has not changed significantly over the past few years, totaling nearly 28 percent of total assets in 1996.

TABLE 6

U.S. CORPORATE INCOME AND ASSETS: RUBBER AND PLASTIC

(Monetary values in millions of U.S. dollars)

INCOME AND EXPENSES	1988	1989	1990	1991	1992	1993	1994	1995	1996	CHANGE OR AVERAGE[1]
Sales and receipts	73,264	76,503	76,691	81,338	88,086	86,595	98,126	112,258	119,242	6.28
Depreciation and amortization	(2,297)	(2,437)	(2,640)	(3,074)	(3,269)	(3,199)	(3,446)	(3,994)	(4,574)	8.99
Other operating costs	(66,582)	(70,172)	(70,541)	(74,669)	(79,450)	(77,781)	(87,722)	(101,049)	(105,804)	5.96
Income from operations	4,386	3,894	3,510	3,594	5,366	5,617	6,957	7,215	8,864	9.19
Nonoperating income (expenditures)	(235)	(622)	(1,393)	(2,022)	(3,470)	(2,461)	(1,230)	(1,351)	(2,768)	....
Income before taxes	4,152	3,273	2,117	1,572	1,896	3,157	5,727	5,865	6,094	4.91
Income after taxes	2,931	2,263	1,369	721	1,535	2,635	4,205	4,572	4,743	6.20
Cash dividends	651	1,404	751	640	951	1,061	1,111	1,078	1,657	12.39
Income retained in business	2,280	860	617	80	584	1,573	3,092	3,494	3,086	3.86
Direct credits (charges)	(2,239)	(654)	(630)	(1,174)	(898)	(602)	(281)	(308)	(518)	....
Ending retained earnings	12,621	11,276	10,060	9,077	10,319	9,714	12,760	17,549	17,609	4.25
ASSETS, END OF YEAR:										
Total	50,059	51,896	56,305	61,884	61,090	62,524	71,017	81,895	83,603	6.62
Accounts receivable	9,993	9,693	9,795	10,938	11,054	11,295	13,177	14,872	14,979	5.19
Inventories	9,525	9,497	9,847	10,072	9,915	9,968	11,435	13,219	13,729	4.68
Net property, plant and equipment	16,777	18,839	20,824	24,169	23,703	23,994	26,349	30,739	30,816	7.90
RATIOS, PERCENT:										
INCOME TO SALES:										
Before tax	5.67	4.28	2.76	1.93	2.15	3.65	5.84	5.22	5.11	4.07
After tax	4.00	2.96	1.79	0.89	1.74	3.04	4.29	4.07	3.98	2.97
INCOME TO STOCKHOLDERS' EQUITY:										
Before tax	23.12	16.98	10.61	7.35	8.71	14.21	21.44	17.82	17.81	15.34
After tax	16.32	11.74	6.86	3.37	7.05	11.86	15.74	13.89	13.86	11.19
INCOME TO TOTAL ASSETS:										
Before tax	8.29	6.31	3.76	2.54	3.10	5.05	8.06	7.16	7.29	5.73
After tax	5.86	4.36	2.43	1.17	2.51	4.21	5.92	5.58	5.67	4.19
AS A PERCENT OF TOTAL ASSETS:										
Property, plant and equipment	33.51	36.30	36.98	39.06	38.80	38.38	37.10	37.53	36.86	37.17
Short-term debt	10.05	8.72	9.39	7.21	7.15	6.25	5.69	5.61	5.46	7.28
Long-term debt	24.59	24.45	24.81	23.94	22.09	22.10	21.49	22.21	22.18	23.10
Stockholders' equity	35.87	37.14	35.44	34.55	35.65	35.54	37.62	40.19	40.92	36.99

1. For income and asset amounts, compound annual growth rate; for ratios, average of ratios for the years shown.

Source: U.S. Bureau of the Census, Quarterly Financial Report.

Notes: Parentheses ( ) indicate negative items, e.g., net expenses, charges, or losses. Net property, plant, and equipment is net of accumulated depreciation. Because the samples used to collect the data change, retained earnings at the end of a given year will not exactly equal the previous year's retained earnings plus the current year's retained income and credits.

CANADA

Canada's rubber and plastic products industries had 1,326 establishments and 73,239 employees in 1993 (Table 7). Plastic products manufacturing is by far the largest of these two sectors, with 69 percent of the industries' employment in 1993 and 67 percent of industry shipments. Hourly earnings in the plastic products sector averaged Can$11.96 in 1993, while those for rubber products averaged Can$15.67.

Shipments by Canada's rubber and plastic products industry totaled $10.5 billion in 1994, compared with $9.3 billion the previous year and $7.6 billion in 1987 (Table 8). After dropping back in 1990-1993, employment rose to 76,970 in 1994—the highest level since the 78,410 of 1989. Production worker employment totaled about 79 percent of the workforce during most of that period. Average hourly earnings of production workers were Can$13.19 in 1994, compared with Can$11.10 in 1988, and the average workweek in 1994 was 40.6 hours.

TABLE 7

CANADA: COMPONENT INDUSTRIES OF RUBBER PRODUCTS AND PLASTIC PRODUCTS INDUSTRIES (CSIC 15 AND 16), 1993

(Monetary values in Canadian dollars)

INDUSTRY NAME	CSIC	ESTABLISH-MENTS (NUMBER)	EMPLOYMENT		VALUE OF SHIPMENTS (MILLIONS)	AVERAGE HOURLY EARNINGS[1]
			NUMBER	PERCENT OF INDUSTRY TOTAL		
RUBBER AND PLASTICS INDUSTRIES[2]	15+16	1,326	73,239	100.0	CAN$9,279.7	CAN$13.03
RUBBER PRODUCTS	15	173	22,804	31.1	3,086.9	15.67
Tires and tubes	151	13	9,837	13.4	1,457.2	18.43
Rubber hose and belting	152	26	2,075	2.8	272.3	13.86
Other rubber products	159	134	10,892	14.9	1,357.4	13.54
PLASTIC PRODUCTS	16	1,153	50,435	68.9	6,192.8	11.96
Foamed and expanded plastic products	161	94	3,658	5.0	503.0	12.00
Plastic pipe and pipe fittings	162	64	2,931	4.0	512.2	12.29
Plastic film and sheeting	163	64	4,712	6.4	841.5	14.37
Other plastic products	169	931	39,134	53.4	4,336.0	11.66
Plastic bags	169	116	6,324	8.6	826.0	13.06
Other plastic products, n.e.c.	169	815	32,810	44.8	3,510.1	11.40

1. Including overtime.

2. Canadian Rubber industry, CSIC 15, and Plastics industry, CSIC 16, are combined for easier comparison to the U.S. industry.

Source: Adapted from Statistics Canada, *Manufacturing Industries of Canada* (Cat. No. 31-203).

TABLE 8

CANADIAN EMPLOYMENT AND SHIPMENTS: RUBBER AND PLASTIC PRODUCTS, 1987-1994

(Monetary values in Canadian dollars)

	1987	1988	1989	1990	1991	1992	1993	1994	CHANGE[1]
All employees	68,888	76,717	78,410	76,708	73,661	72,529	73,239	76,970	1.60
Establishments	1,291	1,439	1,450	1,472	1,379	1,329	1,326	1,307	0.18
Employees per establishment	53	53	54	52	53	55	55	59	1.42
Production workers per establishment	.....	42	43	40	42	43	44	47	1.73
PRODUCTION WORKERS:									
Total	.....	60,593	62,349	59,357	57,979	57,336	57,852	60,999	0.11
Percent of all employees	.....	79.0	79.5	77.4	78.7	79.1	79.0	79.3	.....
Male	.....	44,911	45,888	43,786	43,100	.....	.....	.....	.....
Female	.....	15,682	16,461	15,571	14,879	.....	.....	.....	.....
Percent of all production workers	.....	25.9	26.4	26.2	25.7	.....	.....	.....	.....
Average hourly earnings	.....	11.10	11.51	12.15	12.36	12.70	13.03	13.19	2.92
Average weekly earnings	.....	443.45	461.67	481.63	489.83	507.24	525.24	535.12	3.18
Average weekly hours	.....	40.0	40.1	39.6	39.6	39.9	40.3	40.6	0.26
Shipments (millions)	7,573	8,588	8,965	8,555	8,191	8,432	9,280	10,514	4.80

1. Compound annual growth rate.

Source: Adapted from Statistics Canada, *Manufacturing Industries of Canada* (Cat. No. 31-203).

MEXICO

Mexico's rubber industry in 1993 had 792 production units and 33,265 employees (Table 9). The plastics products industry had 3,249 units and 125,018 employees. Annual income (wages plus benefits) of employees averaged 34,936 ($11,184) for the rubber industry and 20,507 ($6,565) for plastics products. Employment in rubber and plastics combined rose at an annual rate of 3.11 percent between 1988 and 1995, to 149,280 (Table 10). The peak of 160,287 employees was reached in 1994.

TABLE 9

MEXICO: COMPONENT INDUSTRIES OF RUBBER AND PLASTIC INDUSTRIES (CMAP 3550 AND 3560), 1993

(Monetary values in 1993 Mexican New Pesos)

			ALL WORKERS										
							PAID WORKERS					
							PRODUCTION WORKERS		NONPRODUCTION EMPLOYEES		BENEFITS	UNPAID
INDUSTRY	CMAP	NUMBER OF UNITS	NUMBER	PERCENT OF INDUSTRY TOTAL	AVERAGE DAYS WORKED	REMUN- ERATION[1]	NUMBER	WAGES AND SALARIES	NUMBER	WAGES AND SALARIES	PER PAID EMPLOYEE	WORKERS, NUMBER
Rubber industry	3550	792	33,265	21	276	34,936	25,700	19,607	6,919	37,345	11,566	646
Plastics products	3560	3,249	125,018	79	278	20,507	94,814	10,239	27,495	31,468	5,495	2,709

1. Average annual remuneration including benefits.

Source: INEGI, Censos Economicos 1994.

TABLE 10

MEXICAN EMPLOYMENT: RUBBER AND PLASTIC, 1988-1995

	1988	1989	1990	1991	1992	1993	1994	1995	CHANGE[1]
TOTAL EMPLOYMENT: Rubber and plastic	120,448	129,823	136,674	143,132	150,009	157,510	160,287	149,280	3.11

1. Compound annual growth rate.

Source: Sistema de Cuentas Nacionales de Mexico, INEGI.

INTERNATIONAL TRADE

United States. Global U.S. exports of rubber and plastic products almost doubled between 1990 and 1996 to $12.1 billion (Table 11). Imports rose by more than two-thirds to $16.9 billion. The trade deficit declined through 1991 and then increased for three straight years before easing again, to $4.8 billion in 1996. Canada took almost a third of U.S. exports and supplied about 20 percent of U.S. imports in 1996. Mexico received 22 percent of U.S. exports but supplied only 4 percent of U.S. imports that year. The European Union and Japan are among the other trading partners, for both imports and exports.

Canada. U.S. rubber and plastic products exports to Canada reached $3.8 billion in 1996, compared with $2.3 billion in 1990 (Table 11). Canadian exports to the United States more than doubled to $3.4 billion during that period, leaving a U.S. trade surplus in 1996 of just under $400 million. Canadian exports to Mexico totaled only about $9 million in 1996.

Mexico. Mexican exports of rubber and plastics products to the United States rose 137 percent between 1990 and 1996, to $699 million (Table 11). U.S. exports to Mexico rose 184 percent to $2.6 billion, resulting in a 1996 trade surplus with Mexico of about $1.9 billion. Mexico shipped $32 million worth of rubber and plastics products to Canada in 1996, compared with only $4 million in 1990.

NAFTA. While its global trade deficit remained high, the United States saw considerable improvement in its balance of trade with NAFTA during 1990-1996 (Table 11). The U.S. trade surplus grew from $1.3 billion in 1990 to $1.9 billion in 1993 (the year before implementation of NAFTA) and $2.3 billion in 1996. Canada's trade deficit declined from $635 million in 1990 to $411 million in 1996, while Mexico's deficit rose from $630 million in 1990 to $1.3 billion in 1993 and $1.9 billion in 1996.

TABLE 11

INTERNATIONAL TRADE, RUBBER AND PLASTICS

(Millions of U.S. dollars)

	1989[1]	1990	1991	1992	1993	1994	1995	1996
GLOBAL TRADE, U.S.								
IMPORTS								
Value	9,841.5	10,036.3	10,223.7	11,739.2	13,052.5	14,392.7	15,972.8	16,891.0
Ratio to new supply[2]	9.2	9.1	9.4	9.6	9.9	9.9	.....	.....
Ratio to apparent consumption[3]	9.7	9.7	10.0	10.3	10.6	10.7	.....	.....
EXPORTS								
Value	4,914.6	6,323.1	6,975.9	7,803.7	8,554.3	9,942.1	11,024.4	12,092.6
Ratio to comparable domestic shipments	5.1	6.3	7.0	7.1	7.2	7.6	.....	.....
TRADE BALANCE	(4,926.9)	(3,713.2)	(3,247.8)	(3,935.5)	(4,498.2)	(4,450.6)	(4,948.4)	(4,798.4)
BILATERAL TRADE: NAFTA[4]								
U.S. exports to Canada	1,174.4	2,303.4	2,457.5	2,630.9	2,873.0	3,214.6	3,591.5	3,804.8
Canadian exports to U.S.	1,574.2	1,667.2	1,761.0	2,054.7	2,277.5	2,710.8	3,060.9	3,416.6
U.S. exports to Mexico	783.3	923.1	1,054.5	1,411.7	1,631.7	2,245.1	2,116.3	2,624.8
Mexican exports to U.S.	294.4	294.0	328.0	355.1	362.5	451.3	597.7	698.6
Canadian exports to Mexico	5.7	5.2	2.6	3.3	2.4	3.9	5.7	9.3
Mexican exports to Canada	4.1	4.4	7.7	7.8	12.2	17.0	23.2	31.6
TRADE BALANCES WITHIN NAFTA[5]								
Canada	401.4	(635.4)	(701.6)	(580.7)	(605.3)	(516.9)	(548.1)	(410.5)
Mexico	(490.5)	(629.9)	(721.4)	(1,052.1)	(1,259.4)	(1,780.7)	(1,501.1)	(1,903.9)
United States	89.1	1,265.3	1,423.0	1,632.8	1,864.7	2,297.6	2,049.2	2,314.4

1. 1989 and earlier data on U.S. exports to Canada for manufacturing total and manufacturing industries are not comparable with data for 1990 and later years because of a change in the reporting system. The NAFTA trade balances for the U.S. and Canada also are affected.

2. New supply equals comparable domestic shipments plus imports for consumption.

3. Apparent consumption equals comparable domestic shipments plus imports for consumption less exports.

4. Amounts less than U.S. $100,000 shown as zero.

5. Parentheses indicate an excess of imports over exports. Because of commodity coding and other data differences among the three countries, these trade balances are only rough estimates and should be used with caution.

Source for U.S. Global Trade: U.S. Department of Commerce, International Trade Administration.

Source for U.S. -Canada and U.S.-Mexico Bilateral Trade: U.S. Bureau of the Census.

Source for Canada-Mexico and Mexico-Canada Bilateral Trade: Statistics Canada, Foreign Trade Division, Special tabulation, March 1997, converted to U.S. dollars by the editors.

STONE, CLAY, AND GLASS

THE UNITED STATES

Products and Processes. The stone, clay, and glass industry ranked 16th among U.S. manufacturing industries in value of 1995 shipments. Most of its products are used in construction, where strong growth recently has bolstered demand for building materials. The group also includes housewares such as glassware and glass containers, pottery, and vitreous china.

TABLE 1

UNITED STATES: COMPONENT INDUSTRIES OF STONE, CLAY, AND GLASS PRODUCTS (SIC 32), 1992

(Monetary values in millions of U.S. dollars)

| INDUSTRY | SIC | ESTABLISH-MENTS | SHIPMENTS | | VALUE ADDED BY MANUFACTURE | NEW CAPITAL EXPENDI-TURES | EMPLOY-MENT[1] | PAYROLL |
			VALUE	PERCENT BY 4 LARGEST COMPANIES				
STONE, CLAY, GLASS, AND CONCRETE PRODUCTS	32	16,254	$62,520.6	....	$34,641.2	$2,457.6	468,800	$13,113.1
Flat glass	321	35	2,072.8	81	1,310.9	147.9	11,800	451.3
Glass and glassware, pressed or blown	322	525	9,033.0		5,900.1	576.4	66,100	2,074.9
Glass containers	3221	76	4,859.6	84	3,038.4	233.0	32,300	1,052.4
Pressed and blown glass and glassware, n.e.c.	3229	449	4,173.4	48	2,861.8	343.4	33,800	1,022.5
Products of purchased glass	323	1,567	6,903.9	28	3,756.9	276.0	54,800	1,369.4
Cement, hydraulic	324	218	4,050.8	35	2,149.3	226.2	17,000	594.9
Structural clay products	325	547	2,857.2	....	1,695.2	121.7	30,900	733.9
Brick and structural clay tile	3251	219	1,110.4	34	725.5	42.9	14,100	313.8
Ceramic wall and floor tile	3253	118	731.3	59	458.1	48.9	8,900	196.9
Clay refractories	3255	145	886.8	40	435.7	24.6	6,200	183.8
Structural clay products, n.e.c.	3259	65	128.8	35	75.9	5.3	1,700	39.4
Pottery and related products	326	1,091	2,816.7	....	1,994.8	88.0	36,500	862.6
Vitreous plumbing fixtures	3261	61	902.1	71	658.5	14.3	8,400	216.8
Vitreous china food utensils	3262	39	315.6	81	239.1	15.8	5,300	118.2
Fine earthenware food utensils	3263	29	45.2	85	28.6	1.5	900	17.0
Porcelain electrical supplies	3264	128	884.4	36	601.1	34.3	9,700	278.9
Pottery products, n.e.c.	3269	834	669.4	25	467.4	21.9	12,200	231.7
Concrete, gypsum, and plaster products	327	9,679	23,023.6	....	11,008.1	634.7	174,000	4,740.6
Concrete brick and block	3271	1,071	2,055.6	7	1,033.3	58.5	16,500	430.7
Concrete products, except brick and block	3272	3,111	5,949.0	9	3,364.9	171.3	58,900	1,513.8
Ready-mixed concrete	3273	5,256	12,015.0	6	5,345.8	313.3	82,400	2,293.0
Lime	3274	88	903.7	46	460.4	47.9	5,600	171.2
Gypsum products	3275	153	2,100.3	75	803.6	43.8	10,600	331.8
Cut stone and stone products	328	923	1,006.6	23	604.4	36.9	12,200	281.7
Miscellaneous nonmetallic mineral products	329	1,669	10,755.9	....	6,221.6	349.8	65,500	2,003.7
Abrasive products	3291	411	3,748.1	....	2,072.3	120.0	20,900	631.4
Asbestos products	3292	11	69.6	88	39.9	2.1	600	19.7
Minerals and earth's, ground or treated	3295	368	1,774.4	28	1,081.2	47.1	9,500	299.1
Mineral wool	3296	225	3,241.2	64	1,917.7	115.3	19,200	630.9
Nonclay refractories	3297	143	1,203.8	36	650.6	44.9	8,100	249.3
Nonmetallic mineral products, n.e.c.	3299	511	718.8	20	459.9	20.4	7,100	173.4

1. Employment numbers from the economic censuses differ in definition and classification from the Bureau of Labor Statistics estimates in Table 2. Year-to-year comparisons between Table 1 and Table 2 are not appropriate.

Source: U.S. Bureau of the Census, 1992 Census of Manufactures.

Table 1 shows the major product categories in this group in 1992 (the latest year for which economic census data are available). Concrete, gypsum, and plaster products comprised the largest single category, accounting for almost 37 percent of industry shipments that year. Next in size were miscellaneous nonmetallic mineral products such as abrasives, ground or treated minerals and earth, and mineral wool (about 17 percent of the total); glass and glassware (14 percent); products of purchased glass (11 percent); and hydraulic cement (6 percent).

Table 2 gives a breakdown of 1993 employment by product groups, along with projected employment for the year 2005. Employment totaled 517,000 in 1993 and is projected to decline 16 percent to 433,900 by 2005. The concrete, gypsum, and plaster products industry—the largest employer—is projected to have 171,500 employees in 2005 compared with 188,500 employees in 1993. Hourly earnings of production workers averaged $11.85 in 1993, but there was considerable variation within the subindustries. Workers producing flat glass had the highest average earnings ($17.55), while those producing concrete products n.e.c. had the lowest ($10.19).

TABLE 2

U.S. EMPLOYMENT AND EARNINGS: STONE, CLAY, AND GLASS PRODUCTS

INDUSTRY	SIC	1993 EMPLOYMENT[1] NUMBER OF PERSONS	1993 EMPLOYMENT[1] PERCENT OF INDUSTRY TOTAL	1993 AVERAGE HOURLY EARNINGS (U.S. DOLLARS)[2]	2005 PROJECTED EMPLOYMENT[3]
STONE, CLAY, AND GLASS PRODUCTS	32	517,000	100.0	$11.85	433,900
Glass and glass products	321,2,3	127,800	....	....	125,000
Flat glass	321	14,600	2.8	17.55	....
Glass and glassware, pressed or blown	322	77,700	15.0	13.33	....
Glass containers	3221	35,500	6.9	13.78	....
Pressed and blown glass, n.e.c.	3229	42,200	8.2	12.88	....
Products of purchased glass	323	59,300	11.5	10.29	....
Cement, hydraulic	324	17,900	3.5	15.12	14,000
Structural clay products	325	32,100	6.2	10.34	....
Pottery and related products	326	39,100	7.6	10.15	....
Concrete, gypsum, and plaster products	327	188,500	36.5	11.34	171,500
Concrete block and brick	3271	16,300	3.2	10.67	....
Concrete products, n.e.c.	3272	62,600	12.1	10.19	....
Ready-mixed concrete	3273	92,800	17.9	12.02	....
Miscellaneous nonmetallic mineral products	329	74,200	14.4	12.39	....
Abrasive products	3291	19,600	3.8	10.69	....
Asbestos products	3292	3,100	0.6	13.73	....
Mineral wool	3296	22,300	4.3	....	....
Stone, clay, and miscellaneous mineral products	325,6,8,9	....	....	....	124,000

1. Total payroll employment. Employment data from the economic censuses, shown in Table 1, differ in definition and classification from the Bureau of Labor Statistics estimates in this table. Year-to-year comparisons between Table 1 and Table 2 are not appropriate.

2. Earnings of production workers, including overtime.

3. Number of persons, moderate projection by the U.S. Bureau of Labor Statistics.

Source: Bureau of Labor Statistics.

FIGURE 1

U.S. EMPLOYMENT IN STONE, CLAY, AND GLASS

Percent distribution by region, 1995

The Southeast is the largest regional employer for the industry, with about 26 percent of total employment in 1995. Next in importance are the Great Lakes region (20 percent), and the Mid-Atlantic States (16 percent).

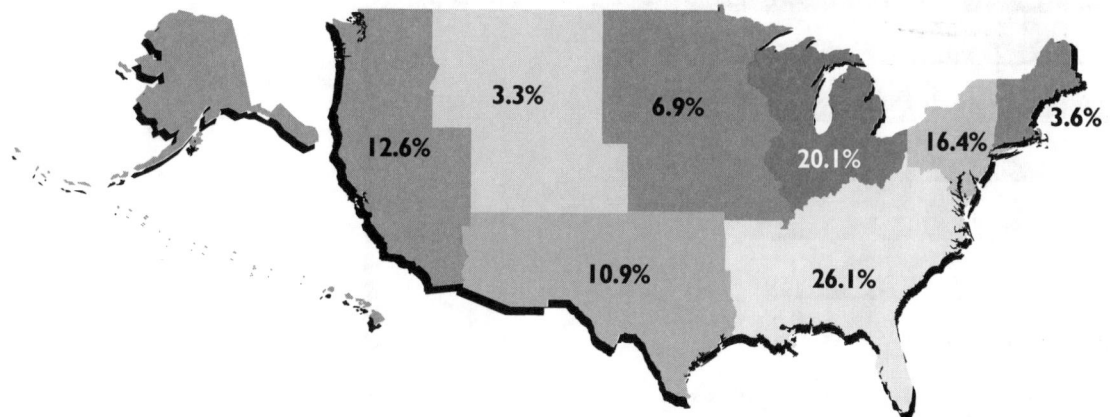

Source: U.S. Department of Commerce, Bureau of Economic Analysis.

What's New. The stone, clay, and glass industry has benefited from growth in construction during the past few years. For example, according to the National Association of Home Builders, a 2,085 square foot single-family home requires 14 tons of concrete. U.S. government estimates of construction activity show a mixed picture for 1997. Residential building permits issued during the first 7 months of 1997 were down 2 percent from the same months of 1996; the rate in August was 2 percent below July's and 1 percent below the August 1996 level. Housing starts slipped 3 percent during January-July and then in August fell 5 percent to an annual rate of 1.36 million units—the slowest rate since December 1996 and 10 percent below the August 1996 pace. However, total U.S. new construction during the first seven months of 1997 was about 6.5 percent above the year-earlier period, not very different from the average over the past several years. Gains occurred in both residential and nonresidential spending, with construction of nonresidential buildings showing a particularly strong 12 percent gain.

In Canada, new home building is forecast to rise nearly 20 percent in 1997 and another 7 percent in 1998, according to the Canada Mortgage and Housing Corp. in its third-quarter national housing outlook. Total housing starts are forecast at 148,100 units in 1997 (compared with 124,713 in 1996) and 158,800 in 1998. Starts of single detached houses are forecast to rise 19.4 percent to 93,100 units in 1997, and starts of multiple units are forecast up 17.7 percent to 55,000. Strong sales of existing homes and rising prices/shrinking supply in some areas have given impetus to the building boom.

FIGURE 2

U.S. EMPLOYMENT AND SHIPMENTS: STONE, CLAY, AND GLASS

Total payroll employment and manufacturers' inflation-adjusted shipments

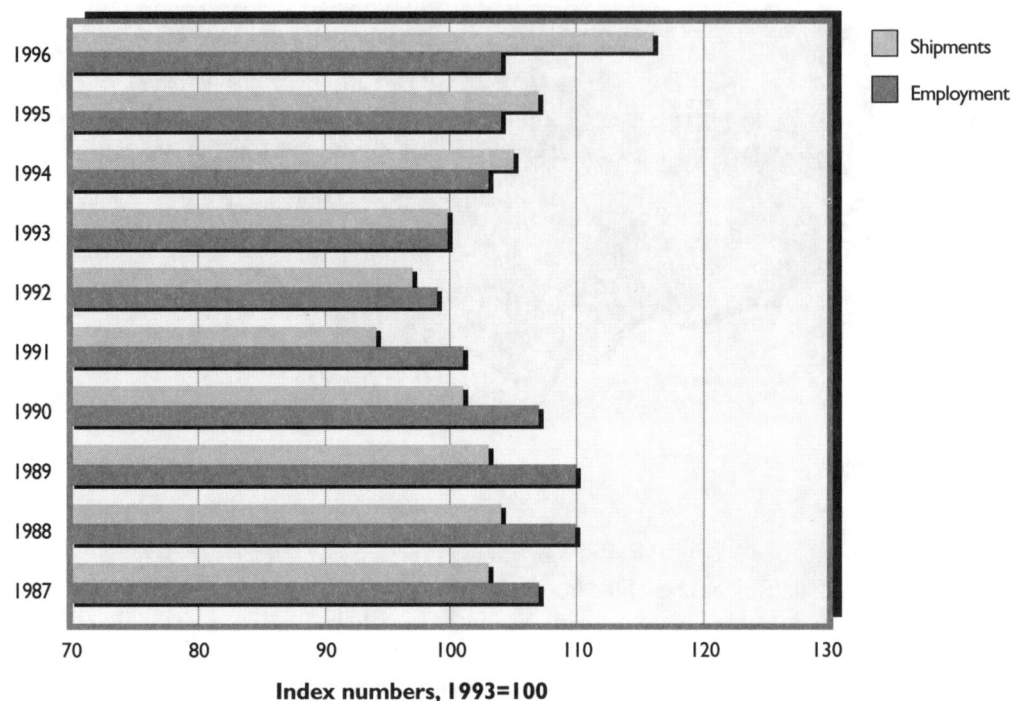

Source: U.S. Bureau of Labor Statistics, U.S. Department of Commerce, and estimates by the editors.

Output. Constant-dollar industry shipments of stone, clay, and glass declined abruptly during the recession in 1991 and then reversed course with an especially strong gain in 1996. Employment followed a similar trend, but with a more modest increase in 1993-1996. (Figure 2). Current-dollar value of industry shipments was $83.1 billion in 1996, compared with $76.0 billion in 1995 and $61.5 billion in 1987 (Table 3). The average rate of growth for the 10-year period was 3.4 percent (1.4 percent in inflation-adjusted dollars).

Investment. New capital expenditures reached a record $3.37 billion in 1995, compared with $2.42 billion in 1987. However, research and development spending, at $553 million in 1994 (latest year for which data are available), was well below the $985 million level for 1987 (Table 3). Capacity utilization in 1996 was 79.4 percent, slightly less than in 1995 but above that in 1990-1993.

Prices. Producer prices for the industry's products rose only slightly in 1996 after relatively large gains in the previous two years (Table 3). The annual rate of increase for the 10-year period beginning in 1987 was 2.09 percent.

TABLE 3

U.S. OUTPUT, INVESTMENT, AND PRICES: STONE, CLAY, AND GLASS

(Millions of U.S. dollars, except as noted)

	1987	1988	1989	1990	1991	1992	1993	1994	1995	1996	GROWTH RATE 1987-1996[1]
VALUE OF SHIPMENTS:											
BY INDUSTRY:											
Current dollars	61,477	63,146	63,729	63,727	59,957	62,521	65,610	71,230	75,990	83,053	3.40
Constant 1992 dollars	65,906	66,828	66,107	65,056	60,175	62,521	64,164	67,160	68,844	74,345	1.35
BY PRODUCT:											
Current dollars	58,015	59,333	59,908	59,885	56,143	58,930	61,819	66,986	71,194	77,812	3.32
Constant 1992 dollars	62,141	62,740	62,088	61,091	56,321	58,930	60,461	63,179	64,507	69,662	1.28
OTHER OUTPUT MEASURES:											
Industrial production, 1993=100	102.6	105.3	105.2	102.8	95.2	97.9	100.0	105.7	106.9	108.6	0.63
Gross domestic product:											
Current dollars	23,687	23,961	24,891	24,836	22,932	25,076	25,660	27,925	.....	.....	.....
Percent of total GDP	0.5	0.5	0.5	0.4	0.4	0.4	0.4	0.4	.....	.....	.....
Rank in manufacturing	13	14	15	15	15	16	15	14	.....	.....	.....
Chained (1992) dollars	23,504	24,556	25,643	25,513	22,916	25,076	24,992	26,213	.....	.....	.....
INVESTMENT-RELATED MEASURES:											
Capacity utilization, percent	79.8	81.7	81.1	78.4	72.2	74.2	75.6	79.4	79.5	79.4	.....
New capital expenditures	2,417	2,269	2,924	2,804	2,481	2,458	2,415	2,834	3,366	.....	.....
Research and development spending	985	697	615	538	455	479	529	553	.....	.....	.....
Producer prices, 1993=100[2]	90.5	91.7	93.5	95.3	97.4	97.8	100.0	103.6	107.7	109.0	2.09

1. Compound annual growth rate.

2. Prices received by domestic producers.

Sources: Shipments and new capital expenditures: U.S. Department of Commerce for 1987-1995, editor's estimates for constant dollar data for 1987-88 and all shipments data for 1996; Industrial production and capacity utilization: Federal Reserve Board of Governors; GDP: Bureau of Economic Analysis; Research and development spending: National Science Foundation; Producer prices: Bureau of Labor Statistics.

Workforce and Employment. Employment in the stone, glass, and clay industry decreased at an annual rate of 0.26 percent from 1987 through 1996 (Table 4). The slight yearly gains during 1993-1996 (to 541,000 employees) were not enough to offset declines in the previous three years. Employment in the glassware industry was one area showing a decrease after implementation of NAFTA, probably reflecting the lowering of the rather high U.S. tariff on glassware. Employment of production workers showed little net change during the 10-year period, ending up at 421,000, or 77.8 percent of the total, in 1996. Employment of women declined slightly; their share of the workforce was 18.9 percent in 1996. Average hourly earnings of production workers totaled $12.82 in 1996, having risen at a 2.52 percent annual rate since 1987. However, this translates into a decline of 1.01 percent per year when adjusted for inflation. The average workweek was up slightly in 1996, to 43.3 percent.

TABLE 4

U.S. EMPLOYMENT, HOURS, AND EARNINGS: STONE, CLAY, AND GLASS

(Monetary values in U.S. dollars)

	1987	1988	1989	1990	1991	1992	1993	1994	1995	1996	CHANGE[1]
NUMBER OF EMPLOYEES, IN THOUSANDS:											
Total	554	567	568	556	522	513	517	532	540	541	-0.26
Production workers	429	443	444	432	403	396	399	411	418	421	-0.20
Percent of total	77.4	78.1	78.1	77.7	77.1	77.2	77.1	77.2	77.4	77.8	.....
Women	109	107	110	109	105	104	103	104	104	102	-0.78
Percent of total	19.7	18.9	19.4	19.7	20.1	20.2	19.9	19.5	19.3	18.9	.....
HOURS AND EARNINGS OF PRODUCTION WORKERS:											
Average hourly earnings, U.S. dollars[2]											
Current dollars	10.25	10.56	10.82	11.12	11.36	11.60	11.85	12.13	12.41	12.82	2.52
1992 dollars[3]	12.59	12.47	12.20	11.92	11.69	11.60	11.53	11.51	11.45	11.50	-1.01
Average weekly hours	42.3	42.3	42.3	42.0	41.7	42.2	42.7	43.4	43.0	43.3	0.26
Average weekly earnings, current U.S. dollars	433.58	446.69	457.69	467.04	473.71	489.52	506	526.44	533.63	555.11	2.78

1. Compound annual growth rate, 1987-1996.

2. Including overtime.

3. Converted to 1992 dollars using Consumer Price Index for Urban Wage Earners and Clerical Workers.

Source: Bureau of Labor Statistics.

FIGURE 3

U.S. OCCUPATIONAL INJURY AND ILLNESS RATES: STONE, CLAY, AND GLASS, 1995

Nonfatal illnesses and injuries in the industry during 1995 averaged 12.3 cases per 100 workers, compared with 11.6 cases for all manufacturing industries.

Incidence of nonfatal injuries and illnesses per 100 full-time workers

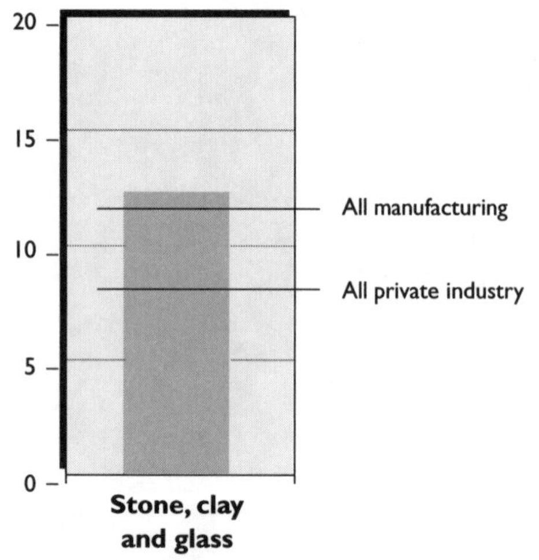

Source: U.S. Bureau of Labor Statistics.

TABLE 5

U.S. EMPLOYMENT PROJECTIONS BY MAJOR OCCUPATIONAL GROUP: STONE, CLAY, AND GLASS

OCCUPATION	1994		PROJECTIONS, 2005			
	NUMBER OF EMPLOYEES	PERCENT OF INDUSTRY TOTAL	NUMBER OF EMPLOYEES			PERCENT OF INDUSTRY TOTAL, MODERATE PROJECTIONS
			LOW	MODERATE	HIGH	
Total, all occupations	532,600	100.0	412,500	433,900	463,400	100.0
Executive, administrative, and managerial	39,857	7.5	31,335	32,947	35,180	7.6
Professional specialties	9,101	1.7	8,356	8,849	9,506	2.0
Technicians and related support	7,663	1.4	5,322	5,621	6,027	1.3
Marketing and sales	16,419	3.1	13,057	13,732	14,678	3.2
Administrative support including clerical	47,366	8.9	33,255	34,948	37,298	8.1
Service	4,586	0.9	2,968	3,130	3,353	0.7
Agriculture, forestry, and fisheries occupations	95	0.0	75	78	83	0.0
Precision production, craft, and repair	112,884	21.2	84,914	89,250	95,230	20.6
Operators, fabricators, assemblers	294,629	55.3	233,217	245,345	262,045	56.5

Source: Bureau of Labor Statistics, November 1995.

Projections for industry employment (moderate assumptions) in 2005 foresee a decline of nearly 100,000 workers from the 1994 level of 532,600 (Table 4). All occupational categories are expected to show declines.

FIGURE 4

U.S. CORPORATE INCOME AND WORKER EARNINGS: STONE, CLAY, AND GLASS

Corporate operating income and aggregate production worker earnings

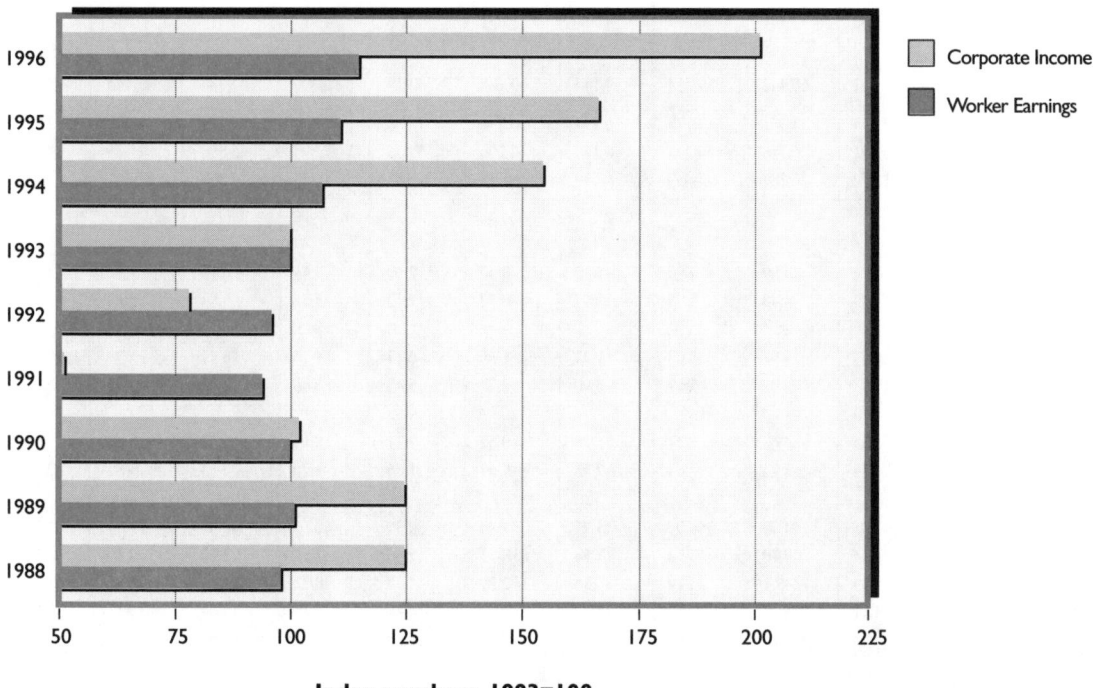

Index numbers, 1993=100

Source: U.S. Bureau of Labor Statistics, U.S. Bureau of the Census, and estimates by the editors.

Finance. The industry's operating earnings fell steadily from 1989 through the recession year of 1991 and then reversed course for the next five years, with especially steep gains in 1994 and again in 1996. Production worker earnings, on the other hand, showed steady but extremely slow growth during most of the period (Figure 4).

Increasing at an annual rate of 6.22 percent for the nine-year period, operating earnings reached a record $6.97 billion in 1996. This compares with $5.77 billion the year before and a low of $1.75 billion in 1991 (Table 6). After-tax income rose at a 5.79 percent annual rate during 1988-1996, ending up at $3.85 billion in a strong recovery from the loss of $1.53 billion in 1991. After-tax income in 1996 amounted to 5.47 percent of sales and 16.74 percent of stockholders' equity. Inventories in 1996 were up slightly from 1995 and above any other year during the period. Debt, largely long-term, amounted to over 31 percent of total assets.

TABLE 6

U.S. CORPORATE INCOME AND ASSETS: STONE, CLAY, AND GLASS

(Monetary values in millions of U.S. dollars)

INCOME AND EXPENSES	1988	1989	1990	1991	1992	1993	1994	1995	1996	CHANGE OR AVERAGE[1]
Sales and receipts	54,636	57,299	55,662	51,075	51,838	51,666	57,333	61,577	70,387	3.22
Depreciation and amortization	(2,389)	(2,633)	(2,650)	(2,581)	(2,636)	(2,556)	(2,629)	(2,738)	(3,099)	3.31
Other operating costs	(47,949)	(50,367)	(49,496)	(46,741)	(46,534)	(45,668)	(49,370)	(53,069)	(60,321)	2.91
Income from operations	4,299	4,299	3,515	1,752	2,669	3,441	5,333	5,769	6,967	6.22
Nonoperating income (expenditures)	(784)	(1,499)	(1,867)	(3,691)	(2,982)	(2,200)	(2,229)	(1,604)	(1,681)	....
Income before taxes	3,516	2,800	1,648	(1,939)	(312)	1,242	3,104	4,165	5,286	5.23
Income after taxes	2,453	1,968	1,087	(1,525)	(374)	1,094	1,932	2,959	3,849	5.79
Cash dividends	2,798	514	674	386	566	501	505	667	1,037	-11.67
Income retained in business	(345)	1,452	413	(1,910)	(941)	594	1,426	2,292	2,813	....
Direct credits (charges)	(1,781)	(585)	(862)	(342)	(559)	1,387	114	(456)	(1,476)	....
Ending retained earnings	8,406	7,787	6,327	4,276	3,091	4,328	4,973	6,319	6,738	-2.73
ASSETS, END OF YEAR:										
Total	51,311	60,440	59,414	59,174	60,184	58,919	60,300	62,487	65,446	3.09
Accounts receivable	7,295	7,581	7,179	6,711	6,996	7,208	7,724	8,132	9,185	2.92
Inventories	5,791	6,358	6,295	6,179	6,206	5,483	5,893	6,698	7,335	3.00
Net property, plant and equipment	21,042	26,887	27,339	26,579	24,675	23,153	24,223	25,351	27,841	3.56
RATIOS, PERCENT:										
INCOME TO SALES:										
Before tax	6.44	4.89	2.96	-3.80	-0.60	2.40	5.41	6.76	7.51	3.55
After tax	4.49	3.43	1.95	-2.99	-0.72	2.12	3.37	4.81	5.47	2.44
INCOME TO STOCKHOLDERS' EQUITY:										
Before tax	20.09	13.97	8.48	-11.31	-1.86	6.17	14.24	18.19	22.99	10.11
After tax	14.01	9.82	5.59	-8.90	-2.23	5.43	8.86	12.92	16.74	6.92
INCOME TO TOTAL ASSETS:										
Before tax	6.85	4.63	2.77	-3.28	-0.52	2.11	5.15	6.67	8.08	3.61
After tax	4.78	3.26	1.83	-2.58	-0.62	1.86	3.20	4.74	5.88	2.48
AS A PERCENT OF TOTAL ASSETS:										
Property, plant and equipment	41.01	44.49	46.01	44.92	41.00	39.30	40.17	40.57	42.54	42.22
Short-term debt	4.14	3.78	3.53	3.58	3.71	2.60	2.11	3.20	3.19	3.31
Long-term debt	35.34	34.61	33.79	30.58	32.75	31.37	28.21	27.11	27.86	31.29
Stockholders' equity	34.11	33.16	32.70	28.97	27.80	34.17	36.15	36.64	35.13	33.20

1. For income and asset amounts, compound annual growth rate; for ratios, average of ratios for the years shown.

Source: U.S. Bureau of the Census, Quarterly Financial Report.

Notes: Parentheses ( ) indicate negative items, e.g., net expenses, charges, or losses. Net property, plant, and equipment is net of accumulated depreciation. Because the samples used to collect the data change, retained earnings at the end of a given year will not exactly equal the previous year's retained earnings plus the current year's retained income and credits.

CANADA

Canada's nonmetallic mineral products industry had 1,519 establishments and 42,661 employees in 1993 (Table 7). Its largest category is ready-mix concrete (which accounted for 25 percent of industry shipments in 1993), followed by glass and glass products (19.8 percent), and other nonmetallic mineral products (19.7 percent). Concrete products (13.1 percent in 1993) and cement (12.6 percent) account for most of the remaining shipments.

Industry shipments during 1987-1994 hit their high of Can$8.0 billion in 1989, fell to a low of Can$6.0 billion in 1992, and then edged up to Can$6.7 billion in 1994 (Table 8). Employment declined from 1988 onward, falling to 41,913 by 1994, for a 4.25 percent annual rate of decline during 1987-1994. Production worker numbers fell at an even faster rate, which reduced their share of the workforce to 77 percent in 1994 from 80 percent in 1988. Production worker earnings averaged Can$15.84 in 1994, compared with Can$13.35 in 1988, and the average workweek was 40.6 hours.

TABLE 7

CANADA: COMPONENT INDUSTRIES OF NON-METALLIC MINERAL PRODUCTS (CSIC 3500), 1993

(Monetary values in Canadian dollars)

INDUSTRY NAME	CSIC	ESTABLISH-MENTS (NUMBER)	EMPLOYMENT		VALUE OF SHIPMENTS (MILLIONS)	AVERAGE HOURLY EARNINGS[1]
			NUMBER	PERCENT OF INDUSTRY TOTAL		
NON METALLIC MINERAL PRODUCTS INDUSTRIES	35	1,519	42,661	100.0	CAN$6,226.7	CAN$15.68
Clay products	351	51	1,686	4.0	184.8	14.29
Clay products (from domestic clay)	3511	17	779	1.8	90.9	14.87
Clay products (from imported clay)	3512	34	907	2.1	93.9	13.88
Cement	352	21	2,786	6.5	787.0	21.30
Concrete products	354	360	7,387	17.3	817.1	14.27
Concrete pipe	3541	42	1,287	3.0	170.0	15.34
Structural concrete products	3542	64	2,100	4.9	226.3	15.62
Other concrete products	3549	254	4,000	9.4	420.9	13.17
Ready-mix concrete	355	647	10,438	24.5	1,562.4	15.59
Glass and glass products	356	155	9,676	22.7	1,234.7	15.93
Primary glass and containers	3561	19	4,354	10.2	606.3	16.91
Glass products (except containers)	3562	136	5,322	12.5	628.4	15.16
Abrasives	357	30	1,395	3.3	238.7	14.27
Lime	358	13	731	1.7	173.6	19.11
Other non-metallic mineral products	359	242	8,562	20.1	1,228.4	15.31
Refractories	3591	28	1,644	3.9	205.3	15.46
Asbestos products	3592	7	230	0.5	22.2	10.43
Gypsum products	3593	29	1,825	4.3	357.2	17.04
Non-metal mineral insulating material	3594	34	2,370	5.6	385.0	16.00
Other non-metal mineral products n.e.c.	3599	144	2,493	5.8	258.7	13.73

1. Including overtime.

Source: Adapted from Statistics Canada, *Manufacturing Industries of Canada* (Cat. No. 31-203).

TABLE 8

CANADIAN EMPLOYMENT AND SHIPMENTS: NON-METALLIC MINERAL INDUSTRY, 1987-1994

(Monetary values in Canadian dollars)

	1987	1988	1989	1990	1991	1992	1993	1994	CHANGE[1]
All employees	56,822	57,837	57,317	54,605	49,334	45,055	42,661	41,913	-4.25
Establishments	1,547	1,663	1,688	1,691	1,593	1,550	1,519	1,522	-0.23
Employees per establishment	37	35	34	32	31	29	28	28	-4.03
Production workers per establishment	.....	28	27	26	24	22	22	21	-4.29
PRODUCTION WORKERS:									
Total	.....	45,974	46,019	43,482	38,756	34,711	32,919	32,344	-5.69
Percent of all employees	.....	79.5	80.3	79.6	78.6	77.0	77.2	77.2	.....
Male	.....	42,367	42,273	39,837	35,828	.....	.....	.....	.....
Female	.....	3,607	3,746	3,645	2,928	.....	.....	.....	.....
Percent of all production workers	.....	7.8	8.1	8.4	7.6	.....	.....	.....	.....
Average hourly earnings	.....	13.35	13.91	14.47	14.76	15.30	15.68	15.84	2.89
Average weekly earnings	.....	546.42	573.09	589.94	596.75	619.65	636.61	642.63	2.74
Average weekly hours	.....	40.9	41.2	40.8	40.4	40.5	40.6	40.6	-0.15
Shipments (millions)	7,444	7,804	7,984	7,392	6,252	5,980	6,227	6,698	-1.50

1. Compound annual growth rate.

Source: Adapted from Statistics Canada, Manufacturing Industries of Canada (Cat. No. 31-203).

MEXICO

Mexico's nonmetallic products industry includes pottery and ceramics, clay for construction, glass products, cement and other (Table 9). The industry in 1993 included 24,361 production units and 183,868 employees—113,561 production workers, 29,502 nonproduction employees, and 40,805 unpaid (family) workers. Employees worked an average of 250 days a year and paid workers received an annual average income (salary plus benefits) of 26,487 new pesos ($8,479). Earnings of production workers averaged 12,957 new pesos ($4,148) a year, compared with 39,778 ($12,734) for nonproduction employees. Industry employment between 1988 and 1995 declined by 0.68 a year, to 150,304 (Table 10). The industry gross domestic product rose 2.21 percent a year during that period, to $5.2 billion (constant 1993 dollars) in 1995.

TABLE 9

MEXICO: COMPONENT INDUSTRIES OF NON-METALLIC MINERALS (CMAP 36), 1993

(Monetary values in 1993 Mexican New Pesos)

						ALL WORKERS						
							PAID WORKERS					
				PERCENT	AVERAGE		PRODUCTION WORKERS		NONPRODUCTION EMPLOYEES		BENEFITS	UNPAID
		NUMBER		OF INDUSTRY	DAYS	REMUN-		WAGES AND		WAGES AND	PER PAID	WORKERS,
INDUSTRY	CMAP	OF UNITS	NUMBER	TOTAL	WORKED	ERATION[1]	NUMBER	SALARIES	NUMBER	SALARIES	EMPLOYEE	NUMBER
Non-metallic products	36	24,361	183,868	100	250	26,487	113,561	12,957	29,502	39,778	7,999	40,805
Pottery and ceramics	3611	5,967	19,931	11	276	12,821	7,746	8,545	919	27,473	2,268	11,266
Clay for construction	3612	9,100	47,426	26	229	21,606	23,322	11,455	5,894	32,684	5,868	18,210
Glass products	3620	785	35,181	19	271	34,536	26,326	15,297	7,915	49,245	11,392	940
Cement and other	3691	8,509	81,330	44	253	26,282	56,167	13,092	14,774	38,302	7,940	10,389

1. Average annual remuneration including benefits.

Source: INEGI, Census Economics 1994.

TABLE 10

MEXICAN GROSS DOMESTIC PRODUCT AND EMPLOYMENT: NON-METALLIC MINERALS, 1988-1995

	1988	1989	1990	1991	1992	1993	1994	1995	CHANGE[1]
GROSS DOMESTIC PRODUCT:									
Millions of constant 1993 new pesos	13,920.4	14,582.0	15,526.7	16,078.3	17,093.8	17,557.1	18,358.2	16,226.2	2.21
Millions of constant 1993 U.S. dollars[2]	4,456.4	4,668.2	4,970.6	5,147.2	5,472.3	5,620.6	5,877.1	5,194.6	2.21
TOTAL EMPLOYMENT:									
Nonmetallic minerals	157,668	167,832	178,737	179,074	183,210	183,108	174,841	150,304	-0.68
Glass	34,255	36,037	38,391	38,174	37,673	35,631	33,168	32,551	-0.73
Cement	16,088	16,128	14,985	14,238	13,634	12,434	11,683	10,155	-6.36
Non-metallic mineral based products	107,325	115,667	125,361	126,662	131,903	135,043	129,990	107,598	0.04

1. Compound annual growth rate.

2. Converted at 3.1237 new pesos to the U.S. dollar.

Source: Sistema de Cuentas Nacionales de Mexico, INEGI.

INTERNATIONAL TRADE

United States.   Global U.S. exports of stone, clay, and glass rose from $3.2 billion in 1990 to $5.1 billion in 1996, while imports climbed from $5.8 billion to $9.1 billion (Table 11).   The export gain was insufficient to offset import growth, resulting in a 1996 trade deficit of $4.0 billion, compared with $2.6 billion in 1990.   In 1996, Canada received about 34 percent of U.S. exports and supplied 15 percent of U.S. imports.   Mexico accounted for about 10 percent of both U.S. exports and imports that year.

Canada.   Canadian exports to the United States rose from $774 million in 1990 to $1.4 billion in 1996, while U.S. exports to Canada went from $1.2 billion to $1.7 billion (Table 11). This resulted in a U.S. trade surplus with Canada of $294 million in 1996, down from $434 million in 1990.

Mexico.   Mexican exports to the United States climbed from $501 million to $971 million during the 1990-1996 period, and U.S. exports to Mexico rose from $318 million to $478 million (Table 11).   Mexico's surplus in trade with the United States thus grew from $183 million in 1990 to almost $500 million in 1996.   Mexican exports to Canada more than doubled between 1990 and 1996, to $55 million, while Canada's shipments to Mexico totaled only $3 million in 1996.

NAFTA.   During the 1990-1996 period, trade balances of the three NAFTA countries changed considerably.   The U.S. balance went from surpluses in 1990 through 1994 ($211 million that year) to a deficit of $199 million in 1996 (Table 11).   Canada's deficit during 1990-1996 declined from $459 million to $346 million, while Mexico's surplus rose from $209 million to $545 million.

TABLE 11

INTERNATIONAL TRADE, STONE, CLAY AND GLASS

(Millions of U.S. dollars)

	1989[1]	1990	1991	1992	1993	1994	1995	1996
GLOBAL TRADE, U.S.								
IMPORTS								
Value	5,758.3	5,812.6	5,522.2	5,906.9	6,431.0	7,593.7	8,497.6	9,088.4
Ratio to new supply[2]	8.8	8.9	9.0	9.1	9.4	10.2	.....	.....
Ratio to apparent consumption[3]	9.1	9.3	9.5	9.7	10.0	10.8	.....	.....
EXPORTS								
Value	2,529.4	3,166.7	3,384.8	3,671.1	3,844.1	4,215.2	4,796.3	5,097.0
Ratio to comparable domestic shipments	4.2	5.3	6.0	6.2	6.2	6.3	.....	.....
TRADE BALANCE	(3,228.9)	(2,645.9)	(2,137.4)	(2,235.8)	(2,586.9)	(3,378.5)	(3,701.3)	(3,991.4)
BILATERAL TRADE: NAFTA[4]								
U.S. exports to Canada	739.6	1,207.1	1,294.3	1,339.9	1,426.1	1,543.7	1,619.5	1,701.5
Canadian exports to U.S.	793.6	773.5	730.6	767.3	916.4	1,072.2	1,260.7	1,407.7
U.S. exports to Mexico	188.5	317.8	348.7	412.2	364.0	474.7	415.5	478.2
Mexican exports to U.S.	512.8	501.4	502.9	542.3	590.0	735.2	814.1	970.6
Canadian exports to Mexico	2.2	2.1	2.3	2.5	4.2	2.7	3.2	3.1
Mexican exports to Canada	19.5	27.3	36.2	36.7	45.0	53.7	49.7	55.2
TRADE BALANCES WITHIN NAFTA[5]								
Canada	36.7	(458.8)	(597.6)	(606.8)	(550.5)	(522.5)	(405.3)	(345.9)
Mexico	341.6	208.8	188.1	164.3	266.8	311.5	445.1	544.5
United States	(378.2)	250.0	409.5	442.5	283.7	211.0	(39.8)	(198.6)

1. 1989 and earlier data on U.S. exports to Canada for manufacturing total and manufacturing industries are not comparable with data for 1990 and later years because of a change in the reporting system. The NAFTA trade balances for the U.S. and Canada also are affected.

2. New supply equals comparable domestic shipments plus imports for consumption.

3. Apparent consumption equals comparable domestic shipments plus imports for consumption less exports.

4. Amounts less than U.S. $100,000 shown as zero.

5. Parentheses indicate an excess of imports over exports. Because of commodity coding and other data differences among the three countries, these trade balances are only rough estimates and should be used with caution.

Source for U.S. Global Trade: U.S. Department of Commerce, International Trade Administration.

Source for U.S. -Canada and U.S.-Mexico Bilateral Trade: U.S. Bureau of the Census.

Source for Canada-Mexico and Mexico-Canada Bilateral Trade: Statistics Canada, Foreign Trade Division, Special tabulation, March 1997, converted to U.S. dollars by the editors.

TEXTILE MILL PRODUCTS

THE UNITED STATES

Products and Processes. The textile industry generally ranks only 14th or 15th among U.S. manufacturing industries in terms of industry shipments, but it is of much greater importance in the Southeast, where four-fifths of the industry now is concentrated. The products of the industry are as diverse as the consumer's need for apparel, home furnishings, cordage, yarn, thread, and numerous other items that can be produced from natural and manmade fibers.

Table 1 gives a profile of the industry in 1992 (latest year for which economic census data are available). The major components of the textile industry are knitting mills (with 24 percent of industry shipments in 1992), yarn and thread mills (almost 16 percent), and carpet and rug mills (almost 14 percent). Broadwoven fabric mills for cotton, manmade fiber and silk, and wool had relatively small shares individually but together accounted for 23 percent of 1992 shipments. The industry also includes textile finishing mills, narrow fabric mills, and producers of coated fabrics, tire cord and fabric, nonwoven fabrics, and cordage and twine. Raw materials for the industry include natural fibers like cotton, wool, and silk and synthetics such as rayon, nylon, polyester, acrylic, olefin, and spandex.

Employment in the industry is on a downward track as a result of relatively slow growth, stiff foreign competition, and improving productivity. Projections to the year 2005 show the industry workforce declining by more than 100,000 from the 1993 level to around 568,100 employees (Table 2). The only employment increase projected is for carpet and rug manufacturing. Average hourly earnings of production workers, at $8.88 in 1993, are among the lowest in manufacturing. The highest 1993 earnings, $10.45 per hour, were in miscellaneous textile goods.

TABLE 1

UNITED STATES: COMPONENT INDUSTRIES OF TEXTILE MILL PRODUCTS (SIC 22), 1992

(Monetary values in millions of U.S. dollars)

INDUSTRY	SIC	ESTABLISH-MENTS	SHIPMENTS VALUE	SHIPMENTS PERCENT BY 4 LARGEST COMPANIES	VALUE ADDED BY MANUFACTURE	NEW CAPITAL EXPENDI-TURES	EMPLOY-MENT[1]	PAYROLL
TEXTILE MILL PRODUCTS	22	5,886	$70,753.0	....	$30,059.6	$2,224.8	616,400	$12,397.6
Broadwoven fabric mills, cotton	221	321	5,810.8	....	2,503.5	168.1	55,900	1,147.2
Weaving mills, cotton	2211	321	5,810.8	39	2,503.5	168.1	55,900	1,147.2
Broadwoven fabric mills, manmade fiber and silk	222	421	8,767.1	....	4,008.1	357.0	87,200	1,849.9
Weaving mills, synthetics	2221	421	8,767.1	22	4,008.1	357.0	87,200	1,849.9
Broadwoven fabric mills, wool	223	99	1,612.4	....	690.5	32.7	13,700	279.4
Weaving and finishing mills, wool	2231	99	1,612.4	....	690.5	32.7	13,700	279.4
Narrow fabric mills	224	258	1,273.5	....	705.9	48.9	16,900	322.9
Narrow fabric mills	2241	258	1,273.5	22	705.9	48.9	16,900	322.9
Knitting mills	225	2,097	16,985.0	....	8,051.9	525.6	195,000	3,399.9
Women's hosiery, except socks	2251	151	1,843.0	55	977.5	65.0	25,300	398.0
Hosiery, n.e.c.	2252	447	2,575.3	20	1,258.1	66.1	38,000	598.9
Knit outerwear mills	2253	677	4,170.3	46	2,291.1	117.0	52,600	871.2
Knit underwear mills	2254	69	891.1	64	498.8	35.5	12,000	190.2
Circular knit fabric mills	2257	390	4,957.7	30	1,903.6	160.3	43,900	862.8
Lace and warp knit fabric mills	2258	279	2,311.8	36	999.8	75.9	20,000	418.1
Knitting mills, n.e.c.	2259	84	235.8	58	123.0	5.8	3,200	60.7
Textile finishing, except wool	226	485	7,088.7	....	2,785.6	188.7	50,900	1,143.2
Finishing plants, cotton	2261	171	2,577.2	49	828.7	60.5	16,000	346.3
Finishing plants, synthetics	2262	181	3,437.6	36	1,531.1	104.4	25,000	601.1
Finishing plants, n.e.c.	2269	133	1,073.9	32	425.9	23.8	9,900	195.8
Carpets and rugs	227	446	9,828.3	40	3,479.6	144.5	49,400	1,087.6
Yarn and thread mills	228	596	11,274.0	....	4,059.4	401.2	92,200	1,744.4
Yarn spinning mills	2281	396	7,668.6	26	2,890.6	294.0	68,700	1,288.4
Throwing and winding mills	2282	135	2,768.4	68	840.3	85.2	17,400	340.6
Thread mills	2284	65	837.0	75	328.4	22.0	6,200	115.4
Miscellaneous textile goods	229	1,163	8,113.3	....	3,775.1	358.0	55,200	1,423.2
Coated fabrics, not rubberized	2295	194	1,573.4	20	628.4	48.5	9,500	279.3
Tire cord and fabric	2296	15	975.5	75	399.5	37.2	5,100	111.8
Nonwoven fabrics	2297	169	3,029.5	39	1,394.1	166.5	16,700	472.7
Cordage and twine	2298	210	672.0	31	349.8	21.5	6,700	138.6
Textile goods, n.e.c.	2299	575	1,862.8	18	1,003.3	84.4	17,200	420.7

1. Employment numbers from the economic censuses differ in definition and classification from the Bureau of Labor Statistics estimates in Table 2. Year-to-year comparisons between Table 1 and Table 2 are not appropriate.

Source: U.S. Bureau of the Census, 1992 Census of Manufactures.

TABLE 2

U.S. EMPLOYMENT AND EARNINGS: TEXTILE MILL PRODUCTS

| INDUSTRY | SIC | 1993 | | | 2005 |
| | | EMPLOYMENT[1] | | AVERAGE HOURLY EARNINGS (U.S. DOLLARS)[2] | PROJECTED EMPLOYMENT[3] |
		NUMBER OF PERSONS	PERCENT OF INDUSTRY TOTAL		
TEXTILE MILL PRODUCTS	22	675,100	100.0	$8.88	568,100
Weaving, finishing, yarn and thread mills	221-4,6,8	361,000	53.5		281,200
Broadwoven fabric mills, cotton	221	83,800	12.4	9.25	....
Broadwoven fabric mills, synthetics	222	69,500	10.3	9.69	....
Broadwoven fabric mills, wool	223	17,300	2.6	9.40	....
Narrow fabric mills	224	22,100	3.3	8.20	....
Knitting mills	225	202,900	30.1	8.11	173,000
Women's hosiery, except socks	2251	28,500	4.2	7.59	....
Hosiery, n.e.c.	2252	39,400	5.8	7.79	....
Knit outerwear mills	2253	59,500	8.8	7.73	....
Knit underwear mills	2254	26,300	3.9	8.12	....
Weft knit fabric mills	2257	27,700	4.1	9.16	....
Textile finishing, except wool	226	71,300	10.6	9.18	....
Finishing plants, cotton	2261	32,200	4.8	9.08	....
Finishing plants, synthetics	2262	24,700	3.7	9.66	....
Carpets and rugs	227	59,900	8.9	8.91	65,000
Yarn and thread mills	228	97,000	14.4	8.61	....
Yarn spinning mills	2281	76,100	11.3	8.57	....
Throwing and winding mills	2282	14,200	2.1	8.94	....
Miscellaneous textile goods	229	51,200	7.6	10.45	48,900

1. Total payroll employment. Employment data from the economic censuses, shown in Table 1, differ in definition and classification from the Bureau of Labor Statistics estimates in this table. Year-to-year comparisons between Table 1 and Table 2 are not appropriate.

2. Earnings of production workers, including overtime.

3. Number of persons, moderate projection by the U.S. Bureau of Labor Statistics.

Source: Bureau of Labor Statistics.

FIGURE 1

U.S. EMPLOYMENT IN TEXTILE MILL PRODUCTS

Percent distribution by region, 1995

The textile industry is the most geographically concentrated of all the manufacturing industries except tobacco, with about 80 percent of its total employment in the Southeast.

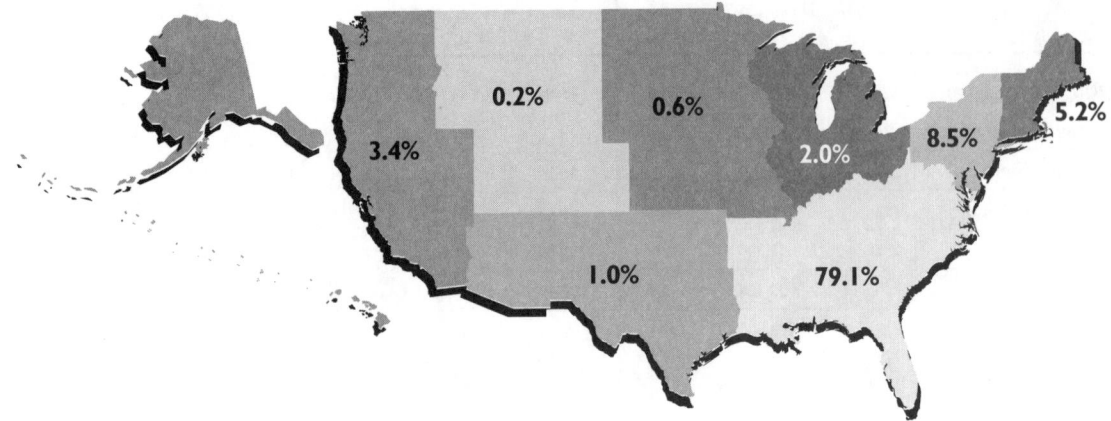

Source: U.S. Department of Commerce, Bureau of Economic Analysis.

What's New.[1] Industry performance in 1997 received a boost from a 9 percent gain in new orders during the fourth quarter of 1996, compared to year-earlier figures. Unfilled orders also rose in late 1996, while inventories held steady.

Consumption changes of note in 1996 included a shift from natural to manmade fibers. Consumption of manmade fibers rose 1.6 percent as that of wool tumbled 13 percent and cotton declined slightly. Denim production in 1996 dipped 1 percent, its first decline since 1990. New orders for carpets in 1996 stayed well ahead of shipments, and unfilled orders as of December 1996 were 40 percent above those in December 1995. Upholstery production has been growing steadily since 1992.

In the trade arena, the growing export of narrow fabrics, trimmings, and cut-fabric pieces for assembly in the Caribbean, Mexico, and Asia is an important trend that affects both the textile and apparel industries.

Output. Inflation-adjusted textile industry shipments reached their highest levels in 1994 and 1995 and then declined moderately in 1996. The trend in industry shipments is almost the reverse of that for employment, which has declined during most of the past 10 years (Figure 2). Shipments increased at an annual rate of 2.52 percent in current dollars (0.96 when adjusted for inflation) from 1987 to 1996 (Table 3). The dip in 1996 shipments, to $78.5 billion from $79.7 billion in 1995, reflected slow growth early in the year.

According to industry reports, mill fiber consumption in 1996 rose about 1 percent from 1995 to 15.97 billion pounds as consumption jumped 7 percent above year-earlier levels in the final quarter. All the gain was in manmade fibers as demand for natural fibers tumbled. Production of broad-woven fabric in 1996 declined 4 percent from 1995 to 15.7 billion square yards, despite a pickup in the final quarter. Carpet shipments in 1996 rose 1.5 percent over the previous year's, and production of upholstery rose 5.4 percent to 534 million square yards.

Investment. New capital expenditures by the industry (Table 3) grew between 1991 and 1994, but then declined slightly in 1995 to $2.9 billion. Research and development spending also trended upward during those years. Capacity utilization was 82.1 percent in 1996, down

[1] *Information in this section includes data from the American Textile Manufacturers Institute.*

FIGURE 2

U.S. EMPLOYMENT AND SHIPMENTS: TEXTILE MILL PRODUCTS

Total payroll employment and manufacturers' inflation-adjusted shipments

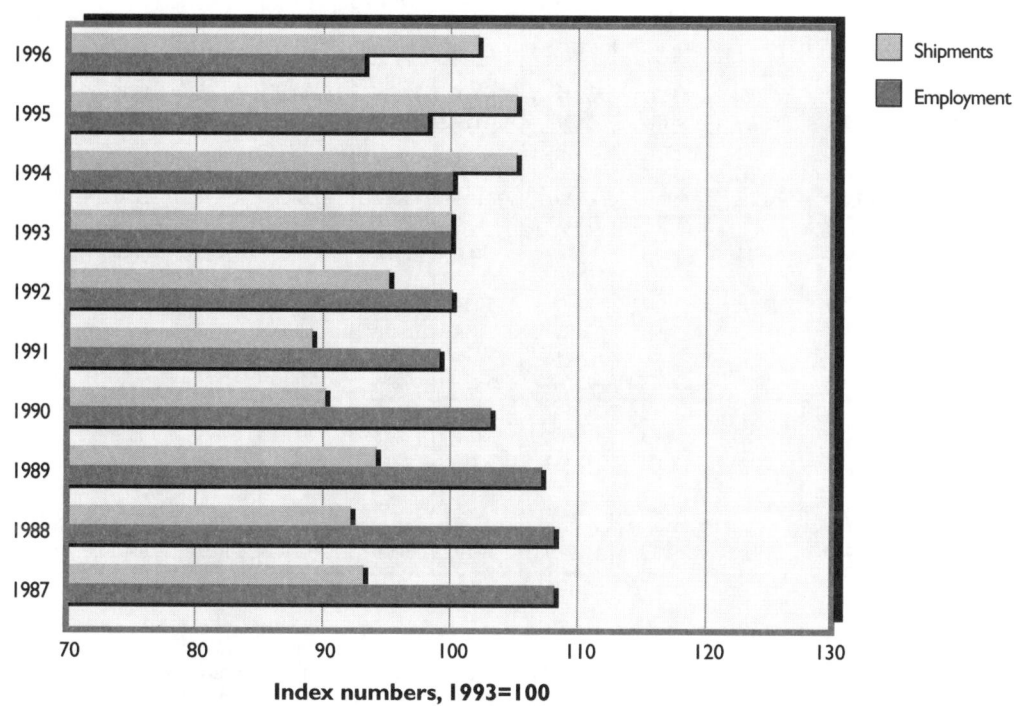

Index numbers, 1993=100

Source: U.S. Bureau of Labor Statistics, U.S. Department of Commerce, and estimates by the editors.

sharply from the recent peak of 91.6 percent in 1994, indicating that investment in plant and equipment may slow in the future.

Prices. Producer prices for textiles rose at an annual rate of 1.58 percent between 1987 and 1996. Most of that gain was in 1987-1990 and 1995-1996 (Table 3).

Workforce and Employment. Reflecting industry restructuring and competition from foreign suppliers, textile industry employment has declined at an annual rate of 1.65 percent during the past 10 years (Table 4). Production workers accounted for 84.6 percent of total employment in 1996, slightly less than the 86.8 percent recorded in 1987. The share of women in the workforce during that time slipped from 48.5 percent in 1987 to 46.6 percent in 1996.

The average workweek was 40.6 hours in 1996, about the midpoint of the narrow 10-year range (Table 4). However, the industry reports that the workweek in the fourth quarter of 1996 was more than 2 percent above that in the same 1995 period as a result of increased orders for textile mill products.

The decline in employment during a period of generally increasing production and shipments indicates that industry productivity has increased over the past 10 years. Outsourcing, which has been increasing among all industries, is another likely factor behind the employment decline.

Hourly earnings of production workers have risen at an annual rate of 3.40 percent since 1987, reaching $9.69 in 1996. When adjusted for inflation, however, average hourly earnings declined at a 0.15 percent rate (Table 4).

TABLE 3

U.S. OUTPUT, INVESTMENT, AND PRICES: TEXTILE MILL PRODUCTS

(Millions of U.S. dollars, except as noted)

	1987	1988	1989	1990	1991	1992	1993	1994	1995	1996	GROWTH RATE 1987-1996[1]
VALUE OF SHIPMENTS:											
BY INDUSTRY:											
Current dollars	62,787	64,627	67,264	65,532	65,439	70,753	73,955	78,027	79,742	78,533	2.52
Constant 1992 dollars	69,340	68,562	69,731	66,645	65,979	70,753	74,409	78,451	77,780	75,569	0.96
BY PRODUCT:											
Current dollars	61,518	63,610	65,747	64,986	65,266	70,008	73,216	77,249	79,092	79,092	2.83
Constant 1992 dollars	67,998	67,484	68,213	66,125	65,807	70,008	73,662	77,686	77,130	76,092	1.26
OTHER OUTPUT MEASURES:											
Industrial production, 1993=100	91.3	90.0	91.5	88.3	87.9	94.8	100.0	105.0	104.2	101.0	1.13
Gross domestic product:											
Current dollars	20,127	20,487	20,916	21,742	22,279	25,434	25,519	25,585	....	....	....
Percent of total GDP	0.4	0.4	0.4	0.4	0.4	0.4	0.4	0.4	....	....	....
Rank in manufacturing	16	16	16	16	16	15	16	16	....	....	....
Chained (1992) dollars	21,795	21,466	21,875	22,573	23,068	25,434	25,858	27,251	....	....	....
INVESTMENT-RELATED MEASURES:											
Capacity utilization, percent	90.5	88.0	87.9	83.4	81.7	87.1	89.8	91.6	87.4	82.1	....
New capital expenditures	2,028	2,261	2,390	2,372	2,183	2,225	2,450	2,961	2,879	....	....
Research and development spending[2]	243	215	....	260	236	261	286	316	....	....	....
Producer prices, 1993=100[3]	90.3	94.0	96.2	98.2	99.0	100.0	100.0	100.0	102.6	104.0	1.58

1. Compound annual growth rate.

2. Also includes apparel (SIC 23).

3. Prices received by domestic producers.

Sources: Shipments and new capital expenditures: U.S. Department of Commerce for 1987-1995, editor's estimates for constant dollar data for 1987-88 and all shipments data for 1996; Industrial production and capacity utilization: Federal Reserve Board of Governors; GDP: Bureau of Economic Analysis; Research and development spending: National Science Foundation; Producer prices: Bureau of Labor Statistics.

TABLE 4

U.S. EMPLOYMENT, HOURS, AND EARNINGS: TEXTILE MILL PRODUCTS

(Monetary values in U.S. dollars)

	1987	1988	1989	1990	1991	1992	1993	1994	1995	1996	CHANGE[1]
NUMBER OF EMPLOYEES, IN THOUSANDS:											
Total	725	728	720	691	670	674	675	676	663	624	-1.65
Production workers	630	632	622	593	574	577	575	575	560	528	-1.93
Percent of total	86.8	86.8	86.4	85.8	85.7	85.6	85.1	85.0	84.5	84.6	.....
Women	352	352	350	336	325	324	322	321	312	291	-2.09
Percent of total	48.5	48.3	48.6	48.6	48.6	48.1	47.7	47.4	47.1	46.6	.....
HOURS AND EARNINGS OF PRODUCTION WORKERS:											
Average hourly earnings, U.S. dollars[2]											
Current dollars	7.17	7.38	7.67	8.02	8.3	8.6	8.88	9.13	9.41	9.69	3.40
1992 dollars[3]	8.81	8.71	8.65	8.60	8.54	8.60	8.64	8.66	8.68	8.69	-0.15
Average weekly hours	41.8	41.0	40.9	39.9	40.6	41.1	41.4	41.6	40.8	40.6	-0.32
Average weekly earnings, current U.S. dollars	299.71	302.58	313.7	320.00	336.98	353.46	367.63	379.81	383.93	393.41	3.07

1. Compound annual growth rate, 1987-1996.

2. Including overtime.

3. Converted to 1992 dollars using Consumer Price Index for Urban Wage Earners and Clerical Workers.

Source: Bureau of Labor Statistics.

FIGURE 3

U.S. OCCUPATIONAL INJURY AND ILLNESS RATES:
TEXTILE MILL PRODUCTS, 1995

Incidence of nonfatal injuries and illnesses per 100 full-time workers

The nonfatal illnesses and injuries rate in the textile industry in 1995 was 8.2 cases per 100 workers, compared with 11.6 for all manufacturing.

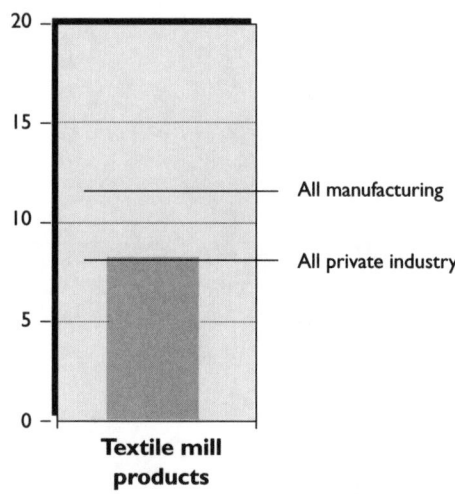

Source: U.S. Bureau of Labor Statistics.

TABLE 5

U.S. EMPLOYMENT PROJECTIONS BY MAJOR OCCUPATIONAL GROUP:
TEXTILE MILL PRODUCTS

Projections to the year 2005 indicate that employment in the textile industry will slide further. Declines are forecast for all occupational areas except professional specialties.

| OCCUPATION | 1994 | | PROJECTIONS, 2005 | | | |
| | NUMBER OF EMPLOYEES | PERCENT OF INDUSTRY TOTAL | NUMBER OF EMPLOYEES | | | PERCENT OF INDUSTRY TOTAL, MODERATE PROJECTIONS |
			LOW	MODERATE	HIGH	
Total, all occupations	673,200	100.0	520,500	568,100	608,200	100.0
Executive, administrative, and managerial	29,921	4.4	23,961	25,981	27,708	4.6
Professional specialties	7,678	1.1	7,195	7,824	8,354	1.4
Technicians and related support	5,698	0.9	4,304	4,677	4,994	0.8
Marketing and sales	8,303	1.2	6,934	7,445	7,910	1.3
Administrative support including clerical	53,600	8.0	38,108	41,362	44,174	7.3
Service	9,596	1.4	6,320	6,912	7,406	1.2
Agriculture, forestry, and fisheries occupations	85	0.0	67	73	78	0.0
Precision production, craft, and repair	117,620	17.5	102,066	111,710	119,714	19.7
Operators, fabricators, assemblers	440,700	65.5	331,544	362,116	387,864	63.7

Source: Bureau of Labor Statistics, November 1995.

Finance. Corporate income of the textile industry in 1996 improved considerably over the 1995 level but still was below the recent high achieved in 1992; changes have been less dramatic in production worker earnings (Figure 4).

While industry sales and receipts during the past 10 years grew at an annual rate of 4.13 percent, operating income rose only 3.12 percent, to $4.3 billion in 1996. After-tax income rose at an even slower 2.10 percent annual rate, to $1.8 billion in 1996, with wide year-to-year fluctuations (Table 6). After-tax income in 1996 averaged 2.67 percent of sales and 9.57 percent of stockholders' equity. Inventories rose at an annual rate of 4.67 percent during the past 10 years, but dipped in 1996 after reaching a peak $11.2 billion in 1995. Long-term debt as a percentage of total assets declined in 1996 to 30.81 percent, the lowest level since 1992, while short-term debt rose slightly to 3.45 percent.

FIGURE 4

U.S. CORPORATE INCOME AND WORKER EARNINGS: TEXTILE MILL PRODUCTS

Corporate operating income and aggregate production worker earnings

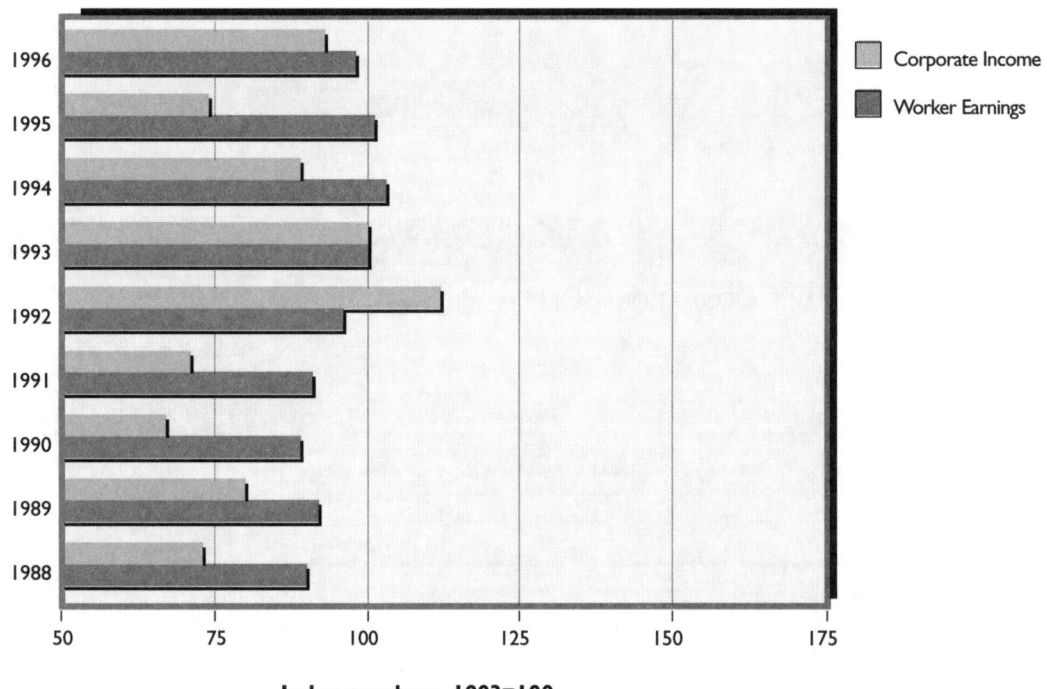

Index numbers, 1993=100

Source: U.S. Bureau of Labor Statistics, U.S. Bureau of the Census, and estimates by the editors.

TABLE 6

U.S. CORPORATE INCOME AND ASSETS: TEXTILE MILL PRODUCTS

(Monetary values in millions of U.S. dollars)

INCOME AND EXPENSES	1988	1989	1990	1991	1992	1993	1994	1995	1996	CHANGE OR AVERAGE[1]
Sales and receipts	49,863	57,185	54,696	55,721	60,942	62,419	63,161	66,329	68,918	4.13
Depreciation and amortization	(1,562)	(1,880)	(2,007)	(2,101)	(2,206)	(2,268)	(2,395)	(2,635)	(2,654)	6.85
Other operating costs	(44,971)	(51,660)	(49,641)	(50,419)	(53,635)	(55,619)	(56,736)	(60,303)	(62,007)	4.10
Income from operations	3,330	3,646	3,049	3,201	5,102	4,533	4,032	3,390	4,258	3.12
Nonoperating income (expenditures)	(1,029)	(2,287)	(2,103)	(1,784)	(1,829)	(1,985)	(1,251)	(1,770)	(1,590)	....
Income before taxes	2,300	1,359	945	1,417	3,271	2,546	2,781	1,622	2,668	1.87
Income after taxes	1,560	742	433	829	2,102	1,441	1,757	891	1,842	2.10
Cash dividends	438	544	682	388	604	681	702	560	679	5.63
Income retained in business	1,122	197	(249)	441	1,498	761	1,055	332	1,163	0.45
Direct credits (charges)	(765)	(453)	(52)	(301)	(563)	61	(500)	(83)	(278)	....
Ending retained earnings	9,903	8,141	8,829	9,049	11,551	10,886	10,655	11,094	11,780	2.19
ASSETS, END OF YEAR:										
Total	33,440	40,322	41,147	40,744	42,639	43,364	44,735	48,513	48,000	4.62
Accounts receivable	6,610	7,401	7,404	7,738	7,840	8,002	8,298	8,824	8,975	3.90
Inventories	7,301	8,451	8,500	8,461	8,977	9,326	10,093	11,244	10,518	4.67
Net property, plant and equipment	11,244	13,739	14,699	13,756	14,658	15,267	17,091	18,316	17,670	5.81
RATIOS, PERCENT:										
INCOME TO SALES:										
Before tax	4.61	2.38	1.73	2.54	5.37	4.08	4.40	2.45	3.87	3.49
After tax	3.13	1.30	0.79	1.49	3.45	2.31	2.78	1.34	2.67	2.14
INCOME TO STOCKHOLDERS' EQUITY:										
Before tax	17.89	11.05	7.01	9.84	17.32	13.80	15.80	8.56	13.86	12.79
After tax	12.14	6.03	3.21	5.76	11.13	7.81	9.98	4.70	9.57	7.81
INCOME TO TOTAL ASSETS:										
Before tax	6.88	3.37	2.30	3.48	7.67	5.87	6.22	3.34	5.56	4.96
After tax	4.67	1.84	1.05	2.03	4.93	3.32	3.93	1.84	3.84	3.05
AS A PERCENT OF TOTAL ASSETS:										
Property, plant and equipment	33.62	34.07	35.72	33.76	34.38	35.21	38.20	37.75	36.81	35.50
Short-term debt	4.02	3.83	3.45	3.24	5.82	2.96	2.75	3.18	3.45	3.63
Long-term debt	33.26	39.60	38.60	33.40	26.79	31.31	34.39	34.14	30.81	33.59
Stockholders' equity	38.44	30.50	32.78	35.34	44.30	42.54	39.34	39.06	40.11	38.04

1. For income and asset amounts, compound annual growth rate; for ratios, average of ratios for the years shown.

Source: U.S. Bureau of the Census, Quarterly Financial Report.

Notes: Parentheses ( ) indicate negative items, e.g., net expenses, charges, or losses. Net property, plant, and equipment is net of accumulated depreciation. Because the samples used to collect the data change, retained earnings at the end of a given year will not exactly equal the previous year's retained earnings plus the current year's retained income and credits.

CANADA

Canada's textile mill industries in 1993 included 928 establishments, 46,022 employees, and industry shipments valued at Can$5.6 billion. The industries consist of two main categories—primary textiles and textile products. The primary textile category in 1993 had 184 establishments and 18,346 employees (Table 7). Its largest component is spun yarn and woven cloth (with over half of total industry shipments in 1993), followed by manmade fiber and filament yarn (about one-fourth), and broad knitted fabric (15 percent).

The textile products subindustry (Table 7) had 744 establishments with 27,676 employees in 1993. The largest component, with 72 percent of textile products shipments in 1993, is other textile products, including narrow fabric, contract dyeing and finishing, household products, and hygiene products. The other categories include carpets, mats, and rugs (14.3 percent), canvas and related products (9.2 percent), and natural fibers and felt products (6.4 percent).

Industry shipments in 1994 improved to Can$6.2 billion from low levels of the previous two years; however, this was not enough to match levels reached in 1987-1989 (Table 8). Employment rose to 46,730 from its low 1993 level but also was well below levels of the late 1980s. Production workers accounted for 80 percent of the workforce in 1994. Average hourly earnings in the industry were Can$11.75 in 1994, and the average workweek was 40.6 hours.

TABLE 7

CANADA: COMPONENT INDUSTRIES OF TEXTILE MILL INDUSTRIES (CSIC 18 AND 19), 1993

(Monetary values in Canadian dollars)

INDUSTRY NAME	CSIC	ESTABLISH-MENTS (NUMBER)	EMPLOYMENT		VALUE OF SHIPMENTS (MILLIONS)	AVERAGE HOURLY EARNINGS[1]
			NUMBER	PERCENT OF INDUSTRY TOTAL		
TEXTILE MILL INDUSTRIES[2]	18+19	928	46,022	100.0	CAN$5,609.0	CAN$11.65
PRIMARY TEXTILE INDUSTRIES	18	184	18,346	39.9	2,733.3	13.44
Manmade fibre and filament yarn	181	25	4,601	10.0	909.9	15.95
Spun yarn and woven cloth	182	95	10,946	23.8	1,338.8	13.06
Wool yarn and woven cloth	1821	24	2,628	5.7	278.9	14.23
Other spun yarn and woven cloth	1829	71	8,318	18.1	1,059.9	12.73
Broad knitted fabrics	183	64	2,799	6.1	484.7	10.91
TEXTILE PRODUCTS INDUSTRIES	19	744	27,676	60.1	2,875.7	10.48
Natural fibres and felt products	191	32	1,783	3.9	244.5	12.20
Carpets, mats, and rugs	192	28	3,952	8.6	736.3	12.61
Canvas and related products	193	147	2,003	4.4	140.8	9.78
Other textile products	199	537	19,938	43.3	1,754.1	9.97
Narrow fabric industry	1991	36	1,532	3.3	118.5	9.63
Contract textile dyeing and finishing	1992	147	4,280	9.3	278.3	10.48
Household products of textile material	1993	167	6,480	14.1	575.5	9.03
Hygiene products of textile material	1994	12	1,510	3.3	232.5	15.02

1. Production worker earnings, including overtime.

2. CSIC 18, Canadian primary textile industry, and CSIC 19, textile products industries, are combined for easier comparison to the U.S. industry.

Source: Adapted from Statistics Canada, *Manufacturing Industries of Canada* (Cat. No. 31-203).

TABLE 8

CANADIAN EMPLOYMENT AND SHIPMENTS: TEXTILE MILL INDUSTRIES, 1987-1994

(Monetary values in Canadian dollars)

	1987	1988	1989	1990	1991	1992	1993	1994	CHANGE[1]
All employees	60,704	61,890	59,588	56,040	52,927	46,166	46,022	46,730	-3.67
Establishments	1,077	1,200	1,136	1,183	1,063	979	928	856	-3.23
Employees per establishment	56	52	52	47	50	47	50	55	-0.46
Production workers per establishment	.....	42	43	38	39	37	39	43	0.65
PRODUCTION WORKERS:									
Total	.....	50,097	48,598	45,271	41,936	36,241	36,488	37,158	-4.86
Percent of all employees	.....	80.9	81.6	80.8	79.2	78.5	79.3	79.5	.....
Male	.....	29,677	28,918	26,743	24,351	.....	.....	.....	.....
Female	.....	20,420	19,680	18,528	17,585	.....	.....	.....	.....
Percent of all production workers	.....	40.8	40.5	40.9	41.9	.....	.....	.....	.....
Average hourly earnings	.....	9.67	9.88	10.61	10.83	11.43	11.65	11.75	3.30
Average weekly earnings	.....	387.28	408.14	427.48	433.20	453.54	467.28	477.52	3.55
Average weekly hours	.....	40.1	41.3	40.3	40.0	39.7	40.1	40.6	0.24
Shipments (millions)	6,376	6,584	6,624	6,143	5,735	5,486	5,609	6,243	-0.30

1. Compound annual growth rate.

Source: Adapted from Statistics Canada, *Manufacturing Industries of Canada* (Cat. No. 31-203).

MEXICO

Mexico's textiles, garments, and leather industries had 44,126 units (establishments) and 547,290 employees in 1993. Employees worked an average of 271 days a year, and their yearly earnings plus benefits averaged 16,258 new pesos (about $5,204). Production workers numbered 409,938 and had average annual earnings of 9,709 new pesos ($3,108), while there were 80,224 nonproduction employees with earnings of 24,101 new pesos ($7,715). Textile-related subindustries are the strong fiber and cord industry; spinning, weaving, and finishing of soft fibers; manufacture using textiles; and fabrication of cloth. In 1993, they had 227,782 employees (including 168,109 production workers) and 14,232 establishments (Table 9).

Total gross domestic product (GDP) of the textiles, garments, and leather industry rose at a rate of 0.67 percent per year between 1988 and 1995 to the equivalent of $5.8 billion (in 1993 dollars). Another measurement shows that employment in the textiles subindustry declined at the annual rate of 1.98 percent between 1988 and 1995 from 191,900 workers to 166,823 (Table 10). Despite the overall slow GDP growth and declining employment, Mexico has greatly increased its textile exports to the United States (see the International Trade section that follows).

TABLE 9

MEXICO: COMPONENT INDUSTRIES OF TEXTILES, GARMENTS, AND LEATHER (CMAP 32), 1993

(Monetary values in 1993 Mexican New Pesos)

			ALL WORKERS									
							PAID WORKERS					
							PRODUCTION WORKERS		NONPRODUCTION EMPLOYEES		BENEFITS	UNPAID
INDUSTRY	CMAP	NUMBER OF UNITS	NUMBER	PERCENT OF INDUSTRY TOTAL	AVERAGE DAYS WORKED	REMUN-ERATION[1]	NUMBER	WAGES AND SALARIES	NUMBER	WAGES AND SALARIES	PER PAID EMPLOYEE	WORKERS, NUMBER
Textiles, garments and leather	32	44,126	547,290	100	271	16,258	409,938	9,709	80,224	24,101	4,193	57,128
Strong fiber and cord industry	3211	2,171	8,991	2	297	14,121	4,199	8,254	862	23,634	3,247	3,930
Spinning, weaving, and finishing of soft fibers	3212	5,461	116,753	21	301	22,372	88,191	12,841	21,694	28,707	6,398	6,868
Manufacture using textiles	3213	4,968	63,458	12	289	18,717	46,727	9,112	10,030	28,332	6,209	6,701
Fabrication of cloth	3214	1,632	38,580	7	245	17,034	28,992	10,528	7,354	22,161	4,152	2,234
Garments	3220	22,560	209,623	38	361	11,720	155,599	7,451	26,095	19,576	2,527	27,929
Leather (excluding footwear)	3230	2,348	26,855	5	275	16,345	20,041	10,424	3,889	23,823	3,744	2,925
Footwear	3240	4,986	83,030	15	260	16,173	66,189	10,782	10,300	23,273	3,709	6,541

1. Average annual remuneration including benefits.

Source: INEGI, Censos Economicos 1994.

TABLE 10

MEXICAN GROSS DOMESTIC PRODUCT AND EMPLOYMENT: TEXTILES, GARMENTS, AND LEATHER INDUSTRY, 1988-1995

	1988	1989	1990	1991	1992	1993	1994	1995	CHANGE[1]
GROSS DOMESTIC PRODUCT:									
Millions of constant 1993 new pesos	17,407.8	18,250.7	19,306.0	19,810.9	19,792.9	19,256.8	19,459.9	18,237.4	0.67
Millions of constant 1993 U.S. dollars[2]	5,572.8	5,842.6	6,180.5	6,342.1	6,336.4	6,164.8	6,229.8	5,838.4	0.67
TOTAL EMPLOYMENT:									
Textiles, garments, and leather	522,032	527,761	527,607	531,034	518,280	515,872	497,454	481,961	-1.13
Textiles	191,900	198,715	199,305	197,452	189,808	184,100	173,561	166,823	-1.98
Garments (Apparel)	217,984	217,746	219,949	221,290	220,586	230,609	231,336	231,619	0.87
Leather	112,148	111,300	108,353	112,292	107,886	101,163	92,557	83,519	-4.12

1. Compound annual growth rate.

2. Converted at 3.1237 new pesos to the U.S. dollar.

Source: Sistema de Cuentas Nacionales de Mexico, INEGI.

INTERNATIONAL TRADE

United States. U.S. textile industry exports to all countries between 1990 and 1996 rose faster than imports, resulting in a 21 percent reduction in the textile trade deficit (Table 11). Exports totaled almost $6.2 billion in 1996, or 70 percent more than in 1990. Imports in 1996 were almost $7.2 billion, up 47 percent from 1990. The textile trade deficit thus was $992 million in 1996, compared with $1.25 billion in 1990.

In addition to large gains in shipments to Mexico and Canada (see below), exports to the nations of the Caribbean Basin Initiative (CBI) rose 13 percent in 1996 and accounted for 8 percent of total U.S. textile exports, according to the American Textile Manufacturers Institute. The CBI region now ranks fourth behind Canada, Mexico, and the European Union as a market for U.S. textile products. CBI nations import narrow fabric pieces and related products like thread and trimmings that are shipped with cut fabric for apparel assembly there.

According to the Institute, the slow (3 percent) growth in U.S. imports of textiles in 1996 came largely because of a 14 percent decline in imports from China. Two explanations for the slowdown include borrowing by China from 1996 U.S. import quotas to compensate for overshipments in 1995 and the U.S. government's tightening of certain quotas as a penalty for illegal transshipments by China. Another reason given was the Chinese government's delay in paying export subsidies until the fourth quarter of 1996.

Canada. Textile trade between Canada and the United States more than doubled from 1990 to 1996. U.S. exports to Canada rose 81 percent during the seven-year period to $1.72 billion in 1996 (Table 11). Canadian exports to the United States climbed 220 percent to $918 million. Canadian-Mexican trade is relatively insignificant, although Mexican exports to Canada more than doubled between 1990 and 1996 to $57 million.

Mexico. U.S.-Mexican trade also has grown rapidly (Table 11). U.S. textile exports to Mexico rose over the 1990-1996 period by 144 percent, with an especially large gain in 1996, when they surpassed $1 billion for the first time. The gain reflected, in part, large U.S. exports of trimmings, elastic, sewing thread, and other products shipped with cut fabric for apparel assembly in Mexico. At the same time, Mexican textile exports to the United States jumped from $104 million in 1990 to $483 million in 1996.

NAFTA. Under NAFTA, tariffs are being phased out over a 10-year period for North American products that meet NAFTA rules of origin (textiles and apparel must be produced from yarn made in a NAFTA country in order to benefit fully from the Agreement). The rules of NAFTA also provide for temporary relief for producers seriously damaged by increased imports of textiles and apparel from member countries.

The trade data strongly suggest that NAFTA (and, before that, the Canadian-U.S. Free Trade Agreement) has already stimulated North American textile trade (Table 11). Trade balances within NAFTA show a growing surplus for the United States until 1994, after which it fell slightly. The U.S. trade surplus in 1996 was $1.36 billion, compared with $985 million in 1990. Canada's trade deficit rose from $686 million in 1990 to a peak $876 million in 1995 before declining slightly in 1996. Mexico's deficit rose from $300 million in 1990 to a high of $626 million in 1994 and then settled back to $499 million by 1996. These figures, of course, mask the fact that some of the textile products shipped to Mexico are coming back into the United States as components of apparel made with U.S. cut fabric pieces, thread, and trimmings.

TABLE 11

INTERNATIONAL TRADE, TEXTILE MILL PRODUCTS

(Millions of U.S. dollars)

	1989[1]	1990	1991	1992	1993	1994	1995	1996
GLOBAL TRADE, U.S.								
IMPORTS								
Value	4,786.1	4,887.7	5,374.7	5,842.5	6,161.2	6,534.0	6,964.6	7,169.0
Ratio to new supply[2]	8.3	8.6	9.4	9.5	9.7	9.7	.....	.....
Ratio to apparent consumption[3]	8.7	9.2	10.1	10.3	10.5	10.5	.....	.....
EXPORTS								
Value	2,803.0	3,635.6	4,101.0	4,466.5	4,687.1	5,150.9	5,696.2	6,177.0
Ratio to comparable domestic shipments	5.3	7.0	7.9	8.1	8.2	8.5	.....	.....
TRADE BALANCE	(1,983.1)	(1,252.1)	(1,273.7)	(1,376.0)	(1,474.1)	(1,383.1)	(1,268.4)	(992.0)
BILATERAL TRADE: NAFTA[4]								
U.S. exports to Canada	515.3	952.2	1,090.5	1,139.3	1,253.7	1,404.0	1,582.2	1,724.7
Canadian exports to U.S.	265.6	287.0	320.8	415.1	490.0	630.0	755.5	918.3
U.S. exports to Mexico	320.0	423.6	441.1	583.0	642.6	799.6	795.9	1,034.7
Mexican exports to U.S.	83.4	103.8	121.9	112.5	119.1	146.5	291.7	482.6
Canadian exports to Mexico	7.2	5.2	4.2	7.8	3.6	5.0	2.4	3.8
Mexican exports to Canada	33.7	25.9	27.7	27.1	28.7	32.4	51.9	57.1
TRADE BALANCES WITHIN NAFTA[5]								
Canada	(276.2)	(685.9)	(793.2)	(743.5)	(788.8)	(801.4)	(876.2)	(859.7)
Mexico	(210.1)	(299.1)	(295.7)	(451.2)	(498.4)	(625.7)	(454.7)	(498.8)
United States	486.3	985.0	1,088.9	1,194.7	1,287.1	1,427.1	1,330.9	1,358.5

1. 1989 and earlier data on U.S. exports to Canada for manufacturing total and manufacturing industries are not comparable with data for 1990 and later years because of a change in the reporting system. The NAFTA trade balances for the U.S. and Canada also are affected.

2. New supply equals comparable domestic shipments plus imports for consumption.

3. Apparent consumption equals comparable domestic shipments plus imports for consumption less exports.

4. Amounts less than U.S. $100,000 shown as zero.

5. Parentheses indicate an excess of imports over exports. Because of commodity coding and other data differences among the three countries, these trade balances are only rough estimates and should be used with caution.

Source for U.S. Global Trade: U.S. Department of Commerce, International Trade Administration.

Source for U.S. -Canada and U.S.-Mexico Bilateral Trade: U.S. Bureau of the Census.

Source for Canada-Mexico and Mexico-Canada Bilateral Trade: Statistics Canada, Foreign Trade Division, Special tabulation, March 1997, converted to U.S. dollars by the editors.

TOBACCO PRODUCTS

THE UNITED STATES

Products and Processes. Tobacco products in 1996 ranked as the smallest U.S. manufacturing industry in terms of employment and was the second smallest (next to leather) in value of industry shipments. The industry's products include cigarettes, chewing and smoking tobacco, and cigars. These products are manufactured from tobacco types such as flue-cured, fire-cured, air-cured, burley, oriental, and cigar wrapper.

Although listed in the U.S. Standard Industrial Classification as a separate industry, most tobacco product manufacturing today is carried out by business conglomerates that produce a wide variety of food and related products. As a result, financial data for tobacco are included within the totals for food and beverages (see Table 6 in the Food and Beverage chapter).

In 1992 (the latest year for which economic census data are available), only 114 establishments, with a combined payroll of $1.5 billion, were engaged in tobacco production (Table 1). Cigarette production accounted for 85 percent of the $35.2 billion worth of industry shipments that year. The tobacco stemming and redrying category was a distant second with about 10 percent of the total.

Employment by the industry is in a steep downtrend, reflecting cost cutting and the impact of tightening restrictions on smoking and the sale of tobacco products.   Projections to the year 2005 show employment falling nearly 40 percent below the 1993 level to 26,300 people (Table 2). Hourly earnings in the industry are the highest in manufacturing; in 1993, they averaged $16.89 for the industry as a whole and $21.04 for workers engaged in cigarette manufacturing.

TABLE 1

UNITED STATES: COMPONENT INDUSTRIES OF TOBACCO PRODUCTS (SIC 21), 1992

(Monetary values in millions of U.S. dollars)

INDUSTRY	SIC	ESTABLISH-MENTS	SHIPMENTS VALUE	SHIPMENTS PERCENT BY 4 LARGEST COMPANIES	VALUE ADDED BY MANUFACTURE	NEW CAPITAL EXPENDI-TURES	EMPLOY-MENT[1]	PAYROLL
TOBACCO PRODUCTS	21	114	$35,197.8	....	$27,206.6	$389.3	38,000	$1,524.4
Cigarettes	211	11	29,746.1	93	24,801.9	322.5	25,400	1,205.0
Cigars	212	27	286.8	74	190.1	3.0	2,600	53.3
Chewing and smoking tobacco	213	30	1,608.4	87	1,212.5	15.1	3,200	91.8
Tobacco stemming and redrying	214	46	3,556.5	72	1,002.0	48.6	6,800	174.2

1. Employment numbers from the economic censuses differ in definition and classification from the Bureau of Labor Statistics estimates in Table 2. Year-to-year comparisons between Table 1 and Table 2 are not appropriate.

Source: U.S. Bureau of the Census, 1992 Census of Manufactures.

TABLE 2

U.S. EMPLOYMENT AND EARNINGS: TOBACCO PRODUCTS

INDUSTRY	SIC	1993			2005
		EMPLOYMENT[1]		AVERAGE HOURLY EARNINGS (U.S. DOLLARS)[2]	PROJECTED EMPLOYMENT[3]
		NUMBER OF PERSONS	PERCENT OF INDUSTRY TOTAL		
TOBACCO PRODUCTS	21	43,700	100.0	$16.89	26,300
Cigarettes	211	30,400	69.6	21.04	....

1. Total payroll employment. Employment data from the economic censuses, shown in Table 1, differ in definition and classification from the Bureau of Labor Statistics estimates in this table. Year-to-year comparisons between Table 1 and Table 2 are not appropriate.

2. Earnings of production workers, including overtime.

3. Number of persons, moderate projection by the U.S. Bureau of Labor Statistics.

Source: Bureau of Labor Statistics.

FIGURE 1

U.S. EMPLOYMENT IN TOBACCO PRODUCTS

Percent distribution by region, 1995

Manufacturing of tobacco products is concentrated in the Southeast, where most U.S. tobacco is grown (North Carolina, Kentucky, Virginia, and Tennessee being the primary producers there). This region accounted for 92 percent of industry employment in 1995. The next most important area, with 5 percent of total product manufacturing, was the Mid-Atlantic region, where Maryland is a sizable tobacco producer.

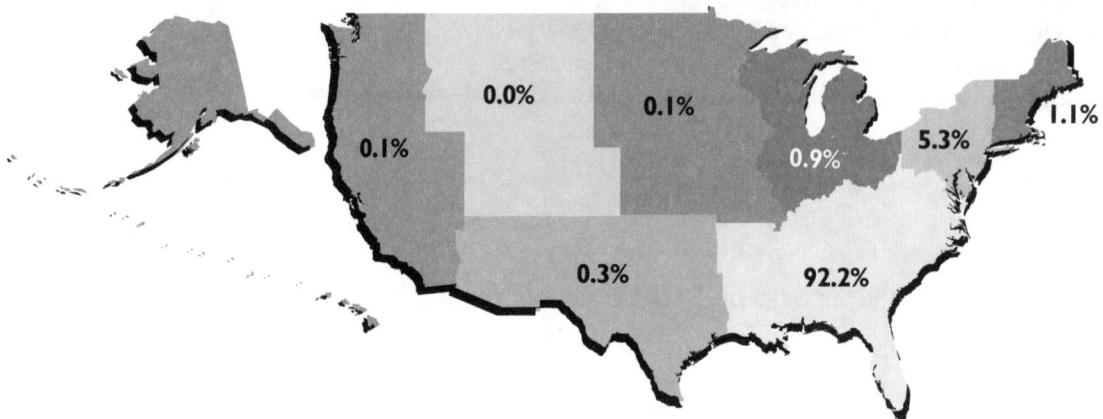

Source: U.S. Department of Commerce, Bureau of Economic Analysis.

What's New. The tax cut and balanced-budget agreement signed in July 1997 calls for an increase of 10 cents per pack in the federal tax on cigarettes in the year 2000 and another five cents in 2002. The federal tax currently is 24 cents per pack.

How high do cigarette prices have to go to achieve a 30-percent cut in smoking by teenagers within five years and 60 percent in 10 years? This was a key question in the extended debate over the tentative $368.5 billion settlement negotiated in June 1997 between the tobacco industry and states seeking to recoup smoking-related Medicaid costs (but subject to approval by the President and Congress). A study by the Council of Economic Advisers and the Treasury Department estimated that to cover costs of the original settlement, the tobacco industry would have to boost cigarette prices by 62 cents per pack. This increase, the study concluded, would result in a reduction of 28 percent in the number of teens that smoke, to 2.7 million by 2002, from levels that would otherwise have occurred. Some sources, however, said that an increase of $1.50 or more would be needed to bring the called-for reductions within an age group where smoking is still fashionable.

President Clinton, in his September 17 assessment of the proposed agreement, endorsed the latter view, saying that industry payments and penalties must boost cigarette prices by $1.50 a pack over the next 10 years. In addition, President Clinton called for compensation to tobacco growers—two-thirds of whom are in North Carolina and Kentucky—who would be hurt by resulting production cuts. Clinton did not specify how the price increase would be brought about. He also did not endorse the original agreement's protection for the industry from punitive damages and other class-action lawsuits, leaving these and most other details to Congress to work out. How soon that might happen, if at all, was still up in the air as of press time. Yet without the settlement, the number of teen smokers is forecast to rise to 3.7 million by 2002 from 3.5 million currently. The greater impact of any settlement, moreover, will be on adult smokers, who outnumber teen smokers by more than 14 to 1 and are more easily persuaded by health concerns and antismoking campaigns than are teens.

Terms of the tentative settlement reached in June 1997 by the tobacco industry and state attorneys general include:

- $368.5 billion in payments by the industry over the next 25 years and then $15 billion a year for an indefinite period in return for some immunity from lawsuits. Much of the money would go toward settling lawsuits by states seeking compensation for smoking-related Medicaid outlays. Money also would be used to help individual smokers kick the habit and for antismoking campaigns, health care for uninsured children, attorney fees, and costs related to enforcement of the new regulations.

- Prohibitions on advertising directed toward young people, billboard and sporting event advertising, all vending machine sales of cigarettes, and most smoking in public places and in workplaces without specially ventilated smoking areas. The proposed settlement further requires stronger warning labels to the effect that cigarettes are addictive, can cause cancer, and can cause fatal lung diseases in nonsmokers.

- Fines to be paid by cigarette manufacturers if smoking by young people fails to drop 30 percent in five years, 50 percent in seven years, and 60 percent in 10 years.

- Food and Drug Administration regulation of nicotine as a drug, although nicotine use cannot be banned before the year 2009.

- Limitations on class-action suits that may be brought against tobacco manufacturers, on consolidation of multiple suits, and on punitive damages for past conduct. The tentative pact also restricts lawsuits by insurers seeking to recover outlays related to smoking.

Meanwhile, some state lawsuits are moving forward. On August 25, 1997, Florida and the major tobacco companies reached a milestone settlement requiring tobacco companies to pay the state $11.3 billion during the next 25 years and to take actions to discourage underage smoking. The money will be used to reimburse state Medicaid expenses; settle other Florida claims; and cover the cost of punitive damages, educational campaigns against smoking, substance abuse programs, and children's health care. The companies also must initially eliminate advertising of tobacco products near schools, eventually cease all billboard and transit advertising, and cooperate in the passage of laws limiting cigarette vending machines to adult-only areas and in strengthening civil penalties against the sale of tobacco to minors and possession by minors. The agreement is similar to a $3.6 million settlement with Mississippi and has been called possibly the largest approved legal settlement in history.

Even as the United States moved to restrict cigarette sales and consumption, Canada's largest cigarette maker, Imperial Tobacco, was preparing to introduce its first U.S. cigarette brand, according to an August 18, 1997, article in *USA Today*. The new brand, Mercer, is promoted as a natural cigarette without additives (but not nicotine-free). It was to be test marketed in Portland, Oregon, beginning September 15, 1997. Imperial Tobacco apparently made the move because restrictions on tobacco sales in Canada are even tougher than those pending in the United States.

FIGURE 2

U.S. EMPLOYMENT AND SHIPMENTS, TOBACCO PRODUCTS

Total payroll employment and manufacturers' inflation-adjusted shipments

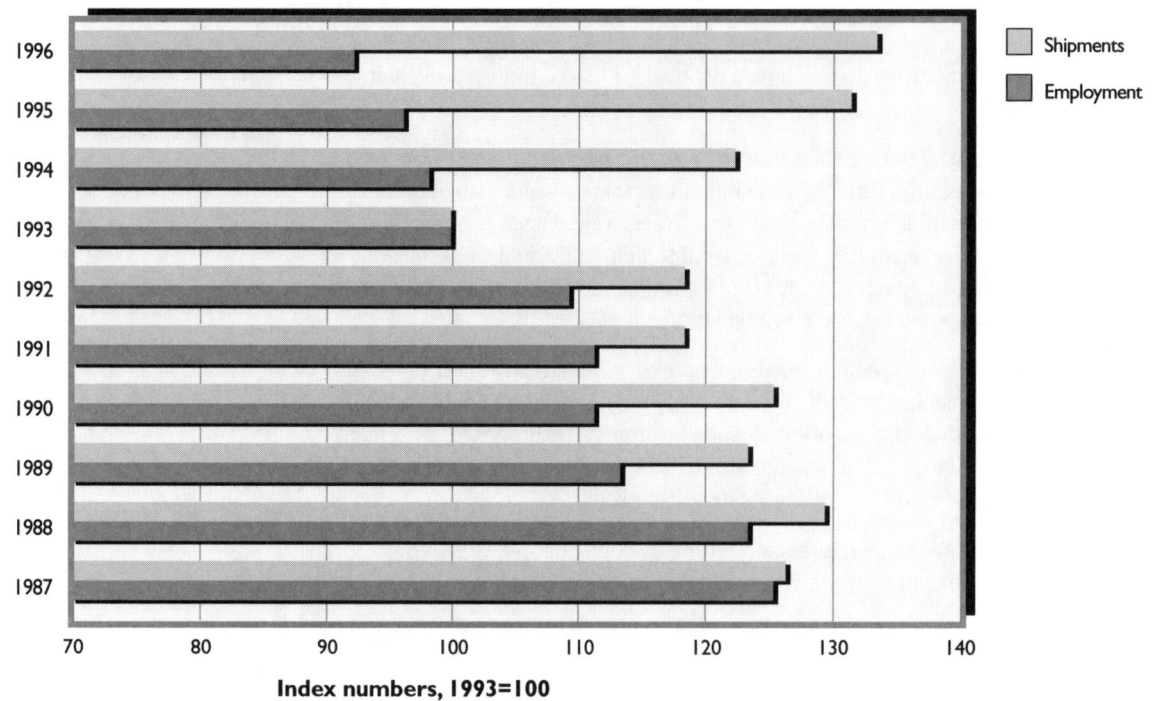

Source: U.S. Bureau of Labor Statistics, U.S. Department of Commerce, and estimates by the editors.

Output. The value of tobacco product shipments (in constant dollars) followed a downward trend between 1988 and 1993, only to rise sharply in 1994 and continue higher in the next two years; in contrast, employment has declined steadily since 1987 (Figure 2). In current-dollar terms, industry shipments reached a peak of $35.2 billion in 1992, fell sharply in 1993, and then rose in each of the following years to end at $34.5 billion in 1996 (Table 3). Shipment growth over the 10-year period was at a compound annual average rate of 5.8 percent in current dollars, but only 0.6 percent in inflation-adjusted dollars.

Investment. New capital expenditures by the industry have declined from their peak level of $464 million in 1987 (Table 3). They hit a low of $278 million in 1990 but rebounded quickly to the $400-million range.

Prices. Producer prices for tobacco products have shown extreme fluctuations during the past 10 years, rising about 82 percent between 1987 and 1992 and then giving up about 16 percent of that gain by 1996 (Table 3). Cost cutting by major producers may account for some of the recent decline.

TABLE 3

U.S. OUTPUT, INVESTMENT, AND PRICES: TOBACCO PRODUCTS

(Millions of U.S. dollars, except as noted)

	1987	1988	1989	1990	1991	1992	1993	1994	1995	1996	GROWTH RATE 1987-1996[1]
VALUE OF SHIPMENTS:											
By INDUSTRY:											
Current dollars	20,757	23,809	25,875	29,856	31,943	35,198	28,383	30,021	32,984	34,492	5.80
Constant 1992 dollars	37,562	38,470	36,740	37,343	35,276	35,198	29,779	36,425	38,972	39,548	0.57
By PRODUCT:											
Current dollars	20,153	23,249	25,229	29,208	31,136	34,360	27,729	29,215	32,204	33,676	5.87
Constant 1992 dollars	36,443	37,541	35,795	36,523	34,398	34,360	29,091	35,442	38,056	38,619	0.65
OTHER OUTPUT MEASURES:											
Industrial production, 1993=100	124.6	126.8	125.5	125.5	117.7	119.0	100.0	123.5	126.4	125.7	0.10
Gross domestic product:											
Current dollars	13,129	14,279	14,894	16,380	17,790	18,365	16,517	16,550	....	....	....
Percent of total GDP	0.3	0.3	0.3	0.3	0.3	0.3	0.3	0.2	....	....	....
Rank in manufacturing	19	19	19	18	18	18	19	19	....	....	....
Chained (1992) dollars	31,806	30,730	27,176	24,851	21,527	18,365	17,452	22,005	....	....	....
INVESTMENT-RELATED MEASURES:											
New capital expenditures	464	410	401	278	405	389	388	387	411	....	....
Producer prices, 1993=100[2]	58.1	65.0	74.0	84.1	95.1	105.6	100.0	86.2	88.6	91.3	5.15

1. Compound annual growth rate.

2. Prices received by domestic producers.

Sources: Shipments and new capital expenditures: U.S. Department of Commerce for 1987-1995, editor's estimates for constant dollar data for 1987-88 and all shipments data for 1996; Industrial production and capacity utilization: Federal Reserve Board of Governors; GDP: Bureau of Economic Analysis; Research and development spending: National Science Foundation; Producer prices: Bureau of Labor Statistics.

Workforce and Employment. Employment in the tobacco products industry declined by 3.2 percent a year between 1987 and 1996, from 55,000 employees to 41,000 (Table 4). Production worker employment fell at a slightly slower annual pace of 3.0 percent and accounted for 78 percent of the workforce in 1996. Employment of women declined by 3.7 percent a year to 13,000, or 30.5 percent of the workforce, in 1996. Production worker earnings averaged $19.41 in 1995, falling slightly to $19.34 in 1996. In both years, tobacco narrowly exceeded petroleum ($19.36 in 1995 and $19.32 in 1996) to record the highest hourly earnings for all manufacturing. The average workweek in 1996 was 40 hours, slightly higher than in past years.

TABLE 4

U.S. EMPLOYMENT, HOURS, AND EARNINGS: TOBACCO PRODUCTS

(Monetary values in U.S. dollars)

	1987	1988	1989	1990	1991	1992	1993	1994	1995	1996	CHANGE[1]
NUMBER OF EMPLOYEES, IN THOUSANDS:											
Total	55	54	50	49	49	48	44	43	42	41	-3.21
Production workers	42	41	37	36	36	36	33	33	32	32	-2.98
Percent of total	76.4	0.8	74.0	74.1	74.1	74.4	74.5	76.7	76.0	78.0	.....
Women	18	18	17	17	16	16	14	14	13	13	-3.73
Percent of total	32.0	33.0	33.2	33.7	33.3	32.9	32.7	31.4	29.8	30.5	.....
HOURS AND EARNINGS OF PRODUCTION WORKERS:											
Average hourly earnings, U.S. dollars[2]											
Current dollars	14.07	14.67	15.31	16.23	16.77	16.92	16.89	19.07	19.41	19.34	3.60
1992 dollars[3]	17.29	17.32	17.26	17.40	17.25	16.92	16.43	18.09	17.91	17.35	0.04
Average weekly hours	39.0	39.8	38.6	39.2	39.1	38.6	37.4	39.3	39.6	40.0	0.28
Average weekly earnings, current U.S. dollars	548.73	583.87	590.97	636.22	655.71	653.11	631.69	749.45	768.64	773.60	3.89

1. Compound annual growth rate, 1987-1996.

2. Including overtime.

3. Converted to 1992 dollars using Consumer Price Index for Urban Wage Earners and Clerical Workers.

Source: Bureau of Labor Statistics.

FIGURE 3

U.S. OCCUPATIONAL INJURY AND ILLNESS RATES: TOBACCO PRODUCTS, 1995

Nonfatal occupational injuries and illnesses in the tobacco products industry averaged 5.6 cases per 100 workers in 1995, one of the lowest levels in manufacturing.

Incidence of nonfatal injuries and illnesses per 100 full-time workers

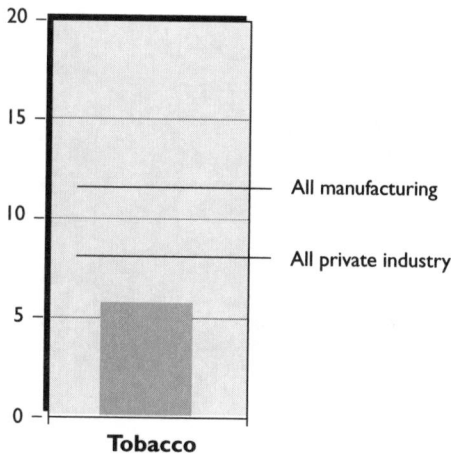

Source: U.S. Bureau of Labor Statistics.

TABLE 5

U.S. EMPLOYMENT PROJECTIONS BY MAJOR OCCUPATIONAL GROUP: TOBACCO PRODUCTS

Industry employment by the year 2005 is projected to be 38 percent below the 42,200 of 1994, with declines in all occupational areas.

OCCUPATION	1994		PROJECTIONS, 2005			
	NUMBER OF EMPLOYEES	PERCENT OF INDUSTRY TOTAL	NUMBER OF EMPLOYEES			PERCENT OF INDUSTRY TOTAL, MODERATE PROJECTIONS
			Low	MODERATE	HIGH	
Total, all occupations	42,200	100.0	28,200	26,300	25,600	100.0
Executive, administrative, and managerial	4,421	10.5	3,069	2,862	2,786	10.9
Professional specialties	2,090	5.0	1,739	1,622	1,579	6.2
Technicians and related support	1,286	3.1	838	782	761	3.0
Marketing and sales	2,358	5.6	1,610	1,502	1,462	5.7
Administrative support including clerical	3,776	9.0	2,199	2,051	1,996	7.8
Service	709	1.7	417	389	379	1.5
Agriculture, forestry, and fisheries occupations	157	0.4	107	100	98	0.4
Precision production, craft, and repair	9,234	21.9	6,400	5,969	5,810	22.7
Operators, fabricators, assemblers	18,169	43.1	11,820	11,024	10,730	41.9

Source: Bureau of Labor Statistics, November 1995.

Finance. Financial data are not broken out for the tobacco products industry, but rather are included with those for food and beverages.

CANADA

Canada's tobacco industry in 1993 had 17 establishments, 4,778 employees, and shipments valued at Can$2 billion (Table 7). The industry is divided into two subindustries—leaf tobacco and tobacco products. Shipments by the tobacco products industry totaled Can$1.66 billion in 1993, compared with only Can$348 million for leaf tobacco.

As in the United States, employment in the small Canadian tobacco industry declined through 1994, while industry shipments continued to rise (Table 8). Tobacco product shipments reached Can$2.5 billion in 1994, a record high some 23 percent above the previous year's shipments and 45 percent above 1987's, reflecting price increases as a result of a hike in taxes on tobacco. Employment during that period fell to 4,600 in 1994 from 5,948 in 1987. Production workers have generally accounted for about 56 percent of the workforce. Average hourly wages of production workers in 1994 were Can$27.98, and the average workweek was 36.1 hours.

TABLE 7

CANADA: COMPONENT INDUSTRIES OF TOBACCO PRODUCTS INDUSTRIES (CSIC 12), 1993

(Monetary values in Canadian dollars)

INDUSTRY NAME	CSIC	ESTABLISH-MENTS (NUMBER)	EMPLOYMENT		VALUE OF SHIPMENTS (MILLIONS)	AVERAGE HOURLY EARNINGS[1]
			NUMBER	PERCENT OF INDUSTRY TOTAL		
TOBACCO PRODUCTS INDUSTRY	12	17	4,778	100.0	CAN$2,006.5	CAN$25.12
Leaf tobacco	121	6	565	11.8	347.7	17.58
Tobacco products	122	11	4,213	88.2	1,658.7	26.71

1. Including overtime.

Source: Adapted from Statistics Canada, *Manufacturing Industries of Canada* (Cat. No. 31-203).

TABLE 8

CANADIAN EMPLOYMENT AND SHIPMENTS: TOBACCO PRODUCTS, 1987-1994

(Monetary values in Canadian dollars)

	1987	1988	1989	1990	1991	1992	1993	1994	CHANGE[1]
All employees	5,948	5,501	5,153	4,928	4,810	4,930	4,778	4,600	-3.60
Establishments	25	19	19	18	16	17	17	17	-5.36
Employees per establishment	238	290	271	274	301	290	281	271	1.86
Production workers per establishment	.....	159	151	154	170	166	157	152	-0.79
PRODUCTION WORKERS:									
Total	.....	3,024	2,874	2,780	2,714	2,818	2,675	2,580	-2.61
Percent of all employees	.....	55.0	55.8	56.4	56.4	57.2	56.0	56.1	.....
Male	.....	1,846	1,770	1,717	1,721	.....	.....	.....	.....
Female	.....	1,178	1,104	1,063	993	.....	.....	.....	.....
Percent of all production workers	.....	39.0	38.4	38.2	36.6	.....	.....	.....	.....
Average hourly earnings	.....	21.30	23.48	24.23	26.63	26.40	25.12	27.98	4.65
Average weekly earnings	.....	742.02	791.44	851.61	935.49	904.00	899.12	1010.36	5.28
Average weekly hours	.....	34.83	33.70	35.14	35.13	34.24	35.79	36.11	0.60
Shipments (millions)	1,707	1,779	1,818	1,883	1,963	2,046	2,006	2,471	5.43

1. Compound annual growth rate.

Source: Adapted from Statistics Canada, *Manufacturing Industries of Canada* (Cat. No. 31-203).

MEXICO

Mexico's tobacco products industry in 1993 (latest year for which industry data are available) had 7,778 employees and 38 units (establishments). The employees worked an average of 279 days a year and their incomes (earnings plus benefits) averaged 48,763 new pesos (about $15,611 a year). Production workers numbered 5,489 and had average annual wages of 11,722 new pesos (about $3,753 a year), while the 2,261 nonproduction employees earned an average of about 62,472 new pesos ($20,000) annually (Table 9). Another measurement shows employment in the industry declining at an annual rate of 8.68 percent between 1988 and 1995, from 20,726 employees to 10,978 (Table 10).

The Mexican tobacco products industry is expected to recover some in 1997 as the economy is improving and the domestic market for cigarettes is growing moderately. All but about 3,000 tons of the leaf tobacco used in Mexican tobacco products is grown domestically, according to the U.S. Department of Agriculture's Foreign Agricultural Service. Burley is the leading tobacco type produced, and the United States takes most of the roughly 13,000 tons of burley exported each year.

TABLE 9

MEXICO: TOBACCO PRODUCTS (CMAP 3140), 1993

(Monetary values in 1993 Mexican New Pesos)

			ALL WORKERS									
							PAID WORKERS					
							PRODUCTION WORKERS		NONPRODUCTION EMPLOYEES		BENEFITS	UNPAID
INDUSTRY	CMAP	NUMBER OF UNITS	NUMBER	PERCENT OF INDUSTRY TOTAL	AVERAGE DAYS WORKED	REMUN-ERATION[1]	NUMBER	WAGES AND SALARIES	NUMBER	WAGES AND SALARIES	PER PAID EMPLOYEE	WORKERS, NUMBER
Tobacco products	3140	38	7,778	100	279	48,763	5,489	11,722	2,261	62,472	22,234	28

1. Average annual remuneration including benefits.

Source: INEGI, Census Economics 1994.

TABLE 10

MEXICAN EMPLOYMENT: TOBACCO, 1988-1995

	1988	1989	1990	1991	1992	1993	1994	1995	CHANGE[1]
TOTAL EMPLOYMENT: Tobacco	20,726	17,226	12,591	12,803	12,015	15,719	12,473	10,978	-8.68

1. Compound annual growth rate.

Source: Sistema de Cuentas Nacionales de Mexico, INEGI.

INTERNATIONAL TRADE

United States. U.S. tobacco product exports totaled $5.2 billion in 1996, about the same as the previous year's and slightly above 1990's (Table 11). Exports amounted to 20.2 percent of domestic shipments in 1994, the highest ratio for the six-year period. Imports have fluctuated considerably during the past six years but overall are small, totaling only $245 million in 1996.

U.S. Department of Agriculture and Bureau of the Census data show exports of cigarettes totaling 244 billion pieces valued at $4.7 billion in 1996 and those of bulk smoking tobacco totaling 50,062 metric tons valued at $381 million. Shipments are forecast to remain close to these levels in 1997.

Canada. U.S. tobacco product exports to Canada in 1996 were a relatively small $20.8 million, up slightly from the previous year but more than double the 1990 level (Table 11). Canadian exports to the United States in 1996 totaled $26.2 million, down from $36.8 million the year before and a record high of $510.5 million reached in 1993 after Canada's imposition of punitive tobacco taxes (which were later rescinded). The U.S. deficit in tobacco product trade with Canada was $5.4 million in 1996.

Mexico. Like Canada, Mexico is not a major market for U.S. tobacco products, but shipments there have increased considerably. Exports to Mexico in 1996 reached $38.3 million, up two-thirds from the previous year and more than 14 times the level for 1990 (Table 11). Mexican tobacco product exports to the United States amounted to only $10.8 million in 1996, compared with $6.1 million the year before. In contrast, the United States is Mexico's leading market for unmanufactured burley tobacco.

NAFTA. Tobacco-product trade balances of NAFTA members fluctuated widely between 1990 and 1996. The United States had a positive trade balance of $22.1 million in 1996, in contrast with deficits in all other years except 1994 (Table 11). Canada had a positive trade balance of only $5.3 million in 1996, compared with a record surplus of $499.4 million in 1993, when unusually large quantities moved across the Canada-U.S. border. Mexico has had negative trade balances since 1992, and in 1996 the deficit totaled $27.4 million.

TABLE 11

INTERNATIONAL TRADE, TOBACCO PRODUCTS

(Millions of U.S. dollars)

	1989[1]	1990	1991	1992	1993	1994	1995	1996
GLOBAL TRADE, U.S.								
IMPORTS								
Value	87.9	94.2	199.5	284.5	467.2	162.7	168.5	245.2
Ratio to new supply[2]	0.4	0.4	0.7	0.9	1.9	0.6	.....	.....
Ratio to apparent consumption[3]	0.5	0.4	0.8	1.1	2.2	0.8	.....	.....
EXPORTS								
Value	3,632.3	5,040.3	4,574.1	4,509.4	4,253.3	5,367.3	5,221.4	5,238.3
Ratio to comparable domestic shipments	15.9	18.9	16.1	14.5	17.1	20.2	.....	.....
TRADE BALANCE	3,544.4	4,946.1	4,374.6	4,224.9	3,786.1	5,204.6	5,052.9	4,993.1
BILATERAL TRADE: NAFTA[4]								
U.S. exports to Canada	10.8	8.8	13.6	14.6	11.1	19.9	19.5	20.8
Canadian exports to U.S.	32.2	38.5	138.0	262.0	510.5	50.6	36.8	26.2
U.S. exports to Mexico	2.2	2.7	3.8	6.5	21.7	41.6	23.0	38.3
Mexican exports to U.S.	4.9	4.0	3.8	3.4	3.7	4.2	6.1	10.8
Canadian exports to Mexico	0.0	0.0	0.0	0.0	0.0	0.0	0.0	0.1
Mexican exports to Canada	0.0	0.0	0.0	0.0	0.0	0.0	0.1	0.2
TRADE BALANCES WITHIN NAFTA[5]								
Canada	21.4	29.6	124.4	247.4	499.4	30.7	17.2	5.3
Mexico	2.8	1.3	0.0	(3.1)	(18.0)	(37.4)	(16.8)	(27.4)
United States	(24.1)	(31.0)	(124.4)	(244.2)	(481.4)	6.8	(0.4)	22.1

1. 1989 and earlier data on U.S. exports to Canada for manufacturing total and manufacturing industries are not comparable with data for 1990 and later years because of a change in the reporting system. The NAFTA trade balances for the U.S. and Canada also are affected.

2. New supply equals comparable domestic shipments plus imports for consumption.

3. Apparent consumption equals comparable domestic shipments plus imports for consumption less exports.

4. Amounts less than U.S. $100,000 shown as zero.

5. Parentheses indicate an excess of imports over exports. Because of commodity coding and other data differences among the three countries, these trade balances are only rough estimates and should be used with caution.

Source for U.S. Global Trade: U.S. Department of Commerce, International Trade Administration.

Source for U.S. -Canada and U.S.-Mexico Bilateral Trade: U.S. Bureau of the Census.

Source for Canada-Mexico and Mexico-Canada Bilateral Trade: Statistics Canada, Foreign Trade Division, Special tabulation, March 1997, converted to U.S. dollars by the editors.

TRANSPORTATION EQUIPMENT

THE UNITED STATES

Products and Processes. The transportation equipment industry encompasses virtually all modes of transportation—ranging from bicycles to autos to space vehicles. Because of this broad scope, it is the second largest industry in manufacturing, with more than 15 percent of industry shipments by that sector in 1996. It also ranked first in terms of sales and receipts and was the second largest employer next to the machinery and computer equipment industry.

Motor vehicles and equipment made up about three-fifths of the value of transportation equipment shipments in 1992 (latest year for which economic census data are available). Aerospace equipment (aircraft and parts and guided missiles and space vehicles) accounted for around one-third of the total (see Table 1). Other components of the industry are ship

TABLE 1

UNITED STATES: COMPONENT INDUSTRIES OF TRANSPORTATION EQUIPMENT (SIC 37), 1992

(Monetary values in millions of U.S. dollars)

INDUSTRY	SIC	ESTABLISH-MENTS	SHIPMENTS		VALUE ADDED BY MANUFACTURE	NEW CAPITAL EXPENDI-TURES	EMPLOY-MENT[1]	PAYROLL
			VALUE	PERCENT BY 4 LARGEST COMPANIES				
TRANSPORTATION EQUIPMENT	37	11,287	$399,269.3	.....	$158,325.6	$11,038.20	1,646,900	$62,733.7
Motor vehicles and motor vehicle equipment	371	4,869	238,383.7	.....	80,934.6	6,755.00	702,800	26,212.5
Motor vehicles and passenger car bodies	3711	452	151,682.1	84	45,982.9	2,987.90	227,800	10,434.1
Truck and bus bodies	3713	676	4,626.5	24	1,822.3	71.2	34,900	868.5
Motor vehicle parts and accessories	3714	3,255	75,058.4	48	31,074.1	3,645.20	400,000	13,955.4
Truck trailers	3715	339	3,551.1	33	1,098.1	30.9	23,500	566.6
Motor homes	3716	147	3,465.7	53	957.3	19.9	16,700	387.9
Aircraft and parts	372	1,746	104,858.3	.....	47,660.5	3,369.80	548,100	22,646.7
Aircraft	3721	182	62,940.1	79	23,107.2	1,660.20	264,600	11,493.0
Aircraft engines and engine parts	3724	448	22,407.5	77	11,725.9	598.1	120,400	4,966.4
Aircraft parts and auxiliary equipment, n.e.c.	3728	1,116	19,510.6	44	12,827.4	1,111.50	163,100	6,187.3
Ship and boat building and repairing	373	3,050	15,248.5	.....	8,560.1	191.7	162,800	4,633.9
Ship building and repairing	3731	597	10,600.9	53	6,537.8	128	118,200	3,630.7
Boat building and repairing	3732	2,453	4,647.6	32	2,022.3	63.6	44,500	1,003.2
Railroad equipment	374	206	4,713.5	.....	2,015.1	96.3	28,300	899.8
Railroad equipment	3743	206	4,713.5	53	2,015.1	96.3	28,300	899.8
Motorcycles, bicycles, and parts	375	249	2,133.6	65	890.9	62	12,800	342.9
Guided missiles and space vehicles and parts	376	137	26,508.4	.....	15,246.0	467.1	145,900	6,780.3
Guided missiles and space vehicles	3761	38	19,423.1	71	10,939.0	312.6	97,700	4,637.2
Guided missile and space propulsion units parts	3764	40	5,121.4	71	3,044.5	120.7	32,000	1,481.2
Space vehicle equipment, n.e.c.	3769	59	1,963.9	75	1,262.5	33.8	16,200	661.9
Miscellaneous transportation equipment	379	1,030	7,423.4	.....	3,018.3	96.3	46,200	1,217.7
Travel trailers and campers	3792	303	2,118.3	41	782.3	18.4	15,200	348.9
Tanks and tank components	3795	42	2,228.8	88	1,128.0	16.7	11,400	414.6
Transportation equipment, n.e.c.	3799	685	3,076.2	36	1,108.0	61.3	19,700	454.2

1. Employment numbers from the economic censuses differ in definition and classification from the Bureau of Labor Statistics estimates in Table 2. Year-to-year comparisons between Table 1 and Table 2 are not appropriate.

Source: U.S. Bureau of the Census, 1992 Census of Manufactures.

and boat building and repair; railroad equipment; motorcycles, bicycles, and parts; travel trailers and campers; and military tanks and tank components. (Discussions in this section focus primarily on motor vehicles and aerospace equipment.)

Table 2 gives a profile of the industry's 1993 employment and prospective employment for the year 2005. The industry's payroll in 1993 included 1.76 million employees, slightly less than half of whom were in the motor vehicle and equipment industry. Employment projections indicate that almost 200,000 fewer people will be on the industry payroll in 2005 than in 1993. The largest decline from 1993 was projected for aerospace (aircraft and parts and guided missiles, space vehicles, and parts); most of that anticipated decline already had taken place by 1996 (see Table 4).

TABLE 2

U.S. EMPLOYMENT AND EARNINGS: TRANSPORTATION EQUIPMENT

| | | 1993 | | | 2005 |
| INDUSTRY | SIC | EMPLOYMENT[1] | | AVERAGE HOURLY EARNINGS (U.S. DOLLARS)[2] | PROJECTED EMPLOYMENT[3] |
		NUMBER OF PERSONS	PERCENT OF INDUSTRY TOTAL		
TRANSPORTATION EQUIPMENT	37	1,756,200	100.0	$15.80	1,567,400
Motor vehicles and equipment	371	836,600	47.6	16.10	775,100
Motor vehicles and car bodies	3711	319,700	18.2	19.44	....
Truck and bus bodies	3713	35,400	2.0	14.10	....
Motor vehicle parts and accessories	3714	432,500	24.6	14.74	....
Truck trailers	3715	30,300	1.7	9.77	....
Aircraft and parts	372	542,000	30.9	17.23	457,800
Aircraft	3721	301,400	17.2	18.43	....
Aircraft engines and engine parts	3724	109,200	6.2	16.70	....
Aircraft parts and equipment, n.e.c.	3728	131,400	7.5	15.72	....
Ship and boat building and repairing	373	159,100	9.1	12.34	130,500
Ship building and repairing	3731	112,600	6.4	13.44	....
Boat building and repairing	3732	46,500	2.6	9.82	....
Railroad equipment	374	31,000	1.8	14.90	35,000
Guided missiles, space vehicles, and parts	376	123,700	7.0	16.80	94,000
Guided missiles and space vehicles	3761	88,900	5.1	17.43	....
Miscellaneous transportation equipment	379	46,200	2.6	11.19	....
Travel trailers and campers	3792	18,700	1.1	10.80	....
All other transportation equipment	375,9	....	....	....	75,000

1. Total payroll employment. Employment data from the economic censuses, shown in Table 1, differ in definition and classification from the Bureau of Labor Statistics estimates in this table. Year-to-year comparisons between Table 1 and Table 2 are not appropriate.

2. Earnings of production workers, including overtime.

3. Number of persons, moderate projection by the U.S. Bureau of Labor Statistics.

Source: Bureau of Labor Statistics.

FIGURE 1A

U.S. EMPLOYMENT IN MOTOR VEHICLES

Percent distribution by region, 1995

The Great Lakes region, and Michigan in particular, still is the center of motor vehicle manufacturing, with 57 percent of all workers in 1995. The Southeast was the second largest employer, with 18 percent of the 1995 total.

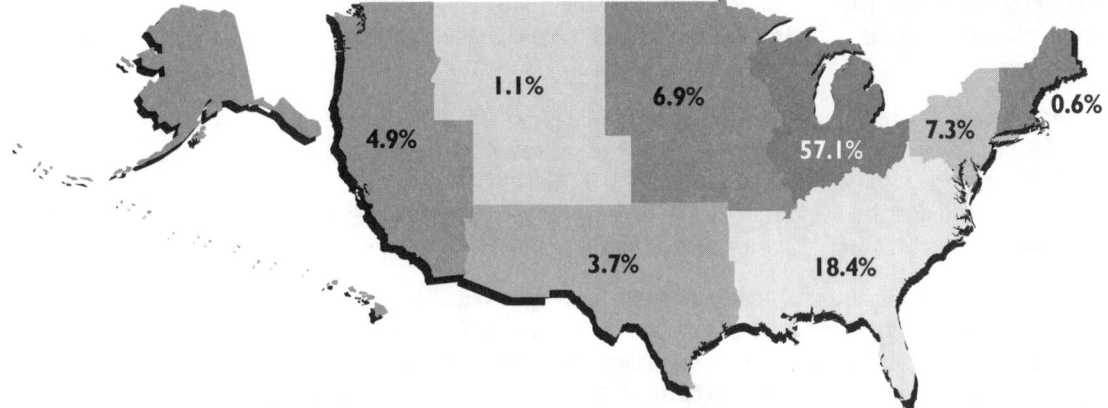

Source: U.S. Department of Commerce, Bureau of Economic Analysis.

FIGURE 1B

U.S. EMPLOYMENT IN TRANSPORTATION EQUIPMENT, EXCEPT MOTOR VEHICLES

Percent distribution by region, 1995

Employment in transportation equipment excluding motor vehicles is more evenly distributed than in the motor vehicle industry, with 28 percent of 1995 employment in the Pacific region (primarily Washington and California), 22 percent in the Southeast, and 11 percent in the Southwest.

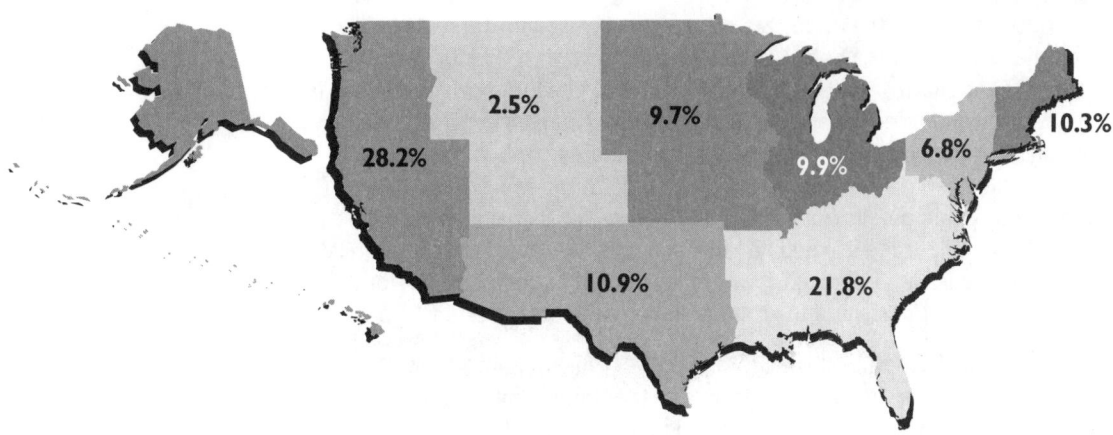

Source: U.S. Department of Commerce, Bureau of Economic Analysis.

What's New. Following a prolonged growth streak that has accompanied the U.S. economy's recovery from the 1991 recession, the **motor vehicle** industry appears headed for a period of relatively flat sales and increased competition. The "Big-3" U.S. producers— General Motors, Ford, and Chrysler—still dominate motor vehicle production, employment, and sales in the United States, particularly in the rapidly growing production of light trucks. At the same time, the huge demand and, in some cases, lower labor costs in the United States are bringing foreign manufacturers into the North American industry. Japan continues to transfer production to NAFTA countries, especially the United States; two German firms have built plants in the United States; and a South Korean manufacturer is starting production here.

Abroad, the opening of once-closed Communist markets and rapid growth in many developing countries have created a host of export opportunities; however, U.S. motor vehicle exporters will face strong competition in these markets, as well as trade barriers erected to protect domestic industries. Additionally, the large motor vehicle companies will continue to shift production to low-wage countries such as Mexico.

Meanwhile, sales of new cars and light trucks in the United States remain sluggish. According to the U.S. Department of Commerce, sales volume in the first half of 1997 totaled 10.27 million vehicles, or 0.8 percent less than in the same period of 1996. This followed a 3 percent sales gain in 1996. While sales of vehicles from all of NAFTA dropped 2.5 percent, to 8.96 million vehicles in the first half of 1997, those from Japan rose 13.1 percent to 870,000.

Car prices also weakened in 1997. Average producer prices for passenger cars in May, June, and July 1997 were down 2.4 percent from those in the same 1996 period, and prices for light trucks were off 0.7 percent. Consumer prices for new cars were slightly above those of a year earlier. As a result, American auto companies reduced prices on a number of 1998 models. In addition, General Motors has announced plans to eliminate at least 42,000 jobs by 2003; still GM had record third-quarter 1997 results in terms of operating income, reflecting continued cost cutting.

Manufacturers also are pushing hard to modernize and expand overseas operations and boost export sales, according to industry statements and press reports. This effort involves both building of new plants and restructuring and cost-cutting in existing ones, especially in Western Europe, which has lagged the United States in restructuring and still has a glut of motor vehicles on the market. For example, GM has launched a study to identify ways of cutting excess capacity and shaving $200-$400 million off costs in its European operations in 1998. The company also announced in early September that its Adam Opel AG unit will invest $9.8 billion in Germany over the next five years and will restructure its European dealer outlets and set up a new distribution network for parts. At the same time, GM has moved to expand production in developing countries. The company's goal is to boost production outside North America to five million units annually over the next 10 years. GM sales outside of North America are estimated at $36 billion for 1997 and $38 billion for 1998, compared with $35.3 billion (21 percent of the company's corporate revenues) in 1996.

GM introduced its 1998 Cadillac Seville at the September 1997 Frankfurt auto show, the company's first introduction of an American brand outside the United States. The car will be available in two sizes and has been redesigned with handling and safety features that meet European luxury standards.

Chrysler Corp. has tried a different approach, introducing its latest prototype of a low-cost, low-weight car specially designed for developing countries. The prototype Composite Concept Vehicle, also unveiled at the Frankfurt auto show, is made of four recyclable plastic pieces manufactured from resins similar to those used in soda bottles and mounted on a structural steel frame chassis. The car is easy to make, weighs only 1,200 pounds (less than half the weight of most subcompacts), and, with eight inches of ground clearance, can traverse rugged terrain and unpaved roads. Yet it is spacious enough to accommodate five passengers and has a canvas top that rolls back to become a convertible. The car, estimated to cost $6,000, is powered by a 25 horsepower engine that has a top speed of 70 miles an hour and gets 50 miles to the gallon. Chrysler still has a number of technical problems to resolve and has not made a final decision about building the car.

The **aerospace industry (aircraft and parts and guided missiles)** only recently began recovering from its worst recession in 40 years. Sales by the industry rose in 1996 for the first time in five years and increased further in 1997. Virtually all of the growth has been in shipments of commercial aircraft, engines, and parts to the general aviation and airline industries, where profits are improving following a rough few years. Demand has been so strong, in fact, that the industry has a huge backlog of orders, and Boeing posted a $696 million loss in the third quarter of 1997 as it struggled to boost production. On the other hand, sales of military aircraft, space vehicles and parts, and missiles slowed further as the Department of Defense cut purchases and NASA also bought less. Aerospace sales to the Department of Defense already had fallen from 56 percent of the total in 1987 to just over a third in 1996 with the shift in emphasis from defense spending to budget balancing.

FIGURE 2

U.S. EMPLOYMENT AND SHIPMENTS, TRANSPORTATION EQUIPMENT

Total payroll employment and manufacturers' inflation-adjusted shipments

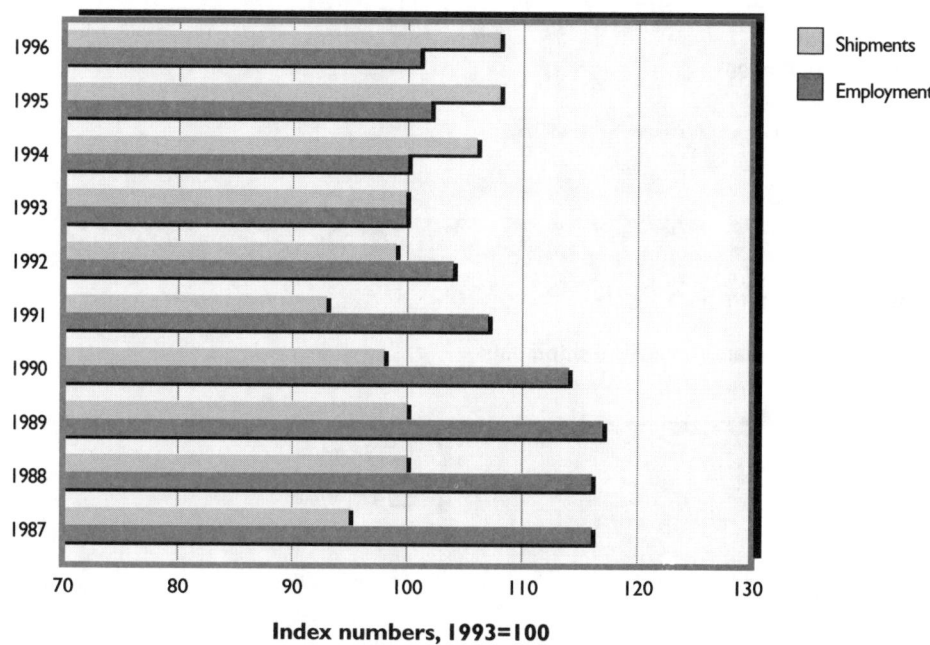

Index numbers, 1993=100

Source: U.S. Bureau of Labor Statistics, U.S. Department of Commerce, and estimates by the editors.

FIGURE 2A

FIGURE 2A

U.S. EMPLOYMENT AND SHIPMENTS, MOTOR VEHICLES

Total payroll employment and manufacturers' inflation-adjusted shipments

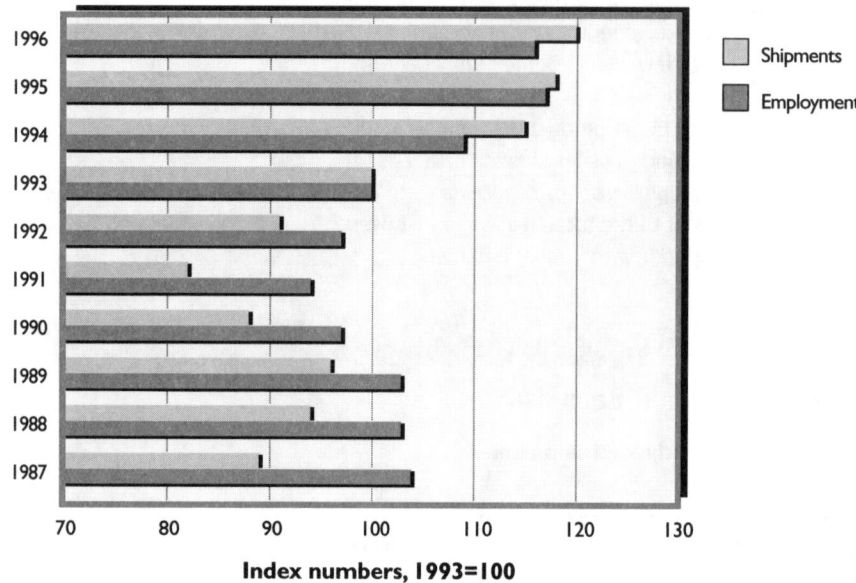

Index numbers, 1993=100

Source: U.S. Bureau of Labor Statistics, U.S. Department of Commerce, and estimates by the editors.

FIGURE 2B

U.S. EMPLOYMENT AND SHIPMENTS, AIRCRAFT AND PARTS

Total payroll employment and manufacturers' inflation-adjusted shipments

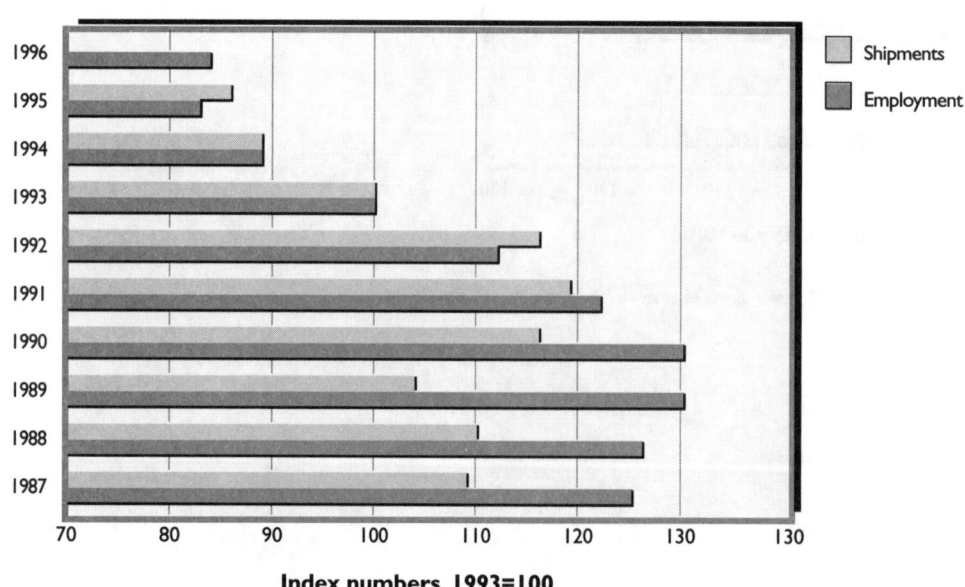

Index numbers, 1993=100

Source: U.S. Bureau of Labor Statistics, U.S. Department of Commerce, and estimates by the editors. Shipments data for 1996 are not available.

FIGURE 2C

U.S. EMPLOYMENT AND SHIPMENTS, GUIDED MISSILES AND SPACE VEHICLES

Total payroll employment and manufacturers' inflation-adjusted shipments

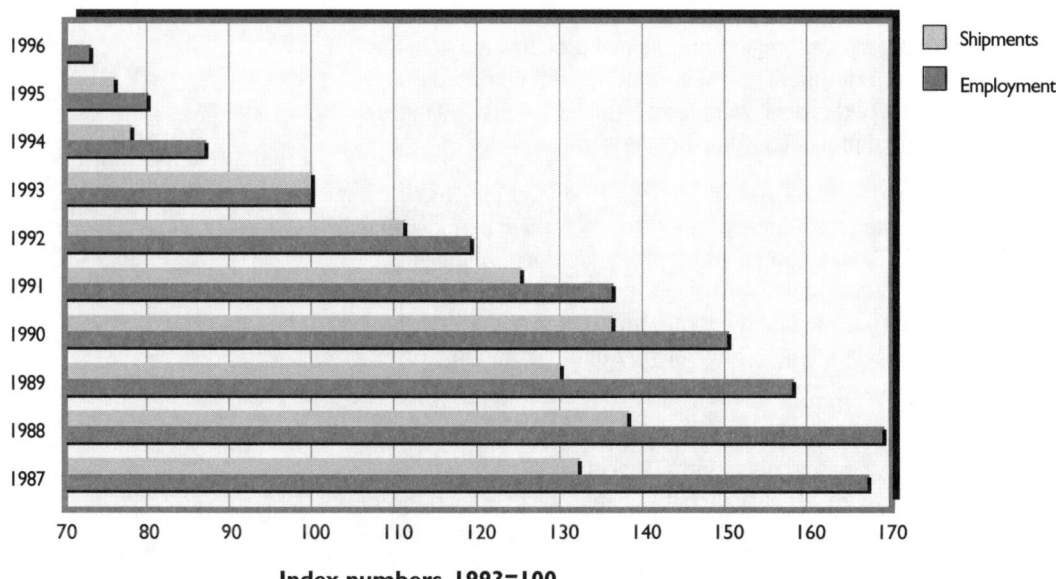

Index numbers, 1993=100

Source: U.S. Bureau of Labor Statistics, U.S. Department of Commerce, and estimates by the editors. Shipments data for 1996 are not available.

Output. Shipments and employment by the transportation equipment industry followed divergent paths during 1989-1996. Shipments by the industry declined from 1988 through 1991 and then rose steadily until a leveling off in 1996, while industry employment was in a downward trend before rising slightly in 1994 and 1995 (Figure 2). The gain in shipments was due almost entirely to growth in the motor vehicle industry, where employment also rose in most years after the 1991 recession (Figure 2A). Shipments of both aircraft and parts and missiles and space vehicles rose at the beginning of the past decade before declining steadily through 1995; employment in both subindustries also headed down after initial gains (Figures 2B and 2C).

Transportation equipment industry shipments totaled $472.0 billion in 1996, compared with $332.9 billion 10 years earlier. The annual growth rate was 3.95 percent in current dollars but only 1.44 percent when adjusted for inflation (Table 3).

U.S. **motor vehicle** shipments were $335.1 billion in 1996, compared with $205.9 billion in 1987 and little more than that in 1991 (Table 3). The motor vehicle industry, in fact, staged a remarkable turnaround from the depths of recession in 1991 to record production and profits in 1995.

The industry includes the Big-3 American producers, two affiliates of German companies, and seven affiliates of Japanese companies. There are five large and about 100 other vehicle assemblers.

Virtually all of the production and sales growth has been in trucks (light trucks, vans, and sport utility vehicles), which recently have accounted for 44 percent of the domestic motor vehicle market, against only 29 percent in 1986. Moreover, U.S. manufacturers by 1996 had increased their share of the truck market to over 86 percent (from 79 percent in 1986).

Because of this dominance, U.S. producers held a near-record 73 percent of the light vehicle market in 1996, despite declines in their share of passenger car sales. However, competition may increase as several new foreign brands of sport utility vehicles are scheduled to be introduced over the next few years.

Production of automotive parts hit a record $134 billion in 1994. This industry includes about 5,000 firms, including some 500 Japanese, European, and Canadian affiliates.

The motor vehicle industry's recent good performance has helped prolong growth in the U.S. economy. The industry alone accounts for more than a sixth of U.S. durable goods shipments and takes over 15 percent of the steel, 25 percent of the aluminum, 30 percent of the iron, and 75 percent of the natural rubber consumed domestically.

Shipments of **aerospace equipment** in 1996 edged up from the 1995 level to $103.6 billion, the first gain since 1992 (Table 3). The growth rate for the entire 1987-1996 period was zero in current dollars and a negative 2.72 percent when adjusted for inflation. Shipments of aircraft and parts through 1995 rose at an annual rate of 1.02 percent in current dollars (but declined 2.91 percent annually when adjusted for inflation), while those of guided missiles and space vehicles declined 4.19 percent annually (and fell 6.72 in inflation-adjusted dollars).

Most of the recent growth was in civil aircraft, engines, and parts, which, according to the Aerospace Industries Association (AIA), rose more than 13 percent to $27.7 billion in 1996. Sales value increased in all three categories of civil aircraft—general aviation (with over five-eighths of the total), commercial transports, and civil helicopters. Military aircraft gained some because of larger exports, and increases also occurred in related products and services (defense electronics and air traffic control equipment) and space vehicles and equipment. The only decline was in production of missiles, which has plunged more than 60 percent since 1990. The AIA estimates that orders soared 18 percent in 1996, the third successive gain, as demand for commercial transport aircraft picked up. Industry backlog of unfilled orders in 1996 was an estimated $215.6 billion—the fifth highest level recorded.

Investment. After an initial decline, new capital expenditures by the **transportation equipment industry** rose steadily between 1988 and 1995 (latest year for which data are available) to $13.1 billion (Table 3). Research and development (R&D) spending through 1994 gained in every year but 1990, ending up at $17.7 billion.

Motor vehicle and equipment producers accounted for most of the investment and growth in investment. After declining sharply in 1988, new capital expenditures more than tripled between that year and 1995, when they hit $10.3 billion. R&D expenditures also grew significantly, from $7.2 billion in 1987 to $12 billion in 1994. Reflecting the expansion in plant and equipment, capacity utilization by the industry has fallen in the last two years to 72.4 percent in 1996.

New capital expenditures by the **aerospace industry**, in a long-term decline, fell to $2.2 billion in 1995, compared with $2.4 billion the previous year and $3.6 billion in 1987. Of the 1995 total, $1.8 billion was for aircraft and parts and $380 million was for guided missiles and space vehicles. Consolidation and mergers have affected capital expenditures in this sector and led to the closure of many R&D and production facilities. R&D emphasis today is on acquiring and using advanced technology to improve product quality, cut costs and design-to-market time, and increase efficiency. A prospective decline in funding for NASA through the year 2000 will have a negative effect on future capital spending on missiles, space vehicles, and equipment.

Prices. Producer prices in the **transportation equipment industry** rose at an annual rate of 2.67 percent between 1987 and 1996 (Table 3). Prices of motor vehicles rose at a slower annual rate of 2.29 percent, while the rate for **aerospace equipment** was considerably higher at 3.93 percent.

TABLE 3

U.S. OUTPUT, INVESTMENT, AND PRICES: TRANSPORTATION EQUIPMENT

(Millions of U.S. dollars, except as noted)

	1987	1988	1989	1990	1991	1992	1993	1994	1995	1996	GROWTH RATE 1987-1996[1]
TRANSPORTATION EQUIPMENT											
VALUE OF SHIPMENTS:											
BY INDUSTRY:											
Current dollars	332,935	354,849	369,675	370,329	367,236	399,269	414,694	450,809	462,616	472,012	3.95
Constant 1992 dollars	383,301	401,504	402,228	393,415	376,425	399,269	402,993	427,800	433,463	436,020	1.44
BY PRODUCT:											
Current dollars	322,169	345,209	354,071	353,167	349,776	384,369	401,922	436,377	446,965	456,042	3.94
Constant 1992 dollars	369,545	389,187	383,848	373,893	357,503	384,369	390,285	413,808	418,634	421,103	1.46
OTHER OUTPUT MEASURES:											
Industrial production, 1993=100	92.7	97.5	101.4	98.6	93.1	96.4	100.0	103.6	101.3	102.3	1.10
Gross domestic product:											
Current dollars	113.5	115.2	110.7	106.6	104.3	109.3	119.4	131.7	....	....	....
Percent of total GDP	2.4	2.3	2.1	1.9	1.7	1.7	1.8	1.9	....	....	....
Rank in manufacturing	1	1	2	3	3	2	2	2	....	....	....
Chained (1992) dollars	144.3	150.8	136.7	125.9	110.8	109.3	112.2	117.9	....	....	....
INVESTMENT-RELATED MEASURES:											
Capacity utilization, percent	77.5	80.6	81.8	77.7	71.7	73.2	75.3	76.3	72.4	71.8	....
New capital expenditures	10,780	7,241	9,937	10,860	11,022	11,038	11,416	11,751	13,109	....	....
Research and development spending	13,462	13,910	14,596	14,264	14,858	16,292	16,640	17,695	....	....	....
Producer prices, 1993=100[2]	83.8	85.3	88.7	91.5	94.8	97.4	100.0	103.0	104.7	106.2	2.67
MOTOR VEHICLES											
VALUE OF SHIPMENTS:											
BY INDUSTRY:											
Current dollars	205,923	222,352	233,232	217,296	209,210	238,384	267,365	314,637	326,181	335,053	5.56
Constant 1992 dollars	231,063	246,428	251,450	230,214	214,157	238,384	260,935	299,510	307,450	312,516	3.41
By product:											
Current dollars	201,667	217,902	220,811	207,207	199,231	232,702	261,541	307,887	319,464	328,153	5.56
Constant 1992 dollars	226,160	241,362	237,927	219,546	203,921	232,702	255,283	293,006	301,098	306,059	3.42
OTHER OUTPUT MEASURES:											
Industrial production, 1993=100	83.5	88.1	89.0	83.8	77.8	88.0	100.0	114.1	113.0	111.8	3.30
Gross domestic product:											
Current dollars	57,920	59,634	53,003	46,102	42,328	52,848	66,160	84,064	....	....	....
Percent of total GDP	1.2	1.2	1.0	0.8	0.7	0.8	1.0	1.2	....	....	....
Chained (1992) dollars	69,940	74,239	64,220	56,840	46,784	52,848	60,573	72,763	....	....	....
INVESTMENT-RELATED MEASURES:											
Capacity utilization, percent	76.8	81.2	79.5	71.6	64.0	69.9	77.3	83.5	76.9	72.4	....
New capital expenditures	6,578	3,314	5,705	6,864	7,170	6,755	8,170	8,782	10,261	....	....
Research and development spending	7,167	7,783	8,756	8,594	9,063	9,132	10,659	11,950	....	....	....
Producer prices, 1993=100[2]	86.0	87.0	89.5	91.3	94.8	97.4	100.0	103.0	104.3	105.4	2.29
AEROSPACE											
VALUE OF SHIPMENTS:											
BY INDUSTRY:											
Current dollars	103,589	107,955	110,603	125,822	132,182	131,367	116,346	103,316	102,532	103,554	0.00
Constant 1992 dollars	129,811	132,314	124,854	136,522	137,510	131,367	113,891	98,739	95,744	101,278	-2.72
BY PRODUCT:											
Current dollars	97,185	102,242	106,320	118,141	124,109	122,800	110,312	96,968	95,248	96,197	-0.11
Constant 1992 dollars	121,390	124,899	119,628	127,856	129,081	122,800	107,971	92,664	88,983	97,388	-2.42
New capital expenditures	3,612	3,386	3,727	3,485	3,400	3,837	2,725	2,363	2,156	....	....
New capital expenditures	3,612	3,386	3,727	3,485	3,400	3,837	2,725	2,363	2,156	....	....
Producer prices, 1993=100[2]	77.2	78.9	85.7	90.1	93.6	96.6	100.0	103.3	106.8	109.2	3.93

TABLE 3 (CONTINUED)

U.S. OUTPUT, INVESTMENT, AND PRICES: TRANSPORTATION EQUIPMENT

(Millions of U.S. dollars, except as noted)

	1987	1988	1989	1990	1991	1992	1993	1994	1995	1996	GROWTH RATE 1987-1996[1]
AIRCRAFT AND PARTS											
VALUE OF SHIPMENTS:											
BY INDUSTRY:											
Current dollars	77,304	79,727	81,891	95,163	103,078	104,858	92,330	84,603	83,865	....	1.02
Constant 1992 dollars	98,514	99,361	94,001	104,264	107,666	104,858	90,100	80,282	77,768	....	-2.91
BY PRODUCT:											
Current dollars	74,354	77,177	80,729	91,547	99,117	99,442	87,685	79,742	77,762	....	0.56
Constant 1992 dollars	94,610	96,039	92,534	100,255	103,552	99,442	85,561	75,673	72,158	....	-3.33
OTHER OUTPUT MEASURES:											
Industrial production, 1993=100	102.5	105.6	114.7	116.0	116.3	110.4	100.0	88.5	82.8	91.6	-1.24
INVESTMENT-RELATED MEASURES:											
New capital expenditures	2,536	2,359	2,659	2,614	2,814	3,370	2,307	1,969	1,776	....	....
GUIDED MISSILES AND SPACE MISSILES											
VALUE OF SHIPMENTS:											
BY INDUSTRY:											
Current dollars	26,285	28,229	28,712	30,659	29,105	26,508	24,016	18,713	18,667	....	-4.19
Constant 1992 dollars	31,355	32,932	30,853	32,258	29,844	26,508	23,791	18,456	17,976	....	-6.72
BY PRODUCT:											
Current dollars	22,832	25,065	25,591	26,594	24,992	23,358	22,628	17,226	17,486	....	-3.28
Constant 1992 dollars	26,836	28,810	27,094	27,601	25,529	23,358	22,410	16,991	16,826	....	-5.67
INVESTMENT-RELATED MEASURES:											
New capital expenditures	1,075	1,027	1,068	871	586	467	418	395	380	....	....

1. Compound annual growth rate.

2. Prices received by domestic producers.

Sources: Shipments and new capital expenditures: U.S. Department of Commerce for 1987-1995, editor's estimates for constant dollar data for 1987-88 and all shipments data for 1996; Industrial production and capacity utilization: Federal Reserve Board of Governors; GDP: Bureau of Economic Analysis; Research and development spending: National Science Foundation; Producer prices: Bureau of Labor Statistics.

Workforce and Employment. The number of employees in the transportation equipment industry during 1987-1996 declined at an annual rate of 1.43 percent, to 1,781,000 in 1996 (Table 4). All of this decline was in aircraft and guided missiles/space vehicles manufacturing, which had annual decreases of 4.22 and 8.77 percent, respectively. Both also had even sharper declines in employment of production workers and women. Conversely, employment in the motor vehicle industry rose at an annual rate of 1.19 percent. Growth in employment of production workers (to 78.9 percent of the total workforce in 1996) and women (to 21 percent) exceeded that pace.

Overall, the transportation equipment industry had the third highest number of workers certified by the U.S. Department of Labor as having been displaced by NAFTA. As of June 18, 1997, 10,100 workers were so certified, including 9,251 displaced because of job losses to Mexico, 439 because of losses to Canada, and 410 to countries unspecified. This amounted to 0.6 percent of the transportation equipment industry's total workforce.

Average hourly earnings in the **transportation equipment industry** rose at a yearly rate of 3.21 percent to $17.20 in current dollars, but when adjusted for inflation, they declined by 0.33 percent a year (Table 4). **Motor vehicle industry** employees earned an average of $17.75 an hour in 1996, up from $17.34 the previous year and $13.53 in 1987. Still, average earnings for the period in inflation-adjusted dollars declined by 0.48 percent a year. The highest-paid workers were in the **aircraft and parts industry**, $18.58 per hour in 1996; those producing **missiles and space vehicles** were close behind at $18.51. In these latter two areas, wage growth during the 10-year period was positive in both current and inflation-adjusted dollars.

TABLE 4

U.S. EMPLOYMENT, HOURS, AND EARNINGS: TRANSPORTATION EQUIPMENT

(Monetary values in U.S. dollars)

	1987	1988	1989	1990	1991	1992	1993	1994	1995	1996	CHANGE[1]
TRANSPORTATION EQUIPMENT											
NUMBER OF EMPLOYEES, IN THOUSANDS:											
Total	2,028	2,036	2,052	1,989	1,890	1,830	1,756	1,761	1,790	1,781	-1.43
Production workers	1,278	1,273	1,278	1,224	1,169	1,147	1,120	1,154	1,200	1,206	-0.64
Percent of total	63.0	62.5	62.3	61.5	61.9	62.7	63.8	65.5	67.0	67.7	.....
Women	393	396	408	406	385	371	355	356	362	363	-0.87
Percent of total	19.4	19.4	19.9	20.4	20.4	20.3	20.2	20.2	20.2	20.4	.....
HOURS AND EARNINGS OF PRODUCTION WORKERS:											
Average hourly earnings, U.S. dollars[2]											
Current dollars	12.94	13.29	13.67	14.08	14.75	15.20	15.80	16.51	16.74	17.20	3.21
1992 dollars[3]	15.90	15.69	15.41	15.09	15.17	15.20	15.37	15.66	15.44	15.43	-0.33
Average weekly hours	42.0	42.7	42.4	42.0	41.9	41.8	43.0	44.3	43.8	44.0	0.52
Average weekly earnings, current U.S. dollars	543.48	567.48	579.61	591.36	618.03	635.36	679.40	731.39	733.21	756.80	3.75
MOTOR VEHICLES											
NUMBER OF EMPLOYEES, IN THOUSANDS:											
Total	866	856	859	812	789	813	837	909	971	963	1.19
Production workers	673	667	664	617	602	622	642	704	761	760	1.36
Percent of total	77.7	77.9	77.3	76.0	76.3	76.5	76.7	77.4	78.4	78.9	.....
Women	150	150	156	153	151	158	168	186	201	202	3.39
Percent of total	17.3	17.5	18.1	18.9	19.2	19.5	20.0	20.4	20.7	21.0	.....
HOURS AND EARNINGS OF PRODUCTION WORKERS:											
Average hourly earnings, U.S. dollars[2]											
Current dollars	13.53	13.99	14.25	14.56	15.23	15.45	16.10	17.02	17.34	17.75	3.06
1992 dollars[3]	16.62	16.52	16.07	15.61	15.67	15.45	15.66	16.15	16.00	15.92	-0.48
Average weekly hours	42.2	43.5	43.1	42.4	42.3	42.4	44.3	46.0	44.9	44.9	0.69
Average weekly earnings, current U.S. dollars	570.97	608.57	614.18	617.34	644.23	655.08	713.23	782.92	778.57	796.98	3.77

TABLE 4 (CONTINUED)

U.S. EMPLOYMENT, HOURS, AND EARNINGS: TRANSPORTATION EQUIPMENT

(Monetary values in U.S. dollars)

	1987	1988	1989	1990	1991	1992	1993	1994	1995	1996	CHANGE[1]
AIRCRAFT AND PARTS											
NUMBER OF EMPLOYEES, IN THOUSANDS:											
Total	678	684	711	712	669	612	542	482	451	460	-4.22
Production workers	339	331	344	345	324	291	253	222	208	218	-4.77
Percent of total	49.9	48.5	48.3	48.4	48.4	47.6	46.6	.....	46.1	47.4	.....
Women	145	148	157	161	150	135	116	101	93	96	-4.48
Percent of total	21.4	21.6	22.1	22.6	22.4	22.1	21.4	.....	20.6	20.9	.....
HOURS AND EARNINGS OF PRODUCTION WORKERS:											
Average hourly earnings, U.S. dollars[2]											
Current dollars	13.17	13.55	14.17	14.79	15.60	16.53	17.23	17.95	18.02	18.58	3.90
1992 dollars[3]	16.18	16.00	15.98	15.85	16.05	16.53	16.76	17.03	16.62	16.66	0.33
Average weekly hours	42.4	42.4	41.9	42.3	41.7	41.7	41.6	42.1	42.0	43.2	0.21
Average weekly earnings, current U.S. dollars	558.41	574.52	593.72	625.62	650.52	689.30	716.77	755.70	756.84	802.66	4.11
GUIDED MISSILES AND SPACE VEHICLES											
NUMBER OF EMPLOYEES, IN THOUSANDS:											
Total	206	208	194	185	168	146	124	108	98	90	-8.77
Production workers	67	63	60	57	48	40	35	31	28	25	-10.30
Percent of total	32.4	30.1	30.8	30.7	28.9	27.5	28.2	28.6	28.5	27.8	.....
Women	55	54	50	48	43	37	32	27	25	22	-9.48
Percent of total	26.7	25.8	25.8	26.0	25.7	25.1	25.5	25.3	24.9	24.9	.....
HOURS AND EARNINGS OF PRODUCTION WORKERS:											
Average hourly earnings, U.S. dollars[2]											
Current dollars	12.73	13.13	13.70	14.39	14.90	15.99	16.80	17.48	17.74	18.51	4.25
1992 dollars[3]	15.64	15.50	15.45	15.42	15.33	15.99	16.34	16.58	16.37	16.60	0.67
Average weekly hours	42.5	43.2	43.0	42.5	42.4	40.8	41.4	42.2	43.1	42.7	0.05
Average weekly earnings, current U.S. dollars	541.03	567.22	589.1	611.58	631.76	652.39	695.52	737.66	764.59	790.38	4.30

1. Compound annual growth rate, 1987-1996.

2. Including overtime.

3. Converted to 1992 dollars using Consumer Price Index for Urban Wage Earners and Clerical Workers.

Source: Bureau of Labor Statistics.

FIGURE 3

U.S. OCCUPATIONAL INJURY AND ILLNESS RATES:
TRANSPORTATION EQUIPMENT, 1995

Incidence of nonfatal injuries and illnesses per 100 full-time workers

Nonfatal occupational illnesses and injuries in the transportation equipment industry during 1995 averaged 18.6 cases per 100 workers, the highest level in manufacturing.

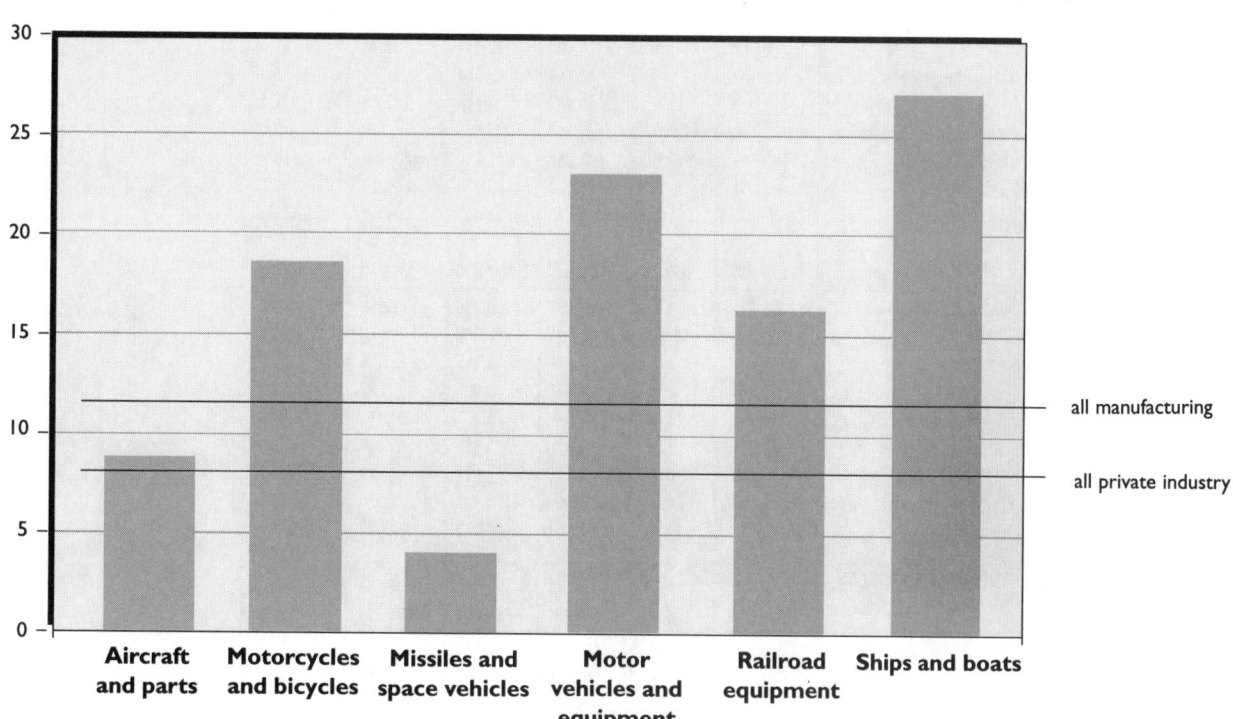

Source: U.S. Bureau of Labor Statistics.

TABLE 5

U.S. EMPLOYMENT PROJECTIONS BY MAJOR OCCUPATIONAL GROUP: TRANSPORTATION EQUIPMENT

	1994		PROJECTIONS, 2005			
	NUMBER OF EMPLOYEES	PERCENT OF INDUSTRY TOTAL	NUMBER OF EMPLOYEES			PERCENT OF INDUSTRY TOTAL, MODERATE PROJECTIONS
OCCUPATION			LOW	MODERATE	HIGH	
TRANSPORTATION EQUIPMENT						
Total, all occupations	1,749,000	100.0	1,455,100	1,567,400	1,744,200	100.0
Executive, administrative, and managerial	176,029	10.1	152,328	163,729	181,653	10.5
Professional specialties	219,643	12.6	223,521	239,745	265,584	15.3
Technicians and related support	70,014	4.0	53,249	57,245	63,544	3.7
Marketing and sales	20,155	1.2	17,198	18,543	20,664	1.2
Administrative support including clerical	154,690	8.8	113,833	122,395	135,541	7.8
Service	24,733	1.4	17,843	19,220	21,414	1.2
Agriculture, forestry, and fisheries occupations	340	0.0	286	308	343	0.0
Precision production, craft, and repair	429,195	24.5	338,678	364,603	403,516	23.3
Operators, fabricators, assemblers	654,201	37.4	538,163	581,613	651,941	37.1
MOTOR VEHICLES						
Total, all occupations	898,600	100.0	715,300	775,100	882,600	100.0
Executive, administrative, and managerial	69,949	7.8	58,099	62,956	71,688	8.1
Professional specialties	64,534	7.2	66,110	71,636	81,572	9.2
Technicians and related support	27,098	3.0	20,475	22,187	25,264	2.9
Marketing and sales	12,577	1.4	10,192	11,044	12,576	1.4
Administrative support including clerical	60,872	6.8	42,740	46,314	52,737	6.0
Service	13,072	1.5	8,987	9,738	11,088	1.3
Agriculture, forestry, and fisheries occupations	178	0.0	144	156	178	0.0
Precision production, craft, and repair	186,759	20.8	133,941	145,139	165,268	18.7
Operators, fabricators, assemblers	463,561	51.6	374,612	405,930	462,229	52.4
AIRCRAFT AND PARTS						
Total, all occupations	479,500	100.0	428,845	457,800	501,937	100.0
Executive, administrative, and managerial	68,987	14.4	62,093	66,286	72,676	14.5
Professional specialties	106,761	22.3	112,025	119,589	131,118	26.1
Technicians and related support	27,194	5.7	21,877	23,355	25,606	5.1
Marketing and sales	3,133	0.7	2,815	3,005	3,295	0.7
Administrative support including clerical	56,036	11.7	43,519	46,457	50,936	10.2
Service	6,976	1.5	5,476	5,846	6,409	1.3
Agriculture, forestry, and fisheries occupations	122	0.0	110	117	129	0.0
Precision production, craft, and repair	134,172	28.0	117,969	125,934	138,076	27.5
Operators, fabricators, assemblers	76,117	15.9	62,961	67,212	73,691	14.7
GUIDED MISSILES AND SPACE VEHICLES						
Total, all occupations	107,500	100.0	88,055	94,000	103,063	100.0
Executive, administrative, and managerial	18,263	17.0	15,688	16,747	18,361	17.8
Professional specialties	39,523	36.8	36,616	39,088	42,856	41.6
Technicians and related support	8,638	8.0	5,824	6,218	6,817	6.6
Marketing and sales	274	0.3	217	232	255	0.3
Administrative support including clerical	13,008	12.1	8,660	9,245	10,136	9.8
Service	1,613	1.5	1,123	1,199	1,314	1.3
Agriculture, forestry, and fisheries occupations	.....	......	.....	.....	.....	......
Precision production, craft, and repair	18,783	17.5	14,250	15,212	16,678	16.2
Operators, fabricators, assemblers	7,384	6.9	5,666	6,049	6,632	6.4

Source: Bureau of Labor Statistics, November 1995.

Transportation-equipment industry employment is projected to total 1,567,400 in 2005. The only areas expected to experience gains in their industry shares over 1994 levels (moderate projections) are executive, administrative, and managerial positions (to 10.5 percent of total employment) and professional specialties (15.3 percent). **Motor vehicle industry** *employment is projected to fall to 775,100 by 2005, with declines in all areas but professional specialties. Slight declines from 1994 are anticipated for employment in* **aerospace (aircraft and missiles/space vehicles)** *where considerable downsizing already has taken place.*

FIGURE 4

U.S. CORPORATE INCOME AND WORKER EARNINGS: TRANSPORTATION EQUIPMENT INDUSTRY

Corporate operating income and aggregate production worker earnings

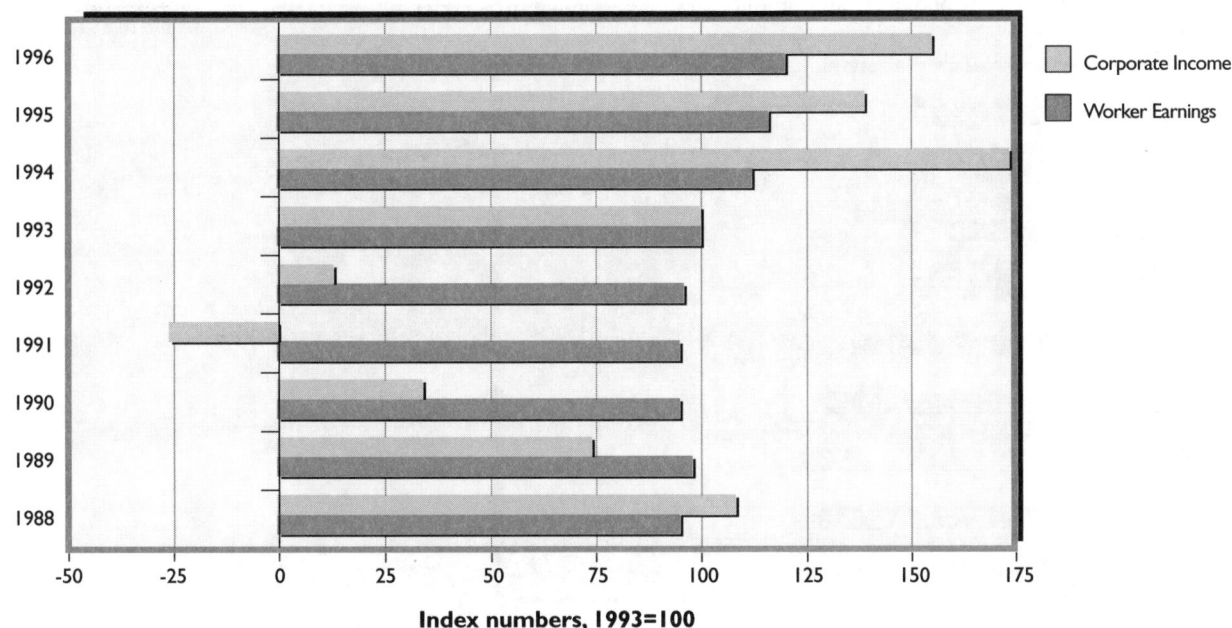

Source: U.S. Bureau of Labor Statistics, U.S. Bureau of the Census, and estimates by the editors.

FIGURE 4A

U.S. CORPORATE INCOME AND WORKER EARNINGS: MOTOR VEHICLE INDUSTRY

Corporate operating income and aggregate production worker earnings

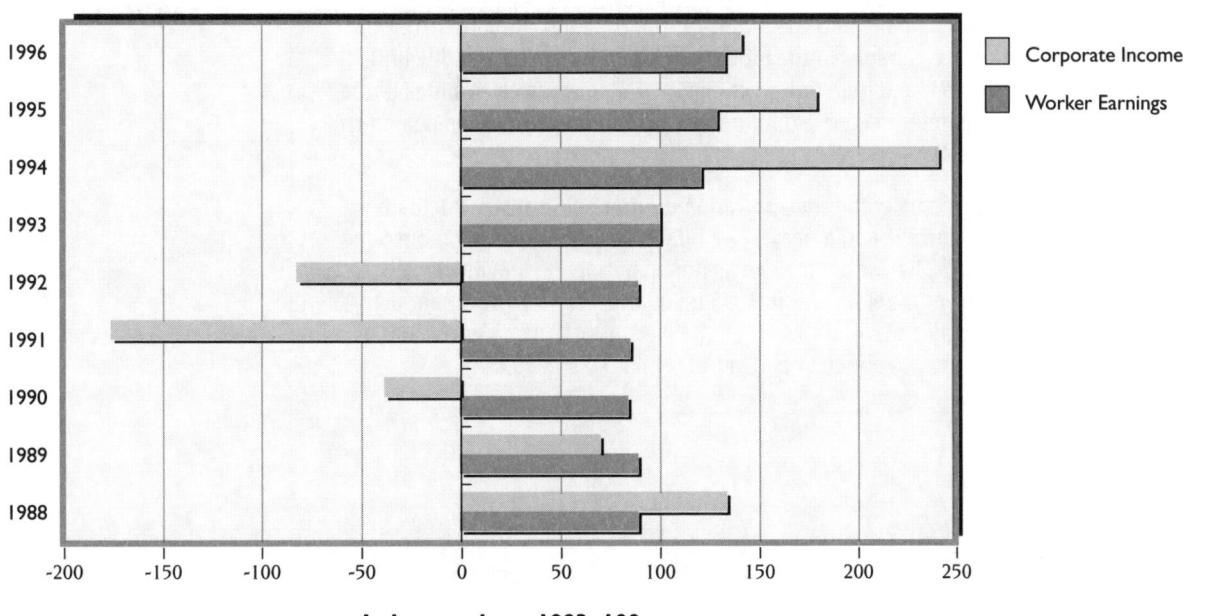

Source: U.S. Bureau of Labor Statistics, U.S. Bureau of the Census, and estimates by the editors.

FIGURE 4B

U.S. CORPORATE INCOME AND WORKER EARNINGS: AIRCRAFT AND PARTS, AND GUIDED MISSILES AND SPACE VEHICLES

Corporate operating income and aggregate production worker earnings

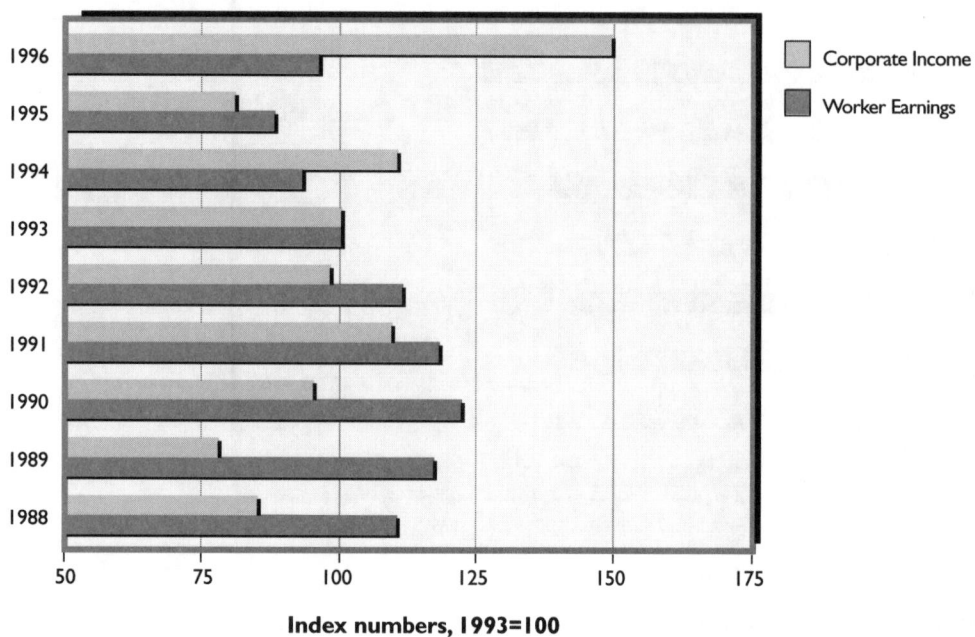

Index numbers, 1993=100

Source: U.S. Bureau of Labor Statistics, U.S. Bureau of the Census, and estimates by the editors.

Finance. Corporate income in the **transportation equipment industry** and its sub-industries has improved significantly from 1991 while little change has occurred in production worker earnings (Figures 4-4B). For the industry as a whole, corporate earnings varied radically from year to year, falling into the red in 1991 and then soaring to a 10-year high three years later. Corporate earnings in the **motor vehicle industry** fell steadily until 1991, climbed to a record in 1994, and then tailed off (Figure 4A). Corporate earnings in the **aerospace industry** charted an uneven course during most of the period and then soared to their best level in 1996 (Figure 4B).

During 1988-1996, operating income of the **transportation equipment industry** fluctuated between a loss of $3.8 billion in 1991 and a peak $25.2 billion achieved in 1994 (Table 6). After-tax income hit its high of $24.4 billion in 1996, as nonoperating income increased. After-tax income was 4.96 percent of total sales in 1996 (in contrast to -8.74 at the industry's nadir in 1992); it was 17.83 percent of stockholders' equity (versus –41.18 percent in 1992). Debt, largely long-term, amounted to about 14 percent of total assets in 1996.

TABLE 6

U.S. CORPORATE INCOME AND ASSETS: TRANSPORTATION EQUIPMENT

(Monetary values in millions of U.S. dollars)

INCOME AND EXPENSES	1988	1989	1990	1991	1992	1993	1994	1995	1996	CHANGE OR AVERAGE[1]
Sales and receipts	343,228	348,269	352,872	340,721	370,718	402,444	445,703	475,513	492,177	4.61
Depreciation and amortization	(12,174)	(12,571)	(13,301)	(13,846)	(14,514)	(14,860)	(15,798)	(17,302)	(18,159)	5.13
Other operating costs	(315,433)	(325,006)	(334,673)	(330,639)	(354,287)	(373,061)	(404,673)	(438,078)	(451,544)	4.59
Income from operations	15,620	10,692	4,899	(3,765)	1,917	14,524	25,232	20,132	22,472	4.65
Nonoperating income (expenditures)	7,789	5,920	195	(2,836)	(48,698)	(5,926)	6,090	8,351	10,149	....
Income before taxes	23,409	16,611	5,094	(6,602)	(46,782)	8,597	31,321	28,484	32,621	4.24
Income after taxes	17,493	13,111	4,589	(4,825)	(32,402)	7,791	22,882	21,438	24,416	4.26
Cash dividends	4,926	6,158	5,912	4,447	4,886	6,441	5,426	6,973	12,499	12.34
Income retained in business	12,569	6,953	(1,324)	(9,273)	(37,287)	1,348	17,456	14,463	11,917	-0.66
Direct credits (charges)	(1,982)	(2,193)	561	(1,103)	(3,465)	(4,013)	2,036	1,230	(2,508)	....
Ending retained earnings	89,476	92,923	92,122	81,821	42,320	37,575	57,300	70,814	79,880	-1.41
ASSETS, END OF YEAR:										
Total	293,229	309,652	328,951	337,038	358,886	382,659	398,450	427,543	468,453	6.03
Accounts receivable	52,348	56,174	51,809	49,409	46,874	38,216	40,255	42,508	44,792	-1.93
Inventories	64,348	66,316	68,366	68,332	62,178	60,744	60,633	62,372	63,257	-0.21
Net property, plant and equipment	72,900	78,593	83,685	85,786	87,079	88,142	91,882	107,799	109,721	5.24
RATIOS, PERCENT:										
INCOME TO SALES:										
Before tax	6.82	4.77	1.44	-1.94	-12.62	2.14	7.03	5.99	6.63	2.25
After tax	5.10	3.76	1.30	-1.42	-8.74	1.94	5.13	4.51	4.96	1.84
INCOME TO STOCKHOLDERS' EQUITY:										
Before tax	21.12	14.38	4.42	-5.93	-59.45	10.61	29.82	22.51	23.82	6.81
After tax	15.78	11.35	3.99	-4.34	-41.18	9.62	21.78	16.94	17.83	5.75
INCOME TO TOTAL ASSETS:										
Before tax	7.98	5.36	1.55	-1.96	-13.04	2.25	7.86	6.66	6.96	2.63
After tax	5.97	4.23	1.40	-1.43	-9.03	2.04	5.74	5.01	5.21	2.13
AS A PERCENT OF TOTAL ASSETS:										
Property, plant and equipment	24.86	25.38	25.44	25.45	24.26	23.03	23.06	25.21	23.42	24.46
Short-term debt	1.42	2.45	3.17	2.34	1.68	2.16	1.13	1.38	1.43	1.91
Long-term debt	15.16	15.22	16.36	16.39	14.85	10.94	11.43	11.41	12.54	13.81
Stockholders' equity	37.80	37.31	35.00	33.02	21.93	21.17	26.36	29.60	29.23	30.16

1. For income and asset amounts, compound annual growth rate; for ratios, average of ratios for the years shown.

Source: U.S. Bureau of the Census, Quarterly Financial Report.

Notes: Parentheses ( ) indicate negative items, e.g., net expenses, charges, or losses. Net property, plant, and equipment is net of accumulated depreciation. Because the samples used to collect the data change, retained earnings at the end of a given year will not exactly equal the previous year's retained earnings plus the current year's retained income and credits.

Operating income of the **motor vehicle industry** rose at an annual rate of 0.70 percent during 1988-1996, but this masks considerable improvement made from the low of 1991, when it was $12 billion in the red, to $9.6 billion in 1996. After-tax income since 1988 has ranged from minus $30.7 billion in 1992 to a peak of $16.5 billion in 1994; in 1996, it stood at $15.3 billion (Table 6A). After-tax income was 4.67 percent of sales and 19.08 percent of stockholders' equity in 1996. Debt totaled a little over 9 percent of total sales in 1996.

TABLE 6A

U.S. CORPORATE INCOME AND ASSETS: MOTOR VEHICLES AND PARTS

(Monetary values in millions of U.S. dollars)

INCOME AND EXPENSES	1988	1989	1990	1991	1992	1993	1994	1995	1996	CHANGE OR AVERAGE[1]
Sales and receipts	219,300	217,850	206,206	190,228	220,868	257,282	306,704	323,774	328,187	5.17
Depreciation and amortization	(8,104)	(8,229)	(8,712)	(9,033)	(9,571)	(9,869)	(10,816)	(12,210)	(12,727)	5.80
Other operating costs	(202,115)	(204,880)	(200,093)	(193,120)	(216,843)	(240,622)	(279,521)	(299,396)	(305,855)	5.31
Income from operations	9,082	4,743	(2,599)	(11,925)	(5,545)	6,791	16,367	12,168	9,606	0.70
Nonoperating income (expenditures)	7,448	5,818	698	614	(39,749)	(5,552)	5,908	8,135	9,963	....
Income before taxes	16,529	10,561	(1,901)	(11,310)	(45,293)	1,238	22,276	20,302	19,568	2.13
Income after taxes	12,474	8,801	(548)	(7,605)	(30,731)	2,758	16,547	15,429	15,313	2.60
Cash dividends	3,442	4,194	4,036	2,647	3,107	2,964	3,377	4,505	9,769	13.93
Income retained in business	9,031	4,607	(4,583)	(10,252)	(33,838)	(207)	13,169	10,925	5,544	-5.92
Direct credits (charges)	(1,550)	(1,214)	744	(417)	(1,713)	(2,990)	2,088	911	(1,437)	....
Ending retained earnings	61,354	63,530	59,944	49,852	13,241	8,942	24,514	35,579	39,079	-5.48
ASSETS, END OF YEAR:										
Total	170,639	174,479	185,482	195,554	218,137	236,768	252,389	267,279	288,019	6.76
Accounts receivable	31,217	30,862	28,630	29,199	28,682	20,146	21,052	22,407	22,859	-3.82
Inventories	16,278	15,078	16,283	16,727	16,026	16,151	19,151	20,032	20,495	2.92
Net property, plant and equipment	47,904	51,443	54,486	55,685	55,529	56,472	61,381	71,849	74,873	5.74
RATIOS, PERCENT:										
INCOME TO SALES:										
Before tax	7.54	4.85	-0.92	-5.95	-20.51	0.48	7.26	6.27	5.96	0.55
After tax	5.69	4.04	-0.27	-4.00	-13.91	1.07	5.40	4.77	4.67	0.83
INCOME TO STOCKHOLDERS' EQUITY:										
Before tax	21.94	13.81	-2.64	-16.66	-113.85	3.10	37.26	26.85	24.38	-0.65
After tax	16.56	11.51	-0.76	-11.21	-77.25	6.90	27.67	20.41	19.08	1.43
INCOME TO TOTAL ASSETS:										
Before tax	9.69	6.05	-1.02	-5.78	-20.76	0.52	8.83	7.60	6.79	1.32
After tax	7.31	5.04	-0.30	-3.89	-14.09	1.16	6.56	5.77	5.32	1.43
AS A PERCENT OF TOTAL ASSETS:										
Property, plant and equipment	28.07	29.48	29.38	28.48	25.46	23.85	24.32	26.88	26.00	26.88
Short-term debt	1.39	1.92	3.90	2.71	1.71	2.30	0.83	0.88	1.00	1.85
Long-term debt	16.80	15.95	16.23	16.20	14.37	7.97	9.47	8.87	8.28	12.68
Stockholders' equity	44.14	43.83	38.79	34.71	18.24	16.89	23.69	28.29	27.86	30.71

1. For income and asset amounts, compound annual growth rate; for ratios, average of ratios for the years shown.

Source: U.S. Bureau of the Census, Quarterly Financial Report.

Notes: Parentheses ( ) indicate negative items, e.g., net expenses, charges, or losses. Net property, plant, and equipment is net of accumulated depreciation. Because the samples used to collect the data change, retained earnings at the end of a given year will not exactly equal the previous year's retained earnings plus the current year's retained income and credits.

The **aerospace industry's** income from operations rose by 7.2 percent annually during 1988-1996 to $10.4 billion (Table 6B). After-tax income in 1996 soared nearly 70 percent above the previous year's to $7.3 billion as sales of commercial aircraft took off and cost cutting and industry restructuring began to pay off. The ratios of after-tax income to sales (5.67 percent) and to stockholders' equity (16.16 percent) also hit their highest levels in 1996. Debt rose slightly in 1996.

TABLE 6B

U.S. CORPORATE INCOME AND ASSETS: AIRCRAFT, GUIDED MISSILES AND PARTS

(Monetary values in millions of U.S. dollars)

INCOME AND EXPENSES	1988	1989	1990	1991	1992	1993	1994	1995	1996	CHANGE OR AVERAGE[1]
Sales and receipts	112,846	118,363	133,618	135,152	134,420	128,633	120,629	120,103	129,161	1.70
Depreciation and amortization	(3,775)	(4,016)	(4,250)	(4,353)	(4,443)	(4,472)	(4,501)	(4,068)	(4,270)	1.55
Other operating costs	(103,098)	(108,876)	(122,678)	(123,188)	(123,075)	(117,148)	(108,422)	(110,337)	(114,471)	1.32
Income from operations	5,972	5,471	6,692	7,612	6,900	7,011	7,705	5,695	10,419	7.20
Nonoperating income (expenditures)	739	(37)	(544)	(3,432)	(8,666)	(307)	372	148	(27)	....
Income before taxes	6,711	5,434	6,147	4,179	(1,766)	6,704	8,078	5,843	10,393	5.62
Income after taxes	4,883	3,861	4,487	2,482	(1,836)	4,618	5,647	4,347	7,326	5.20
Cash dividends	1,465	1,807	1,823	1,678	1,610	3,279	1,832	1,909	2,071	4.42
Income retained in business	3,417	2,054	2,665	804	(3,449)	1,337	3,814	2,440	5,255	5.53
Direct credits (charges)	(156)	(930)	(350)	(707)	(1,673)	(758)	4	97	(1,269)	....
Ending retained earnings	27,490	28,255	30,386	30,555	26,424	26,063	30,380	30,344	34,294	2.80
ASSETS, END OF YEAR:										
Total	109,545	121,892	131,823	130,886	127,770	132,704	132,423	123,443	144,136	3.49
Accounts receivable	16,102	18,732	19,620	17,801	15,762	15,982	16,928	17,310	18,954	2.06
Inventories	45,558	49,944	50,423	49,957	44,010	42,260	39,227	32,064	32,308	-4.20
Net property, plant and equipment	22,211	24,506	26,161	26,542	27,483	27,689	26,457	25,913	26,325	2.15
RATIOS, PERCENT:										
INCOME TO SALES:										
Before tax	5.95	4.59	4.60	3.09	-1.31	5.21	6.70	4.86	8.05	4.64
After tax	4.33	3.26	3.36	1.84	-1.37	3.59	4.68	3.62	5.67	3.22
INCOME TO STOCKHOLDERS' EQUITY:										
Before tax	19.81	14.72	15.41	10.39	-5.12	18.41	19.99	14.40	22.93	14.55
After tax	14.42	10.46	11.25	6.17	-5.33	12.68	13.97	10.71	16.16	10.05
INCOME TO TOTAL ASSETS:										
Before tax	6.13	4.46	4.66	3.19	-1.38	5.05	6.10	4.73	7.21	4.46
After tax	4.46	3.17	3.40	1.90	-1.44	3.48	4.26	3.52	5.08	3.09
AS A PERCENT OF TOTAL ASSETS:										
Property, plant and equipment	20.28	20.10	19.85	20.28	21.51	20.87	19.98	20.99	18.26	20.23
Short-term debt	1.25	3.12	2.03	1.48	1.36	1.53	1.40	1.17	1.35	1.63
Long-term debt	11.36	13.28	15.92	15.80	15.06	15.40	14.92	15.61	20.19	15.28
Stockholders' equity	30.92	30.29	30.26	30.74	26.97	27.44	30.52	32.88	31.45	30.16

1. For income and asset amounts, compound annual growth rate; for ratios, average of ratios for the years shown.

Source: U.S. Bureau of the Census, Quarterly Financial Report.

Notes: Parentheses ( ) indicate negative items, e.g., net expenses, charges, or losses. Net property, plant, and equipment is net of accumulated depreciation. Because the samples used to collect the data change, retained earnings at the end of a given year will not exactly equal the previous year's retained earnings plus the current year's retained income and credits.

CANADA

Canada's **transportation equipment industry** consisted of 1,349 establishments and 209,879 employees in 1993 (Table 7). The largest subindustry is motor vehicles, with 59 percent of total industry shipments in 1993, while motor vehicle parts and accessories had another 26 percent of the total. The aircraft and aircraft parts industry accounted for only 7.5 percent of industry shipments in 1993. Hourly earnings by the industry in 1993 averaged Can$18.08, with the highest (Can$22.65) earned by workers in motor vehicle production.

Shipments by the transportation equipment industry were valued at Can$76.1 billion in 1994, compared with Can$64.1 billion the previous year and Can$43.3 billion in 1987 (Table 8). Industry employment in 1994, at 217,198, was not much changed from the 1987 level but was about 10 percent under the 1989 high. Production worker employment declined from the late 1980s, but their share of the workforce rose slightly to almost 80 percent in 1993 and 1994. Hourly earnings of production workers averaged Can$18.62 in 1994, compared with Can$14.47 in 1988. The average workweek was 43.1 hours in 1994.

Canada's **motor vehicle industry** (including parts and accessories and truck and bus bodies and trailers) had shipments valued at Can$66.1 billion in 1994, 79 percent more than in 1987 (Table 8). However, employment during that period grew only slightly from 154,003 in 1987

TABLE 7

CANADA: COMPONENT INDUSTRIES OF TRANSPORTATION EQUIPMENT (CSIC 32), 1993

(Monetary values in Canadian dollars)

INDUSTRY NAME	CSIC	ESTABLISH-MENTS (NUMBER)	EMPLOYMENT NUMBER	EMPLOYMENT PERCENT OF INDUSTRY TOTAL	VALUE OF SHIPMENTS (MILLIONS)	AVERAGE HOURLY EARNINGS[1]
TRANSPORTATION EQUIPMENT INDUSTRIES	32	1,349	209,879	100.0	CAN$64,112.8	CAN$18.08
Aircraft and aircraft parts	321	182	36,238	17.3	4,796.0	17.96
Motor vehicles	323	31	54,192	25.8	37,802.5	22.65
Trucks and bus bodies and trailers	324	288	10,856	5.2	1,259.1	13.47
Trucks and bus bodies	3241	118	4,407	2.1	456.2	14.15
Commercial trailers	3242	89	3,010	1.4	324.9	13.95
Noncommercial trailers	3243	63	1,878	0.9	279.2	12.20
Mobile homes	3244	18	1,561	0.7	198.8	12.39
Motor vehicle parts and accessories	325	554	87,974	41.9	16,931.9	15.86
Motor vehicle engine and parts	3251	33	6,625	3.2	2,447.0	18.52
Motor vehicle wiring assemblies	3252	26	4,898	2.3	836.0	12.46
Motor vehicle stampings	3253	74	13,372	6.4	2,823.5	16.30
Motor vehicle steering and suspensions	3254	43	6,857	3.3	1,113.2	16.09
Motor vehicle wheels and brake	3255	50	6,971	3.3	1,106.7	14.60
Motor vehicle plastic parts	3256	68	11,595	5.5	1,420.0	12.93
Motor vehicle fabric accessories	3257	31	6,892	3.3	1,636.1	16.96
Other motor vehicle accessories and parts	3259	229	30,764	14.7	5,549.4	16.78
Railroad rolling stock	326	22	6,520	3.1	1,212.3	18.70
Shipbuilding and repairs	327	52	9,122	4.3	1,185.6	20.15
Boatbuilding and repairs	328	198	2,639	1.3	225.3	12.69
Other transportation equipment	329	22	2,338	1.1	700.0	14.04

1. Including overtime.

Source: Adapted from Statistics Canada, *Manufacturing Industries of Canada* (Cat. No. 31-203).

TABLE 8

CANADIAN EMPLOYMENT AND SHIPMENTS: TRANSPORTATION EQUIPMENT INDUSTRIES, 1987-1994

(Monetary values in Canadian dollars)

	1987	1988	1989	1990	1991	1992	1993	1994	CHANGE[1]
TRANSPORTATION EQUIPMENT									
All employees	218,368	232,735	240,838	226,712	208,145	213,009	209,879	217,198	-0.08
Establishments	1,514	1,674	1,699	1,599	1,472	1,400	1,349	1,336	-1.77
Employees per establishment	144	139	142	142	141	152	156	163	1.72
Production workers per establishment	.....	109	111	110	110	120	124	129	2.90
PRODUCTION WORKERS:									
Total	.....	182,229	188,887	175,200	161,624	168,493	166,985	172,685	-0.89
Percent of all employees	.....	78.3	78.4	77.3	77.6	79.1	79.6	79.5	.....
Male	.....	153,472	158,248	146,002	135,702	.....	.....	.....	.....
Female	.....	28,757	30,639	29,198	25,922	.....	.....	.....	.....
Percent of all production workers	.....	15.8	16.2	16.7	16.0	.....	.....	.....	.....
Average hourly earnings	.....	14.47	15.16	15.96	16.85	17.26	18.08	18.62	4.29
Average weekly earnings	.....	608.52	633.68	652.03	683.88	705.10	753.89	802.53	4.72
Average weekly hours	.....	42.1	41.8	40.9	40.6	40.9	41.7	43.1	0.41
Shipments (millions)	43,333	51,718	53,783	51,655	48,180	52,785	64,113	76,132	8.38
MOTOR VEHICLES AND PARTS									
All employees	154,003	162,272	167,834	154,778	143,137	148,313	153,022	159,247	0.48
Establishments	894	1001	1082	984	926	885	873	873	-0.34
Employees per establishment	172	162	155	157	155	168	175	182	0.82
Production workers per establishment	.....	134	129	129	128	141	148	153	2.24
PRODUCTION WORKERS:									
Total	.....	134,240	139,327	127,235	118,229	124,474	128,836	133,709	-0.07
Percent of all employees	.....	82.7	83.0	82.2	82.6	83.9	84.2	84.0	.....
Male	.....	108,915	112,228	101,615	95,194	.....	.....	.....	.....
Female	.....	25,325	27,099	25,620	23,035	.....	.....	.....	.....
Percent of all production workers	.....	18.9	19.4	20.1	19.5	.....	.....	.....	.....
Average hourly earnings	.....	14.48	15.14	15.84	16.74	17.25	18.10	18.60	4.26
Average weekly earnings	.....	619.16	637.85	648.49	678.97	703.46	756.76	807.24	4.52
Average weekly hours	.....	42.8	42.1	40.9	40.6	40.8	41.8	43.4	0.25
Shipments (millions)	36,884	44,394	44,793	42,552	39,817	44,769	55,994	66,120	8.70
AIRCRAFT AND PARTS									
All employees	40,157	43,771	44,976	46,412	42,635	42,127	36,238	36,310	-1.43
Establishments	185	202	194	199	199	189	182	177	-0.63
Employees per establishment	217	217	232	233	214	223	199	205	-0.80
Production workers per establishment	.....	143	150	15.:	139	146	127	130	-1.57
PRODUCTION WORKERS:									
Total	.....	28,938	29,133	30,179	27,701	27,571	23,071	23,065	-3.71
Percent of all employees	.....	66.1	64.8	65.0	65.0	65.4	63.7	63.5	.....
Male	.....	26,260	26,378	27,250	25,294	.....	.....	.....	.....
Female	.....	2,678	2,755	2,929	2,407	.....	.....	.....	.....
Percent of all production workers	.....	9.3	9.5	9.7	8.7	.....	.....	.....	.....
Average hourly earnings	.....	15.04	15.93	16.73	17.63	17.17	17.96	20.99	5.72
Average weekly earnings	.....	605.45	649.75	687.89	723.76	719.78	751.91	889.86	6.63
Average weekly hours	.....	40.3	40.8	41.1	41.1	41.9	41.9	42.4	0.86
Shipments (millions)	3,702	4,309	5,112	5,699	5,391	4,862	4,796	5,744	6.48

1. Compound annual growth rate.

Source: Adapted from Statistics Canada, *Manufacturing Industries of Canada* (Cat. No. 31-203).

to 159,247 in 1994. Production workers accounted for about 84 percent of the workforce in 1994. Their hourly wages that year averaged Can$18.60, versus Can$14.48 in 1988, and the average workweek was 43.4 hours.

Shipments by the Canadian aircraft industry totaled Can$5.7 billion in 1994, compared with Can$3.7 billion in 1987 (Table 8). Employment in the industry rose until 1990 but then fell steadily, to 36,310 people in 1994. That year, production workers accounted for almost 64 percent of the workforce, and their hourly earnings averaged Can$20.99. The average workweek in 1994 was 42.4 hours.

MEXICO

Motor vehicle production is far the largest component of Mexico's transportation equipment industry. According to Mexico's 1994 economic census, the automobile industry in 1993 had 167,221 employees, including 125,301 production workers, 40,880 nonproduction employees, and 1,040 unpaid (family) workers (Table 9). Earnings in 1993 averaged 17,478 new pesos ($5,595) for production workers and 45,561 new pesos ($14,586) for nonproduction employees. The "aircraft and other" industry had 14,151 employees, including 11,023 production workers, and 3,030 nonproduction employees. Production workers earned an average of 11,482 new pesos ($3,675) a year, and nonproduction employees earned 36,520 new pesos ($11,691). Table 10, which has more comprehensive industry data, shows total employment in the transportation equipment industry at 331,338 in 1995 and an annual growth rate of 3.09 percent for the 1988-1995 period.

TABLE 9

MEXICO: COMPONENT INDUSTRIES OF TRANSPORTATION EQUIPMENT INDUSTRIES (CMAP 3841 AND 3842), 1993

(Monetary values in 1993 Mexican New Pesos)

			ALL WORKERS									
							PAID WORKERS					
							PRODUCTION WORKERS		NONPRODUCTION EMPLOYEES		BENEFITS	UNPAID
INDUSTRY	CMAP	NUMBER OF UNITS	NUMBER	PERCENT OF INDUSTRY TOTAL	AVERAGE DAYS WORKED	REMUN- ERATION[1]	NUMBER	WAGES AND SALARIES	NUMBER	WAGES AND SALARIES	PER PAID EMPLOYEE	WORKERS, NUMBER
Automobile industry	3841	1,401	167,221	92	281	37,377	125,301	17,478	40,880	45,561	12,991	1,040
Aircraft and other	3842	171	14,151	8	277	22,322	11,023	11,482	3,030	36,520	5,442	98

1. Average annual remuneration including benefits.

Source: INEGI, Censos Economicos 1994.

TABLE 10

MEXICAN EMPLOYMENT: TRANSPORTATION EQUIPMENT, 1988-1995

	1988	1989	1990	1991	1992	1993	1994	1995	CHANGE[1]
TOTAL EMPLOYMENT: Transportation equipment	267,742	313,448	342,837	335,396	386,370	348,058	338,755	331,338	3.09

1. Compound annual growth rate.

Source: Sistema de Cuentas Nacionales de Mexico, INEGI.

INTERNATIONAL TRADE

United States. Global U.S. exports of transportation equipment totaled $92.9 billion in 1996, or 38 percent more than shipments in 1990 (Table 11). Imports during that period rose 43 percent to $129.2 billion. The resulting trade deficit of $36.3 billion was exceeded only by the $39.6 billion of 1995 and was more than three and a half times the low point reached in 1992. About a third of U.S. exports in 1996 went to Canada, which supplied a slightly larger share of U.S. imports. Mexico received about 6 percent of U.S. exports and supplied about 12 percent of the imports.

According to the U.S. Department of Commerce, U.S. exports of new and used motor vehicles totaled $13.6 billion in the first half of 1997, or 7 percent more than in the same period of 1996. However, imports rose 11.7 percent to $44.2 billion, boosting the U.S. trade deficit to $30.6 billion. U.S. trade balances with Canada and Mexico improved slightly, while the balance with Japan deteriorated. Exports to Canada jumped 19.3 percent to $7.7 billion, as imports from Canada rose 5.7 percent to $18.8 billion, leaving a U.S. trade deficit of $11.2 billion. U.S. exports to Mexico increased 41.3 percent to $800 million and imports from Mexico rose 1.9 percent to $5.8 billion, resulting in a U.S. trade deficit with Mexico of $5 billion. The deficit with Japan reached $10.3 billion in the first half as imports from Japan rose 15.4 percent to $11.3 billion and exports to it fell 37.7 percent to $1 billion.

South Korea also is increasing its share of U.S. motor vehicle imports, and soon will have one affiliate producing in the United States. In 1995, the United States and South Korea signed a U.S.-Korea Automotive Memorandum of Understanding to Increase Market Access for Foreign Passenger Vehicles in the Republic of Korea. In 1996, however, Korea imported less than 3,900 vehicles from the Big-3 American auto manufacturers, compared with a total Korean market of 1.6 million vehicles.

U.S. exports of automotive parts between 1992 and 1995 grew at an average annual rate of 12 percent, from $28 billion to $40 billion. This included a 58 percent increase in shipments to Japan, to $1.6 billion.

Canada. U.S. exports of transportation equipment to Canada totaled $32.4 billion in 1996, while Canadian shipments to the United States were $48 billion (Table 11). The U.S. trade deficit with Canada that year was $15.6 billion, compared with $10.4 billion in 1990. Canada's still-small exports to Mexico rose by two-thirds between 1990 and 1996.

Mexico. U.S. exports of transportation equipment to Mexico were valued at $5.7 billion in 1996, about 50 percent higher than in 1990 (Table 11). Mexico's exports to the United States, however, rose almost fourfold between 1990 and 1996, to $15.4 billion, reflecting increased sourcing of motor vehicle and parts production to Mexico. The U.S. trade deficit with Mexico thus rose from $196 million in 1990 to $9.7 billion in 1996. Canada's trade deficit with Mexico also grew dramatically, from $590 million in 1990 to almost $2.2 billion in 1996, as Mexico's exports to Canada almost tripled during that period to $2.4 billion.

NAFTA. The U.S. deficit with Canada and Mexico rose almost 140 percent between 1990 and 1996, to $25.3 billion (Table 11). Most of this increase occurred after 1993. Canada's NAFTA trade surplus rose from $9.8 billion in 1990 to $13.4 billion in 1996, while Mexico's climbed from $786 million to $11.9 billion. (See the Workforce and Employment section and this book's feature, "NAFTA-The First Four Years," for information on U.S. workers certified to have lost their jobs because of NAFTA.)

TABLE 11

INTERNATIONAL TRADE, TRANSPORTATION EQUIPMENT

(Millions of U.S. dollars)

	1989[1]	1990	1991	1992	1993	1994	1995	1996
Global trade, U.S.								
Imports								
Value	87,855.1	90,139.1	88,608.3	92,708.5	102,259.2	115,998.0	122,343.8	129,235.2
Ratio to new supply[2]	20.8	21.3	21.1	20.1	21.0	21.5	.....	.....
Ratio to apparent consumption[3]	24.0	25.3	25.7	24.6	25.2	25.5	.....	.....
Exports								
Value	56,211.2	67,469.4	75,498.3	82,546.0	80,196.1	85,068.6	82,699.5	92,886.8
Ratio to comparable domestic shipments	16.8	20.2	22.7	22.5	20.9	20.1	.....	.....
TRADE BALANCE	(31,643.9)	(22,669.7)	(13,110.0)	(10,162.5)	(22,063.1)	(30,929.4)	(39,644.3)	(36,348.4)
BILATERAL TRADE: NAFTA[4]								
U.S. exports to Canada	18,019.0	20,135.7	20,660.4	21,104.4	24,358.3	28,788.0	30,894.9	32,416.4
Canadian exports to U.S.	29,896.2	30,491.0	29,530.6	31,861.8	36,672.3	42,646.7	45,421.4	48,006.2
U.S. exports to Mexico	2,693.9	3,801.9	4,329.7	5,440.3	5,112.5	6,363.4	4,755.0	5,693.2
Mexican exports to U.S.	2,941.8	3,997.4	4,518.6	5,328.6	6,311.7	7,961.8	11,596.3	15,398.4
Canadian exports to Mexico	118.1	127.9	150.7	150.2	141.6	155.3	188.9	213.0
Mexican exports to Canada	566.0	718.2	1,425.6	1,328.5	1,749.8	2,018.1	2,226.9	2,369.0
TRADE BALANCES WITHIN NAFTA[5]								
Canada	11,429.3	9,765.0	7,595.3	9,579.1	10,705.8	11,995.9	12,488.5	13,433.8
Mexico	695.8	785.8	1,463.8	1,066.6	2,807.4	3,461.2	8,879.3	11,861.2
United States	(12,125.1)	(10,550.8)	(9,059.0)	(10,645.7)	(13,513.1)	(15,457.1)	(21,367.8)	(25,295.0)

1. 1989 and earlier data on U.S. exports to Canada for manufacturing total and manufacturing industries are not comparable with data for 1990 and later years because of a change in the reporting system. The NAFTA trade balances for the U.S. and Canada also are affected.

2. New supply equals comparable domestic shipments plus imports for consumption.

3. Apparent consumption equals comparable domestic shipments plus imports for consumption less exports.

4. Amounts less than U.S. $100,000 shown as zero.

5. Parentheses indicate an excess of imports over exports. Because of commodity coding and other data differences among the three countries, these trade balances are only rough estimates and should be used with caution.

Source for U.S. Global Trade: U.S. Department of Commerce, International Trade Administration.

Source for U.S. -Canada and U.S.-Mexico Bilateral Trade: U.S. Bureau of the Census.

Source for Canada-Mexico and Mexico-Canada Bilateral Trade: Statistics Canada, Foreign Trade Division, Special tabulation, March 1997, converted to U.S. dollars by the editors.

BUSINESS AND PROFESSIONAL SERVICES

THE UNITED STATES

This chapter presents data on three United States industries that provide services to business and are significantly represented in U.S.international trade—the "business services" industry, legal services, and engineering and management services. The three U.S. industry groups have not been combined, and some data are shown for business services only.

Products and Processes. *Business services* includes firms involved in a broad range of activities. The industry is growing very rapidly as firms move to outsource aspects of business that once took place in-house. Evidence of this is found in the growth in temporary staffing and data processing industries. The expanding role of computers in the workplace and the growth of the internet promise to sustain industry growth into the future.

Business services is divided into eight major subindustries: advertising; consumer credit reporting agencies, mercantile reporting agencies, and adjustment and collection agencies; mailing, reproduction, commercial art and photography, and stenographic services; services to dwellings and other buildings; miscellaneous equipment rental and leasing; personnel supply services; computer programming, data processing, and other computer related services; and miscellaneous business services. Computer services led the industry with $101.1 billion in sales in 1992; personnel supply services had the most employees, with a workforce of 1,974,732.

TABLE 1

UNITED STATES: COMPONENT INDUSTRIES OF BUSINESS AND PROFESSIONAL SERVICES (SIC 73, 81, AND 87), 1992

(Monetary values in millions of U.S. dollars)

INDUSTRY NAME	SIC	ESTABLISH-MENTS	SALES Value	SALES Percent by 4 Largest Companies	EMPLOY-MENT[1]	PAYROLL
Business services	73	306,551	274,892	3.9	5,542,417	109,299
Advertising	731	19,023	19,456	10.1	195,757	7,223
Consumer credit reporting agencies, mercantile reporting agencies, and adjustment and collection agencies	732	7,472	6,151	21.5	98,452	2,163
Mailing, reproduction, commercial art and photography, and stenographic services	733	32,086	18,339	8.1	234,595	5,522
Services to dwellings and other buildings	734	57,649	19,003	9.9	817,944	9,164
Miscellaneous equipment rental and leasing	735	24,816	21,778	10.1	199,912	4,905
Personnel supply services	736	31,166	38,163	9.8	1,974,732	26,436
Computer programming, data processing, and other computer related services	737	59,052	101,073	10.4	885,791	35,598
Miscellaneous business services	738	75,287	50,929	6.5	1,135,234	18,288
Legal services	81	151,737	101,114	.....	923,617	39,328
Engineering and management services	87, except 8733	232,885	192,819	.....	2,271,478	79,344
Engineering, architectural, and surveying	871	68,127	78,770	.....	824,608	32,745
Accounting, auditing, and bookkeeping services	872	79,097	34,038	.....	520,603	14,001
Research, developing, testing, except noncommercial	873, except 8733	13,531	22,690	.....	282,315	9,227
Management and public relations services	874	72,130	57,321	.....	643,952	23,371

1. Employment numbers from the economic censuses differ in definition and classification from the Bureau of Labor Statistics estimates in Table 2. Year-to-year comparisons between Table 1 and Table 2 are not appropriate.

Source: U.S. Bureau of the Census, 1992 Census of Services.

The *legal services* industry employed nearly a million persons in 1992 and had $101.1 billion in receipts.

Engineering and management services employed more than two million persons in 1992 and took in $192.8 billion. The largest of the four component industries was engineering, architectural, and surveying services, with 824,608 employees and $78.8 billion in receipts (Table 1).

Employment in business services is projected to increase from 5,734,700 employees in 1993 to more than 10 million by the year 2005. Much of the growth will come in personnel supply services, which are expected to experience an increase of 1,657,900 employees. Miscellaneous business services, services to buildings, and computer and data processing services will also employ many more people in 2005.

Employment in legal services is expected to grow by 346,000 from 1993 to 2005. For engineering and management services, close to a million new jobs are expected (Table 2).

TABLE 2

U.S. EMPLOYMENT AND EARNINGS: BUSINESS AND PROFESSIONAL SERVICES

INDUSTRY	SIC	1993			2005
		EMPLOYMENT[1]		AVERAGE HOURLY EARNINGS (U.S. DOLLARS)[2]	PROJECTED EMPLOYMENT[3]
		NUMBER OF PERSONS	PERCENT OF INDUSTRY TOTAL		
Business Services	73	5,734,700	100.0	10.12	10,031,501
Advertising	731	223,700	3.9	15.03	250,000
Credit reporting and collection	732	116,100	2.0	.....	159,289
Mailing, reproduction, and stenographic services	733	243,200	4.2	.....	325,929
Services to buildings	734	823,000	14.4	7.41	1,350,000
Miscellaneous equipment rental and leasing	735	208,200	3.6	10.64	325,000
Personnel supply services	736	1,906,100	33.2	.....	3,564,000
Computer and data processing services	737	892,800	15.6	16.46	1,610,500
Miscellaneous business services	738	1,321,600	23.0	8.68	2,446,783
Legal services	81	924,000	100.0	15.20	1,270,000
Engineering and management services	87	2,520,900	100.0	15.01	3,450,660
Engineering, architectural, and surveying services	871	757,100	30.0	16.27	1,043,500
Accounting, auditing, and bookkeeping services	872	507,900	20.1	13.01	612,860
Research, development, and testing services	873	567,500	22.5	16.07	745,000
Management and public relations services	874	688,400	27.3	13.90	1,049,300

1. Total payroll employment. Employment data from the economic censuses, as shown in Table 1, differ in definition and classification from the Bureau of Labor Statistics estimates in this table. Year-to-year comparisons between Table 1 and Table 2 are not appropriate.

2. Earnings of nonsupervisory workers, including overtime.

3. Number of persons, moderate projection by the U.S. Bureau of Labor Statistics.

Source: Bureau of Labor Statistics.

FIGURE 1

U.S. EMPLOYMENT IN BUSINESS SERVICES

Percent distribution by region, 1995

The regional distribution of employment in the business services industry was consistent with the overall distribution of employment in the United States. The Southeast had the highest share of industry employment at 23.6 percent; the Pacific region was the second largest with 17.9 percent.

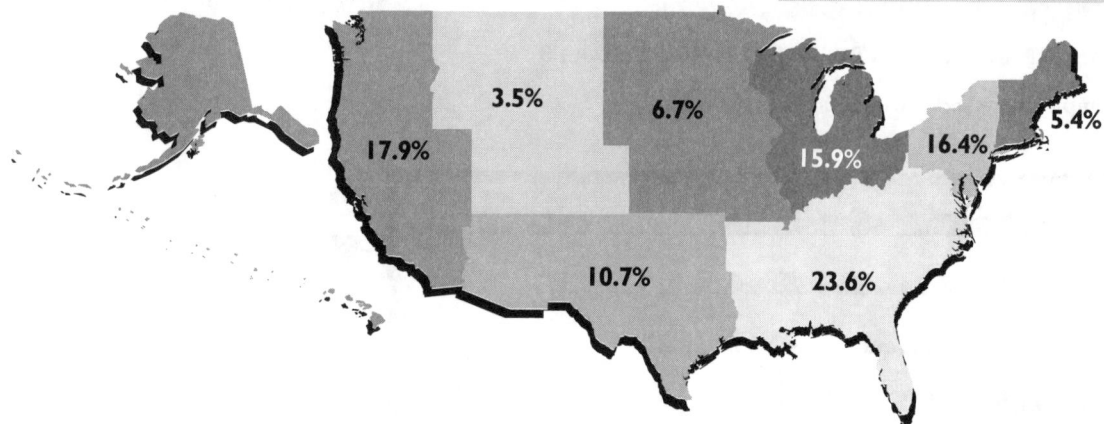

Source: U.S. Department of Commerce, Bureau of Economic Analysis.

What's New. *Advertising* on the internet is beginning to show signs of explosive growth, according to *BusinessWeek* magazine. In the first quarter of 1997, spending on advertising on the World Wide Web reached $133 billion, five times the spending in the same period for 1996. Analysts predict that spending on internet advertising will approach $1 billion by the end of 1997. One of the reasons cited for the growth is that Web advertising is no longer exclusively for technology firms. Now, consumer brand advertisers are beginning to advertise on the Web as well.

Personnel Supply Services. According to the National Association of Temporary and Staffing Services, more than 90 percent of U.S. businesses use external staffing services. The percentage of the workforce employed in temporary jobs has gone from 0.7 percent in 1985 to 1.78 percent in 1995. In 1996, the temporary staffing industry had revenues of more than $47 billion.

Computer Services. In 1996, software and software-related services had $102.8 billion in sales, according to the Business Software Alliance. Of this, $24.1 billion was accounted for by packaged business software sales. The software industry spends more than 7 percent of its revenues on research and development, compared with the 2.5 percent of GDP that goes to research and development for the economy as a whole.

Software piracy is a major concern for the industry with estimated 1996 losses of $11.2 billion worldwide due to illegal distribution, according to a joint study by the Business Software Alliance and the Software Publishers Association. They estimate that of the 523 million new software applications used throughout the world in 1996, 225 million units were pirated. Among the countries with the highest rates of piracy (i.e. percent of new applications that were pirated) were: Vietnam (99 percent), China (96 percent), and Russia (91 percent). The United States had the lowest piracy rate worldwide, at 27 percent, but the largest revenue loss of any country, at $2.3 billion. Canada's piracy rate fell from 44 percent in 1995 to 42 percent in 1996.

The millenium bug, an error in computer programs that will have some systems miscalculating the year 2000 as 1900, is a concern for producers and consumers of software. Estimates of the cost and difficulty of reprogramming computers vary widely, with some estimates of the total cost ranging as high as $600 billion.

FIGURE 2

U.S. EMPLOYMENT AND GROSS PRODUCT, BUSINESS SERVICES

Total payroll employment and constant dollar gross product

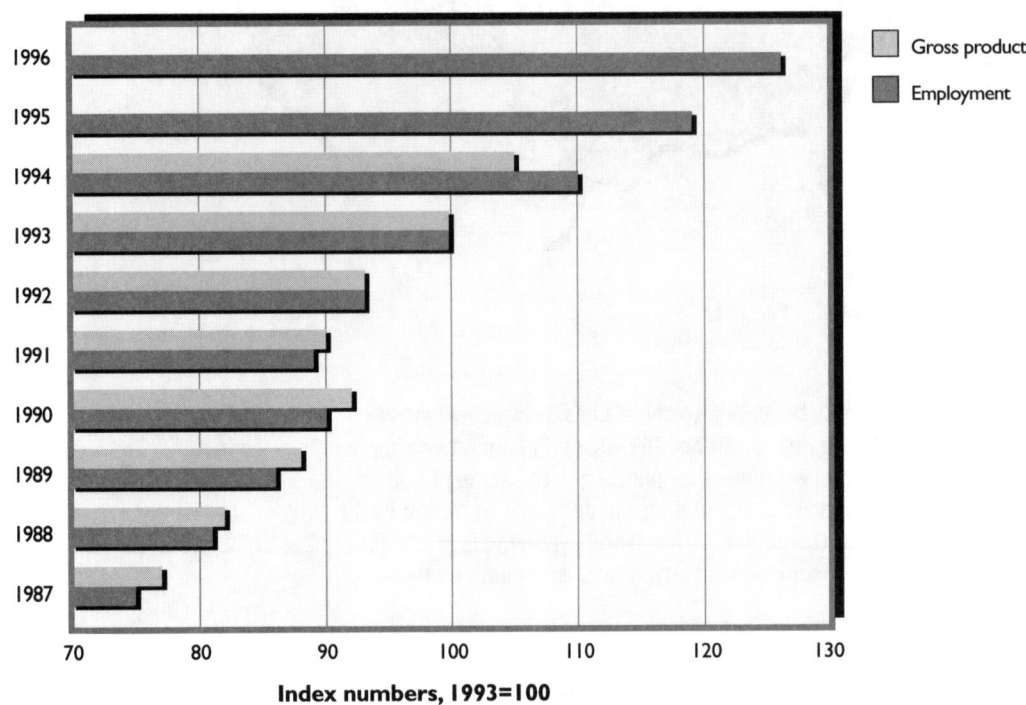

Index numbers, 1993=100

Source: U.S. Bureau of Labor Statistics, U.S. Department of Commerce, and estimates by the editors.

Output. Employment in business services increased every year from 1987 to 1996, except for a small decline in 1991. Gross product originating in business services, in constant 1992 dollars, grew in step with employment over the 1987-1994 period, rising every year (Figure 2). Business services output, as measured by sales, grew from $188.8 billion in 1987 to $424.3 billion in 1995, at an annual rate of 10.7 percent (Table 3). Current-dollar industry GDP grew at a slightly slower 8.59 percent per year from 1987 to 1994, but much faster than the growth rate for the economy as a whole. Even when GDP is adjusted for inflation (1992 dollars), it still increased at 4.7 percent per year. As a result of the industry's rapid GDP growth, its share of total GDP grew from 3.0 percent in 1987 to 3.7 percent in 1994.

Employment growth was slower but steady in legal services. Real output actually declined between 1990 and 1994, as measured by constant-dollar gross domestic product originating in the industry. Legal services were about unchanged as a percent of GDP in current dollars.

Employment in engineering and management services grew at a 3.1 percent annual rate from 1988 to 1996. Output in "other services," whose major component is this industry, rose at a similar pace from 1987 to 1994.

TABLE 3

U.S. OUTPUT: BUSINESS AND PROFESSIONAL SERVICES

(Millions of U.S. dollars, except as noted)

	1987	1988	1989	1990	1991	1992	1993	1994	1995	1996	GROWTH RATE
RECEIPTS OF TAXABLE FIRMS:											
Business services	188,856	223,369	251,658	280,699	287,214	309,439	336,491	374,850	424,322	.....	10.65
Legal services	72,115	81,636	89,144	97,640	100,027	108,443	111,749	113,787	114,357	.....	5.93
Engineering and management services	139,897	160,446	183,528	198,395	202,696	215,624	224,710	238,940	269,718	.....	8.55
OTHER OUTPUT MEASURES:											
Gross domestic product, Business services:											
Current dollars	142,385	163,345	178,995	198,996	197,728	218,911	233,395	253,482	.....	.....	.....
Percent of total GDP	3.0	3.2	3.3	3.5	3.3	3.5	3.6	3.7	.....	.....	.....
Chained (1992) dollars	179,651	191,291	205,304	216,502	210,401	218,911	234,272	246,957	.....	.....	.....
Gross domestic product, Legal services:											
Current dollars	61,137	69,365	74,170	80,698	83,653	90,147	92,282	94,446	.....	.....	.....
Percent of total GDP	1.3	1.4	1.4	1.4	1.4	1.4	1.4	1.4	.....	.....	.....
Chained (1992) dollars	83,336	90,545	91,151	91,463	88,777	90,147	87,901	86,710	.....	.....	.....
Gross domestic product, Other services[2]											
Current dollars	103,135	118,401	134,557	147,831	149,586	162,181	171,162	179,991	.....	.....	.....
Percent of total GDP	2.2	2.3	2.5	2.6	2.5	2.6	2.6	2.6	.....	.....	.....
Chained (1992) dollars	130,678	144,364	158,356	160,374	158,784	162,181	167,515	170,612	.....	.....	.....

1. Compound annual growth rate.

2. Museums, etc., Engineering and Management Services, and Services n.e.c.

Source: Receipts: U.S. Bureau of the Census, Annual Survey of Services; GDP: Bureau of Economic Analysis.

Workforce and Employment. Employment in business services increased from 4,278,000 in 1987 to 7,254,000 in 1996, at a rate of 6 percent per year (Table 4). The percentage of nonsupervisory workers in the industry increased from 85.8 percent in 1987 to 88.9 percent in 1996. This is a significant increase and might suggest a proportional decline in supervisors, but it is probably due to growth in the personnel supply industry in which employees are supervised on customers' sites by customers' supervisory employees. Though the number of women working in the industry increased over the period, their percentage of industry employment fell slightly to 47.1 percent in 1996.

Average hourly earnings of nonsupervisory workers increased from $8.61 per hour in 1988 to $11.21 in 1996, at a rate of 3.4 percent per year. The increases in hourly earnings over the period did not outpace inflation, so in inflation-adjusted dollars hourly earnings actually fell a little from 1987 to 1996. Average weekly hours worked in the industry remained roughly constant over the period at about 33 hours per week, considerably less than the traditional 40 hour workweek because of this industry's use of part-time workers.

Computer services employment almost doubled over the period, going from 629,000 employees in 1987 to 1,208,000 employees in 1996 (Table 4). Nonsupervisory workers' share of employment went up slightly from 78.5 percent to 79.9 percent, while women's share of employment fell from 43.9 percent to 41.9 percent.

Average hourly earnings of nonsupervisory workers in computer services increased from $12.29 in 1987 to $18.72 in 1996, at an annual rate of 4.79 percent. Even when adjusted for inflation, average hourly earnings in the industry increased at a rate of 1.2 percent per year. This contrasts with average inflation-adjusted hourly earnings for nonsupervisory and production workers in the United States, which fell throughout the late 1980s and early 1990s. It is an example of the widely noted trend for highly skilled workers' wages to diverge increasingly from those of the less skilled. Average weekly hours increased slightly to 37.7 hours per week in 1996, well above the figure for the business services industry as a whole.

In legal services, nonsupervisory workers and women both declined as a share of total employment. Average hourly earnings, at $16.60 in 1996, were relatively high but unchanged in real terms from 1988.

Engineering and management services had rapid employment growth from 1988 to 1990, paused in 1991-1992, and then sped up again. As with legal services, hourly earnings were high but about unchanged in real terms.

TABLE 4

U.S. EMPLOYMENT, HOURS, AND EARNINGS: BUSINESS AND PROFESSIONAL SERVICES

(Monetary values in U.S. dollars)

	1987	1988	1989	1990	1991	1992	1993	1994	1995	1996	CHANGE[1]
BUSINESS SERVICES:											
NUMBER OF EMPLOYEES, IN THOUSANDS:											
Total	4,278	4,638	4,941	5,139	5,086	5,315	5,735	6,281	6,812	7,254	6.04
Nonsupervisory workers	3,670	4,093	4,356	4,522	4,460	4,684	5,090	5,602	6,069	6,451	6.47
Percent of total	85.8	88.3	88.2	88.0	87.7	88.1	88.7	89.2	89.1	88.9	.....
Women	.....	2,201	2,345	2,443	2,378	2,504	2,714	2,958	3,196	3,415	5.64
Percent of total	.....	47.5	47.5	47.5	46.8	47.1	47.3	47.1	46.9	47.1	.....
HOURS AND EARNINGS OF NONSUPERVISORY WORKERS:											
AVERAGE HOURLY EARNINGS, U.S. DOLLARS[2]											
Current dollars	.....	8.61	9.08	9.48	9.76	9.97	10.12	10.31	10.71	11.21	3.35
1992 dollars[3]	.....	10.17	10.24	10.16	10.04	9.97	9.84	9.78	9.88	10.05	-0.14
Average weekly hours	.....	33.3	33.2	33.1	33.0	33.0	33.0	33.1	33.1	33.2	-0.04
Average weekly earnings, current U.S. dollars	.....	286.71	301.46	313.79	322.08	329.01	333.96	341.26	354.50	372.17	3.31
COMPUTER SERVICES:											
Number of employees, in thousands:											
Total	629	673	736	772	797	836	893	959	1,090	1,208	7.53
Nonsupervisory workers	494	522	573	603	627	669	725	778	879	965	7.73
Percent of total	78.5	77.6	77.8	78.1	78.7	80.1	81.2	81.1	80.6	79.9	.....
Women	276	308	334	345	352	369	390	410	459	506	6.97
Percent of total	43.9	45.7	45.4	44.7	44.1	44.2	43.7	42.7	42.1	41.9	.....
HOURS AND EARNINGS OF NONSUPERVISORY WORKERS:											
AVERAGE HOURLY EARNINGS, U.S. DOLLARS[2]											
Current dollars	12.29	13.21	14.19	15.11	15.57	15.81	16.46	17.17	17.79	18.72	4.79
1992 dollars[3]	15.10	15.60	16.00	16.20	16.02	15.81	16.01	16.29	16.41	16.79	1.19
Average weekly hours	37.5	37.8	38.0	38.1	38.0	38.1	38.1	37.8	37.8	37.7	0.06
Average weekly earnings, current U.S. dollars	460.88	499.34	539.22	575.69	591.66	602.36	627.13	649.03	672.46	705.74	4.85
LEGAL SERVICES:											
NUMBER OF EMPLOYEES, IN THOUSANDS:											
Total	800.9	844.5	880.4	907.7	911.9	913.5	924.0	924.0	921.4	929.9	1.67
Nonsupervisory workers	672.7	706.5	729.9	748.4	744.4	738.8	743.8	740.1	735.8	742.1	1.10
Percent of total	84.0	83.7	82.9	82.5	81.6	80.9	80.5	80.1	79.9	79.8	.....
Women	576.6	605.0	627.6	648.0	651.7	651.5	656.5	656.7	654.7	661.9	1.54
Percent of total	72.0	71.6	71.3	71.4	71.5	71.3	71.0	71.1	71.1	71.2	.....
HOURS AND EARNINGS OF NONSUPERVISORY WORKERS:											
AVERAGE HOURLY EARNINGS, U.S. DOLLARS[2]											
Current dollars	12.00	12.64	13.44	14.16	14.50	14.96	15.20	15.56	16.06	16.60	3.67
1992 dollars[3]	.....	14.92	15.15	15.18	14.92	14.96	14.79	14.76	14.82	14.89	-0.03
Average weekly hours	34.5	34.6	34.9	34.9	34.8	34.9	34.7	34.7	34.8	34.8	0.10
Average weekly earnings, current U.S. dollars	414.00	437.34	469.06	494.18	504.60	522.10	527.44	539.93	558.89	577.68	3.77
ENGINEERING AND MANAGEMENT SERVICES:											
NUMBER OF EMPLOYEES, IN THOUSANDS:											
Total	.....	2,230.4	2,389.2	2,477.6	2,433.4	2,470.8	2,520.9	2,578.5	2,731.1	2,846.4	3.10
Nonsupervisory workers	.....	1,727.5	1,839.4	1,885.7	1,853.1	1,884.4	1,928.0	1,981.6	2,098.4	2,184.9	2.98
Percent of total	.....	77.5	77.0	76.1	76.2	76.3	76.5	76.9	76.8	76.8	.....
Women	.....	926.6	1,002.6	1,045.8	1,035.5	1,055.2	1,074.1	1,093.5	1,163.4	1,221.9	3.52
Percent of total	.....	41.5	42.0	42.2	42.6	42.7	42.6	42.4	42.6	42.9	.....
HOURS AND EARNINGS OF NONSUPERVISORY WORKERS:											
AVERAGE HOURLY EARNINGS, U.S. DOLLARS[2]											
Current dollars	.....	12.36	13.00	13.56	14.08	14.60	15.01	15.36	15.79	16.36	3.57
1992 dollars[3]	.....	14.59	14.66	14.53	14.49	14.60	14.60	14.57	14.57	14.67	0.07
Average weekly hours	.....	37.4	37.4	37.3	37.3	37.3	37.1	37.2	37.2	37.1	-0.10
Average weekly earnings, current U.S. dollars	.....	462.26	486.20	505.79	525.18	544.58	556.87	571.39	587.39	606.96	3.46

1. Compound annual growth rate for years shown.

2. Including overtime.

3. Converted to 1992 dollars using Consumer Price Index for Urban Wage Earners and Clerical Workers.

Source: Bureau of Labor Statistics.

FIGURE 3

U.S. OCCUPATIONAL INJURY AND ILLNESS RATES:
BUSINESS SERVICES, 1995

The incidence of occupational illness and injury in business services was 4.6 cases per 100 workers, well below the all-services average of 6.4 cases per 100 workers.

Incidence of nonfatal injuries and illnesses per 100 full-time workers

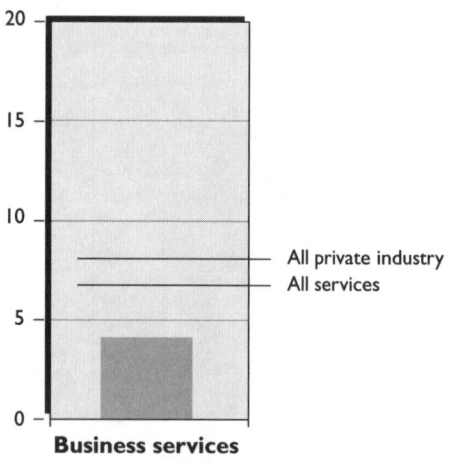

Source: U.S. Bureau of Labor Statistics.

TABLE 5

U.S. EMPLOYMENT PROJECTIONS BY MAJOR OCCUPATIONAL GROUP: BUSINESS AND PROFESSIONAL SERVICES

OCCUPATION	1994		PROJECTIONS, 2005			
	NUMBER OF EMPLOYEES	PERCENT OF INDUSTRY TOTAL	NUMBER OF EMPLOYEES			PERCENT OF INDUSTRY TOTAL, MODERATE PROJECTIONS
			LOW	MODERATE	HIGH	
BUSINESS SERVICES						
Total, all occupations	6,239,100	100.0	9,796,000	10,031,501	10,313,000	100.0
Executive, administrative, and managerial	560,931	9.0	866,848	892,358	922,867	8.9
Professional specialties	507,816	8.1	1,020,619	1,063,454	1,115,020	10.6
Technicians and related support	332,586	5.3	465,372	484,247	507,075	4.8
Marketing and sales	456,772	7.3	832,405	851,370	873,770	8.5
Administrative support including clerical	1,761,254	28.2	2,238,418	2,286,953	2,345,471	22.8
Service	1,486,606	23.8	2,401,980	2,446,266	2,497,719	24.4
Agriculture, forestry, and fisheries occupations	18,660	0.3	30,964	31,518	32,183	0.3
Precision production, craft, and repair	287,622	4.6	496,666	507,656	520,803	5.1
Operators, fabricators, assemblers	826,853	13.3	1,442,728	1,467,678	1,498,093	14.6
COMPUTER SERVICES						
Total, all occupations	950,000	100.0	1,515,800	1,610,500	1,724,700	100.0
Executive, administrative, and managerial	169,124	17.8	249,263	264,835	283,615	16.4
Professional specialties	242,858	25.6	581,097	617,401	661,181	38.3
Technicians and related support	169,063	17.8	242,983	258,163	276,469	16.0
Marketing and sales	68,338	7.2	115,737	122,967	131,687	7.6
Administrative support including clerical	247,991	26.1	249,298	264,873	283,656	16.5
Service	3,670	0.4	4,846	5,149	5,514	0.3
Agriculture, forestry, and fisheries occupations	232	0.0	310	329	353	0.0
Precision production, craft, and repair	36,866	3.9	55,559	59,030	63,216	3.7
Operators, fabricators, assemblers	11,860	1.3	16,708	17,751	19,010	1.1
LEGAL SERVICES						
Total, all occupations	926,800	100.0	1,240,000	1,270,000	1,299,700	100.0
Executive, administrative, and managerial	31,574	3.4	47,173	48,314	49,444	3.8
Professional specialties	306,297	33.1	429,686	440,082	450,374	34.7
Technicians and related support	119,004	12.8	184,311	188,770	193,185	14.9
Marketing and sales	222	0.0	340	348	356	0.0
Administrative support including clerical	461,462	49.8	567,570	581,302	594,896	45.8
Service	7,612	0.8	10,067	10,310	10,551	0.8
Agriculture, forestry, and fisheries occupations	132	0.0	183	187	192	0.0
Precision production, craft, and repair	462	0.1	618	633	648	0.1
Operators, fabricators, assemblers						
ENGINEERING AND MANAGEMENT SERVICES						
Total, all occupations	2,567,100	100.0	3,388,975	3,450,660	3,520,760	100.0
Executive, administrative, and managerial	685,794	26.7	941,959	959,082	978,212	27.8
Professional specialties	682,375	26.6	999,812	1,019,917	1,043,210	29.6
Technicians and related support	308,033	12.0	382,003	390,250	399,855	11.3
Marketing and sales	79,236	3.1	120,841	122,090	123,460	3.5
Administrative support including clerical	616,657	24.0	696,140	707,789	720,795	20.5
Service	64,750	2.5	83,841	84,854	85,958	2.5
Agriculture, forestry, and fisheries occupations	7,087	0.3	9,494	9,573	9,657	0.3
Precision production, craft, and repair	86,916	3.4	105,398	106,852	108,496	3.1
Operators, fabricators, assemblers	36,252	1.4	49,488	50,254	51,116	1.5

Source: Bureau of Labor Statistics, November 1995.

Business services (including computer services) is projected to employ 3,792,401 more people by the year 2005 than in 1994. Leading the growth is the service occupation with almost a million new employees expected. Computer services is projected to add 660,500 more employees by the year 2005. The fastest growing occupation will be professional specialties which includes programmers. For legal, engineering, and management services, professionals will lead the job growth.

CANADA

Business services—which in Canada includes legal, engineering, and management—had 555,578 employees in 1993 (Table 7). Among the Canadian subindustries that are included in the U.S. business services industry, employment agencies and personnel suppliers had 59,701 employees; computer and related services, 55,141; and advertising services, 26,027.

Employment in Canada's business services increased from 535,131 people in 1987 to 683,761 in 1996, at a rate of 2.8 percent per year (Table 8). Most of the growth took place after 1992, when the industry had 536,111 employees. Average weekly earnings rose steadily throughout the period from Can$412.24 in 1987 to Can$651.64 in 1996. When adjusting for inflation (1992 Canadian dollars), average weekly earnings increased from Can$505.82 in 1987 to Can$615.60 in 1996. The value of industry output, as measured by receipts, grew from Can$18.8 billion in 1987 to Can$26.6 billion in 1996, at a rate of 3.9 percent per year.

TABLE 7

CANADA: COMPONENT INDUSTRIES OF BUSINESS SERVICES (CSIC 7700), 1993

		EMPLOYMENT	
INDUSTRY NAME	CSIC	NUMBER	PERCENT OF INDUSTRY TOTAL
BUSINESS SERVICES	7700	555,578	100.0
Employment agencies and personnel suppliers	7710	59,701	10.7
Computer and related services	7720	55,141	9.9
Accounting and bookkeeping services	7730	60,619	10.9
Advertising services	7740	26,027	4.7
Architecture, engineering, and other scientific services	7750	95,307	17.2
Offices of lawyers and notaries	7760	57,355	10.3
Management consulting services	7770	75,796	13.6
Other business services	7790	125,633	22.6

Source: Statistics Canada: CANSIM.

TABLE 8

CANADIAN EMPLOYMENT AND RECEIPTS: BUSINESS SERVICES (CSIC 7700), 1987-1996

(Monetary values in Canadian dollars)

	1987	1988	1989	1990	1991	1992	1993	1994	1995	1996	CHANGE[1]
BUSINESS SERVICES											
All employees	535,131	546,131	595,290	615,314	567,042	536,111	555,578	586,990	631,465	683,761	2.76
Nonsupervisory workers:											
Average weekly earnings	412.24	448.48	489.46	533.22	556.45	583.02	585.25	604.33	621.43	651.64	5.22
Receipts (millions)	18,800	20,917	22,326	22,365	22,067	22,118	22,824	23,754	25,225	26,583	3.92
COMPUTER SERVICES											
All employees	42,365	44,923	51,037	52,692	48,579	55,232	55,141	62,514	68,904	82,729	7.72
Nonsupervisory workers:											
Average weekly earnings	521.13	560.29	615.54	676.7	721.7	739.25	727.09	795.4	801.71	829.54	5.30

1. Compound annual growth rate.

Source: Statistics Canada: CANSIM.

Canada's computer services employment almost doubled during 1987 to 1996, from 42,365 employees to 82,729. The annual growth rate for the period was 7.7 percent per year. Average weekly earnings in computer services increased from $521.13 in 1987 to $829.54 in 1996, at a rate of 5.3 percent per year. In constant 1992 Canadian dollars, average weekly earning grew by 2.3 percent per year.

MEXICO

Data on output and employment for Mexico's business services industry were not available separately; such activity is reported in the commerce sector.

INTERNATIONAL TRADE

The United States had large and growing trade surpluses in computer and engineering and management services over the 1987-95 period. Of the five groups identified as part of this business and professional services group, only advertising had a deficit and it was small. The United States had surpluses with both Canada and Mexico in 1992-1995.

TABLE 11

INTERNATIONAL TRADE, BUSINESS AND PROFESSIONAL SERVICES

(Millions of U.S. dollars)

	1987	1988	1989	1990	1991	1992	1993	1994	1995
GLOBAL TRADE, U.S.									
IMPORTS									
Advertising	128	188	228	243	301	450	646	725	686
Computer and data processing services	74	107	46	44	116	141	304	244	462
Database and other information services	25	39	31	54	51	72	110	141	155
Legal services	56	98	81	111	244	311	321	388	406
Engineering and management services	484	726	794	646	946	945	1,090	1,150	1,227
EXPORTS									
Advertising	109	145	145	130	274	315	338	489	510
Computer and data processing services	649	1,198	978	1,031	1,738	1,902	2,308	2,724	2,823
Database and other information services	133	196	205	283	442	641	694	1,113	1,278
Legal services	147	272	397	451	1,309	1,358	1,442	1,614	1,568
Engineering and management services	1,503	1,680	1,957	2,197	3,481	3,650	4,129	4,799	5,267
TRADE BALANCE[1]									
Advertising	(19)	(43)	(83)	(113)	(27)	(135)	(308)	(236)	(176)
Computer and data processing services	575	1,091	932	987	1,622	1,761	2,004	2,480	2,361
Database and other information services	108	157	174	229	391	569	584	972	1,123
Legal services	91	174	316	340	1,065	1,047	1,121	1,226	1,162
Engineering and management services	1,019	954	1,163	1,551	2,535	2,705	3,039	3,649	4,040
U.S.-NAFTA TRADE:									
U.S. exports to Canada	.....	.....	.....	.....	.....	953	1,056	1,327	1,304
Canadian exports to U.S.	.....	.....	.....	.....	.....	435	458	549	553
U.S. exports to Mexico	.....	.....	.....	.....	.....	421	495	620	553
Mexican exports to U.S.	.....	.....	.....	.....	.....	154	214	157	190

1. Parentheses indicate an excess of imports over exports.

Source: U.S. Department of Commerce, Bureau of Economic Analysis.

CONSUMER SERVICES

THE UNITED STATES

Products and Processes. Consumer services is a growing area of business with increasing revenues and employment. It includes five subindustries: personal services; automotive repair, services, and parking; miscellaneous repair services; motion pictures; and amusement and recreation services.

The largest of the subindustries in terms of employment was personal services, with 1,217,634 employees in 1992 (Table 1). Within personal services, the biggest category in terms of sales and employment was laundry, cleaning, and garment services with $17.1 billion in sales and 425,829 employees. Automotive repair, services, and parking had the highest sales of the five subindustries with $70.0 billion; most of the sales were split between repair shops and rental and leasing.

A remarkable characteristic of this industry is the low concentration of sales by the four largest companies. None of the subindustries for which concentration data were available had a concentration greater than 40 percent of sales by the four largest companies. The greatest business concentration was in motion picture theaters, where the four largest companies had almost a third of sales.

Employment in consumer services has been projected to increase from 4,080,500 employees in 1993 to 5,553,300 by the year 2005. The two areas that are expected to grow the most are amusement and recreation services (by 585,500 employees) and auto repair, services, and parking (by 420,400 employees).

TABLE 1

UNITED STATES: COMPONENT INDUSTRIES OF CONSUMER SERVICES (SIC 72, 75, 76, 78, AND 79), 1992

(Monetary values in millions of U.S. dollars)

INDUSTRY NAME	SIC	ESTABLISH-MENTS	SALES		EMPLOY-MENT[1]	PAYROLL
			VALUE	PERCENT BY 4 LARGEST COMPANIES		
Personal services total, including nonemployer firms	72	1,320,920	$59,597.5	.....	.....	.....
Personal services[2]	72	197,101	43,279.8	4.8	1,217,634	$14,378.5
Laundry, cleaning, and garment services	721	55,760	17,140.4	11.0	425,829	5,587.7
Photographic studios, portrait	722	11,381	3,191.1	32.5	66,822	852.7
Beauty shops	723	82,768	9,906.6	6.4	387,249	4,237.2
Barber shops	724	4,902	440.4	11.5	14,504	190.5
Shoe repair shops and shoeshine parlors	725	2,702	275.8	3.9	6,397	72.4
Funeral service and crematories	726	15,647	7,145.1	8.5	88,328	1,855.9
Miscellaneous personal services	729	23,941	5,180.4	23.2	228,505	1,582.1
Automotive repair, services, and parking total, including nonemployer firms	75	454,317	78,511.6	.....	.....	.....
Automotive repair, services, and parking[2]	75	171,970	70,032.6	9.4	863,856	15,550.0
Automotive rental and leasing, without drivers	751	10,566	20,573.7	31.8	132,323	2,757.4
Automobile parking	752	10,171	3,666.0	23.8	51,563	679.1
Automotive repair shops	753	128,738	39,746.0	1.6	519,503	10,337.2
Automotive services, except repair	754	22,495	6,046.9	6.5	160,467	1,776.3
Miscellaneous repair services total, including nonemployer firms	76	269,751	35,237.1	.....	.....	.....
Miscellaneous repair services[2]	76	71,576	30,731.8	8.9	428,103	9,694.9
Electrical repair shops	762	21,199	10,667.4	19.8	161,864	3,706.7
Watch, clock and jewelry repair	763	1,662	274.7	12.4	5,141	78.8
Reupholstery and furniture repair	764	6,731	980.4	1.6	21,249	311.1
Miscellaneous repair shops and related services	769	41,984	18,809.4	5.3	239,849	5,598.3
Motion pictures total, including nonemployer firms	78	95,884	45,663.5	.....	.....	.....
Motion pictures[2]	78	41,857	43,953.7	.....	478,084	.....
Motion picture production and allied services	781	11,364	21,148.3	.....	228,890	7,208.3
Motion picture distribution and allied services	782	1,603	11,913.6	.....	20,335	.....
Motion picture theaters	783	6,892	5,816.5	32.7	105,188	788.0
Video tape rental	784	21,998	5,075.3	22.9	123,671	943.9
Amusement and recreation services[2]	79	72,514	48,770.1	.....	900,455	.....
Dance studios, schools, and halls	791	4,839	594.8	2.6	23,790	168.0
Theatrical producers (except motion picture), bands, orchestras, and entertainers	792	10,086	8,625.5	6.3	68,998	2,895.0
Bowling centers	793	6,093	2,845.0	13.1	95,701	803.7
Commercial sports	794	3,751	7,594.2	9.0	90,439	4,022.3
Miscellaneous amusement and recreation services	799	47,745	29,110.5	.....	621,527	.....

1. Employment numbers from the economic censuses differ in definition and classification from the Bureau of Labor Statistics estimates in Table 2. Year-to-year comparisons between Table 1 and Table 2 are not appropriate.

2. These 2-digit industry figures, and their 3-digit component industries, refer only to taxable establishments with payroll (employer firms), excluding establishments with no paid employees (nonemployer firms).

Source: U.S. Bureau of the Census, 1992 Census of Services.

TABLE 2

U.S. EMPLOYMENT AND EARNINGS: CONSUMER SERVICES

INDUSTRY	SIC	1993 EMPLOYMENT[1] NUMBER OF PERSONS	1993 EMPLOYMENT[1] PERCENT OF INDUSTRY TOTAL	1993 AVERAGE HOURLY EARNINGS (U.S. DOLLARS)[2]	2005 PROJECTED EMPLOYMENT[3]
CONSUMER SERVICES	72,75,76, 78,79	4,080,500	100	.....	5,553,300
Personal services	72	1,137,100	27.9	.....	1,374,000
Laundry, cleaning, and garment services	721	420,300	10.3	7.22	495,000
Photographic studios, portrait	722	73,700	1.8	.....	.....
Beauty shops	723	385,300	9.4	7.83	451,087
Funeral services and crematories	726	86,700	2.1	.....	100,000
Miscellaneous personal services	729	151,600	3.7	7.39	.....
Auto repair, services, and parking	75	924,700	22.7	9.33	1,345,100
Automotive rentals, without drivers	751	165,300	4.1	9.31	226,600
Automobile parking	752	61,000	1.5	6.88	80,000
Automotive repair shops	753	522,300	12.8	10.28	704,500
Miscellaneous repair services	76	348,500	8.5	11.06	400,000
Electrical repair shops	762	107,200	2.6	.....	125,000
Motion pictures	78	412,000	10.1	12.32	590,500
Motion picture production and services	781	152,700	3.7	18.85	.....
Motion picture theaters	783	110,600	2.7	.....	118,052
Video tape rental	784	132,400	3.2	5.6	165,000
Amusement and recreation services	79	1,258,200	30.8	8.32	1,843,700
Bowling centers	793	87,400	2.1	6.57	72,500

1. Total payroll employment. Employment data from the economic censuses, as shown in Table 1, differ in definition and classification from the Bureau of Labor Statistics estimates in this table. Year-to-year comparisons between Table 1 and Table 2 are not appropriate.

2. Earnings of nonsupervisory workers, including overtime.

3. Number of persons, moderate projection by the U.S. Bureau of Labor Statistics.

Source: Bureau of Labor Statistics.

FIGURE 1

U.S. EMPLOYMENT IN CONSUMER SERVICES

Percent distribution by region, 1995

The Southeast region of the United States employed 22.6 percent of the consumer services industry in 1995. The Pacific region had 19.8 percent of the industry's total employment.

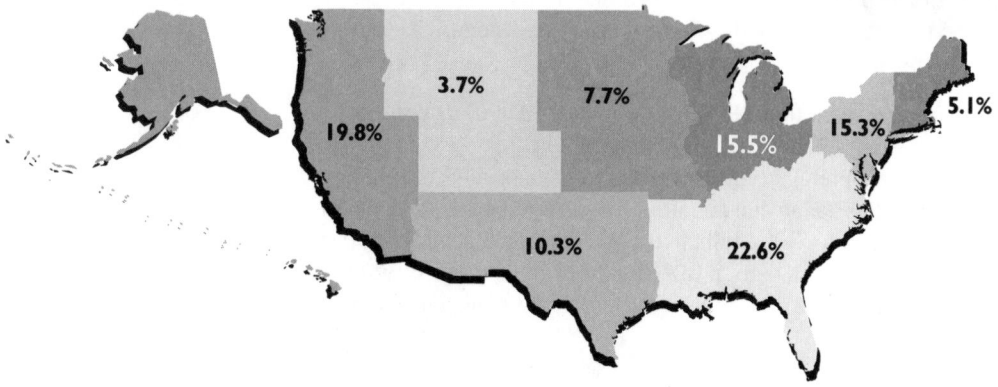

Source: U.S. Department of Commerce, Bureau of Economic Analysis.

What's New. *Personal Services.* New legislation in the House of Representatives proposed by Rep. Joe Barton, a Texas Republican, attempts to clarify the federal safety standards for dry cleaning chemicals in soil and groundwater. Currently, there is no federal standard for the amount of perchloroethylene ("perc"), the principal solvent used in dry cleaning, allowed in soil or groundwater. There is a drinking water standard established by the EPA for "perc," and it is sometimes applied as the cleanup level for soil or groundwater. This standard is very strict compared to the standards applied by Occupational Safety and Health Administratin (OSHA) for workplace exposure to "perc." The goal of the Barton Bill is to redress the discrepancy between the standards of OSHA and the Environmental Protection Agency. Firms in the cleaning industry feel that the Barton Bill will help them to resolve conflicts with regulators and landlords over their potential liability for cleanup costs.

Automotive Repair, Services, and Parking. According to an October 1997 article in *Collision Repair Industry Insight*, an automotive repair trade publication, consolidation in the auto body repair industry will be a major concern in the years to come. Though the pace of consolidation is not very fast now, it is expected to accelerate as firms push to gain market share and boost efficiency through economies of scale. Another reason for consolidation is to improve repair shops' ability to bargain with insurance companies over prices.

Motion Pictures. Domestic box office receipts through October 1997 were $4.58 billion, up 5.8 percent from figures for the same time period of 1996. The growth of the Internet has raised concerns in the film industry about an increase in intellectual property piracy. In the future, illegal copies of films may be distributed throughout the globe via the Internet. This not only threatens the domestic market for motion pictures, but also the international market, where the enforcement of intellectual property rights is already more lax. To address this issue, The Motion Picture Association of America (MPAA) has been lobbying Congress on behalf of two new treaties protecting intellectual property on the Internet. Online service providers are seeking amendments to the treaties limiting their liability for intellectual property theft on their services. The MPAA is critical of limitations on online service providers liability because they fear it will increase intellectual property theft.

Amusement and Recreation Services. According to the International Health, Racquet, and Sportsclub Association's *Profiles of Success*, net income before taxes in the health, racquet, and sportsclub industry increased 22 percent from 1995 to 1996. Since total revenues grew by only 2.4 percent, most of the growth in pre-tax income was caused by reductions in payroll and operating expenses. Membership in the industry's clubs increased 9.1 percent over the 1995 level.

Commercial Sports. Women's professional basketball was in the news in 1996 and 1997, with two competing leagues playing their first games. The first of the two leagues to begin play was the American Basketball League (ABL), in the fall of 1996. Despite its head start, the ABL received less notice than its competitor, the Women's National Basketball Association (WNBA), which profited from its association with the National Basketball Association and from national network television exposure on NBC. Overall attendance for the WNBA surpassed one million fans, and the league averaged 9,669 fans per game. The ABL averaged about 3,600 fans per game for its first season.

Output. Consumer services employment from 1988 to 1996 increased in every year but 1991. Receipts from sales, in constant 1992 dollars, grew considerably from 1987 to 1995, despite a decline in sales in 1991 (Figure 2). In current dollars, consumer services receipts increased every year from 1987 to 1995, at an annual rate of 7.8 percent (Table 3). In 1995, receipts were $346.4 billion, compared to $190.5 billion in 1987. Consumer services GDP was also growing over this time period. Its share of total GDP rose from 2.7 percent in 1987 to 3 percent in 1994. This reflected a faster rate of price increase, since real growth in this industry lagged the national average.

FIGURE 2

U.S. EMPLOYMENT AND SALES RECEIPTS, CONSUMER SERVICES

Total payroll employment and inflation-adjusted sales receipts

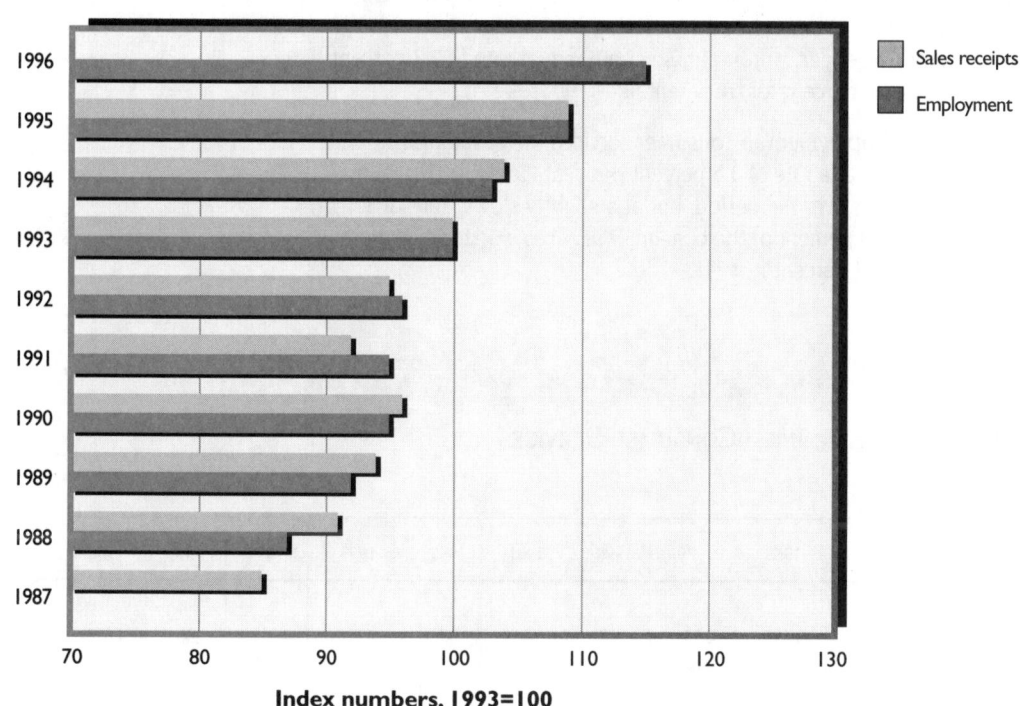

Source: U.S. Bureau of Labor Statistics, U.S. Bureau of the Census, and estimates by the editors.

TABLE 3

U.S. OUTPUT: CONSUMER SERVICES

(Millions of U.S. dollars, except as noted)

	1987	1988	1989	1990	1991	1992	1993	1994	1995	1996	GROWTH RATE 1987-1995[1]
Receipts[2]	190,524	215,059	233,569	251,414	253,055	276,707	296,250	318,474	346,366	.....	7.76
OTHER OUTPUT MEASURES: Gross domestic product:											
Current dollars	126,373	141,352	153,291	164,177	166,989	177,429	188,517	200,305	.....	.....	.....
Percent of total GDP	2.7	2.8	2.8	3.0	2.8	2.9	2.8	3.0	.....	.....	.....
Chained (1992) dollars	161,607	173,324	179,339	182,058	175,348	177,429	179,984	183,607	.....	.....	.....

1. Compound annual growth rate.

2. Receipts of taxable employer and nonemployer firms.

Source: Receipts: Census Bureau, Service Annual Survey; GDP: Bureau of Economic Analysis.

Prices. Though price information for all consumer services is not available, there are data on prices for selected subindustries. Annual increases in the consumer price index from 1987 to 1996 included 3.4 percent for laundry and dry cleaning, 3.4 percent for personal care services (beauty shops and barbershops), 5.2 percent for funeral expenses, 4.3 percent for entertainment services (motion pictures and amusement and recreation services), and 3.6 percent for automobile maintenance and repair. This compares with 3.7 percent annually for the CPI-U (all urban wage earners and clerical workers) during 1987-1996. From 1992 to 1996, the producer price index for passenger car rental rose at an annual rate of 2.7 percent, more than twice the annual rate of 1.3 percent for truck rentals.

Workforce and Employment. Employment in consumer services increased from 3,557,000 in 1988 to 4,678,000 in 1996, at a rate of 3.5 percent per year (Table 4). The number of women in the industry increased over the period, but at a slightly slower rate of 3.4 percent. In 1996, women made up 44.3 percent of the consumer services workforce, compared with a high for the period of 45.2 percent in 1991.

TABLE 4

U.S. EMPLOYMENT, HOURS, AND EARNINGS: CONSUMER SERVICES

(Monetary values in U.S. dollars)

	1987	1988	1989	1990	1991	1992	1993	1994	1995	1996	CHANGE[1]
NUMBER OF EMPLOYEES, IN THOUSANDS:											
Total	.....	3,557	3,752	3,875	3,867	3,934	4,081	4,222	4,464	4,678	3.48
Women	....	1,591	1,666	1,722	1,748	1,770	1,835	1,889	1,987	2,071	3.35
Percent of total	....	44.7	44.4	44.4	45.2	45.0	45.0	44.7	44.5	44.3	.....

1. Compound annual growth rate, 1988-1996.

Data on earnings and on numbers and hours of nonsupervisory workers are not available.

Source: Bureau of Labor Statistics.

FIGURE 3

U.S. OCCUPATIONAL ILLNESS AND INJURY RATES:

SELECTED CONSUMER SERVICES, 1995

Incidence of nonfatal injuries and illnesses per 100 full-time workers

Personal services, auto repair, and the movie industry had below-average illness and injury rates, while amusement and recreation services had an above-average rate of 9.5 per 100 workers.

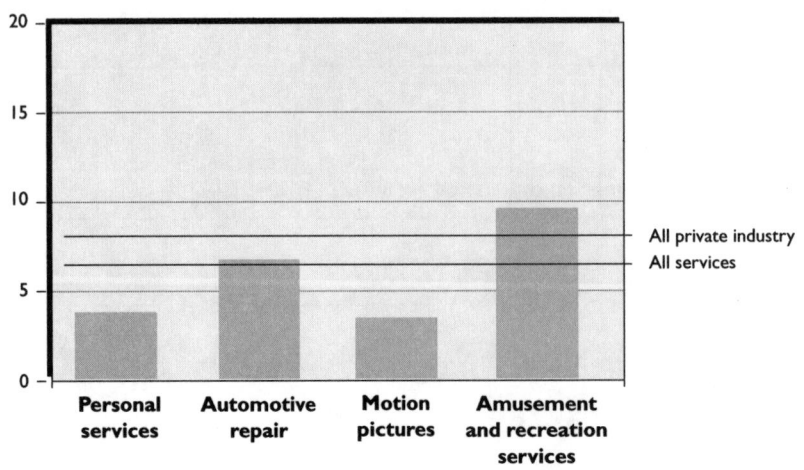

Source: U.S. Bureau of Labor Statistics.

TABLE 5

U.S. EMPLOYMENT PROJECTIONS BY MAJOR OCCUPATIONAL GROUP: CONSUMER SERVICES

OCCUPATION	1994		PROJECTIONS, 2005			
	NUMBER OF EMPLOYEES	PERCENT OF INDUSTRY TOTAL	NUMBER OF EMPLOYEES			PERCENT OF INDUSTRY TOTAL, MODERATE PROJECTIONS
			LOW	MODERATE	HIGH	
Total, all occupations	4,259,100	100.0	5,503,700	5,553,300	5,592,799	100.0
Executive, administrative, and managerial	363,415	8.5	484,338	485,993	487,212	8.8
Professional specialties	388,470	9.1	565,106	561,339	559,140	10.1
Technicians and related support	31,249	0.7	39,220	38,859	38,620	0.7
Marketing and sales	609,454	14.3	808,645	820,723	833,463	14.8
Administrative support including clerical	408,286	9.6	496,531	497,455	497,826	9.0
Service	1,053,706	24.7	1,313,472	1,314,921	1,317,475	23.7
Agriculture, forestry, and fisheries occupations	77,354	1.8	87,671	86,695	86,325	1.6
Precision production, craft, and repair	728,974	17.1	925,666	946,401	960,317	17.0
Operators, fabricators, assemblers	598,188	14.0	783,054	800,914	812,421	14.4

Source: Bureau of Labor Statistics, November 1995.

The consumer services industry has been projected to grow by 1,294,200 employees from 1994 to 2005 (moderate projections). The fastest growing occupation in the industry is professional specialties, with employment expected to rise by 44 percent over the period.

CANADA

Canada's consumer services industry had 2,276,618 employees in 1993 (Table 7). However, consumer services in Canada include several subindustries that are not part of the industry in the United States. The industries that are comparable to U.S. consumer services subindustries are amusement and recreational services (171,857 employees) and personal services (102,894 employees).

TABLE 7

CANADA: COMPONENT INDUSTRIES OF CONSUMER SERVICES (CSIC 8500, 9100, 9200, 9600-9900), 1993

INDUSTRY NAME	CSIC	EMPLOYMENT	
		NUMBER	PERCENT OF INDUSTRY TOTAL
CONSUMER SERVICES	8500, 9100, 9200, 9600-9900	2,276,618	100.0
Educational services	8510-8530	897,193	39.4
Libraries, museums and other educational services	8540-8590	39,022	1.7
Accomodation services	9100	176,723	7.8
Food and beverage services	9200	586,713	25.8
Amusement and recreational services	9600	171,857	7.5
Personal services	9700	102,894	4.5
Membership organizations	9800	100,757	4.4
Other services	9900	201,459	8.8

Source: Statistics Canada: CANSIM.

MEXICO

(comparable consumer services data for Mexico are not available.)

FINANCE, INSURANCE, AND REAL ESTATE

UNITED STATES

Products and Processes. Finance, insurance, and real estate includes firms and agents involved in diverse financial services. The industries together employed more than 6.5 million people and had gross revenues of $1.8 trillion in 1992. Recently, there has been a trend toward consolidation in the sector as firms within each industry offer more and more different services. The lines that separate the functions of an investment bank from a commercial bank or an insurer from a savings institution are becoming blurred as deregulation and industry consolidation progress.

Finance includes depository institutions (e.g., commercial banks, savings institutions, credit unions); nondepository institutions (personal and business credit institutions, mortgage bankers, and loan brokers); security and commodity brokers, dealers, exchanges, and services; and holding and other investment offices. In 1992, the finance industry employed 3.1 million people and had $851.6 billion in revenues (Table 1). Depository institutions ranked as the largest subindustry, with more than two-thirds of finance industry employment and 62 percent of industry revenues.

Insurance includes carriers of all types: life insurance; accident and health insurance; fire, marine, and casualty insurance; surety insurance; title insurance; and other insurance. Insurance agents and brokers are also part of the insurance industry. With revenues of $856.8 billion in 1992, insurance was similar in size to finance, but employed fewer people, with 2.2 million employees (Table 1). Life insurance carriers are the biggest part of the industry in terms of revenue with $378.4 billion, or 44 percent of industry revenues. Employment is distributed more evenly across the industry than are revenues. The three largest employers are: insurance agents, brokers, and services (635,536 employees); life insurance carriers (609,237 employees); and fire, marine, and casualty insurance carriers (588,333 employees).

Real estate includes operators and lessors; real estate agents and managers; title abstract offices; and land subdividers and developers. It is considerably smaller than finance or insurance, with revenues of $229.3 billion and 1.2 million employees in 1992. The subindustry of real estate agents and managers accounted for the majority of industry employment, while operators and lessors brought in the most revenue.

Employment in finance, insurance, and real estate has been projected to increase from 6,757,000 employees in 1993 to 7,372,500 in 2005 (Table 2). While all other parts of the industry are expected to grow, employment in depository institutions is projected to fall by more than 200,000 people by 2005. Employment among security and commodity brokers is projected to grow the fastest, with 228,400 more employees expected by 2005.

TABLE 1

UNITED STATES: COMPONENT INDUSTRIES OF FINANCE, INSURANCE, AND REAL ESTATE (SIC 60-65, 67), 1992

(Monetary values in millions of U.S. dollars)

INDUSTRY NAME	SIC	ESTABLISH-MENTS	REVENUE	PERCENT BY 4 LARGEST COMPANIES	EMPLOY-MENT[1]	PAYROLL
FINANCE, INSURANCE, AND REAL ESTATE		585,580	$1,831,526.5	.....	6,509,591	$211,568.8
Depository institutions	60	105,122	532,163.0	.....	2,100,089	57,339.4
Commercial banks	602	62,761	318,076.8	20.7	1,506,055	41,206.5
National commercial banks	6021	31,360	185,985.7	32.2	852,039	23,188.9
State commercial banks	6022	31,401	132,091.0	20.3	654,016	18,017.6
Savings institutions	603	20,544	92,322.2	12.4	341,920	8,445.6
Savings institutions, federally chartered	6035	13,963	63,934.2	17.5	233,266	5,788.4
Savings institutions, not federally chartered	6036	6,581	28,388.0	9.2	108,654	2,657.1
Credit unions	606	15,665	21,390.4	4.7	139,762	2,872.0
Credit unions, federally chartered	6061	9,631	13,031.4	.....	85,622	1,771.5
Credit unions, not federally chartered	6062	6,034	8,359.0	.....	54,140	1,100.5
Other depository institutions	601,8,9	5,535	100,267.6	18.0	112,352	4,815.3
Central reserve depository institutions	601	67	29,571.7	.....	26,334	870.4
Federal reserve banks	6011	42	20,262.4	.....	23,819	782.5
Central reserve depository institutions, n.e.c.	6019	25	9,309.4	.....	2,515	87.9
Foreign banking and branches and agencies of foreign banks	608	632	62,689.7	.....	,310	2,263.5
Branches and agencies of foreign banks	6081	561	58,525.2	.....	31,060	2,096.1
Foreign trade and international banking institutions	6082	71	4,164.5	.....	3,250	167.4
Functions related to depository banking	609	4,836	8,006.1	.....	51,708	1,681.3
Nondeposit trust facilities	6091	410	3,094.2	.....	19,497	877.9
Functions related to depository banking, n.e.c.	6099	4,426	4,911.9	.....	32,211	803.4
Nondepository credit institutions	61	57,249	136,199.2	.....	445,590	15,481.4
Personal credit institutions	614	16,900	47,668.4	50.0	158,790	4,281.4
Other nondepository credit institutions	611,5,6	22,539	87,718.5	27.7	286,800	11,200.0
Federal and federally-sponsored credit agencies	611	1,349	28,092.0	80.9	21,298	833.1
Business credit institutions	615	5,038	36,552.8	22.6	86,526	3,459.2
Short-term business credit institutions, except agricultural	6153	2,370	17,101.6	.....	54,847	1,991.7
Miscellaneous business credit institutions	6159	2,668	19,451.2	.....	31,679	1,467.5
Mortgage bankers and brokers	616	16,152	23,073.7	12.0	178,976	6,907.7
Mortgage bankers and loan correspondents	6162	9,995	19,855.7	13.9	146,614	5,765.4
Loan brokers	6163	6,157	3,218.1	2.8	32,362	1,142.4
Security and commodity brokers, dealers, exchanges and services	62	77,781	110,795.1	.....	406,444	33,833.5
Security and commodity brokers, dealers, and flotation companies	621,2	44,285	92,090.0	.....	312,846	26,959.2
Security brokers, dealers, and flotation companies	621	38,893	89,275.0	.....	299,953	26,252.8
Commodity contracts brokers and dealers	622	5,392	2,815.0	.....	12,893	706.5
Security and commodity exchanges and allied services	623,8	33,496	18,705.2	.....	93,598	6,874.3
Security and commodity exchanges	623	35	993.5	.....	6,739	311.8
Services allied with the exchange of securities or commodities	628	11,905	17,138.8	.....	86,859	6,562.5
Investment advice	6282	11,520	14,806.4	.....	68,763	5,845.8
Services allied with the exchange of securities or commodities, n.e.c.	6289	385	2,332.4	.....	18,096	716.7
Insurance carriers	63	39,630	796,099.5	.....	1,516,643	50,518.7
Life insurance	631	13,424	378,401.7	24.5	609,237	19,410.7
Accident and health insurance and medical service plans	632	2,846	148,259.5	18.4	250,236	7,545.3
Accident and health insurance	6321	1,100	23,446.3	.....	53,599	1,466.6
Hospital and medical service plans	6324	1,746	124,813.2	.....	196,637	6,078.7
Fire, marine, and casualty insurance	633	19,002	258,394.7	26.5	588,333	21,182.6
Title insurance	636	1,532	4,883.6	70.7	34,473	1,168.4
Other insurance carriers	635,7,9	2,173	6,085.5	24.8	34,364	1,211.7
Surety insurance	635	548	4,005.4	37.7	11,167	518.9

TABLE 1 (CONTINUED)

UNITED STATES: COMPONENT INDUSTRIES OF FINANCE, INSURANCE, AND REAL ESTATE (SIC 60-65, 67), 1992

(Monetary values in millions of U.S. dollars)

INDUSTRY NAME	SIC	ESTABLISH-MENTS	REVENUE	REVENUE PERCENT BY 4 LARGEST COMPANIES	EMPLOY-MENT[1]	PAYROLL
Pension, health, welfare funds; and insurance carriers, n.e.c.	637,9	1,625	2,080.1	18.2	23,197	692.8
Pension, health and welfare funds	637	1,491	1,379.4	.....	20,374	596.9
Insurance carriers, n.e.c.	639	134	700.7	.....	2,823	95.9
Insurance agents, brokers, and servies	64	444,442	60,734.0	.....	635,536	18,921.1
Real estate	65	1,545,669	229,293.9	.....	1,231,471	26,245.1
Real estate operators (except developers) and lessors	651	684,903	134,627.2	.....	462,564	8,257.8
Operators of nonresidential buildings	6512	605,572	96,981.6	.....	168,138	3,691.6
Operators of apartment buildings	6513	48,330	29,373.8	2.6	228,270	3,550.0
Other real estate operators and lessors	6514,5,7,9	21,652	7,827.1	2.3	66,156	1,016.2
Operators of dwellings other than apartment buildings	6514	9,271	3,162.9	.....	29,660	416.5
Operators of residential mobile home sites	6515	9,572	3,607.7	.....	29,270	430.0
Lessors of other real property	6517,9	12,158	1,501.3	.....	7,226	169.6
Real estate agents and managers	653	784,680	73,115.1	.....	646,561	14,859.5
Other real estate	654,5	20,054	13,856.7	5.3	122,346	3,127.8
Title abstract offices	654	8,251	2,431.1	.....	33,742	880.1
Land subdividers and developers	655	67,835	19,120.6	.....	88,604	2,247.7
Land subdividers and developers, except cemeteries	6552	8,848	9,219.7	6.5	48,502	1,452.6
Cemetery subdividers and developers	6553	6,490	2,299.6	17.9	40,102	795.0
Holding and other investment offices	67	196,763	72,396.3	.....	173,818	9,229.6
Holding offices	671	10,381	43,634.1	10.1	108,235	5,934.2
Offices of bank holding companies	6712	2,256	11,126.1	.....	26,741	1,257.5
Offices of holding companies, n.e.c.	6719	8,125	32,508.0	.....	81,494	4,676.8
Investment offices	672	829	3,826.6	40.1	16,752	1,106.5
Management investment offices, open end	6722	561	3,438.3	.....	15,648	1,027.9
Unit investment trusts, certificate offices, and closed-end management investments	6726	268	388.3	1,104	78.6	
Miscellaneous investing	679	9,117	18,356.8	9.7	48,831	2,188.9
Oil royalty traders	6792	746	686.7	.....	2,228	92.7
Patent owners and lessors	6794	1,514	5,412.5	.....	17,409	689.3
Real estate investment trusts	6798	655	2,507.5	.....	4,771	181.8
Investors, n.e.c.	6799	6,202	9,750.1	.....	24,423	1,225.1

1. Employment numbers from the economic censuses differ in definition and classification from the Bureau of Labor Statistics estimates in Table 2. Year-to-year comparisons between Table 1 and Table 2 are not appropriate.

Source: U.S. Bureau of the Census, 1992 Census of Finance, Insurance, and Real Estate.

TABLE 2

U.S. EMPLOYMENT AND EARNINGS: FINANCE, INSURANCE, AND REAL ESTATE

INDUSTRY	SIC	1993			2005
		EMPLOYMENT[1]		AVERAGE HOURLY EARNINGS (U.S. DOLLARS)[2]	PROJECTED EMPLOYMENT[3]
		NUMBER OF PERSONS	PERCENT OF INDUSTRY TOTAL		
FINANCE, INSURANCE, AND REAL ESTATE	60-65, 67	6,757,000	100.0	11.35	7,372,500
Depository institutions	60	2,088,800	30.9	9.10	1,885,800
Nondepository institutions	61	454,900	6.7	12.38	664,800
Personal credit institutions	614	128,600	1.9	9.94	176,600
Mortgage bankers and brokers	616	224,800	3.3	.....	347,600
Security and commodity brokers	62	471,600	7.0	.....	700,000
Security brokers and dealers	621	359,200	5.3	.....	540,435
Insurance carriers	63	1,529,000	22.6	13.14	1,632,700
Life insurance	631	571,900	8.5	12.28	594,700
Medical service and health insurance	632	280,500	4.2	12.66	323,700
Fire, marine, and casualty insurance	633	544,000	8.1	14.10	557,400
Insurance agents, brokers, and services	64	668,000	9.9	.....	702,000
Real estate	65	1,322,000	19.6	.....	1,481,600
Real estate operators and lessors	651	563,200	8.3	.....	606,400
Real estate agents and managers	653	613,800	9.1	.....	724,700
Holding and other investment offices	67	222,600	3.3	.....	305,600

1. Total payroll employment. Employment data from the economic censuses, as shown in Table 1, differ in definition and classification from the Bureau of Labor Statistics estimates in this table. Year-to-year comparisons between Table 1 and Table 2 are not appropriate.

2. Earnings of nonsupervisory workers, including overtime.

3. Number of persons, moderate projection by the U.S. Bureau of Labor Statistics.

Source: Bureau of Labor Statistics.

FIGURE 1

U.S. EMPLOYMENT IN FINANCE, INSURANCE, AND REAL ESTATE

Percent distribution by region, 1995

The Mid-Atlantic region had the highest proportion of finance, insurance, and real estate employment in 1995, with 20.5 percent of total industry employees. The Southeast was second largest with 19.8 percent of industry employment.

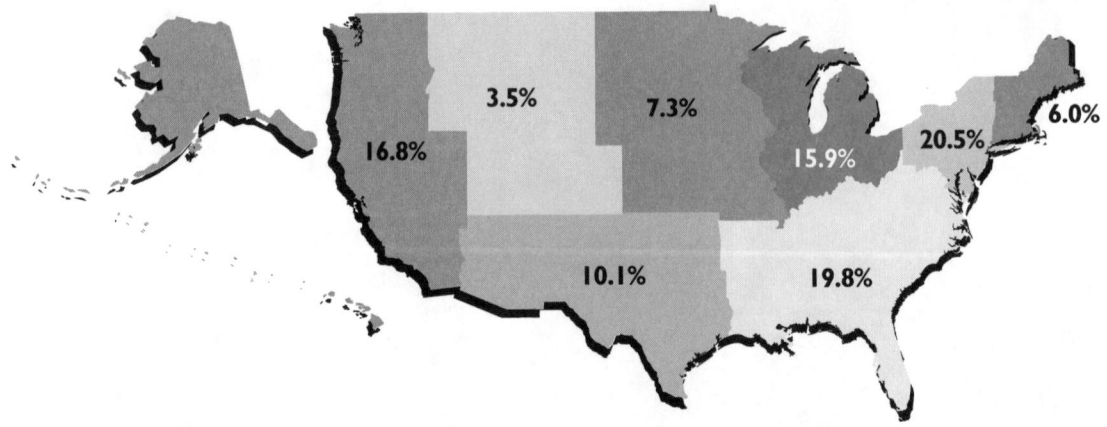

Source: U.S. Department of Commerce, Bureau of Economic Analysis.

What's New. *Finance.* Mergers and consolidation are changing the makeup of the financial services industry. On September 24, 1997, Traveler's Group Inc. announced a deal to purchase Salomon Inc. for $9 billion. Travelers already owned Smith Barney, a large retail brokerage firm. With the addition of Salomon, Travelers can offer a fuller range of financial services. Earlier in the year, Morgan Stanley Group Inc. and Dean Witter, Discover & Co. merged to form a full-service firm with a market capitalization of $21 billion.

Commercial banks were also active in mergers and acquisitions. On June 9, 1997 BankAmerica Corporation announced a $540 million merger agreement with Robertson Stephens & Company Group, L.L.C., a San Francisco-based investment banking firm. The move will help BankAmerica expand its own investment banking activities. On June 30, 1997, First Union Corporation and Signet Corporation announced a merger agreement through which First Union would pay approximately $3.25 billion to acquire Signet. On August 29, 1997, NationsBank Corporation announced that it would purchase Barnett Banks, Inc., of Florida, for $15.5 billion. The merger will make NationsBank the third largest banking company in the United States.

Growth in the online brokerage business promises to change the way small investors make trades, and the way brokerage firms earn profits, according to a *Wall Street Journal* article. Online trading has dramatically reduced the commissions on trades of 1,000 shares of stock from $100 through a regular account at a big discount-brokerage firm to $15 to $20 online. Industry analysts predict a 129 percent increase in online broker commissions for 1997, up to $614 million from $268 million in 1996. Soon, full-service brokers may be forced to adapt to the changing environment by offering online trading of their own.

Insurance. The United States property and casualty insurance industry's consolidated net income after tax increased to $18.1 billion in the first six months of 1997, a 53.7 percent increase from $11.8 billion in the first six months of 1996, according to a joint report of the Insurance Services Office, Inc. and the National Association of Independent Insurers. Net written premiums for the first half of 1997 totaled $139.1 billion, up 4.1 percent from $133.6 billion in the same period in 1996. The industry's consolidated surplus, its assets minus liabilities, rose from $255.5 billion at the end of 1996 to $286.8 billion as of June 30, 1997, an increase of 12.3 percent over six months.

According to Weiss Ratings, Inc., profits from core operations for life and health insurers fell 6 percent in the first quarter of 1997 compared to the same period the previous year. Overall income was up 4.9 percent compared to 1996's first quarter, largely because the insurers chose to cash in on some of their capital gains. The industry had a record-breaking year in 1996, with all-time high profits of $19.3 billion.

In April 1997, a class action lawsuit was filed on behalf of Holocaust survivors and their families who between 1920 and 1945 bought life, property, and casualty insurance policies. The defendants in the case are several European insurance companies charged with profiting from the seized assets of victims of the Holocaust without ever paying out on policies. In September, 1997, the National Association of Insurance Commissioners appointed a working group to determine the role of state regulators in protecting the rights of consumers who have filed the insurance claims of Holocaust survivors and their families.

Real estate. Existing home sales in August 1997 were estimated to be 4.23 million units (seasonally adjusted annual rate), up from the record 4.09 million unit sales of 1996. A tight labor market and low borrowing costs are cited as explanations for the robust sales figures the last few years.

According to a September 1, 1997, article in *Barron's*, some of the most overvalued housing in the United States lies in the Pacific Northwest and Northern California. According to experts' estimates, housing prices are 39 percent above fair value in Portland, Oregon; 15 percent in Seattle; and 13 percent in San Francisco. The estimates are based on a comparison of the overall pace of economic activity in a region with the movement in housing prices in the region. If housing price inflation outpaces the rate of economic growth in an area, then the housing is said to be overvalued. Among the most undervalued cities for housing in the United States are Fort Worth, Texas; West Palm Beach, Florida; and New Haven, Connecticut.

The Building Owners and Managers Association predicts that suburban office properties will offer the biggest returns to commercial real estate investors in the next 5 to 10 years. In 1996, average downtown office rent was $20.55 per rentable square foot, while suburban office rent was $16.52 per square foot. Washington, D.C., had the most expensive downtown office rents; San Jose, California, had the highest suburban office rents.

FIGURE 2A

U.S. EMPLOYMENT AND GROSS PRODUCT, FINANCE

Total payroll employment and inflation-adjusted gross product

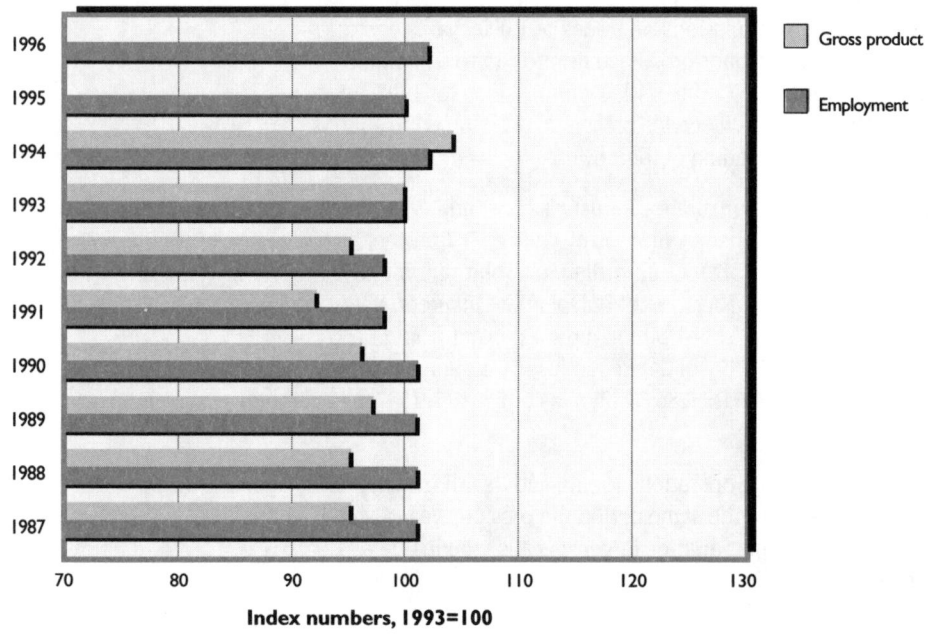

Index numbers, 1993=100

Source: U.S. Bureau of Labor Statistics, U.S. Department of Commerce, and estimates by the editors.

FIGURE 2B

U.S. EMPLOYMENT AND GROSS PRODUCT, INSURANCE

Total payroll employment and inflation-adjusted gross product

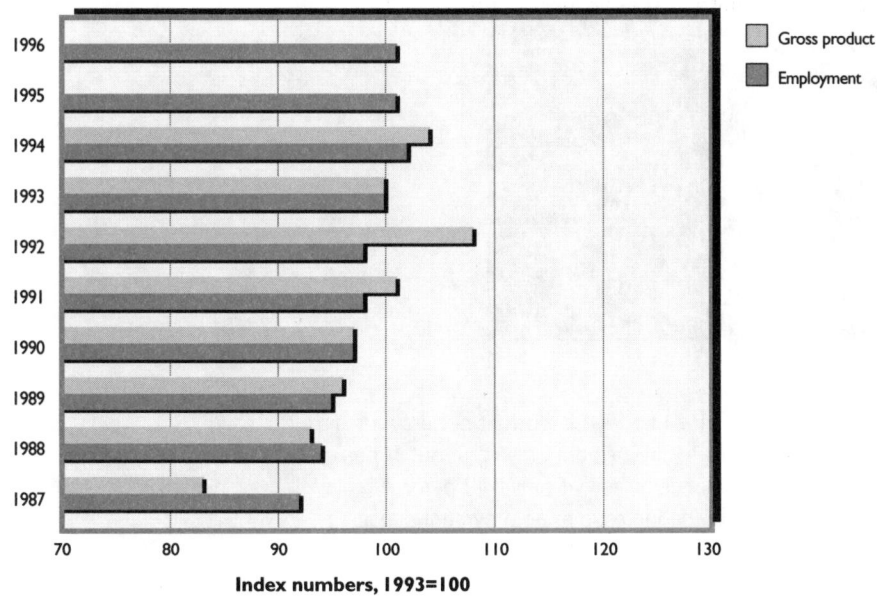

Source: U.S. Bureau of Labor Statistics, U.S. Department of Commerce, and estimates by the editors.

FIGURE 2C

U.S. EMPLOYMENT AND GROSS PRODUCT, REAL ESTATE

Total payroll employment and inflation-adjusted gross product

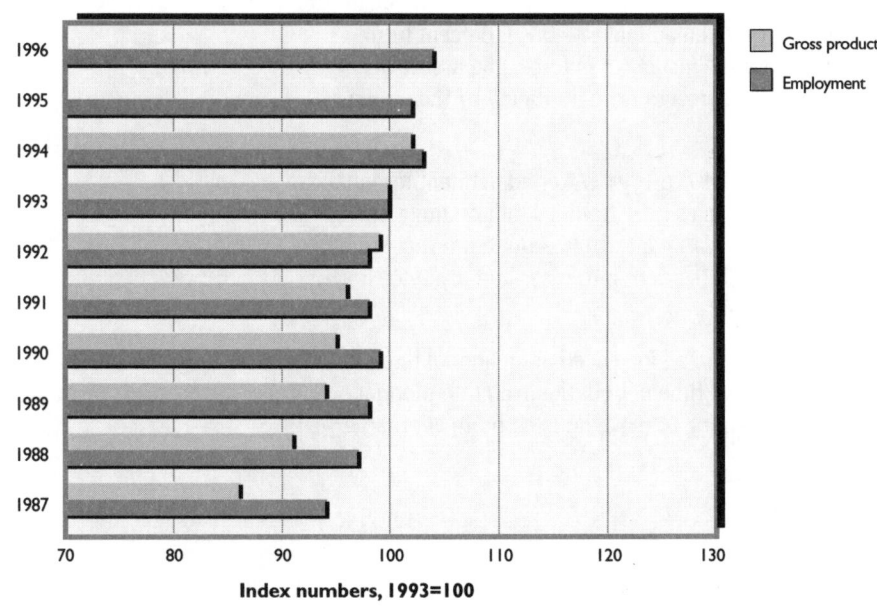

Source: U.S. Bureau of Labor Statistics, U.S. Department of Commerce, and estimates by the editors.

Output. The industry grew at a 6.3 percent rate from 1984 to 1994 in current dollars and at 2.3 percent after inflation, as measured by industry GDP. Employment grew at about 1 percent per annum in real estate and insurance, but in finance it grew at only 0.13 percent. (Figure 2). The increase in real output at about double the increase in employment suggests productivity growth, perhaps a result of the very high levels of investment in computers and communications technology in the industry.

Finance. The industry grew at a 5.9 percent annual rate from 1987 to 1994 and at a 1.3 percent rate after adjustment for inflation, as measured by industry GDP. In 1994 the industry generated GDP of $322 billion or 4.6 percent of the national total. Assets of commercial banks increased from 1988 to 1996, at an annual rate of 5.2 percent. Deposits grew at a similar rate of 5 percent. Loans and leases lagged behind other asset categories, growing 3.7 percent per year.

Insurance. Industry GDP increased from $80.1 billiion in 1987 to $149.4 billion in 1994, an annual rate of 9.3 percent. In real terms, output growth was 3.2 percent per year. The industry accounted for 2.2 percent of total GDP in 1994, up from 1.7 percent in 1987. At life insurance companies, life/health insurance receipts grew at an annual rate of 6.0 percent from 1987 to 1995, slightly slower than rate of growth for life insurance in force. The assets of insurers grew faster over this period (at a rate of 9.4 percent per year), fueled by the strong performance of U.S. financial markets.

Real estate. GDP grew at a 6 percent annual rate from 1987 to 1994. After adjustment for inflation, it grew at a 2.5 percent rate. Sales of existing homes grew from 3.4 million units in 1987 to 4.1 million in 1996—a 2 percent annual rate. Actual growth was quite uneven. From 1988 to 1990, housing sales declined as the United States went into recession. By 1992, however, activity in real estate had regained its 1988 level.

Prices. In *real estate*, the median price for an existing home increased at an annual rate of 3.6 percent from 1987 to 1996 (Table 3). Over the same time period, the fixed rate mortgage interest rate fell from 10.2 percent to 7.8 percent, helping to make housing more affordable.

TABLE 3

U.S. OUTPUT: FINANCE, INSURANCE, AND REAL ESTATE

(Millions of U.S. dollars, except as noted)

	1987	1988	1989	1990	1991	1992	1993	1994	1995	1996	GROWTH RATE[1]
FINANCE											
OUTPUT MEASURES:											
Gross domestic product:											
Current dollars	215,298	206,158	222,439	245,827	265,217	290,253	309,958	321,957	.....	.....	.....
Percent of total GDP	4.6	4.1	4.1	4.3	4.5	4.7	4.7	4.6	.....	.....	.....
Chained (1992) dollars	291,457	290,174	296,122	294,029	283,805	290,253	306,849	318,581	.....	.....	.....
Assets, commercial banks (billions)	.....	2,940.3	3,139.4	3,297.5	3,382.4	3,484.6	3,644.2	3,872.3	4,197.0	4,420.0	5.23
Loans and leases, commercial banks (billions)	.....	2,117.2	2,242.2	2,340.1	2,470.5	2,503.8	2,533.4	2,528.7	2,670.8	2,832.0	3.70
Deposits, commercial banks (billions)	.....	1,873.8	2,024.4	2,117.8	2,111.2	2,113.3	2,194.8	2,373.9	2,608.1	2,782.9	5.07
INSURANCE											
OUTPUT MEASURES:											
Gross domestic product:											
Current dollars	80,116	96,733	101,489	106,399	121,734	122,802	141,643	149,411	.....	.....	.....
Percent of total GDP	1.7	1.9	1.8	1.8	2.0	1.9	2.1	2.2	.....	.....	.....
Chained (1992) dollars	94,600	106,600	110,200	111,000	114,900	122,802	114,200	118,200	.....	.....	.....
Life insurance company data:											
Premium receipts, life and health insurance	212,963	229,115	244,366	264,010	263,791	282,058	319,551	326,342	339,212	.....	5.99
Life insurance in force	7,452,498	8,020,159	8,694,015	9,392,597	9,986,336	10,405,792	11,104,741	11,673,621	12,576,677	.....	6.76
Total assets	1,044,459	1,166,870	1,299,756	1,408,208	1,551,201	1,664,531	1,839,127	1,942,273	2,143,544	.....	9.40
REAL ESTATE[2]											
OUTPUT MEASURES:											
Existing home sales (thousand units)	3,436	3,513	3,346	3,211	3,220	3,520	3,802	3,946	3,802	4,090	1.95
Gross domestic product[2]:											
Current dollars	535,295	589,533	636,714	672,956	695,730	735,771	762,389	802,310	.....	.....	.....
Percent of total GDP	11.4	11.7	11.7	11.7	11.8	11.8	11.6	11.6	.....	.....	.....
Chained (1992) dollars	637,436	677,327	698,466	706,798	708,486	735,771	740,447	758,375	.....	.....	.....
PRICES:											
Existing home, median (dollars)	85,600	89,300	93,100	95,500	100,300	103,700	106,800	109,800	112,900	118,000	3.63
Fixed rate mortgage interest rate (percent)	10.2	10.3	10.3	10.1	9.3	8.4	7.3	8.4	8.0	7.8	.....

1. Compound annual growth rate for years shown.

2. A significant part of the gross product originating in the Real Estate industry is the imputed rent from owner-occupied housing, which has no counterpart in the industry employment statistics. Therefore, these GDP figures are not comparable in magnitude with the employment data. For a detailed accounting of the gross product of the housing industry, see "non-farming services", Table B11-Housing Sector Output, "Gross Product, and National Income", in most issues of the *Survey of Current Business*, Bureau of Economic Analysis. U.S. Department of Commerce.

Sources: GDP: Bureau of Economic Analysis; Assets, loans and leases, deposits: Federal Reserve Board of Governors; Life insurance company data: American Council of Life Insurance; Existing home sales: National Association of Realtors, Mortgage interest rate: Federal Home Loan Mortgage Corporation.

Workforce and Employment. Finance, insurance, and real estate employment grew from 6.5 million in 1987 to 6.9 million in 1996 at a moderate rate of 0.6 percent per year (Table 4). Average hourly earnings of nonsupervisory workers increased from $8.73 per hour in 1987 to $12.79 per hour in 1996, at an annual rate of 4.3 percent. In inflation-adjusted 1992 dollars, the rate of growth was slower, but still positive at about 0.8 percent per year. Average weekly hours worked stayed roughly constant over the period, ending up at 35.9 hours per week in 1996.

Employment in *Finance* was relatively stable from 1987 to 1996. At the end of the period, industry employment was 3.3 million, only slightly above its 1987 level. Similarly, the number of women in the finance industry, and their percentage of total industry employment remained essentially unchanged over the decade. Women made up the majority of the finance workforce, with 67.5 percent of total employment in 1996.

Insurance employment increased from 2 million in 1987 to 2.2 million in 1996. Women's share of industry employment rose slightly from 64.4 percent to 65.8 percent over the period. Increasing industry GDP and virtually unchanged employment suggests increasing productivity.

Real estate employment grew from 1,242,000 in 1987 to 1,381,000 in 1996. Of the 139,000 new employees, 112,000 were women. Consequently, women's share of employment increased from 44.5 percent in 1987 to 48.2 percent at the end of the period.

FIGURE 3

U.S. OCCUPATIONAL INJURY AND ILLNESS RATES:
FINANCE, INSURANCE, AND REAL ESTATE, 1995

Finance, insurance, and real estate had the lowest illness and injury rate of any major industry group—2.6 per 100 workers.

Incidence of nonfatal injuries and illnesses per 100 full-time workers

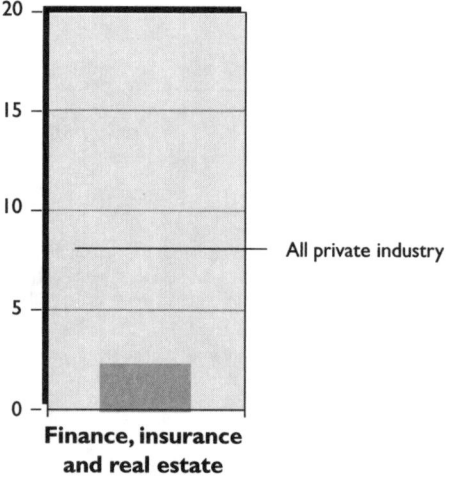

All private industry

Finance, insurance and real estate

Source: U.S. Bureau of Labor Statistics.

TABLE 4

U.S. EMPLOYMENT, HOURS, AND EARNINGS: FINANCE, INSURANCE, AND REAL ESTATE

(Monetary values in U.S. dollars)

	1987	1988	1989	1990	1991	1992	1993	1994	1995	1996	GROWTH RATE[1]
FINANCE, INSURANCE, AND REAL ESTATE											
NUMBER OF EMPLOYEES, IN THOUSANDS:											
Total	6,533	6,630	6,668	6,709	6,646	6,602	6,757	6,896	6,806	6,899	0.61
Nonsupervisory workers	4,797	4,811	4,829	4,860	4,795	4,772	4,908	5,018	4,961	5,034	0.54
Percent of total	73.4	72.6	72.4	72.4	72.1	72.3	72.6	72.8	72.9	73.0	.....
Women	4,076	4,134	4,188	4,239	4,215	4,192	4,279	4,354	4,295	4,352	0.73
Percent of total	62.4	62.4	62.8	63.2	63.4	63.5	63.3	63.1	63.1	63.1	.....
HOURS AND EARNINGS OF NONSUPERVISORY WORKERS:											
AVERAGE HOURLY EARNINGS, U.S. DOLLARS[2]											
Current dollars	8.73	9.06	9.53	9.97	10.39	10.82	11.35	11.83	12.32	12.79	4.33
1992 dollars[3]	10.72	10.71	10.73	10.68	10.69	10.82	11.03	11.22	11.36	11.46	0.75
Average weekly hours	36.3	35.9	35.8	35.8	35.7	35.8	35.8	35.8	35.9	35.9	-0.12
Average weekly earnings, current U.S. dollars	316.90	325.25	341.17	356.93	370.92	387.36	406.33	423.51	442.29	459.16	4.21
FINANCE											
NUMBER OF EMPLOYEES, IN THOUSANDS:											
Total	3,264	3,274	3,283	3,268	3,187	3,160	3,238	3,299	3,231	3,301	0.13
Women	.....	2,215	2,231	2,238	2,191	2,168	2,209	2,237	2,187	2,229	0.08
Percent of total	.....	67.7	68.0	68.5	68.7	68.6	68.2	67.8	67.7	67.5	.....
INSURANCE											
NUMBER OF EMPLOYEES, IN THOUSANDS:											
Total	2,027	2,075	2,090	2,126	2,161	2,152	2,197	2,236	2,225	2,217	1.00
Women	1,305	1,345	1,362	1,392	1,418	1,411	1,438	1,461	1,460	1,459	1.25
Percent of total	64.4	64.8	65.2	65.5	65.6	65.6	65.4	65.4	65.6	65.8	.....
REAL ESTATE											
NUMBER OF EMPLOYEES, IN THOUSANDS:											
Total	1,242	1,280	1,296	1,315	1,299	1,290	1,322	1,361	1,351	1,381	1.19
Women	553	574	595	608	606	613	631	656	648	665	2.07
Percent of total	44.5	44.8	45.9	46.2	46.7	47.5	47.7	48.2	48.0	48.2	.....

1. Compound annual growth rate for years shown.

2. Including overtime.

3. Converted to 1992 dollars using Consumer Price Index for Urban Wage Earners and Clerical Workers.

Source: Bureau of Labor Statistics.

TABLE 5

U.S. EMPLOYMENT PROJECTIONS BY MAJOR OCCUPATIONAL GROUP: FINANCE, INSURANCE, AND REAL ESTATE

OCCUPATION	1994		PROJECTIONS, 2005			
	NUMBER OF EMPLOYEES	PERCENT OF INDUSTRY TOTAL	NUMBER OF EMPLOYEES			PERCENT OF INDUSTRY TOTAL, MODERATE PROJECTIONS
			LOW	MODERATE	HIGH	
Total, all occupations	6,933,100	100.0	7,075,900	7,372,500	7,720,600	100.0
Executive, administrative, and managerial	1,592,453	23.0	1,813,659	1,880,364	1,957,115	25.5
Professional specialties	239,661	3.5	348,795	358,322	368,407	4.9
Technicians and related support	140,694	2.0	139,959	144,946	150,659	2.0
Marketing and sales	780,155	11.3	883,660	917,545	956,549	12.5
Administrative support including clerical	3,467,607	50.0	3,175,320	3,281,437	3,398,605	44.5
Service	353,201	5.1	343,281	378,544	424,894	5.1
Agriculture, forestry, and fisheries occupations	89,075	1.3	78,563	87,499	99,360	1.2
Precision production, craft, and repair	248,299	3.6	269,877	299,437	338,523	4.1
Operators, fabricators, assemblers	21,955	0.3	22,786	24,405	26,488	0.3

Finance, insurance, and real estate are projected to employ 439,400 more people by the year 2005 than in 1994 (moderate assumptions). Declining employment in administrative support, the largest occupation, will be more than compensated for by increases in the number of executives, professionals, and sales persons employed in the industry.

CANADA

Canada's finance, insurance, and real estate industry employed 688,032 people in 1993 (Table 7). *Finance* and *insurance* (excluding agencies) account for almost three-quarters of industry employment. The largest subindustry in terms of employment is deposit accepting intermediaries, with a workforce of 285,862 people. It is difficult to compare the number of employees working in insurance and real estate to those in the U.S. industries since insurance agencies are combined with real estate agencies in the Canadian data.

Employment in finance, insurance, and real estate increased from 675,394 in 1987 to a 1990 peak of 737,432 (Table 8). Employment then fell to 669,981 in 1995, before rising slightly to 679,947 in 1996. Average weekly earnings in finance, insurance, and real estate increased every year from 1987 to 1996. In 1996, average weekly earnings for the industry were Can$704.54 per week. Receipts for the industry increased at an annual rate of 0.9 percent per year from 1987 to 1996. From 1987 to 1991, receipts actually fell, so the rate of growth from 1991 to 1996 was considerably faster, at 2.1 percent per year.

TABLE 7

CANADA: COMPONENT INDUSTRIES OF FINANCE, INSURANCE, AND REAL ESTATE (CSIC 7000-7600), 1993

		EMPLOYMENT	
INDUSTRY NAME	CSIC	NUMBER	PERCENT OF INDUSTRY TOTAL
FINANCE, INSURANCE, AND REAL ESTATE	7000-7600	688,032	100.0
Finance and insurance	7000-7400	500,750	72.8
Deposit accepting intermediaries	7000	285,862	41.5
Consumer and business financing intermediaries	7100	19,829	2.9
Investment intermediaries	7200	59,562	8.7
Insurance (excluding agencies)	7300	105,188	15.3
Other financial intermediaries	7400	30,309	4.4
Real estate	7500, 7600	187,281	27.2
Real estate operators (exc. developers)	7500	87,209	12.7
Insurance and real estate agencies	7600	100,072	14.5

Source: Statistics Canada: CANSIM.

TABLE 8

CANADIAN EMPLOYMENT AND RECEIPTS: FINANCE, INSURANCE, AND REAL ESTATE (CSIC 7000-7600), 1987-1996

(Monetary values in Canadian dollars)

	1987	1988	1989	1990	1991	1992	1993	1994	1995	1996	CHANGE[1]
All employees	675,394	718,965	733,140	737,432	722,295	700,079	688,032	670,484	669,981	679,947	0.07
Nonsupervisory workers:											
Average weekly earnings	483.12	511.94	544.36	546.29	568.62	603.22	633.26	644.24	658.41	704.54	4.28
Receipts (millions)	29,929	30,855	31,613	30,895	29,292	29,643	30,469	32,029	32,322	32,537	0.93

1. Compound annual growth rate.

Source: Statistics Canada: CANSIM

MEXICO

Finance, insurance, and real estate employment grew from 494,769 in 1988 to 548,605 in 1995, at an annual rate of 1.5 percent (Table 10). In 1988, more people were employed in financial services than in insurance and real estate, but by 1995 the roles were reversed. Insurance and real estate employment grew at a rate of 4.6 percent per year, while financial services employment fell by 2 percent per year.

Output for Mexican finance, insurance, and real estate increased from 146.8 billion constant 1993 new pesos ($47.0 billion 1993 U.S. dollars) in 1988 to 192.5 billion constant 1993 new pesos ($61.6 billion 1993 U.S. dollars) in 1995. There was a slight decline in output from 1994 to 1995, in line with the general economic downturn in Mexico.

TABLE 10

MEXICAN GROSS DOMESTIC PRODUCT AND EMPLOYMENT: FINANCE, INSURANCE, AND REAL ESTATE, 1988-1995

	1988	1989	1990	1991	1992	1993	1994	1995	CHANGE[1]
GROSS DOMESTIC PRODUCT:									
Millions of constant 1993 new pesos	146,785.2	151,916.5	158,670.4	166,125.4	173,740.2	183,208.1	193,145.8	192,526.5	3.95
Millions of constant 1993 U.S. dollars[2]	46,990.8	48,633.5	50,795.6	53,182.3	55,620.0	58,651.0	61,832.4	61,634.1	3.95
TOTAL EMPLOYMENT:									
Financial services, insurance, real estate	494,769	503,262	511,118	529,206	538,479	546,811	556,090	548,605	1.49
Financial services	257,570	252,530	248,999	252,676	250,027	246,112	242,059	223,376	-2.01
Insurance and real estate	237,199	250,732	262,119	276,530	288,452	300,699	314,031	325,229	4.61

1. Compound annual growth rate.

2. Converted at 3.1237 new pesos to the U.S. dollar.

Source: Sistema de Cuentas Nacionales de Mexico, INEGI.

INTERNATIONAL TRADE

In Table 11, data are presented on U.S. trade in financial services and insurance. Caution should be used in interpreting these numbers, since they do not correspond exactly to the industry classifications of finance and insurance. Financial services includes funds management, credit card services, explicit fees and commissions on securities transactions, fees on credit related activities, implicit fees from bond trading, and other miscellaneous financial services. Insurance includes premiums received and paid for, primary insurance and reinsurance; losses paid by U.S. insurers and losses recovered from foreign insurers are netted against the premiums.

From 1987 to 1995, the United States maintained a positive trade balance with the rest of the world in financial services. Because of a change in the procedure used to estimate financial services trade, figures for years prior to 1992 are not directly comparable to the numbers for 1992 and beyond. Since 1992, overall trade in financial services has been expanding. Exports have been growing more than imports; consequently, in 1995, the United States had a $4.4 billion trade surplus, compared to the $3.0 billion surplus of 1992.

The United States had a trade deficit in net insurance payments every year from 1987 to 1995. The largest deficit of the period, $3.1 billion, occurred in 1995. Because the net insurance figure depends on the size of losses, which can be very unpredictable, it is useful to look at premiums to get an idea of how the magnitude of trade in insurance has changed over time. Premiums paid by U.S. citizens to foreign insurers have increased substantially from $8.5 billion in 1987 to $13.7 billion in 1995. Foreigners were also increasing spending on U.S. insurance from 1987 to 1995, as premiums paid to U.S. insurers increased from $3.6 billion to $5.6 billion. In 1995, foreign insurers received $8.1 billion more in premiums from U.S. citizens than U.S. insurers received from foreigners.

TABLE 11

INTERNATIONAL TRADE, FINANCE, INSURANCE AND REAL ESTATE

(Millions of U.S. dollars)

	1987	1988	1989	1990	1991	1992	1993	1994	1995
GLOBAL TRADE, U.S.									
IMPORTS									
Financial services[1]	2,077	1,656	2,056	2,475	2,669	986	1,371	1,611	1,707
Insurance, net	3,241	2,628	823	1,910	2,467	1,324	3,095	3,781	4,481
Premiums	8,538	8,954	9,909	10,222	11,207	11,738	12,093	13,861	13,710
Losses	5,297	6,326	9,086	8,312	8,740	10,414	8,998	10,080	9,230
EXPORTS									
Financial services[1]	3,731	3,831	5,036	4,417	5,012	4,034	4,999	5,626	6,109
Insurance, net	1,573	847	103	230	491	682	1,020	1,506	1,395
Premiums	3,615	3,534	3,117	3,388	3,365	3,852	3,981	4,944	5,575
Losses	2,042	2,687	3,015	3,158	2,874	3,170	2,961	3,437	4,180
TRADE BALANCE[2]									
Financial services[1]	1,654	2,175	2,980	1,942	2,343	3,048	3,628	4,015	4,402
Insurance, net	(1,668)	(1,781)	(720)	(1,680)	(1,976)	(642)	(2,075)	(2,275)	(3,086)
Premiums	(4,923)	(5,420)	(6,792)	(6,834)	(7,842)	(7,886)	(8,112)	(8,917)	(8,135)
Losses	(3,255)	(3,639)	(6,071)	(5,154)	(5,866)	(7,244)	(6,037)	(6,643)	(5,050)

1. There is a break in the series in 1992.

2. Parentheses indicate an excess of imports over exports.

Source: U.S. Department of Commerce, Bureau of Economic Analysis.

HEALTH SERVICES

Overview. Virtually all North Americans are consumers of health care services throughout their lives. Health care is a significant part of private and national budgets and a major employer in all three countries. However, the three countries have taken significantly different approaches to health care in both financing and delivery.

The U.S. health care industry is an amalgam of public and private (profit making and not-for-profit) institutions. The U.S. health care system relies heavily on private insurance, with about three-quarters of the population covered by private insurance provided by employers or purchased individually. The government has two large public financing programs— Medicare, primarily for the elderly, and Medicaid for low income persons—and several smaller ones such as those operated by the Public Health Service and the Veterans Administration. About 14 percent of the population has no health insurance at all. The government also operates major medical research facilities and finances extensive private medical research. Private hospitals and medical schools attract patients and students from around the world. Most Americans believe they have the best health care in the world, although they acknowledge that, for the most part, the quality of that care is dependent on one's ability to pay.

The Canadian health system is called Medicare, but it is for everyone, not just for seniors. The Canada Health Act[1] mandates an insurance monopoly for basic health services, and no private company may offer insurance covering the proscribed services, nor may any private purveyor accept payment of any kind for those services except from the government insurance system. All Canadians are eligible for care under the system; there are no deductibles, copayments, or forms for patients to complete. The system relies heavily on primary care physicians (about 63 percent of the total) who provide most care, but make referrals to specialists. Costs are shared by the federal and provincial governments with no explicit health tax or service fees. The provincial and territorial governments negotiate contracts with hospitals, medical associations, and other service providers and pay all bills for basic care. Medical services are delivered almost entirely by private or nonprofit community entities, and most physicians are private practitioners who are paid on a fee-for-service basis. Most Canadians are proud of their "single payer" system, believing it supports the values of fairness, compassion, and respect of the dignity of all.[2]

The Mexican health care system is a mixture of public and private sector delivery systems. Eight government institutes operate hospitals; hire doctors, nurses, and other health professionals; and deliver health care to specific eligible groups. The social security system serves both government and covered private sector workers and their families—about 55 percent of the population.[3] Other government institutes serve specific clientele (e.g., the Mexican petroleum monopoly PEMEX has its own medical service). The remainder of the population is served by the private sector. The Pan American Health Organization estimates that about 6 percent of the population lacks health care of any kind because of geographic, economic, or cultural accessibility problems. The Mexican health system has steadily improved over recent years as indicated by improving life expectancy and infant mortality figures. The Mexican Secretary of Health has recently initiated a health system reform program called Health 1995-2000.[4]

---

[1] The Canada Health Act was passed in 1984, but the existing system had many similarities.

[2] A general description of the Canadian health system is available in "Canada's Health System" on the Internet from the Health Policy Division at www.hwc.ca

[3] See, "Employment, Wages and Benefits," for a description of the "formal" and "informal" labor markets.

[4] El Programa de Reforma del Sector Salud 1995—2000.

THE UNITED STATES

Services and Economic Significance. The U.S. health care industry has a huge impact on the economy. In 1996, nearly one in 10 U.S. nonfarm private sector workers were in health care. Expenditures for health care totaled almost $1 trillion in 1995, or more than 13 times those in 1970 and an estimated 13.6 percent of the U.S. gross domestic product (GDP). Spending grew at a torrid 11.9 percent compound annual rate from 1970 to 1990 before decelerating to a still-rapid 5.5 percent rate in 1995, adding fuel to the debate over health care financing and sparking new trends in delivery of services.

Among these trends has been the shift toward managed health care plans such as health maintenance organizations (HMOs), although growing dissatisfaction with HMOs has been reported recently. HMOs offer prepaid plans covering most health care services obtained through their networks of doctors, clinics, and approved hospitals and pharmacies. Similar in concept are the preferred provider organizations (PPOs), which allow patients to use non-plan providers (physicians and hospitals) but charge less when patients use participating providers. Managed care, in short, exercises greater control over costs by negotiating lower fees with participating doctors, controlling patients' use of specialists and other high-priced practitioners, and making cost a factor in prescribing drugs and treatment regimens. Currently, managed care organizations service more than one-fourth of the U.S. population, and many traditional fee-for-service insurance plans use some managed care features, such as preferred providers. Cost reductions and more specific treatment also are being realized through home health care, hospices, continuing care retirement communities (CCRCs), and other approaches.

In 1996, the health services industry had some 9.5 million employees (Table 1). Hospitals accounted for 40.3 percent of industry employment, followed by nursing and personal care facilities (18.3 percent) and doctors' offices and clinics (17.7 percent). Industry hourly earnings averaged $12.85 in 1996, with hospitals having the highest average earnings at $14.69.

What's New. The Health Insurance Portability and Accountability Act—also known as the Kassebaum-Kennedy Act—was passed and signed into law on August 21, 1996. The Act makes it possible for workers to continue their insurance coverage when they change jobs and also restricts the ability of insurance carriers to refuse insurance to those with previous histories of illness. It is not expected to have a significant effect on the health care industry.

Cost containment continues to be a major concern, and privately financed care seems to be making progress. In 1995, the latest year for which complete data are available, expenditures on the privately financed side decelerated to a 2.8 percent rate of growth; whereas expenditures in publicly financed care continued to rise at an 8.6 percent rate.

Assets held by the Medicare Hospital Insurance Trust Fund fell another 4.1 percent in 1996 following a decline in 1995. Bruce C. Vladick, Administrator of the Health Care Finance Administration, has stated he expects the Trust Fund to run dry early in 2001.[5] This ensures that pressure will continue on the industry to reduce costs for Medicare patients. Congress may also continue efforts to modify Medicare charges and eligibility rules.

Another important development is the downward pressure on hospital revenues—they increased only 1.2 percent in 1996, one of the lowest rates on record. Total inpatient hospital admissions declined in 1996, explaining, perhaps, the recent apparent increase in hospital advertising.

Early in 1998, President Clinton proposed that early retirees, laid-off workers, and other uninsured Americans between the ages of 55 and 64 be permitted to enroll in Medicare by paying $3,600 to $5,000 per year in premiums. The Administration indicated that the plan

---

[5] HCFA press release, Jan. 27, 1997.

TABLE 1

U.S. EMPLOYMENT AND EARNINGS: PRIVATE SECTOR HEALTH SERVICES, 1996

INDUSTRY	SIC	EMPLOYMENT[1]		AVERAGE HOURLY EARNINGS (U.S. DOLLARS)[2]
		THOUSANDS OF PERSONS	PERCENT OF INDUSTRY TOTAL	
TOTAL HEALTH SERVICES	80	9,468.9	100.0	12.85
Offices and clinics of doctors of medicine	801	1,678.5	17.7	13.17
Offices and clinics of dentists	802	609.2	6.4	12.89
Offices and clinics of other health practioners	804	414.2	4.4	11.94
Offices and clinics of chiropractors and optometrists	8041, 8042	160.9	1.7	.....
Nursing and personal care facilties	805	1,732.2	18.3	9.01
Skilled nursing care facilities	8051	1,289.1	13.6	.....
Intermediate care facilities	8052	212.2	2.2	8.38
Nursing and personal care facilties, n.e.c.	8059	230.9	2.4	.....
Hospitals	806	3,813.5	40.3	14.69
General medical and surgical hospitals	8062	3,517.0	37.1	.....
Psychiatric hospitals	8063	87.3	0.9	.....
Specialty hospitals, except psychiatric	8069	209.2	2.2	.....
Medical and dental laboratories	807	196.2	2.1	.....
Home health care services	808	665.4	7.0	11.18

1. Total payroll employment, private.
2. Earnings of nonsupervisory workers, including overtime.
Source: Bureau of Labor Statistics.

FIGURE 1

U.S. EMPLOYMENT IN HEALTH SERVICES

Percent distribution by region, 1995

Health services employment was highest in the Southeast, which had 22.1 percent of the total or slightly less than its 23.7 percent share of all U.S. employment. In contrast, the Mid-Atlantic region had 20 percent of health care employment, but only 16.5 percent of total U.S. employment. The Great Lakes region was next in importance, with 17.4 percent of the health care total, followed by the Pacific region with 13.5 percent.

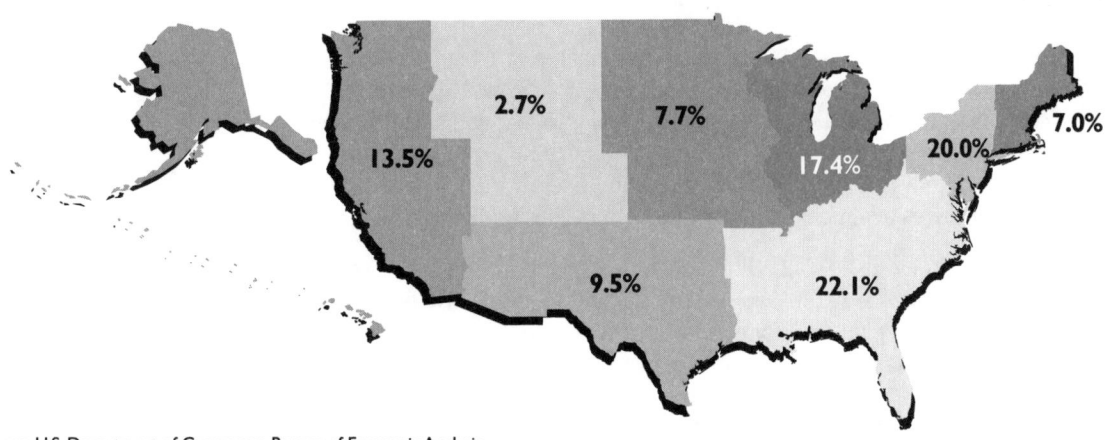

Source: U.S. Department of Commerce, Bureau of Economic Analysis.

FIGURE 2

U.S. EMPLOYMENT AND GROSS PRODUCT, HEALTH SERVICES

Total payroll employment and inflation-adjusted gross product

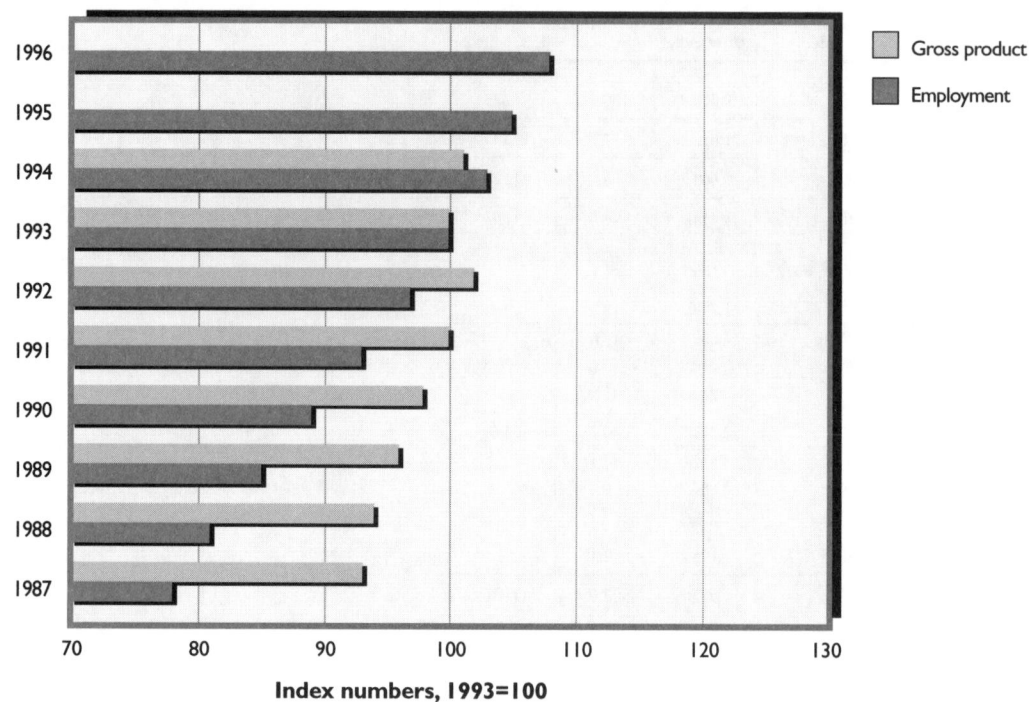

Index numbers, 1993=100

Source: U.S. Bureau of Labor Statistics, U.S. Department of Commerce, and estimates by the editors.

would be self-financing. But according to the *New York Times* (January 20, 1998), a number of experts including Robert Myers, chief actuary of Social Security for 23 years, do not believe the plan would pay for itself, in part because only people with severe medical problems would apply.

Output. The gross domestic product for health care rose about 9 percent between 1987 and 1994 with most of the growth from 1987 to 1992, whereas employment grew by almost a third during that period (Figure 2).

National health expenditures totaled $988.5 billion in 1995, compared with $697.5 billion in 1990, $247.2 billion in 1980, and only $26.9 billion in 1960 (Table 2). The industry employs some of the most complex and advanced equipment and procedures. Yet home health care services, which use some techniques available since the beginning of time, ranked as the fastest growing subindustry from 1970 until 1994. That year, it was overtaken by other personal health care, which includes a number of "alternative" approaches to medicine.

Some of that growth came at the expense of traditional forms of health care such as hospitals and physicians services, which, while the two largest expenditure areas, have been the most affected by cost-cutting. Hospital care, for example, accounted for $350 billion or 35 percent of 1995 health care expenditure, but year-to-year growth has been under 6 percent since 1993 (Table 2). Growth here has been checked by an excess of hospital beds, brought on in part by economy measures such as shorter stays and increased use of outpatient facilities. Outlays for physician services ($201.6 billion in 1995) also have risen at less than 6 percent a year since 1993, although there was a noticeable pickup in 1995 (to 5.8 percent from 4.4 percent the previous year).

Table 3 shows national health expenditures by type and source of funds in 1995. That year, personal health care accounted for $878.8 billion of total expenditures, including $486.7 billion in private outlays and $392.1 billion in federal, state, and local government expenditures. Government's share of total expenditures was highest for other personal health care (87 percent), hospitals (61 percent), and nursing home care (58 percent). The private sector's share was highest for dental services (96 percent), drugs and other medical nondurables (86 percent), other professional services (76 percent), and physician services (68 percent). Spending on program administration and net cost of private health insurance totaled $47.7 billion in 1995, and that on government public health activities was $31.4 billion.

TABLE 2

U.S. NATIONAL HEALTH EXPENDITURES BY TYPE, 1960-1995

(Billions of U.S. dollars; percent)

TYPE OF EXPENDITURE	1960	1970	1980	1990	1991	1992	1993	1994	1995
National health expenditures	26.9	73.2	247.2	697.5	761.7	834.2	892.1	937.1	988.5
Health services and supplies	25.2	67.9	235.6	672.9	736.8	806.7	863.1	906.7	957.8
Personal health care	23.6	63.8	217.0	614.7	676.6	740.5	786.9	827.9	878.8
Hospital care	9.3	28.0	102.7	256.4	282.3	305.4	323.3	335.0	350.1
Physician services	5.3	13.6	45.2	146.3	159.2	175.7	182.7	190.6	201.6
Dental services	2.0	4.7	13.3	31.6	33.3	37.0	39.2	42.1	45.8
Other professional services	0.6	1.4	6.4	34.7	38.3	42.1	46.3	49.1	52.6
Home health care	0.1	0.2	2.4	13.1	16.1	19.6	23.0	26.3	28.6
Drugs and other medical nondurables	4.2	8.8	21.6	59.9	65.6	71.2	75.0	77.7	83.4
Vision products and other medical durables	0.6	1.6	3.8	10.5	11.2	11.9	12.5	12.9	13.8
Nursing home care	0.8	4.2	17.6	50.9	57.2	62.3	67.0	72.4	77.9
Other personal health care	0.7	1.3	4.0	11.2	13.6	15.4	17.9	21.7	25.0
Program administration and net cost of private health insurance	1.2	2.7	11.8	38.6	38.8	42.7	50.9	50.6	47.7
Government public health activities	0.4	1.3	6.7	19.6	21.4	23.4	25.3	28.2	31.4
Research and construction	1.7	5.3	11.6	24.5	24.9	27.5	29.0	30.4	30.7
Research[1]	0.7	2.0	5.5	12.2	12.9	14.2	14.5	15.8	16.6
Construction	1.0	3.4	6.2	12.3	12.0	13.4	14.5	14.6	14.0
AVERAGE ANNUAL PERCENT CHANGE FROM PREVIOUS YEAR SHOWN									
National health expenditures	.....	10.6	12.9	10.9	9.2	9.5	6.9	5.1	5.5
Health services and supplies	.....	10.4	13.2	11.1	9.5	9.5	7.0	5.1	5.6
Personal health care	.....	10.5	13.0	11.0	10.1	9.5	6.3	5.2	6.1
Hospital care	.....	11.7	13.9	9.6	10.1	8.2	5.9	3.6	4.5
Physician services	.....	9.9	12.8	12.5	8.8	10.4	4.0	4.4	5.8
Dental services	.....	9.1	11.1	9.0	5.6	11.0	6.0	7.3	8.9
Other professional services	.....	8.8	16.3	18.5	10.4	10.0	10.0	6.1	7.0
Home health care	.....	14.5	26.9	18.6	22.4	22.3	17.1	14.4	8.6
Drugs and other medical nondurables	.....	7.6	9.4	10.7	9.4	8.6	5.4	3.6	7.3
Vision products and other medical durables	.....	9.6	8.8	10.7	7.0	6.3	5.1	2.8	7.2
Nursing home care	.....	17.4	15.4	11.2	12.2	9.0	7.6	8.1	7.5
Other personal health care	.....	6.5	12.0	10.8	20.7	13.3	16.4	21.6	14.9
Program administration and net cost of private health insurance	.....	8.9	15.8	12.6	0.4	10.2	19.1	-0.5	-5.8
Government public health activities	.....	13.9	17.5	11.3	9.2	9.3	7.9	11.6	11.3
Research and construction	.....	12.2	8.1	7.7	1.7	10.5	5.3	4.9	0.8
Research[1]	.....	10.9	10.8	8.4	5.8	9.8	2.2	9.3	5.0
Construction	.....	12.9	6.2	7.1	-2.4	11.2	8.7	0.5	-3.8

1. Research and development expenditures of drug companies and other manufacturers and providers of medical equipment and supplies are excluded from research expenditures, but are included in the expenditure class in which the product falls.

NOTE: May not add to totals because of rounding.

SOURCE: Health Care Financing Administration, Office of the Actuary: Data from the Office of National Health Statistics.

TABLE 3

U.S. NATIONAL HEALTH EXPENDITURES BY SOURCE OF FUNDS AND TYPE OF EXPENDITURE, 1995

(Millions of U.S. dollars, except as noted)

YEAR AND TYPE OF EXPENDITURE	TOTAL	PRIVATE					GOVERNMENT		
		ALL PRIVATE FUNDS	CONSUMERS			OTHER	TOTAL	FEDERAL	STATE AND LOCAL
			TOTAL	OUT OF POCKET	PRIVATE INSURANCE				
National health expenditures	988.5	532.1	493.2	182.6	310.6	38.9	456.4	328.4	128.0
Health services and supplies	957.8	521.2	493.2	182.6	310.6	28.0	436.7	314.4	122.2
Personal health care	878.8	486.7	459.3	182.6	276.8	27.3	392.1	303.6	88.5
Hospital care	350.1	135.8	124.5	11.4	113.1	11.3	214.3	175.3	39.0
Physician services	201.6	137.6	133.9	36.9	97.0	3.7	64.0	50.9	13.1
Dental services	45.8	44.0	43.8	21.8	22.0	0.2	1.8	1.0	0.8
Other professional services	52.6	39.9	36.0	20.2	15.8	3.9	12.7	9.6	3.1
Home health care	28.6	12.8	9.3	6.0	3.3	3.4	15.8	13.8	2.0
Drugs and other medical nondurables	83.4	72.0	72.0	49.8	22.1	.....	11.4	5.9	5.6
Vision products and other medical durables	13.8	8.7	8.7	7.8	0.9	.....	5.1	5.0	0.1
Nursing home care	77.9	32.6	31.1	28.6	2.5	1.5	45.3	29.3	16.0
Other personal health care	25.0	3.3	.....	.....	.....	3.3	21.7	12.8	8.9
Program administration and net cost of private health insurance	47.7	34.5	33.9	.....	33.9	0.6	13.2	7.1	6.1
Government public health activities	31.4	.....	.....	.....	.....	.....	31.4	3.8	27.6
Research and construction	30.7	10.9	.....	.....	.....	10.9	19.7	14.0	5.7
Research	16.6	1.4	.....	.....	.....	1.4	15.2	12.9	2.3
Construction	14.0	9.6	.....	.....	.....	9.6	4.5	1.1	3.4

NOTE: Research and development expenditures of drug companies and other manufacturers and providers of medical equipment and supplies are excluded from research expenditures, but are included in the expenditure class in which the product falls. Numbers may not add to totals because of rounding.

SOURCE: Health Care Financing Administration, Office of the Actuary: Data from the Office of National Health Statistics.

Investment. Construction of new health care facilities increased in each year but one (1991) from 1990 to 1994 but has since declined, possibly because of the drop in hospital admissions and deceleration of hospital revenues (Table 2). Health research increased at a 5.3 percent compound annual rate over the 1990-1995 period, reaching $16.6 billion in 1995 (Table 2).   Federal, state, and local governments accounted for 92 percent of all research expenditures in 1995 but only 32 percent of the construction spending (Table 3).

Workforce and Employment. The health care industry has been an important source of new jobs, growing through recessions and recoveries. From 1988 to 1996, private employment in the industry increased at a steady 3.7 percent compound annual rate, but employment in government hospitals was virtually unchanged over the same period (Table 4); the industry's share of all nonfarm jobs rose from 4.5 percent in 1967 to 9.5 percent in 1996. Women dominate, accounting for a steady 82 percent of wage and salary workers. There are also a higher proportion of part-time and multiple job holding employees than in most other industries. The average workweek for all employees was 32.7 hours in 1996, compared with 34.4 hours for all of the nonfarm private sector.

Average hourly earnings of wage and salary workers from 1988 to 1996 increased at a 4.26 percent compound annual rate in current dollars (0.7 percent after adjustment for inflation). In comparison, wages for all nonfarm private sector workers rose at a 3.07 annual rate (but fell by 0.4 percent when adjusted for inflation) over the same period.

TABLE 4

U.S. EMPLOYMENT, HOURS, AND EARNINGS: PRIVATE SECTOR HEALTH SERVICES, 1988-1996

(Monetary values in U.S. dollars)

TYPE OF ESTABLISHMENT	1988	1989	1990	1991	1992	1993	1994	1995	1996	CHANGE[1]
TOTAL EMPLOYMENT, THOUSANDS:										
Nonfarm private sector, total	87,824	90,117	91,115	89,854	89,959	91,889	95,044	97,892	100,094	1.65
Health services	7,105	7,463	7,814	8,183	8,490	8,756	8,992	9,230	9,469	3.65
Offices and clinics of physicians	1,199	1,268	1,338	1,404	1,463	1,506	1,545	1,609	1,679	4.29
Offices and clinics of dentists	484	500	513	528	541	556	574	592	609	2.93
Nursing homes	1,311	1,356	1,415	1,493	1,533	1,585	1,649	1,691	1,732	3.55
Private hospitals	3,294	3,438	3,549	3,655	3,750	3,779	3,763	3,772	3,814	1.85
Home health care services	216	244	291	345	398	469	559	629	665	15.09
NONSUPERVISORY EMPLOYMENT, THOUSANDS:										
Nonfarm private sector, total	71,106	73,034	73,800	72,650	72,930	74,777	77,610	80,123	81,998	1.80
Health services	6,311	6,636	6,948	7,276	7,546	7,770	7,966	8,178	8,396	3.63
Offices and clinics of physicians	988	1,047	1,105	1,155	1,202	1,231	1,261	1,315	1,377	4.23
Offices and clinics of dentists	424	437	450	464	473	487	501	517	534	2.94
Nursing homes	1,184	1,226	1,279	1,347	1,385	1,431	1,487	1,526	1,560	3.51
Private hospitals	3,010	3,145	3,248	3,353	3,442	3,464	3,441	3,450	3,491	1.87
Home health care services	199	225	269	319	369	435	518	582	616	15.18
AVERAGE WEEKLY HOURS:										
Nonfarm private sector, total	34.7	34.6	34.5	34.3	34.4	34.5	34.7	34.5	34.4	-0.09
Health services	32.4	32.5	32.5	32.5	32.8	32.8	32.8	32.8	32.7	0.11
Offices and clinics of physicians	31.6	31.9	31.8	31.9	32.2	32.2	32.4	32.5	32.9	0.51
Offices and clinics of dentists	28.5	28.5	28.4	28.3	28.4	28.3	28.1	28.0	28.2	-0.13
Nursing homes	31.6	31.8	32.1	32.2	32.3	32.2	32.3	32.5	32.4	0.33
Private hospitals	34.0	34.0	34.2	34.2	34.4	34.6	34.7	34.6	34.4	0.15
Home health care services	26.5	25.4	25.3	26.1	27.4	27.8	28.2	28.6	28.0	0.69
AVERAGE HOURLY EARNINGS, U.S. DOLLARS:										
Nonfarm private sector, total	9.28	9.65	10.01	10.32	10.57	10.83	11.12	11.44	11.82	3.07
Health services	9.21	9.83	10.40	10.96	11.39	11.78	12.10	12.45	12.85	4.26
Offices and clinics of physicians	9.07	9.78	10.58	11.14	11.42	11.89	12.26	12.54	13.17	4.78
Offices and clinics of dentists	8.82	9.41	10.14	10.62	11.02	11.44	11.97	12.41	12.89	4.85
Nursing homes	6.33	6.80	7.24	7.56	7.86	8.17	8.50	8.77	9.01	4.52
Private hospitals	10.51	11.21	11.79	12.50	13.03	13.46	13.83	14.30	14.69	4.28
Home health care services	7.30	7.85	8.70	9.38	10.00	10.41	10.67	10.91	11.18	5.47
ADDENDA: TOTAL HOSPITAL EMPLOYMENT, THOUSANDS:										
Total	4,600	4,740	4,853	4,958	5,068	5,100	5,077	5,080	5,116	1.34
Private	3,294	3,438	3,549	3,655	3,750	3,779	3,763	3,772	3,814	1.85
Public	1,306	1,302	1,304	1,303	1,318	1,321	1,314	1,308	1,302	-0.04
Federal	241	227	232	234	235	234	234	232	227	-0.72
State	446	442	426	417	419	414	407	397	383	-1.89
Local	619	632	646	653	665	673	673	679	692	1.39

1. Compound annual growth rate, 1988-1996.

Source: Bureau of Labor Statistics.

FIGURE 3

U.S. OCCUPATIONAL INJURY AND ILLNESS RATES: HEALTH SERVICES, 1995

Incidence of nonfatal injuries and illnesses per 100 full-time workers

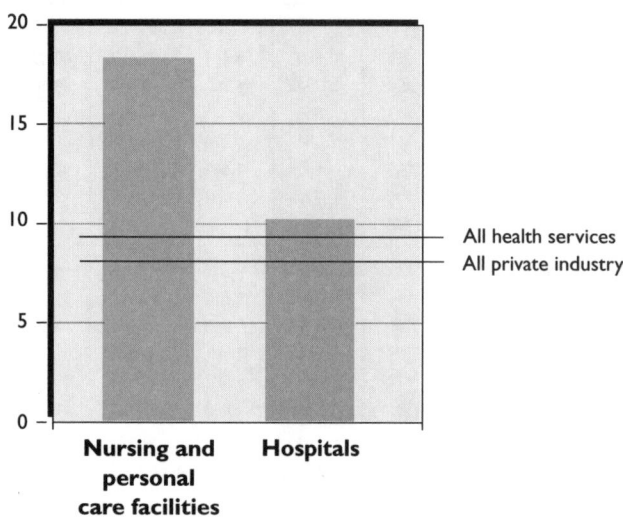

In 1995, the nonfatal illness and injury rate for health services was 9.2 cases per 100 workers, which is higher than for services as a whole and for many manufacturing industries. Within health services, nursing and personal care facilities has the highest rate, 18.2 incidences per 100 workers. The average tenure of health care production workers with their current employers was 7.3 years in 1991, the last year for which data are available.

Source: U.S. Bureau of Labor Statistics.

TABLE 5

U.S. EMPLOYMENT PROJECTIONS BY MAJOR OCCUPATIONAL GROUP: HEALTH SERVICES

OCCUPATION	1994		PROJECTIONS, 2005			
	NUMBER OF EMPLOYEES	PERCENT OF INDUSTRY TOTAL	NUMBER OF EMPLOYEES			PERCENT OF INDUSTRY TOTAL, MODERATE PROJECTIONS
			LOW	MODERATE	HIGH	
Total, all occupations	10,081,800	100.0	12,979,200	13,165,000	13,523,300	100.0
Executive, administrative, and managerial	542,119	5.4	695,205	707,362	729,792	5.4
Professional specialties	2,854,578	28.3	3,707,544	3,772,347	3,891,692	28.7
Technicians and related support	1,579,310	15.7	2,015,829	2,046,776	2,106,026	15.6
Marketing and sales	45,214	0.5	59,923	60,543	61,617	0.5
Administrative support including clerical	1,920,845	19.1	2,232,501	2,250,428	2,285,036	17.1
Service	2,860,446	28.4	3,990,331	4,044,143	4,155,230	30.7
Agriculture, forestry, and fisheries occupations	13,926	0.1	16,118	16,324	16,768	0.1
Precision production, craft, and repair	160,825	1.6	156,718	160,132	166,339	1.2
Operators, fabricators, assemblers	104,537	1.0	105,033	106,944	110,801	0.8

Note: Includes government hospitals.
Source: Bureau of Labor Statistics, November 1995.

Projections to 2005 call for overall employment to increase at a 2.5 percent annual rate to 13,165,000 (moderate projections) from the 1994 level. Increases are expected in all areas but precision workers. The largest gains overall and in share of the workforce will be in service workers and professional specialties (nurses and physicians), also the two largest categories.

Finance. Health care financing is virtually unique in the U.S. economy in that only 18 percent of health care expenditures are paid directly "out-of-pocket" by health care consumers. Private insurance pays 31 percent; the federal government, 33 percent; and state and local governments, 13 percent (Table 3). The fact that third parties pay the bulk of the cost and are often not directly involved in the "purchase decision" is thought by many to be the root of the difficulty in health care cost containment.[6]

Since the passage of Medicare and Medicaid in 1965, health care financing has been a major line item in the federal budget. In 1970, per capita private spending for health care was $212 and public spending was $129 (Table 6). In 1995, private per capita spending was $1,949 and public spending was $1,672 (federal, $1,203; and state and local governments, $469). But the increases in health care spending are decelerating, particularly in the private sector. Over the 1990 to 1995 period, private per capita spending increased at a 5.2 percent rate, while the annual rate for public spending was 9.9 percent. In 1995, the rate of increase in private spending had slowed to 2.9 percent; federal spending was at 8.8 percent, and state and local spending, at 8.4 percent.

TABLE 6

U.S. NATIONAL HEALTH EXPENDITURES AGGREGATE AND PER CAPITA AMOUNTS, PERCENT DISTRIBUTION, AND AVERAGE ANNUAL PERCENT GROWTH, BY SOURCE OF FUNDS: SELECTED YEARS, 1970-1995

	1970	1980	1985	1990	1991	1992	1993	1994	1995
NATIONAL HEALTH EXPENDITURES, BILLIONS OF U.S. DOLLARS:									
Total	73.2	247.2	428.2	697.5	761.7	834.2	892.1	937.1	988.5
Private	45.5	142.5	253.9	413.1	441.4	478.8	505.5	517.2	532.1
Public	27.7	104.8	174.3	284.3	320.3	355.4	386.5	419.9	456.4
Federal	17.8	72.0	123.3	195.8	224.4	253.9	277.6	301.9	328.4
State and local	9.9	32.8	51.0	88.5	95.9	101.6	108.9	118.0	128.0
NATIONAL HEALTH EXPENDITURES, PER CAPITA AMOUNT, U.S. DOLLARS:									
Total	341	1,052	1,733	2,683	2,901	3,145	3,330	3,465	3,621
Private	212	606	1,027	1,589	1,681	1,805	1,887	1,913	1,949
Public	129	446	705	1,094	1,220	1,340	1,443	1,553	1,672
Federal	83	306	499	753	855	957	1,036	1,116	1,203
State and local	46	140	206	341	365	383	407	436	469
PERCENT OF TOTAL NATIONAL HEALTH EXPENDITURES:									
Total	100.0	100.0	100.0	100.0	100.0	100.0	100.0	100.0	100.0
Private	62.2	57.6	59.3	59.2	58.0	57.4	56.7	55.2	53.8
Public	37.8	42.4	40.7	40.8	42.0	42.6	43.3	44.8	46.2
Federal	24.3	29.1	28.8	28.1	29.5	30.4	31.1	32.2	33.2
State and local	13.5	13.3	11.9	12.7	12.6	12.2	12.2	12.6	12.9
NATIONAL HEALTH EXPENDITURES AS A PERCENT OF GROSS DOMESTIC PRODUCT:	7.1	8.9	10.2	12.1	12.9	13.4	13.6	13.5	13.6
COMPOUND ANNUAL GROWTH RATE FROM PREVIOUS YEAR SHOWN (1970 FROM 1960):									
Total national health expenditures	10.6	12.9	11.6	10.2	9.2	9.5	6.9	5.1	5.5
Private	8.5	12.1	12.3	10.2	6.8	8.5	5.6	2.3	2.9
Public	15.3	14.2	10.7	10.3	12.7	11.0	8.7	8.6	8.7
Federal	19.8	15.0	11.4	9.7	14.6	13.1	9.4	8.7	8.8
State and local	10.2	12.7	9.2	11.6	8.3	6.0	7.2	8.4	8.4

SOURCE: HCFA, Office of the Actuary: Data from the Office of National Health Statistics.

---

[6] David R.H. Hines "Health Services: The Real Jobs Machine," *Monthly Labor Review*, November 1992, p.3.

CANADA

Canadian health care costs (public and private) grew from Can$22.4 billion in 1980 to an estimated Can$75.2 billion in 1996, a 7.9 percent annual rate. Private expenditures for health care were about 24 percent of the total in 1980 and rose to about 28 percent in 1994, the latest year for which details are available (Table 7).

Many observers believe the Canadian "single payer" system offers the best means to control health costs. Health care costs—as measured by the ratio of health care costs to GDP—rose in the early 1990s, reaching a high of 10.1 percent in 1992 and 1993. But these costs have apparently been contained as they fell to an estimated 9.5 percent of GDP in 1995 and 1996. It is estimated that 1996 total Canadian health expenditures were Can$75.2 billion, or Can$2,510 per capita (US$2,057). The government at the federal, provincial (territorial) or municipal level pays for about 72 percent of Canada's health expenditures. The rest is paid by private expenditures financed through supplementary insurance, employer sponsored benefits, or directly out-of-pocket. Table 7 provides some historical data. Per capita costs are substantially less that those in the United States, and by some measures (e.g., life expectancy and infant mortality), the Canadian system seems to be better than that in the United States. Critics argue that patients have more choices under the U.S. system.

TABLE 7

CANADA: HEALTH CARE EXPENDITURE, TOTAL AND BY SOURCE, CANADIAN AND U.S. DOLLARS

	1980	1990	1991	1992	1993	1994	1995e	1996e
TOTAL PUBLIC AND PRIVATE HEALTH CARE EXPENDITURE								
TOTAL, MILLIONS OF DOLLARS								
Canadian dollars	22,398	61,042	66,290	70,032	71,775	72,463	73,900	75,200
U.S. dollar equivalent[1]	.....	46,955	51,388	55,143	56,965	57,970	60,081	61,639
As a percent of gross domestic product	.....	9.1	9.8	10.1	10.1	9.7	9.5	9.5
PER CAPITA, DOLLARS								
Canadian dollars	911	2,196	2,358	2,463	2,496	2,478	2,496	2,510
U.S. dollar equivalent[1]	.....	1,690	1,828	1,939	1,981	1,982	2,029	2,057
PUBLIC HEALTH CARE EXPENDITURE								
TOTAL, MILLIONS OF DOLLARS								
Canadian dollars	16,952	45,517	49,442	51,878	52,452	52,061	.....	.....
U.S. dollar equivalent[1]	.....	35,013	38,327	40,849	41,628	41,649	.....	.....
PER CAPITA, DOLLARS								
Canadian dollars	689	1,638	1,758	1,824	1,824	1,780	.....	.....
U.S. dollar equivalent[1]	.....	1,260	1,363	1,437	1,448	1,424	.....	.....
PRIVATE HEALTH CARE EXPENDITURE								
TOTAL, MILLIONS OF DOLLARS								
Canadian dollars	5,447	15,524	16,848	18,154	19,323	20,401	.....	.....
U.S. dollar equivalent[1]	4,667	11,942	13,061	14,295	15,336	16,321	.....	.....
PER CAPITA, DOLLARS								
Canadian dollars	221	559	599	638	672	698	.....	.....
U.S. dollar equivalent[1]	.....	430	465	503	533	558	.....	.....

e=Estimated.

1. Converted to U.S. dollars using OECD Purchasing Power Parity.

Source: Health Canada, Policy and Consultation Branch, Canada's Health System, May 1997.

MEXICO

The Mexican government is working to improve the health of the Mexican people in ways distinct from those of the United States or Canada. The approach has been to establish government-operated health care institutions serving specific sectors of the population and then expand coverage to include larger numbers of workers and families. The Secretary of Health has recently begun a new program called Health 1995-2000 which, among other things, is intended to decentralize the government health system and to improve the quality of health care in the more remote parts of Mexico. It is recognized that both the quality and the coverage of the indigenous population are deficient, and efforts are being made to bring about improvements. The Mexican government is proud that life expectancy has increased to 72 years and that infant mortality is now the lowest in 25 years.[7]

Table 8 shows the distribution of resources to the eight public sector institutions in 1994 (the latest year for which detailed information is available). As measured by the number of doctors and dentists, the two social security institutions account for about 58 percent of total public sector health care. There were 114,329 physicians and dentists practicing under the public sector system in 1994. Accurate data on the private sector are not available, but figures from the Secretary of Health suggest there were about 58,000 private sector physicians in 1994, many of them specialists.

Table 9 shows the growth in the public sector from 1987 to 1994, with some data for 1995. As measured by the number of practicing physicians, the system grew at a 5.5 percent compound annual rate from 1987 to 1994; as measured by the number of hospital beds, it grew at a 3.3 percent rate over the same period.

TABLE 8

MEXICO: HEALTH CARE, PUBLIC SECTOR DELIVERY SYSTEMS, 1994

	TOTAL	SECRETARY OF HEALTH	SOCIAL SECURITY INSTITUTE (NON-GOVERNMENT)	SOCIAL SECURITY SERVICES INSTITUTE (GOVERNMENT)	PETROLEUM MEXICO	SECRETARY OF DEFENSE	SECRETARY OF MARITIME AFFAIRS	DEPT. OF THE FEDERAL DISTRICT	STATE SERVICES
Units of medical service	14,947	7,508	5,240	1,192	153	277	131	143	303
Hospitals	879	252	324	88	22	30	28	31	104
Hospital beds (eligible for census)	74,891	23,160	30,249	6,465	1,101	3,483	602	2,111	7,720
Outpatient facilities	14,068	7,256	4,916	1,104	131	247	103	112	199
Doctors and dentists	114,329	32,889	51,330	15,311	2,510	1,445	703	2,758	7,383
Percent of total	100	29	45	13	2	1	1	2	6
General practitioners	31,692	8,238	15,409	4,673	997	353	209	617	1,196
Specialists	35,707	8,264	14,055	6,753	1,234	609	285	1,138	3,369
Visiting doctors	14,453	7,675	4,840	958	.....	48	44	221	667
Dentists	5,549	1,995	1,840	790	129	358	59	171	207
Not in contact with patients	17,295	2,853	12,778	731	150	39	42	311	391
Others	9,633	3,864	2,408	1,406	.....	38	64	300	1,553
Rightholders in institutions	47,850	.....	36,554	9,102	696	317	223	.....	959

Note: Detail lines may not add to totals.
Source: Anuario Estadistico, INEGI 1995.

---

[7] Secretary of Health, "El Programa de Reforma del Sector Salud 1995—2000," [I]

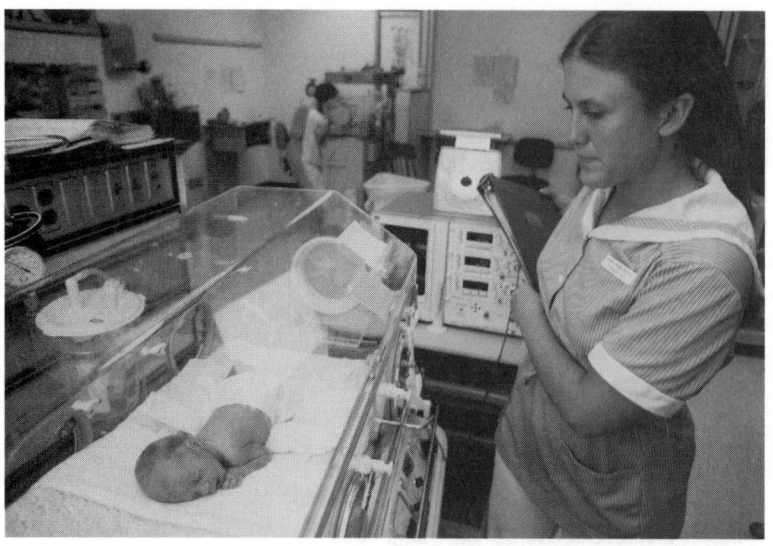

TABLE 9

MEXICO: HEALTH CARE, PUBLIC SECTOR RESOURCES AND OUTPUT, 1987-1995

(Monetary values in 1993 Mexican New Pesos)

	1987	1988	1989	1990	1991	1992	1993	1994	1995
Units of medical service	11,320	11,964	12,702	13,191	13,812	14,172	14,456	14,947	.....
Hospitals	655	665	676	715	772	833	847	879	.....
Hospital beds, eligible for census	59,615	59,552	61,251	63,122	67,703	71,500	72,683	74,891	.....
Outpatient facilities	10,665	11,299	12,026	12,476	13,040	13,339	13,472	14,068	.....
Medical personnel	77,678	89,130	84,568	89,842	97,971	103,356	107,495	114,329	119,434
Total personnel in contact with patients	66,590	70,954	72,049	74,056	82,251	86,487	89,936	97,034	.....
General practitioners	20,568	22,844	24,228	25,440	36,492	39,578	30,102	31,692	31,995
Specialists	23,007	26,401	28,390	29,518	28,220	29,796	41,625	45,089	36,997
Obstetricians	2,911	3,187	3,380	3,603	4,044	4,263	4,770	5,002	.....
Pediatricians	2,990	3,450	3,649	3,731	4,352	4,548	5,092	5,212	.....
Other	17,106	19,764	21,361	22,184	19,824	20,985	31,763	34,875	.....
Visiting doctors	17,379	16,567	14,234	14,765	12,939	12,383	12,039	14,453	.....
Dentists	4,586	5,142	5,197	4,333	4,600	4,730	5,170	5,612	7,517
Not in contact with patients	11,088	18,176	12,519	15,786	15,720	16,869	17,559	17,295	17,759
Paramedical	163,680	172,206	178,279	186,812	193,635	202,114	209,948	223,679	.....
Nurses	118,008	123,919	127,100	130,620	141,404	148,957	154,852	166,644	.....
Other paramedical	45,672	48,287	51,179	56,192	52,231	53,157	55,096	57,035	.....
Hospital patient days (thousands)	13,982	14,157	14,309	15,471	16,000	17,288	17,692	18,549	.....
Immunizations (millions)	58	59	63	81	91	94	90	75	....

Note: Detail lines may not add to totals.

Source: Anuario Estadistico, 1995. Data from 1995 from Secretary of Health Mexico Internet.

TRANSPORTATION, COMMUNICATIONS, AND UTILITIES

THE UNITED STATES

Products and Processes. The transportation, communications, and utilities (electric, gas, and sanitary services) division of the SIC, is a broad classification including firms involved in diverse business areas. All three major components had expanding output in the early nineties in line with developments in the rest of the economy.

Transportation is divided into seven smaller industries: railroad transportation; local and suburban transit and interurban highway passenger transportation; motor freight transportation and warehousing; water transportation; transportation by air; pipelines, except natural gas; and transportation services. In terms of revenue, motor freight transportation and warehousing was the largest industry within transportation in 1992 (the latest year for which economic census data are available), accounting for 43.9 percent of total transportation revenue (Table 1). Transportation by air was next, with 25.2 percent of total revenue.

Communications includes the subindustries of telephone communications; telegraph and other message communications; radio and television broadcasting stations; cable and other pay television services; and communications services. Of these, telephone communications was the largest in 1992 with 74 percent of communications revenues, next was radio and television broadcasting stations (12.2 percent), followed by cable and other pay television services (11.9 percent).

Electric, gas, and sanitary services includes a variety of utilities. Electric services (46.8 percent of revenues), gas production and distribution (24.3 percent), and combination electric and gas utilities (22.7 percent) account for almost all of the industry's revenues. The subindustries of water supply; sanitary services; steam and air conditioning supply; and irrigation systems account for the remainder.

Employment in transportation, communications, and utilities is projected to increase from 5,811,000 in 1993 to 6,431,000 in 2005 (Table 2). Virtually all of the projected growth will come in the transportation industry. Within transportation, employment is expected to increase substantially in trucking and warehousing, transportation services, and local and interurban passenger transportation. Rail and air transportation employment are projected to decline.

TABLE 1

UNITED STATES: COMPONENT INDUSTRIES OF TRANSPORTATION[1], COMMUNICATIONS, AND UTILITIES (SIC 40-42, 44-49), 1992

(Monetary values in millions of U.S. dollars)

INDUSTRY NAME	SIC	ESTABLISH-MENTS	REVENUE Revenue	REVENUE Percent by 4 Largest Companies	EMPLOY-MENT[2]	PAYROLL
TOTAL TRANSPORTATION, COMMUNICATIONS, AND UTILITIES		.....	869,251.4	.....	5,566,120	178,424.5
Total transportation		.....	327,623.0	.....	3,356,872	92,211.4
Railroad transportation	40	.....	28,348.9		197,421	8,752.9
Transit and interurban highway passenger transportation	41	17,805	12,649.3	11.3	354,913	5,191.1
Local and suburban passenger transportation	411	8,275	5,968.0	7.5	153,278	2,623.8
Local and suburban transit	4111	1,135	1,364.0	23.8	37,653	837.7
Local passenger transportation, n.e.c.	4119	7,140	4,604.0	7.0	115,625	1,786.1
Taxicabs	412	3,337	992.4	10.1	26,338	305.9
Intercity and rural bus transportation	413	607	1,092.0	.....	20,404	483.2
Bus charter service	414	1,307	1,269.1	4.7	24,604	393.8
Local bus charter service	4141	429	375.2	11.2	7,699	124.6
Bus charter service, except local	4142	878	893.9	6.7	16,905	269.1
School buses	415	4,260	3,315.3	28.0	130,093	1,380.0
Terminal and service facilities	417	19	12.5	94.6	196	4.5
Motor freight transportation and warehousing	42	110,908	143,794.4	16.4	1,580,095	39,895.7
Trucking and courier services, except air	421	101,169	135,437.0	17.4	1,484,655	37,760.0
Local trucking without storage	4212	49,870	33,554.4	12.1	354,742	8,043.5
Trucking, except local	4213	40,821	78,357.5	10.6	758,435	20,974.5
Local trucking with storage	4214	4,512	4,190.7	8.1	64,417	1,346.0
Courier services except by air	4215	5,966	19,334.3	.....	307,061	7,396.1
Public warehousing and storage	422	9,718	8,329.9	14.1	95,145	2,127.3
Farm product warehousing and storage	4221	584	656.5	20.9	6,497	129.6
Refrigerated warehousing and storage	4222	929	1,744.8	28.3	18,963	463.9
General warehousing and storage	4225	6,753	3,919.2	19.0	49,091	983.1
Special warehousing and storage, n.e.c.	4226	1,452	2,009.5	26.6	20,594	550.6
Trucking terminal facilities.	423	21	27.5	74.8	295	8.4
Water transportation	44	8,147	29,207.2	20.8	171,314	5,170.2
Water transportation of freight	441-4	836	14,704.2	35.5	37,229	1,522.6
Deep sea foreign and domestic freight	441-2	615	11,948.1	40.6	26,798	1,147.9
Deep sea foreign transportation of freight	4412	334	8,490.5	56.4	13,334	629.2
Deep sea domestic transportation of freight	4424	281	3,457.7	40.2	13,464	518.6
Freight transportation on the Great Lakes-St.Lawrence seaway	4432	26	559.2	73.0	1,255	81.3
Water transportation of freight, n.e.c.	4449	195	2,196.9	46.6	9,176	293.4
Water transportations of passengers	448	1,033	4,132.9	53.0	23,308	507.8
Ferries	4482	118	154.7	27.3	1,791	50.8
Deep sea transportation of passengers, except by ferry	4481	72	3,268.5	67.0	12,503	275.1
Water transportation of passengers, n.e.c.	4489	843	709.8	21.8	9,014	181.9
Services incidental to water transportation	449	6,278	10,370.1	15.0	110,777	3,139.8
Marine cargo handling	4491	871	5,066.2	26.7	58,840	1,841.4
Towing and tugboat services	4492	941	2,681.9	30.4	24,639	689.1
Marinas	4493	3,348	1,651.4	3.6	17,913	345.9
Water transportation services, n.e.c.	4499	1,118	970.6	22.2	9,385	263.4
Transportation by air	45	.....	82,670.3	.....	707,148	24,530.2
Transportation by air, except airports and services	451pt.,2	.....	76,502.8	.....	627,195	22,733.8
Air transportation, scheduled	4512	.....	62,057.5	.....	505,029	19,090.5
Air courier services	4513	2,639	11,012.7	86.5	99,021	2,935.3
Air transportation, nonscheduled	452	1,791	3,432.7	23.8	23,145	708.1
Airports, flying fields and airport terminal services	458	3,252	6,167.6	24.8	79,953	1,796.3

TABLE 1 (CONTINUED)

UNITED STATES: COMPONENT INDUSTRIES OF TRANSPORTATION[1], COMMUNICATIONS, AND UTILITIES (SIC 40-42, 44-49), 1992

(Monetary values in millions of U.S. dollars)

INDUSTRY NAME	SIC	ESTABLISH-MENTS	REVENUE	REVENUE PERCENT BY 4 LARGEST COMPANIES	EMPLOY-MENT[2]	PAYROLL
Pipelines, except natural gas	46	844	7,063.0	41.3	16,779	821.1
Refined petroleum pipelines	4613	358	2,010.0	55.2	5,578	251.9
Crude petroleum pipelines	4612	405	4,409.2	60.3	10,355	531.1
Pipelines, n.e.c.	4619	81	643.8	87.7	846	38.0
Transportation services	47	46,593	23,889.9	8.2	329,202	7,850.3
Arrangement of passenger transportation	472	31,793	10,572.8	13.9	192,981	3,921.2
Travel agencies	4724	27,688	6,964.4	12.7	149,140	2,835.5
Tour operators	4725	3,008	1,864.8	12.4	30,519	690.2
Arrangement of passenger transportation, n.e.c.	4729	1,097	1,743.7	71.7	13,322	395.5
Arrangement of transportation of freight and cargo	473	12,553	9,158.6	5.7	106,979	3,232.9
Other transportation services	474,8	2,247	4,158.5	41.0	29,242	696.3
Rental of railroad cars	474	125	1,881.1	78.9	1,926	84.5
Miscellaneous services incidental to transportation	478	2,122	2,277.3	25.8	27,316	611.7
Packing and crating	4783	835	522.5	17.5	8,123	154.5
Fixed facilities inspection and weighing services	4785	263	221.0	63.2	2,810	65.0
Transportation services, n.e.c.	4789	1,024	1,533.8	36.9	16,383	392.2
Communications	48	39,244	230,667.2	34.5	1,294,236	47,057.9
Telephone communications	481	24,730	171,580.1	46.0	928,245	35,900.6
Radiotelephone communications	4812	3,063	12,269.7	41.2	61,077	2,091.4
Telephone communications, except radiotelephone	4813	21,667	159,310.4	47.8	867,168	33,809.2
Telegraph and other message communications	482	489	988.1	66.8	5,536	217.8
Communication services, n.e.c.	489	1,008	2,357.9	61.4	9,737	404.5
Radio and television broadcasting stations	483	8,549	28,228.9	38.3	221,755	6,976.4
Radio broadcasting stations	4832	6,956	6,865.4	12.1	112,385	2,547.7
Television broadcasting stations	4833	1,593	21,363.5	48.3	109,370	4,428.7
Cable and other pay television services	484	4,468	27,512.1	36.6	128,963	3,558.7
Electric, gas, and sanitary services	49	20,049	310,961.2	10.7	915,012	39,155.2
Electric services	491	5,374	145,585.7	19.4	425,285	18,818.3
Gas production and distribution	492	3,968	75,742.3	18.8	147,923	6,172.2
Natural gas transmission	4922	515	8,739.6	66.6	12,928	618.0
Natural gas transmission and distribution	4923	1,648	29,313.7	28.4	69,311	3,000.2
Natural gas distribution	4924	1,734	37,152.4	21.0	65,239	2,536.7
Mixed, manufactured, or liquefied petroleum gas	4925	71	536.7		445	17.2
Combination electric and gas, and other utility services	493	1,814	70,702.9	35.2	222,223	10,597.2
Electric and other services combined	4931	1,589	68,726.0	36.2	216,032	10,369.9
Gas and other services combined	4932	124	1,474.0	85.0	4,459	148.9
Combination utilities, n.e.c.	4939	101	502.9	0.0	1,732	78.5
Water supply	494	3,453	3,188.3	33.8	23,681	620.0
Sanitary services	495	5,064	15,156.0	40.0	92,467	2,839.5
Sewerage systems	4952	470	351.9	30.0	3,470	82.5
Refuse systems.	4953	3,317	14,101.7	42.6	80,917	2,577.9
Sanitary services, n.e.c.	4959	1,277	702.4	30.0	8,080	179.1
Steam and air-conditioning supply	496	69	479.8	59.5	1,647	69.8
Irrigation systems	497	307	106.2	27.1	1,786	38.2

1. Transportation, except for the U.S. Postal Service.

2. Employment numbers from the economic censuses differ in definition and classification from the Bureau of Labor Statistics estimates in Table 2. Year-to-year comparisons between Table 1 and Table 2 are not appropriate.

Source: U.S. Bureau of the Census, 1992 Census of Transportation, Communications, and Utilities.

TABLE 2

U.S. EMPLOYMENT AND EARNINGS: TRANSPORTATION, COMMUNICATIONS, AND UTILITIES

INDUSTRY	SIC	1993			2005
		EMPLOYMENT[1]		AVERAGE HOURLY EARNINGS (U.S. DOLLARS)[2]	PROJECTED EMPLOYMENT[3]
		NUMBER OF PERSONS	PERCENT OF INDUSTRY TOTAL		
ALL TRANSPORTATION, COMMUNICATIONS,UTILITIES	40-42,44-49	5,811,000	100	13.55	6,431,000
All Transportation	40-42,44-47	3,598,000	61.9	.....	4,251,000
Railroad transportation	40	248,300	4.3	.....	185,900
Local and interurban passenger transit	41	379,400	6.5	10.04	490,000
Local and suburban transportation	411	176,100	3.0	10.73	252,600
School buses	415	121,500	2.1	.....	142,000
Trucking and warehousing	42	1,443,600	24.8	12.26	2,000,000
Public warehousing and storage	422	127,800	2.2	10.01	160,000
Water transportation	44	168,200	2.9	.....	165,000
Water transportation services	449	107,600	1.9	17.13	.....
Transportation by air	45	988,200	17	.....	870,000
Airports, flying fields, and services	458	101,700	1.8	.....	130,000
Pipelines, except natural gas	46	18,400	0.3	19.51	14,700
Transportation services	47	351,700	6.1	11.03	525,400
Passenger transportation arrangement	472	187,300	3.2	10.2	255,000
Freight transportation arrangement	473	129,900	2.2	12.31	217,895
Communications	48	1,269,100	21.8	14.91	1,235,000
Telephone communications	481	879,000	15.1	15.62	800,000
Radio and television broadcasting	483	229,500	3.9	14.31	225,000
Cable and other pay television services	484	136,200	2.3	11.43	200,000
Electric, gas, and sanitary services	49	944,400	16.3	16.71	945,000
Electric services	491	428,200	7.4	17.34	400,049
Gas production and distribution	492	161,000	2.8	16.3	145,657
Combination utility services	493	188,900	3.3	19.86	169,294

1. Total payroll employment. Employment data from the economic censuses, as shown in Table 1, differ in definition and classification from the Bureau of Labor Statistics estimates in this table. Year-to-year comparisons between Table 1 and Table 2 are not appropriate.

2.Earnings of nonsupervisory workers, including overtime.

3.Number of persons, moderate projection by the U.S. Bureau of Labor Statistics.

Source: Bureau of Labor Statistics.

FIGURE 1

U.S. EMPLOYMENT IN TRANSPORTATION, COMMUNICATIONS, AND UTILITIES

Percent distribution by region, 1995

Consistent with the distribution of total U.S. employment and population, employment in transportation, communications, and utilities is highest in the Southeast (24.3 percent of the total in 1995). It is lowest in the Rocky Mountain states (3.6 percent).

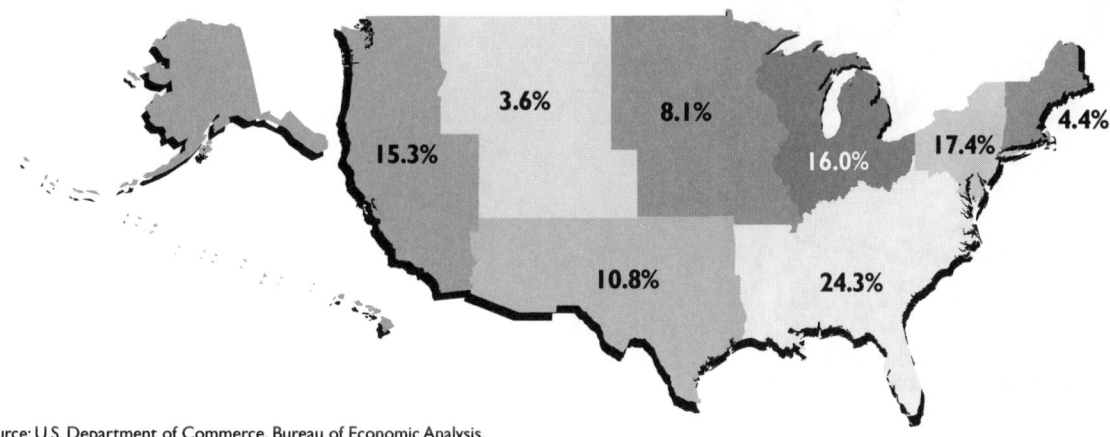

Source: U.S. Department of Commerce, Bureau of Economic Analysis.

What's New. Deregulation is an important issue for transportation, communications, and utilities in the nineties. Recently enacted trade and communications legislation and recent regulatory decisions will force changes in the way these industries conduct business. Some industry segments face markedly increased competition; others face challenges of rapid growth and the need to attract new employees.

Air Transportation. U.S. airlines are expected to achieve record net profits of $4.5 billion for 1997, according to the Air Transport Association. These figures represent a substantial increase over the $2.8 billion of profits in 1996 and the $2.2 billion in 1995. The industry's recent performance is particularly impressive considering that it follows five straight years of losses from 1990 to 1994. Profits are expected in 1998, but at $3.3-$3.5 billion will be below 1997.

Trucking. The trucking industry is struggling to deal with its worst driver shortage in a decade, according to the *Wall Street Journal.* To attract the 400,000 new drivers needed, trucking firms will spend an estimated $750 million on recruiting in 1997, up 20 percent from five years ago. Industry efforts to boost employment are complicated by the industry's high rate of attrition, 50,000 drivers per year, and high mobility within the industry. More than 300,000 drivers are reported to switch jobs each year.

There was friction in 1996 and 1997 between Mexico and the United States over President Clinton's decision on December 18, 1995 to delay the implementation of provisions in NAFTA allowing Mexican trucks to operate in border states and allowing Mexicans to purchase interests in U.S. trucking companies. The reason given for the delay is concern over the safety of Mexican trucks driving in the United States. Critics of the delay include U.S. trucking industry representatives, Mexican officials, and border state governors. The critics argue that the decision was politically motivated as a favor to U.S. labor. According to the U.S. Department of Commerce, 85 percent of U.S. trade with Mexico is transported over land, with a large percentage of that carried by trucks.

Telecommunications. According to a *Wall Street Journal* article, industry sources expect the cellular phone market will grow from 48.9 million users in 1997 to 185.7 million users by the year 2007. The average cost per minute of cellular phone time will decrease from 15 cents per minute in 1997 to 3 cents per minute in 2007. Industry experts predict tough competition in the future among cellular phone providers, as well as competition with traditional wired companies.

In September 1997, the U.S. Congress held hearings on why the Telecommunications Act of 1996 has not led to the increased competition in the telephone business that had been expected. The Telecommunications Act was supposed to open up local phone business to long distance companies and allow local providers to offer long distance service of their own. So far, this has not occurred. Long distance carriers blame the local phone companies for excluding them from their markets; the local companies claim that the long distance companies do not want to enter the local phone business.

Radio Broadcasting. The Telecommunications Act of 1996 has changed the nature of the radio industry. Under the new law, there is no restriction on the number of radio stations any one company can own nationwide. This has led to a number of new acquisitions and mergers. According to press reports, Hicks, Muse, Tate, & Furst Inc., a Dallas-based broadcasting company, has built itself into the biggest radio group in the country through consolidation, including a $2.1 billion deal to take over SFX Broadcasting Inc. of New York.

Utilities. On April 24, 1996, the Federal Energy Regulatory Commission (FERC) issued Order No. 888, requiring electric utilities to open their transmission systems to power generated by other companies. Since this decision by the FERC, competition in the utilities industry has become intense. According to press reports, utility companies are now resorting to telemarketing in attempts to lure new customers away from competitors.

The Energy Information Administration reported in July 1997 that it expected a rise in demand for natural gas in the second half of 1997. U.S. total gas demand is expected to be up 1.2 percent for the year, 3.5 percent in the second half compared to last year's figures. Nuclear power plant outages, higher air conditioning use this summer, a thriving economy, and the gradual decline of hydroelectric output from record highs are all contributing to the increased demand.

FIGURE 2A

U.S. EMPLOYMENT AND GROSS PRODUCT, TRANSPORTATION

Total payroll employment and inflation-adjusted gross product

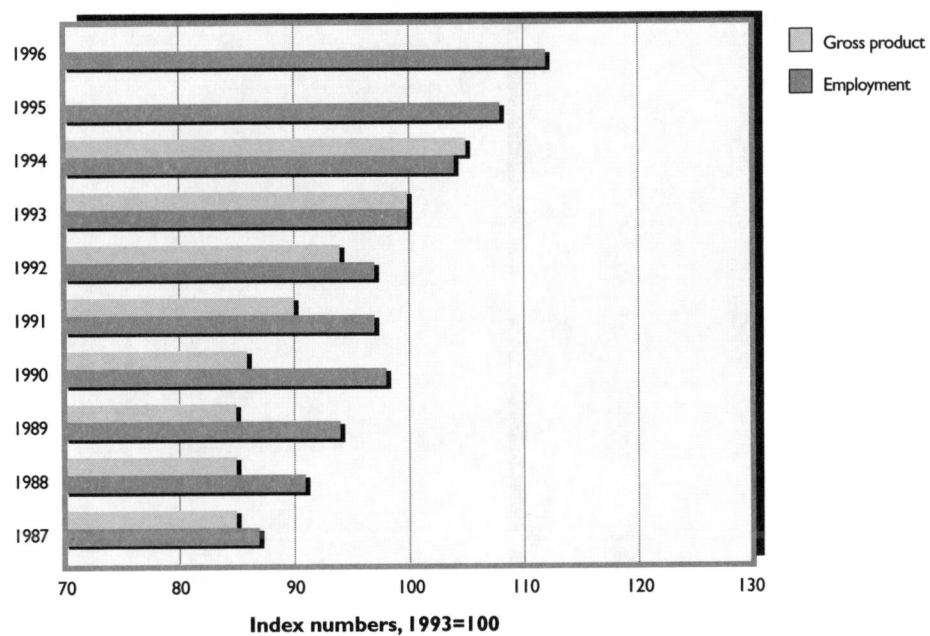

Index numbers, 1993=100

Source: U.S. Bureau of Labor Statistics, U.S. Department of Commerce, and estimates by the editors.

FIGURE 2B

U.S. EMPLOYMENT AND GROSS PRODUCT, COMMUNICATIONS

Total payroll employment and inflation-adjusted gross product

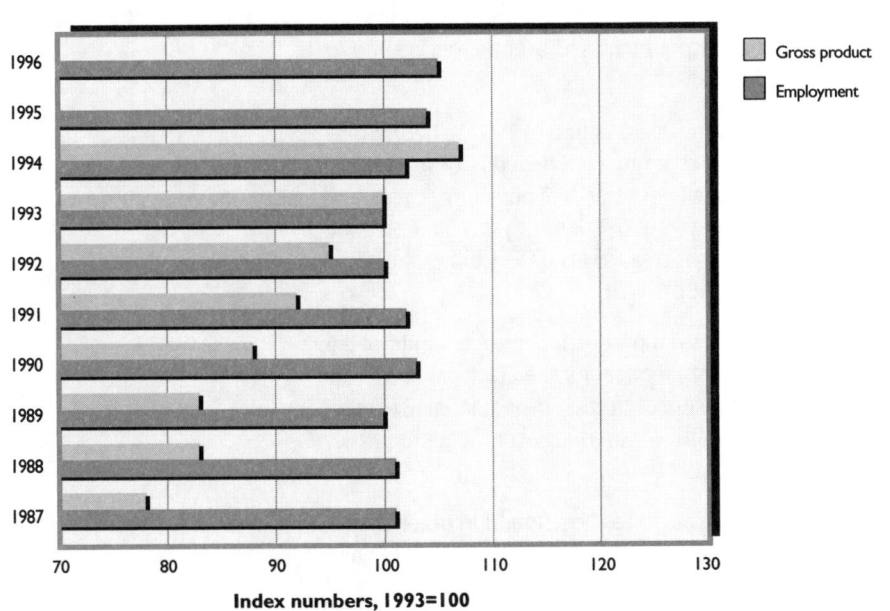

Index numbers, 1993=100

Source: U.S. Bureau of Labor Statistics, U.S. Department of Commerce, and estimates by the editors.

FIGURE 2C

U.S. EMPLOYMENT AND GROSS PRODUCT, UTILITIES

Total payroll employment and inflation-adjusted gross product

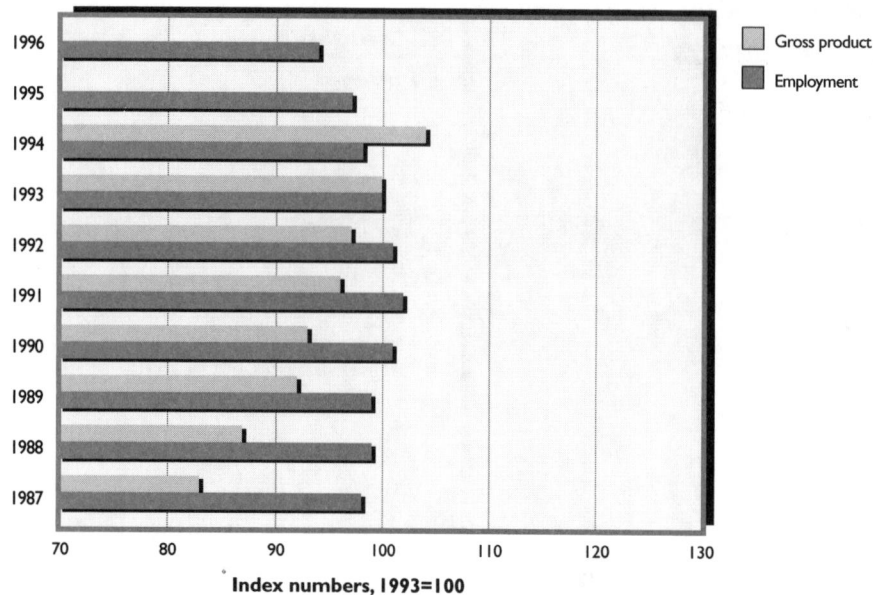

Source: U.S. Bureau of Labor Statistics, U.S. Department of Commerce, and estimates by the editors.

Output. Transportation, communications, and utilities all had increasing GDP from 1987 to 1994 (Figure 2). Changes in employment in the industries were more variable, with increases in transportation and communications and an overall reduction in employment for the utilities during 1987-1996.

Output in the *transportation* industry, as measured by industry gross domestic product (GDP), increased from $157.9 billion in 1987 to $222.8 billion in 1994. This amounted to a growth rate of 5 percent per year. In constant 1992 dollars, output increased over the period at a slightly slower rate of 3 percent per year (Table 3).

Revenues in the *communications* industry expanded from $206.6 billion in 1989 to $287.7 billion in 1995, an annual rate of 5.7 percent. Within the communications industry, revenues of telegraph and other communications services grew the fastest, at 15.7 percent per year, and radio and television broadcasting had the slowest growth, at 3.7 percent per year. Constant dollar gross product originating from communications increased from $133 billion in 1987 to $182 billion in 1994, at an annual rate of 4.6 percent per year.

Real output of *gas and electric utilities*, measured by industrial production, grew at a rate of 2.6 percent per year from 1987 to 1996. Growth was almost identical for the electric services and gas production and distribution subindustries. A measure of output for industrial use, electric power use in mining and manufacturing, grew slightly less rapidly over the period at a rate of 1.9 percent per year.

Investment. Time series data on investment, comparable to those found in other chapters, are not available for transportation, communications, and utilities. However, there are recent data from the U.S. Census Bureau's Annual Capital Expenditures Survey for 1995 for firms with five employees or more. New capital expenditures for the *transportation* industry were $30.4 billion in 1995. Most of this expenditure, $24 billion, went toward new equipment with the remainder, $6.4 billion, going to new structures.

TABLE 3

U.S. OUTPUT, INVESTMENT, AND PRICES: TRANSPORTATION, COMMUNICATIONS, ELECTRIC, GAS AND SANITARY SERVICES

(Millions of U.S. dollars, except as noted)

	1987	1988	1989	1990	1991	1992	1993	1994	1995	1996	GROWTH RATE[1]
TRANSPORTATION											
OUTPUT MEASURES:											
Gross domestic product:											
Current dollars	157,904	168,467	170,800	176,424	185,834	192,800	207,614	222,790	.....	.....	.....
Percent of total GDP	3.4	3.3	3.1	3.1	3.1	3.1	3.2	3.2	.....	.....	.....
Chained (1992) dollars	175,269	173,820	173,781	176,738	185,539	192,800	205,125	215,507	.....	.....	.....
COMMUNICATIONS											
REVENUE (RECEIPTS)											
Current dollars	.....	.....	206,574	216,294	221,466	232,241	246,058	264,714	287,710	.....	5.68
Telephone communications	.....	.....	154,474	160,482	164,738	171,578	181,700	195,333	209,963	.....	5.25
Radio and television broadcasting	.....	.....	29,012	29,707	28,741	29,853	30,383	33,089	36,035	.....	3.68
Cable and other pay television services	.....	.....	.....	23,192	24,954	27,465	30,209	31,535	35,664	.....	9.0
Telegraph and other communications services, n.e.c.	.....	.....	.....	2,913	3,033	3,345	3,766	4,757	6,048	.....	15.7
OUTPUT MEASURES:											
Gross domestic product:											
Current dollars	124,942	132,281	136,272	146,590	154,143	161,001	173,364	188,251	.....	.....	.....
Percent of total GDP	2.7	2.6	2.5	2.6	2.6	2.6	2.6	2.7	.....	.....	.....
Chained (1992) dollars	133,303	140,763	140,421	149,254	156,537	161,001	170,105	182,068	.....	.....	.....
ELECTRIC, GAS, AND SANITARY SERVICES											
OUTPUT MEASURES:											
Industrial production, 1993=100	86	90.4	93.5	94.6	96.6	96.2	100	101.3	105	108.5	2.62
Electric services, utilities	86.1	90.2	93.3	95.6	97.5	96.3	100	101.6	105.5	108.6	2.61
Gas production and distribution	85.3	90.6	94.1	90.5	93.3	95.9	100	100.3	103	108.2	2.68
Electric power use, mining and manufacturing, 1993=100	88.8	92.9	96.1	98.2	97.4	99.6	100	103.7	105.2	105.3	1.91
Gross domestic product:											
Current dollars	137,873	142,844	154,048	159,329	171,822	175,030	185,205	195,313	.....	.....	.....
Percent of total GDP	2.9	2.8	2.8	2.8	2.9	2.8	2.8	2.8	.....	.....	.....
Chained (1992) dollars	149,424	157,792	165,508	168,689	172,603	175,030	180,608	187,990	.....	.....	.....
INVESTMENT-RELATED MEASURES:											
Capacity utilization, percent	82.5	84.9	86.3	85.7	86.3	84.6	87.2	87.3	89.1	90.3	.....
Electric services, percent	86.1	87.8	89.4	89.6	89.1	86.8	88.8	89.2	91.1	91.4	.....
Gas production and distribution, percent	69.9	73.7	75.7	72.9	75.1	77.2	80.4	80.4	82.2	85.9	.....
Consumer prices, piped gas and electricity, 1993=100	87.6	88.3	90.7	92.2	95	96.9	100	100.6	100.6	103	1.82

1. Compound annual growth rate over the years shown.

Sources: GDP: Bureau of Economic Analysis; Communications Revenue: U.S. Census Bureau; Industrial Production, Electric Power Use, and Capacity Utilization: Federal Reserve Board of Governors; Consumer Prices: Bureau of Labor Statistics.

Though the *communications* industry employs fewer people than transportation, its new capital expenditures in 1995 were substantially higher. The industry purchased $45.7 billion of new plant and equipment: $36.3 billion for new equipment, $9.3 billion for new structures. Most of this spending was done by the telecommunications industry, which had $37.4 billion of new capital expenditures for the year.

The *utilities* industry invested $37 billion in new plant and equipment in 1995. This was split more evenly between new equipment and new structures than in the communications or transportation industries; $20.8 billion was spent on new equipment, $16.2 billion on new structures.

Prices. Though price data for the *transportation* industry as a whole are not available, for certain subindustries there are recent data on producer prices. In the motor freight and transportation industry, prices increased at an annual rate of 2.1 percent over the period 1994-1996. Water transportation prices grew at a rate of 1.3 percent from 1993 to 1996; air transportation prices grew at a rate of 4.7 percent per year; and the price index for pipelines grew at a rate of 0.7 percent per year. Consumer prices for piped gas and electricity grew at an annual rate of 1.8 percent from 1987 to 1996 (Table 3).

For communications, industry level data on prices are not available. Producer prices for cable and other pay television services increased at a rate of 3.2 percent per year from 1994 to 1996. Consumer prices for cable television grew almost twice as fast, increasing at a rate of 6.3 percent per year from 1987 to 1996. In radio broadcasting, the price index for commercial airtime grew at 3.1 percent per year from 1989 to 1995. Consumer prices during 1989-1996 increased at a 1.6 percent rate for local telephone charges; 0.4 percent for interstate long-distance telephone tolls, and 0.9 percent for telephone services. Prices for intrastate long-distance telephone tolls fell from 1987 to 1996, at a rate of 1.7 percent per year.

Workforce and Employment. Employment in the transportation industry increased from 3,156,000 in 1987 to 4,038,000 in 1996, at a rate of 2.78 percent per year (Table 4). The growth in employment was fairly consistent throughout the period except for 1990-1992, when employment hit a temporary plateau. The percent of women employed in the industry rose from 23.7 percent in 1987 to 26.6 percent in 1996. Data on hours and earnings of nonsupervisory workers are not available for the transportation industry.

Communications industry employment grew moderately from 1,282,000 in 1987 to 1,338,000 in 1996, at an annual rate of 0.48 percent. The share of nonsupervisory workers in the industry rose from 75.8 percent in 1987 to 78.4 percent in 1996. Though the number of women employed in the industry increased from 585,000 in 1987 to 608,000 in 1996, their share of industry employment was virtually unchanged at 45.4 percent.

Average hourly earnings for nonsupervisory workers in communications increased from $12.45 an hour in 1987 to $16.02 in 1996, at a rate of 2.84 percent per year. Wage growth did not keep pace with inflation over the period, however, as real wages (in 1992 dollars) fell from $15.29 an hour in 1987 to $14.37 in 1996. Average weekly hours worked in the industry fell slightly from 40 hours in 1987 to 39.2 hours in the recession year of 1991 before increasing to 40.4 hours per week in 1996.

Electric, gas, and sanitary services employment followed a countercyclical course from 1987 through 1996. Employment grew from 925,000 in 1987 to a peak of 961,000 in 1991, a recession year, before falling for the next five years (years of overall economic growth) to the lowest level of employment for the decade in 1996 at 885,000. The percent of nonsupervisory workers in the industry stayed roughly constant over the period at around 79 percent. The number of women working in the industry decreased slightly, but increased as a percent of total industry employment from 21.5 percent to 22.4 percent.

Average hourly earnings in the industry increased from $13.79 per hour in 1987 to $18.28 per hour in 1996. Constant dollar wages (1992 dollars) edged downward over the period, falling from $16.94 per hour in 1987 to $16.39 in 1996. Average weekly hours increased a little, from 41.5 hours per week in 1987 to 42.2 in 1996.

TABLE 4

U.S. Employment, Hours, and Earnings: Transportation; Communications; and Electric, Gas, and Sanitary Services

(Monetary values in U.S. dollars)

	1987	1988	1989	1990	1991	1992	1993	1994	1995	1996	Change[1]
TRANSPORTATION											
Number of employees, in thousands:											
Total	3,156	3,303	3,415	3,527	3,501	3,498	3,615	3,769	3,904	4,038	2.78
Nonsupervisory workers	2,741	2,875	2,979	3,071	3,043	3,047	3,149	3,288	3,413	3,514	2.80
Percent of total	86.9	87.0	87.2	87.1	86.9	87.1	87.1	87.2	87.4	87.0	.....
Women	747	807	838	880	882	890	932	975	1,024	1,073	4.10
Percent of total	23.7	24.4	24.5	24.9	25.2	25.4	25.8	25.9	26.2	26.6	.....
COMMUNICATIONS											
Number of employees, in thousands:											
Total	1,282	1,280	1,272	1,309	1,299	1,269	1,269	1,295	1,318	1,338	0.48
Nonsupervisory workers	972	951	950	978	986	981	985	993	1,017	1,049	0.86
Percent of total	75.8	74.3	74.7	74.7	75.9	77.3	77.6	76.7	77.2	78.4	.....
Women	585	583	583	608	599	575	569	580	591	608	0.42
Percent of total	45.7	45.6	45.8	46.5	46.1	45.3	44.8	44.8	44.8	45.4	.....
Hours and earnings of nonsupervisory workers:											
Average hourly earnings, U.S. dollars[2]											
Current dollars	12.45	12.85	13.18	13.51	13.96	14.42	14.91	15.24	15.56	16.02	2.84
1992 dollars[3]	15.29	15.17	14.86	14.48	14.36	14.42	14.5	14.46	14.35	14.37	-0.69
Average weekly hours	40	39.8	39.4	39.4	39.2	39.4	39.6	39.6	39.8	40.4	0.11
Average weekly earnings, current U.S. dollars	498.00	511.43	519.29	532.29	547.23	568.15	590.44	603.50	619.29	647.21	2.95
ELECTRIC, GAS, AND SANITARY SERVICES											
Number of employees, in thousands:											
Total	925	931	938	957	961	954	944	928	911	885	-0.49
Nonsupervisory workers	733	736	742	759	762	753	744	734	719	700	-0.51
Percent of total	79.3	79.1	79.1	79.3	79.3	78.9	78.8	79.0	79.0	79.1	.....
Women	199	202	204	210	211	211	210	206	203	198	-0.07
Percent of total	21.5	21.7	21.8	22.0	21.9	22.1	22.2	22.2	22.3	22.4	.....
Hours and earnings of nonsupervisory workers:											
Average hourly earnings, U.S. dollars											
Current dollars	13.79	14.27	14.72	15.23	15.69	16.08	16.71	17.24	17.68	18.28	3.18
1992 dollars	16.94	16.85	16.60	16.32	16.14	16.08	16.25	16.36	16.31	16.39	-0.36
Average weekly hours	41.5	41.5	41.9	41.6	41.6	41.9	42.3	42.4	42.4	42.2	0.19
Average weekly earnings, current U.S. dollars	572.29	592.21	616.77	633.57	652.70	673.75	706.83	730.98	749.63	771.42	3.37

1. Compound annual growth rate for years shown.

2. Including overtime.

3. Converted to 1992 dollars using Consumer Price Index for Urban Wage Earners and Clerical Workers.

Source: Bureau of Labor Statistics. Data on hours and earnings of nonsupervisory transportation workers not available.

FIGURE 3A

U.S. OCCUPATIONAL INJURY AND ILLNESS RATES:
TRANSPORTATION, 1995

The highest rate of incidence of illnesses and injuries in the transportation industry was 13.8 cases per 100 workers for trucking and warehousing, compared to the 8.1 cases per 100 workers for all private industry. Incidence rates were also above average for air transportation (13.7 cases per 100 workers), passenger transit (10.3 cases per 100 workers), and water transportation (9.0 cases per 100 workers).

Incidence of nonfatal injuries and illnesses per 100 full-time workers

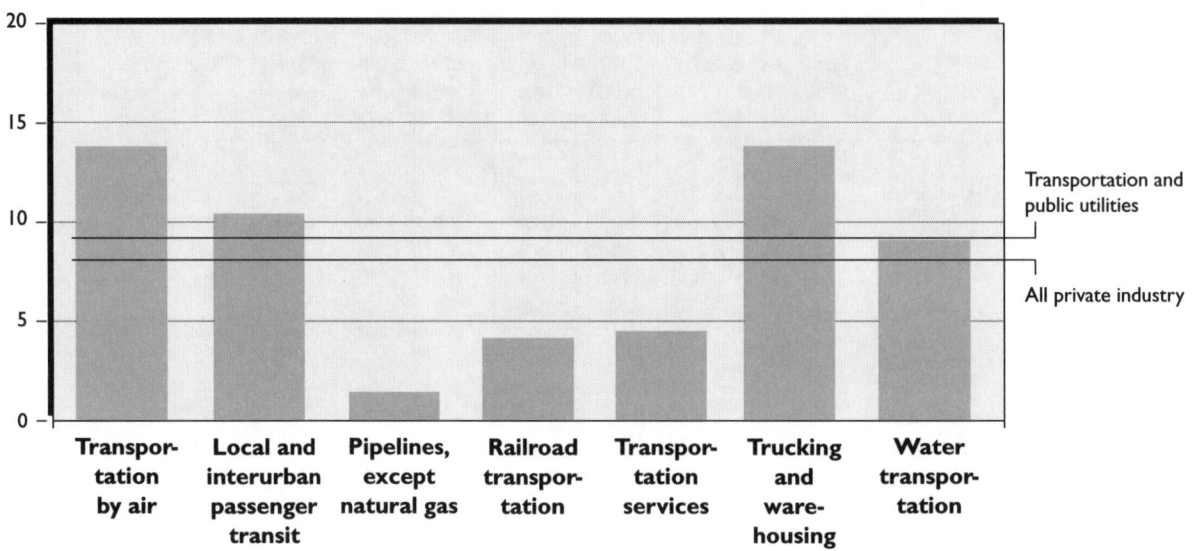

Source: U.S. Bureau of Labor Statistics.

FIGURE 3B

U.S. OCCUPATIONAL INJURY AND ILLNESS RATES: COMMUNICATIONS, 1995

Incidence of nonfatal injuries and illnesses per 100 full-time workers

The incidence rate of illnesses and injuries in the communications industry, at 3.3 cases per 100 workers, was well below the average of 8.1 cases per 100 workers for all private industry.

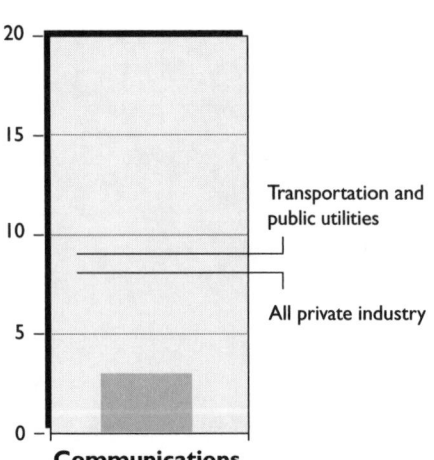

Source: U.S. Bureau of Labor Statistics.

FIGURE 3C

U.S. OCCUPATIONAL INJURY AND ILLNESS RATES: ELECTRIC, GAS, AND SANITARY SERVICES 1995

Incidence of nonfatal injuries and illnesses per 100 full-time workers

The incidence rate of illnesses and injuries in the utilities industry, at 7.5 cases per 100 workers, was just below the average of 8.1 cases per 100 workers for all private industry.

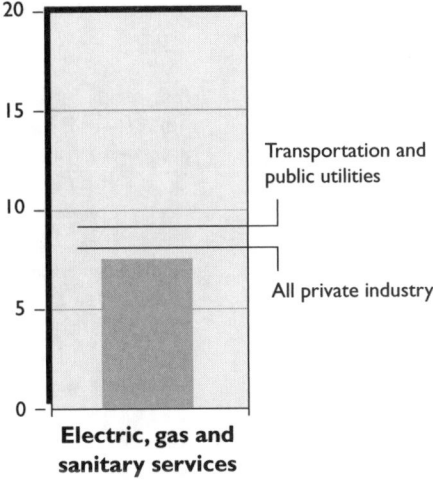

Transportation and public utilities

All private industry

Electric, gas and sanitary services

Source: U.S. Bureau of Labor Statistics.

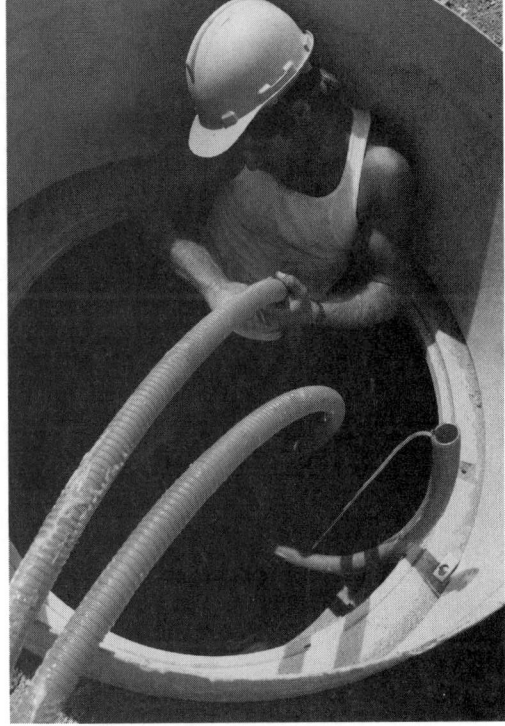

TABLE 5

U.S. EMPLOYMENT PROJECTIONS BY MAJOR OCCUPATIONAL GROUP: TRANSPORTATION; COMMUNICATIONS; AND ELECTRIC, GAS, AND SANITARY SERVICES

| OCCUPATION | 1994 | | PROJECTIONS, 2005 | | | |
| | NUMBER OF EMPLOYEES | PERCENT OF INDUSTRY TOTAL | NUMBER OF EMPLOYEES | | | PERCENT OF INDUSTRY TOTAL, MODERATE PROJECTIONS |
			LOW	MODERATE	HIGH	
TRANSPORTATION						
Total, all occupations	3,774,900	100.0	4,060,300	4,251,000	4,437,900	100.0
Executive, administrative, and managerial	265,502	7.0	272,518	284,471	296,247	6.7
Professional specialties	42,174	1.1	58,925	61,660	64,406	1.5
Technicians and related support	158,712	4.2	180,361	187,867	194,184	4.4
Marketing and sales	193,766	5.1	225,233	238,371	251,072	5.6
Administrative support including clerical	745,060	19.7	738,839	770,727	802,217	18.1
Service	185,614	4.9	215,056	225,210	235,035	5.3
Agriculture, forestry, and fisheries occupations	3,660	0.1	4,035	4,228	4,424	0.1
Precision production, craft, and repair	415,743	11.0	421,207	442,302	463,253	10.4
Operators, fabricators, assemblers	1,764,671	46.8	1,944,128	2,036,165	2,127,062	47.9
COMMUNICATIONS						
Total, all occupations	1,304,500	100.0	1,189,899	1,235,000	1,278,500	100.0
Executive, administrative, and managerial	149,709	11.5	159,804	165,861	171,703	13.4
Professional specialties	165,860	12.7	182,427	189,342	196,011	15.3
Technicians and related support	67,415	5.2	62,386	64,751	67,031	5.2
Marketing and sales	103,430	7.9	114,849	119,203	123,401	9.7
Administrative support including clerical	434,738	33.3	386,581	401,233	415,366	32.5
Service	7,416	0.6	7,452	7,735	8,007	0.6
Agriculture, forestry, and fisheries occupations	70	0.0	68	71	73	0.0
Precision production, craft, and repair	368,637	28.3	268,842	279,032	288,861	22.6
Operators, fabricators, assemblers	7,225	0.6	7,489	7,773	8,047	0.6
ELECTRIC, GAS, AND SANITARY SERVICES						
Total, all occupations	926,500	100.0	895,099	945,000	1,006,800	100.0
Executive, administrative, and managerial	113,441	12.2	112,794	119,081	126,869	12.6
Professional specialties	76,015	8.2	84,676	89,399	95,243	9.5
Technicians and related support	42,868	4.6	38,614	40,768	43,433	4.3
Marketing and sales	18,747	2.0	19,281	20,355	21,687	2.2
Administrative support including clerical	212,608	23.0	181,169	191,267	203,777	20.2
Service	16,235	1.8	15,701	16,577	17,661	1.8
Agriculture, forestry, and fisheries occupations	1,780	0.2	1,782	1,881	2,004	0.2
Precision production, craft, and repair	327,678	35.4	314,291	331,812	353,512	35.1
Operators, fabricators, assemblers	117,126	12.6	126,791	133,859	142,614	14.2

Source: Bureau of Labor Statistics, November 1995.

The transportation industry is projected to employ 476,100 more people by the year 2005 (moderate assumptions). The occupation of operators, fabricators, and assemblers will account for most of the employment growth, with over 271,000 new workers by the year 2005. Employment in the communications industry is projected to decrease by 69,500 employees by the year 2005. The occupations of "Precision, production, craft, and repair" and "Administrative support and clerical" will see the sharpest declines in employment, while professional specialties and executive occupations will have growing employment. The utilities industry is projected to employ an additional 18,500 people by the year 2005. Despite the growth in employment for the industry as a whole, the occupation of administrative support is expected to lose more than 30,000 employees by 2005.

CANADA

Canada's transportation industry had 440,353 employees in 1993 (Table 7). Truck transport was the largest employer among transportation subindustries, with 127,724 employees. The communications industry in Canada had a workforce of 252,154 people in 1993. Canadian postal and courier service accounted for 102,874 of these employees. In the U.S. classification system, courier service is considered a part of transportation, not communications, and the U.S. Postal Service is not included in employment and output for the industry. Of the remaining 149,280 employees outside of postal and courier services, more than two-thirds are in the telecommunication carriers industry. Canada's utilities employed 134,147 people in 1993. Electric power systems made up the bulk of the industry workforce with 95,040 employees.

Transportation industry revenues fell from Can$19.3 billion in 1988 to Can$17.3 billion in 1991, then increased over the next five years to a decade-long high of Can$19.4 billion in 1996 (Table 8). Employment in the industry rose to a peak of 490,936 in 1990, but dropped in 1991 to 451,137. At the end of the period, industry employment stood at 434,923, falling over the decade at a rate of 0.5 percent per year. Earnings in the industry went from Can$541.79 per week in 1987 to Can$695.05 per week in 1996, increasing at a rate of 2.8 percent per year.

From 1987 to 1996, communications industry revenues increased every year, rising from Can$14.1 billion in 1987 to Can$24.4 billion in 1996 (Table 8). This amounted to a growth rate of 6.24 percent per year for revenues. Employment in communications rose at the beginning of the period from 251,666 in 1987 to 267,475 in 1990, but fell each of the next three years and since has fluctuated. In 1996, industry employment was at 255,651. Average weekly earnings in the industry grew at a rate of 2.4 percent per year from Can$562.47 in 1987 to Can$696.10 in 1996. Inflation-adjusted earnings fell by 0.5 percent per year during the period.

Canadian utilities revenues increased from Can$15.8 billion in 1987 to Can$17.2 billion in 1996, at an annual rate of one percent. Following a path similar to the U.S. utilities industry, Canadian utilities employment rose from 116,287 in 1987 to 135,466 in 1992 before falling to 124,427 employees in 1996. Average weekly earnings in the industry increased from Can$715.44 in 1987 to Can$941.96 in 1996, increasing at a rate of 3.1 percent per year. Inflation-adjusted earnings actually fell slightly over the period at a rate of 0.1 percent per year.

TABLE 7

CANADA: COMPONENT INDUSTRIES OF TRANSPORTATION, COMMUNICATIONS, AND UTILITIES (CSIC 4500-4900), 1993

INDUSTRY NAME	CSIC	EMPLOYMENT	
		NUMBER	PERCENT OF INDUSTRY TOTAL
TRANSPORTATION, COMMUNICATIONS, AND UTILITIES	4500-4900	850,514	100.0
Transportation	4500	440,353	51.8
Air transport	4510	50,477	5.9
Services incidental to air transport	4520	5,838	0.7
Railway transportation and related services	4530	59,638	7.0
Water transport	4540	14,281	1.7
Services incidental to water transport	4550	12,391	1.5
Truck transport	4560	127,724	15.0
Public passenger transit systems	4570	90,301	10.6
Transportation, n.e.c.	4580	79,702	9.4
Pipeline transport	4600	8,347	1.0
Storage and warehousing	4700	15,513	1.8
Grain elevators	4710	5,941	0.7
Other storage and warehousing	4790	9,572	1.1
Communication	4800	252,154	29.6
Telecommunication broadcasting	4810	41,806	4.9
Telecommunication carriers	4820	105,577	12.4
Other telecommunications	4830	1,898	0.2
Postal and courier services	4840	102,874	12.1
Utilities (electric, gas, and water)	4900	134,147	15.8
Electric power systems	4910	95,040	11.2
Gas distribution systems	4920	15,908	1.9
Water systems	4930	8,672	1.0
Other utilities n.e.c.	4990	14,527	1.7

Source: Statistics Canada: CANSIM.

TABLE 8

CANADIAN EMPLOYMENT AND REVENUES: TRANSPORTATION, COMMUNICATIONS, AND OTHER UTILITIES (CSIC 4500, 4800, 4900), 1987-1996

(Monetary values in Canadian dollars)

	1987	1988	1989	1990	1991	1992	1993	1994	1995	1996	CHANGE[1]
TRANSPORTATION											
All employees	455,544	462,103	480,786	490,936	451,137	441,908	440,353	443,089	439,200	434,923	-0.51
Nonsupervisory workers:											
Average weekly earnings	541.79	572.49	591.06	601.86	634.56	646.19	658.46	669.92	684.44	695.05	2.81
Revenues (millions)	18,539	19,297	18,955	18,417	17,267	17,407	17,664	18,721	19,236	19,449	0.53
COMMUNICATIONS											
All employees	251,666	254,877	265,243	267,475	262,777	259,686	252,154	258,375	264,904	255,651	0.17
Nonsupervisory workers:											
Average weekly earnings	562.47	566.31	603.01	621.85	654.20	679.58	678.53	683.46	697.41	696.10	2.40
Revenues (millions)	14,140	15,223	16,836	18,044	18,725	19,282	19,835	21,284	22,833	24,389	6.24
ELECTRIC, GAS AND SANITARY SERVICES											
All employees	116,287	120,862	125,268	131,780	134,783	135,466	134,147	133,006	128,646	124,427	0.75
Nonsupervisory workers:											
Average weekly earnings	715.44	745.65	769.93	816.19	873.52	905.68	921.24	923.65	938.04	941.96	3.10
Revenues (millions)	15,756	16,004	15,736	14,948	15,774	15,607	16,033	16,780	16,819	17,216	0.99

1. Compound annual growth rate.

Source: Statistics Canada: CANSIM.

MEXICO

Combined constant dollar gross product originating for Mexico's communications and transportation industries, as measured by gross domestic product (1993 monetary units), for the two industries increased from 87.5 billion new pesos ($28 billion) in 1988 to 116.8 billion new pesos ($37.4 billion) in 1994 before falling to 111.1 billion new pesos ($35.6 billion) in 1995 (Table 10). Despite the fall off in 1995, over the nine year period output grew at an annual rate of 3.47 percent.

Employment data are available separately for transportation and communications. Employment grew faster in the transportation industry, at a rate of 2.76 percent per year from 1988 to 1995, than the annual rate of 1.17 percent for the communications industry.

Output and employment in Mexico's utilities industry both increased from 1988 to 1995. Growth in output, at 2.85 percent per year over the period, outpaced growth in employment, which grew at a rate of 1.68 percent per year. In contrast to other industries in Mexico, there was no decline in output or employment from 1994 to 1995, despite the peso crisis and associated economic downturn.

TABLE 10

MEXICAN GROSS DOMESTIC PRODUCT AND EMPLOYMENT: TRANSPORTATION AND COMMUNICATIONS; ELECTRICITY, GAS, AND WATER, 1988-1995

	1988	1989	1990	1991	1992	1993	1994	1995	CHANGE[1]
TRANSPORTATION AND COMMUNICATIONS									
GROSS DOMESTIC PRODUCT:									
Millions of constant 1993 new pesos	87,505.3	91,602.7	94,872.6	98,124.8	103,317.1	107,480.1	116,842.2	111,081.2	3.47
Millions of constant 1993 U.S. dollars[2]	28,013.3	29,325.1	30,371.9	31,413.0	33,075.2	34,407.9	37,405.0	35,560.8	3.47
TOTAL EMPLOYMENT:									
Transportation and communications	1,267,531	1,337,521	1,438,371	1,485,112	1,488,660	1,498,679	1,579,353	1,520,974	2.64
Transportation	1,162,487	1,233,564	1,332,189	1,378,164	1,380,868	1,388,282	1,467,964	1,407,024	2.76
Communications	105,044	103,957	106,182	106,948	107,792	110,397	111,389	113,950	1.17
ELECTRICITY, GAS, AND WATER									
GROSS DOMESTIC PRODUCT:									
Millions of constant 1993 new pesos	16,114	16,835	17,270	17,337	17,869	18,327	19,201	19,614	2.85
Millions of constant 1993 U.S. dollars[2]	5,159	5,389	5,529	5,550	5,720	5,867	6,147	6,279	2.85
TOTAL EMPLOYMENT:									
Electricity, gas, and water	132,962	136,330	142,252	145,523	146,901	148,030	146,558	149,406	1.68

1. Compound annual growth rate.
2. Converted at 3.1237 new pesos to the U.S. dollar.

Source: Sistema de Cuentas Nacionales de Mexico, INEGI.

INTERNATIONAL TRADE

United States. In Table 11, data are presented on U.S. global trade in travel, passenger fares, other transportation, and telecommunications. Travel, as measured here, is the purchase of services and goods by U.S. travelers abroad and by foreign visitors to the United States. Passenger fares are fares paid by residents of one country to residents in other countries. Other transportation is the charges for transportation of goods by ocean, air, waterway, pipeline, and rail carriers to and from the United States.

Trade in all these areas increased over the time period for which data were available. Exports in travel and passenger fares almost doubled from 1989 to 1996, while other transportation and telecommunications experienced more moderate export growth. Imports were growing, as well, over these eight years, more slowly than exports in travel and passenger fares and more rapidly than exports in other transportation and telecommunications.

Consequently, the United States had increasingly strong positive trade balances in travel, which rose from $2.8 billion in 1989 to $21.2 billion in 1996, and in passenger fares, from $2.4 billion in 1989 to $4.8 billion in 1996. The trade balance in other transportation was negative and did not change substantially from 1989 to 1996. The negative trade balance in telecommunications grew from $2.7 billion in 1987 to almost $5 billion in 1996.

Canada. Canada's trade balance with the United States was positive from 1992 to 1996 for other transportation, while it was consistently negative for travel and passenger fares from 1989 to 1996. The deficit in travel was least stable, expanding from –$2.0 billion in 1989 to –$4.8 billion in 1991, then declining gradually to –$1.9 billion in 1995. In 1996, the trade balance in travel was –$2.2 billion. Fluctuations in Canadian imports, rather than changes in Canada's exports, caused the variation in the trade balance.

Mexico. Mexico's trade balance with the United States in travel went from a deficit of $229 million in 1990 to $2.97 billion surplus in 1996. Over this period, spending by citizens of the

United States in Mexico was increasing steadily, while spending by Mexicans in the United States fell substantially from $5.7 billion in 1992 to $3.0 billion in 1996. Mexico had trade surpluses in passenger fares from 1990 to 1992, and 1995; and trade deficits in 1993, 1994, and 1996. For other transportation, Mexico had trade deficits from 1992 to 1996, except for 1995.

NAFTA. The United States had a favorable balance of trade in travel with its NAFTA partners until 1995. In 1995 and 1996, there were trade deficits in travel, largely due to changes in U.S. exports to Mexico. The trade balance in passenger fares was positive throughout the entire period and increased slightly from $623 million in 1990 to $969 million in 1996. There was a trade deficit for other transportation throughout the period.

TABLE 11

INTERNATIONAL TRADE, TRANSPORTATION AND TELECOMMUNICATIONS

(Millions of U.S. dollars)

	1989	1990	1991	1992	1993	1994	1995	1996
GLOBAL TRADE, U.S.								
IMPORTS								
Travel[1]	33,416	37,349	35,322	38,552	40,713	43,782	46,053	48,739
Passenger fares	8,249	10,531	10,012	10,556	11,313	12,885	14,433	15,776
Other transportation	22,260	25,168	25,204	25,459	26,558	27,255	28,249	28,453
Telecommunications	5,172	5,583	6,608	6,052	6,193	6,928	7,773	8,385
EXPORTS								
Travel[1]	36,205	43,007	48,385	54,742	57,875	58,417	63,395	69,908
Passenger fares	10,657	15,298	15,854	16,618	16,611	17,083	19,125	20,557
Other transportation	21,106	22,745	23,331	23,691	23,983	24,941	27,412	27,216
Telecommunications	2,519	2,735	3,291	2,885	2,784	2,865	3,183	3,405
TRADE BALANCE[2]								
Travel[1]	2,789	5,658	13,063	16,190	17,162	14,635	17,342	21,169
Passenger fares	2,408	4,767	5,842	6,062	5,298	4,198	4,692	4,781
Other transportation	(1,154)	(2,423)	(1,873)	(1,768)	(2,575)	(2,314)	(837)	(1,237)
Telecommunications	(2,653)	(2,848)	(3,317)	(3,167)	(3,409)	(4,063)	(4,590)	(4,980)
BILATERAL TRADE: NAFTA								
U.S. exports to Canada (Travel)[1]	5,385	7,093	8,500	8,182	7,458	6,251	6,207	6,763
U.S. exports to Canada (Passenger fares)	811	979	1,040	1,099	1,191	1,133	1,284	1,331
U.S. exports to Canada (Other transportation)	.....	.....	.....	2,210	2,159	2,293	2,688	2,889
Canadian exports to U.S. (Travel)[1]	3,396	3,541	3,705	3,554	3,692	3,914	4,319	4,606
Canadian exports to U.S. (Passenger fares)	224	255	249	227	260	302	306	391
Canadian exports to U.S. (Other transportation)	.....	.....	.....	2,792	2,911	3,200	3,357	3,607
U.S. exports to Mexico (Travel)[1]	.....	5,108	5,367	5,696	5,119	4,866	2,857	3,001
U.S. exports to Mexico (Passenger fares)	.....	464	514	527	554	733	515	647
U.S. exports to Mexico (Other transportation)	.....	.....	.....	466	509	589	473	603
Mexican exports to U.S. (Travel)[1]	.....	4,879	5,111	5,160	5,162	5,334	5,316	5,971
Mexican exports to U.S. (Passenger fares)	.....	565	531	635	541	601	569	618
Mexican exports to U.S. (Other transportation)	.....	.....	.....	358	356	476	481	525
U.S TRADE BALANCE WITH NAFTA[2]								
Travel[1]	.....	3,781	5,051	5,164	3,723	1,869	(571)	(813)
Passenger fares	.....	623	774	764	944	963	924	969
Other transportation	.....	.....	.....	(474)	(599)	(794)	(677)	(640)

1. Travel expenses in the U.S. international trade accounts cover purchases of goods and services by persons traveling abroad for business or personal reasons for less than one year, including lodging, food, entertainment, local transportation, and gifts, but not passenger fares which are tabulated separately.

2. Parentheses indicate an excess of imports over exports.

Source: U.S. Department of Commerce, Bureau of Economic Analysis.

Wholesale and Retail Trade

The United States

Products and Processes. The wholesale and retail trade industries are essential to the distribution of goods in our economy. Wholesalers take the products of manufacturers and distribute them to retailers, other wholesalers, contractors, or other business users. Retailers sell goods and provide services incidental to the sale of goods. They are the final step in the distribution process, selling directly to individuals for personal or household consumption.

Wholesale trade is divided into two parts: durable and nondurable goods. Industry sales in 1992 were almost equally divided between durable goods, with $1.59 trillion, and nondurable goods, with $1.64 trillion (Table 1). Despite the similarity in sales figures, durable goods employment (3,349,064) was substantially larger than nondurable goods employment (2,442,200). Of the nine durable goods subindustries, motor vehicles had the highest sales, with $394 billion. The biggest employers in durable goods were professional and commercial equipment and supplies (685,092); machinery, equipment, and supplies (689,680), and motor vehicles (488,602). Within wholesale trade of nondurable goods, trade in groceries and related products had the highest sales ($504.6 billion) and employment (811,902). Merchant wholesalers, wholesalers who take title to the goods they sell, account for 79 percent of industry employment and 84 percent of industry establishments, but only 57 percent of industry sales.

In 1992, *retail trade* had sales of $1.95 trillion and employed 18,407,453 people, nearly one fifth of the total U.S. labor force. The industry is divided into eight subindustries: building materials, hardware, garden supply, and mobile home dealers; general merchandise stores; food stores; automotive dealers and gasoline service stations; apparel and accessory stores; home furniture, furnishings, and equipment stores; eating and drinking places; and miscellaneous retail. Automotive dealers and gasoline service stations ranked first in terms of sales, with $543.9 billion. Eating and drinking places led in employment with 6,547,908 employees, more than twice the level of the next largest subindustry, food stores (2,969,317).

Employment in wholesale trade has been projected to increase from 5,981,000 employees in 1993 to 6,558,500 employees by the year 2005 (Table 2). Retail trade is projected to grow by more than 3.3 million employees by the year 2005; more than 1.2 million of the new employees will be in "eating and drinking places."

TABLE 1

UNITED STATES: COMPONENT INDUSTRIES OF WHOLESALE AND RETAIL TRADE (SIC 50-59), 1992

(Monetary values in millions of U.S. dollars)

INDUSTRY NAME	SIC	ESTABLISH-MENTS	SALES		EMPLOY-MENT[1]	PAYROLL
			VALUE	PERCENT BY 4 LARGEST COMPANIES		
WHOLESALE TRADE	50, 51	495,457	$3,238,520.4	5.5	5,791,264	$173,272.1
Merchant wholesalers[2]	50, 51	414,836	1,847,273.6	3.6	4,587,877	127,986.8
Durable goods	50	313,464	1,593,873.9	11.2	3,349,064	105,155.0
Motor vehicles	501	47,274	394,104.4	43.9	488,602	12,064.8
Furniture and home furnishings	502	16,457	58,926.6	9.4	161,460	4,612.3
Lumber and other construction materials	503	19,546	89,764.1	10.9	210,726	6,059.9
Professional and commercial equipment and supplies	504	46,792	262,974.5	19.0	685,092	26,380.1
Metals and minerals, except petroleum	505	11,248	118,321.9	13.6	138,042	4,683.7
Electrical goods	506	39,303	227,784.5	11.4	435,700	15,069.9
Hardware, and plumbing and heating equipment and supplies	507	24,674	76,088.1	7.1	241,043	7,105.8
Machinery, equipment, and supplies	508	73,865	230,004.0	7.6	689,680	21,266.7
Miscellaneous durable goods	509	34,305	135,906.0	13.6	298,719	7,911.7
Nondurable goods	51	181,993	1,644,646.6	3.9	2,442,200	68,117.1
Paper and paper products	511	19,661	106,580.4	13.6	269,038	6,938.6
Drugs, drug proprietaries, and druggists' sundries	512	6,069	129,306.3	21.8	157,855	5,368.0
Apparel, piece goods, and notions	513	19,553	109,202.9	8.2	196,149	6,521.7
Groceries and related products	514	42,874	504,566.8	11.2	811,902	21,722.8
Farm-product raw materials	515	11,551	136,869.4	16.5	108,710	2,100.4
Chemicals and allied products	516	14,193	132,471.2	24.5	147,010	5,595.7
Petroleum and petroleum products	517	16,061	281,585.1	15.2	168,519	4,446.7
Beer, wine, and distilled alcoholic beverages	518	5,259	59,487.3	9.2	141,821	4,669.6
Miscellaneous nondurable goods	519	46,772	184,577.0	12.3	441,196	10,753.7
RETAIL TRADE	52-59	2,671,715	1,949,192.7	6.8	18,407,453	222,867.9
Building materials, hardware, garden supply, and mobile home dealers	52	104,916	100,837.2	16.0	665,747	11,789.8
Lumber and other building materials dealers	521	35,868	68,930.3	23.2	386,260	7,519.5
Paint, glass, and wallpaper stores	523	14,672	6,427.5	29.5	48,944	903.1
Hardware stores	525	25,052	12,728.5	9.7	136,230	1,871.4
Retail nurseries, lawn and garden supply stores	526	22,062	6,772.7	15.4	71,499	1,017.7
Mobile home dealers	527	7,262	5,978.2	9.7	22,814	478.2
General merchandise stores	53	62,616	246,420.0	47.3	2,078,530	24,502.7
Department stores	531	11,001	190,784.9	.....	1,719,276	20,135.7
Variety stores	533	22,509	9,516.2	54.8	115,861	1,088.5
Miscellaneous general merchandise stores	539	29,106	50,481.2	57.6	243,393	3,278.5
Food stores	54	277,629	377,098.3	15.4	2,969,317	37,227.8
Grocery stores	541	185,762	358,147.7	16.1	2,682,153	34,425.3
Retail bakeries	546	30,546	5,731.8	7.4	157,136	1,407.1
Other food stores	542-5, 9	61,321	13,218.8	.....	130,028	1,395.3
Automotive dealers and gasoline service stations	55	88,604	543,885.8	1.5	1,942,613	39,376.3
Motor vehicle dealers (new and used)	551	24,380	333,801.4	1.5	860,139	24,421.3
Motor vehicle dealers (used only)	552	92,003	25,511.5	1.1	62,793	1,131.8
Auto and home supply stores	553	63,040	29,816.8	15.5	269,069	4,683.1
Gasoline service stations	554	119,582	136,950.0	7.2	675,080	7,569.1
Miscellaneous automotive dealers	555-7, 9	27,283	17,806.2	2.4	75,532	1,570.9

TABLE 1 (CONTINUED)

UNITED STATES: COMPONENT INDUSTRIES OF WHOLESALE AND RETAIL TRADE (SIC 50-59), 1992

(Monetary values in millions of U.S. dollars)

| INDUSTRY NAME | SIC | ESTABLISH-MENTS | SALES | | EMPLOY-MENT[1] | PAYROLL |
			VALUE	PERCENT BY 4 LARGEST COMPANIES		
Apparel and accessory stores	56	220,806	104,210.7	17.9	1,144,587	12,038.5
Men's and boy's clothing and accessory stores	561	19,296	10,196.6	20.0	104,520	1,439.9
Women's clothing stores	562	64,652	31,827.9	27.6	423,022	3,690.3
Women's accessory and specialty stores	563	21,962	3,921.6	37.7	43,919	479.5
Family clothing stores	565	32,842	33,222.0	35.3	309,516	3,468.9
Shoe stores	566	41,502	18,121.7	38.6	184,415	2,184.5
Other apparel and accessory	564, 9	40,552	6,920.9	28.8	79,195	775.4
Home furniture, furnishings, and equipment stores	57	189,068	96,947.2	9.7	702,164	11,868.7
Home furniture and furnishings stores	571	111,437	52,348.2	.....	413,372	7,189.8
Household appliance stores	572	16,154	8,407.2	.....	53,782	964.7
Radio, television, consumer electronics, and music stores	573	61,477	36,191.8	25.8	235,010	3,714.1
Radio/TV/electronics stores	5731	27,856	20,274.8	44.3	121,115	2,111.9
Computer and software stores	5734	15,359	7,120.1	26.2	29,852	607.1
Music stores	5735,6	18,262	8,796.9	.....	84,043	995.1
Eating and drinking places	58	557,879	200,163.5	7.9	6,547,908	52,569.7
Eating places	5812	474,298	187,757.7	8.4	6,243,862	50,306.7
Drinking places	5813	83,581	12,405.8	0.9	304,046	2,263.0
Miscellaneous retail	59	932,513	279,630.1	5.4	2,356,587	33,494.4
Drug stores and proprietary stores	591	51,173	77,788.2	24.7	587,943	9,060.3
Liquor stores	592	40,197	21,698.3	8.2	132,989	1,522.8
Used merchandise stores	593	123,675	8,219.2	9.8	93,267	1,124.0
Miscellaneous shopping goods stores	594	311,182	71,650.1	13.8	749,947	8,562.5
Nonstore retailers	596	115,974	52,789.9	10.9	339,134	6,280.4
Fuel dealers	598	15,206	14,202.0	13.2	81,506	1,928.0
Retail stores, n.e.c.	599	275,106	33,282.4	.....	371,801	5,016.4

1. Employment numbers from the economic censuses differ in definition and classification from the Bureau of Labor Statistics estimates in Table 2. Year-to-year comparisons between Table 1 and Table 2 are not appropriate.

2. Merchant wholesalers take title to the goods they sell, as opposed to sales branches and sales offices or agents and brokers.

Source: U.S. Bureau of the Census, 1992 Census of Retail and Wholesale Trades.

TABLE 2

U.S. EMPLOYMENT AND EARNINGS: WHOLESALE AND RETAIL TRADE

| INDUSTRY | SIC | 1993 | | | 2005 |
| | | EMPLOYMENT[1] | | AVERAGE HOURLY EARNINGS (U.S. DOLLARS)[2] | PROJECTED EMPLOYMENT[3] |
		NUMBER OF PERSONS	PERCENT OF INDUSTRY TOTAL		
WHOLESALE AND RETAIL TRADE	50-59	25,755,000	100.0	8.49	29,652,600
Wholesale trade	50-51	5,981,000	23.2	11.74	6,558,500
Durable goods	50	3,433,000	13.3	12.10	.....
Motor vehicles, parts, and supplies	501	451,300	1.8	10.62	500,253
Machinery, equipment, and supplies	508	730,100	2.8	11.94	821,571
Nondurable goods	51	2,549,000	9.9	11.25	.....
Groceries and related products	514	847,000	3.3	11.47	911,376
Petroleum and petroleum products	517	162,800	0.6	10.59	174,255
Retail trade	52-59	19,773,000	76.8	7.29	23,094,100
Building materials and garden supplies	52	779,000	3.0	8.66	850,779
Lumber and other building materials	521	450,600	1.7	9.00	519,173
Paint, glass, and wallpaper stores	523	65,100	0.3	9.26	66,022
Hardware stores	525	154,600	0.6	7.44	160,554
Retail nurseries and garden stores	526	82,100	0.3	7.56	105,030
General merchandise stores	53	2,488,300	9.7	7.29	2,585,362
Department stores	531	2,140,100	8.3	7.29	2,280,760
Food stores	54	3,224,100	12.5	7.80	3,929,810
Grocery stores	541	2,883,700	11.2	7.89	3,526,175
Meat and fish markets	542	45,700	0.2	.....	46,516
Retail bakeries	546	166,600	0.6	6.85	195,065
Automotive dealers and service stations	55	2,013,800	7.8	9.66	2,252,252
Auto and home supply stores	553	340,200	1.3	8.31	397,633
Gasoline service stations	554	617,200	2.4	6.67	622,708
Apparel and accessory stores	56	1,143,600	4.4	7.01	1,341,447
Shoe stores	566	210,300	0.8	7.23	228,076
Home furniture and equipment stores	57	827,500	3.2	9.46	1,033,845
Home furniture and furnishings stores	571	443,700	1.7	9.28	501,167
Eating and drinking places	58	6,821,400	26.5	5.35	8,089,100
Miscellaneous retail establishments	59	2,475,500	9.6	7.93	3,011,505
Drug stores and proprietary stores	591	595,000	2.3	8.09	672,224
Liquor stores	592	112,600	0.4	.....	111,037
Miscellaneous shopping goods stores	594	864,900	3.4	7.24	1,171,891

1. Total payroll employment. Employment data from the economic censuses, as shown in Table 1, differ in definition and classification from the Bureau of Labor Statistics estimates in this table. Year-to-year comparisons between Table 1 and Table 2 are not appropriate.

2. Earnings of nonsupervisory workers, including overtime.

3. Number of persons, moderate projection by the U.S. Bureau of Labor Statistics.

Source: Bureau of Labor Statistics.

FIGURE 1

U.S. EMPLOYMENT IN WHOLESALE AND RETAIL TRADE

Percent distribution by region, 1995

The distribution of wholesale and retail trade employment across the country is consistent with the overall distribution of employment. The Southeast region employs 24.1 percent of the industry's workers, followed by the Great Lakes region with 17.3 percent.

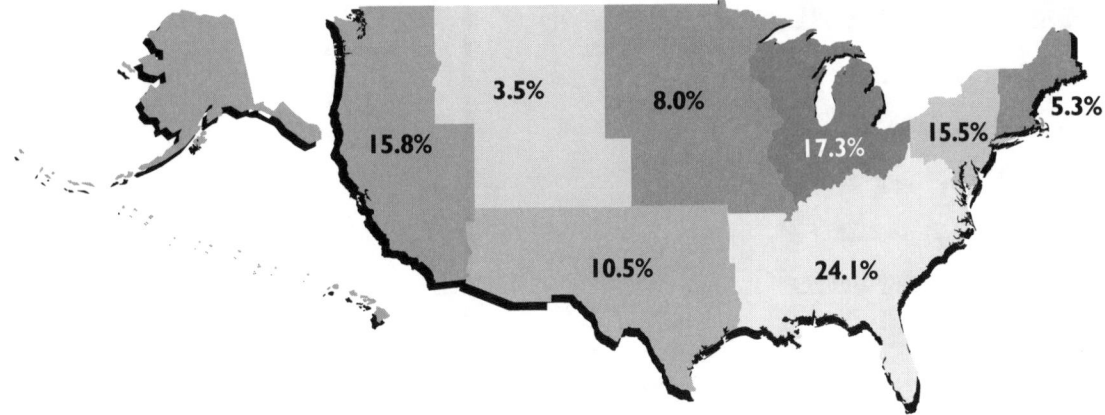

Source: U.S. Department of Commerce, Bureau of Economic Analysis.

What's New. *Retail Trade.* During the first 10 months of 1997, retail sales averaged 4.2 percent above the corresponding 1996 period, indicating annual current dollar 1997 growth below 1996's 6.8 percent. Consumer prices for goods rose very little during 1997, however. (The 1997 Consumer Price Index for all commodities averaged only 1.4 percent above 1996.) Thus the current dollar sales growth of 4 percent or so represents solid real growth. The same conclusion is implied by the BEA estimates of personal consumption expenditure, which show real consumer spending on goods rising 3.7 percent from the third quarter of 1996 to the third quarter of 1997.

In an attempt to boost market share and name recognition, wireless phone companies are opening retail stores of their own. Wireless firms believe that they can gain new customers less expensively through their own outlets. They also think that by offering a higher level of service at retail stores, customers will be less likely to cancel services in the future. Criticism of the strategy focuses on the high cost of establishing a retail outlet and the poor record of phone-company retailing in the past. So far this year, company-owned stores accounted for 22 percent of total wireless distribution, up from 19 percent for all of last year.

According to the National Restaurant Association, sales by limited-service (fast-food) restaurants were projected to grow to $103.5 billion in 1997, with inflation-adjusted growth of 2.5 percent over 1996. Full-service restaurants' sales were expected to reach $104.4 billion, an increase of 1.3 percent in real terms over 1996. Menu prices are projected to rise 2.7 percent in 1997, higher then the 2.4 percent rate of menu-price inflation in 1996.

Wholesale Trade. Seasonally adjusted sales by merchant wholesalers were $208.8 billion in August 1997, down 1.1 percent from the July level but 3.0 percent above the August 1996 level. Durable goods sales fell two percent from July, but were up 4.5 percent from August 1996. The current dollar value of inventories was $264.8 billion at the end of August, 3.4 percent above the August 1996 level.

The purchase of Bergen Brunswig Corp. by Cardinal Health Inc. for $2.8 billion will create the biggest drug distribution company in the nation. The resulting company will distribute 25 percent of all prescription drugs sold domestically. The merger allows for cost cutting and consolidation that should save $100 million annually by the third year after the merger.

FIGURE 2A

U.S. EMPLOYMENT AND SALES RECEIPTS, WHOLESALE TRADE

Total payroll employment and inflation-adjusted sales receipts

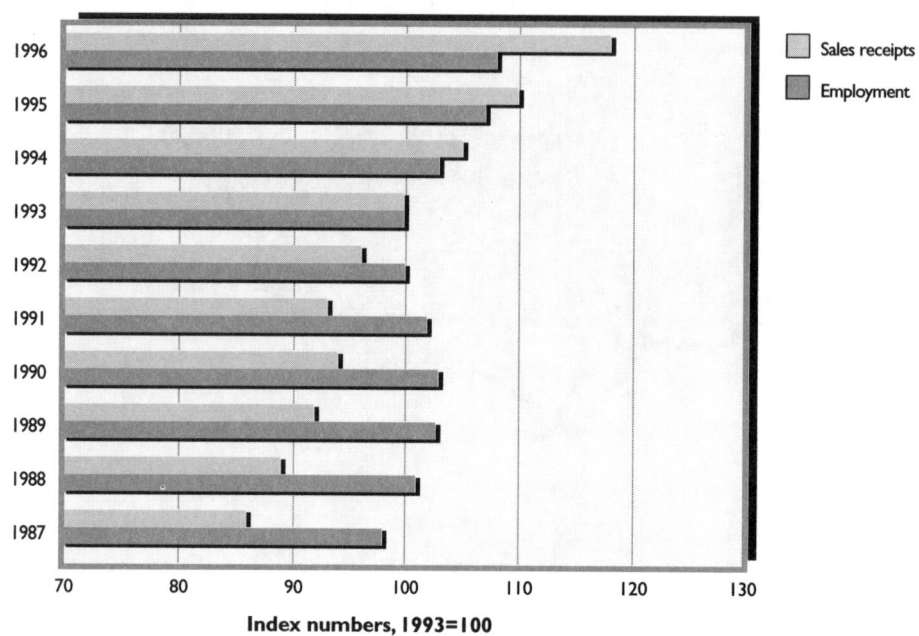

Index numbers, 1993=100

Source: U.S. Bureau of Labor Statistics, U.S. Department of Commerce, and estimates by the editors.

FIGURE 2B

U.S. EMPLOYMENT AND SALES RECEIPTS, RETAIL TRADE

Total payroll employment and inflation-adjusted sales receipts

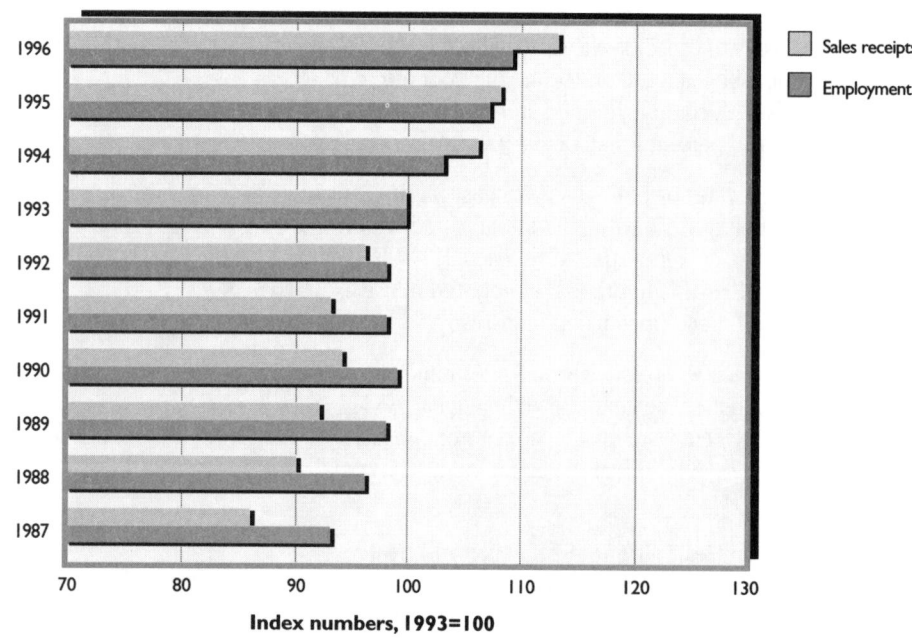

Index numbers, 1993=100

Source: U.S. Bureau of Labor Statistics, U.S. Department of Commerce, and estimates by the editors.

Output. Sales receipts and employment (constant 1992 dollars) for wholesale and retail trade followed similar patterns over the 1987-1996 period (Figure 2). In each industry, sales and employment increased in the late 1980s and then fell slightly in the early 1990s, before resuming growth for the rest of the period.

The gross product originating in the *wholesale trade industry* (merchant wholesalers and non-merchant wholesalers) increased by 6.3 percent annually during 1987-1994, from $300.9 billion to $461.9 billion, and accounted for 6.7 percent of total gross domestic product (GDP) in 1994; in constant 1992 dollars, it grew from $322.9 billion in 1987 to $450.0 billion in 1994 for an annual growth rate of 4.9 percent. Sales by merchant wholesalers increased from $1.48 trillion in 1987 to $2.42 trillion in 1996, at an annual rate of 5.7 percent.

Retail trade gross domestic product originating from 1987 to 1994 grew at a rate of 4.9 percent per year. In constant 1992 dollars, gross product originating increased 2.3 percent annually from 1987 to 1994, despite a slight decline in 1991. Retail sales increased from $1.54 trillion in 1987 to $2.45 trillion in 1996, at a rate of 5.3 percent per year.

Prices. The implicit price deflator for wholesale trade's nonfarm inventories increased at an annual rate of 2.0 percent from 1987 to 1996. The implicit prices of nondurable goods inventories rose at a rate of 3.1 percent per year, substantially faster than the 1.3 percent rate of increase for durable goods. The implicit price deflator for retail trade inventories grew at a rate of 2.1 percent per year. Prices of durable goods grew slightly faster (2.4 percent annually), than nondurable goods prices (1.9 percent).

TABLE 3

U.S. OUTPUT, INVESTMENT, AND PRICES: WHOLESALE AND RETAIL TRADE

(Millions of U.S. dollars, except as noted)

	1987	1988	1989	1990	1991	1992	1993	1994	1995	1996	GROWTH RATE 1987-1996[1]
WHOLESALE TRADE											
SALES (MERCHANT WHOLESALERS[2])	1,475,613	1,614,249	1,725,123	1,794,072	1,779,673	1,849,798	1,940,175	2,075,678	2,265,732	2,420,679	5.65
OTHER OUTPUT MEASURES: Gross domestic product:											
Current dollars	300,968	336,485	356,411	367,292	388,168	406,493	423,074	461,863	.....	.....	.....
Percent of total GDP	6.4	6.7	6.6	6.4	6.6	6.5	6.5	6.7	.....	.....	.....
Chained (1992) dollars	322,895	343,904	366,438	360,597	381,255	406,493	418,631	449,975	.....	.....	.....
IMPLICIT PRICE DEFLATOR FOR NONFARM INVENTORIES (1992=100):											
All wholesale trade	90.0	94.1	97.3	99.1	99.3	100.0	101.2	103.2	107.4	107.2	1.96
Durable goods	92.4	95.5	97.7	98.6	99.3	100.0	101.2	103.3	105.7	104.0	1.32
Nondurable goods	85.5	91.3	96.2	99.6	99.2	100.0	100.9	102.9	109.9	112.3	3.07
Merchant wholesalers	89.7	94.1	97.2	98.8	99.3	100.0	101.4	103.5	107.7	107.4	2.02
RETAIL TRADE											
SALES	1,541,299	1,656,202	1,758,971	1,844,611	1,855,937	1,951,589	2,072,788	2,227,325	2,324,038	2,445,296	5.26
OTHER OUTPUT MEASURES: Gross domestic product:											
Current dollars	435,823	459,330	490,191	503,471	517,447	544,316	571,095	609,908	.....	.....	.....
Percent of total GDP	9.3	9.1	9.0	8.8	8.7	8.7	8.7	8.8	.....	.....	.....
Chained (1992) dollars	509,230	537,616	553,429	546,355	534,122	544,316	563,185	595,361	.....	.....	.....
IMPLICIT PRICE DEFLATOR FOR NONFARM INVENTORIES (1992=100):											
All retail trade	88.0	91.0	94.1	96.2	98.0	100.0	102.0	103.8	106.2	106.5	2.14
Durable goods	89.1	91.8	94.3	95.5	97.7	100.0	103.4	106.3	106.8	109.9	2.35
Nondurable goods	86.9	90.1	94.0	97.2	98.4	100.0	100.7	101.4	105.7	103.0	1.90

1. Compound annual growth rate.

2. Merchant wholesalers take title to the goods they sell as opposed to sales offices and sales branches of manufacturers or trade agents and brokers.

Source: Sales: Bureau of the Census; implicit price deflators and GDP: Bureau of Economic Analysis.

Workforce and Employment. Employment in *wholesale trade* increased from 5.85 million in 1987 to 6.19 million in 1989 (Table 4). From 1989 to 1993, employment in the industry gradually fell by about 200,000 workers as the economy went into recession. The recovery in wholesale trade employment lagged behind the rebound in the overall economy; industry employment did not regain its 1989 level until 1995. Nonsupervisory workers' share of wholesale trade employment increased slightly from 80.1 percent of industry employment in 1987 to 80.8 percent in 1996. Women's share of industry employment also had a modest gain, up from 29.7 percent in 1987 to 30.8 percent in 1996.

Average hourly earnings of nonsupervisory workers increased in current dollars from $9.59 in 1987 to $12.87 in 1996, at a rate of 3.3 percent per year. In constant 1992 dollars, however, average hourly earnings declined by 0.23 percent annually, from $11.78 in 1987 to $11.54 in 1996. Average hours worked in the industry were roughly constant over the period, ending up at 38.3 hours per week in 1996.

Employment in *retail trade* grew from 18.4 million people in 1987 to 21.6 million people in 1996, at a rate of 1.8 percent per year, slightly faster than the rate of growth for wholesale trade (Table 4). Retail trade employment was also affected by the recession, falling from 1990 to 1991, but the effects were short lived and by 1993 the industry had surpassed the 1990 level of employment. Nonsupervisory workers' share of employment fell slightly from

TABLE 4

U.S. EMPLOYMENT, HOURS, AND EARNINGS: WHOLESALE AND RETAIL TRADE

(Monetary values in U.S. dollars)

	1987	1988	1989	1990	1991	1992	1993	1994	1995	1996	CHANGE[1]
WHOLESALE TRADE											
NUMBER OF EMPLOYEES, IN THOUSANDS:											
Total	5,848	6,030	6,187	6,173	6,081	5,997	5,981	6,140	6,378	6,483	1.15
Nonsupervisory workers	4,685	4,857	4,981	4,959	4,872	4,817	4,823	4,972	5,163	5,239	1.25
Percent of total	80.1	80.5	80.5	80.3	80.1	80.3	80.6	81.0	81.0	80.8	.....
Women	1,736	1,815	1,891	1,892	1,864	1,837	1,827	1,889	1,959	1,999	1.58
Percent of total	29.7	30.1	30.6	30.6	30.7	30.6	30.5	30.8	30.7	30.8	.....
HOURS AND EARNINGS OF NONSUPERVISORY WORKERS:											
AVERAGE HOURLY EARNINGS, U.S. DOLLARS[2]											
Current dollars	9.59	9.98	10.39	10.79	11.15	11.39	11.74	12.06	12.43	12.87	3.32
1992 dollars[3]	11.78	11.78	11.71	11.56	11.47	11.39	11.42	11.44	11.47	11.54	-0.23
Average weekly hours	38.1	38.1	38.0	38.1	38.1	38.2	38.2	38.4	38.3	38.3	0.06
Average weekly earnings, current U.S. dollars	365.38	380.24	394.82	411.10	424.82	435.10	448.47	463.10	476.07	492.92	3.38
RETAIL TRADE											
NUMBER OF EMPLOYEES, IN THOUSANDS:											
Total	18,422	19,023	19,475	19,601	19,284	19,356	19,773	20,437	21,187	21,625	1.80
Nonsupervisory workers	16,378	16,869	17,262	17,358	17,006	17,048	17,427	18,056	18,639	19,025	1.68
Percent of total	88.9	88.7	88.6	88.6	88.2	88.1	88.1	88.3	88.0	88.0	.....
Women	9,764	10,113	10,384	10,445	10,304	10,312	10,471	10,834	11,169	11,387	1.72
Percent of total	53.0	53.2	53.3	53.3	53.4	53.3	53.0	53.0	52.7	52.7	.....
HOURS AND EARNINGS OF NONSUPERVISORY WORKERS:											
AVERAGE HOURLY EARNINGS, U.S. DOLLARS[2]											
Current dollars	6.12	6.31	6.53	6.75	6.94	7.12	7.29	7.49	7.69	7.99	3.01
1992 dollars[3]	7.52	7.45	7.36	7.23	7.14	7.12	7.09	7.11	7.09	7.17	-0.53
Average weekly hours	29.2	29.1	28.9	28.8	28.6	28.8	28.8	28.9	28.8	28.8	-0.15
Average weekly earnings, current U.S. dollars	178.70	183.62	188.72	194.40	198.48	205.06	209.95	216.46	221.47	230.11	2.85

1. Compound annual growth rate for years shown.
2. Including overtime.
3. Converted to 1992 dollars using Consumer Price Index for Urban Wage Earners and Clerical Workers.
Source: Bureau of Labor Statistics.

88.9 percent in 1987 to 88.0 percent in 1996, but was still quite high when compared to most industries. Women's share of employment was slightly above half in 1996, at 52.7 percent, slightly below its 1987 level.

Average hourly earnings of nonsupervisory workers in retail trade increased from $6.12 per hour in 1987 to $7.99 per hour in 1996, at a rate of 3 percent per year. Hourly earnings fell slightly in constant 1992 dollars over the period at a rate of 0.5 percent per year. Hourly earnings and average weekly hours worked (28.8 hours in 1996) were very low, reflecting the part-time nature of many of the industry's jobs. Consequently, average weekly earnings, at $230.11 in 1996, were less than half the level of average weekly earnings in wholesale trade, $492.92.

TABLE 5

U.S. EMPLOYMENT PROJECTIONS BY MAJOR OCCUPATIONAL GROUP: WHOLESALE AND RETAIL TRADE

OCCUPATION	1994		PROJECTIONS, 2005			
	NUMBER OF EMPLOYEES	PERCENT OF INDUSTRY TOTAL	NUMBER OF EMPLOYEES			PERCENT OF INDUSTRY TOTAL, MODERATE PROJECTIONS
			LOW	MODERATE	HIGH	
WHOLESALE TRADE						
Total, all occupations	6,139,900	100.0	6,389,200	6,558,500	6,765,400	100.0
Executive, administrative, and managerial	755,327	12.3	798,243	819,396	845,244	12.5
Professional specialties	135,386	2.2	191,622	196,703	202,905	3.0
Technicians and related support	113,759	1.9	120,818	124,022	127,932	1.9
Marketing and sales	1,514,754	24.7	1,699,722	1,744,764	1,799,803	26.6
Administrative support including clerical	1,679,701	27.4	1,583,197	1,625,153	1,676,417	24.8
Service	60,035	1.0	59,299	60,869	62,790	0.9
Agriculture, forestry, and fisheries occupations	70,287	1.1	85,671	87,942	90,716	1.3
Precision production, craft, and repair	560,194	9.1	626,946	643,553	663,861	9.8
Operators, fabricators, assemblers	1,250,457	20.4	1,223,681	1,256,098	1,295,732	19.2
RETAIL TRADE						
Total, all occupations	20,437,500	100.0	22,780,802	23,094,100	23,416,499	100.0
Executive, administrative, and managerial	1,309,253	6.4	1,489,730	1,508,628	1,528,099	6.5
Professional specialties	275,941	1.4	336,851	347,222	357,765	1.5
Technicians and related support	125,574	0.6	149,713	154,668	159,699	0.7
Marketing and sales	7,372,707	36.1	8,280,701	8,518,037	8,759,674	36.9
Administrative support including clerical	2,586,836	12.7	2,620,109	2,700,307	2,781,908	11.7
Service	6,506,381	31.8	7,615,946	7,512,306	7,410,135	32.5
Agriculture, forestry, and fisheries occupations	35,866	0.2	47,310	48,725	50,148	0.2
Precision production, craft, and repair	1,028,240	5.0	1,028,978	1,061,678	1,094,892	4.6
Operators, fabricators, assemblers	1,196,702	5.9	1,211,464	1,242,529	1,274,179	5.4

Source: Bureau of Labor Statistics, November 1995.

Wholesale trade is projected to add more than 400,000 employees (moderate projections) from 1994 to 2005. Marketing and sales is the occupation expected to grow the most, while administrative support including clerical is expected to have a slight reduction in employment by the year 2005. Retail trade employment is projected to increase by more than 2.5 million by the year 2005. The marketing and sales and service occupations are each expected to add more than one million employees from 1994 to 2005.

FIGURE 3

U.S. OCCUPATIONAL INJURY AND ILLNESS RATES: TRADE, 1995

Incidence of nonfatal injuries and illnesses per 100 full-time workers

The incidence rate of illnesses and injuries was 7.5 cases per 100 workers in both wholesale and retail trade.

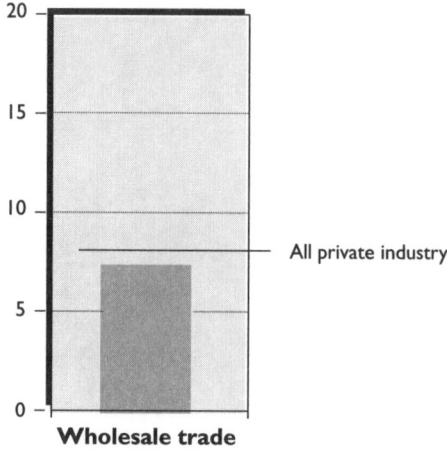

Wholesale trade

All private industry

Retail trade

All private industry

Source: U.S. Bureau of Labor Statistics.

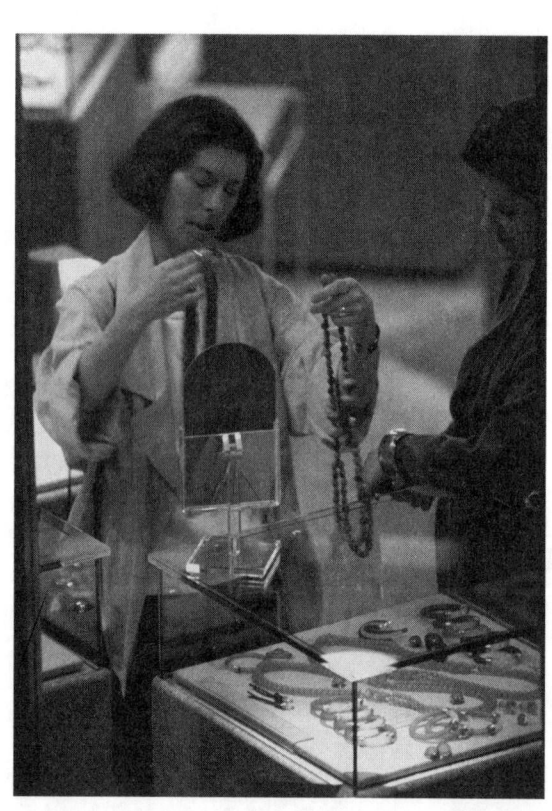

FIGURE 4A

U.S. CORPORATE INCOME AND WORKER EARNINGS: WHOLESALE TRADE

Corporate operating income and aggregate nonsupervisory worker earnings

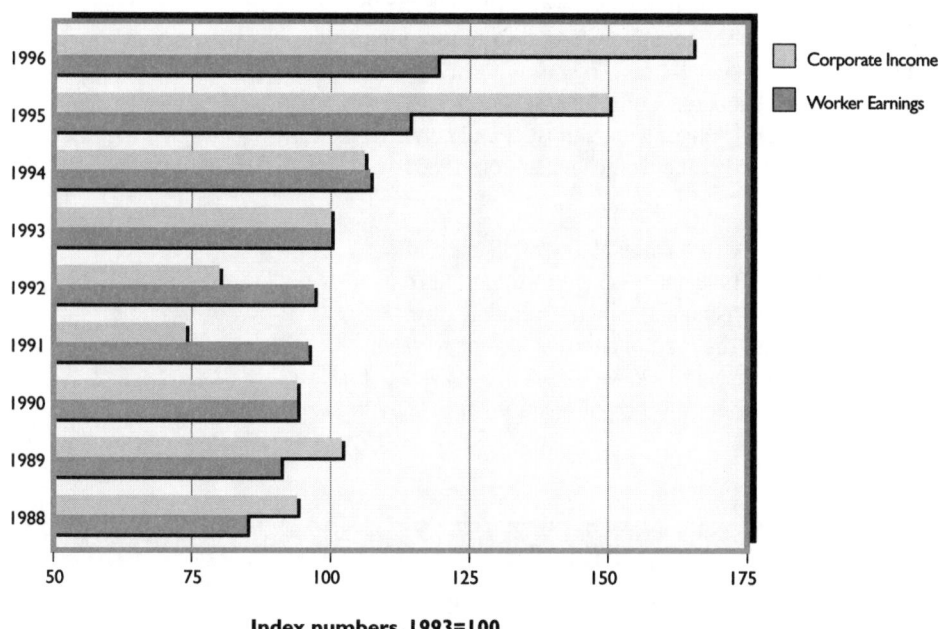

Index numbers, 1993=100

Source: U.S. Bureau of Labor Statistics, U.S. Bureau of the Census, and estimates by the editors.

FIGURE 4B

U.S. CORPORATE INCOME AND WORKER EARNINGS: RETAIL TRADE

Corporate operating income and aggregate nonsupervisory worker earnings

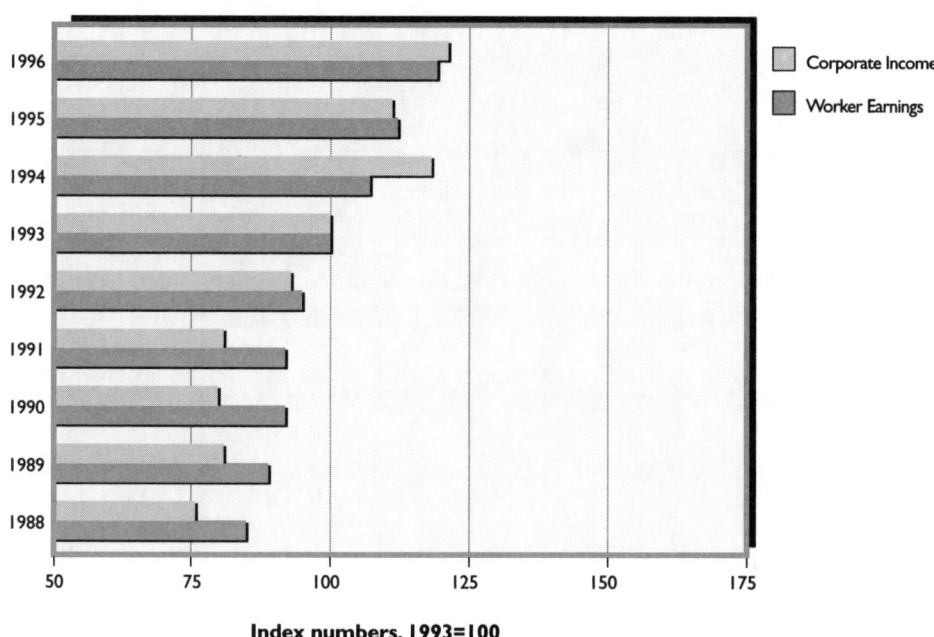

Index numbers, 1993=100

Source: U.S. Bureau of Labor Statistics, U.S. Bureau of the Census, and estimates by the editors.

Finance. Operating income of the *wholesale trade* industry increased at an annual rate of 7.2 percent per year over the 1988-1996 period, despite a substantial decrease during the 1991 recession (Table 6). After-tax income grew at an annual rate of 8.5 percent from 1988 to 1996, but actually decreased from 1988 to 1994, before jumping from $5.7 billion in 1994 to $14.6 billion in 1996. The ratios of after-tax income to sales (1.4 percent) and after-tax income to stockholders' equity (10.1 percent) reached their highest levels in 1996. Over the period, the industry's composition of debt moved away from short-term debt toward long-term debt. Short-term debt as a percent of total assets fell from 17.5 percent in 1988 to 13.9 percent in 1996, while long-term debt increased as a percent of total assets from 15.3 percent in 1988 to 18.4 percent in 1996. Because these changes were almost completely offsetting, the overall debt as a percent of assets remained virtually unchanged from 1988 to 1996.

Operating income of the *retail trade* industry increased at an annual rate of 6.1 percent per year over the 1988-1996 period, despite declines in 1990 and 1995 (Table 6). After-tax income was unstable during the period, alternately rising and falling. Overall, it grew at a rate of 6.5 percent, but fell in five of the nine years. The ratio of after-tax income to sales (1.9 percent) and to stockholders' equity (11.1 percent) in 1996 were each above average for the period, but neither were peaks. Total debt fell from 37.5 percent of assets in 1988 to 30.2 percent of assets in 1996.

TABLE 6

U.S. CORPORATE INCOME AND ASSETS: WHOLESALE AND RETAIL TRADE[1]

(Monetary values in millions of U.S. dollars)

	1988	1989	1990	1991	1992	1993	1994	1995	1996	CHANGE OR AVERAGE[2]
WHOLESALE TRADE										
INCOME AND EXPENSES										
Sales and receipts	603,270	689,223	730,909	713,358	752,566	774,415	841,886	937,854	1,035,364	6.98
Depreciation and amortization	(5,343)	(6,461)	(5,974)	(6,577)	(6,936)	(7,892)	(8,786)	(9,401)	(10,125)	8.32
Other operating costs	(585,280)	(669,112)	(712,388)	(696,961)	(734,944)	(753,195)	(819,019)	(908,331)	(1,003,180)	6.97
Income from operations	12,646	13,652	12,548	9,820	10,684	13,328	14,081	20,122	22,059	7.20
Nonoperating income (expenditures)	(818)	(2,423)	(3,983)	(2,579)	(2,216)	(2,815)	(3,453)	(2,909)	623	......
Income before taxes	11,829	11,228	8,566	7,242	8,468	10,515	10,627	17,214	22,682	8.48
Income after taxes	7,583	7,275	4,415	3,916	5,121	6,717	5,698	11,245	14,586	8.52
Cash dividends	2,395	2,786	2,485	2,301	2,720	3,159	3,457	3,675	4,231	7.37
Income retained in business	5,188	4,489	1,932	1,616	2,401	3,559	2,241	7,569	10,356	9.02
Direct credits (charges)	(1,980)	(1,299)	(971)	(1,456)	(3,314)	(2,606)	(2,404)	(1,742)	(2,824)	......
Ending retained earnings	42,339	47,700	44,000	44,651	41,751	47,190	50,649	60,386	68,613	6.22
ASSETS, END OF YEAR										
Total	239,466	269,402	285,322	299,775	318,143	343,031	382,765	422,176	453,511	8.31
Accounts receivable	58,368	64,129	67,518	68,454	71,145	76,933	88,503	101,538	106,276	7.78
Inventories	61,335	65,404	70,169	72,570	74,064	80,770	89,552	98,647	99,928	6.29
Net property, plant and equipment	44,417	53,232	50,648	53,556	55,103	61,039	65,693	75,530	81,823	7.94
RATIOS, PERCENT:										
Income to sales:										
Before tax	1.96	1.63	1.17	1.02	1.13	1.36	1.26	1.84	2.19	1.51
After tax	1.26	1.06	0.60	0.55	0.68	0.87	0.68	1.20	1.41	0.92
Income to stock holders' equity:										
Before tax	15.34	12.95	9.41	7.58	8.72	9.99	9.34	13.37	15.69	11.38
After tax	9.83	8.39	4.85	4.10	5.27	6.38	5.01	8.73	10.09	6.96

TABLE 6 (CONTINUED)

U.S. CORPORATE INCOME AND ASSETS: WHOLESALE AND RETAIL TRADE[1]

(Monetary values in millions of U.S. dollars)

	1988	1989	1990	1991	1992	1993	1994	1995	1996	CHANGE OR AVERAGE[2]
WHOLESALE TRADE (Continued)										
Income to total assets:										
Before tax	4.94	4.17	3.00	2.42	2.66	3.07	2.78	4.08	5.00	3.57
After tax	3.17	2.70	1.55	1.31	1.61	1.96	1.49	2.66	3.22	2.18
As a percent of total assets:										
Property, plant and equipment	18.55	19.76	17.75	17.87	17.32	17.79	17.16	17.89	18.04	18.01
Short-term debt	17.47	17.01	17.23	17.55	16.40	16.31	15.27	14.63	13.90	16.20
Long-term debt	15.30	16.27	15.89	16.59	18.92	19.79	20.24	19.52	18.40	17.88
Stockholders' equity	32.20	32.18	31.90	31.89	30.54	30.68	29.73	30.50	31.87	31.28
RETAIL TRADE										
INCOME AND EXPENSES										
Sales and receipts	534,266	589,966	647,503	684,476	740,387	783,445	845,739	911,584	970,051	7.74
Depreciation and amortization	10,227	11,408	13,059	14,165	15,071	15,961	16,931	18,470	19,662	8.51
Other operating costs	499,557	552,578	608,723	644,302	695,359	735,127	790,909	857,276	911,125	7.80
Income from operations	24,480	25,983	25,721	26,010	29,958	32,356	37,901	35,838	39,265	6.08
Nonoperating income (expenditures)	-8,144	-10,758	-12,950	-12,712	-17,497	-12,667	-8,263	-10,951	-9,802	.....
Income before taxes	16,335	15,224	12,772	13,299	12,461	19,688	29,637	24,887	29,461	7.65
Income after taxes	10,961	8,380	7,192	6,798	6,170	11,357	18,144	14,855	18,158	6.51
Cash dividends	8,062	4,475	4,036	4,111	4,802	4,884	5,220	4,880	4,766	-6.36
Income retained in business	2,900	3,906	3,155	2,688	1,367	6,471	12,924	9,974	13,392	21.08
Direct credits (charges)	-7,186	-2,362	-2,497	-714	-893	-1,486	-990	-8,693	-3,715	.....
Ending retained earnings	60,895	62,214	62,600	62,266	68,395	76,925	93,883	98,863	107,276	7.33
ASSETS, END OF YEAR:										
Total	294,866	316,289	343,867	367,739	384,276	400,942	433,301	459,308	488,238	6.51
Accounts receivable	41,686	42,452	42,651	43,077	40,711	45,720	50,480	53,394	54,613	3.43
Inventories	73,309	82,012	87,140	93,290	100,093	106,938	121,690	131,870	137,426	8.17
Net property, plant and equipment	99,461	109,908	122,703	130,522	141,476	152,269	166,662	180,904	191,633	8.54
RATIOS, PERCENT:										
Income to sales:										
Before tax	3.06	2.58	1.97	1.94	1.68	2.51	3.50	2.73	3.04	2.56
After tax	2.05	1.42	1.11	0.99	0.83	1.45	2.15	1.63	1.87	1.50
Income to stockholders' equity:										
Before tax	18.64	17.80	14.59	13.48	10.96	15.81	20.39	16.18	17.93	16.20
After tax	12.51	9.80	8.21	6.89	5.43	9.12	12.48	9.66	11.05	9.46
Income to total assets:										
Before tax	5.54	4.81	3.71	3.62	3.24	4.91	6.84	5.42	6.03	4.90
After tax	3.72	2.65	2.09	1.85	1.61	2.83	4.19	3.23	3.72	2.88
As a percent of total assets:										
Property, plant and equipment	33.73	34.75	35.68	35.49	36.82	37.98	38.46	39.39	39.25	36.84
Short-term debt	3.42	4.60	4.47	3.42	4.45	3.06	3.78	3.76	2.72	3.74
Long-term debt	34.06	34.22	36.43	35.54	30.65	29.88	27.33	27.80	27.51	31.49
Stockholders' equity	29.72	27.04	25.46	26.83	29.58	31.06	33.54	33.49	33.65	30.04

1. Corporations with assets of $50 million and above.

2. For income and asset amounts: compound annual growth rate; for ratios, average of ratios for the years shown.

Source: U.S. Bureau of the Census, Quarterly Financial Report.

Notes: Parentheses ( ) indicate negative items, e.g., net expenses, charges, or losses. "Net property, plant, and equipment" is net of accumulated depreciation. Because the samples used to collect the data change, retained earnings at the end of a given year will not exactly equal the previous year's retained earnings plus the current year's retained income and credits.

CANADA

Canada's *wholesale trade* industry had 594,739 employees in 1993 (Table 7). The largest subindustry was machinery, equipment, and supplies, with 30.7 percent of wholesale industry employment. The Canadian *retail trade* industry employed approximately 1.36 million people in 1993. The largest subindustries were food, beverage, and drug with 32.4 percent of retail trade employment, and auto vehicles, parts and accessories, sales and service, with 23.1 percent of employment.

Canada's wholesale trade industry sales increased from Can$25.1 billion in 1987 to Can$34.6 billion in 1996, at an annual rate of 3.6 percent per year (Table 8). The growth was interrupted by the recession in 1991, and sales did not regain their 1990 level until 1993. Employment in the industry grew at a more modest rate of 1.8 percent per year. Employment took longer to recover from the recession than output, decreasing from 1990 to 1993. Average weekly earnings of nonsupervisory workers increased at an annual rate of 3.3 percent per year. In inflation-adjusted (1992) dollars, growth in average weekly earnings was more modest at 0.3 percent per year.

Retail trade sales grew less rapidly than wholesale trade shipments, increasing at 0.9 percent per year (Table 8). Retail trade was also hit by the recession with declining sales in 1990 and 1991 and declining employment in 1991 and 1992. Overall, employment grew only 0.1 percent per year over the period. Average weekly earnings of nonsupervisory workers increased from Can$270.23 in 1987 to Can$348.05 in 1996, at a rate of 2.9 percent per year, but were virtually unchanged in constant 1992 Canadian dollars.

TABLE 7

CANADA: COMPONENT INDUSTRIES OF WHOLESALE AND RETAIL TRADE (CSIC 5000-6900), 1993

INDUSTRY NAME	CSIC	EMPLOYMENT Number	PERCENT OF INDUSTRY TOTAL
WHOLESALE TRADE	5000-5900	594,739	100.0
Farm products	5000	10,872	1.8
Petroleum products	5100	27,824	4.7
Food, beverages, drugs, and tobacco	5200	94,828	15.9
Apparel and dry goods	5300	15,435	2.6
Household goods	5400	18,998	3.2
Motor vehicles, parts, and accessories	5500	57,732	9.7
Metals, hardware, and building materials	5600	97,758	16.4
Machinery, equipment, and supplies	5700	182,635	30.7
Other wholesale products	5900	88,657	14.9
RETAIL TRADE	6000-6900	1,357,360	100.0
Food, beverages, and drugs	6000	439,297	32.4
Shoes, apparel, fabric, and yarn	6100	126,987	9.4
Household furniture, appliances, and furnishings	6200	76,656	5.6
Auto vehicles, parts & access., sales & service	6300	313,070	23.1
General retail merchandising	6400	191,749	14.1
Other retail n.e.c., nonstore retail industries	6500	209,601	15.4

Source: Statistics Canada: CANSIM.

TABLE 8

CANADIAN EMPLOYMENT AND RECEIPTS: WHOLESALE AND RETAIL TRADE (CSIC 5000-5900), 1987-1996

(Monetary values in Canadian dollars)

	1987	1988	1989	1990	1991	1992	1993	1994	1995	1996	CHANGE[1]
WHOLESALE TRADE											
All employees	571,125	591,279	619,542	637,828	613,162	601,621	594,739	608,136	647,604	669,426	1.78
Nonsupervisory workers:											
Average weekly earnings	470.09	487.39	516.77	538.79	557.65	579.26	591.02	605.62	622.06	628.47	3.28
Receipts (millions)	25,132	26,972	28,111	28,435	27,692	27,985	29,510	32,232	33,172	34,644	3.63
RETAIL TRADE											
All employees	1,364,813	1,399,058	1,434,175	1,517,679	1,392,608	1,332,892	1,357,360	1,352,738	1,386,411	1,378,383	0.11
Nonsupervisory workers:											
Average weekly earnings	270.23	280.72	292.71	306.75	317.80	320.75	329.26	339.09	342.21	348.05	2.85
Receipts (millions)	29,929	30,855	31,613	30,895	29,292	29,643	30,469	32,029	32,322	32,537	0.93

1. Compound annual growth rate.

Source: Statistics Canada: CANSIM.

MEXICO

Mexico's commerce industry had 3.2 million employees in 1993, but almost half of them were unpaid workers (Table 9). Average remuneration for paid workers including benefits in the industry was 18,079 new pesos ($5,788). Industry gross domestic product for commerce, hotels, and restaurants (similar to the U.S. classification of wholesale and retail trade, except for hotels) increased from 202.5 billion constant 1993 new pesos in 1988 ($64.8 billion) to 268.7 billion new pesos ($86.0 billion) in 1994 (Table 10). From 1994 to 1995, industry GDP fell 16 percent to 226.9 billion new pesos ($72.6 billion) as Mexico went into recession following the collapse of the peso.

TABLE 9

MEXICO: COMPONENT INDUSTRIES OF COMMERCIAL SECTOR, 1993

(Monetary values in 1993 Mexican New Pesos)

			ALL WORKERS							
					PAID WORKERS					
INDUSTRY	CMAP	NUMBER OF UNITS	NUMBER	PERCENT OF INDUSTRY TOTAL	REMUNERATION[1]	MANUAL WORKERS, NUMBER	WHITE-COLLAR EMPLOYEES, NUMBER	BENEFITS PER PAID EMPLOYEE	UNPAID WORKERS, NUMBER
Commerce	60	1,210,184	3,212,873	100	18,079	306,397	1,334,957	3,641	1,571,519
Wholesale trade	61	70,545	679,331	21	23,754	160,646	459,766	4,764	58,919
Retail trade	62	1,139,639	2,533,542	79	11,672	145,751	875,191	2,958	1,512,600

1. Average annual remuneration including benefits.
Source: INEGI, Censos Economicos, 1994.

TABLE 10

MEXICAN GROSS DOMESTIC PRODUCT AND EMPLOYMENT: COMMERCE, HOTELS AND RESTAURANTS, 1988-1995

	1988	1989	1990	1991	1992	1993	1994	1995	CHANGE[1]
GROSS DOMESTIC PRODUCT:									
Millions of constant 1993 new pesos	202,530.5	211,892.4	225,058.2	238,749.8	251,401.7	251,628.7	268,696.1	226,896.2	1.64
Millions of constant 1993 U.S. dollars[2]	64,836.7	67,833.8	72,048.6	76,431.7	80,482.0	80,554.7	86,018.5	72,637.0	1.64
TOTAL EMPLOYMENT:									
Commerce, restaurants, and hotels	3,921,757	4,149,849	4,505,159	4,772,226	4,976,645	5,024,695	5,176,745	5,184,770	4.07
Commerce	2,811,668	2,932,564	3,135,707	3,259,106	3,393,363	3,406,969	3,459,665	3,495,782	3.16
Restaurants and hotels	1,110,089	1,217,285	1,369,452	1,513,120	1,583,282	1,617,726	1,717,080	1,688,988	6.18

1. Compound annual growth rate.

2. Converted at 3.1237 new pesos to the U.S. dollar.

Source: Sistema de Cuentas Nacionales de Mexico, INEGI.

APPENDICES

APPENDIX A: OPERATION AND EFFECT OF THE NAFTA:

REPORT BY THE PRESIDENT OF THE UNITED STATES TO THE CONGRESS, JULY 1997

EXECUTIVE SUMMARY[1]

PURPOSE OF THE REPORT

The North American Free Trade Agreement (NAFTA) entered into force on January 1, 1994. In accordance with Section 512 of the NAFTA Implementation Act, this Study provides a comprehensive assessment of the operation and effects of the NAFTA, including the economic effects in aggregate and in selected manufacturing sectors and agriculture, and the implementation of the NAFTA environmental and labor agreements. This Study reviews the findings from a variety of outside studies and analyzes Mexican and U.S. data, attempting wherever possible to isolate the effects of the NAFTA from other factors, as stipulated in the statute.

TRADE IN NORTH AMERICA

U.S. trade with Canada and Mexico is much larger relative to the size of these economies than with any other trading partners, in large part reflecting shared land borders and geographical proximity.

- In 1996, nearly one-third of U.S. two-way trade in goods with the world was with Canada and Mexico ($421 billion). Two-way trade with our NAFTA partners has grown 44 percent since the NAFTA was signed, compared with 33 percent for the rest of the world. Mexico and Canada accounted for 53 percent of the growth in total U.S. exports in the first four months of 1997.

- Canada was in 1993 — and remains today — our largest trading partner, accounting for $290 billion in two-way trade in 1996. Between 1993 and 1996, U.S. goods exports to Canada were up by 33.6 percent to $134.2 billion.

- U.S. exports to Mexico grew by 36.5 percent (or $15.2 billion) from 1993 to a record high in 1996, despite a 3.3 percent contraction in Mexican domestic demand over the same period.

- Exports to Canada and Mexico supported an estimated 2.3 million jobs in 1996; this represents an increase of 311,000 jobs since 1993, 189,000 supported by exports to Canada and 122,000 by exports to Mexico.

- Exports to Mexico were up by 54.5 percent in the first four months of 1997 relative to the same period in 1993. In the first four months of 1997, U.S. exports to Mexico virtually equaled U.S. exports to Japan, our second largest market — even though Mexico's economy is one twelfth the size of Japan's.

---

[1] The full text of this report is available from the U.S. Government Printing Office (jacket #42788) and may also be found on the U.S. Trade Representative web site (www.ustr.gov).

NAFTA'S EFFECT ON TRADE BARRIERS

Under NAFTA, Mexico has reduced its trade barriers on U.S. exports significantly and dismantled a variety of protectionist rules and regulations, while the United States — which started with much lower tariffs — has made only slight reductions.

- Before NAFTA was signed, Mexican applied tariffs on U.S. goods averaged 10 percent. U.S. tariffs on Mexican imports averaged 2.07 percent, and over half of Mexican imports entered the United States duty-free. (Figure 1.)

- Since NAFTA was signed, Mexico has reduced its average applied tariffs on U.S. imports by 7.1 percentage points, compared with a reduction of 1.4 percentage points in the United States. The United States would have made some of these tariff reductions under the Uruguay Round even in the absence of NAFTA.

FIGURE 1

AVERAGE APPLIED TARIFF LEVELS IN U.S. AND MEXICO IN 1993 AND 1996

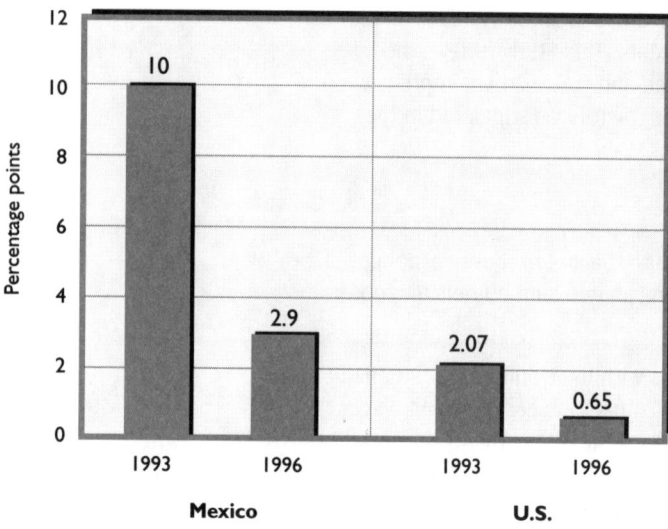

NAFTA'S EFFECTS ON THE U.S. ECONOMY

Several studies conclude that NAFTA contributed to America's economic expansion. NAFTA had a modest positive effect on U.S. net exports, income, investment and jobs supported by exports.

- It is challenging to isolate NAFTA's effects on the U.S. economy, since NAFTA has only been in effect for three years, and events such as the severe recession in Mexico, the depreciation of the Mexican peso, and U.S. tariff reductions under the Uruguay Round have taken place during the same period.

- Nonetheless, several outside studies conclude that NAFTA has resulted in a modest increase in U.S. net exports, controlling for other factors. A new study by DRI estimates that NAFTA boosted real exports to Mexico by $12 billion in 1996, compared to a smaller real increase in imports of $5 billion, controlling for Mexico's financial crisis. An earlier study by the Dallas Federal Reserve finds that NAFTA raised exports by roughly $7 billion and imports by roughly $4 billion. The relatively greater effect on exports partly reflects the fact that under NAFTA Mexico reduced its tariffs roughly 5 times more than the United States.

- DRI estimates that NAFTA contributed $13 billion to U.S. real income and $5 billion to business investment in 1996, controlling for Mexico's financial crisis.

- These estimates suggest that NAFTA has boosted jobs associated with exports to Mexico between roughly 90,000 and 160,000. The Department of Commerce estimates that the jobs supported by exports generally pay 13 to 16 percent more than the national average for non-supervisory production positions.

NAFTA'S EFFECTS ON THE MEXICAN ECONOMY

In 1995, Mexico experienced its most severe economic recession since the 1930s. Comparing Mexico's recovery in 1996 with Mexico's recovery from its last financial crisis in 1982, when NAFTA was not in effect, reveals that both the Mexican economy and American exports recovered more rapidly following the 1995 crisis than the 1982 crisis, in part because of the economic reforms locked in by NAFTA. Mexico's strong economic adjustment program and bilateral and multilateral financial support were also important.

FIGURE 2

NAFTA QUICKENS U.S. EXPORT RECOVERY FROM MEXICAN PESO CRISIS

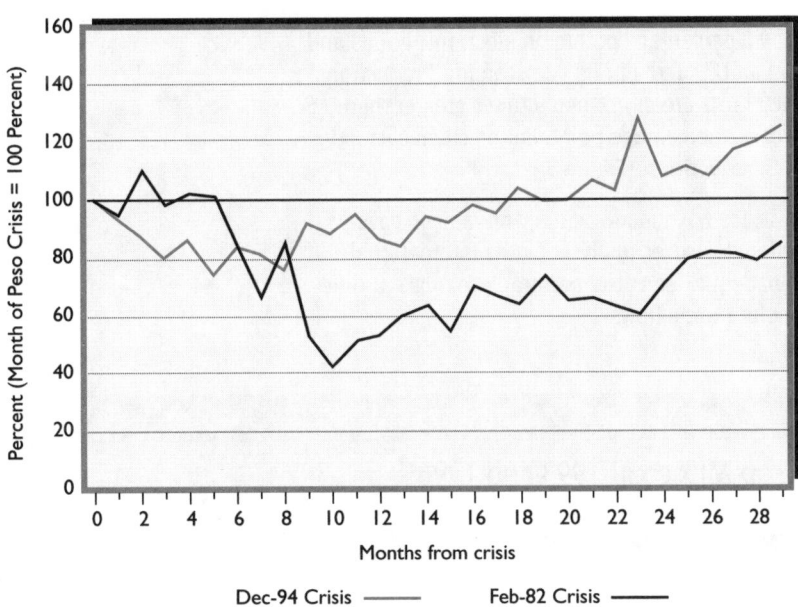

Dec-94 Crisis ——— Feb-82 Crisis ———

- Following Mexico's 1982 financial crisis, Mexican output drifted down for nearly two years before rising again and did not recover to pre-crisis levels for five years. Although Mexican economic output dropped more quickly in 1995, it also rebounded more quickly, reaching pre-crisis peaks by the end of 1996. Similarly, following the 1982 crisis, it took Mexico 7 years to return to international capital markets, while in 1995, it took 7 months.

- Following Mexico's 1982 financial crisis, Mexico raised tariffs by 100 percent, and American exports to Mexico fell by half and did not recover for seven years. (Figure 2.) In 1995, Mexico continued to implement its NAFTA obligations even as it raised tariffs on imports from other countries. As a result, American exports recovered in 18 months and were up nearly 37 percent by the end of 1996 relative to pre-NAFTA levels, even though Mexican consumption was down 3.3 percent.

NAFTA'S EFFECTS IN KEY SECTORS

U.S. suppliers hold dominant shares of Mexico's import markets and in many sectors have expanded their shares significantly under NAFTA, at the expense of suppliers from other countries. In almost all sectors, Mexico has made large reductions in tariff barriers under NAFTA, compared with only slight U.S. reductions.

- Increases in the U.S. share of Mexico's import market are indicative of NAFTA's effects, since they control for factors that affect all foreign suppliers similarly, such as Mexico's recession. Since NAFTA went into effect, U.S. suppliers have seen their share of Mexico's import market grow from 69.3 percent to 75.5 percent, reflecting a 10 percentage point average tariff advantage over foreign suppliers. Mexico's share of American imports has risen from 6.9 percent to 9.3 percent. (Figure 3.)

- Reductions in Mexican barriers in key sectors have led to U.S. share gains in Mexican import markets. Since NAFTA was signed, the U.S. share of Mexican imports is up 17.2 percentage points to 86.4 percent in the textiles sector, where Mexico has cut tariffs by 10.7 percentage points under NAFTA. The U.S. share is up 19.2 percentage points to 83.1 percent in the transport equipment sector, where Mexico has cut tariffs 10.2 percentage points under NAFTA. And the U.S. share is up 5.7 percentage points to 74.3 percent in the electronic goods and appliances sector, where Mexico has cut tariffs by 9.0 percentage points under NAFTA.

- Under NAFTA, Mexican tariff reductions of 9.0 percentage points on electronic goods and appliances are more than 4 times greater than U.S. reductions; Mexican tariff reductions on transport equipment of 10.2 percentage points are more than 9 times greater than U.S. reductions; and Mexican tariff reductions of 6.2 percentage points in the chemicals industry are more than 10 times greater than U.S. reductions. (Figure 5.)

- Since NAFTA was signed, U.S. exports to Mexico have made significant gains in several sectors, despite the severe Mexican recession. However, analysis by the International Trade Commission (ITC) shows that data inadequacies at the sectoral level make it difficult to isolate the effects of NAFTA on absolute trade flows.

FIGURE 3

IMPORT MARKET SHARE FOR THE U.S. AND MEXICO IN 1993 AND 1996

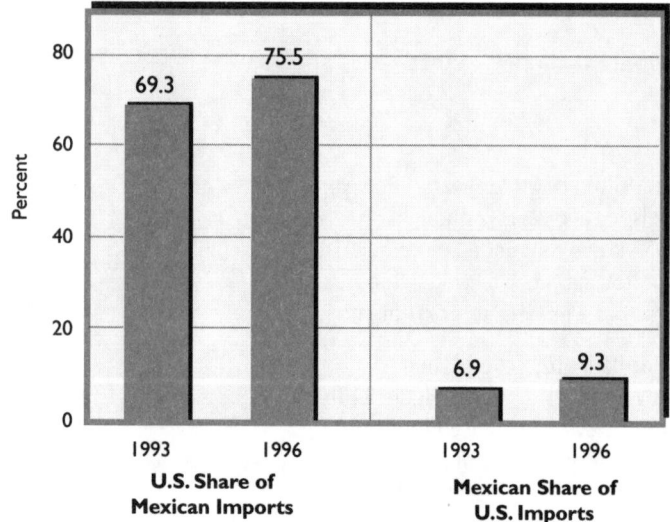

FIGURE 4

U.S. SHARE OF MEXICAN IMPORTS BY SECTOR IN 1996

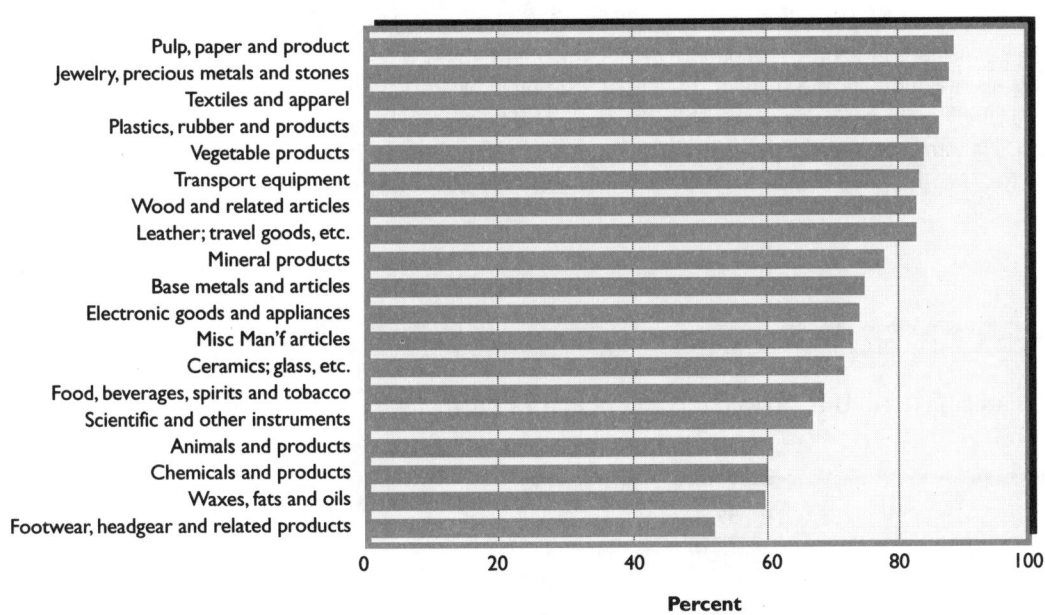

FIGURE 5

CHANGES IN MEXICAN AND U.S. TARIFFS RATES: U.S. SECTORS WITH GREATEST DOLLAR INCREASE IN EXPORTS AND IMPORTS, 1993-96

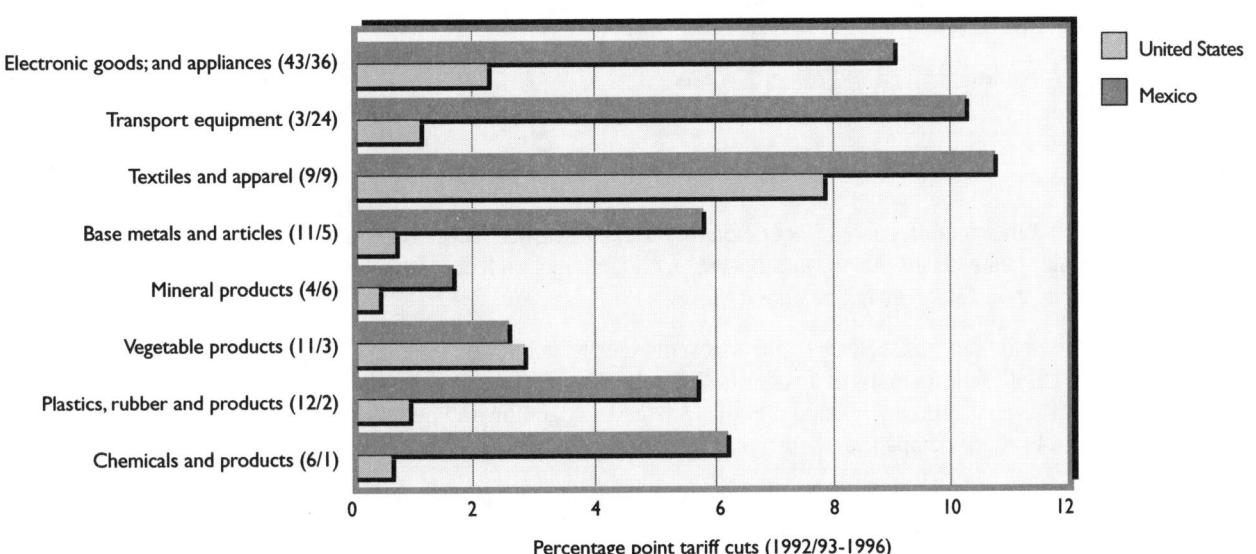

Note: Between parentheses is the share of total 1993-96 percentage change in exports/imports to/from Mexico. These sectors represent over 90 percent of total 1993-96 export and import change.

- In industries such as autos, chemicals, textiles and electronics, NAFTA is permitting American companies to achieve synergies across the North American market, improving their strategic positions abroad and contributing to strong growth in employment, production, and investment at home.

- In several industries that have experienced strong import growth from Mexico, Mexican imports have largely displaced imports from other regions, which have lower U.S. domestic content. In the apparel industry, the share of U.S. imports supplied by Mexico rose from 4.4 percent in 1993 to 9.6 percent in 1996, while the share of U.S. imports from China, Hong Kong, Taiwan and Korea fell from 39 percent in 1993 to 30 percent in 1996. (Figure 6.) Close to 2/3 of the value of Mexican apparel imports in 1996 was comprised of U.S. content.

FIGURE 6

MEXICAN AND ASIAN SHARE OF U.S. APPAREL IMPORTS IN 1993 AND 1996

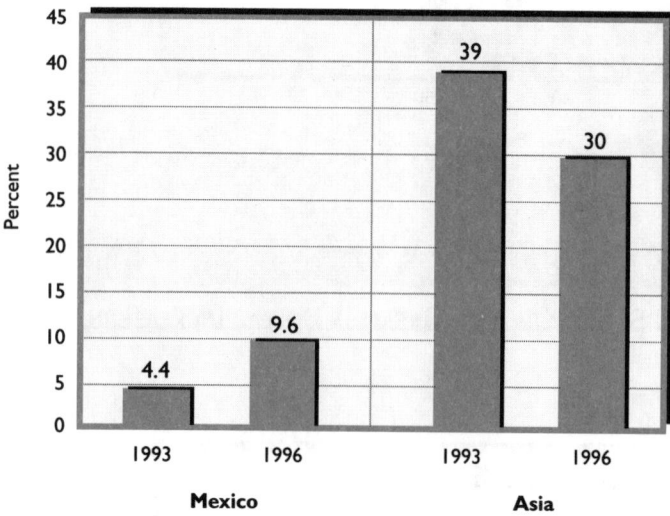

LABOR PROTECTION

The North American Agreement on Labor Cooperation (NAALC) established by the NAFTA has, for the first time, created North American cooperation on fundamental labor issues and has enhanced oversight and enforcement of labor laws.

- The NAALC submission process subjects member governments to public and international attention for alleged violations of labor laws. The submission process has resulted in such outcomes as recognition of a union previously denied recognition and permitting secret union ballots at two companies where union votes previously were not secret.

- Between 1993 and 1996, Mexico's Secretariat of Labor and Social Welfare increased funding for enforcement of labor laws by almost 250 percent.

- Mexico reports a 30 percent reduction in the number of workplace injuries and illnesses since the NAFTA was signed.

- Under the NAALC, the Canadian, Mexican, and U.S. governments have initiated cooperative efforts on a variety of labor issues, including occupational safety and health, employment and training, industrial relations, worker rights and child labor and gender issues.

Environmental Protection

NAFTA includes mechanisms to address environmental problems that have long challenged communities along the 2000-mile shared border with Mexico. NAFTA's environmental agreements are also encouraging regional cooperation on broader environmental issues and improved enforcement of Mexican environmental laws.

- Environmental institutions established under NAFTA are certifying and financing infrastructure projects designed to improve the environment along the U.S.-Mexico border. To date, 16 projects have been certified with a combined cost of nearly $230 million. Construction has already begun on seven projects, including a water treatment facility in Brawley, California and a water supply project in Mercedes, Texas. The NADBank will be able to leverage its capital into $2 to $3 billion in lending.

- The NAFTA Commission for Environmental Cooperation (CEC) has strengthened trilateral cooperation on a broad range of environmental issues, including illegal trade in hazardous wastes, endangered wildlife, and the elimination of certain toxic chemicals and pesticides.

- Through the CEC, Mexico has agreed to join the United States and Canada in banning the pesticides DDT and chlordane, ensuring that these long-lived, toxic substances no longer cross our border.

- The United States and Mexico have launched a Border XXI program establishing five-year objectives for achieving a clean border environment and a blueprint for meeting these objectives. U.S. and Mexican officials are now working to abate emissions from vehicles at border crossings, tracking transboundary shipments of hazardous wastes, and operating a U.S.-Mexico Joint Response Team to minimize the risk of chemical accidents, to name just a few activities.

- Mexico has established a voluntary environmental auditing program, which has completed audits of 617 facilities to date. Of these, 404 have signed environmental compliance Action Plans representing more than $800 million in environmental investments in Mexico.

- Mexico reports a 72 percent reduction in serious environmental violations in the maquiladora industry since the NAFTA was signed, and a 43 percent increase in the number of maquiladora facilities in complete compliance.

APPENDIX B: THE NORTH AMERICAN INDUSTRY CLASSIFICATION SYSTEM[1]

The United States, Canada, and Mexico have developed a common North American Industrial Classification System (NAICS). The revised system recognizes the information industries as a major economic sector and expands the classifications for service industries. In the United States, economic census data for 1997 will be collected in 1998 using the new classifications; publication of these data will begin in 1999. Full implementation of the NAICS by all the U.S. statistical agencies will take until 2004 or longer.

The North American Industry Classification System (NAICS) replaces the existing U.S. Standard Industrial Classification (SIC) system, the Mexican *Clasificacíon Mexicana de Actividads y Productos* (CMAP), and the Canadian Standard Industrial Classification (CSIC). The new system was officially adopted early in 1997, and the first publication of U.S. economic census data based on the new classifications is scheduled for early 1999.

BACKGROUND

For more than 50 years, the SIC system has been used by U.S. federal agencies—and many private sources—to classify establishments by industry and to collect, tabulate, and publish statistical information. The purpose has been to provide analytically useful standardized groupings and to promote comparability of data from different sources.

Despite periodic revisions, the basic structure of the SIC has remained substantially the same over the past half-century. In recent years, the SIC has been criticized for having an over-emphasis on manufacturing, inadequate service categories, and a lack of adequate classifications for new industries.

In 1992 U.S. statistical agencies began working with their Canadian and Mexican counterparts to develop a common North American classification system. The objectives of this effort were much broader than for previous revisions of the U.S. SIC. Not only were new industries to be identified, but the system was to be reorganized according to a more consistent economic principle—according to types of production activities performed—rather than the mixture of production-based and market-based categories in the SIC. Most importantly, the system was to accommodate the industrial classification needs of the three North American countries and provide them with a common basis for analyzing industrial structure and performance.

The new NAICS classifications now have been officially adopted by all three countries. The new U.S. code has been published in the Federal Register, and an official printed manual is scheduled for release by the Office of Management and Budget (OMB) early in 1998. Background papers explaining the principles on which the new system is based also have been made available.[2] The tasks that now remain—and they are daunting—are the actual implementation of the new system by the statistical agencies and the transition to the new concepts by suppliers and users of economic data.

---

[1] Much of the information in this article is adapted from Paul T. Zeisset and Mark E. Wallace, How NAICS Will Affect Data Users, U.S. Bureau of the Census, 1997. This and many other documents pertaining to NAICS may be found on the Bureau of the Census web site at the following address: http://www.census.gov/epcd/www/naics.html

[2] The Federal Register Notice containing the NAICS structure was published on April 9, 1997. This and previous notices and the background papers are available on the Bureau of the Census web site referenced in the note above.

TABLE 1

NAICS Sectors and their Corresponding SIC Divisions

Code	NAICS Sector	SIC Divisions Making the Largest Contributions
11	Agriculture, Forestry, Hunting, and Fishing	Agriculture, Forestry and Fishing Manufacturing
21	Mining	Mineral Industries
22	Utilities	Transportation, Communications, and Utilities
23	Construction	Construction Industries
31-33	Manufacturing	Manufacturing
43	Wholesale Trade	Wholesale Trade
44-45	Retail Trade	Retail Trade Wholesale Trade
48-49	Transportation and Warehousing	Transportation, Communications, and Utilities
51	Information	Transportation, Communications, and Utilities Manufacturing Service Industries
52	Finance and Insurance	Finance, Insurance, and Real Estate
53	Real Estate and Rental and Leasing	Finance, Insurance, and Real Estate Service Industries
54	Professional, Scientific, and Technical Services	Service Industries
55	Management of Companies and Enterprises	Finance, Insurance, and Real Estate Auxiliary establishments in all industries
57	Administrative and Support, Waste Management and Remediation Services	Service Industries Transportation, Communications, and Utilities Manufacturing Construction Industries
61	Education Services	Service Industries
62	Health Care and Social Assistance	Service Industries
71	Arts, Entertainment, and Recreation	Service Industries Retail Trade Finance, Insurance, and Real Estate
72	Accommodation and Food Services	Retail Trade Service Industries
81	Other Services (except Public Administration)	Service Industries Finance, Insurance, and Real Estate
93	Public Administration	Public Administration Service Industries

THE NAICS STRUCTURE

The NAICS classifications incorporate major changes from the familiar SIC. A number of new major sectors are created, and a new 6-digit industry numbering system is used.

The NAICS sectors. NAICS groups the economy into 20 broad sectors, compared to the 10 divisions of the SIC system (Table 1). Many of the new sectors consist largely of recognizable parts of SIC divisions. The transportation sector, for example, is broken out from the SIC Transportation, Communications, and Utilities division. Similarly, the SIC division for Service Industries has been subdivided to form several sectors, including Professional, Scientific, and Technical Services; Education Services; and Health and Social Assistance.

Other sectors represent combinations of pieces from more than one SIC Division. The new Information sector includes major components from Transportation, Communications, and Utilities (broadcasting and telecommunications), Manufacturing (publishing), and Services Industries (software publishing, data processing, information services, motion picture, and sound recording). The Accommodations and Food Services sector brings together hotels and other lodging places from Service Industries and eating and drinking places from Retail Trade.

The NAICS numbering system. NAICS industries are identified by a 6-digit code, in contrast to the 4-digit SIC code. The longer code accommodates the larger number of sectors and allows more flexibility in designating subsectors. It also provides for additional detail not necessarily appropriate for all three NAICS countries. The international NAICS agreement fixes only the first five digits of the code. The sixth digit, where used, identifies subdivisions of NAICS industries that accommodate user needs in individual countries. Thus, 6-digit U.S. codes may differ from counterparts in Canada or Mexico, but at the 5-digit level they are standardized.

Table 2 illustrates the hierarchic structure of the NAICS codes.

TABLE 2

EXAMPLES OF NAICS HIERARCHY

NAICS LEVEL	NAICS CODE	DESCRIPTION
EXAMPLE #1		
Sector	31-33	Manufacturing
Subsector	334	Computer and electronic product manufacturing
Industry group	3346	Manufacturing and reproduction of magnetic and optical media
Industry	33461	Manufacturing and reproduction of magnetic and optical media
U.S. Industry	334611	Reproduction of software
EXAMPLE #2		
Sector	51	Information
Subsector	513	Broadcasting and telecommunications
Industry group	5133	Telecommunications
Industry	51332	Wireless telecommunications carriers, except satellite
U.S. Industry	513321	Paging transmissions services

DATA COMPARABILITY

Because the NAICS is so different from the SIC, users wanting to construct historical time series may face substantial difficulties with respect to some industries. Data for two-thirds of all 4-digit SICs will be derivable from the NAICS data, either because the industry is not being changed (other than in code) or because new industries are being defined as subdivisions of old ones. For the remaining industries, however, there will be breaks in series, and the broad sectors like manufacturing and retailing that we use to describe our economy in everyday conversation will lose some of their historical comparability.

The problem of data comparability was recognized, but the government committee working on the new industrial classification concluded that "it is unproductive to collect and maintain time series data that have questionable value. Thus, it may be preferable to accept a onetime break in historical continuity if the benefits of conversion to a new classification structure are apparent and accepted by users."[3]

Ideally, it would be desirable to retabulate historical data, such as the results of the 1992 U.S. Economic Censuses, using the new classifications. This will not be possible for all industries. Many of the new classifications require information that is not available from the 1992 Census questionnaires. However, as part of its publication plans for the 1997 Economic Censuses, the Census Bureau plans to construct bridge tables and comparative statistics tables to assist data users in making the best possible historical comparisons.[4]

DATA COLLECTION AND PUBLICATION PLANS: THE UNITED STATES

The first data collection using the new classifications will begin early in 1998. The first U.S. data publication is planned for 1999, but full implementation by all the statistical agencies will take until 2004 or longer.

The economic censuses. Early in 1998 the Census Bureau will begin the collection of data for the 1997 Economic Censuses, that is, data pertaining to the year 1997. The questionnaires will be designed to enable the bureau to classify each establishment according to both the SIC and the NAICS.

In early 1999, in its first "advance" report covering the entire U.S. economy, the bureau plans to publish national data for 1997 on a NAICS basis (3-digit sector detail), and comparative statistics for 1997 and 1992 on a 1987 SIC basis (2-digit detail). State level data also will be published, but in less detail; only data for the NAICS 2-digit sectors and comparative statistics for the 10 SIC divisions will be shown.

Roughly a year later, in early 2000, the bureau plans to publish detailed bridge tables covering all industries at the national level, and comparative statistics for all industries at both state and national levels. All other data will be published only on a new, NAICS basis. No comparability tables will be available for metropolitan areas, counties, or cities. All substate data from the 1997 Census will be published on a NAICS basis only.

The Census Bureau's ability to provide comparative and bridge tables is constrained not only by the inherent limitations of the available data, but also by the need for disclosure-avoidance procedures. Federal statistical agencies protect the confidentiality of the information provided by businesses by avoiding the publication of any data that could be identified with an individual establishment or company. Some of the SIC-to-NAICS comparisons may contain so few establishments that the comparisons are dominated by individual companies that could be identified. This would preclude publication of some parts of the comparative and bridge tables, even at the national level.

---

[3] U.S. Economic Classification Policy Committee Issue Paper Number 5 "The Impact of Classification Revisions on Time Series," July 1993.

[4] "Comparative statistics" tables present new data according to the old system, along with data from one or more earlier censuses based on the same system for comparison. "Bridge" tables take interrelating the old and new classifications one step farther. They present new data cross-tabulated by both old and new classification systems at the same time, identifying the most detailed level of comparison between the two systems.

TABLE 3

TENTATIVE U.S. PUBLICATION SCHEDULE FOR SELECTED NAICS-BASED DATA

BUREAU OF THE CENSUS	
1997 Economic Census Reports	1999-2001
Export/Import Data Conversion	1998
County Business Patterns	2000
Annual Survey of Manufactures	2000
Other Current Economic Surveys	2001
BUREAU OF ECONOMIC ANALYSIS	
Direct Investment Surveys	1999-2002
Benchmark Input-Output Accounts	2002
Corporate Profits	2001
State Personal Income	2001
Gross Product Originating by Industry	2002
Real Inventories and Sales	2002
Gross State Product by Industry	2003
BUREAU OF LABOR STATISTICS	
Employment and Wages Report	2001
Current Employment Statistics Survey	2003
Occupational Employment Statistics	2003
Producer Price Index/1997 Net Output Indexes	2004

Budgetary limitations also constrain the ability of the Census Bureau and other statistical agencies to move quickly to fully implement the NAICS. For example, the agricultural services, forestry, and fisheries division of the SIC is not covered by the economic censuses. NAICS moves some activities from this division into other economic sectors. Veterinary services and landscape design, for example, are moved to the Professional, Scientific and Technical Services sector. Summaries for that sector in the economic censuses will be incomplete until funding is available to cover the industries not previously included.

Data collection and publication plans: other U.S. statistical programs. The introduction of NAICS will have a far-reaching impact on the entire U.S. statistical system. The Census Bureau's many annual and monthly economic statistics, the national accounts statistics from the Bureau of Economic Analysis, the Federal Reserve Board's industrial production statistics, and the employment, price, and productivity statistics from the Bureau of Labor Statistics all must be converted to the new system. Implementation will, at best, take several years. Table 3 summarizes agencies present time schedule for publishing NAICS-based data from some of the major statistical programs. Difficulties in obtaining funding could cause current conversion plans to be further stretched out.

Among presently-planned implementation activities are the following.

The Census Bureau will accelerate its business sample revision for the monthly and annual surveys of retail trade, wholesale trade, and service industries. This sample revision has occurred five years after the reference year for recent censuses; this time it is hoped to do it in three years to allow earlier implementation of NAICS for these current economic surveys.

The Census Bureau, in consultation with the Bureau of Economic Analysis (BEA) and other agencies, is considering possibilities for redefining the scope of its economic surveys. For example, Retail Sales will cover fewer industries under NAICS, particularly since eating and drinking places are moving to the Accommodations Sector. The Census Bureau may combine retail and service surveys so as to be able to report monthly changes in "personal consumption expenditures," consistent with concepts used by BEA in the national accounts. BEA's ability to maintain the quality of their estimates of national account aggregates will be dependent on continuing to receive economic survey data from the Census Bureau that is at least as comprehensive as that presently available, despite the shifts in the sectoral classifications for some industries.

The Bureau of Economic Analysis will use the 1997 Census data to develop NAICS-based input-output tables for 1997 and hopes to complete this process by 2002. In its surveys of foreign direct investment, BEA will begin data collection using the NAICS categories in 1998, with publication scheduled for the summer of 1999.

The Bureau of Labor Statistics (BLS) plans to have both NAICS and SIC codes assigned to all establishments in its employment and wages (ES-202) program by the end of the year 2000, assuming funding can be provided to states to accomplish the manual coding of 3.5 million establishments in industries being redefined. The dual-coded database will serve as the foundation for converting a number of other BLS programs. Converting the BLS productivity time series is dependent on the availability of NAICS-based input from Census and BEA, hence publication of these data is not expected until 2004.

CANADA

In Canada, the first data collection will be for the reference year 1997, and the first data publication is planned for 1999. The NAICS Canada manual is to be released in printed form early in 1998; a sample electronic version is available on the Statistics Canada web site.[5]

Statistics Canada has completed its initial conversion of their Business Register, the basic mailing lists for their surveys. The final conversion to NAICS is planned for December 1998. Annual surveys, beginning with the 1997 reference year, will be collected on the NAICS Canada basis. Monthly surveys and the national accounts will be converted in calendar year 2000. Publication of data using the NAICS system is expected to begin in the 1999-2000 period.[6]

TABLE 4

TENTATIVE CANADIAN PUBLICATION SCHEDULE FOR NAICS-BASED DATA

PROGRAM	IMPLEMENTATION DATE
BUSINESS REGISTER	INITIAL CONVERSION JULY 1997 FINAL CONVERSION DECEMBER 1998
ANNUAL BUSINESS SURVEYS	1997 REFERENCE YEAR ON NAICS BASIS
MONTHLY/QUARTERLY SURVEYS	CALENDAR YEAR 2000
SYSTEM OF NATIONAL ACCOUNTS	CALENDAR YEAR 2000

MEXICO

Mexico will use the new NAICS for the first time in its next National Economic Censuses. Data will be collected during 1999 and will pertain to the reference year 1998.[7]

The transition from the individual classification systems of the three NAFTA countries to NAICS is requiring major efforts on the part of the statistical agencies, and the transition can occur only at the cost of some loss of historical comparability in economic data. However, the conversion to a common updated system is a crucial step toward a strong foundation for statistical information in coming decades.

---

[5] Http://www.statcan.ca/english/Standards/stand.htm

[6] Communication with Mr. Kim Farrall, Standards Division, Statistics Canada, December 2, 1997.

[7] Http://www.inegi.gob.mx

APPENDIX C: GOVERNMENTAL STRUCTURE—CANADA, MEXICO, AND THE UNITED STATES

The following information on the governmental structure of Canada, Mexico, and the United States has been excerpted from U.S. government sources as noted.

CANADA[1]

GOVERNMENT

Type of Government	Confederation with parliamentary democracy.
Independence	July 1, 1867.
Constitution	The amended British North America Act of 1867 patriated to Canada on April 17, 1982, Charter of Rights and Freedoms, and unwritten custom.
Executive	Queen Elizabeth II (head of state, represented by a governor general), prime minister (head of government), cabinet.
Legislative	bicameral parliament (301-member House of Commons, 104-member Senate).
Judicial	Supreme Court.
Political parties	Liberal Party, Reform Party, Bloc Quebecois, New Democratic Party, Progressive Conservative Party.
Subdivisions	10 provinces, 2 territories.

Canada is a constitutional monarchy with a federal system, a parliamentary government, and strong democratic traditions. Many of the country's legal practices are based on unwritten custom, but the federal structure resembles the U.S. system. The 1982 Charter of Rights guarantees basic rights in many areas.

Queen Elizabeth II, as Queen of Canada, serves as a symbol of the nation's unity. She appoints a governor general on the advice of the prime minister of Canada, usually for a five-year term. The prime minister is the leader of the political party in power and is the head of the cabinet. The cabinet remains in office as long as it retains majority support in the House of Commons on major issues.

Canada's parliament consists of an elected House of Commons and an appointed Senate. Legislative power rests with the 301-member Commons, which is elected for a period not to exceed five years. The prime minister may ask the governor general to dissolve parliament and call new elections at any time during that period. Federal elections were last held in June 1997. Vacancies in the 104-member Senate, whose members serve until the age of 75, are filled by the governor general on the advice of the prime minister. Recent constitutional initiatives have sought unsuccessfully to strengthen the Senate by making it elective and assigning it a greater regional representational role.

[1] Excerpted from the U.S. Department of State Background Notes, October 1997.

Head of State . . . . .Queen Elizabeth II

Governor General . . . . .Roméo LeBlanc

Prime Minister . . . . .Jean Chrétien

Minister of Foreign Affairs . . . . .Lloyd Axworthy

Ambassador to the United States . . . . .Raymond Chretién

Ambassador to the United Nations . . . . .Robert Fowler

Canada maintains an embassy in the United States at 501 Pennsylvania Avenue, NW, Washington, D.C. 20001 (tel. 202-682-1740).

Criminal law, based largely on British law, is uniform throughout the nation and is under federal jurisdiction. Civil law is also based on the common law of England, except in Quebec, which has retained its own civil code patterned after that of France. Justice is administered by federal, provincial, and municipal courts.

Each province is governed by a premier and a single, elected legislative chamber. A lieutenant-governor appointed by the governor general represents the Crown in each province.

Political Conditions

Prime Minister Jean Chretién's liberal government was elected to a second term on June 2, 1997, winning 155 of parliament's 301 seats. These results reflected slippage from the Liberals' 1993 total, when the party took 178 of 295 seats. In the 1997 vote, the sovereigntist Bloc Quebecois (with 44 seats), which constituted Canada's official opposition from 1993-97, was displaced by the western-based Reform Party, which won 60 seats. Canada's two historic opposition parties—the Progressive Conservative Party and the New Democratic Party— regained official party status in the 1997 election with 20 and 21 seats respectively, after their near total eclipse in the 1993 poll.

Federal-provincial interplay is a central feature of Canadian politics: Quebec wishes to preserve and strengthen its distinctive nature; western provinces desire more control over their abundant natural resources, especially energy reserves; industrialized central Canada is concerned with economic development; and the Atlantic provinces have resisted federal claims to fishing and mineral rights off their shores.

The Chretién government has responded to these different regional needs by seeking to rebalance the Canadian confederation, giving up its spending power in areas of provincial jurisdiction, while attempting to strengthen the federal role in other areas. The Federal government has reached agreement with a number of provinces returning to them authority over job training programs and is embarked on similar initiatives in other fields. Meanwhile, it has attempted to strengthen the national role on interprovincial trade, while also seeking national regulation of securities.

National Unity

Key to the national unity debate is the ongoing issue of Quebec separatism. Following the failure of two constitutional initiatives in the last decade, Canada is still seeking a constitutional settlement that will satisfy the aspirations of the French-speaking province of Quebec.

The issue has been a fixture in Canadian history, dating back to the 18th-century rivalry between France and Britain. For more than a century, Canada was a French colony. Although New France came under British control in 1759, it was permitted to retain its religious and civil code.

The early 1960s brought a Quiet Revolution to Quebec, leading to a new assertiveness and heightened sense of identity among the French-speaking Quebecois, who make up about one-quarter of Canada's population. In 1976, the separatist Parti Quebecois won the provincial election and began to explore a course for Quebec of greater independence from the rest of Canada.

In a 1980 referendum, the Parti Quebecois sought a mandate from the people of Quebec to negotiate a new status of sovereignty-association, combining political independence with a continued economic association with the rest of Canada. Sixty percent of Quebec voters rejected the proposal.

Subsequently, an agreement between the federal government and all provincial governments except Quebec, led to Canada in 1982 assuming from the United Kingdom full responsibility for its own constitution. Quebec objected to certain aspects of the new arrangement, including a constitutional amending formula that did not require consensus among all provinces. The 1987 Meech Lake Accord sought to address Quebec's concerns and bring it back into Canada's constitutional fold. Quebec's provincial government, then controlled by federalists, strongly endorsed the accord, but lack of support in Newfoundland and Manitoba prevented it from taking effect. Rejected in its bid for special constitutional recognition, Quebec's provincial government authorized a second sovereignty referendum.

Intense negotiations among Quebec, the federal government, and other provinces led to a second proposed constitutional accord in 1992—the Charlottetown Accord. Despite near-unanimous support from the country's political leaders, this second effort at constitutional reform was defeated in Quebec and the rest of Canada in an October 1992 nationwide referendum.

Tired of the country's constitutional deadlock, many Canadians prefer to focus on economic issues. Nonetheless, the election of the sovereigntist Bloc Quebecois as Canada's official opposition in 1993 and the subsequent election of the separatist Parti Quebecois as Quebec's provincial government in September 1994 kept national unity in the forefront of political debate and resulted in a second referendum on the issue.

This referendum, held in Quebec on October 30, 1995, resulted in a narrow 50.56 to 49.44 percent victory for federalists over sovereigntists. Quebec's status thus remains a serious political issue in Canada, and the province's Parti Quebecois government remains committed to calling a third referendum if it wins a second term in provincial elections that must be held before the end of 1999.

U.S.-Canada Relations

The bilateral relationship between the United States and Canada is perhaps the closest and most extensive in the world. It is reflected in the staggering volume of trade—over US$1 billion a day—and people- nearly 100 million a year-crossing the U.S.-Canadian border. In fields ranging from environmental cooperation to free trade, the two countries have set the standard by which many other countries measure their own progress.

In addition to their close bilateral ties, Canada and the U.S. also work closely through multilateral fora. Canada—a charter signatory to the United Nations and the North Atlantic Treaty Organization (NATO)—has continued to take an active role in the United Nations, including peacekeeping operations. It is also an active participant in discussions stemming from the Organization for Security and Cooperation in Europe (OSCE). Canada joined the Organization of American States (OAS) in 1990 and has been an active member. It seeks to expand its economic ties across the Pacific through membership in the Asia-Pacific Economic Cooperation forum (APEC)—of which the U.S. is also a member—and which it will host in 1997.

Although Canada views its relationship with the U.S. as crucial to a wide range of interests, it also occasionally pursues policies at odds with the United States. This is particularly true of Cuba, with regard to which the U.S. and Canada have pursued divergent policies for nearly 40 years, even while sharing the common goal of a peaceful democratic transition.

U.S. defense arrangements with Canada are more extensive than with any other country. The Permanent Joint Board on Defense, established in 1940, provides policy-level consultation on bilateral defense matters. The United States and Canada share NATO mutual security commitments. In addition, U.S. and Canadian military forces have cooperated since 1958 on continental air defense within the framework of the North American Aerospace Defense Command (NORAD).

The two countries also work closely to resolve transboundary environmental issues, an area of increasing importance in the bilateral relationship. A principal instrument of this cooperation is the International Joint Commission (IJC), established as part of the Boundary Waters Treaty of 1909 to resolve differences and promote international cooperation on boundary waters. The Great Lakes Water Quality Agreement of 1972 is another historic example of joint cooperation in controlling transboundary water pollution. The two governments also consult semiannually on trans-boundary air pollution. Under the Air Quality Agreement of 1991, both countries have made substantial progress in coordinating and implementing their acid rain control programs.

PRINCIPAL U.S. EMBASSY OFFICIALS

Ambassador	Gordon D. Giffin
Deputy Chief of Mission	Mary Ann Peters
Minister	Counselor for Political Affairs—Christine Shelly
Minister-Counselor for Economic Affairs	Vladimir Sambaiew
Minister-Counselor for PublicAffairs	Gail Gulliksen
Minister-Counselor for CommercialAffairs	Dale Slaght

The U.S. embassy in Canada is located at 100 Wellington Street, Ottawa (tel. 613-238-5335), directly across from Parliament Hill.

UNITED MEXICAN STATES[2]

GOVERNMENT

Type of Government	Federal republic.
Independence	First proclaimed September 16, 1810; republic established 1824.
Constitution	February 5, 1917.
Executive	President (chief of state and head of government).
Legislative	Bicameral.
Judicial	Supreme Court, local and federal systems.
Political parties	Institutional Revolutionary Party (PRI), National Action Party (PAN), Party of the Democratic Revolution(PRD), Green Ecological Party (PVEM), Labor Party (PT), and several small parties. Suffrage: Universal at 18.
Administrative subdivisions	31 states and a federal district.

[2] Excerpted from the U.S. Department of State, Background Notes, April 1997.

The 1917 constitution provides for a federal republic with powers separated into independent executive, legislative, and judicial branches. In practice, the executive is the dominant branch, with power vested in the president, who promulgates and executes the laws of the Congress. The president also legislates by executive decree in certain economic and financial fields, using powers delegated from the Congress. The president is elected by universal adult suffrage for a six-year term and may not hold office a second time. There is no vice president; in the event of the removal or death of the president, a provisional president is elected by the Congress.

The Congress is composed of a Senate and a Chamber of Deputies. Consecutive re-election is prohibited. Senators are elected to six-year terms. Implementing constitutional changes made in 1996,for the first time on July 6, 1997, 32 of the 128 seats in the Senate will be elected by proportional representation from party lists on a national basis. With this change, some states may have more Senators than others. The 32 Senators elected in 1997 will only serve three-year terms, in order to bring the entire Senate back into the same cycle in the year 2000. Deputies serve three-year terms. In the lower chamber, 300 Deputies are directly elected to represent single-member districts, and 200 are selected by a modified form of proportional representation from five electoral regions created for this purpose across the country. The 200 proportional representation seats were created to help smaller parties gain access to the Chamber.

The judiciary is divided into federal and state court systems, with federal courts having jurisdiction over most civil cases and those involving major felonies. Under the constitution, trial and sentencing must be completed within 12 months of arrest for crimes that would carry at least a two-year sentence. Practice often does not meet this requirement. Trial is by judge, not jury, in most criminal cases. Defendants have a right to counsel, and public defenders are available. Other rights include defense against self-incrimination, the right to confront one's accusers, and the right to a public trial. Supreme Court Justices are appointed by the President and approved by the Senate.

PRINCIPAL MEXICAN GOVERNMENT OFFICIALS

President . . . . .Ernesto ZEDILLO Ponce de Leon

Foreign Minister . . . . .Jose Angel GURRIA Trevino

Ambassador to the U.S. .Jesus REYES Heroles

Ambassador to the United Nations . . . . .Manuel TELLO Macias

Ambassador to the OAS .Carmen MORENO de del Cueto

Mexico maintains an embassy in the United States at 1911 Pennsylvania Ave. NW, Washington, DC 20006 (tel. 202-728-1600).
Consular offices are located at 2827 16th St. NW, 20009 (tel. 202-736-1012), and the trade office is co-located at the embassy (tel. 202-728-1686).

Consulates general are located in Chicago, Dallas, Denver, El Paso, Houston, Los Angeles, Miami, New Orleans, New York, San Antonio, San Diego, and San Francisco; consulates are (partial listing) in Atlanta, Boston, Detroit, Philadelphia, Seattle, St. Louis, and Tucson.

Political Conditions

Ernesto Zedillo Ponce de Leon was sworn in on December 1, 1994, as the President of Mexico. A trained economist with degrees from Yale, Zedillo served as Secretary of Programming and Budget and Secretary of Education in the Salinas Administration prior to being elected.

President Zedillo continued the process already underway of opening Mexico's political system, reforming the justice system, curtailing corruption, strengthening the fight against narcotics trafficking, and furthering Mexico's market-oriented economic policies. A severe financial crisis occupied much of the Zedillo Administration's attention in 1995-96, creating a need for difficult emergency economic stabilization policies and intensified longer-term economic restructuring. Significant progress has been achieved in some areas.

Political Scene. Unexpected and traumatic events in early 1994 convulsed the Mexican political scene. In January 1994, peasants in the state of Chiapas briefly took up arms against the government, protesting alleged oppression and governmental indifference to poverty. The government and the Zapatista Army of National Liberation (EZLN) have negotiated on topics such as granting greater autonomy to indigenous peoples since then, reaching several partial accords. There have been no clashes since the government's unilaterally declared cease-fire in 1994, and the two sides remain committed to a negotiated peace settlement.

In March 1994, PRI presidential candidate Luis Donaldo Colosio was assassinated. In September 1994, PRI Secretary General Jose Francisco Ruiz Massieu was also assassinated. Although the gunmen in both murders and co-conspirators in the Ruiz Massieu murder were tried and convicted, the Mexican public is not satisfied that all the truth behind these crimes has been uncovered.

Investigations into the murders resulted in the apprehensions in February 1995 of a second gunman in the Colosio murder, the arrest of the brother of former president Carlos Salinas as a suspected mastermind behind the second crime, and the filing of charges in March 1995 against the brother of Ruiz Massieu for obstructing investigations into the murder. Additional charges, including illegal enrichment for amassing multi-million dollar fortunes in overseas bank accounts, were filed against both men and investigations were widened to include their associates.

This has led to a flurry of public scandals regarding supposed attempts at obstruction of justice and allegations of major corruption in police, judicial, military and other authorities, as well as big business, including allegations of ties to narcotics trafficking. The atmosphere of scandal around former President Carlos Salinas has turned him into something of an arch-villain in the popular mind.

A new group of uncertain origin and size, the Popular Revolutionary Army (EPR), made its appearance in southern Mexico on June 28, 1996. The Government considers the EPR a terrorist organization and has vowed to bring the group to justice. This and the assassination of senior law enforcement officers by suspected drug traffickers in northern Mexico also has contributed to increased attention and concern over public safety.

Recent Elections and Electoral Reform. A record 78 percent of registered voters cast ballots in the August 21, 1994, elections. Election officials declared Zedillo of the PRI the winner with 49 percent of the vote, followed by National Action Party (PAN) candidate Diego Fernandez de Cevallos with 26 percent and Cuauhtemoc Cardenas of the Party of the Democratic Revolution (PRD) with 17 percent. Despite isolated incidents of irregularities and problems, there was no evidence of systematic attempts to manipulate the elections or their results, and critics concluded that the irregularities which did occur did not alter the outcome of the presidential vote. Civic organizations fielded more than 80,000 trained electoral observers; foreigners — many from the United States — were invited to witness the process, and numerous independent "quick count" operations and exit polls validated the official vote tabulation.

These extraordinary electoral observation measures were needed to overcome public suspicions that electoral fraud might be committed. Over the years, the PRI has relied on extensive patronage and massive government and party organizational resources to maintain its continuance in power. In many cases, the party has been accused of fraud. However, as numerous electoral reforms implemented since 1989 have aided in the further opening of the Mexican political system, opposition parties have made historic gains in elections at all levels. Most of the concerns shifted from fraud to campaign fairness issues.

During 1995-96 the political parties negotiated constitutional amendments to address electoral campaign fairness issues, which passed unanimously. In these negotiations, the parties were supported by consultations with civic organizations. It proved a disappointment when implementing legislation could not also be passed by consensus due primarily to disagreements over levels of public funding for political parties. The package of laws passed by the PRI majority in congress did include, however, major points of consensus that had been worked out with the opposition parties. The thrust of the new laws is to have public financing predominate over private contributions to political parties, to tighten procedures for auditing the political parties, and to strengthen the authority and independence of electoral institutions.

Even before the new electoral law was passed, opposition parties obtained an increasing voice in Mexico's political system. A substantial number of candidates from opposition parties won election to the Chamber of Deputies and Senate. Many municipalities were governed by opposition mayors, and the PAN won the governorships of four states.

The court system was also given greatly expanded authority to hear civil rights cases on electoral matters brought by individuals or groups. In short, a serious effort was made to "level the playing field" for the parties.

Mid-term elections held July 6, 1997 saw large gains for opposition parties and marked a significant step in Mexico's political transformation. For the first time in its 68-year history, the PRI lost its absolute majority in the Chamber of Deputies. The opposition majority is split among four parties: the PRD, the PAN and two small parties, the Labor Party (PT), and the Green Ecological Party (PVEM). The opposition also gained ground in the Senate, where the PRI still retains an overall majority but fell below the two-thirds majority important in constitutional amendments.

In another important electoral development, the PRD candidate, Cuauhtemoc Cardenas, won the first modern election for mayor of Mexico City (this post was previously appointed by the Mexican president). In state elections, the PAN won two additional governorships, giving it a total of six. More than 40% of Mexico's population is now governed by an opposition party at the state or municipal level.

Other Reforms. To help reorganize the Mexican justice system, President Zedillo appointed as Attorney General a respected member of the opposition PAN party, the first time an opposition member has held a cabinet post in Mexico. (Attorney General Antonio Lozano was dismissed in late 1996 amid controversy regarding investigations into prominent murder and corruption cases.) Constitutional and legal changes were adopted to improve the performance and accountability of the Supreme Court and the Office of the Attorney General and the administration of federal courts. The Supreme Court, relieved of administrative duties for lower courts, was given responsibilities for judicial review of certain categories of law and legislation. A variety of laws was also passed in 1995-96 to help control organized crime.

Although the constitution provides for three branches of government, the Mexican presidency traditionally occupies a dominant position. In order to overcome this "presidentialism," the Zedillo Administration has sought to develop a greater role for the Congress, notably by inviting the participation of a multi-party legislative commission in the Chiapas peace negotiations and seeking congressional approval of the financial assistance package signed by the U.S. and Mexico in February 1995. The judicial reforms mentioned above are in part designed to allow the judicial branch of government to become a more effective counterweight to the other two branches. The Zedillo Administration has also promoted a "New Federalism" to devolve more power to state and local governments, starting with pilot programs in education and health.

Education

Although educational levels in Mexico have improved substantially in recent decades, the country still faces daunting problems. Education is one of the Government of Mexico's highest priorities and it has increased the education budget 7.2 percent over 1996 to $15 billion for 1997 — one-fourth of the total budget. Education in Mexico is also being decentralized from federal to state authority in order to improve accountability.

Education is mandatory from ages six through 18. The increase in school enrollments during the past two decades has been dramatic. By 1994, an estimated 59 percent of the population between the ages of six and 18 were enrolled in school. Primary (including preschool) enrollment in public schools from 1970 through 1994 increased from less than 10 million to 17.5 million. Enrollment at the secondary public school level rose from 1.4 million in 1972 to as many as 4.5 million in 1994. A rapid rise also occurred in higher education. Between 1959 and 1994, college enrollments rose from 62,000 to more than 1.2 million.

Although education spending has risen dramatically, given increased enrollment, a net decline occurred in per student expenditures. The Mexican Government concedes that despite this progress, 2 million children still do not have access to basic education, and hopes to provide access to half of those children by the year 2000.

UNITED STATES OF AMERICA[3]

Government

The early American way of life encouraged democracy. The colonists were inhabiting a land of forest and wilderness. They had to work together to build shelter, provide food, and clear the land for farms and dwellings. This need for cooperation strengthened the belief that, in the New World, people should be on an equal footing, with nobody having special privileges.

The urge for equality affected the original 13 colonies' relations with the mother country, England. The Declaration of Independence in 1776 proclaimed that all men are created equal, that all have the right to "Life, Liberty, and the Pursuit of Happiness."

The Declaration of Independence, and the Constitution after it, combined America's colonial experience with the political thought of such philosophers as England's John Locke to produce the concept of a democratic republic. The government would draw its power from the people themselves and exercise it through their elected representatives. During the Revolutionary War, the colonies had formed a national congress to present England with a united front. Under an agreement known as the Articles of Confederation, a postwar congress was allowed to handle only problems that were beyond the capabilities of individual states.

The Constitution

The Articles of Confederation failed as a governing document for the United States because the states did not cooperate as expected. When it came time to pay wages to the national army or the war debt to France, some states refused to contribute. To cure this weakness, the congress asked each state to send a delegate to a convention. The so-called Constitutional Convention met in Philadelphia in May of 1787, with George Washington presiding.

The delegates struck a balance between those who wanted a strong central government and those who did not. The resulting master plan, or Constitution, set up a system in which some powers were given to the national, or federal, government, while others were reserved for the states. The Constitution divided the national government into three parts, or branches: the legislative (the Congress, which consists of a House of Representatives and a Senate), the executive (headed by the president), and the judicial (the federal courts). Called

---

[3] Excerpted from "Portrait of the USA," U.S. Information Agency, International Homepage

"separation of powers," this division gives each branch certain duties and substantial independence from the others. It also gives each branch some authority over the others through a system of "checks and balances."

Here are a few examples of how checks and balances work in practice:

> If Congress passes a proposed law, or "bill," that the president considers unwise, he can veto it. That means that the bill is dead unless two-thirds of the members of both the House and the Senate vote to enact it despite the resident's veto.

> If Congress passes, and the president signs, a law that is challenged in the federal courts as contrary to the Constitution, the courts can nullify that law. (The federal courts cannot issue advisory or theoretical opinions, however; their jurisdiction is limited to actual disputes.)

The president has the power to make treaties with other nations and to make appointments to federal positions, including judgeships. The Senate, however, must approve all treaties and confirm the appointments before they can go into effect.

Recently some observers have discerned what they see as a weakness in the tripartite system of government: a tendency toward too much checking and balancing that results in governmental stasis, or "gridlock."

Bill of Rights

The Constitution written in Philadelphia in 1787 could not go into effect until it was ratified by a majority of citizens in at least 9 of the then 13 U.S. states. During this ratification process, misgivings arose. Many citizens felt uneasy because the document failed to explicitly guarantee the rights of individuals. The desired language was added in 10 amendments to the Constitution, collectively known as the Bill of Rights.

The Bill of Rights guarantees Americans freedom of speech, of religion, and of the press. They have the right to assemble in public places, to protest government actions, and to demand change. There is a right to own firearms. Because of the Bill of Rights, neither police officers nor soldiers can stop and search a person without good reason. Nor can they search a person's home without permission from a court to do so. The Bill of Rights guarantees a speedy trial to anyone accused of a crime. The trial must be by jury if requested, and the accused person must be allowed representation by a lawyer and to call witnesses to speak for him or her. Cruel and unusual punishment is forbidden. With the addition of the Bill of Rights, the Constitution was ratified by all 13 states and went into effect in 1789.

Since then 17 other amendments have been added to the Constitution. Perhaps the most important of these are the Thirteenth and Fourteenth, which outlaw slavery and guarantee all citizens equal protection of the laws, and the Nineteenth, which gives women the right to vote.

The Constitution can be amended in either of two ways. Congress can propose an amendment, provided that two-thirds of the members of both the House and the Senate vote in favor of it. Or the legislatures of two-thirds of the states can call a convention to propose amendments. (This second method has never been used.) In either case a proposed amendment does not go into effect until ratified by three-fourths of the states.

Executive Branch

The chief executive of the United States is the president, who together with the vice president is elected to a four-year term. As a result of a constitutional amendment that went into effect in 1951, a president may be elected to only two terms. Other than succeeding a president who dies or is disabled, the vice president's only official duty is presiding over the Senate. The vice president may vote in the Senate only to break a tie.

The president's powers are formidable but not unlimited. As the chief formulator of national policy, the president proposes legislation to Congress. As mentioned previously, the president may veto any bill passed by Congress. The president is commander-in-chief of the armed forces. The president has the authority to appoint federal judges as vacancies occur, including justices of the Supreme Court. As head of his political party, with ready access to the news media, the president can easily influence public opinion.

Within the executive branch, the president has broad powers to issue regulations and directives carrying out the work of the federal government's departments and agencies. The president appoints the heads and senior officials of those departments and agencies. Heads of the major departments, called "secretaries," are part of the president's cabinet. The majority of federal workers, however, are selected on the basis of merit, not politics.

Legislative Branch

The legislative branch — the Congress — is made up of elected representatives from each of the 50 states. It is the only branch of U.S. government that can make federal laws, levy federal taxes, declare war, and put foreign treaties into effect.

Members of the House of Representatives are elected to two-year terms. Each member represents a district in his or her home state. The number of districts is determined by a census, which is conducted every 10 years. The most populous states are allowed more representatives than the smaller ones, some of which have only one. In all, there are 435 representatives in the House.

Senators are elected to six-year terms. Each state has two senators, regardless of population. Senators' terms are staggered, so that one-third of the Senate stands for election every two years. There are 100 senators.

To become a law, a bill must pass both the House and the Senate. After the bill is introduced in either body, it is studied by one or more committees, amended, voted out of committee, and discussed in the chamber of the House or Senate. If passed by one body, it goes to the other for consideration. When a bill passes the House and the Senate in different forms, members of both bodies meet in a "conference committee" to iron out the differences. Groups that try to persuade members of Congress to vote for or against a bill are called "lobbies." They may try to exert their influence at almost any stage of the legislative process. Once both bodies have passed the same version of a bill, it goes to the president for approval.

Judicial Branch

The judicial branch is headed by the U.S. Supreme Court, which is the only court specifically created by the Constitution. In addition, Congress has established 13 federal courts of appeals and, below them, about 95 federal district courts. The Supreme Court meets in Washington, DC, and the other federal courts are located in cities throughout the United States. Federal judges are appointed for life or until they retire voluntarily; they can be removed from office only via a laborious process of impeachment and trial in the Congress.

The federal courts hear cases arising out of the Constitution and federal laws and treaties, maritime cases, cases involving foreign citizens or governments, and cases in which the federal government is itself a party.

The Supreme Court consists of a chief justice and eight associate justices. With minor exceptions, cases come to the Supreme Court on appeal from lower federal or state courts. Most of these cases involve disputes over the interpretation and constitutionality of actions taken by the executive branch and of laws passed by Congress or the states (like federal laws, state laws must be consistent with the U.S. Constitution).

The Court of Last Resort

Although the three branches are said to be equal, often the Supreme Court has the last word on an issue. The courts can rule a law unconstitutional, which makes it void. Most such rulings are appealed to the Supreme Court, which is thus the final arbiter of what the Constitution means. Newspapers commonly print excerpts from the justices' opinions in important cases, and the Court's decisions are often the subject of public debate. This is as it should be: The decisions may settle long-standing controversies and can have social effects far beyond the immediate outcome. Two famous, related examples are Plessy v. Ferguson (1896) and Brown v. Board of Education of Topeka (1954).

In Plessy the issue was whether blacks could be required to ride in separate railroad cars from whites. The Court articulated a "separate but equal" doctrine as its basis for upholding the practice. The case sent a signal that the Court was interpreting the Thirteenth and Fourteenth Amendments narrowly and that a widespread network of laws and custom treating blacks and whites differently would not be disturbed. One justice, John Marshall Harlan, dissented from the decision, arguing that "the Constitution is color-blind."

Almost 60 years later the Court changed its mind. In Brown the court held that deliberately segregated public schools violated the Fourteenth Amendment's equal protection clause. Although the Court did not directly overrule its Plessy decision, Justice Harlan's view of the Constitution was vindicated. The 1954 ruling applied directly only to schools in the city of Topeka, Kansas, but the principle it articulated reached every public school in the nation. More than that, the case undermined segregation in all governmental endeavors and set the nation on a new course of treating all citizens alike.

The Brown decision caused consternation among some citizens, particularly in the South, but was eventually accepted as the law of the land. Other controversial Supreme Court decisions have not received the same degree of acceptance. In several cases between 1962 and 1985, for example, the Court decided that requiring students to pray or listen to prayer in public schools violated the Constitution's prohibition against establishing a religion. Critics of these decisions believe that the absence of prayer in public schools has contributed to a decline in American morals; they have tried to find ways to restore prayer to the schools without violating the Constitution. In Roe v. Wade (1973), the Court guaranteed women the right to have abortions in certain circumstances — a decision that continues to offend those Americans who consider abortion to be murder. Because the Roe v. Wade decision was based on an interpretation of the Constitution, opponents have been trying to amend the Constitution to overturn it.

Political Parties and Elections

Americans regularly exercise their democratic rights by voting in elections and by participating in political parties and election campaigns. Today, there are two major political parties in the United States, the Democratic and the Republican. The Democratic Party evolved from the party of Thomas Jefferson, formed before1800. The Republican Party was established in the 1850s by Abraham Lincoln and others who opposed the expansion of slavery into new states then being admitted to the Union.

The Democratic Party is considered to be the more liberal party, and the Republican, the more conservative. Democrats generally believe that government has an obligation to provide social and economic programs for those who need them. Republicans are not necessarily opposed to such programs but believe they are often too costly to taxpayers. Republicans put more emphasis on encouraging private enterprise in the belief that a strong private sector makes citizens less dependent on government.

Both major parties have supporters among a wide variety of Americans and embrace a wide range of political views. Members, and even elected officials, of one party do not necessarily agree with each other on every issue. Americans do not have to join a political party to vote or to be a candidate for public office, but running for office without the money and campaign workers a party can provide is difficult.

Minor political parties — generally referred to as "third parties" — occasionally form in the United States, but their candidates are rarely elected to office. Minor parties often serve, however, to call attention to an issue that is of concern to voters, but has been neglected in the political dialogue. When this happens, one or both of the major parties may address the matter, and the third party disappears.

At the national level, elections are held every two years, in even-numbered years, on the first Tuesday following the first Monday in November. State and local elections often coincide with national elections, but they also are held in other years and can take place at other times of year.

Americans are free to determine how much or how little they become involved in the political process. Many citizens actively participate by working as volunteers for a candidate, by promoting a particular cause, or by running for office themselves. Others restrict their participation to voting on election day, quietly letting their democratic system work, confident that their freedoms are protected.

PRINCIPAL U.S. OFFICIALS [4]

Executive

President . . . . William J. Clinton (Democrat)

Vice President . . . . Albert Gore, Jr. (Democrat)

Department of State . . . . Secretary, Madeliene K. Albright

Department of Defense . . . . Secretary, William S. Cohen

Department of the Treasury . . . . Secretary, Robert E. Rubin

Department of Justice . . . . Attorney General, Janet Reno

Department of Commerce . . . . Secretary, William M. Daley

Department of Agriculture . . . . Secretary, Daniel Glickman

Department of Labor . . . . Secretary, Alexis M. Herman

Department of the Interior . . . . Secretary, Bruce Babbitt

Department of Energy . . . . Secretary, Frederico Pena

Department of Education . . . . Secretary, Richard W. Riley

Department of Health and Human Services . . . . Secretary, Donna E. Shalala

Department of Transportation . . . . Secretary, Rodney E. Slater

Department of Housing and Urban
    Development . . . . Secretary, Andrew Cuomo

Department of Veterans Affairs . . . . Secretary, Hershel W. Gober (Acting)

Legislature

House of Representatives with 435 members

Speaker of the House . . . . Newt Gingrich of Georgia (Republican.)

Senate with 100 members (two for each state) called Senators;

Majority Leader . . . . Trent Lott of Mississippi (Republican).

Judiciary

Supreme Court . . . . Chief Justice, William H. Rehnquist

---

[4] Current as of January 1, 1998..

Ambassadors

Canada   Ambassador (vacant)

Ottawa, Ontario, 100 Wellington Street K1P 5T1

Telephone: . . . . (613) 238-5335

Fax   . . . . (613) 238-5720

Mexico   Ambassador (vacant)

Mexico City (E), Paseo de la Reforma 305,06500

Telephone |52| (5) 211-0042

Fax . . . .|52| (5) 208-3373

Chile   Ambassador Gabriel Guerra-Mondragon

Santiago (E), Av. Andres Bello 2800

Telephone . . . .|56| (2) 232-2600

Fax . . . .|56| (2) 330-3710

APPENDIX D: SYNOPSIS OF THE PROPOSED NORTH AMERICAN FREE TRADE AGREEMENT

PREPARED BY THE GOVERNMENTS OF CANADA, THE UNITED MEXICAN STATES AND THE UNITED STATES OF AMERICA, AUGUST 12, 1992

INTRODUCTION

This document provides a synopsis of the proposed North American Free Trade Agreement.

On August 12, 1992, Canadian Minister of Industry, Science and Technology and Minister for International Trade Michael Wilson, Mexican Secretary of Trade and Industrial Development Jaime Serra and United States Trade Representative Carla Hills completed negotiations on a proposed North American Free Trade Agreement (NAFTA). Officials of the three governments have been directed to complete work on the final text of the Agreement as soon as possible. The final text will be made public when completed. The following description does not itself constitute an agreement between the three countries and is not intended as an interpretation of the final text.

For ease of reference a summary of significant environmental provisions of the NAFTA is included at the end of this document.

TABLE OF CONTENTS

11. TECHNICAL STANDARDS

    1. Basic Rights and Obligations

    2. International Standards

    3. Compatibility

    4. Conformity Assessment

    5. Procedural Transparency

    6. Technical Cooperation

    7. Committee on Standards Related Measures

12. EMERGENCY ACTION

    1. Bilateral Safeguard

    2. Global Safeguard

    3. Procedural Requirements

13. REVIEW OF ANTIDUMPING AND COUNTERVAILING DUTY MATTERS

    1. Panel Process

    2. Retention of AD and CVD Laws

    3. Extraordinary Challenge Procedure

    4. Special Committee to Safeguard the Panel Process

14. GOVERNMENT PROCUREMENT

    1. Coverage

    2. Procedural Obligations

    3. Technical Cooperation

    4. Future Negotiations

15. CROSSBORDER TRADE IN SERVICES

    1. National Treatment

    2. Most-Favored-Nation Treatment

    3. Local Presence

    4. Reservations

    5. Non-Discriminatory Quantitative Restrictions

    6. Licensing and Certification

    7. Denial of Benefits

    8. Exclusions

16. LAND TRANSPORTATION

    1. Liberalization of Restrictions

        1. Bus and Trucking Services

        2. Rail Services

        3. Port Services

    2. Technical and Safety Standards

    3. Access to Information

    4. Review Process

21. INTELLECTUAL PROPERTY

    1. Copyright

    2. Patents

    3. Other Intellectual Property Rights

    4. Enforcement Procedures

22. TEMPORARY ENTRY FOR BUSINESS PERSONS

    1. Consultations

    2. Provision of Information

    3. Non-Compliance

23. INSTITUTIONAL ARRANGEMENTS AND DISPUTE SETTLEMENT PROCEDURES

    1. Institutional Arrangements

        1. Trade Commission

        2. Secretariat

    2. Dispute Settlement Procedures

        1. Consultations

        2. The Role of the Commission

        3. Initiation of Panel Proceedings

    3. Forum Selection

    4. Panel Procedures

    5. Implementation and Non-Compliance

    6. Alternate Dispute Resolution of Private Commercial Disputes

24. ADMINISTRATION OF LAWS

    1. Procedural Transparency

    2. Contact Points

25. EXCEPTIONS

    1. General Exceptions

    2. National Security

    3. Taxation

    4. Balance of Payments

    5. Cultural Industries

26. FINAL PROVISIONS

    1. Entry into Force

    2. Accession

    3. Amendments and Withdrawal

27. SUMMARY OF ENVIRONMENTAL PROVISIONS

PREAMBLE

The Preamble to the NAFTA sets out the principles and aspirations on which the Agreement is based. It affirms the three countries' commitment to promoting employment and economic growth in each country through the expansion of trade and investment opportunities in the free trade area and by enhancing the competitiveness of Canadian, Mexican and U.S. firms in global markets, in a manner that protects the environment. The Preamble confirms the resolve of the NAFTA partners to promote sustainable development, to protect, enhance and enforce workers' rights and to improve working conditions in each country.

OBJECTIVES AND OTHER OPENING PROVISIONS

The opening provisions of the NAFTA formally establish a free trade area between Canada, Mexico and the United States, consistent with the General Agreement on Tariffs and Trade (GATT). They set out the basic rules and principles that will govern the Agreement and the objectives that will serve as the basis for interpreting its provisions.

The objectives of the Agreement are to eliminate barriers to trade, promote conditions of fair competition, increase investment opportunities, provide adequate protection for intellectual property rights, establish effective procedures for the implementation and application of the Agreement and for the resolution of disputes and to further trilateral, regional and multilateral cooperation. The NAFTA countries will meet these objectives by observing the principles and rules of the Agreement, such as national treatment, most-favored-nation treatment and procedural "transparency".

Each country affirms its respective rights and obligations under the GATT and other international agreements. For purposes of interpretation, the Agreement establishes that the NAFTA takes priority over other agreements to the extent there is any conflict, but provides for exceptions to this general rule. For example, the trade provisions of certain environmental agreements take precedence over NAFTA, subject to a requirement to minimize inconsistencies with the Agreement.

The opening provisions also set out a general rule regarding the application of the Agreement to sub-federal levels of government in the three countries. In addition, this section defines terms that apply to the whole Agreement, to ensure uniform and consistent usage.

RULES OF ORIGIN

NAFTA eliminates all tariffs on goods originating in Canada, Mexico and the United States over a "transition period". Rules of origin are necessary to define which goods are eligible for this preferential tariff treatment.

This section of the Agreement is designed to:

- ensure that NAFTA benefits are accorded only to goods produced in the North American region-not goods made wholly or in large part in other countries;

- provide clear rules and predictable results; and

- minimize administrative burdens for exporters, importers and producers trading under NAFTA.

The rules of origin specify that goods originate in North America if they are wholly North American. Goods containing non-regional materials are also considered to be North American if the non-regional materials are sufficiently transformed in the NAFTA region so as to undergo a specified change in tariff classification. In some cases, goods must include a specified percentage of North American content in addition to meeting the tariff classification requirement. The rules of origin section also contains a provision similar to one in the Canada-United States Free Trade Agreement (FTA) that allows goods to be treated as originating when the finished good is specifically named in the same tariff subheading as its parts and it meets the required value content test.

Regional value content may be calculated using either the "transaction-value" or the "net-cost" method. The transaction-value method is based on the price paid or payable for a good; this avoids the need for complex cost accounting systems. The net-cost method is based on the total cost of the good less the costs of royalties, sales promotion, and packing and shipping. Additionally, the net-cost method sets a limitation on allowable interest. Although producers generally have the option to use either method, the net-cost method must be used where the transaction value is not acceptable under the GATT Customs Valuation Code, and must also be used for certain products, such as automotive goods.

In order to qualify for preferential tariff treatment, automotive goods must contain a specified percentage of North American content (rising to 62.5 percent for passenger automobiles and light trucks as well as engines and transmissions for such vehicles, and to 60 percent for other vehicles and automotive parts) based on the net-cost formula. In calculating the content level of automotive goods, the value of imports of automotive parts from outside the NAFTA region will be traced through the production chain to improve the accuracy of the content calculation. Regional content averaging provisions afford administrative flexibility for automotive parts producers and assemblers.

A de minimis rule prevents goods from losing eligibility for preference solely because they contain minimal amounts of "non-originating" material. Under this rule, a good that would otherwise fail to meet a specific rule of origin will nonetheless be considered to be North American if the value of non-NAFTA materials comprises no more than seven percent of the price or total cost of the good.

CUSTOMS ADMINISTRATION

In order to ensure that only goods satisfying the rules of origin are accorded preferential tariff treatment under the Agreement, and to provide certainty to and streamlined procedures for importers, exporters and producers of the three countries, the NAFTA includes a number of provisions on customs administration. Specifically, this section provides for:

- uniform regulations to ensure consistent interpretation, application and administration of the rules of origin;

- a uniform Certificate of Origin as well as certification requirements and procedures for importers and exporters that claim preferential tariff treatment;

- common record-keeping requirements in the three countries for such goods;

- rules for both traders and customs authorities with respect to verifying the origin of such goods;

- importers, exporters and producers to obtain advance rulings on the origin of goods from the customs authority of the country into which the goods are to be imported;

- the importing country to give exporters and producers in other NAFTA countries substantially the same rights of review and appeal of its origin determinations and advance rulings as it provides to importers in its territory;

- a trilateral working group to address future modifications of the rules of origin and the uniform regulations; and

- specific time periods to ensure the expeditious resolution of disputes regarding the rules of origin between NAFTA partners.

TRADE IN GOODS

National Treatment

The NAFTA incorporates the fundamental national treatment obligation of the GATT. Once goods have been imported into one NAFTA country from another NAFTA country, they must not be the object of discrimination. This commitment extends to provincial and state measures.

Market Access

These provisions establish rules governing trade in goods with respect to customs duties and other charges, quantitative restrictions, such as quotas, licenses and permits, and import and export price requirements. They improve and make more secure the access for goods produced and traded within North America.

Elimination of Tariffs: The NAFTA provides for the progressive elimination of all tariffs on goods qualifying as North American under its rules of origin. For most goods, existing customs duties will either be eliminated immediately or phased out in five or 10 equal annual stages. For certain sensitive items, tariffs will be phased out over a period of up to 15 years. Tariffs will be phased out from the applied rates in effect on July 1, 1991, including the U.S. Generalized System of Preferences (GSP) and the Canadian General Preferential Tariff (GPT) rates. Tariff phase-outs under the Canada-U.S. FTA will continue as scheduled under that Agreement. The NAFTA provides that the three countries may consult and agree on a more rapid phase-out of tariffs.

Import and Export Restrictions: All three countries will eliminate prohibitions and quantitative restrictions applied at the border, such as quotas and import licenses. However, each NAFTA country maintains the right to impose border restrictions in limited circumstances, for example, to protect human, animal or plant life or health, or the environment. Special rules apply to trade in agriculture, autos, energy and textiles.

Drawback: NAFTA establishes rules on the use of "drawback" or similar programs that provide for the refund or waiver of customs duties on materials used in the production of goods subsequently exported to another NAFTA country.

Existing drawback programs will terminate by January 1, 2001, for Mexico-U.S. and Canada-Mexico trade; the Agreement will extend for two years the deadline established in the Canada-U.S. FTA for the elimination of drawback programs. At the time these programs are eliminated, each NAFTA country will adopt a procedure for goods still subject to duties in the free trade area to avoid the "double taxation" effects of the payment of duties in two countries.

Under these procedures, the amount of customs duties that a country may waive or refund under such programs will not exceed the lesser of:

- duties owed or paid on imported, non-North American materials used in the production of a good subsequently exported to another NAFTA country; or

- duties paid to that NAFTA country on the importation of such good.

Customs User Fees: The three countries have agreed not to impose new customs user fees similar to the U.S. merchandise processing fee or the Mexican customs processing fee ("derechos de tr‡mite aduanero"). Mexico will eliminate by June 30, 1999, its existing customs processing fee on North American goods. The United States will eliminate its current merchandise processing fee on goods originating in Mexico by the same date. For goods originating in Canada, the United States currently is phasing down and will eliminate this fee by January 1, 1994, as provided in the Canada/U.S. FTA.

Waiver of Customs Duties: The NAFTA prohibits any new performance based customs duty waiver or duty remission programs. Existing programs in Mexico will be eliminated by January 1, 2001. Consistent with the obligations of the Canada-U.S. FTA, Canada will end its existing duty remission programs by January 1, 1998.

Export Taxes: The NAFTA prohibits all three countries from applying export taxes unless such taxes are also applied on goods to be consumed domestically. Limited exceptions allow Mexico to impose export taxes in order to relieve critical shortages of foodstuffs and basic goods.

Other Export Measures: When a NAFTA country imposes an export restriction on a product, it must not reduce the proportion of total supply of that product made available to the other NAFTA countries below the level of the preceding three years or other agreed period, impose a higher price on exports to another NAFTA country than the domestic price or require the disruption of normal supply channels. Based on a reservation that Mexico has taken, these obligations do not apply as between Mexico and the other NAFTA countries.

Duty Free Temporary Admission of Goods: The Agreement allows business persons covered by NAFTA's "temporary entry" provisions to bring into a NAFTA country professional equipment and "tools of the trade" on a duty free, temporary basis. These rules also cover the importation of commercial samples, certain types of advertising films, and goods imported for sports purposes or for display and demonstration. Other rules provide that by 1998 all goods that are returned after repair or alteration in another NAFTA country will re-enter duty-free. The United States undertakes to clarify what ship repairs done in other NAFTA countries on U.S.flagged vessels qualify for preferential duty treatment.

Country-of-Origin Marking: This section also provides principles and rules governing country-of-origin marking. These provisions are designed to minimize unnecessary costs and facilitate the flow of trade within the region, while ensuring that accurate information about the country of origin remains available to purchasers.

Alcoholic Beverages - Distinctive Products: The three countries have agreed to recognize Canadian Whiskey, Tequila, Mezcal, Bourbon Whiskey and Tennessee Whiskey as "distinctive products" and to prohibit the sale of products under these names unless they meet the requirements of their country of origin.

TEXTILES AND APPAREL

This section provides special rules for trade in fibers, yarns, textiles and clothing in the North American market. The NAFTA textiles and apparel provisions take precedence over those of the Multifiber Arrangement and other agreements between NAFTA countries applicable to textile products.

Elimination of Tariff and Non-Tariff Barriers

The three countries will eliminate immediately or phase out over a maximum period of 10 years their customs duties on textile and apparel goods manufactured in North America that meet the NAFTA rules of origin. In addition, the United States will immediately remove import quotas on such goods produced in Mexico, and will gradually phase out import quotas on Mexican textile and apparel goods that do not meet such rules. No NAFTA country may impose any new quota, except in accordance with specified "safeguards" provisions.

Safeguards

If textile or apparel producers face serious damage as a result of increased imports from another NAFTA country, the importing country may, during the "transition period", either increase tariffs or, with the exception of Canada-U.S. trade, impose quotas on the imports to provide temporary relief to that industry, subject to specific disciplines. In the case of goods that meet NAFTA's rules of origin, the importing country may take safeguard actions only in the form of tariff increases.

Rules of Origin

Specific rules of origin in the NAFTA define when imported textile or apparel goods qualify for preferential treatment. For most products, the rule of origin is "yarn forward", which means that textile and apparel goods must be produced from yarn made in a NAFTA country in order to benefit from such treatment. A "fiber forward" rule is provided for certain products such as cotton and man-made fiber yarns. Fiber forward means that goods must be produced from fiber made in a NAFTA country. In other cases, apparel cut and sewn from certain imported fabrics that the NAFTA countries agree are in short supply, such as silk, linen and certain shirting fabrics, can qualify for preferential treatment.

Additional provisions, responsive to the needs of North American industry, include "tariff rate quotas" (TRQ's), under which yarns, fabrics and apparel that are made in North America, but that do not meet the rules of origin, can still qualify for preferential duty treatment up to specified import levels. The TRQ's for Canada that were included in the Canada-U.S. FTA have been increased and provided an annual growth rate for at least the first five years.

The NAFTA countries will undertake a general review of the textile and apparel rules of origin prior to January 1, 1998. In the interim, they will consult on request on whether specific goods should be made subject to different rules of origin, taking into account availability of supply within the free trade area. In addition, the three countries have established a process to permit annual adjustments to TRQ levels.

Labeling Requirements

A joint government and private sector Committee on Labeling for Textile Products will recommend ways to eliminate unnecessary obstacles to textile trade resulting from different labeling requirements in the three countries through a work program to develop uniform labeling requirements, for example regarding pictograms and symbols, care instructions, fiber content information and methods for attachment of labels.

AUTOMOTIVE GOODS

The NAFTA will eliminate barriers to trade in North American automobiles, trucks, buses and parts ("automotive goods") within the free trade area, and eliminate investment restrictions in this sector, over a 10-year transition period.

Tariff Elimination

Each NAFTA country will phase out all duties on its imports of North American automotive goods during the transition period. Most trade in automotive goods between Canada and the United States is conducted on a duty-free basis under the terms of either the Canada-U.S. FTA or the Canada-U.S. "Autopact".

Vehicles: Canada and the United States eliminated tariffs on their trade in vehicles under the Canada-U.S. FTA. Under the NAFTA, for its imports from Mexico, the United States will:

- eliminate immediately its tariffs on passenger automobiles;

- reduce immediately to 10 percent its tariffs on light trucks and phase out the remaining tariffs over five years; and

- phase out its tariffs on other vehicles over 10 years.

For imports from Canada and the United States, Mexico will:

- reduce immediately by 50 percent its tariffs on passenger automobiles and phase out the remaining tariffs over 10 years;

- reduce immediately by 50 percent its tariffs on light trucks and phase out the remaining tariffs over five years; and

- phase out its tariffs on all other vehicles over 10 years.

Canada will eliminate its tariffs on vehicles imported from Mexico on the same schedule as Mexico will follow for imports from Canada and the United States.

Parts: Each country will eliminate its remaining tariffs on certain automotive parts immediately and phase out duties on other parts over five years and a small portion over 10 years.

Rules of Origin

The NAFTA rules of origin section provides that in order to qualify for preferential tariff treatment, automotive goods must contain a specified percentage of North American content (rising to 62.5 percent for passenger automobiles and light trucks as well as engines and transmissions for such vehicles, and to 60 percent for other vehicles and automotive parts) based on the net-cost formula. In calculating the content level of automotive goods, the value of imports of automotive parts from outside the NAFTA region will be traced through the production chain to improve the accuracy of the content calculation.

Mexican Auto Decree

The Mexican Auto Decree will terminate at the end of the transition period. Over this period, the restrictions under the Auto Decree will be modified by:

- eliminating immediately the limitation on imports of vehicles based on sales in the Mexican market;

- amending its "trade balancing" requirements immediately to permit assemblers to reduce gradually the level of exports of vehicles and parts required to import such goods, and eliminating, at the end of the transition period, the requirement that only assemblers in Mexico may import vehicles;

- changing its "national value-added" rules by reducing gradually the percentage of parts required to be purchased from Mexican parts producers; by counting purchases from certain in-bond production facilities ("maquiladoras") toward this percentage; by ensuring that Canadian, Mexican and U.S. parts manufacturers may participate in the growing Mexican market on a competitive basis, while requiring assemblers in Mexico during the transition period to continue to purchase parts from Mexican parts producers; and by eliminating at the end of the transition period the national value added requirement.

Mexican Auto-Transportation Decree

The Mexican Auto-Transportation Decree covering trucks (other than light trucks) and buses will be eliminated immediately, and replaced with a transitional system of quotas in effect for five years.

Imports of Used Vehicles

Canada's remaining restrictions on the import of used motor vehicles from the United States will be eliminated on January 1, 1994, in accordance with the Canada-U.S. FTA. Beginning 15 years after the NAFTA goes into effect, Canada will phase out over 10 years its prohibition on imports of Mexican used motor vehicles. Mexico will phase out its prohibition on imports of North American used vehicles over the same period.

Investment Restrictions

In accordance with the NAFTA's investment provisions, Mexico will immediately permit "NAFTA investors" to make investments of up to 100 percent in Mexican "national suppliers" of parts, and up to 49 percent in other automotive parts enterprises, increasing to 100 percent after five years. Mexico's thresholds for the screening of takeovers in the automotive sector will be governed by NAFTA's investment provisions.

Corporate Average Fuel Economy Fleet Content

Under the NAFTA, the United States will modify the fleet content definition found in its Corporate Average Fuel Economy ("CAFE") rules, so that vehicle manufacturers may choose to have those Mexican-produced parts and vehicles they export to the United States classified as domestic. After 10 years, Mexican production exported to the United States will receive the same treatment as U.S. or Canadian production for purposes of CAFE. Canadian-produced automobiles currently may be classified as domestic for CAFE purposes. The NAFTA does not change the minimum fuel economy standards for vehicles sold in the United States.

Automotive Standards

The NAFTA creates a special intergovernmental group to review and make recommendations on federal automotive standards in the three countries, including recommendations to achieve greater compatibility in such standards.

Energy and Basic Petrochemicals

This section sets out the rights and obligations of the three countries regarding crude oil, gas, refined products, basic petrochemicals, coal, electricity and nuclear energy.

In the NAFTA, the three countries confirm their full respect for their constitutions. They also recognize the desirability of strengthening the important role that trade in energy and basic petrochemical goods plays in the North American region and of enhancing this role through sustained and gradual liberalization.

The NAFTA's energy provisions incorporate and build on GATT disciplines regarding quantitative restrictions on imports and exports as they apply to energy and basic petrochemical trade. The NAFTA provides that under these disciplines a country may not impose minimum or maximum import or export price requirements, subject to the same exceptions that apply to quantitative restrictions. The NAFTA also makes clear that each country may administer export and import licensing systems, provided that they are operated in a manner consistent with the provisions of the Agreement. In addition, no country may impose a tax, duty or charge on the export of energy or basic petrochemical goods unless the same tax, duty or charge is applied to such goods when consumed domestically.

This section also provides that import and export restrictions on energy trade will be limited to certain specific circumstances, such as to conserve exhaustible natural resources, deal with a short supply situation or implement a price stabilization plan.

Further, when a NAFTA country imposes any such restriction, it must not reduce the proportion of total supply made available to the other NAFTA countries below the level of the preceding three years or other agreed period, impose a higher price on exports to another NAFTA country than the domestic price or require the disruption of normal supply channels. Based on a reservation that Mexico has taken, these obligations do not apply as between Mexico and the other NAFTA countries.

This section also limits the grounds on which a NAFTA country may restrict exports or imports of energy or basic petrochemical goods for reasons of national security. However, based on a reservation that Mexico has taken, energy trade between Mexico and the other NAFTA countries will not be subject to this discipline, but will instead be governed by the Agreement's general national security provision, described in the "Exceptions" section below.

The NAFTA confirms that energy regulatory measures are subject to the Agreement's general rules regarding national treatment, import and export restrictions and export taxes. The three countries also agree that the implementation of regulatory measures should be undertaken in a manner that recognizes the importance of a stable regulatory environment.

In the NAFTA, Mexico reserves to the Mexican State goods, activities and investments in Mexico in the oil, gas, refining, basic petrochemicals, nuclear and electricity sectors.

The NAFTA energy provisions recognize new private investment opportunities in Mexico in non-basic petrochemical goods and in electricity generating facilities for "own use", co-generation and independent power production by allowing NAFTA investors to acquire, establish and operate facilities in these activities. Investment in non-basic petrochemical goods is governed by the general provisions of the Agreement.

To promote cross-border trade in natural gas and basic petrochemicals, NAFTA provides that state enterprises, end users and suppliers have the right to negotiate supply contracts. In addition, independent power producers, CFE (Mexico's state-owned electricity firm) and electric utilities in other NAFTA countries also have the right to negotiate power purchase and sale contracts.

Each country will also allow its state enterprises to negotiate performance clauses in their service contracts.

Certain specific commitments relating to special aspects of Canada-U.S. energy trade, set out in the Energy Chapter of the Canada-U.S. FTA, will continue to apply between the two countries.

AGRICULTURE

The NAFTA sets out separate bilateral undertakings on cross-border trade in agricultural products, one between Canada and Mexico, and the other between Mexico and the United States. Both include a special transitional safeguard mechanism. As a general matter, the rules of the Canada-U.S. FTA on tariff and non-tariff barriers will continue to apply to agricultural trade between Canada and the United States. Trilateral provisions in the NAFTA address domestic support for agricultural goods and agricultural export subsidies.

Tariffs and Non-Tariff Barriers

Trade between Mexico and the United States: When the Agreement goes into effect, Mexico and the United States will eliminate immediately all non-tariff barriers to their agricultural trade, generally through their conversion to either "tariff-rate quotas" (TRQ's) or ordinary tariffs.

The TRQ's will facilitate the transition for producers of import-sensitive products in each country. No tariffs will be imposed on imports within the quota amount. The quantity eligible to enter duty-free under the TRQ will be based on recent average trade levels and will grow generally at three percent per year. The over-quota duty-initially established at a level designed to equal the existing tariff value of each non-tariff barrier-will progressively decline to zero during either a 10- or 15-year transition period, depending on the product.

Under the NAFTA, Mexico and the United States will eliminate immediately tariffs on a broad range of agricultural products. This means that roughly one-half of U.S.-Mexico bilateral agricultural trade will be duty-free when the Agreement goes into effect. All tariff barriers between Mexico and the United States will be eliminated no later than 10 years after the Agreement takes effect, with the exception of duties on certain highly sensitive products-including corn and dry beans for Mexico, and orange juice and sugar for the United States. Tariff phase-outs on these few remaining products will be completed after five more years.

Mexico and the United States will gradually liberalize bilateral trade in sugar. Both countries will apply TRQ's of equivalent effect on third country sugar by the sixth year after the Agreement goes into effect. All restrictions on trade in sugar between the two countries will be eliminated by the end of the 15-year transition period, except that sugar exported under the U.S. Sugar Re-Export Programs will remain subject to most-favored-nation (MFN) tariff rates.

Trade between Canada and Mexico: Canada and Mexico will eliminate all tariff and non-tariff barriers on their agricultural trade, with the exception of those in the dairy, poultry, egg and sugar sectors.

Canada will immediately exempt Mexico from import restrictions covering wheat, barley and their products, beef and veal, and margarine. Canada and Mexico will eliminate immediately or phase out within five years tariffs on many fruit and vegetable products, while tariffs on remaining fruit and vegetable products will be phased out over 10 years. A small number of these products will be subject to the special transitional safeguard described below.

Other than in the dairy, poultry and egg sectors, Mexico will replace its import licenses with tariffs, for example on wheat, or TRQ's, for example respecting corn and barley. These tariffs will generally be phased out over a 10-year period.

Special Safeguard Provision

During the first 10 years the Agreement is in effect, the NAFTA provides a special safeguard provision that applies to certain products within the scope of the bilateral undertakings described above. A NAFTA country may invoke the mechanism where imports of such products from the other country reach "trigger" levels set out in the Agreement. In such circumstances, the importing country may apply the tariff rate in effect at the time the Agreement went into effect or the then-current MFN rate, whichever is lower. This tariff rate may be applied for the remainder of the season or the calendar year, depending on the product. The trigger levels will increase over this 10-year period.

Domestic Support

Recognizing both the importance of domestic support measures to their respective agricultural sectors and the potential effect of such measures on trade, each of the NAFTA countries will endeavor to move toward domestic support policies that are not trade-distorting. In addition, the three countries recognize that a country may change its domestic support mechanisms so long as such change is in compliance with applicable GATT obligations.

Export Subsidies

Recognizing that the use of export subsidies within the free trade area is inappropriate except to counter subsidized imports from a non-NAFTA country, the Agreement provides that:

- a NAFTA exporting country must give three-days' notice of its intent to introduce a subsidy on agricultural exports to another NAFTA country;

- when an exporting NAFTA country believes that another NAFTA country is importing non-NAFTA agricultural goods that benefit from export subsidies, it may request consultations on measures the importing country could take against such subsidized imports; and

- if the importing country adopts mutually agreed measures to counter that subsidy, the NAFTA exporting country will not introduce its own export subsidy.

Building on the bilateral discipline on export subsidies in the Canada-U.S. FTA, the three countries will work toward the elimination of export subsidies in North American agricultural trade in pursuit of their objective of eliminating such subsidies worldwide.

Agricultural Marketing Standards

The NAFTA provides that when either Mexico or the United States applies a measure regarding the classification, grading or marketing of a domestic agricultural product, it will provide no less favorable treatment to like products imported from the other country for processing.

Resolution of Commercial Disputes

The three countries will work toward development of a mechanism for resolving private cross-border commercial disputes involving agricultural products.

Committee on Agricultural Trade

A trilateral committee on agricultural trade will monitor the implementation and administration of this section. In addition, a Mexico-U.S. working group and a Canada-Mexico working group will be established under the committee to review the operation of grade and quality standards.

SANITARY AND PHYTOSANITARY MEASURES

This section imposes disciplines on the development, adoption and enforcement of sanitary and phytosanitary (SPS) measures, namely those taken for the protection of human, animal or plant life or health from risks arising from animal or plant pests or diseases, food additives or contaminants. These disciplines are designed to prevent use of SPS measures as disguised restrictions on trade, while safeguarding each country's right to take SPS measures to protect human, animal or plant life or health.

Basic Rights and Obligations

The NAFTA confirms the right of each country to establish the level of SPS protection that it considers appropriate and provides that a NAFTA country may achieve that level of protection through SPS measures that:

- are based on scientific principles and a risk assessment;
- are applied only to the extent necessary to provide a country's chosen level of protection; and
- do not result in unfair discrimination or disguised restrictions on trade.

International Standards

To avoid creating unnecessary barriers to trade, the NAFTA encourages the three countries to use relevant international standards in the development of their SPS measures. However, it permits each country to adopt more stringent, science-based measures when necessary to achieve its chosen level of protection.

The NAFTA partners will promote the development and review of international SPS standards in such international and North American standardizing organizations as the Codex Alimentarius Commission, the International Office of Epizootics, the Tripartite Animal Health Commission, the International Plant Protection Convention and the North American Plant Protection Organization.

Harmonization and Equivalence

The three countries have agreed to work toward equivalent SPS measures without reducing any country's chosen level of protection of human, animal or plant life or health. Each NAFTA country will accept SPS measures of another NAFTA country as equivalent to its own, provided that the exporting country demonstrates that its measures achieve the importing country's chosen level of protection.

Risk Assessment

The NAFTA establishes disciplines on risk assessment, including for evaluating the likelihood of entry, establishment or spread of pests and diseases. SPS measures must be based on an assessment of risk to human, animal or plant life or health, taking into account risk assessment techniques developed by international or North American standardizing organizations. A NAFTA country may grant a phase-in period for compliance by goods from another NAFTA country where the phase-in would be consistent with ensuring the importing country's chosen level of SPS protection.

Adaptation to Regional Conditions

This section also establishes rules for the adaptation of SPS measures to regional conditions, in particular regarding pest- or disease-free areas and areas of low pest or disease prevalence. An exporting country must provide objective evidence whenever it claims that goods from its territory originate in a pest- or disease-free area or area of low pest or disease prevalence.

Procedural Transparency

The NAFTA requires public notice in most cases prior to the adoption or modification of any SPS measure that may affect trade in North America. The notice must identify the goods to be covered, and the objectives of and reasons for the measure. All SPS measures must be published promptly. Each NAFTA country will ensure that a designated inquiry point provides information regarding such measures.

Control, Inspection and Approval Procedures

The NAFTA also establishes rules governing procedures for ensuring the fulfillment of SPS measures. These rules allow for the continued operation of domestic control, inspection and approval procedures, including national systems for approving the use of additives or for establishing tolerances for contaminants in foods, beverages or feedstuffs, subject to such disciplines as national treatment, timeliness and procedural transparency.

Technical Assistance

The three countries will facilitate the provision of technical assistance concerning SPS measures either directly or through appropriate international or North American standardizing organizations.

Committee on Sanitary and Phytosanitary Measures

A Committee on Sanitary and Phytosanitary Measures will facilitate the enhancement of food safety and sanitary conditions in the free trade area, promote the harmonization and equivalence of SPS measures and facilitate technical cooperation and consultations, including consultations regarding disputes involving SPS measures.

TECHNICAL STANDARDS

This section applies to standards-related measures, namely standards, governmental technical regulations and the procedures used to determine that these standards and regulations are met. It recognizes the crucial role of these measures in promoting safety and protecting human, animal and plant life and health, the environment and consumers. The three countries have agreed not to use standards-related measures as unnecessary obstacles to trade, and will cooperate and work towards the enhancement and compatibility of these measures in the free trade area.

Basic Rights and Obligations

The NAFTA affirms that each country maintains the right to adopt, apply and enforce standards-related measures, to choose the level of protection it wishes to achieve through such measures and to conduct assessments of risk to ensure that those levels are achieved. In addition, the NAFTA affirms each country's rights and obligations under the GATT Agreement on Technical Barriers to Trade and other international agreements, including environmental and conservation agreements.

The NAFTA also sets out certain disciplines on the use of standards-related measures, with a view to facilitating trade between the NAFTA partners. For example, each country must ensure that its standards-related measures provide both national treatment and most-favored-nation treatment. That is, they must ensure that goods or specified services from the other two countries are treated no less favorably than like goods or services of national origin, and like goods or services from non-NAFTA countries.

International Standards

Each NAFTA country will use international standards as a basis for its standards-related measures if those standards are an effective and appropriate means to fulfill the country's objectives. However, each country retains the right to adopt, apply and enforce standards-related measures that result in a higher level of protection than would be achieved by measures based on international standards.

Compatibility

The NAFTA countries will work jointly to enhance safety, health and environmental and consumer protection. They will also seek to make their standards-related measures more compatible, taking into account international standard-setting activities, so as to facilitate trade and to reduce the additional costs that arise from having to meet different requirements in each country.

Conformity Assessment

Conformity assessment procedures are used to determine that the requirements set out in technical regulations or standards are fulfilled. The Agreement sets out a detailed list of rules governing these procedures to ensure that they do not create unnecessary obstacles to trade between the NAFTA countries.

Procedural Transparency

The NAFTA requires public notice in most cases prior to the adoption or modification of standards-related measures that may affect trade in North America. The notice must identify the goods or services to be covered and the objectives of and the reasons for the measure. Other NAFTA countries and anyone interested in a particular standards-related measure will be allowed to comment on it. Each NAFTA country will ensure that designated inquiry points are able to respond to questions and provide information regarding standards-related measures to other NAFTA countries and any interested person.

Technical Cooperation

Each country will, on request, provide to another NAFTA country technical advice, information and assistance on mutually agreed terms and conditions to enhance their standards-related measures. The Agreement encourages cooperation between the standardizing bodies of the NAFTA countries.

Committee on Standards-Related Measures

A Committee on Standards-Related Measures will monitor the implementation and administration of this section of the Agreement, facilitate the attainment of compatibility, enhance cooperation on developing, applying and enforcing standards-related measures and facilitate consultations regarding disputes in this area. Subcommittees and working groups will be created to deal with specific topics of interest. The Agreement provides that these subcommittees and working groups may invite the participation of scientists and representatives of interested nongovernmental organizations from the three countries.

EMERGENCY ACTION

This section of the Agreement establishes rules and procedures under which a NAFTA country may take "safeguard" actions to provide temporary relief to industries adversely affected by surges in imports. A transitional bilateral safeguard mechanism applies to emergency actions taken against import surges that result from tariff reductions under the NAFTA. A global safeguard applies to import surges from all countries.

The Agreement's procedures governing safeguard actions provide that relief may be imposed for only a limited period of time and require that the NAFTA country taking the action must compensate the NAFTA country against whose good the action is taken. If the countries are not able to agree on the appropriate compensation, the exporting country may take trade measures of equivalent effect to compensate for the trade effect of the safeguard.

Bilateral Safeguard

During the transition period, if increases in imports from another NAFTA country cause or threaten to cause serious injury to a domestic industry, a NAFTA country may take a safeguard action that temporarily suspends the agreed duty elimination or re-establishes the pre-NAFTA rate of duty. The injury must result from the elimination of duties under the NAFTA. Such a safeguard action may be taken only once, and for a maximum period of three years. In the case of certain extremely sensitive goods, a country may extend the safeguard action for a fourth year. Bilateral safeguard actions may be taken after the transition period only with the consent of the country whose good would be affected by such action.

Global Safeguard

The Agreement provides that where a NAFTA partner undertakes a safeguard action on a global or multilateral basis (in accordance with Article XIX of the GATT, which permits both tariff and quota-based safeguard measures), each NAFTA partner must be excluded from the action unless its exports:

- account for a substantial share of total imports of the good in question; and

- contribute importantly to the serious injury or the threat of injury.

The Agreement stipulates that a NAFTA country normally will not be considered to account for a substantial share of imports if it does not fall among the top five suppliers of the good. For a NAFTA country's goods to be deemed not to contribute importantly to injury, the rate of growth of imports of the goods entering from that country must be appreciably lower than that of total imports of those goods. Even if a NAFTA country is initially excluded from a safeguard action, the country taking the action has the right subsequently to include it in the action if a surge in imports from that country undermines the effectiveness of the action.

Procedural Requirements

This section also provides detailed procedures to guide the administration of safeguard measures, including:

- entrusting injury determinations to a specified administrative authority; and

- requirements for the form and content of petitions, the conduct of investigations, including public hearings to allow all interested parties an opportunity to present views, and notification and publication of investigations and decisions.

REVIEW OF ANTIDUMPING AND COUNTERVAILING DUTY MATTERS

The NAFTA establishes a mechanism for independent binational panels to review final antidumping (AD) and countervailing duty (CVD) determinations by administrative authorities in each country. Each country will make those changes to its law necessary to ensure effective panel review. This section also sets out procedures for panel review of future amendments to each country's antidumping and countervailing duty laws. In addition, it establishes an "extraordinary challenge" procedure to deal with allegations that certain actions may have affected a panel's decision and the panel review process. Finally, the NAFTA creates a safeguard mechanism designed to remedy instances in which application of a country's domestic law undermines the functioning of the panel process.

Panel Process

Binational panels will substitute for domestic judicial review in cases in which either the importing or exporting country seeks panel review of a determination based on a request by a person entitled to judicial review of that determination under the domestic law of the importing country.

Each panel will comprise five qualified individuals from the countries involved, drawn from a roster maintained by the three countries. Each country involved will select two panelists, with the fifth selected by agreement of those countries or, in the absence of agreement, by the agreement of the four designated panelists or by lot.

A panel must apply the domestic law of the importing country in reviewing a determination. The three countries will develop rules of procedure for panels. The panel will either uphold the determination or remand it to the administrative authority for action not inconsistent with the panel's decision. Panel decisions will be binding.

Retention of AD and CVD Laws

The NAFTA explicitly preserves the right of each country to retain its AD and CVD laws. Each country may amend its AD and CVD laws after the NAFTA takes effect. Any such amendment, to the extent it applies to imports from another NAFTA country, may be subject to panel review for inconsistency with the object and purpose of the Agreement, the GATT or the relevant GATT codes. If a panel finds such an inconsistency, and consultations fail to resolve the matter, the country that requested the review may take comparable legislative or administrative action or terminate the Agreement.

Extraordinary Challenge Procedure

The NAFTA also provides for an extraordinary challenge procedure and establishes certain grounds for invoking this procedure. Following a panel decision, either of the countries involved may request the establishment of a three-person extraordinary challenge committee, comprising judges or former judges from those countries. If it determines that one of the grounds for the extraordinary challenge has been met, it will vacate the original panel decision. In such event, a new panel will be established.

Special Committee to Safeguard the Panel Process

This section provides a safeguard mechanism to ensure that the panel process functions as intended. A NAFTA country may request a "special committee" to determine if the application of another country's domestic law has:

- prevented the establishment of a panel;

- prevented a panel from rendering a final decision;

- prevented the implementation of a panel's decision or denied it binding force and effect; or

- failed to provide opportunity for judicial review of the basis for the disputed administrative determination by an independent court applying the standards set out in the country's domestic law.

If a special committee makes an affirmative finding on any of these grounds, the countries involved will attempt to resolve the matter in the light of the special committee's finding. If they are unable to do so, the complaining country may suspend the binational panel system with respect to the other country or may suspend other benefits under the Agreement. If the complaining country suspends the panel system, the country complained against may take reciprocal action. Unless the countries involved resolve the matter, or unless the country complained against demonstrates to the special committee that it has taken the necessary corrective action, any suspension of benefits may remain in effect.

GOVERNMENT PROCUREMENT

The Agreement opens a significant portion of the government procurement market in each NAFTA country on a non-discriminatory basis to suppliers from the other NAFTA countries for goods, services and construction services.

Coverage

The NAFTA covers procurements by specified federal government departments and agencies and federal government enterprises in each NAFTA country.

The NAFTA applies to procurements by federal government departments and agencies of:

- over US$50,000 for goods and services; and

- over US$6.5 million for construction services.

For federal government enterprises, the NAFTA applies to procurements of:

- over US$250,000 for goods and services; and

- over US$8 million for construction services.

For procurements covered by the Canada-U.S. FTA, the dollar thresholds of that Agreement will continue to apply.

Mexico will phase in its coverage over a transition period.

This section does not apply to the procurement of arms, ammunition, weapons and other national security procurements. Each country reserves the right to favor national suppliers for procurements specified in the Agreement.

Procedural Obligations

In addition to requiring national and most-favored NAFTA country treatment, the Agreement imposes procedural disciplines on covered procurements that:

- promote transparency and predictability by providing rules for technical specifications, qualifications of suppliers, setting of time limits and other aspects of the procurement process;

- prohibit offset practices and other discriminatory buy-national requirements; and

- require each country to establish a bid protest system that allows suppliers to challenge procedures or awards.

Technical Cooperation

The three countries will exchange information regarding their procurement systems to assist suppliers in each country to take advantage of the opportunities created by this section.

A Committee on Small Business will assist NAFTA small businesses to identify procurement opportunities in NAFTA countries.

Future Negotiations

Recognizing that improvements to NAFTA's procurement section are desirable, the three countries will endeavor to extend the coverage of this section to state and provincial governments that, after consultations, voluntarily accept its commitments.

CROSSBORDER TRADE IN SERVICES

The NAFTA expands on initiatives in the Canada-U.S. FTA and the Uruguay Round of multilateral trade negotiations to create internationally-agreed disciplines on government regulation of trade in services. The cross-border trade in services provisions establish a set of basic rules and obligations to facilitate trade in services between the three countries.

National Treatment

The Agreement extends to services the basic obligation of national treatment, which has long been applied to goods through the GATT and other trade agreements. Under NAFTA's national treatment rule, each NAFTA country must treat service providers of the other NAFTA countries no less favorably than it treats its own service providers in like circumstances.

With respect to measures of a state or province, national treatment means treatment no less favorable than the most favorable treatment that the state or province accords to the service providers of the country of which it forms a part.

Most-Favored-Nation Treatment

The Agreement also applies another basic GATT obligation to services: that of most-favored-nation treatment. This rule requires each NAFTA country to treat service providers of the other NAFTA countries no less favorably than it treats service providers of any other country in like circumstances.

Local Presence

Under the Agreement, a NAFTA country may not require a service provider of another NAFTA country to establish or maintain a residence, representative office, branch or any other form of enterprise in its territory as a condition for the provision of a service.

Reservations

Each NAFTA country will be able to keep certain current laws and other measures that do not comply with the rules and obligations described above. Such federal, state and provincial measures will be listed in the Agreement. Each NAFTA country will have up to two years to complete the list of state and provincial measures of this kind. All such measures currently in force at the municipal and other local government level may be retained.

Each NAFTA country may renew or amend its non-conforming measures provided that the renewal or amendment does not make a measure more inconsistent with the rules and obligations described above.

Non-Discriminatory Quantitative Restrictions

Each country will also list its existing non-discriminatory measures that limit the number of service providers or the operations of service providers in a particular sector. Any other NAFTA country will be able to request consultations on such measures with a view to negotiating their liberalization or removal.

Licensing and Certification

The NAFTA provisions related to professional licensing and certification are designed to avoid unnecessary barriers to trade. Specifically, each country must seek to ensure that its licensing and certification requirements and procedures are based on objective and transparent criteria such as professional competence, are no more burdensome than is necessary to ensure the quality of the service and are not in themselves a restriction on the provision of the service. This section also provides a mechanism for the mutual recognition of licenses and certifications, but does not require a NAFTA country automatically to recognize the credentials of service providers of another country. In particular, the three countries will undertake a work program with a view to liberalizing the licensing of foreign legal consultants and the temporary licensing of engineers.

Commencing two years after implementation of the Agreement, a NAFTA country will remove any citizenship or permanent residency requirement for the licensing and certification of professional service providers in its territory. Any failure to comply with this obligation will entitle the other NAFTA countries to maintain or reinstate equivalent requirements in the same service sector.

Denial of Benefits

A NAFTA country may deny the benefits of this section to a specific firm if the services involved are provided through an enterprise of another NAFTA country that is owned or controlled by persons of a non-NAFTA country and the enterprise has no substantive business activities in the free trade area. In addition, for transportation cargo services, a NAFTA country may deny benefits to a firm if these services are provided with equipment that is not registered by any of the NAFTA countries.

Exclusions

The services section does not apply to a number of matters dealt with in other parts of the Agreement, including government procurement, subsidies, financial services and energy-related services. The rules described above also will not affect most air services, basic telecommunications, social services provided by the government of any NAFTA country, the maritime industry except for certain services between Canada and Mexico and sectors currently reserved by the Mexican Constitution to the Mexican State and Mexican nationals. Each NAFTA country maintains the right to take action necessary to enforce measures of general application that are consistent with the Agreement, such as regarding deceptive practices.

LAND TRANSPORTATION

The NAFTA provides a timetable for the removal of barriers to the provision of land transportation services between the NAFTA countries and for the establishment of compatible land transport technical and safety standards. It provides for the phase out of restrictions on cross-border land transportation services among the three countries in order to create equal opportunities in the North American international land transportation market. The provisions are designed to ensure that the land transportation services industries of the three countries will have a full opportunity to enhance their competitiveness without being placed at a disadvantage during the transition to liberalized trade.

Liberalization of Restrictions

Bus and Trucking Services: When the NAFTA goes into effect, the United States will amend its moratorium on grants of truck and bus operating authority by allowing full access for Mexican charter and tour bus operators to its cross-border market. Mexico will grant equivalent rights to U.S. and Canadian charter and tour bus operators. Canadian truck and bus companies are not subject to the U.S. moratorium. Canada will continue to permit U.S. and Mexican truck and bus operators to obtain operating authority in Canada on a national treatment basis.

Three years after signature of the Agreement, Mexico will allow U.S. and Canadian truck operators to make cross-border deliveries to, and pick up cargo in, Mexican border states, and the United States will allow Mexican truck operators to perform the same services in U.S. border states. At the same time, Mexico will allow 49 percent Canadian and U.S. investment in bus companies and in truck companies providing international cargo services (including point-to-point distribution of such cargo within Mexico). The United States and Canada will permit Mexican truck companies to distribute international cargo as well. The United States will maintain its moratorium on grants of operating authority for truck carriage of domestic cargo and for domestic passenger service, continuing to allow Mexicans to hold a noncontrolling interest in U.S. companies.

Three years after the Agreement goes into effect, the United States will allow bus firms from Mexico to begin scheduled cross-border bus service to and from any part of the United States. At the same time, Mexico will provide the same treatment to bus firms from Canada and the United States.

Six years after the Agreement goes into effect, the United States will provide crossborder access to its entire territory to trucking firms from Mexico. Mexico will provide the same treatment to trucking firms from Canada and the United States.

Seven years after the Agreement goes into effect, Mexico will allow 51 percent Canadian and U.S. investment in Mexican bus companies and in Mexican truck companies providing international cargo services. At the same time, the United States will lift its moratorium on domestic operating authority for Mexican bus companies.

Ten years after the Agreement goes into effect, Mexico will permit 100 percent investment in truck and bus companies in Mexico. No NAFTA country will be required to remove restrictions on truck carriage of domestic cargo.

Rail Services: Under the Agreement and consistent with a Mexican reservation taken pursuant to its Constitution, Canadian and U.S. railroads will continue to be free to market their services in Mexico, operate unit trains with their own locomotives, construct and own terminals and finance rail infrastructure. Mexico will continue to enjoy full access to the Canadian and U.S. railroad systems. The Agreement does not affect each NAFTA country's immigration law requirements for crews to change at or near their borders.

Port Services: The Agreement also liberalizes landside aspects of marine transport. Mexico will immediately allow 100 percent Canadian and U.S. investment in, and operation of, port facilities such as cranes, piers, terminals and stevedoring companies for enterprises that handle their own cargo. For enterprises handling other companies' cargo, 100 percent Canadian and U.S. ownership will be allowed after screening by the Mexican Foreign Investment Commission. Canada and the United States will continue to permit full Mexican participation in these activities.

Technical and Safety Standards

Consistent with their commitment to enhance safety, health and environmental and consumer protection, the NAFTA partners will endeavor to make compatible, over a period of six years, their standards-related measures with respect to motor carrier and rail operations, including:

- vehicles, including equipment such as tires and brakes, weights and dimensions, maintenance and repair and certain aspects of emission levels;

- non-medical testing and licensing of truck drivers;

- medical standards for truck drivers;

- locomotives and other rail equipment and operating personnel standards relevant to cross-border operations;

- standards relating to the transportation of dangerous goods; and

- road signs and supervision of motor carrier safety compliance.

Access to Information

Each NAFTA country will designate contact points to provide information regarding land transportation matters such as those related to operating authorizations and safety requirements.

Review Process

Beginning five years after the Agreement goes into effect, a committee of government officials will consider the effectiveness of liberalization in the land transportation sector, including any specific problems or unanticipated effects liberalization might have on each country's motor carrier industry. No later than seven years after the Agreement goes into effect, consultations will also address possible further liberalization. The results of these consultations will be forwarded to the NAFTA Trade Commission for appropriate action.

TELECOMMUNICATIONS

NAFTA provides that public telecommunications transport networks (public networks) and services are to be available on reasonable and nondiscriminatory terms and conditions for firms or individuals who use those networks for the conduct of their business. These uses include the provision of enhanced or value-added telecommunications services and intracorporate communications. However, the operation and provision of public networks and services have not been made subject to the NAFTA.

Access to and Use of Public Networks

The three countries will ensure that reasonable conditions of access and use include the ability to:

- lease private lines;

- attach terminal or other equipment to public networks;

- interconnect private circuits to public networks;

- perform switching, signaling and processing functions; and

- use operating protocols of the user's choice.

Moreover, conditions on access and use may be imposed only if necessary to safeguard the public service responsibilities of network operators or to protect the technical integrity of public networks. Provided that these criteria are met, such conditions on access and use may include restrictions on resale or shared use of public telecommunications transport services, requirements to use specified technical interfaces with public networks or services and restrictions on the interconnection of private circuits to provide public networks or services.

Rates for public telecommunications transport services must reflect economic costs, and private leased circuits must be available on a flat-rate pricing basis. However, NAFTA does not prohibit cross-subsidization between public telecommunications transport services. In addition, firms or individuals may use public networks and services to move information within a country and across NAFTA borders.

The provisions in this section do not apply to measures affecting the distribution of radio or television programming by broadcast stations or cable systems, which will have continued access to and use of public networks and services.

Exclusions and Limitations

The three countries are not required to authorize a person of another NAFTA country to provide or operate telecommunications transport networks or services and may prohibit operators of private networks from providing public networks and services.

Enhanced Telecommunications

The NAFTA provides that each country will ensure that its licensing or other authorization procedures for the provision of enhanced or value-added telecommunications services are transparent, nondiscriminatory and applied expeditiously. Enhanced providers of the three countries will not be subject to obligations that are normally imposed on providers of public networks and services, such as providing services to the public generally or costjustifying their rates.

Standards Related Measures

The NAFTA limits the types of standards-related measures that may be imposed on the attachment of telecommunications equipment to public networks. Such measures must be necessary to prevent technical damage to, and interference with, public networks and services, to prevent billing equipment malfunctions and to ensure user safety and access. In addition, any technically qualified entity will be permitted to test equipment to be attached to public networks. This section also establishes procedures in each country to permit the acceptance of equipment test results conducted in the other NAFTA countries.

Monopoly Provision of Services

The NAFTA recognizes that a country may maintain or designate a monopoly provider of public networks or services. Each country will ensure that any such monopoly does not abuse its monopoly position by engaging in anti-competitive conduct outside its monopoly that adversely affects a person of another NAFTA country.

Provision of Information

Information affecting access to and use of public networks and services must be made publicly available, including:

- tariffs and other terms and conditions of service;

- specification of network and service technical interfaces;

- information on standardizing organizations;

- conditions for the attachment of terminal or other equipment; and

- notification, permit, registration or licensing requirements.

Technical Cooperation

The NAFTA countries will cooperate in the exchange of technical information and in the development of government-to-government training programs. Recognizing the importance to global telecommunications of international standards, they will also promote such standards through the work of the International Telecommunications Union, the International Organization for Standardization and other relevant international organizations.

INVESTMENT

The NAFTA removes significant investment barriers, ensures basic protections for NAFTA investors and provides a mechanism for the settlement of disputes between such investors and a NAFTA country.

Coverage

This section covers investments in one country by NAFTA investors from another NAFTA country. NAFTA investors include all enterprises with substantial business activities in a NAFTA country. Investment covers all forms of ownership and interests in a business enterprise, tangible and intangible property and contractual investment interests.

Non-Discriminatory and Minimum Standards of Treatment

Each country will treat NAFTA investors and their investments no less favorably than its own investors-national treatment-and investors of other countries-most-favored-nation treatment. With respect to measures of a state, provincial or local government, national treatment is defined to mean treatment no less favorable than the most favorable treatment accorded to investors of the country of which it forms a part. In addition, each country must provide investments of NAFTA investors treatment in accordance with international law, including fair and equitable treatment and full protection and security.

Performance Requirements

No NAFTA country may impose specified "performance requirements" in connection with any investments in its territory, namely specified export levels, minimum domestic content, preferences for domestic sourcing, trade balancing, technology transfer or product mandating. However, these disciplines do not apply to any NAFTA country's government procurement, export promotion or foreign aid activities.

Transfers

NAFTA investors will be able to convert local currency into foreign currency at the prevailing market rate of exchange for earnings, proceeds of a sale, loan repayments or other transactions associated with an investment. Each NAFTA country will ensure that such foreign currency may be freely transferred.

Expropriation

No NAFTA country may directly or indirectly expropriate investments of NAFTA investors except for a public purpose, on a non-discriminatory basis and in accordance with principles of due process of law. Compensation to the investor must be paid without delay at the fair market value of the expropriated investment, plus any applicable interest.

Dispute Settlement

This section sets out a detailed mechanism for the resolution of investment disputes involving a breach of the NAFTA investment rules by the host country. A NAFTA investor, at its option, may seek either monetary damages through binding investor-state arbitration or the remedies that are available in the host country's domestic courts.

Country-Specific Commitments and Exceptions

The NAFTA includes explicit country-specific liberalization commitments and exceptions to the national treatment, MFN and performance requirement rules. In the case of Mexico, these exceptions take into account constitutional requirements reserving certain activities to the Mexican State. Each country will specify exceptions for state and provincial measures within two years. Exceptions may not be made more restrictive and, if liberalized, may not subsequently be made more restrictive. However, a few sectors, such as basic telecommunications, social services and maritime services, are not subject to this constraint.

Canada may review acquisitions as provided in the Canada-U.S. FTA. Mexico may review acquisitions with an initial threshold of $25 million phased up to $150 million in the tenth year after the Agreement goes into effect. Threshold levels will be indexed.

Exceptions

The investment provisions do not apply to government procurement and subsidies. Other provisions of the Agreement address exceptions related to national security and to Canada's cultural industries.

Investment and the Environment

The NAFTA provides that no country should lower its environmental standards to attract an investment and that the countries will consult on the observance of this provision. The Agreement also specifies that a country may take action consistent with the NAFTA's investment provisions to protect its environment.

COMPETITION POLICY, MONOPOLIES, AND STATE ENTERPRISES

The NAFTA includes provisions on anti-competitive government and private business practices, in recognition that disciplines in this area will help fulfill the objectives of the Agreement.

Competition Policy

Each NAFTA country will adopt or maintain measures against anticompetitive business practices and will cooperate on issues of competition law enforcement and other competition issues.

Monopolies and State Enterprises

State Enterprises: The Agreement requires any enterprise owned or controlled by a federal, provincial or state government to act in a manner consistent with that country's NAFTA obligations when exercising regulatory, administrative or other governmental authority, such as the granting of licenses.

Monopolies: The NAFTA imposes certain additional disciplines on current and future federal government-owned monopolies and on any privately-owned monopoly that a NAFTA country may designate in the future. When buying or selling a monopoly good or service, the monopoly must follow commercial considerations, consistent with the terms of its government mandate, and must not discriminate against goods or businesses of the other NAFTA countries. NAFTA provides that each country must ensure that such monopolies do not use their monopoly positions to engage in anti-competitive practices in non-monopoly markets in that country's territory.

Trade and Competition Committee

A trilateral committee will consider issues concerning the relationship between competition laws and policies and trade in the free trade area.

FINANCIAL SERVICES

The NAFTA establishes a comprehensive principles-based approach to disciplining government measures regulating financial services. This section covers measures affecting the provision of financial services by financial institutions in the banking, insurance and securities sectors as well as other financial services. The section also sets out certain country-specific liberalization commitments, transition periods for compliance with the agreed principles and certain reservations listed by each country.

Principles

Commercial Presence and Cross-Border Services: Under the Agreement, financial service providers of a NAFTA country may establish in any other NAFTA country banking, insurance and securities operations as well as other types of financial services. Each country must permit its residents to purchase financial services in the territory of another NAFTA country. In addition, a country may not impose new restrictions on the cross-border provision of financial services in a sector, unless the country has exempted that sector from this obligation.

Non-Discriminatory Treatment: Each country will provide both national treatment, including treatment respecting competitive opportunities, and most-favored-nation treatment to other NAFTA financial service providers operating in its territory. Under the Agreement, any measure that does not disadvantage financial service providers of another NAFTA country in their ability to provide financial services, by comparison to domestic providers, is deemed to provide equality of competitive opportunity.

Procedural Transparency: In processing applications for entry into its financial services markets, each country will:

- inform interested persons of its requirements for completing applications;

- provide information on the status of an application on request;

- make an administrative determination on a completed application within 120 days, where possible;

- publish measures of general application no later than their effective date and, where practicable, allow interested persons the opportunity to comment on proposed measures; and

- establish one or more inquiry points to answer questions about its financial services measures.

Prudential and Balance of Payments Measures: The NAFTA ensures that each country retains the right to take reasonable prudential measures notwithstanding any other provision of the Agreement. It also provides that a country may take measures for balance-of-payment purposes under limited circumstances.

Consultations

The Agreement provides specific procedures for NAFTA countries to consult on financial services matters.

Country-Specific Commitments

Canada: Under the Canada-U.S. FTA, U.S. firms and individuals are exempt from the non-resident provisions of Canada's "10/25" rules. Under the NAFTA, Canada will extend this exemption to Mexican firms and individuals who will thus be exempt from Canada's prohibition against non-residents collectively acquiring more than 25 percent of the shares of a federally-regulated Canadian financial institution. Mexican banks will also not be subject to the combined 12 percent asset ceiling that applies to non-NAFTA banks, nor will they be required to seek the approval of the Minister of Finance as a condition of opening multiple branches in Canada.

Mexico: Mexico will permit financial firms organized under the laws of another NAFTA country to establish financial institutions in Mexico, subject to certain market share limits that will apply during a transition period ending by the year 2000. Thereafter, temporary safeguard provisions may be applicable in the banking and securities sectors.

Banking and Securities: During the transition period, Mexico will gradually increase the aggregate market share limit in banking from eight percent to 15 percent. For securities firms, the limit will increase from 10 percent to 20 percent over the same period. Mexico will apply individual market share caps of 1.5 percent for banks and four percent for securities dealers during the transition period. After the transition period, bank acquisitions will remain subject to reasonable prudential considerations and a four percent market share limit on the resulting institution.

Insurance: Under the NAFTA, Canadian and U.S. insurers may gain access to the Mexican market in two ways. First, firms that form joint ventures with Mexican insurers may increase their foreign equity participation in such ventures in steps from 30 percent in 1994 to 51 percent by 1998, and to 100 percent by the year 2000. These firms will not be subject to aggregate or individual market share limits. Second, foreign insurers may establish subsidiaries, subject to aggregate limits of six percent of market share, gradually increasing to 12 percent in 1999, and subject to individual market share caps of 1.5 percent. These limits will be eliminated on January 1, 2000. Canadian and U.S. firms that currently have an ownership interest in Mexican insurers may increase their equity participation to 100 percent by January 1, 1996. Intermediary and auxiliary insurance services companies will be permitted to establish subsidiaries with no ownership or market share limits when the Agreement goes into effect.

Finance Companies: Mexico will permit Canadian and U.S. finance companies, on terms no less favorable than those accorded to Mexican institutions, to establish separate subsidiaries in Mexico to provide consumer lending, commercial lending, mortgage lending or credit card services. However, during the transition period, the aggregate assets of such subsidiaries may not exceed three percent of the sum of the aggregate assets of all banks in Mexico plus the aggregate assets of all types of limited-scope financial institutions in Mexico. Lending by affiliates of automotive companies with respect to the vehicles such companies produce will not be subject to, or taken into account in, the three percent limit.

Other Firms: NAFTA factoring and leasing companies will be subject to transition limits on aggregate market share in Mexico of the same duration and magnitude as those applying to securities firms, except that they will not be subject to individual market share limits. NAFTA warehousing and bonding companies, foreign exchange houses and mutual fund management companies will be permitted to establish subsidiaries with no ownership or market share limits when the Agreement goes into effect.

United States: The United States will permit any Mexican financial group that has lawfully acquired a Mexican bank with operations in the United States to continue to operate a securities firm in the United States for five years after the acquisition. The acquisition must occur before the NAFTA goes into effect and the bank and securities firm involved must have been operating in the U.S. market on January 1, 1992 and June 30, 1992, respectively. The securities firm may not expand the scope of its activities or acquire other securities firms in the United States, and will be subject to nondiscriminatory restrictions on transactions between it and its affiliates. Other than these provisions, nothing in this commitment will affect the U.S. banking operations of a Mexican financial group.

Canada-United States: Financial services commitments of Canada and the United States to each other under the Canada-U.S. FTA will be incorporated into the NAFTA.

INTELLECTUAL PROPERTY

Building on the work done in the GATT and various international intellectual property treaties, NAFTA establishes a high level of obligations respecting intellectual property. Each country will provide adequate and effective protection of intellectual property rights on the basis of national treatment and will provide effective enforcement of these rights against infringement, both internally and at the border.

The Agreement sets out specific commitments regarding the protection of:

- copyrights, including sound recordings;

- patents;

- trademarks;

- plant breeders' rights;

- industrial designs;
- trade secrets;
- integrated circuits (semiconductor chips); and
- geographical indications.

Copyright

For copyright, the Agreement's obligations include requirements to:

- protect computer programs as literary works and databases as compilations;
- provide rental rights for computer programs and sound recordings; and
- provide a term of protection of at least 50 years for sound recordings.

Patents

The NAFTA provides protection for inventions by requiring each country to:

- provide product and process patents for virtually all types of inventions, including pharmaceuticals and agricultural chemicals;
- eliminate any special regimes for particular product categories, any special provisions for acquisition of patent rights and any discrimination in the availability and enjoyment of patent rights made available locally and abroad; and
- provide patent owners the opportunity to obtain product patent protection for pharmaceutical and agricultural chemical inventions for which product patents were previously unavailable.

Other Intellectual Property Rights

This section also provides rules for protecting:

- service marks to the same extent as trademarks;
- encrypted satellite signals against illegal use;
- trade secrets generally, as well as for protecting from disclosure by the government test data submitted by firms regarding the safety and efficacy of pharmaceutical and agrichemical products;
- integrated circuits, both directly and in goods that incorporate them; and
- geographical indications so as to avoid misleading the public, while protecting trademark owners.

Enforcement Procedures

The NAFTA also includes detailed obligations regarding:

- procedures for the enforcement of intellectual property rights, including provisions on damages, injunctive relief and general due process issues; and
- enforcement of intellectual property rights at the border, including safeguards to prevent abuse.

TEMPORARY ENTRY FOR BUSINESS PERSONS

Taking account of the preferential trading relationship between the NAFTA countries, this section sets out commitments by the three countries to facilitate on a reciprocal basis temporary entry into their respective territories of business persons who are citizens of Canada, Mexico or the United States.

The NAFTA does not create a common market for the movement of labor. Each NAFTA country maintains its rights to protect the permanent employment base of its domestic labor force, to implement its own immigration policies and to protect the security of its borders.

This section's rules governing entry of business persons, constructed along the lines of similar provisions of the Canada-U.S. FTA, are tailored to meet the needs of all NAFTA partners.

Each country will grant temporary entry to four categories of business persons:

- business visitors engaged in international business activities for the purpose of conducting activities related to research and design, growth, manufacture and production, marketing, sales, distribution, after-sales service and other general services;

- traders who carry on substantial trade in goods or services between their own country and the country they wish to enter, as well as investors seeking to commit a substantial amount of capital in that country, provided that such persons are employed or operate in a supervisory or executive capacity or one that involves essential skills;

- intra-company transferees employed by a company in a managerial or executive capacity or one that involves specialized knowledge and who are transferred within that company to another NAFTA country; and

- certain categories of professionals who meet minimum educational requirements or who possess alternative credentials and who seek to engage in business activities at a professional level in that country.

Mexico and the United States have agreed to an annual numerical limit of 5,500 Mexican professionals entering the United States. This number is in addition to those admitted under a similar category in U.S. law that is subject to a global limitation of 65,000 professionals, but which remains unaffected by the NAFTA. The numerical limit of 5,500 may be increased by agreement between the United States and Mexico, and will expire 10 years after the Agreement goes into effect unless the two countries decide to remove the limit earlier. Canada has not set a numerical limit with respect to Mexico.

Consultations

The three countries will consult through a specialized working group on temporary entry matters. As part of its work, the group will consider providing temporary entry to spouses of business persons granted entry under NAFTA for periods of one year or more as traders and investors, intra-company transferees and professionals.

Provision of Information

Each country will publish clear explanatory material on procedures that business persons must follow to take advantage of the NAFTA temporary entry provisions.

Non-Compliance

The dispute settlement provisions of the Agreement may be invoked only if a country claims, on the basis of repeated practices, that another country has not complied with the temporary entry provisions.

Institutional Arrangements and Dispute Settlement Procedures

Institutional Arrangements

This section establishes the institutions responsible for implementing the Agreement, ensuring its joint management and for avoiding and settling any disputes between the NAFTA countries regarding its interpretation and application.

Trade Commission: The central institution of the Agreement is the Trade Commission, comprising Ministers or cabinet-level officers designated by each country. Regular meetings are to be held annually, although the day-to-day work of the Commission will be carried out by officials of the three governments participating in the various committees and working groups mandated by the Agreement, operating on the basis of consensus.

Secretariat: The NAFTA establishes a Secretariat to serve the Commission as well as other subsidiary bodies and dispute settlement panels. The administrative and technical support that the Secretariat will provide is designed to assist the Commission to ensure effective and joint management of the free trade area.

Dispute Settlement Procedures

The dispute settlement procedures of the NAFTA provide expeditious and effective means for the resolution of disputes.

Consultations: Whenever any matter arises that could affect a country's rights under the Agreement, it may request consultations and the countries concerned will promptly consult on the matter. The NAFTA places priority on reaching an amicable settlement. The third country may participate, or may seek its own consultations.

The Role of the Commission: Should the consultations fail to resolve the matter within 30 to 45 days, any country may call a meeting of the Trade Commission with all three countries present. The NAFTA directs the Commission to seek to settle the dispute promptly. The Commission may use good offices, mediation, conciliation or other means of alternative dispute resolution to this end.

Initiation of Panel Proceedings: If the countries concerned are unable to reach a mutually satisfactory resolution through the Commission, any consulting country may initiate panel proceedings.

Forum Selection

If a dispute could be brought under both the GATT and the NAFTA, the complaining country may choose either forum. If the third NAFTA country wants to bring the same case in the other forum, the two complaining countries will consult, with a view to agreement on a single forum. If those countries cannot agree, the dispute settlement proceeding normally will be heard by a NAFTA panel. Once selected, the chosen forum must be used to the exclusion of the other.

If a dispute involves factual issues regarding certain standards-related environmental, safety, health or conservation measures or if the dispute arises under specific environmental agreements, the responding country may elect to have the dispute considered by a NAFTA panel. The rules also set out procedures for addressing disputes relating to matters covered by the Canada-U.S. FTA.

Panel Procedures

If the complaining country elects to have the matter heard through NAFTA procedures, it may request the establishment of an arbitral panel. The third country may either join as a complaining country or limit its participation to oral and written submissions. The panel will typically be charged with making findings of fact and determining whether the action taken by the defending country is inconsistent with its obligations under the NAFTA, and may make recommendations for resolution of the dispute.

Panels will be composed of five members, who will normally be chosen from a trilaterally agreed roster of eminent trade, legal and other experts, including from countries outside the NAFTA. The NAFTA provides for a special roster of experts for disputes involving financial services.

The panel will be chosen through a process of "reverse selection" to ensure impartiality: the chair of the panel will be selected first, either by agreement of the disputing countries or, failing agreement, by designation of one disputing side, chosen by lot. The chair may not be a citizen of the side making the selection, and may be a non-NAFTA national. Each side will then select two additional panelists who are citizens of the country or countries on the other side. Whenever an individual not on the roster of panelists is nominated, any other disputing NAFTA country may exercise a peremptory challenge against that individual.

Rules of procedure, to be more fully elaborated by the Commission, provide for written submissions, rebuttals and at least one oral hearing. There are strict time limits to ensure prompt resolution. A special procedure permits scientific boards to provide expert advice to panels on factual questions related to the environment and other scientific matters.

Unless the disputing countries decide otherwise, within 90 days of a panel's selection, it will present to them a confidential initial report. They will then have 14 days in which to provide comments to the panel. Within 30 days of the presentation of its initial report, the panel will present its final report to the countries concerned. The report will then be transmitted to the Commission, which will normally publish it.

Implementation and Non-Compliance

Upon receiving the panel's report, the disputing countries are to agree on the resolution of the dispute, which will normally conform to the recommendations of the panel. If a panel determines that the responding country has acted in a manner inconsistent with its NAFTA obligations, and the disputing countries do not reach agreement within 30 days or other mutually agreed period after receipt of the report, the complaining country may suspend the application of equivalent benefits until the issue is resolved. Any country that considers the retaliation to be excessive may obtain a panel ruling on this question.

Alternate Dispute Resolution of Private Commercial Disputes

Special provisions, described in the investment section, set out procedures for international arbitration of disputes between investors and NAFTA governments. The NAFTA countries will also encourage and facilitate the use of alternative dispute resolution as a means of settling international commercial disputes between private parties in the NAFTA region. The three countries will provide for the enforcement of arbitral agreements and arbitral awards. The Agreement establishes an advisory committee concerning the use of alternative dispute resolution for such disputes.

ADMINISTRATION OF LAWS

Procedural Transparency

This section provides rules designed to ensure that laws, regulations and other measures affecting traders and investors will be accessible and will be administered fairly and in accordance with notions of due process by officials in all three countries. Each country will also ensure, under its domestic laws, independent administrative or judicial review of government action relating to matters covered by the NAFTA.

The NAFTA's notification and exchange of information provisions will allow each government the opportunity to consult on any action taken by another country that could affect the operation of the Agreement. These provisions are designed to assist the three countries to avoid or minimize potential disputes.

Contact Points

Each country will designate a contact point to facilitate communications between NAFTA countries.

EXCEPTIONS

The NAFTA includes provisions that ensure that the Agreement does not constrain a country's ability to protect its national interests.

General Exceptions

This provision permits a country to take measures otherwise inconsistent with its obligations affecting trade in goods to protect such interests as public morals, human, animal or plant life or health or national treasures, to conserve exhaustible natural resources or to take enforcement measures regarding such matters as deceptive practices or anticompetitive behavior. However, such measures must not result in arbitrary discrimination or disguised restrictions on trade between NAFTA countries.

National Security

Nothing in the Agreement will affect a NAFTA country's ability to take measures it considers necessary for the protection of its essential security interests.

Taxation

The NAFTA provides that, as a general matter, taxation questions will be governed by applicable double taxation agreements between the NAFTA countries.

Balance of Payments

Under the Agreement, a NAFTA country may take trade-restrictive measures to protect its balance of payments only in limited circumstances and in accordance with the rules of the International Monetary Fund.

Cultural Industries

The rights of Canada and the United States with respect to cultural industries will be governed by the Canada-U.S. FTA. Each country reserves the right to take measures of equivalent commercial effect in response to any action regarding cultural industries that would have been a violation of the Canada-U.S. FTA but for the cultural industries provisions. Such compensatory measures will not be limited by the obligations imposed by the NAFTA.

The rights and obligations between Canada and Mexico regarding cultural industries will be identical to those applying between Canada and the United States.

FINAL PROVISIONS

Entry into Force

This section provides that the Agreement will enter into force on January 1, 1994, upon completion of domestic approval procedures.

Accession

The NAFTA provides that other countries or groups of countries may be admitted into the Agreement if the NAFTA countries agree, and subject to terms and conditions that they require and to the completion of domestic approval procedures in each country.

Amendments and Withdrawal

This section also provides for amendments to the Agreement, subject to domestic approval procedures. Any country may withdraw from the Agreement on six-months' notice.

SUMMARY OF ENVIRONMENTAL PROVISIONS

The three NAFTA countries have committed in the NAFTA to implementing the Agreement in a manner consistent with environmental protection and to promoting sustainable development. Specific provisions throughout the Agreement build upon these commitments. For example:

- The trade obligations of the NAFTA countries under specified international environmental agreements regarding endangered species, ozone-depleting substances and hazardous wastes will take precedence over NAFTA provisions, subject to a requirement to minimize inconsistency with the NAFTA. This ensures that the NAFTA will not diminish a country's right to take action under these environmental agreements.

- The Agreement affirms the right of each country to choose the level of protection of human, animal or plant life or health or of environmental protection that it considers appropriate.

- NAFTA also makes clear that each country may maintain and adopt standards and sanitary and phytosanitary measures, including those more stringent than international standards, to secure its chosen level of protection.

- The NAFTA countries will work jointly to enhance the protection of human, animal and plant life and health and the environment.

- The Agreement provides that no NAFTA country should lower its health, safety or environmental standards for the purpose of attracting investment.

- When a dispute regarding a country's standards raises factual issues concerning the environment, that country may choose to have the dispute submitted to NAFTA dispute settlement procedures rather than under the procedures of other trade agreements. This same option is available for disputes concerning trade measures taken under specified international environmental agreements.

- NAFTA dispute settlement panels may call on scientific experts, including environmental experts, to provide advice on factual questions related to the environment and other scientific matters.

- In dispute settlement, the complaining country bears the burden of proving that another NAFTA country's environmental or health measure is inconsistent with the NAFTA.